Fodor's 5th Edition

W9-CUZ-798

The Rockies

The Guide for All Budgets, Completely Updated, with Many Maps and Travel Tips

Where to Stay, Eat,
and Explore

On and Off
the Beaten Path

When to Go,
What to Pack

Post-it® Flags,
Web Sites, and More

Fodor's Travel Publications • New York, Toronto, London, Sydney, Auckland
www.fodors.com

Fodor's Rockies

EDITOR: Christina Knight

Editorial Contributors: Jean Arthur, Kate Boyes, Lori Cumpston, Janet Lowe, Jeanne McGovern, Candy Moulton, Sharon Niederman, Eric Peterson, Gregory Robl, Kristin Rodine

Editorial Production: Taryn Luciani

Maps: David Lindroth, *cartographer;* Rebecca Baer and Robert P. Blake, *map editors*

Design: Fabrizio La Rocca, *creative director;* Guido Caroti, *art director;* Jolie Novak, *senior picture editor;* Melanie Marin, *photo editor*

Cover Design: Pentagram

Production/Manufacturing: Colleen Ziemba

Cover Photograph: Galen Rowell

Copyright

Fifth Edition

ISBN 0-676-90217-0

ISSN 1527-3210

Important Tip

Although all prices, opening times, and other details in this book are based on information supplied to us at press time, changes occur all the time in the travel world, and Fodor's cannot accept responsibility for facts that become outdated or for inadvertent errors or omissions. So **always confirm information when it matters,** especially if you're making a detour to visit a specific place.

Special Sales

Fodor's Travel Publications are available at special discounts for bulk purchases for sales promotions or premiums. Special editions, including personalized covers, excerpts of existing guides, and corporate imprints, can be created in large quantities for special needs. For more information, contact your local bookseller or write to Special Markets, Fodor's Travel Publications, 280 Park Avenue, New York, NY 10017. Inquiries from Canada should be directed to your local Canadian bookseller or sent to Random House of Canada, Ltd., Marketing Department, 2775 Matheson Boulevard East, Mississauga, Ontario L4W 4P7. Inquiries from the United Kingdom should be sent to Fodor's Travel Publications, 20 Vauxhall Bridge Road, London SW1V 2SA, England.

PRINTED IN THE UNITED STATES OF AMERICA

10 9 8 7 6 5 4 3 2 1

CONTENTS

ON THE ROAD WITH FODOR'S

The more you know before you go, the better your trip will be. A fascinating frontier history museum, an esteemed art gallery, or the best steak house in the Rockies could be just around the corner from your hotel, but if you don't know it's there, it might as well be on the other side of the globe. That's where this book comes in. It's a great step toward making sure your next trip lives up to your expectations. As you plan, check out the Web as well. Guidebooks have been helping smart travelers find the special places for years; the Web is one more tool. Whatever reference you consult, be savvy about what you read, and always consider the source. Images and language can be massaged to make places appear better than they are. And one traveler's quaint is another's grimy. Here at Fodor's, and at our on-line arm, Fodors.com, our focus is on providing you with information that's not only useful but accurate and on target. Every day Fodor's editors put enormous effort into getting things right, beginning with the search for the right contributors—people who have objective judgment, broad travel experience, and the writing ability to put their insights into words. There's no substitute for advice from a like-minded friend who has just come back from where you're going, but our writers, having seen all corners, peaks, and valleys of the Rockies, are the next best thing. They're the kind of people you'd poll for tips yourself if you knew them.

Jean Arthur writes for travel and adventure publications from her Montana home. Her nonfiction books include *Timberline* and *A Century of Skiing on Mount Hood, Hellroaring: Fifty Years on The Big Mountain, and Winter Trails Montana.* She is a regular contributor to *Ski Trax* magazine, *Horizon Air* magazine, and *Montana Magazine* and numerous newspapers such as the *Christian Science Monitor.* When not writing, she travels Montana's front country and back country by boot, bicycle, or back-country ski.

Kate Boyes has lived in Utah since 1982, where she spends her free time hiking, biking, skiing, whitewater rafting, and gathering ideas for screenplays. Her commentaries on life in the Rockies air regularly on Utah Public Radio, and her essays on art, nature, and outdoor recreation appear in numerous magazines and anthologies, including *Great & Peculiar Beauty* and *American Nature Writing.* In 1999, she gave up her teaching job at Southern Utah University to serve as a visiting writer in public schools, especially those on the Navajo Reservation in the Four Corners region. Her home base is Smithfield, Utah.

Lori Cumpston is a native of Colorado. After spending a decade as a broadcast journalist in Missoula, Montana, Bismarck, North Dakota, and Phoenix, Arizona, she has turned her talents to print where she works full-time as a freelance journalist covering stories in the West. Prior to freelancing, she worked as a humor columnist, entertainment, and feature writer for a Cox-owned newspaper. She has won awards from North Dakota AP Broadcasters, Colorado Associated Press Editors and Reporters Association, and Society of Professional Journalists. Her work has appeared in *The Washington Times, The Atlanta Journal Constitution, The Denver Post, Denver Rocky Mountain News,* and various other print and on-line publications. She lives in Grand Junction, Colorado.

Janet Lowe began exploring the southwest in 1985 and relocated to Moab, Utah, a few years later to head up the publications and operations department for Canyonlands Natural History Association. Now a full-time writer, she has published two books on Arches and Canyonlands national parks as well as *Into the Mystery: A Driving Guide to Moab Area Rock Art.* Her local color essays appeared for six years in *Moab Happenings,* she writes restaurant reviews for a local newspaper, and is a regular contributor to *Canyon Legacy,* the Dan O'Laurie History Museum journal. A published poet, she serves on the literary advisory board for the Utah State Arts Council. She is at work on a Moab area history and cookbook as well as a collection of her essays.

Jeanne McGovern left Southern California for the Colorado Rockies over 15 years ago, and has called Aspen home for the past 11 years. The former executive director of the Aspen Writers' Foundation, McGovern now works for the *Aspen times* and *Soujourner* magazine, as well as other local, regional, and national publications.

Candy Moulton has spent years traveling through Wyoming—her native state—researching her nonfiction books: *Roadside History of Wyoming; Legacy of the Tetons: Homesteading in Jackson Hole; The Grand Encampment: Settling the High Country; Wagon Wheels: A Contemporary Journey on the Oregon Trail; Writer's Guide to Everyday Life in the Wild West From 1840 to 1900; Writer's Guide to Everyday Life: Native Americans in the 1800s;* and *Steamboat: Legendary Bucking Horse.* She has also written *Roadside History of Nebraska* and *Salt Lake City Uncovered.* She is the editor of *Roundup,* the official publication of Western Writers of America, and she is a regular contributor to Fodor's. Moulton makes her home near Encampment, Wyoming.

Sharon Niederman is the author of six books on Southwest travel, cuisine, history, and culture. A full-time writer who travels the backroads and high mountain passes of Colorado and New Mexico, she loves dining in small-town cafés and soaking in the hot springs of Ouray, Durango, and Pagosa. She is a regular contributor to *Sunset* magazine and other regional Western publications. She lived in Colorado for ten years, where she was a professor at Metropolitan State College in Denver. Two of her books, including *A Quilt of Words: Women's Diaries, Letters & Original Accounts of Life in the Southwest, 1860–1960,* received the Border Regional Library Association Southwest Book Award for literary excellence. She lives in Albuquerque, New Mexico.

Eric Peterson is a Denver-based freelance writer who covers travel, business, and music for local and national publications.

Gregory Robl has lived on Colorado's Front Range for more than 30 years and has seen the urban corridor grow into a blend of striking, sophisticated cities and verdant open-space buffers. His publications include a handbook about German-American genealogy, and a series of newspaper articles about the fall of the Berlin Wall. A passionate traveler, he is always happy to return home to Colorado's relaxed lifestyle, and for the cycling, hiking, and camping, and to usher at the Colorado Shakespeare Festival each summer.

Kristin Rodine, a lifelong resident of the Northwest, is Communities editor of the *Idaho Statesman* in Boise, Idaho and a veteran contributor to Fodor's. A couple of decades in Idaho and Montana as a reporter and editor have honed her desire to explore and share the sights and experiences of the region. Her articles have appeared in Northwest and national publications, and she has won state and regional awards for feature writing, investigative reporting, editorial writing, and coordinating special reports.

Don't Forget to Write

Your experiences—positive and negative—matter to us. If we have missed or misstated something, we want to hear about it. We follow up on all suggestions. Contact the Rockies editor at editors@fodors.com or c/o Fodor's, 280 Park Avenue, New York, New York 10017. And have a fabulous trip!

Karen Cure

Karen Cure
Editorial Director

The United States

CANADA

ONTARIO
QUÉBEC
NEW BRUNSWICK
Fredericton
Québec
MAINE
Augusta
Montréal
Montpelier
Ottawa
VT. Concord
N.H. Boston
MINNESOTA
Duluth
MICHIGAN
Lake Superior
Lake Huron
Toronto
Lake Ontario
Albany
MASS.
R.I.
Providence
WISCONSIN
St. Paul Green Bay
Lake Michigan
Buffalo
NEW YORK
Hartford
CONN.
New York
Minneapolis
Milwaukee
Lansing
Lake Erie
Cleveland
PENNSYLVANIA
N.J.
Trenton
Madison
Detroit
Harrisburg
Philadelphia
IOWA
Chicago
OHIO
Pittsburgh
Baltimore
MD. Dover
DEL.
Des Moines
ILLINOIS
INDIANA
Columbus
WEST VIRGINIA
Annapolis
Washington, D.C.
Omaha
Springfield
Indianapolis
Charleston
Richmond
Topeka
St. Louis
Cincinnati
Louisville
Frankfort
VIRGINIA
Norfolk
Kansas City
Jefferson City
KENTUCKY
Raleigh
MISSOURI
Ohio R.
NORTH CAROLINA
Nashville
TENNESSEE
Tulsa
ARKANSAS
Memphis
Tennessee R.
Columbia
SOUTH CAROLINA
Little Rock
Mississippi R.
Savannah R.
ATLANTIC OCEAN
Birmingham
Atlanta
GEORGIA
MISSISSIPPI
Savannah
Jackson
Montgomery
ALABAMA
Jacksonville
Baton Rouge
Mobile
Tallahassee
FLORIDA
Houston
New Orleans
LOUISIANA
Orlando
Gulf of Mexico
Bahama Islands
Miami
Nassau

N
0   500 miles
0   800 km

ESSENTIAL INFORMATION

AIR TRAVEL

BIKES IN FLIGHT

Most airlines accommodate bikes as luggage, provided they are dismantled and boxed. For bike boxes, often free at bike shops, you'll pay about $15 (at least $100 for bike bags) from airlines. International travelers can sometimes substitute a bike for a piece of checked luggage at no charge; otherwise, the cost is about $100. Domestic and Canadian airlines charge $80–$160.

BOOKING

When you book **look for nonstop flights** and **remember that "direct" flights stop at least once.** Try to avoid connecting flights, which require a change of plane. For more booking tips and to check prices and make on-line flight reservations, log on to www.fodors.com.

CARRIERS

Chances are, you'll fly into one of the hub cities of Denver or Salt Lake City. Connecting flights all across the Rockies are available most frequently from these two cities. During ski season, some of the major resort towns have increased service, and direct flights may be available.

➤ MAJOR AIRLINES: Air Canada (☎ 888/247–2262, WEB www.aircanada. com). American Airlines (☎ 800/433–7300, WEB www.aa.com). British Airways (☎ 800/247–9297, WEB www. ba.com). Continental (☎ 800/525–0280, WEB www.continental.com). Delta (☎ 800/221–1212, WEB www. delta.com). Northwest (☎ 800/225–2525, WEB www.nwa.com). TWA (☎ 800/221–2000). United Airlines (☎ 800/241–6522, WEB www.united. com). US Airways (☎ 800/428–4322, WEB www.usair.com).

➤ SMALLER AIRLINES: America Trans Air (☎ 800/225–2995). America West (☎ 800/235–9292).Frontier (☎ 800/432–1359). Horizon Air (☎ 800/547–

9308). Mesa Airlines (☎ 800/637–2247). Midwest Express (☎ 800/452–2022). SkyWest (☎ 800/453–9417). Southwest (☎ 800/435–9792).

CHECK-IN & BOARDING

Most domestic carriers require you to check in two hours before your scheduled departure time, 2½ to 3 hours for international carriers. If you're traveling during snow season, **allow extra time for the drive** to the airport, as weather conditions can slow you down. If you'll be checking skis, arrive even earlier.

CUTTING COSTS

Always **check different routings** and look into using different airports. Travel agents, especially low-fare specialists (☞ Discounts & Deals), are helpful.

Consolidators are another good source. They buy tickets for scheduled international flights at reduced rates from the airlines, then sell them at prices that beat the best fare available directly from the airlines, usually without restrictions. Sometimes you can even get your money back if you need to return the ticket. Carefully read the fine print detailing penalties for changes and cancellations, and **confirm your consolidator reservation with the airline.**

➤ CONSOLIDATORS: Cheap Tickets (☎ 800/377–1000). Discount Airline Ticket Service (☎ 800/576–1600). Unitravel (☎ 800/325–2222). Up & Away Travel (☎ 212/889–2345). World Travel Network (☎ 800/409–6753).

HOW TO COMPLAIN

If your baggage goes astray or your flight goes awry, complain right away. Most carriers require that you **file a claim immediately.**

➤ AIRLINE COMPLAINTS: U.S. Department of Transportation Aviation Consumer Protection Division (✉

C-75, Room 4107, Washington, DC
20590, ☎ 202/366–2220, WEB www.
dot.gov/airconsumer). **Federal Aviation Administration Consumer Hotline** (☎ 800/322–7873).

AIRPORTS

The major gateways to the Rockies
include, in Colorado, Denver International Airport; in Idaho, Boise Air
Terminal; in Montana, Missoula
Airport and Glacier Park International Airport in Kalispell; in Utah,
Salt Lake City International Airport;
and in Wyoming, Jackson Hole
Airport. Flights to smaller, resort
town airports generally connect
through one of these hubs.

➤ AIRPORT INFORMATION: **Boise Air
Terminal** (☎ 208/383–3110). **Denver
International Airport** (☎ 303/342–
2200; 800/247–2336; 800/688–1333
TTY). **Glacier Park International
Airport** (☎ 406/257–5994). **Jackson
Hole Airport** (☎ 307/733–3039).
Missoula International Airport (☎
406/728–4381). **Salt Lake City Inter-
national Airport** (☎ 801/575–2400).

BUS TRAVEL

Greyhound Lines has regular intercity
routes throughout the region, with
connections from Denver to Grand
Junction, Cheyenne, Rawlings, Boise,
Salt Lake City, Bozeman, and Missoula. Smaller bus companies provide
service within state and local areas.

➤ BUS INFORMATION: **Boise-Win-
nemucca Northwestern Bus Lines**
(Idaho, ☎ 800/448–5692). **Colorado
Mountain Express** (☎ 800/525–
6363). **Greyhound Lines** (☎ 800/
231–2222). **Powder River Transportation** (Wyoming, ☎ 800/442–
3682). **Rimrock/Trailways** (Montana,
☎ 406/549–2339 or 800/255–7655).
Springs Transit Management (Colorado Springs, ☎ 719/385–7433).

BUSINESS HOURS

Most retail stores are open from 9 AM
or 9:30 AM until 6 PM or 7 PM daily in
downtown locations and until 9 or 10
in suburban shopping malls and in
resort towns during high season.
Downtown stores sometimes stay open
later Thursday night. Normal banking
hours are weekdays 9–5; some
branches are also open on Saturday
morning.

CAMERAS & PHOTOGRAPHY

Photographers love the Rockies—and
with good reason. The scenery is
America's best, and every season offers
a multitude of breathtaking images.
When you're at Native American sites,
be sure to ask if taking pictures is
appropriate. The *Kodak Guide to
Shooting Great Travel Pictures*
(available at bookstores everywhere)
is loaded with tips.

Wild Eyes Photo Adventures in
Columbia Falls, Montana conducts
workshops that put professional and
amateur photographers up close to
tigers, wolves, mountain lions, and
other animals in outdoor, natural
settings. All animals are well-cared
for by professional, loving handlers.

➤ PHOTO HELP: **Kodak Information
Center** (☎ 800/242–2424).

➤ PHOTO WORKSHOP: **Wild Eyes
Photo Adventures** (☎ 888/330–5391,
WEB www.wildeyes-USA.com).

EQUIPMENT PRECAUTIONS

**Don't pack film and equipment in
checked luggage,** where it is much
more susceptible to damage. X-ray
machines used to view checked luggage are becoming much more powerful and therefore are much more
likely to ruin your film. Always **keep
film and tape out of the sun.** Carry an
extra supply of batteries, and **be
prepared to turn on your camera or
camcorder** to prove to security personnel that the device is real. Always
ask for hand inspection of film, which
becomes clouded after repeated
exposure to airport X-ray machines,
and **keep videotapes away from
metal detectors.**

CAR RENTAL

Rates in most major cities run about
$35 a day and $175 a week for an
economy car with air-conditioning,
an automatic transmission, and
unlimited mileage. This does not
include tax on car rentals, which is
12.95% in Denver, 5% in Boise,
13.6% in Salt Lake City, and 6% in
Jackson Hole. There is no tax in
Montana, but if you rent from an
airport location, there is an airport
concession fee.

➤ MAJOR AGENCIES: **Alamo** (☎ 800/327–9633; 020/8759–6200 in the U.K., WEB www.alamo.com). **Avis** (☎ 800/331–1212; 02/9353–9000 in Australia; 800/879–2847 in Canada; 09/525–1982 in New Zealand; 0870/606–0100 in the U.K., WEB www.avis.com). **Budget** (☎ 800/527–0700; 0870/156–5656 in the U.K., WEB www.budget.com). **Dollar** (☎ 800/800–4000; 02/9223–1444 in Australia; 0124/622–0111 in the U.K., WEB www.dollar.com). **Hertz** (☎ 800/654–3131; 02/9669–2444 in Australia; 800/263–0600 in Canada; 09/256–8690 in New Zealand; 020/8897–2072 in the U.K., WEB www.hertz.com). **National Car Rental** (☎ 800/227–7368; 020/8680–4800 in the U.K., WEB www.nationalcar.com).

CUTTING COSTS

To get the best deal, **book through a travel agent who will shop around.** Also **price local car-rental companies,** although the service and maintenance may not be as good as those of a major player. Remember to ask about required deposits, cancellation penalties, and drop-off charges if you're planning to pick up the car in one city and leave it in another. If you're traveling during a holiday period, also make sure that a confirmed reservation guarantees you a car.

INSURANCE

When driving a rented car you are generally responsible for any damage to or loss of the vehicle as well as for any property damage or personal injury that you may cause. Before you rent, see what coverage your personal auto-insurance policy and credit cards provide.

For about $15 to $20 per day, rental companies sell protection, known as a collision- or loss-damage waiver (CDW or LDW), that eliminates your liability for damage to the car.

In most states you don't need a CDW if you have personal auto insurance or other liability insurance. However, **make sure you have enough coverage to pay for the car.** If you do not have auto insurance or an umbrella policy that covers damage to third parties, purchasing liability insurance and a CDW or LDW is highly recommended.

REQUIREMENTS & RESTRICTIONS

In the Rockies you must be 25 to rent a car with a valid driver's license; most companies also require a major credit card. You'll pay extra for child seats (about $3 per day), which are compulsory for children under five, and for additional drivers (about $2 per day). Non-U.S. residents will need a reservation voucher, a passport, a driver's license, and a travel policy that covers each driver, in order to pick up a car.

SURCHARGES

Before you pick up a car in one city and leave it in another, **ask about drop-off charges or one-way service fees,** which can be substantial. Note, too, that some rental agencies charge extra if you return the car before the time specified in your contract. To avoid a hefty refueling fee, **fill the tank just before you turn in the car,** but be aware that gas stations near the rental outlet may overcharge.

CAR TRAVEL

You'll seldom be bored driving through the Rockies. The most mountainous terrain is in Colorado, but this state is also the region's most populated and accessible. Idaho is home to the rockiest and most rugged stretch of the mountains, with an extraordinarily wild beauty. It is impossible to travel directly through the heart of the state—only two routes go from north to south. Montana's interstate system is more driver-friendly, connecting soaring summits, rivers, glacial valleys, forests, lakes, and vast stretches of prairie, all capped by that endless "Big Sky." It is practically impossible to get around Utah without a car. There are more national parks here than in any other states but Alaska and California, although their interiors are not always accessible by car. Wyoming's interstate links classic, open-range cowboy country and mountain-range vistas with the geothermal wonderland of Yellowstone National Park. In Wyoming, everything is separated by vast distances, so be sure to leave each major city with a full tank of gas and be prepared to see lots of wildlife and few other people.

Before setting out on any driving trip, it's important to **make sure your vehicle is in top condition.** It is best to have a complete tune-up. At the least, you should check the following: lights, including brake lights, backup lights, and emergency lights; tires, including the spare; oil; engine coolant; windshield-washer fluid; windshield-wiper blades; and brakes. For emergencies, take along flares or reflector triangles, jumper cables, an empty gas can, a fire extinguisher, a flashlight, a plastic tarp, blankets, water, and coins or a calling card for phone calls (cell phones don't always work in high mountain areas).

BORDER CROSSING

Driving a car across the U.S.–Canadian border is simple. Personal vehicles are allowed entry into the neighboring country, provided they are not to be left behind. Drivers must have owner registration and proof of insurance coverage handy. If the car isn't registered in your name, carry a letter from the owner that authorizes your use of the vehicle. Drivers in rental cars should **bring along a copy of the rental contract when crossing the border,** bearing an endorsement stating that the vehicle is permitted to cross the border.

GASOLINE

In major cities throughout the Rockies, gas prices are roughly similar to the rest of the continental United States; in rural and resort towns, prices are considerably higher. Although gas stations are relatively plentiful in many areas, you can drive more than 100 mi on back roads without finding gas.

ROAD CONDITIONS

The Rockies offer some of the most spectacular vistas and challenging driving in the world. Roads range from multilane blacktop to barely graveled backcountry trails; from twisting switchbacks considerably marked with guardrails to primitive campgrounds with a lane so narrow that you must back up to the edge of a steep cliff to make a turn. Scenic routes and lookout points are clearly marked, enabling you to slow down and pull over to take in the views.

One of the more unpleasant sights along the highway are roadkills—animals struck by vehicles. Deer, elk, and even bears may try to get to the other side of a road just as you come along, so **watch out for wildlife on the highways.** Exercise caution, not only to save an animal's life, but also to avoid possible extensive damage to your car.

➤ ROAD CONDITION INFORMATION: **Colorado** (☎ 303/639–1111 within a 2-hr drive of Denver; 303/639–1234 statewide). **Idaho** (☎ 208/336–6600). **Montana** (☎ 406/444–6339 or 800/332–6171). **Utah** (☎ 801/964–6000 in the Salt Lake City area; 800/492–2400 within Utah). **Wyoming** (☎ 307/772–0824).

RULES OF THE ROAD

You'll find highways and the national parks crowded in summer, and almost deserted (and occasionally impassable) in winter. Follow the posted speed limit, drive defensively, and **make sure your gas tank is full.** The law requires that drivers and front-seat passengers **wear seat belts;** in Montana, Utah, and Wyoming **rear seat occupants must also wear seat belts.**

Always **strap children under age 4 or under 40 pounds into approved child-safety seats.** You may turn right at a red light after stopping if there is no sign stating otherwise and no oncoming traffic. When in doubt, wait for the green.

SPEED LIMITS

The speed limit on U.S. interstates is 75 mph in rural areas and 65 mph in urban zones.

WINTER DRIVING

Modern highways make mountain driving safe and generally trouble free even in cold weather. Although winter driving can occasionally present some real challenges, road maintenance is good and plowing is prompt. However, in mountain areas, tire chains, studs, or snow tires are essential. If you're planning to drive into high elevations, be sure to **check the weather forecast and call for road conditions** beforehand. Even main highways can close. Be prepared for stormy weather: **carry an emergency kit** containing warm clothes, a flashlight, some food and water, and blankets. It's also good to carry a cell phone, but be aware that the mountains can disrupt service. If you do get stalled by deep snow, **do not leave your car.** Wait for help, running the engine only if needed, and remember that assistance is never far away. Winter weather isn't confined to winter months in the high country (it's been know to snow on July 4th), so be prepared year-round.

CHILDREN IN THE ROCKIES

The Rockies are tailor-made for family vacations, offering dude ranches; historic railroads; mining towns; the extreme natural features of national parks such as Yellowstone, Mesa Verde, and Arches; large wildlife; rafting; and many other outdoor activities. Visitor centers and lodgings are often good at recommending places to spend time with children. Attractions sometimes offer reduced family admission tickets, particularly in Utah.

The guides issued by the tourism offices of Colorado, Utah, and Wyoming have sections geared toward children. Idaho and Montana have a small flyer for kids as well as more extensive information on children's activities in their state travel brochures.

If you are renting a car, don't forget to **arrange for a car seat** when you reserve. For general advice about traveling with children, consult *Fodor's FYI: Travel with Your Baby* (available in bookstores everywhere).

LODGING

Most hotels in the Rockies allow children under a certain age to stay in their parents' room at no extra charge, but others charge for them as extra adults; be sure to **find out the cutoff age for children's discounts.**

Although most dude ranches are ideal for children of all ages, be sure you know not only the activities a ranch offers but also which are emphasized before booking your vacation. A few ranches may have age restrictions excluding very young children.

OUTDOOR ACTIVITIES AND SPORTS

Altitude can be even more taxing on small lungs than on adult lungs, so **be conservative** when evaluating what level of activity your child will enjoy.

Some trip organizers arrange backpacking outings for families with small children, especially for family groups of eight or more. Short half-day or full-day bike trips with plenty of flat riding are possible at many Rocky Mountain resorts. Among the better resorts for this sort of activity are Aspen and Steamboat Springs, in Colorado; Sun Valley, Idaho; and Park City, Utah. Winter Park resort in Colorado has good instructional programs. Ask at local bike shops for recommended rides for children.

It is not advisable to take children under seven on any extended rafting trip, except those specifically geared toward young children. Before taking an extended trip, you might want to test the waters with a half-day or one-day excursion. For families with younger children, trips aboard larger, motorized rafts are probably safest. Floating the gentle Snake River in Wyoming is best for young children. The Green River in Utah is also a fairly gentle river in most places. Outfitters designate some trips as "adults only," with the cutoff usually being 16 years old.

SIGHTS & ATTRACTIONS

Places that are especially appealing to children are indicated by a rubber-duckie icon (☺) in the margin.

CONSUMER PROTECTION

Whenever shopping or buying travel services in the Rockies, **pay with a major credit card,** if possible, so you can cancel payment or get reimbursed if there's a problem. If you're doing business with a particular company for the first time, **contact your local Better Business Bureau and the attorney general's offices** in your state and (for U.S. businesses) the company's home state as well. Have any complaints been filed? Finally, if you're buying a package or tour, always **consider travel insurance** that includes default coverage (☞ Insurance).

➤ BBBs: **Council of Better Business Bureaus** (✉ 4200 Wilson Blvd., Suite 800, Arlington, VA 22203, ☎ 703/276–0100, FAX 703/525–8277, WEB www.bbb.org).

CUSTOMS & DUTIES

When shopping, **keep receipts** for all purchases. Upon reentering the country, **be ready to show customs officials what you've bought.** If you feel a duty is incorrect or object to the way your clearance was handled, note the inspector's badge number and ask to see a supervisor. If the problem isn't resolved, write to the appropriate authorities, beginning with the port director at your point of entry.

IN AUSTRALIA

Australian residents who are 18 or older may bring home $A400 worth of souvenirs and gifts (including jewelry), 250 cigarettes or 250 grams of tobacco, and 1,125 ml of alcohol (including wine, beer, and spirits). Residents under 18 may bring back $A200 worth of goods. Prohibited items include meat products. Seeds, plants, and fruits need to be declared upon arrival.

➤ INFORMATION: **Australian Customs Service** (Regional Director, ✉ Box 8, Sydney, NSW 2001, Australia, ☎ 02/9213–2000, FAX 02/9213–4000, WEB www.customs.gov.au).

IN CANADA

Canadian residents who have been out of Canada for at least seven days may bring home C$750 worth of goods duty-free. If you've been away fewer than seven days but more than 48 hours, the duty-free allowance drops to C$200; if your trip lasts 24–48 hours, the allowance is C$50. You may not pool allowances with family members. Goods claimed under the C$750 exemption may follow you by mail; those claimed under the lesser exemptions must accompany you. Alcohol and tobacco products may be included in the seven-day and 48-hour exemptions but not in the 24-hour exemption. If you meet the age requirements of the province or territory through which you reenter Canada, you may bring in, duty-free, 1.14 liters (40 imperial ounces) of wine or liquor *or* 24 12-ounce cans or bottles of beer or ale. If you are 19 or older you may bring in, duty-free, 200 cigarettes and 50 cigars. Check ahead of time with the Canada Customs Revenue Agency or the Department of Agriculture for policies regarding meat products, seeds, plants, and fruits.

You may send an unlimited number of gifts worth up to C$60 each duty-free to Canada. Label the package UNSOLICITED GIFT—VALUE UNDER $60. Alcohol and tobacco are excluded.

➤ INFORMATION: **Canada Customs Revenue Agency** (✉ 2265 St. Laurent Blvd. S, Ottawa, Ontario K1G 4K3, Canada, ☎ 204/983–3500 or 506/636–5064; 800/461–9999 in Canada, WEB www.ccra-adrc.gc.ca).

IN NEW ZEALAND

Homeward-bound residents 17 or older may bring back $700 worth of souvenirs and gifts. Your duty-free allowance also includes 4.5 liters of wine or beer; one 1,125-ml bottle of spirits; and either 200 cigarettes, 250 grams of tobacco, 50 cigars, or a combination of the three up to 250 grams. Prohibited items include meat products, seeds, plants, and fruits.

➤ INFORMATION: **New Zealand Customs** (Custom House, ✉ 50 Anzac Ave., Box 29, Auckland, New Zealand, ☎ 09/300–5399, FAX 09/359–6730, WEB www.customs.govt.nz).

IN THE U.K.

From countries outside the European Union, including the United States, you may bring home, duty-free, 200 cigarettes or 50 cigars; 1 liter of spirits or 2 liters of fortified or sparkling wine or liqueurs; 2 liters of still table wine; 60 ml of perfume; 250 ml of toilet water; plus £145 worth of other goods, including gifts and souvenirs. If returning from outside the EU, prohibited items include meat products, seeds, plants, and fruits.

➤ INFORMATION: **HM Customs and Excise** (✉ St. Christopher House, Southwark, London SE1 OTE, U.K., ☎ 020/7928–3344, WEB www.hmce.gov.uk).

IN THE U.S.

➤ INFORMATION: **U.S. Customs Service** (✉ 1300 Pennsylvania Ave. NW, Room 6.3D, Washington, DC 20229, WEB www.customs.gov; inquiries ☎ 202/354–1000; complaints c/o ✉ 1300 Pennsylvania Ave. NW, Room 5.4D, Washington, DC 20229; registration of equipment c/o Office of Passenger Programs, ☎ 202/927–0530).

DINING

Dining in the Rockies is generally casual. Menus are becoming more varied with such regional specialties as trout, elk, or buffalo, but you can nearly always order a hamburger or a steak. Authentic ethnic food is hard to find outside of cities. Dinner hours are from 6 PM to 9 PM. Outside the large cities and resort towns in the high seasons, many restaurants close by 10 PM.

The restaurants we list are the cream of the crop in each price category. Properties indicated by an ✕☒ are lodging establishments whose restaurant warrants a special trip.

RESERVATIONS & DRESS

Reservations are always a good idea: we mention them only when they're essential or are not accepted. Book as far ahead as you can, and reconfirm as soon as you arrive. We mention dress only when men are required to wear a jacket or a jacket and tie— which is almost never in the casual Rockies—but there are some restaurants where men may simply feel more dressed for the occasion by wearing a jacket.

SPECIALTIES

While you can find all types of cuisine in the major cities and resort towns, don't forget to try native dishes like trout, elk, and buffalo (the latter two have less fat than beef and are just as tasty); organic fruits and vegetables are also readily available. When in doubt, go for a steak, forever a Rocky Mountain mainstay.

Rocky Mountain Oysters, simply put, are cow testicles (although they've been known to come from bulls, pigs, and even turkeys!). They're generally served fried, although you can get 'em lots of different ways. You can find them all over the West, usually at down-home eateries, county fairs, and the like.

WINE, BEER & SPIRITS

You'll find renowned breweries throughout the Rockies, including, of course, Coors. (Those in the know will also check out the smaller, resort town breweries of Colorado.) Although the region is not known for its wines, there are some wineries to visit, too—those in Idaho have been highly touted of late.

DISABILITIES & ACCESSIBILITY

The Rockies are home to countless recreational opportunities for travelers with disabilities. Most ski areas offer adaptive ski programs (Winter Park in Colorado is home to the National Sports Center for the Disabled— which offers year-round activities— and Park City Mountain Resort in Utah has excellent ski lesson programs). DREAM—Adaptive Recreation, Inc. serves the ski areas of Big Mountain and Blacktail in Montana.

The majority of United States Forest Service campgrounds have wheelchair-accessible sites. Many resort towns have created opportunities for all types of visitors (on Independence Pass in Colorado, for example, is a short trail with sights marked in Braille for the visually impaired). Access Tours leads nine-day trips for people who use wheelchairs or walk slowly and can customize trips for groups of four or more.

Relay Colorado allows a person with a TTY machine to call someone without a TTY machine (and vice-versa) by relaying a message on the customer's behalf.

➤ LOCAL RESOURCES: **Denver Commission for People with Disabilities** (☎ 303/640–3056). **DREAM— Adaptive Recreation, Inc.** (✉ Box 4085, Whitefish MT 59937, ☎ 406/ 862–1817). **Grand Teton National Park** (accessibility coordinator, Robin Gregory, ☎ 307/739–3300; 307/733– 2053 TDD). **National Sports Center for the Disabled** (✉ Winter Park CO, ☎ 970/726–1540). **Relay Colorado** (☎ 800/659–3656; 800/659–2656 TDD). **Rocky Mountain National Park** (accessibility coordinator, Dana

Leavitt, ☎ 970/586–1206; 970/586–8506 TDD). **Utah Travel Council** (☎ 801/538–1030). **Wilderness on Wheels** (✉ 3131 Vaughn Way, Suite 305, Aurora, CO 80014, ☎ 303/751–3959). **Wyoming Tourist Commission** (☎ 307/777–7777). **Yellowstone National Park** (accessibility coordinator, Doug Madsen, ☎ 307/344–7381).

➤ TOUR OPERATOR: **Access Tours** (✉ Box 499, Victor, ID 83455, ☎ 800/929–4811, FAX 208/787–2332).

LODGING

RESERVATIONS

When discussing accessibility with an operator or reservations agent, **ask hard questions.** Are there any stairs, inside *or* out? Are there grab bars next to the toilet *and* in the shower/tub? How wide is the doorway to the room? To the bathroom? For the most extensive facilities meeting the latest legal specifications, **opt for newer accommodations.**

TRAVEL AGENCIES

In the United States, the Americans with Disabilities Act requires that travel firms serve the needs of all travelers. Some agencies specialize in working with people with disabilities.

➤ COMPLAINTS: **Aviation Consumer Protection Division** (☞ Air Travel) for airline-related problems. **Civil Rights Office** (✉ U.S. Department of Transportation, Departmental Office of Civil Rights, S-30, 400 7th St. SW, Room 10215, Washington, DC 20590, ☎ 202/366–4648, FAX 202/366–9371, WEB www.dot.gov/ost/docr/index.htm) for problems with surface transportation. **Disability Rights Section** (✉ U.S. Department of Justice, Civil Rights Division, Box 66738, Washington, DC 20035-6738, ☎ 202/514–0301 or 800/514–0301; 202/514–0383 TTY; 800/514–0383 TTY, FAX 202/307–1198, WEB www.usdoj.gov/crt/ada/adahom1.htm) for general complaints.

➤ TRAVELERS WITH MOBILITY PROBLEMS: **Access Adventures** (✉ 206 Chestnut Ridge Rd., Scottsville, NY 14624, ☎ 716/889–9096, dltravel@prodigy.net), run by a former physical-rehabilitation counselor. **Accessible**

Vans of America (✉ 9 Spielman Rd., Fairfield, NJ 07004, ☎ 877/282–8267, FAX 973/808–9713, WEB www.accessiblevans.com). **CareVacations** (✉ No. 5, 5110–50 Ave., Leduc, Alberta T9E 6V4, Canada, ☎ 780/986–6404 or 877/478–7827, FAX 780/986–8332, WEB www.carevacations.com), for group tours and cruise vacations. **Flying Wheels Travel** (✉ 143 W. Bridge St., Box 382, Owatonna, MN 55060, ☎ 507/451–5005 or 800/535–6790, FAX 507/451–1685, WEB www.flyingwheelstravel.com).

DISCOUNTS & DEALS

Be a smart shopper and **compare all your options** before making decisions. A plane ticket bought with a promotional coupon from travel clubs, coupon books, and direct-mail offers or on the Internet may not be cheaper than the least expensive fare from a discount ticket agency. And always keep in mind that what you get is just as important as what you save.

DISCOUNT RESERVATIONS

To save money, **look into discount reservations services** with toll-free numbers, which use their buying power to get a better price on hotels, airline tickets, even car rentals. When booking a room, always **call the hotel's local toll-free number** (if one is available) rather than the central reservations number—you'll often get a better price. Always ask about special packages or corporate rates.

➤ AIRLINE TICKETS: ☎ 800/AIR–4LESS.

➤ HOTEL ROOMS: **Accommodations Express** (☎ 800/444–7666, WEB www.accommodationsexpress.com). **Players Express Vacations** (☎ 800/458–6161, WEB www.playersexpress.com). **RMC Travel** (☎ 800/245–5738, WEB www.rmcwebtravel.com). **Turbotrip.com** (☎ 800/473–7829, WEB www.turbotrip.com).

PACKAGE DEALS

Don't confuse packages and guided tours. When you buy a package, you travel on your own, just as though you had planned the trip yourself. Fly/drive packages, which combine airfare and car rental, are often a good deal.

ECOTOURISM

Although neither the Bureau of Land Management (BLM) nor the National Park Service has designated any particular parts of the Rockies to be endangered ecosystems, many areas are open only to hikers; vehicles, mountain bikes, and horses are banned. It is wise to respect these closures, as well as the old adage—**leave only footprints, take only pictures.** Recycling is taken seriously throughout the Rockies and you will find yourself very unpopular if you litter or fail to recycle your cans and bottles (locals can be strident about protecting their wilderness).

All archaeological artifacts, including rock etchings and paintings, are protected by Federal law and must be left untouched and undisturbed.

➤ CONTACTS: **U.S. Bureau of Land Management** (☎ 303/239–3600). **National Park Service** (☎ 800/436–7275).

GAY & LESBIAN TRAVEL

Most resort towns are gay-friendly. Events of note are Gay Ski Week, held in Aspen every January; Boulder's Gay and Lesbian Film Festival in November; and PrideFest parades in most larger cities. For details about the gay and lesbian scene, consult *Fodor's Gay Guide to the USA* (available in bookstores everywhere).

➤ GAY- & LESBIAN-FRIENDLY TRAVEL AGENCIES: **Different Roads Travel** (✉ 8383 Wilshire Blvd., Suite 902, Beverly Hills, CA 90211, ☎ 323/651–5557 or 800/429–8747, FAX 323/651–3678, lgernert@tzell.com). **Kennedy Travel** (✉ 314 Jericho Turnpike, Floral Park, NY 11001, ☎ 516/352–4888 or 800/237–7433, FAX 516/354–8849, WEB www.kennedytravel.com). **Now Voyager** (✉ 4406 18th St., San Francisco, CA 94114, ☎ 415/626–1169 or 800/255–6951, FAX 415/626–8626, WEB www.nowvoyager.com). **Skylink Travel and Tour** (✉ 1006 Mendocino Ave., Santa Rosa, CA 95401, ☎ 707/546–9888 or 800/225–5759, FAX 707/546–9891, WEB www.skylinktravel.com), serving lesbian travelers.

GUIDEBOOKS

Plan well and you won't be sorry. Guidebooks are excellent tools—and you can take them with you. You may want to check out the individual *Compass American Guides* to Colorado, Idaho, Montana, Utah, and Wyoming, which are thorough on culture and history, and include color photographs.

For hikers, a good guidebook for the specific region you plan to explore—no matter how well marked the trails are—can be extremely helpful. Most hikers' guidebooks provide fairly detailed trail descriptions, including length and elevation gains and recommended side trips.

➤ HIKING GUIDEBOOKS: **Adventurous Traveler Bookstore** (☎ 802/860–6667 or 800/282–3963). **Falcon Books** (☎ 800/725–8303). **The Mountaineers** (✉ 300 3rd Ave. W, Seattle, WA 98119, ☎ 206/284–6310). **Sierra Club Books** (✉ 85 2nd St., 4th floor, San Francisco, CA 94105, ☎ 415/977–5500).

HOLIDAYS

Major national holidays include New Year's Day (January 1); Martin Luther King, Jr., Day (third Monday in January); President's Day (third Monday in February); Memorial Day (last Monday in May); Independence Day (July 4); Labor Day (first Monday in September); Thanksgiving Day (fourth Thursday in November); Christmas Eve and Christmas Day (December 24 and 25); and New Year's Eve (December 31). Businesses in major cities generally close on these holidays, but resort town retailers often stay open to serve vacationers.

INSURANCE

The most useful travel-insurance plan is a comprehensive policy that includes coverage for trip cancellation and interruption, default, trip delay, and medical expenses (with a waiver for preexisting conditions).

Without insurance you will lose all or most of your money if you cancel your trip, regardless of the reason. Default insurance covers you if your tour operator, airline, or cruise line goes out of business. Trip-delay covers expenses that arise because of bad weather or mechanical delays. Study the fine print when comparing policies.

Always **buy travel policies directly from the insurance company**; if you buy them from a cruise line, airline, or tour operator that goes out of business you probably will not be covered for the agency or operator's default, a major risk. Before making any purchase, **review your existing health and home-owner's policies** to find what they cover away from home.

➤ TRAVEL INSURERS: In the United States: **Access America** (✉ 6600 W. Broad St., Richmond, VA 23230, ☎ 800/284–8300, FAX 804/673–1491, WEB www.etravelprotection.com), **Travel Guard International** (✉ 1145 Clark St., Stevens Point, WI 54481, ☎ 715/345–0505 or 800/826–1300, FAX 800/955–8785, WEB www. travelguard.com).

FOR INTERNATIONAL TRAVELERS

For information on customs restrictions, *see* Customs & Duties.

CAR TRAVEL

Highways are well paved. Interstate highways—limited-access, multilane highways whose numbers are prefixed by "I-"—are the fastest routes. Interstates with three-digit numbers encircle urban areas, which may have other limited-access expressways, freeways, and parkways as well. Tolls may be levied on limited-access highways. So-called U.S. highways and state highways are not necessarily limited-access but may have several lanes.

Along larger highways, roadside stops with rest rooms, fast-food restaurants, and sundries stores are well spaced. State police and tow trucks patrol major highways and lend assistance. If your car breaks down on an interstate, pull onto the shoulder and wait for help, or have your passengers wait while you walk to an emergency phone. If you carry a cell phone, dial *55, noting your location on the small green roadside mileage markers.

Bookstores, gas stations, convenience stores, and rest stops sell maps (about $3) and multiregion road atlases (about $10).

CURRENCY

The dollar is the basic unit of U.S. currency. It has 100 cents. Coins include the copper penny (1¢); the silvery nickel (5¢), dime (10¢), quarter (25¢), and half-dollar (50¢); and the golden $1 coin, replacing a now-rare silver dollar. Bills are denominated $1, $5, $10, $20, $50, and $100, all green and identical in size; designs vary. The exchange rate at press time was US$.50 per Australian dollar, US$1.48 per British pound, US$.64 per Canadian dollar, and US$.91 per Euro.

ELECTRICITY

The U.S. standard is AC, 110 volts/60 cycles. Plugs have two flat pins set parallel to each other.

EMERGENCIES

For police, fire, or ambulance, **dial 911** (0 in rural areas).

INSURANCE

Britons and Australians need extra medical coverage when traveling overseas.

➤ INSURANCE INFORMATION: In Australia: **Insurance Council of Australia** (✉ Level 3, 56 Pitt St., Sydney, NSW 2000, ☎ 02/9253–5100, FAX 02/9253–5111, WEB www.ica.com.au). In Canada: **RBC Insurance** (✉ 6880 Financial Dr., Mississauga, Ontario L5N 7Y5, Canada, ☎ 905/816–2400 or 800/668–4342 in Canada, FAX 905/816–2498, WEB www.royalbank.com). In New Zealand: **Insurance Council of New Zealand** (✉ Level 7, 111–115 Customhouse Quay, Box 474, Wellington, New Zealand, ☎ 04/472–5230, FAX 04/473–3011, WEB www.icnz.org.nz). In the United Kingdom: **Association of British Insurers** (✉ 51–55 Gresham St., London EC2V 7HQ, U.K., ☎ 020/7600–3333, FAX 020/7696–8999, WEB www.abi.org.uk).

MAIL & SHIPPING

You can buy stamps and aerograms and send letters and parcels in post offices. Stamp-dispensing machines can occasionally be found in airports, bus and train stations, office buildings, drugstores, and the like. You can also deposit mail in the stout, dark blue, steel bins at strategic locations everywhere and in the mail chutes of large buildings; pickup schedules are posted.

For mail sent within the United States, you need a 34¢ stamp for first-class letters weighing up to 1 ounce (23¢ for each additional ounce) and 21¢ for domestic postcards. For overseas mail, you pay 80¢ for 1-ounce airmail letters, 70¢ for airmail postcards, and 35¢ for surface-rate postcards. For Canada and Mexico you need a 60¢ stamp for a 1-ounce letter and 50¢ for a postcard. For 70¢ you can buy an aerogram—a single sheet of lightweight blue paper that folds into its own envelope, stamped for overseas airmail.

To receive mail on the road, have it sent c/o General Delivery at your destination's main post office (use the correct five-digit zip code). You must pick up mail in person within 30 days and show a driver's license or passport.

PASSPORTS & VISAS

When traveling internationally, **carry your passport** even if you don't need one (it's always the best form of I.D.) and **make two photocopies of the data page** (one for someone at home and another for you, carried separately from your passport). If you lose your passport, promptly call the nearest embassy or consulate and the local police.

Visitor visas are not necessary for Canadian citizens, or for citizens of Australia and the United Kingdom who are staying fewer than 90 days.

➤ AUSTRALIAN CITIZENS: **Australian Passport Office** (☎ 131–232). **U.S. Office of Australia Affairs** (⌂ MLC Centre, 19-29 Martin Pl., 59th floor, Sydney, NSW 2000, Australia).

➤ CANADIAN CITIZENS: **Passport Office** (☎ 819/994–3500; 800/567–6868 in Canada).

➤ NEW ZEALAND CITIZENS: **New Zealand Passport Office** (☎ 04/494–0700 for application procedures; 0800/225–050 in New Zealand for application-status updates). **U.S. Office of New Zealand Affairs** (⌂ 29 Fitzherbert Terr., Thorndon, Wellington, New Zealand).

➤ U.K. CITIZENS: **London Passport Office** (☎ 0870/521–0410) for application procedures and emergency passports. **U.S. Consulate General** (⌂ Queen's House, Queen St., Belfast BTI 6EO, Northern Ireland). **U.S. Embassy Visa Branch** (⌂ 5 Upper Grosvenor Sq., London W1A 1AE, U.K.); send a self-addressed, stamped envelope. **U.S. Embassy Visa Information Line** (☎ 01891/200–290).

TELEPHONES

All U.S. telephone numbers consist of a three-digit area code and a seven-digit local number. Within most local calling areas, dial only the seven-digit number. Within the same area code, dial "1" first. To call between area-code regions, dial "1" then all 10 digits; the same goes for calls to numbers prefixed by "800," "888," and "877"—all toll-free. For calls to numbers preceded by "900" you must pay—usually dearly.

For international calls, dial "011" followed by the country code and the local number. For help, dial "0" and ask for an overseas operator. The country code is 61 for Australia, 64 for New Zealand, 44 for the United Kingdom. Calling Canada is the same as calling within the United States. Most local phone books list country codes and U.S. area codes. The country code for the United States is 1.

For operator assistance, dial "0." To obtain someone's phone number, call directory assistance, 555–1212 or occasionally 411 (free at public phones). To have the person you're calling foot the bill, phone collect; dial "0" instead of "1" before the 10-digit number.

At pay phones, instructions are usually posted. Usually you insert coins in a slot (25¢–35¢ for local calls) and wait for a steady tone before dialing. When you call long-distance, the operator will tell you how much to insert; prepaid phone cards, widely available in various denominations, are easier. Call the number on the back, punch in the card's personal identification number when prompted, then dial your number.

LODGING

Accommodations in the Rockies vary from the very posh resorts in ski areas such as Vail, Aspen, Sun Valley, and Jackson Hole, to basic chain hotels and independent motels. Dude and guest ranches often require a one-week stay, and the cost is all-inclusive. Bed-and-breakfasts can be found throughout the Rockies.

The lodgings we list are the cream of the crop in each price category. We always list the facilities that are available—but we don't specify whether they cost extra: When pricing accommodations, always ask what's included and what costs extra. Properties indicated by an ✕⊡ are lodging establishments whose restaurant warrants a special trip.

Assume that hotels operate on the **European Plan** (EP, with no meals) unless we specify that they use either the **Continental Plan** (CP, with a Continental breakfast), **Breakfast Plan** (BP, with a full breakfast) or the **Modified American Plan** (MAP, with breakfast and dinner), or the **Full American Plan** (FAP, with all meals).

General InformationColorado Hotel and Lodging Association (⊠ 999 18th St., Suite 1240, Denver, CO 80202, ☎ 303/297–8335). **Idaho Division of Travel Promotion** (⊠ Idaho Department of Commerce, 700 W. State St., Boise, ID 83720, ☎ 800/ 635–7820). **Travel Montana** (⊠ Department of Commerce, 1424 9th Ave., Helena, MT 59620, ☎ 406/ 444–2654; 800/548–3390 in Montana; 800/847–4868 nationwide). **Utah Hotel and Lodging Association** (⊠ 9 Exchange Pl., Suite 115, Salt Lake City, UT 84114, ☎ 801/359– 0104). **Wyoming Division of Tourism** (⊠ I–25 at College Dr., Cheyenne, WY 82002, ☎ 307/777–7777 or 800/ 225–5996).

APARTMENT & VILLA RENTALS

If you want a home base that's roomy enough for a family and comes with cooking facilities **consider a furnished rental.** These can save you money, especially if you're traveling with a group. Home-exchange directories sometimes list rentals as well as exchanges. Also see the A to Z sections at the end of state chapters for local business that arrange cabin, house, and condo rentals.

➤ INTERNATIONAL AGENTS: **Hideaways International** (⊠ 767 Islington St., Portsmouth, NH 03801, ☎ 603/ 430–4433 or 800/843–4433, FAX 603/ 430–4444, WEB www.hideaways.com; membership $129).

B&BS AND INNS

Charm is the long suit of these establishments, which generally occupy a restored older building with some historical or architectural significance. They're generally small, with fewer than 20 rooms. Breakfast is usually included in the rates.

➤ INFORMATION: **Bed & Breakfast Inns of Utah** (⊠ Box 2639, Park City, UT 84060, FAX 801/595–0332, WEB www.bbin.com). **Distinctive Inns of Colorado** (⊠ Box 10472, Colorado Springs, CO 80932, ☎ 800/866–0621, WEB www.bedandbreakfastinns.org). **Montana Bed & Breakfast Association** (⊠ 5557 U.S. 93 S, Somers, MT 59932, ☎ 800/453–8870, WEB www .mtbba.com). **Montana Innkeepers Association** (⊠ Box 1272, Helena, MT 59624, ☎ 406/449–8408, WEB www.visitmt.worldres.com).

CAMPING

Camping is invigorating and inexpensive. Colorado, Idaho, Montana, Utah, and Wyoming are full of state and national parks and forests with sites that range from rustic (pit toilets and cold running water), to campgrounds with bathhouses with hot showers, paved trailer pads that can accommodate even jumbo RVs, and full hookups. Fees vary, from $6 to $10 a night for tents and up to $21 for RVs, but are usually waived once the water is turned off for the winter.

Sometimes site reservations are accepted, and then only for up to seven days (early birds reserve up to a year in advance); more often, they're not. Campers who prefer a more remote setting may camp in the backcountry; it's free but you might need a permit, available from park visitor centers and ranger stations. If you're visiting in summer, **plan well ahead.**

The facilities and amenities at privately operated campgrounds are usually more extensive (swimming pools are common), reservations are more widely accepted, and nightly fees are higher: $7 and up for tents, $23 for RVs.

➤ INFORMATION: *The National Parks: Camping Guide* (Superintendent of Documents, ⊠ U.S. Government Printing Office, Washington, DC 20402; $3.50; ☎ 800/365–2267).

GUEST RANCHES

If the thought of sitting around a campfire after a hard day on the range makes your heart beat faster, consider playing dude on a guest ranch. These range from wilderness-rimmed working ranches that accept guests and encourage them to pitch in with chores and other ranch activities to luxurious resorts on the fringes of a small city, with an upscale clientele, swimming pools, tennis courts, and a lively roster of horse-related activities such as breakfast rides, moonlight rides, and all-day trail rides. Rafting, fishing, tubing, and other activities are usually available; at working ranches, you even may be able to participate in a cattle roundup. In winter, cross-country skiing and snowshoeing keep you busy. Lodgings can run the gamut from charmingly rustic cabins to the kind of deluxe quarters you expect at a first-class hotel. Meals may be gourmet or plain but hearty. Many ranches offer packages and children's and off-season rates. The various state tourism offices also have information on dude ranches. *See* Dude Ranches *in* Outdoor Activities & Sports.

➤ INFORMATION: **Colorado Dude/ Guest Ranch Association** (⊠ Box 2120, Granby, CO 80446, ☎ 970/ 887–3128). **Dude Ranchers' Association** (⊠ Box F-471, LaPorte, CO 80535, ☎ 970/223–8440). **Idaho Guest and Dude Ranch Association** (⊠ HC 72 K, Cascade, ID 83611, ☎ 208/382–4336 or 208/382–3217). **Old West Dude Ranch Vacations** (⊠ c/o American Wilderness Experience, 10055 Westmoor Dr., #215, Westminster, CO 80021, ☎ 303/444– 2622 or 800/444–3833).

HOME EXCHANGES

If you would like to exchange your home for someone else's, **join a home-exchange organization,** which will send you its updated listings of available exchanges for a year and will include your own listing in at least one of them. It's up to you to make specific arrangements.

➤ EXCHANGE CLUBS: **HomeLink International** (⊠ Box 47747, Tampa, FL 33647, ☎ 813/975–9825 or 800/ 638–3841, ℻ 813/910–8144, WEB www.homelink.org; $106 per year). **Intervac U.S.** (⊠ Box 590504, San Francisco, CA 94159, ☎ 800/756– 4663, ℻ 415/435–7440, WEB www. intervacus.com; $93 yearly fee includes one catalog and on-line access).

HOSTELS

Hostelling through the Rockies is an inexpensive way to see the vast mountains, especially since many hostels are located in resort towns and near National Parks. The only problem is that they are few and far between, with only one or two in every state but Colorado, which has 10 in such prime locations as Crested Butte, Breckenridge, and Glenwood Springs.

No matter what your age, you can **save on lodging costs by staying at hostels.** In some 4,500 locations in more than 70 countries around the world, Hostelling International (HI), the umbrella group for a number of national youth-hostel associations, offers single-sex, dorm-style beds and, at many hostels, rooms for couples and family accommodations. Membership in any HI national hostel association, open to travelers of all ages, allows you to stay in HI-affiliated hostels at member rates; one-year membership is about $25 for adults ($30 in Australia, C$26.75 in Canada, $30 in New Zealand, and £9.30 in the United Kingdom); hostels run about $10–$25 per night. Members have priority if the hostel is full; they're also eligible for discounts around the world, even on rail and bus travel in some countries.

HI is also an especially helpful organization for road cyclists.

➤ ORGANIZATIONS: **Hostelling International—American Youth Hostels**

(✉ 733 15th St. NW, Suite 840, Washington, DC 20005, ☎ 202/783–6161, FAX 202/783–6171, WEB www.hiayh.org). **Hostelling International—Canada** (✉ 400–205 Catherine St., Ottawa, Ontario K2P 1C3, Canada, ☎ 613/237–7884; 800/663–5777 in Canada, FAX 613/237–7868, WEB www.hostellingintl.ca). **Youth Hostel Association Australia** (✉ 10 Mallett St., Camperdown, NSW 2050, Australia, ☎ 02/9565–1699, FAX 02/9565–1325, WEB www.yha.com.au). **Youth Hostel Association of England and Wales** (✉ Trevelyan House, 8 St. Stephen's Hill, St. Albans, Hertfordshire AL1 2DY, U.K., ☎ 0870/870–8808, FAX 01727/844126, WEB www.yha.org.uk). **Youth Hostels Association of New Zealand** (✉ Level 3, 193 Cashel St., Box 436, Christchurch, New Zealand, ☎ 03/379–9970, FAX 03/365–4476, WEB www.yha.org.nz).

HOTELS

Most big-city hotels cater to business travelers, with such facilities as restaurants, cocktail lounges, swimming pools, exercise equipment, and meeting rooms. Room rates usually reflect the range of amenities offered. Most cities also have less expensive hotels that are clean and comfortable but have fewer facilities. A new accommodations trend is the all-suite hotel, which gives you more room for the money; examples include Courtyard by Marriott and Embassy Suites. In resort towns, hotels are decidedly more deluxe, with every imaginable amenity in every imaginable price range; rural areas generally offer simple, and sometimes rustic, accommodations.

Many properties offer special weekend rates, sometimes up to 50% off regular prices. However, these deals are usually not extended during peak summer months, when hotels are normally full. The same discounts generally hold true for resort town hotels in the off-seasons.

All hotels listed have private bath unless otherwise noted.

➤ TOLL-FREE NUMBERS: **Best Western** (☎ 800/528–1234, WEB www.bestwestern.com). **Choice** (☎ 800/221–2222, WEB www.choicehotels.com). **Colony** (☎ 800/777–1700, WEB www.colony.com). **Comfort** (☎ 800/228–5150, WEB www.comfortinn.com). **Days Inn** (☎ 800/325–2525, WEB www.daysinn.com). **Doubletree and Red Lion Hotels** (☎ 800/222–8733, WEB www.doubletree.com). **Embassy Suites** (☎ 800/362–2779, WEB www.embassysuites.com). **Fairfield Inn** (☎ 800/228–2800, WEB www.marriott.com). **Hilton** (☎ 800/445–8667, WEB www.hilton.com). **Holiday Inn** (☎ 800/465–4329, WEB www.basshotels.com). **Howard Johnson** (☎ 800/654–4656, WEB www.hojo.com). **Hyatt Hotels & Resorts** (☎ 800/233–1234, WEB www.hyatt.com). **La Quinta** (☎ 800/531–5900, WEB www.laquinta.com). **Marriott** (☎ 800/228–9290, WEB www.marriott.com). **Radisson** (☎ 800/333–3333, WEB www.radisson.com). **Ramada** (☎ 800/228–2828, WEB www.ramada.com). **Sheraton** (☎ 800/325–3535, WEB www.starwoodhotels.com). **Westin Hotels & Resorts** (☎ 800/228–3000, WEB www.westin.com).

MOTELS

The once-familiar roadside motel is fast disappearing from the American landscape. In its place are chain-run motor inns at highway intersections and in rural areas off-the-beaten path. Some of these establishments offer very basic facilities; others provide restaurants, swimming pools, and other amenities.

➤ MOTEL CHAINS: **Motel 6** (☎ 800/466–8356). **Quality Inn** (☎ 800/228–5151). **Rodeway Inns** (☎ 800/228–2000). **Shilo Inn** (☎ 800/222–2244). **Super 8 Motels** (☎ 800/800–8000). **Travelodge** (☎ 800/578–7878).

RESORTS

Ski towns throughout the Rockies are home to dozens of resorts in all price ranges; the activities lacking in any individual property can usually be found in the town itself—in summer as well as winter. Off the slopes, there are both wonderful rustic and luxurious resorts in the national parks: Jackson Lake Lodge and Jenny Lake Lodge in Grand Teton National Park, and Old Faithful Lodge in Yellowstone.

MONEY MATTERS

First-class hotel rooms in Denver, Salt Lake City, Boise, Missoula, and Cheyenne cost from $75 to $175 a night, although some "value" hotel rooms go for $40–$60, and, as elsewhere in the United States, rooms in national budget chain motels go for around $40 nightly. Weekend packages, offered by most city hotels, cut prices up to 50% (but may not be available in peak winter or summer seasons). As a rule, costs outside cities are lower, except in the deluxe resorts. In cities and rural areas, a cup of coffee costs between 50¢ and $1, the price for a hamburger runs between $3 and $5, and a beer at a bar generally is between $1.50 and $3; expect to pay double in resort towns. Prices throughout this guide are given for adults. Substantially reduced fees are almost always available for children, students, and senior citizens. For information on taxes, *see* Taxes.

CREDIT CARDS

Throughout this guide, the following abbreviations are used: **AE**, American Express; **D**, Discover; **DC**, Diners Club; **MC**, MasterCard; and **V**, Visa.

➤ REPORTING LOST CARDS: **American Express** (☎ 800/528–4800). **Discover** (☎ 800/347–2683). **MasterCard** (☎ 800/307–7309). **Visa** (☎ 800/847–2911).

NATIONAL PARKS

Look into discount passes to save money on park entrance fees. The National Parks Pass ($50) gets you and your companions free admission to all parks for one year. (Camping and parking are extra.) A percentage of the proceeds from sales of the pass will fund National Parks projects. Both the Golden Age Passport ($10), for those 62 and older, and the Golden Access Passport (free), for travelers with disabilities, entitle holders to free entry to all national parks, plus 50% off fees for the use of many park facilities and services. You must show proof of age and of U.S. citizenship or permanent residency (such as a U.S. passport, driver's license, or birth certificate) and, if requesting Golden Access, proof of disability. The Golden Age and Golden Access passes are available at all national parks wherever entrance fees are charged. The National Parks Pass is available by mail or through the Internet.

➤ PASSES BY MAIL: **National Park Service** (✉ National Park Service/Department of Interior, 1849 C St. NW, Washington, DC 20240, ☎ 202/208–4747, WEB www.nps.gov). **National Parks Pass** (✉ 27540 Ave. Mentry, Valencia, CA 91355, ☎ 888/GO–PARKS, WEB www.nationalparks.org).

OUTDOOR ACTIVITIES & SPORTS

The Rockies is one of America's greatest playgrounds, and many area residents make exercise a high priority. Within an hour of leaving their homes and offices, Rockies jocks can do their thing in the midst of exquisite scenery—not boxed in at a gym watching ceiling-mounted televisions.

ADVENTURE TRIP OUTFITTERS

Many trip organizers specialize in only one type of activity; however, a few companies guide a variety of active trips. (In some cases, these larger companies also act essentially as a clearinghouse or agent for smaller trip outfitters.) Be sure to sign on with a reliable outfitter; getting stuck with a shoddy operator can be disappointing, uncomfortable, and even dangerous. Some sports—whitewater rafting and mountaineering, for example—have organizations that license or certify guides, and you should be sure that the guide you're with is properly accredited.

➤ OUTFITTER LISTINGS: **America Outdoors** (✉ Box 10847, Knoxville, TN 37939, ☎ 423/558–3597 or 800/524–4814, WEB www.americaoutdoors.org). **Colorado Outfitters Association** (✉ Box 1949, Rifle, CO 81650, ☎ 970/876–0543, WEB www.coloradooutfitters.org). **Idaho Outfitters and Guides Association** (✉ Box 95, Boise, ID 83701, ☎ 208/342–1919, WEB www.ioga.org). **Montana Board of Outfitters** (✉ 111 N. Jackson St., Helena, MT 59620, ☎ 406/444–3738). **Utah Travel Council** (✉ 300 N. State St., Salt Lake City, UT 84114, ☎ 801/

538–1030, WEB www.utah.com).
**Wyoming Outfitters and Guides
Association** (✉ Box 2284, Cody,
WY 82414, ☎ 307/527–7453,
WEB www.wyoga.org).

➤ OUTFITTERS: **American Wilderness
Experience** (✉ 10055 Westmoor Dr.,
#215, Westminster, CO 80021, ☎
800/444–0099, WEB www.gorp.com).
Sierra Club Outings (✉ 85 2nd St.,
San Francisco, CA 94105, ☎ 415/
977–5500, WEB www.sierraclub.org).
The World Outdoors (✉ 2840
Wilderness Pl. F, Boulder, CO 80301,
☎ 303/413–0938 or 800/488–8483,
WEB www.theworldoutdoors).

BIKING

High, rugged country puts a premium
on fitness. Even if you can ride 40 mi
at home without breaking a sweat,
you might find yourself struggling
terribly on steep climbs and in elevations often exceeding 10,000 ft. If you
have an extended tour in mind, you
might want to come a couple of days
early to acclimate yourself to the
altitude and terrain. Pretrip conditioning is likely to make your trip
more enjoyable.

On tours where the elevation may
vary 4,000 ft or more, the climate can
change dramatically. Although the
valleys may be scorching, high-mountain passes may still be lined with
snow in summer. Pack clothing accordingly. (Bicycle racers often stuff
newspaper inside their jerseys when
descending from high passes to shield
themselves from the chill.) Although
you shouldn't have much problem
renting a bike (trip organizers can
usually arrange rentals), it's a good
idea to bring your own pair of sturdy,
stiff-bottom cycling shoes to make
riding easier, and your own helmet.
Some experienced riders bring not
only their own shoes but their pedals
if they use an interlocking shoe-and-
pedal system. If you do decide to
bring your own bike, be prepared to
spend as much as $150 in special
luggage handling. Summer and early
fall are the best times to plan a trip; at
other times, snow and ice may still
obstruct high-terrain roads and trails.

Guided bike trips generally range in
price between $80 and $150 a day,
depending on lodging and meals. The
Adventure Cycling Association is
perhaps the best general source of
information on biking in the Rockies—including detailed maps and
information on trip organizers. They
also guide trips stretching along the
Continental Divide. Hostelling-Inter-
national (HI; ☞ Lodging) is a good
connection for cycling tours as well.
Also, when you're in a ski resort town,
check if lifts service mountain bikes.
Remember that biking is not permitted
in National Wilderness areas.

For serious road riders, especially
would-be racers, the Carpenter/Phin-
ney Bike Camps are conducted in
Summit County and near Boulder in
Colorado by 1984 Olympic road
champion Connie Carpenter and her
husband, Davis Phinney, also an
Olympic medalist and professional
racer. One-week sessions focus on
riding technique, training methods,
and bicycle maintenance.

➤ CONTACTS: **Adventure Cycling
Association** (✉ Box 8308, Missoula,
MT 59807, ☎ 406/721–1776
or 800/755–2453, WEB www.
adventurecycling.org). **Carpenter/
Phinney Bike Camps** (☎ 303/442–
2371, WEB www.bikecamp.com).
**Kaibab Mountain Outfitters and
Cyclery** (✉ Box 339, Moab, UT
84532, ☎ 800/451–1133). **Timberline Adventures** (✉ 7975 E. Harvard, Suite J, Denver, CO 80231,
☎ 303/759–3804 or 800/417–2453).

DUDE RANCHES

Most dude ranches don't require any
previous experience with horses,
although a few working ranches
reserve weeks in spring and fall—
when the chore of moving cattle is
more intensive than in summer—for
experienced riders. No special equipment is necessary, although if you
plan to do much fishing, you're best
off bringing your own tackle (some
ranches have tackle to loan or rent).
Be sure to check with the ranch for a
list of items you might be expected to
bring. If you plan to do much riding,
a couple of pairs of sturdy pants,
boots, a wide-brimmed hat to shield
you from the sun, and outerwear as
protection from the possibility of rain
or chill should be packed. Expect to

spend at least $125 per day. Depending on the activities you engage in, as well as accommodations, the price can exceed $250 a day. *See* Guest Ranches *in* Lodging, as well.

FISHING

Field and Stream magazine is a leading source of information on fishing travel, technique, and equipment. For lists of guides to various rivers and lakes of the Rockies, contact the state tourism departments.

Fishing licenses, available at tackle shops and a variety of local stores, are required in all Rocky Mountain states. The fishing season may vary from state to state, and from species to species. A few streams are considered "private" streams, in that they are privately stocked by a local club, other rivers are fly-fishing or catch-and-release only, so be sure you **know the rules before making your first cast.** Tribal fishing licences are necessary on reservation land.

Rocky Mountain water can be cold, especially at higher elevations and especially in spring and fall (and winter, of course). You'd do well to **bring waterproof waders** or buy them when you arrive in the region. Outfitters and some tackle shops rent equipment, but you're best off bringing your own gear. Lures are another story, though: Whether you plan to fish with flies or other lures, local tackle shops can usually give you a pretty good idea of what works best in a particular region, and you can buy accordingly.

In the mid-1990s, whirling disease—a parasitic infection that afflicts trout—began to reduce fish populations in some Rocky Mountain streams dramatically. Efforts to curb the spread of the disease have met with some success, but some waters are still suffering from a smaller fish population.

A guide will cost about $250 per day and can be shared by two anglers if they are fishing from a boat and possibly by three if they are wading. Lunch will probably be included and flies might be, although there may be an extra $15–$20 charge for these.

Orvis Fly Fishing Schools runs one of the most respected fishing instructional

programs in the country and endorses other instructional programs. Summertime 2½-day programs take place in Evergreen, Colorado, and Coeur d'Alene, Idaho.

➤ INFORMATION AND LICENSES: **Colorado Division of Wildlife** (⌧ 6060 Broadway, Denver, CO 80216, ☎ 303/297–1192, WEB www.wildlife.state.co.us). **Idaho Department of Fish and Game** (⌧ Box 25, 600 S. Walnut St., Boise, ID 83707, ☎ 208/334–3700, WEB www2.state.id.us/fishgame). **Montana Department of Fish, Wildlife, and Parks** (⌧ 1420 E. 6th St., Helena, MT 59620, ☎ 406/444–2535, WEB www.fwp.state.mt.us). **Utah Division of Wildlife Resources** (⌧ 1596 W. North Temple St., Salt Lake City, UT 84116, ☎ 801/538–4700, WEB www.nr.utah.gov/dwr/dwr.htm). **Wyoming Game and Fish Department** (⌧ 5400 Bishop Blvd., Cheyenne, WY 82006, ☎ 307/777–4600, WEB www.gf.state.wy.us).

➤ INSTRUCTION: **Bud Lilly's Trout Shop** (⌧ 39 Madison Ave., Box 530, West Yellowstone, MT 59758, ☎ 406/646–7801 or 800/854–9559, WEB www.budlilys.com). **Jan's Mountain Outfitters** (⌧ 1600 Park Ave., Box 280, Park City, UT 84060, ☎ 801/649–4949 or 800/745–1020, WEB www.jans.com). **Orvis Fly Fishing Schools** (☎ 800/239–2074 ext. 784, WEB www.orvis.com). **Telluride Outside** (⌧ 1982 W. Rte. 145, Box 685, Telluride, CO 81435, ☎ 970/728–3895 or 800/831–6230, WEB www.tellurideoutside.com).

GROUP TRIPS

Group sizes for organized trips vary considerably, depending on the organizer and the activity. Often, if you are planning a trip with a large group, trip organizers or outfitters will sometimes offer discounts of 10% and more, and are willing to customize trips. For example, if you're with a group specifically interested in photography or in wildlife, trip organizers have been known to get professional photographers or naturalists to join the group. Recreating as a group gives you leverage with the organizer, and you should use it.

One way to travel with a group is to join an organization before going. Conservation-minded travelers might want to contact the Sierra Club, a nonprofit organization, which offers both vacation and work trips. Hiking trails tend to be maintained by volunteers (this is more often done by local hiking clubs). Park or forest rangers are the best source of information for groups involved in this sort of work.

Individuals or groups wanting to test their mettle can learn wilderness skills through "outdoor schools."

➤ CONTACTS: **Boulder Outdoor Survival School** (✉ Box 1590, Boulder, CO 80305, ☎ 303/444–9779 or 800/335–7404, WEB www.boss-inc.com). **National Outdoor Leadership School** (✉ 288 Main St., Lander, WY 82520, ☎ 307/332–5300, WEB www.nols.edu). **Sierra Club** (✉ 85 2nd St., San Francisco, CA 94105, ☎ 415/977–5500, WEB www.sierraclub.org).

HIKING

See Guidebooks for guidebook sources. *Backpacker* magazine (Rodale Press) is the leading national magazine that focuses on hiking and backpacking and each region in the Rockies has great local publications on places to hike. Organized-trip costs can be as little as $30 a day.

➤ CONTACT: **American Hiking Society** (✉ Box 20160, Washington, DC 20041, ☎ 301/565–6704, WEB www.americanhiking.org).

KAYAKING

The streams and rivers of the Rockies tend to be better suited to kayaking than canoeing. Steep mountains and narrow canyons usually mean fast-flowing water in which the maneuverability of kayaks is a great asset. A means of transport for less experienced paddlers is the inflatable kayak. Central Idaho and southern Colorado and Utah are where the best rivers for kayaking are found. Cascade Kayak School features Idaho river trips and instruction, including special kid's classes, by former world-class competitors and coaches. Dvorak Expeditions (☞ Rafting) leads trips on the rivers of southwestern Colorado, Idaho, Wyoming, and eastern Utah and conducts clinics, including certification courses, for kayakers of all abilities. River Travel Center (☞ Rafting) arranges trips in Idaho and Utah, among other destinations.

To minimize environmental impact as well as ensure a sense of wilderness privacy (riverside campgrounds are often limited to one party per night), a reservation policy is used for many rivers of the West. Often, the reserved times—many of the *prime* times—are prebooked by licensed outfitters, limiting your possibilities if you're planning a self-guided trip. For those rivers with restricted-use policies, it's best to reserve through a guide company several months or more in advance. Also, try to be flexible about when and where to go; you might find that the time you want to go is unavailable, or you may find yourself closed out altogether from your river of choice. If you insist on running a specific river at a specific time, your best bet is to sign on with a guided trip (which will cost at least $100 a day).

Outfitters provide life jackets and, if necessary, paddles and helmets; they often throw in waterproof containers for cameras, clothing, and sleeping bags. Bring bug repellent as well as a good hat, sunblock, and warm clothing for overnight trips. The sun on the river can be intense, but once it disappears behind canyon walls, the temperature can drop 30° or more. The best footwear is either a pair of water-resistant sandals or old sneakers.

➤ INSTRUCTION AND TRIPS: **Cascade Kayak School** (✉ Rte. 1, Box 117-A, Horseshoe Bend, ID 83629, ☎ 800/292–7238, WEB www.cascaderaft.com).

MAPS

If you plan to do much traveling where trails might not be well marked or maintained, you'll need maps and a compass. Topographical maps are sold in well-equipped outdoor stores (REI or Eastern Mountain Sports, for example). Maps in several different scales are available from the U.S. Geological Survey. Before ordering, you will need to request the free index and catalog, from which you can order the specific maps you need. Many local camping, fishing, and hunting stores carry U.S.G.S. and other detailed maps of the surrounding region.

The U.S. Forest Service and the BLM also publish useful maps.

➤ MAPS: **U.S. Geological Survey** (✉ Distribution Center, Box 25286, Federal Center, Denver, CO 80225, ☎ 303/202–4700 or 888/275–8747).

PACK TRIPS AND HORSEBACK RIDING

Horsemanship is not a prerequisite for most trips, but it is helpful. If you aren't an experienced rider (and even if you are), you can expect to experience some saddle discomfort for the first day or two. If you're unsure of how much of this sort of thing you can put up with, sign up for a shorter trip (one to three days) before taking on an adventure of a week or longer. Another option is to spend a few days at a dude or guest ranch to get used to life in the saddle, then try a shorter, overnight pack trip organized by the ranch.

Clothing requirements are minimal. A sturdy pair of pants, a wide-brim sun hat, and outerwear to protect against rain are about the only necessities. Ask your outfitter for a list of items you'll need. You might be limited in the gear (extra clothing) or luxuries (alcoholic beverages) an outfitter will let you bring along. Trip costs typically range between $120 and $180 per day.

Pack trips tend to be organized by local outfitters or ranches rather than national organizations. Local chambers of commerce can usually provide lists of outfitters who work in a particular area.

➤ OUTFITTERS: **All Round Ranch** (✉ Box 153, Jenson, UT 84035, ☎ 800/603–8069, FAX 435/798–5902, WEB www.allaroundranch.com). **Glacier Wilderness Guides** (✉ Box 535, West Glacier, MT 59936, ☎ 800/521–7238, FAX 406/387–5656, WEB www.glacierguides.com). **Rocky Mountain Outdoor Center** (✉ 10281 Hwy. 50, Howard, CO 81233, ☎ 800/255–5784, FAX 719/942–3215, WEB www.americanadventure.com).

RAFTING

Unless you are an expert, **pick a recognized outfitter** if you're going into white water. Even then, you should be a good swimmer and in solid general health. Different companies are licensed to run different rivers, although there may be several companies working the same river. Some organizers combine river rafting with other activities: pack trips, mountain-bike excursions, extended hikes, fishing.

"Raft" can mean any of a number of things: an inflated raft in which passengers do the paddling; an inflated raft or wooden dory in which a licensed professional does the work; a motorized raft on which some oar work might be required. Be sure you know what kind of raft you'll be riding—or paddling—before booking a trip. Day trips typically run between $30 and $60 per person. Expect to pay between $80 and $120 per day for multiday trips. Raft Utah publishes a comprehensive directory with full descriptions of all of Utah's rivers, and the outfitters who run them.

➤ OUTFITTER LISTINGS: **Colorado River Outfitters Association** (✉ CROA, c/o Johnson Communications, 730 Burbank St., Broomfield, CO 80020, ☎ 303/280–2554, WEB www.croa.org). **Raft Utah** (☎ 800/200–1160). **River Travel Center** (✉ Box 6, Point Arena, CA 95468, ☎ 800/882–7238, WEB www.rivers.com).

➤ OUTFITTERS: **Adrift Adventures** (✉ Box 192, Jensen, UT 84035, ☎ 800/824–0150). **ARTA River Trips** (✉ 24000 Casa Loma Rd., Groveland, CA 95321, ☎ 800/323–2782, WEB www.arta.org). **Dvorak Expeditions** (✉ 17921 U.S. 285, Nathrop, CO 81236, ☎ 800/824–3795, WEB www.dvorakexpeditons.com). **ECHO: The Wilderness Company** (✉ 6529 Telegraph Ave., Oakland, CA 94609, ☎ 510/652–1600 or 800/652–3246, WEB www.echotrips.com). **Glacier Raft Company** (✉ Box 210C, West Glacier, MT 59936, ☎ 406/888–5454 or 800/235–6781, WEB www.glacierraftco.com). **OARS** (✉ Box 67, Angels Camp, CA 95222, ☎ 800/346–6277, WEB www.oars.com).

ROCK CLIMBING AND MOUNTAINEERING

Before you sign on with any trip, be sure to clarify to the trip organizer your climbing skills, experience, and physical condition. Climbing tends to be a team sport, and overestimating your capabilities can endanger not only yourself but other team members. A fair self-assessment of your abilities also helps a guide choose an appropriate climbing route; routes (not unlike ski trails) are rated according to their difficulty. The way to a summit may be relatively easy or brutally challenging, depending on the route selected. You may want to get some instruction at a climbing wall before a trip to the Rockies.

Guide services usually rent such technical gear as helmets, pitons, ropes, and axes, and be sure to ask what equipment and supplies you'll need to bring along. (Outfitters usually rent equipment on a per-item, per-day basis.) Some mountaineering stores rent climbing equipment. As for clothing, temperatures can fluctuate dramatically at higher elevations. Bringing several thin layers of clothing, including a sturdy, waterproof/ breathable outer shell, is the best strategy for dealing with weather variations.

Organized trip costs can vary considerably, depending on group size, length of climb, instruction rendered, and equipment supplied. Count on spending at least $80 a day. However, the cost of a small-group multiday instructional climb can push $200 a day. The American Alpine Institute leads trips around the world, ranging from training climbs to expeditionary first ascents. It is one of the most respected climbing organizations in the country.

➤ INSTRUCTIONAL PROGRAMS AND OUTFITTERS: **American Alpine Institute** (⊠ 1515 12th St., N-4, Bellingham, WA 98225, ☎ 360/671–1505, WEB www.aai.cc). **Colorado Mountain School** (⊠ Box 1846, Estes Park, CO 80517, ☎ 970/586–5758, FAX 970/ 586–5798, WEB www.cmschool.com). **Exum School of Mountaineering** (⊠ Box 56, Moose, WY 83012, ☎ 307/ 733–2297, WEB www.exumguides. com). **Fantasy Ridge Alpinism** (⊠ Nugget Bldg., Suite 204, Box 1679, Telluride, CO 81435, ☎ 970/728– 3546). **Jackson Hole Mountain Guides** (⊠ Box 7477, Jackson, WY 83001, ☎ 800/239–7642, WEB www.jhmg.

com). **The Wilderness School** (⊠ 72 W. 500 North St., Orem, UT 84057, ☎ 801/221–0398, WEB www. highangletechnologies.com).

TOUR COMPANIES

Off The Beaten Path customizes trips within the Rockies that combine outdoor activities and learning experiences. Many trips cross the Montana-Wyoming border, but there are itineraries for Colorado and Utah as well. Timberline Adventures lead hiking and biking tours in the bigger national parks such as Glacier, Yellowstone, Zion, and Rocky Mountain National Park.

➤ CONTACTS: **Off The Beaten Path** (⊠ 27 E. Main St., Bozeman, MT 59715, ☎ 800/445–2995, FAX 406/ 587–4147, WEB www.offthebeatenpath. com). **Timberline Adventures** (⊠ 7975 E. Harvard, Suite J, Denver, CO 80231, ☎ 303/759–3804 or 800/417– 2453, WEB www.timberlinetours.com).

PACKING

Informality reigns here; jeans, sport shirts, and T-shirts fit in almost everywhere, for both men and women. The few restaurants and performing-arts events where dressier outfits are required, usually in resorts and larger cities, are the exception.

If you plan to spend much time outdoors, and certainly if you go in winter, **choose clothing appropriate for cold and wet weather.** Cotton clothing, including denim—although fine on warm, dry days—can be uncomfortable when it gets wet and when the weather's cold. A better choice is clothing made of wool or any of a number of new synthetics that provide warmth without bulk and maintain their insulating properties even when wet.

In summer, you'll want shorts during the day. But because early morning and night can be cold, and high passes windy, pack a sweater and a light jacket, and perhaps also a wool cap and gloves. Try layering—a T-shirt under another shirt under a jacket—and peel off layers as you go. For walks and hikes, you'll need sturdy footwear. To take you into the wilds, boots should have thick soles and plenty of ankle support; if your shoes are new and you plan to spend much time on the trail, break them in at home. Bring a day pack for short hikes, along with a canteen or water bottle, and don't forget rain gear, a hat, sunscreen, and insect repellent.

In winter, prepare for subzero temperatures with good boots, warm socks and liners, long johns, a well-insulated jacket, and a warm hat and mittens. Dress in layers so you can add or remove clothes as the temperatures fluctuate.

If you attend dances and other events at Native American reservations, dress conservatively—skirts or long pants for women, long pants for men—or you may be asked to leave.

When traveling to mountain areas, **remember that sunglasses and a sun hat are essential at high altitudes**; the thinner atmosphere requires sunscreen with a greater SPF than you might need at lower elevations.

In your carry-on luggage, **pack an extra pair of eyeglasses or contact lenses and enough of any medication** you take to last the entire trip. You may also ask your doctor to write a spare prescription using the drug's generic name, since brand names may vary from country to country. In luggage to be checked, **never pack prescription drugs or valuables.** To avoid customs delays, carry medications in their original packaging. And don't forget to carry with you the addresses of offices that handle refunds of lost traveler's checks. Check *Fodor's How to Pack* (available in bookstores everywhere) for more tips.

CHECKING LUGGAGE

You are allowed one carry-on bag and one personal article, such as a purse or a laptop computer. Make sure that everything you carry aboard will fit under your seat or in the overhead bin. Get to the gate early, so you can board as soon as possible, before the overhead bins fill up. Note that if you have a seat at the back of the plane, you'll probably board first, while the overhead bins are still empty.

If you are flying internationally, note that baggage allowances may be determined not by piece but by weight—generally 88 pounds (40 kilograms) in first class, 66 pounds (30 kilograms) in business class, and 44 pounds (20 kilograms) in economy.

Airline liability for baggage is limited to $1,250 per person on flights within the United States. On international flights it amounts to $9.07 per pound or $20 per kilogram for checked baggage (roughly $640 per 70-pound bag) and $400 per passenger for unchecked baggage. You can buy additional coverage at check-in for about $10 per $1,000 of coverage, but it excludes a rather extensive list of items, shown on your airline ticket.

Before departure, **itemize your bags' contents** and their worth, and label the bags with your name, address, and phone number. (If you use your home address, cover it so potential thieves can't see it readily.) Inside each bag, **pack a copy of your itinerary**. At check-in, **make sure that each bag is correctly tagged** with the destination airport's three-letter code. If your bags arrive damaged or fail to arrive at all, file a written report with the airline before leaving the airport.

PASSPORTS & VISAS

Idaho and Montana border Canada, and if you plan to enter Canada have the proper papers with you (☞ Car Travel, as well). Citizens and legal residents of the United States do not need a passport or a visa to enter Canada, but proof of citizenship (a birth certificate or valid passport) and some form of photo identification will be requested. Naturalized U.S. residents should carry their naturalization certificate. Permanent residents who are not citizens should carry their "green card." Citizens of the United Kingdom need only a valid passport to enter Canada for stays of up to six months.

The best time to apply for a passport or to renew is in fall and winter. Before any trip, check your passport's expiration date, and, if necessary, renew it as soon as possible.

SAFETY

Regardless of the outdoor activity or your level of skill, safety must come first. Remember: **know your limits!**

Many trails are at high altitudes, where oxygen is scarce. They're also frequently desolate. Hikers and bikers should **carry emergency supplies** in their backpacks. Proper equipment includes a flashlight, a compass, waterproof matches, a first-aid kit, a knife, and a light plastic tarp for shelter. Backcountry skiers should add a repair kit, a blanket, an avalanche beacon, and a lightweight shovel to their lists. Always **bring extra food and a canteen of water** as dehydration is a common occurrence at high altitudes. **Never drink from streams or lakes,** unless you boil the water first or purify it with tablets. Giardia, an intestinal parasite, may be present.

Always **check the condition of roads and trails, and get the latest weather reports** before setting out. In summer, **take precautions against heat stroke or exhaustion** by resting frequently in shaded areas; in winter, **take precautions against hypothermia** by layering clothing. Ultimately, proper planning, common sense, and good physical conditioning are the strongest guards against the elements.

ALTITUDE

You may feel dizzy and weak and find yourself breathing heavily—signs that the thin mountain air isn't giving you your accustomed dose of oxygen. Take it easy and **rest often for a few days until you're acclimatized.** Throughout your stay drink plenty of water and watch your alcohol consumption. If you experience severe headaches and nausea, see a doctor. It is easy—especially in Colorado, where highways climb to 12,000 ft and higher—to go too high too fast. The remedy for altitude-related discomfort is to go down quickly, into heavier air. Other altitude-related problems include dehydration and overexposure to the sun due to the thin air.

FLASH FLOODS

Flash floods can strike at any time and any place with little or no warning. The danger in mountainous terrain is piqued when distant rains are channeled into gullies and ravines, turning a quiet streamside campsite or wash into a rampaging torrent in seconds; similarly, desert terrain can become dangerous when heavy rains falls on land that is unable to absorb the water and thus floods quickly. Check weather reports before heading into the backcountry and be prepared to head for higher ground if the weather turns severe.

WILD ANIMALS

One of the most wonderful parts of the Rockies is the abundant wildlife. And while a herd of grazing elk or a bighorn sheep high on a hillside is most certainly a Kodak moment, an encounter with a bear or mountain lion is not. To avoid such an unpleasant situation while hiking, **make plenty of noise, keep dogs on a leash and small children between adults.** While camping, be sure to store all food, utensils, and clothing with food odors far away from your tent, preferably high in a tree (also far from your tent). If you do come across a bear or big cat, **do not run.** For bears, back away quietly; for lions, make yourself look as big as possible. In either case, be prepared to fend off the animal with loud noises, rocks, sticks, etc. And, like the saying goes, do not feed the bears—or any wild animals, whether they're dangerous or not.

When in any park, **give all animals their space and never attempt to feed any of them.** If you want to take a photograph, use a long lens rather than a long sneak to approach closely. This is particularly important for winter visitors. Approaching an animal can cause stress and affect its ability to survive the sometimes brutal climate. In all cases remember that the animals have the right-of-way; this is their home, you are the visitor.

SENIOR-CITIZEN TRAVEL

To qualify for age-related discounts, **mention your senior-citizen status up front** when booking hotel reservations (not when checking out) and before you're seated in restaurants (not when paying the bill). When renting a car, ask about promotional car-rental discounts, which can be cheaper than senior-citizen rates.

➤ EDUCATIONAL PROGRAMS: **Elderhostel** (✉ 11 Ave. de Lafayette, Boston, MA 02111-1746, ☎ 877/426–8056, FAX 877/426–2166, WEB www.elderhostel.org).

SHOPPING

While there are plenty of modern shopping malls across the Rockies, a trip through the West is an opportunity to buy authentic memorabilia and clothing—choose from cowboy boots, cowboy hats, bolero ties, and the like. It's also a great place to find Native American crafts. Small artisan colonies often neighbor ritzy resorts. These enclaves of creative souls produce some of the finest hand-crafted wares anywhere; look for local galleries and boutiques that showcase their work.

STUDENTS IN THE ROCKIES

➤ I.D.s & SERVICES: **Council Travel** (CIEE; ✉ 205 E. 42nd St., 15th floor, New York, NY 10017, ☎ 212/822–2700 or 888/268–6245, FAX 212/822–2699, WEB www.councilexchanges.org) for mail orders only, in the United States. **Travel Cuts** (✉ 187 College St., Toronto, Ontario M5T 1P7, Canada, ☎ 416/979–2406 or 800/667–2887, FAX 416/979–8167, WEB www.travelcuts.com).

TAXES

SALES TAX

Sales taxes are as follows: 2.9% in Colorado, 5% in Idaho, 4.75% in Utah, and 4% in Wyoming. Montana has no sales tax. Some areas have additional local sales and lodging taxes, which can be quite significant.

If you are crossing the border into Canada, be aware of Canada's goods and services tax (better known as the GST). This is a value-added tax of 7%, applicable on virtually every purchase except basic groceries and a small number of other items. Visitors to Canada, however, may **claim a full rebate of the GST** on any goods taken out of the country as well as on short-term accommodations. Rebates can be claimed either immediately on departure from Canada at participating duty-free shops or by mail within 60 days of leaving Canada. Rebate forms can be obtained from certain retailers, duty-free shops, customs officials, or by writing to Revenue Canada (☞ Customs & Duties). Purchases made during multiple visits to Canada can be grouped together

for rebate purposes. Instant cash rebates up to a maximum of $500 are provided by some duty-free shops when leaving Canada, and most provinces do not tax goods that are shipped directly by the vendor to the purchaser's home. Always **save your original receipts** from stores and hotels (not just credit-card receipts), and **be sure the name and address of the establishment is shown on the receipt.** Original receipts are not returned. To be eligible for a refund, receipts must total at least $200, and each individual receipt must show a minimum purchase of $50.

TELEPHONES

Cell phones are generally unreliable in the backcountry, especially in canyons and in remote locations where cell towers are not within reach.

AREA & COUNTRY CODES

The telephone area codes for the Rocky Mountain region are 303, 970, 720, and 719 for Colorado; 208 for Idaho; 406 for Montana; 801 and 435 for Utah; and 307 for Wyoming.

LOCAL CALLS

Pay telephones cost 35¢ for local calls. Charge phones, also common, may be used to charge a call to a telephone-company calling card or a credit card, or for collect calls.

Many hotels place a surcharge on local calls made from your room and include a service charge on long-distance calls. It may be cheaper for you to make your calls from a pay phone in the hotel lobby rather than from your room.

TIME

Idaho, Montana, Utah, and Wyoming are all in the Mountain Time Zone, as is most of Colorado. The southeastern portion of Colorado, east of the Rockies, is in the Central Time Zone. Mountain time is two hours earlier than Eastern time and one hour later than Pacific time. It is one hour earlier than Chicago, seven hours earlier than London, and 17 hours earlier than Sydney. Central time is one hour earlier than New York, two hours later than Los Angeles, six hours earlier than London, and 16 hours earlier than Sydney.

TIPPING

It is customary to tip 15% at restaurants; 20% in resort towns is increasingly the norm. For coat checks and bellman, $1 per coat or bag is the minimum. Taxi drivers expect 10% to 15%, depending on where you are. In resort towns, ski technicians, sandwich makers, coffee baristas, and the like also appreciate tips.

TOURS & PACKAGES

Because everything is prearranged on a prepackaged tour or independent vacation, you spend less time planning—and often get it all at a good price.

BOOKING WITH AN AGENT

Travel agents are excellent resources. But it's a good idea to collect brochures from several agencies as some agents' suggestions may be influenced by relationships with tour and package firms that reward them for volume sales. If you have a special interest, **find an agent with expertise in that area**; the American Society of Travel Agents (ASTA; ☞ Travel Agencies) has a database of specialists worldwide.

Make sure your travel agent knows the accommodations and other services of the place being recommended. Ask about the hotel's location, room size, beds, and whether it has a pool, room service, or programs for children, if you care about these. Has your agent been there in person or sent others whom you can contact?

Do some homework on your own, too: local tourism boards can provide information about lesser-known and small-niche operators, some of which may sell only direct.

BUYER BEWARE

Each year consumers are stranded or lose their money when tour operators—even large ones with excellent reputations—go out of business. So **check out the operator.** Ask several travel agents about its reputation, and try to **book with a company that has a consumer-protection program.** (Look for information in the company's brochure.) In the United States, members of the National Tour Association and the United States Tour Operators Association are required to set aside funds to cover your payments and travel arrangements in the event that the company defaults. It's also a good idea to choose a company that participates in the American Society of Travel Agents' Tour Operator Program (TOP); ASTA will act as mediator in any disputes between you and your tour operator.

Remember that the more your package or tour includes the better you can predict the ultimate cost of your vacation. Make sure you know exactly what is covered, and **beware of hidden costs.** Are taxes, tips, and transfers included? Entertainment and excursions? These can add up.

➤ Tour-Operator Recommendations: **American Society of Travel Agents** (☞ Travel Agencies). **National Tour Association** (NTA; ⊠ 546 E. Main St., Lexington, KY 40508, ☎ 859/226–4444 or 800/682–8886, WEB www.ntaonline.com). **United States Tour Operators Association** (USTOA; ⊠ 342 Madison Ave., Suite 1522, New York, NY 10173, ☎ 212/599–6599 or 800/468–7862, FAX 212/599–6744, WEB www.ustoa.com).

TRAIN TRAVEL

Amtrak connects the Rockies to both coasts and all major American cities, with trains that run through Boise, Salt Lake City, Cheyenne, and Denver, and other stops in between. Amtrak trains also run through northern Montana, with stops in Essex and Whitefish, near Glacier National Park. Connecting bus services to Yellowstone National Park are provided in the summer from Amtrak's stop in Pocatello, Idaho.

Canada's passenger service, VIA Rail Canada, stops at Jasper, near the Canadian entrance to Waterton/Glacier International Peace Park.

➤ Contacts: **Amtrak** (☎ 800/872–7245, WEB www.amtrak.com). **VIA Rail Canada** (☎ 800/561–3949).

SCENIC TRAIN TRIPS

Several Rocky Mountain states have restored unused stretches of track and refurbished turn-of-the-20th-century touring cars. These give you the chance to scout out places beyond the reach of any four-lane freeway.

The American Orient Express Railway Company operates several trips—including one that visits a few national parks—aboard its luxury cars.

The Colorado Railroad Museum has details on journeys to Pikes Peak on the highest cog railway in the world, and the celebrated Durango & Silverton narrow-gauge mining-train trip along the Animas River.

On the Heber Valley Historic Railroad in Utah, you can catch the *Heber Creeper*, a turn-of-the-20th-century steam engine train that rides the rails from Heber City across Heber Valley, alongside Deer Creek Reservoir, down Provo Canyon to Vivian Park.

➤ CONTACTS: **The American Orient Express Railway Company** (✉ 5100 Main St., Downers Grove, WA 60515, ☎ 206/441–2725 or 888/759–3944). **Colorado Railroad Museum** (✉ 17155 W. 44th Ave., Box 10, Golden, CO 80402, ☎ 800/365–6263, FAX 303/279–4229). **Heber Valley Historic Railroad** (✉ 450 S. 600 West St., Heber City, UT 84032, ☎ 435/654–5601).

TRAVEL AGENCIES

A good travel agent puts your needs first. Look for an agency that has been in business at least five years, emphasizes customer service, and has someone on staff who specializes in your destination. In addition, **make sure the agency belongs to a professional trade organization.** The American Society of Travel Agents (ASTA)—the largest and most influential in the field with more than 26,000 agents in some 170 countries—maintains and enforces a strict code of ethics and will step in to help mediate any agent-client disputes if necessary. ASTA (whose motto is "Without a travel agent, you're on your own") also maintains a Web site that includes a directory of agents. (If a travel agency is also acting as your tour operator, *see* Buyer Beware *in* Tours & Packages.)

➤ LOCAL AGENT REFERRALS: **American Society of Travel Agents** (ASTA; ✉ 1101 King St., Suite 200, Alexan-

dria, VA 22314 ☎ 800/965–2782 24-hr hot line, FAX 703/739–7642, WEB www.astanet.com). **Association of British Travel Agents** (✉ 68–71 Newman St., London W1T 3AH, U.K., ☎ 020/7637–2444, FAX 020/7637–0713, WEB www.abtanet.com). **Association of Canadian Travel Agents** (✉ 130 Albert St., Suite 1705, Ottawa, Ontario K1P 5G4, Canada, ☎ 613/237–3657, FAX 613/237–7052, WEB www.acta.net). **Australian Federation of Travel Agents** (✉ Level 3, 309 Pitt St., Sydney, NSW 2000, Australia, ☎ 02/9264–3299, FAX 02/9264–1085, WEB www.afta.com.au). **Travel Agents' Association of New Zealand** (✉ Level 5, Paxus House, 79 Boulcott St., Box 1888, Wellington 10033, New Zealand, ☎ 04/499–0104, FAX 04/499–0827, WEB www.taanz.org.nz).

VISITOR INFORMATION

➤ TOURIST INFORMATION: **Colorado Tourism Office** (✉ 1625 Broadway, #1700, Denver, CO 80202, ☎ 800/265–6723, WEB www.colorado.com). **Idaho Travel Council** (✉ Department of Commerce, 700 W. State St., Box 83720, Boise, ID 83720, ☎ 208/334–2470 or 800/635–7820, FAX 208/334–2175, WEB www.visitid.org). **Travel Montana** (✉ Department of Commerce, 1424 9th Ave., Helena, MT 59620, ☎ 406/444–2654 or 800/847–4868, FAX 406/444–1800, WEB www.visitmt.com or www.wintermt.com). **Utah Travel Council** (✉ Council Hall, Capitol Hill 300 North State St., Salt Lake City, UT 84114, ☎ 801/538–1030; 800/200–1160 for brochures; 801/521–8102 for ski reports, FAX 801/538–1399, WEB www.utah.com). **Wyoming Tourist Office** (✉ I–25 at College Dr., Cheyenne, WY 82002, ☎ 307/777–7777 or 800/225–5996, FAX 307/777–6904, WEB www.wyomingtourism.org).

WEB SITES

Do check out the World Wide Web when planning your trip. You'll find everything from weather forecasts to virtual tours of famous cities. Be sure to **visit Fodors.com** (www.fodors.com), a complete travel-planning site. You can research prices and book plane tickets, hotel rooms, rental cars, vacation packages, and more. In addition, you can post your pressing questions in the Travel Talk section. Other planning tools include a currency converter and weather reports, and there are loads of links to travel resources.

Also keep in mind that many towns, parks, and attractions have their own Web site, often jam-packed with pertinent information. Park sites are particularly helpful to read for safety precautions, as many Rocky Mountain area parks are true wilderness.

WHEN TO GO

Hotels in tourist destinations book up early, especially in July and August, and hikers crowd the backcountry from June through Labor Day. Temperatures rarely rise above the 80s.

Ski resorts buzz from December to early April, especially during Christmas and President's holiday weeks.

If you don't mind sometimes-capricious weather, spring and fall are opportune seasons to visit. Rates drop and crowds are nonexistent. You may even enjoy a corner of Yellowstone all to yourself. Spring's pleasures are somewhat limited, since snow usually blocks the high country well into June, and mountain-pass roads, such as the famous Going-to-the-Sun Road in Glacier National Park, stay closed into June. But spring is a good time for fishing, rafting on rivers swollen with snowmelt, bird-

ing, and wildlife-viewing. In fall, aspens splash the mountainsides with gold, and wildlife come down to lower elevations. The fish are spawning, and the angling is excellent.

CLIMATE

Summer in the Rockies begins in late June or early July. Days are warm, with highs often in the 80s, while nighttime temperatures fall to the 40s and 50s. Afternoon thunderstorms are common over the higher peaks. Fall begins in September, often with a week of unsettled weather around mid-month, followed by four–six gorgeous weeks of Indian summer—frosty nights and warm days. Winter creeps in during November, and deep snows have arrived by December. Temperatures usually hover near freezing by day, thanks to the surprisingly warm mountain sun, dropping considerably overnight, occasionally as low as -60°F. Winter tapers off in March, though snow lingers into April on valley bottoms and into July on mountain passes. The Rockies have a reputation for extreme weather, but that cuts two ways: No condition ever lasts for long.

➤ FORECASTS: **Weather Channel Connection** (☎ 900/932–8437), 95¢ per minute from a Touch-Tone phone.

What follows are the average daily maximum and minimum temperatures for the region.

ASPEN, CO

Jan.	33F	1C	May	64F	18C	Sept.	71F	22C
	6	−14		32	0		35	2
Feb.	37F	3C	June	73F	23C	Oct.	60F	16C
	8	−13		37	3		28	− 2
Mar.	42F	6C	July	80F	27C	Nov.	44F	7C
	15	− 9		44	7		15	− 9
Apr.	53F	12C	Aug.	78F	26C	Dec.	37F	3C
	24	− 4		42	6		8	−13

BOISE, ID

Jan.	37F	3C	May	71F	22C	Sept.	75F	24C
	21	− 6		44	7		46	8
Feb.	42F	6C	June	80F	27C	Oct.	64F	18C
	26	− 3		51	11		39	4
Mar.	53F	12C	July	89F	32C	Nov.	50F	10C
	33	1		57	14		30	− 1
Apr.	62F	17C	Aug.	87F	31C	Dec.	39F	4C
	37	3		55	13		24	− 4

HELENA, MT

Jan.	28F	– 2C	May	62F	17C	Sept.	66F	19C
	12	–11		41	5		44	7
Feb.	32F	0C	June	71F	22C	Oct.	55F	13C
	15	– 9		48	9		35	2
Mar.	42F	6C	July	80F	27C	Nov.	41F	5C
	23	– 5		53	12		24	– 4
Apr.	53F	12C	Aug.	78F	26C	Dec.	32F	0C
	33	1		53	12		17	– 8

SALT LAKE CITY, UT

Jan.	35F	2C	May	73F	23C	Sept.	78F	26C
	17	– 8		44	7		48	9
Feb.	41F	5C	June	82F	28C	Oct.	66F	19C
	24	– 4		51	11		39	4
Mar.	51F	11C	July	91F	33C	Nov.	48F	9C
	30	– 1		60	16		28	– 2
Apr.	62F	17C	Aug.	89F	32C	Dec.	39F	4C
	37	3		60	16		21	– 6

SHERIDAN, WY

Jan.	33F	– 1C	May	66F	19C	Sept.	71F	22C
	6	–14		39	4		41	5
Feb.	35F	2C	June	75F	24C	Oct.	60F	16C
	10	–12		48	9		30	– 1
Mar.	46F	8C	July	86F	30C	Nov.	46F	8C
	21	– 6		53	12		19	– 7
Apr.	55F	13C	Aug.	84F	29C	Dec.	35F	2C
	30	– 1		50	10		10	–12

FESTIVALS AND SEASONAL EVENTS

➤ DEC.: Christmas celebrations blanket most Rockies towns. For the holidays, many ski areas mount **torchlight parades,** with large groups of torch-bearing ski instructors tracing patterns down the mountainside. Contact specific resorts for details.

Colorado: Denver hosts the **World's Largest Christmas Lighting Display** (☎ 303/892–1112), with 40,000 floodlights washing civic buildings in reds, greens, blues, and yellows. Silverton searches for a yule log at its **Yule Log Celebration** (☎ 970/387–5522 or 800/752–4494). Georgetown hosts the **Christmas Market** (☎ 800/472–8230), a small-town Christmas fair with sleigh rides through town. The **Vail Festival of Lights** (☎ 970/479–1394) promotes a whole range of attractions, including Dickensian carolers, brilliant lighting displays, and Christmas ice-skating spectaculars.

Idaho: Sun Valley sparkles as a winter wonderland throughout the month of December with **Christmas in Sun Valley** (☎ 208/726–3423) festivities. The torchlight parade with the ski-school instructors is a decades-old tradition followed by fireworks on Christmas Eve. Sandpoint becomes "Santapoint" for the **Hometown Christmas** (☎ 208/263–0887), a 10-day festival of winter activities.

Montana: Bozeman's **Christmas Stroll** (☎ 406/586–4008) features sleigh rides, carolers, hot-chocolate stands, holiday lights, and late shopping hours.

Utah: Salt Lake City's show is the **Christmas Lights** ceremony (☎ 801/521–2822) at Temple Square.

Wyoming: Members of Company I, 3rd U.S. Volunteer Infantry and the museum at **Fort Caspar Historic Site** (☎ 307/235–8462) celebrate Christmas with candlelight tours.

➤ JAN.: *Colorado:* Denver's two-week **National Western Stock Show and Rodeo** (☎ 303/297–1166), the world's largest livestock show, is one of the month's big events. Ski celebrations such as the **Steamboat Springs**

Annual Cowboy Downhill (☎ 970/879–6111), the Aspen Winterskol (☎ 970/925–1940), and Breckenridge's Ullr Fest (☎ 970/453–6018) keep ski areas lively with races, torchlight skiing, and other events.

Idaho: Sandpoint Winter Carnival (☎ 208/263–0887) is a 10-day festival of winter activities. Winter Olympics Week (☎ 800/634–3347) in Sun Valley has celebrity ski racing, a food fair, and dances. McCall (☎ 208/634–7631) stages a huge winter carnival that stretches into February. You'll find world-class ice sculptures as well as the usual parades, dogsled races, and fireworks.

Utah: The annual Sundance Film Festival (☎ 801/225–4107 or 800/892–1600) based in Park City, lures film aficionados as well as industry executives to seminars, workshops, and previews of films from around the world.

Wyoming: Wild West Winter Carnival (☎ 800/325–2732 or 800/645–6233) at Boysen State Park, near Shoshoni, has dog races, a demolition derby, softball, and golf, all on ice, as well as snowmobile races, and a "snowdeo."

➤ FEB.: *Colorado:* Steamboat Springs hosts the oldest continuous Winter Carnival (☎ 970/879–0880) west of the Mississippi. Summit County is home to the Skijoring World Championships (☎ 970/668–2051). The Ice Fishing Contest (☎ 970/723–4600) in Walden consists of fishing on four lakes for the eight largest fish. Leadville puts on an Ice Fishing Derby (☎ 970/486–8363).

Idaho: The Lionel Hampton Jazz Festival (☎ 208/885–6765) in Moscow attracts some of the world's top jazz musicians.

Montana: Race to the Sky (☎ 406/442–4008 or 800/847–4868), in Helena, is a 350-mi, six-day dogsled race in mid-February that crisscrosses the Continental Divide at elevations of up to 7,000 ft.

Wyoming: On Presidents' Day weekend horses race down the track pulling two-wheel carts at the Donald E. Erickson Memorial Chariot Races (☎ 307/326–8855), near Saratoga.

➤ MAR.: *Colorado:* More than 70 tribes convene for the Denver Pow-wow (☎ 303/892–1112 or 800/393–8559) with Native American dancers, artisans, and musicians. Charity and celebrity events rope them in at many ski areas, including the Special Olympics Colorado's (☎ 303/592–1361) winter events at Copper Mountain. Jimmie Heuga's Ski Express for MS (☎ 970/926–1290 or 800/367–3101) raises money to fight Multiple Sclerosis. The charity event in Vail, the American Ski Classic (☎ 970/949–1999), is hosted by former president Gerald Ford.

Idaho: In Pocatello, the Dodge National Circuit Finals Rodeo (☎ 208/233–1525) draws the top two cowboys from each of 12 national circuits for four days of bareback-riding, roping, and steer-wrestling competitions.

Montana: Irish folk and other wearers of the green flock to Butte for one of the West's largest and most rollicking St. Patrick's Day (☎ 406/723–3177) parades and for other Irish-accented events. Collectors from around the world attend the C. M. Russell Auction of Original Western Art (☎ 406/761–6453 or 800/803–3351) held in Great Falls.

➤ APR.: *Colorado:* The ski towns of Aspen, Breckenridge, and Copper Mountain put on events to celebrate spring. A Taste of Vail (☎ 970/926–1494) showcases that area's superlative restaurants. The mountain bike racing event during the Fruita Fat Tire Festival (☎ 970/858–3894) lets riders experience the world famous Kokopelli Trail and the majestic Bookcliffs.

Idaho: The citywide Dogwood Festival (☎ 208/799–2243) in Lewiston features a rodeo, concerts, and plays.

Montana: The International Wildlife Film Festival (☎ 406/728–9380) in Missoula is one of two such film festivals in the world. The Rendezvous cross-country ski race (☎ 406/646–7701) attracts 700 skiers and an entourage 1,500 strong to the 50-km (and other) races at West Yellowstone.

Utah: The Jeep Safari (☎ 435/259–7625) during Easter week is a must-see event especially for 4X4 enthusiasts. Nearly 2,000 four-wheel-drive vehicles descend on Moab to challenge their driving skills on the backcountry roads that surround the area. The annual **Pond Skimming Competition** (what skiers and snowboarders do when the snow starts to melt) is held at The Canyons (☎ 888/226–9667), near Park City.

Wyoming: **Cowboy Songs and Range Ballads** (☎ 307/587–4771) in Cody includes concerts, jam sessions, and a symposium all about cowboy music.

➤ MAY: *Colorado*: The **Kinetic Conveyance Race** (☎ 303/444–5226, WEB www.kbco.com) draws crowds to the Boulder Reservoir to see whose kinetic contraption can slip over the land and slog through the water to win the race and the $1,000 booty. Top international runners, along with 45,000 ordinary citizens, race 10 km through the streets of town during Memorial Day's **Bolder Boulder** (☎ 303/444–7223, WEB www.bolderboulder.com). Square dancers, belly dancers, and classical string quartets provide sideline entertainment for about 100,000 spectators. Don't forget to register your rubber duck for the "Great Rubber Duck Race" if you go to the **Boulder Creek Festival** (☎ 303/449–3825; 303/413–7216 for duck race, WEB www.bouldercreekfestival.com) on Memorial Day weekend. The outdoor festival along Boulder Creek downtown offers art and crafts for sale, food, and live entertainment. In Fruita, **Mike the Headless Chicken Festival** (☎ 970/858–3894) throws together a microbrew festival, a chicken dance marathon, a 5-km race, and more fun and food.

Idaho: Sandpoint marks summer's beginning with a **Waterfest** (☎ 208/263–2161), including a sand-sculpture contest, a regatta, and waterskiing events. The entire town of Wallace, in north central Idaho's silver-mining district, is listed on the National Register of Historic Places, and the town's **Depot Day** (☎ 208/263–2161) celebrates Wallace's heritage with music and a car show in early May.

Montana: At the annual **Big Timber Bull-A-Rama** (☎ 406/932–6228 or 406/932–6697) the West's top bull

riders test their skills and spurs on 1,800-pound bucking-mad bulls. In Miles City, rodeo stock for the upcoming season is auctioned off at the **Bucking Horse Sale** (☎ 406/232–7700). The horses demonstrate their bucking prowess in rodeo competitions, and the event also features bull riding, a wild-horse race, and street dances. St. Ignatius hosts the **Buffalo Feast and Powwow** (☎ 406/745–2951) with three days of dancing and games capped by a free feast of pit-roasted buffalo. You can sample fine beers from Montana and the Northwest at the **Garden City Micro B.R.I.W. Fest** (☎ 406/721–6061) in Missoula.

Utah: Bring your boat and travel 184 mi down the Green River to the confluence of the Colorado River on the annual **Friendship Cruise** (☎ 435/564–8144, 435/564–3432, or 435/564–8227, WEB www.ecso.com/friendship). This two- to three-day event has been running for over 40 years.

Wyoming: The huge **Flaming Gorge Fishing Derby** (☎ 307/362–3771) in Rock Springs draws 350 teams of anglers. Dubois hosts **Pack Horse Races** (☎ 307/455–2556 or 307/455–2174) where teams break camp, pack up on horses, and run an obstacle course.

➤ JUNE: *Colorado*: The **Silly Home Built River Raft Race** (☎ 719/456–0453) held in Las Animas on the Arkansas River keeps spectators guessing which improbable floating contraptions will reach the finish line. The season of music festivals and cultural events gets into swing with Telluride's weekend-long **Bluegrass Festival** (☎ 800/624–2422), the **Aspen Music Festival** (☎ 970/925–3254), **Jazz Aspen** (☎ 970/920–4996) in Snowmass, and Breckenridge's **Genuine Jazz** (☎ 970/453–6018). **Steamboat's Annual Cowboy Roundup Days** (☎ 970/879–0880) combines rodeo events, a country-music festival, chili cook-off, a Cowboy Poetry gathering, and more. Glenwood Springs puts on **Strawberry Days** (☎ 970/945–6589). Grand Junction's **Country Jam** (☎ 800/530–3020) brings four days of country music and camp-outs during the third or fourth weekend of June. The **Food-Wine Classic** (☎ 970/925–1940) in Aspen is an epicurean extravaganza. Fort Collins's **Annual Colorado Brewers' Festival** (☎ 970/484–6500) comes to Old Town to show off the fermented products of 45 Colorado brewers. Boulder's **Colorado Shakespeare Festival** (☎ 303/492–0554), one of the three most popular Bard fests in the country, stages comedies and tragedies under the stars from mid-June through mid-August. Crested Butte's **Fat Tire Festival** (☎ 970/349–6817), held the third week in June, is an outstanding mountain biking event with guided tours, clinics, and a competitive cross-country race.

Idaho: The **Boise River Festival** (☎ 208/338–8887) has a nighttime parade with lit, animated floats; six stages of continuous entertainment; and 300 other events the last week of June. The **International Women's Challenge** (☎ 208/345–7223), statewide, is the nation's premier cycling race for women. Weiser's **National Old-Time Fiddlers Contest** (☎ 208/549–0452) draws the nation's best to compete.

Montana: The **Lewis and Clark Festival** (☎ 406/761–4434 or 800/735–8535) in Great Falls highlights the expedition across the West two centuries ago. Tours, kids' day camp, float trips, and courses mark the five-day event. On the third or fourth weekend in June, Great Falls puts on the **Montana Traditional Dixieland Jazz Festival** (☎ 406/771–1642). The **Augusta Rodeo** (☎ 406/562–3477) is one of the largest one-day rodeos in Montana and features the old-time Wild Cow Milking and parade. **Custer's Last Stand Reenactment** (☎ 406/665–3577 or 888/450–3577) in Hardin enlists more than 200 riders.

Wyoming: **Bozeman Trail Days** (☎ 307/684–7687 or 307/684–7629) has tours and programs about Bozeman Trail travel and Indian wars. On the third full weekend in June, competing lumberjacks make wood chips fly at the **Woodchoppers Jamboree & Rodeo** (☎ 307/326–8855) in Encampment.

Utah: At the **Utah Arts Festival** (☎ 801/322–2438), local, national, and international artists provide four days of entertainment in downtown Salt Lake City. From late June through October, the **Utah Shakespearean Festival** (☎ 435/586–7880 or 800/752–9849, WEB www.bard.org) is held at Southern Utah University in Cedar City. Lectures and seminars supplement the productions, puppet shows, and feasts. Three nights of PRCA rodeo, a parade, and wild West gunfights are all a part of the fun during **Butch Cassidy Days** (☎ 435/259–6226) in Moab.

➤ JULY: *Colorado:* Arts events galore run throughout July, including Winter Park's **Jazz and American Music Festivals** (☎ 970/726–4118), and Vail's **Bravo! Colorado Music Festival** (☎ 970/827–5700). In Denver, the **Cherry Creek Arts Festival** (☎ 303/355–2787, WEB www.cherryarts.org) is a juried outdoor arts festival held in early July. There are guided walks and a host of seminars on identification, photography, and cooking at Crested Buttes's **Wildflower Festival** (☎ 970/349–6438 or 800/545–4505).

Idaho: Thirty to forty hot-air balloons are a colorful sight over the mountains at the **Teton Valley Hot-Air Balloon Races** (☎ 208/354–2500) in Driggs, Idaho, around Independence Day. The **Snake River Stampede** (☎ 208/466–8497) in Nampa, just west of Boise, is one of the top 20 rodeos in the nation. The largest concentration of Basques in the United States has called southern Idaho home since the 1800s, and the small town of Gooding celebrates Basque heritage with music, dancing, and food during the **Gooding Basque Association Picnic** (☎ 208/934–4402 or 208/886–2982). The **Idaho Shakespeare Festival** (☎ 208/336–9221) in Boise runs all summer, presenting the bard's work under the stars. The **Festival at Sandpoint** (☎ 208/263–0887), the last two weeks of July and the first two weeks of August, is a celebration of music that includes classical, pop, and jazz. The **Sun Valley Ice Shows** (☎ 208/622–4111) feature former Olympians and professional figure skaters carving the ice from June through September.

Montana: The Grant-Kohrs National Historic Site in Deer Lodge, Montana, celebrates cowboy lore and skills during **Western Heritage Days** (☎ 406/846–2070 or 406/846–3388) with roping, branding, chuck-wagon cooking, and traditional cowboy music and poetry. And don't miss the **Montana State Fair** (☎ 406/727–8900) in Great Falls at the end of the month.

Utah: The **Railroaders Festival** (☎ 800/255–8824), held in Ogden, commemorates the completion of America's first transcontinental railroad. Pioneer Day is July 24th and a week of events surrounding it is called **Days of '47** (801/521–2822). Parades, rodeos, fireworks, and other festivities throughout the state celebrate the arrival of Mormons in the Salt Lake valley in 1847. At the end of the month, the **Festival of the American West** (☎ 800/225–3378), featuring Native American, mountain man, pioneer, and military reenactments and displays, is held at the American West Heritage Center in Cache Valley.

Wyoming: The old-fashioned **Cody Stampede** (☎ 307/587–5155 or 800/207–0744) in Buffalo Bill Cody's eponymous hometown is one of the Rockies' larger July 4th celebrations, complete with rodeos. The **Green River Rendezvous** (☎ 307/367–2242), near Pinedale, stages a reenactment of 1830s mountain life. For the king of outdoor rodeos, see the world's largest, **Cheyenne Frontier Days** (☎ 800/227–6336), in late July. For something in a more arty line, check out the **Grand Teton Music Festival** (☎ 307/733–1128) in Teton Village.

➤ AUG.: *Colorado*: Rodeos are typical late-summer fare; witness the **Pikes Peak or Bust Rodeo** (☎ 719/635–7506; 800/368–4748 outside the state) in Colorado Springs, Colorado's largest rodeo. Country fairs are also big business, especially Pueblo's star-studded **state fair** (☎ 800/876–4567). For more high-minded fare, Vail hosts the **International Festival of Dance** (☎ 970/949–1999 or 970/476–2918), set amid the wildflowers in the outdoor Ford Amphitheater. Other top music events include Denver's **Festival of Mountain and Plain: A Taste of Colorado** (☎ 303/295–6330) and Telluride's **Jazz Celebration** (☎ 970/728–7009). The **Wild Mushroom Festival**

(☎ 970/728–4431 or 800/525–3455) sponsors seminars on cooking and medicinal uses and forays into the woods around Telluride. Visitors from as far away as the East Coast and Alaska join the corn-eating contest and corn cook-off of the **Olathe Sweet Corn Festival** (☎ 877/858–6006, WEB www.olathesweetcornfest.com). Olathe lies between Grand Junction and Montrose on Highway 50.

Idaho: As common as rodeos this month are Native American events that showcase traditional songs, dances, and crafts, such as the **Shoshone-Bannock Indian Festival** (☎ 208/238–3700) in Fort Hall. The **Three Island Crossing** (☎ 208/366–2394), at Glenns Ferry on the first weekend in August, is a re-creation of the pioneers' treacherous Snake River crossing. Boise's **Western Idaho Fair** (☎ 208/376–3247) is the state's biggest and brings in a slate of nationally known entertainers. **Art on the Green** (☎ 208/664–3194), in Coeur d'Alene the first weekend in August, has arts, crafts, and dance and is one of Idaho's largest festivals.

Montana: The **Crow Fair and Rodeo** (☎ 406/638–2601) takes place in Crow Agency—the self-styled tepee capital of the world. The Crow Indian Reservation is off I–90, 45 mi southeast of Billings. At the **Montana Cowboy Poetry Gathering** (☎ 406/538–8278) in Lewiston, U.S. and Canadian performers share verses about a man and a horse following a cow.

Utah: During the first week of the month, quaff a frosty raspberry milk shake, and enjoy other lakeside food and fun during the **Bear Lake Raspberry Days** (☎ 800/448–2327). In Salt Lake City the **Belly Dancing Festival** (☎ 801/521–2822), held in a local park, is the largest outdoor Middle Eastern dance festival in the nation.

➤ SEPT.: *Colorado*: Major **film festivals** (☎ 970/925–6882, 970/453–6200, or 603/643–1255) take place in Aspen, Breckenridge, and Telluride. Estes Park's annual **Longs Peak Scottish/Irish Highland Festival** (☎ 970/586–6308 or 800/903–7837, WEB www.scotfest.com, www.irishscotfest.com) draws more than 60,000 visitors the weekend after Labor Day. Events include parades, clan and living history exhibits; seminars on Gaelic language; athletic, pipe band, and jousting competitions; folk concerts; and the *Ceilidh*—the Celtic New Year bash. Musical performances by well-known outfits such as the Royal Ulster Constabulary Pipe Band, the Royal Canadian Artillery Band, and the U.S. Air Force Honor Drill Team are perennial highlights. A bike tour of vineyards, grape stomping, wine tasting, entertainment, food from area chefs, and more are part of the **Colorado Mountain Wine Festival** (☎ 800/764–3667).

Idaho: You'll find lumberjack competitions at the **Clearwater County Fair and Lumberjack Days** (☎ 208/476–4335) in Orofino. **Idaho Spud Day** (☎ 208/357–3390) in Shelley sponsors the World Spud-Picking Championship. The **Nez Percé Cultural Day** (☎ 208/843–2261), in Spalding, celebrates Native American heritage. Bands from around the country come to the **Pocatello Dixieland Jamboree** (☎ 208/233–1525).

Montana: Libby's four-day **Nordicfest** (☎ 406/293–6430) celebrates Scandinavian food, costumes, music, dance, and crafts. The **Running of the Sheep** (☎ 406/326–2288) in Reedpoint is a surrealistic version of Pamplona's running of the bulls, with hundreds of sturdy Montana-bred woollies charging down Main Street. Seventeen species of raptors and magnificent golden eagles soar over the Bridger Mountains' knife-edge ridge during their southern migration. The **Bridger Raptor Festival** (☎ 406/585–1211) is arranged around the event.

Utah: The state's Native American, pioneer, and agricultural heritage are highlighted, along with big-name bands, during the **Utah State Fair** (☎ 801/538–8400) in Salt Lake City. The **Lotoja** (☎ 435/752–5131), a grueling bike race from Logan to Jackson Hole, Wyoming, follows a course through some of the most

spectacular scenery in the West. **Moab Music Festival** (☎ 435/259–7003, WEB www.moabmusicfestival.org) welcomes classical musicians from all over the world to play music throughout canyon country. Concerts are staged in a dome set amid the red-rock cliffs. The Colorado River Concert features a boat ride 33-mi downriver for a performance at the grotto. Eat all the watermelon you can stand—free—during Green River's **Melon Days** (☎ 435/564–3526). Talent shows, craft booths, square dancing, and a fiddling contest make up the old-fashioned American fun.

Wyoming: The **Jackson Hole Fall Arts Festival** (☎ 307/733–3316) marks the season with concerts, art, poetry, dance, and crafts workshops and lectures throughout the valley.

➤ OCT.: *Colorado*: Oktoberfests and harvest celebrations dominate October, most notably Carbondale's **Potato Days** (☎ 970/963–1890), and the **Cedaredge Applefest** (☎ 800/436–3041). The **Great American Beer Festival** (☎ 303/447–0816) in Denver is the country's largest beer fest, offering samples of more than 1,000 brews.

Idaho: The **Swing 'N' Jazz Jamboree** (☎ 208/726–3423) in Sun Valley presents both big-band and Dixieland music.

Montana: The four-day **Glacier Jazz Stampede** (☎ 406/758–2800) belts out ragtime, Dixieland, swing, modern and big band jazz in Kalispell.

➤ NOV.: *Colorado*: Look for Creede's **Chocolate Festival** (☎ 719/658–2374 or 800/327–2102), which puts chocolates of every size, shape, and description imaginable in every corner of the town.

Idaho: Steelhead are the quarry at Idaho's **Great Snake Lake Steelhead Derby** (☎ 208/743–3531 or 800/473–3543) in Lewiston.

1 DESTINATION: THE ROCKIES

Between a Rock and a High Place

What's Where

Pleasures and Pastimes

Fodor's Choice

BETWEEN A ROCK AND A HIGH PLACE

THE ROCKY MOUNTAINS DEFINE America, in both literal and symbolic ways. The sawtooth crest of the Rockies is the backbone of the continent—hence the Continental Divide—and emanating from it are many of America's great rivers, born from trickles of snowmelt that gradually join forces to flow east and west like veins feeding a single, massive organism.

The Rockies also demarcate a line where the East ends and the West begins, a line where old-world principles segue into a still simmering ethos of manifest destiny. From 40,000 ft in transcontinental flight, you can witness in the landscape the earmarks of a cultural transformation. To the east, the orderly mosaic of wheat fields and farmlands represents a rootedness in a stay-at-home, hard-work ethic. To the west, the vast and jumbled open spaces of Colorado, Utah, and Idaho—largely public lands, largely undeveloped—suggest in spirit (if not always in fact) that there is still room in the American Dream for the buffalo to roam and for the antelope to play.

And somewhere within the Rockies themselves resides the essential, unflagging soul of American ruggedness. The country may be hell-bent on urbanizing, modernizing, and multiplying, and in such Rocky Mountain cities as Denver and Salt Lake City urban sprawl may be spreading like an incurable pox. But that won't stop Americans from hanging on to an intuitive, collective belief in a land of rough-and-tumble vigor at the edge of the frontier. That's where the Rockies come in—rough-and-tumble geology still harboring the American frontier myth.

If there are three geographical features an American ought to see as a rite of citizenship, they are the Atlantic Ocean, the Pacific Ocean, and the Rocky Mountains. Seemingly as vast and mysterious as the oceans by virtue of their size, these big and beautiful mountains invoke a primordial spirit of wilderness and timelessness. The Rockies can inspire an appreciation that escapes logic, that comes on when alpenglow is the last light of day or when new snow highlights each feathered ledge in a band of rock cliffs. It occurs when the wild bloom of high-alpine meadows exceeds any fair description of color. The sentiment is something close to faith.

It is also something beyond accurate representation. On relief maps, the 2-billion-year-old Rockies are often drawn as a single string of mountains—forming blisters on the page—and are defined primarily by the dotted line of the Continental Divide. The plains are over and the mountains begin, and that's that.

But that's *not* that. The Rockies (and here things can get fuzzy, confused by which mountain ranges geologists choose to consider part of the Rockies) cut a swath several hundred miles wide in places and constitute multiple ranges and spurs, each with slightly or markedly differing characteristics. The Colorado Rockies are the highest of the bunch, with most peaks exceeding 14,000 ft, but ironically they might not seem so because the timberline (the point above which trees won't grow) is unusually high. In short, the Rockies aren't, as the maps might suggest, one big strip of interchangeable rock.

All of these ranges do, however, share a similar history. Uplift (the pressure inflicted by the movements and swelling of ancient oceans through aeons of time) preyed upon weaknesses in the land mass (weaknesses known appropriately if unsympathetically as "faults"); the land squeezed thus could go nowhere but *up*. Couple that phenomenon with volcanic activity and mountains were the result.

Thereafter came the sculpting effects of erosion, with water in various forms (ice, snow, rain, fog, and waterfalls) being the primary chisels. Over the long, long haul, the characteristic formations that we identify as elemental to mountain structure have taken shape: peaks, ridges, bowls, cirques, arêtes, scree slopes, and so on. On lower slopes, depending on the quality and availability of soil as well as the harshness of weather, trees have grown: mainly cottonwoods and aspens (or "quakies," as the cowboys dubbed them because of the shimmering illusion created by their leaves in the sun and wind); higher up, Douglas fir, lodgepole pine, and Engelmann spruce.

Although there are those rare events when the Earth shrugs and mountains heave with cataclysmic suddenness, the Rockies are essentially a stationary spectacle, or, as they appeared to settlers from the East in the 1800s, a stationary obstacle. One can only imagine the thoughts of the pioneers and railroaders on seeing the Rockies for the first time: a mix, presumably of awe and annoyance; inspired by the mountains' beauty yet flustered by the impending (and inevitable) difficulties in finding passage to the other side.

It is somewhat easier to tap the mind-set of prospectors who, after word spread of the discovery of the Comstock lode in western Nevada in the 1850s, came to the Rockies with visions of vast wealth. It's uncertain whether the mountains imposed a ruggedness on the miners and railroad workers, the vanguard of settlement in the Rockies, or whether it was the other way around. Probably a bit of both. These were rowdy men in a rugged country: Civil War deserters, ex-cons, bushwhackers, and miners whose previous claims had come up empty in California, Nevada, or British Columbia. As Glenn Chesney Quiett put it in *They Built the West,* "It was a rough, dangerous, dirty, sweating, hardworking, hard-drinking, free-spending life."

It was not a life made any more comfortable by Native American tribes residing in the mountains—the Cheyenne, the Crow, the Blackfoot, and others—whose homelands had been invaded by these interlopers pick-axing the countryside. Confrontations were numerous; Quiett relates one story in which the natives killed a man by lighting a bonfire on his chest, suggesting—quite obviously—that some natives were going around in very ill humor in regards to the whole idea of the white man's settlement.

Mining, railway construction, lawbreaking, opportunism: the early settlement of the Rockies began taking shape. The route of the railway dictated which Rocky Mountain outposts would become major cities and which wouldn't; that Denver, Colorado, rather than Cheyenne, Wyoming, became the central metropolis of the eastern slope of the Rockies was due largely

to politicking by Denver's business elite. It was due also to the paying of a hefty sum to the railroad for the right to have the rail route pass through town. Miners came, established towns, settled in (or some did, anyway), and left their mark and legacy. Indeed, towns that have become popular resorts in the latter half of the 20th century—Aspen, Breckenridge, and Telluride in Colorado and Park City in Utah, for example—have their roots in mining.

UNLIKE GEOLOGY IN ITS incomprehensible slowness, human activity in the Rockies has evolved and changed in a hurry. It has all transpired in little more than 100 years, which isn't even a hiccup's worth of geological time. As precious-metal mining has ebbed (due as much to a swoon in metal prices as a lack of ore) as a mainstay of the Rocky Mountain economy in the last few decades, a boom in tourism has more than filled the gap. Before the 1960s, visitors who spent time in the Rockies were likely to be bohemians, artists, die-hard sportsmen, and national-park visitors in Winnebagos and Airstreams; or passersby broken down in transit—axle busted en route to California and the American Dream. Today the region hosts families and tourists of all means.

As much as any single event in the region, the creation of Vail (the ski resort 100 mi west of Denver) in 1964 issued an evangelical message to the world that tourism in the Rockies was for everyone. In 1963, Vail was an empty valley; today it is a tourism machine generating hundreds of millions of dollars a year in summer and winter business, but not including real-estate turnover, which is hardly small potatoes. No wonder other Rockies resorts, following the Vail model in varying degrees, have sprung up since the mid-1960s to tap the mighty tourism dollar.

Anyone who spends any time in the Rockies is destined to be touched by the exquisite landscape supporting an intricately entwined network of ecosystems. The high Rockies are full of amazements; for example, on south-facing slopes in April, microscopic buds of wildflowers can be found incubating under shards of warm shale, while the snow on north-facing slopes is likely to be still several feet deep. The lesson here, miraculous as it is, is also quite simple: the land, severe as it is, takes care of itself. It regenerates all on its own. Things work. Unfortunately, once you accept the premise that you are in the presence of nature efficiently and dispassionately going about its own business— a premise that invariably comes in one form or another to anyone who visits or lives in the Rockies—you tend then to proceed to the next obvious question: What to do about it? Here, things turn troublesome.

IN THE LAST DECADE or so the Rocky Mountain states have become the political focus of land grabbers, tree huggers, civilization escapees, resort developers, ranchers, sportspeople, seasonal workers, and the "Hollywood element." Each group has its own sense of righteous propriety and feelings about how the land should be best managed. For whatever reason—and a sheer, alpine beauty comes immediately to mind—almost everyone who comes to the Rockies for any length of time develops an instinctive (if imagined) sense of aboriginal belonging. It's funny: you hear people who have spent barely a year or two of their lives in the Rockies talk wistfully of "the way things used to be," as if their families had lived there for generations. Such reminiscence, of course, implies an attitude about the way things *ought* to be. The upshot is a messy collision of territorial imperatives: each group is sure it *knows* what is best for the land, and how to defend it against the greed, shortsightedness, or harebrained thoughtlessness of others. This can lead to such wacky scenarios as ardent wildlife preservationists stalking hunters, who in turn are stalking animals, the idea being that when the hunter gets lined up for a shot, the preservationists make a holy racket, alerting the animal and averting the kill. It is environmental politics right out of *Caddyshack*.

The issues are impossibly, hopelessly complex. In simplest terms the question is: what's the proper formula for balancing the interest of people, the integrity of the land and its resources, and the needs of wildlife? It is a question inevitably muddled in morality, pragmatism, science, self-interest, and the indisputable fact that nobody really knows for sure. As yet, there is no single Grand Unifying Theory. The result, in part, has been a balkanized checkerboard: private land, wilderness areas, national parks, national forests, national monuments, state parks, state forests, wildlife preserves, Native American reservations. Tread carefully. The rules change from one land type to the next, and the borders aren't always obvious (except, mysteriously, to wild animals, who seem to know more accurately than surveyors where national-park borders are, and within which hunting is prohibited). For example, hunting and campfires are legal in national forests but not in national parks; some private landowners are good sports about rights of way, some charge fees, some will have you arrested for just contemplating trespassing. And so on.

When 323,291 acres of forest land burned in Yellowstone in the summer of 1988, fire control was a bitter issue: would it be better to allow a fire to burn its natural course, even if it might threaten wildlife and human settlements? Fire, the argument goes, is part of a forest's natural way of replenishing itself. Or would it be more correct to fight the fire with every resource at one's disposal, snuffing it out as quickly as possible?

Are mountain resorts scars upon the landscape, as some environmentalists might suggest, or nodes of economic sustenance producing, in most respects, less environmental hazard and impact than mining, ranching, or lumbering? Do visitors to the resorts simply overpopulate an environmentally sensitive region? Or, inspired by the beauty of the land, does their visiting heighten their own environmental sensitivity? And do they then pass that new sensitivity on to others?

The ultimate question is: Who knows?

Fortunately, the Rockies are still big country. There is a lot of room for people to do a lot of shouting, hand-wringing, and placard-waving without upsetting, in any measurable way, the balance of the universe. For all the shouting, for all the resort development that boomed in the '80s and '90s; for all the ranchers fencing in land and upsetting animal migratory patterns; for all the Hollywooders moving to Aspen or to Livingston, Montana, and wrecking the neighborhood, as some residents imply; for all the environmentalists militating against growth—for all of that, and above and beyond all of that, the Rockies remain relatively uncongested, undeveloped country, where the air above 12,000 ft is still clean.

The population density of Colorado, by far the most populous of the Rocky Mountain states, is about 42 people per square mile. Compare that, for example, with 217 people per square mile in California or more than 1,135 per square mile (gasp!) in New Jersey. There are more people living in the borough of Brooklyn, New York, than in the states of Idaho, Montana, and Wyoming combined.

Wandering around in these open spaces, one comes occasionally across the relics of human failure, most likely old mining encampments, now rotting and rusting on their slow way toward vanishing into total decay. They are small reminders that however abusive or misguided people are and have been in their use of this land, the land has the patience to heal itself. Patience that people, with life spans of infinitesimal shortness in geologic terms, can't fathom. If the mountains had a voice in all the land-management yakkety-yak, they would be saying something like: "We can wait. We don't care."

And in the shorter term, the Rockies have one other ace in the hole in withstanding the incursion of man: their own magisterial presence, their ruggedness. The Rockies were the last part of the country to be "settled" and may be the only part of the country that will never be broadly developed. One doesn't build cities on 40-degree slopes raked by rock slides and avalanches. The land is too severe and the growing seasons too short to sustain viable commercial cultivation (except, to some degree, timber crops). In other words, the high-mountain wilderness is a great place to visit but you wouldn't want to live there. And a great place, too, in the summer sun, when the thin air steals breath and the dust settles on old roads, to imagine an America still youthful and inchoate, at the edge of an unexplored frontier.

— Peter Oliver

WHAT'S WHERE

Colorado

With the Rocky Mountains as its enormous spine, and deep canyons carved by its three main rivers, Colorado is a state of sharp contrasts. The Colorado Rockies offer every possible skiing experience, from the glitter and gossip of Aspen to the skiing purism of Crested Butte. Denver, the Mile High City, has transformed its cow-town aura with a downtown arts district and bustling business centers. To the southwest is Black Canyon of the Gunnison National Park, whose walls narrow so severely that little sunlight can reach the bottom. At Mesa Verde the mysterious cliff dwellings of the ancestral Puebloan peoples excite the imagination. Near Colorado Springs stands Pikes Peak, the state's most indelible landmark. Katherine Lee Bates wrote "America the Beautiful" while gazing out from its summit.

Idaho

In Idaho, it often seems as if state creed dictates that there is no admittance unless you do something outdoors. Mountain biking, rock climbing, and skiing rank among the most popular pursuits, and the Gem State provides plenty of challenging terrain. That terrain, however, might not seem too hospitable at first. Southern Idaho's flat plains are broken by geysers, hot springs, sand dunes, and lava craters, along with taller-than-Niagara waterfalls and the great gash of the Snake River canyon. In contrast to these stark natural wonders are the plush Sun Valley ski resort and upwardly mobile Boise, with its wine bars, corporate headquarters, and stately mansions warmed by natural hot springs. Northern Idaho has its own extremes in Hells Canyon, a cleft even deeper (though narrower) than the Grand Canyon, and the Salmon River, the longest wild river left in the lower 48 states.

Montana

The moniker "Big Sky Country" only tells half the story; as the nation's fourth-largest state, Montana has the land to match. More than 30% of this land is publicly owned, making it a gold mine of national forests and parks. The best trout fishing in the country is found at the Yellowstone, Missouri, Madison, Beaverhead, Gallatin, and Bighorn rivers. Montana's mountainous western half bears the "Crown of the Continent," Glacier National Park, which retains vestiges of the great glaciers that scraped across this majestic landscape, leaving behind impressive lakes, waterfalls, and knife-edge ridges. East of the Continental Divide, rugged mountain country yields to the flowing plains and ranch land that inspired the name "Big Sky Country." The Divide marks a stark separation for more than just topography: ranching, conservative politics, hunting, and distrust of government regulation continue to dominate the way of life in eastern Montana's far-flung small towns, where locals consider the mountain-bike-and-espresso-set an aberration in their state. Western Montana is generally more liberal and recreation-oriented, with avid environmentalists battling those who strive to preserve the logging and mining economies that built the region's towns.

Utah

Few states can match Utah's topography. In the south, sculpted red-rock desert is showcased in five national parks. In the north, the Wasatch Range stretches from the Idaho border to central Utah and is peppered with ski and summer resorts. Most of Utah's major cities line the base of these mountains, including the capital, Salt Lake City, founded by Mormon pioneers in 1847. Salt Lake City still maintains strong religious ties. Far to the southeast, Moab, along the Colorado River, is headquarters for religion of another kind: mountain biking. With both history and adventure to offer statewide, Utah delivers a surprising blend of recreation and cultural charm.

Wyoming

For most people, Wyoming conjures up images of its northwestern area, dominated by Yellowstone National Park and the Grand Teton mountains. Yellowstone is recovering well from the fires of 1988, and visitors can examine first-hand the ecological renewal process. Not to be entirely outdone by its neighbor, the Teton range harbors one of America's most challenging ski resorts, Jackson Hole. In the southeastern corner of the state, Laramie and Cheyenne still possess a strong frontier flavor—even if they're no longer exactly "hell on wheels."

PLEASURES AND PASTIMES

Cycling

Mountain biking has a huge following in the Rockies and is more popular in the region than touring on paved roads. Moab, Utah, has become the mountain biker's mecca, with its fortuitous spreads of smooth sandstone, or slickrock, formations. (The Slickrock Trail has both a practice and a main loop.) For an expedition-length ride, the 100-mi White Rim Trail near Moab offers spectacular views of Canyonlands National Park. In Colorado, Crested Butte vies with Moab as the mountain biking center of the Rockies; the trip over the demanding Pearl Pass is supposedly how the biking craze originated. As for road cycling, the San Juan Mountains loop is as beautiful a ride as there is in the country. Valley roads tend to be clear of snow by mid- to late-April; roads and trails at higher elevations may not be clear until several months later and may be snow-covered again by early October.

The Montana-based Adventure Cycling Association has mapped interconnecting back roads, logging and forest-service roads, and trails stretching from Canada to Mexico. Few people, of course, ride the whole route, which covers close to 2,500 mi. But it's easy to pick a segment to suit any rider's stamina, thirst for challenge, or preferences in mountain scenery. While the route does follow, very approximately, the Continental Divide, the riding is not necessarily all big-mountain climbing and descending. Portions of the trip are negotiable by children as young as 10. The Adventure Cycling Association leads tours or can provide detailed maps (complete with lodging and/or camping options), information, and advice for self-guided trips.

Dining

In 1944, a Denver drive-in owner named Louis Ballast grilled a slice of cheese on top of a hamburger and became famous for patenting his invention, the cheeseburger. It has been suggested that Rocky Mountain cuisine consists of the three *B*s: beef, buffalo, and burritos. Although these items certainly will appear on menus throughout the region, restaurant chefs rise to the challenge and head to market to round out the offerings with seasonal and local specialties.

In addition to mouthwatering steak and tender lamb, this is prime hunting and fishing territory, so antelope, elk, venison, and grouse are no strangers to the Rockies palate. Rainbow trout, salmon, and bass pulled from someone's favorite (and maybe secret) fishing spot find their way onto almost every menu. Colorado's Rocky Mountain oysters (fried bull testicles) are famous—some would say infamous—for their size and taste.

On the savory side of things, Colorado's sugar-sweet Rocky Ford cantaloupe has passionate admirers. Utah's raspberries and cherries make incredible pies, and huckleberries from Montana or Idaho are used in everything from muffins to ice cream. Apples, peaches, and pears from roadside stands are deliciously tree-ripened. And don't forget about potatoes—natives will tell you that if it's not from Idaho, it's just a spud.

With such high-end resort towns as Vail and Aspen, Colorado's dining scene is quite sophisticated. Idaho and Wyoming reputedly have the best steaks; no ties are needed, as almost all establishments are casual—this holds true for Montana as well. Utah's fine restaurants are primarily centered in Salt Lake City and Park City. Microbreweries are enjoying increasing recognition throughout the area. Often located in or connected with a local pub, some of these breweries produce only enough specialty beers (called microbrews) for their own establishments. Colorado has more microbreweries than any other state, and some of their brews, such as Crested Butte's Fat Tire Ale, are available from regular beer outlets. Other strong entries in the microbrew market are Montana's Black Dog and Idaho's Table Rock.

Dude Ranches

Dude ranches fall roughly into two categories: working ranches and guest ranches. Working ranches, in which guests participate in such activities as roundups and cattle movements, sometimes require horsemanship experience. Guest ranches, with a wide range of activities in addition to horseback riding, rarely do. The slate of possible activities can vary widely from ranch to ranch. At most establishments,

guests will be given some taste of the working-ranch experience with demonstrations of rodeo skills and the like. Fishing tends to be given second priority, and after that, almost anything goes. At a typical dude ranch, guests stay in log cabins and are served meals family-style in a lodge or ranch house. Colorado, Utah, and Wyoming have ranches on both ends of the spectrum.

Fishing

Trout, whether they be cutthroat, brown, rainbow, Mackinaw, brook, or lake, are the prime game fish in the Rockies. This isn't exactly trophy-fish country, but what they lack in size they make up in volume, especially in stocked waters. Western Montana, the setting of Norman Maclean's fishing-permeated book *A River Runs Through It* and the subsequent film, is teeming with fishing holes along the Blackfoot, Madison, Gallatin, and Yellowstone rivers. Just over the state line in eastern Idaho, anglers in drift boats ply the water for trout at Henry's Fork. Silver Creek, a precious little stretch of spring water in the high country of south central Idaho's Picabo Desert, is revered among dry-fly anglers. Provo Canyon in Utah is also an excellent, if overhyped, fishing spot, and the Snake River in Wyoming has its own unique cutthroat trout strain. Only at Lake Pend Oreille in the far northern reaches of Idaho's Panhandle do anglers catch 30-pound Kamloops trout. Catercorner across the state, in the southeastern corner, is Bear Lake, the only place that Bonneville cisco, also known as Bear Lake sardines, call home. Folks head there with dip nets (it's the only place where net fishing is allowed in the state) for the winter runs.

Fishing licenses, ranging in term from daily to annual, are required in each state and are available in many convenience stores and sporting-goods shops. Local tackle shops are a good place to feel out a region's most effective lures. It's quite common to hire a knowledgeable guide or sign on with an outfitter for the best experience.

Hiking

There are literally thousands of miles of hiking trails in the Rockies. The national parks have particularly well-marked and well-maintained trails, and admittance to all trails is free. In fact, hiking is sometimes the only way to get close to certain highlights on protected land; for example, the famed Mesa Arch rock formation in Canyonlands National Park, Utah, can be reached only on foot. Hiking in the south is usually best in spring, when water is plentiful and before the heat of summer sets in. Primarily for safety reasons, overnight hikers are usually expected to register with park or forest rangers. Also keep in mind that run-ins with bears and mountain lions have become increasingly common, especially in northern regions.

Horse-Pack Trips

Horse-pack trips are a great way to visit the Rockies' backcountry, since horses can travel distances and carry supplies that would be impossible for hikers. Montana's Bob Marshall Wilderness is the perfect example; as the largest stretch of roadless wilderness in an already spacious state, a horse-packing trip is almost the only way to travel the huge expanses. Although horsemanship isn't required for most trips, it is helpful, and even an experienced rider can expect to be a little sore for the first few days. June through August is the peak period for horse-packing trips; before signing up with an outfitter, inquire about the skills they expect.

National Parks

Together, the Rocky Mountain states have a phenomenal amount of national-park land (not to mention the national monuments, national forests, and state parks). Most national parks are open 365 days a year and charge an entrance fee, which varies according to the kind of vehicle. Tight budgets and overcrowding are bringing changes to the national parks. Fees at some parks (such as Yellowstone and Grand Teton) have been increased substantially to raise funds for park upkeep.

COLORADO➤ Rocky Mountain National Park is home to 355 mi of hiking trails and sweeping vistas of high-country lakes, meadows, pine forests, alpine tundra, and snow-dusted peaks dotted with small glaciers. Trees grow at right angles, whipped into shape by high winds, and there are minuscule tundra versions of familiar wildflowers. Long's Peak, the highest point in the park, is a surprisingly accessible hike for those in good shape.

IDAHO➤ Unlike every other Rocky Mountain state, Idaho claims no national parks per se. The state does have its share of National Park Service properties and other nationally prominent places, though. Among those is the centerpiece of Hells Canyon National Recreation Area, a chasm even deeper than the Grand Canyon. The Main Salmon River and its Middle Fork are surrounded by the 2-million-acre Frank Church–River of No Return Wilderness Area, the largest such area in the lower 48 states. Selected as a training site for U.S. astronauts owing to its striking, lunarlike appearance, Craters of the Moon National Monument covers 83 square mi near Arco with black-lava spatter cones, caves, and other eerie volcanic-formed features. Other National Park Service properties include: Nez Percé National Historical Park, Hagerman Fossil Beds National Monument, and City of Rocks National Reserve.

MONTANA➤ Glacier National Park is dominated by the Continental Divide, where pure mountain streams form the headwaters of the Columbia and Missouri rivers. Glaciers, pine forests, craggy mountaintops, and lush meadows can all be seen from the serpentine Going-to-the-Sun Road, which provides dizzying views. The Crown of the Continent is one of the last grizzly bear territories; the park is also home to mountain goats, bighorn sheep, gray wolves, and more than 1,000 species of flowers. Montana also boasts the most awe-inspiring entryway to Yellowstone National Park; the Beartooth Scenic Highway has breathtaking views en route to the park's northeast corner.

UTAH➤ The southern half of this state holds five national parks. Arches National Park preserves a 73,378-acre fantasy landscape. Wind and water have eroded the red rock into more than 2,000 "windows" and freestanding arches, the largest collection of such formations in the world. Canyonlands National Park offers views down to the Green and Colorado rivers, as well as red-rock pinnacles, cliffs, and spires. Much of the park can be explored only on foot, or by mountain bike or four-wheel drive. In Capitol Reef National Park, a striated reeflike wall juts up 1,000 ft over ground level, with domelike features reminiscent of the U.S. Capitol building. Visitors can pick fruit at the park's large orchards, drive along the base of the "reef," or hike down the canyons to see the 1,000-year-old Fremont Petroglyphs. Bryce Canyon National Park is a series of natural amphitheaters and is famed for the pink-and-cream-color spires that reflect the sun's glow. Ebenezer Bryce, the Mormon settler for whom the park is named, is said to have exclaimed that the area was "a hell of a place to lose a cow!" Zion National Park, one of the nation's oldest national parks, is famous for its sheer, 2,500-ft-high sandstone walls and its complex desert ecology. The 147,000-acre park includes Zion Canyon and the Gateway to the Narrows, a squeak-through passageway carved by the Virgin River.

WYOMING➤ In the northwestern part of the state, just below Yellowstone National Park, is Grand Teton National Park. (Grand Teton, the highest peak in the Teton Range, was named by French-speaking trappers who thought the mountains resembled breasts.) A handful of glacier-scooped lakes, including Jackson and Jenny lakes, offer ample fishing, canoeing, and even windsurfing possibilities. The majority of visitors, however, are pulled toward Yellowstone National Park, which has two entrances in Wyoming. There are 370 mi of public roads within the park, providing (in theory) access to the park's exceptional sights—the trade-offs are the crawling traffic during tourist season and the fraying road conditions. The Grand Canyon of the Yellowstone has two towering waterfalls; the mercurial Norris Geyser Basin changes every year, as new steam vents erupt and older ones fizzle out. With more than 10,000 geysers, hot springs, fumaroles, and mud pots, the park is the world's largest thermal area. The stunted landscape surrounding a hydrothermal point can seem almost otherworldly, especially in winter, when the skeletons of trees scorched by the heat glitter with icicles. The wealth of animal life is equally awesome—spotting trumpeter swans, grazing bison, or herds of elk is a wonderfully common occurrence.

Rock Climbing and Mountaineering

Climbing in its various forms—mountaineering, rock climbing, ice climbing—is a year-round sport in the Rockies. Many "fourteeners" (peaks over 14,000 ft), such as Long's Peak in Colorado, are a relatively easy (although long) ascent for the well conditioned and well prepared, but there are also dozens of highly technical climbs, such as the spires of El Dorado Canyon

in Colorado, the City of Rocks in Idaho, and the jagged Grand Teton in Wyoming. In many areas, especially in the national parks, climbing permits are required, primarily for safety reasons. Rangers want to be sure that you have the experience and skill necessary to undertake the challenge at hand.

Generally speaking, the Rockies do not call for great expeditionary preparation. The range is very accessible and the climbs, by alpine standards, relatively short. Long hikes with heavy packs in order to establish a base are rare, and climbs that typically involve less than 6,000 vertical ft are not like dealing with the 10,000 or more vertical ft involved in climbing, say, Mt. Rainier in Washington. There are few major climbs in the Rockies that can't be accomplished in a day or two. Avalanche risks can persist even into May at higher elevations, and winter can begin in earnest by October. The best months, weather-wise, are June and July; the risk of afternoon thunderstorms (also possible earlier in the summer) throw an additional hazard into August climbing.

Shopping

The Rocky Mountain region combines a frontier reverence for nature and the country's past with a fascination for ski-resort glitz and a modern love of megamalls and discount-outlet shopping centers. Boutiques, galleries, and malls are either right in or nearby the many resort towns and cities throughout all five states covered in this book.

ANTIQUES➤ In downtown Denver, South Broadway is the main drag as far as antiques are concerned; western and Native American collectibles are also scattered all over the southwestern part of the state. Idaho is an antiquer's dream, as entire towns can fit the bill; most small towns are rife with old-time street signs, utensils, and other western goods. In Ogden, Utah, 25th Street (the town's version of a red-light district in the 1870s), is now a chichi shopping district with its fair share of antiques stores.

CRAFTS➤ Remarkable crafts—particularly Native American work—can be bought throughout this part of the country. In Denver, the LoDo district is a good place to track down impressive weavings, pottery, jewelry, kachinas, and painting. Southwestern Colorado is generally rumored to be the best place to find both western and Native American arts and crafts, especially basketry, weaving, and beadwork adapted from Native American methods. As for more esoteric choices, in Coeur d'Alene, Idaho, you can select a custom-made tepee or yurt. High-quality western gear, such as cowboy hats and saddles, can also be found in Montana. King's Ropes and Saddlery in Sheridan, Wyoming, is where real cowboys come from all over the world for everything a rancher could wish for.

Skiing

Downhill skiing is the most popular activity by a large margin, although cross-country skiing and snowboarding have loyal followings. Resorts offer an ever-increasing range of special-interest programs, such as classes for women skiers, for skiers with disabilities, or for recreational racing. Rockies resorts may open their lifts as early as October and close as late as July; the ski season, however, usually runs from December until early April. Christmas through New Year's Day and the month of March tend to be the busiest periods for most ski areas. The slower months of January and February often yield good package deals, as do the early and late ends of the season. Cross-country skiing generally has a shorter season owing to lack of snow, but as avalanche risks lessen in April, backcountry skiers may take advantage of the sun-baked snow. Overall, ski resorts are each area's best source of information on everything from lodging to snow conditions.

CHILD CARE➤ Day care can be found at almost all ski areas, often accepting children under a year old. Parents pay a premium for this service, but what they get is peace of mind. Most resorts have a high caretaker-to-children ratio and even offer beepers to parents who want to be notified if their child is unhappy. Normally, parents must supply bottles and diapers for infants, and some young children may want to bring their favorite toys. "Pre-ski" programs (more play than serious instruction) may be offered for children at age three.

EQUIPMENT RENTAL➤ Rental equipment is available at all ski areas and at ski shops around resorts or in other cities. It's usually more expensive to rent right at the resort where you'll be skiing, but then it's easier to go back to the shop if something doesn't fit or you want to upgrade. Experienced skiers can "demo" (try out) premium equipment to get a feel for new technology before upgrading. Usually the cost of the rental is deducted if you decide to buy.

LESSONS➤ In the United States, the Professional Ski Instructors of America (PSIA) has devised a progressive teaching system that is used with relatively little variation at most ski schools. This allows skiers to take lessons at schools at different ski areas based on the same principles. Classes range in length from 1½ hours to all-day workshops. Many ski areas now offer specialized programs such as powder-skiing courses, mogul clinics, or lessons for women. Of note are the children's ski schools at Vail and Beaver Creek, Colorado; the skiers with disabilities program at Winter Park, Colorado; the "extreme skiing" lessons at Jackson, Wyoming; and the Mountain Experience Program for challenging, off-trail skiing at Snowbird, Utah.

Most ski schools have adopted the PSIA teaching approach for children, and many also incorporate SKIwee, another standardized teaching technique that includes progress certificates. Classes for children are arranged by ability and age group; often the ski instructor chaperons a meal during the teaching session. Children's ski instruction has come a long way in the last 10 years; instructors specially trained in teaching children, and equipment designed for little bodies now mean that most children can start skiing successfully as young as three or four.

Ask about special beginners' programs. Packages normally include basic equipment (rental skis with bindings, ski boots, ski poles), a lesson lasting at least an hour, and a lift ticket that may be valid only on beginners' slopes.

LIFT TICKETS➤ The more popular the resort, the higher the lift ticket's price. Single-day, adult, holiday-weekend passes cost the most, but better bargains can be had through off-site purchase locations, multiple-day passes, stretch weekends (a weekend including a Monday or a Friday), season-long tickets, or other options. You can always call a particular resort's central reservations line to ask where discount lift tickets can be purchased.

Occasionally, lift tickets are included in the price of lodging.

LODGING> Most ski areas offer several kinds of accommodations—lodges, condominiums, hotels, motels, inns, bed-and-breakfasts—close to or a short distance away from the action. For longer vacations, request the resort area's accommodations brochure, since a package rate may offer the best deal. Combinations can include rooms, meals, lift tickets, ski lessons, rental equipment, parties, or other features.

TRAIL RATING> Ski areas have designed fairly accurate standards for rating and marking trails and slopes. Trails are rated Easier (green circle), Intermediate (blue square), Advanced (black diamond), and Expert (double black diamond). Remember that trail difficulty is measured in relation to the other trails *at the same ski area,* not in comparison to trails in other areas; for example, a black-diamond trail in one area may be labeled as a blue square in another area close by.

Water Sports

Spring, when rivers are flushed with snowmelt, is the best time of year for white-water enthusiasts. April through June is the best time to run rivers in the south; June through August are the principal months on rivers farther north. In general (except on dammed rivers), the flow of water lessens as the season wears on. River runners seeking the maximum white-water thrills should come early; families and those who want a gentler float should come later.

To prevent overcrowding, almost all major rivers require rafters or kayakers to have permits. For individuals planning their own trips, permits on popular rivers (such as the Middle Fork of the Salmon River or the Selway River in Idaho) can be extremely hard to come by. Permits tend to be awarded first to reputable outfitters, so signing up with an appropriate company is a good way to insure access.

FODOR'S CHOICE

Dining
Lone Mountain Ranch, Big Sky, Montana. Firelight casts a romantic glow across the lodge's Indian artifacts, and guests have their table for the entire evening. Seasonal menus emphasize Montana beef and game like bison medallions. $$$$

Metropolitan, Salt Lake City, Utah. Consistent awards for ambience, service, and world-class cuisine confirm that this is the place to dine when only the best will do. Caribou and lobster specialties, an extensive tasting menu, and exquisite desserts await you. $$$–$$$$

The Tree Room, Sundance, Utah. For Utah natives, Sundance is as well known for The Tree Room as it is for the annual film festival. Fresh is the keyword here; dishes change with the seasons. $$$–$$$$

Antares, Steamboat Springs, Colorado. An exciting, eclectic cuisine inspired by America's rich ethnic stew is served in this landmark Victorian building. $$–$$$$

Café Alpine, Breckenridge, Colorado. A perfect reflection of the town itself, this outstanding restaurant weaves together Victorian romance, in the intimate dining room, with resort town hipness, at the casually chic tapas and dessert bar. $$$

Center Café, Moab, Utah. Owners Paul and Zee McCarrol show their creativity in the flavor, color, and presentation of every dish they prepare. The menu changes seasonally and the wine list is the best for miles around. $$–$$$

Marianne's at the Wilma, Missoula, Montana. Built when vaudeville was king, this elegant eatery is known for New York strip steak au poivre and the 1,000-seat theater on the banks of the Clark Fork River. $$–$$$

Rustique Bistro, Aspen, Colorado. Within the French bistro of renowned chef and restaurateur Charles Dale, small plates, enticing entrées, and an outstanding wine list bring together an authentic, and surprisingly affordable, bistro experience. $$–$$$

Showthyme!, Bigfork, Montana. Chef Blu Funk celebrates dining with entrées like fresh Chilean sea bass, seared and roasted in a mild Thai red curry sauce. Seating is unique: outside, overlooking Flathead Lake, inside the century-old bank building, or downstairs in the snug bank vault. $$–$$$

The Bunnery, Jackson, Wyoming. The breakfasts here are irresistible, and it shows in the brief wait and the elbow-to-elbow seating on busy mornings. $–$$

Buffalo Café, Twin Falls, Idaho. This tiny café produces an enormous amount of food for breakfast, including the dauntingly sized but delicious Buffalo Chip (an egg, potato, and cheese concoction). $

Lodging

The Big EZ, Big Sky, Montana. The most opulent lodge under the Big Sky, this mountain-top retreat is fully wired for business and comfort. Suites have stone fireplaces, king-size beds, and 40-mi views. Fun includes an on-site putting course, fly-fishing, and exploring in Yellowstone National Park. $$$$

The Broadmoor, Colorado Springs, Colorado. One of America's truly great hotels, the Broadmoor almost seems like a village unto its own. Besides its luxurious accommodations, it commands a private lake, three world-class championship golf courses, nine restaurants, and a spa. $$$$

Brown Palace, Denver, Colorado. This is the grande dame of Colorado hotels. Scrupulous attention is paid to the details, and the formal restaurant, the Palace Arms, has won several awards. $$$$

Grand America, Salt Lake City, Utah. Staying at the Grand, which opened in 2001, is reason enough to visit Utah. Imported marble, rugs, and chandeliers, and original art—some of it centuries old—in the ballrooms, hallways, and guest rooms create an oasis of European elegance. $$$$

Hotel Jerome, Aspen, Colorado. Built in 1889, the Hotel Jerome is a deep draft of Victorian grandeur. If you tend toward the lavish, the rose damask curtains of the public rooms alone should satisfy. $$$$

Hyatt Regency Beaver Creek, Beaver Creek, Colorado. The list of indulgences goes on and on at this ski-in/ski-out, full-service retreat with a posh lobby, countless whirlpools, a pampering spa, and an outdoor fire pit. $$$$

Wort Hotel, Jackson, Wyoming. Locals congregate around the Silver Dollar Bar, named for the 2,032 silver dollars embedded in the S-shape bar counter. The hotel seems to have been around as long as the Tetons, but it feels fresh inside. $$$$

Gold Lake Mountain Resort & Spa, Ward, Colorado. The tranquility and seclusion here defines the rustic mountain resort experience. The indulgent dining and European-style, environmentally conscious spa make this a hallmark of the "New West." $$$–$$$$

The Idaho Rocky Mountain Ranch, Stanley, Idaho. This guest ranch has retained its decades-old character and classic western-lodge splendor and offers up awesome views of the spectacular Sawtooth Mountain range across the valley floor. $$$–$$$$

B&Bs on North Main Street, Breckenridge, Colorado. This B&B offers two options: an unabashedly romantic miner's cottage and a collection of western primitive rooms in a barnlike structure overlooking the river. The innkeepers are unfailingly generous with their homemade muffins and skiing tips. $$–$$$$

Teton Ridge Ranch, Tetonia, Idaho. This guest ranch, standing tall and proud in the shadow of the 12,000-ft Grand Tetons, has built luxury into each of its seven suites—and charges accordingly for a slice of private paradise in the Wild West. $$$

Clark House on Hayden Lake, Coeur d'Alene, Idaho. Originally a millionaire's eccentric extravagance and once a near–ruin the building was transformed into a giant, sumptuous wedding cake of a place. $$–$$$

Lake Yellowstone Hotel, Yellowstone National Park, Wyoming. This property is one of the oldest and most elegant park resorts. Old-style luxury tourism in the "wilderness" is recalled by the afternoon chamber music in the lobby. $$–$$$

Mountain Lake Lodge, Bigfork, Montana. The view from private balconies or patios of each suite spans much of the 27-mi-long Flathead Lake. On site are two restaurants and an art gallery. $$–$$$

Boulder Mountain Lodge, Boulder, Utah. Halfway between Capitol Reef and Bryce Canyon national parks on gorgeous Highway 12 is tiny Boulder, Utah. This first-class retreat lies near a 5-acre wetland. The restaurant uses organic foods for its Puebloan, Mormon, and cowboy dishes. $$

Desert Pearl Inn, Springdale, Utah. Just outside the entrance to Zion National Park, this contemporary inn is a delight to the senses. Towering cliffs surround you and the Virgin River is only a few feet from your doorstep. $$

Ski Resorts

Aspen Highlands, Colorado, for the Highland Bowl. Not for the faint of heart, the hike to the upper reaches of the Bowl pays major dividends for those in the know. Nowhere else will you find controlled terrain with such awesome views, pristine powder, gnarly steeps, and generally outrageous extreme skiing.

Crested Butte, Colorado, for both its rolling intermediate slopes and its Extreme Limits runs. The main trail network has easy, maneuverable terrain, while Extreme Limits has several hundred acres of steep bowls, tough chutes, and tight tree skiing.

Vail, Colorado, for its back bowls and resort amenities. On powder days, the back bowls can offer intermediate and expert skiers a small slice of heaven. The resort village is crafted to anticipate every need (or desire).

Sun Valley, Idaho, for bestowing the royal treatment on Baldy Mountain. A whole host of multimillion-dollar improvements, including new high-speed quad lifts, computerized snowmaking, luxurious new day lodges, and mountaintop dining, let the grand dame of U.S. ski resorts reclaim her ranking as queen.

Alta, Utah, for its chance to explore. Sharing Snowbird's exceptional snowfall, Alta's layout may seem confusing at first. However, Alta is made for exploration, and new discoveries can be made year after year.

Snowbird, Utah, for its expert runs. The open bowls are already challenging, but even these pale in comparison to chutes such as Upper Cirque. What makes this bearable is the legendary quantity of powder.

Jackson Hole, Wyoming, for its endless variations. Jackson has literally thousands of skiable routes from top to bottom—all it takes is a little imagination. Its stunning backcountry terrain is some of the most diverse in the United States.

Views

First glimpse of Vail's sweeping back bowls, Colorado. The Valhalla of skiers, the back bowls seem like an endless expanse of beckoning snow. In summer, the bowls' enormous cradle works the same magic for mountain bike fanatics.

The cliff dwellings of the ancestral Puebloan people at Mesa Verde, Colorado. These haunting villages were built into the cliff walls more than 600 years ago, then mysteriously abandoned.

The black basalt columns in Hells Canyon, Idaho. Deeper than the Grand Canyon, and much narrower, Hells Canyon is flanked with rock formations resembling giant black pencils. By floating or rafting through the chasm, you can also see Native American pictographs along the smooth canyon walls.

The shimmering northern lights in Montana. Take your pick of open spaces from which to see this exquisite summer phenomenon—sometimes delicately tinting the night sky, other times blazing until dawn.

The views from Going-to-the-Sun Road in Glacier National Park, Montana. This serpentine, 52-mi-long highway has some of the best views in the world. It crests at Logan Pass, where you can take a short hike to the crystalline Hidden Lake.

Snow clinging to the rock formations in Bryce Canyon National Park, Utah. The Martianlike landscape of the ruddy pinnacles and spires is incredibly beautiful when dusted with snow. The bristlecone pines along the amphitheaters' rims heighten the colors' effect.

Route 12 between Capitol Reef National park and Escalante, Utah. Pine, spruce, and aspen line a climb toward Boulder Mountain that every now and then reveals a stunning vista across southern Utah. Once past the town of Boulder, a narrow hogback allows 360-degree views into the Grand Staircase-Escalante National Monument.

Jackson as seen from the top of Signal Mountain, Wyoming. A matchless view of the whole of Jackson Hole can be seen from the summit of Signal Mountain.

Erupting geysers and hissing steam vents at the Norris Geyser Basin in Yellowstone National Park, Wyoming. Norris is the oldest and hottest of Yellowstone's geyser basins; every year its roster of live hydrothermal features changes.

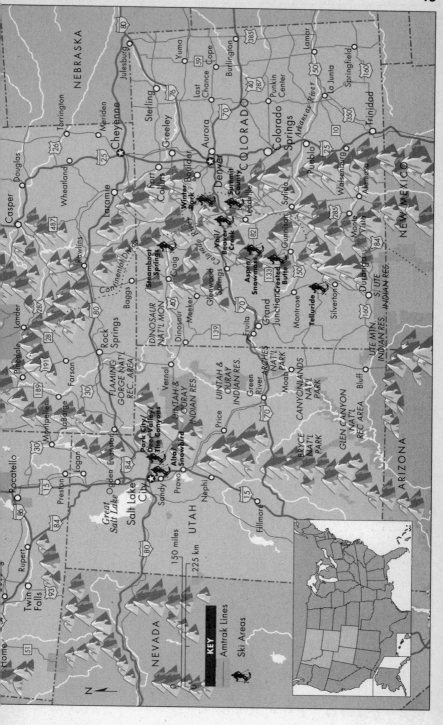

KEY

Amtrak Lines

Ski Areas

150 miles

225 km

2 COLORADO

Theodore Roosevelt spoke of Colorado
as "scenery to bankrupt the English
language." Walt Whitman wrote that
its beauty "awakens those grandest and
subtlest elements in the human soul." For
more than 200 years pioneers, poets,
and presidents alike have rhapsodized
over what an increasing number of "out-of-
towners" are learning: that Colorado is one
of America's prime chunks of real estate.

COLORADO IS A STATE OF STUNNING CONTRASTS. The Rockies create a mountainous spine that's larger than Switzerland, with 52 eternally snowcapped summits towering higher than 14,000 ft. Yet its eastern third is a sea of hypnotically waving grasslands, and its southwest, a vibrant multihue desert, carved with pink and mauve canyons, vaulting cinnamon spires, and gnarled red-rock monoliths. Its mighty rivers, the Colorado, Arkansas, and Gunnison, etch deep, yawning chasms every bit as impressive as the shimmering blue-tinged glaciers and jagged peaks of the San Juan, Sangre de Cristo, and Front ranges. Add to this glittering sapphire lakes and jade forests, and you have an outdoor paradise second to none.

Much of the state's visual appeal can also be attributed to the legacy of the frontier and mining days, when gold, silver, and railroad barons left an equally rich treasure trove of Victorian architecture in the lavish monuments they built to themselves. The Old West comes alive in Colorado, where you're practically driving through the pages of a history book.

The first Europeans to explore the area were the Spanish, who left their imprint in the lyrical names and distinctive architecture of the southern part of the state. They were followed by trappers, scouts, and explorers, including some of the legendary names in American history—Zebulon Pike, Kit Carson, Stephen Long, and William Bent—intent on exploiting some of the area's rich natural resources, including vast lodes of gold and silver. In so doing they displaced—and often massacred—the original settlers: Pawnee; Comanche; Ute; and Pueblo, whose ancestors fashioned the haunting cliff dwellings of Mesa Verde National Park.

Along with feisty independence, be it right- or left-wing, Coloradans have always displayed an eccentric, even ostentatious streak. State history is animated by stories of fabulous wealth and equally dramatic ruin in the bountiful precious-metal mines. The discovery of gold in 1859 spurred the first major settlement of Colorado, followed by the inevitable railroad lines for transport. When the lodes petered out, many of the thriving communities became virtual ghost towns, until the discovery of black gold in the oil-shale reserves of northwest Colorado and, especially, white gold on the ski slopes.

Today Colorado is a state of unabashed nature lovers and outdoors enthusiasts. Though most people associate the state with skiing, residents have a saying, "We came for the winters, but we stayed for the summers." In addition to skiing and snowmobiling in winter, they climb, hike, bike, fish, and camp in the summer, making Colorado one of America's premier four-season destinations. As a visitor, you'll find plenty to occupy yourself year-round.

Pleasures and Pastimes

Dining

The dining scene in Colorado is quite sophisticated, especially in Denver and the resort towns. Still, restaurants in smaller areas such as Crested Butte rank among the country's most vibrant and creative. Livestock are a main source of livelihood on the eastern plains, where billboards proclaim "Nothing satisfies like beef." However, the calorie- and cholesterol-conscious will appreciate the fresh fish that sometimes appear on menus. Beef, buffalo, and burritos are available in many of the restaurants throughout the state, but a dazzling range of international cuisine from southwestern to classic French, Italian, and Thai can be found just as easily.

CATEGORY	COST*
$$$$	over $30
$$$	$20–$30
$$	$15–$20
$	under $15

*per person for a main course at dinner excluding drinks, tax, and tip

Lodging

Take your pick from the numerous selections across the state: resorts, chain hotels, dude ranches, bed-and-breakfasts, guest houses. Colorado has all sorts of accommodations to match any budget. In many parts of Colorado, particularly the ski areas, condominiums often represent an excellent alternative to the pricier hotels, especially for families and groups. In certain resorts, such as Steamboat, Copper Mountain, and Winter Park, they are often the best lodging, period.

CATEGORY	COST*
$$$$	over $225
$$$	$150–$225
$$	$75–$150
$	under $75

*All prices are for a standard double room in high season, excluding tax and service.

Shopping

You'll find outlets of many top designers in Denver's malls and department stores, as well as in chic resorts such as Aspen and Vail. But the real buys in Colorado are indigenous artifacts, crafts, and specialties. Western and Native American art galleries, ceramics and jewelry shops, and stores specializing in western memorabilia and cowboy clothing dot the landscape, especially in the Southwest. Beware of the numerous "authentic trading posts" that line the roads. Although they're fun and kitschy, they're usually tourist traps with second-rate merchandise.

Ski Areas

Residents and travelers alike claim that the state's snow—champagne powder—is the lightest and fluffiest anywhere. With Aspen lifting its ban on snowboarding at the end of the 2000/2001 ski season, all Colorado ski areas permit snowboarding. Many offer special half pipes for performing tricks, in addition to their skiable terrain. In summer, more and more ski areas are opening their chairlifts to mountain bikers. There are numerous trails winding through the mountain passes, with arduous ascents and exhilarating descents.

Exploring Colorado

Colorado's capital city, Denver, lies smack in the middle of the state. To the west, the High Rockies are home to most of Colorado's many ski resorts. To the east is flat terrain more similar to Kansas than what one typically thinks of as Colorado. The main interest of visitors to eastern Colorado lies in retracing the paths of the pioneers. The southwestern corner of the state has jaggedly beautiful mountains, as well as deserts, canyons, and mesas. The state's second-largest city, Colorado Springs, is found in the South Central area. Farther south is the San Luis Valley, home to the Great Sand Dunes National Monument as well as some of the region's oldest towns. The North Central region contains the state's most progressive city—the university town of Boulder—as well as the spectacular alpine scenery of Rocky Mountain National Park. Northwest Colorado is known primarily as dinosaur country.

Numbers in the text correspond to numbers in the margin and on the Denver, North Central Colorado, I–70 and the High Rockies, Southwest Colorado, Colorado Springs Vicinity, South Central Colorado, and Northwest Colorado maps.

Great Itineraries

IF YOU HAVE 3 DAYS

Spend a day and an evening exploring the many attractions of **Denver** ①–⑯. The next day, head up to **Rocky Mountain National Park** ㉑ to take in some alpine scenery and wildlife, and spend the evening in the hip, colorful town of **Boulder** ⑰. The third day, you can head to **Golden,** home of the Coors Brewery; **Central City,** where you can try your hand at gambling or just tour this gold-mining town returned to its glory days; and **Georgetown** ㉕, a charming old silver mining town with a well-preserved downtown. From here, it's just an hour back to Denver.

IF YOU HAVE 7 DAYS

Follow the above itinerary for the first three days, spending the third night in **Georgetown** ㉕. The fourth day, head to **Breckenridge** ㉘—considered by some to be Colorado's prettiest town. No trip to Colorado would be complete without a visit to **Vail** ㉜, so stop there for lunch. Your afternoon destination is **Aspen** ㊲—in summer, you can head south through **Leadville** ㉛ and over Independence Pass; in winter, when the pass is closed, drive west to **Glenwood Springs** ㉟ and south to Aspen. Both are scenic drives with interesting towns along the way; the Glenwood Springs route takes about an hour longer. The next day, when you can tear yourself away from Aspen's chic charms, head north past Carbondale and south to **Redstone** ㊱. In summer, if you have a four-wheel-drive vehicle, you could cut through Kebler Pass for a quick trip to the funky mountain town of **Crested Butte** ㊴ (you can even hike from Aspen to Crested Butte in a day, through the vibrant wildflower meadows of the Maroon Bells Wilderness), but in winter, it's a four-hour drive. Continue on to **Montrose** ㊶ and **Ridgway** ㊷ and into **Telluride** ㊸, a perfectly preserved National Historic District in a stunning box canyon. The sixth day, take your time driving the San Juan Skyway—perhaps the most scenic drive in a state known for breathtaking scenery—through **Dolores** ㊹, **Cortez** ㊺, **Mancos, Durango** ㊼, and **Silverton** ㊿. Each of these towns merits exploring, and if you have time, you'll want to stop at **Mesa Verde National Park** ㊻ for a look at the haunting Native American cliff dwellings. Spend the night in **Ouray** (51), take a soak in the hot springs, and the next day head back to Denver through **Gunnison** ㊵, **Salida** (80), **Buena Vista** (79), and Fairplay.

When to Tour Colorado

Colorado is known for its winter pastimes, but what keeps most locals here are the summers, when meadows are blanketed with wildflowers and snowcapped peaks shimmer in the sunlight. In winter, keep in mind that driving conditions can be treacherous, and you may not be able to cover as much ground as in summer. Of course, if you're a skier, you'll want to spend at least a full day in such resorts as Vail, Aspen, and Telluride to experience some of the best skiing in the country. In summer, you can time your trip to coincide with some of the state's many festivals: June's Shakespeare Festival in Boulder and Bluegrass Festival in Telluride; Crested Butte's Fat Tire Festival in late June and Wildflower Festival in July; the Aspen Music Festival all summer long. Temperatures are warmest and wildflowers are at their peak in July and August, and amazingly, resorts are still uncrowded and prices

20

Colorado

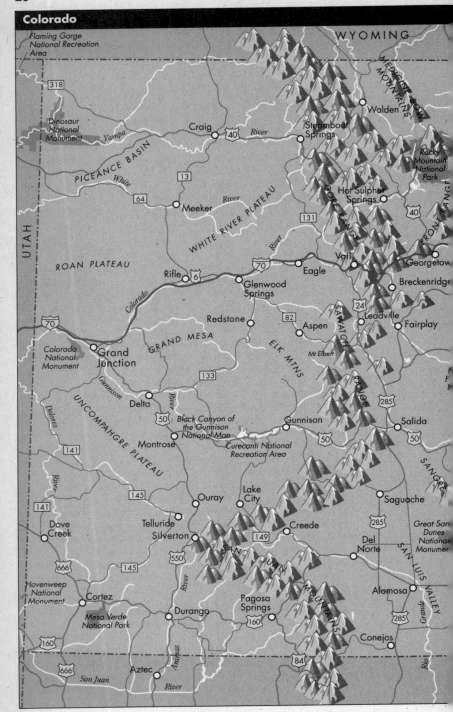

WYOMING

Flaming Gorge
National Recreation
Area

318

Dinosaur
National
Monument

Craig

40

River

Walden

Steamboat
Springs

Rocky
Mountain
National
Park

PICEANCE BASIN

Yampa

White

13

64

Meeker

River

WHITE RIVER PLATEAU

Hot Sulphur
Springs

131

40

ROAN PLATEAU

River

70

Rifle

6

Glenwood
Springs

Eagle

Vail

Georgetow

Breckenridge

Colorado

GORE RANGE

FRONT RANGE

Redstone

82

Aspen

24

Leadville

Fairplay

70

Colorado
National
Monument

Grand
Junction

GRAND MESA

ELK MTNS

Mt Elbert

SAWATCH RANGE

Gunnison

133

Delta

River

285

Salida

UNCOMPAHGRE PLATEAU

141

50

Black Canyon of
the Gunnison
National Mon

Montrose

Curecanti National
Recreation Area

Gunnison

50

50

UTAH

Dolores

River

141

145

Ouray

Lake
City

Creede

Saguache

285

Great San
Dunes
National
Monumer

SANGRE

Dove
Creek

Telluride

Silverton

550

149

Del
Norte

SAN LUIS VALLEY

666

145

River

SAN JUAN MOUNTAINS

Hovenweep
National
Monument

Cortez

Durango

160

Pagosa
Springs

Alamosa

285

Conejos

Mesa Verde
National Park

160

Animas

84

Rio

666

San Juan

River

Aztec

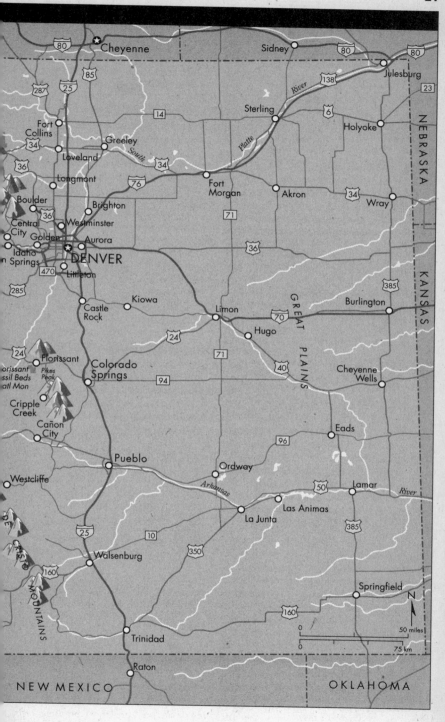

off-peak, since most tourists still don't think of Colorado as a summer destination. Real bargains can be had in spring and fall, but you can count on iffy weather, with at least some snow. Many residents say their favorite month is September, when the changing aspen leaves set the hillsides ablaze with gold.

DENVER

Denver's buildings jut jaggedly into the skyline, creating an incongruous setting in a state that prides itself on its pristine wilderness. Denver has finally shed its cow-town image, and the new sophistication is more than skin deep. Throughout the 1960s and '70s, when the city mushroomed on a huge surge of oil and energy revenues, Denverites hustled to discard evidence of their western past to prove their modernity. As the city has emerged as a telecommunications hub in the last decade, an influx of young, well-educated professionals have contributed to this new cosmopolitan vibe, lured by Colorado's outdoor mystique and encouraged by the megalopolis's business prospects. That Denver is a city of cherished and cared-for neighborhoods extends a feeling of community throughout the city and makes it a particularly interesting place to explore. Economic diversity has freed Denver from its historical boom-and-bust cycle and the city has settled into a period of prosperity and optimism. The two-time Super Bowl champion Denver Broncos have given the city an unparalleled sense of civic pride.

Most Denverites are unabashed nature lovers whose weekends are often spent skiing, camping, hiking, biking, or fishing. (Perhaps as a result of this active lifestyle, Denver is the "thinnest" city in the United States, with only 20% of the adult population overweight.) For Denverites, preserving the environment and the city's rich mining and ranching heritage are of equally vital importance to the quality of life. Areas such as LoDo—the historic lower downtown—buzz with jazz clubs, restaurants, and art galleries housed in carefully restored century-old buildings. The culturally diverse populace avidly supports the Denver Art Museum, the Denver Museum of Nature and Science, the Colorado History Museum, and the Museo de las Americas. The Denver Performing Arts Complex is the nation's second-largest theatrical venue, bested in capacity only by New York's Lincoln Center. An excellent public transportation system, including a popular, growing light rail and 400 mi of bike paths, make getting around easy.

Those who don't know Denver may be in for a few big surprises. Although one of its monikers is the "Mile High City," another is "Queen City of the Plains." Denver is flat, with the Rocky Mountains as a backdrop; this combination keeps the climate delightfully mild. Denverites do not spend their winters digging out of fierce snowstorms and skiing out their front doors, though snow may arrive early and leave late. They take advantage of a comfortable climate (over 300 days of sunshine a year), historic city blocks, a cultural center, and sky's-the-limit outdoor adventures just minutes from downtown. All of these factors make this appealing city more than just a layover between home and the Rockies.

Downtown

Denver's downtown is an intriguing mix of well-preserved monuments from the state's frontier past and modern high-tech marvels. You'll often catch the reflection of an elegant Victorian building in the mirrored glass of a skyscraper. Hundreds of millions of dollars have been poured into the city in the past decade, in such projects as the Coors Field, the downtown home of Denver's baseball Rockies; the relocation of Six Flags Elitch Gardens—the first amusement park in the country to relocate into a downtown urban area; and an expansion of the light-rail system, which now runs from downtown into the south suburbs. Lower Downtown, or LoDo, is a Victorian warehouse district revitalized by the new ballpark, loft condominiums, and numerous brewpubs, nightclubs, and restaurants. Downtown is remarkably compact and can be toured on foot, but a car is recommended for exploring outside of downtown proper.

Numbers in the text correspond to numbers in the margin and on the Denver map.

A Good Tour

Denver presents its official face to the world at the **Civic Center,** a three-block-long park that runs from Bannock Street to Broadway south of Colfax Avenue and north of 14th Avenue. To the east, lawns, gardens, and a Greek amphitheater form a serene backdrop for the **State Capitol** ①. Southeast of the Civic Center on Broadway is the vibrant **Colorado History Museum** ②. Walk west one block on 13th Avenue to reach the **Denver Public Library's Central Library** ③, and cross over Acoma Plaza (or take the underground walkway) to the **Denver Art Museum** ④. The **Byers-Evans House** ⑤, a snapshot of Denver's Victorian beginnings, is just south of here on Bannock Street. Head back to 14th Avenue and turn left to reach the **U.S. Mint** ⑥, the source of all those coins stamped with a *D*. From the mint, continue north on Cherokee Street to Tremont Place and the **Denver Firefighters Museum** ⑦. A block away on 14th Street is the **Trianon Museum and Art Gallery** ⑧.

Continue on Tremont Place to **The Denver Pavilions** ⑨, an open-air shopping and entertainment complex. Farther up the street is the historic **Brown Palace** ⑩ hotel. Walk or catch a free shuttle up the pedestrian-only **16th Street Mall.** As you head north you'll see the **Daniels and Fisher Tower** ⑪. Just past it is the festive **Tabor Center** ⑫ mall. Across 16th Street from Tabor Center is **Writer Square,** whose shops line the entrance to classy **Larimer Square** ⑬. **LoDo** ⑭, the hip arts district, is northwest of Larimer Square. Head southeast on 14th Street to reach the **Denver Performing Arts Complex** ⑮.

TIMING

Although Denver's downtown is easily covered on foot in an hour or less, you'll want to set aside some time to explore its many fine cultural attractions. The Denver Art Museum merits at least two to three hours and the Colorado History Museum can be covered in an hour or two. Once you've done the museum rounds, save some time for browsing and people-watching along the 16th Street Mall and Larimer Square. LoDo is a 30-block-square area that takes several hours to meander through. By day, the art galleries and shops are the attraction. At night the many brewpubs and cafés hop, especially in summer baseball season.

Sights to See

⑩ **Brown Palace.** Denver's hotel empress was built in 1892 and is still considered the city's most prestigious address. Reputedly this was the first atrium hotel in the United States: its ornate lobby and nine stories are crowned by a Tiffany stained-glass window. ✉ *321 17th St.,* WEB *www.brownpalace.com.*

⑤ **Byers-Evans House.** This elaborate redbrick Victorian was built in 1883 and is restored to its pre–World War I condition. Offering a glimpse into Denver's past, the house is filled with many original furnishings

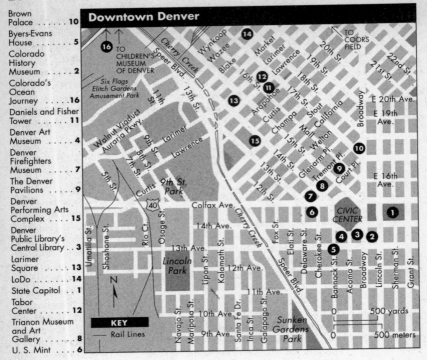

once owned by the Evans family at the turn of the 20th century. ✉ *1310 Bannock St.,* ☎ *303/620–4933,* WEB *www.coloradohistory.org.* 🎫 *$3.* ⊙ *Tues.–Sun. 11–3.*

Civic Center. You'll find a peaceful respite in this three-block park in the cultural heart of downtown, site of the State Capitol. A Greek amphitheater is set in the middle of one of the city's largest flower gardens. Festivals such as Cinco de Mayo and the People's Fair keep things lively here throughout the spring and summer. ✉ *Bannock St. to Broadway south of Colfax Ave. and north of 14th Ave.*

② **Colorado History Museum.** The state's frontier past is vibrantly depicted here. Changing exhibits highlight eras from the days of native cultures to those of the 20th century. Permanent displays include Conestoga wagons, great old touring cars, and an extraordinary time line called "The Colorado Chronicle 1800–1950," which depicts the state's history in amazing detail. The mixed media display stretches 112 ft, 6 inches, and dedicates 9 inches to each year. It's crammed with artifacts from rifles to land-grant surveys and old daguerreotypes. ✉ *1300 Broadway,* ☎ *303/866–3682,* WEB *www.coloradohistory.org.* 🎫 *$5.* ⊙ *Mon.–Sat. 10–4:30, Sun. noon–4:30.*

⑪ **Daniels and Fisher Tower.** This 330-ft-high structure emulates the campanile of St. Mark's Cathedral in Venice, and it was the highest building west of the Mississippi when it was built in 1909. Today, it's the city's most convenient clock tower and particularly striking when viewed in concert with the fountains in the adjacent Skyline Park. ✉ *16th and Arapahoe Sts.*

★ ☺ ④ **Denver Art Museum.** Superlative, uniquely displayed holdings in Asian, pre-Columbian, Spanish Colonial, and Native American art are the hallmarks of this model of museum design, which also has extensive spe-

HOW TO
USE THIS GUIDE

Great trips begin with great planning, and this guide makes planning easy. It's packed with everything you need—insider advice on hotels and restaurants, cool tools, practical tips, essential maps, and much more.

COOL TOOLS

Fodor's Choice Top picks are marked throughout with a star.

Great Itineraries These tours, planned by Fodor's experts, give you the skinny on what you can see and do in the time you have.

Smart Travel Tips A to Z This special section is packed with important contacts and advice on everything from how to get around to what to pack.

Good Walks You won't miss a thing if you follow the numbered bullets on our maps.

Need a Break? Looking for a quick bite to eat or a spot to rest? These sure bets are along the way.

Off the Beaten Path Some lesser-known sights are worth a detour. We've marked those you should make time for.

POST-IT® FLAGS

Dog-ear no more!

"Post-it" is a registered trademark of 3M.

Favorite restaurants • Essential maps • Frequently used numbers • Walking tours • Can't-miss sights • Smart Travel Tips • Web sites • Top shops • Hot nightclubs • Addresses • Smart contacts • Events • Off-the-beaten-path spots • Favorite restaurants • Essential maps • Frequently used numbers • Walking tours • Can't-miss sights • Smart Travel Tips • Web sites • Top shops • Hot nightclubs • Addresses • Smart contacts • Events • Off-the-beaten-path spots • Favorite restaurants • Essential maps • Frequently used numbers • Walking tours •

ICONS AND SYMBOLS

Watch for these symbols throughout:

★   Our special recommendations

✕   Restaurant

🏠   Lodging establishment

✕🏠   Lodging establishment whose restaurant warrants a special trip

☾   Good for kids

☞   Sends you to another section of the guide for more information

✉   Address

☎   Telephone number

FAX   Fax number

WEB   Web site

🎟   Admission price

🕐   Opening hours

$-$$$$ Lodging and dining price categories, keyed to strategically sited price charts. Check the index for locations.

①❶   Numbers in white and black circles on the maps, in the margins, and within tours correspond to one another.

ON THE WEB

Continue your planning with these useful tools found at **www.fodors.com**, the Web's best source for travel information.

"Rich with resources." —*New York Times*

"Navigation is a cinch." —*Forbes* "Best of the Web" list

"Put together by people bursting with know-how."
                 —*Sunday Times* (London)

Create a Miniguide Pinpoint hotels, restaurants, and attractions that have what you want at the price you want to pay.

Rants and Raves Find out what readers say about Fodor's picks—or write your own reviews of hotels and restaurants you've just visited.

Travel Talk Post your questions and get answers from fellow travelers, or share your own experiences.

On-Line Booking Find the best prices on airline tickets, rental cars, cruises, or vacations, and book them on the spot.

About our Books Learn about other Fodor's guides to your destination and many others.

Expert Advice and Trip Ideas From what to tip to how to take great photos, from the national parks to Nepal, Fodors.com has suggestions that'll make your trip a breeze. Log on and get informed and inspired.

Smart Resources Check the weather in your destination or convert your currency. Learn the local language or link to the latest event listings. Or consult hundreds of detailed maps—all in one place.

cial exhibits. With dazzling mountain views as a bonus, it's highly accessible and thoughtfully lit. Children will love the imaginative hands-on exhibits and video corners. The Adventures in Art Center offers hands-on art classes and exploration for both children and adults. The on-site restaurant, Palettes, serves excellent contemporary American food. ⊠ *100 W. 14th Ave. Pkwy.,* ☎ *720/865–5000,* WEB *www. denverartmuseum.org.* ☞ *$6; free Sat. for Colorado residents.* ☉ *Tues.–Sat. 10–5 (Wed. until 9), Sun. noon–5.*

☺ ❼ **Denver Firefighters Museum.** Occupying the space of Denver's first firehouse, all the original items of the trade are displayed here, including uniforms, nets, fire carts and trucks, bells, and switchboards. ⊠ *1326 Tremont Pl.,* ☎ *303/892–1436,* WEB *www.firedenver.org/museum.* ☞ *$3.* ☉ *Mon.–Sat. 10–2.*

❾ **The Denver Pavilions.** Denver's newest retail and entertainment center anchors the newly abuzz southeast corner of downtown. This two-city-block complex, with an assortment of restaurants, bookstores, movie theaters, and shops, is located along the 16th Street Mall adjacent to the Adam's Mark Hotel. ⊠ *Along the 16th St. Mall near Court Pl.,* ☎ *303/260–6000,* WEB *www.denverpavilions.com.*

⓯ **Denver Performing Arts Complex.** A huge, impressively high-tech group of theaters is connected by a soaring glass archway to a futuristic symphony hall. The complex hosts more events than any other performing arts center in the world. Guided tours for groups of five or more are available by appointment only. ⊠ *14th and Curtis Sts.,* ☎ *303/ 893–4000,* WEB *www.denvercenter.org.*

❸ **Denver Public Library's Central Library.** This Michael Graves–designed building houses a world-renowned collection of books, photographs, and newspapers that chronicle the American West, as well as original paintings by Remington, Russell, Audubon, and Bierstadt. The children's library is notable for its captivating design and its unique, child-friendly multimedia computer catalog. The library is the cornerstone of the Civic Center Cultural Complex, intended to be a center for western Americana, with shared exhibits and collections with the Denver Art Museum and Colorado History Museum. ⊠ *10 W. 14th Ave. Pkwy.,* ☎ *720/865–1111,* WEB *www.denver.lib.co.us.* ☉ *Mon.–Wed. 10– 9, Thurs.–Sat. 10–5:30, Sun. 1–5.*

OFF THE
BEATEN PATH
FORNEY TRANSPORTATION MUSEUM – Uprooted in 1999 from its Platte River Valley location, this museum is a trivia-laden gem. It reopened in 2001 outside of the downtown loop (north on Brighton Boulevard, adjacent to the Denver Coliseum on the south side of I–70) with a much-improved layout and most of the same exhibits. Inside a converted warehouse are an 1898 Renault coupe, Teddy Roosevelt's tour car, Amelia Earhart's immaculately maintained "Goldbug," and a Big Boy steam locomotive, among many other former denizens of the country's railroads and highways. Other exhibits consist of antique bicycles, cable cars, experimental car-planes, and even the "Zabeast," a 1975 Pontiac entirely covered in bumper stickers. Anyone who grew up on model cars or Lionel trains will wander this eccentric museum in a happy daze. ⊠ *4303 Brighton Blvd.,* ☎ *303/297–1113,* WEB *www.forneymuseum.com.* ☞ *$6.* ☉ *Mon.–Sat. 8–5.*

⓭ **Larimer Square.** Larimer Square is on the oldest street in the city, immortalized by Jack Kerouac in his seminal book, *On the Road.* It was saved from the wrecker's ball by a determined preservationist in the 1960s, when the city went demolition-crazy in its eagerness to present a more youthful image. Much has changed since Kerouac's wanderings, as Larimer Square's rough edges have been cleaned up in favor of upscale retail and chic restaurants. At **Writer Square** shops line the entrance to the arched redbrick courtyards of Denver's most charming shopping district, where some of the city's oldest retail buildings and toniest specialty shops, such as Overland Sheepskin and Tewksbury & Co., do business. ⊠ *Larimer and 15th Sts.,* ☎ *303/685–8143,* WEB *www.larimersquare.com.*

⑭ LoDo. The historic lower downtown area is home to art galleries, nightclubs, and restaurants ranging from Denver's most upscale to its most down-home. This part of town was once the city's thriving retail center, then it fell into disuse and slid into slums. Since the early 1990s, LoDo has metamorphosed into the city's cultural center, thanks to its resident avant-garde artists, retailers, and loft dwellers who have taken over the old warehouses and redbricks. The handsome **Coors Field** (⊠ Blake and 20th Sts.), home of baseball's Colorado Rockies, has further galvanized the area. Its old-fashioned brick and grillwork facade, ornamented with 41 blue, green, and white terra-cotta columbines (the state flower), was designed to blend in with the surrounding Victorian warehouses. ⊠ *From Larimer St. to the South Platte River, between 14th and 22nd Sts.,* WEB *www.lodo.org.*

OFF THE **MUSEO DE LAS AMERICAS** – The region's first museum dedicated to the
BEATEN PATH   achievements of Latinos in the Americas has a permanent collection as well as rotating exhibits that cover everything from Hispanics in the state legislature to Latin American women artists in the 20th century. ⊠ *861 Santa Fe Dr.,* ☎ *303/571–4401.* ☞ *$3.* ⊙ *Tues.–Sat. 10–5.*

★ 16th Street Mall. Outdoor cafés, historic buildings, and tempting shops line this pedestrians-only 12-block thoroughfare, shaded by red oak and locust trees. You'll find Denver's best people-watching here, with more than 1,000 chairs set out along its length so you can take in the sights. The rose-and-gray granite mall is scrubbed clean every day. Catch one of the free shuttle buses that run the length of downtown.

❶ State Capitol. Built in 1886, the capitol was constructed mostly of materials indigenous to Colorado, including marble, granite, and rose onyx. Especially inspiring is the gold-leaf dome, a reminder of the state's mining heritage. Visitors can climb to the dome's interior balcony for a panoramic view of the Rockies, or merely to the 18th step, which is exactly 1 mi high (above sea level). ⊠ *200 E. Colfax Ave.,* ☎ *303/866–2604.* ☞ *Free.* ⊙ *Jan.–May, weekdays 9–2:30; June–Sept., weekdays 9:30–3:30, Sat. 9:30–2; Oct.–Dec., weekdays 9:30–2:30; tours every 30 min.*

⑫ Tabor Center. Undergoing a major renovation through 2002, this festive shopping mall has about 55 stores and attractions, including fast-food eateries, strolling troubadours, jugglers and fire-eaters, and splashing fountains. The latest addition is an ESPN Zone sports-themed restaurant. A concierge desk at the Lawrence Street entrance is staffed with friendly people who offer free walking tours around the city. ⊠ *Larimer and Arapahoe Sts. on 16th St.,* ☎ *303/572–6868.*

❽ Trianon Museum and Art Gallery. This tranquil museum houses a collection of 18th- and 19th-century European furnishings and objets d'art dating from the 16th century onward. Guided tours are offered on the hour. ⊠ *335 14th St.,* ☎ *303/623–0739.* ☞ *$1.* ⊙ *Mon.–Sat. 10–4.*

❻ U.S. Mint. Free tours of this facility give a glimpse of the coin-making process, as presses spit out thousands of coins a minute. There are also several exhibits on the history of money and a restored version of Denver's original mint, prior to numerous expansions. More than 14 billion coins are minted yearly, and the nation's second-largest hoard of gold is stashed away here. ✉ *W. Colfax Ave. and Cherokee St.,* ☎ *303/405–4761,* WEB *www.usmint.gov.* 🎫 *Free.* ☉ *Tours weekdays 8–3 every 20 min, except during inventory (usually last wk in June and first wk in July).*

Platte River Valley

Just west of downtown is the booming Platte River Valley. Once the cluttered heart of Denver's railroad system, it is now overflowing with attractions. The imposing glass facade of the NFL Broncos' new Invesco Field at Mile High, the stately Pepsi Center sports arena, the Ocean Journey aquarium, and the flagship REI outdoors store are but four more crowd-pleasers to add to the growing list in Denver. The sights are so popular that the city plans to complete a light rail system that will connect the attractions with downtown by the end of the decade.

A Good Tour

Leave I–25 at exit 211 (23rd Avenue). Take the first right east of the interstate (Children's Museum Drive) to get to the Children's Museum, which has its own parking lot. Get back on 23rd Avenue, where you'll see the aquarium and REI down the street. To reach Six Flags, get back on I–25 going south, exit on Speer Boulevard south, and take a right at the sign for the park.

TIMING

The Platte River Valley can be a destination for an entire day if you're interested in riding the roller coasters at Six Flags, and touring the aquarium and the Children's Museum require about two hours each. You'll have to tour the area by car.

Sights to See

★ ♺ **Children's Museum of Denver.** This is one of the finest museums of its kind in North America, offering constantly changing hands-on exhibits that engage children in discovery. The Maze-eum is a walk-through musical maze; children can build a car on an assembly line and send it careening down a test ramp at the "Inventions" display; at "Arts á la carte," kids paint, dance, sing, and otherwise develop their creative talents. One of the biggest attractions is the new Center for the Young Child, a 3,700-square-ft playscape aimed at newborns through four-year-olds and their caregivers. A trolley ($2) clatters and clangs the 2 mi down the South Platte River from the museum to the REI flagship store, which has some interactive fun for the kids, too. The trolley also connects to the Ocean Journey aquarium. ✉ *2121 Crescent Dr., off Exit 211 of I–25,* ☎ *303/433–7444,* WEB *www.cmdenver.org.* 🎫 *$6.50; free the 1st Fri. of every month.* ☉ *June–Aug., daily 10–5; Sept.–May, Tues.–Sun. 10–5.*

⓰ **Colorado's Ocean Journey.** On the north side of the Platte River across from Six Flags Elitch Gardens, Ocean Journey is the only million-gallon aquarium between Chicago and the West Coast. It has four sections that show water and aquatic life in all its forms, from the seas to the ocean's headwaters in the Colorado mountains. The mountain-to-ocean journeys of two great rivers—the Colorado River and Indonesia's Kampar River—are depicted by a pair of multisensory exhibits in the 106,500-square-ft aquarium. Other major displays include "Depths of the Pacific," "Sea Otter Cove," and a rotating seasonal exhibit. ✉ *700 Water St., off Exit 211 of I–25,* ☎ *303/561–4450,* WEB *www.oceanjourney.org.* 🎫 *$14.95.* ☉ *June–Aug., daily 10–6; Sept.–May, daily 10–5.*

♺ **Six Flags Elitch Gardens.** This was a Denver family tradition long before its 1995 relocation from northwest Denver to its current home

on the outskirts of downtown. The park's highlights include several
hair-raising roller coasters (including one ranked in the nation's top
10) and thrill rides; a hand-carved, antique carousel; and a 100-ft-high
Ferris wheel that provides sensational views of downtown. A 10-acre
water adventure park is included in the standard entry fee. ✉ *I–25 and
Speer Blvd.,* ☎ *303/595–4386,* WEB *www.sixflags.com/elitchgardens.*
✎ *$33 unlimited ride pass.* ☉ *June–Labor Day, daily; Apr., May,
Sept., and Oct., Fri.–Sun.; hrs vary so call ahead.*

East of Downtown

The area east of downtown is home to two of the city's finest parks,
as well as some grand old residential neighborhoods.

A Good Tour

You'll need transportation on this tour, as it covers an area more
spread out than downtown. If you don't have a car, Denver has an excellent bus system. Head east from the **Civic Center** on 14th Avenue to
the flamboyant **Molly Brown House.** Continue east on 14th and south
on York for a peaceful interlude at the **Denver Botanic Gardens.** Denver's most impressive public space is **City Park,** reached by heading north
on York Street. Go east on 23rd Avenue for the main entrance to the
Denver Zoo. From here it's a short walk across the park (or a drive,
on Colorado Boulevard south), to the **Denver Museum of Nature and
Science.** Finish up your day with a stop at the **Black American West
Museum and Heritage Center** by getting back on York Street north and
going west on 31st Avenue.

TIMING

You'll want to set aside a full day to do these sights justice. If you have
children or are an animal lover, you could easily spend half a day in
City Park, exploring the Denver Zoo and the Denver Museum of Nature and Science. Garden enthusiasts could spend half a day in the Denver Botanic Gardens in summer, when the many theme gardens are in
full bloom; in the off-season, the conservatory is still a good respite
for an hour. There are often evening hours and musical performances
in the Denver Botanic Gardens in summer, and the Denver Museum
of Natural History stays open late on Friday night. The Molly Brown
House and the Black American West Museum and Heritage Center are
worthy of at least an hour each. In the off-season (October through
April), both are closed Monday and have shortened hours on Sunday.

Sights to See

Black American West Museum and Heritage Center. The revealing documents here depict the vast contributions that African-Americans
made to opening up the West. Nearly a third of the cowboys and
many pioneer teachers and doctors were African-Americans. One floor
is devoted to black cowboys; another to military troops such as the
Buffalo Soldiers. Changing exhibits focus on topics such as the history
of black churches in the West. ✉ *3091 California St.,* ☎ *303/292–2566.*
✎ *$4.* ☉ *May–Sept., daily 10–5; Oct.–Apr., Wed.–Fri. 10–2, week-
ends 10–5.*

★ **City Park.** Denver's largest public space contains rose gardens, lakes,
a golf course, tennis courts, a huge community-built children's playground, and two of the city's most popular attractions: the Denver Zoo
and the Denver Museum of Natural and Science. A shuttle runs between the two.

Denver Botanic Gardens. The horticultural displays in thoughtfully
laid-out theme gardens are at their peak during summer, but the
tropical conservatory alone is worth a visit in the off-season. Spring

brings a brilliant display of wildflowers to the world-renowned rock alpine garden. Tea ceremonies take place some summer weekends in the tranquil Japanese garden. ⊠ *1005 York St.,* ☎ *720/865–3500,* WEB *www.botanicgardens.org.* ⊡ *$6.50.* ⊙ *Daily 9–5; selected evening hrs in summer.*

★ ⊙ **Denver Museum of Nature and Science.** Formerly known as the Denver Museum of Natural History, this facility is one of the country's largest, holding a rich combination of traditional collections—dinosaur remains, animal dioramas, a mineralogy display, an Egyptology wing—and intriguing hands-on exhibits. In the "Hall of Life," you can test your health and fitness on various contraptions and receive a personalized health profile. Another permanent exhibit, "Prehistoric Journey," covers the seven stages of the earth's development, with each "envirorama" representing the sights and sounds of a specific area of North America or Australia at a particular time. The massive complex also includes an IMAX movie theater and the Gates Planetarium, which reopened in 2002 after a two-year renovation. Slated to open in 2003, the planetarium's "Space Odyssey" will offer the sensory experiences of space travel. ⊠ *2001 Colorado Blvd.,* ☎ *303/322–7009 or 800/925–2250,* WEB *www.dmns.org.* ⊡ *Museum $7, IMAX $7; $11 for a joint museum/IMAX pass.* ⊙ *Daily 9–5, 9–7 on Tuesdays Memorial Day–Labor Day.*

⊙ **Denver Zoo.** The nation's fourth–most visited zoo got even bigger in 2000 with the grand opening of the world's largest Komodo dragon exhibit, featuring the man-eating reptiles in a lush recreation of a cavernous riverbank. In 2001, the **Conservation Carousel** ($1) began rotating in the center of the zoo, featuring handcrafted endangered species as mounts. Also of note is the 7-acre **Primate Panorama,** which houses 31 species of primates in state-of-the-art environments that simulate the animals' natural habitats. Other highlights include a nursery for baby animals; seal shows; the world's only painting rhinoceros, Mshindi; and the electric *Safari Shuttle,* which snakes through the property as guests are treated to a lesson on the zoo's inhabitants. ⊠ *E. 23rd Ave. between York St. and Colorado Blvd.,* ☎ *303/376–4800,* WEB *www.denverzoo.org.* ⊡ *$7 Oct.–Mar., $9 Apr.–Sept.* ⊙ *Oct.–Mar., daily 10–5; Apr.–Sept., daily 9–6.*

Molly Brown House. This Victorian confection, on Pennsylvania Street between East 13th and 14th avenues, not far from the capitol, celebrates the life and times of the scandalous, "unsinkable" Molly Brown, heroine of the *Titanic* who courageously saved several lives and continued to provide assistance to survivors back on terra firma. Costumed guides and period furnishings in the museum, including flamboyant gilt-edge wallpaper, lace curtains, tile fireplaces, and tapestries, evoke bygone days. A bit of trivia: Margaret Tobin Brown was known as Maggie, not Molly, during her lifetime. Meredith Willson, the composer-lyricist of the musical, *The Unsinkable Molly Brown,* based on Brown's life, thought Molly was easier to sing. Tours run every half hour. ⊠ *1340 Pennsylvania St.,* ☎ *303/832–4092,* WEB *www.mollybrown.org.* ⊡ *$6.50.* ⊙ *June–Aug., Mon.–Sat. 10–3:30, Sun. noon–3:30; Sept.–May, Tues.–Sat. 10–3:30, Sun. noon–3:30.*

Dining

As befits a multiethnic crossroads, Denver lays out a dizzying range of eateries: head for LoDo, 32nd Avenue in the Highland District, or 17th Street for the more inventive kitchens; try Federal Street for cheap ethnic eats—especially Mexican, Thai, and Vietnamese. Throughout Denver, however, you'll find many trendy restaurants offering New American cuisines with an emphasis on indigenous regional ingredients and light, healthful preparations. Denver's hotels also have some fine restaurants.

American

$$–$$$ ✕ **Denver ChopHouse & Brewery.** This is the best of the many LoDo brewpubs and restaurants surrounding the Coors Field ballpark. Housed in the old Union Pacific Railroad warehouse, the restaurant has a clubby atmosphere, with dark wood paneling and exposed brick. The food is basic American, and there's plenty of it: steaks, seafood, and chicken served with hot corn bread and honey butter, and "bottomless" salads tossed at the table. ✉ 1735 19th St., ☎ 303/296–0800. AE, DC, MC, V.

$–$$ ✕ **Rocky Mountain Diner.** In the heart of the downtown business district, you can come in and sample all-American fill-ups of cowboy steak, pan-charred rib eye served with crisp onions, or the very popular buffalo meat loaf. Don't miss the real mashed potatoes, gravy, and all the fixings. ✉ 800 18th St., ☎ 303/293–8383. AE, D, DC, MC, V.

$–$$ ✕ **Wazee Supper Club.** Denverites flock to this hip hole for hot jazz and the best pizza in town—crisp yet gooey and bursting with flavor. The exposed brick walls, jet-black tables, and maroon Naugahyde chairs convey an ultracool tone. This is one of the few LoDo holdovers that has survived since Coors Field arrived. ✉ 1600 15th St., ☎ 303/623–9518. AE, MC, V.

$–$$ ✕ **Wynkoop Brewing Co.** This trendy yet unpretentious local institu-
★ tion was Denver's first brewpub, and it's still the best. Try the terrific shepherd's pie or charbroiled elk medallions with brandy peppercorns. Wash it down with one of the Wynkoop's trademark microbrews—try either the exemplary Railyard Ale or the spicy chili beer. Then check out the gallery, pool hall, and cabaret for a full night of entertainment. ✉ 1634 18th St., ☎ 303/297–2700. AE, DC, MC, V.

$ ✕ **Hotcakes.** This jumping Capitol Hill spot is a breakfast and lunch hangout. Weekend brunch draws crowds of bicyclists and newspaper readers in search of the croissant French toast, "health nut" pancakes, colossal omelets, and scrumptious skillets. ✉ 1400 E. 18th Ave., ☎ 303/830–1909. MC, V. No dinner.

Brazilian

$$ ✕ **Cafe Brazil.** Worth the trip to an outlying neighborhood known as Highlands (just over the viaduct from LoDo), this humble but festive, always-packed spot is the place for shrimp and scallops sautéed with fresh herbs, coconut milk, and hot chiles; *feijoda completa*, the Brazilian national dish of black bean stew and smoked meats, accompanied with fried bananas; or grilled chicken breast in a sauce of palm oil, red chile, shallots, and coconut milk. This not-quite hole-in-the-wall is favored by locals in the know. ✉ 3611 Navajo St., ☎ 303/480–1877. No credit cards. Reservations essential. Closed Sun. and Mon. No lunch.

Chinese

$–$$ ✕ **Imperial Chinese.** Papier-mâché lions greet you at the entrance of this sleek Szechuan stunner, probably the best Chinese restaurant in a 500-mi radius. Seafood is the specialty. Try the steamed sea bass in ginger or the spicy, fried Dungeness crab. ✉ 431 S. Broadway, ☎ 303/698–2800. AE, DC, MC, V. No lunch Sun.

Contemporary

$$–$$$$ ✕ **Strings.** This light, airy restaurant with its wide-open kitchen resembles an artist's loft. It's a preferred hangout for Denver's movers and shakers as well as for visiting celebs, whose autographs on head shots, napkins, and program notes hang on the walls. The specialties include pan-roasted sea bass in a citrus-cashew crust and penne with chicken, mushrooms, and broccoli in a tomato-cream sauce. ⊠ *1700 Humboldt St., ☎ 303/831–7310. Reservations essential. AE, D, DC, MC, V. No lunch Sun.*

$$–$$$ ✕ **Mel's Bar and Grill.** Taking its moniker from proprietor Mel Mas-
★ ters, this cheery Cherry Creek bistro is a perennial favorite of local and national critics. Italian and French traditions are injected with the occasional Asian spin, and the seasonal menu can always be counted on for its delectable mussels "La Cagouille," award-winning Caesar salad, and exceptional grilled salmon and beef tenderloin dinners. The atmosphere is gracious and unpretentious, with a jazz combo performing on a nightly basis. The bar here doubles as a laid-back neighborhood hangout and serves up some of Denver's best (and biggest) burgers. ⊠ *235 Fillmore St., ☎ 303/333–3979. Reservations essential. AE, D, DC, MC, V. No lunch Sun.*

Continental

$$–$$$ ✕ **Janleone.** In Colfax Avenue's historic—and supposedly haunted— Colmar Mansion (1889), proprietor and chef Janette Leone serves up variations of Continental standards, often with a contemporary twist. The predominate influences are French and Italian, but many of Leone's dishes are infused with eclectic touches, from Japanese to Cajun. The resulting fare is uniformly fresh and spiced to perfection; you can't go wrong with the filet of beef with mushrooms and Gorgonzola-wine sauce or the rich seafood lasagna. Brunch is served on Sunday and the desserts, prepared by Janette's daughter Mara, are the best in town. ⊠ *1509 Marion St., ☎ 303/863–8433. Reservations essential. AE, D, DC, MC, V. Closed Mon. No dinner Sun. No lunch.*

French

$$$–$$$$ ✕ **Tante Louise.** This longtime Denver favorite, just 15 minutes from downtown by car, resembles an intimate French country home. Fireplaces, candlelight, and classical music attract a decidedly mature crowd. About one-third of chef Duy Phan's seasonally changing menu is French, one-third is New American, and one-third features low-fat dishes. If available, try the Maine sea scallops served with caramelized foie gras butter or any of the superlative lamb specials. ⊠ *4900 E. Colfax Ave., ☎ 303/355–4488. AE, D, DC, MC, V. Closed Sun. No lunch.*

$$ ✕ **Le Central.** This homey bistro serves excellent mussel dishes and
★ provincial French specialties, including beef Bourguignonne, salmon en croûte, and steak au poivre. A real find, you can depend on Le Central for fabulous food, great service, and a surprisingly low tab. ⊠ *112 E. 8th Ave., ☎ 303/863–8094. AE, D, DC, MC, V.*

Italian

$$–$$$ ✕ **Barolo Grill.** This restaurant looks like a chichi farmhouse, as if Martha
★ Stewart went gaga over an Italian count. Dried flowers in brass urns, hand-painted porcelain, and straw baskets are everywhere. The food isn't pretentious in the least, however. It's more like Santa Monica meets San Stefano—bold yet classic, healthful yet flavorful. Choose from duckling stewed in red wine, fresh pastas, and gnocchi, all well made and fairly priced. ⊠ *3030 E. 6th Ave., ☎ 303/393–1040. Reservations essential. AE, D, DC, MC, V. Closed Sun. and Mon. No lunch.*

$ ✕ **Pasquini's Pizzeria.** Come to this informal, popular spot to indulge in fresh, homemade pastas, pizzas, and calzones. Individual pizzas are the house specialty. Don't miss the bakery's fresh Italian breads. ⊠ *1310 S. Broadway, ☎ 303/744–0917. D, DC, MC, V. No dinner Sun.*

Japanese

$$–$$$ ✕ **Domo.** As Domo's owners pride themselves on fresh flavors and painstaking preparation of "Japanese country foods," this traditional eatery is open only three days a week. It's worth the wait: this is where you'll find some of Denver's best seafood, curry dishes, and vegetarian fare. The house specialty is *wankosushi*—three to five servings of sushi accompanied by rice, soup, and six of Domo's tantalizing side dishes. The restaurant also houses a cultural education center, a museum, and a Japanese garden. ⊠ *1365 Osage St.,* ☎ *303/595–3666. MC, V. Closed Sun.–Wed.*

Mexican

$–$$ ✕ **Tosh's Hacienda.** At the northernmost light-rail stop, Tosh's dishes out Mexican fare both hearty and healthy in a festive atrium bedecked in tile and southwestern art. Specialties include stuffed *sopaipillas* (puffy deep-fried bread pockets), spinach enchiladas, and a whole host of seafood offerings. Kids can order off the children's menu. The service is brisk and attentive at this 50-year-old eatery, and the margaritas spiced with prickly pear cactus are decidedly different. ⊠ *3090 Downing St.,* ☎ *303/295–1861. Reservations not accepted. AE, D, DC, MC, V.*

$ ✕ **Blue Bonnet Café and Lounge.** Its location out of the tourist loop, in a fairly seedy neighborhood southeast of downtown, doesn't stop the crowds (mostly tourists) from lining up early for this restaurant. The early western, Naugahyde decor and fantastic jukebox set an upbeat mood for killer margaritas and some of the best burritos and green chili in town. ⊠ *457 S. Broadway,* ☎ *303/778–0147. Reservations not accepted. MC, V.*

Steak/Western

$$$–$$$$ ✕ **The Fort.** This adobe structure, complete with flickering luminarias
★ and a piñon bonfire in the courtyard, is a perfect replica of Bent's Fort, a Colorado fur trade center. Buffalo meat and game are the specialties; the elk with huckleberry sauce and tequila-marinated quail are especially good. Intrepid eaters might try the buffalo bone-marrow appetizer, jalapeños stuffed with peanut butter, or Rocky Mountain oysters. Costumed characters from the fur trade wander the restaurant, playing the mandolin and telling tall tales. ⊠ *U.S. 285 and Rte. 8,* ☎ *303/697–4771. AE, D, DC, MC, V.*

$$$–$$$$ ✕ **Palm Restaurant.** This Denver outpost of the longtime New York steak house serves meat, seafood, pork chops, and other American dishes à la carte. While the walls are bedecked with caricatures of local celebrities, there's a chance you might see one in person—the restaurant is a favorite of local politicians, executives, and athletes, and with good reason: the steaks and the portions are both superlative. ⊠ *1672 Lawrence St.,* ☎ *303/825–7256. AE, D, DC, MC, V. No lunch weekends.*

$$–$$$$ ✕ **Buckhorn Exchange.** If hunting makes you queasy, don't enter this Denver landmark, a shrine to taxidermy where 500 pairs of eyes stare down at you from the walls. The handsome men's-club decor—with pressed-tin ceilings, burgundy walls, red-checker tablecloths, rodeo photos, shotguns, and those trophies—probably looks the same as it did when the Buckhorn first opened in 1893. Rumor has it Buffalo Bill was to the Buckhorn what Norm Peterson was to *Cheers*. The dry-aged, prime-grade Colorado steaks are huge, juicy, and magnificent, as is the game. For an appetizer, try the smoked buffalo sausage or navy bean soup. ⊠ *1000 Osage St.,* ☎ *303/534–9505. AE, D, DC, MC, V. No lunch weekends.*

Lodging

Denver has lodging choices ranging from the stately Brown Palace to the commonplace YMCA, with options such as bed-and-breakfasts and business hotels in between. Unless you're planning a quick escape to the mountains, consider staying in or around downtown, where most of the city's attractions are within walking distance. Most of the hotels cater to business travelers, with accordingly lower rates on weekends (many establishments slash their rates in half on Friday and Saturday).

$$$$ ★ ⌶ **Brown Palace.** This grande dame of Colorado lodging has housed numerous public figures from President Eisenhower to the Beatles since it first opened its doors in 1892. The details are exquisite: a dramatic nine-story lobby is topped with a glorious stained-glass ceiling, and the Victorian rooms have sophisticated wainscoting and art deco fixtures. In 2000 the hotel put the finishing touches on a five-year, $14 million renovation, availing guests with such high-tech features as high-speed Web access, business services, and cordless telephones. The Palace Arms, its formal restaurant, has won numerous awards, including one from *Wine Spectator* magazine. The Churchill cigar bar sells rare cigars and single-malt scotches. ⊠ *321 17th St., 80202,* ☎ *303/297–3111 or 800/321–2599,* ℻ *303/312–5900,* ⒲ *www.brownpalace.com. 230 rooms, 25 suites. 4 restaurants, 2 bars, in-room data ports, in-room fax, gym, laundry service, concierge, business services, parking (fee). AE, D, DC, MC, V.*

$$$–$$$$ ★ ⌶ **Hotel Teatro.** Black-and-white photographs, costumes, and scenery from plays that were staged in the Denver Performing Arts Complex across the street are displayed in the several grand public areas of this hotel. The earth-tone rooms are sleek, simple, and stylish, featuring the latest in technology, spacious bathrooms with separate tubs and showers, and top-of-the-line amenities. The ninth-floor rooms have balconies. There are two highly regarded restaurants here: a casual bistro, Jou Jou, and the contemporary and elegant Restaurant Kevin Taylor. ⊠ *1100 14th St., 80202,* ☎ *303/228–1100 or 888/727–1200,* ℻ *303/ 228–1101,* ⒲ *www.hotelteatro.com. 104 rooms, 6 suites. 2 restaurants, bar, in-room data ports, in-room fax, gym, laundry service, concierge, business services, parking (fee). AE, D, DC, MC, V.*

$$$–$$$$ ★ ⌶ **Westin Tabor Center.** This sleek, luxurious high-rise opens right onto the 16th Street Mall and all the downtown action. Rooms are oversize and done in grays and taupes, with white duvets, piles of cushy pillows, and contemporary prints on the walls. The fourth-floor pool has one of the best views of the Rockies in all of downtown. Each room has an iron and ironing board, a large working desk, a dual-line speaker phone with voice mail, and cable TV and in-room movies. The hotel even buys blocks of tickets for weekend shows at the Denver Performing Arts Complex for guests' exclusive use. The Palm, a branch of the Manhattan-based steak house, is a favorite eating and drinking spot for local luminaries. ⊠ *1672 Lawrence St., 80202,* ☎ *303/572–9100 or 800/937–8461,* ℻ *303/572–7288,* ⒲ *www.westin.com. 430 rooms. 2 restaurants, 2 bars, in-room data ports, room service, pool, health club, racquetball, laundry service, concierge, business services, parking (fee). AE, D, DC, MC, V.*

$$–$$$$ ⌶ **Adam's Mark.** The city's first convention-headquarters hotel is composed of two distinct structures: a former Radisson designed by I. M. Pei and the onetime May D&F Department Store across the street. The glittering glass hotel—among the 25 largest in the country—includes more than 1,000 rooms and 130,000 square ft of meeting space. The location, at one end of the 16th Street Mall, is ideal. ⊠ *1550 Court Pl., 80202,* ☎ *303/893–3333 or 800/444–2326,* ℻ *303/626–2543,* ⒲ *www.adamsmark.com/denver. 1,225 rooms, 100 suites. 3 restaurants, 3 bars, in-room data ports, room service, pool, sauna, steam room, hair salon, health club, dry cleaning, laundry service, concierge, business services, convention center, parking (fee). AE, D, DC, MC, V.*

$$–$$$$ 🏨 **Warwick Hotel.** This stylish business hotel, ideally located on the edge of downtown, underwent a monumental $20 million renovation that was completed in 2001. The money was well spent: the stylish, oversize rooms and suites are some of the nicest in town, featuring brass and mahogany furnishings and the latest in high-tech perks. All rooms contain wet bars and private terraces with exceptional city views. A restaurant, Randolph's, serves contemporary American cuisine three meals daily. ✉ *1776 Grant St., 80203,* ☎ *303/861–2000 or 800/525–2888,* FAX *303/839–8504,* WEB *www.warwickhotels.com/denver. 220 rooms, 20 suites. Restaurant, 2 bars, in-room data ports, in-room safes, minibars, room service, pool, health club, concierge, business services, parking (fee). AE, D, DC, MC, V.*

$$$ 🏨 **Hotel Monaco.** Visiting celebrities and business travelers check into
★   this hip property with modern perks and art deco–meets–classic-French style. The unabashedly colorful guest rooms feature original art, custom headboards, glass-fronted armoires, and CD players. The service is similarly a cut above: room service is available 24 hours, pets are welcome, and guests without pets are given the complimentary company of a goldfish. The hotel's mascot, a Jack Russell terrier named Lily Sopris, has quickly become one of Denver's best-known canines. ✉ *1717 Champa St., 80202,* ☎ *303/296–1717 or 800/397–5380,* FAX *303/296–1818,* WEB *www.monaco-denver.com. 157 rooms, 32 suites. Restaurant, bar, in-room data ports, in-room fax, minibars, room service, spa, health club, laundry service, concierge, business services, parking (fee). AE, D, DC, MC, V.*

$$–$$$ 🏨 **Burnsley.** This 16-story, Bauhaus-style tower is a haven for executives seeking peace and quiet close to downtown. The tastefully appointed accommodations are all suites and have balconies and full kitchens. Marble foyers and old-fashioned riding prints decorate the rooms. Many suites have a sofa bed, making this a good bet for families. The swooningly romantic restaurant is a perfect place to pop the question. ✉ *1000 Grant St., 80203,* ☎ *303/830–1000 or 800/231–3915,* FAX *303/830–7676,* WEB *www.burnsley.com. 80 suites. Restaurant, bar, pool, laundry service, concierge. AE, D, DC, MC, V.*

$$–$$$ 🏨 **Castle Marne.** This historic B&B, just east of downtown, sits in a shabbily genteel area. Its balconies, four-story turret, and intricate stone and woodwork present a dramatic facade. Rooms are richly decorated with antiques and artwork. Birdcages, butterfly cases, and old photos of the house are displayed throughout. Most rooms have brass or mahogany beds, throw rugs, tile fireplaces (nonworking), a profusion of dried and fresh flowers, and claw-foot tubs; a few have hot tubs or whirlpool baths. There's a TV in the common room. A full gourmet breakfast—served in the dining room—is included in the room rate, as is afternoon tea. ✉ *1572 Race St., 80206,* ☎ *303/331–0621 or 800/926–2763,* FAX *303/331–0623,* WEB *www.castlemarne.com. 10 rooms, 1 suite. Dining room, lounge, business services. MC, V. BP.*

$$–$$$ 🏨 **Holiday Chalet B&B.** Stained-glass windows and homey touches throughout make this 1896 Victorian brownstone exceptionally charming. It's also conveniently situated in Capitol Hill, the neighborhood immediately east of downtown. Many of the rooms are furnished with overstuffed Victorian armchairs in light floral fabrics and such historic touches as furniture once owned by Baby Doe Tabor. Some units have tile fireplaces, others have small sitting rooms. Each room has a full kitchen, a holdover from the home's days as an apartment, and full breakfast is included. Across a surprisingly serene courtyard, the Oak & Berries Tea Room serves a light lunch with tea Thursday through Sunday. ✉ *1820 E. Colfax Ave., 80218,* ☎ *303/321–9975 or 800/626–4497,* FAX *303/377–6556,* WEB *www.bbonline.com/co/holiday. 10 rooms. Dining room, kitchenettes. AE, D, DC, MC, V. BP.*

$$–$$$
★ 🖫 **Loews Denver Hotel.** The 12-story steel-and-black-glass facade conceals the unexpected and delightful Italian baroque motif within. Rooms are spacious and elegant, with earth tones and blond wood predominating, and such lovely touches as fresh flowers, fruit baskets, and Renaissance-style portraits. The formal Tuscany restaurant serves sumptuous Italian cuisine. Guests may use a nearby health club, and a Continental breakfast is included on Sunday. The only drawback of this property is its location: halfway between downtown and the Denver Tech Center, with little in the immediate vicinity. ✉ *4150 E. Mississippi Ave., 80222,* ☎ *303/782–9300 or 800/345–9172,* 𝖥𝖠𝖷 *303/758–6542,* 𝖶𝖤𝖡 *www.loewshotels.com. 183 rooms, 19 suites. Restaurant, bar, in-room data ports, in-room fax, minibars, room service, health club, laundry service, concierge, business services, free parking. AE, D, DC, MC, V.*

$$–$$$ 🖫 **Merritt House.** This beautifully run, antiques-filled 1889 Queen Anne Victorian B&B in Capitol Hill serves a full breakfast with a different selection of made-to-order items each day. Originally designed by Brown Palace architect Frank Edbrooke, the inn's rooms are replete with interesting interior angles, original hardwood floors, and an assortment of antiques and reproductions. Large bay windows with window seats frame the third-story room's four-poster bed and vaulted ceiling. Five of the rooms have double whirlpool baths. Locals put their guests up at this find only 10 blocks from downtown. ✉ *941 E. 17th Ave., 80218,* ☎ *303/861–5230 or 877/861–5230,* 𝖶𝖤𝖡 *www.merritthouse.com. 10 rooms. AE, D, DC, MC, V. BP.*

$$–$$$
★ ✕🖫 **Oxford Hotel.** During the Victorian era this hotel was an elegant fixture on the Denver landscape. Rooms are uniquely furnished with French and English period antiques, while the Cruise Room bar re-creates an art deco ocean liner. The hotel's location is perfect for those seeking a different, artsy environment. Complimentary shoe shines, afternoon sherry, and morning coffee are among the civilized touches offered here. Although the Oxford is a notch down from the Brown Palace in most respects, it's also less expensive and is home to McCormick's Fish and Oyster House, Denver's premier seafood restaurant. ✉ *1600 17th St., 80202,* ☎ *303/628–5400 or 800/228–5838,* 𝖥𝖠𝖷 *303/628–5413,* 𝖶𝖤𝖡 *www.theoxfordhotel.com. 80 rooms. Restaurant, 2 bars, in-room data ports, room service, hair salon, spa, health club, parking (fee). AE, D, DC, MC, V.*

$$–$$$
★ 🖫 **Queen Anne Inn.** Occupying two adjacent Victorians north of downtown in the regentrified Clements historic district (some of the neighboring blocks have yet to be reclaimed), this is a delightful, romantic getaway for B&B mavens. Both houses have handsome oak wainscoting and balustrades, 10-ft vaulted ceilings, numerous bay or stained-glass windows, and such period furnishings as brass and canopy beds, cherry and pine armoires, and oak rocking chairs. The best accommodations are the four "gallery suites" dedicated to Audubon, Rockwell, Calder, and Remington. A full breakfast and afternoon tastings of Colorado wines are offered daily. ✉ *2147 Tremont Pl., 80205,* ☎ *303/296–6666 or 800/432–4667,* 𝖥𝖠𝖷 *303/296–2151,* 𝖶𝖤𝖡 *www.queenannebnb.com. 10 rooms, 4 suites. Dining room. AE, D, DC, MC, V. BP.*

$$ 🖫 **Comfort Inn/Downtown.** The advantages of this well-used hotel are its reasonable rates and its location in the heart of downtown. Rooms are somewhat cramped, but the corner rooms on the upper floors feature wraparound windows with panoramic views. A complimentary deluxe Continental breakfast is included in the rate. ✉ *401 17th St., 80202,* ☎ *303/296–0400 or 800/237–1431,* 𝖥𝖠𝖷 *303/297–0774,* 𝖶𝖤𝖡 *www.comfortinn.com. 231 rooms. Restaurant, bar, laundry service, parking (fee). AE, D, DC, MC, V. CP.*

Nightlife and the Arts

Friday's *Denver Post* and *Denver Rocky Mountain News* both pub-lish calendars of the week's events, as does the slightly alternative *Westword,* which is free and published on Wednesday. Downtown and LoDo are where most Denverites make the nightlife scene. Downtown features more mainstream entertainment, whereas LoDo is home to fun, funky rock clubs and small theaters. Remember that Denver's al-titude can intensify your reaction to alcohol.

The ubiquitous **TicketMaster** (☎ 303/830–8497) is Denver's prime agency, selling tickets to almost all concerts, sporting events, and plays that take place in the Denver area. **TicketMan** (⊠ 6800 N. Broadway, ☎ 303/430–1111 or 800/200–8497) sells tickets to major events, ei-ther by phone or at their office north of downtown. On the theatrical side of the spectrum, the **Ticket Bus** (☎ no phone), on the 16th Street Mall at Curtis Street, sells tickets from 10 until 6 weekdays, and half-price tickets on the day of the performance.

Fiddler's Green (⊠ 6350 Greenwood Plaza Blvd., ☎ 303/220–7000) hosts larger outdoor concerts in the summer. Downtown, the **Paramount Theater** (⊠ 1631 Glenarm Pl., ☎ 303/623–0106) is the venue for many large-scale rock concerts. The exquisite 9,000-seat **Red Rocks Am-phitheater** (⊠ Morrison, off U.S. 285 or I–70, ☎ 303/640–2637), nes-tled among majestic geological formations in nearby Morrison, is renowned for its natural acoustics. Red Rocks will be closed for ren-ovations until June 2002.

BARS

Denver's numerous brewpubs are always abuzz with activity: **Rock Bot-tom Brewery** (⊠ 1001 16th St., ☎ 303/534–7616) is a perennial fa-vorite, thanks to its rotating special brews and reasonably priced pub grub. **Rock Island** (⊠ Wazee and 15th Sts., ☎ 303/572–7625) caters to the young and hip.

CABARET

The **Impulse Theater** (⊠ 1634 18th St., downstairs in the Wynkoop Brewpub, ☎ 303/297–2111) hosts everything from top-name jazz acts to up-and-coming stand-up comedians to cabaret numbers.

COMEDY CLUBS

Three area improv groups make their home at **Bovine Metropolis The-ater** (⊠ 1527 Champa St., ☎ 303/758–4722), which also stages satir-ical productions. Denver comics have honed their skills at **Comedy Works** (⊠ 1226 15th St., ☎ 303/595–3637) for 20 years. Well-known per-formers often drop by.

COUNTRY MUSIC CLUBS

The legendary **Grizzly Rose** (⊠ I–25 at Exit 215, ☎ 303/295–1330) has miles of dance floor, national bands, and gives two-step dancing lessons. **Stampede Grill & Dance Emporium** (⊠ 2430 S. Havana St., Aurora, ☎ 303/337–6909) is another cavernous boot-scooting spot.

DANCE CLUBS

Deadbeat Club (⊠ 4040 E. Evans Ave., ☎ 303/758–6853), a cavernous building with three dance floors, is where the cool college crowd goes to get carded.

DINNER THEATER

The **Country Dinner Playhouse** (⊠ 6875 S. Clinton St., ☎ 303/799–1410) serves a meal before the performance, which is usually a Broad-way-style show.

Charlie's (✉ 900 E. Colfax Ave., ☏ 303/839–8890) offers country-western atmosphere and music. **The Grand** (✉ 538 E. 17th Ave., ☏ 303/839–5390) is an upscale piano bar that specializes in martinis and cocktails.

Brendan's Pub (✉ 1624 Market St., ☏ 303/595–0609) attracts local and national blues talents. **El Chapultepec** (✉ 1962 Market St., ☏ 303/295–9126) is a cramped, fluorescent-lit, bargain-basement Mexican dive. Still, the limos parked outside hint at its enduring popularity: this is where visiting musicians, from former visits of Ol' Blue Eyes to the Marsalis brothers, jam after hours. Hidden in the back of a parking lot, the hipster favorite **Herb's Hideout** (✉ 2057 Larimer St., ☏ 303/299–9555) is a gloriously nostalgic bar with dim lighting and checkerboard floors, featuring smooth jazz and blues acts onstage as well as the occasional DJ. LoDo's slickly contemporary **Sambuca Jazz Café** (✉ 1320 15th St., ☏ 303/629–5299) serves up live jazz and Mediterranean cuisine on a nightly basis. **Vartan's Jazz Club** (✉ 1800 Glenarm Pl., ☏ 303/399–1111) is a comfortable place to listen to a variety of jazz.

There are a number of smoky hangouts in this city, the most popular being the regally restored **Bluebird Theater** (✉ 3317 E. Colfax Ave., ☏ 303/322–2308) which showcases local and national acts, emphasizing rock, hip-hop, ambient, and the occasional evening of cinema. **Cricket on the Hill** (✉ 1209 E. 13th Ave., ☏ 303/830–9020) is a somewhat seedy Denver institution, presenting a mix of rock, blues, acoustic, and alternative music. Down-home **Herman's Hideaway** (✉ 1578 S. Broadway, ☏ 303/777–5840) showcases mostly local rock, with a smattering of reggae and blues thrown in to keep things lively. The **Mercury Café** (✉ 2199 California St., ☏ 303/294–9281) triples as a health-food restaurant (sublime tofu fettuccine), fringe theater, and rock club specializing in acoustic sets, progressive, and newer wave music.

The **Colorado Symphony Orchestra** performs at Boettcher Concert Hall (✉ 13th and Curtis Sts., ☏ 303/986–8742). **Opera Colorado** (☏ 303/778–5100) has a spring season, often with internationally renowned artists, at the Denver Performing Arts Complex. The **Colorado Ballet** (☏ 303/837–8888) specializes in the classics; performances are staged at the Denver Performing Arts Complex.

The **Bug Theatre Company** (✉ 3654 Navajo St., ☏ 303/477–9984) produces primarily cutting-edge, original works in Denver's Highlands neighborhood. **Denver Center Attractions** (✉ 14th and Curtis Sts. at DPCA's Temple Buell and Auditorium theaters, ☏ 303/893–4100) brings Broadway road companies to town. The **Denver Center Theater Company** (✉ 14th and Curtis Sts., ☏ 303/893–4100) presents high-caliber repertory theater, including new works by promising playwrights, at the Bonfils Theatre Complex (part of the Denver Performing Arts Complex). The **Denver Performing Arts Complex** (✉ 14th and Curtis Sts., ☏ 303/893–4000) houses a good chunk of the city's large concert and theater venues, with eight different stages of varying capacities centered around an open-air galleria with a high glass ceiling. Both the ballet and opera have their seasons here, and dozens of theater groups produce everything from experimental drama to Broadway musicals. **El Centro Su Teatro** (✉ 4725 High St., ☏ 303/296–0219) is a Latino-Chicano company that puts on mostly original works and a variety of festivals during its May to September season. **Hunger Artists Ensemble Theater** (⊠ Denver Civic Theater, 721 Santa Fe Dr., ☎ 303/893–5438) presents dramas, comedies, and adaptations of works from the likes of Shakespeare, James Joyce, and Tom Stoppard.

Outdoor Activities and Sports

Participant Sports

CYCLING AND JOGGING

The **Denver Parks Department** (☎ 303/964–2500) has suggestions for biking and jogging paths throughout the metropolitan area's 250 parks, including the popular Cherry Creek and Chatfield Reservoir State Recreation areas. With more than 400 mi of off-road paths in and around the city, cyclists can move easily between urban and rural settings. The well-kept **Cherry Creek Bike Path** runs from Cherry Creek Shopping Center to Larimer Square downtown alongside the peaceful creek of its name. The scenic **Highline Canal** has 70 mi of mostly dirt paths through the metro area running an almost completely level grade. **Platte River Greenway** is a 20-mi-long path for in-line skating, bicycling, and jogging that runs alongside Cherry Creek and the Platte River. Much of it runs through downtown Denver. There are 12 mi of paved paths along the **South Platte River** heading into downtown. West of the city, paved paths wind through **Matthews-Winters Park,** just south of I–70 on Colorado 26, dotted with plaintive pioneer graves amid the sun-bleached grasses, thistle, and columbine. The **Deer Creek Canyon** trail system is popular with mountain bikers, running through forested foothills southwest of Denver near the intersection of C–470 and Wadsworth Avenue.

Just south of downtown, **The Bicycle Doctor** (⊠ 860 Broadway, ☎ 303/831–7228) offers repairs and rents street and mountain bikes for $10 to $40 a day. Pick out a mountain bike at **Bicycle Village** (⊠ 6435 E. Hampden Ave., ☎ 303/691–1921), which rent for about $25 each 24-hour rental period. **Blazing Saddles Bicycle Rentals** (⊠ 1432 Market St., ☎ 303/534–5255) rents bikes by the day ($25) and hour ($5). They also provide trail maps for five different urban tours and rent bikes with the latest in high-tech cycling gadgetry.

FITNESS

Denver has more fitness clubs per capita than any other American city. **Bally's Total Fitness** (⊠ 720 S. Colorado Blvd., ☎ 303/782–9424), featuring a wide array of exercise equipment, including stationary bikes and weight machines, offers free passes to out-of-town visitors. The state-of-the-art **Colorado Athletic Club** (⊠ 1630 Welton St., ☎ 303/623–2100) is a 40,000-square-ft, full-service facility featuring more than 60 aerobics and yoga classes weekly. The club has cardiovascular and fitness equipment; weight training; racquetball and basketball courts; and a running track, among other features. Complimentary day passes are available to guests of many major hotels. The City of Denver operates 29 **Recreation Centers** (☎ 303/964–2500), many of which have indoor pools, weight rooms, basketball courts, and other amenities. A nonresident day pass is $6.

GOLF

Six courses are operated by the City of Denver and are open to the public. Green fees for all range from $17 to $24. For same-day tee times, visitors can call the starters at an individual course, but for advance reservations golfers must call the **main reservation system** (☎ 303/784–4000) up to three days in advance. **City Park** (⊠ E. 25th Ave. and York St., ☎ 303/295–4420) is a fairly plain course near downtown with a few good skyline views. The 69-par **Evergreen** (⊠ 29614 Upper Bear

Creek, Evergreen, ☎ 303/674–4128) features undulating fairways in a mountainous, forested setting. **Kennedy** (✉ 10500 E. Hampden Ave., ☎ 303/751–0311) is a popular spot with three 9-hole courses as well as a par-3 course. Fairly flat **Overland Park** (✉ S. Santa Fe Dr. and Jewell Ave., ☎ 303/698–4975) has quite a few bunkers. Donald Ross designed **Wellshire** (✉ 3333 S. Colorado Blvd., ☎ 303/692–5636) with small, subtly breaking greens and tree-lined fairways. **Willis Case** (✉ W. 50th Ave. and Vrain St., ☎ 303/458–4877) is hilly and wide open.

Arrowhead Golf Club (✉ 10850 W. Sundown Trail, Littleton, ☎ 303/973–9614), 45 minutes from downtown in Roxborough State Park, was designed by Robert Trent Jones and is set impressively among red sandstone spires. **The Ridge at Castle Pines** (✉ 1414 Castle Pines Pkwy., Castle Rock, ☎ 303/688–0100) is an 18-hole Tom Weiskopf–designed course with great mountain views and dramatic elevation changes. It is ranked among the nation's top 100 public courses.

HIKING

Mt. Falcon Park looks down on Denver and across at Red Rocks. It's amazingly tranquil, laced with meadows and streams and shaded by conifers. The trails are very well marked. ✉ *Off Rte. 8, Morrison exit, or U.S. 285, Parmalee exit.*

Just 15 mi southwest of Denver, **Red Rocks Park and Amphitheater** is a breathtaking, 70-million-year-old wonderland of vaulting oxblood-and-cinnamon-color sandstone spires. The outdoor music stage is set in a natural 9,000-seat amphitheater (with perfect acoustics, as only nature could have designed) that has awed the likes of Leopold Stokowski and the Beatles. Tickets to concerts are available through Ticketmaster, but hiking in this metro Denver park is free. (However, the amphitheater will be closed for concerts until June 2002 for renovations.) ✉ *Off U.S. 285 or I–70 in Morrison.*

Roxborough State Park has an easy 2-mi loop trail through rugged rock formations, offering beautiful vistas and a unique look at metro Denver and the plains. This trail is handicap accessible. ✉ *I–25 south to Santa Fe exit, take Santa Fe Blvd., south to Titan Rd. Turn right, and follow signs.*

TENNIS

The city has 28 parks with tennis courts. For information call the **Denver Parks Department** (☎ 303/964–2522).

WATER SPORTS

Chatfield and Cherry Creek marinas rent sailboats, powerboats, and Jet Skis (April–October at Cherry Creek and Memorial day–Labor Day at Chatfield). **Chatfield Marina** (✉ Chatfield State Park, Littleton, ☎ 303/791–5555 or 303/791–6104) is on the fringes of the Rocky Mountains 15 mi south of downtown and attracts wakeboarders, water-skiers, and tubers. Southeast of Denver, the **Cherry Creek Marina** (✉ Cherry Creek State Park, Aurora, ☎ 303/779–6144) serves the 850-acre reservoir of the same name, a sailing hot spot.

Spectator Sports

The Colorado Avalanche of the National Hockey League are wildly popular in Denver, winning the Stanley Cup in 1996 and beating the New Jersey Devils for an encore in 2001. The Denver Nuggets of the National Basketball Association are something of an ugly duckling in Denver's professional sports scene. Both the Nuggets and Avalanche play at the **Pepsi Center** (✉ 1000 Chopper Pl., ☎ 303/405–8555), a 19,000-seat arena that opened in 1999. The Colorado Rockies, Denver's National League baseball team, plays April–October in **Coors Field** (✉ 2001 Blake St., ☎ 303/292–0200 or 800/388–7625). The National Football League's Denver Broncos play September–December at the $400-million-dollar **Invesco Field at Mile High** (✉ 1900 Eliot St., Exit 210B off I–25, ☎ 303/433–7466). Broncos owner Pat Bowlen footed the one-million-dollar bill for the seven larger-than-life bronze horses running up the hill next to the stadium's south entrance. As every game has sold out for 30 years, tickets are not easy to come by.

Horse racing takes place June through August at **Arapahoe Park** (✉ 26000 E. Quincy Ave., ☎ 303/690–2400). **Bandimere Speedway** (✉ 3051 S. Rooney Rd., Morrison, ☎ 303/697–6001) features NHRA Championship Drag Racing from April through October.

Shopping

Denver may be the best place in the country for shopping for recreational gear. Sporting-goods stores hold legendary ski sales around Labor Day. The city's selection of books and western fashion is also noteworthy.

MALLS AND SHOPPING DISTRICTS

The **Cherry Creek** shopping district features an enclosed mall and several surrounding retail-oriented blocks 2 mi from downtown in a pleasant, predominantly residential neighborhood. On one side of First Avenue at Milwaukee Street is the **Cherry Creek Shopping Mall**(✉ 3000 E. 1st Ave., ☎ 303/388–3900), a granite-and-glass behemoth that holds some of the nation's top retailers among its 160 stores, including: Abercrombie & Fitch, Eddie Bauer, Banana Republic, Burberry's, Tiffany & Co., Lord & Taylor, Louis Vuitton, Neiman Marcus, Polo/Ralph Lauren, and Saks Fifth Avenue. Just north of the Cherry Creek Shopping Mall is the **Cherry Creek North** shopping district (✉ between 1st and 3rd Aves. from University Blvd. to Steele St., ☎ 303/394–2904), an open-air development of tree-lined streets and shady plazas, with art galleries, specialty shops, and fashionable restaurants.

The **Denver Pavilions** (✉ 16th St. Mall between Tremont and Welton Sts.) is downtown Denver's newest shopping and entertainment complex, a three-story, open-air structure that houses national stores like Barnes & Noble, NikeTown, Ann Taylor, Talbot's, and a Virgin Records Megastore. There are also several restaurants, including Denver's Hard Rock Cafe, and a 15-screen movie theater. Historic **Larimer Square** (✉ 14th and Larimer Sts.) houses distinctive shops and restaurants. Some of the square's retail highlights are the new Vespa scooter dealership; Earthzone, a gallery featuring art fashioned from fossils and minerals; and John Atencio Designer Jewelry. **Tabor Center** (✉ 16th St. Mall) is a light-filled atrium whose 20 specialty shops and restaurants include the ESPN Zone theme restaurant and Sunglass Hut. Others, such as the Best of Denver store, showcase uniquely Coloradan merchandise and souvenirs. **Writer Square** (✉ 1512 Larimer St.) has Tiny Town— a doll-size village inhabited by Michael Garman's inimitable figurines— as well as shops and restaurants.

The upscale **Park Meadows** mall (✉ I–25, 5 mi south of Denver at County Line Rd.) was designed to resemble a ski resort, with a 120-ft-high log-beam ceiling anchored by two massive stone fireplaces. In addition to Colorado's first Nordstrom, the center includes more than 100 specialty shops. On snowy days, "ambassadors" scrape your windshield while free hot chocolate is served inside.

Between Denver and Colorado Springs, **Prime Outlets at Castle Rock** (✉ Exit 184 off I–25) offers 25%–75% savings on everything from appliances to apparel at its more than 50 outlets.

ANTIQUES DEALERS

South Broadway between First Avenue and Evans Street, as well as the side streets off this main drag, is chockablock with dusty antiques stores, where patient browsing could net some amazing bargains. More than 80 dealer showrooms fill the **Antique Mall of Lakewood** (⊠ 9635 W. Colfax Ave., ☎ 303/238–4914).

BOOKS

The Tattered Cover (⊠ 1st Ave. at Milwaukee St., ☎ 303/322–7727; ⊠ 1628 16th St., ☎ 303/436–1070) is a must for all bibliophiles. It may be the best bookstore in the United States, not only for the near-endless selection of volumes (more than 400,000 on four stories at the Cherry Creek location and 300,000 in LoDo) and helpful, knowledgeable staff, but also for the incomparably refined atmosphere. Treat yourself to the overstuffed armchairs, reading nooks, and afternoon readings and lectures.

CRAFT AND ART GALLERIES

LoDo has the trendiest galleries, many in splendidly and stylishly restored Victorian warehouses.

African Experiences (⊠ 2850 E. 2nd St., ☎ 303/595–0965) sells South African imports, including astonishing masks. One of the oldest and best photography galleries between the east and west coasts, **Camera Obscura Gallery** (⊠ 1309 Bannock St., ☎ 303/623–4059) carries images both contemporary and vintage. **David Cook/Fine American Art** (⊠ 1637 Wazee St., ☎ 303/623–8181) specializes in historic Native American art and regional paintings, particularly Santa Fe modernists. The **Mudhead Gallery** (⊠ 555 17th St., across from the Hyatt, ☎ 303/293–0007; ⊠ 321 17th St., in the Brown Palace, ☎ 303/293–9977) sells museum-quality southwestern art, with an especially fine selection of Santa Clara and San Ildefonso pottery, and Hopi kachinas.

Native American Trading Company (⊠ 1301 Bannock St., ☎ 303/534–0771) carries an outstanding collection of weavings, pottery, jewelry, and regional paintings. **Old Santa Fe Pottery**'s (⊠ 2485 S. Santa Fe Dr., ☎ 303/871–9434) 20 rooms are crammed with Mexican masks, pottery, rustic Mexican furniture—even a chip dip and salsa room. Cherry Creek has its share of chic galleries, including **Pismo** (⊠ 235 Fillmore St., ☎ 303/333–2879), which showcases exquisite handblown-glass art.

DEPARTMENT STORES

The nine **Foley's** department stores throughout metropolitan Denver offer good values; their main store (⊠ 15 S. Steele St., ☎ 303/333–8555) is in the Cherry Creek Shopping Mall.

SPORTING GOODS

Gart Brothers Sports Castle (⊠ 1000 Broadway, ☎ 303/861–1122) is a huge, multistory shrine to Colorado's love of the outdoors. Entire floors are given over to a single sport at this and the many other branches throughout Denver. Denver's new **REI Flagship Store** (⊠ 1416 Platte St., ☎ 303/756–3100), one of three such shops in the country, is yet another testament to the city's adventurous spirit. Located in an historic building, the store's 94,000 square ft are packed with all stripes of outdoors gear and some special extras: a climbing wall, a mountain bike track, a white-water chute, and a "cold room" for gauging the protection offered by coats and sleeping bags.

WESTERN PARAPHERNALIA

At Larimer Square, **Cry Baby Ranch** (⊠ 1422 Larimer St., ☎ 303/623–3979) has a rambunctious assortment of 1940s and '50s cowboy kitsch. **Denver Buffalo Company Trading Post** (⊠ 1109 Lincoln St., ☎ 303/832–0884) sells western duds and high-quality souvenirs. Its restaurant specializes in buffalo. There's also a gourmet deli serving BuffDogs (hot dogs made with buffalo meat), corned buffalo, and other such specialties.

Side Trips West of Denver

Less than a half-hour's drive from Denver is Golden, which is also a good jumping-off point for the gambling towns of Central City and Black Hawk.

Golden

Golden, 15 mi west of Denver via I–70 or U.S. 6 (West 6th Avenue), was once the territorial capital of Colorado. City residents have smarted ever since losing that distinction to Denver by "dubious" vote in 1867, but in 1994, then-Governor Roy Romer restored "ceremonial" territorial-capital status to Golden. Today, the city is one of Colorado's fastest-growing, boosted by the high-tech industry as well as longtime employers Coors Brewery and Colorado School of Mines.

A GOOD TOUR

Start at the **Coors Brewery** and take the free tour and tasting. Then walk west on **12th Street**, a National Historic District that includes **Clear Creek History Park.** Go south on Arapahoe one block to the Armory, and then continue on Arapahoe into the **Colorado School of Mines.** From here you'll need a car; take 10th Street east out of town about 2 mi to the **Colorado Railroad Museum.** If there are children in the group, get on I–70 West to Colfax Avenue West (U.S. 40) to the rides of **Heritage Square.** Otherwise, get off on 6th Avenue West (U.S. 6) to 19th Street to the **Buffalo Bill Grave and Museum.** (From Heritage Square, take Heritage Road [Route 93] north to U.S. 6 west.)

Timing: Golden is a 25-minute drive from Denver, and you can see downtown and the Colorado School of Mines in an hour or two. The Coors Brewery tour takes about an hour. To drive to and visit the Colorado Railroad Museum and Buffalo Bill Grave and museum will take one to two hours.

SIGHTS TO SEE

Buffalo Bill Grave and Museum. Contrary to popular belief, Bill Cody—Pony Express rider, cavalry scout, and tireless promoter of the West—never expressed a burning desire to be buried here: The *Denver Post* bought the corpse from Bill's sister, and bribed her to concoct a teary story about his dying wish. Apparently, rival towns were so outraged that the National Guard had to be called in to protect the grave from robbers. Adjacent to the grave is a small museum with art and artifacts detailing Cody's life and times, as well as a run-of-the-mill souvenir shop. The drive up **Lookout Mountain** to the burial site offers a sensational panoramic view of Denver that alone is worth the price of admission. You can also hike up Lariat Look, a winding trail that leads to Buffalo Bill's Grave, starting at 19th Avenue in west Golden. The trail leads to other trailheads branching out from the Jefferson County Nature Center at the peak. Two-thirds of the way up, find the Stapleton Trail that takes you up Lookout Mountain. ⊠ *Rte. 5 off I–70 Exit 256, or 19th Ave. out of Golden,* ☎ *303/526–0747,* WEB *www.buffalobill.org.* ⊡ *$3.* ☉ *May–Oct., daily 9–5; Nov.–Apr., Tues.–Sun. 9–4.*

Clear Creek History Park. This park in the National Historic District interprets the Golden area circa 1843–1900 via restored structures and replicas, including a tepee, prospector's camp, schoolhouse, and cabins.

⊠ *11th and Arapahoe Sts.,* ☎ *303/278–3557.* ☒ *$3; $4 for park and Astor House.* ☉ *Mid-May–mid-Oct., Wed.–Sun. 11–4; tours on the hr.*

Colorado Railroad Museum. Just outside Golden is this must-visit for any choo-choo lover. More than 50 vintage locomotives and cars are displayed outside. Inside the replica-1880 masonry depot are historical photos and puffing Billy (nickname for steam trains) memorabilia, along with an astounding model train set that steams through a miniature, scale version of Golden. New for 2001 was a roundhouse where visitors can witness a train's restoration in progress. ⊠ *17155 W. 44th Ave.,* ☎ *303/279–4591,* WEB *www.crrm.org.* ☒ *$6.* ☉ *Daily 9–5.*

Colorado School of Mines. The nation's largest and foremost school of mineral engineering has a lovely campus containing an outstanding **geology museum** displaying minerals, gemstones, and fossils from around the world and a reproduction of a gold mine. Guided tours are available Tuesday through Thursday when student volunteers are available. Also on campus is the prominent **U.S.G.S. National Earthquake Center** (⊠ 1711 Illinois St., ☎ 303/273–8500) which is responsible for pinpointing seismic activity all over the country. Tours are by appointment Tuesday–Thursday 9–11 and 1–3. ⊠ *16th and Maple Sts.,* ☎ *303/273–3815,* WEB *www.mines.edu.* ☒ *Free.* ☉ *Mon.–Sat. 9–4, Sun. 1–4; closed Sun. May–Aug.*

Coors Brewery. Thousands of beer lovers make the pilgrimage to this venerable brewery each year. One of the world's largest, it was founded in 1873 by Adolph Coors, a 21-year-old German stowaway. The free tour lasts a half hour and explains not only the brewing process, but also how "Rocky Mountain mineral water" is packaged and distributed locally. Informal tastings are held at the end of the tour for those 21 and over; souvenirs are available at the gift shop. ⊠ *13th and Ford Sts.,* ☎ *303/277–2337,* WEB *www.coors.com.* ☒ *Free.* ☉ *Mon.–Sat. 10–4. Children under 18 must be accompanied by an adult.*

☺ **Heritage Square.** This re-creation of an 1880s frontier town has an opera house, a narrow-gauge railway train ride, a Ferris wheel, a water slide, a bungee-jumping tower, specialty shops, and a music hall that stages original comedies and musicals as well as traditional melodramas. A vaudeville-style review ends each evening's entertainment. ⊠ *U.S. 40 and Rte. 93,* ☎ *303/279–2789.* ☒ *Entrance to park is free; admission varies per ride.* ☉ *Shops open Memorial Day–Labor Day, Mon.–Sat. 10–8, Sun. noon–6; Labor Day–Memorial Day, Mon.–Sat. 10–6, Sun. noon–6. Rides open weekends Mar.–May and Sept.–Oct.; daily June–Sept. Hours vary.*

12th Street. This National Historic District has a row of handsome 1860s brick buildings. Among the monuments is the **Astor House** (⊠ corner of 12th and Arapahoe Sts., ☎ 303/278–3557; ☒ $3; ☉ Tues.–Sat. 10–4:30), a museum with period furnishings. Colorado's first **National Guard Armory** (⊠ corner of 13th and Arapahoe Sts.) was built in 1913 and is the largest cobblestone building in America.

Central City and Black Hawk
18 mi from Golden via U.S. 6 west and Rte. 119 north.

When limited-stakes gambling was introduced in 1991 to the beautifully preserved old mining towns of Central City and Black Hawk, howls of protest were drowned out by cheers from struggling townspeople. Fortunately, strict zoning laws were legislated to protect the towns' architectural integrity, and by and large the laws have successfully handled the steady stream of tour buses. Gaming here is restricted to blackjack, poker, and slots, and the maximum bet is $5.

There are nearly 40 casinos in Black Hawk and Central City. All are in historic buildings dating to the 1860s—from jails to mansions—and their plush interiors have been lavishly decorated to re-create the Old West era—a period when this town was known as the "Richest Square Mile on Earth." They all serve meals and offer some entertainment. The most popular are Bullwhackers and Harrah's Glory Hole. While no longer a casino, the Teller House is one of the most historic buildings in either town.

A GOOD TOUR

Both towns can be explored on foot. Starting in Central City, park in one of the pay parking lots in town and begin at the west end of town, at the **Thomas House Museum.** Walk a block down Eureka Street to the **Central City Opera House** and Teller House. Take a detour on Main Street to browse the shops and casinos, and then head back down Eureka Street. Just before the Central Palace casino, you'll see a set of steep stairs; take them directly up to the **Gilpin County Historical Society Museum.** Go back down the stairs and walk the downhill mile to Black Hawk, to the **Mountain City Historic Park** on Gregory Street. If you don't feel like walking back uphill to Central City, catch a free shuttle in front of the Bull Durham or Eureka casinos.

Timing: Both towns are about a 45-minute drive from Denver. Bus transportation is also available from Denver and Golden through most of the casinos and the Opera House. You can cover Central City and Black Hawk's main attractions in a few hours. If you're the gaming type, set aside extra time to try your luck. Although the casinos are open year-round, the museums are open only in the summer.

SIGHTS TO SEE

Central City Opera House. Opera has been staged here almost every year since opening night in 1878. Lillian Gish has acted, Beverly Sills has sung, and many other greats have performed in the Opera House. Because there's no central heating, performances are held in summer only. ✉ *200 Eureka St., Central City,* ☎ *303/292–6700 Denver box office,* WEB *www.centralcityopera.org.*

Gilpin County Historical Society Museum. Photos and reproductions, as well as vintage pieces from different periods of Gilpin County history, paint a richly detailed portrait of life in a typical rowdy mining community. ✉ *228 E. High St., Central City,* ☎ *303/582–5283.* ✍ *$3; $5 in conjunction with admission to the Thomas House Museum.* ☉ *June–Sept., daily 11–4; Oct.–May, by appointment only.*

Mountain City Historic Park. Apart from the casinos, this city block is the prime attraction in Black Hawk, consisting of a dozen historic homes and commercial structures from the town's heyday. It's a nice stroll that offers a glimpse of intermingling Victorian and Gothic architectural styles. ✉ *Gregory St., Black Hawk,* ☎ *303/582–5221.* ✍ *Free.* ☉ *Daily 24 hrs.*

Thomas House Museum. This 1874 house is an example of Victorian mountain elegance. It depicts the life of a middle-class turn-of-the-20th-century family through family photos and heirlooms such as period quilts and feather hats. ✉ *209 Eureka St., Central City,* ☎ *303/582–5283.* ✍ *$3; $5 in conjunction with admission to the Gilpin County Historical Society Museum.* ☉ *June–Sept., Fri.–Mon. 11–4; Oct.–May, by appointment only.*

DINING AND LODGING

Virtually every casino has a restaurant with the usual mediocre $4.99 daily specials and all-you-can-eat buffets. The only restaurant outside a casino is the Teller House, which is open in accordance with opera season.

$$–$$$$ ✕ **White Buffalo Grille.** Regarded as the best casino restaurant in the area, the White Buffalo serves up steaks and seafood with southwestern panache. The steaks are mesquite-broiled and served with poblano bordelaise and shallot jam; another good bet is the chile-glazed swordfish with kiwi-pineapple salsa. The atmosphere is upscale and the views from the all-glass enclosure on a bridge above Richmond Street are divine. ✉ *240 Main St. in the Lodge Casino, Black Hawk,* ☎ *303/ 582–1771. AE, D, DC, MC, V. Closed Mon. No lunch.*

$ ✕ **Teller House.** This edifice was once one of the West's ritziest hotels, but it now serves as a casual restaurant during Central City's summer opera season. The grub here is simple and fresh, a mix of sandwiches, salads, and burgers. The floor of the famous Face Bar is adorned with the portrait of a mystery woman named Madeline, painted in 1936 by Herndon Davis. Some say it was created as a lark, others bet it was done for the price of a drink. ✉ *120 Eureka St., Central City,* ☎ *303/ 292–6500. AE, D, MC, V. Closed mid-Aug.–late June.*

$–$$ 🏠 **Golden Rose Victorian Hotel.** On the second floor of a historic bank building (1875), this establishment is a departure from the standard casino accommodations. Each room is named after a luminary from Central City's mining era: the Madam Lou Bunch Room is decorated a bit more aggressively than your typical historic inn—with red wallpaper and a "kissing couch"—but the accommodations are otherwise mellow, equipped with antiques, reproductions, and details down to period wallpaper. ✉ *101 Main St., Central City 80427,* ☎ *303/582– 3737. 5 rooms. Bar. AE, MC, V.*

Denver A to Z

AIRPORTS AND TRANSFERS

Denver International Airport, or DIA, is located 15 mi northeast of downtown. It is served by most major domestic carriers and many international ones, including Air Canada, American, America West, Continental, Delta, Frontier, Mesa, Northwest, Sun Country, TWA, United, and USAir.

Between the airport and downtown, Super Shuttle makes door-to-door trips. The region's public bus service, Regional Transportation District (RTD) runs SkyRide to and from DIA; the trip takes 50 minutes, and the fare is $6. There is a transportation center in the airport just outside baggage claim. A taxi ride costs $43–$55 to downtown from DIA.

➤ AIRPORT INFORMATION: **Denver International Airport** (☎ 800/247– 2336, WEB www.flydenver.com).

➤ TAXIS AND SHUTTLES: **Regional Transportation District** (☎ 303/299– 6000 for route and schedule information; 303/299–6700 for other inquiries, WEB www.rtd-denver.com). **Super Shuttle** (☎ 303/370–1300).

BUS TRAVEL TO AND FROM DENVER

Greyhound Lines serves Denver.

➤ BUS INFORMATION: **Greyhound Lines** (✉ 1055 19th St., ☎ 800/231– 2222).

BUS TRAVEL WITHIN DENVER

The region's public bus service, RTD, is comprehensive, with routes throughout the metropolitan area. The service also links Denver to outlying towns such as Boulder, Longmont, and Nederland. You can buy bus tokens at grocery stores or pay with exact change on the bus. Fares vary according to time and zone. Within the city limits, buses cost $1.25

during peak hours (6 AM–9 AM, 4 PM–6 PM), 75¢ at other times. You can also buy a Cultural Connection Trolley ticket for $3 at several convenient outlets throughout downtown, from the trolley driver, or from most hotel concierges. The trolley operates daily, every half hour 9–6, linking 18 prime attractions from the Denver Performing Arts Complex downtown to the Denver Museum of Nature and Science in City Park. Tickets are good for the entire day.

➤ BUS INFORMATION: **Cultural Connection Trolley** (☎ 303/299–6000). RTD (☎ 303/299–6000 or 800/366–7433, WEB www.rtd-denver.com).

CAR RENTAL

Rental car companies include Advantage, Alamo, Avis, Budget, Dollar, Enterprise, Hertz, and National. All have airport and downtown representatives.

CAR TRAVEL

Reaching Denver by car is fairly easy, except during rush hour when the interstates (and downtown) get congested. Interstate Highways 70 and 25 intersect near downtown; an entrance to I–70 is just outside the airport.

Broadway runs north–south through Denver. Speer Boulevard runs alongside Cherry Creek from northwest to southeast through downtown; numbered streets run parallel to Speer. Colfax Avenue (U.S. 287) runs east–west through downtown; numbered avenues run parallel to Colfax. (It gets confusing—numbered streets intersect numbered avenues at a right angle at Broadway. When you're looking for an address, make sure you know whether it's a street or avenue. Most numbered streets are one-way.) Other main thoroughfares include Colorado Boulevard (north–south) and Alameda Avenue (east–west). Try to avoid driving in the area during rush hour, when traffic gets heavy.

PARKING

Finding an open meter has become increasingly difficult in downtown Denver, especially during peak times such as Rockies games and weekend nights. Additionally, most meters have two-hour limits until 10 PM. However, there is no shortage of pay lots ($5 to $25 per day).

EMERGENCIES

Concentra Medical Center is a full medical clinic. HealthOne and Health Advisors offer a free referral service. Rose Medical Center refers patients to doctors from 8 to 5:30 and is open 24 hours for emergencies. Exempla St. Joseph Hospital is open 24 hours. Walgreens and King Soopers pharmacies are both open around the clock.

➤ DENTISTS: **Affordable Dentist USA** (☎ 888/657–6453). **Dental Referral Service** (☎ 800/428–8773).

➤ HOSPITALS: **Concentra Medical Centers** (✉ 1860 Larimer St., Suite 100, ☎ 303/296–2273). **Exempla St. Joseph Hospital** (✉ 1835 Franklin St., ☎ 303/837–7111). **Health Advisors** (☎ 303/777–6877). **HealthOne** (☎ 877/432–5846). **Rose Medical Center** (✉ 4567 E. 9th Ave., ☎ 303/320–2121).

➤ 24-HOUR PHARMACIES: **King Soopers** (✉ 3100 S. Sheridan Blvd., ☎ 303/937–4404). **Walgreens** (✉ 2000 E. Colfax Ave., ☎ 303/331–0917).

MEDIA

NEWSPAPERS AND MAGAZINES

The *Denver Post* and the *Denver Rocky Mountain News,* now under a joint operating agreement, are Denver's two daily newspapers. *Westword* is an alternative, liberal-leaning weekly that's published every Wednesday, focusing on local politics, media, and entertainment. The bimonthly *5280 Magazine* is a light lifestyle/arts/entertainment publication.

SAFETY

While Denver is a generally peaceful city, the crime rate has increased slightly in recent years as the population has boomed. There are a few shadier areas on the outskirts of downtown, but violent crimes are few and far between. As always, paying attention to your surroundings is your best defense.

TAXIS

Cabs are available by phone and at the airport and can generally be hailed outside major hotels, for $1.60 minimum, $1.60 per mi. However, at peak times—during major events and at 2 AM when the bars close—taxis are very hard to come by.

➤ TAXI COMPANIES: **Metro Taxi** (☎ 303/333–3333). **Yellow Cab** (☎ 303/777–7777). **Zone Cab** (☎ 303/444–8888).

TOURS

BUS TOURS

Gray Line Tour of Denver offers a two-hour city tour, a Denver mountain parks tour, and other regional excursions. Tours range from $30 to $70 per person. Actually Quite Nice Brew Tours' 23-seat Brewmobile hauls beer aficionados to the best microbreweries in Metro Denver, which it touts as the "Napa Valley of Brewing."

➤ FEES AND SCHEDULES: **Actually Quite Nice Brew Tours** (☎ 303/431–1440). **Gray Line Tour** (☎ 303/289–2841).

WALKING TOURS

Gunslingers, Ghosts and Gold conducts humorous and trivia-filled walking tours of downtown ($15) that focus on both the historic and the supernatural and cover a few miles in two hours. Lower Downtown District, Inc. offers guided tours of historic Denver. Self-guided walking-tour brochures are available from the Denver Metro Convention and Visitors Bureau.

➤ FEES AND SCHEDULES: **Gunslingers, Ghosts and Gold** (☎ 303/860–8687). **Lower Downtown District, Inc.** (☎ 303/628–5428).

TRAIN TRAVEL

Union Station has Amtrak service. RTD's Light Rail service's original 5⅓-mi track links southwest and northeast Denver to downtown. In 2000, RTD extended the tracks down to the city's southern suburbs; the peak fare is $1.25 within the city limits.

➤ TRAIN INFORMATION: **RTD Light Rail** (☎ 303/299–6000, WEB www.rtd-denver.com). **Union Station** (✉ 17th Ave. at Wynkoop St., ☎ 303/534–2812).

TRANSPORTATION AROUND DENVER

In downtown Denver, free shuttle-bus service operates about every 10 minutes until 1 AM, running the length of the 16th Street Mall (which bisects downtown) and stopping at two-block intervals. If you plan to spend much time outside downtown, a car is advised, although Denver has one of the best city bus systems in the country and taxis are available.

VISITOR INFORMATION

The Denver Metro Convention and Visitors Bureau, open weekdays 8–5 and Saturday 9–1, is located downtown above the Wolf Camera store on California Street. It provides information and free maps, magazines, and brochures, as does an information center at the Tabor Center (same hours).

➤ TOURIST INFORMATION: **Denver Metro Convention and Visitors Bureau** (✉ 1555 California St., Denver 80202, ☎ 303/892–1112 or 800/

393–8559, FAX 303/892–1636, WEB www.denver.org). **Visitor Informa-tion Center** (✉ 1668 Larimer St. at the Tabor Center).

NORTH CENTRAL COLORADO

Updated by
Gregory Robl

North Central Colorado is an appealing blend of Old West and New Age. More a ranching than a mining area, it's strewn with rich evo-cations of pioneer life, as well as turn-of-the-20th-century resort towns such as Estes Park and Grand Lake. Yet the region is anchored by Boul-der, one of the country's most progressive cities and a town virtually synonymous (some might say obsessed) with environmental concern and physical fitness. As the local joke goes, even the dogs jog.

Boulder residents take full advantage of the town's glorious natural setting, nestled against the peaks of the Front Range, indulging in everything from rock climbing to mountain biking. A short drive south brings them to the ski areas along I–70. To the west and north, the Roo-sevelt and Arapaho national forests and the Great Lakes of Colorado provide a host of recreational opportunities from hiking to fishing to cross-country skiing and snowmobiling. Estes Park is the gateway to America's alpine wonderland: Rocky Mountain National Park, which spans three ecosystems that 900 species of plants, 250 species of birds, and 25 species of mammals—including elk, deer, moose, bobcats, and even black bears—call home.

Boulder

🕖 *25 mi northwest of Denver via U.S. 36.*

No place in Colorado better epitomizes the state's outdoor mania than Boulder. Boulder started taxing itself in 1967 in order to buy greenbelts and in 2000 had a referendum (failed) on the ballot to provide free pub-lic transportation for city residents. There are nearly as many bikes as cars in this uncommonly beautiful and beautifully uncommon city em-broidered with 30,000 acres of parks and greenbelts and laced with more than 200 mi of trails for hiking, walking, jogging, and biking.

In this vibrant and liberal city, personal styles run the gamut from the latest trends out of Los Angeles and New York to the punkish look of neon blue hair and an armor of body piercings. Natty professorial togs are still common in this university town as well as the proverbial Boul-der three-piece suit: a T-shirt, fleece vest, and shorts, completed by Birken-stock sandals. The city is home to the Buddhist Naropa University, the National Institute of Standards and Technology, the Boulder College of Massage Therapy, the University of Colorado at Boulder, the Na-tional Center for Atmospheric Research, and the nationally popular *E-Town* radio show.

Pearl Street between 8th and 20th streets is the city's hub, an eclectic collection of classy boutiques, consignment shops, eccentric book-stores, art galleries, cafés, bars, and restaurants. A few national retailers have hung out their signs among the home-grown businesses along the four-block pedestrian mall, but beyond 11th Street to the west and 15th Street to the east, the milieu evokes the early days of the Pearl Street Mall. The **Boulder Museum of Contemporary Art** hosts local and in-ternational contemporary art exhibits. ✉ *1750 13th St.,* ☎ *303/443–2122.* 🎫 *$4.* ◷ *Tues.–Sat. 10–6.*

Three blocks north of Pearl Street and west of Broadway is **Mapleton Historic District,** a charming neighborhood of turn-of-the-20th-century homes and shady trees. **Historic Boulder** (✉ 646 Pearl St., ☎ 303/444–

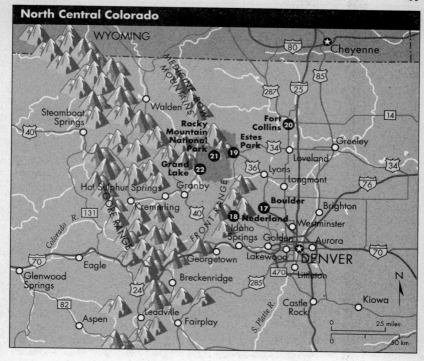

5192) sponsors both guided and self-guided tours of the area during summer and the Christmas season.

South of downtown is the **University of Colorado at Boulder** campus. Red sandstone buildings with tile roofs (built in the "Rural Italian" architectural style that Charles Z. Klauder created in the early 1920s) outline the campus's green lawns and small ponds. The **Norlin Quadrangle** (on the National Register of Historic Places), a broad lawn where students sun themselves or play a quick round of Frisbee between classes, is the center of the original campus that was begun in 1875 with the construction of Old Main. The **CU Heritage Center** (⊠ Old Main Bldg. on Norlin Quadrangle, ☎ 303/492–6329; 💲 free; ⊙ weekdays 10–4, Sat. 10–2) preserves the history of the university—including notable student pranks and a lunar sample on long-term loan from NASA—and displays the personal memorabilia of alumni such as Marilyn Van Derbur, Robert Redford, Glenn Miller, and CU's 12 astronauts, among them Ellison Onizuka, who was killed aboard the *Challenger* space shuttle in 1986. The natural history collection at the **University of Colorado Museum** (⊠ Henderson Bldg., ☎ 303/492–6892; 💲 free; ⊙ weekdays 9–5, Sat. 9–4, Sun. 10–4) includes dinosaur relics and has permanent and changing exhibits. ⊠ *University Memorial Center, ☎ 303/492–1411; 303/492–6301 to reserve a tour,* WEB *www.colorado.edu. ⊙ Campus tours year-round, weekdays 10:30 and 2:30, Sat. 10:30. Reservations required.*

The university's **Fiske Planetarium/Sommers-Bausch Observatory** present star shows Friday at 7:30 PM and laser shows set to the music of well-known bands on Fridays at 10 PM and selected Saturdays at 2 PM during the academic year. The observatory is open Friday evenings, weather permitting. ⊠ *Regent Dr., ☎ 303/492–5001,* WEB *www.colorado.edu/fiske.* 💲 *$4. ⊙ Year-round. Closed on university holidays.*

A favorite college student hangout is the bohemian neighborhood called **The Hill** (13th St. between Pennsylvania St. and College Ave.), which is home to eateries, music venues, record shops, bars, coffeehouses, and hip boutiques. The actor Robert Redford worked at **The Sink** (⊠ 1165 13th St., ☎ 303/444–7465) during his student years. The restaurant has served great pizza, burgers, beer, and other student dietary staples since 1949.

The prettiest views of town can be had by following Baseline Drive (off Broadway) up to **Chautauqua Park** (⊠ 900 W. Baseline Rd.), site of the Colorado Music Festival, and a favorite oasis of locals on weekends. Continue farther up Flagstaff Mountain to Panorama Point and Boulder Mountain Park, where people jog, bike, and climb. The admirable park system includes the trademark red sandstone **Flatirons.** These massive structures, so named for their flat rock faces, are popular among rock climbers and hikers. They can be seen from almost every vantage point in town.

The scents of hops fill the air during the free tours and tastings at the **Rockies Brewing Company.** ⊠ *2880 Wilderness Pl.,* ☎ *303/444–8448.* ⊡ *Free.* ☉ *Tours Mon.–Sat. 2* PM.

Celestial Seasonings, North America's largest herbal-tea producer (8 million tea bags per 24-hour period) offers free tours of its factory. Before the tour, you can sample from more than 60 varieties of tea and view the sewing machine used to sew the company's first 10,000 tea bags in 1969. The famous "Mint Room" will clear your tear ducts and sinuses. Teas, foodstuffs, teapots, and T-shirts are sold in the gift shop. The café, open weekdays, serves breakfast 7:30 AM–9:30 AM and lunch 11–2:30. ⊠ *4600 Sleepytime Dr., 8 mi northeast of downtown Boulder,* ☎ *303/581–1202.* ⊡ *Free.* ☉ *Tours Mon.–Sat. 10–3, hourly; Sun. 11–3, hourly.*

The **Leanin' Tree Museum of Western Art**—brought to you by the folks who make popular and humorous western-theme greeting cards—is one of the country's largest privately owned collections of post-1950 cowboy and western art. More than 200 paintings of western landscapes, wildlife, and the pioneers' ranch life and 85 bronze sculptures by renowned, contemporary artists including Bill Hughes and Frank McCarthy, recall an era in the Boulder Valley before lattés and herbal tea. The superlative collection ranges from traditionalists in the Remington and Bierstadt manner to stylistic innovators of the western genre. One room is devoted to the paintings of the original greeting-card genius, Lloyd Mitchell. ⊠ *6055 Longbow Dr.,* ☎ *303/530–1442,* WEB *www.leanintree.com.* ⊡ *Free.* ☉ *Weekdays 8–4:30, Sat. 10–4.*

Dining and Lodging

Boulderites dine out at over 300 restaurants whose cuisines include ethnic surprises like Nepalese, Indian, Ethiopian, and Moroccan. Prices vary, but most are reasonable and geared to the large student population. Smoking is banned in all Boulder workplaces, restaurants, and bars.

$$$$ ✕ **Flagstaff House.** This refined restaurant on Flagstaff Mountain is
★ one of Colorado's finest. Sit on the enclosed patio and drink in the sublime views of Boulder while enjoying a selection from the remarkably comprehensive wine list. Chef Mark Monette is noted for his exquisite combinations of ingredients and fanciful, playful presentations. The menu changes daily, but sample inspirations might include lobster ravioli and shrimp in shiitake broth; potato roll of smoked rabbit and duck with sautéed foie gras; mesquite-smoked alligator and rattlesnake; and elk dumplings with ginger and sweet onion. ⊠ *1138 Flagstaff Rd.,* ☎ *303/442–4640. Reservations essential. AE, DC, MC, V.*

$$–$$$$ ✕ **Red Lion Inn.** A local institution for natives and travelers, this beautiful inn resides up in Boulder Canyon. For a feeling of the Alps, ask to be seated in the original dining room—with its fireplace, antlers, Austrian murals, red tablecloths, and white napery. The stone walls and potbellied stove in the bar make it a cozy place to wait for a table. The Red Lion is revered for its excellent game: start with rattlesnake cakes or wild game sausage, then try the elk or caribou steak. Or order a satisfying old-fashioned specialty, such as steak Diane or one of the specials. ⊠ *Boulder Canyon Dr.,* ☎ *303/442–9368. Reservations essential. AE, D, MC, V. No lunch.*

$$$ ✕ **Gold Hill Inn.** This humble log cabin hardly looks like a bastion of
★ haute cuisine, but the six-course, $26 prix-fixe dinner is something to rave about. Sample entrées may be broiled, stuffed trout; paella; or lamb venison marinated for four days in buttermilk, juniper berries, and cloves. The inn also hosts occasional "murder mystery" nights using professional actors. ⊠ *Sunshine Canyon, 10 mi from Boulder,* ☎ *303/443–6461. No credit cards.* ☺ *Closed Nov.–Apr. and Tues. No lunch.*

$$–$$$ ✕ **Da Gabi Cucina.** It's well worth the quest to find this jewel of a stylish restaurant in an out-of-the-way strip mall. Both the food and personal, knowledgeable service are exquisite. Tapas such as calamari fritti, mussels, and bruschetta are tasty starters. Try the homemade black ravioli stuffed with salmon and served in a tomato cream sauce, the chicken marsala, or the gnocchi in walnut-Gorgonzola cream sauce. Whether you're looking for low light and romance or simply a nice place to meet a friend, you'll find it here. ⊠ *3970 N. Broadway,* ☎ *303/786–9004. AE, DC, MC, V. No lunch.*

$$–$$$ ✕ **Mediterranean Café.** After work, when all of Boulder shows up to enjoy tapas, "The Med" becomes a real scene (you may feel quite closed in, despite the restaurant's light and airy design). The decor is Portofino meets Santa Fe, with abstract art, terra-cotta floors, and brightly colored tile. The open kitchen turns out daily specials such as barbecued mahimahi and horseradish-crusted tuna—dishes complemented by an extensive, well-priced wine list. Come here for a dose of local attitude and pretty people. During happy hour from 4 to 6:30, various tapas are just a buck or two. ⊠ *1002 Walnut St.,* ☎ *303/444–5335. AE, D, DC, MC, V.*

$$–$$$ ✕ **Sunflower.** Storefront-size windows allow plenty of sun into the room where chefs/owners Jon Pell and Alison McDonald serve savory meals like golden masuman curry, tempeh scallopini, and a bamboo steamer that are based on fresh, organic ingredients. Even the nonvegetarian entrées are exclusively organic and free-range, such as the sesame-crusted salmon and the corn-and-sage–stuffed chicken breast. Organic selections are even available on the wine list. End your lunch or dinner with a creamy, decadent, chocolate dessert prepared without dairy products, refined sugar, or eggs. Mr. Pell spent 16 years developing the dessert; he won't share the recipe. Brunch is served on Sunday. ⊠ *1701 Pearl St.,* ☎ *303/440–0220. AE, MC, V.*

$$–$$$ ✕ **Zolo Grill.** David Query, who once served Malcolm Forbes as his
★ personal chef, now serves happy patrons of Zolo Grill superlative southwestern cuisine. Its huge picture windows overlook an active shopping center and the Flatirons beyond. Blond-wood furnishings, striking abstract art, and a high-tech open kitchen complete the urbane decor. The inventive menu offers tortilla-crusted ahi tuna served with chipotle beurre blanc. The margaritas, which may be sipped on the open patio, are sassy, and there's a short but fairly priced wine list (about half the wines are available by the glass). ⊠ *2525 Arapahoe Blvd.,* ☎ *303/449–0444. AE, MC, V.*

$$ ✕ **Boulder Dushanbe Teahouse.** A unique sight in Colorado, this stunning teahouse is a gift from Boulder's sister city, Dushanbe, in Tajikistan. More than 40 artisans handcrafted the building in the traditional Tajik style including the exterior, ceramic Islamic art and the carved, painted ceiling. The menu presents a culinary cross section of the world that includes Cajun gumbo, Persian lamb kabob, Tajik *plov* (a rice dish with beef and vegetables), Balinese fried fish, and Tibetan kongpo beef. The house-tea gingerbread is a favorite. Staff are knowledgeable about the more than 80 tea varieties and can recommend one for any palate. Patio dining is available with views of the park. The teahouse is also open for breakfast weekdays. ⊠ *1770 13th St.,* ☎ *303/442–4993,* WEB *www.boulderteahouse.com. AE, D, MC, V.*

$$ ✕ **Mataam Fez.** Eat with your hands at this lavish Moroccan restaurant that looks as if it came straight from *The Arabian Nights.* The prix-fixe dinner ($25) includes five courses, with such fragrant dishes as lamb with honey and almonds and hare paprika couscous. There are branches in Denver, Colorado Springs, and Vail, but this is the original. ⊠ *2226 Pearl St.,* ☎ *303/440–4167. AE, D, DC, MC, V. No lunch.*

$$ ✕ **Sushi Zanmai.** The restaurant section is a cool, sleek place to enjoy
★   delectable seafood and very good hibachi items. But the action's really at the zany sushi bar, where the chefs periodically burst into song: "If you knew Sushi" is a popular request. There's always karaoke here, although the official night is Saturday. ⊠ *1221 Spruce St.,* ☎ *303/440–0733. AE, MC, V. No lunch weekends.*

$$$–$$$$ ✕▥ **Gold Lake Mountain Resort & Spa.** There are no exercise machines
★   or in-room phones and TVs at this casual, environmentally responsible resort where you can dip into four lakeside hot pools. Come here to revive your body and soul with activities like canoeing, fly-fishing, snowshoeing, and hiking—and luxurious spa treatments (including an herbal remedy for altitude sickness). You'll slumber peacefully beneath a huge, goose-down comforter in a rustic, 1920s lakeside cabin with period antiques and slate and zinc bathrooms. Executive Chef Eric Skokan at Alice's Restaurant ($$$$) has a gift for drawing savory and indulgent three- or seven-course spa meals out of simple, organic ingredients like quince, partridge, persimmons, and truffles. Ask the knowledgeable servers to pair wines with the courses of your dinner; they never miss. ⊠ *3371 Gold Lake Rd., Ward, 80481, 32 mi northwest of Boulder,* ☎ *303/459–3544 or 800/450–3544,* FAX *303/459–3541,* WEB *www.goldlake.com. 18 cabins. Restaurant, bar, hot tub, sauna, spa, hiking, horseback riding, mountain bikes, ice-skating, cross-country skiing, recreation room. D, MC, V.*

$$$–$$$$ ▥ **Hotel Boulderado.** The gracious lobby of this elegant 1909 beauty
★   has a soaring stained-glass ceiling, and the mezzanine beckons with romantic nooks galore. When choosing a room, opt for the old building, with spacious quarters filled with period antiques and reproductions. The new wing is plush and comfortable but has less Victorian character. Mountain views and smoking rooms are available on request. The restaurant, Q's, serves the stylish New American cuisine of John Platt. The Catacombs Blues Bar is always hopping. Guests have access to the nearby health club, The Pulse. Business travelers can benefit from the 24-hour, complimentary services. ⊠ *2115 13th St., 80302,* ☎ *303/442–4344 or 800/433–4344,* FAX *303/442–4378. 160 rooms. 3 restaurants, 2 bars, in-room data ports, business services, meeting rooms. AE, D, DC, MC, V.*

$$$ ▥ **Coburn House.** Designer-architect Scott Coburn wanted to create a tasteful lodging providing the services of a hotel and the intimacy of an inn, and he succeeded. The "no shoes" policy protects guests from the tapping of hard-soled shoes on the hardwood floors. Modern western furnishings like hand-carved wood and iron beds, work desks, and pine armoires lend a warm elegance to the oversize rooms. A "green" hotel, the Coburn uses low-flush toilets, reduced-flow showerheads,

and 100% cotton linens. The self-serve breakfast buffet is as light or filling as guests like and features coffee cake, fruit, yogurt, juice, and coffee. ✉ *2040 16th St., 80302,* ☎ *303/545–5200 or 800/585–5811,* FAX *303/440–6740,* WEB *www.coburnhouse.com. 12 rooms. Breakfast room, in-room data ports, business services, meeting rooms. AE, MC, V. CP. No children under 14.*

$$$ ★ 🏨 **Victoria B&B.** This ideally situated, 1870s Victorian has the most exquisite accommodations in the area. Large rooms, each named after a present or former owner, run toward the English country-home look. Brass beds, down comforters, terry-cloth robes, lace curtains, rocking chairs, dried flowers, and period antiques complete the picture. In addition to the complimentary Continental breakfast, baked goods (try the scones or gingersnaps) and tea are served every afternoon in a sunny parlor scented with potpourri. ✉ *1305 Pine St., 80302,* ☎ *303/938–1300. 7 rooms. Breakfast room. AE, MC, V. CP.*

$$–$$$ 🏨 **Briar Rose B & B.** Innkeeper Margaret Weisenbach makes guests feel completely at home in this appealing B&B. There are six rooms in the sturdy, 1890s brick main house and four in the adjacent carriage house. The individually decorated rooms abound in froufrou, such as floral carpeting and flowers stenciled above the headboards. All rooms have down comforters and private baths; the most expensive have wood-burning fireplaces. ✉ *2151 Arapahoe Ave., 80302,* ☎ *303/442–3007. 10 rooms. AE, DC, MC, V. BP.*

$$–$$$ 🏨 **Earl House Historic Inn.** You'll find this 1882 stone Gothic Revival mansion only four blocks from the Pearl Street Mall. Each room has a whirlpool tub or steam shower. Enjoy homemade baked goods at breakfast and afternoon tea, served on marble-top tables near the fireplace. The luxury here is in the details, so much that you may find it difficult to leave your room to sightsee. The Continental breakfast buffet includes a hot dish. ✉ *2429 Broadway, 80304,* ☎ *303/938–1400,* FAX *303/938–9710,* WEB *www.bouldervictoria.com. 6 rooms. Breakfast room. AE, D, MC, V. CP.*

$$–$$$ 🏨 **Inn on Mapleton Hill.** Tall trees shade this impressive redbrick Victorian with jade trim. The sunny, individually decorated guest rooms are just as elegant, with hardwood or brass beds, rocking chairs or armoires, throw rugs, lace curtains, and hand-stenciled walls; two also have marble gas-burning fireplaces. The location, on a quiet residential street two blocks from the Pearl Street Mall, is ideal. Owners Judi and Ray are happy to share their local expertise with guests. Lasting friendships have been made over breakfasts of homemade granola, cinnamon French toast, and great coffee. ✉ *1001 Spruce St., 80302,* ☎ *303/449–6528,* FAX *303/415–0470,* WEB *www.innonmapleton.com. 7 rooms. AE, MC, V. BP. No children under 12.*

$$–$$$ ★ 🏨 **Millennium Hotel Boulder.** This relatively large property has an unusual semicircular design, set amid immaculate gardens dotted with splashing fountains. Spacious rooms are done up in light woods and pastel colors, and some have full baths with a mountain view. In keeping with Boulder's environmental concerns, the 269 rooms have been designated as ecologically sound, with all trash recycled and water treated and recirculated. ✉ *1345 28th St., 80302,* ☎ *303/443–3850 or 800/545–6285,* FAX *303/443–1480,* WEB *www.millennium-hotels.com. 269 rooms. Restaurant, bar, indoor-outdoor pool, hot tubs, 15 tennis courts, basketball, gym, playground, laundry service, business services, meeting rooms, travel services, car rental. AE, D, DC, MC, V.*

$$ 🏨 **Pearl Street Inn.** The decor is reserved and refined at this B&B, favoring fresh flowers, light colors like sage, plush carpeting, watercolors of Colorado scenery, antiques, and brass or mahogany four-poster beds. The dining alcove and garden courtyard with the fountain are fine places to enjoy the full breakfasts with crispy waffles and home-

made granola. Guests can enjoy an evening drink or a complimentary glass of wine at the mahogany, copper-top bar. ⊠ *1820 Pearl St., 80302,* ☎ *303/444–5584 or 888/810–1302. 8 rooms. Bar, breakfast room. AE, MC, V. BP.*

$$　🏨 **Quality Inn & Suites Boulder Creek.** The independently owned inn, just a 10-minute walk from downtown Pearl Street and five minutes from CU, provides the personal attention and services of a B&B, including a complimentary, hot breakfast buffet. The caring staff have been known to scrape ice off guests' car windshields. The well-lighted, spacious rooms with custom iron lamps and wood and leather furniture in rich earth tones create a sophisticated, yet comfortable feel. Rooms have kitchenettes with microwaves, refrigerators, and granite countertops. ⊠ *2020 Arapahoe Ave., 80302,* ☎ *303/449–7550 or 888/449–7550,* FAX *303/449–7082,* WEB *www.qualityinnboulder.com. 40 rooms, 6 suites. Breakfast room, in-room data ports, kitchenettes, indoor pool, hot tub, sauna, gym, laundry service, business services. AE, D, MC, V. BP.*

$–$$　🏨 **Colorado Chautauqua Association.** The association was founded in 1898 as part of the Chautauqua movement and still fulfills its charge to provide a venue for recreation and cultural and educational enrichment. Guests enjoy lectures, concerts, and silent films accompanied by a pianist. The simple lodge rooms and cabins are fully furnished, including linens and cooking utensils (in rooms with kitchens), but no phones, TVs, or daily housekeeping. The green is a terrific spot for a picnic before a concert or before the annual Independence Day fireworks. Cabins are also available and run $68–$185 nightly. ⊠ *900 Baseline Rd. 80302,* ☎ *303/442–3282,* FAX *303/449–0790,* WEB *www.chautauqua.bouldernet.com. 16 rooms, 69 cabins. Restaurant, 2 tennis courts, hiking, concert hall, playground. MC, V.*

$–$$　🏨 **Foot of the Mountain.** This series of connecting wood cabins is con-
★　veniently located near the mouth of Boulder Canyon and the Boulder Creek Path. It seems far from Boulder's bustle, yet it's only a few minutes' walk from downtown. Each cozy cabin has either a mountain or stream view and is outfitted with TV, phone, heater, minirefrigerator, and large bath—but no air-conditioning. Pets can board too for an extra charge. ⊠ *200 Arapahoe Ave., 80302,* ☎ *303/442–5688,* FAX *303/442–5719,* WEB *www.footofthemountainmotel.com. 18 rooms. Refrigerators. AE, D, MC, V.*

Nightlife and the Arts

BARS AND LOUNGES

The **Corner Bar** (⊠ 2115 13th St., ☎ 303/442–4344) in the Hotel Boulderado is a contemporary American pub with outdoor seating. It's a popular place for a business lunch or an after-work cocktail. **The Foundry** (⊠ 1109 Walnut St., ☎ 303/447–1803) is where the hip hang out—in front is an espresso bar (open weekdays at 7 AM); in back is a cigar bar and smoking parlor; in between is the main bar with 11 pool tables and a mezzanine overlooking all the action. The **Mediterranean Café** (⊠ 1002 Walnut St., ☎ 303/444–5335) is the place to see and be seen. Bartenders at **Rio Grande Mexican Restaurant** (⊠ 1101 Walnut St., ☎ 303/444–3690) make Boulder's best margaritas (no frilly variations—just classic margs). The **West End Tavern** (⊠ 926 Pearl St., ☎ 303/444–3535), with its rooftop deck, is a popular after-work hangout serving fine pub grub.

DINNER SHOW

Boulder's Dinner Theater (⊠ 5501 Arapahoe Ave., ☎ 303/449–6000 or 800/448–5501) presents Broadway-style musicals.

The microbreweries are popular places where friends meet for a fresh brew. The **Oasis Brewery** (✉ 1095 Canyon Blvd., ☎ 303/449–0363) is the locals' favorite. **Rockies Brewing Company** (✉ 2880 Wilderness Pl., ☎ 303/444–8448) has a bar. Good beer and upscale pub fare are served at the **Walnut Brewery** (✉ 1123 Walnut St., ☎ 303/447–1345).

MUSIC AND DANCE CLUBS

The Broker (✉ 555 30th St., ☎ 303/449–1752) has Bentley's Lounge, with salsa, swing, and tango. Free lessons are given Thursday nights ($5 cover). In the Hotel Boulderado, the **Catacombs Blues Bar** (✉ 2115 13th St., ☎ 303/443–0486) presents local and national blues and rock talent Wednesday through Saturday. The **Fox Theater** (✉ 1135 13th St., ☎ 303/447–0095) is an art deco movie palace that now hosts top touring bands as well as the occasional Disco Inferno. **Soma** (✉ 1915 Broadway, ☎ 303/938–8600), one of Colorado's most popular dance clubs, pulsates nightly to the high-energy beat of hip-hop, underground, and techno—all spun by nationally known DJs. Tuesday through Saturday, dancers at the **Trilogy Wine Bar** (✉ 2017 13th St., ☎ 303/473–9463) move to everything from toe-tapping Cajun ditties to the smooth, silky Latin beat of South American music. Class rock acts like Flash Cadillac appear at **Tulagi** (✉ 1129 13th St., ☎ 303/938–8090), also the venue for hip-hop dance nights.

PERFORMANCES

The Boulder Philharmonic (✉ University of Colorado, Macky Auditorium and Old Main Theatre, ☎ 303/449–1343) presents its own concert season, as well as chamber music concerts, the Boulder Ballet Ensemble, and special performances by visiting divas such as Kathleen Battle. **The Boulder Theater** (✉ 2032 14th St., ☎ 303/786–7030, WEB www.bouldertheater.com) is a venue for top touring bands and the radio show that features environmental speakers and folk musicians, *E-Town*. Concerts take place throughout the summer at Boulder's peaceful **Chautauqua Community Hall** (✉ 900 Baseline Rd., ☎ 303/442–3282).

The superb **College of Music** (☎ 303/492–8008, WEB www.cuconcerts.org) at CU presents concerts year-round, including performances by the internationally renowned Takás String Quartet. National dance companies teach and perform at the **Colorado Dance Festival** (☎ 303/442–7666, WEB www.cdf-dance.org) from late June to late July. CU's Mary Rippon outdoor theater is the **Colorado Shakespeare Festival**'s (☎ 303/492–0554, WEB www.coloradoshakes.org) annual venue for the bard's comedies and tragedies from mid-June to mid-August. The **Dept. of Theater and Dance** at the University of Colorado (☎ 303/492–8181, WEB www.colorado.edu/TheatreDance) stages excellent student productions throughout the year.

Outdoor Activities and Sports

Memorial Day brings the annual 10-km **Bolder Boulder** (☎ 303/444–7223, WEB www.bolderboulder.com), when top international runners, along with 45,000 others, run in the country's fourth-largest race.

CYCLING

The **Boulder Creek path** winds through town for about 16 mi from the mouth of Fourmile Canyon west of Boulder to Arapahoe and 55th streets, connecting to over 200 mi of city and greenbelt trails and paths. For more strenuous mountain biking, head west out of town to **Walker Ranch** (✉ 8 mi west of town on Flagstaff Rd.); the 7½-mi loop has great views of the Indian Peaks. To get there take Baseline Road west; it becomes Flagstaff Road at the sharp curve before the steep incline. For less technical cycling but a scenic 7.2-mi, two-hour ride nonetheless, the **Be-**

tasso Preserve Loop is 3 mi west of Broadway on Canyon Boulevard. Look for the trailhead turnout on the left. The **Foothills Trail,** accessed off North 4th Street, offers an 8-mi ride out to Boulder Reservoir. To test your quadriceps, take the **Switzerland Trail,** a 9–13-mi ride with a nice drop to the town of Sunset, and a climb up to Gold Hill. From Broadway drive west 5 mi on Canyon Boulevard and turn right onto Sugarloaf Road. After 5 mi turn right at Sugarloaf Mountain Road. The parking area is 1 mi farther.

You can rent a mountain bike for four hours to three days at **Full Cycle** (⊠ 1211 13th St., ☏ 303/440–7771). **University Bicycles** (⊠ 839 Pearl St., ☏ 303/444–4196) rents bikes (including a helmet and a map) for four hours to one week.

FISHING

Kinsley Outfitters (⊠ 1155 13th St., ☏ 303/442–6204 or 800/442–7420), endorsed by Orvis, licensed and insured, arranges half- and full-day guided fishing trips that include meals and gear.

GOLF

In Boulder, **Flatirons Golf Course** (⊠ 5706 Arapahoe Ave., ☏ 303/442–7851) is an 18-hole public course within view of the eponymous mountains. Local favorite **Indian Peaks Golf Course** (⊠ 2300 Indian Peaks Trail, Lafayette, Baseline Rd. to Indian Peaks Trail, 10 mi east of Boulder, ☏ 303/666–4706) is an 18-hole course with fine views.

HIKING

For information on the easy to moderate hiking in the Boulder Mountain parks, including Chautauqua Park and Sunshine Canyon, call the **City of Boulder Parks and Recreation Department** (☏ 303/413–7200). Locals love the **Chautauqua Trail/Bluebell Mesa Trail** (⊠ 900 W. Baseline Rd.) loop that leads southwest from Chautauqua Park to the Flatirons (2½-mi round-trip, about 1½ hours) with great views of the city. **Green Mountain** rewards ambitious hikers with beautiful vistas of the Front Range. To get there drive west on Baseline Road and turn left at the sharp curve. The Gregory Canyon, Ranger, E.M. Greenman, and Saddle Rock trails create a 3-mi loop that takes about three hours to hike. To get to Green Mountain's summit (8,144 ft), stay on the Ranger trail to the intersection with the Green Mountain West Ridge trail. Head east to the summit and descend along the E.M. Greenman trail after taking in the view. The 5½-mi hike will take about four hours. Carry a picnic to the **Red Rocks** and relax with lunch and the views of Boulder (1½ mi round-trip, about one hour). From the intersection of Broadway and Mapleton, drive 1 mi west to the parking area. **Flagstaff Mountain** offers hikers a walk to May's Point (1¼ mi, about one hour) for a look at the Indian Peaks. Drive west on Baseline Road to the sharp curve that is Flagstaff Road, and then turn right at Summit Road. The trail starts at the amphitheater.

INNER-TUBING

The **Conoco** gas station (⊠ 1201 Arapahoe Ave., at Broadway, ☏ 303/442–6293) sells inner tubes ($12–$16) for floating down the nearby Boulder Creek. It's open from 7 AM until 8:30 PM.

Shopping

The Hill, centered around 13th Street between College Avenue and Pennsylvania Street, near the university, is a great place for hip duds and CDs. The metropolitan area's newest shopping center is **Flatiron Crossing** (U.S. 36 between Boulder and Denver, ☏ 720/887–9900) near Broomfield. Shoppers can hit stores such as Nordstrom's, Coach, and Sharper Image, browse at a few jewelers and galleries, and take a break in the food court or in one of the popular, fine restaurants. Boulder's **Pearl Street Mall** (⊠ Pearl St. between 11th and 15th Sts.) is both a shopping extravaganza, with upscale boutiques, art galleries, and craft boutiques, and a venue for street musicians and buskers.

ANTIQUES DEALERS

Boulder County's most beautiful collection of antiques is east of the city at **West's Antiques** (⊠ 401 S. Public Rd., Lafayette, ☎ 303/666–7200). From Boulder drive east about 11 mi on Baseline Road and turn right on Public Road.

The town of Niwot, 10 mi northeast of downtown Boulder, is a mecca for antiques hunters, and **Wise Buys Antiques** (⊠ 190 2nd Ave., Niwot, ☎ 303/652–2888) has a good selection.

BOUTIQUES

Alpaca Connection (⊠ 1326 Pearl St., ☎ 303/447–2047) offers Indian silks, Bolivian alpaca, and Ecuadorian merino wool garments. **Chico's** (⊠ 1200 Pearl St., ☎ 303/449–3381) traffics in funky jewelry and natural fibers and fabrics from around the globe. **Fresh Produce** (⊠ 1218 Pearl St., ☎ 303/442–7507) is a Boulder-based company that makes brightly colored and whimsically designed cotton clothing for adults and children.

CHILDREN'S ITEMS

Boulder kids' favorite toy store is **Grandrabbit's Toy Shoppe** (⊠ 2525 Arapahoe Ave., ☎ 303/443–0780). **Little Mountain** (⊠ 1136 Spruce St., ☎ 303/443–1757) carries outdoor clothing for children, and rents child-carrier backpacks and all-terrain strollers. **The Printed Page** (⊠ 1219 Pearl St., ☎ 303/443–8450) sells unique and exquisite old-fashioned toys.

CRAFT AND ART GALLERIES

Art Source International (⊠ 1237 Pearl St., ☎ 303/444–4080) is Colorado's largest antique print and map dealer. **Artesanias** (⊠ 1468 Pearl St., ☎ 303/442–3777) sells Zapotec rugs, Mexican santos, decorative iron, and handcrafted furniture. **Boulder Arts & Crafts Cooperative** (⊠ 1421 Pearl St., ☎ 303/443–3683), owned by 45 local artists, is popular for pottery and photography. The approximately 150 Colorado artists represented create everything from hand-painted silk scarves and handwoven garments to glass art and furniture. **Handmade in Colorado** (⊠ 2010 10th St., ☎ 303/938–8394) sells only the best Colorado-made goods. **Hangouts** (⊠ 1328 Pearl St., ☎ 303/442–2533) carries Mayan- and Brazilian-design handmade hammocks. **McLaren Markowitz Gallery** (⊠ 1011 Pearl St., ☎ 303/449–6807) features fine jewelry, sculpture, paintings, and pottery—primarily with a southwestern feel—and has a branch in the Flatiron Crossing mall. For meditation gear, silk clothes, yoga mats, or a tarot card reading, head to **Namaste** (⊠ 840 Pearl St., ☎ 303/443–2993).

FOOD

Alfalfa's (⊠ 1651 Broadway at Arapahoe St., ☎ 303/442–0909) is an organic supermarket, with everything from "cruelty-free" cosmetics and herbal and homeopathic remedies to glorious produce and picnic supplies. At the deli, the "three-salad plate" is a lunch bargain for $5.99—choose from the selection of healthy, fresh salads like salmon penne, curried turkey, or green lentil. The store has a self-serve salad bar, a juice bar, and a coffee bar and also sells its own sushi, pizza, panini, and baked goods.

From April through October the **Boulder Farmers' Market** (⊠ 13th St. between Canyon Blvd. and Arapahoe St.) sells baked goods, bedding plants, and seasonal produce on Wednesday and Saturday until 2 PM.

GIFT STORES

Two Hands Paperie (✉ 803 Pearl St., ☎ 303/444–0124), also in the Flatiron Crossing mall, carries elegant European stationary, handmade paper, and handcrafted, leather-bound journals. Try out an antique or new fountain pen, and select a well of emerald or havana ink to fill it. **Where the Buffalo Roam** (✉ 1320 Pearl St., ☎ 303/938–1424) sells quirky T-shirts, CU and Colorado souvenirs, and tacky trinkets.

HOME AND GARDEN

The store to visit for the finest selection in cookware, table linen, and kitchen utensils, as well as gourmet food items and cookbooks, is **Peppercorn** (✉ 1235 Pearl St., ☎ 303/449–5847 or 800/447–6905).Gardeners will find their treasures at **The West End Gardener** (✉ 777 Pearl St., ☎ 303/938–0607), purveyors of vintage garden tools and accessories.

OUTDOOR GEAR

McGuckin Hardware (✉ Village Shopping Center, 2525 Arapahoe St., ☎ 303/443–1822) is a Boulder institution that features a mind-boggling array of outdoor merchandise and salespeople who know where everything is. **Mountain Sports** (✉ 2835 Pearl St., ☎ 303/442–8355; ✉ 821 Pearl St., ☎ 303/443–6770) offers the gear to tackle those athletic pursuits that Boulderites revel in.

Nederland

⑱ *16 mi west of Boulder via Canyon Blvd. (CO Rte. 119).*

A funky mountain hamlet at the top of Boulder Canyon and on the scenic Peak-to-Peak Highway, "Ned" is the gateway to skiing at Eldora Mountain Resort and summer hiking in the Indian Peaks Wilderness. A small downtown retains the character of gold-mining days and has several good bars and restaurants. Shops sell gemstones, minerals, and natural products.

Dining and Lodging

$$–$$$ ✕ **Black Forest Restaurant.** One of Colorado's premier wild-game and fowl restaurants, the Black Forest's meal presentations and dining room—replete with heavy wood furniture, a stone fireplace, and Biedermeier-style landscape paintings—are somewhat reminiscent of a southern German restaurant. Specialties are elk, goose, duck, and traditional German fare, all good and filling. Lunch in the atrium is accompanied by a 20-ft waterfall and panoramic views of the snowcapped peaks of the Continental Divide. A smoking parlor and full bar are on the premises. ✉ *24 Big Springs Dr.,* ☎ *303/279–2333 or 303/582–9971. AE, D, MC, V.*

$ ✕ **Neapolitan's.** The meat-filled or vegetarian calzones are monstrous in size, and included in the price are a salad dripping with Gorgonzola and toasted rolls redolent of garlic. If you're a glutton for punishment, you'll want to order the hot fudge sundae topped with homemade sauce that's made with Ghiradelli chocolate. The tiny, rustic restaurant is a favorite with locals and skiers. ✉ *1 First St.,* ☎ *303/258–7313. AE, D, MC, V. No lunch weekdays.*

$$ ▥ **Best Western Lodge at Nederland.** Built in 1994 and ultramodern within, the lodge is constructed of rough-hewn timber, giving it a rustic feel. All rooms are no-smoking and spacious and have refrigerators, coffeemakers, hair dryers, and cable TV; rooms upstairs have cathedral ceilings, and those downstairs have gas fireplaces. The enthusiastic staff will help to arrange any outdoor activity you desire—and the possibilities are just about endless. An excellent choice for those who want to be central, the property is within a half-hour's drive of Boulder, Eldora ski area, and Central City. ✉ *55 Lakeview Dr., 80466,* ☎ *303/ 258–9463 or 800/279–9463,* FAX *303/258–0413,* WEB *www.nedlodge.com. 23 rooms, 1 suite. Refrigerators, no-smoking rooms, hot tub. AE, D, DC, MC, V.*

Nightlife and the Arts

Garnering attention in *Acoustic* magazine, Nederland's only brewpub, the **Wolf Tongue Brewery** (✉ 35 E. 1st St., ☎ 303/358–7001), is the springboard to fame for many local music groups. Live acid-jazz every Monday night and live music by both local and national talent Thursday through Saturday nights draws locals and out-of-towners alike. The food is standard pub fare, but the calzones are popular for their size and flavor. Patrons quaff either the bar's own brews (the coffee porter is a gold-medal winner) or the featured foreign beer of the week, all on tap.

Outdoor Activities and Sports

There is easily accessible hiking and overnight camping (June 1 to September 15) in the **Indian Peaks Wilderness.** Contact the Boulder Ranger District Office for information and permits (☎ 303/444–6600).

SKIING

With a 1,400-ft vertical rise (the longest run is 3 mi), **Eldora Mountain Resort** has expanded to 53 trails, 12 lifts, and 680 acres; 45 km (28 mi) of groomed Nordic track; and a one-half pipe terrain park for snowboarding. The resort rents skis, snowboards, and snowshoes and provides lessons. The new skier services day lodge will have a cafeteria-style restaurant and a sit-down restaurant. ✉ *5 mi west of Nederland on Rte. 119,* ☎ *303/440–8700,* WEB *www.eldora.com.* ☉ *Early Nov.–mid-Apr., daily 9–4; weekends and holidays during the season, 8:30–4.*

The **Peak-to-Peak Highway,** which winds from Central City, through Nederland, to Estes Park, is not the quickest route to the eastern gateway to Rocky Mountain National Park but is certainly the most scenic. You'll pass through the old mining towns of Ward and Allenspark and be rewarded with spectacular mountain vistas and, in the fall, golden stands of aspen.

Lyons

14 mi north of Boulder on U.S. 36.

Lyons is the Front Range's ideal feng shui town according to resident Timothy Oakes, professor and expert in the geography of China—a quirky description for this down-to-earth community in the red sandstone foothills. This pleasant town of cafés, restaurants, ice-cream shops, and antiques stores offers plenty of recreation opportunities.

Dining

$–$$ ✕ **Gateway Café.** Locals head here to enjoy upscale, yet unpretentious, versions of Asian and western cuisines in a casual atmosphere. Elk chili with roasted poblanos, vegetarian *gyozas* (filled dumplings), and smoked tofu are delicious variations of classics. Chicken, leg of lamb, beefsteak, and buffalo short ribs are just a few of the succulent meats smoked and then grilled. The cozy dining room is filled with paintings, stained glass, and a huge wood-framed mirror. ✉ *432 Main St.,* ☎ *303/823–5144. AE, MC, V. No lunch.*

Outdoor Activities and Sports

Hall Ranch (¾ mi west of Lyons on Hwy. 7; marked trailhead on right) is open to hikers, mountain bikers, and equestrians alike. The 10½-mi loop provides mountain views and an interpretive display about the area's ecosystem and the roles that prairie dogs and raptors play in it.

Start on the Bitterbrush trail and connect to the Nelson loop at 3½ mi, all the while ascending and descending through stands of pine trees, rock outcroppings, and crossing meadows.

Ornithologists gather at **Bohn Park** at sunrise and sunset in order to spot some of the many species of songbirds that reside along St. Vrain Creek. Golden eagles have been sited in the red cliffs on the southwest side of town. From northbound U.S. 36, turn left onto Park Street and then left onto 2nd Street to reach the park.

Estes Park

⑲ *22 mi from Lyons via U.S. 36 northwest; 40 mi from Nederland via Rte. 72 and Rte. 7 (the Peak-to-Peak Hwy.).*

The scenery on the U.S. 36 approach to Estes Park gives little hint of the grandeur to come. If ever there was a classic picture-postcard Rockies view, Estes Park has it. Even the McDonald's has glorious views and a facade that complements its surroundings, thanks to strict zoning laws that require all businesses to present a rustic exterior. The town itself is very family-oriented, albeit somewhat kitschy: many of the small hotels lining the country roads are mom-and-pop outfits that have been passed down through several generations.

As a resort town, Estes attracted the attention of genius entrepreneur F.O. Stanley, inventor of the Stanley Steamer automobile and several photographic processes. In 1905, having been told by his doctors he would soon die of tuberculosis, he constructed the regal **Stanley Hotel** on a promontory overlooking the town. Stanley went on to live another 30-odd years, an extension that he attributed to the fresh air. The hotel soon became one of the most glamorous resorts in the Rockies, a position it holds to this day. Incidentally, the hotel was the inspiration for Stephen King's horror novel, *The Shining,* part of which he wrote while staying at the hotel.

Archeological evidence displayed at the **Estes Park Area Historical Museum** makes an eloquent case that Native Americans used the area as a summer resort. The museum also has an assortment of pioneer artifacts and changing exhibits. ⌧ *200 4th St.,* ☎ *970/586–6256.* ⌧ *$2.50.* ☉ *May–Oct., Mon.–Sat. 10–5, Sun. 1–5; Nov.–Apr., Fri.–Sat. 10–5, Sun. 1–5.*

The **MacGregor Ranch Museum,** on the National Register of Historic Places, offers views of the Twin Owls and Long's Peak (towering more than 14,000 ft). Although the original ranch was homesteaded in 1873, the present house was built in 1896, and it provides a well-preserved record of typical ranch life. ⌧ *MacGregor Ave., off U.S. 34,* ☎ *970/586–3749.* ⌧ *Free.* ☉ *June–Aug., Tues.–Fri. 10–4.*

Dining and Lodging

$$–$$$ ✕ **Dunraven Inn.** The bar at the inn is "wallpapered" with more than 12,000 $1 bills autographed by diners during the years that Dale has owned the restaurant. The casual establishment serves dependably good food and specializes in Italian cuisine, good steaks, and fresh fish. This popular dining spot in a canyon just outside town sports an old-English ceiling, tartan carpet, and dark wood paneling embellished with many copies of Da Vinci's *Mona Lisa,* all nicely visible in the low light. ⌧ *2470 Hwy. 66,* ☎ *970/586–6409. AE, D, MC, V. No lunch.*

$$–$$$ ✕ **Nicky's Cattleman Restaurant.** Elegant wood beams, oak paneling, maroon carpeting and upholstery, and a huge picture window fronting the mountain and river make this one of the most sophisticated dining spots in town. The steak house ages and cuts its own meat, and

specialties include sensational sirloin prepared Greek style with onions, peppers, and feta, and prime rib broiled in rock salt. Nicky's also offers motor-lodge rooms, cabins, and condominiums. ⊠ *1350 U.S. 34,* ☎ *970/586–5376. AE, D, DC, MC, V.*

$–$$ ✕ **Ed's Cantina.** Huge burritos and tasty burgers are reliable choices at this popular locals' hangout. Lighthearted antiques adorn the walls. ⊠ *362 E. Elkhorn Ave.,* ☎ *970/586–2919. AE, D, MC, V.*

$–$$ ✕ **Estes Park Brewery.** The homemade beer chili is the specialty here. The menu otherwise includes the usual pizza, burgers, sandwiches, and chicken or steak dinners. ⊠ *470 Prospect Village Dr.,* ☎ *970/586–5421. AE, D, MC, V.*

$–$$ ✕ **Sweet Basilico Café.** This tiny, homey place is a local favorite for basic Italian classics like lasagna, manicotti, and eggplant Parmesan. Sandwiches made with homemade focaccia are delicious, and the homemade minestrone satisfies wonderfully. ⊠ *401 E. Elkhorn Ave.,* ☎ *970/586–3899. MC, V.*

$$$–$$$$ ⊞ **Stanley Hotel.** Perched regally on a hill commanding the town, the ★ Stanley is one of Colorado's great old hotels. As is often the case, the sunny rooms, decorated with antiques and period reproductions, are not as sumptuous as they once were. Still, there is an incomparable air of history to this 1909 hotel, along with all the modern conveniences. The MacGregor Room is the classiest ballroom in town. Outdoor seating by the waterfall is available at the restaurant, The Cascade. ⊠ *333 Wonderview Ave., 80517,* ☎ *970/586–3371 or 800/976–1377,* FAX *970/586–3673,* WEB *www.stanleyhotel.com. 135 rooms. Restaurant, bar, pool, meeting room. AE, D, DC, MC, V.*

$$$ ⊞ **Aspen Lodge at Estes Park Ranch Resort and Conference Center.** The ★ main building is the largest log structure in Colorado, with cathedral ceilings, antler chandeliers, and a vaulted stone fireplace. Rustic lodge rooms (variously decorated with Native American weavings and original art) have balconies and thrilling mountain views. There are also 23 nicely appointed cabins with gingerbread trim. Rides are offered to a 2,000-acre working ranch, and you can two-step or square dance in the homey lounge after an excellent dinner. There are many outdoor activities available, including snowshoeing and ice hockey on the lake in winter. ⊠ *6120 Rte. 7, 80517,* ☎ *970/586–8133 or 800/332–6867,* WEB *www.aspenlodge.net. 52 rooms. Restaurant, bar, pool, hot tub, sauna, 2 tennis courts, basketball, gym, horseback riding, racquetball, fishing, ice-skating, cross-country skiing, children's programs, laundry service, convention center. AE, D, DC, MC, V. AP in summer. 3-night minimum.*

$$$ ⊞ **Lake Shore Lodge.** This open, lodge-style building is the only hotel on Lake Estes. Rooms have either lake or mountain views and are generously appointed with amenities, replica brass light fixtures, blond-wood furniture, and an easy chair or couch. The suites have a fireplace, Jacuzzi, kitchenette, and balcony that overlooks the lake. A 1-mi bike-and walking path provides easy access to town. An upstairs lounge is a quiet place to read. ⊠ *1700 Big Thompson Ave., 80517,* ☎ *970/ 577–6400 or 800/332–6867,* WEB *www.estesvalleyresorts.com. 48 rooms. Bar, restaurant, lounge, in-room data ports, indoor pool, hot tub, sauna, health club, recreation room, children's programs, meeting rooms. AE, D, MC, V.*

$$–$$$ ⊞ **Boulder Brook.** Luxury suites at this secluded spot on the river are tucked in the pines, yet close to town. All feature full kitchen or kitchenette, private deck, gas fireplace, double-headed showers, cable TV, and VCR. Half the units have whirlpool tubs, for which you'll pay a great deal more. ⊠ *1900 Fall River Rd., 80517,* ☎ *970/586–0910 or 800/239–0910. 16 suites. Kitchenettes. AE, D, MC, V.*

$$–$$$ ⊡ **Estes Park Center/YMCA of the Rockies.** This self-contained property is so huge it's easy to get lost. It even has its own zip code (and roller-skating rink)! Both lodge rooms and the 200 cabins are simple, clean, and attractive, and all are constructed of sturdy oak. Three meals per day are included in the lodge rates. The two- to four-bedroom cabins also have full kitchens. The Barclay Reunion Lodge can house up to 72 people in 17 rooms. ⊠ *2515 Tunnel Rd., 80511,* ☎ *970/586–3341 or 303/443–4743,* FAX *303/449–6781,* WEB *www.ymcarockies.org. 688 rooms, 220 2–4 bedroom cabins. Restaurant, indoor pool, basketball, gym, playground, meeting room. MC, V. MAP.*

$$–$$$ ⊡ **Lake Estes Inn & Suites.** All the well-maintained rooms are decorated in burgundy and forest green with light, sand-color walls and dark-stain or blond-wood furniture. The family units have two sleeping rooms and sleep up to eight. The newer chalet suites have updated baths, sitting rooms with fireplaces, oak cabinets, Jacuzzis, and kitchens. All rooms include a minirefrigerator and hair dryers, as well as the usual amenities. Ask for a unit with a lake view. ⊠ *1650 Big Thompson Ave., Hwy. 34, 80517,* ☎ *970/586–3386. 58 rooms. Refrigerators, pool, hot tub, sauna, playground, coin laundry. AE, D, DC, MC, V.*

Nightlife and the Arts

The summertime **Estes Park Music Festival** takes place on Sunday afternoons in various locations around town, often at the Stanley Hotel.

The **Gaslight Pub** (⊠ Gaslight Sq., ☎ 970/586–0994) has occasional live music. The locals' favorite after-work hangout is **J. R. Chapins Lounge** (⊠ Holiday Inn, 101 S. St. Vrain St., ☎ 970/586–2332). Blues and country bands play at **Lonigans** (⊠ 110 W. Elkhorn Ave., ☎ 970/586–4346) on weekends. The venerable **Wheel Bar** (⊠ 132 E. Elkhorn Ave., ☎ 970/586–9381) is among the choice watering holes.

Outdoor Activities and Sports

Camping facilities abound in the 800,000 acres of **Roosevelt National Forest** (⊠ Canyon Lakes Ranger District Visitor Center, 1311 S. College, Fort Collins, 80524, ☎ 970/498–2770), and there's excellent cycling and hiking here, too. **Sombrero Ranch** (☎ 970/586–4577) offers trail rides through the Estes Park region, including Rocky Mountain National Park. Good fishing can be found in the **Big Thompson River** near Estes Park. **Rocky Mountain Adventures** (☎ 970/586–6191 or 800/858–6808) offers guided fly- and float-fishing as well as white-water rafting on the Cache la Poudre River.

Estes Park Golf Club (⊠ 1080 S. St. Vrain St., ☎ 970/586–8146) is one of the oldest and prettiest 18-hole courses in the state where the grazing elk seldom allow golfers to play through.

A-1 Wildwater (☎ 970/224–3379 or 800/369–4165) provides white-water rafting on the Cache la Poudre River. **Rapid Transit Rafting** (☎ 970/586–8852 or 800/367–8523) arranges river-rafting trips on both the Colorado and Cache la Poudre rivers.

Shopping

Although shopping in Estes Park includes many run-of-the-mill trinket, T-shirt, and souvenir shops typical of resort towns, the number of classy galleries is increasing as Estes Park becomes a more upscale resort.

CRAFT AND ART GALLERIES
The cooperative **Earthwood Artisans** (⊠ 145 E. Elkhorn Ave., ☎ 970/586–3545) features the work of stained-glass artists, photographers, jewelers, sculptors, and potters. **Glassworks** (⊠ 323 Elkhorn Ave., ☎ 970/586–8619) offers glassblowing demonstrations and sells a rainbow of glass creations. **Michael Ricker Pewter** (⊠ 2050 Big Thomp-

son, 2 mi east of town on U.S. 34, ☎ 970/586–2030) gives free tours of its production area and museum, where you can see the world's largest pewter sculpture. **Spectrum** (⊠ No. 8 Park Theater Mall, Elkhorn Ave., ☎ 970/586–2497 or 888/553–3421) sells fine arts and crafts exclusively by Colorado studio artists, including spectacular nature photography, hand-thrown and signed pottery, and hand-turned wood crafts made from mesquite, aspen, or cedar.

The Christmas Shoppe (⊠ Park Theatre Mall, Elkhorn Ave., ☎ 970/586–2882) delights children of all ages with every conceivable Noël-related ornament, doll, curio, and knickknack from around the world.

Rustic Mountain Charm (⊠ 116, 165, and 344 E. Elkhorn Ave., ☎ 970/586–0512) has home accessories with the lodge look, including furniture, quilts, baskets, and throws; one clothing store; and local foodstuffs. Permeated by the pungent aroma of leather, **Stage Western Family Clothing** (⊠ 104 Moraine Ave., ☎ 970/586–3430) offers imaginative cowboy hats, boots, and belts.

Fort Collins

20 *50 mi from Estes Park via U.S. 34 east and I–25 north; 72 mi from Denver International Airport via I–70, I–270, and I–25.*

The old neighborhoods of Fort Collins still have elm tree–lined streets thanks to the agricultural scientists at Colorado State University who were able to keep the vicious Dutch Elm disease at bay. The city was originally established to protect traders from the natives, while the former negotiated the treacherous Overland Trail. After the flood of 1864 swept away Camp Collins—a cavalry post near today's town of La-Porte—Colonel Will Collins established a new camp on 6,000 acres where Fort Collins stands today. The town grew on two industries: education (Colorado State University was founded here in 1879) and agriculture (rich crops of alfalfa and sugar beets). With six microbreweries crafting ales, lagers, and stouts in Fort Collins, the city has the most microbreweries per capita in the state. The Fort Collins Convention & Visitors Bureau has designated a historic walking tour of more than 20 buildings, including the original university structures and the stately sandstone **Avery House.** ⊠ *328 W. Mountain Ave.,* ☎ *970/221–0533.* ⊡ *Free.* ⊙ *Wed. and Sun. 1–3.*

Old Town Square (⊠ Mountain and College Aves.), a National Historic District, is a pedestrian zone with sculptures and fountains. The restored buildings house shops, cafés, galleries, and bars. During the summer local musicians, bands, and theater groups entertain Tuesday at noon and Thursday evenings.

The **Fort Collins Museum** includes an 1860s cabin from the original military camp and a 1905 vintage schoolhouse on the grounds. The collection contains artifacts representing Fort Collins history, from the Native Americans through the fur trappers to CSU professor Donald Sutherland, held hostage by terrorists in Beirut during the 1980s. ⊠ *200 Matthews St.,* ☎ *970/221–6738,* WEB *www.fcgov.com/museum/.* ⊡ *Free.* ⊙ *Tues.–Sat. 10–5, Sun. noon–5.*

Colorado State University's **Environmental Learning Center** is a 1.2-mi trail loop within a 200-acre nature preserve. The raptor cages and the walk through wetland animal habitat are an excellent educational family activity and fun for anyone curious about animal habitats. Staff conduct special walks like the full-moon hike, Saturday picnics with naturalists, and sunrise bird-watching strolls. The learning center loop is 1 mi east of the Timberline and Drake Road intersection, on Drake Road. ✉ *Information Center, 3745 E. Prospect Rd.,* ☎ *970/491–1661,* WEB *www.cnr.colostate.edu/elc/.* 🎫 *Free.* ⏲ *Information center: Mid-May–Aug., daily 10–5; Sept.–Apr., weekends 10–5. Learning Center: year-round, dawn–dusk.*

The **Swetsville Zoo** is the unique creation of a dairy farmer insomniac who stayed up nights fashioning more than 150 dinosaurs, birds, insects, and other fantastic creatures from old farm equipment. ✉ *4801 E. Harmony Rd., ¼ mi east of I–25,* ☎ *970/484–9509.* 🎫 *Free.* ⏲ *Daily dawn–dusk.*

Learn lots of facts about the large-scale brewing process at **Anheuser-Busch** during a free tour. Tours start every 45 minutes (every half-hour on weekends) and last 1 hour and 20 minutes. ✉ *2351 Busch Dr.,* ☎ *970/490–4691,* WEB *www.budweisertours.com.* 🎫 *Free.* ⏲ *June–Aug., daily 9:30–6; Sept., daily 10–4; Oct.–May, Thurs.–Mon. 10–4.*

Dining and Lodging

Lodging in Fort Collins is mainly franchise hotels and inns. However, the city has several enchanting B&Bs that are either close to downtown or within easy access of town and outdoor activities.

$$$–$$$$ ✕ **Nico's Catacombs.** The chefs here excel in traditional Continental cuisine—including table-side cooking—with no trendy versions or fluffy variations on the classics. Diners savor the house specialties (Dover sole, bouillabaisse, Châteaubriand, and rack of lamb) in subterranean brick caverns outfitted with wood tables and dark upholstery—the appropriate old-world ambience for a restaurant that features more than 500 wines. Daily specials may be fresh sea bass, elk loin, or veal. Reservations are strongly recommended. Shorts are not allowed. ✉ *115 S. College Ave.,* ☎ *970/482–6426. AE, D, DC, MC, V. No lunch.*

$$–$$$ ✕ **Canino's.** Hearty Italian specialties are served in this historic, four-square house that still has a few stained-glass windows. Appetizers like the bruschetta and entrées such as cioppino, pollo cacciatora, eggplant parmigiano, and veal marsala are made in the classic Italian style. The menu is rounded out with pizzas and pasta dishes like baked mostaccioli and spinach lasagna. Tables are set in the enclaves of the house's wood-trimmed rooms that have hardwood floors with carpets. Homemade cheesecake, tiramisu, or gelato paired with a robust espresso finish dinner on a sweet note. ✉ *613 S. College Ave.,* ☎ *970/493–7205. AE, D, DC, MC, V.*

$$ ✕ **Rio Grande Mexican Restaurant.** One of the best Mexican restaurants in the area, the Rio Grande always satisfies with such old favorites as sopaipillas, burritos, and Mexican steak, as well as more fiery Tex-Mex fare. Minimargaritas cost $2.50, and they're strong enough to impart a pleasant buzz. ✉ *143 W. Mountain Ave.,* ☎ *970/224–5428. MC, V.*

$ ✕ **Starry Night.** Espresso drinkers sip their sustenance under the night-blue ceiling while reading, chatting, or mulling over the sunflowers and the mural "Starry Night over Fort Collins" inspired by Van Gogh. Beyond breakfast, there's soups, salads, and sandwiches at lunch and dinnertime. ✉ *112 S. College Ave.,* ☎ *970/493–3039. MC, V.*

$$–$$$ 🏨 **Edwards House B&B.** This quiet Victorian inn with hardwood floors and light, birchwood trim is four blocks from downtown attractions. At actor Adolph Menjou's dining room table, guests enjoy gourmet breakfasts that include espresso drinks and an entrée such as gingerbread pancakes or eggs Florentine. The parlor has an extensive video collection and the library is well stocked for those who forego relaxing on the large front porch. Rooms exude an old-fashioned elegance without being fussy and are variously appointed with sleigh or canopy beds, gas stoves, hot tubs or claw-foot tubs, comfortable sitting chairs, writing desks, and slate fireplaces. ✉ *402 W. Mountain Ave., 80521,* ☎ *970/493–9191 or 800/281–9190,* FAX *970/484–0706,* WEB *www.edwardshouse.com. 8 rooms. Dining room, library, meeting room. AE, D, MC, V. BP.*

$$ 🏠 **Raindrop.** Secreted away on 26 peaceful acres in the red sandstone foothills at the mouth of the Poudre Canyon, this B&B is still only 15 minutes from Fort Collins. The lofty ranch house and artist's studio has an eclectic mix of beautiful antiques and modern art. Guests read in the sunny atrium or relax in the hot tub under the night sky while listening to the coyotes sing. The spacious, light rooms are done in white, Wedgwood blue, or terra-cotta and have hardwood floors or carpet. Owner Tara prepares a fresh, hearty breakfast with excellent coffee. ✉ *6901 McMurry, Bellvue, 80512,* ☎ *970/493–0799,* WEB *bbonline.com/co/ raindrop. 4 rooms. Outdoor hot tub, massage. No credit cards. BP.*

$–$$ 🏠 **Elizabeth Street Guest House.** Guests wake up to the inviting aroma of Sheryl's home-baked muffins and breads at this turn-of-the-20th-century, brick four-square with oak woodwork and leaded glass windows. The parlor and the bedrooms are furnished with family antiques and folk art, including a three-story dollhouse in the front room. Only one guest room has a private bath and shower; the others share a bath but have sinks in the room. Louie, the dog, gladly accompanies guests on walks. The house is nine blocks from downtown and one block from Colorado State University. ✉ *202 E. Elizabeth, 80524,* ☎ *970/493– 2337,* FAX *970/416–0826,* WEB *www.bbonline.com/co/elizabeth. 3 rooms, 1 with bath. Breakfast room. AE, MC, V. BP.*

$–$$ 🏠 **Fort Collins Plaza Inn.** This locally owned establishment is unspectacular, but it's a better buy than the nearby franchise competitors. Rooms have cable TV and are simple and standard: beige walls, veneered furniture, and queen- or king-size beds. ✉ *3709 E. Mulberry St., 80524,* ☎ *970/ 493–7800 or 800/434–5548,* FAX *970/493–1826,* WEB *www.plaza-inn.com. 135 rooms. Restaurant, bar, indoor-outdoor pool, hot tub, sauna, dry cleaning. AE, D, DC, MC, V.*

$–$$ 🏠 **Mariposa on Spring Creek.** The calming atmosphere in the two-story tropical atrium will give your travels another dimension and inspire sighs of ease. Also an Aveda Concept Spa, this B&B is a beautiful retreat that's close to the downtown scene. You'll get plenty of sunlight in the rooms, which are outfitted with pastel hues, minimal patterning and decoration, and uncomplicated furniture. Guests breakfast on scones, apple French toast, or tortilla eggs, or can opt for the lighter spa meals such as smoothies, oatmeal, and fruit. ✉ *706 E. Stuart St., 80525,* ☎ *970/495–0789 or 800/495–9604,* WEB *www.mariposaspa.com. 6 rooms. Breakfast room, hot tub, spa, hiking. AE, D, MC, V. BP.*

Nightlife and the Arts

BARS AND LOUNGES

The sports bar **C, B & Potts** (✉ 1415 W. Elizabeth St., ☎ 970/221–1139) is famous for its burgers and international selection of beers. The establishment has both its own brewery and a pool hall with six tables and a full bar. A place to hang (usually with the college crowd) is **Coopersmith's Pub & Brewery** (✉ 5 Old Town Sq., ☎ 970/498–0483). Coopersmith's own pool hall just outside the front door at 7 Old Town Square has 12 tables and a pizza oven for hungry billiard players. College students line the bar at **Lucky Joe's Sidewalk Saloon** (✉ 25 Old Town Sq., ☎ 970/493–2213).

ROCK CLUBS

Several clubs in Fort Collins jam with the hottest rock, folk, and blues in the area. **Lindens Brewing Co.** (✉ 214 Linden St., ☎ 970/482– 9291) has live music Wednesday, Friday, and Saturday. Past acts include Wide Spread Panic and Bo Didley. The kitchen serves creole specialties and pub fare. **Mishawaka Inn** (✉ 13714 Poudre Canyon, 25 mi north of Fort Collins, ☎ 970/482–4420), an outdoor amphitheater on the banks of the Poudre River, usually corrals some name bands.

Outdoor Activities and Sports

BICYCLING

Both paved-trail cycling and single-track mountain biking are within easy access of town. The **Poudre River Trail** (17-mi round-trip) is an easy riparian jaunt within Fort Collins. The **Spring Creek Trail** (13-mi round-trip) is another easy spin through town. For short, single-track rides close to town, Pineridge and Maxwell trails do not disappoint and connect to other trails for longer adventures: head west on Drake Road to where it bends right and becomes Overland Trail; turn left on County Road 42C and drive almost 1 mi to the posted fence opening. Serious gearheads crank at **Horsetooth Mountain Park** on the southwest side of Horsetooth Reservoir. Several single tracks and Jeep trails provide any level of desired challenge. **Lee's Cyclery** (✉ 202 W. Laurel, ☎ 970/482–6006 or 800/748–2453) rents city cruisers, tandems, kid trailers, and hard-tail and full-suspension mountain bikes for five hours to seven days.

FISHING

Horsetooth Reservoir, Red Feather Lakes, and Cache la Poudre River are locally renowned for excellent fishing. The knowledgeable chaps at **St. Peter's Fly Shop** (✉ 202 Remington St., ☎ 970/498–8968 or 888/211–7250) arrange half-day to full-day guided or instructional wade and float trips that can include permits for waters not open to the public. They gladly provide information on conditions for independent fishermen, too.

GOLF

Collindale Golf Course (✉ 1441 E. Horsetooth St., ☎ 970/221–6651) is an 18-hole public golf course.

HIKING, HORSEBACK RIDING

Twenty-eight miles of trails in **Horsetooth Mountain Park** (☎ 970/679–4570, WEB www.co.larimer.co.us/parks) offer easy to difficult hikes and rides all with views of the mountains to the west and the plains to the east. Drive west on Harmony Road to Taft Hill Road; head down County Road 38E to the park entrance, where you should purchase a permit. West of Fort Collins, in truly unspoiled surroundings, the **Colorado State Forest State Park** (☎ 970/723–8366) offers superb hiking.

NORDIC SKIING

Never Summer Nordic (✉ Box 1983, Fort Collins 80522, ☎ 970/482–9411) is a hut-to-hut system for cross-country skiers in the Colorado State Forest State Park.

Shopping

The shopkeepers at the **Children's Mercantile Company** (✉ 111 N. College Ave., ☎ 970/484–9946 or 888/326–8465) enjoy playing with the toys as much as the young customers. The shop carries books, CDs, imported toys like Lego and Rokenbok, and classics like marbles, dolls, and stuffed animals. Western furniture is individually hand-crafted and signed at **Mountain Woods Furniture** (✉ 11 Old Town Sq., ☎ 970/416–0701). Throws, pillows, blankets, and other accessories—all handmade by artisans—complement the aspen, birch, and pine furnishings. Shipping is available. Fort Collins's **Old Town Square** (✉ at College and Mountain Aves. and Jefferson St.) and adjacent Linden Street have a pleasant collection of historic buildings that house galleries, bookshops, cafés, brewpubs, intriguing shops, and a martini bar.

Trimble Court Artisans (✉ 118 Trimble Ct., ☎ 970/221–0051), a co-op with more than 40 members, sells paintings, jewelry, clothing, weavings, stained glass, and pottery.

Rocky Mountain National Park

㉑ *5 mi from Estes Park via U.S. 36 or U.S. 34; 55 mi from Fort Collins via I–25 south and U.S. 34 west.*

A savage clawing of the earth by volcanic uplifts and receding glaciers has resulted in a majestic landscape of three distinct ecosystems in this national park: verdant mountain valleys towering with proud ponderosa pines and Douglas firs; higher and colder subalpine mountains with wind-whipped trees (krummholz) that grow at right angles; and harsh, unforgiving alpine tundra with dollhouse-size versions of familiar plants and wildflowers. The park teems with wildlife, from beaver to bighorn sheep. Lectures, slide shows, and displays on the park's geology and botany are part of the **Moraine Park Museum.** ✉ *Bear Lake Rd., off U.S. 36.* ⊞ *Free.* ⊙ *May–Sept., daily 9–5.*

The world's highest continuous paved highway, **Trail Ridge Road** (U.S. 34), runs 48 mi across the park and accesses several hikes along its meandering way, through terrain filigreed with silvery streams and turquoise lakes. The views around each bend—of moraines and glaciers, and craggy hills framing emerald meadows carpeted with columbine and Indian paintbrush—are truly awesome: nature's workshop on an epic scale. **Many Parks Curve** affords breathtaking views of the crest of the Continental Divide and of the **Alluvial Fan,** a huge gash created in 1982 by a vicious flood after an earthen dam broke. Erosion occurred immediately, rather than over the millions of years that nature usually requires, and today it resembles a lonely lunar landscape. Trail Ridge Road is open only from June to mid-October. A loop up 11-mi-long Old Fall River Road to the Alpine Visitor Center (11,796-ft elevation) and back down along Trail Ridge Road is a scenic alternative to backtracking on Trail Ridge Road. Start at **West Horseshoe Park,** which has the park's largest concentrations of sheep and elk, and head up the one-way, paved and gravel Old Fall River Road, passing **Chasm Falls.** Early visitors to the park traveled Old Fall River Road before Trail Ridge Road was built. A caveat for car travelers: expect extensive road reconstruction through 2003.

The twisting, 9-mi-long **Bear Lake Road** winds past shimmering waterfalls perpetually shrouded with rainbows. The drive offers superlative views of Long's Peak (14,255-ft summit) and the glaciers surrounding Bear Lake. The park has five visitor centers: **Beaver Meadows** (✉ Park Headquarters, U.S. 36 southwest of Estes Park); **Alpine** (✉ Trail Ridge Rd. at Fall River Pass); **Lily Lake** (✉ CO Rte. 7 south of Estes Park); **Fall River** (✉ U.S. 34 west of Estes Park); and **Kawuneeche** (✉ U.S. 34 near Grand Lake). All offer maps, brochures, newsletters, and comprehensive information on the park and its facilities. ✉ *Rocky Mountain National Park, Estes Park, 80517,* ☎ *970/586–1206,* ⓦⓔⓑ *www.nps.gov.* ⊞ *$15 per vehicle for 1- to 7-day pass.* ⊙ *Year-round.*

Camping

Five top-notch campgrounds in the park accommodate tents, trailers, and RV's (only two accept reservations; the others fill up on a "first come, first served" basis). **Aspenglen Campground** is for summer camping only. **Glacier Basin Campground** (☎ 800/365–2267) accepts reservations and is open in summer. **Long's Peak Campground** is open year-round. **Moraine Park Campground** (☎ 800/365–2267) accepts reservations and is open year-round. **Timber Creek Campground** is open year-

Rocky Mountain National Park

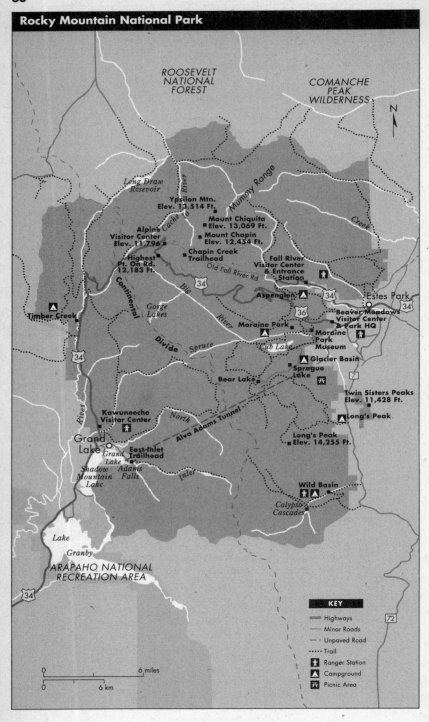

ROOSEVELT
NATIONAL
FOREST

COMANCHE
PEAK
WILDERNESS

N

Long Draw
Reservoir

Ypsilon Mtn.
Elev. 13,514 Ft.

Mummy Range

Mount Chiquita
Elev. 13,069 Ft.

Alpine
Visitor Center
Elev. 11,796 ft.

Mount Chapin
Elev. 12,454 Ft.

Chapin Creek
Trailhead

Highest
Pt. On Rd.
12,183 Ft.

Old Fall River Rd.

Fall River
Visitor Center
& Entrance
Station

34

Aspenglen

34

Estes Park

34

36

Beaver Meadows
Visitor Center
& Park HQ

Timber Creek

Continental

Gorge
Lakes

Big

Thompson

River

Moraine Park

Moraine
Park
Museum

34

Divide

Spruce

Cub Lake

Glacier Basin

Sprague
Lake

7

Bear Lake

Twin Sisters Peaks
Elev. 11,428 Ft.

Kawuneeche
Visitor Center

North

Alva Adams Tunnel

Long's Peak

Long's Peak
Elev. 14,255 Ft.

Grand
Lake

River

Grand
Lake

East Inlet
Trailhead

Adams
Falls

Shadow
Mountain
Lake

Inlet

Wild Basin

Calypso
Cascades

Lake
Granby

ARAPAHO NATIONAL
RECREATION AREA

34

72

0   6 miles

0   6 km

KEY

Highways
Minor Roads
Unpaved Road
Trail
Ranger Station
Campground
Picnic Area

round. Backcountry camping requires advance reservations or a day-of-trip permit, so contact **Backcountry Permits, Rocky Mountain National Park** (☎ 970/586–1206 or 970/586–1242).

Outdoor Activities and Sports

There are 78 peaks in the park that rise above 12,000 ft, several of which require no technical skills to reach the summit. Even the summit of Long's Peak, the highest point in the park at 14,255 ft, has a walkable route leading to it. The ease of access to trails makes the park relatively crowded in summer; as many as 800 hikers and climbers have registered to ascend Long's Peak on a single day. The elevation can steal one's breath away, but with mountain bases above 9,000 ft, ascents of even the 14,000-footers become relatively short climbs. Most hikers ignore trails on the park's west side, leaving the footpaths less trafficked for those seeking more solitude in nature. A good guide to hiking the park is *Rocky Mountain National Park: Classic Hikes and Climbs,* by Gerry Roach (Fulcrum). The **Colorado Mountain Club** (☎ 970/586–6623) sponsors day and overnight trips into the park.

The **Bear Lake Nature Trail** is a point of departure for several easy-to-strenuous walks and hikes ranging in length from .6 mi to 8½ mi. A jaunt from **Cub Lake** is of moderate difficulty and just 2.3 mi long. Hikers with the stamina for challenging hiking at altitude head up **Long's Peak,** 8 mi one-way and an 4,855-ft gain in elevation. Sunrise at the **Keyhole** is a treat, and the views from the top are singularly awesome. Nontechnical access is limited to mid-July to early September. Inquire with a ranger about conditions before starting out. A walk to the summits of the **Twin Sisters Peaks** (11,428 ft) provides a strenuous but shorter (3.7-mi one-way) hike than Long's Peak, and has great views of both Long's Peak and the Front Range. Another favorite but tough hike starts at the **Chapin Pass Trailhead** about 7 mi up Old Fall River Road. It's 3½ mi one-way and a 2,874-ft gain in elevation to the summit of **Ypsilon Mountain**; you'll bag the summits of Mount Chapin and Mount Chiquita on the way. Gaze out across the park's lower valleys before hiking back to the car. On the west side of the park, the **Colorado River Trail** is a moderate, 3.7-mi one-way walk to the ghost town of **Lulu City,** excellent for families looking for the bighorn sheep, elk, and moose that reside in the area. Part of the trail is the former stagecoach route that went from Granby to Walden. Adams Falls are quickly accessed by the **East Inlet Trail,** just .3 mi one-way.

Wintertime offers easy to strenuous hiking, snowshoeing, and cross-country skiing on all of the park's 347 mi of trails, including ski touring trails that start at the park's western entrance. Shorter trips of 1½ to 3 mi in length to destinations like Chasm Falls, Cub Lake, and Spruce Lake are fun on a crisp, sunny winter day. Inquire about conditions ahead of time and plan to have the proper gear with you as though you were spending the night.

Grand Lake

㉒ *54 mi from Estes Park via U.S. 34 (Trail Ridge Rd.—closed in winter); 109 mi from Denver via U.S. 40 and 34.*

Grand Lake is the western gateway to Rocky Mountain National Park, and it, too, enjoys an idyllic setting, on the shores of the state's largest natural lake of the same name. This is the highest-altitude yacht anchorage in America. According to Ute legend, the fine mists that shroud the lake punctually at dawn are the risen spirits of women and children whose raft capsized as they were fleeing a marauding party of Cheyennes and Arapahoes. Grand Lake feeds into two much larger man-made reservoirs, Lake Granby and Shadow Mountain Lake, forming the "Great Lakes of Colorado." The entire area is a paradise for hikers and fishermen, and for snowmobilers in winter. Even the town, although it has the usual assortment of souvenir shops and motels, seems less spoiled than many other resort communities.

Dining and Lodging

$$ ✕ **Mountain Inn.** Fine, family-style meals are served in this rustic, vertical-log restaurant with a pleasant, woodsy feel. Á-la-carte selections are also available. The food ranges from fine Rocky Mountain oysters to flavorful prime rib, beer-batter shrimp, and salmon and trout specialties. The real standouts are the chicken-fried steak and fried chicken that are cooked in cast-iron skillets for homemade flavor. ⊠ *612 Grand Ave.,* ☎ *970/627–3385. MC, V.*

$–$$ ✕ **Sagebrush BBQ & Grill.** The barbecue ribs, chicken, and catfish draw local and out-of-town attention. The homey café serves up filling meals that can be sized appropriately for larger or smaller appetites. Comforting sides like baked beans, corn bread, coleslaw, and potatoes top off the large plates. ⊠ *1101 Grand Ave.,* ☎ *970/627–1404. AE, D, DC, MC, V.*

$$ ✕⊡ **Rapids Lodge.** This handsome lodgepole-pine structure is one of ★ the oldest hotels in the area. Lodge rooms—each with cable TV and ceiling fan—are frilly, with dust ruffle quilts, floral wallpaper and fabrics, and such mismatched furnishings as old plush chartreuse armchairs, claw-foot tubs, and carved hardwood beds. Cabins, all with kitchenettes, are more rustic. The delightful restaurant ($$–$$$) is Grand Lake's most romantic, with stained glass, timber beams, and views of the roaring Tonahatu River. The kitchen turns out sumptuous Italian cuisine. ⊠ *209 Rapids La., 80447,* ☎ *970/627–3707,* WEB *www.rapidslodge.com. 6 lodge rooms, 20 suites. Restaurant, bar. AE, MC, V. Closed Nov.*

$–$$ ⊡ **Bighorn Lodge.** This downtown motel has a rustic look, which helps it blend in well with its surroundings. Pride is reflected in the spotless rooms, all with cable TV, phones, ceiling fans, soundproof walls, maroon carpeting, sailing prints, and pastel fabrics and wallpaper. ⊠ *613 Grand Ave., 80447,* ☎ *970/627–8101. 20 rooms. Hot tub. AE, D, DC, MC, V.*

$–$$ ⊡ **Grand Lake Lodge.** This rustic retreat, built of lodgepole pine in 1921, calls itself "Colorado's favorite front porch," thanks to its stupendous views of Grand and Shadow Mountain lakes. The restaurant offers the same gorgeous vistas, in addition to fish and wild game specialties. Cabins are cozy, clean, and comfortably but simply furnished—no TVs or phones. The resort abuts Rocky Mountain National Park and offers foot-trail access to the park. ⊠ *Box 569, 80447, off U.S. 34, north of Grand Lake,* ☎ *970/627–3967,* FAX *970/627–9495,* WEB *www.grandlakelodge.com. 54 cabin units. Restaurant, bar, pool, hot tub, horseback riding. AE, D, MC, V. Closed mid-Sept.–May.*

$–$$ ⊡ **Western Riviera.** This friendly motel books up far in advance, thanks to the low prices, affable owners, and comfortable accommodations. Even the cheapest units—although small—are pleasant, done in mauve and earth tones. All rooms face the lake and have cable TV. ⊠ *419 Garfield Ave., 80447,* ☎ *970/627–3580,* FAX *970/627–3320,* WEB *www.westernriv.com. 15 rooms. Hot tub. MC, V.*

Nightlife

The hands-down local favorite is the **Stagecoach Inn** (⊠ 920 Grand Ave., on the Boardwalk, ☎ 970/627–8079), as much for its cheap booze and good eats as for the live entertainment on weekends.

Outdoor Activities and Sports

BOATING AND FISHING

Grand Lake and Lake Granby are the premier boating and fishing centers. Contact the **Grand Lake Recreation District** (⊠ Box 590, 80447, ☎ 970/627–8872) for information. **Beacon Landing** (⊠ 1 mi off Hwy. 34 on County Rd. 64, ☎ 970/627–3671) arranges boat rentals. Call the **Trail Ridge Marina** (⊠ Shadow Mountain Lake, ☎ 970/627–3586) for information on renting pontoon boats.

GOLF

Grand Lake Golf Course (⊠ County Rd. 48, ☎ 970/627–8008) is an 18-hole course 8,420 ft above sea level.

HIKING

In Grand County, near Lake Granby, **Indian Peaks Wilderness Area** (☎ 970/887–4100) is a prime location for hiking.

NORDIC SKIING

For cross-country skiing, the **Grand Lake Metropolitan Recreation Center** (☎ 970/627–8008) offers 29 km (18 mi) of trails with breathtaking vistas of the Never Summer Range and the Continental Divide.

SNOWMOBILING

Grand Lake is considered by many to be Colorado's snowmobiling capital, with more than 130 mi of trails, many winding through virgin forest. There are several rental and guide companies in the area. **Alpine Arctic Cat** (⊠ 902 Grand Ave., ☎ 970/627–8866). **Grand Lake Motor Sports** (⊠ 10438 Hwy. 34, ☎ 970/627–3806). **Lone Eagle Rentals** (⊠ 712 Grand Ave., ☎ 970/627–3310). **Spirit Lake Rentals** (⊠ 829 Grand Ave., ☎ 970/627–9288).

Shopping

Shopping in Grand Lake tends toward the usual panoply of resort-town souvenir shops, although a handful stand out. **Grand Lake Art Gallery** (⊠ 1117 Grand Ave., ☎ 970/627–3104) purveys superlative weavings, pottery, stained glass, gourds, and landscapes, primarily by regional artists. **Humphrey's Cabin Fever** (⊠ 1100 Grand Ave., ☎ 970/627–8939), the log building with the green roof, sells upscale cabin collectibles, rustic home furnishings, clothes, bedding, and ceramics in all price ranges. For outdoor gear and clothing, head for **Never Summer Mountain Products** (⊠ 919 Grand Ave., ☎ 970/627–3642), which also rents cross-country skis and snowshoes.

Grand County

20 mi (Granby), 30 mi (Hot Sulphur Springs), and 47 mi (Kremmling) from Grand Lake via U.S. 34 south and U.S. 40 west; 100 mi (Hot Sulphur Springs) and 117 mi (Kremmling) from Denver via I–70 west and U.S. 40 north.

The area west of Grand Lake along U.S. 40 is populated by a number of small towns and some interesting resorts and dude ranches. Hot Sulphur Springs is a faded resort town whose hot springs attracted Hollywood types in the 1950s. Kremmling is known as a sportsman's paradise for its year-round recreation, including mountain biking, river rafting, hunting, fishing, and cross-country skiing. The pools at the **Hot Sulphur Springs Resort&Spa** are open if you want a long soak in the invigorating hot springs after a day cycling, horseback riding, or cross-country skiing. ⊠ U.S. 40, Hot Sulphur Springs, 80451, 9 mi west of Granby, ☎ 970/725–3306 or 800/510–6235. ☞ $13.50. ☉ Daily 8 AM–10 PM.

Dining and Lodging

$–$$ ✕ **Longbranch Restaurant.** *The* restaurant in Granby, this stylish, western coffee shop with a warming fireplace, wood paneling, and wagon-wheel chandeliers offers German, Mexican, Continental, and American dishes. Not surprisingly, the quality is uneven. Stick to what the German owners do best—goulash, schnitzel, and sauerbraten, with heavenly homemade spaetzle. ⊠ *185 E. Agate Ave. (U.S. 40), Granby,* ☎ *970/887–2209. MC, V.*

$ ✕🏨 **Riverside Hotel.** Colorado is full of fun and funky finds, such as this historic 1903 hotel that you enter through a jungle of plants. The lobby, dominated by a magnificent fieldstone fireplace with cluttered mantel, leads into a grand old mirrored bar and a cozy dining room ($–$$) with a huge potbellied stove, a piano, landscape paintings of the kind charitably called folk art, and views of the Colorado River. Steaks are simple but well prepared and fish is fresh as can be. The upstairs rooms are filled with iron or oak beds, floral quilts, heavy oak dressers or armoires, and washbasins or sinks. Corner rooms are the sunniest and most spacious. ⊠ *509 Grand Ave., Hot Sulphur Springs 80451,* ☎ *970/725–3589. 17 rooms with shared baths. Restaurant, bar. No credit cards.*

$$$$ 🏨 **C Lazy U Guest Ranch.** This deluxe dude ranch attracts an international clientele, including both Hollywood royalty and the real thing.
★   You enjoy your own personal horse, luxurious western-style accommodations (with hair dryers, coffeemakers, and humidifiers), fine meals, live entertainment, and any outdoor activity you can dream up. The instructors are top-notch, the ratio of guests to staff is nearly one to one, and the children's programs are unbeatable. The ranch seeks to provide the ultimate in hedonism without ostentation, and it succeeds admirably. During the summer, the minimum stay is a week; in winter, it's two nights. All meals are included. ⊠ *Box 379, Granby 80446,* ☎ *970/887–3344. 19 rooms, 20 cabins. Restaurant, bar, pool, hot tub, sauna, 2 tennis courts, gym, horseback riding, racquetball, fishing, cross-country skiing, children's programs. No credit cards. Closed Apr.–June and Oct.–Dec. 21. FAP.*

$$$$ 🏨 **Latigo Ranch.** Considerably more down-to-earth than many other Colorado guest ranches, Latigo has a caring staff that does everything it can to give you an authentic ranch experience. Accommodations are in comfortable, carpeted, one- to three-bedroom, contemporary log cabins fitted with wood-burning stoves. Although providing fewer amenities than comparable properties, the ranch offers views of the Indian Peaks range, complete seclusion (17 mi—and 30 minutes on heart-stopping roads—to the nearest town), and superb cross-country trails. Owner Jim Yost was an anthropologist, and Randy George, a chemical engineer, now engineers the "nouvelle ranch cuisine" (BYOB). ⊠ *County Rd. 1911, Box 237, Kremmling 80459,* ☎ *970/724–9008 or 800/227–9655,* 🌐 *www.latigotrails.com. 10 cabins. Dining room, pool, hot tub, horseback riding, fishing, cross-country skiing, tobogganing, recreation room, coin laundry. No credit cards. Closed Apr.–May and mid-Oct.–mid-Dec. FAP.*

North Central Colorado A to Z

AIRPORTS

The northern Front Range and Grand County are served by Denver International Airport, from which regular shuttles are available. Estes Park Shuttle carries passengers from Denver and Boulder to Rocky Mountain National Park; Super Shuttle serves Boulder; Shamrock Airport Shuttle serves Fort Collins; and Home James serves Grandby, Grand

Lake, and guest ranches. There are municipal airports in Boulder, Fort Collins, and Grand County.

➤ AIRPORT SHUTTLE INFORMATION: **Estes Park Shuttle** (☎ 970/586–5151). **Home James** (☎ 970/726–5060 or 800/359–7536). **Shamrock Airport Shuttle** (☎ 970/686–9999, WEB www.shamrockshuttle.com). **Super Shuttle** (☎ 303/227–0000).

BUS TRAVEL

Greyhound Lines serves most of the major towns in the region. The excellent network of the Regional Transportation District (RTD) includes service from Denver and Denver International Airport to and within Boulder, Lyons, and Nederland. Transfort serves Fort Collins's main thoroughfares.

➤ BUS INFORMATION: **Regional Transportation District** (RTD, ☎ 303/299–6000 or 800/366–7433, WEB www.rtd–Denver.com). **Transfort** (☎ 970/221–6620).

CAR TRAVEL

The region is easily reached via I–25, which runs north–south. U.S. 36 North accesses Boulder and Estes Park from Denver. Fort Collins and Longmont can be reached from Denver, via I–25 North. The main thoroughfare through Rocky Mountain National Park, connecting Grand Lake with Estes Park, is U.S. 34, which is partially closed mid-October through May. Grand Lake can also be reached by U.S. 40 into U.S. 34, from Georgetown on I–70.

EMERGENCY SERVICES

➤ CONTACTS: **AAA Colorado** (☎ 303/753–8800).

ROAD CONDITIONS

➤ CONTACTS: **Rocky Mountain National Park** (☎ 970/586–1333). **State of Colorado** (☎ 303/639–1111 or 877/315–7623).

EMERGENCIES

➤ CONTACTS: **Boulder Community Hospital** (✉ 1100 Balsam Ave., Boulder, ☎ 303/440–2037). **Estes Park Medical Center** (✉ 555 Prospect Ave., Estes Park, ☎ 970/586–2317). **Fort Collins: Poudre Valley Hospital** (✉ 1024 S. Lemay Ave., Fort Collins, ☎ 970/495–7000).

LODGING

CABIN AND CONDO RENTALS

Range Property Management rent properties in the Estes Park area; RE/MAX Resorts of Grand County arranges rentals around Grand Lake.

➤ LOCAL AGENTS: **Range Property Management** (✉ Box 316, Estes Park, 80517, ☎ 970/586–7626 or 888/433–5211, FAX 970/577–8881, WEB www.rangeprop.com). **RE/MAX Resorts of Grand County** (✉ Box 39, Grand Lake, 80447, ☎ 970/627–8001 or 800/982–2155, WEB www.remax-grandlake-co.com).

TAXIS

➤ LOCAL COMPANIES: **Boulder Yellow Cab** (☎ 303/442–2277). **Shamrock Taxi & Transportation** (✉ Fort Collins, ☎ 970/226–6886).

TRAIN TRAVEL

Amtrak serves Granby from Denver and from points east and west.

VISITOR INFORMATION

➤ TOURIST INFORMATION: **Boulder Convention & Visitors Bureau** (✉ 2440 Pearl St., Boulder 80302, ☎ 303/442–2911 or 800/444–0447, FAX 303/938–8837, WEB www.bouldercoloradousa.com). **Estes Park Area Chamber of Commerce** (✉ 500 Big Thompson Ave., Estes Park 80517, ☎ 970/586–4431 or 800/443–7837, FAX 970/586–2816, WEB www.

estesparkresort.com). **Fort Collins Area Convention & Visitors Bureau** (⊠ 3745 E. Prospect Rd. #200, Fort Collins 80525, ☎ 970/491–3388 or 800/274–3678, FAX 970/491–3389, WEB www.ftcollins.com). **Granby Chamber of Commerce** (⊠ Box 35 Granby 80446, ☎ 970/887–2311 or 800/325–1661, FAX 970/887–3895, WEB www.granbychamber.com). **Grand Lake Chamber of Commerce** (⊠ Box 57, Grand Lake 80447, ☎ 970/627–3372 or 800/531–1019, FAX 970/627–8007, WEB www. grandlakechamber.com).

I–70 AND THE HIGH ROCKIES

Updated by
Jeanne
McGovern

I–70 is the major artery that fearlessly slices the Continental Divide, passing through or near many of Colorado's most fabled resorts and towns: Aspen, Vail, Breckenridge, Steamboat, Keystone, Snowmass, Copper Mountain, Beaver Creek, Winter Park. True powder hounds intone those names like a mantra to appease the snow gods, speaking in hushed tones of the gnarly mogul runs, the wide-open bowls on top of the world. Here is the image that lingers when most people think of Colorado: a Christmas paperweight come to life, with picture-postcard mining towns and quasi-Tyrolean villages framed by cobalt skies and snowcapped peaks. To those in the know, Colorado is as breathtaking the rest of the year, when meadows are woven with larkspur and columbine, the maroon mountains flecked with the jade of juniper and the white of aspen.

Like most of Colorado, the High Rockies region is a blend of old and new, of tradition and progress. It is historic towns such as Leadville, whose muddy streets still ring with the lusty laughter from saloons, of flamboyant millionaires who built grandiose monuments to themselves before dying penniless. It's also modern resorts such as Vail, whose history began a mere 30 years ago, yet whose founding and expansion involved risk-taking and egos on as monumental a scale. The High Rockies is fur trappers and fur-clad models, rustlers and Rastafarians, heads of cattle and heads of state. One thing links all the players together: a love of the wide-open spaces. Here, those spaces are as vast as the sky.

Most visitors on their way to the magnificent ski resorts along I–70 whiz through the Eisenhower Tunnel and cross the Continental Divide without paying much attention to the extraordinary engineering achievements that facilitate their journey. Interstate 70 and the tunnel are tributes to human ingenuity and endurance: before their completion in the 1970s, crossing the High Rockies evoked the long, arduous treks of the pioneers.

Idaho Springs

❷❸ *33 mi west of Denver via I–70; 13 mi west of Denver via U.S. 6.*

Colorado prospectors struck their first major vein of gold here on January 7, 1859. The quaint old town recalls its mining days, especially along downtown's National Historic Landmark District **Miner Street,** where pastel Victorians will transport you back to a century giddy with all that glitters.

During the gold rush days, ore was ferried from Central City via a 22,000-ft tunnel to Idaho Springs. The **Argo Gold Mill** explains the milling process and runs public tours. ⊠ *2350 Riverside Dr.,* ☎ *303/ 567–2421,* WEB *www.historicargotours.com.* ⌦ *$9.* ☉ *Daily 9–6, weather permitting.*

Just outside town is the **Phoenix Gold Mine,** still a working site. A seasoned miner leads visitors underground, where they can wield 19th-

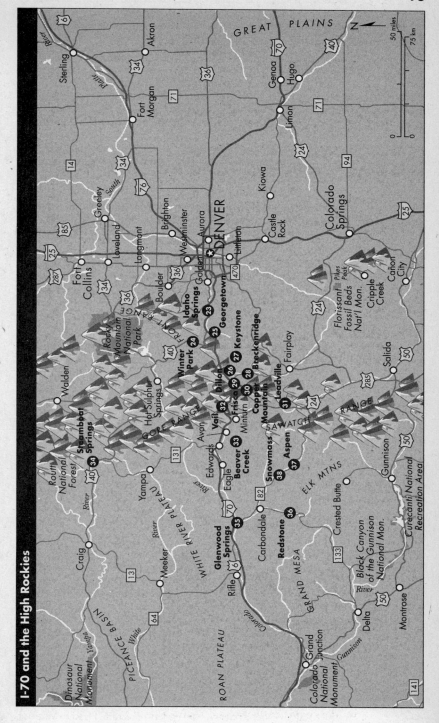

I-70 and the High Rockies

century excavating tools, and dig or pan for gold. Whatever riches you find are yours to keep. ⊠ *Off Trail Creek Rd.,* ☎ *303/567–0422.* 🖃 *$9; $5 for gold-panning only.* ⊙ *Daily 10–6, weather permitting.*

Idaho Springs presently prospers from its hot springs, at **Indian Springs Resort** (⊠ 302 Soda Creek Rd., ☎ 303/567–2191, WEB www.indianspringsreort.com). Around the springs, known to the Ute natives as the "healing waters of the Great Spirit," are geothermal caves that were used by several tribes as a neutral meeting site. Hot baths and a mineral-water swimming pool are the primary draws for the resort, but the scenery is equally fantastic. Within sight of the resort is the state's highest waterfall, Bridal Veil Falls. The imposing **Charlie Tayler Water Wheel**—the largest in the state—was constructed in the 1890s by a miner who attributed his strong constitution to that fact that he never shaved, took baths, or kissed women.

A vision of alpine splendor is **St. Mary's Glacier** (⊠ Fall River Rd.). In summer the sparkling sapphire lake makes a pleasant picnic spot; in winter, intrepid extreme skiers and snowboarders hike up the glacier and bomb down.

The Mt. Evans Scenic and Historic Byway—the highest paved auto road in America—leads to the summit of the 14,264-ft-high **Mt. Evans.** The pass winds through scenery of incomparable grandeur: past several placid lakes, one after another every few hundred feet; and vegetation galore, from towering Douglas firs to stunted dwarf bristlecone pines.

Dining

$–$$ ✕ **Beau Jo's Pizza.** No doubt about it, this always-hopping pizzeria is the original après-ski destination. Perfectly situated en route to Denver from the I–70 ski resorts, a stop here is mandatory—as is the roasted garlic cream pizza sauce served on Beau Jo's famous olive oil and honey pizza crust. ⊠ *1517 Miner St.,* ☎ *303/567–4376. AE, D, MC, V.*

$–$$ ✕ **Buffalo Bar and Restaurant.** No surprise as to the specialty here: steaks, burgers, fajitas, chili, Philly steak sandwiches—all made with choice buffalo. It's all part of the western theme, with walls jam-packed with frontier artifacts and memorabilia. The ornate bar dates from 1886. There's often great live music. ⊠ *1617 Miner St.,* ☎ *303/567–2729. AE, D, DC, MC, V.*

Winter Park

② *36 mi from Idaho Springs or 67 mi from Denver, via I–70 west and U.S. 40 north.*

Denverites have come to think of Winter Park as their own personal ski area. Although it's owned by the City of Denver and makes a favorite day trip (it's a 1½-hour drive), it is a destination resort on its own. Winter Park is easily accessible, the skiing and setting are superb, and it offers the best value of any major ski area in the state. It's equally popular in summer for hiking and biking. Winter Park has traditionally had few tourist attractions outside its natural beauty. Change is on the horizon, though, as the planned Village at Winter Park—a base area development anchored by the Zephyr Mountain Lodge, a slope-side minivillage comprised of condominiums, restaurants, bars, and shops—comes to fruition.

The three interconnected mountains—Winter Park, Mary Jane, and Vasquez Ridge—offer a phenomenal variety of terrain. Head to Vasquez Ridge for splendid intermediate cruising; Mary Jane for some of the steepest, most thrilling bumps in Colorado; and Winter Park for a pleasing blend of both.

Dining and Lodging

$$$$ ✕ **The Dining Room at Sunspot.** This striking log-and-stone structure
★ at the top of the Winter Park ski area is reached via gondola. Rough-
hewn log beams and furniture are accented with southwestern rugs hung
on the walls, but the real stunner is the view, so be sure to arrive early
enough to catch a glimpse of it. The five-course prix-fixe menu offers
game and fish paired with side dishes such as wild rice and potatoes
roasted in olive oil and herbs. ⊠ *Top of Zephyr Express Lift,* ☎ 970/
726–1446. *Reservations essential. AE, D, DC, MC, V. No dinner
Mar.–Oct. Lunch closures vary.*

$–$$$ ✕ **Deno's Mountain Bistro.** Deno's seems like a casual drinking estab-
★ lishment (there's a sizable selection of beers from around the world),
and it is by far the liveliest spot in town, yet it also has an impressive
international wine list that's comprehensive and fairly priced, which
is a bit of a rarity in low-key Winter Park. The wine is a labor of love
to Deno himself, a charismatic, energetic powerhouse. The menu is as
surprising as the wine list, from double-cut pork chops to grilled Rocky
Mountain trout to the best burgers in town, all well prepared and served
by a friendly staff, most of whom have been working here for years.
⊠ *78911 U.S. 40,* ☎ *970/726–5332. AE, D, MC, V.*

$ ✕ **Last Waltz.** This very homey place is festooned with hanging plants
and warmed by a crackling fireplace. The huge, family-friendly menu
jumps from seafood to burritos. The south-of-the-border dishes are best:
zesty *calientitas* (fried jalapeños filled with cream cheese and served
with salsa) and authentic chiles rellenos with home-roasted chiles are
especially noteworthy. Breakfast and brunch will power you for those
mogul runs. ⊠ *78336 U.S. 40,* ☎ *970/726–4877. Reservations not ac-
cepted. AE, D, DC, MC, V.*

$$ ✕🏨 **Gasthaus Eichler.** This small hotel holds Winter Park's most ro-
★ mantic dining spot ($$), with quaint Bavarian decor, antler chande-
liers, and stained glass, all glowing in the candlelight as Strauss lilts
softly in the background. Featured are veal and grilled items, in addi-
tion to scrumptious versions of German classics such as sauerbraten.
The *Rahmschnitzel*—tender veal in a delicate wild mushroom and
brandy cream sauce—is extraordinary, as are the feathery-light potato
pancakes. The cozy, old-world guest rooms, with down comforters, lace
curtains, armoires, cable TV, and Jacuzzis, are quite economical when
you consider that the rate includes breakfast and dinner. Rates with-
out meals included are considerably lower. ⊠ *78786 U.S. 40, 80482,*
☎ *970/726–5133 or 800/543–3899. 15 rooms. Restaurant. AE, MC,
V. MAP.*

$–$$ ✕🏨 **Peck House.** This snug, red-and-white, barnlike inn, Colorado's
oldest continually operating hostelry, is actually in the quirky town of
Empire. It began in 1860 as a boardinghouse for wealthy mine investors,
and the dining room ($$–$$$) is crammed with period antiques, in-
cluding the original etched-glass, gaslight lamp shades from the state
capitol, and tinted lithographs. Game is the house specialty: expertly
prepared quail and venison (try it with cabernet sauce) are among the
standouts. The charming rooms (with Jacuzzis but no TVs) are awash
in Victorian splendor. A Sunday brunch is offered in July and August.
⊠ *U.S. 40, 2 mi north of I–70, Box 428, Empire 80438,* ☎ *303/569–
9870,* FAX *303/569–2743,* WEB *www.thepeckhouse.com. 11 rooms, 10
with bath. Restaurant. AE, D, DC, MC, V. CP.*

$$$$ 🏨 **Iron Horse Resort Retreat.** This ski-in/ski-out hotel and condominium complex is the deluxe address in Winter Park. There are studios and one- and two-bedroom units; all except the lodge rooms have
a full kitchen and balcony and are furnished in an attractive, modern
rustic style. ⊠ *Iron Horse Dr., Box 1286, 80482,* ☎ *970/726–8851
or 800/621–8190,* FAX *970/726–2321,* WEB *www.ironhorse-resort.com.*

113 *rooms. Restaurant, bar, pool, 4 hot tubs, steam room, health club, ski shop. AE, D, DC, MC, V.*

$$–$$$$ ⊞ **Grand Victorian.** This luxury B&B is a three-story neo-Victorian in downtown Winter Park. Amenities include robes, slippers, and potpourri sachets in the rooms and an afternoon happy hour featuring Colorado wines and beers and the "grand après-ski" fondue party. The huge breakfast may include potato pancakes, quiches, or delectable macadamia-nut waffles. ⊠ *78542 Fraser Valley Pkwy., 80482, ☎ 970/726–5881 or 800/204–1170. 11 rooms. Breakfast room, meeting room. AE, D, DC, MC, V.*

$$$ ⊞ **Woodspur Lodge.** This classic log-cabin lodge is on the edge of the Arapahoe National Forest, about 1½ mi from Winter Park. The small rooms are more rustic than posh, with furnishings handmade from local lodgepole pines, and the emphasis is on mingling in the common areas. "All you can eat" breakfast, dinner, and afternoon snacks is included in the room rate, and are served in a dining area with a giant fireplace and a soaring roof. Many rooms have adjoining access. ⊠ *111 Van Anderson Dr., Box 249, 80482, ☎ 970/726–8417 or 800/626–6562, 瓰 970/726–8553, 瓁 www.woodspur.com. 32 rooms. Dining room, 2 outdoor hot tubs, sauna, recreation room. D, MC, V. FAP.*

$$ ⊞ **Anna Leah.** You'll feel like you're staying at a good friend's house at this B&B, thanks to the congenial owner, Patricia Handel, who will accommodate almost any request. The inn is just past the town of Fraser, about 5 mi from the ski area. With balconies overlooking the national forest and the Continental Divide, it has a wonderfully serene feel. A full breakfast and evening desserts are included in the price. ⊠ *1001 County Rd. 8, Fraser 80442, ☎ 970/726–4414, 瓰 970/726–5033, 瓁 www.annaleah.com. 5 rooms. Hot tub. No credit cards. BP.*

$$ ⊞ **Vintage Hotel.** This well-run hotel is Winter Park's other premier resort, offering spacious, comfortable rooms mostly decorated in soothing earth or mountain tones. Configurations range from standard hotel rooms (some with kitchenette and fireplace) to studios (with kitchens) and two-bedroom suites. ⊠ *Box 1369, 80482, ☎ 970/726–8801 or 800/472–7017, 瓰 970/726–9250, 瓁 www.vintagehotel.com. 118 rooms. Restaurant, bar, kitchenettes (some), pool, hot tub, sauna, gym. AE, D, DC, MC, V.*

$–$$ ⊞ **Sundowner Motel.** This is probably the nicest motel on the strip, and a great bargain, considering the free shuttle to the ski area. The rooms, recently renovated or within the new wing, are decorated in earth tones and have the standard amenities. ⊠ *78869 U.S. 40, Box 221, 80482, ☎ 970/726–9451 or 970/726–5452, 瓰 970/726–5452, 瓁 www.thesundownermotel.com. 38 rooms. Indoor pool, hot tub. AE, D, DC, MC, V.*

CONDOMINIUMS

The one-, two- and three-bedroom condos at the new **Zephyr Mountain Lodge** (⊠ 201 Zephyr Way, 80482, ☎ 970/726–8664, 瓰 970/726–6582) are ski-in/ski-out. Part of the grand Village at Winter Park, these units are equally impressive with every imaginable amenity and sweeping views of the surrounding mountains. The condominiums managed by **Condominium Management Co.** (⊠ Box 3095, 80482, ☎ 970/726–9421 or 800/228–1025, 瓰 970/726–8004) are an especially good value. Many feature recreational centers (including pool and hot tub) and laundry facilities. They run the gamut in price.

Nightlife

For a bit of local color, head down the road a ways to Fraser and the **Crooked Creek Saloon** (⊠ 401 Zerex St., ☎ 970/726–9250), where the motto is "Eat till it hurts; drink till it feels better." **The Slope**

(✉ 1161 Winter Park Dr., ☎ 970/726–5727) is Winter Park's most raucous venue, staging everything from rock to jazz to rockabilly.

Outdoor Activities and Sports

CYCLING

Winter Park is one of the leading mountain biking destinations in the Rockies, with some 50 mi of trails crisscrossing the ski area, and hundreds of miles off-the-beaten path. The **Winter Park Resort** (☎ 970/726–5514) offers complimentary mountain biking tips and tours every day in summer.

FISHING

The **Sulphur Ranger District** (✉ 9 Ten Mile Dr., Granby, ☎ 970/887–4100) can provide information about fishing in Winter Park and the surrounding region.

GOLFING

Winter Park's **Pole Creek Golf Club** (✉ County Rd. 51, ☎ 970/726–8847), a 7,000-yard, par-72, 27-hole course designed by Denis Griffiths, is consistently ranked in the top 75 public courses by *Golf Digest*.

HORSEBACK RIDING

For leisurely horseback riding tours of the Fraser Valley by day and hay-wagon rides by night, contact **Grand Adventure Stables** (☎ 970/726–9247).

SNOWMOBILING

Rentals and guided tours are available from **Trailblazer Snowmobile Tours** (☎ 970/726–8452 or 800/669–0134). Rates range from $40 per hour to $165 for a full-day tour.

SNOW TUBING

A lift-serviced snow-tubing hill? Yes, and it's lit at night, no less. The **Fraser Snow Tubing Hill** (☎ 970/726–5954) has two lifts, groomed trails, and a warming hut to make your inner tube riding most enjoyable. The rate is $12 per hour.

Downhill Skiing and Snowboarding

Winter Park is really three interconnected ski areas: Winter Park, flanked by Mary Jane and Vasquez Ridge. Skiers can spread out, but it's easy to lose your skiing partners, and once that happens, it's hard to find them.

The skiing at Winter Park and Vasquez Ridge leans heavily toward ultrawide, groomed intermediate trails. It's terrific skiing for families, groups, and schussboomers who enjoy testing the ski patrol's resolve by skiing too fast. On busy weekends, Vasquez Ridge is the best place for escaping crowds, partly because it's difficult to figure out how to get there. For experts *really* trying to escape crowds, the chutes and headwalls of Vasquez Cirque are the place to run to.

Mary Jane is 2,610 vertical ft of unrelenting moguls, with a couple of groomed runs (if you want groomed, there are more choices at Winter Park). The Timberline lift behind Mary Jane provides access to the above-tree-line skiing of Parsenn Bowl. The pitch is moderate, making the bowl a terrific place for intermediates to try their luck at powder and crud-snow skiing.

FACILITIES

3,060-ft vertical drop; 2,886 skiable acres; 9% beginner, 35% intermediate, 56% advanced; 8 high-speed quad chairs, 4 triple chairs, 7 double chairs.

LESSONS AND PROGRAMS

For adult skiers and snowboarders, the **Winter Park Skier and Rider Improvement Center** (☎ 970/726–1551) offers half-day lessons starting at $25. All-day children's programs, which include lunch, start at $70. Winter Park has the best program for skiers with disabilities in the country (303/316–1540).

LIFT TICKETS

$54. Savings of up to 25% on multiday tickets.

RENTALS

Winter Park Resort (☎ 970/726–5514) has rental packages starting at $20 at West Portal Rental and Repair at its base and Slopeside Gear and Sport in the Zephyr Mountain Lodge. Rental equipment is also available from several shops in downtown.

Nordic Skiing

BACKCOUNTRY SKIING

Berthoud Pass (Hwy. 40 at summit of Berthoud Pass, ☎ 800/754–2378), just south of Winter Park, is a hard place to define. As a ski area, it has been opened, closed, and reopened so often that lifts may or may not be running at any given time. Even when they are, only a portion of the skiing is truly lift-serviced. Much of the best terrain must be hiked to, and skiers and snowboarders get back to the ski-area base via shuttle buses from pickup points along the highway. Whatever the means of going up and down, Berthoud is well worth a visit for well-conditioned, expert skiers and riders.

TRACK SKIING

The closest groomed tracks to Winter Park are at **Devil's Thumb Ranch,** 7 mi from Winter Park, with a trail system totaling more than 105 km (65 mi). Some skiing is along tree-lined trails, some with more ups and downs and open views. The ranch offers lodging, a restaurant, rentals, lessons, and backcountry tours. ⊠ *Box 750, Tabernash 80478,* ☎ *970/726–5632 or 800/933–4339.* 🎿 *Trail fee $12.*

Snow Mountain Ranch is 12 mi northwest of Winter Park in Tabernash. The 100-km (62-mi) trail system includes 3 km (almost 2 mi) lit for night skiing. The ranch is a YMCA facility (with discounts for YMCA members) that has such added bonuses as a sauna and an indoor pool. Lessons, rentals, and on-site lodging are available. ⊠ *Box 169, Winter Park 80482,* ☎ *970/887–2152.* 🎿 *Trail fee $10.*

Shopping

Cooper Creek Square (⊠ 47 Cooper Creek Way, ☎ 970/726–8891) has souvenir shops and fine jewelers, delightful eateries and local hangouts, plus live entertainment in summer in the courtyard. **Crestview Place Mall** (⊠ 78737 U.S. 40, ☎ 970/276–9421) is home to fine shopping, though not as extensive a selection as Cooper Creek.

Georgetown

㉕ *50 mi from Denver via I–70 west; 41 mi from Winter Park via U.S. 40 south and I–70 west.*

Georgetown rode the crest of the silver boom during the second half of the 19th century. Most of its elegant, impeccably maintained brick buildings, which make up a five-square-block National Historic District, date from that period. Fortunately, Georgetown hasn't been tarted up at all, so it provides a true sense of what gracious living meant in those rough-and-tumble times. Just east of the Continental Divide, and just west of the I–70/U.S. 40 junction, Georgetown is close enough to be a day trip from Denver, but its quiet charms warrant more than a hurried visit.

The **Hamill House,** home of the silver magnate William Arthur Hamill, is a Gothic Revival beauty that displays most of the original wall coverings and furnishings; there's also a unique curved glass conservatory. ⊠ *3rd and Argentine Sts.,* ☎ *303/569–2840,* WEB *www. historicgeorgetown.org.* ᪥ *$5.* ⊘ *June–Sept., daily 10–5; Oct.–Dec., weekends noon–4; Jan.–May, by appointment.*

The elaborate **Hotel de Paris,** built almost single-handedly by Frenchman Louis Dupuy in 1878, was one of the Old West's preeminent hostelries. Now a museum, the hotel depicts how luxuriously the rich were accommodated: Tiffany fixtures, lace curtains, and hand-carved furniture re-create an era of opulence. ⊠ *409 6th St.,* ☎ *303/569–2311.* ᪥ *$4.* ⊘ *June–Sept., daily 10–5; Oct.–May, weekends 10–5.*

Hop on the **Georgetown Loop Railroad,** a 1920s narrow-gauge steam train that connects the town with the equally historic community of Silver Plume. The 6-mi round-trip excursion takes about 70 minutes and winds through vast stands of pine and fir before crossing the 95-ft-high Devil's Gate Bridge, where the track actually loops back over itself as it gains elevation. In Silver Plume, you can tour the Lebanon Silver Mill and Mine. ⊠ *100 Loop Dr.,* ☎ *303/569–2403 or 800/691–4386,* WEB *gtownloop.com.* ᪥ *$14.50.* ⊘ *Train operates June–Sept., daily 9:20–4.*

OFF THE BEATEN PATH	**GUANELLA PASS SCENIC BYWAY –** Get in the car and drive the 23-mi loop of Routes 381 and 62 for vistas of the Mt. Evans Wilderness Area. Then park yourself at the wildlife viewing station by Georgetown Lake, from where you can catch a glimpse of the state's largest herd of rare bighorn sheep.

Dining and Lodging

$–$$ ✕ **Red Ram.** This Georgetown landmark has been serving food since the 1950s, in a building dating from almost 100 years before that. Black-and-white photos of Georgetown's heydays bedeck the walls; there's a small cigar bar downstairs and live entertainment on weekends. The fare is basic western: burgers, ribs, and such Mexican specialties as fajitas. ⊠ *606 6th St.,* ☎ *303/569–2300. AE, D, MC, V.*

$$–$$$ ⌂ **Alpine Hideaway B & B.** Innkeeper Dawn Janov's refers to her romantic retreat as a "memory maker," and she's couldn't be more exact. The cozy rooms, all with private bath, fireplace and spectacular views, are furnished by theme—the Mountain Contemporary with black-and-white tile and gold fixtures; the Scandinavian with down-filled comforts; the Country Irish with landscape scenes of Ireland adorning the walls. With a homemade breakfast of quiche, fruit, and other delectables delivered to your door each morning, the Hideaway is a reasonably priced escape. ⊠ *Box 788, 80444,* ☎ *303/569–2800 or 800/490–9011. 3 rooms. MC, V.*

Downhill Skiing

The **Loveland Ski Area** is considered small-fry, but only because of its proximity to the megaresorts of Summit County. Actually, Loveland—the nearest ski area to Denver (62 mi, just before the Eisenhower Tunnel)—offers a respectable 1,365 acres serviced by 11 lifts and spread out over two mountains: Loveland Valley for beginners, and Loveland Basin for everyone else. Basin has some excellent glade and open-bowl skiing and snowboarding, with a 2,410-ft vertical drop. Best of all, it opens early and usually stays open later than any other area except Arapahoe Basin (A-Basin). ⊠ *Exit 216 off I–70, 12 mi west of Georgetown,* ☎ *303/569–3203,* WEB *www.skiloveland.com.* ⊘ *Mid-Oct.–May, weekdays 9–4, weekends 8:30–4.*

Shopping

The **Georgetown Antique Emporium** (✉ 501 Rose St., ☎ 303/569–2727) specializes in oak and brass items. The **Trading Post** (✉ 510 6th St., ☎ 303/569–3375) carries western paraphernalia, from pottery to jewelry to moccasins.

En Route   The western slope of the Rockies past the Continental Divide is where the most—and fluffiest—snow falls. As you travel west along I–70, you'll reach one of the world's engineering marvels, the 8,941-ft-long **Eisenhower Memorial Tunnel.** Most people who drive through take its presence for granted, but until the first lanes were opened in 1973, the only route west was the perilous Loveland Pass, a twisting, roller coaster of a ride. Snow, mud, and a steep grade proved the downfall of many an intrepid motorist. In truly inclement weather, it was impassable, and the east and west slopes were completely cut off from each other. Authorities first proposed the Eisenhower in 1937 (under a different name, of course). At that time, most geologists warned about unstable rock; for more than three decades their direst predictions came true as rock walls crumbled, steel girders buckled, and gas pockets caused mysterious explosions. When the project was finally completed, more than 500,000 cubic yards of solid granite had been removed from Mt. Trelease. The original cost estimate in 1937 was $1 million. By the time the second bore was completed in 1979, the tunnel's cost had skyrocketed to $340 million.

Dillon/Silverthorne

㉖   *23 mi from Georgetown or 73 mi from Denver via I–70 west.*

Founded in the 1870s as a stagecoach stop and trading post for miners, Dillon has had to pack up and move itself twice since its conception. In the 1880s Dillon was moved closer to the railroad line. Then, in 1955, plans were drawn up to dam the Blue River, hence forming a reservoir to quench Denver's growing thirst. Dillon would end up submerged under 150 ft of water. Once again the town was moved, this time to pine-blanketed hills mirrored in sapphire water. Residents agreed that no building in the new location would be higher than 30 ft, so as not to obstruct the view of the reservoir—now gratefully called Dillon Reservoir, or Lake Dillon. There's no pretension to Dillon, just nature lovers and sports enthusiasts who take advantage of all the recreational opportunities their idyllic home affords. The neighboring town of Silverthorne, which straddles I–70, offers recreation of a different sort in its many factory outlet shops.

Dining

$$–$$$ ✕ **Historic Mint.** Built in 1862, this raucous eatery originally served as a bar and brothel. The old days are still evident in the bar's brass handles and hand-carved wood, as well as in the antiques and vintage photographs covering the walls of the dining area. Red meat reigns here, although you will find chicken and fish on the menu; either way, you cook your own on lava rocks sizzling at 1,100°F. A well-stocked salad bar complements your entrée. If you prefer to leave the cooking to the chef, there's a prime rib special. ✉ *347 Blue River Pkwy., Silverthorne,* ☎ *970/468–5247. MC, V.*

$ ✕ **Blue Moon Bakery.** In addition to its excellent bagels, this stylish deli has some tasty soups and pastas and a good selection of cold cuts and cheeses. Breakfast features homemade granola, scones, muffins, turnovers, and one of the best breakfast burritos in Summit County. You can eat in at one of the five tables or take out, but just get there before closing, at 5 PM. ✉ *253 Summit, Summit Plaza Shopping Center, Silverthorne,* ☎ *970/468–1472. MC, V.*

Outdoor Activities and Sports

FISHING

Summit Guides (✉ Box 2489, Dillon, ☎ 970/468–8945) offers full- and half-day fishing trips.

HORSEBACK RIDING

There's horseback riding in summer and sleigh rides in winter at **Bar T Outfitters** (✉ Silverthorne, ☎ 970/468–6916).

Shopping

Dillon Factory Stores Complex (✉ 765 Anemone Tr., Exit 205 off I–70, Silverthorne, ☎ 970/468–6765) features shops like Timberland, Coach, and Donna Karan. **Silverthorne Factory Stores Complex** (✉ 145 Stevens Way, Exit 205 off I–70, Silverthorne, ☎ 970/468–5780) includes discount wares from J.Crew, Geoffrey Beene, Liz Claiborne, Jones New York, Bass Shoe, Nike, and many others.

En Route Dillon is the gateway to a string of superb ski areas in **Summit County**, where four mega-areas—Keystone, Arapahoe Basin (A-Basin), Breckenridge, and Copper Mountain—attract skiers from all over the world. There's a saying among Summit County residents: Copper for skiing, Breck for lodging, and Keystone for food. The adage is accurate. So popular is Summit County, thanks to its incomparable setting, incredible variety of ski terrain, multitude of summer activities, and easy accessibility from Denver, that it welcomes more visitors annually than Aspen and Vail combined. Unfortunately, this creates terrible traffic snarls along I-70, especially on weekends and holidays.

Keystone

❷❼ *8 mi from Dillon via U.S. 6 east.*

Keystone was designed to be cruisers' nirvana. With just enough flash to compete with the glamorous resorts, Keystone is quiet and popular with families, and probably wins the Summit County prize for the most genuine mountain resort. For the most part, its planners were sensitive to the environment, favoring mountain colors and materials that blend inconspicuously with the natural surroundings. Keystone has pursued an aggressive policy of expansion, opening the tougher terrain on North Peak (mogul heaven) and the Outback (glade skiing) in an attempt to change its "easy" reputation and provide a balanced ski experience. Keystone has one drawback: its sprawling base area. To improve this situation, an ambitious $700 million redevelopment plan is modernizing each base area and creating more accommodations at the mountain itself, especially at upscale River Run. Plus, just about every restaurant, lodge room, and activity in the resort is operated by Keystone, which makes planning a vacation here a one-stop shopping experience. Keystone is becoming a magnet in summer, too, with a small lake for water sports and a top-ranked golf course.

Dining and Lodging

$$$$ ✕ **Alpenglow Stube.** Without a doubt, this is the finest on-mountain
★ restaurant in Colorado. The decor is warmly elegant, with exposed wood beams, a stone fireplace, and floral upholstery. At night, the gondola ride you take to get here is alone worth the cost of the meal. Dinner is a six-course extravaganza, starting with the signature pine cone pâté, followed perhaps by rack of caribou in Poire William sauce. Lunch is equally delectable, with particularly fine pasta specials. (Removing your ski boots at lunch and putting on the plush slippers reserved for diners is a nice touch.) ✉ *North Peak, the Outpost,* ☎ *970/496–4386 or 800/354–4386. Reservations essential. AE, D, DC, MC, V. No lunch mid-Apr.–mid-Nov.*

$$$$ ✕ **Keystone Ranch.** This glorious 1930s ranch homestead was once part
  ★   of a working cattle ranch, and cowboy memorabilia is strewn throughout, nicely blending with stylish throw rugs and western craftwork.
The gorgeous and massive stone fireplace is a cozy backdrop for sipping an aperitif or after-dinner coffee. Chef Christopher Wing's rotating,
seasonal six-course menu emphasizes indigenous ingredients, including farm-raised game and fresh fish. You're in luck if the menu includes
elk with wild mushrooms in juniper sauce and quince relish or Gorgonzola flan. Finish your meal with a Grand Marnier soufflé drizzled
with pistachio cream sauce. ⊠ *Keystone Ranch Golf Course,* ☎ 970/
*496–4386 or 800/354–4386. Reservations essential. AE, D, DC, MC,
V. No lunch Oct.–May.*

$$$$ ✕ **Ski Tip Lodge.** In this original ski lodge circa 1800s, almost every-
  ★   thing on the menu will melt in your mouth. The four-course, prix-fixe
dinner is a favorite in the area for its American cuisine with a Colorado
twist. The main course may be a wood-grilled pork tenderloin or roast
African pheasant with game sausage, or Pacific style seafood fricassee
with coconut and lime. The delicious homemade bread and soup are
a meal in themselves. Adjourn to the cozy lounge for the decadent desserts
and special coffees. ⊠ *0764 Montezuma Rd., 1 mi off U.S. 6,* ☎ 970/
496–4386 or 800/354–4386. AE, D, DC, MC, V.

$$ ✕ **Kickapoo Tavern.** This rustic bar and grill features Colorado mi-
crobrews on tap and big portions of home-style American food such
as Mountain Momma's beef stew, hearty sandwiches, and burritos "as
big as a barn." The central location, outdoor patio, and TVs tuned to
favorite sporting events keep the place hopping both après ski and après
night-ski. ⊠ *Jackpine Lodge, River Run Plaza,* ☎ 970/496–4386 or
800/354–4386. AE, MC, V.

$–$$ ✕ **Gassy Thompson's Food & Spirits.** Imagine a sports bar crossbred
with a hunting lodge, and you'll get an idea of the ambience and decor
of this popular mountain-base hangout. Gassy Thompson was an
1880s miner said to have made his living by swindling other miners.
In his namesake restaurant, hearty American fare is served up in generous portions. Pork barbecue is the specialty, with burgers and extra-
large sandwiches vying for second place. Memorabilia from Colorado's
mining days—picks, buckets, lamps, and drawings—keeps Gassy's
spirit alive despite the honest dealings. ⊠ *Mountain House,* ☎ 970/
*496–4386 or 800/354–4386. Reservations not accepted. AE, D, DC,
MC, V. Closed mid-Apr.–mid-Nov..*

$$$–$$$$ ▥ **Keystone Lodge.** The ugly cinder-block structure gives no hint of
  ★   the gracious, pampered living within this member of Preferred Hotels.
Rooms with king-size beds are on the small side, while rooms with two
queen-size beds are enormous, with terraces. All units are beautifully
appointed in rich mountain colors, with all the amenities. ⊠ *Keystone
Resort, Box 38, 80435,* ☎ 970/496–4500 or 877/753–9786, Ⅸ 970/
468–4343, Ⓦ *www.keystoneresort.com. 152 rooms. 3 restaurants, bar,
outdoor pool, 2 hot tubs, 2 tennis courts, health club, children's pro-
grams, convention center. AE, D, DC, MC, V.*

$$–$$$ ▥ **Ski Tip Lodge.** The rooms at this charming, elegant log cabin have
  ★   quaint names such as Edna's Eyrie. They're uniquely decorated with
homespun furnishings and accessories such as quilts and hand-knitted
throw rugs. Some rooms have four-poster beds. Breakfast is included
in the room rate, and the Ski Tip's prix-fixe dinner vies for best in Sum-
mit County with the Alpenglow Stube and Keystone Ranch. ⊠ *Key-
stone Resort, Box 38, 80435,* ☎ 970/496–4500 or 877/753–9786, Ⅸ
970/468–4343, Ⓦ *www.keystoneresort.com. 11 rooms, 2 suites.
Restaurant. AE, D, DC, MC, V. BP.*

CONDOMINIUMS

Keystone Resort Corporation (☎ 970/496–4500 or 877/753–9786) operates all the lodging facilities at the resort, which range from hotel-style accommodations at Keystone Lodge to various condominium properties.

Nightlife

Kickapoo Tavern (✉ Jackpine Lodge, River Run Plaza, ☎ 970/496–4386 or 800/354–4386) is a popular Keystone hangout. The older set relaxes at **RazzBerry's Lounge** (✉ The Inn at Keystone, Hwy. 6, ☎ 970/496–4386), where wingback chairs, Tiffany lamps, and live jazz create a warm and welcoming atmosphere. Live music with rockabilly leanings makes the **Snake River Saloon** (✉ 23074 U.S. 6, 1 mi east of Keystone, ☎ 970/468–2788) a good spot to drink beer if you like a loud, music-driven environment. The crowd is generally under 30.

Outdoor Activities and Sports

GOLFING

Keystone Ranch Course (✉ 22010 Rte. 6, ☎ 970/496–4250) is listed as one of the top 50 resort courses in America by *Golf Digest*. The 7,090-yard, par-72 course, designed by Robert Trent Jones Jr., winds through mountain scenery. **Keystone River Course** (✉ 21196 Rte. 6, ☎ 970/496–4250) is a 6,886-yard stunner. The par-71 Hurdzan-Fry–designed course is a challenge for all players, with views that make it all worthwhile.

ICE-SKATING

Keystone boasts the largest maintained outdoor **ice-skating lake** (☎ 970/496–4386 or 800/354–4386) in North America, with skate, sled, and hockey-stick rentals and lessons from late November to early March, daily 10–10.

Downhill Skiing and Snowboarding

It's hard to get a good read on **Keystone** at first, especially since the slopes you see from the base lodge look quite steep—and they are—but they are not indicative of the rest of the trails. About 75% of Keystone Mountain is geared toward novice and lower-intermediate skiing. Yet Keystone Mountain isn't all there is to Keystone. Slip off the back side, and you've got North Peak and the Outback, with skiing for more skilled intermediates and advanced skiers. None of it is real knock-your-socks-off expert terrain, but Keystone has never tried to market itself as an expert's ski area. It's great for families, for people who ski once or twice a year, and for those in search of an all-around resort experience. Better skiers prefer to toss the boards in the car and head for either Copper or Arapahoe, 6 mi up the road. ✉ *Hwy. 6,* ☎ *970/468–2316,* WEB *www.keystoneresort.com.* ☉ *Late Oct.–early May, daily 8:30 AM–8 PM.*

FACILITIES

2,900-ft vertical drop; 1,861 skiable acres; 12% beginner, 29% intermediate, 59% advanced; 2 gondolas, 1 super six lift, 5 high-speed quad chairs, 1 quad chair, 2 triple chairs, 5 double chairs, 7 surface lifts and carpets.

LESSONS AND PROGRAMS

Keystone offers a variety of instructional programs, from half-day group lessons to special clinics, notably mogul clinics and women's seminars. One of the better children's programs is at Keystone, with day care and ski groups for children from 2 months to 16 years old. A special program of note is the Mahre Training Center at Keystone, intensive three- or five-day clinics hosted by either Phil or Steve Mahre, both Olympic medalists.

Tickets are $57 at Keystone and are good at Arapahoe Basin and Breckenridge (but unfortunately not at Copper, which is under different ownership). Multiday ticket savings can exceed 20% and are good at Vail and Beaver Creek. Twilight tickets (2 PM–8 PM) are $39; night skiing (4 PM–8 PM) is $33.

Rental packages (skis, boots, and poles) start at $18 per day. Considerable savings can be found by bargain shopping at ski stores in Breckenridge, Dillon, Frisco, and Silverthorne.

Nordic Skiing

The **Keystone Cross-Country Center** (☎ 970/496–4386 or 800/354–4386) has 57 km (35 mi) available for track skiing, skate skiing, and snowshoeing.

Shopping

Edgewater Mall and Argentine Plaza, both on the shore of the lake at Keystone Village, have basic shops such as Rocky Mountain Chocolate Factory and Shirt Off My Back. **River Run** at the base of the River Run Gondola is a bit more upscale, with shops like the ski-clothing boutique Gorsuch, Mother Moose children's store, and Inxpot, an eclectic bookstore, coffeehouse, and bar.

Arapahoe Basin

7 mi from Dillon via U.S. 6 east.

Arapahoe was the first ski area to be built in Summit County, in the late 1940s. Some say it hasn't changed since; the dig refers, in part, to some of Colorado's slowest lifts. Still, most of A-Basin's dedicated skiers wouldn't have it any other way. It's America's highest ski area, with a *base* elevation of 10,800 ft (and a summit of 13,050 ft). Most of the runs are above timberline, giving it an almost otherworldly feel. Aficionados love the short lift lines, the literally breathtaking views (and altitudes), the whopping 85% intermediate and expert terrain, and the wide-open bowls that stay open into June (sometimes July). A-Basin has remained true to its resolutely un-chic, gnarly self, and its late-season, on-mountain partying spirit has become legendary. Of course if you're looking for slope-side accommodations or fine dining, look elsewhere: A-Basin is only a ski hill, with cafeteria food and après entertainment, at best. You'll have to set up base camp in nearby Keystone, Breckenridge, Frisco, Dillon, or Silverthorne and shuttle in for the day.

Outdoor Activities and Sports

Mountain bikers in **Arapahoe National Forest** cycle over Loveland Pass and along the Blue River Bikeway and the Tenmile Canyon National Recreation Trail.

Downhill Skiing and Snowboarding

What can make **Arapahoe** delightful is also what damns it in bad weather: its elevation. Most of Arapahoe's skiing is above tree line and when a storm moves in, you can't tell up from down. When the storm passes, skiing can be limited because of avalanche problems.

But if that sounds dreadful, consider the other side of the coin: On sunny spring days, Arapahoe is probably *the* place to be skiing in Colorado. It feels more like skiing in the Alps than Summit County, Colorado, with craggy peaks surrounded by treeless, rolling terrain. Intermediates can have a great time here, although "A-Basin" is best known for its expert challenges: the East Wall, a steep open face with great powder-skiing possibilities; Pallavicini, a wide, steep, tree-lined gutter of a run; and the West Wall cornice, from which young bucks, with varying degrees of bravado and sobriety, like to launch themselves. A typical spring day at Arapahoe: ski frantically hard in the morning; kick back, catch rays, and swill beers in the afternoon. ⊠ *Box 8787, 80435,* ☎ *970/468–0718,* WEB *www.arapahoebasin.com.* ☉ *Mid-Nov.–mid-June, daily 9–4.*

FACILITIES
2,250-ft vertical drop; 490 skiable acres; 15% beginner, 45% intermediate, 40% advanced; 1 triple chair, 4 double chairs.

LESSONS AND PROGRAMS
Contact **central reservations** (☎ 970/468–0718) for information on instructional programs.

LIFT TICKETS
Tickets cost $28–$44, depending on the time of season. Multiday ticket savings can exceed 20%.

RENTALS
Rental packages (skis, boots, and poles) start at $18 per day. Considerable savings can be found by bargain shopping at ski stores in Breckenridge, Dillon, Frisco, and Silverthorne.

Breckenridge

❷❽ *22 mi from Keystone via U.S. 6 west, I–70 west, and Rte. 9 south.*

Many people consider Breckenridge the prettiest Colorado town. Gold was discovered here in 1859, and for the next several decades Breckenridge's fortunes rose and fell as its lodes of gold and then silver were mined and exhausted. It's the oldest continuously occupied town on the western slope. Much of its architectural legacy from the mining era remains, yet Breckenridge has become so built up over the years (close to 25,000 beds) that it comes off as the most thoroughly developed resort of Summit County.

The **downtown** comprises one of Colorado's largest National Historic Districts, with 254 buildings in the National Register of Historic Places. The district is roughly a compact 12 square blocks, bounded by Main, High, and Washington streets and Wellington Road. The **Breckenridge Activity Center** (⊠ 201 S. Main St., ☎ 970/453–5579) and **Summit Historical Society** (⊠ 309 N. Main St., ☎ 970/453–9022, WEB www.summithistorical.org) publish guided tours of more than 40 prominent structures, which range from simple log cabins to false-fronts to Victorians with lacy gingerbread trim, all lovingly restored and painted.

Dining and Lodging

$$–$$$$ ✕ **Poirrier's at the Wellington.** A welcome alternative to resort town burgers and uptown pasta, this spicy spot cooks up authentic Cajun cuisine under the capable guidance of Louisiana chef James Allen Graham. Start with the Tabasco jack shrimp, followed by the crawfish enchiladas. Or, for an afternoon escape, hit the gumbo bar. ⊠ *200 N. Main St.,* ☎ *970/453–1877. AE, MC, V.*

$$$ ✕ **Café Alpine.** This bright, cheerful place serves terrific soups, salads, ★ and sandwiches at lunch (summer only), and more substantial regional American cuisine on a menu that changes daily at dinner. Try the cilantro seared California snapper with red pepper; cheddar cheese quesadillas and mole negro; or the grilled tenderloin of beef stuffed with blue cheese and wrapped in boar bacon. At the tapas bar (served after 5 PM) you can sample global cuisine, including kibbeh with tahini aioli, clams casino, seared tuna sashimi, rock shrimp, and yucca fritters with mango. The recipient of a Wine Spectator Award of Excel-

lence since 1994, Café Alpine serves 20 wines by the glass. ⊠ *106 E. Adams Ave.,* ☎ *970/453–8218. AE, D, MC, V.*

$–$$ ✕ **Blue Moose.** Locals flock here for the hearty breakfasts: eggs, oatmeal, pancakes, and more. At lunch, choose from one of the sandwiches, burritos, pastas, or salads. Nothing here is fancy—food or decor—but a meal here will hit the spot. ⊠ *540 S. Main St.,* ☎ *970/453–4859. MC, V. No dinner.*

$$$–$$$$ ⊞ **Village at Breckenridge.** The word "village" puts it mildly, at this sprawling, self-contained resort spread over 14 acres, offering several varieties of accommodation from lodge-style rooms to three-bedroom condominiums, all ski-in, ski-out. The decor runs from southwestern color schemes to gleaming chrome-and-glass units. Studios and efficiencies have fireplaces and kitchenettes. ⊠ *Box 8329, 80424,* ☎ *970/453–2000 or 800/800–7829,* ℻ *970/453–3116,* ⓦⓔⓑ *www.villageatbreckenridge.com. 295 rooms. 4 restaurants, bar, kitchenettes (some), indoor-outdoor pool, 9 hot tubs, sauna, health club, ice-skating, 3 ski shops, theater, meeting rooms. AE, D, DC, MC, V.*

$$–$$$$ ⊞ **B&Bs on North Main Street.** Innkeepers Fred Kinat and Diane Jaynes
   ★ offer accommodations in three adjacent buildings. They restored and expanded the 1885 miner's cottage, which was once their home. The Willoughby Cottage next door is a romantic retreat for two, complete with a gas-burning fireplace, hot tub, kitchenette, and rustic antique furnishings. A river streams past the modern, timber-frame Barn Above the River, which has five country rooms. Best of all the affable hosts are avid skiers ("Cold cereal on powder days," they warn), and take guests to their secret ski spots. ⊠ *303 N. Main St. 80424,* ☎ *970/453–2975 or 800/795–2975,* ℻ *970/453–5258,* ⓦⓔⓑ *www.breckenridge-inn.com. 12 rooms. AE, DC, MC, V. BP.*

$$–$$$$ ⊞ **Lodge & Spa at Breckenridge.** This special property has the disadvantage of being outside town, though shuttle service is provided to the town and ski area. The compensation is the breathtaking panoramas of the Tenmile Range from nearly every angle. Huge, strategically placed picture windows allow full vantage. The look is mountain chalet, with a rustic-modern decor. The well-lit, spacious rooms all have cable TV and full bath. Minisuites also feature fireplace and kitchenette. Continental breakfast is included. The complete spa and health club facility is a bonus. ⊠ *112 Overlook Dr., 80424,* ☎ *970/453–9300 or 800/736–1607,* ℻ *970/453–0625,* ⓦⓔⓑ *thelodgeatbreck.com. 45 rooms. Restaurant, indoor pool, 2 indoor hot tubs, 2 outdoor hot tubs, spa, health club, meeting room. AE, D, DC, MC, V. CP.*

$$$ ⊞ **Allaire Timbers Inn.** Nestled in a wooded area, this stone-and-timber log cabin inn has a great room anchored by a huge stone fireplace, as well as a reading loft and a sunroom with a green slate floor and handcrafted log furniture. The main deck and hot tub offer spectacular views of the Tenmile Range. A hearty breakfast is included, as is an afternoon happy hour. ⊠ *9511 S. Main St., 80424,* ☎ *970/453–7530 or 800/624–4904,* ℻ *970/453–8699. 8 rooms, 2 suites. Outdoor hot tub. AE, D, MC, V.*

$$$ ⊞ **Great Divide Lodge.** This property is just 50 yards from the base of Peak 9. The only full-service hotel in Breckenridge, it was planned as a condo development, but management ran out of financing. This pays dividends in the enormous bedrooms, which have pleasing contemporary southwestern decor. Amenities include hair dryers, bathrobes, and gourmet coffee for the coffeemakers. The one surprising omission: air-conditioning (though it's hardly necessary). ⊠ *550 Village Rd., 80424,* ☎ *970/453–4500 or 800/321–8444,* ℻ *970/453–0212,* ⓦⓔⓑ *www.greatdividelodge.com. 208 rooms. Restaurant, bar, in-room data ports, indoor pool, 2 hot tubs, health club, ski shop, meeting room. AE, D, DC, MC, V.*

Breckenridge Accommodations (⌧ Box 1931, 80424, ☎ 970/453–9140 or 800/872–8789, FAX 970/453–8686). **Breckenridge Central Lodging** (⌧ Box 709, 80424, ☎ 970/453–2160 or 800/858–5885, FAX 970/453–4163). **Breckenridge Resort Chamber Central Reservation System** (☎ 800/221–1091). **East West Resorts** (⌧ Box 2009, 80424, ☎ 970/457–1330 or 800/525–2258, FAX 970/453–0698). **Summit County Central Reservations** (⌧ Box 1069, Silverthorne 80498, ☎ 970/468–7851 or 800/365–6365, FAX 970/262–0993).

Nightlife

Breckenridge is generally the choice of a young, lively crowd. The skiing focuses mainly on cruising, and so does the nightlife.

BARS AND LOUNGES

Breckenridge Brewery (⌧ 600 S. Main St., ☎ 970/453–1550), brews up six premium homemade beers. It's a great après-ski spot. **Cecilia's** (⌧ La Cima Mall, lower level, ☎ 970/453–2243) is a martini lounge offering a cigar parlor. Decorated with maroon velour walls and lace curtains, **Hearthstone** (⌧ 130 S. Ridge St., ☎ 970/453–1148) shows its bordello roots. Skiers and locals scarf down the addictive happy-hour special, jalapeño-wrapped shrimp. The **Olive Nightclub** (⌧ La Cima Mall, upper level, ☎ 970/453–9181) has a wide selection of single malt scotches and tap beer.

MUSIC CLUBS

You can take free dance lessons at **Salt Creek Saloon** (⌧ 110 E. Lincoln Ave., ☎ 970/453–4959), where the occasional live C&W band gives you something to practice to. **Sherpa and Yeti's** (⌧ 318 S. Main St., ☎ 970/547–9299) is the hot spot for rock, acoustic, blues, Cajun, and reggae sets. **Tiffany's** (⌧ 20 Village Rd., ☎ 970/453–6000 ext. 8732) has a DJ and dancing nightly, and is the ultimate gathering place for thirtysomething tourists.

Outdoor Activities and Sports

FISHING

Mountain Anglers (⌧ Breckenridge, ☎ 970/453–4665) organizes fishing trips throughout Summit County.

FITNESS

Breckenridge Recreation Center (⌧ Kingdom Park, ☎ 970/453–1734) is a state-of-the-art, 62,000-square-ft facility that has a fully equipped health club, two swimming pools, and indoor tennis and racquetball courts.

GOLFING

Breckenridge Golf Club (⌧ 200 Clubhouse Dr., ☎ 970/453–9104), a municipally owned Jack Nicklaus–designed course, is a 7,279-yard, par-72 beauty. Dramatically situated, it resembles a nature reserve, with woods and beaver ponds lining the fairways.

HORSEBACK RIDING

For horseback riding, try **Breckenridge Stables** (☎ 970/453–4438).

RAFTING

Performance Tours Rafting (☎ 970/453–0661 or 800/328–7238) leads rafting trips on the Arkansas, Blue, and Colorado rivers for families and experienced rafters ready for extremes.

SNOWMOBILING

Good Times (⌧ Breckenridge, ☎ 970/453–7604) will get you snowmobiling on more than 40 mi of groomed trails, through open meadows, or along the Continental Divide to Georgia Pass at an elevation of 11,585 ft.

Downhill Skiing and Snowboarding

For the most part, **Breckenridge** is the sort of area where you can close your eyes and let your skis run; intermediate cruising is the name of the game. It is ideal for people who like a relaxed day on the slopes without overworking the challenge meter. Still, there is some more adventurous, above-tree-line bowl skiing, accessible either by hiking or by a hard-to-ride T-bar. When that high-country skiing is good, it's great, but because of Breck's exposure to stormy weather, conditions can often be less than ideal.

Breckenridge's chief drawback is its horizontal layout, spreading across the flanks of four main peaks of the Tenmile Range, named—with great imagination—Peaks 7, 8, 9, and 10. There are bowls and chutes on Peak 7 and 8, which are above timberline; gentle sweeping runs on Peak 9; and roller-coaster steeps on Peak 10. Consistent with the town's proud heritage, many runs are named for the old mines, including Bonanza, Cashier, Gold King, and Wellington. Want to get from the base of Peak 8 to the summit of Peak 10? A couple of lift rides are necessary, and navigational aids would be helpful.

Breck has developed a reputation for embracing the new: it was one of the first areas to permit snowboarding, and it has hosted the annual World Cup Freestyle Classic. Also, for one week each January the town declares itself an independent kingdom during the wild revel called Ullr Fest, which honors the Norse god of snow. ☎ 970/453–5000, WEB *www.breckenridge.com.* ☉ *Late Oct.–late May, daily 8:30–4.*

FACILITIES

3,398-ft vertical drop; 2,031 skiable acres; 14% beginner, 26% intermediate, 60% advanced; 1 high-speed six-person lift, 5 high-speed quad chairs 1 triple chair, 7 double chairs.

LESSONS AND PROGRAMS

Contact the **Breckenridge Ski Resort ski school** (☎ 888/576–2754) for information about instructional programs such as the $60 all-day class-lesson rate.

LIFT TICKETS

The $57 tickets at Breckenridge are good at Keystone and Arapahoe Basin (but not at Copper). Multiday ticket savings can exceed 20% and are also good at Vail and Beaver Creek.

RENTALS

Rental packages (skis, boots, and poles) start at $18 per day. Shop around at the ski stores to get the best deal.

Nordic Skiing

BACKCOUNTRY SKIING

Despite widespread development in Summit County, there are still plenty of opportunities to escape into the backcountry and get away from it all. They don't call it Summit County for nothing; mountain passes above 10,000 ft allow for relatively easy access to high-country terrain and good, high-country snow. This recommendation comes, however, with a word of caution: Avalanche-related deaths are all too common in Summit County (more often involving snowmobilers than skiers). Easy access often attracts backcountry travelers whose snow-safety awareness is not what it should be. For information on snow conditions, contact the **Dillon Ranger District Office** (☎ 970/468–5400).

Among the easier, and safer, touring routes is the trip to Boreas Pass, just south of Breckenridge. The trail (about 20 km/12 mi round-trip) follows a former rail route, with good views of distant peaks along the way. Summit County is also developing a system of backcountry huts that will be linked to Aspen's 10th Mountain Hut and Trail System. The first of these huts is Janet's Cabin, about a 10-km (6-mi) ski in from the trailhead off I–70 west of Copper Mountain. For information and reservations, contact the **10th Mountain Hut and Trail System** (☎ 970/925–5775).

TRACK SKIING

The Breckenridge terrain is probably the gentlest in Summit County. The **Breckenridge Nordic Center** (☎ 970/453–6855) has 30 km (18½ mi) of groomed tracks.

Shopping

At the intersection of Main Street and Lincoln Avenue there's an abundance of shopping—from tourist traps and high-end boutiques to ski shops and art galleries—so it's wise to spend an evening window-shopping before breaking out your wallet. **La Cima Mall** (⊠ Main St. between Jefferson and Ridge Sts.) offers an upscale shopping experience.

The **Bay Street Company** (⊠ 232 S. Main St., ☎ 970/453–6303) carries colorful hand-painted furniture and collectibles in a quaint Victorian house. **Skilled Hands Gallery** (⊠ 110 S. Main St., ☎ 970/453–7818) is the largest arts-and-crafts gallery in Summit County, offering everything from wood carvings to wind chimes.

Frisco

㉙ *9 mi from Breckenridge via Rte. 9 north.*

Funky, low-key Frisco contains an odd hodgepodge of strip malls near the interstate and a charming downtown district trimmed with restored bed-and-breakfasts and hell-raising bars. The town is a sane, moderate alternative to the glitzier, pricier resorts in Summit County. It's worth exploring even if you're staying elsewhere.

The **Frisco Historic Park** re-creates the boom days with a fully outfitted one-room schoolhouse, jail, and log chapel among the seven authentic 19th-century buildings. ⊠ *Main and 2nd Sts.,* ☎ *970/668–3428.* 🎟 *Free.* ☉ *Year-round Tues.–Sat. 11–4; also Sun. 11–4 Memorial Day–Labor Day.*

Dining and Lodging

$–$$ ✕ **El Rio.** On a sunny deck overlooking Tenmile Creek and Gore Range, you can down great margaritas and very fresh south-of-the-border specialties, such as blackened fish tacos, or Taos tacos: a soft flour tortilla with cheese, pinto beans, and roasted vegetables. ⊠ *450 W. Main St.,* ☎ *970/668–5043. AE, DC, MC, V.*

$–$$ ✕ **Frisco's Bar & Grill.** You'll find no frills here, just juicy burgers (nine varieties), hellacious nachos, Buffalo wings, and a boisterous crowd in this classic pub with neon signs on the walls and sawdust on the floor. ⊠ *720 Granite St., Boardwalk Blvd.,* ☎ *970/668–5051. Reservations not accepted. AE, D, MC, V.*

$$–$$$ 🏨 **Hotel Frisco.** The lobby soars 2½ stories in this mountain-charming, central lodge on historic Main Street. Easy access to Copper Mountain, Breckenridge, Keystone, and Vail/Beaver Creek, in addition to nearby river rafting, hiking, and fly-fishing, make this hotel a find in any season. Toast your toes by the river-rock fireplace after a day on the slopes. The owner, a former Colorado ski patroller, happily shares tips. ⊠ *308 Main St., 80443,* ☎ *970/668–5009 or 800/262–1002,* ℻ *970/668–0695,* 🌐 *www.hotelfrisco.com. 14 rooms. In-room data ports, hot tub. AE, MC, V.*

Nightlife

Backcountry Brewery (⊠ Main St. at Hwy. 9, ☎ 970/668–2337) is home to the Great American Beer Festival's gold medal-winner, Telemark IPA, and a half dozen other handcrafted brews. The **Moose Jaw** (⊠ 208 Main St., ☎ 970/668–3931) is definitely a locals' hangout. Pool tables beckon the unwary, and a plethora of old photographs, trophies, and newspaper articles makes the barn-wood walls all but invisible.

Outdoor Activities and Sports

Timber Ridge Adventures (⊠ Frisco, ☎ 970/668–8349 or 800/282–9070) runs snowmobiling trips.

Nordic Skiing

The **Frisco Nordic Center** (☎ 970/668–0866) has 45 km (27 mi) of groomed trails.

Shopping

The **Cactus Patch** (⊠ 401 Main St., ☎ 970/668–1240) showcases the work of local artists, from hand-dyed silk scarves to whimsical wood-workings. Odds and ends fill the **Junk-Tique Antique Barn** (⊠ 313 Main St., ☎ 970/668–3040).

Copper Mountain

③⓪ *7 mi from Frisco via I–70 south.*

Copper Mountain is dedicated to skiing, although it's picking up as a summer resort. Many skiers think the award-winning design, perfectly contoured to the natural terrain, is one of the world's best. The layout is ideal: beginner runs are concentrated on the right side (facing the mountain) of the area, intermediate runs in the center, and expert terrain to the left. Weaker skiers can't get into trouble unless they look for it. Copper lacks a real town, and hasn't much in the way of personality, although the resort's new owners, the ski development juggernaut Intrawest, is sinking some $250 million into a complete overhaul of the mountain's base area. Still under construction, plans call for a pedestrians-only village filled with shops, restaurants, open plazas and a variety of lodging options, as well as sports-related amenities like a climbing wall and tubing hill.

Dining and Lodging

$$–$$$ ✕ **Double Diamond.** A staple of Copper Mountain's restaurant scene and a favorite among locals, this casual, rustic eatery serves up the best steak and seafood in the Village. Try the classic prime rib au jus or the fresh catch of the day (it's flown in weekly from a "secret" connection on the big island of Hawaii), or just kick back with a cold beer and a shrimp cocktail. ⊠ *East Village,* ☎ *970/968–2880. AE, D, DC, MC, V.*

$$–$$$ ✕ **Molly B's Saloon.** This lively American bistro serves fresh and flavorful contemporary dishes. Try the rotisserie chicken, hickory-smoked pork chop with a sun-dried cherry vinaigrette, barbecue chicken pizza, and pan-roasted mussels. ⊠ *102 Wheeler Circle,* ☎ *970/968–2318, Ext. 83062. AE, D, DC, MC, V.*

$$–$$$$ 🏨 **Copper Mountain Resort.** The resort runs just about every lodging facility in the base area, ranging from hotel-style units to condos. All include use of the Copper Mountain Racquet and Athletic Club. The new Village at Copper is the most conveniently located, within easy walking distance of the lifts, and the most favored by families and those in search of a happening ski vacation. The hustling, modern complex features one- to four-bedroom units; most have a fireplace and a balcony. Two small subdivisions, East Village (which provides easy access to the mountain's more challenging terrain) and Union Creek (at the base of the ski school), have some of the largest and most upscale accommodations at the resort, with three or four bedrooms, full kitchens, dining areas, patios, garages, and some private hot tubs. ⊠ *Copper Mountain Resort, 209 Tenmile Circle, Box 3001, 80443,* ☏ *970/968–2882 or 800/458–8386,* FAX *970/968–6227,* WEB *www.ski-copper.com. 800 rooms. 5 restaurants, 3 cafeterias, coffee shop, pool, hot tub, sauna, 18-hole golf course, 8 tennis courts, health club, hiking, horseback riding, racquetball, ice-skating, cross-country skiing, ski shop, playground, business services, convention center. AE, D, DC, MC, V.*

Nightlife

BARS AND LOUNGES

Club Med (⊠ 50 Beeler Pl., ☏ 970/968–2161) offers an international dinner buffet that includes bar games, nightly entertainment, and admission to its disco. You can forgo dinner and just hit the show and disco. Grab a cocktail and kick back on **Copper Beach** (⊠ base of the American Eagle lift), a snowy oasis of lawn chairs and sunshine. In the Village, **Jack's** (⊠ Camp One base lodge, ☏ 970/968–2882) is the place to be for après ski, with live entertainment and a raucous crowd. **Molly B's Saloon** (⊠ 102 Wheeler Circle, base of B-Lift, ☏ 970/968–2318, Ext. 83062) is the spot to drink beer after a long day on the bumps under the Super Bee lift. Local fave Moe Dixon gets 'em dancing on the tables.

Outdoor Activities and Sports

CYCLING

For serious road riders, especially would-be racers, the **Carpenter/Phinney Bike Camps** (☏ 303/442–2371) are conducted in Frisco and near Boulder by 1984 Olympic road champion Connie Carpenter and her husband, Davis Phinney, also an Olympic medalist and professional racer. One-week sessions focus on riding technique, training methods, and bicycle maintenance.

FISHING

Vail Fishing Guides (☏ 970/476–3296) provides gear as well as guided tours.

GOLFING

Copper Creek Golf Club (⊠ Wheeler Circle, Copper Mountain, ☏ 970/968–2882), at 9,650 ft, is the highest 18-hole course in North America. Designed by Pete and Perry Dye, the par-70, 6,094-yard course follows the twisting, narrow, natural terrain of Copper's valley.

Downhill Skiing and Snowboarding

Copper Mountain has perhaps the best variety of skiing among the Summit County areas: good, long cruisers, satisfying mogul runs, above-tree-line bowl skiing, tight tree skiing, and a terrific cluster of lower-intermediate terrain. Furthermore, the layout is such that there's minimal contact (literally) between skiers of differing abilities. One reason for this is that Copper, like Breckenridge, is a horizontal spread, with novice skiers tending toward the right, intermediates in the middle, and experts toward the left. It's a great choice for a family or group of friends with widely varying skills. In recent years, Copper has been pushing out its boundaries to include open bowls and chutes that add an almost backcountry character to the layout. The runs are relatively short, but that does little to dampen the above-tree-line, high-alpine drama.

The area also provides the "Extreme Experience" on 350 acres of guided adventure skiing. For cross-country, Copper Mountain/Trak Cross-Country Center offers 25 km (15½ mi) of groomed track and skate lanes. ⊠ *Copper Mountain Resort, 209 Tenmile Circle, Box 3001, 80443,* ☏ *970/968–2882 or 800/458–8383,* FAX *970/968–6227,* WEB *www.ski-copper.com.* ⊘ *Mid-Nov.–late Apr., daily 8:30–4.*

FACILITIES

2,601-ft vertical drop; 2,433 skiable acres; 20% beginner, 24% intermediate, 56% advanced; 1 high-speed six-person chair, 4 high-speed
quad chairs, 5 triple chairs, 5 double chairs, 8 surface lifts.

LESSONS AND PROGRAMS

Copper Mountain's **ski program** (☎ 866/656–1541) has excellent
courses for children that are based out of the schoolhouse at the beginner area at Union Creek. There are programs and lessons for adults
as well.

LIFT TICKETS

Tickets are $55 per day at Copper. Multiday ticket savings can ex-
ceed 20%.

RENTALS

Rental packages (skis, boots, and poles) start at $20 per day.

Nordic Skiing

Copper Mountain terrain is the most challenging for Nordic, track,
and backcountry skiing. The **Copper Mountain Cross-Country Center**
(☎ 970/968–2882) has 25 km (15½ mi) of groomed trails.

Leadville

③ *24 mi from Copper Mountain via Rte. 91 south; 31 mi from Vail via
U.S. 24 south; 57 mi from Aspen via Rte. 82 east and Rte. 24 north
(summer only).*

In the history of Colorado mining, perhaps no town looms larger than
Leadville—at 10,152 ft, America's highest incorporated town. (In
summer the drive on Route 82 from Aspen over Independence Pass is
spectacular.) Two of the state's most fascinating figures are immortalized in Leadville: larger-than-life multimillionaire Horace Tabor and
his wife Baby Doe (Elizabeth Doe McCourt), the subject of John La-
Touche's Pulitzer Prize–winning opera *The Ballad of Baby Doe*.

Tabor amassed a huge fortune (by 1880s standards) of $12 million,
much of which he spent building monuments throughout the state to
himself and Baby. His power peaked when he purchased a U.S. Senate seat and replaced Senator Henry Teller, who had been appointed
Secretary of the Interior, well into his term. Baby Doe was his ambitious mistress and eventual second wife, after he dumped his first, the
faithful Augusta. They made enemies and incurred the scorn of "high
society" as only those who throw their money and weight around can.
But in 1893 the repeal of the Sherman Act demonetized silver and, like
so many other mining magnates, Tabor was ruined. He died a pauper
in 1899, admonishing Baby to "hang on to the Matchless," his most
famous mine, which he was convinced would once again restore her
fortunes. It never did. Baby became a recluse, rarely venturing forth
from her tiny unheated cabin beside the Matchless. She froze to death
in 1935.

Their legacy can be found in several attractions in town. The **Tabor Home**
(✉ 116 E. 5th St., ☎ 719/486–2092) is the modest dwelling where
Horace lived with Augusta. Admission is $2. Call to arrange a tour,
only for groups of 10 or more.

The redbrick **Tabor Opera House** opened in 1879 and can be toured
in summer. ✉ *308 Harrison St., ☎ 719/486–3900.* ◪ *$4.* ☉ *Memo-
rial Day–Labor Day, Sun.–Fri. 9–5:30.*

The **Matchless Mine** and squalid Baby Doe's Cabin are 2 mi east of downtown. Stroll around the mine and peer into the mine shaft, then pay a visit

to the small museum, a tribute to the tragic love story of Horace and Baby Doe Tabor. ⊠ *7th St.,* ☎ *719/486–1899.* 🎟 *$4.* ☉ *Daily 9–5.*

The **Mining Hall of Fame and Museum** covers virtually every aspect of mining, including displays of various ores, tools, equipment, and dioramas explaining the extraction processes. ⊠ *120 W. 9th St.,* ☎ *719/486–1229.* 🎟 *$3.50.* ☉ *May–Oct., daily 9–5; Nov.–Apr., weekdays 9–3.*

A museum complex on Harrison Street comprises the **Healy House** and the Dexter Cabin—an 1878 Greek Revival clapboard house and an 1879 log cabin—two of Leadville's earliest houses. The lavishly decorated rooms yield clues as to how the upper crust such as the Tabors lived and played. ⊠ *912 Harrison St.,* ☎ *719/486–0487.* 🎟 *$3.50.* ☉ *Memorial Day–Labor Day, daily 10–4:30.*

The **Heritage Museum** paints a vivid portrait of life in Leadville at its zenith, with dioramas depicting the old mines as well as furniture, clothing, and toys from the Victorian era. ⊠ *120 E. 9th St.,* ☎ *719/486–1878.* 🎟 *$2.50.* ☉ *June–Sept., daily 10–6.*

Eccentricity is still a Leadville trait, as witnessed by the annual **International Pack Burro Race** over Mosquito Pass. The race, held the first weekend of August, ends in Fairplay, another quirky old mining town. The event is immortalized with T-shirts and bumper stickers that read, "Get Your Ass Over the Pass."

Dining and Lodging

$–$$ ✕ **The Grill.** This locals' favorite has been run by the Martinez family since 1965 (and has been in business since 1938). Traditional Mexican specialties are homemade, from the hand-roasted green chili to the stuffed sopaipillas. In summer, you can sip margaritas on the patio while you toss horseshoes. ⊠ *715 Elm St.,* ☎ *719/486–9930. MC, V.*

$$ 🏨 **Ice Palace Inn Bed & Breakfast.** The original Leadville Ice Palace (1895–96) is the inspiration for this inn, a refurbished Victorian built in 1900 with lumber taken from the icy original (the grandiose palace was built with some 5,000 tons of ice with ice sculpture adorning most rooms). Rooms today are warmly decorated with period antiques and luxurious featherbeds, and innkeepers Giles and Kami Kolakowski are just as inviting. A full breakfast and afternoon tea are included in the room rate. But don't forget your slippers: no shoes are allowed on the inn's plush carpets. ⊠ *813 Spruce St., 80461,* ☎ *719/486–8272 or 800/ 754–2840,* FAX *719/486–0345,* WEB *icepalaceinn.com. 5 rooms. Dining room, no-smoking rooms. AE, D, DC, MC, V. BP.*

$–$$ 🏨 **Delaware Hotel.** This beautifully restored 1888 Victorian is on the National Register of Historic Places. The lobby is graced with period antiques, brass fixtures, crystal chandeliers, and oak paneling. The comfortable rooms have lace curtains and antique heirloom quilts, in addition to modern conveniences such as private bath and cable TV. A Continental breakfast is included in the rate. ⊠ *700 Harrison Ave., 80461,* ☎ *719/486–1418 or 800/748–2004,* FAX *719/486–2214,* WEB *www.delawarehotel.com. 36 rooms. Hot tub. AE, D, DC, MC, V. CP.*

Outdoor Activities and Sports

There's snowmobiling at **2 Mile Hi Ski-Doo** (⊠ 400 E. 6th St., ☎ 719/ 486–1183).

At **Ski Cooper,** 70% of the 385 skiable acres are rated beginner or intermediate but the area—with a 1,200-ft vertical drop—also runs Sno-Cat tours into 2,400 acres of pristine backcountry powder. ⊠ *9 mi west of Leadville on Rte. 24,* ☎ *719/486–3684,* WEB *www.skicooper.com.* ☉ *Late-Nov.–early Apr., daily 9–4.*

Vail

③② *20 mi from Copper Mountain or 100 mi from Denver via I–70 west.*

Just a hop, skip, and a jump west of Summit County on I–70 is one of the nation's leading ski destinations, consistently ranked the finest ski resort in North America, if not the world: Vail. The four-letter word means Valhalla for skiers and conjures up images of the rich and famous indulging their privileges. Actually, Vail is one of the least likely success stories in skiing. Seen from the village, the mountain doesn't look all that imposing. There are no glowering glaciers, no couloirs and chutes slashed from the rock, not even an Olympian summit shrouded in clouds. Even local historians admit that the Gore Creek Valley in which Vail regally sits was an impoverished backwater, too isolated to play a prominent or colorful role in Colorado history, until the resort's opening in 1962.

In truth, the men who lent their names to the valley and resort deserved more notoriety than notice. Sir St. George Gore was a swaggering, filthy rich, drunken lout of a baronet who went on a three-year bacchanal in the 1850s and butchered every herd of elk and buffalo in sight. Charles Vail, the otherwise obscure chief engineer of the Colorado Highway Department from 1930 to 1945 was—according to townspeople who dealt with him—an ornery cuss who was rumored to accept kickbacks from contractors.

Then, two visionaries appeared on the scene: Pete Seibert, a veteran of the 10th Mountain Division that prepared for alpine warfare in the surrounding Gore and Sawatch ranges during World War II, and Earl Eaton, a uranium prospector who had grown up in and surveyed these very ranges. In 1957 they ascended the mountain now known as Vail, and upon attaining the summit discovered what skiers now salivate over: the back bowls, over 3,000 acres of open glades formed when the Ute Indians set "spite fires" to the timberland in retaliation for being driven out by ranchers and miners. After five years of bureaucratic red tape and near financial suicide, Seibert's dream became reality, and the Vail resort was created.

Vail is an almost perfect example of mountain-and-village design. The development is remarkably compact, divided into the residential East Vail, the upscale Vail Village, and the more modest utilitarian Lionshead. Vail resembles a quaint Bavarian hamlet, with homey inns and lodges nestled against cozy A-frame chalets and clock towers. This, along with a heavy European bias among both the population and clientele, gives Vail perhaps the most international flavor and flair of any Colorado resort. It's crafted to anticipate a guest's every need, so you'll find a wealth of dining, shopping, and entertainment options at your fingertips. Everyone here is thoroughly professional: friendly without being familiar, knowing their business but not yours. Despite its tony reputation, the resort actively courts the family trade in recent years. Children love the 12 specially designed adventure zones, like Chaos Canyon and Fort Whippersnapper, where they can explore ski-through tepee villages, gold mines, and other attractions. The whole family can get in on the action at brand-new Adventure Ridge, an on-mountain mecca for nonskiing fun, including thrill sledding, snowmobile tours, tubing, ski-biking, and laser tag.

Although the mountain has the sheer exhilarating edge in size over nearly every other North American ski area, it's brilliantly and clearly linked by a well-placed network of lifts and trails. There are 1,220 acres of immensely varied runs on the front side and 645 acres of intermediate-to-advanced adventure skiing in the new Blue Sky Basin, but the back bowls are truly skiers' heaven: with more than twice the skiable terrain accessed from the front, the back side has eye-popping expanses of fluffy white snow that make both intermediates and experts feel they can ski for days and not run into a single soul. Those same slopes have become a mecca for mountain bike fanatics in summer, and the village now hosts a wide variety of festivals year-round.

At cosmopolitan Vail the emphasis is on luxury, although the prefab buildings are beginning to show their age. Weekends have become almost too busy, with folks from the Front Range flocking here in droves. The best sightseeing is window-shopping, ogling the deluxe merchandise and the consumers—a delightful rather than daunting experience. While you're here, there are two tourist attractions worth visiting. The **Betty Ford Alpine Gardens** (✉ Ford Park, adjacent to the Ford Amphitheater, ☎ 970/476–0103, WEB www.bettyfordalpinegardens.org), open daily from snowmelt (around Memorial Day) to snowfall (around Labor Day), are an oasis of forsythia, heather, wild roses, and shrubs, and have the distinction of being the highest public botanic gardens in North America.

The **Colorado Ski Museum/Ski Hall of Fame** traces the development of the sport throughout the world, with an emphasis on Colorado's contributions. On display are century-old skis and tows, early ski fashions, and an entire room devoted to the 10th Mountain Division. ✉ *231 S. Frontage Rd.,* ☎ *970/476–1876,* WEB *skimuseum.net.* ☜ *$1.* ☉ *Tues.–Sun. 10–5.*

Vail Valley is also composed of solid working-class towns such as Avon, Eagle, Edwards, and **Minturn,** which is enjoying a renaissance thanks to the influx of savvy artists and entrepreneurs who have opened several superb galleries and the **Minturn Cellars winery** (✉ 107 Williams St., ☎ 970/827–4065).

Dining and Lodging

$$$$ ✕ **Game Creek Club.** Catch a heated gondola and then a Sno-Cat to Vail's exclusive on-mountain lunch club, now open to the public for dinner and for an outstanding summertime Sunday brunch. Be prepared to linger over a four-course prix-fixe meal in this Bavarian-style lodge. You might start with a yellowfin tuna tartare and petite mesclun salad with toasted goat cheese followed by chili-dusted salmon roulade, or annatto-dipped Colorado lamb rack. If you're really feeling decadent, opt for the seven-course grand tasting menu, with or without wine parings. ✉ *600 Lionshead Circle,* ☎ *970/479–4275. Reservations essential. AE, D, DC, MC, V. No lunch.*

$$$$ ✕ **Sweet Basil.** The understated decor—blond-wood chairs and muted ★ teal and buff walls—is enlivened by towering floral arrangements and abstract art. Chef Bruce Yim serves American cuisine with Mediterranean and Asian influences. Try the grilled mahimahi with Asian spring roll or the grilled beef tenderloin with foie gras ravioli and wild mushroom barley ragout. Pair with a selection from the restaurant's extensive, award-winning wine list. ✉ *193 E. Gore Creek Dr.,* ☎ *970/ 476–0125. AE, MC, V.*

$$$–$$$$ ✕ **Chap's Grill & Chophouse.** This authentic steak house is a welcome addition to the Vail Valley. With deep wood walls, burlap window coverings, horsehair upholstery, and wrought-iron accents, the restaurant screams Old West. And the menu follows suit, with grilled specialties such as a 20-ounce T-bone, double-cut pork chop, and the Colorado trio (elk, lamb, and venison) leading the way. ✉ *Vail Cascade Resort, 1300 Westhaven Dr.,* ☎ *970/479–7014. AE, D, DC, MC, V.*

$$$–$$$$ ✕ **Terra Bistro.** In the Vail Mountain Lodge & Spa, this sleek, airy space, ★ with a warm fireplace contrasting with black wood chairs and black-

and-white photographs, is a sterling addition to the Vail dining scene. The upscale menu combines seasonal ingredients with Asian, Mediterranean, and Southwest influences. White bean and delicata squash sauté and peppered beef tenderloin in a cabernet reduction with herbed Yukon gold potatoes are headliners. Organic produce and free-range meat and poultry are used whenever possible. ⊠ 352 E. Meadow Dr., ☎ 970/476–6836. AE, D, MC, V.

$$–$$$ ✕ **Alpenrose Restaurant & Patisserie.** Peter Haller's restaurant began as a tearoom and bakery in 1976. The pink, frilly decor is just as sugarcoated. This is rich, luscious, love-handle cuisine with tons of calories, drowning in butter: so good and so bad for you. The schnitzels, steak tartare, and fresh seafood specials are all home cooking at its best. ⊠ 100 E. Meadow Dr., ☎ 970/476–3194. AE, MC, V. No lunch Tues.

$$–$$$ ✕ **Minturn Country Club.** This rustic, homey joint is a favorite hangout of racers during World Cup ski competitions, when they literally hang from the rafters. Steaks, prime rib, fish, and chicken preparations vary wildly, but you have only yourself to blame if you wanted it medium rare and it comes out well done: you cook everything yourself. ⊠ Main St., Minturn, ☎ 970/827–4114. Reservations not accepted. MC, V. No lunch.

$–$$$ ✕ **Blu's.** This fun, casual, constantly hopping place is a Vail institution, with an eclectic, affordable menu. The food is fresh and zippy, from authentic jambalaya to kick-ass California chicken rellenos to Aunt Bea's meat loaf. Blu's is open for breakfast (try the green eggs and ham), lunch, and dinner. Breakfast and lunch are much cheaper than dinner. Blu's is a lively spot, more bistro than restaurant, and enjoys a great location in the heart of Vail Village. ⊠ 193 E. Gore Creek Dr., ☎ 970/476–3113. Reservations not accepted. AE, DC, MC, V.

$–$$$ ✕ **Hubcap Brewery and Kitchen.** Vail's first microbrewery offers five regular beers (Vail Pale Ale and Beaver Tail Brown Ale are standouts) and rotating specials. The decor is upscale-diner, with gleaming chrome hubcaps (owner Lance Lucy welcomes additions) adorning the walls. The food is mostly superior pub grub, such as cream-cheese-and-crab-stuffed won tons, chicken wings, and quesadillas, but there are a few upscale offerings such as the linguine con granchio and an excellent walnut-and-basil-crusted ahi tuna. ⊠ Crossroads Shopping Center, ☎ 970/476–5757. AE, D, MC, V.

$–$$ ✕ **Fiesta's!** The Marquez sisters, Debbie and Susan, use family recipes brought to Colorado by their great-grandparents to create Fiesta's southwestern cuisine. Among the menu favorites are chicken enchiladas in a white jalapeño sauce and blue corn enchiladas, served Santa Fe–style with an egg on top. The handmade corn tamales are stuffed with pork and smothered in a classic New Mexican chile sauce. Fiesta's is brightly decorated with lots of New Mexican folk art and paintings. More than 20 tequilas keep the bar—and patrons—hopping. ⊠ 57 Edwards Access Rd., Edwards Plaza, 4 mi west of Beaver Creek, ☎ 970/926–2121. AE, D, MC, V.

$–$$ ✕ **The Saloon.** Skiers in the know do the "Minturn Mile" at the end of the day, bushwhacking out the bottom of Game Creek Bowl and ending up a few steps from this venerable gathering place. (Warning: this is not ski area–maintained terrain, and there is no transportation back. Of course, you can always drive here.) The reward is margaritas made with real lime juice, Mexican food in an Old West atmosphere, a children's menu, serve-yourself chips and homemade salsa, such specialties as chili rellenos and the steak and quail plate, and a bar that's always packed with locals. ⊠ 146 N. Main St., Minturn, ☎ 970/827–5954. Reservations not accepted. AE, MC, V. No lunch.

$$$$ 🏨 **Lodge at Vail.** The first hotel to open in Vail remains one of its swankiest. "Location, location, location" translates to ski-in, ski-out status. The medium-size rooms are frilly and floral, a riot of pastels, with mahogany and teak furnishings and marble baths. The suites are individually owned and decorated condos, but they must meet rigorous standards set by management. Mickey's piano bar is a favored après-ski spot. ⊠ *174 E. Gore Creek Dr., 81657,* ☎ *970/476–5011 or 800/ 331–5634,* FAX *970/476–7425,* WEB *www.lodgeatvail.com. 76 rooms, 49 suites. 2 restaurants, bar, pool, hot tub, sauna, spa, gym, ski shop. AE, D, DC, MC, V.*

$$$$ ☆ ⚑ **Sonnenalp.** This property, in the midst of a pseudo-Bavarian village, impresses as the real thing, and for good reason: the owning Fassler family has been in the hotel business in Germany for generations. The Swiss Hotel and Spa is quaint, with Bavarian pine armoires and secretaries and down comforters; and the large, sunny Sonnenalp Resort at Vail suites have an elegant lodge look, with stucco walls, wood beams, and heated marble floors. The superb restaurants include the western saloon Bully Ranch (great barbecue), the Swiss Chalet (sensational fondue), and the elegant, Continental Ludwig's. ⊠ *20 Vail Rd., 81657,* ☎ *970/476–5656 or 800/654–8312,* FAX *970/ 476–1639,* WEB *www.sonnenalp.com. 93 rooms, 93 suites. 3 restaurants, bar, in-room data ports, 2 indoor pools, 2 indoor hot tubs, outdoor hot tub, 2 spas, 3 gyms. AE, DC, MC, V.*

$$$$ ⚑ **Vail Cascade Resort.** Down-to-earth yet glamorous is the best way to describe this ski-in, ski-out hotel that manages—despite its fairly large size—to maintain an intimate feel, thanks to the expert staff. Rooms in the older wing are done in mountain colors; those in the newer Terrace Wing have rich, deep plaid and floral fabrics, wicker beds, and wrought-iron lamps. Chap's Grill & Chophouse has garnered acclaim for its outstanding grilled foods and fine selection of wines. Guests also have access to the adjoining Cascade Spa and Club, a full-service facility. ⊠ *1300 Westhaven Dr., 81657,* ☎ *970/476–7111,* FAX *970/479–7020,* WEB *www.vailcascade.com. 291 rooms, 28 suites, 78 condominiums. Restaurant, bar, pool, hair salon, 2 hot tubs, spa, 4 indoor tennis courts, health club, 2 ski shops, cinema, meeting room. AE, DC, MC, V.*

$$$–$$$$ ⚑ **Sitzmark Lodge.** This cozy lodge brims with European ambience, thanks to many repeat international guests (it's often booked months in advance). The good-size rooms look out onto either the mountain or Gore Creek, and are wonderfully clean, thanks in part to the lodge's no-smoking-anywhere policy. Decor is a hodgepodge, ranging from dark to blond woods and rose, teal, or floral fabrics. Each unit has a balcony, refrigerator, cable TV, hair dryer, and humidifier; some deluxe rooms have gas-burning fireplaces. The staff is ultrafriendly, encouraging guests to congregate in the sunny, split-level living room for complimentary mulled wine. A Continental breakfast is gratis in winter; the French Left Bank restaurant serves up dinner in high season. ⊠ *183 Gore Creek Dr., 81657,* ☎ *970/476–5001,* FAX *970/476–8702,* WEB *www.sitzmarklodge.com. 35 rooms. Restaurant, refrigerators, pool, indoor and outdoor hot tub, sauna. D, MC, V.*

$$–$$$$ ⚑ **Minturn Inn.** This 1915 three-story home is older than the town of Vail. The owners, who also operate two other B&Bs in the area, have painstakingly restored it into a charming inn with theme rooms. The Angler has carved wooden fish and fly-fishing paraphernalia, while the 10th Mountain Division is decorated with skis and snowshoes. The beds are handmade of logs, with quilt coverings. Most rooms have mountain and river views; some have Jacuzzis. The four rooms in the newer lodge across the alley have private decks or patios overlooking Eagle River. Hearty breakfasts and afternoon wine and cheese are served around a river-rock fireplace. ⊠ *442 Main St., Box 186, Minturn 81645,* ☎ *970/827–9647 or 800/646–8876,* FAX *970/827–5590,* WEB *www.minturninn.com. 13 rooms, 2 with shared bath. Sauna. AE, D, MC, V. BP.*

$$–$$$ 🏨 **Gasthof Gramshammer.** Pepi Gramshammer, a former Austrian Olympic ski racer, is one of Vail's most beloved and respected citizens, whose labor of love—Wedel Weeks—ranks among the country's best intensive ski programs. His charming rooms are done up in pastels, with original oil paintings and fluffy down comforters. Pepi's and Antlers, the property's two fine restaurants, have a European ambience, with stucco walls, wood-beam ceilings, and waitresses in dirndls. ⊠ *231 E. Gore Creek Dr., 81657,* ☎ *970/476–5626 or 800/610–7374,* FAX *970/476–8816,* WEB *www.pepis.com. 40 rooms. 2 restaurants, bar, 2 hot tubs, sauna, gym, ski shop. AE, MC, V.*

$$
★ 🏨 **Roost Lodge.** Situated on I–70 and advertising economical rates, comfortable rooms, and a heated pool, this accommodation is true to its promise—and then some, considering the price. The airy rooms are pleasing, many with four-poster beds, all with basic amenities. The staff is helpful, and complimentary Continental breakfast and afternoon wine and cheese are served daily in ski season. A free shuttle drops you at the base of the slopes. ⊠ *1783 N. Frontage Rd. W, 81657,* ☎ *970/476–5451 or 800/873–3065,* FAX *970/476–9158,* WEB *www.roostlodge.com. 70 rooms, 2 suites. Pool, hot tub, sauna. AE, D, DC, MC, V.*

CONDOMINIUMS

Vail/Beaver Creek Reservations (☎ 800/525–2257) can handle all calls, requests, and bookings. Among the recommended Vail properties are Cascade Village, Manor Vail, Vail Village Inn, and Simba Resort (all of which have several extras, including restaurants and shops on site). Vail Village Inn is especially notable for the unusual Dieter Menzel–designed woodwork throughout the property. Top Beaver Creek facilities, also with the above extras, include the Poste Montane, St. James Place, and the Charter. The **Vail Valley Tourism and Convention Bureau** (☎ 800/824–5737) also helps with condominium bookings and information.

Nightlife and the Arts

BARS AND LOUNGES

Garfinkel's (⊠ 536 W. Lionshead Mall, ☎ 970/476–3789) is a sports bar open until 2 AM. The pianist plays soothing pop standards at **Mickey's** (⊠ Lodge at Vail, 174 E. Gore Creek Dr., ☎ 970/476–5011) for the après-ski crowd. The **Red Lion** (⊠ top of Bridge St., ☎ 970/476–7676), a Vail tradition, attracts a more sedate crowd, with mellow live acts and a wildly popular deck. **Sarah's** (⊠ Christiania at Vail, 356 E. Hanson Ranch Rd., ☎ 970/476–5641) showcases Helmut Fricker, a Vail institution who plays accordion while yodeling up a storm. A young crowd scarfs down excellent, cheap pizzas until 2 AM at **Vendetta's** (⊠ 291 Bridge St., ☎ 970/476–5070).

DANCE

The **Vail International Festival of Dance** (☎ 970/949–1999), in August, hosts ballet and modern dance performers from around the world in the alpine splendor of the Ford Outdoor Amphitheater.

MUSIC AND DANCE CLUBS

The saloon **Cassidy's Hole in the Wall** (⊠ 82 E. Beaver Creek Blvd., Avon, ☎ 970/949–9449) puts on live country bands nightly, to go with the mouthwatering barbecue. **Club Chelsea** (⊠ 304 Bridge St., ☎ 970/476–5600) has it all: a quiet piano bar that feels like a speakeasy, a fevered disco, and a cigar-smoking room complete with leopard-skin couches around the fire. **8150** (⊠ Crossroads Mall, ☎ 970/479–0607) is the place to catch live rock—with a crowd that rocks. **Sheika's** (⊠ Gasthof Gramshammer, 231 E. Gore Creek Dr., ☎ 970/476–1515) is where the young are restless on the dance floor.

Outdoor Activities and Sports

The **Activities Desk of Vail** (☎ 970/476–9090) can arrange a variety of nonskiing activities, including dogsledding, hot-air ballooning, and Sno-Cat skiing.

CYCLING

Shrine Mountain Adventure (✉ Red Cliff, ☎ 970/827–5363) offers backcountry mountain bike tours, as well as hikes, through the Vail Valley.

FITNESS

The ultimate place in Vail to both workout and relax is at the **Vail Cascade Spa & Club** (✉ in the Vail Cascade Resort, ☎ 970/476–7400). **Vail Mountain Athletic Club** (✉ 352 E. Meadow Dr., ☎ 970/476–7960) is a full-service health club with Vail's only indoor climbing wall.

GOLFING

The Vail Valley is home to nearly a dozen golf courses. Among the best is the **Sonnenalp Golf Club** (✉ 1265 Berry Creek Rd., Edwards, Vail Valley, ☎ 970/328–5111), a 7,059-yard, par-71 course, that's a perennial top-50 resort course, according to *Golf Digest*.

HORSEBACK RIDING

A. J. Brink Outfitters (✉ Sweetwater, north of Vail off Exit 133 of I–70, ☎ 970/524–9301), a full-service outfitter on scenic Sweetwater Lake, offers day and overnight horseback excursions high in the Flat Tops Wilderness. **Piney River Ranch** (✉ 12 mi north of Vail, ☎ 970/476–3941) offers pony rides for kids, and guided one-hour horseback rides around the property for adults.

SNOWMOBILING

Adventure Ridge at Eagle's Nest (☎ 970/476–9090), at the top of Vail's Lionshead, offers twilight snowmobile excursions, snow inner-tubing, a lighted snowboard terrain garden and half-pipe, and ice-skating. **Nova Guides** (☎ 970/949–4232) offers guided and unguided snowmobile rentals. **Timber Ridge Adventures** (☎ 970/668–8349) has miles of riding on groomed trails.

TREKKING

Paragon Guides (☎ 970/926–5299) runs day and overnight llama treks in and around the Vail Valley.

Downhill Skiing and Snowboarding

Vail logs more "skier days" (the ski industry's measure of ticket sales) than any other resort in the country. Now, with the merger of Vail with Keystone and Breckenridge, it is the world's largest ski company. Vail is perhaps best known for its back bowls, a vast expanse (over 3,000 acres) of open-bowl skiing that can be sensational on powder days but generally only so-so at other times, after the fresh snow has been tracked up and worked on by sun and wind. For the most part, the back bowls are not extraordinarily steep, and are good places for intermediates to learn how to ski powder.

Skiing on the front side of the mountain is a markedly different experience. There's lots of wide-trail skiing, heavily skewed toward groomed intermediate runs. Vail is an ideal mountain for those in the intermediate- and advanced-skier audience who ski a week or two a season and want to be reminded each year that they do know how to turn a ski. Vail skiing has a way of boosting egos, especially with the addition of Blue Sky Basin, a vast area touted as "intermediate-to-advanced adventure skiing" that makes anyone feel like they can ski the backcountry. There are a few steep and long mogul runs for experts, but Vail's true expert terrain represents a relatively small chunk of the huge Vail pie. ☎ 970/476–5601, WEB *www.vail.com.* ☼ *Mid-Nov.–mid-Apr., daily 8:30–4.*

FACILITIES

3,335-ft vertical drop; 5,289 skiable acres; 18% beginner, 29% inter-mediate, 53% expert (the majority of this terrain is in the back bowls); 1 gondola, 14 high-speed quad chairs, 1 regular quad, 3 triple chairs, 5 double chairs, 9 surface lifts.

LESSONS AND PROGRAMS

Half-day group lessons start at $70; full-day lessons start at $80. The ski schools at Vail and Beaver Creek are among the best in the country, with several specialty classes and excellent children's programs. For more information, call the **Vail and Beaver Creek Ski School** (☎ 970/476–3239).

LIFT TICKETS

$59. Multiday tickets (up to seven days) are available, although per-day savings are minimal. Tickets are good at both Vail and Beaver Creek, as well as at Breckenridge and Keystone.

RENTALS

Base Mountain Sports (ski rentals) and **One Track Mind** (snowboard) have more than 10 locations in the Vail/Beaver Creek area. Full rental packages go for as low as $16 a day for multiday rentals. Call ☎ 800/544–6648 for advanced reservations. For high-performance rentals, a good choice is **Kenny's Double Diamond** (✉ 520 Lionshead Mall , Vail, ☎ 970/476–5500 or 800/466–2704).

Nordic Skiing

BACKCOUNTRY SKIING

The **10th Mountain Hut and Trail System** (☎ 970/925–5775) reaches far into Vail's backcountry; one route continues to Aspen. Maps, equipment, and other information are available and hut reservations should be made at least a month in advance. Rates range between $22 and $32 per person per night. If you aren't familiar with the trail system, hiring a guide is highly recommended. In Vail, contact **Paragon Guides** (☎ 970/926–5299).

TRACK SKIING

For cross-country, **Vail/Beaver Creek Cross-Country Ski Centers** (☎ 970/845–5313) provide information on the many trails in the Vail Valley.

To reach Beaver Creek's cross-country trail network, **McCoy Park** (☎ 970/845–5313), you must ride the Strawberry Park chairlift. This is a bonus, for it gets you far enough from the resort village that you get a rare sense (around Vail, anyway) that you're in a pristine mountain environment. The 32 km (20 mi) of groomed tracks have a fair amount of ups and downs—or perhaps because the elevation is above 9,500 ft, it just seems that way. The trail fee is $17 for a full day. Lessons, rentals, and snowshoe tours are available through the Vail ski school. The cross-country skiing at the **Vail Nordic Center** (☎ 970/476–9090) is less inspiring—a network laid out on what in the summer is a golf course—but it's also free.

Shopping

The boutiques and galleries along Bridge Street or Gore Creek Drive make for excellent window-shopping. **Crossroads Shopping Center** (✉ South Frontage Rd., just east of the roundabout) has everything you might need, from souvenir shops and a liquor store to art galleries and movie theaters.

BOUTIQUES

Gorsuch (✉ 263 Gore Creek Dr., Vail, ☎ 970/476–2294; ✉ 70 Promenade, Beaver Creek, ☎ 970/949–7115) is far more than a boutique or a sporting goods store: it stocks everything from buffalo coats to pottery and potpourri. **Pepi's Sports** (⊠ 231 Bridge St., ☎ 970/476–5202) sells chic ski clothes and accessories, as well as evening wear from Armani to Ralph Lauren.

CRAFT AND ART GALLERIES

Aboriginal Arts (⊠ 5124 Grouse La., ☎ 970/476–7715) stocks ethnic jewelry, resin-cast wood carvings, and feather masks from around the South Pacific and the Americas. **Laughing Monkey** (⊠ 223 E. Gore Creek Dr., ☎ 970/476–8809) has Mexican ceramics and women's clothing. **Menzel** (⊠ 12 S. Frontage Rd., ☎ 970/476–6617) specializes in fanciful, intricate furniture and interiors crafted from 200-year-old pine. **Two Elk Gallery** (⊠ 102 Main St., Minturn, ☎ 970/827–5307) showcases a dizzying array of home furnishings, including items by Colorado artists, from coonskin caps to lodgepole-pine furniture. **Windwood Galleries** (⊠ 151 Main St., Minturn, ☎ 970/827–9232) specializes in Colorado artists, as well as ceramics and artifacts.

SPORTING GOODS

Gore Range Mountain Works (⊠ Gore Creek Dr., across from the Children's Fountain, ☎ 970/476–7625) carries mountaineering gear for the truly hard core, as well as mountain fashions for everyone else.

Beaver Creek

③③ *12 mi from Vail or 110 mi from Denver via I–70 west.*

Beaver Creek is an exclusive four-season development that gives even Utah's ultraposh Deer Valley a run for its cash flow. It's been open since 1980 and has fully emerged from big sister Vail's shadow. With 38% of its terrain rated advanced, skiers flock here on powder days to seek out Grouse and famed runs such as Birds of Prey. Beginners and intermediates can still find the same pampering on the slopes they receive elsewhere in the resort, which is often blissfully uncrowded even on Vail's most congested days. Linkage with nearby Arrowhead and the Bachelor Gulch area has created one of the state's finest family areas.

Beaver Creek's sublime setting, luxurious accommodations, fine restaurants, Vilar Center for the Arts, and world-class golf course designed by Robert Trent Jones Jr. make the resort equally popular in summer, especially with families and couples. Elegant without being ostentatious, Vail's quietly glamorous little sister appeals to a select, settled crowd, and everything at Beaver Creek lives up to its billing.

Dining and Lodging

$$$$ ✗ **Beano's Cabin.** Perhaps the ultimate wilderness dining experience is traveling in a snowmobile-drawn sleigh to this Beaver Creek hunting lodge. During your 2-mi ride, the sled host fills you in on some mountain history. Your destination is a midmountain Montana pine-log cabin, warmed inside by a crackling fire and live dinner music. (In summer, you can reach Beano's by horseback or shuttle van.) Choose from among seven seasonally rotating entrées and six courses. Pair the pan-seared buffalo carpaccio with wood-grilled venison, and top it off with bourbon pecan torte. The convivial setting can't be matched. ⊠ *Larkspur Bowl, ☎ 970/949–9090. Reservations essential. AE, MC, V.*

$$$$ ✗ **Splendido.** This ultraposh eatery with marble columns and statu-
★ ary and custom-made Italian linens is the height of decadence. Chef David Walford is a master of New American cuisine, borrowing merrily from several different traditions. He is equally adept at turning out rack of lamb with rosemary and carrot-cardamom souffle. Retire to the classic piano bar, featuring the talented Taylor Kundolf, for a nightcap. ⊠ *17 Chateau La., ☎ 970/845–8808. AE, D, DC, MC, V. No lunch.*

$$$–$$$$ ✕ **Mirabelle.** From the fireplace to the burgundy and pink linens, this
    ★   award-winning restaurant has the ultimate in romantic, French-country decor. Belgian Daniel Joly is the superb chef who offers as close to contemporary French haute cuisine as you'll get in Colorado. His preparations are a perfect blend of colors, flavors, and textures. Try hot foie gras with caramelized golden apples, grilled salmon with littleneck clams jus and yellow corn succotash, or Colorado rack of lamb with flageolets ragout casserole. Fairly priced wine recommendations are listed beneath each entrée. Depending on your perspective, desserts are either sheer heaven or sinful. ⊠ *Entrance to Beaver Creek,* ☎ *970/949–7728. AE, D, MC, V. Closed Sun. No lunch.*

$$$–$$$$ ✕ **TraMonti.** This breezy trattoria in The Charter at Beaver Creek showcases the vibrant progressive cuisine of chef Curtis Cooper. He loves experimenting with bold juxtapositions of flavors and is most successful with creative pizzas such as the spicy shrimp with fennel, roasted peppers, basil, feta, and infused garlic oil. Try the lobster ravioli in saffron cream sauce, spaghetti puttanesca, or the osso buco. ⊠ *The Charter at Beaver Creek,* ☎ *970/949–5552. AE, MC, V. No lunch.*

$–$$$ ✕ **The Gashouse.** This classic local hangout, in a 1930s log cabin with trophy-covered walls, draws up-valley crowds who swear by the steaks, delicious ribs, and fresh salmon. Stop in for a brew and some heavenly Buffalo shrimp (a close cousin to wings) and watch how the Vail Valley kicks back. ⊠ *Rte. 6, Edwards,* ☎ *970/926–3613. AE, MC, V.*

$$ ✕ **Cassidy's Hole in the Wall.** If you're looking for *the* burger, you're in the right place: the Big-Bob one-pounder should satisfy. Sandwiches, Mexican dishes, and specialties such as chicken-fried steak and a 2-ft-long rack of ribs head the menu (made of newsprint, of course) in this western saloon that spans two floors. Looking for the action? Stay at ground zero. If you're partial to watching rather than participating, you'll want to be upstairs. ⊠ *82 E. Beaver Creek Blvd., Avon,* ☎ *970/ 949–9449. AE, D, MC, V.*

$$$$ ▥ **Beaver Creek Lodge.** An atrium centerpiece highlights this all-suite property that's charmingly decorated in European alpine style. The units have a sky-blue and forest-green color scheme, and each features a kitchenette and gas-burning fireplace. The traditionally hearty Beaver Creek Chophouse is the perfect place to fuel up after a day on the slopes. ⊠ *26 Avondale La., 81620,* ☎ *970/845–9800,* 🖷 *970/845–8242,* 🕸 *www.beavercreeklodge.com. 72 suites. Restaurant, bar, kitchenettes, indoor-outdoor pool, hot tub, spa, health club, ski shop, meeting room. AE, MC, V.*

$$$$ ▥ **Hyatt Regency Beaver Creek.** The lobby at this slope-side hotel, with
    ★   a magnificent antler chandelier and huge oriel windows opening onto the mountain, manages to be both cozy and grand. Rooms are sizable and have an inviting ski lodge theme, with coffeemakers and heated towel racks. The full spa and health club and nearby golf course (with guest tee times) make it popular with nonskiers, but perhaps the ultimate in pampering is stepping out of the hotel and into your warmed and waiting ski boots and skis. Once those ski boots are off, warm up with a hot toddy by the outdoor fire pit. ⊠ *136 E. Thomas Pl., 81620,* ☎ *970/949–1234 or 800/233–1234,* 🖷 *970/949–4164,* 🕸 *www.beavercreek.hyatt.com. 275 rooms, 31 suites. 3 restaurants, 2 bars, deli, in-room data ports, pool, 8 hot tubs, spa, health club, 5 tennis courts, children's programs, meeting room. AE, D, DC, MC, V.*

$$$$ ▥ **Lodge & Spa at Cordillera.** Surrounded by a pristine wilderness area,
    ★   this isolated lodge offers sweeping vistas. The rooms are old world, in burgundy, buff, and hunter green, with burled-pine furnishings. An air of quiet luxury prevails: prints by Picasso and Miró adorn the pine-paneled or exposed-brick walls, and ceilings are of carved recessed wood. You can luxuriate in the spa after a hard day's hiking or cross-coun-

try skiing, then sit down to a meal in one of the superlative restaurants serving healthful spa cuisine. The lodge operates a shuttle to the lifts. ✉ *Box 1110, Edwards 81632,* ☎ *970/926–2200 or 800/877–3529,* FAX *970/926–2486,* WEB *www.cordilleravail.com. 56 rooms. 4 restaurants, bar, indoor-outdoor pool, 3 hot tubs, spa, health club, 3 18-hole golf courses, cross-country skiing, meeting room. AE, D, MC, V.*

$$$$ 🏨 **Pines Lodge.** This small, ski-in, ski-out Beaver Creek winner combines posh digs with unpretentious atmosphere. The rooms are spacious and light with blond-wood furnishings and pale pink ceilings. Each room has a TV/VCR; several have balconies overlooking the ski area and mountain range. The air of quiet pampering is furthered by such little extras as afternoon tea by the lobby fireplace, and a ski concierge who arranges complimentary guided mountain tours and a free wax for your skis. The Grouse Mountain Grill serves up superb New American cuisine in an unparalleled setting with huge picture windows. ✉ *Box 36, Avon 81620,* ☎ *970/845–5990 or 800/859–8242,* FAX *970/ 845–7809,* WEB *www.vbcrp.com. 60 rooms, 12 suites. Restaurant, bar, lobby lounge, in-room data ports, in-room VCR, refrigerators, pool, hot tub, spa, gym, laundry service. AE, D, MC, V.*

Nightlife and the Arts

After attacking the moguls, relax at the Hyatt's **Crooked Hearth Tavern** (✉ 136 E. Thomas Pl., ☎ 970/949–1234) and enjoy the lively guitar entertainment. **McCoy's** (☎ 970/949–1234), at the base of the mountain, has live music après-ski. Drink your hot toddy outdoors at the **Slopeside Firepit** (☎ 970/949–1234).

The **Vilar Center for the Arts** (✉ 68 Avondale La., ☎ 970/949–8497) has a 518-seat theater that plays host to everything from classical ballet to musical theater to pop concerts. It also includes more than a half dozen art galleries in the Market Square pedestrian plaza at the base of the ski area.

Outdoor Activities and Sports

The **Beaver Creek Resort Concierge** (☎ 970/845–9090) can arrange a variety of nonskiing activities, including dogsledding, hot-air ballooning, and Sno-Cat skiing.

GOLFING

Beaver Creek Golf Course (✉ 100 Offerson Rd., ☎ 970/845–5775), befitting the resort's reputation, is a 6,400-yard, par-70 stunner designed by Robert Trent Jones Jr. **Golf Course at Cordillera** (✉ Lodge at Cordillera, Edwards, ☎ 970/926–2200) is actually three courses. One designed by Hale Irwin is a par-72, 7,444-yard course with open meadows, ponds, and stands of pine and aspen trees. The Dave Pelz short course, par 3, offers irons practice, and the Valley Course, designed by Tom Fazio, is a par-71, 7,500-yard course. Among the challenges of the full courses are wandering elk and brown bears.

Downhill Skiing and Snowboarding

Neither Vail nor Beaver Creek is renowned for expert terrain. Although **Beaver Creek** has the less of the two in terms of acreage, many locals prefer "the Beave" and the steep, bumped up runs of Grouse Mountain because far fewer people ski there than Vail, leaving plenty of fresh tracks to be found. But the Beave's strong suit remains that it is one of the best ski areas in America for lower intermediates. The top third of the mountain features a large trail cluster of almost exclusively easygoing stuff, and any skier who doesn't feel up to the slightly steeper lower section of the mountain can ride the lift down to the base. The linking of Beaver Creek's trail system with that of neighboring Arrowhead Resort, and Bachelor Gulch, a new area between the two, has added 30% more novice and intermediate terrain to the area, and has created a European-style "village-to-village" ski experience. ☎ 970/476–5601, WEB *www.vail.com.* ☉ *Late Nov.–mid-Apr., daily 8:30–4.*

FACILITIES

4,040-ft vertical drop; 1,625 skiable acres; 27% beginner, 39% intermediate, 34% advanced; 6 high-speed quad chairs, 3 triple chairs, 4 double chairs, 1 surface lift.

LESSONS AND PROGRAMS

Beaver Creek and Vail share its ski programs. For more information, call the **Vail and Beaver Creek Ski School** (☎ 970/476–3229).

LIFT TICKETS

$61. Multiday tickets (up to seven days) are available, although per-day savings are minimal. Tickets are good at both Vail and Beaver Creek, as well as at Breckenridge and Keystone.

En Route   A few miles west, past the town of Edwards, the narrow, winding Route 131 squirrels north from I–70 through the **Yampa Valley.** The lush, wide-open spaces and vistas are both gorgeous and lonely, relieved only by the occasional odd rock formation thrusting up from the ground. This is cattle country, a land of jade forests, jagged outcroppings, and silvery streams skirting the Flat Tops Wilderness Area—a high, flat mountaintop crowned with a lava dome that glaciers sculpted into a series of steep cliffs and deep gashes.

Steamboat Springs

㉞   *86 mi from Beaver Creek via I–70 west and U.S. 131 north; 170 mi from Denver via I–70 west, Rte. 9 north, and U.S. 40 north.*

Steamboat is aptly nicknamed Ski Town, U.S.A., since the town has "sent" more athletes—several dozen—to the Winter Olympics than any other ski resort in the nation. The most famous in Steamboat Mountain Village is probably 1972 slalom silver medalist Billy Kidd, whose irrepressible grin and 10-gallon hat are instantly recognizable. When he's around, Kidd conducts daily tours of the mountain. The entrance to Steamboat is roughly marked by the amusingly garish 1950s neon sign from the Rabbit Ears Motel, and the unmistakable stench of sulphur. The town got its name from French trappers who, after hearing the bubbling and churning hot springs, mistakenly thought a steamboat was chugging up the Yampa River.

When sizing up the mountain, keep in mind that the part that's visible from the base area is only the tip of the iceberg, and much more terrain lies concealed in back. Steamboat is famed for its eiderdown-soft snow; in fact, the term "champagne powder" was coined here to describe the area's unique feathery dumps, the result of Steamboat's fortuitous position between the arid desert to the west and the moisture-magnet of the Continental Divide to the east, where storm fronts duke it out.

If you're looking for hellacious steeps and menacing couloirs, you won't find them in Steamboat, but you will find perhaps the finest tree skiing in America. Beginners and intermediates rave about the wide-open spaces of Sunshine Bowl and Storm Peak. Steamboat also earns high marks for its comprehensive children's programs and the Kidd Center for Performance Skiing (where you can learn demanding disciplines such as powder, mogul, and tree skiing).

The modern Steamboat Mountain Village is attractive enough, if lacking in personality amid the maze of upscale condos, boutiques, and bars.

It's a bit too spread out—or still too new—to have developed much ski-town character. To its credit, though, this increasingly "hot" destination has retained its down-home, western friendliness, providing the trappings while avoiding the trap of a premium resort. That may have to do with Steamboat Springs itself, a mere 10-minute drive away, where Stetson hats are sold for use and not for souvenirs, and the Victorian buildings, most of them fronting Lincoln Avenue, the main drag, were built to be functional, not ornamental.

Steamboat's 1800s origins are as a ranching and farming community, setting it apart from the mining history of a Breckenridge or an Aspen. In fact, these early cowboy settlers were also responsible for the advent of skiing in the area, as they strapped wooden boards (vaguely resembling skis) to their feet so they could get around the neighborhood in winter. Later, Steamboat was one of the first ski areas to be developed in the West.

The **Tread of Pioneers Museum,** in a beautifully restored federal building, is an excellent spot to bone up on local history, and includes ski memorabilia dating back to the turn of the 20th century, when Carl Howelsen opened Howelsen Hill, still the country's preeminent ski-jumping facility. ⌧ *8th and Oak Sts.,* ☎ *970/879–2214.* 🎫 *$3.* ⊙ *Apr.–Oct., Tues.–Sat. 11–5; Nov.–Mar., Mon.–Sat. 11–5.*

There are more than 100 hot springs in the area; the **Steamboat Visitor Center** (⌧ 1255 S. Lincoln Ave., ☎ 970/879–0882) publishes a fun and informative walking-tour guide that describes many of the spots. The springs may not be as restorative as legend claims, but the inspiring views of the surrounding pristine forest certainly are. Two springs are the most famous.

Downtown, **Steamboat Springs Health and Recreation Hot Springs** gets its waters from the all-natural Steamboat Hot Springs. The modern facility has a lap pool, relaxation pool, water slide, locker rooms, and a health club. ⌧ *3rd and Lincoln Ave.,* ☎ *970/879–1828.* 🎫 *$6.* ⊙ *Daily 7 AM–9:45 PM.*

The **Strawberry Park Natural Hot Springs** is a bit remote and rustic. In fact, after dark, clothing is optional and you have to bring your own flashlight to find your way to the small pools. ⌧ *Strawberry Park Rd., 7 mi west of town,* ☎ *970/879–0342.* 🎫 *$5; $10 after 5 PM and on weekends.* ⊙ *Daily 10 AM–10:30 PM.*

In summer, Steamboat serves as the gateway to magnificent **Medicine Bow/Routt National Forest,** which offers a wealth of activities from hiking to mountain biking to fishing. Among the nearby attractions are the 283-ft **Fish Creek Falls** and the splendidly rugged **Mt. Zirkel Wilderness Area.** To the north, two sparkling man-made lakes, **Steamboat** and **Pearl,** offer a variety of water sports, including fishing and sailing.

Dining and Lodging

$$$–$$$$ ✕ **L'Apogée.** This expert French restaurant is Steamboat's most intimate, with rose-color walls, flickering candlelight, and hanging plants. The classic food, with subtle Asian influences, is well crafted, especially the half roast duckling glazed with orange-blossom honey; the Alaskan King crab cakes; and the foie gras pan seared and topped with warm chèvre. Still, the menu takes a back seat to the admirable wine list. Oenophile alert: owner Jamie Jenny is a collector whose magnificent wine cellar—cited by *Wine Spectator* as one of America's best—contains more than 750 labels (10,000 bottles). ⌧ *911 Lincoln Ave.,* ☎ *970/879–1919. AE, DC, MC, V.*

$$–$$$$ ✕ **Antares.** The co-owners of this superlative eatery cut their culinary
★   teeth at Steamboat's finest restaurants, Harwig's and L'Apogée. With
      fieldstone walls, frosted windows, pressed-tin ceilings, and stained
      glass, all eyes turn to the splendid Victorian building itself before the
      meal arrives. Paul LeBrun's exciting, eclectic cuisine is inspired by
      America's rich ethnic stew. Hence, you might feast on elk medallions
      with a Bing cherry–merlot sauce, or Maine lobster over chili pepper
      linguine. Doug's encyclopedic knowledge of wines is reflected in the
      comprehensive, fairly priced list. ✉ 57½ 8th St., ☎ 970/879–9939. Reser-
      vations essential. AE, MC, V. No lunch.

$$–$$$ ✕ **Harwig's Grill.** This popular eatery is next door to L'Apogée, and
★   it's run by the same team. The bar offers 40 wines by the glass, including
      many lesser-known labels, and you can order from L'Apogée's wine
      list. The menu here reflects owner Jamie Jenny's love of travel, with
      confidently prepared specialties from around the world: home-cured
      salmon pastrami to raclette, jambalaya to dim sum. The desserts are
      predictably sinful. ✉ 911 Lincoln Ave., ☎ 970/879–1980. AE, MC,
      V. No lunch.

$$–$$$ ✕ **Riggio's.** This local favorite is in a dramatic space, whose industrial
      look (black-and-white tile, exposed pipes) is softened by tapestries, mu-
      rals, and landscape photos. The menu offers tasty pizzas (gourmet top-
      pings include goat cheese and clams) and lighter pastas (the sciocca,
      with rock shrimp, eggplant, tomatoes, and basil, is superb). Standards
      such as manicotti, chicken cacciatore, and saltimbocca are also well
      prepared. ✉ 1106 Lincoln Ave., ☎ 970/879–9010. AE, D, DC, MC,
      V. No lunch.

$–$$$ ✕ **La Montana.** This Mexican/southwestern establishment is among
★   Steamboat's most popular restaurants. The kitchen incorporates in-
      digenous specialties into the traditional menu. Among the standouts
      are pepita-crusted tuna with a margarita buerre blanc; enchiladas lay-
      ered with Monterey Jack and goat cheese and roasted peppers; and elk
      loin crusted with pecan nuts and bourbon cream sauce. ✉ Après Ski
      Way and Village Dr., ☎ 970/879–5800. AE, D, MC, V. No lunch.

$$ ✕ **Yama Chan's.** Most people think you can't get good sushi in Col-
      orado: wrong. Somehow, the fish tastes fresher in the crisp mountain
      air at this simple, superlative Japanese restaurant. The rest of the menu
      is equally well presented and prepared. ✉ Old Town Sq., 635 Lincoln
      Ave., ☎ 970/879–8862. AE, MC, V. Closed Mon. year-round; closed
      Sun. mid-Nov.–mid-Apr. No lunch weekends.

$–$$ ✕ **Steamboat Smokehouse.** The loud, raucous scene, brick-and-wood
      decor, and occasional live music might fool you into thinking this joint
      is just a bar. Once you try the phenomenal barbecue or hickory-smoked
      brisket and turkey, however, you'll realize that this is a place where
      they really know their beans about home cooking. ✉ 912 Lincoln Ave.,
      ☎ 970/879–5570. AE, D, DC, MC, V.

$$$$ ⌂ **Home Ranch.** You won't be roughing it at this all-inclusive retreat
★   (with a seven-night minimum stay), a Relais & Chateaux property nes-
      tled among towering stands of aspen outside Clark (just north of
      Steamboat). The living room, with a magnificent fieldstone fireplace
      surrounded by plush leather armchairs and sofa, is cozy; the dining room,
      where Clyde Nelson turns out gourmet southwestern fare, homey. Ac-
      commodations are in the main lodge or in individual cabins with hot
      tubs and terraces. Decor leans toward Native American rugs and
      prints, lace curtains, terra-cotta tile or hardwood floors, and stenciled
      walls. ✉ 54880 County Rd. 129, Box 822, Clark 80428, ☎ 970/879–
      1780, WEB www.homeranch.com. 6 rooms, 8 cabins. Dining room,
      lounge, pool, hot tub, horseback riding, fishing, cross-country skiing,
      ski shop. AE, D, MC, V. Closed late-Mar.–early June and early Oct.–
      late-Dec. FAP.

$$$$
★ ⊞ **Vista Verde Guest Ranch.** Offering similarly deluxe digs and just as many activities as Home Ranch in Clark, Vista Verde has lower rates (available in three-, five- and seven-night packages) and a more authentic western ambience. Lodge rooms are huge and beautifully appointed, with lace curtains, western art, and lodgepole furniture. Cabins are more rustic, with pine paneling and old-fashioned wood-burning stoves, plus refrigerators, coffeemakers, and porches. Chef Jonathon Gillespie serves up sumptuous country repasts, which include wild game and fresh produce from his herb and vegetable garden. ⊠ *3100 County Rd. 64, Box 770465, 80477,* ☎ *970/879–3858 or 800/526–7433,* ꜰᴀx *970/879–1413,* ᴡᴇʙ *www.vistaverde.com. 3 rooms, 9 cabins. Dining room, 10 hot tubs, sauna, gym, horseback riding, fishing, cross-country skiing. No credit cards. Closed mid-Mar.–May and Oct.–Nov. FAP.*

$$–$$$$
⊞ **Sheraton Steamboat Resort & Conference Center.** This bustling deluxe hotel is Steamboat's only true ski-in, ski-out property. Rooms are Sheraton standard, fair-size, with muted decor and most comforts. The amenities are classic resort town, with a ski shop, golf course, and four rooftop hot tubs with sweeping views of the surrounding ski slopes. ⊠ *2200 Village End Court, Box 774808, 80477,* ☎ *970/879–2220 or 800/848–8877,* ꜰᴀx *970/879–7686,* ᴡᴇʙ *www.steamboat-sheraton.com. 317 rooms. 2 restaurants, bar, pool, 4 hot tubs, sauna, steam room, 18-hole golf course, ski shop, meeting room. AE, D, DC, MC, V.*

$$–$$$
⊞ **Best Western Ptarmigan Inn.** Convenience and comfort are the keynotes of this appealing property situated on the slopes. The modest rooms, decorated in pleasing pastels and earth tones, have cable TV, balcony, and full bath. ⊠ *2304 Après Ski Way, Box 773240, 80477,* ☎ *970/879–1730 or 800/538–7519,* ꜰᴀx *970/879–6044,* ᴡᴇʙ *www.bestwestern.com. 77 rooms. Restaurant, bar, in-room data ports, in-room VCRs, refrigerators, pool, hot tub, sauna, ski shop. AE, D, DC, MC, V.*

$$
★ ⊞ **Harbor Hotel and Condominiums.** This charming, completely refurbished 1940s hotel is smack in the middle of Steamboat's historic district. The inviting brick-and-wood-panel lobby sets the tone, and nifty artifacts, such as the old switchboards, dot the interior of the property. Each room is individually decorated with period furniture, combined with modern amenities for comfort. The property also runs an adjacent motel and condo complex. ⊠ *703 Lincoln Ave., 80477,* ☎ *970/879–1522 or 800/543–8888,* ꜰᴀx *970/879–1737. 113 rooms. 2 hot tubs, sauna, steam room. AE, D, DC, MC, V.*

$$
⊞ **Rabbit Ears Motel.** The playful, pink-neon bunny sign outside this motel has been a local landmark since 1952, making it an unofficial gateway to Steamboat Springs. The location is ideal for those who want the springs (across the street); the ski area (the town bus stops outside); and the downtown shops, bars, and restaurants. All the rooms are clean and attractive and are equipped with minirefrigerators and coffeemakers. Most have balconies with views of the Yampa River. Continental breakfast is included in the rate. ⊠ *201 Lincoln Ave., 80477,* ☎ *970/879–1150 or 800/828–7702,* ꜰᴀx *970/870–0483,* ᴡᴇʙ *www.rabbitearsmotel.com. 66 rooms. AE, D, DC, MC, V. CP.*

$$
⊞ **Sky Valley Lodge.** This homey property is a few miles from downtown, amid glorious scenery that contributes to the get-away-from-it-all feel of the inn. Warm English country–style rooms are decorated in mountain colors. Continental breakfast is included. ⊠ *31490 E. U.S. 40, 80477,* ☎ *970/879–7749 or 800/538–7519,* ꜰᴀx *970/879–7752. 24 rooms. Restaurant, hot tub. AE, D, DC, MC, V. CP.*

$$
⊞ **Steamboat B&B.** This custard-and-blue Victorian was originally a church that owner Gordon Hattersley converted into the area's nicest B&B in 1989, cleverly retaining the arched doorways and stained-glass windows. The cozy, comfy rooms have floral wallpaper, lace curtains,

landscape photos, potted geraniums, polished hardwood floors, and period antiques and reproductions. A full breakfast is included. ⊠ *442 Pine St., 80477,* ☎ *970/879–5724,* FAX *970/870–8787. 7 rooms. Dining room, hot tub. AE, D, MC, V. BP.*

CONDOMINIUMS

Mountain Resorts (⊠ 2145 Resort Dr., Suite 100, 80487, ☎ 800/525–2622, FAX 970/879–3228). Torian Plum, one of the properties managed by **Steamboat Premier Properties** (⊠ 1855 Ski Time Sq., 80487, ☎ 970/879–8811 or 800/228–2458, FAX 970/879–8485), offers elegant one- to three-bedroom units in a ski-in, ski-out location. Each condo has a private balcony, and indoor and outdoor hot tubs are available. **Steamboat Resorts** (⊠ Box 2995, 80477, ☎ 800/525–5502, FAX 970/879–8060).

Nightlife

The **Old Town Pub** (⊠ 600 Lincoln Ave., ☎ 970/879–2101) has juicy burgers and local flavor, with some great live bands. **Steamboat Brewery** (⊠ 5th St. and Lincoln Ave., ☎ 970/879–2233) serves superior pub grub and pours an assortment of homemade ales, lagers, porters, and stouts. The Loft section of the **Ore House** restaurant (⊠ U.S. 40 and Pine Grove Rd., ☎ 970/879–1190) ropes 'em in for juicy steaks and boot-scooting country music. On the mountain, **The Tugboat** (⊠ Ski Time Sq., ☎ 970/879–7070) features loud live rock acts, pool, and video games.

Outdoor Activities and Sports

Dogsledding, hot-air ballooning, and snowmobiling can be arranged by calling the activities department at **central reservations** (☎ 800/922–2722).

BOBSLEDDING

The term "bobsledding" might be stretching things, since this isn't quite the 80-mph rush down a twisting gutter of ice that you've seen at the Olympics. However, when riding a soft-shell, four-person sled down the course at **Howelsen Hill** (☎ 970/879–2170), the ski-jumping hill just outside town, it's possible to reach speeds of nearly 50 mph—plenty fast for most people. The cost is $10 per run.

GOLFING

Sheraton Steamboat Golf Club (⊠ 2000 Clubhouse Dr., ☎ 970/879–1391) is a 6,906-yard, par-72, 18-hole championship course designed by Robert Trent Jones, Jr.

HORSEBACK RIDING

The Yampa and Elk river valleys have a long and continuing ranching history. Steamboat has successfully used its cowboy heritage as a way of promoting tourism; the area is full of not only real cowboys but also visitors trying to act the part. Horseback riding is a spectator sport as well as a participant sport here. Riding, instruction, and extended pack trips are offered at a number of ranches in the area, although some may require minimum stays of a week. One ranch that offers the full gamut, from hour-long rides to rides of several days into the surrounding mountains, **Del's Triangle 3 Ranch** (⊠ Box 333, Clark, CO 80428, ☎ 970/879–3495), is about 20 mi north of Steamboat via Highway 129. Every weekend in summer, evening rodeos are held at the **Steamboat Rodeo Grounds** (☎ 970/879–1818). **Steamboat Stables** (⊠ 835 River Rd., ☎ 970/879–2306) offers one-hour guided tours.

ICE DRIVING

Here's one for anyone who's either been intimidated by snowy roads or gotten teenage thrills from executing doughnuts on icy shopping-mall parking lots. The **Bridgestone Winter Driving School** (☎ 970/879–6104 or 800/949–7543) offers half-day and full-day winter driving courses, as well as special, women-only programs.

RAFTING

High Adventures (☎ 970/879–8747) runs rafting excursions to various rivers. Half-day to two-week trips are available for all levels.

SLEIGH RIDES

Several ranches in the area offer horse-drawn sleigh rides, dinner rides being the most popular. Call the Steamboat central reservations number for details.

SNOWMOBILING

Explore the forests and meadows of the Medicine Bow/Routt National Forest with **Steamboat Powder Cats** (☎ 970/879–5188). **Steamboat Snowmobile Tours** (☎ 970/879–6500) has guided tours.

Downhill Skiing and Snowboarding

Steamboat is perhaps best known for its tree skiing and "cruising" terrain—the latter term referring to intermediate skiing on wide, groomed runs. The abundance of cruising terrain has made Steamboat immensely popular with intermediates and families who ski only a few times a year and who aren't looking for diabolical challenges to tax their abilities. Set on a predominantly western exposure—most ski areas are situated on north-facing exposures—the resort benefits from intense sun, which contributes to the cruising quality. Moreover, one of the most extensive lift systems in the West allows skiers to take a lot of fast runs without having to spend much time in line. The Storm Peak and Sundown high-speed quads, for example, each deliver about 2,000 vertical ft in less than seven minutes. Do the math, and you can figure that a day of more than 60,000 vertical ft is entirely within the realm of diehards.

All this is not to suggest, however, that Steamboat lacks challenge entirely. Steamboat is renowned as a breeding ground for some of the country's top mogul skiers, and for good reason. The mogul runs might not be steep, but they're numerous. There are also some real steeps, such as Chute One, but they're few and not especially long. The 950-acre Morningside Park expansion encompasses advanced and intermediate terrain. If you're looking for challenging skiing at Steamboat, take on the trees. The ski area has done an admirable job of clearing many gladed areas of such nuisances as saplings, underbrush, and fallen timber, making Steamboat tree skiing a much less hazardous adventure than it can be at some areas. The trees are also where advanced skiers—as well as, in some places, confident intermediates—can find the best of Steamboat's ballyhooed powder. Statistically, Steamboat doesn't report significantly more snowfall than other Colorado resorts, but somehow its numbers seem literally to stack up better than the others. Ask well-traveled Colorado skiers, and they'll confirm that when it comes to consistently good, deep snow, Steamboat is hard to beat. ⊠ *2305 Mt. Werner Circle,* ☎ *970/879–6111,* WEB *www.steamboat.com.* ☺ *Late-Nov.–mid-Apr., daily 9–4.*

The **Howelsen Ski Area,** a tiny historic area right in Steamboat Springs, is Colorado's oldest. Its three lifts, 15 trails, and 440-ft vertical aren't impressive, but it *is* the largest ski-jumping complex in America, and it's a major Olympic training ground. ⊠ *845 Howelsen Pkwy.,* ☎ *970/ 879–8499.* ☺ *Dec.–Mar., Mon. 11–6, Tues.–Fri. 11–9, weekends 9–4:30.*

FACILITIES

3,668-ft vertical drop; 2,939 skiable acres; 14% beginner, 56% intermediate, 30% advanced; one 8-passenger gondola, 4 high-speed quad chairs, 1 quad chair, 6 triple chairs, 6 double chairs.

Two-hour adult group lessons begin at $38; all-day lessons are $57. Clinics in moguls, powder, snowboarding, and "hyper-carving"— made possible by the relatively new shaped skis—are available. For general **ski school** information, call ☎ 970/879–6111 ext. 531. Intensive two- and three-day "training camps" are offered in racing and advanced skiing through the **Billy Kidd Center for Performance Skiing** (☎ 970/879–6111 ext. 543). Children's programs (lessons and/or day care) are offered for kids 6 months–15 years old through the **Kids' Vacation Center** (☎ 970/879–6111 ext. 218).

Sno-Cat skiing is the "poor man's" version of helicopter skiing, although at close to $200 a day, it's not exactly skiing for the lunch-pail crowd. But Sno-Cat users don't have to worry about landing and can get to places in bad weather that would be inaccessible by helicopter. Buffalo Pass, northeast of Steamboat, is reputed to be one of the snowiest spots in Colorado, and that's where **Steamboat Powder Cats** (☎ 970/879–5188 or 800/288–0543) operates. The basics are included: open-meadow skiing, deep powder, and a maximum of only 24 skiers.

$52. Savings of 5% or less on multiday tickets.

Equipment packages are available at the gondola base as well as at ski shops in town. Packages (skis, boots, and poles) average about $16 a day, less for multiday rentals. Call **central reservations** (☎ 970/879–4070 or 800/922–2722) for rental information.

Nordic Skiing

The most popular area for backcountry skiing is Rabbit Ears Pass southeast of town, the last pass you must cross if you drive from Denver to Steamboat. Much of its appeal is the easy access to high country; trails emanate from the U.S. 40 roadside. There are plenty of touring routes possible, with limited telemarking opportunity. Arrangements for backcountry tours can be made through the **Steamboat Ski Touring Center** (☎ 970/879–8180).

A popular backcountry spot is Seedhouse Road, north of the town of Clark and about 25 mi north of Steamboat. A marked trail network covers rolling hills, with good views of distant peaks. For maps, trail suggestions, and information on snow conditions and stability, contact the **Hahn's Peak Ranger Office** (✉ 57 10th St., Box 771212, Steamboat Springs 80477, ☎ 970/879–1870).

Touring and telemarking rentals are available at various ski shops in the Steamboat area. One of the best is the **Ski Haus** (✉ 1450 Lincoln Ave., ☎ 970/879–0385).

The main center for cross-country skiing is the **Steamboat Ski Touring Center,** where most of the 30-km (18½-mi) trail network—laid out on or alongside the Sheraton Steamboat Golf Club—is relatively gentle. The inspiration behind the center is Sven Wiik, a seminal figure in the establishment of cross-country skiing in the United States. A good option for a relaxed afternoon of skiing is to pick up some eats at the Picnic Basket in the touring center building and enjoy lunch at the picnic area along the Fish Creek Trail, a 5-km (3-mi) loop that winds through pine and aspen groves. Rental packages (skis, boots, and poles) are available. ✉ *Box 775401, Steamboat Springs 80477,* ☎ *970/879–8180.* 🎿 *Trail fee $10.*

Some guest ranches in the area also have groomed track networks. **Home Ranch** (⊠ Box 822, Clark 80428, ☎ 970/879–1780), 20 mi north of Steamboat, has 40 km (25 mi) of groomed tracks. **Vista Verde Guest Ranch** (⊠ Box 465, Steamboat Springs 80477, ☎ 970/879–3858 or 800/526–7433) also has a groomed trail network, as well as access to adjacent national forest land for touring.

Shopping

On the mountain, at the base of the ski area are three shopping centers—Ski Time Square, Torian Plum Plaza, and Gondola Square. Steamboat's **Old Town Square** (⊠ 7th St. and Lincoln Ave.) is a collection of upscale boutiques and retailers.

BOOKS

Off the Beaten Path (⊠ 56 7th St., ☎ 970/879–6830) is a throwback to the beat generation, with poetry readings, lectures, and concerts. It has an excellent selection of New Age works, in addition to the usual best-sellers and guides.

BOUTIQUES

Amallama (⊠ Old Town Sq., ☎ 970/879–9127) offers folk art, jewelry, and clothing from around the world, including Balinese cradle watchers, carved wooden figures believed to keep evil spirits away from sleeping children. You can make your own earrings at the bead counter. **Old Town Leather** (⊠ 929 Lincoln Ave., ☎ 970/879–3558) sells every conceivable leather item, most of them handmade.

CRAFT AND ART GALLERIES

Art Quest (⊠ 511 Lincoln Ave., ☎ 970/879–1989) carries a variety of works in silver, glass, paper, ceramics, and alabaster, as well as furniture and jewelry. A wide range of Native American art from Alaska to Mexico is featured. **White Hart Gallery** (⊠ 843 Lincoln Ave., ☎ 970/879–1015) is a magnificent clutter of western and Native American paintings and objets d'art.

SPORTING GOODS

Rent or buy ski equipment at **Christy Sports** (⊠ 1724A Mt. Werner Circle, ☎ 970/879–9001). **Sport Stalker** (⊠ Ski Time Sq., ☎ 970/879–2445) sells the latest fashions and gear.

WESTERN PARAPHERNALIA

F. M. Light and Sons (⊠ 830 Lincoln Ave., ☎ 970/879–1822), owned by the same family for four generations, caters to the Marlboro man in us all. If you're lucky you'll find what you're looking for cheaply—how about cowboy hats for $4.98? **Into the West** (⊠ 807 Lincoln Ave., ☎ 970/879–8377) is owned by Jace Romick, a former member of the U.S. ski team and a veteran of the rodeo circuit. He crafts splendid, beautifully textured lodgepole furniture, and sells anything tasteful to do with the West: antiques (even ornate potbellied stoves), collectibles, cowhide mirrors, and new handicrafts, such as Native American drum tables and fanciful candleholders made from branding irons. **Two Rivers Gallery** (⊠ 56 9th St., ☎ 970/879–0044) sells such cowboy collectibles as antler chandeliers and cow-skull lamps, as well as vintage photographs, prints, sculpture, and paintings.

En Route Head west on I–70 to reach the natural and man-made 15-mi-long **Glenwood Canyon.** Nature began the work as the Colorado River carved deep buff-tint granite, limestone, and quartzite gullies—brilliantly streaked with lavender, rose, and ivory. This process took a half billion years. Then man stepped in, seeking a more direct route west. In 1992, the work on I–70 through the canyon was completed at a cost of almost $500 million. Much of the expense was attributable to the effort to preserve the natural landscape as much as possible. When contractors blasted cliff faces, for example, they stained the exposed rock to simulate nature's weathering. Biking trails were also created, providing easy access to the hauntingly beautiful **Hanging Lake Recreation Area.** Here Dead Horse Creek sprays ethereal flumes from curling limestone tendrils into a startlingly turquoise pool, as jet-black swifts dart to and fro. It's perhaps the most transcendent of several idyllic spots now reachable on bike or foot. The intrepid can scale the delicate limestone cliffs, pocked with numerous caverns and embroidered with pastel-hue gardens.

Glenwood Springs

🏵 *110 mi from Steamboat Springs via U.S. 131 south and I–70 west; 160 mi from Denver via I–70 west.*

Interstate 70 snakes through the canyon on its way to a famed spa that forms the western apex of a triangle with Vail and Aspen. Once upon a time, Glenwood Springs was every bit as tony as those chic resorts are today, attracting a faithful legion of the pampered and privileged who came to enjoy the waters (the world's largest natural hot springs), said to cure everything from acne to rheumatism.

Today the entrance to town and its once-splendid prospects of a fertile valley fringed by massive peaks is marred by the proliferation of malls, motels, and fast-food outlets. Remnants of her glory days can still be seen in the grand old **Hotel Colorado** (✉ 526 Pine St.), regally commanding the vaporous pools from a patrician distance. Modeled after the Villa de Medici in Italy, the property opened its doors in 1893 to become the fashionable retreat of its day. Teddy Roosevelt even made it his unofficial "Little White House" in 1905.

The **Hot Springs Pool,** formerly called the Yampah Hot Springs, were discovered by the Ute Indians (Yampah is Ute for "Big Medicine"). Even before the heyday of the hotel, western notables from Annie Oakley to Doc Holliday came to take the curative waters. In Doc's case, however, the cure didn't work, and six months after his arrival in 1887 he died broke, broken down, and tubercular. (He lies in Linwood Cemetery, ½ mi east of town.) The smaller pool is 100 ft long and maintained at 104°F. The larger is more than two city blocks long (405 ft), and contains in excess of a million gallons of constantly filtered water that is completely refilled every six hours and maintained at a soothing 90°F. ✉ *401 N. River Rd.,* ☎ *970/945–7131,* WEB *www.hotspringspool.com.* 🎫 *$9.50.* ☉ *Memorial Day–Labor Day, daily 7:30 AM–10 PM; Labor Day–Memorial Day, daily 9 AM–10 PM.*

The **Yampah Spa and Vapor Caves** is a series of three natural underground steam baths. The same 124-°F springs that supply the pool flow under the cave floors. Each chamber is successively hotter than the last; you can scoop mud from the walls for a cleansing facial, as you purify your body (and soul, according to Ute legend). A variety of spa treatments from massages to body wraps is also available. ✉ *709 E. 6th St.,* ☎ *970/945–0667,* WEB *www.yampahhotsprings.com.* 🎫 *$8.75 for caves, more for various treatments.* ☉ *Daily 9–9.*

Glenwood is home to many caves, including the famed **Fairy Caves,** whose subterranean caverns, grottos, and labyrinths are truly a marvel of nature. Take one of two cavern tours: a two-hour, family-friendly walk; or a more extensive, crawl-on-your-belly spelunking adventure. ✉ *508 Pine St.,* ☎ *970/945–4228,* WEB *www.glenwoodcaverns.com.* 🎫 *$12; $50 for extended tour.* ☉ *Apr. 15–Nov. 1, daily 9–5.*

Dining and Lodging

$$–$$$ ✕ **Florinda's.** The peach walls of this handsome space are graced by changing art exhibits. The chef has a deft hand with northern and southern Italian dishes. Try the veal chops sautéed with shiitake mushrooms in marsala or the nightly specials, which are always extensive and superb. ⊠ *721 Grand St.,* ☎ *970/945–1245. MC, V. Closed Sun. No lunch Sat.*

$–$$ ✕ **The Bayou.** "Food so good you'll slap yo' mama," trumpets the menu
★ at this casual eatery, whose most distinctive attribute is its frog awning (two bulbous eyes beckon you in). Choose from "pre-stuff, wabbit stuff, udder stuff," such as lip-smacking gumbo that looks like mud (and is supposed to), étouffée and blackened fish, or lethal Cajun martinis. And when the menu labels an item as "hurt me" hot, it's no joke. On summer weekends live music is performed on the patio. ⊠ *52103 Rte. 6, at Rte. 24,* ☎ *970/945–1047. AE, MC, V.*

$ ✕ **Daily Bread.** For years, locals have been packing this little café, where you can get some of the best food at the best prices in town. Hearty breakfasts such as the veggie skillet or breakfast burrito are favorites, while lunch features creative sandwiches, soups, and burgers. Many items are low-fat or vegetarian. The bakery also sells their homemade breads to go. ⊠ *729 Grand Ave.,* ☎ *970/945–6253. D, MC, V. No dinner. No lunch Sun.*

$$ 🏨 **Hot Springs Lodge.** This lodge is perfectly located right by the Hot Springs Pool, which is used to heat the property. The attractive rooms, decorated in jade, teal, buff, and rose, stress a southwestern motif. Deluxe rooms offer a minirefrigerator and tiny balcony, in addition to standard conveniences such as cable TV and full bath. ⊠ *415 E. 6th St., 81601,* ☎ *970/945–6571 or 800/537–7946,* FAX *970/947–2950,* WEB *www.hotspringspool.com. 107 rooms. Bar, deli, hot tub. AE, D, DC, MC, V.*

$$ 🏨 **Hotel Colorado.** The exterior of this building, listed in the National Historic Register, is simply exquisite, with graceful sandstone colonnades and Italianate campaniles. The impression of luxury continues in the imposing, yet gracious, marble lobby and public rooms. The sunny, individually decorated rooms and suites—most with high ceilings, fireplaces, gorgeous period wainscoting, and balconies affording superlative vistas—are designed to match. Everyone, whether notable or notorious, from Teddy Roosevelt to Doc Holliday to Al Capone, stayed here in its halcyon days. ⊠ *526 Pine St., 81601,* ☎ *970/945–6511 or 800/544–3998,* FAX *970/945–7030,* WEB *www.hotelcolorado.com. 128 rooms. Restaurant, café, hair salon, gym, meeting room. AE, D, DC, MC, V.*

$$ 🏨 **Hotel Denver.** Although this hotel was originally built in 1806, its most striking features are the numerous art deco touches throughout. Most rooms open onto a view of the springs or a three-story New Orleans–style atrium bedecked with colorful canopies. The accommodations are ultraneat, trim, comfortable, and so quiet it's hard to believe you're only footsteps from the Amtrak train station. Glenwood's only microbrewery—the Glenwood Canyon Brewing Company—is the hotel restaurant. ⊠ *402 7th St., 81601,* ☎ *970/945–6565 or 800/826–8820,* FAX *970/945–2204,* WEB *www.thehoteldenver.com. 78 rooms. Restaurant, bar, hair salon, gym, meeting room. AE, D, DC, MC, V.*

$$ 🏨 **Sunlight Mountain Inn.** This charming traditional ski lodge is a few hundred feet from the Sunlight Mountain Resort lifts. It brims with European country ambience, from the delightful lounge (with a carved fireplace and wrought-iron chandeliers) and western-flair restaurant to the cozily rustic rooms, all with pine-board walls and rough-hewn armoires. The restaurant, open in winter only, specializes in apple dishes, made from local apples whenever possible. Sunlight is a true get-away-from-it-all place, with no TVs in the rooms. A full breakfast is included. ⊠ *10252 County Rd. 117, 81601,* ☎ *970/945–5225 or 800/*

733–4757, FAX 970/947–1900, WEB *www.sunlightinn.com. 20 rooms. Restaurant, bar, hot tub. AE, D, MC, V. BP.*

Outdoor Activities and Sports

FISHING

Roaring Fork Anglers (☎ 970/945–0180) leads wade and float trips throughout the area.

FITNESS

Choose between Nautilus, stationary bikes, treadmills, steam rooms, saunas, and racquetball at **Hot Springs Athletic Club** (✉ 401 N. River Rd., ☎ 970/945–7428).

RAFTING

Blue Sky Adventures (☎ 970/945–6605) offers a unique "pedal and paddle" deal with a half-day raft trip followed by a half-day bike tour. **Rock Garden Rafting** (☎ 970/945–6737) run trips down the Colorado and Roaring Fork rivers, and has a full-service campground on the banks of the Colorado. **Whitewater Rafting** (☎ 970/945–8477) is home of the "double Shoshone," a round-trip through the area's most hair-raising rapids.

Downhill Skiing

Sunlight Mountain Resort, 20 minutes south of Glenwood Springs, has 66 trails, including the super-steep glades of the East Ridge, serviced by four lifts with a drop of 2,010 vertical ft. The varied terrain, sensational views, and lack of pretension make this a local favorite. The ratio of shredders to downhillers here is quite high, as Sunlight has a reputation for "radical air." ✉ *10901 County Rd. 117,* ☎ *970/945–7491 or 800/445–7931,* WEB *www.sunlightmtn.com.* ☉ *Early Dec.–early Apr., daily 9–4.*

Shopping

Glenwood Springs Mall (✉ 51027 U.S. 6, at U.S. 24, ☎ 970/945–1200) has everything from Kmart and JCPenney to factory outlets and specialty shops. The **Watersweeper and the Dwarf** (✉ 717 Grand Ave., ☎ 970/945–2000) sells handicrafts and Americana fashioned from silver, gold, clay, wood, glass, stone, wool, wax, and patience.

En Route   At Carbondale, Route 82 splits and continues southeast, skirting the Roaring Fork River on its way to Aspen. Route 133 veers south on its way to Redstone.

Redstone

36   *29 mi from Glenwood Springs via Rte. 82 south and Rte. 133 south.*

Redstone is a charming artists' colony whose streets are lined with pretty galleries and boutiques, and whose boundaries are ringed by impressive sandstone cliffs from which the town draws its name. Redstone's history dates back to the late 19th century when J. C. Osgood, director of the Colorado Fuel and Iron Company, built Cleveholm Manor, now known as **Redstone Castle** (✉ 58 Redstone Blvd., ☎ 970/704–1430) to entertain the other titans of his day, such as John D. Rockefeller, J. P. Morgan, and Teddy Roosevelt. Among the home's embellishments are gold-leaf ceilings, maroon velvet walls, silk brocade upholstery, marble and mahogany fireplaces, Persian rugs, and Tiffany chandeliers. While the Castle has been closed as a public lodge for several years, you can catch a glimpse of the baronial splendor at luncheon tours, offered sporadically. The Castle is also available for weddings, business conventions, and other special events.

Dining and Lodging

$$ ✕ **SIX89.** Located in a decidedly unglamorous ranching community just north of Redstone, this funky restaurant is well worth a visit. As chef/owner Mark Fisher's attempt to provide an "intelligent alternative" to Aspen's posh eateries, the kitchen and winebar's irreverent menu and whimsical lexicon, coupled with an unusual zinc-topped bar and a "sharing and grazing" philosophy, create a downright delightful dining experience. Pass around the truffled mac and cheese, crispy goat cheese gnocchi, pomegranate glazed Sonoma quail, and a warm chocolate ancho chile brownie and you'll get the picture. Reservations are suggested. ✉ *689 Main St., Carbondale,* ☎ *970/963–6890. AE, D, MC, V. No lunch.*

$–$$ ✕⊡ **Redstone Inn.** The inn was originally designed as an elegant 35-room lodging for the Colorado Fuel and Iron Company's bachelor employees. (Owner J.C. Osgood also constructed one of the first planned communities for his employees, a utopian model in its day.) Eat in the poolside Grill ($–$$$) or the more formal Redstone Dining Room ($$–$$$). Specialties range from tortilla lasagna to duck ravioli to elk in phyllo. The Sunday brunch is famous. You can also stay overnight at the cozy, relaxing inn, where rooms range from antiques-laden, to one-of-a-kind, to those with a veranda view. Don't forget to take advantage of the complimentary wine-and-cheese receptions every afternoon. ✉ *82 Redstone Blvd., 81623,* ☎ *970/963–2526 or 800/748–2524,* ℻ *970/963–2527,* 𝚆𝙴𝙱 *www.redstoneinn.com. 35 rooms. Restaurant, grill, hot tub, pool, spa, tennis court. AE, D, MC, V.*

Aspen/Snowmass

42 mi from Glenwood Springs via Rte. 82 south; 200 mi from Denver via I–70 west and Rte. 82 east; 165 mi from Denver via I–70 west, Rte. 91 south, and Rte. 82 west (summer only).

③⑦ One of the world's fabled resorts, **Aspen** is practically a byword for glitz, glamour, and glorious skiing. To the uninitiated, Aspen and Vail are virtually synonymous. To residents, a rivalry exists, with locals of each claiming rights to the state's most epic skiing, hottest nightlife, and finest resort town lifestyle. Comparisons are admittedly odious and at best superficial, though a few instructive generalizations can be made.

The most obvious distinction is the look: Vail is a faux-Bavarian development, Aspen is an authentic mining town. Vail is politicians—it's where Gerald Ford, Dan Quayle, and John Sununu fled to escape the cares of state. Aspen is recording stars and Hollywood—where Don Johnson and Melanie Griffith remarried (and divorced) and Barbra Streisand took a stand against controversial Amendment 2.

Between galleries, museums, international conferences, and events, there's so much going on year-round in Aspen that even in winter many people come to "do the scene," and don't even ski. Aspen is as much a national icon as it is a town—forever in the news as a litmus test of the American public's tolerance of radical-chic politics, conspicuous consumption, and conspicuous love affairs. It's like a scriptless soap opera shot as cinema verité. It is a place where celebrities have affairs and locals have dogs and mountain bikes. It is weird.

In Aspen, high-end clothing boutiques have been known to serve free Campari-and-sodas après-ski, a practice so brazenly elitist that there's a certain charm to it. At the same time, it's a place where people actually live, send their children to school, and work real jobs that may or may not have to do with skiing. It is, arguably, America's original ski-bum destination, a fact that continues to give the town's character an underlying layer of humor and texture. People can come to Aspen, dress much too expensively, and loudly make fools of themselves, as Donald Trump and Barbra Streisand (among others) have done. But a person can also come to Aspen and have a reasonably straightforward, enjoyable ski vacation, because once you've stripped away the veneer, Aspen is not a bad town or a bad place to ski.

Aspen has always been a magnet for cultural and countercultural types. After all, bad-boy gonzo journalist Hunter S. Thompson is one of the more visible citizens of the nearby community of Woody Creek. One of Aspen's most amusing figures is Jon Barnes, who tools around in his "Ultimate Taxi" (it's plastered with 3-D glasses, crystal disco balls, and neon necklaces and is redolent of dry ice and incense). You'll find everyone from "social X rays" with Vogue exteriors and vague interiors to long-haired musicians in combat boots and fatigues. To be fair, most Aspenites couldn't care less: theirs is a freewheeling, tolerant town that welcomes diversity of personal expression. It's all part of the Aspen mystique. Ultimately, it doesn't matter what you wear here, as long as you wear it with conviction.

Originally called Ute City (after its displaced former residents), Aspen was founded in the late 1870s during a silver rush. The most prominent early citizen was Jerome Wheeler, who in 1889, at the height of Aspen's prosperity, opened two of Aspen's enduring landmarks, the Hotel Jerome and the Wheeler Opera House. The silver market crashed in 1893, and Aspen's population dwindled from 15,000 to 250 by the Depression era. In the late 1930s, the region struck gold when Swiss mountaineer and ski consultant Andre Roche determined that Aspen Mountain would make a prime ski area. By 1941 it had already landed the U.S. Nationals, but Aspen was really put on the world map by Walter Paepcke, who developed the town as a cultural mecca. In 1949, he helped found the Aspen Institute for Humanistic Studies, and he organized an international celebration to mark Johann Wolfgang von Goethe's 200th birthday. This event paved the way for such renowned annual festivities as the Aspen Music Festival and the International Design Conference.

Downtown Aspen is easily explored on foot. It's best to wander without a planned itinerary, although the Aspen Historical Society puts out a walking-tour brochure. You can spend an afternoon admiring the sleek window displays and graceful Victorian mansions, many of which now house fine boutiques and restaurants.

The ornate lobby, bar, and restaurant of the redbrick **Hotel Jerome** (⊠ 330 E. Main St., ☏ 970/920–1000) re-create fashionable turn-of-the-20th-century living. The elegant 1889 **Wheeler Opera House** (⊠ 320 E. Hyman Ave., ☏ 970/920–5770) remains a concert venue today.

You can obtain great insight into Victorian high life at the newly renovated Queen Anne **Wheeler-Stallard House Museum**, which displays period memorabilia collected by the Aspen Historical Society. ⊠ 620 W. Bleeker St., ☏ 970/925–3721, WEB aspenhistory.org. ⊡ $3. ☉ Jan.–Mar. and mid-June–mid-Sept., Tues.–Fri. 1–4.

Top local and national artists are exhibited at the **Aspen Art Museum.** The complimentary wine-and-cheese-session-cum-gallery-tour, held every Thursday at 5, is a lot of fun. ⊠ 590 N. Mill St., ☏ 970/925–8050, WEB www.aspenartmuseum.org. ⊡ $3. ☉ Tues., Wed., Fri., Sat. 10–6; Thurs. 10–7; Sun. noon–6.

Southeast along Route 82 you'll see the turnoffs (Brush Creek or Owl Creek roads) to **Snowmass,** one of four ski areas owned by the Aspen Skiing Company. Snowmass Village has its share of chic boutiques and eateries, but it's more affordable and down-to-earth than Aspen, and it predominantly caters to families. These differences apply equally to the development and to the mountain itself.

Snowmass was built in 1967 as Aspen's answer to Vail—a ski-specific resort—and although it has never quite matched the panache or popularity of Vail, it has gained a certain stature with age. It used to be that if you stayed at Snowmass, dining meant cooking in your condo and entertainment could only be found 15 mi away in Aspen. In recent years, an effort has been made to breathe a little life and pizzazz into Snowmass Village, and the effect has been noticeable. Better restaurants and a livelier après-ski scene give people something to do after the lifts close. In general, Snowmass is the preferred alternative for families with young children, leaving the town of Aspen to a more hard-partying, up-at-the-crack-of-noon kind of crowd. The selling points of Snowmass as an alternative to Aspen are lots of on-slope, ski-in/ski-out lodging, a slow pace, and quiet.

Dining

ASPEN

$$$$ ✕ **Matsuhisa.** Renowned in Los Angeles, New York, London, and Tokyo, Nobu Matsuhisa brings his nouveau-Japanese cuisine to Aspen. While you shouldn't expect to see Nobu in the kitchen, his recipes and techniques greet you at every turn. His jalapeño yellowtail is scrumptious, his anticuchu beef is delicious, his new-style sashimi indescribable, and his prices astronomical. Needless to say, the clientele is appropriately star-studded to match. ⊠ 303 E. Main St., ☎ 970/544–6628. Reservations essential. AE, MC, V.

$$$$ ✕ **Pine Creek Cookhouse.** Cross-country ski or board a horse-drawn sleigh (or hike during the summer) to this homey log cabin—Krabloonik's main competition—where the emphasis is also on game specialties, including quail, elk, and wild boar. Lunch offerings include a hot smoked salmon salad, spinach crêpes, and Hungarian goulash to warm the soul. In winter or summer, shoot for a seat on the deck for breathtaking views of the Elk Mountains. ⊠ 11399 Castle Creek, Aspen, ☎ 970/925–1044. Reservations essential. AE, MC, V.

$$$$ ✕ **Renaissance.** The decor of this stunner is a coolly seductive, abstract ★ rendition of a sultan's tent—one that has a knockout view of Aspen Mountain from the patio. Owner-chef Charles Dale apprenticed as chef saucier to his mentor, Daniel Boulud, at New York's trendiest mineral watering hole, Le Cirque, before opening Renaissance in 1990. Opt for one of his two tasting menus—one vegetarian, one decidedly not—with hand-selected wines to accompany. The menu, as well as the style of preparation, changes seasonally. Among standouts are crispy Chilean sea bass with artichoke, shiitakes, and foie gras, and rack of lamb with an aromatic sauce. Upstairs, the Bistro grants a taste of the kitchen's splendors at down-to-earth prices. ⊠ 304 E. Hopkins St., Aspen, ☎ 970/925–2402. Reservations essential. AE, DC, MC, V. No lunch.

$$$–$$$$ ✕ **Ajax Tavern.** The brains behind Mustards Grill and Tra Vigne, two ★ of Napa Valley's finest eateries, have created this bright, pleasant restaurant with mahogany paneling, diamond-pattern floors, leather banquettes, open kitchen, and an eager, unpretentious waitstaff. You might begin with the grilled spring asparagus with roasted pepper and Kalamata olive tapenade, followed with the braised short ribs with roasted garlic polenta or the grilled double-cut pork chop with sweet potato, Parmesan, and thyme. Try the caramel-apple cobbler for dessert. The wine list, showcasing Napa's best, is almost matched by the fine selection of microbrews. Enjoy outstanding lunch offerings on the spacious, sunny patio, which abuts Aspen Mountain. ⊠ 685 E. Durant Ave., Aspen, ☎ 970/920–9333. Reservations essential. AE, D, DC, MC, V.

$$$-$$$$
★ ✕ **Syzygy.** Personable owner Walt Harris succeeds at providing a harmony of expressive cuisine (the name refers to the alignment of heavenly bodies) thanks to a sterling, unusually helpful waitstaff and the assured, sublimely seasoned creations of chef Morton Oswald. Though the setting is a bit outdated, the restaurant remains outstanding with food that is crisply flavored and sensuously textured, floating from French to Oriental to southwestern influences without skipping a beat. Standouts include the Szechuan tempura lobster with grilled pineapple and Asian vegetable salad to start, followed by such main courses as elk tenderloin with sun-dried fig chutney and ancho chile aioli. The patient and knowledgeable will find a few good buys on the extensive wine list; enjoy a glass while listening to Aspen's best live jazz. ⊠ *520 E. Hyman Ave., Aspen,* ☎ *970/925–3700. Reservations essential. AE, D, DC, MC, V. No lunch.*

$$-$$$$ ✕ **Cache Cache.** Like his predecessor, chef Christopher Lauter is a practitioner of *cuisine minceur*—no butter or cream is used in his preparations. But the sunny flavors of Provence explode on the palate, thanks to the master's savvy use of garlic, tomato, eggplant, fennel, and rosemary. The osso bucco in a marsala sauce is sublime; salads and rotisserie items are sensational; desserts are worth leaving room for. The bar menu offers a budget-conscious way to sample this outstanding cuisine. ⊠ *205 S. Mill St., Aspen,* ☎ *970/925–3835. AE, DC, MC, V.*

$$$ ✕ **L'Hostaria.** Dante Medri and wife Cristina brought over all of the furniture and fixtures for this subterranean hot spot from Italy. The atmosphere is sophisticated, yet rustic with an open-beam farmhouse ceiling, sleek blond-wood chairs, contemporary art, and a floor-to-ceiling glass wine cooler in the center of the room. The menu relies on simple, subtle flavors in specialties such as goat cheese flan on mixed greens, gnocchi with duck ragout, risotto with veal sauce, and a delectable veal Milanese. For a change of pace, check out the carpaccio bar, which features some wonderful cured meats and fishes. ⊠ *620 E. Hyman Ave., Aspen,* ☎ *970/925–9022. AE, MC, V.*

$$-$$$
★ ✕ **Farfalla.** This sleek, L.A.-style northern Italian eatery, well lit and adorned with fine art, is one of the best spots in town. (It was once also one of the hottest spots, but the pretty crowd has moved, leaving behind a few open tables and the same excellent food.) Specialties include homemade tortellini with asparagus and goat cheese in walnut sauce, an outstanding veal chop, wood-fired pizzas, and one of the town's best selections of grappas. Reservations are accepted for parties of six or more. ⊠ *415 E. Main St., Aspen,* ☎ *970/925–8222. AE, DC, MC, V.*

$$-$$$ ✕ **Kenichi.** This Asian restaurant gets the nod as much for the ultra-happening atmosphere as for its delectable bamboo salmon and Oriental roast duck served Peking style. Blackened sea bass is very popular, as is the seared ahi tuna with Cajun spices and anything from the sushi bar. With a crowd? Book one of the private tatami rooms. ⊠ *533 E. Hopkins Ave., Aspen,* ☎ *970/920–2212. AE, D, DC, MC, V. No lunch.*

$$-$$$ ✕ **Poppies Bistro Cafe.** Ask 20 Aspenites where to find the most romantic meal in Aspen, and 19 of them will tell you Poppies (the other one probably works at the Jerome). Its out-of-the-way location, on the tranquil, westernmost edge of town, makes it feel like a secret retreat, and the intimate atmosphere, loaded with Victorian charm, just begs you to play Casanova. The cuisine ranges from classic bistro entrées such as steak au poivre in a cognac cream sauce to house specialties like the spicy Anaheim peppers stuffed with lobster and goat cheese. It's cozy in winter, but even better in summer after an afternoon concert at the nearby music tent. ⊠ *834 W. Hallam St., Aspen,* ☎ *970/ 925–2333. AE, MC, V.*

$$–$$$ ✕ **Rustique Bistro.** Charles Dale, the culinary maestro who made Renaissance the closest thing to a Michelin-starred restaurant in Aspen, has done it again with Rustique Bistro. As you walk into the dining room, you feel as if you've left the Rockies and landed at a French county inn. Carafes of house wine sit on the white-papered tabletops, hinting that you should make a leisurely evening of it. The Weird Dish of the Day is a gastronomic adventure featuring such unusual delicacies as braised veal tongue with potato hash and sauce gribiche. ⊠ *216 S. Monarch St., Aspen,* ☎ *970/920–2555. AE, D, MC, V. No lunch.*

$$–$$$ ✕ **Toppers.** Cheerful Greg Topper, previously the esteemed chef of the
★ Ajax Tavern, has opened a fuss-free café and take-out shop with first-rate American food. He serves fresh salads, soups, and fancy pizzas (think truffle oil), and, undeniably, the best sandwiches in town. Locals love the $9.95 Aspen Bowls: you mix and match main items, such as fennel-spiced pork stew or red snapper and rock shrimp vegetable curry, with various sides. If you come for dinner, get the succulent, slow-braised short ribs. Also popular are venison chili, rotisserie chicken, trout puttanesca, and pappardelle with Colorado lamb. ⊠ *300 Puppy Smith St.,* ☎ *970/920–0069. MC, V.*

$–$$$ ✕ **Little Annie's Eating House.** Everything at this charmer is ultrasimple, from the wood paneling and red-and-white checked tablecloths to the fresh fish, barbecued ribs and chicken, and Colorado lamb. Annie's is a big favorite with locals who like the relaxed atmosphere, dependable food, and reasonable prices, not to mention the Bundt cake and "shot and a beer" special. ⊠ *517 E. Hyman Ave., Aspen,* ☎ *970/925–1098. AE, DC, MC, V.*

$–$$ ✕ **Main Street Bakery & Café.** Perfectly brewed coffee and hot breakfast buns and pastries are served at this café along with a full breakfast menu including homemade granola. During the late season when the sun is out, head out back to the deck for the mountain views. This is also a good spot for lunch and dinner (it's a quiet respite in the heart of the season). Try the Yankee pot roast, chicken potpie, and homemade soups. ⊠ *201 E. Main St., Aspen,* ☎ *970/920–6446. AE, MC, V. No dinner Apr.–June and Sept.–Nov.*

$–$$ ✕ **Rusty's Hickory House.** Tie on your bib and dig in. No one will mind if your hands and face are covered in the secret sauce that tops the slow-cooked meats and chicken. Rusty's hickory-smoked baby back ribs have won more than 40 national competitions. The rustic Hickory House is also home to Aspen's only southern-style breakfast, grits and all. And for a hangover, nothing beats a good helping of ribs and eggs. ⊠ *730 W. Main St., Aspen,* ☎ *970/925–2313. D, MC, V.*

$ ✕ **Boogie's Diner.** This cheerful spot filled with diner memorabilia and an outrageous waitstaff resounds with rock-and-roll faves from the 1950s and '60s. The menu has true diner range—from vegetarian specialties to grilled cheese and half-pound burgers (including turkey). Other items are excellent soups, a monster chef salad, meat loaf and mashed potatoes, and a hot turkey sandwich. There's even a potato bar with one-pound taters and many toppings. Save room for a gigantic milk shake, malted, or float. ⊠ *534 E. Cooper Ave., Aspen,* ☎ *970/925–6610. AE, MC, V.*

$ ✕ **Charcuterie Cheese Market.** This take-out shop has dozens of hot and cold sandwich options, and a wide selection of fine cheeses. Feel free to mix and match ingredients and breads. The store also carries crackers, cookies, jams, and other food items to arm you for your picnic. The shop is near the base of Aspen Mountain, just east of the gondola. Hours are limited in the off-season. ⊠ *665 E. Cooper Ave., Aspen,* ☎ *970/925–8010. AE, MC, V. No dinner.*

$ ✕ **La Cocina.** For good inexpensive eats, follow the locals. They'll lead you to this small Mexican restaurant (although no one can explain the garlic bread that comes with every dish). You'll order by the number and receive some combination of beans, rice, chicken, tortilla, and chile verde. Almost every night the house is packed full. If the wait is too long, you'll likely cop a complimentary bean dip or margarita for your trouble. ⊠ *308 E. Hopkins Ave., Aspen,* ☎ *970/925–9714. Reservations not accepted. MC, V.*

SNOWMASS

$$$$ ✕ **Krabloonik.** Owner Dan MacEachen has a penchant for dogsled rac-
★ ing, and Krabloonik (Eskimo for "big eyebrows," and the name of his first lead dog) helps subsidize his expensive hobby. This cozy rustic-elegant cabin is on the slopes, and while you can drive there, the best—and most memorable—way to arrive is by the restaurant's dogsled. You'll dine sumptuously on some of the best game in Colorado, perhaps carpaccio of smoked caribou with lingonberry vinaigrette; elk loin with marsala and sun-dried cherry glaze; pheasant breast with Gorgonzola; or wild boar medallions with morel cream sauce. The western decor features dogsled memorabilia and throw rugs. ⊠ *4250 Divide Rd., Snowmass,* ☎ *970/923–3953. Reservations essential. AE, MC, V. Closed Apr.–Nov.*

$$–$$$$ ✕ **Butch's Lobster Bar.** Once a lobsterman off Cape Cod, Butch knows
★ his lobster and offers it up a dozen different ways, along with crab legs, shrimp, steamers, and the occasional steak. While the atmosphere and service are not fancy, it's the best place in town to get your seafood fix. ⊠ *Parking Lot 13, Snowmass,* ☎ *970/923–4004. AE, MC, V.*

$$–$$$$ ✕ **Il Poggio.** In the ultracompetitive resort town restaurant market, this fine eatery—possibly the best casual restaurant in the village—is smart enough not to take itself too seriously. Classic Italian food is served in a fun and lively atmosphere. Try the marinated chicken in a honey-spiced glaze, hearth-baked pizzas, and hearty pastas. ⊠ *73 Elbert La., Snowmass,* ☎ *970/923–4292. AE, DC, MC, V. No lunch.*

Lodging

ASPEN

$$$$ 🏠 **Aspen Club Lodge.** This refined, intimate ski-in hotel has a delight-
★ fully European flavor. The rooms are tastefully outfitted in rich mountain colors and desert pastels, with polished pine woodwork and beams. Amenities include hair dryers, minirefrigerators, and cable TV. Higher-priced rooms have French doors opening onto the patio or balcony, down comforters, and in-room data ports. The restaurant serves an excellent breakfast buffet; the bar is always happening; and the on-site ski shop makes hitting the slopes hassle-free. ⊠ *709 E. Durant Ave., Aspen 81611,* ☎ *970/925–6760 or 800/882–2582,* FAX *970/925–6778,* WEB *www. aspenclublodge.com. 84 rooms, 6 suites. Restaurant, bar, refrigerators, pool, hot tub, gym, ski shop, concierge, airport shuttle. AE, MC, V.*

$$$$ 🏠 **Hotel Jerome.** One of the state's truly grand hotels since 1889, this
★ solid, redbrick property is a treasure trove of Victoriana and froufrou. The sumptuous public rooms alone have five kinds of wallpaper, antler sconces, and more than $60,000 worth of rose damask curtains, as well as vintage furnishings, crystal chandeliers, intricate woodwork, and gold-laced floor tiling. Rooms in the original hotel face Aspen Mountain; those in the new portion face Independence Pass or the Red Mountains. All rooms are large, with high ceilings, oversize beds, antique armoires and chests, and huge bathtubs. A six-month advance reservation will get you big savings. The two on-site restaurants are held in high regard, and the J-Bar is downright legendary. ⊠ *330 E. Main St., Aspen 81611,* ☎ *970/920–1000 or 800/331–7213,* FAX *970/925–2784,* WEB *www.hoteljerome.com. 76 rooms, 16 suites. 2 restaurants, 2 bars, minibars, room service, pool, 2 outdoor hot tubs, gym, ski shop, meeting room, airport shuttle. AE, DC, MC, V.*

$$$$ 🏨 **Hotel Lenado.** If the Sardy House is full, head down the block to this equally sumptuous property under the same management. The focal point of this dramatic B&B is a very modern, 28-ft stone-and-concrete fireplace. The smallish but quaint rooms contain either intricate carved apple-wood or Adirondack ironwood beds (*lenado* is Spanish for wood, and the motif appears throughout the hotel), antique armoires, Ralph Lauren linens, even wood-burning stoves, in addition to modern amenities such as cable TV and tile baths. Rates include a full gourmet breakfast, served in the urbane bar area. ⊠ *200 S. Aspen St., Aspen 81611,* ☎ *970/925–6246 or 800/321–3457,* FAX *970/925–3840,* WEB *www.hotellenado.com. 19 rooms. Breakfast room, lobby lounge, hot tub. AE, DC, MC, V. BP.*

$$$$ 🏨 **Little Nell.** The Nell is the only truly ski-in, ski-out property in Aspen, ★ and that alone is worth something. Belgian wool carpets and large, overstuffed down couches surround the massive lobby fireplace. The luxurious rooms have a fireplace, one king-size or two queen-size beds with down comforters, a plush down couch and chair, and a large marble bathroom. Every conceivable amenity and comfort has been thought of, including patio, safe, cable TV, and minibar. Equally superior is the staff, who anticipate your every need. There's even a ski concierge to help guide your way. The unpretentious Montagna restaurant is worth a splurge (or save by ordering the prix fixe menu 6–6:30 PM), and the bar hosts one of Aspen's most fashionable après-ski scenes. ⊠ *675 E. Durant Ave., Aspen 81611,* ☎ *970/920–4600 or 888/843–6355,* FAX *970/ 920–4670,* WEB *www.thelittlenell.com. 77 rooms, 15 suites. 2 restaurants, bar, in-room safes, in-room VCRs, minibars, room service, pool, hot tub, health club, concierge, meeting rooms. AE, D, DC, MC, V.*

$$$$ 🏨 **St. Regis Aspen.** The property is a memorable one, even by Aspen's ★ exacting standards. The august reception area is comfortably furnished with overstuffed leather chairs, suede pillows, leather-topped tables, and rawhide lamp shades. The rooms follow suit with dark-wood furniture, muted colors, and Aspen photos, plus such signature touches as trademark "Heavenly" beds, fruit bowls, bottled water, and Bijan toiletries. The house restaurant is Olives, a venture of celebrity chef Todd English; Whiskey Rocks, a cousin to L.A.'s Sky Bar, is the chic place to imbibe. The property is ski-out, though not quite ski-in. ⊠ *315 E. Dean St., Aspen 81611,* ☎ *970/920–3300 or 888/454–9005,* FAX *970/925–8998,* WEB *www.stregisaspen.com. 231 rooms, 26 suites. Restaurant, bar, lobby lounge, pool, hair salon, indoor and outdoor hot tub, sauna, steam room, health club, ski shop, meeting room. AE, D, DC, MC, V.*

$$$$ 🏨 **Sardy House.** Its easy to imagine a prosperous family living within ★ this Victorian bordered by soaring evergreens. Past the tiny reception area, a narrow winding staircase with a magnificent oak balustrade leads to the elegant rooms, decorated with Axminster carpets from Belfast, cherry armoires and beds, wicker furniture, and such welcome touches as Laura Ashley bedclothes and duvets, and whirlpool tubs. The new wing scrupulously duplicates the authentic Victorian feel of the original house, and throughout, the atmosphere is that of a discreet inn rather than a homey B&B. The restaurant serves exquisite Continental cuisine, and the pool and patio, ringed by huge spruces, is especially inviting. ⊠ *128 E. Main St., Aspen 81611,* ☎ *970/920–2525 or 800/321– 3457,* FAX *970/920–4478,* WEB *www.sardyhouse.com. 14 rooms, 6 suites. Restaurant, pool, hot tub, sauna. AE, DC, MC, V. BP.*

$$–$$$$ 🏨 **Hotel Aspen.** With a location on Main Street, just a few minutes from the mall and the mountain, this hotel is a good find. The modern exterior is opened up with huge windows to take full advantage of the view; inside reveals a southwestern influence. Most rooms have a balcony or terrace and are comfortable, if not luxurious. Four guest rooms have hot tubs. Continental breakfast is included in the room rate, as is après-ski wine and cheese in winter. ✉ *110 W. Main St., Aspen 81611,* ☎ *970/925–3441 or 800/527–7369,* FAX *970/920–1379,* WEB *www.hotelaspen.com. 37 rooms, 8 suites. Pool, 2 hot tubs. AE, D, DC, MC, V. CP.*

$$–$$$ 🏨 **Limelite Lodge.** In the early 1950s this Aspen institution was a nightclub, but in 1958 it was converted to an inn by its present owners. Today it is a good value, particularly because of its prime location, just two blocks from the mall and three blocks from Lift 1A on Aspen Mountain. The guest rooms are furnished with brass or cherrywood beds and wooden furniture. All are accessible from the outside, motel style, which makes the lodge convenient for families. Nine apartments with full kitchens are available at the neighboring Deep Powder, an older ski lodge now owned by the Limelight; ask for one of the two log cabin-style units. ✉ *228 E. Cooper St., Aspen 81611,* ☎ *970/925–3025 or 800/433–0832,* FAX *970/ 925–5120,* WEB *www.limelitelodge.com. 63 rooms, 9 apartments. 2 outdoor pools, 2 outdoor hot tubs, sauna, ski storage. AE, D, DC, MC, V.*

$$–$$$ 🏨 **Skier's Chalet.** One of Aspen's best bargains, Skier's Chalet has been under the same ownership for half a century. The location—100 ft from the ticket office and Chairlift 1A—can't be beat for the price. Basic but snug rooms all have cable TV, private bath, and phone, and the staff and fellow clientele are unfailingly congenial. A complimentary Continental breakfast is served every morning, and the on-site steak house is an Aspen classic. ✉ *233 Gilbert St., Aspen 81611,* ☎ *970/920–2037,* FAX *970/920–6504. 16 rooms. Restaurant, pool. AE, MC, V. Closed late-Apr.–late-Nov. CP.*

$$–$$$ 🏨 **Snowflake Inn.** This motel has a prime downtown location, but the guest rooms, with rough-wood paneling and older furniture, are in need of a face-lift. Nevertheless, it could be an ideal choice for a family on a budget, as many of the rooms are actually suites. The rustic lobby with its stone fireplace and wood beams is a convivial gathering place for the complimentary Continental breakfast and afternoon tea. ✉ *221 E. Hyman Ave., Aspen 81611,* ☎ *970/925–3221 or 800/247–2069,* FAX *970/925–8740,* WEB *www.snowflakeinn.com. 14 rooms, 24 suites. Pool, hot tub, sauna. AE, D, DC, MC, V. CP.*

$$ 🏨 **Boomerang Lodge.** This comfortable, functional property offers a wide range of accommodations, from standard, somewhat drab hotel rooms to smartly appointed studios and deluxe rooms to three-bedroom apartments. There's even a log cabin. The nicest lodgings are the deluxe units, decorated in earth tones and with a southwestern flair, each with a balcony, an enormous marble bath, a fireplace, and a wet bar. The staff is most hospitable. Continental breakfast is included in the rate. ✉ *500 W. Hopkins Ave., Aspen 81611,* ☎ *970/925–3416 or 800/992–8852,* FAX *970/925–3314,* WEB *www.boomeranglodge.com. 32 rooms, 2 apartments. Breakfast room, pool, outdoor hot tub, sauna. AE, D, DC, MC, V. CP.*

SNOWMASS

$$–$$$$ 🏨 **Silvertree Hotel.** This ski-in, ski-out property, under the same management as the Wildwood Lodge next door, is actually built into Snowmass Mountain. It's sprawling, with virtually everything you need on-site. Rooms and suites feature subdued attractive decor, with all the expected amenities of a first-class hotel. Condominium units are also available, with full use of facilities. ✉ *100 Elbert La., Snowmass Village 81615,* ☎ *970/923–3520 or 800/525–9402,* FAX *970/923–5192,* WEB *www.silvertreehotel.com. 240 rooms, 8 suites. 2 restaurants, bar, 2 pools, outdoor hot tub, spa, health club, ski shop, meeting room. AE, D, DC, MC, V.*

$$$ 🏨 **Stonebridge Inn.** Slightly removed from the hustle and bustle of the
★ Village Mall, the Stonebridge is one of the nicer options in Snowmass.

The lobby and bar are streamlined and elegant; the window-ringed restaurant offers regional cuisine as well as outdoor dining in summer. Rooms, all with two queen beds, are not fancy but comfortably appointed and up-to-date. A Continental breakfast is included in winter. The Stonebridge also rents out the adjacent two- and four-bedroom Tamarack Townhouses. ⊠ *300 Carriage Way, Snowmass Village 81615,* ☎ *970/923–2420 or 800/922–7242,* ℻ *970/923–5889,* 🖥 *www.stonebridgeinn.com. 87 rooms, 5 suites. Restaurant, bar, pool, outdoor hot tub, sauna, meeting rooms. AE, D, DC, MC, V.*

CONDOMINIUMS

Aspen Central Reservations (☎ 800/262–7736). **Aspen Alps Condominium Association** (⊠ 700 Ute Ave., Aspen 81611, ☎ 970/925–7820 or 800/228–7820, ℻ 970/920–2528). **Coates, Reid & Waldron** (⊠ 720 E. Hyman Ave., Aspen 81611, ☎ 970/925–1400 or 800/222–7736, ℻ 970/920–3765). **Destination Resort Management** (⊠ 610 W. End St., Aspen 81611, ☎ 970/925–5000 or 800/345–1471, ℻ 970/925–6891). **Frias Properties** (⊠ 730 E. Durant Ave., Aspen 81611, ☎ 970/920–2010 or 800/633–0336, ℻ 970/920–2020). **McCartney Property Management** (⊠ 421-G Aspen Airport Business Center, Aspen 81611, ☎ 970/925–8717 or 800/433–8465, ℻ 970/920–4770).

Snowmass Central Reservations (☎ 800/766–9627). **Snowmass Lodging Company** (⊠ Box 6077, Snowmass Village 81615, ☎ 970/923–3232 or 800/365–0410, ℻ 970/923–5740). **Village Property Management** (⊠ Box 5009, Snowmass Village 81615, ☎ 970/923–4350, ℻ 970/923–5192).

Nightlife and the Arts

The **Aspen Music Festival and School** (☎ 970/925–3254), featuring chamber music to jazz, runs late-June–September. **Jazz Aspen Snowmass** (☎ 970/920–4996) has a June festival and a Labor Day festival, and also sponsors free Thursday-night concerts on Fanny Hill in Snowmass during the summer. Aspen's **Wheeler Opera House** (⊠ 320 E. Hyman Ave., ☎ 970/925–5770) is the venue for big-name classical, jazz, pop, and opera groups, especially in summer.

BARS AND LOUNGES

East Hyman Avenue has a cluster of three nightspots at the same address. Whiskey is the claim to fame of **Eric's Bar** (⊠ 315 E. Hyman Ave., Aspen, ☎ 970/920–6707), a happening little watering hole where you can also find a varied lineup of imported beers on tap. **Cigar Bar** (⊠ 315 E. Hyman Ave., Aspen, ☎ 970/920–4244) is a smoky scene straight from the movies, with overstuffed chairs and sofas, velvet curtains and a dimly lit bar area. **Aspen Billiards** (⊠ 315 E. Hyman Ave., Aspen, ☎ 970/920–6707) is the town's decidedly upscale pool hall.

Tourists now outnumber locals at the **'J' Bar** (⊠ Hotel Jerome, 330 E. Main St., Aspen, ☎ 970/920–1000), but it's still a fun, lively spot and a necessary Aspen experience. For the real thrills (in other words, star-gazing), head to **Whiskey Rocks** (⊠ St. Regis Aspen, 315 Dean St., Aspen, ☎ 970/920–3300).

By its own admission, the **Woody Creek Tavern** (⊠ Woody Creek Plaza, Woody Creek, ☎ 970/923–4585) "has no redeeming features." This may be true, except that it's a great hangout, with a grungy atmosphere, assorted bar games, and notable visitors such as Don Johnson and Hunter S. Thompson.

CABARET

The **Crystal Palace** (⊠ 300 E. Hyman Ave., Aspen, ☎ 970/925–1455) is an Aspen fixture, offering two seatings nightly with fine food and a fiercely funny, up-to-the-minute satirical revue. The **Tower** (✉ Snowmass Mall, Snowmass, ☎ 970/923–4650) hosts hokey but hilarious magic and juggling acts.

MUSIC AND DANCE CLUBS

Thirtysomethings who act like twentysomethings come to **Double Diamond** (✉ 450 S. Galena St., Aspen, ☎ 970/920–6905) for high-energy cruising and dancing to either live entertainment or a DJ. For late-night music, check out **The Grottos** (✉ 320 S. Mill St., Aspen, ☎ 970/925–3775). Live music, and the real twentysomethings, can be found at **Hannibal Brown's** (✉ 424 E. Cooper Ave., Aspen, ☎ 970/920–4004). Jazz entertains at the cozy, but crowded bar at the **Little Nell** (✉ 675 E. Durant Ave., Aspen, ☎ 970/920–4600). **Shooters Saloon** (✉ Galena and Hopkins Sts., Aspen, ☎ 970/925–4567) is the only place in town to get your country-and-western fix. For late-night jazz of truly astounding quality, head to **Syzygy** (✉ 520 E. Hyman Ave., Aspen, ☎ 970/925–3700). **The Tippler** (✉ 535 E. Dean St., Aspen, ☎ 970/925–4977) has been affectionately nicknamed "The Crippler," because happy customers stagger out after such legendary occasions as Tuesday Disco nights, for which fans dress in their best polyester. The Tippler attracts slightly older partiers who don't want young bloods cutting in on their action.

Outdoor Activities and Sports

Aspen Center for Environmental Studies (✉ Hallam Lake Wildlife Sanctuary, 100 Puppy Smith St., Aspen, ☎ 970/925–5756) is a research center and wildlife sanctuary where children and adults alike can take refuge. The facility sponsors snowshoe walks with naturalist guides in winter, and backyard-wildlife workshops that teach children to create a minisanctuary in their own yard. In summer there are bird-watching hikes and Special Little Naturalist programs for four- to seven-year-olds, which include nature walks and arts and crafts.

Aspen is equally popular in summer, with hiking and biking throughout the **White River National Forest.** A favorite jaunt through the forest is to the majestic **Maroon Bells,** twin peaks more than 14,000 ft high, so colorful, thanks to mineral streaking, you'd swear they were blanketed with primrose and Indian paintbrush. It's one of the most photographed spots in the state. Cars are allowed only partway, but the Roaring Fork Transit Agency provides shuttle buses that leave regularly in the summer from the Rubey Park Transportation Center in downtown Aspen.

CYCLING

Blazing Pedals (✉ Aspen, ☎ 970/923–4544, or 800/282–7238) offers downhill bicycle tours through Aspen and the countryside. **The Hub of Aspen** (✉ 315 E. Hyman Ave., ☎ 970/925–7970) rents bicycles and offers mountain biking lessons through the Aspen Cycling School.

DOGSLEDDING

Krabloonik (✉ 4250 Divide Rd., Snowmass, ☎ 970/923–3953), with about 200 dogs at its disposal, can put on a good half-day ride (beginning at 8:30 AM or 12:30 PM). The ride can be preceded or followed by lunch or dinner at the Krabloonik restaurant, among the best in the area.

FISHING

Aspen Sports (✉ 303 E. Durant Ave., Aspen, ☎ 970/925–6332) runs fly-fishing tours of local waterways. In Snowmass, **The Outfitters** (✉ Snowmass Village Mall,, ☎ 970/923–5959) offers equipment rentals and guided tours.

Aspen Athletic Club (⊠ 720 E. Hyman Ave., ☎ 970/925–2531) is fully equipped, and includes a steam room, tanning salon, and massage therapy. The upscale **Aspen Club & Spa** (⊠ 1450 Crystal Lake Rd., ☎ 970/925–8900) has weight-training and cardiovascular equipment, as well as indoor alpine skiing, squash, pools, basketball, a children's playland, and a deluxe, full-service spa.

GOLFING
The Aspen Golf Course (⊠ 39551 Hwy. 82, ☎ 970/925–2145) is a fine municipal course, with 18 holes, a driving range, and pro shop. Drive 30 minutes downvalley to play the new, and stunning, **River Valley Ranch Golf Course** (⊠ 303 River Valley Ranch Dr., ☎ 970/963–0132). **Snowmass Club Golf Course** (⊠ 239 Snowmass Village Circle, ☎ 970/923–3148) is an 18-hole, 6,900-yard championship course designed by Arnold Palmer and Ed Seay.

HORSEBACK RIDING
For day or overnight horseback tours, try **T Lazy Seven Ranch** (☎ 970/925–4614), which offers snowmobiling in the winter.

RAFTING
Blazing Paddles (☎ 970/923–4544 or 800/282–7238) runs trips to various rivers and canyons in the area and beyond. **Colorado Riff Raft** (☎ 970/925–5405 or 800/759–3939) operates mild to wild excursions on the Shoshone, Upper Roaring Fork, and lower Colorado.

Downhill Skiing and Snowboarding

Aspen and Snowmass are really four ski areas rolled into one resort. Aspen Highlands, Aspen (or Ajax) Mountain, Buttermilk, and Snowmass can all be skied with the same ticket.

Aspen Highlands is essentially a long, long ridge with trails dropping off to either side. Over the past few years, the antiquated lift system has been replaced by three high-speed quads, and a massive base-area village has risen from the ground, turning the "maverick" ski hill into a destination in and of itself. Although not quite as hairy as Aspen Mountain, the Highlands offers thrilling descents at Steeplechase, Olympic Bowl, and now, Highland Bowl, a hike-in, off-piste experience unlike any in Colorado. The steep and often bumpy cluster of trails and small bowls of Steeplechase and Highland Bowl make it one of the best places to be in the Aspen area on a powder day. For intermediates, Highlands offers up a wide-open bowl called Thunder, and plenty of lower-mountain blue runs. A big Highlands bonus besides the comparatively short lift lines and some heart-pounding runs is the summit: the panorama of the Maroon Bells and Pyramid Peak is one of the most dramatic views among the four area mountains and anywhere in American skiing. ⊠ *Off Maroon Creek Rd.,* ☎ *970/925–1220 or 800/525–6200,* WEB *www.skiaspen.com.* ☻ *Early Dec.–early Apr., daily 9–4.*

Aspen Mountain (Ajax) is considered a mogul skier's dreamland. Bell Mountain provides some of the best bump skiing anywhere, followed by Walsh's, Hyrup's, and Kristi's. Those wanting cruisers ski the ridge tops or valleys: Ruthie's Run, Buckhorn, and International are the classics. This is a resort where 65% of the trails are rated advanced or expert, and there are no novice runs. A black diamond here might rank as a double diamond elsewhere. The narrow mountain is laid out as a series of steep unforgiving ridges with little room for error. Most Aspen Mountain skiers spend much of their time on intermediate trails off the upper-mountain quad. They also spend their lunchtime on the deck of Bonnie's, the mid-mountain restaurant, which on a sunny day is one of the great people-watching scenes in the world of skiing. After a big snowstorm, there's also Sno-Cat–assisted powder skiing off the back side of the mountain. Aspen Mountain's biggest drawback is that too many trails funnel into Spar Gulch, making the end-of-the-day rush to the bottom chaotic and often dangerous—a situation that might become more hairy as Ajax is no longer snowboard-free. ⊠ *Durant St. in downtown Aspen,* ☎ *970/925–1220 or 800/525–6200,* WEB *www.skiaspen.com.* ⊗ *Late Nov.–mid-Apr., daily 9–4.*

Buttermilk—a place where it is virtually impossible to get into trouble—is terrific for lower intermediates and children. It's a low-key, lighthearted sort of place, an antidote to the kind of skiing machismo you might encounter at Aspen Mountain. Among its featured attractions is a hangout for children named Ft. Frog. The Tiehack section on the east contains several advanced runs (though nothing truly expert), as well as sweeping views of Maroon Creek Valley. It also has superb powder, and deep snow sticks around longer because so few serious skiers realize what they're missing. If you're looking for an escape from the Aspen bustle, spend a day at Buttermilk. ⊠ *Off Rte. 82, accessed by West Buttermilk Rd.,* ☎ *970/925–1220 or 800/525–6200,* WEB *www.skiaspen.com.* ⊗ *Late Nov.–early Apr., daily 9–4.*

Snowmass is a huge sprawl of a ski area, best known for Big Burn, itself a great sprawl of wide-open, intermediate skiing. Snowmass is Aspen Skiing Company's family resort, with 55% of its 3,010 skiable acres designated intermediate, including the renowned classic cruiser runs off Big Burn lift, the stuff of ego massage. However, don't overlook that Snowmass is four times the size of Aspen Mountain, and has triple the black and double black diamond terrain of its famed sister, including several fearsomely precipitous gullies and Hanging Valley, accessible by a short hike. In general, Snowmass is one of the best ski areas in the Rockies for intermediates. The route variations down Big Burn are essentially inexhaustible, and there are many, many other places on the mountain for intermediates to find entertainment. Although only 38% of the terrain is rated advanced or expert, this is a huge mountain, with enough black runs in the Hanging Valley and Cirque areas to satisfy all but the most demanding skier. The novice and lower-intermediate terrain on the lower part of the mountain makes Snowmass a terrific place for young children. ⊠ *Via Brush Creek Rd.,* ☎ *970/925–1220 or 800/525–6200,* WEB *www.skiaspen.com.* ⊗ *Late-Nov.–mid-Apr., daily 9–4.*

FACILITIES

Aspen Highlands: 3,635-ft vertical drop; 680 skiable acres; 20% beginner, 33% intermediate, 47% advanced; 3 high-speed quad chairs, 1 triple chair. **Aspen Mountain:** 3,267-ft vertical drop; 675 skiable acres; 35% intermediate, 35% advanced, 30% expert; one 6-passenger gondola, 1 high-speed quad chair, 2 quad chairs, 1 high-speed double chair, 3 double chairs. **Buttermilk:** 2,030-ft vertical drop; 420 skiable acres; 35% beginner, 39% intermediate, 26% advanced; 1 high-speed quad chair, 5 double chairs, 1 surface lift. **Snowmass:** 4,406-ft vertical drop; 3,010 skiable acres; 7% beginner, 55% intermediate, 18% advanced, 20% expert; 20 lifts.

LESSONS AND PROGRAMS

The **Aspen Skiing Company** (☎ 970/925–1220 or 800/525–6200) gives lessons at all four mountains: half-day group lessons start at $62 (a private half-day lesson will cost you $309), but a noteworthy deal is the three-day guaranteed learn-to-ski or learn-to-snowboard package at Buttermilk, which includes lessons and lift tickets for $249. The company also runs Sno-Cat trips on Aspen Mountain.

Aspen Mountain Powder Tours (☎ 970/925–1220 ext. 3549) provides access to 1,500 acres on the back side of Aspen Mountain via Sno-Cat tours. Most of the terrain is negotiable by confident intermediates, with about 10,000 vertical ft constituting a typical day's skiing. Reservations are required at least a day in advance, but you should book as far in advance as possible during the season. Tours cost $275.

LIFT TICKETS
Lift tickets are $65, but almost nobody pays full price thanks to multiday savings, early- and late-season specials, and pre-purchase discounts.

RENTALS
Numerous ski shops in Aspen and Snowmass rent equipment. Rental packages (skis, boots, and poles) start at around $16 per day; snowboard packages (boots and boards) run about $25. Bargain shopping at stores around town may turn up lower-priced deals. **Aspen Sports** (☎ 970/925–6331 or 970/923–6111) has numerous locations in Aspen and Snowmass. **Pomeroy Sports** (☎ 970/925–7875) at the Aspen Mountain gondola base is conveniently located. Rentals are also available at Aspen Skiing Company–owned shops at the Buttermilk and Aspen Highlands' base lodges.

Nordic Skiing
BACKCOUNTRY SKIING
The **Alfred A. Braun Hut System** is one of Aspen's major backcountry networks. The trailhead leads from the Ashcroft Ski Touring Center into the Maroon Bells/Snowmass Wilderness, and it generally covers terrain more prone to avalanche possibilities than the 10th Mountain Division Trail. Huts sleep seven to 14 people. Huts are open in winter only, and reservations can be made beginning May 1. ✉ *Box 7937, Aspen 81612,* ☎ *970/925–5775.* ⚏ *Hut fees vary from $17.50 to $25 per person per night.*

The **10th Mountain Hut and Trail System,** named in honor of the U.S. Army's skiing 10th Mountain Division, includes 10 huts along the trail connecting Aspen and Vail. The main trail follows a generally avalanche-safe route in altitudes that vary between 8,000 ft and 12,000 ft. This translates to a fair amount of skiing along tree-lined trails and a good bit of high-alpine up and down. You must be in good shape, and some backcountry skiing experience is extremely helpful. The accommodations along the trail are the Hiltons of backcountry huts, supplied with precut wood for wood-burning stoves, mattresses and pillows, and propane stoves and utensils for cooking. Huts sleeps from six to 16 people (more if you're willing to cuddle). Reservations are taken beginning in June; weekends in peak ski season fill up very quickly. ✉ *1280 Ute Ave., Aspen 81611,* ☎ *970/925–5775.* ⚏ *Hut fees range from $22 to $35 per person per night.*

If you're either unfamiliar with the hut system or inexperienced in backcountry travel, you should hire a guide. One reliable recommendation is **Aspen Alpine Guides** (✉ Box 5122, Aspen 81612, ☎ 970/925–6618 or 800/643–8621). **Paragon Guides** (✉ Edwards, ☎ 970/926–5299) arranges tours along the 10th Mountain hut system. In Aspen, the best store for backcountry-gear rentals (including ski equipment, climbing skins, packs, sleeping bags, and mountaineering paraphernalia) is the **Ute Mountaineer** (✉ 308 S. Mill St., ☎ 970/925–2849).

TRACK SKIING
There is something to be said for a wealthy tax base. Subsidized by local taxes (in most towns, public cross-country ski trails would be considered a fiscal extravagance), the **Aspen/Snowmass Nordic Council** (☎ 970/544–9246) charges no fee for the 80 km (48 mi) of maintained

trails (not all interconnected) in the Roaring Fork Valley. Probably the most varied, in terms of scenery and terrain, is the 30-km (18-mi) Snowmass Club trail network. For a longer ski, try the Owl Creek Trail, connecting the Snowmass Club trail system and the Aspen Cross-Country Center trails. More than 16 km (10 mi) long, the trail provides both a good workout and a heavy dosage of woodsy beauty, with many ups and downs across meadows and aspen-gladed hillsides.

Lessons and rentals are available at the **Aspen Cross-Country Center** (⊠ 39551 Rte. 82, at the Aspen Golf Course, ☎ 970/544–9246). Diagonal, skating, racing, and light-touring setups are available. Lessons and rentals are available at the **Snowmass Lodge Cross-Country Touring Center** (⊠ Drawer G-2, Snowmass Village, ☎ 970/923–3148).

Twelve miles from Aspen, the **Ashcroft Ski Touring Center** (⊠ Ashcroft Touring Unlimited, Castle Creek Rd., ☎ 970/925–1971) is sequestered in a high alpine basin up Castle Creek, which runs between Aspen Mountain and Aspen Highlands. The 40 km (25 mi) of groomed trails are surrounded by the high peaks of the Maroon Bells/Snowmass Wilderness. It is truly one of the most dramatic cross-country sites in the Rockies.

Shopping

Downtown Aspen is an eye-popping display of conspicuous consumption. For a eclectic mix of glitz and glamour, T-shirts and trinkets, stroll down Cooper Street. For ultrachic boutiques, check out the **Brand Building** (⊠ Hopkins Ave. between Mill and Galena Sts.), home to Gucci, Louis Vuitton (which shares space with Christian Dior), and Cashmere Aspen, among others. For touristy items, you're best bet is the **Hyman Avenue Mall** (⊠ Hyman Ave. between Mill and Galena Sts.).

ANTIQUES DEALERS

Fetzer Antiques (⊠ 113 Aspen Airport Business Center, ☎ 970/925–5447) carries Aspen's finest antiques, and specializes in 18th- and 19th-century English and Continental goods. **Little Bear Antiques and Uniques** (⊠ 415 Spring St., ☎ 970/925–3750) is jam-packed with European and American antique furniture and accessories.

ART GALLERIES

Anderson Ranch Arts Center (⊠ Snowmass Village, ☎ 970/923–3181) sells the work of resident artists. **Baldwin Gallery** (⊠ 209 S. Galena St., Aspen, ☎ 970/920–9797) is the place to see and be seen at artist receptions. **Hill Gallery of Photography** (⊠ 312 E. Hyman St., Aspen, ☎ 970/925–1836) captures nature's artistry in works by leading American photographers. **Joel Soroka Gallery** (⊠ 400 E. Hyman Ave., Aspen, ☎ 970/920–3152) specializes in rare photos. **Magidson Fine Art** (⊠ 525 E. Cooper Ave., Aspen, ☎ 970/920–1001) is known for its well-rounded collection of contemporary art.

BOUTIQUES

In Aspen, **Boogie's** (⊠ 534 E. Cooper Ave., ☎ 970/925–6111) sells kitschy clothes and jewelry; you can grab a bite in its diner, too. **Chepita's** (⊠ 525 E. Cooper Ave., ☎ 970/925–2871) calls itself a "toy store for adults," and the whimsy continues with kinetic clothing and wood-carved sartorially resplendent pigs, to complement the standard designer watches and jewelry. **Funky Mountain Threads** (⊠ 520 E. Durant Ave., ☎ 970/925–4665) offers just that: ethnic clothes, festive hats, extravagant beadwork, and imaginative jewelry. **Geraniums 'n Sunshine** (⊠ 208 E. Main St., ☎ 970/925–6641) has a delightful display of children's toys and wearable art, as well as colorful gifts for grown-ups. **Gracy's** (⊠ 517 E. Hopkins Ave., ☎ 970/925–5131) has first-class secondhand clothing. **Scandinavian Designs** (⊠ 607 E. Cooper Ave.,

☎ 970/925–7299) features some of Aspen's finest hand-knit sweaters, as well as everything Scandinavian from Swedish clogs to Norwegian trolls.

CRAFTS

Aspen Potters (✉ 231 E. Main St., ☎ 970/925–8726) sells the latest designs from local artisans. **Heather Gallery** (✉ 555 E. Durant Ave., Aspen, ☎ 970/925–6170) features an enchanting mix of merchandise, including Janna Ungone's hand-painted lamp shades and popular pet clocks handmade by an Aspen local. To create your own art, visit the **Kolor Wheel** (✉ 720 E. Durant Ave., Aspen, ☎ 970/544–6191), a paint-it-yourself pottery studio. In Snowmass, **Quilts Unlimited** (✉ Silvertree Plaza Mall, 100 Elbert La., Snowmass, ☎ 970/923–5467) sells superb handmade antique and contemporary quilts, as well as various regional handicrafts.

SPORTING GOODS

Aspen Sports (✉ 408 E. Cooper Ave., ☎ 970/925–6331; ✉ 303 E. Durant Ave., ☎ 970/925–6332; ✉ Snowmass Mall, ☎ 970/923–6111; ✉ Snowmass Center, ☎ 970/923–3566; ✉ Silvertree Hotel, ☎ 970/923–6504) is the biggest store around, with a full line of apparel and equipment for all sports.

I–70 and the High Rockies A to Z

AIRPORTS

Aspen Airport is served daily by United Express, America West Express/Mesa, Northwest Express/Mesaba, and has nonstop United service to Los Angeles in ski season. American, Continental, Northwest, TWA, and United Express fly nonstop from various gateways during ski season to Steamboat Springs' Yampa Valley Airport. The Vail Valley is served by Eagle County Airport, 35 mi west of Vail. During ski season, American, Continental, Delta, United, and Northwest offer nonstop flights from several gateways. United is the only airline that flies year-round.

Most of the I–70 corridor, however, is served via Denver and its airports. This used to be the surer choice because flying into the smaller airports in winter was always iffy, but with jets making nonstop flights to many of those smaller airports now, the decision of which airport to use depends more on where you're coming from and which flights are convenient. There's an extensive list of Denver-based companies that specialize in transportation to the mountain resorts.

➤ AIRPORT INFORMATION: **Aspen Airport** (☎ 970/920–5385). **Denver International Airport** (☎ 800/247–2336). **Eagle County Airport** (☎ 970/524–9490). **Yampa Valley Airport** (☎ 970/276–3669).

AIRPORT SHUTTLES AND TAXIS

To and from Aspen and Snowmass Village, use Roaring Fork Transit Agency, which provides bus service from Aspen Airport to the Rubey Park bus station. Also, Colorado Mountain Express connects Aspen with Denver, Grand Junction, and the Eagle County airport. High Mountain Taxi will also provide charter service outside the Roaring Fork Valley.

To and from Summit County (Breckenridge, Copper Mountain, Dillon, Frisco, Keystone), use Resort Express or Colorado Mountain Express, which have regular service to and from Denver airports. Rainbow Taxi provides local service in Summit County.

To and from Steamboat Springs, take Alpine Taxi or Steamboat Taxi, which offer service from the airport, as well as special rates to Vail, Boulder, and Denver.

To and from Vail and Beaver Creek, try Colorado Mountain Express, or Vail Valley Taxi.

Home James Transportation and Greyhound serves Winter Park from Denver.

➤ SHUTTLE INFORMATION: **Alpine Taxi** (☎ 970/879–2800). **Colorado Mountain Express** (☎ 970/949–4227 or 800/525–6353). **Greyhound Lines** (☎ 800/231–2222). **High Mountain Taxi** (☎ 970/925–8294 or 800/528–8294). **Home James Transportation** (☎ 970/726–5060 or 800/451–4844). **Resort Express** (☎ 970/468–7600 or 800/334–7433). **Rainbow Taxi** (☎ 970/453–8294). **Roaring Fork Transit Agency** (☎ 970/925–8484). **Steamboat Taxi** (☎ 970/879–3335). **Vail Valley Taxi** (☎ 970/476–8294 or 800/882–8872).

BUS AND RESORT SHUTTLE TRAVEL

Greyhound Lines offers regular service from Denver to several towns along I–70. The company also runs intercity bus service. The resort areas offer free or inexpensive shuttles within the town proper, between the town and the slopes, and within Summit County, between ski areas.

➤ ASPEN/SNOWMASS INFORMATION: **Roaring Fork Transit Agency** (☎ 970/925–8484).

➤ STEAMBOAT SPRINGS INFORMATION: **Steamboat Springs Transit** (☎ 970/879–5585).

➤ SUMMIT COUNTY INFORMATION: **Breckenridge Free Shuttle and Trolley** (☎ 970/547–3140). **KAB Express** (☎ 970/468–4200). **Keystone Resort Shuttle Service** (☎ 970/468–2316). **Summit Stage** (☎ 970/668–0999).

➤ VAIL/BEAVER CREEK INFORMATION: **Avon Beaver Creek Transit** (☎ 970/748–4120). **Beaver Creek Dial-A-Ride** (☎ 970/949–1938). **Resort Express** (☎ 970/468–7600). **Town of Vail** (☎ 970/479–2100).

➤ WINTER PARK INFORMATION: **Winter Park Lift** (☎ 970/726–4163).

CAR TRAVEL

All major sights in this tour are either on I–70, which bisects the state east to west, or on clearly marked side routes. I–70 is a fast, convenient superhighway that is remarkably well maintained (the speed limit is 75 mph in many places). Idaho Springs, Summit County, the Vail Valley, and Glenwood Springs are all on I–70. Winter Park is north of I–70, on U.S. 40, which has several hairpin turns (Berthoud Pass on U.S. 40 can be treacherous when winter storms blow in). Leadville and Ski Cooper are south of I–70 along U.S. 24 or Route 91.

Generally speaking, driving to Aspen from Denver in the winter is more trouble than it's worth, unless you are on an extended vacation and plan to stop at other resorts such as Vail. With Independence Pass (Route 82) closed in the winter, the drive west on I–70 and east on Route 82 takes more than three hours at best, depending on road and weather conditions. On the other hand, the drive from the west is relatively easy, with no high-mountain passes to negotiate. Take the Route 82 exit off I–70 at Glenwood Springs.

Steamboat Springs is about a three-hour drive from Denver via I–70 west and U.S. 40 north. The route traverses high-mountain passes, so it's a good idea to check road conditions before you travel.

ROAD CONDITIONS

➤ CONTACTS: **Road Condition Information: Colorado Road Condition Hotline** (☎ 303/639–1111 within a 2-hr drive of Denver; 303/639–1234 statewide).

EMERGENCIES

➤ CONTACTS: **Aspen/Snowmass: Aspen Valley Hospital** (✉ 0401 Castle Creek Rd., ☎ 970/925–1120). **Glenwood Springs: Valley View Hospital** (✉ 1906 Blake St., ☎ 970/945–6535). **Steamboat Springs: Routt Memorial Hospital** (✉ 1024 Central Dr., Steamboat Springs, ☎ 970/879–1322). **Summit County: Summit Medical Center** (✉ Rte. 9 and School Rd., Frisco, ☎ 970/668–3300). **Vail Valley: Beaver Creek Village Medical Center** (✉ 1280 Village Rd., Beaver Creek, ☎ 970/949–0800). **Vail Valley Medical Center** (✉ 181 W. Meadow Dr., Vail, ☎ 970/476–2452). **Winter Park: Seven Mile Medical Center** (✉ Base of Winter Park ski area, Winter Park, ☎ 970/726–8066).

TOURS

A romantic way to orient yourself to the Aspen backcountry is by taking the T Lazy Seven Ranch private sleigh ride. Aspen Carriage Co. offers stagecoach tours around downtown and the historic West End. In summer and through mid-October, narrated bus tours from Aspen to the Maroon Bells are available. The Summit Historical Society offers lively 1½-hour tours of downtown Breckenridge, Colorado's largest National Historic District, Monday–Saturday at 10 AM. Several tour companies include Idaho Springs on their itineraries, and the Idaho Springs Visitor Information Center can supply information. Steamboat's Sweet Pea Tours visits nearby hot springs. Vail's Nova Guides offers Jeep and ATV (all-terrain vehicle) tours, as well as rafting, fishing, snowmobiling, and hiking expeditions. Mad Adventures offers Continental Divide van tours from Winter Park. If rafting is your choice, Mad Adventures can help you shoot the rapids of the North Platte, Colorado, and Arkansas rivers. Timberline Tours runs rafting trips and Jeep tours, throughout the region.

➤ CONTACTS: **Aspen Carriage Co.** (☎ 970/925–3394). **Idaho Springs Visitor Information Center** (✉ 2060 Miner St., ☎ 303/567–4709). **Mad Adventures** (✉ Winter Park, ☎ 970/726–5290 or 800/451–4844). **Maroon Bells Bus Tour** (✉ Aspen, ☎ 970/925–8484). **Nova Guides** (✉ Vail, ☎ 970/949–4232). **Summit Historical Society** (☎ 970/453–9022). **Sweet Pea Tours** (✉ Steamboat Springs, ☎ 970/879–5820). **T Lazy Seven Ranch** (✉ Aspen, ☎ 970/925–4614). **Timberline Tours** (✉ Vail, ☎ 970/476–1414).

TRAIN TRAVEL

Amtrak offers service from Denver's Union Station to the Winter Park Ski Area station in nearby Fraser (where shuttles to the area are available). Glenwood Springs is on the *California Zephyr* route.

The nonstop Ski Train leaves Denver's Union Station every Saturday and Sunday morning, chugging through 29 tunnels before depositing passengers only 50 yards from Winter Park's lifts.

➤ TRAIN INFORMATION: **Amtrak** (☎ 970/726–5587 or 800/872–7245). **Ski Train** (☎ 303/296–4754).

VISITOR INFORMATION

There are Tourist Information Centers in the downtown areas of every resort. Ask any local how to find them.

➤ SNOW REPORTS: ☎ 800/525–6200 for Aspen; 800/789–7669 for Breckenridge; 800/789–7609 or 970/968–2100 for Copper Mountain; 970/468–2316 for Keystone; 970/879–7300 for Steamboat Springs; 970/476–4888 for Vail; 970/726–7669 for Winter Park

➤ TOURIST INFORMATION: **Aspen Chamber Resort Association** (✉ 425 Rio Grande Pl., 81611, ☎ 970/925–1940 or 800/262–7736, WEB aspenchamber.org). **Breckenridge Resort Chamber** (✉ 309 N. Main St., 80424, ☎ 970/453–6018, WEB gobreck.com). **Copper Mountain Re-**

sort (✉ Box 3001, Copper Mountain 80443, ☎ 800/458–8386 or 970/968–2882, WEB ski-copper.com). **Glenwood Springs Chamber Resort Association** (✉ 806 Cooper Ave., 81601, ☎ 970/945–6589 or 800/221–0098, WEB glenwoodchamber.com). **Keystone Resort** (✉ Box 38, Keystone 80435, ☎ 970/468–2316, WEB keystoneresort.com). **Leadville Chamber of Commerce** (✉ 809 Harrison St., 80461, ☎ 719/486–3900, WEB leadvilleusa.com). **Steamboat Ski & Resort Corporation** (✉ 2305 Mt. Werner Circle, Steamboat Springs 80487, ☎ 970/879–6111, WEB steamboat.com). **Steamboat Springs Chamber Resort Association** (✉ 1255 S. Lincoln Ave., 80477, ☎ 970/879–0880 or 800/922–2722, WEB steamboatchamber.com). **Summit County Chamber of Commerce** (✉ Main St., Frisco 80443, ☎ 970/668–5000 or 800/530–3099, WEB summitchamber.org). **Vail Resorts, Inc.** (✉ Box 7, Vail 81658, ☎ 970/476–5601, WEB vail.com). **Vail Valley Tourism and Convention Bureau** (✉ 100 E. Meadow Dr., Vail 81658, ☎ 970/476–1000 or 800/824–5737, WEB visitvailvalley.com). **Winter Park Resort** (✉ Box 36, Winter Park 80482, ☎ 970/726–5514, WEB winterparkresort.com). **Winter Park/Fraser Valley Chamber of Commerce** (✉ Box 3236, Winter Park 80482, ☎ 970/726–4118 or 800/903–7275, WEB winterpark-info.com).

SOUTHWEST COLORADO

Updated by
Sharon
Niederman

"Colorado" is a Spanish word meaning ruddy or colorful—adjectives that clearly describe many regions of the state, but particularly the Southwest. The terrain varies widely—from yawning black canyons and desolate monochrome moonscapes to pastel deserts and mesas, glistening sapphire lakes, and 14,000-ft mountains. It's so rugged in the Southwest that a four-wheel-drive vehicle is necessary to explore the wild and beautiful backcountry. The mostly paved Alpine Loop Scenic Byway joins Lake City with Ouray and Silverton, shimmying through some stunning scenery.

The region's history and people are as colorful as the landscape, from the mysterious ancestral Puebloan peoples (formerly known as Anasazi, meaning "ancient ones"), who constructed impressive cliff dwellings in Mesa Verde National Park to such notorious outlaws as Butch Cassidy, who embarked on his storied career by robbing the Telluride Bank in 1889. Even today, the more ornery, independent locals, disgusted with the political system, periodically talk of seceding. They can be as rough as the country they inhabit.

Southwest Colorado offers such diversity that, depending on where you go, you can have radically different vacations, even during the same season. You can spiral from the towering peaks of the San Juan range to the plunging Black Canyon of the Gunnison, taking in alpine scenery along the way, as well as the eerie remains of old mining camps, before winding through striking desert landscapes, the superlative ancestral Puebloan ruins, and the Old West railroad town of Durango. If you're not here to ski or golf the world-class resorts of Crested Butte, Purgatory, or Telluride (or even if you are), there is much to experience in this part of the state.

Crested Butte

㊴ *90 mi from Glenwood Springs via Rtes. 82 and 133 south and Rte. 135 east (over Kebler Pass, summer only); 110 mi from Aspen via Rte. 82 north, Rte. 133 south, and Rte. 135 (summer only); 190 mi from Glenwood Springs, south via Rtes. 82 and 133 south, Rte. 92 south, U.S. 50 west, and Rte. 135 north; 210 mi from Aspen via Rte. 82 north, south on Rte. 133 south, Rte. 92 south, U.S. 50 west, and Rte. 135 north.*

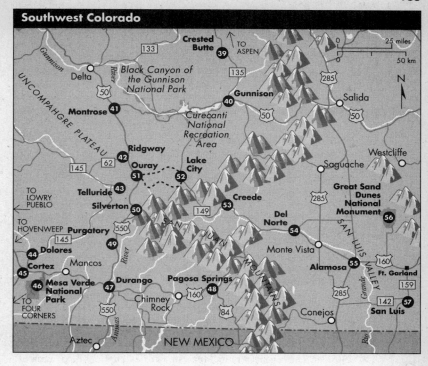

Crested Butte is literally just over the mountain from Aspen, but a 15-minute scenic flight or one-hour drive (or five-hour walk) in summer turns into a four-hour trek by car in winter, when Kebler Pass (on Route 135) is closed. The town of Crested Butte has been declared a National Historic District and, like Aspen, it was once a quaint mining center whose exquisite Victorian gingerbread-trim houses remain—albeit painted in whimsical shades of hot pink, magenta, and chartreuse. Unlike Aspen, however, Crested Butte never became chic. A controversial ad campaign about its ski area touted it as: "Aspen like it used to be, and Vail like it never was."

Locals are proud and independent, and it takes a puckish sense of humor to streak down the mountain nude on the last day of ski season. But like so many other Colorado ski resorts, Crested Butte has become an escape for the wealthy, losing some of its reputation as a holdout of renegades. It has also upgraded its wilder former identity to become a comfortable family resort. The fact remains that no matter what your budget or lifestyle, you'll find Crested Butte is just about the friendliest ski town around.

Free skiing is no longer one of the perks at Crested Butte, but early and late prices are kept low as a compensating gesture. While many resorts are limiting their "out-of-bounds" terrain owing to increasing insurance costs and lawsuits, Crested Butte has steadily increased its extreme skiing terrain to 550 ungroomed acres. The Extreme Limits and The North Face should only be attempted by advanced skiers or experts, but there are plenty of cruisable trails for recreational skiers. In the summer, mountain bikers challenge the hundreds of miles of trails surrounding the town, which are blanketed with columbine and Indian paintbrush. Late August is time for the ever more popular Mushroom Festival.

There is reliable shuttle-bus service between the town of Crested Butte and the resort village, which are about 3 mi apart. However, because most lodging is at the resort village and the better restaurants, shopping, and general atmosphere are in town, you can expect to make many resort-to-town trips, and a car makes the going much easier. The town more or less shuts down in the spring between mid-April and Memorial Day, and again in the fall, between October and the start of ski season around mid-December. Establishments choose to close anywhere from a month to more than two months.

Dining and Lodging

$$$-$$$$
★ ✕ **Soupçon.** Soupçon ("soup's on," get it?) occupies two intimate rooms in a delightful log cabin—and a cozier place doesn't exist in this town. The menu changes daily with innovative variations on classic bistro cuisine. Roast duckling, usually topped with an impeccable Hoisin glaze, and the fresh fish dishes are sublime. Try mango-barbecue glazed Atlantic salmon. Desserts really shine; order the house-made Jack Daniels chocolate ice cream or crème brûlée. ✉ *Just off 2nd St., behind the Forest Queen,* ☎ *970/349–5448. Reservations essential. AE, MC, V. No lunch. Closed Oct.–Dec. 9 and mid.-Apr.–mid-May.*

$$-$$$$
✕ **Timberline.** This handsome Western bar and elegant fine dining establishment serves a respectable fettuccine Alfredo, sesame ahi tuna, and veal chop and risotto with local wild mushrooms, as well as a salmon with chanterelle mushroom sauce. Smoked trout with local tomatoes is a signature dish. ✉ *21 Elk Ave.,* ☎ *970/349–9831. AE, MC, V. No lunch. Closed Sun. and Mon., Labor Day–mid-Dec. and Apr.–June.*

$$$
★ ✕ **Powerhouse.** This enormous barnlike structure has a delightful Gay '90s bar. The cuisine is haute Mexican, with scrumptious tacos and burritos and more exotic dishes, such as soft-shell crab in cornmeal and delectable mesquite-roasted *cabrito* (kid)—a true delicacy. Chef and owner Tim Egelhoff is justly proud of the house-made mozzarella and his reliance on seasonal ingredients. The margaritas are the best in town, complemented by a knockout list of more than 100 tequilas by the glass. ✉ *130 Elk Ave.,* ☎ *970/349–5494. Reservations not accepted. AE, D, DC, MC, V. No lunch.*

$$$
✕ **Swiss Chalet.** The owner duplicates the true Alpine experience, right down to the *Bierstube* (pub) with Paulaner on tap. The *Kalbsgeschnetzeltes* (veal loin sautéed with mushrooms and shallots in whitewine cream sauce), raclette, and fondue are luscious, as are such hard-to-find specialties as *Buendnerfleisch* (savory air-dried beef soaked in wine). ✉ *621 Gothic Rd., Mt. Crested Butte,* ☎ *970/349–5917. AE, MC, V. No lunch. Closed Apr. 15–June 15 and Sept. 15–mid-Nov. or mid-Dec.*

$-$$
★ ✕ **Slogar.** Set in a lovingly renovated Victorian tavern awash in lace and stained glass, this restaurant—run by Mac Bailey—is just plain cozy. Slogar's turns out some of the plumpest, juiciest fried chicken west of the Mississippi. The fixings are sensational: flaky biscuits, creamy mashed potatoes swimming in hearty chicken gravy, and unique sweet-and-sour coleslaw from a Pennsylvania Dutch recipe that dates back nearly two centuries. Served family-style, you get all that and more, including ice cream, for just $13.45, or, if you'd prefer, a steak dinner for $22.95. ✉ *2nd and Whiterock Sts.,* ☎ *970/349–5765. MC, V. Closed late Sept.–Dec. 15 and mid-Apr.–June 10. No lunch.*

$
✕ **Donita's Cantina.** This down-home Mexican restaurant is hard to miss: it's the one in the hot-pink building. The food isn't nearly as showy: simply good, solid standards such as fajitas and enchiladas, and a tangy salsa. It may be owing to either the bargain prices or the killer margaritas, but the crowds here are always jovial. ✉ *330 Elk Ave.,* ☎ *970/349–6674. Reservations not accepted. AE, D, MC, V. No lunch.*

$$$–$$$$ ⊞ **Crested Butte Club.** This quaint, stylish inn is a Victorian dream: each
★   sumptuous, individually furnished room contains a brass or mahogany
           bed, Axminster carpets, and cherry-wood antiques or good-quality re-
           productions. All have spacious modern bathrooms and such little ex-
           tras as footed copper and brass tubs or gas fireplaces. The downstairs
           bar is similarly delightful, but best of all is the full health club on the
           property, so you don't have to go far to soothe your weary muscles
           after a hard day's hiking or skiing. The Continental-plus breakfast is
           complimentary. ⊠ *512 2nd St., 81224,* ☎ *970/349–6655 or 800/815–
           2582,* FAX *970/349–7580,* WEB *www.visitcrestedbutte.com/cbclub. 8
           rooms. Bar, indoor pool, health club. D, MC, V. CP.*

$$–$$$ ⊞ **Sheraton Crested Butte Resort.** This ski-in/ski-out property, only 200
           yards from the lift, offers all the amenities and facilities of other luxury
           hotels at down-to-earth prices. A warm stone-log lobby welcomes guests.
           Huge rooms are decorated in muted earth and pastel tones with copper
           accents. ⊠ *6 Emmons Loop, Mt. Crested Butte 81225,* ☎ *970/349–7561
           or 800/544–8448,* FAX *970/349–8050,* WEB *www.crestedbutteresort.com.
           248 rooms, 106 suites. Restaurant, bar, in-room data ports, indoor-out-
           door pool, outdoor hot tub, gym, recreation room, laundry service,
           meeting room. AE, D, DC, MC, V. Closed mid-Apr.–mid-June and mid-
           Aug.–mid-Dec.*

$$ ⊞ **Cristiana Guesthouse.** This European-style ski lodge with sun deck
           and huge stone fireplace in the beamed lobby provides a cozy, unpre-
           tentious year-round haven for those who love mountain sports. Wood-
           paneled rooms are decorated in soothing neutrals with traditional
           country pine furnishings. The lodge is in a housing development within
           walking distance to the historic downtown, and is close to hiking and
           ski trails. ⊠ *621 Maroon Ave., 81224,* ☎ *800/824–7899,* FAX *970/349–
           1962,* WEB *www.visitcrestedbutte.com/cristiana. 21 rooms. In-room
           data ports, hot tub, sauna. AE, D, MC, V. Closed early Nov.–mid-Nov.
           and mid-Apr.–mid-May. CP.*

$$ ⊞ **Pioneer Guest Cabins.** Only 10 minutes out of town, on 7 acres of
           the Gunnison National Forest, this is a dream getaway. Rustic log cab-
           ins from the 1930s have been appointed with all new appliances, down
           comforters, and antique furnishings. You can hear and see the stream
           that runs through the property from every cabin. Each cabin has its
           own personality and comes with a fully equipped kitchen, as well as
           a fireplace or wood-burning stove. Cement Creek, ½-mi away, is a world-
           class fishing stream. A resident guide conducts mountain bike tours.
           ⊠ *Cement Creek Rd., 81224,* ☎ *970/349–5517,* FAX *970/349–9697.
           8 cabins. Kitchenettes, hiking, cross-country skiing. MC, V.*

CONDOMINIUMS

Crested Butte Vacations (⊠ Box 5700, Mt. Crested Butte 81225, ☎
800/544–8448, FAX 970/349–2270) can make arrangements for all con-
dominiums on the mountain.

Nightlife

Kochevar's (⊠ 127 Elk Ave., ☎ 970/349–6745), a hand-hewn 1896
log cabin, is a classic pool hall–saloon. The popular **Wooden Nickel**
(⊠ 222 Elk Ave., ☎ 970/349–6350) has happy hour daily 4–6. **Rafters**
(⊠ Gothic Bldg., Ski Village, Mt. Crested Butte, ☎ 970/349–2298) is
a big barn with cheap eats, strong drinks, and loud rock music (often
live on weekends).

Outdoor Activities and Sports

For you summer visitors, **Alpine Outside** (⊠ 315 6th St., ☎ 970/349–
5011) can arrange just about every outdoor activity you can think
of between June and mid-September, and also rents bikes from its
storefront.

CYCLING

Crested Butte is probably *the* mountain-biking center of the Rockies (vying with Moab, Utah, for the title), a place where there are more bikes than cars, and probably more bikes than residents, too. Authentic Crested Butte-ites own not one but two mountain bikes: a town bike for hacking around and a performance bike for *serious* hacking around. Mountain-bike chroniclers say that **Pearl Pass** is the route that got the mountain-biking craze started about 20 years ago. A couple of guys, sitting around in Crested Butte without much to do, decided that a great way to entertain themselves would be to ride the rough old road over Pearl Pass to Aspen. Jeeps did it, so why not bikes? They hopped on board their clunky two-wheelers—a far cry from the sophisticated machinery of today—and with that, a sport was born. The 40-mi trip over Pearl Pass can be done in a day, but you must be in excellent condition to do it. Altitude is the chief enemy of fitness here; the pass itself is close to 13,000 ft. Unless you want to ride back from Aspen—a scenic two-day road ride is the alternative to retracing your route over the pass—you'll need to make return shuttle arrangements by car or by plane.

The **Alpineer** bike shop (⊠ 419 6th St., ☎ 970/349–5210) rents bikes and offers guided mountain bike tours through Crested Butte Mountain Guides (970/349–5430). Each summer enthusiasts roll in for the **Fat Tire Bike Week** (⊠ Box 782, Crested Butte, CO 81224, ☎ 970/349–6817), a week of racing, touring, silly events, and mountain-biker bonding.

FISHING

Alpine Outside (⊠ Box 339, Almont, CO 81210, ☎ 970/349–5011) runs fishing trips.

GOLF

The Club at Crested Butte (⊠ 385 Country Club Dr., ☎ 970/349–6127) is a ravishing 18-hole course designed by Robert Trent Jones, Jr., and although it belongs to the country club, it is open to the public.

HORSEBACK RIDING

Fantasy Ranch (⊠ Gothic Rd., .3 mi after road turns to gravel, ☎ 970/349–5425) provides horses for riding tours.

HOT-AIR BALLOONING

The conditions must be just right, but on a clear windless morning, this wide-open basin, surrounded on all sides by mountain ranges, must surely be one of the country's best places to be aloft in a balloon. For information, contact **Big Horn Balloon Company** (☎ 970/596–1008). Flights are $125 per person for a ride of 30–60 minutes; $190 per person for a flight of up to two hours.

TENNIS

Crested Butte and Mt. Crested Butte Town **parks** (☎ 970/349–5338) have free public courts at the intersection of 6th Street and Elk Avenue.

WATER SPORTS

Three Rivers Outfitting (⊠ Box 339, Almont 81225, ☎ 970/641–1303) offers rafting trips and kayaking lessons on the Gunnison from May through September.

Downhill Skiing and Snowboarding

Crested Butte skiing has a split personality, a judgment that is easily made by checking out the skiers who come here. One side of its personality is the primary trail network, characterized by long intermediate and lower-intermediate runs. This is the sort of skiing that attracts vacationers and families. They take advantage of, among other things, a wonderful expanse of easy terrain from the Keystone lift—not just a trail network but rolling, tree-dotted meadows with plenty of opportunities to poke around off the beaten track.

The other side of Crested Butte's personality is the Extreme Limits, several hundred acres of steep bowls, gnarly chutes, and tight tree skiing. Crested Butte has made its mark on the national sporting scene as former winter host in January to ESPN's X Games. Crested Butte annually hosts late in the season both the U.S. Extreme Freeskiing Championship and the U.S. Extreme Borderfest, both nationally televised events. That's not to say you have to be a young hot shot to enjoy Crested Butte's often steep and challenging terrain.

The best skiing on the main trail network is on the front side of the mountain. The Silver Queen high-speed quad shoots you up 2,000 vertical ft in just one quick lift ride. On the other side of the mountain, the Paradise high-speed quad accesses some of the mountain's best intermediate terrain.

The Extreme Limits is backcountry, ungroomed, exciting terrain, and not for the faint of heart. Terrain as steep and rocky as this with good snowfall becomes truly pleasurable. ⊠ *Rte. 135, Box 5700, 17 Emmons Loop, Mt. Crested Butte 81225,* ☎ *970/349–2222,* FAX *970/349–2270,* WEB *www.skicb.com.* ☉ *Open mid-Nov. or mid-Dec.–mid-Apr., daily 9–4.*

FACILITIES

2,775-ft vertical drop; 1,058 skiable acres; 24% beginner, 56% intermediate, 20% advanced; 3 high-speed quad chairs, 3 triple chairs, 3 double chairs, 2 surface lifts and 2 Magic Carpets (beginners' lifts).

LESSONS AND PROGRAMS

The Beginner's Shortcut, which includes one three-hour lesson and lift ticket, is available for $75. The same package is available at $25 during one week in December, most of January, and two weeks in April. Call the **Crested Butte Ski and Snowboard School** (☎ 970/349–2252) for information on additional packages and programs. One special program of note is Kim Reichhelm's **Women's Ski Adventures** (⊠ Skitours, 2335 Honolulu Ave., Montrose CA 91020, ☎ 888/444–8151). Reichhelm, a former world extreme-skiing champion, leads four-day workshops aimed at "breakthrough" experiences for women of all abilities.

LIFT TICKETS

$53. Children under four ski free, and those ages five through 16 "pay their age."

RENTALS

Full rental packages (including skis, boots, and poles), touring, and telemark equipment are available through **Crested Butte Ski and Snowboard Rental** (⊠ base of ski area, ☎ 970/349–2241 or 888/280–5728) and start at $14 per day. Substantial discounts are available for multiday rentals.

Nordic Skiing

BACKCOUNTRY SKIING

Considerable avalanche hazards notwithstanding, Crested Butte abounds with backcountry possibilities, from deep-woods touring to above-treeline telemarking. Keep in mind that this is high-mountain country (the town itself is around 9,000 ft, and things go up from there) and that skiing in certain areas under certain weather conditions can be nothing short of suicidal. To play it safe, your best bet is to arrange a guided tour with the **Crested Butte Nordic Center** (☎ 970/349–1707).

In town, the **Alpineer** (✉ 419 6th St., ☎ 970/349–5210) is not only a good backcountry equipment source but can also provide information on backcountry routes and snow conditions.

Irwin Lodge (✉ Box 457, Crested Butte 81224, off Kebler Pass in the backcountry, ☎ 970/349–9800) is in a high basin about 12 mi from town. In winter, Sno-Cats carry alpine as well as telemark skiers to a ridge offering terrific views of the 14,000-ft peaks of the Maroon Bells/Snowmass Wilderness. From here, it's more than 2,000 vertical ft of bowl and tree skiing back to the lodge. Equally enjoyable is touring on your own (or with a guide) from the lodge.

TRACK SKIING

Three track networks totaling approximately 50 km (31 mi) are maintained by the **Crested Butte Nordic Center.** The largest of the three, the Red Lady Loop, covers mostly flat and rolling terrain across the meadows and through the aspen groves of the valley floor. Views of distant peaks are stunning. The Bench network includes a steep loop through the trees of Gibson Ridge—close to town but seemingly far away in the woods. A groomed trail of 2½ mi links Crested Butte and Mt. Crested Butte. Town Ranch loops allow dogs, as does Slate River Road to Pittsburgh. Besides lessons and rentals, the center can arrange backcountry tours for skiers of all abilities. ✉ 602 2nd St., Box 1269, Crested Butte 81224, ☎ 970/349–1707. ☞ Trail fee: $10.

Shopping

Creekside Pottery (✉ 126 Elk Ave., ☎ 970/349–6459) showcases local artist Mary Jursinovic's pottery and landscape lamps.

En Route   The Route 135 scenic loop goes west from Crested Butte over Kebler Pass to Paonia, and south through banks of cottonwoods (which usually attract several swooping bald eagles).

Gunnison

🐾 *28 mi from Crested Butte via Rte. 135 south.*

At the confluence of the Gunnison River and Tomichi Creek, Gunnison has been a fishing and hunting community ever since the Utes adopted it as their summer hunting grounds. It provides economical lodging and easy access to Crested Butte. **Western State College** loudly states its presence with a 320-by-420–ft whitewashed rock that's shaped like a W on Tenderfoot Mountain, just to the north of the campus. Gunnison's other claim to fame is that the town has recorded some of the coldest temperatures ever reported in the continental United States.

The **Gunnison County Chamber of Commerce** (✉ 500 E. Tomichi Ave., ☎ 970/641–1501) issues an informative historical walking-tour brochure of downtown. Those interested in the region's history can stop by the **Pioneer Museum,** a living history complex that includes several buildings and relics that date from the late 19th century. ✉ U.S. 50 and S. Adams St., ☎ 970/641–4530. ☞ $3. ☉ Memorial Day–Labor Day, Mon.–Sat. 9–5, Sun. noon–5.

Nine miles west of Gunnison is the **Curecanti National Recreation Area** (✉ U.S. 50, ☎ 970/641–2337), set amid a striking eroded volcanic landscape and stretching for more than 60 mi. Dams built during the 1960s created three reservoirs, including **Blue Mesa,** the state's largest body of water, where you can fish, swim, or windsurf. The reservoirs provide a wealth of recreational opportunities, as well as fine camping and hiking. Rangers lead education programs. At the western entrance to the recreation area, the **Cimarron Visitor Center** (✉ U.S. 50, ☎ 970/249–4074), open June–September, daily 8–4:30, displays vintage locomotives, an 1882 trestle listed on the National Register of Historic Places, and a reconstruction of a railroad stockyard.

Dining and Lodging

$–$$ ✕ **Garlic Mike's.** For upscale Italian, a nightly changing menu, and good seafood, give this spot a try. Try the homemade meat ravioli, pizzas, and eggplant Parmesan. The marinated sirloin steak carbonara wins as the house favorite. The menu is a welcome change of pace from the usual burger and fast-food joints that abound in the area. ⊠ 2674 Hwy. 153, ☎ 970/641–2493. AE, D, MC, V. No lunch.

$–$$ 🏠 **Mary Lawrence Inn.** This restored Victorian is an unexpected delight in Gunnison. The large rooms are furnished with tasteful antiques and Victorian touches such as lace curtains, stenciled walls, handmade quilts, vivid local art, and potpourri. A complimentary breakfast is offered each morning, along with a smile and advice for the day's adventures from helpful innkeeper Janette McKinny. ⊠ 601 N. Taylor St., 81230, ☎ 970/641–3343, FAX 970/641–6719, WEB www.commerceteam.com/mary.html. 7 rooms. Hot tub. AE, MC, V. BP

Outdoor Activities and Sports

Lake San Cristobal is about 60 mi south of Gunnison on Route 149. Water comes into play on 17 of the 18 holes at **Dos Rios Golf Club** (⊠ 501 Camino del Rio, 2 mi west of Gunnison, ☎ 970/641–1482).

Lazy F Bar Outfitters (⊠ 2991 County Rd. 738, ☎ 970/641–0193) provides horses for riding tours.

Shopping

Save time to browse the 2,000 sq ft of crafts, pottery, handmade lace, and CDs at **Let's Go Country** (⊠ 234 N. Main St., ☎ 970/641–1638). **The Corner Cupboard** (⊠ 101 N. Main St., ☎ 970/641–0313) has a nifty selection of specialty food items and kitchen wares.

Montrose

🜨 65 mi from Gunnison via U.S. 50 west.

The self-described "Home of the Black Canyon" sits amid glorious surroundings, but it's an otherwise nondescript town with little more than a collection of truck stops, trailer parks, and strip malls. However, Montrose is perfectly placed for exploring Curecanti and the Black Canyon to the east; the San Juans to the south; the world's largest flattop mountain, Grand Mesa, to the north; and the fertile Uncompahgre Plateau to the west.

If you're interested in learning more about the original residents of the area, stop by the excellent **Ute Indian Museum**, 3 mi south of town on U.S. 550. The museum contains several dioramas and the most comprehensive collection of Ute materials and artifacts in Colorado. ⊠ 17253 Chipeta Rd., ☎ 970/249–3098. 🎟 $3. ⊙ June–Oct., Mon.–Sat. 10–5.

★ The Gunnison River slices through one of the West's most awe-inspiring sights, the **Black Canyon of the Gunnison National Park,** a vivid testament to the powers of erosion. This 2,500-ft-deep gash in the earth's crust is 1,300 ft wide at its top and only 40 ft wide at the bottom. The canyon's name comes from the fact that so little sunlight penetrates its depths, and the eternal shadows permit scant plant growth on its steep walls. To reach the south rim of the canyon, take U.S. 50 east from Montrose (or west from Gunnison) and head north on Route 347. The fine visitor center has exhibits on the region's geology, history, and flora and fauna, and schedules nature walks to the canyon's forbidding rim. ⊠ Visitor center: Rte. 347, 6 mi east of Montrose, ☎ 970/249–1914, WEB www.nps.gov/blca. 🎟 $7 per vehicle. ☉ *Park daily 8–5; visitor center June–Sept., daily 8–6, Oct.– May daily 9–4.*

Dining and Lodging

$ ✕ **Sally's Café.** Gum-cracking waitresses serve up huge portions of gravy-laden food at Sally's Café. The menu has it all, from Mexi-burgers, patty melts, chicken-fried steak, and grilled PB&J sandwiches to Duncan Hines cakes and dull-as-dirty-dishwater coffee. The decor, too, reflects a quirky, local flavor, with a reindeer made out of an old clock that hangs on the wall, and Sally's own diverse collection of china ("I like my dishes," says Sally with typical understatement). ⊠ *715 S. Townsend Ave.,* ☎ *970/249–6096. No credit cards. Closed Wed. and Thurs. No dinner.*

$ ✕ **Fiesta Guadalajara.** Authentic Mexican fare like quesadillas, tostadas, and enchiladas in hefty portions, served in a festive atmosphere will make you think you've been transported south of the border. Go for the shrimp fajitas. ⊠ *147 S. Main St.,* ☎ *970/249–2460. AE, MC, V.*

$$ 🏨 **Best Western Red Arrow Motor Inn.** This fully outfitted property is one of the nicest in the area, mainly because of the large, prettily appointed rooms adorned in greens and browns with handsome mahogany furnishings. The full baths include jetted whirlpool tubs. ⊠ *1702 E. Main St., 81401,* ☎ *970/249–9641 or 800/468–9323,* FAX *970/249–8380,* WEB *www.bestwestern.com. 60 rooms. Hot tub, gym, laundry service, meeting room. AE, D, DC, MC, V.*

$ 🏨 **Colorado Inn.** This friendly property offers pleasing, fair-size rooms with all the usual motel amenities, as well as free Continental breakfast. The Colorado Inn offers many of the same facilities as other hotels in town, but at a considerably lower rate. ⊠ *1417 E. Main St., 81401,* ☎ *970/249–4507. 71 rooms. Restaurant, bar, pool, hot tub, sauna, coin laundry. AE, D, DC, MC, V. CP.*

Nightlife and the Arts

The **Montrose Pavilion** (⊠ 1800 Pavilion Dr., ☎ 970/249–7015) includes a 602-seat auditorium where well-known musicians, comedians, dance companies, and regional orchestras often perform.

Outdoor Activities and Sports

For information on back country hiking experiences in the wilderness area of the San Juans and Sangre de Cristo, contact the **Gunnison National Forest** (⊠ Delta, ☎ 970/641–0471). To learn the rules and regulations regarding a fishing license, contact the **Colorado Division of Wildlife** (⊠ 2300 S. Townsend Ave., 81401, ☎ 970/249–3431). Kokanee salmon, rainbow, brown and lake trout are abundant in the area. For lake boating, you can rent a boat at **Elk Creek Marina** (⊠ Montrose, ☎ 970/641–0707).

CANOEING AND KAYAKING

The 12-mi stretch of the Gunnison River through the Black Canyon is so narrow and steep that in some sections the distance from rim to rim at the top is less than the distance from the elevation of the rim to the river. In fact, the Black Canyon earned its name because in places very little sunlight reaches the canyon floor. The stretch of the Gunnison through the canyon is one of the premier kayak challenges in North America, with Class IV and Class V rapids and portages required around bigger drops. It is a section of river that early visitors to the canyon declared unnavigable, and the fact that a few intrepid kayakers are able to make the journey today still stretches belief. This part of the river is only for hardy and experienced paddlers. However, once outside this area designated as a national park, the canyon opens up, the rapids ease considerably, and the trip becomes more of a quiet float (Class I–Class III rapids). The canyon itself is administered by the National Park Service;

surrounding land is administered by the **U.S. Forest Service** (✉ 2465 S. Townsend St., Montrose, 81401, ☎ 970/240–5300).

Gunnison River Expeditions (✉ Box 315, Montrose, 81402, ☎ 970/ 249–4441) specializes in Gunnison River tours.

Shopping
Zappa Pottery (✉ 16367 So. Townsend Ave., ☎ 970/252–0303) showcases the fine stoneware designs of Nick and Joan Zappa.

Ridgway

㊷   *26 mi from Montrose via U.S. 550 south.*

The 19th-century railroad town of Ridgway has been the setting for some classic Westerns, including *True Grit* and *How the West was Won.* It's also home to many swank ranches, including Ralph Lauren's.

Dining and Lodging

$–$$ ✕ **True Grit.** Scenes from the movie "True Grit" were filmed here, and the local hangout is a shrine to the film and its star, John Wayne. A friendly neighborhood pub, it serves standard fare—burgers, chicken fried steak, and nachos. ✉ *123 N. Lena Ave.,* ☎ *970/626–5739. D, MC, V.*

$$ 🏨 **Chipeta Sun Lodge.** Hosts Lyle and Shari Braund are happy to di-
★   rect guests to their favorite hiking, mountain-biking, and cross-country ski trails. Their Southwestern-style adobe inn features rooms with handmade log beds, Mexican tiles, and stunning views from the decks. The hearty complimentary breakfast is served in a sunny solarium. ✉ *304 S. Lena St., 81432,* ☎ *970/626–3737 or 800/633–5868. 20 rooms. Hot tubs. MC, V. BP.*

Nightlife
Boots scuff the 1,000-square-ft dance floor of **The Big Barn** (✉ Trail Town, U.S. 550 and Rte. 62, ☎ 970/626–3600) to the accompaniment of live music (there's free video country dance lessons for city slickers).

Shopping
Unicas Southwest (✉ Ft. Smith Saloon Bldg., ☎ 970/626–5723) has clothing, folk art, and other Southwestern wares for sale.

En Route   U.S. 550 and Route 62 fan out from Ridgway to form one of the country's most stupendously scenic drives, the **San Juan Skyway,** which weaves through a series of "fourteeners" (a Rockies term for peaks reaching more than 14,000 ft) and picturesque mining towns. U.S. 550 continues through historic Ouray and Silverton to Durango. Route 62 and Route 145 reach Durango via the extraordinary Anasazi cliff dwellings of Mesa Verde National Park.

Telluride

㊸   *45 mi from Ridgway via Rte. 62 west and Rte. 145 east.*

Tucked like a jewel in a tiny valley caught between azure sky and gunmetal mountains is Telluride, once so inaccessible that it was a favorite hideout for desperadoes such as Butch Cassidy, who robbed his first bank here in 1889. The savage but beautiful terrain now attracts mountain people of a different sort—alpinists, snowboarders, freestylers, mountain bikers, and freewheeling four-wheelers—who attack any incline, up or down, and do so with abandon.

The town's independent spirit is shaped not only by its mining legacy, but also by the social ferment of the '60s and early '70s. Before the ski area opened in 1971, Telluride had been as remote as it was back in

Cassidy's day. It was even briefly included on the "Ghost Town Club of Colorado" itinerary, but that was before countercultural types moved in, seeking to lose themselves in the wilderness. By 1974 the town's orientation had changed so radically that the entire council was composed of hippies. An enduring Telluride tradition called the Freebox (⊠ Pine St. and Colorado Ave.), where residents can sort through and take whatever used clothing and appliances they need, remains as a momento of those times. (One memorable day, just after a fur shop had the temerity to open in town, surprised residents found a wide selection of minks, sables, and chinchillas at the Box. After the mysterious break-in, the furriers got the point and moved on.)

Despite such efforts at keeping visible signs of wealth away, more and more locals are finding they can no longer afford to live here. Things were fine when the town was isolated, but thanks to the construction of the Telluride Regional Airport in the late 1980s, it has become quite accessible. Today Telluride is positioning itself as an upscale alternative to Vail and Aspen, and celebrities who need only be identified by their first names (Arnold and Oprah, for example) own homes here.

Telluride is chic—and not everyone's happy about it. Many townies deplore the over-the-top Telluride Mountain Village development at the base of the ski area, and some bitterly resent the Peaks at Telluride, a glamorous resort and spa. The ambivalence felt about the influx of wealth and new buildings brings into question whether development is inevitable, whether the pristine can be preserved in this fast-paced world. For better or worse, Telluride is gorgeous. The San Juans loom over town either menacingly or protectively, depending on the lighting.

While the separation of the resort village from the town of Telluride has kept the town's historic integrity intact, you can still travel to and fro via a 2½-mi, over-the-mountain free gondola, one of the most beautiful commutes in Colorado. The gondola makes a car unnecessary for local transportation; both the village and the town are pedestrian-friendly. However, for any out-of-town excursions—and a drive through the spectacular San Juan Mountains is well worthwhile—a car is necessary.

Telluride magazine prints an excellent historic walking tour in its "Visitors' Guide" section. The town offers one pastel Victorian residence or frontier trading post after another. It's hard to believe that the lovingly restored shops and restaurants once housed gaming parlors and saloons known for the quality of their "waitressing." That party-hearty spirit lives on, evidenced by numerous annual events. Highly regarded wine and wild-mushroom festivals alternate with musical performances celebrating everything from bluegrass to jazz to chamber music. And the Telluride Film Festival is one of the world's leading showcases for the latest releases. Telluride has two off-seasons, when most restaurants and many lodgings are closed. Nearly everyone flees town after the ski area shuts down in mid-April, to return sometime in early or mid-June. After the summer season, the town closes up from late-September or early October until ski season gets going in late November to early December.

The 1887 brick **San Miguel County Courthouse** (⊠ Colorado Ave., between Fir and Aspen Sts.) was the county's first courthouse, and it still operates as one today. William Jennings Bryan spoke at the 1895 **New Sheridan Hotel and Opera House** (⊠ 231 W. Colorado Ave., ☎ 970/728–4351) during his 1896 presidential campaign. The opera house, added in 1914 and completely redone in 1996, is now home to the thriving Sheridan Arts Foundation.

Dining and Lodging

$$$$
★

✕ **La Marmotte.** This romantic bistro seems transplanted from Provence, with its brick walls, lace curtains, and baskets overflowing with flowers or garlic bulbs. The fish specials, such as grilled salmon with citrus risotto, are particularly splendid, as is the loin of venison with braised apple and gratinée of artichoke. ⊠ *150 W. San Juan Ave.,* ☎ *970/728–6232. Reservations essential. AE, D, MC, V. No lunch. Closed mid-Apr.–early June and Oct.–late Nov. Closed Tues. mid-June–Sept.*

$$$–$$$$

✕ **Allred's.** After riding the gondola up the mountain, diners are still astounded by the views from Allred's. Colorado native chef Bob Scherner, who worked with Charley Trotter in Chicago, has designed a creative menu for the most discriminating tastebuds. Start with a napoleon of house-cured, tea-smoked salmon with avocado and citrus vinaigrette, then move on to a free-range Canadian veal chop with potato-chanterelle hash or seared yellowfin tuna with vegetable risotto, fried oyster mushrooms, and red pepper au jus. The homemade ice cream and molten Valhrona chocolate cake will send you home smiling. ⊠ *Top of San Sophia Gondola,,* ☎ *970/728–7474. AE, D, MC, V. No lunch. Closed early Apr.–early June and Oct.–late Nov.*

$$$–$$$$

✕ **Cosmopolitan.** The sleek Hotel Columbia at the base of the gondola is home to this elegant eatery, overseen by chef Chad Scothorn. Try the sesame-seared tuna with cucumber salad and mango-vanilla nori roll, the rack of New Zealand lamb, or the coriander-crusted yellowfin tuna. ⊠ *300 W. San Juan Ave.,* ☎ *970/728–1292. Reservations essential. AE, MC, V. No lunch. Closed mid-Apr.–Memorial Day and mid-Oct.–Thanksgiving.*

$$–$$$$
★

✕ **Campagna.** Vincent and Joline Esposito transport diners to a Tuscan farmhouse, from the decor (open kitchen, oak and terra-cotta floors, turn-of-the-20th-century photos of the Italian countryside, and Tuscan cookbooks) to the assured, classically simple food. Most everything is grilled or roasted with garlic, sage, or rosemary in olive oil, allowing the natural juices and flavors to emerge. Whole grilled snapper with fennel and local porcini and chanterelle wild mushroom risotto are among the enticing possibilities. Finish your meal off with a letter-perfect tiramisu or hazelnut torte and a fiery house grappa. ⊠ *435 W. Pacific Ave.,* ☎ *970/728–6190. Reservations essential. MC, V. No lunch. Closed Mon. and mid-Apr.–mid-June and Oct.–late Nov.*

$$–$$$$

✕ **221 South Oak Bistro.** This bistro makes its home in a pretty Victorian cottage with spot-lit peach walls and a blond-wood bar. Soft music wafts through the casually elegant space. Chef-owner Eliza Goodall trained in Paris, New Orleans, and Napa Valley, and cooks up such dishes as Muscovy duck breast with duck confit, spinach, shiitakes, and pine nuts; rack of lamb with potato-chevre ravioli; and halibut with asparagus and fennel. ⊠ *221 S. Oak St.,* ☎ *970/728–9507. AE, MC, V. No lunch. Closed Tues. and early Apr.–mid-June and early Oct.–early Dec.*

$–$$$
★

✕ **The PowderHouse.** Tony Clinco (a former Golden Gloves winner who found another use for his hands) bills his food as "Rocky Mountain Cuisine." In reality, this is classic Italian married to wild game. Among the winners are pheasant ravioli; smoked buffalo sausage; and the game special—stuffed quail, venison chop, and marinated elk, each in its own sauce. ⊠ *226 W. Colorado Ave.,* ☎ *970/728–3622. AE, MC, V. Closed mid-Apr.–mid-May.*

$–$$$

✕ **Roma Bar and Café.** In operation since 1897, this restaurant offers good value and an incomparable air of history. The 1860 Brunswick bar, with 12-ft-high mirrors, has seen everything, including cowboys riding their mounts up to the stools. Flappers even brewed rotgut whiskey in the cellar during Prohibition. The pasta specials are terrific, as are the burgers, pizzas, and fresh salads. ⊠ *133 E. Colorado Ave.,*

☎ 970/728–3669. AE, MC, V. Closed Tues. and Wed. in Nov. No lunch Oct.–May.

$–$$ ✕ **Fat Alley's BBQ.** A few family-style tables and benches, along with some old skis and ceiling fans fill this popular spot. Messy, mouth-watering ribs are complemented by delectable Southern side dishes such as red beans and rice, baked sweet potatoes, and snap-pea and feta salad. A few beers and wines are available, in addition to homemade iced tea and pink lemonade. ✉ 122 S. Oak St., ☎ 970/728–3985. Reservations not accepted. AE, MC, V.

$–$$ ✕ **Honga's Lotus Petal and Tea Room.** A popular local favorite, Honga's serves "super-healthy and fresh" food in the vibrant, elegant setting of a restored Victorian. Though it caters to vegetarians, Honga's also puts free-range chicken and organic beef on the table. Blackened tofu is the signature dish, and the crowds go wild for the crunchy shrimp roll and pineapple coconut curry. Don't leave town without sampling the potstickers. ✉ 133 S. Oak St., ☎ 970/728–5134. AE, MC, V. Closed early Apr.–early June and mid-Oct.–late Nov.

$$$$ ▥ **Camel's Garden.** In a curious contradiction, this ultra-modern, sophisticated lodging that is all gleaming edges and sleek neutral surfaces bears the name of an old mine. Rooms have fireplaces, stereos, and CD players. The Continental breakfast is loaded with fresh-baked pastries from the bakery next door. The hotel is ski-in/ski-out. ✉ 250 W. San Juan Ave., 81435, ☎ 970/728–9300, FAX 970/728–0433, WEB www.camelsgarden.com. 30 rooms, 7 condos. In-room VCRs. AE, D, DC, MC, V. CP. Closed Oct.–Nov.

$$$$ ▥ **Wyndham Peaks Resort and Golden Door Spa.** The pastel-color, somewhat forbidding exterior at this ski-in/ski-out, golf-in/golf-out luxury resort can be forgiven, thanks to its invigorating, revitalizing Golden Door spa facilities, where more than 55 treatments are offered. The setting is glorious, dominated by fourteener Mt. Wilson (the peak on the Coors can). Rooms are sizable, if somewhat sterile, decorated in Norwegian wood and muted shades of green, with all amenities; many have balconies. The sports offerings here are vast. There's even an indoor climbing wall. ✉ 136 Country Club Dr., 81435, ☎ 970/728–6800 or 800/789–2220, FAX 970/728–6567, WEB www.wyndham.com. 145 rooms, 32 suites. 2 restaurants, bar, in-room data ports, indoor-outdoor pool, hair salon, hot tub, sauna, spa, 5 tennis courts, gym, racquetball, squash. AE, DC, MC, V. Closed early Apr.–mid-May and mid-Oct.–mid-Nov.

$$$–$$$$ ▥ **Ice House.** This property offers an appealing blend of Scandinavian and Southwestern decor: blond woods; jade carpets; fabrics in beiges, forest greens, and maroons; Native American tapestries; and polished wood ceilings. The spacious rooms feature cable TV, oversize tubs, balconies, and minibars. The hotel provides a free Continental breakfast and a place to store your skis. Best of all, the Oak Street lift is just a little more than a block away. ✉ 310 S. Fir St., 81435, ☎ 970/728–6300 or 800/544–3436, FAX 970/728–6358, WEB www.icehouselodge.com. 42 rooms, 16 condos. Minibars, pool, hot tub, steam room. AE, D, DC, MC, V. CP. Closed mid-Apr.–early June.

$$$–$$$$ ▥ **New Sheridan Hotel.** William Jennings Bryan delivered his rousing "Cross of Gold" speech in 1896, garnering a presidential nomination in the process. Decor favors exposed brick walls; old tintypes; marble-top dressing tables; faux Tiffany, crystal, or fringed lamps; and red velour love seats. The gorgeous Victorian bar, a local favorite, is the original. A complimentary breakfast and afternoon tea complete the picture of fin de siècle gracious living. ✉ 231 W. Colorado Ave., 81435, ☎ 970/728–4351, FAX 970/728–5024, WEB www.newsheridan.com. 26 rooms, 8 with shared bath; 6 suites. Restaurant, bar, in-room data ports, 2 hot tubs, gym, meeting room. AE, MC, V. BP. Closed mid-Apr.–mid-May and mid-Oct.–mid-Nov.

$$$-$$$$ ★ ▣ **San Sophia B&B.** This is a Victorian-style inn, replete with turrets and gingerbread trim. Pristine mountain light streams into every room, warmly accented with whitewashed oak woodwork. Rooms have contemporary brass beds with handmade quilts, tables and nightstands handcrafted by Colorado artisans, stylish black-and-white landscape photographs, and stained-glass windows over the oversize tubs. The inn is known for its fabulous breakfasts and après-ski treats. Owners Alicia Bixby and Keith Hampton also run a marketing firm in town, put on the annual wine festival, and raise two young children, but they still find time to mingle with the guests. ⊠ *330 W. Pacific St., 81435,* ☏ *970/ 728-3001 or 800/537-4781,* FAX *970/728-6226,* WEB *www.sansophia.com. 16 rooms. Hot tub. AE, MC, V. BP. Closed early Apr.–early May and two weeks in Nov.*

CONDOMINIUMS

Telluride Central Reservations (☏ 800/525-3455) handles all properties at Telluride Mountain Village, and several in town. **Telluride Resort Accommodations** (⊠ Box 100, 81435, ☏ 800/538-7754) offers several top-notch accommodations in town.

Nightlife and the Arts

Telluride offers numerous music festivals during the summer, including the monstrous jazz and bluegrass festivals. The **Telluride Film Festival** (☏ 603/643-1255) in September is considered one of the world's leading showcases of foreign and domestic films.

BARS AND LOUNGES

The House (⊠ 131 N. Fir St., ☏ 970/728-6207) is set in a building once dubbed "The Freak House" for the colorful characters who lived here during the '70s and '80s. These days the atmosphere is more refined, says owner Clay Skinner. While drinking one of the fine ales on tap you can play cribbage, backgammon, Trivial Pursuit, or chess. The nine TVs and $2 daily draft specials tend to make for a lively crowd, especially during Bronco games. Burgers and specials are all under $9, served in a completely no-smoking atmosphere.

Leimgruber's Bierstube and Restaurant (⊠ 573 W. Pacific Ave., ☏ 970/ 728-4663) is arguably Telluride's most popular après-ski hangout, thanks to gemütlich owner Christel Leimgruber; a Bavarian ambience enhanced by barmaids in dirndls; and a clientele that seems on the verge of launching into "The Drinking Song." Leimgruber's offers such traditional Alpine food as mixed German and wild-game sausage plates, mouth-puckering sauerbraten, and, of course, apple strudel. If you only want a brew, stop by to down a Paulaner or hoist a glass boot, which holds more than a liter of beer.

The elegant turn-of-the-20th-century bar at the **New Sheridan Hotel** (⊠ 231 W. Colorado Ave., ☏ 970/728-4351) is a favorite après-ski hangout. Prime time is between 4 and 8 PM. In summer, folks gather to socialize and watch the world go by outside on the main street. On July 4th, a local cowboy named Rowdy is known to ride his horse into the bar and enjoy his drink while astride. The 1899 **Swede-Finn Hall** (⊠ 472 W. Pacific Ave., ☏ 970/728-2085) was the place to go dancing during the gold boom days. Popular with locals for its happy hour, it's known for its sunny deck and great margaritas—in both summer and winter.

ROCK CLUBS

The **Fly Me To The Moon Saloon** (⊠ 132 E. Colorado Ave., ☏ 970/ 728-1942) has live music—jazz, blues, funk, ska, rock, you name it— most nights, and the action gets wild on the spring-loaded dance floor. The **Last Dollar Saloon** (⊠ 100 E. Colorado Ave., ☏ 970/728-4800) has a lively jukebox. **Excelsior Café** (⊠ 200 W. Colorado Ave., ☎ 970/728–4250) is the spot to hear the best in folk rock.

The **Sheridan Arts Foundation** (⊠ 110 Oak St., ☎ 970/728–6363) is a mentoring program that brings top actors to town to perform alongside budding young artists in the Sheridan Opera House. The **Telluride Repertory Theater Company** (☎ 970/728–4539) gives free performances in the town park each summer.

Outdoor Activities and Sports

Telluride Outside (⊠ Box 685, 81435, ☎ 970/728–3895 or 800/831–6230) organizes a variety of winter activities in the Telluride area, among them hot-air ballooning, sleigh rides, snowmobile tours, mountain biking trips, and even winter fly-fishing excursions.

FISHING

Telluride Angler (☎ 970/728–0773), Colorado's second largest fishing guide service, offers guided fly-fishing trips on the beautiful San Miguel and Delores rivers.

GLIDER RIDES

For an unusual look at the San Juans, **Telluride Soaring** (☎ 970/728–5424) operates out of the Telluride Airport. Rates are about $80 per half hour, $130 per hour; rides are offered daily, weather permitting.

GOLF

Telluride Golf Club (⊠ Telluride Mountain Village, ☎ 970/728–6900) has breathtaking views of Mt. Wilson and Mt. Sunshine, which dominate this 7,009-yard course.

HIKING

A good local hiking guidebook is *Telluride Hiking Guide,* by Susan Kees. The peaks of the rugged San Juan Mountains around Telluride require some scrambling, occasionally bordering on real climbing, to get to the top. A local favorite is **Mt. Wilson,** a roughly 4,000-vertical-ft climb for which only the last 400 vertical ft call for a scramble across steep, shale slopes. July and August are the most likely snow-free months on this 8-mi roundtrip hike. Sound a bit too grueling? Try the 13-mi Sneffels Highline Trail through wildflower-covered meadows, or any of numerous other great day hikes in the Telluride area. **Skyline Ranch** (☎ 970/728–3757 or 888/754–1226) will provide guide service up Mt. Wilson for intrepid ranch guests.

The 425-ft liquid diamond **Bridal Veil Falls,** Colorado's highest cascade, tumbles lavishly just a short hike from the end of Colorado Avenue, the main street.

For information and permits, contact **San Juan National Forest** (⊠ 701 Camino del Rio, Durango, CO 81301, ☎ 970/247–4874) and **Uncompahgre National Forest** (⊠ 2250 U.S. Hwy. 50, Delta, CO 81416, ☎ 970/874–6600).

ICE-CLIMBING

Having your body suspended for any extended length of time on a wall of ice would be considered a form of torture by some. For those who think it can be fun, **Fantasy Ridge Alpinism** (⊠ 323 N. Oak, Box 1679, Telluride 81435, ☎ 970/728–3546) offers introductory ice-climbing courses. A three-day course, including three nights of lodging and three days of climbing, costs about $900 per person.

RAFTING

Telluride Whitewater (☎ 970/728–3895) explores the Gunnison, Dolores, Colorado, and Animas rivers.

Telluride Town Park (☎ 970/728–3071) has free public tennis courts.

Downhill Skiing and Snowboarding

Telluride is really two ski areas in one. For many years, it had a reputation as being an experts-only ski area. Indeed, the north-facing trails on the town side are impressively steep and long, and by springtime, the moguls are humongous. The terrain accessed by Chairlift Nine, including the famed Spiral Staircase and The Plunge, is for experts only (although one side of The Plunge is groomed for advanced skiers).

But then there is the other side—literally—of the ski area, the west-facing village, with long, gentle runs excellent for intermediates and beginners. There is the aptly named See Forever, a great, long cruiser and numerous intermediate runs from Lift 5. The addition of Telluride's new Prospect Bowl adds 733 acres of terrain for all ability levels. ⊠ *Rte. 145,* ☎ *970/728–6900 or 800/525–3455,* WEB *www. ski-telluride-colorado.com.* ☉ *Late Nov.–early Apr., daily 8:45–4.*

FACILITIES
3,535-ft vertical drop (3,535 ft lift-serviced); 1,700 skiable acres; 22% beginner, 38% intermediate, 40% advanced/expert; 1 gondola, 7 high-speed quad chairs, 2 triple chairs, 2 double chairs, 1 surface lift. **Snow report:** ☎ 970/728–7425.

LESSONS AND PROGRAMS
The **ski school** (☎ 800/801–4832) gives half-day group clinics beginning at $40. First-time beginner lessons are available for alpine and telemark skiers, as well as snowboarders. A five-hour clinic with rentals and restricted beginner lift tickets is available at $95. The ski school can put people with disabilities in touch with a non-profit organization that runs an adaptive ski program. Free tours of the mountain for skiers or snowboarders depart from the top of Lift 7 at 10 AM.

LIFT TICKETS
$63. On multiday tickets the daily rate can be as low as $43.

RENTALS
Rental packages are available from **Telluride Sports** (☎ 970/728–4477), which has six locations in town and in the Mountain Village. Packages start at around $25.

Nordic Skiing

BACKCOUNTRY SKIING
Among the better backcountry skiing routes in Colorado is the **San Juan Hut System,** leading toward Ridgway along the Sneffels Range. Five huts in the system are about 11 km (7 mi) apart and are well equipped with beds, blankets, wood-burning stoves, and cooking stoves. Previous backcountry experience is not essential (though highly recommended). Rental equipment is available, and reservations are recommended at least two weeks in advance. The system also offers a day-guiding service as an introduction to backcountry groomed tracks. ⊠ *224 E. Colorado Ave. or Box 1663, Telluride 81435,* ☎ *970/626–3033.*

Equipment rentals, for both track skiing and backcountry touring, are available in the Mountain Village at **Paragon Ski and Sport** (⊠ 213 W. Colorado Ave., ☎ 800/903–4525), a local business that specializes in personal service and fitting the right equipment to each individual. **Telluride Nordic Center** (☎ 970/728–1144) provides rentals and 16 km (10 mi) of cross-country trails. The areas around Molas Divide and Mesa Verde National Park are also popular. **Telluride Sports** (⊠ 150 West Colorado Ave., ☎ 800/828–7547) carries the largest variety of equipment.

Shopping

BOOKS

Between the Covers Bookstore and Coffee House (✉ 224 W. Colorado Ave., ☎ 970/728–4504) offers the perfect ambience for browsing through the latest titles while sipping a cappuccino. **Bookworks** (✉ 191 S. Pine St., ☎ 970/728–0700) is an independent bookstore with a knowledgable owner.

BOUTIQUES

The **Bounty Hunter** (✉ 226 W. Colorado Ave., ☎ 970/728–0256) is the spot for leather, especially boots and vests. It also houses an astonishing selection of hats, among them Panama straw, beaver felt, Australian Outback, and just plain outrageous.

CRAFT AND ART GALLERIES

Hellbent Leather and Silver (✉ 209 E. Colorado Ave., ☎ 970/728–6246) is a fine source for Native American arts and crafts. **The Potter's Wheel** (✉ 221 E. Colorado Ave., ☎ 970/728–4912) has decorative and functional pottery crafted by local artisans.

SPORTING GOODS

Telluride Sports (✉ 150 W. Colorado Ave., ☎ 970/728–4477) has equipment and clothing for all seasons.

Dolores

44 *75 mi from Telluride via Rte. 145 south.*

The gentle rising hump to the southwest of town is **Sleeping Ute Mountain,** which resembles the reclining silhouette of a Native American replete with headdress. The site is revered by the Ute Mountain tribe as a great warrior god who, mortally wounded in a titanic battle with the evil ones, lapsed into eternal sleep, his flowing blood turning into the life-giving Dolores and Animas rivers. In town, the enchanting **Galloping Goose Museum** (✉ 5th St. and Rte. 145, ☎ 970/882–7082) is a replica of a Victorian train station that contains an original narrow-gauge locomotive.

In 1968, construction of an irrigation dam on the Dolores River was authorized, forming the **McPhee Reservoir,** a haven for boaters and fishermen. An environmental-impact study was mandated by law, and it concluded that hundreds of potentially valuable archaeological sites would be flooded. This led to massive, federally funded excavations that uncovered the freestanding pueblos and cliff dwellings of ancestral Puebloan peoples. The mysterious and talented people who thrived until 1300 were probably the ancestors of present-day Pueblo tribes. No one knows for sure why they abandoned their homes, although most anthropologists surmise that a combination of drought and overfarming sent them off in search of greener pastures. One current school of thought is that they never really disappeared at all; rather they migrated, and actually still live on in the modern Pueblo Indians. Striking similarities between the artwork and customs of the two cultures seem to support this thinking. The Ute Mountain Tribe lives 12 mi south of Cortez.

★ ℭ The state-of-the-art **Anasazi Heritage Center** houses the finest artifacts culled from more than 1,500 excavations, as well as a theater, a library, a gift shop, and a full-scale replica of an ancestral Puebloan pit-house dwelling that illustrates how the people lived around 850. The complex is particularly notable for its Discovery Center, a series of hands-on, hologramlike interactive displays that enable visitors to weave on a Navajo loom, grind corn, and even generate an ancestral Puebloan village using a computer.

The first white explorers to stumble upon ancestral Puebloan ruins were the Spanish friars Dominguez and Escalante, who set out in 1776 from Santa Fe to find a safe overland route to Monterey, California. The two major ruins at the Anasazi Heritage Center are named for them. The Dominguez site, right next to the parking lot, is unimpressive, although it is of great archaeological interest because extremely rare evidence of a "high-status burial" was found here. The Escalante site, ½ mi away, is a 20-room masonry pueblo standing eerie guard over McPhee Reservoir. ⊠ *27501 Rte. 184, 3 mi west of Dolores,* ☎ *970/882–4811,* WEB *www.co.blm.gov/ahc/hmepge.htm.* ☜ *$3.* ☉ *Mar.–Oct. 9–5; Nov.–Feb. 9–4.*

OFF THE BEATEN PATH	**LOWRY PUEBLO** – The Lowry site has only eight kivas (Native American ceremonial structures, usually partly underground) and 40 rooms, and it may have been a "suburb" of larger communities in the area during its occupation from about 800 to 1110. Of particular note are the Great Kiva, one of the largest such structures ever discovered, and a painted kiva, which provides insight into ancestral Puebloan decorative techniques. A brochure, which details the self-guided tour, is available at the entrance to the site. ⊠ *From Dolores, take Rte. 184 west to U.S. 666, and head west (follow signs) for 9 mi at Pleasant View,* ☎ *no phone.* ☜ *Free.* ☉ *Daily 9–5.*

Outdoor Activities and Sports

Beginning in the San Juan Mountains of southwestern Colorado, the Dolores River runs north for more than 150 mi before joining the Colorado River near Moab, Utah. This is one of those rivers that tend to flow madly in spring and diminish considerably by midsummer, and for that reason rafting trips are usually run between April and June. Sandstone canyons, ancestral Puebloan ruins, and the spring bloom of wildflowers and cacti are trip highlights. For the most part, this is a float, interrupted by rapids that—depending on the flow level—can rate a Class IV.

Cortez

45 *10 mi from Dolores via Rte. 145 south and Rte. 160 west.*

The northern escarpment of Mesa Verde and the volcanic blisters of the La Plata mountains to the west dominate sprawling Cortez. A series of Days Inns, Dairy Queens, and Best Westerns, the town's architecture seems to have been determined by neon-sign and aluminum-siding salesmen of the '50s. Hidden among these, however, are fine galleries and a host of pawn shops that can yield surprising finds.

The exterior of the excellent **Cortez Cultural Center** has been painted to resemble the cliff dwellings of Mesa Verde. Exhibits focus on regional artists and artisans, the Ute Mountain branch of the Ute tribe, and various periods of ancestral Puebloan culture. The **Cultural Park** at the Cortez Cultural Center contains an authentic Navajo hogan and a Ute tepee. The park is open 9–5; admission is free. Summer evenings include Native American dances; sandpainting, rug weaving, and pottery-making demonstrations; and storytelling events. ⊠ *25 N. Market St.,* ☎ *970/565–1151,* WEB *www.cortezculturalcenter.org.* ☜ *Free.* ☉ *June–Aug., Mon.–Sat. 9–10; May and Sept., Mon.–Sat. 10–5:30; Oct.–Apr., weekdays 10–5.*

Visitor information is available at the **Colorado Welcome Center** (⊠ Cortez City Park, 928 E. Main St., ☎ 970/565–3414 or 800/253–1616).

Dining and Lodging

$ ✕ **M&M Family Restaurant and Truck Stop.** Semis and RVs jammed into the parking lot attest that M&M is the real McCoy as truck stops go. If chicken-fried steak, enchiladas, and huge breakfasts (served 24 hours a day) are your fancy, you'll be thrilled to eat here. There are posher restaurants in town, but none better—certainly not for these prices. ⊠ *7006 U.S. 160 S,* ☎ *970/565–6511. Reservations not accepted. AE, MC.*

$ 🏨 **Anasazi Motor Inn.** This is definitely the nicest hotel on the strip, mostly because its air-conditioned rooms are spacious and pleasantly decorated in Southwestern colors. ⊠ *640 S. Broadway, 81312,* ☎ *970/565–3773 or 800/972–6232,* ℻ *970/565–1027. 89 rooms. Restaurant, bar, pool, hot tub, meeting room, airport shuttle. AE, D, DC, MC, V.*

Nightlife

Colorado's first tribal gaming facility, offering limited-stakes gambling—slots, poker (video and live), bingo, and 21—is the **Ute Mountain Casino** (⊠ 3 Weeminuche Dr., at Yellow Hat, Towaoc, ☎ 970/565–8800), 11 mi south of Cortez on U.S. 160/666.

Outdoor Activities and Sports

Conquistador Golf Course (⊠ 2018 N. Dolores Rd., ☎ 970/565–9208) is an 18-hole public course with views of Mesa Verde and Sleeping Ute Mountain.

Shopping

Earth Song Haven (⊠ 34 W. Main St., ☎ 970/565–9125) is a fine bookstore, with an espresso bar and tearoom in back. Cortez seems an unlikely spot for this European touch, but the café makes coffees, sandwiches, and high-calorie desserts such as peanut-butter cream pie. **Mesa Indian Trading/Mesa Verde Pottery** (⊠ 27601 Hwy. 160 E, ☎ 970/565–4492) offers a comprehensive sampling of ceramics from most Southwestern tribes. **Ute Mountain Pottery Plant** (⊠ Rtes. 160 and 666, Towaoc, ☎ 970/565–8548) invites customers to watch the painstaking processes of molding, trimming, cleaning, painting, and glazing, before adjourning to the showroom to buy pieces straight from the source.

OFF THE BEATEN PATH   **FOUR CORNERS MONUMENT –** A stone slab marks the only spot where four states—Colorado, Arizona, Utah, and New Mexico—meet. This is photo-op country. Snacks and souvenirs are sold by Native Americans. To get here, travel south from Cortez on Route 160 for about 40 mi. You can't miss the signs. ⊠ *Rte. 160 (follow signs).* 🎫 *$2 per vehicle.* ☉ *Daily 8–6.*

Mesa Verde National Park

46 *10 mi from Cortez via U.S. 160 east.*

Cortez is the gateway to Mesa Verde National Park, an 80-square-mi area that forms one of the nation's most riveting attractions. In 1888, two ranchers—Richard Wetherill and Charlie Mason—set off in search of stray cattle and stumbled upon the remarkable and perfectly preserved Cliff Palace, apartment-style cliff dwellings built into the canyon walls. By the next day's end they had discovered two more major sites: Spruce Tree House and Square Tower House. Excitement over their find culminated in the 1906 creation of the national park by Congress, making it the first park established to preserve the works of humankind.

Mesa Verde is one of Colorado's highlights, but consider either going off-season (though many of the ruins are closed) or overnighting in the park (after the tour buses have departed) to appreciate its full effect, without the crowds. The park's major attractions were unscathed by the fires in 2000. You can pick up information on the park and accommodations at the entrance on U.S. 160. From here a 15-mi drive corkscrews up the mesa, skirting canyons and plateaus, to the Far View Visitor Center, after which you can head in one of two directions. The scenic route to **Wetherill Mesa**, open Memorial Day–Labor Day, affords vistas of the Shiprock Formation in New Mexico and Monument Valley in Arizona and Utah. A minitram departs every half hour between 8:55 AM and 4:55 PM from the Wetherill parking lot, on a 4-mi loop to view the ruins; self-guided and ranger-led tours of Long House, the second-largest dwelling in the park, are also options. The other Far View route, **Ruins Road**, accesses the major sites on Chapin Mesa in two 6-mi loops. If you don't want to hike down into the canyons to view the ruins up close (which requires a free ticket available at the visitor center), this drive still offers several strategic overlooks.

The first stop on the Ruins Road is the park's informative archaeological museum, which traces the development of ancestral Puebloan culture. It's a short walk from the museum to one of the most extraordinary sites, **Spruce Tree House**, the only ruin open year-round. Climb down into an excavated kiva, symbolic of the womb of Mother Earth, for a better sense of how the ancestral Puebloans worshipped.

From the museum trailhead, one loop leads to the most famous ruin, **Cliff Palace**, the largest dwelling of its kind in the world (accessible by a moderately strenuous 15-minute hike), and to the more remote Balcony House (an arduous trek into the canyon below). Ranger-guided tours are available. The other loop accesses two major ruins, **Sun Temple** and **Square Tower House**, both involving a significant amount of walking and climbing. ⊠ *U.S. 160,* ☎ *970/529–4461 or 970/529–4465,* ⓦⓔⓑ *www.nps.gov/meve.* ⊠ *$10 per vehicle.* ⊙ *Park late May–early Sept., daily 8–6:30; early Sept.–mid-Oct., daily 9–6:30; mid-Oct.–early Apr., daily 9–5; early Apr.–early May, daily 9–6:30. Visitor center May–Sept., daily 8–5.*

OFF THE BEATEN PATH

HOVENWEEP NATIONAL MONUMENT – This site—whose literal translation from Ute means "deserted valley"—contains several major ruins, including imposing square, oval, and circular man-made towers such as Holly, Cajon, Hackberry, and Horseshoe, all of which are accessible only on foot. The most impressive ruin, called the Castle, underscores the site's uncanny resemblance to a medieval fiefdom. Hovenweep is approached via Route 160 west to County Road G (McElmo Canyon Rd.), which enters the red-walled McElmo Canyon along the way. ⊠ *McElmo Canyon Rd.,* ☎ *970/562–4282,* ⓦⓔⓑ *www.nps.gov/hove.* ⊠ *$6 per vehicle; camping entry fee $8.* ⊙ *Daily sunrise–sunset.*

Dining and Lodging

$$ ✕ **Millwood Junction.** Folks come from four states (no fooling) for the 25-item salad bar and phenomenal Friday-night seafood buffet. Steaks and seafood are featured in this upscale Red Lobster/Sizzler–style eatery. ⊠ *U.S. 160 and Main St., Mancos,* ☎ *970/533–7338. MC, V. No lunch.*

$$ 🏠 **Far View Lodge.** The rustic rooms at this lodge include private balconies with panoramas of Arizona, Utah, and New Mexico. Soothing Southwestern pastels predominate. Another draw here is the hotel's enthusiastic arrangement of guided tours. There are also nightly talks for guests by either a local Native American or an author, before a multimedia show on the ancestral Puebloan people is shown. ⊠ *Navajo Hill, 15 mi inside Mesa Verde National Park; Box 277, Mancos 81328,*

☎ 970/529–4421, FAX 970/529–4411, WEB *www.visitmesaverde.com.*
150 rooms. Restaurant, travel services. AE, D, DC, MC, V. Closed mid-Oct.–mid-Apr.

Outdoor Activities and Sports

Rimrock Outfitters (✉ Echo Basin, 1275 County Rd. 44, Mancos
81328, ☎ 970/533–7588) provides horses for riding tours, which
range from one-hour walks to steak dinners to overnight excursions;
rates begin at $18.

CAMPING

Campsites are available in Mesa Verde and Hovenweep; contact the
National Park Service (✉ Mesa Verde National Park, Box 8, Mesa Verde,
81330, ☎ 970/529–4461, WEB www.nps.gov/meve).

En Route   Driving east on U.S. 160 from Mesa Verde will take you past an en-
dearing bit of classic American kitsch, the **Mud Creek Hogan** (✉ U.S.
160, ☎ 970/533–7117). More than a dozen enormous arrows stuck
in the ground mark the spot of this hokey trading post and museum
(where you get the feeling that everything is for sale) adorned with tepees and a giant plastic horse. Beside the shop is a re-creation of a frontier town, replete with saloon, hotel, bank, jail, and livery station. Don't
breathe too hard or you'll blow the town over: The "buildings" are
only fronts. U.S. 160 continues through the lush Mancos Valley to the
small and charming town of **Mancos,** where there are several excellent
crafts shops, such as the **Bounty Hunter** (✉ 119 W. Grand Ave., ☎
970/533–7215), that offer everything from saddles to 10-gallon hats.

Durango

🚗 *45 mi from Cortez via U.S. 160 east.*

Will Rogers had this to say about Durango: "It's out of the way and
glad of it." His crack is a bit unfair, considering that as a railroad town
Durango has always been a cultural crossroads and melting pot (as well
as a place to raise hell). It was founded in 1879 by General William
Palmer (president of the all-powerful Denver & Rio Grande Railroad), when nearby Animas City haughtily refused to donate land for
a depot; within a decade Durango had absorbed its rival completely.
The booming town quickly became the region's main metropolis and
a gateway to the Southwest. A walking tour of the historic downtown
bears eloquent witness to Durango's prosperity during the late 19th
century. The northern end of Main Avenue offers the usual assortment
of cheap motels and fast-food outlets, all evidence of Durango's present
status as the major hub for tourism in the area.

At 13th Avenue and Main Avenue (also known as Main Street)—the beginning of its **National Historic District**—the tenor changes dramatically,
with old-fashioned gas lamps gracing the streets and a superlative collection of Victorians filled with chic galleries, restaurants, and brand-
name outlet stores. The 1882 Train Depot (✉ 4th St. and Main Ave.),
the 1887 Strater Hotel (✉ 7th St. and Main Ave.), and the three-story
sandstone Newman Building (✉ 8th St. and Main Ave.) are among the
elegant edifices restored to their original grandeur. Stop into the Diamond
Belle Saloon (in the Strater Hotel)—awash in velour and lace, with a player
piano, gilt-and-mahogany bar, and scantily clad Gay '90s waitresses—
for an authentic re-creation of an old-time honky-tonk.

The **Third Avenue National Historic District** (known simply as "The Boulevard"), two blocks east of Main Avenue, contains several Victorian residences, ranging from the imposing mansions of railroad and smelting
executives to more modest variations erected by well-to-do merchants.

The hodgepodge of styles veers from Greek Revival to Gothic Revival to Queen Anne to Spanish Colonial and Mission designs.

The most entertaining way to relive those halcyon days of the Old West is to take a ride on the **Durango and Silverton Narrow Gauge Railroad,** an eight-hour, round-trip journey along the 45-mi railway. You'll travel in comfort in restored 1882 parlor cars, and listen to the train's shrill whistle as the locomotive chugs along the fertile Animas River Valley and, at times, clings precariously to the hillside. ✉ *479 Main Ave.,* ☎ *970/247–2733,* WEB *www.durangotrain.com.* ☞ *$53.* ⊘ *Late Nov.–late Oct. daily; times vary.*

Trimble Hot Springs (✉ County Rd. 203, off U.S. 550, 7 mi north of Durango, ☎ 970/247–0111) is a great place to soak your aching bones, especially if you've been doing some hiking.

Dining and Lodging

$$–$$$$ ✕ **Ore House.** Durango is a meat-and-potatoes kind of town, and this is Durango's idea of a steak house, where the aroma of beef smacks you in the face as you walk past. This classic eatery serves enormous slabs of aged Angus—cholesterol heaven hand-cut daily. ✉ *147 E. College Dr.,* ☎ *970/247–5707. D, MC, V.*

$–$$$$ ✕ **The Red Snapper.** If you're in the mood for fresh fish, head to this congenial place, decorated with more than 200 gallons of saltwater aquariums. Try the oysters Durango, with jack cheese and salsa; salmon Wellington; or snapper Monterey with jack cheese and tarragon. Of course, delicious steaks and prime rib are also available. The salad bar is enormous. ✉ *144 E. 9th St.,* ☎ *970/259–3417. AE, MC, V. No lunch.*

$–$$$ ✕ **Ariano's.** This popular Northern Italian restaurant occupies a dimly lit room plastered with local art. It offers pastas made fresh daily and a sure touch with meats. Try the veal scallopini with fresh sage and garlic or the fettucine Alfredo. ✉ *150 E. College Dr.,* ☎ *970/247–8146. AE, D, DC, MC, V. No lunch.*

$–$$ ✕ **Carver's Bakery and Brew Pub.** This microbrewery run by the "Brews Brothers," Bill and Jim Carver, pours about eight tap beers at any given time, including such flavors as Raspberry Wheat Ale, Jackrabbit Pale Ale, and Colorado Trail Nut Brown Ale. There's a patio out back. From breakfast to the wee hours, the place is always hopping. Try the bread bowls filled with either soup or salad. ✉ *1022 Main Ave.,* ☎ *970/259–2545. Reservations not accepted. AE, D, MC, V.*

$–$$ ✕ **937 Main, Ken and Sue's Place.** This might well be Durango's favorite restaurant of the moment. Locals are wild for the artful contemporary cuisine served with a light touch of Asian and Southwestern accents. Try the pistachio nut crusted grouper with vanilla rum butter, or lemon pepper linguine. ✉ *937 Main Ave.,* ☎ *970/259–2616. No lunch weekends. AE, D, DC MC, V.*

$$–$$$ ★ 🏨 **New Rochester Hotel.** This one-time flophouse keeps up a funky chic atmosphere, thanks to mother-and-son team Diane and Kirk Komick, who rescued some of the original furnishings. Steamer trunks, hand-painted settees, wagon-wheel chandeliers, and quilts contribute to the authentic feel. Denver and Rio Grande train windows convert the back porch into a parlor car, and gas lamps under towering maple trees grace the courtyard. The owners also run the nearby Leland House B & B. A full gourmet breakfast is served to guests of both establishments in the lobby of the Rochester Hotel. ✉ *726 E. 2nd Ave., 81301,* ☎ *970/385–1920 or 800/664–1920,* FAX *970/385–1967,* WEB *www.rochesterhotel.com. 17 rooms, 8 suites. Restaurant, kitchenettes, massage. MC, V. BP.*

$$–$$$ ★ 🏨 **Strater Hotel.** This Victorian beauty originally opened in 1887 and has been lovingly restored. Inside, Henry's restaurant and the Diamond Belle Saloon sport crystal chandeliers, beveled windows, original oak

beams, flocked wallpaper, and plush velour curtains. The individually decorated rooms are swooningly exquisite: after all, the hotel owns the largest collection of Victorian walnut antiques in the country and even has its own wood-carving shop on site to create exact period reproductions. Your room might have entertained Butch Cassidy, Gerald Ford, Francis Ford Coppola, Louis L'Amour (he wrote *The Sacketts* here), JFK, or Marilyn Monroe (the latter two at separate times). ⊠ *699 Main Ave., 81301,* ☎ *970/247–4431 or 800/247–4431,* ℻ *970/ 259–2208,* WEB *www.strater.com. 93 rooms. Restaurant, bar, hot tub. AE, D, DC, MC, V.*

$$ ⚏ **Apple Orchard Inn.** This gem of a country inn sits on 5 acres in the
★   lush Animas Valley. The main house and six cottages surround a flower-bedecked pond, complete with friendly geese. There are cherry-wood antiques, feather beds, and handcrafted armoires in the handsome rooms. In the evening, relax on your cottage swing, enjoying views of the surrounding cliffs. The owners' experience at European cooking schools is evident in the breakfasts—and in the "train cookies" sometimes sent along with guests who take the train to Silverton. ⊠ *7758 County Rd. 203, 81301, 8 mi from downtown Durango,* ☎ *970/247–0751 or 800/426– 0751,* ℻ *970/385–6976,* WEB *www.appleorchardinn.com. 10 rooms. Hot tub. D, MC, V. BP.*

$–$$ ⚏ **Comfort Inn.** This is one of the nicer properties along Durango's strip, because it's clean, comfortable, and has sizable rooms. ⊠ *2930 N. Main St., 81301,* ☎ *970/259–5373,* ℻ *970/259–1546,* WEB *www. choicehotel.com/durangohotel.com. 48 rooms. Pool, 2 hot tubs. AE, D, DC, MC, V.*

Nightlife and the Arts

BARS AND CLUBS

The hot spot is the **Diamond Belle Saloon** (⊠ Strater Hotel, 699 Main Ave., ☎ 970/247–4431), whose antique, gold-leaf filigree bar, honky-tonk piano player, and waitresses dressed as 1880s saloon girls pack them in. **Lady Falconburgh's Barley Exchange** (⊠ 640 Main Ave., ☎ 970/382– 9664) is a favorite local pub with more than 140 beers available.

CASINOS

The **Sky Ute Lodge and Casino** (⊠ Ignacio, ☎ 800/876–7017), 25 mi southeast of Durango on Route 172, offers limited-stakes gambling.

DINNER SHOWS

Bar D Chuckwagon (⊠ 8080 County Rd. 250, East Animas Valley, 9 mi from Durango, ☎ 970/247–5753) serves barbecued beef, beans, and biscuits, along with a heaping helping of their Bar D Wranglers singing group.

THEATER

The **Diamond Circle Theater** (⊠ 699 Main Ave., ☎ 970/247–4431) stages rip-roaring melodramas in summer. The **Durango Lively Arts Co.** (⊠ Durango Arts Center, 802 2nd Ave., ☎ 970/259–2606) presents fine community theater productions.

Outdoor Activities and Sports

The **San Juan Public Lands Center** (⊠ 15 Burnett Court, Durango, ☎ 970/247–4874) offers both Forest Service and Bureau of Land Management information on hiking, fishing, camping and other recreational activities. This office also stocks maps and guidebooks. The **San Juan National Forest** (⊠ 701 Camino del Rio, Room 101, Durango, 81301, ☎ 970/247–4874) can provide information and permits for rock-climbing in the San Juan Mountains, as well as information on other outdoor activities.

Mountain Bike Specialists (✉ 949 Main Ave., ☎ 970/247–4066) rents bikes. For information on climbing, contact **SouthWest Adventures** (☎ 970/259–0370). **Duranglers** (☎ 970/385–4081) runs trips to fishing spots in the area. **Southfork Stables** (✉ 28481 U.S. 160, ☎ 970/259–4871) provides horses for riding tours. **Durango Rivertrippers** (☎ 970/259–0289) runs expeditions down the Animas River.

GOLF

Dalton Ranch and Golf Club (✉ U.S. 550, 7 mi north of Durango, ☎ 970/247–7921) is a Ken Dye–designed 18-hole championship course with inspiring panoramas of red-rock cliffs. The restaurant has become a popular hangout for both duffers and skiers, who enjoy watching the resident elk herd on its afternoon stroll.

Hillcrest Golf Course (✉ 2300 Rim Dr., ☎ 970/247–1499) is an 18-hole public course perched on a mesa. **Durango City Park** (☎ 970/385–2950) has free public tennis courts.

Shopping

BOOKS

Maria's Books (✉ 960 Main Ave., ☎ 970/247–1438) specializes in regional literature and nonfiction.

BOUTIQUES

Appaloosa Trading Co. (✉ 501 Main Ave., ☎ 970/259–1994) is one of the best venues for all things leather, from purses to saddles, hats to boots, as well as jewelry, weaving, and other crafts. **O'Farrell Hat Company** (✉ 563 Main Ave., ☎ 970/259–2517) form-fits hats with a "customizer" machine; heads they've fitted include former presidents Bush and Reagan. **Shirt Off My Back** (✉ 680 Main Ave., ☎ 970/247–9644) sells silk-screened T-shirts (choose from more than 60 images or create your own) with images of elk, horses, bears, mountains, and wildflowers.

CRAFT AND ART GALLERIES

The Mexican crafts are remarkably fine at **Artesanos** (✉ 1700 E. 2nd St., ☎ 970/259–5755), which also has a selection of eclectic furnishings from around the world. **Dietz Market** (26345 U.S. 160, ☎ 970/259–5811 or 800/321–6069) carries pottery, metalwork, candles, weavings, and foodstuffs, all celebrating the region. **Hellbent Leather and Silver** (✉ 741 Main Ave., ☎ 970/247–9088) sells Native American arts and crafts.

Toh-Atin Gallery (✉ 145 W. 9th St., ☎ 970/247–8277) has perhaps the best Western, Native American, and Southwestern art gallery in Colorado, offering a wide-ranging selection of paintings, pottery, prints, CD's, and jewelry.

En Route At the junction of U.S. 550 and U.S. 160 you have two options: Pick up U.S. 550 north toward Purgatory, or follow U.S. 160 east toward Pagosa Springs. Thirty-five miles from Durango is **Chimney Rock,** so-named for the distinctive, twin-rock spires that architecturally are more closely related to the Chaco Canyon Anasazi sites in New Mexico than to those in Mesa Verde. Anthropologists debate whether the rocks served as a trading post or as an astronomical observatory of great religious significance. Whatever the origin, many believe that the mystical ruins retain their power and resonance. Access to the site is only possible with a Forest Service guide; reservations are mandatory for the free tour. For information contact the Pagosa Springs Forest Ranger District (☎ 970/264–2268).

Pagosa Springs

48 *62 mi from Durango via U.S. 160 east.*

Although not a large town, Pagosa Springs, 17 mi east of Chimney Rock, is a major outdoor sports center, where hiking, fishing, and cross-country-skiing opportunities abound not far from an excellent but underused ski area, Wolf Creek (which has no lodging facilities). A bonus is the hot mineral baths right in town, where recreationalists can soak sore muscles. **The Springs,** made up of 13 outdoor tubs with temperatures ranging from 90–110 degrees, offer natural mineral waters that heal, soothe, and relax. ⊠ *165 Hot Springs Blvd.,* ☎ *970/264–2284.* 🎫 *$12.* ⊗ *5 AM–1 PM.*

Dining and Lodging

$ ✗ **Elkhorn Café.** Filling and fiery Mexican fare (try the stuffed sopaipillas), burgers and chile fries, makes this a popular drop-in spot. Fill up on a breakfast burrito before attacking the Wolf Creek bowls. ⊠ *438 Main St.,* ☎ *970/264–2146. AE, D, MC, V.*

$$ 🏠 **Davidson's Country Inn B&B.** This three-story log cabin is on a 32-acre working ranch in the middle of Colorado's San Juan mountains, just north of Pagosa Springs. The location is perfect, just 20 minutes from Wolf Creek Ski Area. Rooms are comfortable and crammed with family heirlooms and antiques. ⊠ *2763 U.S. 160 E, 81147,* ☎ *970/264–5863,* 🖷 *970/264–5492. 9 rooms, 4 with shared bath. Recreation room. AE, D, MC, V. BP.*

Outdoor Activities and Sports

Fairfield Pagosa Resort (⊠ U.S. 160, 3 mi west of Pagosa Springs, ☎ 970/731–4123) has both an 18-hole and a 9-hole course.

SKIING

With five lifts, 800 acres, and a 1,425-ft vertical drop, **Wolf Creek** is one of Colorado's best-kept secrets and a powder hound's dream: it's uncrowded with no lift lines, and it gets phenomenal snow (averaging more than 450 inches a year). The 50 trails run the gamut from wide-open bowls to steep glade skiing. ⊠ *U.S. 160, at the top of Wolf Creek Pass,* ☎ *970/264–5629.* ⊗ *Early Nov.–mid-Apr., daily 9–4.*

En Route Double back along U.S. 160 to Durango to continue on to Purgatory. U.S. 550 North from Durango along the section of the San Juan Skyway is also known as the **Million Dollar Highway.** Depending on whom you ask, the name refers to either the million dollars worth of gold and silver mined each mile along the stretch, the low-grade ore from mining residue that was used to pave the road, the cost of the road's construction, or the million-dollar views it offers.

Purgatory Ski Area at Durango Mountain Resort

49 *25 mi from Durango via U.S. 550 north.*

North of the U.S. 160 and U.S. 550 junction are two famous recreational playgrounds: the ravishing golf course and development at Sheraton-Tamarron and the Purgatory Ski Area at Durango Mountain Resort. Purgatory is about as down-home as ski resorts get, with a clientele that runs toward families, cowboys, and college kids on break.

What's unique about Purgatory is its stepped terrain: lots of humps and dips, and steep pitches followed by virtual flats. This profile makes it difficult for skiers to lose control. There are some great powder days on the mountain's back side that will convince anyone that Purgatory isn't just "Pleasant Ridge," as it's derisively known in Crested Butte and Telluride.

Dining and Lodging

$$$$ ✕ **Café Cascade.** Many locals' choice for the best restaurant on the mountain, if not in the region, this intimate split-level eatery features the Southwestern stylings of chef Roy Griffiths. The menu has been made more affordable in recent years. Try roast Colorado lamb with grilled Anasazi beans or grilled elk tenderloin over wild mushrooms in a lingonberry-merlot demiglaze. Rabbit satay with peanut sauce is a sterling appetizer. ✉ *50827 U.S. 550 N (1 mi north of Purgatory), Cascade Village,* ☎ *970/259–3500. AE, D, DC, MC, V. No lunch.*

$$$$ ★ ✕ **Sow's Ear.** It's a toss-up between the Ore House in Durango and this Purgatory watering hole for the "Best Steak House" award. The Sow's Ear gets the edge, though, for its great views of the mountain and show kitchen in the dining area where you can view your meal as it's prepared. The mouthwatering, fresh-baked jalapeño-cheese rolls and honey-wheat rolls, and creative preparations such as blackened filet mignon and the daunting "hodgeebaba"—an 18-ounce rib eye smothered with sautéed mushrooms and onions—are a few more reasons Sow's Ear leads the pack. ✉ *Silver Pick Resort, 48475 U.S. 550,* ☎ *970/247–3527. MC, V. No lunch.*

$$$ ★ **Purgatory Village Hotel.** This luxurious ski-in/ski-out property offers both hotel rooms and condos, all decorated with Southwestern flair, including Native American rugs and prints. The condos include full kitchen, private balcony, whirlpool bath, and wood-burning fireplace. ✉ *5 Skier Pl., 81302,* ☎ *970/385–2100,* FAX *970/382–2248,* WEB *www.durangomountainresort.com. 133 rooms. 2 restaurants, bar, pool, 2 hot tubs. AE, D, MC, V.*

$$$ ★ **Sheraton-Tamarron Resort.** This handsome development, on 750 acres surrounded by the San Juan National Forest, harmonizes beautifully with the environment. The main lodge seems an extension of the cliffs. Units are a blend of frontier architecture and Southwestern decor, and nearly all feature a fireplace, a full kitchen, and a terrace. Tamarron is famed for one of the country's most ravishing championship golf courses, and tennis and horseback riding (and condominium rentals) are also available. ✉ *18 mi north of Durango on U.S. 550; Drawer 3131, 81302,* ☎ *970/259–2000 or 800/678–1000,* FAX *970/382–7822,* WEB *www.tamarron.com. 412 rooms. Restaurant, bar, indoor-outdoor pool, hot tub, spa, 18-hole golf course, 3 tennis courts, horseback riding, children's programs (ages 4–12). AE, D, DC, MC, V.*

CONDOMINIUMS

There are fine condo units at **Cascade Village** (✉ 50827 U.S. 550 N, 81301, ☎ 970/259–3500 or 800/525–0896), a mile and a half north of the ski area.

Nightlife

Check out **Farquahrt's** (✉ Purgatory Mountain Village, ☎ 970/247–9000 Ext. 3123), which attracts a lively, youthful crowd and hosts bands on weekends.

Outdoor Activities and Sports

Sheraton-Tamarron Resort (✉ 40292 U.S. 550 N, ☎ 970/259–2000) is an 18-hole, 6,885-yard course, frequently ranked among *Golf Digest's* top 75 resort courses.

For snowmobiling, contact **Snowmobile Adventure Tours** (☎ 970/247–9000).

SKIING

Durango Mountain Resort (formerly Purgatory) has 75 trails, 11 chairs, 1,200 acres, and a 2,029-ft vertical drop—with a lot of intermediate runs and glade and tree skiing. For cross-country, there are 42 km (26 mi) of machine-groomed scenic trails just outside the ski area. ⊠ *U.S. 550,* ☎ *970/247–9000 or 800/525–0892.* ☉ *Late Nov.–early Apr., daily 9–4.*

Shopping

Honeyville Station (⊠ 33633 U.S. 550 N, Hermosa, ☎ 800/676–7690) south of Purgatory sells jams, jellies (try the chokecherry), condiments, and, of course, honey. You can watch how the bees make honey (in glass hives), and you may be treated to a lecture by a fully garbed beekeeper.

En Route   The tortuous northern route from Purgatory to Silverton begins a dizzying series of switchbacks as it climbs over the Molas Pass, yielding splendid vistas of the Grand Turks, the Needles Range, and Crater Lake. This is prime mountain biking and four-wheeler territory. On the other side of the pass you'll reach the town of Silverton.

Silverton

🔟 *20 mi from Purgatory via U.S. 550 north.*

Glorious peaks ring Silverton, an isolated, unspoiled old mining community. It reputedly got its name when a miner exclaimed, "We ain't got much gold but we got a ton of silver!" The entire town is a National Historic Landmark District. The **Chamber of Commerce** (⊠ 414 Greene St., ☎ 970/387–5654 or 800/752–4494) issues a fact-filled walking-tour brochure that describes—among other things—the most impressive buildings lining Greene Street: **Miners' Union Hall,** the **Teller House, Town Hall, San Juan County Courthouse** (site of the county historical museum), and the **Grand Imperial Hotel.** These structures hold historical significance, but more history was probably made in the raucous red-light district along Blair Street.

Silverton has always been a rowdy town with a hardy populace, and that spirit remains. Every summer evening at 5:30, gunfights are staged at the corner of Blair and 12th streets. But the lawlessness evoked by such events is only part of the heritage that the town wishes to commemorate. If you look north toward Anvil Mountain, you'll see the community's touching tribute to miners—the **Christ of the Mines Shrine**—built in the '50s out of Carrara marble.

Dining and Lodging

$–$$ ✕ **Handlebars.** As much a museum as an eatery, the restaurant is crammed with mining artifacts, antiques, and animal mounts—including a full-size elk. Baby-back ribs are the specialty, basted with the restaurant's own barbecue sauce (bottled to go). The hearty menu also includes steaks, hamburgers, mashed potatoes, and the like. On weekends, the action heats up on the dance floor with live country and western and rock bands. ⊠ *117 13th St.,* ☎ *970/387–5395. D, MC, V. Closed Nov.–Apr.*

$$–$$$ 🛏 **Wyman Hotel & Inn.** This wonderful 1902 red-sandstone building has 24-inch-thick walls, cathedral ceilings, and arched windows. The building is listed on the National Register of Historic Places. The attractive rooms all contain period antiques and pretty wallpapers, brass lamps, and VCRs. Five rooms have whirlpool tubs. A full breakfast and afternoon tea are included. The inn is entirely no-smoking. ⊠ *1371 Greene St., 81433,* ☎ *970/387–5372 or 800/609–7845,* FAX *970/387–5745,* WEB *www.thewyman.com. 13 rooms, 4 suites, 1 carriage house. Breakfast room, in-room VCRs. AE, D, MC, V. BP.*

$ 🛏 **Wingate House Bed & Breakfast.** Owner Judy Graham, a prominent landscape artist, adorns the walls of the inn with her and her friends' works and family photos dating from the Civil War; the entire effect is both sophisticated and homey. The breezy front porch overlooks a majestic "thirteener" (mountain higher than 13,000 ft). Large sunny rooms are filled with antiques and have down pillows, comforters, and an eclectic library culled from Judy's journeys. A well-set dining room table is the scene of breakfast. ✉ *1045 Snowden St., 81433,* ☎ *970/387–5584,* FAX *970/387–5520,* WEB *www.silvertonsaga.com. 5 rooms, 3 with bath. Dining room, hot tub. MC, V. BP.*

Nightlife and the Arts

A Theatre Group (✉ Miners Union Theatre, Greene St., ☎ 970/387–5337) presents a varied repertory season.

Outdoor Activities and Sports

St. Paul Lodge (✉ Box 463, Silverton 81433, ☎ 970/387–5494) is a terrific find for anyone enchanted by remote high country. Above 11,000 ft and about a half-hour ski-in from the summit of Red Mountain Pass between Ouray and Silverton, the lodge (a converted mining camp) provides access to a series of above-tree-line bowls and basins. Included in the lodge rates are guide service (essential in this potentially hazardous area), ski equipment, and telemark lessons if necessary, along with meals and lodging. Though only a few miles as the crow flies from Telluride, a car ride takes about an hour.

Shopping

Blair Street Emporium (✉ 1147 Blair St., ☎ 970/387–5323) specializes in all manner of Christmas ornaments, lights, and decorations. The Victorian gift shop **My Favorite Things** (✉ 1145 Greene St., ☎ 970/387–5643) stocks porcelain dolls; potpourri; antique jewelry; and romantic, lacy wearables.

Ouray

(51) *23 mi from Silverton via U.S. 550 north.*

The town of Ouray is trapped in a narrow, steep-wall valley in the bullying shadow cast by rugged peaks of the San Juan Mountains. It was named for the great Southern Ute chief Ouray, labeled a visionary by the U.S. Army and branded a traitor by his people because he attempted to assimilate the Utes into white society. The mining town is yet another National Historic Landmark District, with a glittering array of lavish old hotels and residences. The town's ultimate glory lies in its surroundings, and it has become an increasingly popular destination for climbers (both mountain and ice varieties), Fat-tire fanatics, and hikers. More than 25 classic edifices are included in the **historic walking-tour** brochure issued by the chamber of commerce (✉ 1222 Main St., ☎ 970/325–4746); among the points of interest are the grandiose **Wright's Opera House**; the **Beaumont, Western,** and **St. Elmo hotels**; and the **Elks Lodge.**

One particularly gorgeous jaunt is to **Box Canyon Falls and Park,** just south of town, off U.S. 550. The turbulent waters of Clear Creek (part of the falls) thunder 285 ft down a narrow gorge. A steel suspension bridge and various well-marked trails afford breathtaking panoramic vistas.

More opportunities to immerse yourself in nature present themselves at the various hot springs in the area. It's hard to tell which is more revivifying: the 104-degree waters or the views of surrounding peaks at the **Ouray Hot Springs Pool.** ✉ *U.S. 550 at the north end of town,* ☎ *970/325–4638.* 🎟 *$6.* ⏲ *Weekdays 1–9, weekends noon–9.*

For a trip to the springs' source, visit the **Wiesbaden Vapor Cave,** an underground chamber where you can soak in the pools and breathe in the hot vapors. Massage and mud wraps are offered at the spa here. ⊠ *625 5th St.,* ☎ *970/325–4347.* ➲ *$9 for vapor cave and pool.* ☉ *Daily 8 AM–9:45 PM.*

Lodging

$$–$$$ ⊞ **China Clipper Inn.** A welcome relief from the typical Western- or Victorian-style inns in this area, the China Clipper is tastefully decorated with Oriental and nautical antiques. Most rooms open onto a charming garden patio and hot tub. The inn was built almost entirely, with great attention to detail, by a retired Navy commander from Louisville, Kentucky. He is warm and interesting without being overly ingratiating. ⊠ *525 2nd St., 81427,* ☎ *970/325–0565 or 800/315–0565,* FAX *970/325–4190,* WEB *www.chinaclipperinn.com. 12 rooms. Hot tub. AE, D, MC, V. BP.*

$$ ⊞ **St. Elmo Hotel.** This tiny 1898 hostelry was originally a haven for "miners down on their luck," or so the story goes, thanks to its original owner Kitty Heit, who couldn't resist a sob story. Her son's ghost reputedly hovers about protectively. The rooms are awash with polished wood, stained glass, brass or mahogany beds, marble-top armoires, and other antiques. A complimentary breakfast buffet is served in a sunny parlor. The Bon Ton restaurant, Ouray's best, serves fine Continental cuisine with an Italian flair and a sophisticated wine list. ⊠ *426 Main St., 81427,* ☎ *970/325–4951,* FAX *970/325–0348,* WEB *www.stelmohotel.com. 7 rooms, 2 suites. Restaurant, breakfast room, hot tub, sauna. AE, D, DC, MC, V. BP.*

$$ ⊞ **Riverside Inn.** A comfortable stop beside the Uncompahgre River, this welcoming motel has recently been completely redecorated and features handmade Western log furniture. Cabins on the premises, which rent for $45 a night, are popular with ice-climbers and other sports hounds. ⊠ *1805 N. Main, 81427,* ☎ *970/325–4061 or 800/432–4170,* FAX *970/325–7302,* WEB *www.ourayriversideinn.com. 18 rooms, 4 suites, 10 cabins. Kitchenettes, laundry. AE, D, MC, V.*

$–$$ ⊞ **Box Canyon Lodge and Hot Springs.** The private mineral spring here was used first by the Ute, then by the Cogar Sanitarium (formerly on site). Soak away your cares in four redwood tubs full of steaming 103-degree to 107-degree water, with mountain views around you. The rooms are nondescript, but modern and comfortable, with all amenities. ⊠ *45 3rd Ave., 81427,* ☎ *970/325–4981 or 800/327–5080,* FAX *970/325–0223,* WEB *www.boxcanyonouray.com. 38 rooms. Hot springs. AE, D, DC, MC, V.*

Outdoor Activities and Sports

Ouray has some of the best four-wheel-drive roads in the country (they lead to ghost towns high in the San Juans), but you should be an experienced off-roader to explore them solo. **Switzerland of America Tours** (☎ 970/325–4484) leads guided tours in open-air, six-passenger Jeeps.

San Juan Skyway Marina (⊠ U.S. 550, ☎ 970/626–5094; 970/626–5538 off-season) rents canoes and boats at the Ridgway State Recreation Area, 12 mi north of town. Free public tennis courts can be found at **Ouray Hot Springs Pool** (⊠ 1220 Main St., ☎ 970/325–4638).

Ouray is gaining fame in ice-climbing circles, with its abundance of frozen waterfalls. **Ouray Mountain Sports** (⊠ 722 Main St., ☎ 970/325–4284) arranges lessons and guided tours.

Shopping

Buckskin Trading Co. (⊠ Beaumont Hotel, 505 Main Ave., ☎ 970/325–4044) has an array of mining, railroading, Native American, and cowboy antiques and collectibles, but the emphasis in on the western book selection. **North Moon** (⊠ 801 Main St., ☎ 970/325–4885) carries irresistible jewelry and art. **Ouray Glassworks** (⊠ 619 Main St., ☎ 800/748–9421) sells exquisite handblown glass by Sam Rushing and leatherwork crafted by Robert Holmes.

Lake City

52 *45 mi from Ouray via the Alpine Loop Scenic Byway (summer only); 55 mi from Gunnison via U.S. 50 south and Rte. 149 north; 49 mi from Creede via Rte. 149 north.*

Lake City is noted for the superb hiking and fishing in Uncompahgre National Forest, especially at Lake San Cristobal. The town—with its collection of lacy gingerbread-trim houses and false-front Victorians—also has the largest National Historic Landmark District in Colorado. But Lake City is best known for the lurid history surrounding a notorious gentleman named Alfred Packer. Packer was a member of a party of six prospectors who camped near Lake San Cristobal during the winter of 1874. That spring, only Packer emerged from the mountains, claiming to have been deserted, and to have subsisted on roots and rabbits. Soon after, a Ute came across a grisly scene: strips of human flesh and crushed skulls. Packer protested his innocence and fled, but a manhunt ensued; Packer was finally caught nine years later, tried, and sentenced to life.

The inspiring **Alpine Loop Scenic Byway** joins Lake City with Ouray and Silverton. This circle is only open in summer and is not paved over Cinnamon and Engineer passes. However, this is four-wheel heaven, dizzily spiraling from 12,800-ft passes to gaping valleys.

Lodging

$$ 🏨 **Old Carson Inn.** This peaceful A-frame log cabin nestled among stands of towering aspen and spruce has seven rooms brimming with rustic charm and nicely appointed with down comforters. The complimentary country breakfast, served family style, should get you off to a good start. ⊠ *Box 144, County Rd. 30, 81235,* ☎ *970/944–2511,* FAX *970/944–0149,* WEB *www.oldcarsoninn.com. 7 rooms. Hot tub. AE, D, MC, V. BP.*

Southwest Colorado A to Z

AIRPORTS

The Durango–La Plata Airport receives daily flights from American, America West Express, Great Lakes Aviation (formerly known as United Express) and Rio Grande Air. Gunnison County Airport, which also serves Crested Butte, has flights by United Express, American Airlines, Delta, and Western Express. Montrose Airport is served by America West, American, Continental, and Great Lakes Aviation. Telluride Regional Airport, 5 mi from the resort town, welcomes flights from America West and Great Lakes Aviation. Telluride is notorious for being one of the hardest ski resorts in the country to fly into, mainly because its airport elevation is well above 9,000 ft. A little turbulence, a few clouds, and the next thing you know, you're landing in Montrose, 67 mi away, and taking a van to Telluride.

➤ AIRPORT INFORMATION: **Durango–La Plata Airport** (☎ 970/247–8143). **Gunnison County Airport** (☎ 970/641–2304). **Montrose Airport** (☎ 970/249–3203). **Telluride Regional Airport** (☎ 970/728–5313).

AIRPORT TRANSFERS

Several companies offer transportation between the airports and the resorts. Shuttles average $15–$20 per person. In Crested Butte, try Alpine Express. In Durango, Durango Transportation. In Montrose,

call Western Express Taxi. Telluride Express and Skip's Taxi service
Telluride's airport.
➤ TRANSFER INFORMATION: **Crested Butte: Alpine Express** (☎ 970/641–
5074 or 800/822–4844). **Durango Transportation** (☎ 970/247–4161
or 800/626–2066). **Montrose: Skip's Taxi** (☎ 970/728–6667). **Telluride
Express** (☎ 970/728–6667). **Montrose: Western Express Taxi** (☎ 970/
249–8880).

BUS TRAVEL
Greyhound Lines serves most of the major towns in the region.

The Crested Butte Mountain Express runs regularly between the town
and the ski area. Durango Lift has regular bus service up and down
Main Street, as well as to Purgatory Ski Area during ski season. The
Galloping Goose provides an in-town loop, while the gondola connects
the town of Telluride with the Mountain Village for free, 7 AM–11 PM.
➤ BUS INFORMATION: **Crested Butte Mountain Express** (☎ 970/349–
5616). **Durango Lift** (☎ 970/259–5438). **The Galloping Goose** (☎ 970/
728–5700).

CAR RENTAL
Avis, Budget, Hertz, and National have counters at Gunnison County
Airport. Budget, Dollar, and Hertz car-rental agencies have offices at
Telluride Regional Airport.

CAR TRAVEL
If you're entering Colorado from the south, U.S. 550, U.S. 160, and
U.S. 666 lead to the Four Corners region. From the east or west, I–70
(U.S. 6) intersects U.S. 50 in Grand Junction; U.S. 50 runs south to the
San Juans and Four Corners area. From the north, take I–25 to I–70
in Denver, for a long drive west to U.S. 50.

The main roads are Route 135 between Crested Butte and Gunnison;
U.S. 50 linking Poncha Springs, Gunnison, Montrose, and Delta; Route
149 between Gunnison, Lake City, and Creede; U.S. 550 from Montrose to Ridgway; Route 62 and Route 145 linking Ridgway with Telluride, Dolores, and Cortez; Route 110 running from Ridgway through
Ouray and Silverton to Durango; and U.S. 160, the closest thing to a
major highway in the area, from Cortez to Durango via the Mesa Verde
National Park north entrance.

Crested Butte is 230 mi southwest of Denver. Take U.S. 285 south to
U.S. 24 south to U.S. 50 west to Gunnison. From Gunnison, take Rte.
134 north to Crested Butte.

Telluride is 330 mi southwest of Denver. There is no such thing as a
direct route, but the fastest is probably U.S. 285 south to U.S. 24 south
to U.S. 50 west to Montrose. Take U.S. 550 south to Ridgway. From
Ridgway, take Route 62 west to Placerville and Route 45 south to
Telluride.
➤ ROAD CONDITIONS: ☎ 877/315–7623.

EMERGENCIES
➤ CONTACTS: **Cortez: Southwest Memorial Hospital** (⊠ 1311 N. Mil-
dred St., Cortez, ☎ 970/565–6666). **Durango: Mercy Medical Center**
(⊠ 375 E. Park Ave., Durango, ☎ 970/247–4311). **Gunnison Valley
Hospital** (⊠ 711 N. Taylor, Gunnison, ☎ 970/641–1456). **Montrose
Memorial Hospital** (⊠ 800 S. 3rd St., Montrose, ☎ 970/249–2211).
Telluride Medical Center (⊠ 500 W. Pacific Ave., Telluride, ☎ 970/
728–3848).

TAXIS

In most cases you'll need to call for a cab; taxis are plentiful and the wait is only about 15 minutes.

➤ LOCAL COMPANIES: **Crested Butte Town Taxi** (☎ 970/349–5543). **Durango Transportation** (☎ 970/259–4818). **Montrose Taxi** (☎ 970/249–8880). **Telluride Shuttle and Taxi** (☎ 970/728–6667). **Telluride Transit** (☎ 970/728–6000).

TOURS

Adventures to the Edge creates customized treks, ski tours, and alpine ascents in the Crested Butte area. ARA Mesa Verde Company runs three- and six-hour tours into Mesa Verde National Park. Durango Transportation arranges tours of Mesa Verde, Chaco Canyon (in New Mexico), and the San Juan Skyway.

Historic Tours of Telluride provides humorous walking tours of this historic town, enlivening them with stories of famed figures such as Butch Cassidy and Jack Dempsey.

Crow Canyon Archaeological Center promotes understanding and appreciation of ancestral Puebloan culture by guiding visitors through excavations and botanical studies in the region. Also included in the weeklong programs are day trips to isolated canyon sites and hands-on lessons in weaving and pottery-making with Native American artisans. Day programs are available on a reservation-only basis to families and groups. Native American guides at Ute Mountain Tribal Park lead grueling hikes into this dazzling primitive repository of ancestral Puebloan ruins, including the majestic Tree House cliff dwelling and enchanting Eagle's Nest petroglyphs. Tours usually start at the Ute Mountain Pottery Plant, 15 mi south of Cortez, on U.S. 666. Overnight camping can also be arranged.

➤ TOUR CONTACTS: **Adventures to the Edge** (✉ Crested Butte, ☎ 970/349–5219). **ARA Mesa Verde Company** (✉ Mancos, ☎ 970/529–4421). **Crow Canyon Archaeological Center** (✉ 23390 County Rd. K, Cortez 81321, ☎ 970/565–8975 or 800/422–8975. **Durango Transportation** (☎ 970/259–4818). **Historic Tours of Telluride** (☎ 970/728–6639). **Ute Mountain Tribal Park** (✉ Towaoc 81334, ☎ 970/565–3751 ext. 282).

VISITOR INFORMATION

➤ CRESTED BUTTE INFORMATION: **Crested Butte central reservations:** ☎ 800/544–8448. **Crested Butte–Mt. Crested Butte Chamber of Commerce** (✉ 601 Elk Ave., 81224, ☎ 970/349–6438 or 800/545–4505, WEB www.crestedbuttechamber.com). **Crested Butte Mountain Resort** (✉ 500 Gothic Rd., Box A, Mount Crested Butte 81225, ☎ 970/349–2378 or 888/223–3530). **Snow report:** (☎ 888/442–8883).

➤ TELLURIDE INFORMATION: **Telluride and Mountain Village Visitor Services** (✉ 666 W. Colorado Ave., Box 653, Telluride 81435, ☎ 800/525–3455). **Telluride Chamber Resort Association** (✉ 666 W. Colorado Ave., 81435, ☎ 970/728–3041, WEB www.telluride.com). **Telluride central reservations:** ☎ 888/605–2573. **Telluride Ski Resort** (✉ 565 Mountain Village Blvd., Telluride 81435, ☎ 970/728–6900). **Snow report:** ☎ 970/728–7425.

➤ TOURIST INFORMATION: **Cortez Area Chamber of Commerce** (✉ 928 E. Main St., 81321, ☎ 970/565–3414, WEB www.mesaverdecountry.com). **Durango Chamber Resort Association** (✉ 111 S. Camino del Rio, 81302, ☎ 970/247–0312 or 800/525–8855, WEB www.durango.org). **Gunnison County Chamber of Commerce** (✉ 500 E. Tomichi Ave., 81230, ☎ 970/641–1501 or 800/274–7580, WEB www.gunnisonchamber.com). **Lake City Chamber of Commerce** (✉ 306 N. Silver St., 81235, ☎ 970/

944–2527, WEB www.lakecityco.com). **Mesa Verde National Park** (✉ Box 8, Supt., Mesa Verde Park 81330, ☎ 970/529–4465, WEB www.nps.gov/meve). **Mesa Verde Country** (✉ Box HH, Cortez 81321, ☎ 800/253–1616, WEB www.mesaverdecountry.com). **Montrose Chamber of Commerce** (✉ 1519 E. Main St., 81401, 970/249–5000; Visitor Information Center, 17253 Chipeta Rd., 81401, ☎ 970/249–1726, WEB www.montrose.org/chamber2). **Ouray County Chamber** (✉ 1222 Main St., 81427, ☎ 970/325–4746 or 800/228–1876, WEB www.ouraycolorado.com). **Pagosa Springs Chamber of Commerce** (✉ 402 San Juan St., 81147, ☎ 303/264–2360 or 800/252–2204, WEB pagosa-springs.com). **Dolores Ranger District and BLM Field Office of the San Juan National Forest** (✉ 100 N. 6th St., Dolores 81323, ☎ 970/882–7296). **Silverton Chamber of Commerce** (✉ 414 Greene St., 81433, ☎ 970/387–5654 or 800/752–4494, WEB www.silverton.org). **Southwest Colorado Travel Region** (☎ 800/933–4340).

THE SAN LUIS VALLEY

At 8,000 square mi, the San Luis Valley is the world's largest alpine valley, nestled between the San Juan Mountains to the west and the Sangre de Cristo range to the east. Despite its average altitude of 7,500 ft, its sheltering peaks help to create a relatively mild climate. The valley is one of Colorado's major agricultural producers, with huge annual crops of potatoes, carrots, canola, barley, and lettuce. It's so self-sufficient that local businessmen threatened to secede in the 1950s to prove that the state couldn't get along without the valley and its valuable produce.

Watered by the mighty Rio Grande and its tributaries, the San Luis Valley also supports a magnificent array of wildlife, including flocks of sandhill cranes and even whooping cranes. The range of terrain is equally impressive, from the soaring fourteener, Mt. Blanca, to the stark moonscape of the Wheeler Geologic Area, to the tawny, undulating Great Sand Dunes National Monument. The natural beauty is simply awe-inspiring.

This highly religious, traditional area was settled first by the Ute, then by the Spanish, who left their indelible imprint in the town names and local architecture. The oldest town (San Luis), the oldest military post (Ft. Garland), and the oldest church (Our Lady of Guadalupe in Conejos) in the state are in this valley.

World-class climbing can be found outside Del Norte in the Penitente Canyon and in the Wheeler Geologic Area outside Creede. The Great Sand Dunes are a favorite hike. The Rio Grande National Forest offers more than a million acres of pristine wilderness. River tours, with trips down the Arkansas, Taylor, and Gunnison, can last for an afternoon or for 10 days, depending on the arrangements.

Numbers in the margin and in the text in the section below refer to bullets on the Southwest Colorado map.

Creede

❺❸ *105 mi from Gunnison via U.S. 50 west and Rte. 149 south; 49 mi from Lake City via Rte. 149 south.*

Creede once earned a reputation as Colorado's rowdiest mining camp and was immortalized in an evocative poem by the local newspaper editor, Cy Warman: "It's day all day in daytime, and there is no night in Creede." Every other building was a saloon or bordello. Bob Ford, who killed Jesse James, was himself gunned down here; other notorious residents included Calamity Jane and Bat Masterson. As delightful as the town is, its location is even more glorious, with the pristine Weminuche Wilderness 30 mi to the south and the Wheeler Geological Area 20 mi to the west, where the unusual rock formations resemble playful abstract sculptures or an M. C. Escher creation.

The **Creede Museum,** occupying the original Denver & Rio Grande Railroad Depot, paints a vivid portrait of those rough-and-tumble days. Highlights include an underground firehouse and mining museum. ⊠ *6th and San Luis Sts.,* ☎ *719/658–2374.* ⌸ *$1.* ☉ *Memorial Day–Labor Day, Mon.–Sat. 10–4.*

Lodging

$–$$ ⌸ **Creede Hotel.** A relic of the silver days, this charming 1890s two-story structure with a street-front balcony has been fully restored, and the rooms offer the usual Victoriana. The gracious dining room serves excellent meals in addition to the complimentary breakfast. ⊠ *120 Main St., 81130,* ☎ *719/658–2608,* FAX *719/658–0725,* WEB *www.creedehotel.com. 4 rooms. Restaurant. AE, D, DC, MC, V. BP.*

En Route   Continue along Route 149—declared the Silver Thread National Scenic Byway—on its impossibly beautiful journey east through South Fork (where Route 149 joins U.S. 160) and the **Rio Grande National Forest.** The route flirts with the Rio Grande, passes near the majestic North Clear Creek Falls, and ambles through numerous ghost towns along the way.

Del Norte

54 *38 mi from Creede via Rte. 149 south and U.S. 160 east.*

In and around Del Norte are several historic sites, one of which is an original 1870s station on the Barlow-Sanderson Stagecoach Line. The **Rio Grande County Museum and Cultural Center** celebrates the region's multicultural heritage with displays of petroglyphs, mining artifacts, early Spanish relics, and rotating shows of contemporary art. ⊠ *580 Oak St.,* ☎ *719/657–2847.* ⌸ *$1.* ☉ *May–Sept., weekdays 10–5, Sat. 1–5; Oct.–Apr., weekdays 11–4.*

Just west of town is the gaping **Penitente Canyon,** which is usually crawling with rock climbers. Several miles north of town, off Route 112, near La Garita, is another marvel—the towering rock formation **La Ventana Natural Arch.**

Shopping

Casa de Madera (⊠ 680 Grand St., ☎ 719/657–2336) sells upscale gifts and pottery. **Haefeli's Honey Farms** (⊠ 0041 S. Rd. 1, Monte Vista, ☎ 719/852–2301), on the way to Alamosa in Monte Vista, sells delectable mountain-bloom honeys.

Outdoor Activities and Sports

The Rio Grande River—between Del Norte and South Fork—teems with rainbows and lunker browns. Gold Medal waters, where special restrictions control the size and type of fish you can hook, abound in the area.

Alamosa

55 *34 mi from Del Norte via U.S. 160 east.*

The San Luis Valley's major city is best known as the Olympic high-altitude training center for long-distance runners. Just outside town is the **Alamosa National Vista Wildlife Refuge.** These natural and man-made wetlands—an anomaly amid the arid surroundings—are an important sanctuary for the nearly extinct whooping crane and its cousin, the sandhill. ✉ *9383 El Rancho La.,* ☎ *719/589–4021.* ☑ *Free.* ☉ *Daily sunrise–sunset.*

The **Adams State College** complex (in town, along Main Street) contains several superlative examples of 1930s, WPA-commissioned murals in its administrative building. The college's **Luther Bean Museum and Art Gallery** displays European porcelain and furniture collections in a handsome, wood-paneled 19th-century drawing room, and changing exhibits of regional arts and crafts. ✉ *Richardson Hall, Richardson and Third Sts.,* ☎ *719/587–7011.* ☑ *Free.* ☉ *Weekdays 1–4:30.*

<table>
<tr><td>OFF THE
BEATEN PATH</td><td>**MANASSA** – Known as the Manassa Mauler, one of the greatest heavy-weight boxing champions of all time is honored at the **Jack Dempsey Museum** (✉ 401 Main St., ☎ 719/843–5207. ☉ Memorial Day–Sept., Mon.–Sat., 9–5). Also in Manassa, **Destiny Pewter** (✉ 419 Main St., ☎ 719/843–0821) fashions seemingly everything—from bolos to belts, charms to figurines—in pewter. The town is 23 mi from Alamosa, south on U.S. 285 and east on Route 142.</td></tr>
</table>

Dining and Lodging

$–$$ ✕ **True Grits.** At this noisy steak house the cuts are predictably good, but that's not the real draw: as the name implies, the restaurant is really a shrine to John Wayne. His portraits hang everywhere: the Duke in action; the Duke in repose; the Duke lost in thought. ✉ *Junction U.S. 160 and Rte. 17,* ☎ *719/589–9954. MC, V.*

$$ ⌂ **Conejos River Guest Ranch.** On the Conejos River, this peaceful, family-friendly retreat 14 mi south of Alamosa offers private fishing. The six cabins—all fully equipped—and eight guest rooms are pleasantly outfitted with ranch-style decor, including lodgepole pine furnishings. Breakfast is complimentary. ✉ *25390 Hwy. 17, Antonito, 81120,* ☎ *719/376–2464,* Ⓦ️ *www.conejosranch.com. 8 rooms, 6 cabins. Restaurant, horseback riding, fishing. D, MC, V. Closed Dec.–Apr. BP.*

$$ ⌂ **Cottonwood Inn B&B.** This pretty cranberry-and-azure, lovingly re-
★   furbished house is owned by host Debbie Donaldson. Public rooms feature both original and reproduction Stickley woodwork and furnishings; regional photographs and watercolors (most of them for sale) grace the walls. In the five sunny rooms with country-French washed walls, there are hand-painted florets, framed knits, weavings, dried flowers, lace curtains, and predominantly wicker furnishings. There are also four suites, two with oak floors and all with claw-foot tubs. A complimentary breakfast is provided. Cooking workshops take place monthly. ✉ *123 San Juan Ave., 81101,* ☎ *719/589–3882 or 800/955–2623,* ℻ *719/589–6437,* Ⓦ️ *cottonwoodinn.com. 5 rooms, 4 suites, 1 carriage house. Breakfast room. AE, DC, MC, V. BP.*

$ ⌂ **Best Western Alamosa Inn.** This sprawling, well-maintained complex, scattered over several blocks, is the best hotel bet in town. Rooms are spacious and offer the standard amenities. ✉ *1919 Main St., 81101,* ☎ *719/589–3567,* ℻ *719/589–0767,* Ⓦ️ *www.bestwestern.com/alamosainn. 120 rooms. Restaurant, bar, indoor pool. AE, D, DC, MC, V.*

Outdoor Activities and Sports

Cattails Golf Course (✉ 6615 N. River Rd., ☎ 719/589–9515) is an 18-hole, par-71 course that wraps scenically around the Rio Grande.

Shopping

Fireworks Gallery (✉ 608 Main St., ☎ 719/589–6064) carries fine art, collectibles, jewelry, weavings and prints. The San Luis Valley is noted for its produce. Mycophiles should stop by the **Rakhra Mushroom Farm** (✉ 10719 Rd. 5 S, ☎ 719/589–5882). **The Turquoise Shop** (✉ 423 San Juan Ave., ☎ 719/589–2631) sells sterling silver and turquoise jewelry and various arts and crafts.

Great Sand Dunes National Monument

56 *35 mi from Alamosa via U.S. 160 east and Rte. 150 north.*

Created by windswept grains from the Rio Grande floor, the sand dunes—which rise up to 700 ft in height—are an improbable, unforgettable sight silhouetted against the sagebrush plains and looming forest slopes of the San Juans. The dunes, as curvaceous as Rubens's nudes, stretch for 55 square mi and are painted with light and shadow that shift through the day. Their very existence seems tenuous, as if they might blow away before your eyes, yet they're solid enough to withstand the stress of hikers and skiers. The sand is as fine and feathery as you'll find anywhere. It's a place for contemplation and repose, the silence broken only by passing birds and the faint rush of water from the Medano Creek. The park is open 24 hours. ✉ *11500 Rte. 150, Mosca,* ☎ *719/378–2312,* WEB *www.nps.gov/grsa.* ⌧ *$3.* ☉ *Monument daily; visitor center daily 9–6.*

Just outside the national monument is the **Great Sand Dunes Oases** (✉ 5400 Hwy. 150, Mosca 81146, ☎ 719/378–2222), with restaurant, gift shop, motel rooms, campground—and the concession for tours of the sand dunes. The two-hour tours are in four-wheel-drive, open-air, sun-shaded, converted trucks and cost $14.

Outdoor Activities and Sports

Great Sand Dunes Country Club (✉ 5303 Rte. 150, Mosca, ☎ 719/378–2357) is an 18-hole course with the billowing dunes as a backdrop.

San Luis

57 *46 mi from Alamosa via U.S. 160 east and Rte. 159 south; 32 mi from Manassa via Rte. 142 east.*

San Luis, founded in 1851, is the oldest incorporated town in Colorado. Murals depicting famous stories and legends of the area adorn the town's gracious tree-lined streets. A latter-day masterpiece is the *Stations of the Cross Shrine,* created by renowned local sculptor Huberto Maestas. Perched above town on a mesa called *La Mesa de la Piedad y de la Misericordia* (Hill of Piety and Mercy), its 15 figures illustrate the last hours of Christ's life. The trail culminates in a tranquil grotto dedicated to the Virgin Mary. San Luis's Hispanic heritage is celebrated in the **San Luis Museum and Cultural Center,** with its extensive collection of *santos* (decorated figures of saints used for household devotions), *retablos* (paintings on wood), and *bultos* (carved religious figures). ✉ *401 Church Pl.,* ☎ *719/672–3611.* ⌧ *$2.* ☉ *Weekdays 8–4:30, weekends 10–3.*

OFF THE
BEATEN PATH

FT. GARLAND – Colorado's first military post, established in 1856 to protect settlers, lies in the Sangre de Cristos (Blood of Christ, after the ruddy color of the peaks at dawn). The legendary Kit Carson commanded the outfit, and the six original adobe structures are still around, composing the Ft. Garland State Museum. The venue features a re-creation of the commandant's quarters, various period military displays, and a rotating local folk-art exhibit. ✉ *South of intersection of U.S. 160 and 159, 16 mi north of San Luis via Rte. 159, 24 mi east of Alamosa via U.S. 160,* ☎ *719/379–3512.* ⌧ *$3.* ☉ *Thurs.–Mon. 9–5.*

San Luis Valley A to Z

CAR TRAVEL
San Luis Valley can be reached by car via U.S. 160 from both the west (direct from Durango) and the east (via I–25 south to U.S. 160), or via U.S. 285 from New Mexico.

EMERGENCIES
➤ CONTACTS: **San Luis Valley Regional Medical Center** (✉ 106 Blanca Ave., Alamosa, ☎ 719/589–2511).

VISITOR INFORMATION
➤ TOURIST INFORMATION: **San Luis Valley Information Center** (✉ 947 1st Ave., Box 165, Monte Vista 81144, ☎ 719/852–0660 or 800/835–7254).

COLORADO SPRINGS AND VICINITY

The contented residents of the Colorado Springs area believe they live in an ideal location, and it's hard to argue with them. To the west, the Rockies form a majestic backdrop. To the east, the plains stretch for miles. Taken together, the setting ensures a mild, sunny climate year-round, and makes skiing and golfing on the same day feasible with no more than a two- or three-hour drive. This easy access to diverse outdoor activities attracts tourists seeking a varied vacation: you can climb the Collegiate Peaks one day, and go white-water rafting on the Arkansas River the next.

Colorado Springs is among the most contemporary cities in the West, with its sleek, shining arts and convention center. The region abounds in natural and man-made wonders, from the eerie sandstone formations of the Garden of the Gods to the space-age architecture of the U.S. Air Force Academy. However, the most indelible landmark is unquestionably Pikes Peak, from whose vantage point Katharine Lee Bates penned "America the Beautiful." The song's lyrics remain an accurate description of south central Colorado's many glories.

Colorado Springs

The Springs has a dazzling array of tourist attractions. Pikes Peak, for instance, is the state's most famous landmark, but only one of the city's many natural and man-made wonders. Other tourist draws include the Cave of the Winds, the Garden of the Gods, and historic neighborhoods such as Manitou Springs and Old Colorado City.

Colorado Springs was created by General William Palmer, president of the Denver & Rio Grande Railroad, as a utopian vision of fine living in the 1870s. The original broad, tree-lined boulevards still grace the southwest quadrant of the city. With the discovery of hot springs in the area, the well-to-do descended on the bustling resort town to take the waters and to enjoy the mild climate and fresh air. It soon earned the monikers "Saratoga of the West" and "Little London," the latter for the snob appeal of its considerable resident and visiting English population. The discovery of gold at nearby Cripple Creek toward the end of the 19th century signaled another boom for the Springs. In the early part of the 1900s, until the mines petered out just before World War I, the residents' per-capita wealth was the highest in the nation.

After World War II, the city fathers invited the military to move in, and the city's personality changed drastically. Today, a large portion of the local economy is derived from Department of Defense contracts, directly or indirectly, from the army's Fort Carson (Colorado's largest military base, just south of downtown Colorado Springs) and the Peterson Air Force Complex.

Colorado Springs, the state's second-largest city, made headlines in 1992 when it was identified as the headquarters for several right-wing groups behind the controversial Colorado state Amendment 2, which outlawed antidiscrimination legislation that gave protection to gays and lesbians. With active and retired military personnel and their families making up nearly a third of the population, it's no surprise that the Springs is staunchly conservative.

A Good Tour

Begin at the **U.S. Air Force Academy** ⑱. Directly across I–25 from the north gate of the academy is the considerable acreage of the **Western Museum of Mining and Industry** ⑲. Continue along I–25 South toward downtown and get off at Exit 147. A bronze rodeo bull lures visitors to the **Pro Rodeo Hall of Fame and Museum of the American Cowboy** ⑳. Now take I–25 or Nevada Avenue to the southern end of the city for a glimpse of its posher neighborhoods, where the **Broadmoor** ㉑ stands. From the Broadmoor, make a left onto Mesa Avenue, and then turn right onto Evans. Continue along Evans, and then take the Cheyenne Mountain Zoo Road to begin the ascent of Cheyenne Mountain. Aside from panoramic views of the city and Pikes Peak in the distance, the road leads to the **Cheyenne Mountain Zoo** ㉒ and then further spirals to the **Will Rogers Shrine of the Sun** ㉓. At the base of the mountain, turn west on Cheyenne Road and follow the signs to **Seven Falls** ㉔. Take Cheyenne Mountain Zoo Road back into town and turn north on Nevada Avenue. Colorado Springs' handsome downtown contains many historically significant buildings, including the **Pioneers Museum** ㉕. A few blocks north is the **Colorado Springs Fine Arts Center** ㉖. Take Nevada Avenue south and Boulder east to the **Olympic Training Center** ㉗. Cross under I–25 to Colorado Avenue and take it west, turning left on 21st Street, which you'll follow to **Ghost Town** ㉘ and the **Van Briggle Art Pottery Factory and Showroom** ㉙. Back on Colorado Avenue you'll find yourself in **Old Colorado City** ㉚, once a separate, rowdier town where miners caroused; today it's a National Historic Landmark District whose restored buildings house the city's choicest galleries and boutiques.

TIMING

You'll need a car, as these attractions are fairly spread out. It takes at least an hour to tour the Air Force Academy. The Olympic Training Center tours last an hour. Save some time to wander around the Broadmoor, and while you're in the neighborhood, at least drive through Seven Falls. The Fine Arts Center also merits at least 45 minutes.

Sights to See

㉑ **Broadmoor.** The pink-stucco, Italianate complex, built in 1918, still stands as one of the world's great luxury resorts, a tribute to the foresight of its original owner, the enterprising Spencer Penrose, one of Colorado Springs' wealthiest (and most conspicuously consuming) philanthropists. Having constructed the zoo, the Cheyenne Mountain Highway, and Pikes Peak Cog Railway, Penrose is credited with making the town the tourist mecca it is today. The free **Carriage House Museum** displays Penrose's prodigious carriage collection, from broughams (closed carriages with driver outside) to opera buses. ⊠ *Lake Circle,* ☎ *719/634–7711 ext. 5353.* ▨ *Free.* ⊙ *Museum Tues.–Sat. 10–noon, 1–5; Sun. 1–5.*

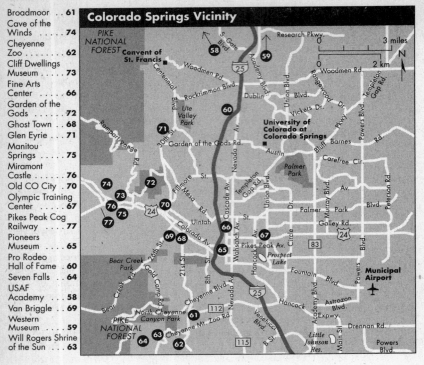

Colorado Springs Vicinity

62 **Cheyenne Mountain Zoo.** America's highest zoo, at 6,800 ft, has more than 500 animals amid mossy boulders and ponderosa pines. Highlights include feeding the giraffes or viewing the primates, wolves, or big cats of Asia. ⊠ *4250 Cheyenne Mt. Zoo Rd.,* ☎ *719/633–9925.* ☞ *$10.* ☺ *June–Sept., daily 9–6; Oct.–May, daily 9–5.*

★ **66** **Colorado Springs Fine Arts Center.** This pueblo-style space includes a performing-arts theater, an art school, and a room devoted to the work and life of famed western artist Charles Russell. Also at the center are a handsome sculpture garden, a surprisingly fine permanent collection of modern art, and rotating exhibits that highlight the cultural contributions of the area's diverse ethnic groups. ⊠ *30 W. Dale St.,* ☎ *719/634–5581,* WEB *www.csfineartscenter.org.* ☞ *$4.* ☺ *Weekdays 9–5, Sat. 10–5, Sun. 1–5.*

☝ **68** **Ghost Town.** You can play a real player piano and nickelodeon at this complete, authentic western town with a sheriff's office, general store, saloon, and blacksmith. ⊠ *400 S. 21st St.,* ☎ *719/634–0696.* ☞ *$5.* ☺ *May–Labor Day, Mon.–Sat. 9–6, Sun. noon–6; Labor Day–Apr., Mon.–Sat. 10–5, Sun. noon–5.*

70 **Old Colorado City.** Once a separate, rowdier town where miners caroused, today it's a National Historic Landmark District whose restored buildings house the city's choicest galleries and boutiques. ⊠ *Colorado Ave.*

67 **Olympic Training Center.** This is where America's hopefuls come to train and be tested, and depending on which teams are in residence at the time, you might catch a glimpse of some future Wheaties-box material. The guided tours every hour begin with a stirring half-hour movie, then take you on a half-hour walk around the facilities. A highlight is the flume—a kind of water treadmill, where swimmers can have every aspect of their stroke analyzed. ⊠ *1750 E. Boulder St.,* ☎ *719/578–4500.* ☐ *Free.* ☉ *Mon.–Sat. 9–4, Sun. 10–4.*

65 Pioneers Museum. Once the Old El Paso Courthouse, this repository of artifacts relating to the entire Pikes Peak area is most notable for the special exhibits it mounts (or are loaned on tour from institutions such as the Smithsonian), such as a quilt competition commemorating the 100th anniversary of the song "America the Beautiful." ⊠ *215 S. Tejon St.,* ☎ *719/385–5990,* WEB *www.cspm.org.* ☐ *Free.* ☉ *May–Oct., Tues.–Sat. 10–5, Sun. 1–5; Nov.–Apr., Tues.–Sat. 10–5.*

60 Pro Rodeo Hall of Fame and Museum of the American Cowboy. Even a tenderfoot would get a kick out of this museum, which includes changing displays of western art; permanent photo exhibits that capture both the excitement of bronco-bustin' and the lonely life of the cowpoke; gorgeous saddles and belt buckles; and multimedia tributes to rodeo's greatest competitors. ⊠ *101 Pro Rodeo Dr. (Exit 147 off I–25),* ☎ *719/528–4764,* WEB *www.prorodeo.com.* ☐ *$6.* ☉ *Daily 9–5.*

★ 64 Seven Falls. The road up to this transcendent series of seven cascades is touted as the "grandest mile of scenery in Colorado." Considering the state's splendors, that may be an exaggeration, but the red-rock canyon *is* amazing—though no more so than the falls themselves, plummeting into a tiny emerald pool. A set of 224 steep steps leads to the top, but there is an elevator too. ⊠ *Cheyenne Blvd.,* ☎ *719/632–0765.* ☐ *$6.50.* ☉ *May–Sept., daily 8 AM–11 PM; Oct.–Apr., daily 9–4.*

58 U.S. Air Force Academy. The academy, which set up camp in 1954, has become one of Colorado's largest tourist attractions. It's partly notable for its striking futuristic design, but even more extraordinary are the 18,000 beautiful acres of land that have been dedicated as a game reserve and sprinkled with antique and historic aircraft. Most of the campus is off-limits to civilians, but there is a ⅓-mi self-guided tour. At the visitor center you'll find photo exhibits, a model of a cadet's room, a gift shop, a snack bar, and a 14-minute film designed to make you want to run out and join up. Other tour attractions include a B-52 display, sports facilities, a planetarium, a parade ground (the impressive cadet review takes place daily at noon; other times of day, watch the freshmen square off their corners), and the chapel. The Air Force chapel is easily recognized by its unconventional design, which features 17 spires that resemble sharks' teeth or billowing sails. Catholic, Jewish, and Protestant services can be held simultaneously, without the congregations disturbing one another. ⊠ *Exit 156B, off I–25 N,* ☎ *719/472–0102,* WEB *www.airforcestore.com.* ☐ *Free.* ☉ *Daily 9–5.*

69 Van Briggle Art Pottery Factory and Showroom. The Van Briggle factory has been in operation since the turn of the 20th century, and its ceramic work is admired for its graceful lines and pure, vibrant glazes. A free tour of the facility is offered, culminating—naturally—in the mind-boggling showroom. ⊠ *600 S. 21st St.,* ☎ *719/633–7729,* WEB *www.vanbriggle.com.* ☐ *Free.* ☉ *Mon.–Sat. 8:30–5, Sun. 1–5.*

59 Western Museum of Mining and Industry. The rich history of mining is represented through comprehensive exhibits of equipment and techniques and hands-on demonstrations, including gold panning. The 27-acre mountain site has several outdoor exhibits, and is a great spot for a picnic. ⊠ *Exit 156A off I–25 N,* ☎ *719/488–0880,* WEB *www.wmmi.org.* ☐ *$6.* ☉ *June–Oct., Mon.–Sat. 9–4, Sun. noon–4; Nov.–May, Mon.–Sat. 9–4.*

63 Will Rogers Shrine of the Sun. This five-story tower was dedicated in 1937 after the tragic plane crash that claimed Rogers's life. Its interior

is painted with all manner of western murals (in which Rogers and
Spencer Penrose figure prominently) and is plastered with photos and
the homespun sayings of America's favorite cowboy. In the chapel on-
site are European pieces of art from the 15th and 16th centuries. ⊠
Cheyenne Mt. Zoo Rd.. ≊ *$10 (free with Cheyenne Mountain Zoo
ticket).* ⊙ *Memorial Day–Labor Day, daily 9–5:30; Labor Day–Memorial Day, daily 9–4:30.*

Manitou Springs and Environs

The home of Manitou Springs mineral water is set in this quaint National Historic Landmark District, which exudes a slightly shabby, but
genteel charm. The chamber of commerce offers free walking tours of
the springs. The springs are all naturally effervescent; you might stop
by Soda Springs for an after-dinner spritz (it tastes and acts just like
Alka-Seltzer), or Twin Springs, sweet-tasting and loaded with lithium
(which, say residents, is why they're always calm and smiling). Antique
trolleys ply the streets in summer. Manitou has a growing artist population; the Manitou Art Project sponsors a year-round public exhibition, and the galleries offer a delightful ArtWalk Thursday evening
in summer.

A Good Tour

Take U.S. 24 west from I–25 and 30th Street north to reach the **Glen
Eyrie** ⑦ estate. Double back on 30th Street to the **Garden of the Gods** ⑦
visitor center. Drive through Garden of the Gods and back onto U.S.
24 west to the **Cliff Dwellings Museum** ⑦ and the **Cave of the Winds** ⑦.
On the left of U.S. 24 headed west is **Manitou Springs** ⑦, home of the
mineral water. Off Ruxton Avenue, just past downtown is the **Miramont Castle Museum** ⑦. Continue down Ruxton Avenue to the **Pikes
Peak Cog Railway** ⑦.

TIMING

Most of Manitou Springs' attractions are clustered in a fairly small area;
you should be able to cover them on foot in an hour. The exceptions
are the Garden of the Gods and the Glen Eyrie estate, which you'll need
to drive to. The Cave of the Winds tours take 45 minutes; the Glen
Eyrie estate tours take about the same. Save some time to hike in the
Garden of the Gods and browse in Manitou Springs' downtown.

Sights to See

⑦ **Cave of the Winds.** Discovered by two boys in 1880, the cave has been
exploited as a tourist sensation ever since. The entrance is through the
requisite "trading post," but once inside the cave you'll forget the hype
and commercialism. You'll pass through grand chambers with such
names as the Crystal Palace, Oriental Garden, the Old Curiosity Shop,
the Temple of Silence, and the Valley of Dreams. The cave contains examples of every major sort of limestone formation, from stalactites and
stalagmites to delicate cave flowers, rare anthracite crystals, flowstone
(rather like candle wax), and cave coral. Enthusiastic guides for the
45-minute tour, most of them members of the Grotto Club (a spelunking group), also run more adventurous cave expeditions, called Wild
Tours. Summer evenings, a laser show transforms Williams Canyon,
the backdrop for the spectacle, into an unsurpassed sound-and-light
show of massively corny, yet undeniably effective, proportions. ⊠
Cave of the Winds Rd., off Hwy. 24, ☎ *719/685–5444.* ≊ *$15.* ⊙
May and Sept., daily 10–5; June–Aug., daily 9–9.

⑦ **Cliff Dwellings Museum.** You can see 40 rooms of prehistoric ruins, featuring ancestral Puebloan cliff dwelling ruins dated to AD 1100. Two
rooms of artifacts offer information on the history of the dwellings.

Native American dancing takes place several times a day during the summer in front of the cliff dwellings. ⊠ *U.S. 24,* ☎ *719/685–5242,* WEB *www.cliffdwellingsmuseum.com.* ☞ *$8,* ☉ *June–Aug., daily 9–8; May and Sept., daily 9–6; Oct.–Apr., daily 9–5.*

㉒ Garden of the Gods. These magnificent, eroded red-sandstone formations—from gnarled jutting spires to sensuously abstract monoliths—were sculpted more than 300 million years ago. The visitor center has several geologic, historic, and hands-on displays. Follow the road as it loops through the Garden of the Gods, past such oddities as the Three Graces, the Siamese Twins, and the Kissing Camels. High Point, near the south entrance, provides camera hounds with the ultimate photo-op: the jagged formations framing Pikes Peak. ⊠ *30th St.,* ☎ *719/634–6666.* ☞ *Free.* ☉ *June–Aug., daily 8–8; Sept.–May, daily 9–5.*

㉑ Glen Eyrie. William Packer's grandiose estate is maintained by a non-denominational fundamentalist sect called the Navigators, which publishes various religious literary works. The original gas lamps and sandstone structures remain, many of whose rocks were hewn with the moss still clinging, to give them an aged look. Try to come here for high tea, or during the Christmas season, when there's an extravagant drive-through nativity scene. ⊠ *North of Garden of the Gods, 3820 30th St.,* ☎ *719/634–0808,* WEB *www.gleneyrie.org.* ☞ *$5.* ☉ *Tours June–Aug., daily at 11 and 1; Sept.–May daily at 1.*

㉕ Manitou Springs. The town grew around the springs, so all nine of them are smack in the middle of downtown. Competitions to design the fountains that bring the spring water to the public ensured that each fountain design is unique. The Chamber of Commerce publishes a free guide to the springs. ☎ *719/685–5089.* ☞ *Free.* ☉ *Daily.*

㉖ Miramont Castle Museum. This Byzantine extravaganza was commissioned in 1895 as the private home of French priest Jean-Baptiste Francolon. The museum is a mad medley of exhibits, with 46 rooms offering a wide variety of displays, from original furnishings to antique doll and railroad collections. ⊠ *9 Capitol Hill Ave.,* ☎ *719/685–1011,* WEB *www.pikes-peak.com.* ☞ *$4.* ☉ *June–Aug., daily 10–5; Sept.–May, daily 11–4.*

㉗ Pikes Peak Cog Railway. The world's highest cog railway departs from Manitou and follows a frolicking stream up a steep canyon, through copses of quaking aspen and towering lodgepole pines, before reaching the timberline and the 14,100-ft summit. ⊠ *Ruxton Ave. (depot),* ☎ *719/685–5401,* WEB *www.cograilway.com.* ☞ *$24.50.* ☉ *May–mid-Nov., daily 9–5; call for winter hrs.*

OFF THE BEATEN PATH
PIKES PEAK HIGHWAY – You can drive the 19-mi Pikes Peak Highway, which rises nearly 7,000 ft in its precipitous, dizzying climb to the Summit House, a pit-stop café and trading post, in approximately three hours, round-trip. This is the same route that leading race-car drivers follow every July in the famed "Race to the Clouds," at 100 mi an hour. ⊠ *Hwy. 24 west to Cascade (4 mi from Manitou Springs),* ☎ *719/684–9383.* ☞ *$8.* ☉ *Summit House: May–Oct., daily 7–7; Nov.–Apr., daily 9–3.*

Dining

$$$–$$$$ ✕ **Margarita.** Plants, adobe walls, terra-cotta tile, and mosaic tables lend an air of refinement to this fine eatery, whose constantly changing menu is an intriguing hybrid of Mexican and Continental influences. ⊠ *7350 Pine Creek Rd.,* ☎ *719/598–8667. AE, D, DC, MC, V. Closed Mon. No lunch weekends.*

\$\$–\$\$\$\$ ✕ **Briarhurst Manor.** The symphony of cherry wainscoting, balustrades,
★   and furnishings; Van Briggle wood-and-ceramic fireplaces; tapestries;
chinoiserie; and hand-painted glass make this one of the most exquisitely
romantic restaurants in Colorado. There are several dining rooms, each
with its own look and mood. Chef-owner Ken Healy serves an international clientele. Start with the house-smoked Rocky Mountain trout
mousse or alligator pear (avocado stuffed with seafood, topped with
both hollandaise and bordelaise sauces), then try the perfectly prepared
Châteaubriand or striped bass. Game is the specialty here, such as the
plains bison and mushroom roulade. ⊠ *404 Manitou Ave.,* ☎ *719/
685–1864. AE, MC, V. Closed Sun. No lunch.*

\$\$–\$\$\$\$ ✕ **Craftwood Inn.** This intimate, restful restaurant regularly hosted such
★   luminaries as Cary Grant, Bing Crosby, and Liberace. The inn is more
than 50 years old, with a delightful Old English feel, with wrought-
iron chandeliers, stained-glass partitions, heavy wood beams, and a majestic stone-and-copper fireplace. To start, try the crab-and-artichoke
bisque, pistachio-pesto ravioli, or warm spinach salad with wild boar
bacon. The mixed game bird and wild grill are particularly memorable
entrées, especially when accompanied by a selection from the well-con-
sidered and fairly priced wine list. ⊠ *404 El Paso Blvd., Manitou Springs,*
☎ *719/685–9000. AE, D, DC, MC, V. No lunch.*

\$\$–\$\$\$ ✕ **La Petite Maison.** This pretty Victorian abode has been divided into
several romantic dining rooms. Pale pink walls, floral tracery, Parisian
gallery posters, and pots overflowing with flowers create the atmosphere
of a French country home. The menu offers an expert balance of old-
fashioned standards and newfangled southwestern fare. Recommended
appetizers include curried shrimp crêpe with banana chutney, and
seared Hudson Valley foie-gras poached with white figs. Top-notch main
courses range from brined half-duck with cinnamon fruit sauce to
rosemary pork tenderloin. ⊠ *1015 W. Colorado Ave.,* ☎ *719/632–
4887. Reservations essential. AE, D, DC, MC, V. Closed Sun. and Mon.*

\$\$–\$\$\$ ✕ **Pepper Tree.** From its hilltop position the Pepper Tree enjoys smash-
ing views of the city that enhance the restaurant's aura of quiet sophistication. Interior decor features a pink-and-maroon color scheme
and a mirror wall. Table-side preparations (including the inevitable and
delectable pepper steak) are its stock-in-trade, though the chef will go
out on a limb with such daily features as calamari stuffed with crab-
meat and bacon. Still, this is one of those old-fashioned places where
flambé is considered the height of both elegance and decadence. The
chicken marsala and lamb chops are superb. Reservations are recommended. ⊠ *888 W. Moreno Ave.,* ☎ *719/471–4888. Jacket and tie.
AE, D, DC, MC, V. Closed Sun. and Mon. No lunch.*

\$ ✕ **Adam's Mountain Café.** With whirring ceiling fans, hanging plants,
floral wallpaper, and old-fashioned hardwood tables and chairs, this
cozy eatery is reminiscent of someone's great-grandmother's parlor. Come
here for smashing breakfasts (wondrous muffins and organic juices);
fine pastas (try the baked penne with peperonata and three cheeses);
great sandwiches (red-chile-rubbed free-range chicken on grilled po-
lenta with red chile sauce and lime sour cream); and yummy desserts.
⊠ *110 Cañon Ave.,* ☎ *719/685–1430. Reservations not accepted. MC,
V. No dinner Sun. and Mon.*

\$ ✕ **El Tesoro.** At the turn of the 20th century, this building served as a
★   brothel, and then for many years it was an atelier for various artists.
Today, it's a restaurant that doubles as an art gallery. The adobe and
exposed brick walls and the tile work are original; rugs, textiles, and
the ubiquitous garlands of chile add color. The sterling northern New
Mexican food is the real thing—a savvy, savory blend of Native American, Spanish, and Anglo-American influences. The *posole* (hominy
with pork and red chile) is magical, the green chile heavenly, and in-

novative originals such as mango quesadillas (a brilliant pairing of sweet and spicy elements) are simply genius. ⊠ *10 N. Sierra Madre St.,* ☏ *719/471–0106. AE, D, MC, V. Closed Sun. No dinner Mon. No lunch Sat.*

$ ✕ **King's Chef.** This original Valentine diner is scarcely recognizable as such, with the pink and purple turrets that have been added to make it resemble a castle. If you finish your order, consisting of a massive mound of real home fries or hash browns, served alongside an omelet or a red-chile cheeseburger, you'll receive a "clean plate" award to mark your achievement. For breakfast all day, humor from behind the counter, and rubbing elbows at the counter with all kinds of locals, check this place out. The food is far from gourmet, but it's substantial and worth the experience. ⊠ *10 E. Costilla Ave.,* ☏ *719/634–9135. No credit cards.*

$ ✕ **Old Chicago.** One of many "concept restaurants" popular throughout Colorado, this one features a sports bar in front and a pleasant enclosed atrium and outdoor patio in back. It's a pizza, pasta, and beer (110 varieties) joint, and it scores on all counts. ⊠ *7115 Commerce Center Dr.,* ☏ *719/593–7678. AE, MC, V.*

Lodging

$$$$ 🏨 **The Broadmoor.** One of America's truly great hotels, the Broadmoor ★ celebrates over eight decades of unwavering deluxe service. Completely self-contained, its 30 buildings sprawl majestically across 3,500 acres. The pink-and-ocher main building, crowned by Mediterranean-style towers, serenely commands a private lake. Rooms in this building are the loveliest, with period furnishings; others are more contemporary in style. The resort is renowned for its three world-class championship golf courses and former Davis Cup coach Dennis Ralston's tennis camps. Three of the nine restaurants (the Tavern, the Penrose Room, and the Charles Court) rank among the state's finest. ⊠ *Lake Circle, Box 1439, 80906,* ☏ *719/634–7711 or 800/634–7711,* FAX *719/577–5700,* WEB *www.broadmoor.com. 607 rooms, 93 suites. 9 restaurants, 3 bars, 2 pools (1 indoor), hair salon, spa, 3 18-hole golf courses, 12 tennis courts, health club, horseback riding, fishing, cinema, children's programs (ages 4–12), meeting room, car rental. AE, D, DC, MC, V.*

$$–$$$ 🏨 **Antlers Adams Mark.** Two previous incarnations of this hotel competed ★ with the Broadmoor for the rich and famous, thanks to its superb, historic location downtown. Built in 1883 by William Jackson Palmer, the founder of Colorado Springs, to house his antler collection, an "Antlers" has stood on this site ever since. The spacious, elegant marble and granite lobby strikes an immediate note of class when you enter, and the deep-cushioned sofas in the lounge make a comfortable place to read the paper or watch the news. The atrium off the lobby holds a day spa. The business traveler will find deluxe accommodations here. ⊠ *4 S. Cascade Ave., 80903,* ☏ *719/473–5600 or 800/444–2326,* FAX *719/444–0417,* WEB *www.adamsmark.com. 277 rooms, 13 suites. 2 restaurants, bar, in-room data ports, room service, indoor pool, indoor hot tub, health club, spa, business services, meeting room. AE, D, DC, MC, V.*

$$ 🏨 **Embassy Suites.** This is one of the original properties in this chain, and it's among the best. The airy atrium lobby, crawling with plants, has a stream running through it, stocked with koi fish. To complete the tropical motif, a waterfall tumbles lavishly into it. Suites are comfortable, favoring teal and dusty rose. The pool deck offers a view of Pikes Peak; jazz groups play here every Thursday night in season. The free breakfast is cooked-to-order. ⊠ *7290 Commerce Center Dr.,*

80919, ☎ 719/599–9100 or 800/362–2779, FAX 719/599–4644, WEB *www.embassysuites.com. 207 suites. Restaurant, bar, indoor pool, hot tub, sauna, gym, meeting room. AE, D, DC, MC, V. BP.*

$$ 🏠 **Holden House.** Innkeepers Sallie and Welling Clark realized their dream when they lovingly restored this 1902 Victorian home and transformed it into a B&B. Two rooms in the main house, two in the adjacent carriage house, and one in the Victorian next door are filled to the brim with family heirlooms and antiques. Fireplaces, oversize or claw-foot tubs in the private baths, and down pillows and quilts make guest rooms cozy. A full breakfast is served in the antique-filled dining room. ✉ *1102 W. Pikes Peak Ave., 80904, ☎ 719/471–3980. 5 rooms. AE, D, DC, MC, V. BP.*

$$ 🏠 **Red Stone Castle.** The Castle was built in the 1890s, and a stay here is a fantasy adventure, where you can have a turret of your own. In fact, the entire third floor, called the "Inspiration Suite," is your domain. A three-course gourmet breakfast is served in the Victorian-appointed dining room. The private 20-acre estate overlooking Manitou Springs has views of the Garden of the Gods and Colorado Springs. ✉ *601 S. Side Rd., 80829, ☎ 719/685–5070. 1 suite. No credit cards. BP.*

$$ 🏠 **Victoria's Keep.** Proud owners Gerry and Donna Anderson preside over this turreted 1891 Queen Anne B&B. The parlor verges on the Dickensian, with its slightly fussy, Victorian clutter. There are carved tile ceilings and intricate tracery. Each Victorian-style room has its own fireplace and some distinguishing feature—a Jacuzzi or a claw-foot tub, stained-glass windows, or thrilling views of Miramont Castle. Full breakfasts and afternoon tea add to the more-than-pleasant guest experience. ✉ *202 Ruxton Ave., 80829, ☎ 719/685–5354 or 800/905–5337, FAX 719/685–5913, WEB www.victoriaskeep.com. 6 rooms. Hot tub, mountain bikes. AE, D, MC, V. BP.*

Nightlife and the Arts

Colorado Springs' **Pikes Peak Center** (✉ 190 S. Cascade Ave., ☎ 719/520–7469) presents the Colorado Springs Symphony, as well as touring theater and dance companies.

BARS AND LOUNGES

The **Golden Bee** (✉ International Center at the Broadmoor, Lake Circle, ☎ 719/634–7711) is an institution. The gloriously old-fashioned bar, with pressed-tin ceilings and magnificent woodwork, features a piano player leading sing-alongs. **Judge Baldwin's** (✉ Antlers Adams Mark, 4 S. Cascade Ave., ☎ 719/473–5600) is a lively brewpub. The singles head to **Old Chicago** (✉ 118 N. Tejon Ave., ☎ 719/634–8812) for brews. **Phantom Canyon Brewing Co.** (✉ 2 E. Pikes Peak Ave., ☎ 719/635–2800), in a turn-of-the-20th-century warehouse, has rotating art exhibits, billiards, and great pub grub (try the pizzas or the sinful black-and-tan cheesecake brownie).

COMEDY CLUB

Laffs Comedy Corner (✉ 1305 N. Academy Blvd., ☎ 719/591–0707) showcases live stand-up comedy; some of the performers here are nationally known.

DINNER SHOWS

The **Flying W Ranch** (✉ 3330 Chuckwagon Rd., ☎ 719/598–4000), open mid-May–October, and weekends during winter, ropes them in for the sensational western stage show and chuck-wagon dinner. The **Iron Springs Chateau** (✉ across from Pikes Peak Cog Railway, ☎ 719/685–5104) stages comedy melodramas along with dinner, February–December.

MUSIC AND DANCE CLUBS

Cowboys (⊠ 3910 Palmer Park Blvd., ☎ 719/596–1212) is for hard-core two-steppers. **Rodeo** (⊠ 3506 N. Academy Blvd., ☎ 719/597–6121) tends to have a young, professional crowd attracted by nightly drink specials, live music, and a dance floor. You can dance part of the night away at the Broadmoor's **Stars** (⊠ 1 Lake Ave., ☎ 719/634–7711), a sleek, intimate boîte with a striking black granite bar, a black marble floor inlaid with gold stars, and walls covered with photos of celebrities who have stayed at the Broadmoor over the years. There is usually live jazz at the Broadmoor's **Tavern** (⊠ 1 Lake Ave., ☎ 719/634–7711) several nights weekly.

Outdoor Activities and Sports

There are numerous trails in the Pikes Peak area, including Barr Trail up the mountain and North Cheyenne Canyon Trail. The Garden of the Gods, outside Colorado Springs, is also popular, especially with rock climbers who test their skills on the stark spires and cliffs. Register at the visitor center if you're climbing. The **El Paso County Parks Department** (☎ 719/520–6375) can provide information about facilities in the Colorado Springs/Pikes Peak area.

The **Academy Riding Stables** (⊠ 4 El Paso Blvd., Colorado Springs, ☎ 719/633–5667) offers trail rides on horseback.

GOLF

The **Broadmoor** (⊠ Lake Circle, ☎ 719/634–7711) offers 54 splendid holes to guests and members. **Colorado Springs Country Club** (⊠ 3333 Templeton Gap Rd., ☎ 719/473–1782) is another fine 18-hole course. The public **Pine Creek Golf Course** (⊠ 9850 Divot Terr., ☎ 719/594–9999) has 18 holes.

Shopping

In Colorado Springs, the areas to shop are Old Colorado City, with numerous charming boutiques and galleries, and the very upscale Broadmoor One Lake Avenue Shopping Arcade. **The Citadel** (⊠ N. Academy Blvd. at E. Platte Ave., Colorado Springs), counts JCPenney and Dillard's among its more than 175 stores. The streets of Manitou Springs and Cripple Creek offer one souvenir shop and gallery after another.

BOUTIQUES

Brok'n Spoke (⊠ 2345 E. Boulder Ave., Colorado Springs, ☎ 719/632–3131) is a bazaar of western regalia, from square dance outfits to saddles. **The Rhinestone Parrot** (⊠ 739 Manitou Ave., Manitou Springs, ☎ 719/685–5333) sells brocaded and appliquéd purses, vests, and jackets; and antique costume jewelry.

CRAFT AND ART GALLERIES

Commonwheel Artists Co-Op (⊠ 102 Cañon Ave., Manitou Springs, ☎ 719/685–1008) exhibits jewelry and fiber, clay, and glass art. The **Dulcimer Shop** (⊠ 740 Manitou Ave., Manitou Springs, ☎ 719/685–9655) sells these stringed instruments. **The Flute Player Gallery** (⊠ 2511 W. Colorado Ave., Colorado Springs, ☎ 719/632–7702) carries southwest Native American art. **Helstrom Studios** (⊠ 712 W. Colorado Ave., Colorado Springs, ☎ 719/473–3620) showcases pottery and ethnic treasures. **Michael Garman Gallery** (⊠ 2418 W. Colorado Ave., Colorado Springs, ☎ 719/471–1600) showcases western-style paintings and contemporary sculpture.

Simpich Character Dolls (⊠ 2413 W. Colorado Ave., Colorado Springs, ☎ 719/636–3272) fashions detailed ceramic figurines and fabric dolls and displays extraordinary marionettes. **Van Briggle Art Pottery Factory and Showroom** (⊠ 600 S. 21st St., Colorado Springs, ☎ 719/633–7729) offers free tours of its world-famous facility that end with a visit to their showroom. Wood-carver Sophie Cowman's evocative pieces—from spoons to sculpture, made out of scrub oak, fragrant cedar, and cottonwood—are for sale at the **Wood Studio** (⊠ 725 Manitou Ave., Manitou Springs, ☎ no phone).

FOOD

Patsy's Candies (⊠ 1540 S. 21st St., Colorado Springs, ☎ 719/633–7215) is renowned for its saltwater taffy and chocolate. **Pikes Peak Vineyards** (⊠ 3901 Janitell Rd., Colorado Springs, ☎ 719/576–0075) offers tastings of its surprisingly fine wines, including merlots and chardonnays. **Rocky Mountain Chocolates** (⊠ 2431 W. Colorado Ave., Colorado Springs, ☎ 719/635–4131) tempts with chocolates of every variety, in delightful seasonal and holiday arrangements.

Colorado Springs and Vicinity A to Z

AIRPORTS AND TRANSFERS
Colorado Springs Airport is served by American, America West, Continental, Delta, Mesa, TWA, and United. The company Ground Transportation offers service from the Colorado Springs airport and downtown. For taxi service, try Yellow Cab.
➤ AIRPORT INFORMATION: **Colorado Springs Airport** (☎ 719/550–1900).
➤ TAXIS AND SHUTTLES: **Ground Transportation** (☎ 719/597–4682). **Yellow Cab** (☎ 719/634–5000).

BUS TRAVEL TO AND FROM COLORADO SPRINGS
Greyhound Lines and TNM&O Coaches both serve Colorado Springs.
➤ BUS INFORMATION: **Greyhound Lines** (☎ 800/231–2222). **TNM&O Coaches** (☎ 719/543–2775).

CAR TRAVEL
Interstate-25, which bisects Colorado and runs north–south from New Mexico to Wyoming, is the major artery giving access to the area. Colorado Springs is 68 mi south of Denver along I–25.

EMERGENCIES
➤ HOSPITALS: **Colorado Springs Memorial Hospital** (⊠ 1400 E. Boulder Ave., Colorado Springs, ☎ 719/365–5000).

LODGING
CAMPING
The Painted Rocks, South Meadows, and Colorado campgrounds are in the ponderosa forests; there are also campgrounds on the Ramparts Reservoir, where boating and fishing are allowed. The Forest Service can provide information.
➤ CONTACTS: **Forest Service** (☎ 719/636–1602).

TOURS
Gray Line offers tours of the Colorado Springs area, including Pikes Peak and Manitou Springs, as well as jaunts to Cripple Creek.
➤ CONTACTS: **Gray Line** (☎ 719/633–1181).

TRANSPORTATION AROUND COLORADO SPRINGS
Colorado Springs Transit serves most of the Colorado Springs metropolitan area, including Manitou Springs.
➤ CONTACTS: **Colorado Spring Transit** (☎ 719/385–7433).

VISITOR INFORMATION

➤ TOURIST INFORMATION: **Colorado Springs Convention and Visitors
Bureau** (⊠ 104 S. Cascade Ave., Suite 104, 80903, ☎ 719/635–7506
or 800/368–4748, WEB www.coloradosprings-travel.com). **Manitou
Springs Chamber of Commerce** (⊠ 354 Manitou Ave., 80829, ☎ 719/
685–5089 or 800/642–2567).

SOUTH CENTRAL COLORADO

South Central Colorado, its territory scouted and explored by the
likes of Kit Carson and Zebulon Pike, has plenty to offer history buffs.
The haunting remains of the Santa Fe Trail, which guided pioneers westward, weave through the southeastern section of the region. Towns such
as Cripple Creek and Trinidad are living history. In fact, residents are
so proud of their mining heritage that, despite economic hard times,
they've earmarked tax revenues to preserve local landmarks.

Between alpine and desert scenery are such thrilling natural attractions
as the Florissant Fossil Beds and Royal Gorge. Outdoorsy types love
the area: camping is superb in the San Isabel and Pike national forests.
For climbers, Collegiate Peaks around Buena Vista and Salida offers
a variety of ascents from moderate to difficult. The Royal Gorge, Redrocks Park, and Garden Park outside Cañon City are alive with intrepid clamberers. Pike, bass, and trout are plentiful in this region: favorite
fishing spots include Trinidad Lake, Spinney Mountain Reservoir (between Florissant and Buena Vista), and the Arkansas and South Platte
rivers.

The most direct route from Colorado Springs to the state's southern
border is I–25, but it's certainly not the most interesting. Instead,
make a loop to the west, starting in Cripple Creek and taking in Florissant Fossil Beds, Buena Vista, Salida, and Cañon City, and ending up
in Pueblo, to hook up with I–25 again. From here, you can detour to
the east to La Junta, and then rejoin I–25 in Trinidad. Finally, travel
west to the lovely Cuchara Valley, and you will have experienced most
of South Central Colorado's charms.

Cripple Creek

78 *46 mi from Colorado Springs via Rte. 24 west and Rte. 67 south.*

Colorado's third legalized gambling town, Cripple Creek once had the
most lucrative mines in the state—and 10,000 boozing, brawling,
bawdy citizens. Today, its old mining structures and the stupendous
curtain of the Collegiate Peaks are marred by slag heaps and parking
lots. Although the town isn't as picturesque as Central City or Black
Hawk, the other gambling hot spots, Cripple Creek—a little rougher
and dustier than the others—feels more authentic.

The **Cripple Creek District Museum** provides a glimpse into mining life
at the turn of the 20th century. ⊠ *East end of Bennett Ave.,* ☎ *719/
689–2634.* ⊡ *$2.50.* ☉ *Late-May–mid-Oct., daily 10–5; mid-Oct.–
late May, weekends noon–4.*

The **Mollie Kathleen Mine Tour** descends 1,000 ft into the bowels of
the earth in a mine that operated continuously from 1892 to 1961. ⊠
Rte. 67 north of town, ☎ *719/689–2466.* ⊡ *$10.* ☉ *Apr.–Oct., daily
10–4; tours every 40 min.*

Imperial Hotel and Casino offers a peek into the era's high life and
a chance spin on the wheel of fortune. ⊠ *123 N. 3rd St.,* ☎ *719/
689–7777.*

South Central Colorado

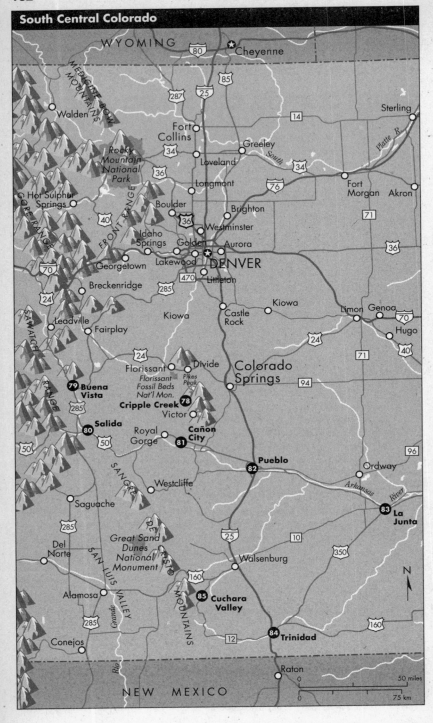

The **Cripple Creek and Victor Narrow Gauge Railroad** weaves past abandoned mines to Cripple Creek's former rival, Victor, 6 mi to the south. In bygone days, more than 50 ore-laden trains made this run daily. Today, however, Victor is a sad town, virtually a ghost of its former self; walking the streets—past several abandoned or partially restored buildings—is an eerie experience that does far more to evoke the mining (and post-mining) days than its tarted-up neighbor. ⊠ *Depot at Cripple Creek District Museum,* ☎ *719/689–2640.* ⊡ *$9.* ⊙ *Memorial Day–Oct., daily 10–5; departs every 45 min.*

Dining and Lodging

$$ ✕🏨 **Victor Hotel.** Listed on the National Register of Historic Places, the Victor Hotel is the nicest place to stay in the Cripple Creek area. Public spaces have been restored to their Victorian splendor, and guest rooms have mountain views. Unfortunately, aside from the original open brickwork and a few old-fashioned tubs and radiators, the decor and furnishings in the rooms are prosaically modern, and bathrooms are tiny. Adeline's Restaurant ($$; open June–September) serves steak and seafood. ⊠ *4th and Victor Sts., Victor 80860,* ☎ *719/689–3553 or 800/748–0870,* ₣₳ₓ *719/689–3979,* ₩ₑ₿ *www.victorhotel.com. 30 rooms. Restaurant. AE, D, MC, V.*

Shopping

Victor Trading Co. & Manufacturing Works (⊠ 114 S. 3rd St., Victor, ☎ 719/689–2346) has everything from beeswax candles to 43 styles of handmade brooms.

OFF THE BEATEN PATH | **FLORISSANT FOSSIL BEDS NATIONAL MONUMENT –** A primeval rain forest was perfectly preserved by volcanic ash 35–40 million years ago, making this little-known site a treasure trove for paleontologists. The visitor center offers guided walks into the monument, or you can follow the well-marked hiking trails and lose yourself in the Oligocene epoch, among 300-ft petrified redwoods. ⊠ *26 mi north of Cripple Creek via Rte. 67 and U.S. 24 (east); 3 mi south of Florissant, off U.S. 24, follow signs,* ☎ *719/748–3253,* ₩ₑ₿ *www.nps.gov/flfo.* ⊡ *$2.* ⊙ *May–Sept., daily 8–7; Oct.–Apr., daily 8–4:30.*

Buena Vista

79 *112 mi from Cripple Creek via Rte. 67 north and U.S. 24 west.*

Sky-scraping mountains, the most impressive being the Collegiate Peaks, ring Buena Vista (or as locals pronounce it, *byoo*-na *vis*-ta). The 14,000-ft giants were first climbed by alumni from Yale, Princeton, Harvard, and Columbia, who named them for their alma maters. A small mining town–turned–resort community, Buena Vista offers the usual historic buildings alternating with motels.

The most compelling reason to visit this area is for the almost unequaled variety of recreational activities, including rafting down the Arkansas River. Hiking, biking, and climbing in the **Collegiate Peaks Wilderness Area** are among the favorite jaunts.

After a full day of activities, check out the **Mt. Princeton Hot Springs** for a restorative soak. The springs have three swimming pools and several "hot spots in the creek." ⊠ *5 mi west of Nathrop, County Rd. 162,* ☎ *719/395–2447.* ⊡ *$6.* ⊙ *Sun.–Thurs. 9–9; Fri.–Sat. 9–11.*

Before leaving downtown Buena Vista, meander through the four rooms of the **Buena Vista Heritage Museum.** Each is devoted to a different aspect of regional history: one to mining equipment and minerals, another to fashions and household utensils, a third to working models of the three railroads that serviced the area in its heyday, and the last to historical photos. ⊠ *E. Main St.,* ☎ *719/395–8458.* ⊡ *$2.* ☉ *Memorial Day–Labor Day, daily 9–5.*

Lodging

$ 🏨 **Adobe Inn.** This adobe hacienda has five charming rooms, each named for its predominant decorative motif: antique, Mexican, Native American, Mediterranean, and wicker. Some rooms have a fireplace. The airy solarium is dominated by a magnificent kiva. The owners—Marjorie, Paul, and Michael Knox—also run the charming Casa del Sol Mexican restaurant next door. ⊠ *303 U.S. 24 N, 81211,* ☎ *719/395–6340. 5 rooms. Hot tub. MC, V. BP.*

Nightlife

Head to the **Green Parrot** (⊠ 304 Main St., ☎ 719/395–8985), which has live music weekends.

Outdoor Activities and Sports

CYCLING

Cycling is popular in the **Collegiate Peaks Wilderness Area,** around Buena Vista and Salida. **American Adventure Expeditions** (⊠ 228 N. F St., Salida, ☎ 719/339–4680) provides mountain-bike rentals and tours.

RAFTING

The rafting and kayaking on the **Arkansas River** can be the most challenging in the state, ranging from Class II to V, depending on the season. Contact **American Adventure Expeditions** (☎ 719/339–4680) or **Dvorak Kayak & Rafting Expeditions** (☎ 800/824–3795).

Salida

⑧⓪ *25 mi from Buena Vista via U.S. 24 and 285 and Rte. 291 south.*

Imposing peaks, including 14,000-plus-ft **Mt. Shavano,** dominate the town of Salida, which is situated along the Arkansas River. Salida draws some of the musicians from the Aspen Music Festival during the summer—classical pianists, brass ensembles, and the like—for its Salida–Aspen Series Concerts, July–August. The town's other big event is the annual (more than 40 years old) kayak and rafting white-water rodeo in June, on a section of river that cuts right through downtown.

Dining and Lodging

$–$$ ✕ **Antero Grill.** Featuring its own brand of "Modern American Cow-
★   boy Cuisine," and plenty of cowboy art, the Antero Grill is one of the best restaurants in the region, with creative combinations of home cooking with southwestern and Latin American flavors. Prickly pear cactus margaritas are the specialty of the house, along with the wrangler's meat loaf with wild mushrooms and green chile in a rich demiglaze, served with garlic mashed potatoes. The New Mexico red chile–seared salmon is worth a try too. Save room for homemade s'mores, a concoction of house-baked graham crackers, chocolate mousse, crème anglaise, and chocolate sauce. ⊠ *14770 Hwy. 285, between Salida and Buena Vista,* ☎ *719/530–0301. MC, V. Closed Mon.*

$ ✕ **First Street Café.** This café in the historic district serves creative heart-healthy and vegetarian specials, in addition to the expected robust Mexican-American fare. Breakfast is available, as are lunch and dinner. ⊠ *137 E. 1st St.,* ☎ *719/539–4759. AE, D, MC, V.*

$ 🏨 **River Run Inn.** On the Arkansas River, this gracious Victorian home has breathtaking mountain prospects. Rooms are filled with antiques and family memorabilia, and a complimentary breakfast is provided. ⊠ *8495 County Rd. 160, 81201,* ☎ *719/539–3818 or 800/385–6925,*

FAX *801/659–1878,* WEB *www.riverruninn.com. 8 rooms, 4 with bath. AE, MC, V. BP.*

Outdoor Activities and Sports

FISHING

The Arkansas River, as it spills out of the central-Colorado Rockies on its course through the south-central part of the state, reputedly supports a brown-trout population exceeding 3,000 fish per mile. Some of the river's canyon's are deep and some of the best fishing locations difficult to access, making a guide or outfitter a near necessity for anyone wanting to get at all those fish. **Browner's Fly Shop and Guide Service** (✉ 3745 Hwy. 50, Salida, CO 81201, ☎ 719/539–9350 or 800/826–6505) is more than a just local fly shop offering good advice. Guided trips on the Arkansas, as well as trips into the backcountry of the Sangre de Cristo Mountains, some of Colorado's most ruggedly beautiful, are among services rendered.

RAFTING

The largest company in the state, specializing in white water rafting on the Arkansas is **River Runners** (☎ 800/525–2081). **Canyon Marine Expeditions** (☎ 719/539–7476) takes families on exciting river expeditions.

SKIING

Monarch has 5 chairlifts, 54 trails, 670 acres, and a 1,170-ft vertical drop. The service is exceptional. Lift lines and lift ticket prices are nominal by most comparative standards. ✉ *U.S. 50 (18 mi west of Salida),* ☎ *719/539–3573.* ⊞ *$36.* ☉ *Mid-Nov.–mid-Apr., daily 9–4.*

Shopping

Art Gallery of the Rockies (✉ 5051 N. Academy Blvd., ☎ 719/260–1873) showcases limited-edition prints and does custom framing.

Cañon City

🟤 *50 mi from Salida via U.S. 50 east.*

Cañon City is an undeniably quirky town—and proud of it. Where else would you find a shop entitled "Fluff 'em, Buff 'em, Stuff 'em"? Would you have guessed the services it provides: hairstyling, car waxing, and taxidermy? From its aggressive, even tacky, strip-mall veneer (softened, fortunately, by some handsome old buildings) you'd think Cañon City existed solely for tourism. Nothing could be further from the truth. Cañon City's livelihood stems from its lordly position as "Colorado's Prison Capital." There are 10 prisons in the vicinity, all of which the citizens lobbied to get! It might seem a perverse source of income to court, but consider that the prisons have pumped nearly $200 million into the local economy, and, as an affable former mayor states, "You got these people walking around Denver and the Springs; here at least they're locked up." Temperate year-round conditions in Cañon City is what draws retirees in droves.

Morbid curiosity seekers and sensationalists will revel in the **Colorado Territorial Prison Museum,** which formerly housed the Women's State Correctional Facility. Now it exhaustively documents prison life in Colorado, through old photos and newspaper accounts, as well as with inmates' confiscated weapons, contraband, and one warden's china set. The individual cell exhibits were funded by local businesses and civic organizations. There's also a video room where you can view titles such as "Prisons Ain't What They Used to Be" and "Drug Avengers." The original gas chamber sits in the courtyard. This museum is grim, grisly, gruesome, and fascinating. ✉ *1st and Macon Sts.,* ☎ *719/269–3015,*

WEB *www.prisonmuseum.org.* ⌑ *$5.* ⊘ *May–Oct., daily 8:30–6; Nov.–Apr., Fri.–Sun. 10–5.*

☾ Not only is **Buckskin Joe Frontier Town** the largest western-style theme park in the region, but it's also actually an authentic ghost town that was literally moved here from its original site 100 mi away. Such famous films as *True Grit* and *Cat Ballou* were shot in this place, which vividly evokes the Old West, especially during the re-created gunfights and hangings that occur daily. Children love the horse-drawn trolley rides, horseback rides, and gold panning, while adults appreciate live entertainment in the Crystal Palace and Saloon. The complex includes its own scenic railway that travels to the rim of Royal Gorge. ⌂ *Cañon City, off U.S. 50,* ☎ *719/275–5149,* WEB *www.buckskinjoe.com.* ⌑ *Combination ticket for all attractions $14.* ⊘ *May–Sept., daily 9–6.*

☾ Cañon City is also the gateway to the 1,053-ft-deep **Royal Gorge,** which was carved by the Arkansas River more than 3 million years ago. The gorge is a commercially-run site and is spanned by the world's highest **suspension bridge.** Near the bridge, hubristic signs trumpet, "Who says you can't improve on Nature?" Never intended for traffic, it was originally constructed in 1929 as tourist attraction. More than half a million visitors come annually, causing a fair amount of exploitation to the area. Families love crossing the bridge, particularly on gusty afternoons when it sways, adding to the thrill.

You can also ride the astonishing aerial tram (2,200 ft long and 1,178 ft above the canyon floor, and across from the bridge) or descend the **Royal Gorge Bridge and Park** (the world's steepest-incline rail line) to stare at the bridge from 1,000 ft below. Also on hand are a theater that presents a 25-minute multimedia show, outdoor musical entertainment in summer, and the usual assortment of food concessions and gift shops.

The famed Royal Gorge War between the Denver & Rio Grande and Santa Fe railroads occurred here in 1877. The battle was over the right-of-way through the canyon, which could only accommodate one rail line. Rival crews would lay tracks during the day and dynamite each other's work at night. The dispute was finally settled in court—the Denver & Rio Grande won. ⌂ *Royal Gorge Bridge, 12 mi west of Cañon City,* ☎ *719/275–7507,* WEB *www.royalgorgebridge.com.* ⌑ *$16.* ⊘ *Daily 8:30–dusk.*

Dining and Lodging

$ ✕ **Janey's Chile Wagon.** Owner Janey Workman is a former New
★ Yorker who fled the big city and made it big. *The National Enquirer* did a feature on her: "Waitress Builds Diner into $350,000 Restaurant!" Her food is haute greasy spoon, with huge portions of delicious burritos and the like, smothered in "green chile that won't stay with you all night, hon." The decor favors neon parrots, velvet paintings, and other tchotchkes, but nothing is as colorful as Janey herself. ⌂ *807 Cyanide Ave.,* ☎ *719/275–4885. No credit cards. Closed Sun. and Mon.*

$ ✕ **Merlino's Belvedere.** This Italian standby has ritzy coffee-shop decor, with floral banquettes, centerpieces, and a rock grotto. Locals swear by the top-notch steaks, seafood, and pasta. It's the usual choice for a big evening out. ⌂ *1330 Elm Ave.,* ☎ *719/275–5558. AE, D, DC, MC, V.*

$$ ⌸ **Cañon Inn.** Some of the famous people who have stayed here—John Belushi, Tom Selleck, Jane Fonda, John Wayne, Glenn Ford, and Goldie Hawn among them—now have their names emblazoned on the door of a hotel room here in their honor. Spacious and ultracomfortable, basic accommodations are offered in two wings. ⌂ *U.S. 50 and Dozier St.,*

81212, ☎ 719/275–8676, FAX 719/275–8675, WEB *www.canoninn.com.*
152 *rooms. 2 restaurants, bar, pool, 6 hot tubs. AE, D, DC, MC, V.*

Outdoor Activities and Sports

Cañon City–owned **Redrocks Park,** 12 mi north of town, offers splendid hiking among the sandstone spires.

RAFTING

Rafting through the **Royal Gorge** is not an experience for the faint of heart, as you pass between narrow canyon walls through rolling Class IV and V waves, with hordes of tourists watching from the suspension bridge above. Several outfitters line U.S. 50.

Pueblo

82 *40 mi from Cañon City via U.S. 50 east; 42 mi from Colorado Springs via I–25 south.*

Pueblo is a city divided: it can't make up its mind whether to promote its historic origins or the active lifestyle it offers, with biking in the mountains and golfing in the desert. A working-class, multiethnic steel town, Pueblo lacks some of the traditional glamour of such towns as Aspen, whose growth mushroomed from gold and silver. Though sizable, it remains in the shadow of Colorado Springs to the north.

Civic leaders have embarked on an ambitious beautification plan, encouraging citizens to volunteer their time and talents. This has especially paid dividends in the extraordinary ongoing **Pueblo Levee Project,** the largest mural in the world. The grass-roots movement began with a lone artist's whimsical "statement," and now includes all manner of witty graffiti and illustrations gracing the levee along the Arkansas River. A splendid riverwalk, completed in late 2000, has been added to the stretch of the Arkansas perpendicular to the Historic Union Avenue District. There you're likely to find street fairs and classic car shows that draw what seems like the entire town.

The **Union Avenue Historic District,** including the glorious 1889 sandstone-and-brick Union Avenue Depot, is a repository of century-old stores and warehouses, now a fashionable commercial district. Among the landmarks are Mesa Junction, which celebrates Pueblo as a crossroads, at the point where two trolleys met; and Pitkin Avenue, lined with fabulous gabled and turreted mansions attesting to the town's more prosperous times. Walking-tour brochures of each district are available at the **Chamber of Commerce** (⊠ 302 N. Santa Fe Ave., ☎ 719/542–1704).

The **El Pueblo Museum** is ostensibly a holding place for the city's history, but it extends its scope to chronicle life on the plains from the prehistoric era onward, as well as Pueblo's role as a cultural and geographic crossroads, beginning when it was a trading post in the 1840s. The museum is located in temporary quarters while the new museum is under construction. ⊠ *119 Central Plaza,* ☎ *719/583–0453,* WEB *www. coloradohistory.org.* ⊡ *$2.50.* ☉ *Mon.–Sat. 10–3, Sun. noon–3.*

★ Unquestionably, the glory of Pueblo is the **Rosemount Victorian Museum,** one of Colorado's finest historical institutions. This splendid 24,000-square-ft, 37-room mansion, showplace of the wealthy Thatcher family, features exquisite maple, oak, and mahogany woodwork throughout, with ivory glaze and gold-leaf trim. Italian marble fireplaces, Tiffany-glass fixtures, and frescoed ceilings complete the expensive look. This museum is the height of opulence, and the rooms seem virtually intact. The top floor—originally the servants' quarters—features the odd Andrew McClelland Collection: objects of curiosity this eccentric philanthropist garnered on his worldwide travels, including an Egyptian mummy. ⊠ *419 W. 14th St.,* ☎ *719/545–5290,* WEB *www.rosemount.org.* ☎ *$5.* ⊙ *Tues.–Sat. 10–4; tours every half hour.*

Pueblo's equally vital concern with the present is documented in the gleaming **Sangre de Cristo Arts Center,** where several rotating exhibits in a well-thought-out space celebrate regional arts and crafts. The center also houses the superb, permanent western art collection donated by Francis King; a performing arts theater; and the brand-new **Buell Children's Museum,** which offers fun, interactive audiovisual experiences. ⊠ *210 N. Santa Fe Ave.,* ☎ *719/543–0130.* ☎ *$4.* ⊙ *Children's Museum Tues.–Sat. 11–4.*

Pueblo has an uncommonly fine **City Park** (⊠ Pueblo Blvd. and Goodnight Ave., ☎ 719/561–9664), which has fishing lakes, playgrounds, kiddie rides, tennis courts, a swimming pool, and the excellent **Pueblo Zoo** (☎ 719/634–7711, ☎ $4, ⊙ Daily 9–4, WEB www.pueblozoo.org)— a Biopark that includes an Ecocenter with a tropical rain forest, black-footed penguins, ring-tail lemurs, and green tree pythons.

At the airport, the **Pueblo-Weisbrod Aircraft Museum** traces the development of American military aviation, with its more than two dozen aircraft in mint condition, ranging from a Lockheed F-80 fighter plane to a Boeing B-29 Super Fortress of atomic bomb fame. ⊠ *31001 Magnuson, Pueblo Memorial Airport,* ☎ *719/948–9219,* WEB *www.co.pueblo.co. us/pwam/.* ☎ *$4.* ⊙ *Weekdays 10–4, Sat. 10–2, Sun. 1–4.*

OFF THE BEATEN PATH

BISHOP'S CASTLE – An elaborate re-creation of a medieval castle replete with turrets, buttresses, and ornamental iron is the prodigious (some might say monomaniacal) one-man undertaking of Jim Bishop, who began construction in 1969 and has hauled nearly 50,000 tons of rock used for the construction. Not yet complete, it soars three stories and nearly 75 ft, and Bishop has plans to build a drawbridge and moat. Bishop finances this enormous endeavor through donations and a gift shop. Anyone can stop by at any time; if you're lucky he'll be there, railing against the establishment (numerous posted signs graphically express his sentiments). To get there take I–25 south from Pueblo, turn west on Route 165 (Exit 74) and follow the signs. ⊠ *Rte. 75,* ☎ *719/485–3050.* ☎ *Free.* ⊙ *Daily, but hrs vary.*

Dining and Lodging

$–$$ ✕ **Café del Rio.** This adobe café has a sunny outdoor patio on the Arkansas River and a festive dining room. The kitchen turns out southwestern and Continental fare for lunch, afternoon "trail snacks," and early dinner (closing is at 9). Three-course prix-fixe dinners are served nightly, with dishes such as fresh grilled salmon and trout. The menu is fairly standard, but the setting on a summer evening makes it worth a stop. ⊠ *5200 Nature Center Blvd.,* ☎ *719/549–2009. AE, D, MC, V. Closed Mon.*

$–$$ ✕ **Irish Brew Pub & Grill.** This bustling, consistently jam-packed hot spot
★   is a bar and grill with a difference: it has a good kitchen. The owner *loves* food, and he has elevated pub grub to an art form. Even the house salad— field greens studded with pine nuts and blue cheese—is imaginative. Among the mouthwatering appetizers is a grilled smoked-duck sausage with goat cheese, topped with a honey-mustard sauce. Sandwiches are equally creative; try the buffalo burger or beaver (yes, beaver) sandwich. The range of entrées, many of them heart-healthy, is astonishing: from a dazzling prime rib to a lip-smacking, "border grill" turkey breast lightly dusted in flour, grilled, and then poached in chicken broth and raspberry vinaigrette. And of course, they brew their own beer—nine varieties. ⊠ *108 W. 3rd St.,* ☎ *719/542–9974. AE, D, DC, MC, V. Closed Sun.*

$–$$　✕ **La Renaissance.** This converted church and parsonage is the most imposing and elegant space in town, and the impeccably attired, unfailingly courteous waitstaff completes the picture. Continental standbys are filet mignon in mushroom sauce, superb baby-back ribs, and New Zealand deep sea bass fillet. The dinner price includes appetizer, soup, salad, and a sinful dessert. ✉ *217 E. Routt Ave.,* ☎ *719/543–6367. AE, D, DC, MC, V. Closed Sun. and Mon. No lunch Sat.*

$–$$　✕ **La Tronica's.** Although it's dressed like a saloon, with mirror beer signs and Christmas lights draping the bar, this sectarian restaurant is real "Mamma Mia" Italian. Waitresses, who invariably call you "sweetheart," have been here for as long as anyone can remember. Steak, seafood, scrumptious fried chicken, and homemade pastas are the lure. ✉ *1143 E. Abriendo Ave.,* ☎ *719/542–1113. AE, D, MC, V. Closed Sun. and Mon. No lunch.*

$　✕ **Grand Prix.** A neon sign announces the location of this authentic Mexican restaurant run by the Montoya family. Red neon lights and a painted false ceiling relieve the otherwise spartan decor. The food is classic: pork and avocado, chorizo, burritos, and Mexican steak, utilizing the flavorful local Pueblo chile and served with heaping helpings of rice and beans. ✉ *615 E. Mesa St.,* ☎ *719/542–9825. MC, V. Closed Mon. No lunch Sat.*

$–$$　▣ **Abriendo Inn.** This exquisite 1906 home, listed on the National Register of Historic Places, overflows with character. Gracious owner Ker-
★　relyn Trent did most of the painting, papering, and refurbishing. The house now gleams with its original, lovingly restored parquet floors, stained glass, and Minnequa oak wainscoting. The 10 no-smoking rooms are richly appointed with antiques, oak armoires, quilts, crocheted bedspreads, and either brass or four-poster beds. Fresh fruit and cookies are left out for guests, and gourmet breakfasts are included in the rate. ✉ *300 W. Abriendo Ave., 81004,* ☎ *719/544–2703,* 𝖥𝖠𝖷 *719/542–6544,* 𝖶𝖤𝖡 *www.abriendoinn.com. 10 rooms. AE, DC, MC, V. BP.*

$　▣ **Inn at Pueblo West Best Western.** This handsome, sprawling resort is a notch above most Best Westerns. Although it's out of the way for those who want to be close to town (about 15 minutes away by car), the golf course and activities on nearby Lake Pueblo keep guests busy. Rooms are large, have terraces, and are done in southwestern earth tones. ✉ *201 S. McCulloch Blvd., 81007,* ☎ *719/547–2111 or 800/448–1972,* 𝖥𝖠𝖷 *719/547–0385. 80 rooms. Restaurant, pool, 4 tennis courts. AE, D, DC, MC, V.*

Nightlife and the Arts

Gus' Place (✉ Elm and Mesa Sts., ☎ 719/542–0756) is a big yuppie hangout that once held a record for the most kegs emptied in an evening. The **Irish Brew Pub & Grill** (✉ 108 W. 3rd St., ☎ 719/542–9974) is always hopping after work hours. **Peppers** (✉ 4109 Club Manor Dr., ☎ 719/542–8629) has something going on every evening, from oldies nights to stand-up comedy.

Broadway Theatre League (✉ 210 N. Santa Fe Ave., ☎ 719/545–4721) presents touring shows and specialty acts. The **Pueblo Symphony** (✉ 2200 Bonfort Blvd., ☎ 719/549–2385) performs music, from cowboy to classical, throughout the year. The **Sangre de Cristo Arts and Conference Center** (✉ 210 N. Santa Fe Ave., ☎ 719/542–1211) presents various local and road shows.

Outdoor Activities and Sports

More than 110 parks, in addition to hiking and biking trails, help to define Pueblo as a sports and recreation center. The **Greenway and Nature Center** (✉ off 11th St., ☎ 719/549–2414), on the Arkansas River, offers fine cycling, hiking, and canoeing. A small interpretive center describes the flora and fauna unique to the area, while a **Raptor Rehabilitation Center,** part of the nature center, cares for injured birds of prey.

There is excellent camping and fishing at **Lake Pueblo State Park** (⊠ off U.S. 50 W, ☎ 719/561–9320), as well as many other outdoor activities. The south shore marina (☎ 719/564–1043) rents pontoon boats. You can hike in relative solitude in **San Isabel National Forest** (☎ 719/ 545–8737), 20 mi southwest of Pueblo.

CYCLING

Pueblo has an extensive **Bike Trail System,** which loops the city, following the Arkansas River part way, then goes out to the reservoir. There are popular in-line skating routes along these trails, too. The Pueblo Parks and Recreation Department (☎ 719/566–1745) can provide information.

GOLF

Desert Hawk Golf Course (⊠ Pueblo West Development, 8 mi west of town on U.S. 50, ☎ 719/547–2280) is an 18-hole championship course. **Pueblo City Golf Course** (⊠ City Park, ☎ 719/561–4946) is a handsome, highly rated 18-hole course. **Walking Stick Golf Course** (⊠ 4301 Walking Stick Blvd., ☎ 719/584–3400), an 18-hole course, is perennially ranked in the top 50 courses by *Golf Digest.*

Shopping

Pueblo's beautifully restored and renovated **Union Avenue Historic District** and **Mesa Junction** contain several fine antiques shops and boutiques. The **Midtown Center** (⊠ 1000 W. 6th St.) mall includes chains such as Sears. There is a flea market every weekend at the **Pueblo Fairgrounds.**

ANTIQUES AND COLLECTIBLES

Tivoli's Antique Gallery (⊠ 325 S. Union Ave., ☎ 719/545–1448) sells antique furniture. Numerous other antiques shops are to be found in the Union Avenue district.

BOUTIQUES

Gotcha Covered (⊠ 111 W. B St., ☎ 719/544–6833) sells unique clothing from around the world. **Razmataz** (⊠ 335 S. Union Ave., ☎ 719/ 544–3721) has creative clothing by local artists.

CRAFT AND ART GALLERIES

John Deaux Art Gallery (⊠ 221 S. Union Ave., ☎ 719/545–8407) specializes in contemporary art by southern Colorado artists. **Latka Pottery** (⊠ 229 Midway St., ☎ 719/543–0720) features the designs of Tom and Jean Latka.

FOOD

See what's possible to cook up with cookware and delicacies from **Seabel's Baskets and Gifts** (⊠ 105 W. C St., ☎ 719/543–2400).

En Route   If you head east on U.S. 50, leaving the Rockies far behind, you'll be traveling toward the eastern plains, where rolling prairies of the northeast give way to hardier desert blooms and the land is stubbled with sage and stunted piñons. One fertile spot—50 mi along the highway— is the town of **Rocky Ford,** dubbed the "Melon Capital of the World" for the famously succulent cantaloupes grown here.

La Junta

 65 mi from Pueblo via U.S. 50 east.

Wholesome La Junta was founded as a trading post in the mid-19th century. The town is notable for its **Koshare Indian Museum,** which contains extensive holdings of Native American artifacts and crafts (Navajo silver, Zuni pottery, Shoshone buckskin clothing), as well as pieces from Anglo artists such as Remington, known for their depictions of Native Americans. The Koshare Indian Dancers (actually a local Boy Scout troop) perform regularly, keeping their precious traditions alive. ⊠ *115 W. 18th St.,* ☎ *719/384–4411,* WEB *www.koshare.org.* ☜ *$2.* ☉ *Daily 10–5.*

The splendid **Bent's Old Fort National Historic Site** is a perfect example of a living museum, with its painstaking re-creation of the original adobe fort. Founded in 1833 by savvy trader William Bent, one of the region's historical giants, the fort anchored the commercially vital Santa Fe Trail, providing both protection and a meeting place for the military, trappers, and traders of the era. The museum's interior includes a smithy and soldiers' and trappers' barracks. The guided tour is most informative. ⊠ *35110 Hwy. 194 E,* ☎ *719/383–5010,* WEB *www.nps.gov/beol.* ☜ *$2.* ☉ *Daily 9–4.*

OFF THE BEATEN PATH

SANTA FE TRAIL'S MOUNTAIN BRANCH – This area of Colorado played a major role in opening up the West, through the Mountain Branch of the Santa Fe Trail. Bent's Fort was the most important stop between the route's origin in Independence, Missouri, and its terminus in Santa Fe, New Mexico. U.S. 50 roughly follows its faded tracks from the Kansas border through the pioneer towns of Lamar and Las Animas to La Junta, where U.S. 350 picks up the trail, traveling southwest to Trinidad. If you detour onto the quiet county roads, you can still discern its faint outline over the gentle hump of swales and the dip of arroyos. Here, amid the magpies and prairie dogs, it takes little imagination to conjure visions of the pioneers, struggling to travel just 10 mi a day by oxcart over vast stretches of territory.

Trinidad

 80 mi from La Junta via U.S. 350 southwest.

Initially founded as a rest-and-repair station along the Santa Fe Trail, Trinidad boomed with the discovery of coal in the area, followed inevitably by the construction of the railroad. The period from 1880 to 1910 saw major building and expansion. The advent of natural gas, coupled with the Depression, ushered in a gradual decline in population, but not of spirit. Trinidad's citizens contribute 1% of a 4% sales tax to the upkeep of the city's rich architectural heritage. That civic pride is clearly demonstrated in the town's four superb museums, a remarkably large number for a town its size. With all the new people moving into town, Trinidad is coming to life, with restaurants, cafés, and galleries opening downtown.

Downtown, called the Corazon de Trinidad, is a National Historic Landmark District containing splendid Victorian mansions, churches, and the glorious, bright red domes and turrets of Temple Aaron, Colorado's oldest ongoing synagogue. The **Chamber of Commerce** (⊠ 309 Nevada St., ☎ 719/846–9285) publishes an excellent walking tour of the neighborhood, which even retains its original paved brick streets.

The **Baca House/Bloom House/Pioneer Museum Complex** represents the most significant aspects of Trinidad's history. Felipe Baca was a prominent Hispanic trader whose 1870 residence—**Baca House**—is replete with original furnishings in the parlor, sitting room, kitchen, dining room, and bedrooms. The displays convey a mix of Anglo (clothes, furniture) and local Hispanic (santos, rosaries, textiles) influences. Next door, **Bloom House** provides an effective contrast to the Baca House. Frank Bloom made his money through ranching, banking, and the railroad, and although he was no wealthier than Baca, his mansion (built in the 1880s) reveals a very different lifestyle. The railroad enabled him to fill his ornate Second Empire–style Victorian (with mansard roof and elaborate wrought ironwork) with fine furnishings and fabrics brought from New York and imported from Europe. The adjacent **Santa Fe Trail Museum** is dedicated to the effect of the Santa Fe Trail on the community. Inside the museum are exhibits covering the days of Trinidad's heyday as a commercial and cultural center through the 1920s. Finish up with a stop at the **Historic Gardens,** a fine example of southwestern vegetable and herb gardens, as tended by the pioneers, with native plants and heirloom, century-old grapevines. ⊠ *Complex: 300 E. Main St.,* ☎ *719/846–7217,* WEB *www.trinidadco.com or www.coloradohistory.org.* ⊠ *$5.* ☉ *May–Sept., daily 10–4.*

The **A. R. Mitchell Memorial Museum and Gallery** celebrates the life and work of the famous western illustrator, whose distinctive oils, charcoal drawings, and watercolors graced the pages of pulp magazines and ranch romances. The museum also has his personal collection of other masters of the genre, such as Larry Heller and Harvey Dunn, as well as a re-creation of his atelier. The community holds Mitchell in great esteem: He was responsible for saving the Baca and Bloom houses from demolition, and he spearheaded numerous campaigns to restore the historic downtown. For a further glimpse into Trinidad history, be sure to see the **Aultman Collection of Photography** in the Memorial Museum Gallery. On display are photos by the Aultman family dating back to 1889; they offer a unique visual record of Trinidad. ⊠ *150 E. Main St.,* ☎ *719/846–4224.* ⊠ *Free.* ☉ *Mid-Apr.–Sept., Mon.–Sat. 10–4.*

On the other side of the Purgatoire River, the **Louden-Henritze Archaeology Museum** takes viewers back millions of years to document the true origins of the region, including early geologic formations, plant and marine animal fossils, and prehistoric artifacts. ⊠ *Trinidad State Junior College,* ☎ *719/846–5508,* WEB *www.tsjc.cccoes.edu.* ⊠ *Free.* ☉ *Jan.–Nov., weekdays 10–4.*

☾ The **Trinidad Children's Museum** is in the delightful Old Firehouse Number 1, and it displays fire-fighting memorabilia, such as a 1936 American LaFrance fire truck (children love clanging the loud bell) and the city's original fire alarm system. Upstairs is a fine re-creation of a Victorian schoolroom. ⊠ *314 N. Commercial St.,* ☎ *719/846–2024.* ⊠ *Free.* ☉ *Apr.–Sept., weekdays 1–4.*

Dining and Lodging

$–$$ ✕ **Black Jack's Saloon and Steak House.** Step inside this 1890s building, where you can toss your peanut shells on the floor while saddled up to the full-service antique bar. Between the bar and the leafy salad kind of bar is an open grill where the most succulent steaks on the Santa Fe Trail are prepared. Those avoiding red meat can go for salmon or swordfish. ⊠ *225 W. Main St.,* ☎ *719/846–9501. AE, MC, V. Closed Mon.–Tues. No lunch.*

$ ✕ **Main Street Bakery.** In a century-old building decorated with sunny interior murals, this homey café serves fresh-baked breads and desserts, a famous potpie, and Reuben sandwiches. The Oriental chicken salad is a thing of beauty, and ample enough for a full meal. Try the Branding Iron sandwich (roast beef and melted Brie on focaccia), or the Michiganer, turkey breast salad mixed with dried cherries. This spot is usually very crowded with locals and visitors both at breakfast and lunch. Don't want a meal? Drop in for a divine cinnamon roll and a cup of strong coffee. ⊠ *121 W. Main St.,* ☎ *719/846–8779. AE, MC, V. No dinner.*

$ ✕ **Nana and Nano's Pasta House.** This tiny eatery is saturated with the tempting aroma of garlic and tomato sauce. Pastas are uniformly excellent, with standards such as homemade ravioli, gnocchi Bolognese, and rigatoni with luscious meatballs among the standouts. If you don't have time for a sit-down lunch, stop at the deli counter for smashing heroes and gourmet sandwiches or takeouts of imported cheeses and olives. Fran Monteleone is your amiable host; it's her secret sauce that will drive you wild. ⊠ *418 E. Main St.,* ☎ *719/846–2696. AE, DC, MC, V. Closed Sun. and Mon.*

$ ⊡ **Best Western Country Club Inn.** To apply the term "country club" is exaggerating this lodging's amenities. Rooms are clean and comfortable and are decorated in warm earth tones. ⊠ *Exit 13A off I–25, 900 W. Adams St., 81082,* ☎ *719/846–2215,* FAX *719/846–2480,* WEB *www.bestwestern.com. 55 rooms. Restaurant, bar, pool, hot tub, gym, coin laundry. AE, D, DC, MC, V.*

Nightlife and the Arts

The Other Place (⊠ 466 W. Main St., ☎ 719/846–9012) hires top local rock bands on weekends to play its intimate classy space.

Outdoor Activities and Sports

There is hiking, fishing, horseback riding, and camping in the Purgatory River valley at the **Trinidad Lake State Recreation Area** (☎ 719/846–6951), 3 mi west of Trinidad on Route 12.

Cuchara Valley

85 *55 mi from Trinidad (to town of Cuchara) via Rte. 12 northwest.*

From Trinidad, Route 12—the scenic **Highway of Legends**—curls north through the Cuchara Valley. As it starts its climb, you'll pass a series of company towns built to house coal miners. **Cokedale** is nestled in Reilly Canyon. The entire town is a National Historic Landmark District, and it is the most significant example of a turn-of-the-20th-century coal/coke camp in Colorado. As you drive through the area note the telltale streaks of black in the sandstone and granite bluffs fronting the Purgatoire River and its tributaries, the unsightly slag heaps, and the spooky abandoned mining camps dotting the hillsides. The impressive **Stonewall Gap,** a monumental gate of rock, roughly marks the end of the mining district.

As you approach Cuchara Pass, several switchbacks snake through rolling grasslands and dance in and out of spruce stands whose clearings afford views of Monument Lake. You can camp, fish, and hike throughout this tranquil part of the **San Isabel National Forest,** which emblazoned with a color wheel of wildflowers in spring and summer. Four corkscrewing miles later, you'll reach a dirt road that leads to the twin sapphires of **Bear and Blue lakes** and the resort town of **Cuchara.** Nestled in a spoon valley ("cuchara" means spoon), the area become popular as a turn-of-the-20th-century camping getaway for Texans and Oklahomans because of its cool temperatures and stunning scenery. Today it is becoming known as one of the undiscovered gems of the Rockies for its outdoor recreational opportunities and unspoiled feel. The quaint western town consists of one main street lined with boardwalks and shops, bars, and restaurants, mostly open in summer only.

In the Cuchara Valley you'll begin to see fantastic rock formations with equally fanciful names, such as Profile Rock, Devil's Staircase, and Giant's Spoon. With a little imagination you can devise your own legends about the names' origins. There are more than 400 of these upthrusts, which radiate like the spokes of a wheel from the valley's dominating landmark, the **Spanish Peaks.** In Spanish they are known as *Dos Her-*

manos, or "Two Brothers"; in Ute, their name *Huajatolla* means "breasts of the world." The haunting formations are considered to be a unique geologic phenomenon for their sheer abundance and variety of rock types.

The Highway of Legends passes through the charming, laid-back resort town of **La Veta** before reaching its junction with I–25 at Walsenburg, another city built on coal, and the largest town between Pueblo and Trinidad. Colorado Springs is 90 mi north on I–25.

Dining

$$–$$$ ✕ **Silver Spoon.** On the banks of the Cuchara River, this elegant restaurant is one of Cuchara's charms. In winter, the candlelit dining room is warmed by a stone fireplace, with rustic sleds and skis completing the decor; in summer, dine outdoors by the river and wander across a small bridge to an island gazebo. The menu includes grilled bacon-wrapped shrimp, French-sauce preparations such as pepper steak with a raspberry and blackberry brandy cream sauce, and chicken with blue-cheese pepper sauce. Save room for the sophisticated homemade desserts. Reservations are essential in summer. ✉ *16984 Hwy. 12, Cuchara,* ☎ *719/742–3764. AE, D, MC, V. No lunch weekdays Nov.–Apr.*

South Central Colorado A to Z

AIRPORTS

The area is served by Pueblo Memorial Airport, which receives about three flights a day from United Express, which operates through Great Lakes Aviation. To summon a taxi from the Pueblo airport, call City Cab.
➤ AIRPORT INFORMATION: **Pueblo Memorial Airport** (☎ 719/948–3355).
➤ AIRPORT TRANSFER: **City Cab** (☎ 719/543–2525).

BUS TRAVEL

Greyhound Lines and TNM&O Coaches serve most of the major towns in the region. Pueblo Transit services Pueblo and outlying areas. The Trinidad Trolley (summer only) stops at parks and historical sites, departing from the parking lot next to City Hall (for information, call the Chamber of Commerce).
➤ BUS INFORMATION: **Greyhound Lines** (☎ 800/231–2222). **Pueblo Transit** (☎ 719/542–4306). **TNM&O Coaches** (☎ 719/544–6295). **Trinidad Trolley** (☎ 719/846–9285).

CAR TRAVEL

Pueblo is on I–25. Florissant and Buena Vista are reached via U.S. 24 off I–25; Cañon City and the Royal Gorge via U.S. 50. Salida can be reached via CO 291 from either U.S. 24 or U.S. 50.

EMERGENCIES

➤ CONTACTS: **Cañon City: St. Thomas More Hospital** (✉ 1338 Phay Ave., Cañon City, ☎ 719/269–2000). **La Junta: Arkansas Valley Regional Medical Center** (✉ 1100 Carson Ave., La Junta, ☎ 719/384–5412). **Pueblo: Parkview Episcopal Medical Center** (✉ 400 W. 16th St., Pueblo, ☎ 719/584–4000). **Salida: Heart of the Rockies Regional Medical Center** (✉ 448 E. 1st St., Salida, ☎ 719/539–6661). **Trinidad: Mt. San Rafael Hospital** (✉ 410 Benedicta St., Trinidad, ☎ 719/846–9213).

LODGING

CAMPING
The U.S. Forest Service operates many campsites in the area.
➤ CONTACTS: **Forest Service Office for the San Isabel National Forest** (✉ 3170 E. Main St., Cañon City, 81212, ☎ 719/269–8500).

TAXIS

➤ CONTACTS: **Pueblo: City Cab**(☎ 719/543–2525). **Trinidad: Your Ride** (☎ 719/859–3344).

TOURS

Arkansas River Tours, Buffalo Joe River Trips, and Echo Canyon River Expeditions are but a few of the reliable rafting outfitters that line U.S. 50, between Cañon City and the Royal Gorge.
➤ RIVER OUTFITTERS: **Arkansas River Tours** (✉ Cotopaxi, ☎ 800/321–4352). **Buffalo Joe River Trips** (✉ Royal Gorge, ☎ 719/395–8757 or 800/356–7984). **Echo Canyon River Expeditions** (✉ Cañon City, ☎ 719/275–3154 or 800/748–2953).

TRAIN TRAVEL

Amtrak stops in Trinidad and La Junta.

VISITOR INFORMATION

➤ TOURIST INFORMATION: **Buena Vista Chamber of Commerce** (✉ 343 Hwy. 24, Buena Vista 81211, ☎ 719/395–6612, WEB www. buenavistacolorado.org). **Cañon City Chamber of Commerce** (✉ 403 Royal Gorge Blvd., Cañon City 81212, ☎ 719/275–2331, WEB www.canoncitychamber.com). **Heart of the Rockies Chamber of Commerce** (✉ 406 W. Rainbow Blvd., Salida 81201, ☎ 719/539–2068, WEB www.salidachamber.org). **Huerfano County Chamber of Commerce** (✉ 400 Main St., Walsenburg 81089, ☎ 719/738–1065). **La Junta Chamber of Commerce** (✉ 110 Santa Fe Ave., La Junta 81050, ☎ 719/384–7411, WEB www.lajuntacochamber.com). **La Veta/Cuchara Chamber of Commerce** (✉ Box 32, La Veta 81055, ☎ 719/742–3676). **Lamar Chamber of Commerce** (✉ 109A E. Beech St., Lamar 81052, ☎ 719/336–4379). **Pueblo Chamber of Commerce and Convention & Visitors Bureau** (✉ 302 N. Santa Fe Ave., Pueblo 81003, ☎ 719/542–1704 or 800/233–3446, WEB www.pueblochamber.org). **Trinidad/Las Animas Chamber of Commerce** (✉ 309 Nevada St., Trinidad 81082, ☎ 719/846–9285, WEB www.trinidadco.com).

NORTHWEST COLORADO

Updated by
Lori Cumpston

As you drive through northwest Colorado, its largely barren terrain sculpted by eons of erosion, it may be difficult to imagine the region as a primeval rain forest. Yet millions of years ago much of Colorado was submerged under a roiling sea. That period left a vivid legacy in three equally precious resources: vast oil reserves, abundant uranium deposits, and one of the world's largest collections of dinosaur remains. Throughout the area the evidence of these buried treasures is made obvious by unsightly uranium tailings, abandoned oil derricks, and the huge mounds of dirt left from unearthing valuable fossils. Some of the important paleontological finds made here have radically changed the fossil record and the way we look at our reptilian ancestors. These discoveries even fueled the imagination of *Jurassic Park* author Michael Crichton: the book's fierce and ferocious predator, velociraptor, was first uncovered here.

Grand Junction makes the ideal hub for exploring the region which includes the starkly beautiful rock formations of the Colorado National Monument; the important petroglyphs of Canyon Pintado; the forest and lakes of Grand Mesa, the world's largest flattop mountain; and the orchards and vineyards of Palisade and Delta to the south and east. Most of the sights are less than a two-hour drive in various directions. Beginning at Grand Junction, you can make the loop from Palisade to

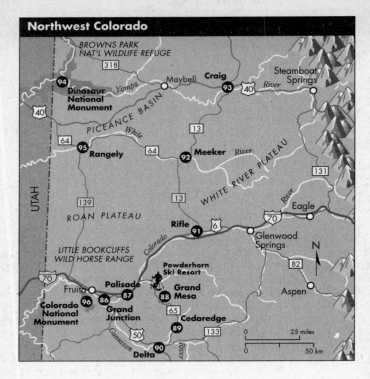

Northwest Colorado

Grand Mesa and Cedaredge to Delta easily in a day. If you want to break up the trip, stop in the lovely town of Cedaredge overnight. The loop in the opposite direction—including Rifle, Craig, Dinosaur National Monument, and Colorado National Monument—is quite a bit longer, but there is decent lodging in any of the stops along the way, with the exception of Dinosaur National Monument (unless you're prepared to camp.)

Grand Junction

86 *255 mi from Denver via I–70 west.*

Grand Junction sits between the picturesque Grand Mesa to the south and the multihued Bookcliffs to the north. As the largest city between Denver and Salt Lake City, it provides a variety of services and facilities to the surrounding populace and offers a fair amount of cosmopolitan sophistication for a comparatively small town.

Grand Junction's cultural sophistication is readily apparent in the Art on the Corner exhibit, a year-round event showcasing leading regional sculptors whose latest works are installed on the Main Street Mall. Each year the community selects and purchases its favorites for permanent display. Art on the Corner is organized by the **The Art Center,** which rotates its fine permanent collection of Native American tapestries and Western contemporary art, including the only complete series of lithographs by noted printmaker Paul Pletka. The fantastically carved doors—done by a WPA artist in the '30s—alone are worth the visit. Take time to enjoy the elegant historic homes along North 7th Street afterward. ⊠ *1803 N. 7th St.,* ☎ *970/243–7337,* WEB *www.gjartcenter.org.* 🎟 *$2.* ⊗ *Tues.–Sat. 9–4.*

The **Museum of Western Colorado** relates the history of the area dating from the 1880s, with an 11-decade time line, a firearms display, and two gorgeous parlor organs. It also runs the Cross Orchards Living History Farm and Dinosaur Journey Museum and oversees paleontological excavations. ⊠ *462 Ute Ave.,* ☎ *970/242–0971,* WEB *www.wcmuseum.org.* ⌾ *$5. Mon.–Sat. 8–4.*

The **Cross Orchards Living History Farm** re-creates a historic agricultural community of the early 20th century on its 24½-acre site, listed on the National Register of Historic Places. A workers' bunkhouse, blacksmith shop, country store, and an extensive collection of vintage farming and road-building equipment are among the exhibits to be seen on the 1½–2 hour tours. ⊠ *3073 F Rd.,* ☎ *970/434–9814,* WEB *www.wcmuseum.org.* ⌾ *$3.* ⊙ *May–Oct., Tues.–Sat. 9–3, Sun. noon–4; Oct.–Dec., Tues.–Sat. 10–4. Tours run mid-May–Nov. 1.*

☾ The entertaining and instructive **Dinosaur Journey** has half-size, moving, roaring replicas of the dinos found in the region. The museum is designed for children and adults alike with numerous hands-on exhibits that emphasize understanding the wealth of the local fossil record. You can handle real fossils in the open storage displays, look into a working laboratory, and talk with the volunteers preparing and cataloguing the latest excavated specimens. Three working sites run by the museum are open to the public: **Riggs Hill, Dinosaur Hill,** and the **Rabbit Valley Trail Through Time.** Each is a self-guided tour that will increase your knowledge and appreciation of paleontology. ⊠ *550 Jurassic Ct.,* ☎ *970/858–7282 or 888/344–3466,* WEB *www.wcmuseum.org.* ⌾ *$6.* ⊙ *Apr.–Sept., daily 9–5; Oct.–Mar., Mon.–Sat. 10–4, Sun. 12–4.*

☾ **Rim Rock Adventures** offers a variety of rafting and horseback-riding expeditions, as well as a petting zoo, a deer park, and a somewhat hoary wildlife museum. ⊠ *Rte. 340, Exit 19, Fruita,* ☎ *970/858–9555 or 888/712–9555,* WEB *www.rradventures.com.* ⌾ *$3.50.* ⊙ *May–Sept., daily 8:30–5:30.*

OFF THE BEATEN PATH

TABEGUACHE/UNAWEEP SCENIC BYWAY – This 150-mi stretch of savage scenery (Route 141) sweeps south from Grand Junction, arcing almost to the Utah border before curling over to Naturita, where you can pick up Route 145 to Telluride. It slices through the Uncompahgre Plateau, an area of great geologic interest. Unaweep means "Canyon with Two Mouths," and the piddling streams seem insufficient to have carved these harsh gashes. Along the way you'll see an engineering marvel: the 7-mi long Hanging Flume, used to transport water, virtually defies gravity by clinging to the sheer cliff. One of Colorado's oddest communities, Nucla, also lies along this route, 3 mi north of Naturita on Route 97. Founded as an early experiment in communal living (though the current conservative residents could hardly be called hippies), Nucla today is famous for one thing: the Top Dog World Prairie Dog Shootout, held every June. Residents justify the carnage by insisting that prairie dogs are only pests and that they run roughshod over the grazing lands.

Dining and Lodging

The Grand Junction dining scene is fairly sophisticated, compared with other towns in the region, though it's hardly fancy or exotic. There's a lot of standard beef and burritos. Grand Junction offers the widest selection of accommodations; outside the town, expect motels and fairly rustic guest ranches.

$$ ✕ **Dolce Vita.** Chef-owner Massimiliano Perucchini is a fourth-generation chef who hails from Verona. His Northern Italian restaurant with its outdoor patio fronting on Main Street provides consistently wonderful cooking. Try the Portobello mushroom marinated in Chianti and served on polenta with red onions and pancetta; the veal picatta; and the chicken with mushrooms, capers, artichoke hearts, and lemon butter on angel-hair pasta. It's a tough call between the homemade cannoli and tiramisu—you may need to try them both. ✉ *336 Main St.,* ☎ *970/242–8482. AE, D, DC, MC, V. Closed Sun.*

$$ ✕ **The Winery.** This is *the* place for the big night out and special occasions. It's very pretty, awash in stained glass, wood beams, exposed brick, and hanging plants. The menu isn't terribly adventuresome, but it does turn out top-notch steak, chicken, prime rib, and shrimp in simple, flavorful sauces and fresh fish specials. ✉ *642 Main St.,* ☎ *970/242–4100. AE, D, DC, MC, V. No lunch.*

$ ✕ **Crystal Café & Bake Shop.** Locals flock to this European-style café for its apple pancakes, scrumptious banana nut french toast, and wonderful array of omelets. The lunch menu has a Greek influence with favorites like the grilled veggie pita with homade feta mayonnaise and the Oriental chicken salad. There are also many delicious items to pick from for the carb-conscious dieter. ✉ *314 Main St.,* ☎ *970/242–8843. No credit cards. No dinner.*

$ ✕ **G. B. Gladstone's.** This local hangout boasts of its own style of turn-of-the-20th-century decor: stained-glass windows, faux-Victorian gas lamps, and antique skis and kayaks on the walls. It's particularly lively on Friday night, but whatever the day, you can enjoy such savory starters as Glad Crabs (won ton's stuffed with crab meat), as well as the freshest seafood, pasta, and steaks in town. Favorites include the prime rib; grilled salmon; and Thai pesto linguine with broiled chicken strips. ✉ *2531 N. 12th St.,* ☎ *970/241–6000. AE, D, DC, MC, V.*

$$–$$$ 🏨 **Los Altos Bed & Breakfast.** Perched on a hill, this B&B offers a 360-degree view; you can see clear to Utah. This cozy lodging—a Victorian inn—feels timeless. Guests enjoy relaxing in the third-floor observatory room or stepping out onto the wraparound deck. Several rooms have French doors leading to private decks. Breakfast includes home-baked muffins, coffee cakes, and multigrain pancakes. Tea is served in the winter. ✉ *375 Hillview Dr., 81503,* ☎ *970/256–0964 or 888/774–0982,* FAX *970/256–0964,* WEB *www.colorado-bnb.com/losaltos. 7 rooms, 3 suites. Breakfast room. AE, D, MC, V. BP.*

$$ 🏨 **Adams Mark Grand Junction.** By far the premier property in the area, ★ the Adams Mark offers quiet pampering at affordable rates, although some of the units could use refurbishing. Rooms are large and have welcome extras, such as a phone *and* TV in the bathroom. The bar and nightclub are longtime local favorites. ✉ *743 Horizon Dr., 81506,* ☎ *970/241–8888,* FAX *970/242–7266,* WEB *www.adamsmark.com. 246 rooms, 14 suites. 2 restaurants, bar, pool, hot tub, 3 tennis courts, gym, recreation room, nightclub, airport shuttle. AE, D, DC, MC, V.*

$$ 🏨 **Grand Vista Hotel.** Management does its utmost to create a warm, ★ inviting ambience, and it succeeds, with plush high-back chairs in the welcoming lobby and a private club look in the main restaurant, Oliver's. Old-fashioned charm and dark mountain colors characterize the rooms. Guests have health club privileges at the Crossroads Fitness Center. ✉ *2790 Crossroads Blvd., 81506,* ☎ *970/241–8411,* FAX *970/241–1077,* WEB *www.grandvistahotel.com. 158 rooms. Restaurant, bar, patisserie, indoor pool, hot tub, nightclub, meeting room, airport shuttle. AE, D, DC, MC, V.*

$$ 🏨 **Hawthorne Suites L.T.D. Hotel.** Grand Junction's newest hotel offers rooms with amenities galore, including microwave, refrigerator, coffeemaker, and complimentary full breakfast. For the business traveler, there is also Internet access and some suites have full kitchens. The plush rooms are decorated in rich shades of green and maroon. A sofa and two oversize chairs offer plenty of room to sit back and relax. ✉ *225 Main St., 81501,* ☎ *970/242–2525,* FAX *970/242–0295. 70 rooms.*

Breakfast room, indoor pool, hot tub, gym, business services. AE, D, DC, MC, V. BP.

$ 🖭 **Budget Host.** The owner continually refurbishes this property (you can occasionally catch him scrubbing the floors), whose gray-and-white exterior seems more country inn than motor lodge. Care is also lavished on the smart, fresh rooms, which have an early-American look with Stanley cherry furniture, burgundy carpets, and floral spreads. ✉ *721 Horizon Dr., 81506,* ☎ *970/243–6050 or 800/888–5736. 55 rooms. Pool. AE, D, DC, MC, V.*

$ 🖭 **The Historic Melrose House.** This funky 100-year-old, brick-red-and-forest-green building functions as both a full-service hotel and a hostel. Most of the hotel rooms are bright and airy, with a smattering of antiques and original woodwork. All of the hotel rooms have cable TV and sinks in the room, however, most share a European-style bath down the hall. This is a great place to connect with students from around the world. The hosts couldn't be more friendly and helpful, full of tips on how to save money in the area. Hostelers enjoy a pleasant common room. Morning coffee and Danish pastry is complimentary. ✉ *337 Colorado St., 81501,* ☎ *970/242–9636,* FAX *970/242–5613,* WEB *www.hotelmelrose.com. 21 rooms, 6 with private bath, 2 dorms. AE, D, DC, MC, V.*

Nightlife and the Arts

Country Jam (☎ 970/244–1480 or 800/530–3020, WEB www.countryjam.com), held annually in June, attracts the biggest name acts, such as Faith Hill and Charlie Daniels. The 65-piece **Grand Junction Symphony** (☎ 970/243–6787, WEB www.gjsymphony.org) is highly regarded and performs in venues throughout the city.

BARS AND LOUNGES

Blue Moon (✉ 120 N. 7th, ☎ 970/242–4506) is everyone's favorite neighborhood bar. The "Cheers"-like atmosphere encourages patrons to nurse their favorite brew while catching up with colleagues or friends. The Adams Mark Grand Junction's **Players Sports Bar** (✉ 743 Horizon Dr., ☎ 970/241–8888, Ext. 121) serves up beverages, appetizers, and light snacks. Occasionally entertainers perform outside on the beer garden stage. The upscale lounge at **G. B. Gladstone's** (✉ 2531 N. 12th St., ☎ 970/241–6000) is a popular watering hole. Take advantage of the outdoor patio. The **Rockslide Brewery** (✉ 401 Main St., ☎ 970/245–2111) has won awards for its ales, porters, and stouts. An open-air patio is available during the summer months.

COFFEEHOUSE

At **Mountain Roasted** (✉ 620 Main St., ☎ 970/242–5282), biscotti, homemade muffins, and pastries are served with gourmet coffees in an arty atmosphere. The local art gracing the walls is also for sale, and live music is offered several evenings a week.

MUSIC AND DANCE CLUBS

Cinnamon's (✉ Holiday Inn, 755 Horizon Dr., ☎ 970/243–6790) has a dance floor and live music. **Club Millennium** (✉ 490 28¼ Rd., ☎ 970/241–2282) is the best variety dance club in Grand Junction with state-of-the-art lights and sound system. Live country western entertainment takes place nightly at **The Rose** (✉ 2993 North Ave., ☎ 970/245–0606).

Outdoor Activities and Sports

Adventure Bound River Expeditions (☎ 970/245–5428) runs trips on the Colorado and Green rivers (the latter through the canyons of Dinosaur National Monument). **Vertical Horizons Rock Guides** (☎ 970/245–8513) offers guided climbs and lessons in the area. For cyclists, **Kokopelli's Trail** links Grand Junction with the famed Slickrock Trail outside Moab,

Utah. The 128-mi stretch winds through high desert and the Colorado River valley before climbing the La Sal Mountains. Those interested in bike tours should get in touch with the **Colorado Plateau Mountain Bike Trail Association** (☎ 970/249–8055). **Rim Rock Deer Park** (✉ 927 17 Rd., Fruita, ☎ 970/858–9555) offers everything from one-hour horseback rides into Colorado National Monument to overnight pack rides.

Tiara Rado Golf Course (✉ 2063 S. Broadway, ☎ 970/245–8085) is an 18-hole championship course set at the foot of the Colorado National Monument.

Shopping

ANTIQUES

A Haggle of Vendors Emporium (✉ 510 Main St., ☎ 970/245–1404) is just what it says. It's as if every attic you'd ever seen had emptied its contents here.

CRAFT AND ART GALLERIES

Frame Works and Gallery (✉ 309 Main St., ☎ 970/243–7074) specializes in local artist's works and carries serigraphs, sculpture, oils, watercolors, etchings and photos. **Working Artists Studio and Gallery** (✉ 520 Main St., ☎ 970/256–9952) has everything from prints to pottery and one of a kind gifts. **Terry Shepherd** (✉ 825 N. 7th St., Grand Junction, ☎ 970/243–4282) sells his own stoneware and salt-vapor designs, in which the salt forms trails on the pottery.

FOOD

Enstrom's (✉ 200 S. 7th St., ☎ 970/242–1655) makes scrumptious candy and is world-renowned for their toffee.

WESTERN PARAPHERNALIA

Champion Boots and Saddlery (✉ 545 Main St., ☎ 970/242–2465), in business since 1936, is the best place in the area for the likes of Tony Lama boots or Minnetonka moccasins.

Palisade

 12 mi east of Grand Junction via I–70.

Palisade is nestled between the wintry Grand Mesa (10,000 ft high and mostly snow-covered year-round) and semiarid terrain. The surprisingly temperate microclimate produces delectable Elberta peaches, apples, plums, pears, and cherries, making Palisade the center of Colorado's orchard and vineyard territory. Plucky wine makers have been experimenting with several varietals since the early '80s, and the results have been encouraging. There are fewer than 20 vineyards in the state; the best are located right here in the Grand Valley.

You can find all the great European grapes here: Riesling, chardonnay, pinot noir, cabernet, merlot. So far, the top results have been obtained with merlot and chardonnay. Wine lovers will appreciate the heady, uncomplicated varietal bouquet and surprising depth and complexity of some of the vintages. Some vineyards are open to the public, offering tours, tastings, and the opportunity to meet wine makers and discuss their craft. The oldest, largest (20 acres), and most commercially successful winery is **Colorado Cellars** (✉ 3553 E Rd., ☎ 970/464–7921. ☺ Weekdays 9–4, Sat. noon–4), founded in 1978. The perfectly manicured grounds are reminiscent of Napa Valley and include a picnic area and grassy knoll that provide a panoramic view of the Grand Valley. There is a tasting room in the retail sales outlet.

Carlson Vineyards (✉ 461 35 Rd., ☎ 970/464–5554. ☺ Daily 11–6) produces wines with names such as Tyrannosaurus Red and Prairie Dog.

Probably the best wines to buy here are those made from fruit (such as the peach pearadactyl). One of the most promising in quality is undoubtedly **Plum Creek Cellars** (⊠ 3708 G Rd., ☎ 970/464–7586. ◷ Daily 9:30–6). Chardonnay and Riesling are among the full selection of fine wines made from 100% Colorado-grown grapes. **Grande River Vineyards** (⊠ 787 Elberta Ave., ☎ 970/464–5867, ◷ Daily 9–5) features award-winning, premium Colorado-grown wines, including chardonnay, merlot, red and white meritage, syrah, and viognier. An annual concert series is also held on the premises from May through September.

Rocky Mountain Meadery/Rocky Mountain Cidery (⊠ 3701 G Rd., ☎ 970/464–7899. ◷ Daily 10–5) is Colorado's exclusive producer of honey wine (mead) and carbonated hard cider made from Colorado fruits and honey. Savor the styles and blends of the Renaissance Era Honey Wines while overlooking Grand Mesa.

The true spirit of the Wild, Wild West can be found at the **Little Bookcliffs Wild Horse Range,** just one of three in the United States specifically set aside for wild horses. It encompasses 30,261 acres of rugged canyons and plateaus in the Bookcliffs northwest of Palisade. There are from 80 to 120 wild horses roaming the sagebrush covered hills. Most are believed to be descendants of horses that escaped from owners in the late 1800s or early 1900s. Most years, new foals can be spotted with their mothers in the spring and early summer on the hillsides just off the main trails. The best season for riding, hiking, or biking the trails is May to September. In the summer you might glimpse some wild horses in Indian Park or North Soda, but it's a matter of luck. Local favorites for riding include the Coal Canyon Trail and Main Canyon Trail, where the herd frequents in winter. Be sure to bring plenty of water. Vehicles are permitted on designated trails. Beware of frequent summer thunderstorms that can result in flash flood conditions making roads slick and impassable. ⊠ *2815 H Rd., approximately 8 mi northeast of Grand Junction,* ☎ *970/244–3000,* WEB *www.co.blm.gov/gjra/lbc.* ☜ *Free.* ◷ *Daily dawn to dusk.*

Dining and Lodging

$ ✕ **Ann Marie's Country Cottage Cafe.** This casual, family friendly restaurant serves up blue plate specials just like grandma's only better. Menu favorites include chicken-fried steak, biscuits and gravy, breakfast burritos, and hamburgers. ⊠ *349 W. 8th,* ☎ *970/464–4600. MC, V. No dinner Sun.*

$ ▦ **The Garden House Bed & Breakfast.** This comfortable B & B with quaint country charm and a touch of elegance is tucked inside a small fruit orchard. Benches and a hammock invite you to relax outdoors and experience the changes of the season. Decorated in French country decor, the tri-level home has a spacious feeling with gorgeous oak floors, bay windows, and high-beamed ceilings. All guest rooms offer designer linens for a cozy night's sleep. Morning beverage tray, afternoon snacks, and evening turndown service are also available. Extra amenities for the business traveler include fax, copier, and portable phone. ⊠ *3587 G Rd., 81526,* ☎ *970/464–4686 or 800/305–4686,* FAX *970/464–4686,* WEB *www.colorado-bnb.com/gardnhse. 4 rooms. Breakfast room, lounge, business services, meeting room. D, MC, V. BP.*

Shopping

Harold and Nola Voorhees (⊠ 3702 G 7/10 Rd., ☎ 970/464–7220) sells a range of dried fruits, including cherries, pears, apricots, and peaches. **Slice-O-Life Bakery** (⊠ 105 W. 3rd St., ☎ 970/464–0577) is run by two of the zaniest bakers in Colorado, Mary and Tim Lincoln.

All the savory, aromatic goodies are baked with whole grains and fresh local fruits. Buy your favorites, grab a bottle of wine at one of the nearby wineries, add in some fresh fruit from an orchard, and you have the makings of a picnic.

Grand Mesa

88 *32 mi from Palisade or 44 mi from Grand Junction via Rte. 65 east and south.*

The world's largest flattop mountain towers 10,000 ft above the surrounding terrain and sprawls an astounding 50 square mi. Grand Mesa's landscape is dotted with more than 200 sparkling lakes—a fisherman's paradise in summer. According to Ute legend, a great eagle carried off a Native American child, and in retaliation the father hurled its eaglets to the base of the mesa, where they were devoured by a serpent. The enraged eagle seized the serpent and tore it into hundreds of pieces, which formed deep pits upon hitting the earth. The eagle's ire caused the mesa to rattle with thunder, and torrents of rain filled the pits, creating lakes.

The stands of golden quakies (aspens) blanketing the mesa are glorious in autumn. Even on brilliantly sunny days, wispy clouds seem to catch and reflect the sun's rays, draping the summit in prismatic light. The views of the Grand Valley and the Bookcliffs (escarpments) are absolutely ravishing here, and an excellent little ski area, **Powderhorn,** takes full advantage of them.

Outdoor Activities and Sports

The **Grand Mesa Lakes** provide some of the best angling opportunities for rainbow, cutthroat, and brook trout in Colorado. For information, contact the **Grand Mesa National Forest** (☎ 970/242–8211) or the **U.S. Forest Service** (☎ 970/242–8211). The **Crag Crest Trail** on top of Grand Mesa affords hikers breathtaking views of the canyons and cliffs below.

SKIING

Powderhorn has 20 trails, 4 lifts, 240 acres, and a 1,650-ft vertical drop. The slopes intriguingly follow the fall line of the mesa, carving out natural bowls, those on the western side being steeper than they first appear. ⊠ *Rte. 65,* ☎ *970/268–5700,* WEB *www.powderhorn.com.* ➟ *Lift ticket $35.* ⊙ *Nov.–mid-Apr., 9–4.*

For cross-country skiing, the acres of untracked powder amid stands of aspen and spruce on Grand Mesa are a Nordic nirvana. For information, contact the Grand Mesa National Forest or the **Grand Mesa Nordic Council** (☎ 970/434–9753).

Cedaredge

89 *15 mi from Grand Mesa or 59 mi from Grand Junction via Rte. 65 south.*

Cedaredge is an exceptionally pretty town in the shadow of the Grand Mesa. The **Grand Mesa Scenic Byway** runs to Cedaredge from Grand Junction along I–70 and Route 65. The town site was originally the headquarters of a cattle spread, the Bar-I Ranch. **Pioneer Town,** a cluster of 23 authentic buildings that re-create turn-of-the-20th-century life, include a country chapel, the Lizard Head Saloon, original silos from the Bar-I Ranch, and a working blacksmith shop. ⊠ *Rte. 65,* ☎ *970/856–7554.* ➟ *$3.* ⊙ *Memorial Day–Labor Day, Mon.–Sat. 10–4, Sun. 1–4.*

Dining and Lodging

$–$$ ✕ **The Divot at DeerCreek Village.** After a day of fun, feed your appetite with a delicious array of Italian and European influenced cuisine. This casual restaurant has a dining room overlooking a golf course, and outdoor patio dining too. Local favorites include the steaks, seafood, and pasta dishes (especially seafood pasta). Reservations are essential on weekends. ⊠ *500 S.E. Jay Ave.,* ☎ *970/856–7782. D, DC, MC, V. No dinner Mon.*

$–$$ 🏨 **Cedars' Edge Llamas B&B.** The pretty cedar house and guest cottage offer four neatly appointed rooms. Breakfast is served privately in your room, in the breakfast room, or on a private deck, which affords astonishing 100-mi views. The best part about staying at Ray and Gail Record's retreat, however, is the llama herd (yes, they accompany guests on picnics). ⊠ *2169 Hwy. 65, 81413,* ☎ *970/856–6836,* FAX *970/856–6846,* WEB *www.llamabandb.com. 4 rooms. AE, MC, V. BP.*

$ 🏨 **Super 8 Motel.** Cedaredge's newest economy motel has the only pool in town and is just a few minutes south of downtown. The Continental breakfast is free, and rooms have cable TV. ⊠ *530 S. Grand Mesa Dr., 81413,* ☎ *970/856–7824,* FAX *970/856–7826,* WEB *www.super8.com. 31 rooms. Pool, hot tub, coin laundry. AE, D, DC, MC, V. CP.*

Shopping

The Apple Shed (⊠ 250 S. Grand Mesa Dr., ☎ 970/856–7007) is a group of galleries that sell an impressive array of Colorado crafts.

Delta

⑳ *15 mi from Cedaredge via Rte. 65 south; 46 mi from Grand Junction via Rte. 50 south.*

Delta is the headquarters of the Grand Mesa, Gunnison, and Uncompahgre national forests. The town is ideally located for exploring the region's natural wonders and also has an interesting public artwork. Seven murals, most of them lining Main Street, were painted by local artists in the late 1980s and celebrate various aspects of life in the area, from wildlife in "Delta County Ark" and ranching in "High Country Roundup," to agriculture in both "A Tribute to Agriculture" and "Labels of Delta County."

At **Ft. Uncompahgre,** docents in period attire guide visitors through this 1826 fur-trading post. ⊠ *Confluence Park,* ☎ *970/874–8349.* 🎟 *$3.50.* ☉ *Apr.–Oct., Tues.–Sat. 10–4.*

The **Delta County Museum** has an eclectic display that includes local dinosaur finds, an 1886 jail, a butterfly collection, and a collection of large bells. ⊠ *251 Meeker St.,* ☎ *970/874–8721.* 🎟 *$2.* ☉ *May–Sept., Tues.–Sat. 10–4; Oct.–Apr., Wed. and Sat. 10–4.*

Shopping

Windfeather Designs (⊠ 1204 Bluff St., ☎ no phone) offers Jean Madole's extraordinary weaving, a reinterpretation of designs from extinct cultures such as the Mimbre.

Rifle

㉑ *58 mi from Grand Junction via I–70 east.*

This unassuming community (which lives up to its name with gun racks outnumbering ski racks on cars) is developing quite a reputation among mountain bikers for the series of high-quality trails along the Roan Cliffs.

Rifle Gap State Park is about 12 mi north of town, and at 6,000 ft in elevation and 1,305 acres (350 of which are water), it offers a variety of activities for the outdoor enthusiast. Even ice climbers head here to clamber up the frozen waterfalls and ice caves. As you gaze at the massive rock window of Rifle Gap, try to imagine a huge, orange nylon curtain billowing between the steep walls. Famed installation artist Christo did; two of his efforts were foiled due to wind, save for one amazing day when his *Valley Curtain* piece was gloriously unfolded for a brief few hours. The road wraps around a tiny reservoir before reaching **Rifle Falls State Park,** a triple flume cascading down moss-covered cliffs. ⊠ *Route 325,* ☎ *970/625–1607,* WEB *www.parks.state.co.us/rifle_gap.* ☜ *$3.* ☉ *Year-round.*

The huge schools of trout at the **Rifle Fish Hatchery** (⊠ Rte. 325, 14 mi north of Rifle, ☎ 970/625–1865. ☜ Free. ☉ Daily 7–4:30) include an intriguing iridescent blue hybrid. The facility raises rainbow and cutthroat trout for the Colorado Division of Wildlife. Visitors are welcome to view troughs of fish in different stages of life.

Dining and Lodging

$$ ✕ **Fireside Inn.** This dining spot has an enormous stone fireplace as its centerpiece. The owner is Italian, and along with Continental favorites such as veal marsala and prime rib au jus, he offers tasty homemade ravioli and chicken Alfredo. The inn serves Sunday brunch, as well as lunch and dinner. ⊠ *1214 Access Rd.,* ☎ *970/625–2233. AE, D, MC, V. No lunch Sat. Closed Mon.*

$ ☷ **Rusty Cannon Motel.** This motor lodge offers spacious accommodations and is plain but clean and comfortable. ⊠ *701 Taughenbaugh Blvd., 81650,* ☎ *970/625–4004. 89 rooms. Pool, sauna. AE, D, DC, MC, V.*

Outdoor Activities and Sports

The **Rifle Gap Reservoir** (☎ 970/625–1607) is plentifully stocked with rainbow trout and walleye pike. **Battlement Mesa Golf Course** (⊠ 3930 N. Battlement Mesa Pkwy., Battlement Mesa, ☎ 970/285–7274) is an 18-hole championship course with ravishing views of the Grand Valley and Grand Mesa in the distance. **Battlement Mesa,** outside Rifle, offers rugged hiking trails.

CLIMBING

The rock faces and ice caves of **Rifle Mountain Park** (⊠ Rte. 325, 13 mi north of Rifle, ☎ 970/625–2121. ☜ $4) are a magnet for rock and ice climbers, depending on the season. There are about 200 routes to climb, many with exhilarating views. The terrain veers from semiarid to subalpine. **Natural Progression Rock Guides** (☎ 877/434–8213) is a highly recommended guide company for climbers.

CYCLING

The biking around Rifle is gaining momentum among aficionados for the variety of trails around the Roan Cliffs, through shale, sagebrush, and piñon, punctuated by panoramic views. Call the **Rifle Chamber of Commerce** (☎ 970/625–2085) for maps and details.

Meeker

🔵 *43 mi from Rifle or 101 mi from Grand Junction via I–70 east and Rte. 13 north.*

Meeker is named for Nathan Meeker, who attempted to "civilize" the Utes with little success. The Utes' resentment of his disregard for their land rights caused a worried Meeker to send for the cavalry. The Utes became further enraged and ambushed the troops in the 1879 Meeker Massacre, which ushered in yet another period of intransigence on the part of the U.S. government. The town is predominantly known as an outdoorsy place, but its handsome historical buildings include the still-operating Meeker Hotel on Main Street. The worthwhile **White River Museum** features pioneer artifacts and historical photos. ⊠ *565 Park St.,* ☎ *970/878–9982.* ☒ *Free.* ☉ *Mid-Apr.–Nov., weekdays 9– 5; Nov.–Apr., weekdays 11–3.*

East of Meeker is the **Flattops Scenic Byway,** an 82-mi gravel road from Meeker to Yampa, through an area shaped by molten lava flows and glaciers that gouged tiny jewel-like lakes in the folds of the mountains.

Dining and Lodging

$–$$ ✕ **Market Street Bar and Grill.** Dine in the days of yesteryear with country furnishings, hardwood floors, antiques, and paintings of the area. This country-style restaurant offers up steaks, baked trout, delicious homemade fruit pies, and bread baked daily. There's a kids' menu and full bar, too. ⊠ *173 First St.,* ☎ *970/878–3193. AE, D, MC, V.*

$–$$ ✕🛏 **Sleepy Cat Lodge and Restaurant.** Owned by the same family since
★ 1964, the huge log structure is filled with gorgeous beveled glass and the requisite trophies and bearskins mounted on the walls. Soup and salad bar accompany the filling dinners ($$) of ribs, huge cuts of steak, teriyaki chicken, and pan-fried trout. The cabins have full kitchens, bathrooms with showers, and fireplaces. The motel units have small refrigerators, coffee makers, and a television in select rooms. ⊠ *County Rd. 8, 16 mi east of Meeker, 81641,* ☎ *970/878–4413. 27 cabins. Restaurant. D, MC, V. Restaurant hrs vary; call ahead.*

Craig

🅖 *48 mi from Meeker via Rte. 13 north; 149 mi from Grand Junction via I–70 east and Rte. 13 north.*

Craig is a growing cow town, made newly prosperous by coal and oil (you'll see billowing white plumes belch from Colorado's largest coal-processing plant, the Colorado-Ute Power Station), but it's also set in pristine wilderness, teeming with wildlife. The **Sandstone Hiking Trail,** an easy ½-mi walk beginning in town along Alta Vista Drive, is a splendid vantage point for viewing the local elk and deer herds, as well as ancient Native American petroglyphs carved on the cliff.

The **Museum of Northwest Colorado** elegantly displays an eclectic collection of everything from arrowheads to a fire truck. The upstairs of this restored county courthouse is devoted to one man's obsession. Bill Mackin, one of the leading traders in cowboy collectibles, has spent a lifetime gathering guns, bits, saddles, bootjacks, holsters, and spurs of all descriptions. It's the largest privately owned collection of working cowboy artifacts in the world. Old photos of the area, books on outlaws and homesteaders, and posters are for sale. ⊠ *590 Yampa Ave.,* ☎ *970/824–6360,* 🆆🅴🅱 *www.museumnwco.org.* ☒ *Free (donations accepted).* ☉ *Mon.–Sat. 9–5.*

Dining and Lodging

$–$$ ✕ **Golden Cavvy.** A "cavvy" is the pick of a team of horses, and this restaurant is certainly the selection in town, for the price. It's a standard coffee shop enlivened by mirrors, hanging plants, faux-antique chandeliers, and the incredible masonry of the original 1900s fireplace of the Baker Hotel (which burned down on this spot). Hearty breakfasts, homemade pies and ice cream, pork chops, and anything deep-fried (try the mesquite-fried chicken) are your best bets. ⊠ *538 Yampa Ave.,* ☎ *970/824–6038. MC, V.*

$–$$ 🛏 **Holiday Inn.** This property is Craig's largest hotel. Amenities include an indoor recreational center equipped with a pool, whirlpool, exercise and game room, all inside a lush atrium setting. The rooms are decorated in teal and floral fabrics and offer electronic key access, irons and ironing boards, and coffeemakers. For the business traveler, there are also work stations equipped with telephones, Internet access, in-room data ports, voicemail, and wake-up service. ✉ *300 Rte. 13 S, 81625,* ☎ *970/824–4000,* FAX *970/824–3950,* WEB *www.basshotels.com. 152 rooms, 19 suites. Restaurant, bar, in-room data ports, indoor pool, hot tub, gym, nightclub, recreation room. AE, D, DC, MC, V.*

Outdoor Activities and Sports

Around Craig and Meeker, the Yampa and Green rivers, Trappers Lake, Lake Avery, and Elkhead Reservoir are known for pike and trout; contact the **Sportsman's Center** (✉ 360 East Victory Way, ☎ 970/824–3046) for information.

Yampa Valley Golf Course (✉ County Rd. 394, ☎ 970/824–3673) is an 18-hole course dotted with copses of willow and cottonwood by the Yampa River. Tracks are groomed for cross-country skiing in winter.

En Route   Outside Craig, U.S. 40 gradually shifts into hillier sagebrush country. This is ideal land for raising cattle, which are about all you'll see for miles on this desolate stretch of highway. The route winds through increasingly minuscule towns every 15 mi or so, including Maybell, Elk Springs, Massadona, Blue Mountain—some not even on the map.

At Maybell, the road forks. If you follow Route 318 northwest for 53 mi you'll reach the **Browns Park Wildlife Refuge,** with lacy waterfalls and canyons carved by the Green River and straddled by a swinging bridge. The area was a notorious hideaway for the likes of Butch Cassidy and the Sundance Kid, Tom Horn, and John Bennett. This is an unspoiled, almost primitive spot, ideal for watching antelope and bighorn sheep, as well as nesting waterfowl such as mallards, redheads, and teal, and the Great Basin Canada goose. You might also see elk, pronghorn, and various songbirds. The marshes are closed during nesting season between March and July 31. The route here is complicated, so call first for directions. The refuge has two primitive campgrounds equipped with pit toilets and are free of charge. Beware: there is no drinking water, firewood, or trash removal. ✉ *1318 Rte. 318,* ☎ *970/365–3613,* WEB *www.r6.fws.gov/refuges/browns.* ✉ *Free.* ☉ *Year-round, 7:30 AM–sunset.*

Pristine campsites are available at **Gates of Lodore Campground** (✉ Rte. 318, 68 mi from Maybell, ☎ 970/374–3000), 2 mi from the border of Browns Park Wildlife Refuge.

Dinosaur National Monument

94 *90 mi from Craig via U.S. 40 west; 106 mi from Grand Junction via I–70 west, Rte. 139 north, Rte. 64 north, and U.S. 40 east (to national monument headquarters).*

On U.S. 40, west of Maybell, you'll note that the earth becomes increasingly creased and furrowed, divided by arroyos and broken by the mauve- and rose-streaked cliffs of Dinosaur National Monument. The **Dinosaur Quarry** is actually located on the Utah side of the monument, but the Colorado section offers some of the finest hiking in the West, along the **Harpers Corner** and **Echo Park Drive** routes, and the ominous-sounding **Canyon of Lodore** (where rafting is available along the rapids of the Green River). The drive is only accessible in summer—even then, four-wheel drive is preferable—and some of the most breathtaking overlooks are well off the beaten track. Still, the 62-mi-round-trip paved Harpers Corner drive will take you past looming buttes and yawning sunbaked gorges etched by the Green and Yampa rivers. It leads to the dirt Echo Park Road, where angular rock formations are stippled with petroglyphs; the route skirts the rim of narrow 3,000-ft-deep crevasses that ripple from beige to black depending on the angle of the sun. Wherever you go, remember this austerely beautiful park is fragile: avoid the rich black soil, which contains actual cryptogams—one-celled creatures that are the building blocks of life in the desert; and don't touch the petroglyphs. The visitor center for Dinosaur Quarry is in Jensen, Utah, 7 mi north of Highway 40. ⊠ *Park Headquarters, 4545 U.S. 40, Dinosaur, 81610, 2 mi east of Dinosaur,* ☎ *970/374–3000,* WEB *www.nps.gov/dino.* ☞ *$10 per vehicle.*

Dinosaur, a few miles west of the monument's headquarters, is a sad little town whose streets are named for the giant reptiles. It offers little more than pit stops and dinky motels. If you've traveled this far, though, you're almost better off camping in the park, which is first-come, first-served, and has no facilities.

Dining

$ ✕ **B&B Family Restaurant.** Capitalizing on its location, this restaurant has a dino emblazoned on the side of the building. The decor is simple: one wall is papered with potato sacks and another is adorned with cheesy wildlife art; there are also still surprisingly beautiful remnants of an old bar with intricate carving and mirrors. The menu is cute. Where else can you get Brontoburgers, Stegosaurus rib-eyes, and Plateosaurus rib-eyes? ⊠ *Ceratosaurus St. and U.S. 40,* ☎ *970/374–2744.*

Camping

Dinosaur National Monument (☎ 970/374–3000) has information on area campgrounds, most of which are filled on a first-come, first-served basis. **Deerlodge Park Campground** is off U.S. 40, between Maybell and Elk Springs. **Echo Park Campground** is off Harper's Corner Rd., 13 mi from the national monument headquarters.

Rangely

⑨⑤ *19 mi from Dinosaur via Rte. 64 south; 96 mi from Grand Junction via I–70 west and Rte. 139 north.*

Rangely proudly touts itself as the "Oil Capital of Colorado." It's also nicknamed Strangely: a perverse sense of humor is required to live in this desolate neck of the woods. The life of oil riggers and uranium miners is a hard one, after all.

Rangely's most compelling sights are the superb Fremont petroglyphs—dating from between 600 and 1300—in Douglas Creek Canyon, south of town along Route 139. This stretch is known as the **Canyon Pintado National Historic District** (WEB www.co.blm.gov) and the examples of rock art are among the best-preserved in the West; half the fun is clambering up the rocks to find them. A brochure listing the sights is available at the Rangely Chamber of Commerce.

Lodging

$–$$ 🏨 **Four Queens Motel.** This motel is 18 mi from the town of Dinosaur. Most of the rooms have queen or kingsize beds, a table, and two chairs. Room amenities include cable TV, refrigerators, and coffeemakers, and a microwave and coin laundry are available in the common area. Guests also have access to the Rangely Recreation Center which is equipped with a pool, sauna, hot tub, weight room, gym, pool tables, and outdoor basketball court. Pets are welcome. ⊠ *206 E. Main,*

81648, ☎ 970/675–5035, 𝖥𝖠𝖷 970/675–5037. *32 rooms. Refrigerators, coin laundry, business services. AE, D, DC, MC, V.*

Colorado National Monument

96 *78 mi from Rangely via Rte. 139 south and I–70 east; 23 mi from Grand Junction via Rte. 340 west.*

The western entrance of the Colorado National Monument is just east of the I–70 and Route 139 junction. The 23-mi Rim Rock Drive climbs this colorful plateau that's been nearly 1 billion years in the making, yielding sterling views of the gaping canyons and gnarled knobby monoliths below. This is dramatic, rugged country, stubbled with stunted piñon trees and junipers; populated by mule deer, gray foxes, and bobcats; and perpetually swept by ravens, swifts, and golden eagles. The starkly beautiful sandstone and shale formations include Balanced Rock, Independence Monument, and the slender, willowy sculptures of the Kissing Couple and Praying Hands. Backcountry camping is permitted. An eccentric visionary named John Otto was instrumental in having the park declared a national monument in 1911. To get his way, the headstrong Otto frequently threatened members of Congress with everything from blackmail to beatings, acts that caused him to be institutionalized on three occasions. But as locals observed, "He's the sanest man in town 'cause he's got the papers to prove it." ⊠ *Fruita,* ☎ *970/858–3617,* 𝖶𝖤𝖡 *www.nps.gov/colm.* ✑ *$5 per car for 7-day pass.* ☉ *Park: daily, 24 hours; visitor center: daily, hours vary.*

West of Colorado National Monument, it's a treacherous 7-mi hike into **Rattlesnake Canyon** (☎ 970/244–3000). The intrepid will be rewarded with thrilling natural arches and spires. The canyon can be reached in summer from the upper end of Rim Rock Drive with four-wheel-drive vehicles.

☺ Dinosaur Journey is a sparkling facility created by the Dinamation International Society, the folks who fabricate robotic dinos. The society's Dr. Robert Bakker advises, "Don't think of T. rex as a 'tyrant lizard,' but as a 10,000-pound roadrunner that could eat a school bus." In addition to the amazingly lifelike robotics (including a hatching egg), there are more than 20 interactive displays. Children can stand in an earthquake simulator, dig up "fossils" in a mock quarry, or make dino prints in dirt (along with reptile and bird tracks for comparison). Kids get a special passport that's stamped as they visit each dinosaur exhibit, and they have the chance to watch local volunteers at work cleaning and preparing fossils for study. ⊠ *550 Jurassic Ct., Fruita, Exit 19 off I–70, opposite western entrance to Colorado National Monument,* ☎ *970/858–7282 or 800/344–3466,* 𝖶𝖤𝖡 *www.dinosaurjourney.com.* ✑ *$5.50.* ☉ *Daily 9–5.*

Northwest Colorado A to Z

AIRPORTS
Walker Field Airport, the only major airport in the region, is served by America West Express, Sky West, and United Express. A Touch With Class has regular limo service into Grand Junction and outlying communities from Walker Field. Sunshine Taxi serves Grand Junction.
➤ AIRPORT INFORMATION: **Walker Field Airport** (⊠ Grand Junction, ☎ 970/244–9100).
➤ TAXIS: **A Touch With Class** (☎ 970/245–5466). **Sunshine Taxi** (☎ 970/245–8294).

BIKE TRAVEL

For three trail maps covering mostly western Colorado and parts of Utah, send $2 to Colorado Plateau Mountain Bike Trail Association. Much useful information is posted on its Web site.

➤ INFORMATION: **Colorado Plateau Mountain Bike Trail Association** (✉ Box 4602, Grand Junction 81502, WEB www.copmoba.com).

BUS TRAVEL

Greyhound Lines serves most of the major towns in the region.

CAR TRAVEL

Interstate 70 (U.S. 6) is the major thoroughfare, accessing Grand Junction, Rifle, and Grand Mesa (via Rte. 65, which runs to Delta). Meeker is reached from Rifle via Route 13 and Rangely and Dinosaur via Route 64. U.S. 40 east from Utah is the best way to reach Dinosaur National Monument and Craig.

GASOLINE

Most gas stations in the smaller towns are open until 10 PM during the summer. Beware, some automated credit card pumps also shut down at 10 PM. Grand Junction does have gas stations that are open 24 hours.

ROAD CONDITIONS

Most roads are paved and in fairly good condition. Summer is peak road construction season, so expect some delays. Be prepared for winter driving conditions at all times, especially in the high country.

ROAD MAPS

Though the roads are straightforward here, if you want a map, most gas stations carry some.

EMERGENCIES

➤ CONTACTS: **Craig Memorial Hospital** (✉ 785 Russell Ave., Craig, ☎ 970/824–9411). **Meeker: Pioneers Hospital** (✉ 345 Cleveland St., Meeker, ☎ 970/878–5047). **St. Mary's Hospital** (✉ 2635 N. 7th St., Grand Junction, ☎ 970/244–2273).

TOURS

Palisade is home to the largest concentration of wineries in the state. By van or chauffered limousine Colorado Wine Country Tours brings you to wineries where you'll learn about the wine-making process, talk with local experts, and taste a variety of Colorado wines. Prices start at $20 per person. For a self-guided tour, print out maps with directions to the wineries from the Web site.

Coopertours specializes in tours for artists and photographers. Eagle Tree Tours runs tours of Colorado National Monument and the Grand Junction area, including some with four-wheel-drive vehicles, hiking, or biking.

Museum of Western Colorado Dinosaur Journey leads five- to six-day paleontological treks that include work in a dinosaur quarry. Meander Tours offers scenic and Western-theme adventures.

➤ CONTACTS: **Coopertours** (✉ Grand Junction, ☎ 970/434–0224). **Colorado Wine Country Tours** (✉ 740 Horizon Dr., Grand Junction 81506, ☎ 970/244–1480, FAX 970/243–7393, WEB www.coloradowine.com). **Museum of Western Colorado Dinosaur Journey** (✉ 550 Jurassic Ct., Fruita 81521, ☎ 970/858–7282). **Eagle Tree Tours** (✉ Grand Junction, ☎ 970/241–4792). **Meander Tours** (✉ 209 Main St., Collbran 81624, ☎ 970/487–3402).

TRAIN TRAVEL

Amtrak stops in Grand Junction.

VISITOR INFORMATION

► TOURIST INFORMATION: **Battlement Mesa Chamber of Commerce** (✉ Box 93, Parachute 81635, ☎ 970/285–7934). **Cedaredge Chamber of Commerce** (✉ Box 278, Cedaredge 81413, ☎ 970/856–6961, FAX 970/856–7292, WEB www.cedaredgecolorado.com). **Delta Chamber of Commerce and Visitors Center** (✉ 301 Main St., Delta 81416, ☎ 970/874–8616 or 800/436–3041, FAX 970/874–8618, WEB www.deltacolorado.org). **Greater Craig Chamber of Commerce** (✉ 360 E. Victory Way, Craig 81625, ☎ 970/824–5689, FAX 970/824–0231, www.craig-chamber.com, WEB www.colorado-go-west.com). **Grand Junction Area Chamber of Commerce** (✉ 360 Grand Ave., Grand Junction 81501, ☎ 970/242–3214 or 800/352–5286, FAX 970/242–3694, WEB gjchamber.org). **Meeker Chamber of Commerce** (✉ Box 869, Meeker 81641, ☎ 970/878–5510, FAX 970/878–0271, WEB www.meekerchamber.com). **Nucla/Naturita Area Chamber of Commerce** (✉ 230 W. Main St., Naturita 81422, ☎ 970/865–2350, FAX 970/865–2100). **Palisade Chamber of Commerce** (✉ 319 Main St., Palisade 81526, ☎ 970/464–7458, FAX 970/464–4757, WEB www.palisadecoc.coc). **Plateau Valley Chamber of Commerce** (✉ 103 Main St., Collbran 81624, ☎ 970/487–3833, WEB www.coloradodirectory.com/plateauvalleycc). **Rangely Chamber of Commerce** (✉ 209 E. Main St., Rangely 81648, ☎ 970/675–5290, FAX 970/675–8471, WEB www.rangely.com). **Rifle Area Chamber of Commerce** (✉ 200 Lions Park Circle, Rifle 81650, ☎ 970/625–2085, FAX 970/625–4757, WEB www.riflechamber.com).

COLORADO A TO Z

To research prices, get advice from other travelers, and book travel arrangements, visit www.fodors.com.

AIR TRAVEL

Denver is the hub airport of Colorado.

CARRIERS

Regional carriers include Delta/SkyWest, Mesa, Midwest Express, and United Express.

BIKE TRAVEL

You can obtain brochures and maps from the Colorado State Office of the U.S. Bureau of Land Management. For general information on mountain biking, contact the International Mountain Bike Association.
► BIKE MAPS: **Colorado State Office of the U.S. Bureau of Land Management** (✉ Dept. of the Interior, 2850 Youngfield St., Lakewood 80215, ☎ 303/239–3600). **International Mountain Bicycling Association** (✉ Box 7578, Boulder 80306, ☎ 303/545–9011, FAX 303/545–9026, WEB www.imba.com).

BUS TRAVEL

Greyhound Lines operates regular intercity routes with connections from Denver. Smaller bus companies provide service within local areas. One such line is Springs Transit Management in Colorado Springs.
► BUS INFORMATION: **Springs Transit Management** (☎ 719/385–7433).

CAR TRAVEL

The U.S. interstate highway network provides quick, easy access to Colorado despite imposing mountain barriers. Denver is served by I–25, running north–south through Colorado Springs and Pueblo; I–70, running east–west via Vail, Glenwood Springs, and Grand Junction; and I–76 running northeast from Denver via Fort Morgan into Wyoming. U.S. 666 flirts with the southwest corner of the state. U.S. 160 traverses southern Colorado, while U.S. 40 accesses the northwest section.

RULES OF THE ROAD
Right turns on red lights (after making a stop) are legal in Colorado.
➤ STATEWIDE ROAD CONDITIONS: ☎ 877/315–7623 within Colorado.

LODGING
The Colorado Directory has reviewed campgrounds, cabins, and rural accommodations for over twenty years. Mail orders of the directory can take up to four weeks.
➤ CONTACT: **The Colorado Directory** (✉ 5101 Pennsylvania Ave. Boulder, CO 80303, ☎ 888/222–4641, FAX 303/499–9333, WEB www.coloradodirectory.com.

TOURS
Gray Line of Denver offers two- to five-day tours of the surrounding areas. Maupintour offers a nine-day rail tour that takes in Colorado and parts of New Mexico. Tauck Tours offers an eight-day tour of the state. If your time is limited or if the entire itinerary doesn't appeal to you, you can take only part of the tour (at least 50%) for a slight surcharge.

The Bureau of Land Management has information on Colorado's sterling trekking opportunities. The U.S. Forest Service is another good source of information. The 500-mi Colorado Trail winds its way from Durango to Denver and is popular with both bikers and hikers. For more information, contact the Colorado Trail.

Rivers such as the Colorado, Arkansas, and Animas abound in Level IV and V rapids, as well as gentler stretches for beginners. For more information, contact the Colorado River Outfitters Association.
➤ CONTACTS: **Bureau of Land Management** (☎ 970/947–2800). **Colorado River Outfitters Association** (✉ 730 Burbank St., Broomfield 80020-1658, ☎ 303/280–2554). **Colorado Trail** (✉ Box 260876, Lakewood 80226, ☎ 303/526–0809). **Gray Line of Denver** (✉ Box 17646, Denver 80217, ☎ 303/289–2841 or 800/348–6877). **Maupintour** (✉ Box 807, Lawrence, KS 66044, ☎ 785/843–1211 or 800/255–4266). **Tauck Tours** (✉ 276 Post Rd. W, Westport, CT 06880, ☎ 203/226–6911 or 800/468–2825). **U.S. Forest Service** (✉ Box 25127, Lakewood 80225, ☎ 303/275–5350; ✉ Arapahoe, ☎ 970/498–1100; ✉ Medicine Bow/Routt, ☎ 970/879–1722; ✉ White River, ☎ 970/945–2521).

TRAIN TRAVEL
Amtrak, the U.S. passenger rail system, has daily service to Denver's Union Station. The railroad, of course, helped to shape and develop the American West, and it's still a way to see the state at leisure. The westbound route to California cuts through the Glenwood Canyon.

VISITOR INFORMATION
Fishing is legal year-round (though several restrictions apply in Rocky Mountain National Park), but you must obtain a license. Fees for nonresidents are $18.25 for a five-day period, and $5.25 for a single day. For more information, including the "Fishing Hotspots" and "Watchable Wildlife" booklets, contact the Colorado Division of Wildlife.

For complete information on more than 30 ski areas in Colorado—
from the large, world-famous resorts to the "Gems of Colorado"
(smaller resorts that would be considered quite large elsewhere)—contact Colorado Ski Country USA.

Contact the Colorado Tourism Office to receive a vacation planner.
➤ TOURIST INFORMATION: **Colorado Division of Wildlife** (✉ 6060
Broadway, Denver 80216, ☎ 303/297–1192, WEB www.wildlife.
state.co.us). **Colorado Golf Association** (✉ 5655 S. Yosemite, Suite 101,
Englewood 80111, ☎ 303/366–4653). **Colorado Golf Resort Association** (✉ 2110 S. Ash St., Denver 80222, ☎ 303/680–9967, WEB
www.coloradogolfresorts.com). **Colorado Ski Country USA** (✉ 1560
Broadway, Suite 2000, Denver 80202, ☎ 303/837–0793, WEB www.
coloradoski.com). **Colorado Tourism Office** (✉ 1625 Broadway, Ste.
1700, Denver 80202, ☎ 800/433–2656, WEB www.colorado.com).

3   IDAHO

Utter the word *Idaho* and inevitably the starchy tuber, a staple of the American dinner table, comes to mind. The potato fields spread out along southeastern Idaho's fertile Snake River plain support the state's largest cash crop and provide the slogan for the state's license plates. But across the state in the Boise basin it's chips of a different (micro) kind that yield a technological cash crop. And deep in the heart of the Gem State is the largest wilderness area in the lower 48 states, nurturing the popular notion that Idaho is the last true vestige of frontier wilderness.

Updated by
Kristin Rodine

WHEN PEOPLE TALK ABOUT IDAHO, they talk about escaping cities for the simple life. They talk about mountain biking in summer on mountains they ski down during winter. They talk about fishing the Salmon and Snake rivers and about rafting the white water through tremendous chunks of wilderness. Outdoor recreation is the unofficial state religion, and it has been embraced by thousands of new immigrants from California, Washington, New York, and elsewhere. It's why they say that if God doesn't live in Idaho, He at least has a vacation home here.

The Gem State's popularity was a long time coming, however. Until the 1980s, Idaho may well have qualified as the most ignored state in the Union. Such Native American tribes as the Nez Percé, the Coeur d'Alene, and the Shoshone-Bannock settled here because they found the rivers full of fish, the land fertile, and the game abundant. But, despite Lewis and Clark's trip through the state in 1805, white folks didn't show up in significant numbers until the 1840s, when pioneers on the Oregon Trail came, saw, and kept heading west. It wasn't until 1860, when a few Mormons came up from Utah at the direction of Brigham Young and settled in Franklin, that a true Anglo settlement was established.

Beginning in the 1940s, J. R. Simplot, patriarch of the potato industry and now a billionaire who lives atop a hill in Boise, masterminded ways to add value to the simple potato by freezing, frying, and drying. Simplot hit pay dirt and transformed the common spud into Idaho's Famous Potatoes, an industry that earns $526 million annually. The savvy Simplot (license plate: Mr. Spud) also sunk his roots into another major Idaho industry, helping found computer- and microchip-giant Micron. Boise, the state's capital and largest city, anchors the southwestern corner of the state with corporate headquarters and thriving businesses that keep the economy vibrant despite a recent downturn in high-tech profits and employment. Venture beyond the potato fields and the tech basin of Boise, and another Idaho takes shape.

The 2-million-acre Frank Church–River of No Return Wilderness Area (the largest such area in the lower 48 states) extends across much of the state's midsection. Here is a rugged wilderness of mountain, forest, and stream so impenetrable that even Lewis and Clark scouts, after catching an eyeful of the frothy, unforgiving Salmon River, turned back and sought a kinder, gentler route over the Continental Divide. At first glance Idaho *is* an inhospitable place. The Snake River plain in southern Idaho is high-plateau desert, a thin layer of soil over the ancient lava flows, and it's *hot* in summer. The Sawtooth Mountains, with peaks as high as 11,800 ft, loom to the north, and there it gets mighty *cold*. Northern Idaho is cloaked in dense forest and glacier-carved lakes that are revealed like jewels when the heavy winter snow melts.

These days, though, we have Gore-Tex and down and waterproofing, and what looked like misery to pioneers looks like fun to us. So, despite the cries of native Idahoans about all the newcomers arriving in their Volvos and bringing their espresso shops with them, people keep coming. Still, Idaho has a little less than 1.3 million people spread over its 82,413 square mi. That's about 16 people per square mile. Considering that more than 500,000 Idahoans live in just 10 towns—168,000 in Boise alone—there's a lot of land out there with nobody on it. Only 0.4% of the state (209,000 acres) is considered urban, and virtually the entire eastern two-thirds is wilderness or national forest. Point all this out to Idahoans, and they'll shoot back that the population increased by a whopping 287,000 from 1990 to 2000 and that you're not from around here, or else you'd feel how crowded it's gotten.

The fact is, Idahoans do feel some pressure. They lived a certain way for nearly 150 years: they fished, hunted, did a little skiing, trapped furbearing animals, mined the hills, and cut down trees. Now people, including many newcomers, are telling them that their way of life is all wrong. There is a palpable cultural rift between new arrivals and old-timers. For now, though—aside from celebrity-filled Sun Valley, which some Idahoans look upon as a different planet—this is a meat-and-potatoes, cowboys and fishermen, back-to-basics kind of place. It is a conservative agricultural state despite the growth of high-tech manufacturing. There are the famous potatoes, of course, but also grains, sugar beets, onions, hops, beans, and a burgeoning wine industry. Idaho raises 70% of the nation's trout, and the dollar value of cattle outstrips even that of potatoes. Lumber, too, is still a tremendous industry in Idaho.

Things still operate very informally here. Unless you are conducting business, it is possible to go into any restaurant sans coat and tie and feel completely at home. This is a state where the lieutenant governor—now a U.S. Congressman—could enter a local tight-jeans contest, win it, travel out of state to the national finals, and hear little more from his constituents than a chuckle.

Pleasures and Pastimes

Dining
It is virtually impossible to go hungry in Idaho, especially if you like basic American cooking. What many restaurants lack in Continental flair, they make up for in volume. Meals are often served on platters big enough to be mistaken for UFOs. But what Idaho does, it does well: a good steak and a hearty breakfast can be found most anywhere. And fine dining and exotic cuisines are growing in popularity and abundance, particularly in Boise, Coeur d'Alene, Sandpoint, and Sun Valley. Dress is predominantly casual.

CATEGORY	COST*
$$$$	over $20
$$$	$15–$20
$$	$10–$15
$	under $10

per person for a main course at dinner

Lodging
Although there are bed-and-breakfasts and lodge-style accommodations, particularly in resort areas, most of the lodging in southern Idaho is in Best Westerns, AmeriTels, Shilo Inns, and other national and regional motel chains on I–84 from Boise to south-central Idaho and along I–86 and I–15 in the southeastern and eastern regions of the state. Boise has more than 3,000 motel rooms, and from the capital north, lodging becomes more diverse: B&Bs, guest ranches, grand old hotels, and resort lodges. Short- and long-term condominium, apartment, and home rentals are available in the Ketchum/Sun Valley area and in many of the other resort areas. Guest and dude ranches near wilderness areas offer complete vacation packages, including horseback riding, rodeos, and even cattle herding.

CATEGORY	COST*
$$$$	over $175
$$$	$110–$175
$$	$70–$110
$	under $70

All prices are for a standard double room, excluding 5% sales tax.

Outdoor Activities and Sports

CANOEING, KAYAKING, AND RAFTING

With more than 3,000 mi of white-water rivers backing their claim, aficionados will tell you there is no better state for white-water kayaking, canoeing, and rafting, with the possible exception of Alaska. Canoe and raft trips range from placid to truly dangerous, and because the state is so outdoor-conscious, the public has access to virtually every body of water. The Payette, Selway, and Lochsa rivers and the Middle Fork of the Salmon River are among the top white-water rafting choices.

Permits from the U.S. Forest Service are usually required to run these rivers, but they're often hard to get and may require waiting periods (two good reasons to use an outfitter). July through September are by far the most popular months; be sure to book rafting and boating trips well in advance.

The Middle Fork is a true rafting legend. Other than the Colorado River's course through the Grand Canyon, the 100-plus-mi Middle Fork offers perhaps the preeminent rafting experience in North America. Despite the number of river runners who come here each summer, the signs of civilization along the undammed and undeveloped river are exceedingly rare. Steep, tree-studded mountainsides, hot springs, and wildlife are trip highlights—along with all those rapids, of course. But perhaps the river that out–white-waters them all—the one that licensed Idaho boaters generally consider the ultimate test of their skill—is the Selway near Riggins. When the snowmelt feeds the river in earnest in June, the Selway can offer true Class V action. By July, it has usually toned down its act to something more like Class IV. The two things you can generally count on from the Selway are that you'll get very wet and that you'll see wildlife. Perhaps the biggest challenge of the Selway, though, is simply getting on it. Permits are issued on a lottery basis, and kayaking groups might have to wait a couple of years before landing a prized permit. (Another possibility is that one of the licensed raft companies that runs the river will agree to allow kayakers to accompany a trip, if space is available.)

FISHING

There's a reason Hemingway liked Idaho so much. It has some of the best fly-fishing in the world, especially in the central Idaho streams, such as Silver Creek in the high desert, the Big Wood River, and Henry's Fork in the Yellowstone/Teton territory—areas the author loved so well. Unfortunately, sockeye salmon have been dammed out of existence, and chinook are barely hanging on. Coeur d'Alene Lake was successfully stocked with chinook a number of years ago, and people have been pulling out some large fish there.

In the northern Panhandle, Lake Pend Oreille is renowned for bull trout and kamloops, a large variety of rainbow trout, and the Middle Fork of the Salmon River is known for cutthroat trout. Significant populations of steelhead, one of the state's largest trophy fish, are found in the Clearwater River and northern sections of the Snake River. The Snake and Kootenai rivers are famous for sturgeon, an ancient species that can grow to well over 6 ft; however, sturgeon may not be removed from the water, even for weighing.

Find America
WITH A COMPASS

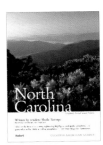
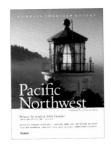

Written by local authors and illustrated throughout with spectacular color images from regional photographers, these companion guides reveal the character and culture of more than 35 of America's most spectacular destinations. Perfect for residents who want to explore their own backyards, and visitors who want an insider's perspective on the history, heritage, and all there is to see and do.

Fodor's COMPASS AMERICAN GUIDES

At bookstores everywhere.

By early July most years, river levels fall and the water clears, making the conditions just about right for fly-fishing. An excellent publication, *The Official Guide to Fishing in Idaho,* details boat ramp locations, regulations (taking undersize fish or not releasing in a catch-and-release area isn't just frowned upon, it's illegal), the best spots for various species, and even filleting instructions. It's available from the Idaho Department of Fish and Game, and information on guided fishing adventures is available from the Idaho Outfitters and Guides Association.

SKIING

Because the state falls in the Northwest's weather pattern, it receives plenty of winter precipitation. But as elsewhere in the West, the snow is often dry and powdery. For skiers, it's the best of both worlds. Idaho, especially Sun Valley, is known for alpine skiing. The popularity of Nordic skiing has soared, however, and many alpine resorts now offer groomed cross-country tracks at their hill's base or near the principal lodge. There are trails in many state parks. Snowshoeing also is rapidly gaining in popularity, and most cross-country areas now offer groomed snowshoe trails and equipment rentals.

The major downhill ski resorts now reach out to both skiers and non-skiers with a full list of activities including snowshoeing, spa and fitness programs, indoor tennis, swimming, and just plain rest and relaxation. Many areas also offer heli and Sno-Cat skiing. Check with the local U.S. Forest Service office or the chamber of commerce and the regional travel association about backcountry yurt-to-yurt ski treks. There are yurt systems in the Sawtooth National Recreation Area north of Sun Valley and the U.S. National Forest systems near Lava Hot Springs in southeastern Idaho. For the most part, though, there is plenty to do within the immediate vicinity of the ski resorts.

Exploring Idaho

Like a crazy quilt, the terrain of Idaho is a colorful patchwork of patterns, textures, and shapes. High desert plateaus, sugary sand dunes, miles of ink-black lava flows, deep river canyons, and sheer mountain wilderness are all stitched together by a lacy web of rivers and streams. In the eastern and southeastern corners of the state, Native Americans', emigrants', and explorers' trails enter the state and fan out westward. Ruts from wagons on the Oregon Trail and historic sites give testament to the frontier spirit that helped shape the face of Idaho. Dipping down and traveling near the state's southern border, the 1,000-mi-long Snake River carves a steady course as it provides the lifeblood to Idaho's famous potato fields. Along the way, waterfalls higher than Niagara Falls, springs gushing from canyon walls, and a gorge deeper than the Grand Canyon remind travelers of the humbling power behind the mighty Snake.

Roughly in the middle of the state, desert and alpine climes converge. Here, on the upper reaches of the Snake River plain, a highly unusual mix of geologic phenomena occur. A great volcanic rift zone ripples across the state, leaving in its wake spatter cones, calderas, and a blackened landscape as far as the eye can see. Then, traveling north like a living brick wall, the 2-million-acre Frank Church–River of No Return Wilderness Area holds its verdant ground. In the thick of this dense wilderness mosaic is the nation's longest wild river, the Salmon, and its Middle Fork of white-water fame. Here is a mountain-and-forest landscape so impenetrable that even cartographers are hard-pressed to sketch roadways across much of it. Fortunately, under the expert guidance of Sacajawea, a Shoshone guide, the Lewis and Clark expedition eventually charted a course across the lower end of Idaho's Panhandle. At the upper end of the Panhandle, mankind has managed to tame much of the lake district, transforming it into a huge watery playground.

This chapter is organized around these three geographical sections of the state: the Boise–Sun Valley loop, where desert and mountain alpine terrain meet to spectacular effect, and Boise and Sun Valley lure travelers; the East–Southeastern Triangle, east and west of the Snake River and extending to the Utah and Wyoming borders; and Northern Idaho, a deeply forested terrain claiming many of the nation's top "natural" honors, such as North America's deepest gorge—the Hells Canyon of the Snake River—and the nation's longest wild river, the Salmon.

Numbers in the text correspond to numbers in the margin and on the Idaho map.

Great Itineraries

IF YOU HAVE 3 DAYS

The giant loop tour connecting Boise to Sun Valley/Ketchum takes in an amazingly diverse mix of terrain, from stretches of arid high desert to pristine mountain settings. On day one, strike out from ▣ **Boise** ① on I–84 for the two-hour drive to ▣ **Twin Falls** ③. Check out Shoshone Falls, and enjoy lunch in the town's charmingly retro downtown area. From there, head north on scenic Route 75 to Ketchum and ▣ **Sun Valley** ④. Depending on your interests and energy level, prowl the Sun Valley Resort's pedestrian mall, browse the shops and galleries along Ketchum's trendy main street, or bask in the scenery along the Wood River Trails, an 18-mi network of paved trails for cycling, in-line skating, and walking. Take advantage of one of the area's fine restaurants, then sample the nightlife in Ketchum.

On day two, head into town for breakfast, then catch the sights you missed the day before. Drive north on Route 75 about 25 mi to Galena Pass, overlooking the southern terminus of the Sawtooth range—worthy of the nickname "America's Alps"—and the beginnings of the Salmon River. All along Route 75 in the Sawtooth/White Cloud valley, near the center of the Sawtooth National Recreation Area, gravel roads lead to trailheads and lakes in the Sawtooths and to the White Cloud range on the eastern side of the valley. Spend the afternoon hiking, cycling, or boating. End the day in the rough-and-tumble town of ▣ **Stanley** ⑤, with its awe-inspiring mountain backdrop.

On day three, head out on yet another gorgeous mountain road, Route 21, through the former gold mining town of Idaho City to Boise. The trip takes about three hours, leaving you plenty of time to sample some of the capital city's offerings, including the Old Idaho Penitentiary and the Morrison-Knudsen Nature Center, a capsulized tour of the area's ecosystems.

IF YOU HAVE 7 DAYS

There are many ways to spend a week in Idaho; we make two suggestions:

South Idaho: From spuds to waterfalls, lava flows to alpine peaks, this trip offers a whirlwind tour of southern Idaho's offerings. Spend your first two days in ▣ **Boise** ①. Check out the city's sights, venture out to the World Center for Birds of Prey, then sample the hands-on science displays of the Discovery Center of Idaho. On day three, strike out for ▣ **Twin Falls** ③, detouring at Gooding for the Thousand Springs Scenic Route, where water gushes from the canyon walls. After checking out the town's namesake falls and charming downtown area, continue on I–84 to ▣ **Pocatello** ⑨ for the night. On day four, continue east on the freeway to Blackfoot, where you can check out the World

Idaho

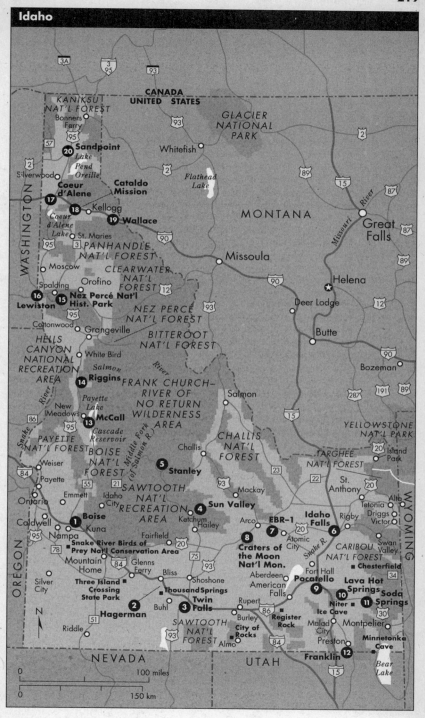

KANIKSU
NAT'L FOREST

Bonners
Ferry

57

20 Sandpoint
Lake
Pend
Oreille

Silverwood

17 Coeur
d'Alene

Cataldo
Mission

18 Kellogg

19 Wallace

Coeur
d'Alene
Lake

St. Maries

3

PANHANDLE
NAT'L FOREST

Moscow

CLEARWATER
NAT'L
FOREST

Spalding
Orofino

16 **15** Nez Percé Nat'l
Lewiston   Hist. Park

Cottonwood

Grangeville

HELLS
CANYON
NATIONAL
RECREATION
AREA

White Bird

NEZ PERCE
NAT'L FOREST

BITTEROOT
NAT'L FOREST

Salmon
River

14 Riggins

FRANK CHURCH–
RIVER OF
NO RETURN
WILDERNESS
AREA

Salmon

New
Meadows

Payette
Lake

13 McCall

Cascade
Reservoir

PAYETTE
NAT'L FOREST

Weiser

86

BOISE
NAT'L
FOREST

CHALLIS
NAT'L
FOREST

Challis

5 Stanley

Payette

55

Emmett

21

Idaho
City

SAWTOOTH
NAT'L
RECREATION
AREA

Mackay

93

Ontario

1 Boise

Kuna

Caldwell

Nampa

78

4 Sun Valley

Ketchum
Hailey

Arco

EBR-1
7

Fairfield

Snake River Birds of
Prey Nat'l Conservation Area

20

8

Craters of
the Moon
Nat'l Mon.

Atomic
City

Silver
City

Mountain
Home

84

Glenns
Ferry

Bliss

75

93

Shoshone

Three Island
Crossing
State Park

Thousand Springs

Aberdeen

American
Falls

2 Hagerman

Buhl

3 Twin
Falls

Rupert

Register
Rock

51

Riddle

SAWTOOTH
NAT'L
FOREST

Burley

City of
Rocks

93

Almo

86

84

N

CANADA
UNITED STATES

93

GLACIER
NATIONAL
PARK

Whitefish

2

Flathead
Lake

MONTANA

Missoula

90

12

93

Deer Lodge

Butte

Bozeman

287   191

Salmon
River

15

23

22

TARGHEE
NAT'L FOREST

St.
Anthony

20

YELLOWSTONE
NAT'L PARK

Island
Park

Idaho
Falls

Rigby

6

Tetonia

Driggs
Victor

Alta

WYOMING

CARIBOU
NAT'L
FOREST

Swan
Valley

34

Chesterfield

Pocatello

9

Lava Hot
10 Springs

Niter
Ice Cave

11

Soda
Springs

30

Malad
City

Montpelier

Preston

Minnetonka
Cave

12 Franklin

Bear
Lake

NEVADA

UTAH

15

3A

3
95

93

Great
Falls

Missouri River

2

89   87

87

15

89

90

12

Helena

0   100 miles

0   150 km

OREGON

WASHINGTON

Potato Exposition and benefit from its "free taters for out-of-staters" policy. Then take U.S. 23 north toward Arco and the land of lava and nuclear energy. From there, turn southwest on U.S. 93 toward the eerie landscape of **Craters of the Moon National Monument** ⑧. Spend a few hours exploring lava caves, learning about *pahoe* and *aa* (types of lava) and other geologic oddities and quirks of the volcanic lexicon. Then head to 🔜 **Sun Valley** ④ via U.S. 93 south to U.S. 20 west and Route 75 north. Sit back, relax, and enjoy dinner outdoors at one of Ketchum's trendy bistros.

Explore the shops and trails of Ketchum/Sun Valley on day five before heading north to the stunning Sawtooth Range and 🔜 **Stanley** ⑤. Spend the sixth day in this rugged mountain town doing outdoorsy things. Options include a Salmon River raft trip or a hiking, horseback, or fishing excursion in the Sawtooths or White Cloud Mountains. The award for the best short trail (under 5 mi round-trip) with a view might go to the Fishhook Trail in the Redfish Lake area of the Sawtooths, which takes hikers on a gentle cruise along Fishhook Creek to a panorama of beaver ponds, a wildflower meadow, and snowcapped peaks. On day seven, head southwest on scenic Route 21 to return to Boise. At the end of this alpine-lava jaunt you may feel that you've been to the moon and back.

Northern Idaho: This seven-day trip spans the chasm dubbed Hell's Canyon as well as three of the state's most scenic lakes—Payette, Coeur d'Alene, and Pend Oreille—each accompanied by a charming resort town. Most of the trip follows U.S. 95. Start in 🔜 **McCall** ⑬, about 108 mi north of Boise via scenic Route 55. Walk the white sand beaches of Payette Lake, play a round of golf, watch other tourists from a sidewalk café, or enjoy one of the many hiking trails in the surrounding forest. On day two, continue north on Route 55 and U.S. 95 to 🔜 **Riggins** ⑭, a tiny town with big recreational options. On the third day, use Riggins as your base for a raft trip on the Salmon or a jet boat or float trip in Hells Canyon National Recreation Area.

On day four, climb north on U.S. 95 over White Bird Summit, overlooking the valley where the Nez Percé War began. From there, the highway plunges rapidly into the Camas Prairie. At **Spalding,** tour the visitor center at the **Nez Percé National Historical Park** ⑮ to learn more about the tribe's history. Continue on to **Lewiston** ⑯, the nation's largest inland port. Or head straight for **Moscow,** a college town with a charming downtown historic district. End the day in 🔜 **Coeur d'Alene** ⑰, where you can spend the next two nights.

Start the fifth day with an early deck-side breakfast along the waterfront. Spend the day exploring the Coeur d'Alene area: stroll the world's longest floating boardwalk, take a boat ride on the lovely lake, check out the town's many shops and galleries, or pedal along the paved Centennial Trail. Make the sixth day a "play day" at **Silverwood Theme Park,** Idaho's one and only such facility, located in Athol 14 mi north of Coeur d'Alene. The park has not only the requisite eight-story roller coaster, but a perfectly reconstructed turn-of-the-20th-century mining town and rides on a narrow-gauge steam train. Wrap up your visit by mid-afternoon, stop by nearby 🔜 **Cataldo Mission** ⑱, then drive north on U.S. 95 to spend the night in 🔜 **Sandpoint** ⑳, nestled next to Lake Pend Oreille.

On day seven, you can take a chairlift to the top of the ski mountain at Schweitzer Mountain Ski Resort—11 mi northwest of Sandpoint—shop in Sandpoint, and end the day with a quiet, relaxing dinner there.

When to Tour Idaho

The best time to visit Idaho and be assured of easy access to most parts of the state and outdoor diversions is during the summer and fall months, when many of the state's premier festivals and special events occur. To be assured of milder weather, the safest bet is to schedule hiking, backpacking, and white-water rafting after July 4. By this date, the snow covering mountain hiking trails is melting and trails are relatively dry underfoot. The water warms up by mid-July as well, making rafting, kayaking, sailing, and other water activities more comfortable.

There are a few exceptions to the summer-fall rule for visiting Idaho. In the arid lava-flow, desert, and Snake River plain areas, summer brings blazing heat, so a late spring visit is best. In August at the volcanic rift zone of Craters of the Moon National Monument, daytime temperatures hover near 100°F and heat reverberates off the pitch-black lava. Similar mid-summer heat is found in the south-central and Owyhee uplands area in the southwestern corner of the state.

Many travelers are lured to Idaho by the powdery snow dumped by winter storms. As a rule, if you come in the winter, be prepared to stay put: sudden snowstorms can close mountain passes and make tire chains a mandatory automotive accessory.

When planning an itinerary, also take into consideration seasonal phenomena. For die-hard anglers, when the snow flies, it means winter runs and prime fishing for steelhead trout in the Middle Fork of the Salmon River, and Bear Lake sardines, known as Bonneville Cisco. Dubbed "Niagara of the West," the 212-ft Shoshone Falls in Twin Falls is at its peak in March and April, before the summer growing season kicks in and irrigation diverts much of the water. Bird-watchers flock to Harriman State Park during the winter, when some 300–400 Rocky Mountain Trumpeter swans make a layover there.

BOISE–SUN VALLEY LOOP

Most Idaho travelers' paths lead to Boise. It's the state's capital, its largest city, corporate headquarters, and cultural center. And it boasts outstanding natural amenities and variety, with a river flowing through it, a ski area just 16 mi away, and cool forests and desert sand dunes each within a short drive. Boise also offers two scenic routes to southern Idaho's other top draw, Sun Valley.

South-central Idaho was a sleepy backwater, home to a few ranchers and Basque shepherds until 1935, when Union Pacific Railroad chief W. Averell Harriman realized he needed more riders for his trains. He hired a European count, who presumably understood what makes for a good ski area, to scout the West and come up with a site for a resort. The chosen spot was Ketchum, Idaho, and the result was Sun Valley. Although Twin Falls and the Magic Valley around it are still largely agricultural, growing beans and hops, there is considerable tourism, spurred by Sun Valley's presence 80 mi north. And the Oregon Trail and scenic Thousand Springs area in the Snake River valley are interesting stops in their own right.

The Boise–Sun Valley Loop tour begins in the state's capital, then follows the Snake River east to Twin Falls before veering north to the Wood River valley, where Sun Valley and Ketchum mark the southernmost reaches of the region's alpine terrain. Stanley, in the Sawtooth Range, marks the northernmost stop on the tour and offers a scenic route back to Boise.

Boise

❶ *108 mi south from McCall via Rte. 55; 131 mi from Twin Falls via I–84 west; 157 mi from Ketchum/Sun Valley via Rte. 77 south, U.S. 26 west, and I–84 west; 43 mi from the Oregon border via I–84 east.*

"It's tough to be the object of so much swooning, so much rosy wooing . . . ," wrote *Idaho Statesman* reporter Marianne Flagg in 1992. "Now please stop writing about us." Nestled against foothills and riverbanks, with a desert to the south and alpine forests to the north, Boise is worried that its "discovery" will bring an end to the very quality of life that is attracting new transplants.

Make no mistake, though: even with 168,000 people and a university, Boise still functions as a small town. People know one another and exchange waves as they whiz by on their in-line skates or mountain bikes. As the state's capital and largest city, Boise has cultural attractions and dining variety found in few communities of its size. The best place to start your exploration of Boise is at the **state capitol,** which is a scale replica of the Capitol in Washington, D.C. You can explore the main rotunda during business hours, and hour-long tours are offered in summer. The rest of the city fans out from the capitol steps. From here, walk northwest to 8th Street, the heart of downtown. Streets on both sides of 8th are lined with cafés, businesses, and shops. After exploring the capitol area, head east on Warm Springs Avenue past mansions heated by underground hot springs. ⊠ *Capitol Blvd. and Jefferson St.,* ☎ *208/334–5174.* ☑ *Free.* ☉ *Weekdays 9–5. Tours June–Aug., daily 10 AM and 1:30 PM and by appointment year-round.*

Warm Springs Avenue, lined by opulent mansions, leads to the **Old Idaho Penitentiary,** one of only three territorial prisons still standing. Built in 1870, the prison was used until 1974 without much improvement in conditions. Things became so intolerable by the 1960s that prisoners staged a series of rebellions. The final revolt, in 1973, triggered the move to a more modern facility. The cell blocks have been left exactly as they were after the riot. Scorched stone walls, tiny cells with calendars still in place, and metal bunks evoke the spirit of the place. A self-guided tour, replete with tales of such colorful inmates as Lady Bluebeard and Diamondfield Jack, takes at least 90 minutes. The Idaho Botanical Gardens next door offer an attractive change of scenery. ⊠ *2445 Old Penitentiary Rd., off Warm Springs Ave.,* ☎ *208/368–6080 or 208/334–2844,* WEB *www.ohwy.com/id/o/oldidpen.html.* ☑ *$4.* ☉ *Labor Day–Memorial Day, daily noon–5; Memorial Day–Labor Day, daily 10–5.*

🐾 The **Morrison-Knudsen Nature Center** behind the Idaho Department of Fish and Game headquarters features a man-made stream in an outdoor natural museum. The stream has been constructed so that you can view trout and salmon from above and below the water's surface. Walking trails pass a sampling of local ecosystems, from a wetlands pond to a high desert plain. ⊠ *600 S. Walnut Ave., off Warm Springs Ave.,* ☎ *208/334–2225,* WEB *www.ohwy.com/id/m/mknatctr.htm.* ☑ *Donations accepted.* ☉ *Daily sunrise–sunset.*

The **Idaho Historical Museum** surveys Idaho's past and includes very detailed reconstructions of building interiors that make accompanying text about the pioneer days come to life; a working wood shop is open Saturday from 11 to 3. Botanical specimens gathered by Lewis and Clark are scheduled for display in 2002. ⊠ *Julia Davis Park, 610 Julia Davis Dr., off Capitol Blvd.,* ☎ *208/334–2120,* WEB *www2.state.id.us/ishs/Museum.html.* ☑ *Free.* ☉ *Mon.–Sat. 9–5, Sun. 1–5.*

On the northern edge of Julia Davis Park, the **Discovery Center of Idaho** is a hands-on science museums for children (and adults who act like children). Almost every exhibit moves, talks, or otherwise acts up in response to a visitor's interaction with it. ✉ *131 Myrtle St.,* ☎ *208/ 343–9895,* WEB *www.scidaho.org.* ⊒ *$4.* ⊙ *Tues.–Sat. 10–5, Sun. noon–5.*

OFF THE
BEATEN PATH

CHATEAU STE. CHAPELLE – Idaho's largest winery, and the oldest of the local grape-growing operations, is about 30 mi west of Boise in the fertile Sunny Slope region. First famed for its Rieslings, the winery also produces award-winning cabernet and merlot. Its hilltop tasting room offers lovely views, a gift shop, and a free sampling of white and red wines. A grassy amphitheater is the scene of blues and jazz concerts each summer Saturday. ✉ *19348 Lowell Rd., Caldwell; from I–84 west of Boise, take the Nampa Blvd. exit and follow signs to Hwy. 55 west; continue 12 mi to Lowell Rd.,* ☎ *208/459–7222.* ⊙ *Mon.–Sat. 10–6, Sun. noon–5.*

WORLD CENTER FOR BIRDS OF PREY – The center, headquarters for a conservation project and educational program run by the Peregrine Fund, has species such as the harpy eagle and peregrine falcon on view. Guided 90-minute tours leave from the visitor center throughout the day. ✉ *5666 W. Flying Hawk La.; take Exit 50 off I–84, head south for 6 mi on South Cole Rd., and follow the signs,* ☎ *208/362–8687.* ⊒ *$4.* ⊙ *Mar.–Oct., daily 9–5; Nov.–Feb., daily 10–4.*

SNAKE RIVER BIRDS OF PREY NATURAL CONSERVATION AREA – This conservation area on 482,640 acres administered by the Bureau of Land Management has become a key stop for those fascinated by North American raptors. Many kinds of eagles, ospreys, hawks, falcons, and owls nest and soar overhead. You can get a closer look at these regal birds, their habitat, and the ancient petroglyphs in the area during free guided hikes. One hike focuses on human history in the area, including ancient petroglyphs; another lets participants help band nestling birds. Float trips through the area cost only $10 and fill up far in advance. Advance reservations (☎ 208/384–3463) are required for all hikes, which are offered mid-April through June. *Take I–84 west to Rte. 69 south; past Kuna, the road is unimproved,* ☎ *208/384–3056 or 208/ 495–2745,* WEB *www.id.blm.gov/bopnca/.* ⊒ *Free.* ⊙ *Open 24 hours.*

Dining and Lodging

$$$ ✕ **Mortimer's Idaho Cuisine.** In the basement of downtown Boise's historic, turreted Belgravia Building, this casually elegant spot veers close to perfection. From the complimentary savory appetizer to the creative and satisfying desserts, food preparation and presentation are superb but never fussy, and the service is as good as it gets. The menu changes nightly, and sample offerings include rack of lamb in lavender-soy marinade, braised duck crêpes with sweet-and-sour blackberry sauce, and cedar-roasted salmon stuffed with rock shrimp. Try the wilted spinach salad with shallots, bacon, and spicy candied macadamia nuts. ✉ *110 S. 5th St.,* ☎ *208/338–6550. AE, MC, V. Closed Sun. and Mon. No lunch.*

$–$$ ✕ **Bardenay.** Billed as "possibly the nation's first distillery pub," this spa-
★ cious, wood-rich restaurant-bar on Boise's "Basque Block" makes its own gin, vodka, and rum. From a great pastrami sandwich to delectable salmon, Bardenay offers well-prepared meals with creative touches and a wide variety of spirits with which to accompany them. The place is noisy and vibrant on weekday evenings, when it is thronged by the after-work crowd. ✉ *610 Grove St.,* ☎ *208/426–0538. AE, MC, V.*

$–$$ ✕ **Doughty's Bistro.** This downtown restaurant's marble entry and high ceiling betray its history as a bank. The muted colors and ample space between tables provide a fine atmosphere for casual, intimate dining. Beautifully prepared dishes offer innovative ingredients and stylish presentations without lapsing into pretentiousness. Chef Joyce Doughty, star of a local radio cooking show, draws on influences from all over the globe, from Thai to Tex-Mex. ✉ *199 N. 8th St.,* ☎ *208/366–7897. MC, V. Closed Sun. and Mon.*

$ ✕ **Gernika Basque Pub & Eatery.** This popular bar and café is a convenient downtown window on Idaho's long history of Basque culture. Many people come for the pimento sandwich, spicy sausages, and other Basque fare, while others opt for burgers or specialty coffees. You may have to squeeze yourself into this narrow, redbrick, corner café if you go on a weekend night. ✉ *202 S. Capitol Blvd., at Grove St.,* ☎ *208/244–2175. AE, MC, V. Closed Sun.*

$ ✕ **Harrison Hollow Brewhouse.** This brewpub is a favorite stop for skiers heading to or returning from Bogus Basin. The building's massive timbers are echoed by huge portions of tasty food, from overstuffed sandwiches to red beans and rice. Cheerful servers haul hot sauces and creative condiments to your table in wooden toolboxes. A central fireplace adds to the ski-lodge atmosphere, and speakers pour forth blues and R&B. Six to nine handcrafted ales are available at all times. ✉ *24555 Harrison Hollow Rd.,* ☎ *208/343–6820. AE, MC, V.*

$ ✕ **Tablerock Brew Pub and Grill.** This microbrewery makes some of the best beer in Idaho, and it has managed to parlay that skill into a happening restaurant, especially on weekend nights. Neon lights; long, high tables; an energetic staff; and loud pop music create a kinetic atmosphere. The casual menu offers hearty portions of varied fare that goes well with beer—from fiery Cajun dishes to British "bangers and mashers." ✉ *705 Fulton St.,* ☎ *208/342–0944. AE, D, DC, MC, V.*

$$–$$$ 🛏 **Owyhee Plaza.** Several Hawaiians got lost in the Idaho wilderness in the 1800s and became local legend. Idahoans, not knowing how to spell Hawaii, settled on Owyhee, now the name of a county and this hotel, built in 1910. Refurbished during the 1950s, the building lost a little of its charm, but its old glory can still be seen in its giant light fixtures and dark wood paneling. The Gamekeeper restaurant specializes in elegant presentations of lamb, duck, and scampi. ✉ *1109 Main St., 83702,* ☎ *208/343–4611 or 800/233–4611,* 𝖥𝖠𝖷 *208/381–0695,* 𝖶𝖤𝖡 *www.owyheeplaza.com. 100 rooms. 2 restaurants, bar, pool, hair salon, meeting room. AE, MC, V.*

$$ 🛏 **Doubletree Riverside.** This attractive modern hotel occupies a prime location just off the freeway but is sheltered from road noise and is adjacent to the Boise River Greenbelt. You'll find fresh chocolate chip cookies in your room at check-in. ✉ *2900 Chinden Blvd., 83714,* ☎ *208/343–1871,* 𝖥𝖠𝖷 *208/344–1079,* 𝖶𝖤𝖡 *www.doubletree.com. 340 rooms. Restaurant, bar, pool, sauna, spa, gym, meeting rooms. AE, D, MC, V.*

$–$$ 🛏 **Idaho Heritage Inn.** Tom and Phyllis Lupher operate this pretty blue
★   B&B in a former governor's residence about 1 mi east of downtown. Each room is very different, but all have names with political themes. The Governor's Suite has a sleigh bed and an enclosed sunporch. Antiques, wallpaper, and old-style bed frames retain an early 1900s feel. The top-floor room, carved out of the attic, is very private. A full breakfast is included. ✉ *109 W. Idaho St., 83702,* ☎ *208/342–8066,* 𝖶𝖤𝖡 *www.idheritageinn.com. 6 rooms. Dining room. AE, D, MC, V. BP.*

Nightlife and the Arts

In addition to the lively Harrison Hollow and Tablerock brewpubs and the distillery pub Bardenay, there are several bars that offer live jazz and pop on weekends in the neighborhood around 6th and West Idaho streets, and in the 8th Street Marketplace area downtown.

The **Blues Bouquet** (⊠ 1010 W. Main St., ☎ 208/345–6605) features a beautiful mahogany bar, a small dance floor, and a diverse sampling of national and local blues artists, from Taj Mahal to Mitch Ryder. **The Interlude** (⊠ 213 N. 8th St., ☎ 208/342–9593) is a capitol hangout affectionately known as "the Tube." One step inside this long, narrow bar will tell you why. This spot draws lawyers, legislators, and other locals to discuss the issues of the day and watch sports on TV.

The **Morrison Center for the Performing Arts** (⊠ 2101 Campus La., ☎ 208/385–1609, WEB mc.boisestate.edu) puts on one of the most extensive arts programs in any city this size. The Boise Opera Company, Ballet Idaho, the Boise Philharmonic, and the Boise Master Chorale all have full season programs, and touring Broadway productions make frequent stops here. In summer, a riverside amphitheater hosts nationally acclaimed productions of the **Idaho Shakespeare Festival** (⊠ 5657 Warm Springs Ave., ☎ 208/336–9221, WEB www.idahoshakespeare.org).

Outdoor Activities and Sports

Julia Davis Park is the spot to catch the Boise Tours train, but perhaps it's most notable as a key gateway to the renowned **Boise River Greenbelt,** which runs along both banks of the river. In all, there are about 19 mi of paved pathways linking parks and attractions. The trails also are favorites of in-line skaters, bicyclists, walkers, and joggers.

CYCLING

The Greenbelt is a great place to cycle. Mountain biking is popular on the hills just outside central Boise. Trails include the 8th Street Extension (north on 8th Street to where the pavement ends) and Cartwright Road (Harrison Boulevard north to Hill Road, to Bogus Basin Road, then left on Cartwright Road). **Idaho Tandem Cyclery** (⊠ 3139 N. Cole Rd., ☎ 208/375–1107) offers bicycles built for two or more. **Wheels R Fun** (⊠ 831 S. 13th St., at Shoreline Park, ☎ 208/343–8228) rents bicycles.

GOLF

Quail Hollow (⊠ 4520 N. 36th St., ☎ 208/344–7807) has 18 holes and spectacular views from Stewart Gulch. Local golfers have rated **Shadow Valley** (⊠ 15711 Rte. 55, ☎ 208/939–6699) the best public golf course four years in a row (1998–2001). Its 18 holes were laid out with an eye for protecting and enjoying wildlife. **Warm Springs** (⊠ 2495 Warm Springs Ave., ☎ 208/343–5661), closest to downtown, is in the midst of a $4 million face-lift.

SKIING

Only 16 mi north of town, **Bogus Basin** (⊠ 2405 Bogus Basin Rd., 83702, ☎ 208/332–5151 or 800/367–4397) is Boise's winter backyard playground. It's known for night skiing, which leads suit-clad executives to climb into their and change into ski gear on the way. There are some serious black diamond runs as well as a healthy proportion of tame beginner trails. The vertical drop is 1,800 ft; six double chairs and four rope tows serve 48 runs, 17 of which are lighted.

TUBING

In summer, thousands of people go tubing—sitting in an inner tube and floating down the river. A special bus service from **Ann Morrison Park** (⊠ Americana Blvd. between Owyhee St. and Capitol Blvd.) carries tubers to Barber Park, about 6 mi to the east. From there, floaters drift back to Ann Morrison Park. Across from the park, Wheels R Fun rents inner tubes.

Shopping

SHOPPING MALLS/DISTRICTS

Antiques shops abound in Hyde Park, around the intersection of 13th and Eastman streets just northwest of the state capitol, and specialty stores with classic awnings and decorated windows vie for your attention.

A rich selection of stores lines 8th Street downtown. The **8th Street Marketplace** (⊠ Capitol Blvd. and Front St.), a brick warehouse converted into more than 30 stores, sits on the east side of 8th Street across from the convention center. The **8th Street Shops** (⊠ 8th St., between Grove and Broad Sts.) spice up a restored turn-of-the-20th-century block with specialty shops and small restaurants. **Boise Factory Outlets** (⊠ Gowen Rd., off I–84, Exit 57, ☎ 208/331–5000) stretches along the interstate in southeast Boise with offerings from London Fog to Corning Revere. On the west side of town, **Boise Towne Square** (⊠ Franklin and Cole Rds., off I–84, Exit 49 or 50, ☎ 208/336–2631), a sprawling 185-store mall, has the usual lineup of large and small retailers including **Pendleton** (☎ 800/743–9606), the Northwest's maker of sought-after woolens. **Capitol Terrace** (⊠ Idaho and Main Sts., ☎ 208/384–3901) resembles a New Orleans French Quarter building with a balcony-level of shops.

SPECIALTY SHOPS

American Nostalgia (⊠ 1517 N. 13th St., ☎ 208/345–8027) specializes in Depression glass, dinnerware, linens, and books.

The **Idaho Angler** (⊠ 1033 W. Bannock St., ☎ 208/389–9957) carries the state's largest selection of fly-fishing equipment, including a broad range of gear to rent. Well-informed staff offer classes, personal instruction, and guided fishing trips.

Hagerman

❷ *91 mi from Boise via I–84 east.*

Hagerman is the proud home of Idaho's state fossil, a complete skeleton of a small Ice Age horse. On the way, look for large, round boulders scattered over the landscape. These "melon rocks" were eroded into that shape and dumped here by the Bonneville flood.

The **Idaho State Bank building** (⊠ State and Hagerman Sts.) dates from 1887 and has served as a general store between stints as a bank. The teller area has been restored to a wooden and brass showplace, just the way a bank would have looked in the 1880s, so it's worth stopping in just to look around or to transact some business.

The **Hagerman Fossil Beds National Monument** covers 4,000 acres and offers a look at fossil beds along the west side of the Snake River canyon. The visitor center, on U.S. 30 across from Hagerman High School, houses more than 150 fossils of the famous Hagerman horse, *Equus simplicidens,* along with fossils from 90 other distinct species, from camels to turtles. Guided tours of the Pliocene Age (3.4 million years old) fossil beds are available. ⊠ 221 N. State St., ☎ 208/837–4793. ☞ Free. ☺ Visitor center: weekdays 8–5.

Frank Lloyd Wright, perhaps the greatest architect of the 20th century, believed that buildings should harmonize with their sites. An excellent example of this philosophy, Idaho's only **Frank Lloyd Wright house** is a private residence about 2½ mi west of Hagerman off U.S. 30. At the Snake River Pottery sign, just west of the Malad River Bridge, turn left and go 1½ mi. It's to the left, a stone masterpiece built into the hillside overlooking the Snake River and its magnificent canyon. For the best view, go as far as the driveway of Snake River Pottery (the oldest producer of pottery in Idaho), then head back up the road. (The house can also be seen from an overlook 1 mi farther uphill on U.S. 30.) Please don't disturb the occupants.

En Route From Hagerman, take U.S. 30 east; the road gradually tumbles into the Snake River canyon until it is nearly level with the river at the Thousand Springs area. Here, dozens of springs literally pour out of the north canyon wall. Geologists think the water comes from mountains to the north and that it may take up to 100 years for it to make the underground journey to the Snake. It's possible to tour the area by boat on 1½-hour excursions offered by Thousand Springs Tours. Boats leave from **Sligar's Thousand Springs Resort** (✉ 18734 U.S. 30, ☎ 208/837–4987)—near where several swimming-pool operators have set up hot-springs pools and river-swimming areas.

Twin Falls

❸ *35 mi from Hagerman via U.S. 30 east.*

Driving into Twin Falls feels like putting on a comfortable sweater. It is perhaps as all-American a city as you'll find anywhere. After a shopping mall was built just on the town side of the Perrine Bridge, downtown merchants banded together to take on the new competition. The result is a downtown straight out of the 1950s, with neon signs, a score of small shops, and some eateries and bars. The downtown's only drawback is its maddening adherence to the classic Mormon street grid. There are, for example, four 3rd avenues, one for each point on the compass. The massive Greek Revival **courthouse** (✉ 425 Shoshone St. N) faces a band shell in the park across the street, home to summertime concerts.

Twin Falls gained fame as the site of two falls: Shoshone Falls, at 212 ft about 50 ft higher than Niagara, and the namesake Twin Falls. Snake River dams have greatly reduced the flow over these once-majestic attractions, but during the height of the spring snowmelt, the falls regain their former glory. Traveling on U.S. 93 south, cross the Snake on the I. B. Perrine Bridge; just after the river look for signs to the right (or west) and follow Canyon Springs Road about ½ mi west to a turnoff for the **Centennial Waterfront Park** (✉ Canyon Springs Rd., ☎ 208/733–3974). The park, open from sunrise to sunset, is the only way to access the river from this area. It provides access to the bridge's pedestrian walkway, which offers outstanding views of the Snake River gorge. To view Shoshone Falls, after the Perrine Bridge travel about 1 mi south to Falls Avenue.

Shoshone Falls Park (✉ 3300 East Rd., ☎ 208/736–2265) is a prime falls-viewing area 2 mi east of Waterfront Park. Entry costs $3 per vehicle. A little farther east than Shoshone Falls Park, Idaho Power Co. maintains a viewing area of Twin Falls, **Twin Falls Park** (✉ 3500 East Rd., ☎ 208/773–3974).

Dining and Lodging

$$–$$$$ ✕ **Rock Creek.** This steak, prime rib, and seafood house west of downtown is a throwback to the days when cholesterol and red meat reigned. With a dark red interior, thick booths, and a massive salad bar, it's known for its wide selection of single-malt whiskeys and vintage ports and for the most comprehensive wine list in town. ✉ *200 Addison Ave. W,* ☎ *208/734–4154. AE, D, MC, V. No lunch.*

$$–$$$ ✕ **A'roma.** Opened by Mark and Dawn Makin in 1985, when downtown Twin Falls was struggling, this small Italian restaurant has become a local favorite by serving such fresh, zesty standards as lasagna, ravioli, and pizza. Tablecloths are plastic and the decor simple, but ser-

vice is friendly and the food reliable. ⊠ *147 Shoshone St. N,* ☎ *208/733–0167. D, MC, V. Closed Sun.*

$ ✕ **Buffalo Café.** Ask anybody in town where to go for breakfast, and
★   you'll get the same answer. This tiny café, with a twin in Sun Valley,
is squeezed next to a tire store, across from a truck lot surrounded by
barbed wire. You can sit at the counter or at one of 10 tables, but if
you go on Sunday, expect to wait. The house specialty is the Buffalo
Chip, a concoction of eggs, fried potatoes, cheese, bacon, peppers, and
onion. (The brave can ask for a Mexi-chip, made with spicy chorizo
sausage.) A half order should fill most stomachs. ⊠ *218 4th Ave. W,*
☎ *208/734–0271. No credit cards. No dinner.*

$$–$$$ 🏨 **Best Western Springs Park Hotel.** This property has very well-kept
rooms that are larger than those at most other motels. Some units
have a balcony with a pool view. ⊠ *1357 Blue Lakes Blvd. N, 83301,*
☎ *208/734–5000 or 800/727–5003,* ꜰᴀx *208/734–5000,* ᴡᴇʙ *www.
bestwestern.com. 112 rooms. Restaurant, bar, pool. AE, D, DC,
MC, V.*

$$ 🏨 **AmeriTel Inn–Twin Falls.** This 1990s motel offers large rooms with
dark wood furnishings and a color scheme of blue-green florals and
mauves. Some units feature whirlpool tubs. Fresh-baked cookies are
served in the evening as is a generous Continental breakfast in the lounge.
⊠ *1377 Blue Lakes Blvd. N, 83301,* ☎ *208/736–8000 or 800/822–
8946,* ꜰᴀx *208/734–7777. 118 rooms. Kitchenettes, indoor pool, hot
tub, gym, meeting room. AE, D, DC, MC, V. CP.*

$–$$ 🏨 **Best Western–Apollo Motor Inn.** This smaller motel offers clean, reliable rooms but no restaurant or lounge. A Continental breakfast is
served in the lobby, and restaurants are a short walk away. ⊠ *296 Addison Ave. W, 83301,* ☎ *208/733–2010 or 800/528–1234,* ᴡᴇʙ
www.bestwestern.com. 50 rooms. Hot tub. AE, D, DC, MC, V. CP.

Nightlife and the Arts

Dunken's (⊠ 102 Main Ave., ☎ 208/733–8114), Tim Jones's homage
to microbreweries, has become a regular stop for downtown workers.
There are 21 taps, covering most of the better Northwest brews. Reg-
ulars come for a beer, some good conversation, and a few games of
cribbage, dominoes, or chess. They also come in for pizzas and sandwiches, especially the New Orleans muffaletta on focaccia bread.

Outdoor Activities and Sports

Canyon Springs (⊠ Canyon Springs Rd., ☎ 208/734–7609) sits on the
south rim of the Snake River canyon with a breathtaking view and 18
holes of golf.

The **City of Rocks National Reserve** (☎ 208/824–5519), 77 mi southeast of Twin Falls via I–84 and Route 27, draws European and American rock climbers to its sheer faces. The rock formations, reaching 100–
300 ft, tower out of the desert floor and are considered some of the
most challenging in the American West.

Shopping

Downtown Twin Falls has a variety of small stores. Shopping along
Main Avenue around the intersection with Shoshone Street is much the
way shopping in small American towns used to be before malls arrived.
If you're hankering for a mall, the **Magic Valley Mall** (⊠ 1485 Pole
Line Rd., ☎ 208/733–3000) is near the Perrine Bridge.

En Route   U.S. 93 crosses the Perrine Bridge just north of Twin Falls. Unsuspecting
travelers may feel a sudden sense of vertigo as they cross the massive
Snake River canyon, justly known for its drama. (A similar effect occurs to travelers over the Hansen Memorial Bridge, by which U.S. 50
crosses the valley a few miles east of town via I–84.) The flat plain to

the north simply falls away into the chasm below. About 15,000 years ago, a massive inland sea, Lake Bonneville (the remnant of which is the Great Salt Lake), crashed through its natural dikes in southeast Idaho and poured into the Snake. For about six weeks, a volume of water many times greater than the flow of the Amazon acted like a giant plow as it thundered down the Snake and carved the canyon.

Sun Valley/Ketchum

④ *82 mi north from Twin Falls via Rte. 75 and U.S. 93.*

Since the late 1930s and especially after World War II, Sun Valley has been one of the premier ski destinations in the country. A model for later resorts, it helped to create the idea that the slopes used for skiing in the winter could also draw visitors for summer fun. Today Sun Valley and its neighbor, Ketchum, are gold-plated resort towns with a gentrified western feel. The nearby Wood River also is a haven for outdoor activities, which residents pursue with manic energy.

Long before there were such movies as *Aspen Extreme* (1993) to take Hollywood skiing, there was *Sun Valley Serenade* (1941). Sun Valley's celebrity lineup of yesteryear—Gary Cooper, Claudette Colbert, Erroll Flynn, and Ernest Hemingway, among others—makes Aspen's present-day luster seem dull in comparison. A lot of this can be attributed to the power of astute marketing: when W. Averell Harriman, chairman of the Union Pacific Railroad in the 1930s, decided that the railroad company needed some western attraction to fill train-car seats with tourists, he had visions of the Saint-Moritz of the Rockies. The location of choice was an old mining town named Ketchum. His PR team came up with the much sexier name of Sun Valley, flew in a host of Hollywooders for the 1936 opening, and the rest is jet-set history.

Sun Valley can still summon up its share of Hollywood glamour, but it would be misleading to suggest that this is what Sun Valley is all about. If anything, it is antiglitter, a place where the stardust settled long ago. The town of Ketchum and its Harriman-crafted satellite, Sun Valley, effectively mix an air of elegance with ski-town funkiness.

Sightseeing in the area is largely limited to mountain vistas, spotting movie stars, and visiting **Hemingway's grave site** in the Ketchum cemetery (⊠ off Rte. 75 near 10th St.). There also is a small memorial to the author just north of the Sun Valley Resort up Sun Valley Road.

Dining and Lodging

$$$$ ✕ **A Winter's Feast.** No doubt about it, this dining establishment is distinctive. The owner calls it gourmet yurt dining. After a scenic sleigh ride, step into this authentic Mongolian yurt—or modern alternative, if you prefer—and indulge in a luscious five-course meal. The illusion of dining in the wilds is a bit marred by lights shining from million-dollar homes on the hill, but the candles and woodstove provide a more enjoyable light. The food is expertly created by Colleen Crain. Entrées include home-smoked salmon, beef tenderloin, and rack of lamb. ⊠ *Warm Springs Golf Course, Warm Springs Rd., 1 mi west of Ketchum, Ketchum,* ☎ *208/788–7655. Reservations essential. MC, V.*

$$$–$$$$ ✕ **Michel's Christiania.** This is as old-line as Sun Valley gets. Hemingway had cocktails here during his final months. Michel Rudigoz, a former U.S. ski-team coach, took over the chalet-style restaurant in 1994, reinvigorating the menu with traditional French cuisine. The atmosphere blends white-linen elegance with old timbers and gigantic wrought-iron chandeliers. Elk, duckling, and trout receive the gourmet treatment with delicious sauces and dramatic presentations. ⊠ *303 Walnut Ave., Ketchum,* ☎ *208/726–3388. AE, D, MC, V.*

$$–$$$ ✕ **Globus.** The menu borrows from Asia with inventive fare spanning the culinary corridor from Thailand and China to India. Diners dive into huge white porcelain bowls mounded with steaming Hunan chili beef, sizzling twice-cooked pork, and pungent vegetarian Thai green curry. Homemade desserts such as five-spice ice cream cool down the palate. ⊠ *291 6th St., Ketchum,* ☎ *208/726–1301. AE, D, MC, V. No lunch.*

$–$$$ ✕ **Gretchen's.** This rustic, cozy restaurant offers breakfast, lunch, and dinner overlooking the ice rink inside the Sun Valley Resort. The menu features well-prepared entrées such as fresh salmon, trout, and zesty pasta dishes, as well as more casual sandwich-and-salad fare. The hamburgers are enormous, and the young staff is very enthusiastic. ⊠ *Lodge, Sun Valley Village,* ☎ *208/622–2144. AE, MC, V.*

$–$$ ✕ **Desperado's.** For well-prepared fresh Mexican food head to this informal restaurant in the heart of Ketchum. Huge fish burritos, black beans, and four kinds of salsa headline the menu, which offers low-fat options. The restaurant also has a steady carry-out business. ⊠ *4th St. and Washington Ave.,* ☎ *208/726–3068. AE, D, MC, V.*

$ ✕ **Perry's.** The Belgian waffles in this café are favorites of local skiers who want a carbohydrate and sugar rush. Hot oatmeal, cereal, yogurt parfaits, and legendary cakelike muffins round out the breakfast menu. Hot and cold sandwiches, soups, and a selection of salads are offered for lunch, which lasts until 5:30 PM. Take-out service is available. ⊠ *131 W. 4th St., Ketchum,* ☎ *208/726–7703. MC, V. No dinner.*

$$$$ ✕🏨 **Knob Hill Inn.** With lots of wood and log furnishings, the interior of this exclusive inn suits Ketchum's western character, but since this is a new building, everything that should be modern is. All rooms have large tubs, wet bars, and balconies with mountain views. Intermediate rooms, suites, and penthouse suites have fireplaces. The intimate Place Restaurant ($$–$$$) serves "seasonal comfort food" with luxurious details and a stellar wine list in an elegant Continental setting. A full buffet breakfast, afternoon refreshments, and fresh baked goods are included. ⊠ *960 N. Main St., Box 800, Ketchum 83340,* ☎ *208/ 726–8010 or 800/526–8010,* ℻ *208/726–2712,* 𝚆𝙴𝙱 *www.knobhillinn. com/info.html. 20 rooms, 4 suites. 2 restaurants, indoor-outdoor pool, sauna, gym. AE, MC, V. BP.*

$$$–$$$$ ✕🏨 **Sun Valley Resort.** Since 1936 this has been the most complete year-round vacation option in Idaho. The "mall" between the lodge and the inn is patterned after an Austrian village, with a lawn and ponds where white swans quietly troll the waters. In winter, with a thick frosting of snow, the place takes on the look of a toy town. The lodge's poured-concrete exterior is almost indistinguishable from wood (from a slight distance), while the interior has a country European feel. Inspired by European traditions, the Lodge Dining Room, a dramatic, circular, two-level room, serves old standards, fresh fish, and a standout Caesar salad prepared tableside. The resort has five restaurants on site and three on the mountain. ⊠ *Sun Valley Rd., Sun Valley 83353,* ☎ *800/786–8259,* ℻ *208/622–3700,* 𝚆𝙴𝙱 *www.sunvalley.com. 234 rooms, 301 suites. 8 restaurants, 3 pools, sauna, 18 tennis courts, bowling, horseback riding, ice-skating, cross-country skiing, downhill and Nordic school, cinema, nightclub. AE, D, DC, MC, V.*

$$$ 🏨 **Elkhorn Resort & Golf Club.** Once known as Sun Valley's "other" resort, this hotel and restaurant complex came into its own with a multi-million dollar remodeling project in 1999. Earth-tone interiors echo the splendid scenery beyond the windows, and hand-tinted historic photos tell of the area's past. Surrounded by condominiums, the resort sits at the base of Dollar Mountain, with a lift up that beginner's slope and shuttles to the more challenging Baldy Mountain. All rooms have refrigerators; many have fireplaces, kitchens, and Jacuzzis. A variety of year-round activities, including jazz concerts on the complex's center terrace and surrounding lawn area, keep guests entertained. A huge river-rock fireplace in the lobby inspires the River Rock Steak House, which offers tender beef and fine wines. The Robert Trent Jones–designed golf course challenges even the best golfers. ✉ *Elkhorn Rd., Box 6009, Sun Valley 83353,* ☎ *208/622–4511 or 800/333–3333,* ℻ *208/ 622–3261,* ᴡᴇʙ *www.elkhornresort.com. 131 rooms. 3 restaurants, bar, pool, refrigerators, 18-hole golf course, 18 tennis courts, horseback riding, nightclub. AE, D, MC, V.*

$–$$ 🏨 **Heidelberg Inn.** This friendly motel offers spacious, attractive rooms with kitchenettes; some have fireplaces. The complimentary Continental breakfast is skimpy, but it is delivered to your room. ✉ *1908 Warm Springs Rd., Ketchum 83340,* ☎ *208/726–5361 or 800/284–4863,* ℻ *208/726–2084. 30 rooms. Kitchenettes, pool. AE, D, MC, V. CP.*

$–$$ 🏨 **Lift Tower Lodge.** Don't let the genuine lift tower and chair outside the front door (just for show—think of it as western-style lawn art) put you off. Half the rooms look toward the ski mountain, the other seven face Route 75 (also known as Ketchum's Main Street). There is a free Continental breakfast and most rooms have remote cable TVs for your downtime pleasure. ✉ *703 S. Main St., Box 185, Ketchum 83340,* ☎ *208/726–5163 or 800/462–8646,* ℻ *208/726–2614. 14 rooms. Refrigerators, outdoor hot tub. AE, D, DC, MC, V. CP.*

CONDOMINIUMS

Premier Resorts at Sun Valley offers a collection of condominiums and homes throughout the Wood River valley in the $$–$$$ range for short- and long-term stays. Premier prides itself in representing top-notch properties, from in-town condominiums for families to ski-to-your-door luxury homes at the base of the ski mountain, coupled with special touches and services that make lodgers feel at home during their stays. ✉ *Box 659, Sun Valley 83353,* ☎ *208/727–4000 or 800/635–4444,* ℻ *208/ 727–4040,* ᴡᴇʙ *www.sunvalley-realestate.com. AE, MC, V.*

Nightlife and the Arts

The nightspot for over a decade has been **Whiskey Jacques** (✉ Main St. and Sun Valley Rd., Ketchum, ☎ 208/726–3200). It's a cross between a nightclub and a cowboy bar. Live music, western dancing, and lots of drinking help to create a rowdy crowd and a few red eyes on ski slopes the next day. The food is popular, too—everything from burgers to hand-thrown pizzas. The Sun Valley Resort's **Duchin Lounge** (✉ Sun Valley Rd., ☎ 208/622–2145) is relatively subdued and features live jazz trios and elegant appetizers.

Outdoor Activities and Sports

A public biking/in-line skating/walking trail runs most of the length of the Wood River valley. It's possible to take the trail all the way from Hailey to a point about 2 mi north of the Sun Valley Resort, a distance of about 18 mi. Maps are available from the **Blaine County Recreation District** (✉ Box 297, Hailey 83333, ☎ 208/726–6662). **Pete Lane's** (✉ Sun Valley Mall, ☎ 208/622–2276) has bike, ski, and skate rentals by the hour or the day, as do other outdoor recreation shops in Ketchum.

GLIDING

For a spectacular bird's eye glimpse of the ski mountain and the valleys below, climb aboard a glider from **Sun Valley Soaring** (☎ 208/ 788–3054). Be prepared for breathtaking views while the pilot banks the plane around the top of Baldy, wowing skiers as they catch a few rays on the outdoor terrace of Seattle Ridge Lodge.

GOLF

Without question, two of Idaho's three premier golf courses are at Sun Valley. Both are expensive (more than $90) and both were designed by Robert Trent Jones. **Elkhorn Resort & Golf Club** makes great use of its spectacular setting and challenging terrain. The course at **Sun Valley Resort,** equally stunning, is nestled along Trail Creek. **Warm Springs Golf Course** (✉ Warm Springs Rd., 1 mi southwest of Ketchum, ☎ 208/726–3715) is a reasonably priced nine-hole course.

FISHING

Right in Ketchum and Sun Valley's backyard is excellent trout fishing. Most of the streams in the **Wood River valley** have 10- to 15-ft easements for fishing along the banks, or they are conducive to wading. Trout are plentiful in all the valley fisheries, including the East Fork of the Big Wood River and Trail and Warm Springs creeks. Various streams have specific rules as to bait, catch-and-release fishing, and trout limits, so it's best to check first and get a fishing map before throwing out a lure. Contact the **Blaine County Recreation District** (✉ 308 N. Main St., Hailey, ☎ 208/788–2117) for more information.

The Sun Valley area on the Wood River (also known as the Big Wood, not to be confused with the Little Wood) and Silver Creek are known worldwide for dry fly-fishing. The high-desert, cold-spring-fed **Silver Creek Preserve,** about 30 mi south of Sun Valley (✉ Silver Creek Preserve Rd., Box 624, Picabo, ☎ 208/788–2203), is a slow-moving, easy-to-wade, yet extremely challenging fishery with huge browns and native rainbows. From the porch of the tiny cabin that houses the visitor center, the squiggle of a stream that sketches a diminutive course across fields of tall grass looks deceivingly mundane. Longtime dry-fly aficionados and veterans of Silver Creek, though, are quick to compare fishing Silver Creek to golfing at Augusta National the very first time out. It's a humbling experience. Nonetheless, its allure is constant and more than 12,000 anglers find their way to Silver Creek each year. Fortunately much of Silver Creek and its feeder creeks are protected by the Nature Conservancy, so only catch-and-release fishing is allowed. The creek is an ecologically unique waterway, a high-desert system formed from a series of cold springs that rise from underground aquifers. Smaller feeder streams serve as the ideal spawning ground for trout. Anglers don chest waders or use float tubes in designated areas and try their hands at the legendary rainbows, browns, and brookies, some reaching 20 or more inches in length. The slow-moving, clear water makes skillful fly presentation and masterful execution of casts such as the reach-mend essential. Some say because the fish have been caught so many times, they are very picky and reluctant to eat just any old fly. Add teeny-tiny flies to the formula, and it is easy to see why typically only the experienced dry-fly fishers prevail there. Nevertheless, even beginners enjoy honing their casting techniques, taking in the view, and catching a glimpse—even if from afar—of some of the biggest dorsal fins around.

Bill Mason Outfitters (✉ Sun Valley Mall, Box 127, Sun Valley, ☎ 208/622–9305) brags that its classes can teach even a novice to fly-fish in just 15 minutes, and it's true. You may not be a champion, but you'll be able to cast and even catch fish. Classes for children (morning and afternoon sessions daily) include equipment, instruction, transportation, and fishing on a private, stocked pond. Reservations are required.

Lost River Outfitters (✉ 171 N. Main St., Ketchum, ☎ 208/726–1706) employees practice what they preach. Avid anglers, they can direct customers to just-fished hot spots in the Lost River mountains and Copper Basin area, Silver Creek, and the Wood River drainage, where rainbows and brookies are rising and—given the right bug presented properly—might be caught. Lost River is quick to point out that with fly-fishing, presentation is everything.

Silver Creek Outfitters (✉ 500 N. Main St., Ketchum, ☎ 208/726–9056 or 800/732–5687) is the Wood River valley's biggest fly-fishing outfitter and also offers bird-hunting trips. Professional guides know every ripple of Hemingway's beloved Silver Creek and the Big Wood River.

ICE-SKATING

Sure, many resorts have a skating rink or two, but the rink at the Sun Valley Resort is special. The original rink dates back to 1937 and has been a training and performance spot for skaters from Sonja Henie to Kristi Yamaguchi. Katarina Witt has reportedly named this her favorite place to skate. Shows featuring some of the world's great skaters are staged here regularly, mainly in the summer. When they aren't being staged, the ice is open to the public. For information, call the **Ice Center** (☎ 208/622–2194).

PARAGLIDING

With some help from **Sun Valley Paragliding** (☎ 208/726–3332), you can catch some air under the wing of a paraglider floating over the bowls, and then, hopefully, depending on which way the wind is blowing, make a slow, soft landing on the River Run side of Baldy.

SLEIGH RIDE/DINNER

Bundle up and take a half-hour moonlight ride aboard a horse-drawn 20-passenger sleigh to dinner at a "log cabin" on the northern end of the Sun Valley Golf Course, which doubles as the Nordic ski system in the winter. Leave around 5 PM, to catch the alpenglow on the way out and the stars on the way back. A blast from Sun Valley's past, **Trail Creek Cabin** was built in 1937 and hosted many a party of Harriman and his Hemingway and movie-star entourage. Today, it maintains its original hunting cabin, outdoorsy decor with stuffed pheasants perched overhead and vintage pictures lining the walls. Diners warm themselves by the fire, then settle in for sumptuous prime rib, Idaho trout, pasta, and barbecued ribs. This is one of those schmaltzy must-do activities while playing tourist in Sun Valley. Make reservations well ahead (Sun Valley Reservations, ☎ 208/622–2135); these sleigh-ride dinners fill up fast, particularly during the Christmas holidays.

SNOWMOBILING

For those who like the thrill of speed using motorized modes of transportation, numerous snowmobile trails wind through the Sawtooth National Recreation Area. Head up over Galena Pass to **Smiley Creek Lodge** (☎ 208/774–3547), 37 mi north of Ketchum, and rent a snowmobile. Smiley Creek is on the southern terminus of the jagged Sawtooth range, also known as "America's Alps." When the summit is passable the view of the Sawtooths is well worth the drive. A guide on Idaho snowmobiling trails is available by contacting **Idaho Snowmobiling** (☎ 800/743–7669) or regional travel associations and chambers of commerce.

Downhill Skiing and Snowboarding

The **Sun Valley** ski area is a well-proportioned mix of trail and open-bowl skiing, easy skiing, and tough stuff. The unfortunate rap on Sun Valley has been a lack of snow; not lying in a natural snowbelt and with parts of the mountain exposed to too much valley sun, the ski area has been more likely than most other western resorts to suffer snow shortages. Recent snowmaking improvements have gone a long way toward solving the problem on 630 of the 2,000 skiable acres. Sun Valley has the largest computer-controlled snowmaking system in the world. Plus, with four high-speed quad lifts and three elegantly furnished log day lodges (one on top and two on the bottom), rounding out the improvements, Sun Valley practically guarantees a good ski. However, seekers of consistently deep powder will have to venture east to Grand Targhee on the Idaho-Wyoming border or south to the Utah resorts.

Dollar Mountain is Sun Valley's original ski hill, but when you compare it with the newer Bald Mountain—"Baldy" for short—you get a good idea of how far skiing has come in almost 60 years. Dollar alone was enough to lure celebrities in the 1930s and '40s, but it's a short beginner's hill by today's standards, utterly dwarfed by Baldy's 3,400 vertical ft. Together they have 75 runs serviced by seven high-speed quads, five triple chairs, five doubles, and seven T-bars. On-hill amenities include three restaurants, and the children's program is among the most comprehensive of any ski resort. Some purists might find Baldy a little crowded with glittery lodge sitters.

Two Baldy attributes are the resort's most noteworthy pluses. First, its vertical drop is continuous, and so are its ski runs—uninterrupted by Sno-Cat tracks, long traverses, or extra lift rides. From the Challenger quad alone, you can cover more than 3,000 vertical ft—a rarity in U.S. skiing. The second plus is Baldy's diverse terrain: plenty of good skiing for intermediates and experts; and impeccably groomed trails as well as a good supply of bump runs. A handful of trails, such as the Seattle Ridge and College trails, are suitable for skilled beginners. In all, though, the appeal of Baldy is challenging terrain that's better suited to intermediate and advanced skiers. Because of the mountain's steep, vertical drop, an intermediate run here might earn a black diamond elsewhere.

Trails reach down three Baldy exposures (east, north, and west), and the key to skiing Sun Valley (at least on sunny days) is to follow the sun around the mountain. The best skiing for novices and lower intermediates is from the Seattle Ridge quad chair, a nice pod of easy skiing set apart from Sun Valley's more challenging terrain. The best skiing for intermediates are long—*very* long—cruisers, such as River Run. For experts, Sun Valley's mogul skiing is famous: Exhibition has long been regarded as one of the premier mogul runs in the United States, although the real mogul action tends to be on the Warm Springs side of the mountain, under the afternoon sun. The quality of Sun Valley bowl skiing can vary dramatically according to snow conditions. After a storm, the skiing—about 1,500 vertical ft of wide-open terrain—can be absolutely exhilarating. Otherwise, depending on the time of day, the snow can be soft, crusty, mushy, or slick. ⊠ *Sun Valley 83353,* ☎ *208/622–6151,* WEB *www.sunvalley.com/winter.asp.* ☺ *Thanksgiving–early Apr., daily 9–4.*

For cross-country and downhill skiing and racing information, contact the **Sun Valley Ski Association** (⊠ Box 2420, Sun Valley 83353, ☎ 208/622–3003).

FACILITIES

3,400-ft vertical drop; 2,054 skiable acres; 36% beginner, 42% intermediate, 22% advanced/expert; 7 high-speed quad chairs, 5 triple chairs, 5 double chairs, 7 T-bars.

LESSONS AND PROGRAMS

Two-hour group lessons are $35; four-hour children's group lessons are $69. Daylong child-care programs are available through Sun Valley Company. Race clinics are $60 for three hours of instruction. Throughout the season, special masters racing, snowboarding, and women's clinics are also offered. For more information, call the **ski school** (☎ 208/622–2248).

$54. Multiday tickets, starting with three-day tickets at $156 (valid three of four consecutive days), offer a slight savings.

Equipment can be rented at a number of shops in Ketchum, Sun Valley, and Warm Springs, and at Sun Valley's base lodges. The **Elephant's Perch** (⊠ 280 N. East Ave., ☎ 208/726–3497) is a good place to get ski equipment. **Backwoods Sports** (⊠ 711 N. Main St., ☎ 208/726–8818) also rents skis and other equipment.

Nordic Skiing

For information on the condition of other trails throughout the valley, call the **Sun Valley/Ketchum Chamber of Commerce** (☎ 800/634–3347).

The **Sawtooth National Recreation Area** (SNRA; HC 64 [on North Fork Rd. just off Hwy. 75], Box 8291, Ketchum 83340, ☎ 208/726–7672) offers plenty of backcountry skiing opportunities. There are several yurts in the Boulder, Smoky, and Sawtooth ranges of the SNRA reached via Route 75 north of Ketchum. There are no roadside signs designating yurt parking areas or trails, so secure maps from the SNRA or cross-country ski shops in town before heading out. Also, check on yurt availability and accessibility (weather and snow conditions can vary considerably between Sun Valley and points north in the SNRA). Guides can be hired for day trips as well as multiday backpack jaunts to the yurts. Once there, skiers can practice their telemark turns or simply tour around frozen alpine lakes and meadows.

Tours for skiers of all abilities, from first-time tourers to seasoned telemarkers, can be arranged through guide and outfitter services, such as **Sun Valley Trekking** (☎ 208/726–1002). Among Sun Valley Trekking's highlight trips are hut-to-hut tours and a strenuous "haute route" tour, comparable to similarly named high-mountain journeys in the French Alps.

The **North Valley Trails** system and some 80 mi of trails all along the Wood River valley are well maintained by the Blaine County Recreation District (☎ 208/788–2117 for trail report). However, KART (the public bus system) does not service these areas, so transportation by car is required. More than 100 mi of trails are groomed for both skating and touring, starting just 3 mi north of Ketchum. Dogs are allowed on designated trails. Daily trail fees are reasonable at $7. Passes are available at local businesses of Galena Lodge. Galena, 22 mi north of Ketchum, is ideal for a daylong ski with rest breaks at **Galena Lodge** (☎ 208/726–4010), a roomy, log day lodge with a huge fireplace, a ski shop with rentals, lessons, tasty lunches, and snacks.

The **Sun Valley Nordic Center** rents cross-country skies and grooms 40 km (24½ mi) of trails on the flatlands and rolling meadows of the Sun Valley Golf Course, and adjacent bench and valley areas along Trail Creek. Challenge is not the strong point here (ups and downs are minimal compared with trail systems at many other resorts), but the groomers do an excellent job of maintaining the tracks for both classical and skating skiers, and instruction is first-rate. Trails are evenly divided among beginner, intermediate, and advanced. Trails for snowshoers have been added. One other noteworthy feature: the center sets some tracks specifically for children—leaving less space between left- and right-ski tracks to account for smaller legs. Because of the open-valley exposure, late-season (late March and onward) trail conditions can be iffy. ⊠ *Sun Valley Resort golf course,* ☎ *208/622–2250.* ☞ *Trail fee $15.*

Shopping

Central Ketchum is packed with small shops, art galleries, and cafés. Everything from Ralph Lauren designs to Native American beadwork beckons from shop windows. For more information on gallery tours, or a map, contact **Sun Valley Gallery Association** (⊠ Box 1241, Sun Valley 83353, ☎ 208/726–2602). **Sun Valley Village,** in the famed resort's pedestrian mall, offers 13 mostly upscale specialty shops ranging from Bill Mason Outfitters to Towne and Park Jewelers.

Stanley

⑤ *61 mi from Ketchum via Rte. 75 north.*

Deep in the heart of south-central Idaho, the Sawtooth range assembles more than 40 gray needlelike spires reaching more than 10,000 ft and marches across the Sawtooth/White Cloud valley floor for more than 35 mi. The 8,700-ft Galena Pass overlook, about 25 mi north of Ketchum on Route 75, marks the southern end of the Sawtooths and the White Cloud Range, which faces the Sawtooths on the east side of the valley. From the turnout at the pass, the headwaters of the Salmon River looks like a squiggly dribble. But by the time the river reaches the town of Stanley, a straight shot about 30 mi north on U.S. 75, the lapping dark-blue waters are some 25 ft wide. In the summer, Stanley hosts a swarm of rafters and kayakers who put in at this point and make the white-water journey down the famed stream. With the jagged Sawtooths as a backdrop, the usually subdued dirt-road town lights up on weekend nights when cowboys and river guides return to saloons in town to unwind doing the "Stanley Stomp," a version of two-steppin'.

Following U.S. 75 east and north from Stanley to Challis, 38 mi away, the roadway mirrors the Salmon River corridor, offering mesmerizing views and earning this stretch of asphalt the title of Salmon River Scenic Byway. U.S. 93 continues the scenic drive along the river north past the town of Salmon, although many travelers may choose to take U.S. 93 south to loop back to the Sun Valley/Ketchum area or head on to Twin Falls.

OFF THE BEATEN PATH

CUSTER MOTORWAY ADVENTURE ROAD – This 35-mi driving tour takes about three hours and follows Forest Service Road 070, from the Sunbeam Dam on U.S. 75, 10 mi east of Stanley. The motorway continues east, terminating in Challis. The narrow dirt road is suitable for high-clearance and four-wheel-drive vehicles. The route had its start when miners rushed to the Yankee Fork gold mines in the 1870s. By 1879, Alex Toponce, an enterprising freighter, had built a toll road from Challis to Bonanza. Town sites, mines, and several "stations" served those venturing along the rugged back road. (Back then, the trip from the Yankee Fork mines to Challis took nine hours and cost $8.) Because of the popularity of the Yankee Fork mining district, the old road was reconstructed by the Civilian Conservation Corps in 1933 and designated the Custer Motorway. On it you can see the remains of a tollgate station; the Custer ghost town site and museum; and the mammoth 112-ft-long, 988-ton Yankee Fork dredge, which dug into the valley to recover gold. A brochure with a map of the motorway is available from the South Central Idaho Travel Association, Idaho Department of Parks and Recreation, **Yankee Fork Ranger District** (⊠ HC 67, Box 650, Clayton 83227, ☎ 208/838–2201), or **Challis Ranger District** (⊠ HC 63, Box 1669, Challis 83227, ☎ 208/879–4321).

Lodging

$$$–$$$$　☒ **Idaho Rocky Mountain Ranch.** Constructed in the 1930s by a New
★　York businessman as an invitation-only guest ranch, the 8,000-square-
ft lodge with its massive rock fireplace remains much the same, with
period photographs on the walls, animal trophies, and even the orig-
inal monogrammed white china. Lodge rooms and most of the duplex
cabins have Oakley stone showers and handcrafted log furniture. A
natural hot-springs pool is a short walk away. At weekend barbecue
dinners on the wide front porch, musicians entertain with toe-tapping
acoustic western music and spin yarns about Idaho cowboys and Saw-
tooth ghosts. All meals are included. ☒ *Off U.S. 75, 9 mi south of Stan-
ley; HC 64, Box 9934, Stanley 83278,* ☎ *208/774–3544,* FAX *208/774–
3477,* WEB *www.idahorocky.com. 2 lodge rooms, 8 duplex cabins. Din-
ing room, hot-springs pool, hiking, horseback riding, horseshoes, vol-
leyball. D, MC, V. Closed May and Oct. FAP.*

$$$　☒ **Twin Peaks Ranch.** One of America's first authentic dude guest
ranches, Twin Peaks was homesteaded in 1923 and then established
as a dude ranch by the E. DuPont family in the mid-1900s. The 2,900-
acre ranch is nestled in a mile-high valley between the Salmon River
and the Frank Church–River of No Return Wilderness Area. A stately
lodge, the original ranch house, cabins, and an apple orchard are set
on several acres of lawn. Learn horsemanship from wranglers in the
full-size rodeo arena, then venture out for a day ride or an overnight
pack trip. By week's end, chances are you'll help with a cattle drive
and take part in a cattle-penning contest. Stocked trout ponds attract
anglers, and fishing and white-water rafting trips can be arranged, with
overnight stays at the ranch's farthest outposts. Closer to your cabin,
you can learn line dancing or take part in a western sing-along. Weekly
rates include meals and all activities. ☒ *Off U.S. 93, 18 mi south of
Salmon; Box 774, Salmon 83467,* ☎ *208/894–2290 or 800/659–
4899,* FAX *208/894–2429,* WEB *www.twinpeaksranch.com. 13 cabins. Dining room, pool, hot tub. MC, V. Closed Jan.–Apr. FAP.*

$　☒ **Jerry's Country Store and Motel.** This pleasant, easy-going motel of-
fers clean, affordable rooms and an excellent view of the Sawtooths.
Rooms have VCRs, and movies can be rented. ☒ *1 mi north of Stanley on U.S. 75; HC 67, Box 300, Stanley 83278,* ☎ *208/774–3566,* FAX
208/774–3518. 9 rooms. Kitchenettes, in-room VCRs. AE, D, MC, V.

Outdoor Activities and Sports

Most lodging services can arrange for guided adventures in the Sawtooth Mountains and on the Salmon River, or coordinate with specific
outfitters or guides for fishing, hiking, pack-horse, mountain-biking,
and river trips. Horse-pack trips can combine other activities such as
fishing and hiking. **Sawtooth Wilderness Outfitters** (☒ Box 8ITG,
Garden Valley 83622, ☎ 208/462–3416 or 208/259–3408) organizes
and leads horse-pack trips in the Sawtooths, ranging from 1 to 10 days.

HIKING

At one time, the Sawtooths were in line to become a national park,
but it didn't happen: in its zeal to create as much bureaucracy as possible, Congress instead divvied the land up into two parcels—a wilderness area and a national recreation area, each with different regulations.
This has not, however, detracted significantly from the beauty of the
landscape of rough-edged peaks (hence the name); and perhaps *because*
this is not a national park, much of the backcountry here is barely visited, even in the summer. There are 180 lakes, but only the two or three
most accessible receive much traffic—mostly locals from the Sun Valley area. Because this is technically national forest, not national park,
don't be surprised to encounter mountain bikes and horses on some
trails. On many trails, however, you won't see much of anyone at all.

The time to trek is between July and September, when trails are generally clear of snow. For trail tips and detailed information, check out the guidebook, *Trails of the Sawtooth and White Cloud Mountains*, by Margaret Fuller.

Fishhook Trail is a gentle trek of less than 5 mi round-trip (sturdy sneakers suffice) along Fishhook Creek, with spectacular views of meadows, beaver ponds, and snowcapped peaks. The trailhead parking area is near Redfish Lake, about 2 mi south of Stanley on Route 75.

A good source of official information is the **Sawtooth National Forest** (✉ 2647 Kimberly Rd. E, Twin Falls, ID 83301, ☎ 208/737–3200). If your desired trail is in the recreation area portion of the Sawtooths, check in with the **Sawtooth National Recreation Area** (✉ Star Rte., Ketchum 83340, ☎ 208/726–7672).

KAYAKING AND RAFTING

As far as kayakers and rafters are concerned, the two branches of the Salmon River of greatest interest are the Middle Fork and the Main. Although the rapids of the 80-mi Main stretch are somewhat less fierce and frequent than the rapids on the Middle Fork, the scenery is possibly even more breathtaking. The Class III Main runs through one of the deepest canyons in the country—narrower, certainly, and in places deeper than the Grand Canyon. Running through the heart of the largest wilderness area in the country, the Salmon is a great river for kayakers who appreciate natural beauty and wildlife as much as white-water conquest. California outfitter **Mountain Travel/Sobek** (✉ 6420 Fairmount Ave., El Cerrito, CA 94530, ☎ 888/687–6235, WEB www.mtsobek.com) makes six-day Middle Fork trips here June through August. Sign up for a trip between June and September with **Salmon River Outfitters** (✉ Box 519, Donnelly, ID 83615, ☎ 800/346–6204).

Boise–Sun Valley Loop A to Z

AIRPORTS AND TRANSFERS

Jet service into Boise Municipal Airport is provided by Delta, Northwest, Southwest, and United. Most flights originate in Salt Lake City, although United flies direct from Chicago and Denver. The commuter carriers America West, Horizon, and SkyWest also serve Boise.

Twin Falls and Sun Valley are served by Horizon and SkyWest. Because the Sun Valley airport, Friedman Memorial—actually in Hailey, south of Ketchum—is at a high elevation, be prepared for delays or diversions. In winter, the same snow that attracts skiers can also close the airport. An alternative route is to land in Twin Falls or Boise and rent a car. Sun Valley hotels often offer guests free shuttle service from Hailey. Ask when making reservations. Sun Valley Express provides van service from the Boise airport to Sun Valley. Sun Valley Bell Service (arrangements made through Sun Valley Reservations) provides complimentary transportation to the resort from Friedman Memorial Airport.

➤ AIRPORT AND TRANSFER INFORMATION: **Boise Municipal Airport** (☎ 208/383–3110). **Friedman Memorial Airport** (☎ 208/788–4956). **Sun Valley Express** (☎ 800/634–6539).

BUS TRAVEL

Boise–Winnemucca Stages serves the U.S. 95 corridor from Nevada to Boise, with stops in towns around Boise. Greyhound Lines has service to the Boise Bus Depot, as well as service into Twin Falls from Boise or Idaho Falls.

In Boise, Boise Urban Stages, called simply "the BUS," runs frequently from the airport to major points around the city. The cost is approximately 75¢ to downtown.

Sun Valley and Ketchum offer free service on KART (Ketchum Area Rapid Transit) to most major lodgings, downtown Ketchum, and the River Run and Warm Springs ski lifts. Buses run about every 20 minutes from Sun Valley and Elkhorn resorts and about every hour from central Ketchum.

Sun Valley Stages is an economical alternative for daily round-trip bus transportation between Twin Falls, Boise, and Sun Valley.
➤ BUS INFORMATION: **Boise Urban Stages** (☎ 208/336–1010). **Boise–Winnemucca Stages** (☎ 208/336–3300). **Greyhound Lines** (✉ 1212 W. Bannock St., ☎ 208/343–3681). **KART** (☎ 208/726–7140). **Sun Valley Stages** (☎ 208/821–9064).

CAR TRAVEL

Avis, Budget, and Hertz rent from all three airports. Twin Falls and Boise are both on I–84. From the north, enter the region on Route 55. From the south, you may find it easier to take U.S. 93 through Jackpot, Nevada, which joins U.S. 30 near Twin Falls, rather than taking the smaller and twisting Routes 225 (Nevada) and 51 (Idaho).

The region's main highway, I–84, stretches from Boise in the west through Twin Falls, and then east and south into Utah. However, a much more scenic route from Boise to Twin Falls is U.S. 30, which turns off at Bliss and follows the Snake River canyon. From Boise to Sun Valley, there are several options. In summer, Routes 21 and 75 through Stanley and the Sawtooth National Recreation Area make for a long but very beautiful drive. In winter, the road is often closed, so be sure to check road conditions. The shortest route from Boise is to head east on I–84 to Mountain Home and then take U.S. 20 east to U.S. 75 north. From Twin Falls or points farther east along I–84, take U.S. 93 and U.S. 75 north (Sun Valley is about 80 mi north of Twin Falls). For the most part, this is the high-desert lava-field area. If there is snow it is cleared or melts quickly.

EMERGENCY SERVICES
➤ CONTACT: **Idaho State Police** (☎ 208/334–2900).

ROAD CONDITIONS
➤ CONTACTS: **Boise** (☎ 208/334–3731)). **Twin Falls** (☎ 208/733–7210).

EMERGENCIES
➤ CONTACTS: **Magic Valley Regional Medical Center** (✉ 650 Addison Ave. W, Twin Falls, ☎ 208/737–2000; 208/737–2114 TTY). **St. Alphonsus Regional Medical Center** (✉ 1055 N. Curtis Rd., Boise, ☎ 208/378–2121; 208/378–2121 emergency room). **St. Luke's Regional Medical Center** (✉ 190 E. Bannock St., Boise, ☎ 208/381–2222; 208/386–2344 emergency room). **Wood River Medical Center** (✉ Sun Valley, adjacent to the east end of Sun Valley Village, near the Inn and resort golf course, ☎ 208/622–3333).

LODGING
➤ CONTACT: **Sun Valley Reservations and Information** (☎ 800/786–8259).

TAXIS
➤ LOCAL COMPANIES: **Boise: Blue Line** (☎ 208/384–1111). **Boise City Taxi** (☎ 208/377–3333). **Metro Cab** (☎ 208/866–0633). **Ketchum and Sun Valley: A-1 Taxi** (☎ 208/726–9351).

TOURS

Boise Tours' bright red tour trolley takes sightseers past key local sights for $5.50, May–October. Sun Valley Stages can arrange tours or charters of the Sun Valley area.

Idaho has a rapidly growing wine industry that proud locals say is catching up to Oregon's and Washington State's, especially in the white varietals. Five of the 12 wineries are west of Boise in Nampa and Caldwell; one is in Hagerman. Entry to all wineries is free. For a map, contact Idaho Grape Growers and Wine Producers Commission.

Thousand Springs Tours runs 1½-hour boat excursions on the Snake River mid-April–September. Reservations are strongly recommended; the fare is $24. Boats leave from Sligar's Thousand Springs Resort on U.S. 30 and stop at various points, including eddies in which the water is a clear green, a favorite attraction for scuba divers.

➤ CONTACTS: **Boise Tours** (✉ Julia Davis Park, ☎ 208/342–4796 or 800/999–5993). **Idaho Grape Growers and Wine Producers Commission** (✉ Box 790, Boise, ☎ 208/334–2227). **Sun Valley Stages** (✉ 119 S. Park Ave. W, Twin Falls, ☎ 208/622–4200). **Thousand Springs Tours** (✉ Box 449, Hagerman 83332, ☎ 208/837–9006 or 800/838–1096).

VISITOR INFORMATION

➤ TOURIST INFORMATION: **Boise Convention and Visitors Bureau** (✉ 312 S. 9th St., Suite 100, 83702, ☎ 208/344–7777 or 800/635–5240, WEB www.boise.org). **South Central Idaho Travel Committee** (✉ Twin Falls Chamber of Commerce, 858 Blue Lakes Blvd. N, Twin Falls 83301, ☎ 800/255–8946, WEB www.rideidaho.com). **Southwest Idaho Travel Association** (✉ Boise Convention and Visitors Bureau, 312 S. 9th St., Box 100, Boise 83702, ☎ 800/635–5240). **Sun Valley snow report:** ☎ 800/635–4150. **Stanley–Sawtooth Chamber of Commerce** (✉ Box 8, Stanley 83278, ☎ 208/774–3411 or 800/878–7950, WEB www.stanleycc.org). **Sun Valley Company** (✉ Sun Valley 83353, ☎ 208/622–4111 or 800/786–8259 for reservations only).

EAST–SOUTHEASTERN TRIANGLE

Westbound pioneers on the Oregon Trail didn't always find their way out of southeastern Idaho, and their crisscrossing routes remain, along with small hamlets that never grew beyond 100 villagers. The settlements represent a kind of time capsule, but with a progressive sense of humor, where women drive pickups with bumper stickers declaring WRANGLER BUTTS DRIVE ME NUTS. One tiny town is locally renowned for its automatic car wash. Collectively known as "Pioneer Country," most of the hamlets were founded by hardy souls from Utah who trapped or hunted or farmed in the area. The close-knit communities remain almost unchanged since the days when folks such as Pegleg Smith opened trading posts. Often the only modern building in town is the local Mormon church.

To the east of the Snake River valley, deep in the forest-and-mountain terrain, tiny towns that are little more than crossroads are chock-full of history, legends, and lore. Henry's Fork, Bear Lake, and other waters attract anglers for blue-ribbon fishing. Hot springs, a geyser, and caves are among the geologic phenomena luring visitors to Lava Hot Springs, Soda Springs, and other small towns tucked in this corner of the state. To the west are eerie sights such as spatter cones, lava flows, and other volcanic features that pockmark the arid Snake River plateau.

If you're coming from Wyoming or you just want to see some beautiful countryside, a good place to start a tour of Pioneer Country is on U.S. 20 in West Yellowstone, Montana, which dips down to Island Park, Idaho. Pristine Lower and Upper Mesa Falls are the main attractions along the Mesa Falls Scenic Byway, Route 47. Continue south and turn on Route 32 (Teton Scenic Byway) to Route 31 through Tetonia, Driggs, and Victor. Strictly farming and ranching towns until the Grand Targhee ski resort was built just across the Wyoming border in 1969, they're now part western ski towns, part ranching communities. Continue south on Route 31 through the Snake River valley, one of the state's most beautiful drives in any season. In winter, hoofprints of elk, deer, and smaller animals zigzag across the hills. In spring and summer, wildflowers coat the mountains. At Swan Valley, you'll meet up with U.S. 26, which crosses the Snake River and continues into Idaho Falls.

Idaho Falls

6 *107 mi from Jackson, Wyoming, via U.S. 191 south, U.S. 26/89 west, and U.S. 91 south; 208 mi from Butte, Montana, via I–15 south; 210 mi from Salt Lake City via I–84 and I–15 north.*

Idaho Falls sits at the edge of the Snake River plain, which arcs across southern Idaho. This town of nearly 50,000 people sprouted when an industrious stagecoach worker figured a bridge across a narrow section of the Snake would be much faster for overland stages than the ferry used upstream. He completed the bridge in 1866, and a community, dubbed Eagle Rock, developed at the site. Later the name was changed to Idaho Falls, despite the lack of natural falls. In 1911 a weir was built in the river to generate power, lending some legitimacy to the name.

The **Bonneville Museum,** housed in a 1916 Andrew Carnegie Library building, is small but more impressive than most small-town museums. Somehow the volunteer historical society that operates it has managed to re-create early Eagle Rock in the basement. The faux street is complete with a dentist's office, dry-goods store, and other facades. Upstairs, displays include objects and photos from the early days of Bonneville County, including an extensive selection of Shoshone-Bannock artifacts. ✉ *200 N. Eastern Ave.,* ☎ *208/522–1400.* 🎫 *$2.* ☉ *Weekdays 10–5, Sat. 1–5 (winter hrs slightly irregular).*

With 222 square mi, **Hell's Half Acre Lava Flows** (about 25 mi south of Idaho Falls on I–15) is a smaller version of Craters of the Moon National Monument. The centerpiece is a vent reaching 5,350 ft and measuring up to 200 ft wide and 730 ft long with 13 pit craters. The area includes a rest stop on the interstate and an interpretive sign explaining the volcanic activity in the area and resulting lava flows.

Dining and Lodging

$$–$$$ ✗ **Sandpiper.** Although the nautical theme may have gone a little overboard, this seafood and steak establishment is one of the better dining spots in town. Because it sits on the bank of the Snake River, there are lovely views from the back windows. ✉ *750 Lindsay Blvd.,* ☎ *208/524–3344. AE, D, DC, MC, V.*

$–$$ ✗ **Snakebite.** This lively, casual eatery dishes out gourmet burgers, vegetarian burgers, steaks, and pasta in an atmosphere that the manager dubs southwestern eclectic. Snakebite has the city's widest selection of microbrewery beers. ✉ *425 River Pkwy.,* ☎ *208/525–2522. MC, V. Closed Sun. No dinner Mon.*

$ ✗ **Mama Inez.** Located downtown, the Idaho Falls outpost of this popular Mexican restaurant chain is considered the best spot for south-of-the-border home-style food. ✉ *344 Park Ave.,* ☎ *208/525–8968. MC, V.*

$ ✕ **Smitty's Pancake House Restaurant.** The waitresses still call you "honey" in this cross between a Big Boy and a roadhouse. The pancakes are meals in themselves, and if you don't want it fancy, the burgers, steaks, and chicken are reliable. Breakfast is served all day in this friendly, bustling eatery. ⊠ *645 W. Broadway,* ☎ *208/523–6450. MC, V.*

$$$ 🏨 **Teton Ridge Ranch.** Built of lodgepole pine, this luxuriously rustic
★ ranch lodge accommodates up to 14 guests seeking the utmost in comfort and service. Both the lodge (with cathedral-beam ceilings, stone fireplaces, and comfy sofas in the library) and the guest suites offer majestic views of the Tetons. Suites are equipped with woodstoves, hot tubs, and steam showers. More than 4,000 acres offer plenty of seclusion. Activities include hiking on 14 mi of marked trails, riding with an experienced wrangler, fishing at two spring-fed stocked ponds, cycling, and shooting at two sporting clay courses. In the winter, guests enjoy cross-country skiing, snowshoeing, sleigh rides, and dogsledding. All meals are included in the lodging price.⊠ *200 Valley View Rd., Tetonia 83452, 83 mi from Idaho Falls via U.S. 26 east and Rtes. 31 and 33 north;* ☎ *208/456–2650,* FAX *208/456–2218,* WEB *www.ranchweb.com/teton. 7 suites. Dining room, hiking, horseback riding, fishing, cross-country skiing, sleigh rides, library. No credit cards. Closed Nov.–Dec. 25, Apr.–May. FAP.*

$$ 🏨 **AmeriTel Inn.** This relatively new motel is the top choice of business travelers. Guest rooms are handsomely decorated in deep hunter green, burgundy, and cream with coordinating print bedspreads; oak armoires hide TVs. Some units feature whirlpool tubs, fireplaces, and kitchen suites. There is a comfortable lounge with plump sofas and a big-screen TV, fitness equipment, and such business amenities as fax and copy facilities, in-room data ports, and two-line speakerphones. A Continental breakfast and fresh-baked cookies in the evening are included in the room charges. ⊠ *645 Lindsay Blvd., 83402,* ☎ *208/523–1400 or 800/528–1234,* FAX *208/523–0004. 126 rooms. Lounge, in-room data ports, kitchenettes, indoor pool, hot tub, gym, business services, meeting room. AE, D, DC, MC, V. CP.*

$$ 🏨 **Best Western Driftwood Inn.** Guest rooms on two levels are dressed in traditional light-pine furnishings, with soft floral bedspreads and curtains. Rooms have coffeemakers, microwaves, and refrigerators. Picture windows look out across the lawn, the Snake River, and the falls, which lie just 74 steps away, and you can take a seat on one of the benches to appreciate the lush garden overflowing in blooms. The Driftwood sits between the Greenbelt and the Lindsay Boulevard motel strip. ⊠ *575 River Pkwy., 83402,* ☎ *208/523–2242 or 800/528–1234,* FAX *208/523–0316,* WEB *www.bestwestern.com. 74 rooms. Refrigerators, coin laundry. AE, D, MC, V.*

Nightlife and the Arts

The **Idaho Falls Symphony** (☎ 208/529–1080) presents a five-concert series each year, often with renowned special guests. Each August the **Shoshone-Bannock Indian Festival,** south of Idaho Falls in Fort Hall, celebrates the culture of the region's original inhabitants; for information, contact the Idaho Falls Arts Council (☎ 208/522–0471) or the Southeastern Idaho Travel Council (☎ 208/776–5273 or 800/423–8597).

Outdoor Activities and Sports

The Idaho Falls Parks and Recreation Department manages more than 50 parks with 1,400 acres of grounds in the area. If the weather is warm and the skies are blue, take a break on the 2⅕-mi pathway that encircles **Greenbelt Park,** spread along both sides of the Snake River between the Broadway Bridge and the John's Hole Bridge. Locals take lunch breaks and bike, walk, or in-line skate along the paved paths, and picnic tables are set up at intervals. For information on bike rentals, call **Idaho Falls City Parks** (☎ 208/529–1480).

BIRD-WATCHING

Bird-watchers should flock to **Harriman State Park,** about 80 mi north of Idaho Falls and 33 mi southwest of West Yellowstone, Montana, off Highway 20. In this 16,000-acre wildlife refuge you'll glimpse Canada geese, osprey, bald eagles, and waterfowl year-round. In winter, a large number (some 300–400) of Rocky Mountain trumpeter swans (the world's heaviest flying bird) make a layover here. ⊠ *Island Park,* ☎ *208/558–7368.*

FISHING

Idaho Falls is the drift-boat manufacturing capital of the world. (A drift boat resembles a banana-shape rowboat.) So it's only natural that drift-boat and bank fishing are the favored modes of fishing Henry's Fork of the Snake River and other local waterways. Area fisheries produce abundant populations of rainbow, brown, and cutthroat trout, Kokanee salmon, and whitefish. The Eastern Idaho Yellowstone/Teton Territory Visitor Information Center can provide information on local fishing.

GOLF

Sage Lakes Golf Course (⊠ 100 E. 65 N, ☎ 208/528–5535) is the newest 18-hole addition to the local golf community. **Sandcreek** (⊠ 5230 Hackman Rd., ☎ 208/529–1115) is a popular spot southeast of the city.

Shopping

Grand Teton Mall (⊠ 2300 E. 17th St., 3 mi east of central Idaho Falls, ☎ 208/525–8300 or 208/525–8301) has a variety of specialty and department stores, including JCPenney, ZCMI, and Made in Idaho, which lives up to its name with a bevy of products from the spud state.

Atomic City

35 mi from Idaho Falls via U.S. 20 west.

Idaho Falls derives most of its income from the **Idaho National Engineering and Environmental Laboratory (INEEL),** on 890 square mi of sage desert northwest of Idaho Springs. When you're driving on U.S. 20 to the site, near the aptly named small town of Atomic City, it's easy to see why makers of B movies thought odd things might crawl out of the desert around nuclear facilities. Here, back in 1951, **EBR-1** became the nation's first nuclear reactor to generate usable amounts of electricity. It is now the site of more nuclear reactors (52) than anywhere else on earth. Research is conducted on subjects ranging from nuclear-powered naval vessels to radioactive-waste management. EBR-1 is now a National Historic Landmark. Tours can be arranged through INEEL Public Affairs. ⊠ *785 DOE Pl., MS 3516, 83401,* ☎ *208/526–0050.* 🎟 *Free.* ☉ *Memorial Day–Labor Day, daily 8–4.*

Craters of the Moon National Monument

❽ *45 mi from Atomic City via U.S. 93 and U.S. 26 west.*

In case movie directors need more inspiration about what the world might look like after a nuclear war, they could visit Craters of the Moon National Monument. Just 15,000 years ago, the earth opened up north of here and poured molten rock over the landscape. The flows pushed the Snake River south and left this part of the Snake River valley a ghostly plain punctuated by lava tubes and mysterious-looking formations. The visitor center, just off the highway 18 mi west of Arco, provides an introduction to the area, but those who want to learn and see more can drive a 7-mi self-guided loop tour beginning at the visitor center. ⊠ *Box 29, Arco 83213,* ☎ *208/527–3257.* 🎟 *Loop $4* *per vehicle.* ☺ *Visitor center: June 15–Labor Day, daily 8–6; Labor Day–June 14, daily 8–4:30. Loop road closed to cars Nov. 1–Apr. 15 (approximately).*

Pocatello

❾ *51 mi from Idaho Falls via I–15 south.*

Trains, trails, and travelers have all figured in Pocatello's history. Spread out along the Snake River in a fertile valley ringed by softly sculpted mountains, Pocatello was once the largest rail center west of the Mississippi. Now the state's second-largest city, with a population of about 52,000, it is still a gateway to the Teton Territory/Yellowstone area, Sun Valley, and the rest of the Rockies. Stroll downtown through the shady streets of Old Town Pocatello, a renovated shopping and commercial district, and glimpse the historic Oregon Short Line Depot and turn-of-the-20th-century houses trimmed with turrets and lovely brick and stone work. On the eastern edge of downtown, coeds scurry across the campus of the 11,000-student Idaho State University.

☙ The **Idaho Museum of Natural History,** on the campus of Idaho State University, has a fine collection of more than 400,000 artifacts and Ice Age fossil specimens of mammoths, mastodons, and other previous residents of what is now Idaho. The Discovery Room gives kids hands-on encounters with fossils and computers. From I–15, take U.S. 91 to Yellowstone Avenue and follow the signs to the campus. ⊠ *S. 5th Ave. and E. Dillon St., Box 8096,* ☎ *208/236–3168 or 208/236–3317.* ☒ *$2.50.* ☺ *Mon.–Sat. 10–4.*

Fort Hall was a major pioneer outpost northeast of Pocatello and it is now within the ½-million acre Fort Hall Native American Reservation. Massive wooden gates open to a museum complex, the **Fort Hall Replica,** representing an historic trading post once located on the Portneuf River and serving as an important stop along the Oregon Trail. ⊠ *Upper Ross Park, Ave. of the Chiefs, off 4th St.,* ☎ *208/234–1795.* ☒ *$2.50.* ☺ *Apr.–May, Tues.–Sat. 10–2; June–Sept. 1, daily 9–7; Sept. 2–30, Tues.–Sat. 10–2.*

OFF THE
BEATEN PATH

REGISTER ROCK – Wagons on their way west often stopped to camp here, just a few miles from what is now Massacre Rocks State Park (☎ 208/548–2672). During the night, pioneers left proof of their passage by painting or carving their names into the stone. Some of their markings date back to the 1860s. The 20-ft-high rock is now protected by a roofed and fenced enclosure. Take I–86 west from Pocatello 8 mi past its junction with Route 37, at which point signs lead you to the rock and surrounding picnic area. A $2 day-use fee is collected on the honor system via a box near the entrance.

Dining and Lodging

$ ✕ **Buddy's.** This bustling family-owned restaurant has been packing 'em in for over 30 years with tasty, affordable Italian food. Takeout is available. ⊠ *626 E. Lewis St.,* ☎ *208/333–1172. MC, V.*

$ ✕ **Frontier Pies Restaurant and Bakery.** Tender corn bread and honey accompany breakfast, lunch, and dinner at this Old West–theme family restaurant, which takes great pride in its pies. High-back booths and home-style cooking keep the crowds coming. ⊠ *1205 Yellowstone Ave.,* ☎ *208/237–7159. D, DC, MC, V.*

$ ▥ **Best Western Cotton Tree Inn.** This efficient motel is conveniently located off I–15. Rooms were recently remodeled; some have whirlpool tubs and kitchenettes. ⊠ *1415 Bench Rd., 83201, Exit 71 (Pocatello Creek Rd.),* ☎ *208/237–7650 or 800/662–6886,* FAX *208/*

238–1355, WEB *www.bestwestern.com. 149 rooms. Restaurant, bar, hot tub, racquetball, coin laundry. AE, D, DC, MC, V.*

Lava Hot Springs

❿ *35 mi from Pocatello via I–15 and U.S. 30 east.*

Lava Hot Springs, population 400, is one of the funkiest little towns in Idaho. It has one main street, turn-of-the-20th-century brick buildings, and some of the most desirable hot springs in the United States. The springs passed from Native American hands to the U.S. Army to the state of Idaho and are now operated by a state foundation, which has turned the area around the pools into a garden spot. The springs have almost no sulfur or chlorine but are rich in other minerals. This attracts people who believe in the powers of mineral springs or simply relish a good, hot soak. ✉ *430 E. Main St.,* ☎ *208/776–5221 or 800/423–8597.* ☞ *$4.* ☉ *Apr.–Sept., daily 8 AM–11 PM; Oct.–Mar., daily 9 AM–10 PM.*

The **World Famous Hot Pools** and **Olympic Swimming Complex** offers five **hot pools** with temperatures ranging from 104°F to 112°F. Two swimming pools, one with ⅓ acre of water surface, are located on each end of the 25-acre landscaped property. Suits, towels, and lockers are available. ☞ *Hot pools or swimming pools $4; both $7.* ☉ *Hot pools: Apr.–Sept., daily 8 AM–11 PM; Oct.–Mar., daily 9 AM–10 PM. Swimming pools: Sun.–Fri. 11–8, Sat. 10–8.*

OFF THE BEATEN PATH	**CHESTERFIELD –** Virtually a ghost town now, Chesterfield was founded in 1880 by Mormons, complete with the Mormon grid system for streets. Many of the original buildings still stand as if waiting for the inhabitants to return. Chesterfield, 20 mi from Lava Hot Springs via U.S. 30 east to Bancroft and Chesterfield Road north, is listed on the National Register of Historic Places.

Dining and Lodging

$–$$ ✕ **Johnny's.** This pleasant, informal place cooks up burgers, steaks, and seafood, plus a hearty breakfast. ✉ *78 E. Main St.,* ☎ *208/776–5562. AE, D, MC, V.*

$$ ✕🏠 **Royal Hotel Bed & Breakfast.** Lisa Toly has turned this old miners' rooming house into a cozy B&B with turn-of-the-20th-century furnishings. Rooms are small, but the second floor has a kitchen area especially for guests to make snacks in, and the honeymoon suite has a whirlpool tub. The full breakfast, including Toly's home-baked apple turnovers and frittata, is the best in town. If you're in time for lunch—and especially if you've got a hungry brood—stop in for pizza, a specialty. ✉ *11 E. Main St., Box 476, 83246,* ☎ *208/776–5216. 3 rooms, 1 suite. Restaurant. AE, D, MC, V. BP.*

$–$$$ 🏠 **Lava Hot Springs Inn.** This grand old building began as a hospital and is now a European-style B&B. (A buffet breakfast is included.) The interior is done in pinks and purples, and the rooms are neat and well appointed. Five suites have private baths with whirlpool tubs; a hot mineral pool, just steps away from the back door, overlooks the Portneuf River. ✉ *94 E. Portneuf Ave., Box 670, 83246,* ☎ *208/776–5830 or 800/527–5830,* WEB *www.lavahotspringsinn.com. 19 rooms, 2 with bath; 5 suites with bath. Dining room, hot springs, library. AE, D, MC, V. BP.*

Outdoor Activities and Sports

Thunder Canyon (✉ *9898 E. Merrick Rd.,* ☎ *208/776–5048*) is a nine-hole golf course.

Soda Springs

⑪ *20 mi from Lava Hot Springs via U.S. 30 east.*

Soda Springs is home to another regional landmark. No, not the Monsanto slag pour, which the town lists as a tourist attraction, but the only **man-made geyser** on earth, a sight that's more reputation than reality. It seems the town fathers were drilling for a swimming pool when they hit carbon dioxide, a gas that permeates this region. The carbon dioxide mixed with groundwater under pressure and started shooting out of the ground. Local boosters capped the geyser with a valve. During daylight hours the Captive Geyser is turned on—unless the wind is coming from the west, which would douse the parking lot. From U.S. 30, turn left onto Main Street; the geyser is right behind the Statesman's Lounge and Enders Café on the left side of the street.

OFF THE
BEATEN PATH

MINNETONKA CAVE – Adventurous travelers may want to take a side trip on U.S. 30 east to Montpelier (31 mi), another interesting pioneer town, and then take U.S. 89 south to St. Charles (18 mi). Just west of St. Charles, first on a county highway and then on a U.S. Forest Service road (both numbered 30012), lies the Minnetonka Cave, a classic nine-room limestone cavern dotted with stalactites and stalagmites. The forest service gives 90-minute tours throughout the summer. Take a jacket. The cavern is a naturally constant 40°F. Nearby Bear Lake, famous for its odd turquoise color, is a local favorite with campers and anglers looking for cutthroat trout. ✉ 1¼ mi west of St. Charles, ☎ 208/847–2407. ☞ $4. ☉ Tours: mid-June–Labor Day (depending on weather), daily 10:30–5, every ½ hr.

En Route U.S. 30 heads west from Soda Springs to Route 34. As you head south on Route 34, there's a small sign 3 mi past the town of Grace that points the way (left onto Ice Cave Road for a very short distance) to **Niter Ice Cave.** This may look like a small hole in the ground, but the cave, used by pioneers to keep food cold, is nearly ½ mi long. You can climb in if you want, but be sure to have a flashlight and be prepared to get dirty. Route 34 continues south through rolling ranch lands that were the object of range wars between farmers, who wanted to put up fences, and shepherds and cattlemen, who wanted an open range.

Franklin

⑫ *43 mi from Soda Springs via U.S. 30 west, Rte. 34 south, and U.S. 91 south (at Preston).*

The oldest town in Idaho was established on April 14, 1860, by order of Brigham Young, who sent settlers north from Utah. At first the pioneers struggled, but eventually a sawmill was installed and more cash flowed in. Today the town, population 478, contains the **Franklin Historic District** along Main Street. Turn left off U.S. 91; the **village hall,** built in 1904, is on the right. Across the street, the **Lorenzo Hatch** house (1870) is a fine example of Greek Revival architecture, popular in many western pioneer towns. The exterior masonry is a marvel, considering how primitive the town was in 1870. Nearby stands the **Franklin Cooperative Mercantile Institution,** a great stone structure; it was built to house the local cooperative store and now contains a museum.

Continue south out of town on U.S. 91, and just before the Utah border you'll see the **town cemetery.** Many grave sites are more than 100 years old.

En Route A nice drive dips into Utah, then loops back toward I–86 and Register Rock. Cross into Utah, take Route 61 to Cornish, and drive north on Route 23 toward Weston, where you pick up Route 36 to Malad

City. If the weather is good and all roads are open, head south on I–15 to Route 38 west, follow it to Holbrook, and turn north on Route 37. This road winds through the Curlew National Grasslands and past abandoned homestead cabins sitting lonely on the rolling hills. When Route 37 meets I–86, drive west to Register Rock.

East–Southeast Triangle A to Z

AIRPORTS
The commuter carriers Horizon and SkyWest have service to Idaho Falls and Pocatello. Delta flies to Idaho Falls.
➤ AIRPORT INFORMATION: **Idaho Falls Regional Airport** (☎ 208/529–1221). **Pocatello Regional Airport** (☎ 208/234–6154).

BUS TRAVEL
Greyhound Lines serves Idaho Falls corridor. To the east, buses run to Rexburg and West Yellowstone, Montana.

Pocatello has an urban bus service, Pocatello Urban Transit. Schedules can be obtained from the Chamber of Commerce.
➤ BUS INFORMATION: **Greyhound Lines** (✉ 215 W. Bonneville St., Idaho Falls, ☎ 208/232–5365 or 800/231–2222). **Pocatello Chamber of Commerce** (☎ 208/233–1525). **Pocatello Urban Transit** (☎ 208/254–2287).

CAR RENTAL
There is an abundance of car-rental companies with booths at the Pocatello and Idaho Falls airports. Be aware, however, that rentals in Idaho, especially during ski season, can be pricey.

CAR TRAVEL
From the south, I–15 connects Salt Lake and other Utah cities to southeastern Idaho; from the north, it comes from western Montana. In Idaho, I–15 runs through Idaho Falls and Pocatello, where it intersects I–86 (the main route west), and along the edge of the pioneer towns in the southeast corner. From the east, the most scenic route into the region descends from Wyoming's Teton Pass and connects with Idaho's Routes 33 and 31 at Victor in the Targhee National Forest. Route 31 runs to Swan Valley and U.S. 26, which goes to Idaho Falls.

ROAD CONDITIONS:
Idaho Falls (☎ 208/522–5141). **Pocatello** (☎ 208/232–1426).

EMERGENCIES
In an emergency, dial **911** except in Franklin County, where you should call ☎ 208/852–1234.
➤ CONTACTS: **Eastern Regional Medical Center** (✉ 3100 Channing Way, Idaho Falls, ☎ 208/529–6111). **Pocatello Regional Medical Center** (✉ 777 Hospital Way, Pocatello, ☎ 208/234–0777).

VISITOR INFORMATION
➤ TOURIST INFORMATION: **Eastern Idaho Visitor Information Center** (✉ 505 Lindsay Blvd., Box 50498, Idaho Falls 83402, ☎ 208/523–1010 or 800/634–3246, WEB www.yellowstoneteton.org). **Southeast Idaho Tourist Information** (✉ Box 669, Lava Hot Springs 83246, ☎ 208/776–5221 or 800/423–8597).

NORTHERN IDAHO

Most Idahoans consider the Salmon River the unofficial boundary between north and south, since it bisects the state almost perfectly and separates the Pacific and Mountain time zones. The Salmon River is also one of the state's great scenic attractions. It is the longest wild river left in the United States, outside of Alaska, and the Middle Fork, which begins as runoff from the Sawtooths and flows through the Frank Church–River of No Return Wilderness Area, is recognized around the world for one of the wildest, most gorgeous river-raft trips on earth. The river system is a magnet for anglers, too. Riggins, near its western end; Stanley, high in the Sawtooths near the Middle Fork; and Salmon, to the east near Montana, are the gateways to the Salmon River and its wilderness.

North of White Bird Summit, Idaho begins to feel more like the Northwest than the West. Lewiston, for example, is an inland port whose traffic comes from the Columbia River; it's also a portal to Hells Canyon, a natural wonder that forms the border between Oregon and Idaho.

The Panhandle of Idaho is a logging region that has been "discovered" by refugees from larger cities in California, Washington State, and elsewhere. The resort towns of Coeur d'Alene and Sandpoint are just the sort of places that compel vacationers to thumb through real estate brochures.

McCall

13 *108 mi from Boise via Rte. north.*

Although the town of McCall is close to Boise and falls within the capital's sphere of influence, it has the alpine feel of the northern half of the state. The 108-mi drive north from Boise on Route 55 is one of the most beautiful in Idaho, if not the country. The road, choked by recreational vehicles in summer, runs along the shore of the Payette River as it rollicks down the mountains, over boulders, and through alpine forests. The arid plains of the Snake River give way to higher and higher mountains covered by tremendous stands of pines.

McCall traces its beginnings to a wagon train and passengers Tom McCall and family, who decided to stay behind. Laid out in 1901, the town blossomed a few years later with the arrival of the Union Pacific Railroad. The area's first ski slope, Little Ski Hill, opened in 1937 with a T-bar carrying skiers up 405 vertical ft, and the film *Northwest Passage* was shot here in 1938. In 1948, a lodge was built on the shore of Payette Lake where the town sits today. Beginning in 1961 with plenty of powdery snow and the construction of Brundage Mountain Resort, McCall experienced a rebirth. Today, the Little Ski Hill is overshadowed by Brundage Mountain, which is still considered modest by ski-area standards, with 1,400 acres of skiable terrain.

During the 1980s, the area was discovered by Californians. Espresso shops and tourist-friendly stores line the streets. The 1948 lodge on Payette Lake was bought by a San Diego developer and has been remodeled and gone upscale. Locals are a little ambivalent about all this, but there's no doubt the changes have made McCall one of the most popular resort destinations in the state. The town hosts a popular Winter Carnival each January featuring massive, intricately detailed ice sculptures.

Dining and Lodging

$$–$$$$ ✕ **The Mill.** This antiques-laden place with heavy wooden beams is a carnivore's dream, dishing out huge portions of steak and prime rib, with seafood options for those who want to go against the flow. The food is good, and so is the service. ⊠ *324 N. 3rd St.,* ☎ *208/634–7683. AE, D, MC, V.*

$ ✕ **Pancake House.** At the south edge of town, this breakfast spot has become a skiers' favorite, thanks to its massive pancakes. You may have a short wait, because everybody in McCall seems to eat here. ✉ *201 N. 3rd St.,* ☎ *208/634–5849. MC, V. No dinner.*

$–$$$$ 🏨 **Hotel McCall.** This hybrid between a hotel and a B&B is in the center of town. The building, constructed in 1939, is more attractive outside than in. Rooms and prices vary widely; six are small, dark, and share a bath, while others are almost grand and have lots of light and antique furnishings. Some have views of Payette Lake. A Continental breakfast is included. ✉ *1101 N. 3rd St., 83638,* ☎ *208/634–8105. 22 rooms, 16 with bath. Dining room. AE, MC, V. CP.*

$ 🏨 **Scandia Inn Motel.** This standard motel stands out for its very clean rooms and quiet location off the highway. Rooms are comfortable; two have kitchens. ✉ *401 N. 3rd St., 83638,* ☎ *208/634–7394. 18 rooms. Sauna. AE, D, MC, V.*

Outdoor Activities and Sports

GOLF

Launched in 1926, **McCall Golf Course** (✉ Davis St., McCall, ☎ 208/ 634–7200) is one of the oldest in the state. Frequently updated, it now has 27 holes in three nine-hole segments.

SKIING

Brundage Mountain might be a small ski area as far as chairlifts and tows are concerned, but the area has ample treed terrain, and lots of powder. Although the runs are a little short, Brundage does have enough to keep intermediates and beginners interested. Advanced skiers find solace in the powder glades. On top of the hill are spectacular views of the Seven Devils peaks and Payette Lake. With a vertical drop of 1,800 ft and 38 runs, Brundage has one quad, two triple chairs, a platter tow, and a handle tow. ✉ *Box 1062, McCall, 8 mi north of McCall,* ☎ *208/ 634–4151.* 🎿 *$34.* ☉ *Thanksgiving–Apr., daily 9:30–4:30.*

Little Ski Hill (✉ Rte. 55, south of McCall, ☎ 208/634–5691) still serves downhill skiers, primarily those who want to make a few telemark turns (with free heel boots and bindings). It also has 49 km (30 mi) of groomed Nordic skating and touring trails and is one of the five U.S. Olympic Committee–sanctioned biathlon courses in the nation.

En Route Route 55 reaches its peak a few miles outside McCall and then gradually snakes its way downhill. It joins U.S. 95 and the Little Salmon River at New Meadows and heads into mining territory, where gold and silver, and rumors of both, drew hundreds of mostly disappointed men.

Riggins

⑭ *45 mi from McCall via Rte. 55 and U.S. 95 north.*

About 33 mi north of the junction of Route 55 and U.S. 95, where the Little Salmon flows into the main Salmon River, the tiny town of Riggins is a wide spot in the road. It's also the last stop in the Mountain Time Zone; across the river, it's an hour earlier. Hunters and anglers flock here for chukar, elk, and steelhead.

Lodging

$$$–$$$$ 🏨 **Lodge at Riggins Hot Springs.** This lodge, named for hot springs that
★ have been harnessed into pools on the bank of the Salmon River, is just over 10 mi upriver from Riggins along a narrow, winding road. Inside, western antiques and Native American crafts abound, and a sitting room is dominated by a large rock fireplace. Rooms have pine paneling and wooden bed frames. Full country breakfasts, snack lunches, and fine dinners, such as lamb in raspberry sauce, are included. The

dining room features a rustic yet glamorous setting with a huge stone fireplace and antler candelabras. The lodge works with outfitters to create tailor-made package excursions for hunters, anglers, and rafters. ✉ *Box 1247, 83549,* ☎ *208/628–3725,* FAX *208/628–3785,* WEB *www.rhslodge.com. 10 rooms. Dining room, pool, hot tub, mineral baths, sauna, billiards, travel services. MC, V. FAP.*

$ 📺 **Salmon River Motel.** The rooms are clean, comfortable, and spare; choose between TV and the sounds of the river. One of Riggins's four restaurants is on site. ✉ *1203 U.S. 95, 83549,* ☎ *208/628–3231 or 888/628–3025. 16 rooms. Restaurant. MC, V.*

Nightlife

Locals hang out at the **Ruby Rapids** (✉ U.S. 95, ☎ 208/622–3914), that rare establishment that gives drinks on credit to folks it knows. Yes, it's a small-town dive, but a dive of the best kind.

En Route Immediately outside Riggins, U.S. 95 crosses the Salmon and begins the 40-mi climb toward **White Bird Summit,** which rises 4,245 ft above sea level. There were no roads from north to south Idaho until 1915, when the White Bird Grade was finished. It climbed nearly 3,000 ft in 14 mi of agonizing hairpins and switchbacks. The new road was finished in 1975. A little more than halfway up the new grade, a small scenic overlook sits above the valley where the Nez Percé War started. In 1877, Chief Joseph and his band of Nez Percé, who had not signed a treaty with the whites (as had other bands), were nevertheless on their way to resettle at the nearby reservation when trouble broke out. About 80 Native Americans decimated a much larger white force without losing a person. The army retreated, but the legendary pursuit of Joseph's band across 1,500 mi of Idaho and Montana began. An interpretive shelter tells the story of the battle. From White Bird Summit, U.S. 95 plunges rapidly into the Camas Prairie and into Grangeville, a farming town. Here, the Nez Percé dug the roots of the camas plant, a dietary staple.

Spalding

90 mi from Riggins via U.S. 95 north.

About 53 mi north of Riggins, U.S. 95 enters the modern Nez Percé native American Reservation, home to treaty and nontreaty Nez Percé. (There is still some minor antagonism between the groups.) **Nez Percé National Historical Park** is really a series of 24 sites spread across three states. Park headquarters is in Spalding (11 mi east of Lewiston), where a visitor center gives a detailed look at the Nez Percé, or Ne-Mee-Poo, as they called themselves, and their history. A 30-minute film details the tribe's contacts with Lewis and Clark and their lives today. A small museum exhibits artifacts from chiefs Joseph and White Bird, including textiles; pipes; and, poignantly, a ribbon and a coin given to the tribe by Meriwether Lewis as thanks for help. ✉ *U.S. 95,* ☎ *208/ 843–2261.* 🎟 *Donation.* ☉ *Memorial Day–Labor Day, daily 8–5:30; Labor Day–Memorial Day, daily 8–4:30.*

Lewiston

🔟 *11 mi from Spalding via U.S. 95 north and U.S. 12 west.*

The hardworking mill town of Lewiston is tucked into the hills at the junction of the Snake and Clearwater rivers. It was once the capital of the Idaho Territory but is now known regionally for its relatively mild temperatures and early golf season. Its blue-collar economy is based on its inland port and the giant paper mill just on its eastern edge.

Lewiston and Clarkston (its twin city in Washington), named for you know whom, are also known as the gateways to **Hells Canyon,** a geologic wonder deeper than the Grand Canyon. Canyon tours have become big business in Lewiston. The hills in the canyon resemble ancient Mayan temples as they rise high above the waterway. Columnar basalt, rock formations that look like giant black pencils, frame the river. In some spots, ancient Native American pictographs can be seen on smooth rock faces. Bald eagles swoop down from cliffs to hunt for fish, and deer scatter along the hillsides.

Miners tried to exploit the area, but they gave up. Today a few hardy sheep and cattle ranchers are all that's left of the pioneers who first settled here. The **Kirkwood Historic Ranch** (☎ 208/628–3916), a long hike past mining-camp sites and petroglyphs or a four-hour jet-boat ride from Lewiston, has been preserved to show how the pioneers lived. Although they make their homes from cut lumber instead of logs, ranchers today live in nearly the same style.

Dining and Lodging

$$ ✕ **Bojack's.** This popular downtown eatery has been pleasing locals with the same menu for 30 years: tasty steaks and seafood with spaghetti as a side dish. Doggie bags are frequently required. There's a dark bar upstairs. ⊠ *311 Main St.,* ☎ *208/746–9532. AE, MC, V. Closed Sun. No lunch.*

$ ✕🏨 **Sacajawea Motor Inn.** The basic motel-type rooms are quiet, and a good bargain. Lots of locals eat at the attached restaurant, the Helm ($), because they know exactly what to expect: good, reliable, simple food for breakfast, lunch, or dinner. It is much like a Denny's with its counter and vinyl booths. The menu carries steaks, burgers, chops, chicken, pancakes, and a variety of sandwiches. ⊠ *1824 Main St., 83501,* ☎ *208/746–1393 or 800/333–1393,* FAX *208/743–3620. 90 rooms. Restaurant, pool, hot tub, gym, coin laundry. AE, D, DC, MC, V.*

$ 🏨 **Inn America.** Many rooms in this cheerful, hilltop motel have views of the Snake River. Rooms are large, and it's easy to access the inn from the highway. ⊠ *702 21st St., 83501,* ☎ *208/746–4600,* FAX *208/748–1050. 61 rooms. Pool. AE, D, DC, MC, V.*

Outdoor Activities and Sports

Sitting high on a hill overlooking the Lewiston/Clarkston Valley and the Snake and Clearwater rivers, the 18-hole **Bryden Canyon Golf Course** (⊠ 445 O'Connor Rd., ☎ 208/746–0863) is open almost year-round.

En Route From Lewiston, U.S. 95 climbs 2,000 ft virtually straight up out of the valley and into rolling farmland. About 40 mi later, it cuts through the middle of **Moscow,** home of the University of Idaho. Students often joke that the university was placed in Moscow because there is absolutely nothing to do here except study. The city does feature a fine set of late-19th-century buildings, however, and in February, the Lionel Hampton Jazz Festival, one of the best jazz festivals in the country.

Coeur d'Alene

🅦 *120 mi from Lewiston via U.S. 95 north.*

Idaho's second-most-famous resort town sits on the shores of lovely Coeur d'Alene Lake, surrounded by evergreen-covered hills. Originally a Native American settlement, then a U.S. Army fort, the town has always attracted visitors. Now it does so with a vengeance, but it retains a pleasant village atmosphere, especially along Sherman Avenue, the main drag. Although primarily known as a summer destination and as Spokane's playground, Coeur d'Alene has boosted its number of winter visitors by promoting Silver Mountain, a ski area about 50 mi to the east.

The Coeur d'Alene Indian Reservation is 10 mi south of Coeur d'Alene on U.S. 95. French-Canadian trappers mingled with the local Native Americans in the early 1800s and found them to be astute traders. Possibly because of their tough bargaining skills, the trappers called them *Coeurs d'Alenes* (Pointed Hearts).

In between shopping, swimming, sailing, and fishing in Coeur d'Alene, visit **Tubbs Hill.** A 2-mi loop trail winds around the hill. Small wooden signs describe plant and rock types found in the area as well as the remnants of historical buildings. An interpretive guide is available from the city's parks department. ⊠ *221 S. 5th St.,* ☎ *208/769–2250.* ⊠ *Free.* ☉ *Daily sunrise–sunset.*

Silverwood Theme Park, 14 mi north of Coeur d'Alene, is Idaho's only amusement park and the biggest such park in the Northwest. It features a perfectly reconstructed turn-of-the-20th-century mining town, with rides on a narrow-gauge steam train or in a vintage biplane, and old-fashioned barnstorming performances. The eight-story, 55 mph, wooden roller coaster dubbed "Tremors" is a prime attraction. ⊠ *26225 N. U.S. 95, Athol,* ☎ *208/683–3400,* WEB *www.silverwood4fun.com/.* ⊠ *$22, plus $4 for parking.* ☉ *Memorial Day–Labor Day, daily; hrs vary.*

Dining and Lodging

$$–$$$ ✕ **Cedars Floating Restaurant.** This restaurant is actually *on* the lake, giving it wonderful views and drawing diners from miles away for seafood and beef and a supper-club atmosphere with a boat dock and outside deck dining. Beer-marinated, charbroiled steak is a specialty. ⊠ *U.S. 95, ¼ mi south of I–90,* ☎ *208/664–2922. AE, DC, MC, V. No lunch.*

$$–$$$ ✕ **Jimmy D's.** This comfortable downtown spot across from the lakefront is a favorite of locals, including several inn owners who have their food catered by Jimmy D's. Redbrick walls decorated with art, candlelit tables, and a small bar forge a bistrolike atmosphere. The menu is uncomplicated but well done: pastas, steaks, chicken, fish, and a seasonal weekend brunch. There is also a strong selection of wines, perhaps because the former owner runs a wine store and nightclub across the street. ⊠ *320 Sherman Ave.,* ☎ *208/664–9774. AE, D, MC, V.*

$–$$ ✕ **T. W. Fisher's—A Brewpub.** Fisher's microbrewery offers daily tours of the brew works and some of the best beer made in Idaho, along with a solid menu of burgers, chicken, salads, and pizza, a specialty. The pub is a lively place, with a TV tuned to sports, a wood-and-brass U-shape bar, and a mostly young crowd. Brewery tours are given at 1:30 and 5:30 daily. ⊠ *204 N. 2nd St.,* ☎ *208/664–2739. AE, D, MC, V.*

$ ✕ **Hudson's Hamburgers.** When they say hamburgers, they mean it. It's burgers, ham and cheese, or egg sandwiches, and that's it. But that's plenty for their devoted fans. These folks have been in business since 1907, and even local rivals have been forced to admit that Hudson's basic burgers are the town favorites. Sit at the counter and watch how burgers used to be made. ⊠ *207 Sherman Ave.,* ☎ *208/664–5444. No credit cards. Closed Sun. No dinner.*

$$$–$$$$ ✕🏨 **Coeur d'Alene Resort.** The modern tower was controversial in 1986, but its effect has been mitigated somewhat by the long floating boardwalk around the marina. Inside, the lobby is full of small eateries, shops, and sunny nooks from which to people-watch. Standard rooms, especially in the former motel, have very basic amenities dating from the 1960s; more expensive tower rooms are spacious and beautiful. Many feature fireplaces or balconies with terrific views of the lake. Atop the tower, with expansive windows, Beverly's ($$–$$$) creates an airy, relaxed setting for a Northwest-inspired menu including grilled salmon drizzled with huckleberry salsa. Tableside preparations are elaborate and entertaining. Ski packages are available. ✉ *2nd and Front Sts., 83814,* ☎ *208/765–4000 or 800/688–5253,* FAX *208/667–2707,* WEB *www.cdaresort.com. 336 rooms. 4 restaurants, 3 bars, lobby lounge, indoor pool, sauna, spa, 18-hole golf course, bowling, health club, beach, shops, recreation room, children's programs (ages 4–14), travel services. AE, D, DC, MC, V.*

$$$ ⬚ **Berry Patch Inn Bed and Breakfast.** On 2 acres of landscaped grounds atop a hill just west of Coeur d'Alene Lake, this 4,500-square-ft cedar chalet has wonderful views of Mt. Spokane and the Cabinet Mountains to the north. Paths through an adjacent forest are perfect for summer strolls. Inside, the spacious living room has a large stone fireplace, and a TV, VCR, and stereo. Decor throughout is country elegant. Breakfasts include an abundance of fresh fruit with poppy-seed dressing and such entrées as griddle cakes stuffed with oats and green apple and topped with huckleberries in sour cream. ✉ *1150 N. Four Winds Rd., 83814,* ☎ *208/775–4994,* FAX *800/667–7336,* WEB *www.berrypatchbb.com. 3 rooms, 1 with bath. Breakfast room. MC, V. BP.*

$$–$$$ ⬚ **Clark House on Hayden Lake.** Half hidden in the trees across the
★ street from Hayden Lake, this ample B&B was modeled after a summer residence of Kaiser Wilhelm in 1910—the owner had been a guest at the Kaiser's island retreat on Lake Constance. By the late 1980s, the local fire department was ready to torch it for practice, but a nearly $1 million restoration has resulted in a giant wedding cake of a place with wide-open rooms, an art deco feel, hardwood floors in public areas, luxurious guest rooms, and an expansive walled garden. The wedding-cake look apparently inspires many couples; it's a popular place for taking vows. A formal, four-course breakfast (included in the room rate) and dinner (reservations essential) are served. ✉ *E. 4550 S. Hayden Lake Rd., Hayden Lake 83835,* ☎ *208/772–3470 or 800/765–4593,* FAX *208/772–6899,* WEB *www.clarkhouse.com. 10 rooms. Dining room. AE, D, DC, MC, V. BP.*

Outdoor Activities and Sports
CYCLING
The premier cycling route is the **Centennial Trail,** a paved path leading from east of Coeur d'Alene all the way to Spokane. Silver and Schweitzer ski areas are renowned for mountain biking. In Coeur d'Alene, rent bikes at the activities desk of the Coeur d'Alene Resort.

GOLF
Avondale-on-Hayden Golf Club (✉ 10745 Avondale Loop, Hayden Lake, ☎ 208/772–5963) offers 18 holes in a scenic setting. The 18-hole course at **Coeur d'Alene Resort** (✉ 900 Floating Green Dr., ☎ 208/765–4000 or 800/688–5253) might just be the only floating green in the nation. **Highlands Golf and Country Club** (✉ 701 N. Inverness Dr., Post Falls, ☎ 208/773–3673) takes pride in its 18-hole course and popular restaurant.

Shopping
Plaza Shops at the Coeur d'Alene (✉ 210 Sherman Ave., at 2nd St., ☎ 208/664–1111) is an enclosed minimall with 22 small shops, several selling merchandise with a Northwest emphasis. There are resort-wear retailers, including United Colors of Benetton and Worn Out West, which specializes in shirts with wildlife designs; an espresso shop; and an Italian bistro-style restaurant, Tito Macaroni's.

Journeys American Indian Arts (✉ 117 S. 4th St., ☎ 208/664–5227) carries beads and other jewelry supplies, as well as a wealth of Native American drums, moccasins, baskets, and books. The **Original Penny**

Candy Store (✉ 325 Sherman Ave., ☎ 208/667–0992), a re-created turn-of-the-20th-century dry-goods and candy store, tempts with exotic candies from around the world, from sour-green-apple balls to strawberry bonbons. Lodge decor reigns at **Partners** (✉ 404 Sherman Ave., ☎ 208/664–4438), where you can find everything from beds to love seats to tables, all made from peeled-pine tree trunks and limbs; decorative birdhouses and Navajo-print pillows are also for sale. Antique lodge furnishings are available at **Sherman Arms Antiques** (✉ 412 Sherman Ave., ☎ 208/667–0527). **Wilson's Variety** (✉ 401 Sherman Ave., ☎ 208/664–8346) carries a wide selection of books about Idaho, including guides on geology and history, and topographical maps.

Silver Valley and Cataldo Mission

24 mi from Coeur d'Alene via I–90 east.

Influenced by trappers and visited by missionaries, a group of Coeur d'Alenes took up Roman Catholicism. In 1850, together with Father Anthony Ravalli, they began construction of **Cataldo Mission,** now the oldest building in Idaho and one of the best historical attractions in the area. The mission church is massive, considering that it was built almost totally by hand with an ax and a few other hand tools. Behind the altar you can see the mud-and-stick construction used on the walls. The giant beams overhead were dragged from the forest, and rock for the foundation was quarried from a hill ½ mi away. The adjacent mission house, home to generations of priests, is furnished the way it would have been at the turn of the 20th century. An interpretive center provides more details about the Coeur d'Alenes and the site, which is accessible to travelers with mobility impairments. ✉ *Old Mission State Park, Exit 39, I–90, Cataldo,* ☎ *208/682–3814.* 🎟 *$2 per vehicle.* ☉ *Memorial Day–Labor Day, daily 8–6; Labor Day–Memorial Day, daily 9–5.*

The historic mining town of **Wallace,** 37 mi east of Coeur d'Alene off I–90, is one of the few towns to be included in its entirety on the National Register of Historic Places. It was first settled in the 1880s mining rush, and today much of the town center looks exactly as it did at the turn of the 20th century.

Dining and Lodging

$ ✕🏨 **The Historic Jameson.** The redbrick, downtown Jameson Building (opened 1908) houses a saloon and restaurant on the first floor, second-floor conference space, and B&B accommodations on the third floor, reached by stairs. Small rooms have been carefully furnished with choice antiques. The softened Victorian decor features warm hues of brown and tan and is spiced up with dainty floral wallpaper. Complimentary Continental breakfast is served in guest rooms or the parlor. The Jameson Restaurant ($–$$) serves classic American cuisine, including steaks and pasta dishes. Ceiling fans, bentwood chairs, polished brass, chandeliers, and Oriental carpets are reminiscent of a fancy Old West saloon and hotel. If you're lucky, one of the Jameson's three resident ghosts may visit! ✉ *314 6th St., Wallace 83873,* ☎ *208/556–1554 or 800/643–2386,* 🖷 *208/753–0981. 6 rooms, 1 with bath. Restaurant, meeting room. MC, V. CP.*

Outdoor Activities and Sports

SKIING

Silver Mountain solved an accessibility problem by installing the world's longest single-stage gondola. Near Kellogg, the hill offers a complete family learning program. Locals think the advanced terrain at Schweitzer is better, but Silver offers some excellent wooded powder skiing and some steep runs. Fifty-two trails cover a vertical drop of 2,200 ft and are reached by a quad, two triple chairs, two double chairs, and a surface lift in addition to the gondola. In January and February there's night skiing until 9 on Friday and Saturday. ⊠ *610 Bunker Ave., Kellogg 83837,* ☎ *208/783–1111.* ⌑ *$32.* ⊙ *Mid-Nov–Apr., Wed.–Sun. 8–4.*

Sandpoint

⓴ *40 mi from Coeur d'Alene via U.S. 95 north.*

Sandpoint lies on the shore of Lake Pend Oreille, the second-deepest lake in the United States. Nestled between the lake and the Selkirk and Cabinet mountain ranges, Sandpoint has been a railroad depot and a mining town, but now it survives on tourism and lumber. The town is small—five blocks of shops and restaurants form its core—and the brick and stone buildings are almost unchanged since the early 1900s. Locals say the town is 20 years behind Coeur d'Alene. They mean it as a compliment. Like Coeur d'Alene, this is a summer destination with fine lake beaches, extensive woodlands, and nearby mountains. However, the local ski hill, Schweitzer, is transforming itself into a first-class ski area. Sandpoint, it has been said, is what places such as Vail, Colorado, and Jackson, Wyoming, were like just before they expanded.

Dining and Lodging

$–$$ ✕ **Hydra.** Wood, stained glass, and greenery decorate this intimate, comfortable restaurant that draws crowds for its pasta, seafood, prime rib, and steak. Sunday brunch is offered, and there's a lunch buffet Tuesday through Friday. ⊠ *115 E. Lake St.,* ☎ *208/263–7123. AE, D, MC, V.*

$$ ✕🖭 **Hawthorn Inn and Suites.** Rooms in this recently expanded motel are clean and tastefully decorated, with special touches such as marbleized wallpaper. Most rooms come with a small refrigerator and two sinks. Family suites offer microwaves. A two-room suite with a whirlpool tub and a wet bar feels downright decadent. A breakfast buffet comes with the room price. The restaurant ($–$$) and lounge are popular with locals as well as guests, providing basic, affordable fare. ⊠ *415 Cedar St., 83864,* ☎ *208/263–9581 or 800/282–0660,* ㏛ *208/263–3395. 70 rooms. Restaurant, lounge, refrigerators, pool, hot tub, meeting room. AE, D, MC, V. BP.*

$–$$$ 🖭 **Green Gables Lodge.** At ski resorts you pay for location, and that's what this lodge 50 yards from the ski lift at Schweitzer's offers. There is a cozy, European-chalet feeling in the public areas. Standard rooms are basic, motel-type units, while more deluxe rooms, with whirlpool tubs, are bigger and have microwaves and minibars. ⊠ *Schweitzer Mountain Resort, Box 815, Sandpoint 83864, 11 mi northwest of Sandpoint off U.S. 95,* ☎ *208/265–0257 or 800/831–8810,* ㏛ *208/263–7961. 82 rooms. 2 restaurants, pool, 2 hot tubs. AE, MC, V.*

$–$$ 🖭 **Sandpoint Quality Inn.** The rooms are clean and pleasant, and units on the second floor have water views. ⊠ *807 N. 5th Ave., 83864,* ☎ *208/263–2111 or 800/635–2534,* ㏛ *208/263–3289. 57 rooms. Restaurant, bar, indoor pool, hot tub. AE, D, MC, V.*

Nightlife

The **Kamloops** (⊠ *302 N. 1st St.,* ☎ *208/263–6715*) often leaves its mike open for blues and R&B musicians during the week, so you never know what you'll hear. On weekends, it has live rock and blues acts.

Outdoor Activities and Sports

Hidden Lakes Country Club (⊠ *8838 Lower Pack River Rd., 8 mi east of Sandpoint,* ☎ *208/263–1621*) has 18 holes and an abundance of water hazards and sand traps on its golf course. You can rent bicycles at **Sandpoint Recreational Rentals** (⊠ 209 E. Superior St., ☎ 208/265–4557).

SKIING

For years, only people in Spokane and Sandpoint knew much about **Schweitzer,** but it's on the way to becoming a top western ski destination. It offers on-hill accommodations, children's programs, and a full-service ski school, in addition to two mountain bowls with spine-tingling black diamond runs so steep your elbows scrape the snow on turns. Open-bowl skiing is available for the intermediate and advanced, and beginners can choose from among half a dozen tree-lined runs. There is a vertical drop of 2,400 ft. A six-person high-speed chair, a quad, and five double chairs access 55 runs. Night skiing takes place daily during Christmas week and on Friday and Saturday between January and March. ⊠ *11 mi northwest of Sandpoint off U.S. 95, Box 815, Sandpoint 83864,* ☎ *800/831–8810.* ☞ *$40.* ☺ *Late-Nov.–early Apr., daily 9–4.*

Shopping

Cabin Fever (⊠ 113 Cedar St., ☎ 208/263–7179; ⊠ 309 1st St., ☎ 208/263–7178) has one of the best assortments of gifts, home-decor items, garden adornments, and curios for cabins in North Idaho. The 1st Street store sells casual, northwestern-style clothing. The only retail outlet for the mail-order **Coldwater Creek** (⊠ 1st and Cedar Sts., ☎ 208/263–2265) took over the Cedar Street Bridge Public Market, which now comprises six stores and restaurants in a split-level arcade of native tamarack and fir timbers spanning a mountain creek. Merchandise includes wildlife-inspired jewelry, posters, and books; bird feeders; and other nature-oriented gifts.

The next time you need a custom Mongolian yurt, try **Little Bear Trading Company** (⊠ 324 1st St., ☎ 208/263–1116). The shop owner, Bear (yes, just Bear), makes tepees and yurts for clients around the country. The small store also carries Native American crafts, beads, and feathers, as well as materials from Africa and Central and South America.

Northern Idaho A to Z

AIRPORTS

Horizon serves Lewiston-Nez Perce County Regional Airport, the only commercial airport north of Boise. Spokane, Washington, a 35-minute drive from Coeur d'Alene, is a popular hub for those traveling to the Idaho Panhandle. The airport is served by Alaska, Delta, Northwest, Southwest, and United.

➤ AIRPORT INFORMATION: **Lewiston-Nez Perce County Regional Airport** (☎ 208/746–7962, WEB www.lcairport.com).

BUS TRAVEL

Greyhound Lines stops at the Coeur d'Alene Bus Depot. Northwestern Greyhound Bus Lines serves Lewiston. Sandpoint's Empire Bus Lines provides service to other cities.

➤ BUS INFORMATION: **Coeur d'Alene Bus Depot** (⊠ 1923½ N. 4th St., Coeur d'Alene, ☎ 208/667–3343). **Empire Bus Lines** (⊠ 402 5th Ave., Sandpoint, ☎ 208/263–7721). **Northwestern Greyhound Bus Lines** (⊠ 1002 Idaho St. Lewiston, ☎ 208/746–8108).

CAR TRAVEL

The primary north–south highway is U.S. 95; I–90 and U.S. 2 run east–west. During the winter, storms can slow interstate travel, but major highways are usually cleared promptly and are rarely closed. From Boise, Route 55 heads north to McCall. From Spokane take U.S. 2 north to Sandpoint. From western Montana, you can take I–90 to Coeur d'Alene and then U.S. 95 north to Sandpoint.

ROAD CONDITIONS
➤ CONTACTS: **Coeur d'Alene** (☎ 208/772–0531). **Lewiston** (☎ 208/743–9546).

EMERGENCIES
➤ CONTACTS: **Bonner General Hospital** (✉ 3rd and Fir Sts., Sandpoint, ☎ 208/263–1441; 208/265–4733 emergency room). **Kootenai Medical Center** (✉ 2003 Lincoln Way, Coeur d'Alene, ☎ 208/667–6441). **St. Joseph Hospital** (✉ 5th Ave. and 6th St., Lewiston, ☎ 208/743–2511).

TOURS
Hells Canyon and other river tours are a thriving business. Most tour operators give historical and geological information on one- or two-day trips on the Snake River in Hells Canyon. Some outfitters run jet boats upriver from Lewiston into the Hells Canyon National Recreation Area, while others put rafts in near Oxbow Dam and float downstream. When booking a trip, make clear whether you'd like a wild float or a white-water adventure. Some trips offer lodging at cabins or lodges along the way or combine river activities with horseback riding and mountain biking.

Beamer's Landing Hells Canyon Tours has the contract to deliver the U.S. mail to remote ranches in the canyon and offers a two-day mail-run jet-boat trip that includes a stop at a sheep ranch. Salmon River Challenge offers half-day to week-long rafting tours of the River of No Return Wilderness, including lodging at a backcountry ranch. ROW plies a number of waters throughout the state, including the Snake River in Hells Canyon, the Middle Fork of the Salmon River, and a Snake/Lochsa rivers combination. Specialized tours cater to senior citizens or parents with teenagers.
➤ CONTACTS: **Beamer's Landing Hells Canyon Tours** (✉ Box 1223, Lewiston 83501, ☎ 800/522–6966). **ROW** (✉ River Odysseys West, Box 579–TO, Coeur d'Alene 83816, ☎ 800/451–6034). **Salmon River Challenge** (✉ Box 1299, Riggins 83549, ☎ 800/727–9977).

TRAIN TRAVEL
Amtrak's *Empire Builder* stops at the Sandpoint Amtrak Depot, bound for Seattle or Chicago.
➤ TRAIN INFORMATION: *Empire Builder* (✉ 409 Railroad Ave., ☎ 800/872–7245).

VISITOR INFORMATION
➤ TOURIST INFORMATION: **Coeur d'Alene Chamber of Commerce** (✉ Box 850, Coeur d'Alene 83816, ☎ 208/664–3194, WEB www.coeurdalene.org). **Lewiston Chamber of Commerce** (111 Main St., Lewiston 83501, ☎ 208-664–3194, WEB www.lewistonchamber.org). **McCall Area Chamber of Commerce** (✉ 116 N. 3rd St., Box D, McCall 83638, ☎ 208/634–7631, WEB www.mccall-idchamber.org). **North Central Idaho Travel Committee** (✉ 111 E. Main St., Lewiston 83501, ☎ 208/743–3531 or 800/473–3543, WEB www.idahonwp.org). **North Idaho Tourism Alliance** (✉ Box 850, Coeur d'Alene 83816, ☎ 208/664–3194 or 888/333–3737, WEB www.visitnorthidaho.com).

IDAHO A TO Z

To research prices, get advice from other travelers, and book travel arrangements, visit www.fodors.com.

AIR TRAVEL
Commuter airlines serve airports in Idaho Falls, Lewiston, Pocatello, Sun Valley, and Twin Falls. Major airlines serve Boise and Spokane,

Washington, a gateway to the Panhandle. In addition, there are many airstrips scattered around Idaho, especially in wilderness areas. These strips, open only in summer and early fall, are used by private planes and those chartered by outfitters.

BUS TRAVEL

Major Idaho towns are served by Greyhound Lines and by Boise–Winnemucca Stages.

➤ BUS INFORMATION: **Boise–Winnemucca Stages** (☎ 208/336–3300).

CAR TRAVEL

The best way to see the state is by car—this is the West, after all, and interesting sights are sometimes spread out. Remember that westerners often have an expanded view of distance. So when an Idahoan says "right around the corner," translate that as under an hour's drive. Interstates and the much more interesting two-lane state and U.S. highways are uncrowded, with rare exceptions (such as Boise to McCall on Friday at 5:30 PM). Best of all, a car allows you to travel the back roads, where some of Idaho's unique sights await. Be sure to keep an eye on your gas gauge; in some parts of the state, the next gas station may be no closer than "right around the corner."

As a rule of thumb, the state's network of improved and unimproved roads are open in the summer and early fall months. Winter travel can be unpredictable, with many state highways and particularly smaller unimproved roads rendered impassable for varying lengths of time. In winter, snowstorms in the mountainous regions can make tire chains mandatory. Many of Idaho's unimproved roads in the backcountry are accessible only by four-wheel-drive vehicles, even in summer, and are shut down for the winter. Major newspapers carry road-condition reports on their weather pages. Or, call the state's road report hot line or hot lines for specific regions.

EMERGENCY SERVICES

➤ CONTACT: **Road Report Hot Line** (☎ 208/336–6600 or 888/432–7623).

RULES OF THE ROAD

In Idaho you may make a right turn on red after stopping, unless there is a sign posted forbidding it.

LODGING

The *Idaho Official Travel Guide* lists accommodations across the state and is available from the Idaho Travel Council. Information on dude and guest ranches, farm vacations, and similar accommodations is available from the Idaho Guest and Dude Ranch Association. The Idaho Department of Agriculture publishes a handy farm and ranch recreation guide.

➤ CONTACTS: **Idaho Department of Agriculture** (✉ Division of Marketing and Development, Box 790, Boise, ID 83701, ☎ 208/334–2227). **Idaho Guest and Dude Ranch Association** (✉ c/o John Muir, 7600 E. Blue Lake Rd., Harrison, ID 83833).

CAMPING

Primitive campsites at Idaho state parks cost $5 per day, basic sites are $7, and developed sites cost $8. Electric and sewer hookups cost an additional $4. There is an entrance fee of $2 for motorized vehicles at most parks, but it is incorporated into camping fees. An annual passport for $25 provides unlimited entrance to all state parks for one calendar year. Group facilities are available at some parks. For a complete guide, contact the Idaho Department of Parks and Recreation.

➤ CONTACT: **Idaho Department of Parks and Recreation** (✉ Box 65, Boise 83720, ☎ 208/334–4199 or 800/635–7820).

TOURS

Most tourism in Idaho is related to the outdoors, and Idaho was one of the first states to license and bond its outfitters and guides. Packagers can combine different sites, such as the Salmon and Snake rivers, or activities, such as fishing and rafting, on their trips. It is against the law for anyone who is not a member of the Idaho Outfitters and Guides Association to provide guiding or outfitting services; contact the association for a free directory of members.

➤ CONTACT: **Idaho Outfitters and Guides Association** (✉ Box 95, Boise 83701, ☎ 208/342–1919 or 800/847–4843, WEB www.ioga.org).

VISITOR INFORMATION

➤ TOURIST INFORMATION: **Idaho Department of Fish and Game** (✉ Box 25, Boise 83707, ☎ 208/334–3700, 208/334–3417, or 800/554–8685 for tags and license orders only). **Idaho Travel Council** (✉ 700 W. State St., Box 83720, Boise 83720–0093, ☎ 208/334–2470 or 800/635–7820, WEB www.visitid.org).

4 MONTANA

They call it Big Sky Country, but that's only part of the story; the land is big, too: the fourth-largest state, Montana stretches from North Dakota on the eastern side to Idaho on the west, 600 and some odd miles. From north to south, meanwhile, is a distance of about 400 mi. Not only is this a massive chunk of land, but it's also sparsely peopled. There are roughly 902,000 Montanans on all this ground, most of them in the major cities of Billings, Bozeman, Great Falls, Missoula, and Helena.

Updated by
Jean Arthur

MONTANA IS DIVIDED INTO TWO REGIONS: the Rocky Mountain cordillera, which enters Montana in the northwest corner, taking up most of the western half of the state with timbered mountains and broad, grassy river valleys; and the plains and rolling hills to the east. When night comes down, the skies are so dark and clear that the stars look like shiny glass beads suspended in a midnight sky. Northern lights shimmer like red and green curtains against velvet black skies and at other times stream across the full scope of the sky, ending only when the light of dawn erases them. If there is a factor that makes Montana so unusual, it is the light. Sometimes it shoots down from behind the clouds in long, radiant spotlight shafts, outlining the clouds in gold. A pink-and-orange light falls gently like dust on western slopes. A brilliant crimson takes over clouds at sunset. The fiery red-and-orange light of sunset in the Rockies illuminates the mountains so intensely they appear to be lit from within like glowing coal.

The land here teems with wildlife. Bald eagles soar by the thousands and zero in on streams flush with fish: rainbow, brown, cutthroat, and brook trout among them. Cougars scream in the night, and grizzlies and wolves move through the darkness. With manes flapping, wild horses gallop over red hillsides. Thousands of elk move from the high country to the lowlands in the fall, and head back to the high country come summer.

Long gone, but not forgotten, are some of Montana's most famous wildlife, whose skeletons remain as evidence of their greatness. Some of the richest dinosaur fossil beds in the world are found in the Rocky Mountain Front Range, where the mountains meet the plains. Recently, discoveries of fossils and dinosaur eggs have challenged the notion that dinosaurs were cold-blooded; it's possible they were warm-blooded animals who cared for their young, closer to mammals than reptiles.

Evidence of early human occupation dates back 12,000 years. For generations before the Europeans arrived here, Native Americans inhabited what is now Montana. In 1805–06, the Lewis and Clark Expedition came through, seeking a transcontinental route to the Pacific, and expanded trade relations with the natives.

Montana remained a remote place, however, through much of the 19th century, and it was valued for its rich trade in buffalo hides and beaver pelts. The discovery of gold at Gold Creek (between Missoula and Helena) in 1858 began to change the region dramatically. After large gold strikes at Grasshopper Creek and Alder Gulch, miners came to the southwest mountains of Montana by the thousands. In 1862, the Territory of Montana was created. Pressure by miners and settlers for native lands in the area was unrelenting; inhabitants were forced from their homelands and restricted to reservations. Major events in the West's Indian wars—the Battle of the Little Bighorn and the Flight of the Nez Percé—were played out in Montana, indelibly shaping the history of this region and the nation.

The state of Montana entered the Union in 1889, and its motto "Oro y Plata" (gold and silver) still stands. With the landscape relatively untouched, history remains alive here. Ranching and farming, mining and logging are still the ways of life, and a small-town atmosphere and friendly outlook greet travelers even in the state's larger cities. The natural splendor, free-running rivers, vast mountain ranges, and large populations of wildlife make this what Montanans call the "Last Best Place."

Pleasures and Pastimes

Dining

No matter where you eat in Montana, dress is casual. Leave your ties at home. Fine steaks and home-style cooking can be found throughout the state, along with a surprising number of upscale eateries with casually chic atmosphere and fine Continental food. Good ethnic cuisine is a rarity.

CATEGORY	COST*
$$$$	over $25
$$$	$15–$25
$$	$10–$15
$	under $10

*per person for a main course at dinner

Lodging

Montana's lodging falls generally into three categories: historic hotels and bed-and-breakfasts; motels along commercial strips; and resort communities offering a wide range of accommodations and a dizzying array of seasonal recreational pursuits.

CATEGORY	COST*
$$$$	over $225
$$$	$150–$225
$$	$75–$150
$	under $75

*Prices are for a standard double room in high season, not including the 4%–8% tax and service.

Outdoor Activities and Sports

FISHING

Montana has the best rainbow, brown, and brook trout fishing in the country. This is the land of *A River Runs Through It,* the popular movie based on the acclaimed book by Norman Maclean. Although the book was set in Missoula, the movie was filmed in the trout-fishing mecca of the southwest, with the Gallatin River playing the role of Maclean's beloved Big Blackfoot. In fact, several rivers run through the region, notably the Madison, Gallatin, and Yellowstone (which run more or less parallel to one another flowing north of Yellowstone National Park), as well as the Big Hole River to the west. All are easily accessible from major roads, which can mean that in summer you might have to drive a ways to find a hole to call your own. However, stream fishing in these parts is a year-round enterprise. Just where the fishing is best along these rivers will vary considerably depending on the source of local knowledge you tap into, but such disagreement no doubt confirms a wealth of opportunity. The Gallatin near Big Sky Ski and Summer Resort; the Madison south of Ennis as well as at its confluence with the Missouri near Three Forks; the Yellowstone south of Livingston: these are among the spots that get mentioned most often, though it is hard to go wrong in these parts. And even if you never catch a fish, the mountain ranges that separate these rivers (or vice versa) are among the most beautiful in the Rockies.

HIKING

Many of the hiking trails involve arduous climbing, changeable weather, and wild animals: it's best to know what you are getting into before you go. *Hiking Montana,* by Bill Schneider, offers useful, basic information and is available at most bookstores. *Hiker's Guide to Glacier National Park,* by the Glacier Natural History Association, details 25 park routes and tips for hiking in this park. The U.S. Forest Service offices often have local maps and trail guides for free or a nominal fee. It is always best to check locally for recent trail closures or changes due to weather, wildlife, land swaps, or maintenance.

Wilderness

This state is home to almost 1,300 species of animals, from deer to dippers, mountain lions, moose, and mollusks. The Montana Department of Fish, Wildlife, and Parks operates a Watchable Wildlife program. Signs along the highways, marked with an icon that represents a pair of binoculars, indicate 100 of the best places to see some of the state's wildlife.

Known by locals simply as "the Bob," the Bob Marshall Wilderness has remained wild enough to have become popular with bears (including a large grizzly population), mountain goats, bighorn sheep, and elk, as well as pack trippers. It is the largest expanse of roadless land in Montana, and although there are trails to hike and rivers to raft, horse-pack trips are the best way to penetrate this huge wilderness. This tends to be big-country riding, best for (though not restricted to) experienced riders, with stretches of more than 20 mi a day common. Among the highlights of the Bob are wildflowers as well as wildlife; mountain scenery; fishing; and the Chinese Wall, a 120-mi-long, reeflike stretch of cliffs, a kind of natural monument to the powers of tectonic forces. There are dozens of outfitters who guide horse-pack trips in the Bob. For a list, contact the Montana Board of Outfitters.

Exploring Montana

To really explore Montana, you must spend a lot of time on the road. Towns and attractions are widely spaced, especially in the east. Most of the state's tourist magnets and awe-inspiring scenery lie along the Rocky Mountains between two of the west's great national parks— Glacier in the north and Yellowstone on the state's southern border. But to get a real feel for Montana, venture through the rolling agricultural plains to Billings and points east.

Numbers in text correspond to numbers in the margin and on the Montana map.

Great Itineraries

IF YOU HAVE 4 DAYS

The mountains and wildlife of western Montana are its most prized attractions, and this tour offers plenty of both. Begin your day in **Missoula** ① with a visit to the **Rocky Mountain Elk Foundation Wildlife Visitor Center,** then head north to the **National Bison Range** ② near Moiese. The self-guided auto tour takes at least two hours, allowing for frequent stops to gaze at bighorn sheep, deer, elk, and the massive mammals that give the range its name. Enjoy a picnic lunch on the grounds or at your next stop, the historic mission in **St. Ignatius** ③. After admiring the mission's 58 frescoes, continue north along the east shore of **Flathead Lake,** the largest freshwater lake west of the Mississippi. Take in the shops and scenery of small, vibrant ⊞ **Bigfork** ⑥, then visit one of the village's fine restaurants and enjoy a production of the Bigfork Summer Playhouse.

Day two takes you to the "Crown of the Continent," **Glacier National Park** ⑨. Take a leisurely stroll along the fragrant, wheelchair-accessible Trail of the Cedars before continuing up steep, scenic Going-to-the-Sun Road, with views of waterfalls and wildlife to the left and an awe-inspiring, precipitous drop to the right. At the summit, **Logan Pass,** stop in at the visitor center. As your eyes strain to focus on mountain goats on the distant cliffs, don't be surprised if one walks past you on

Montana

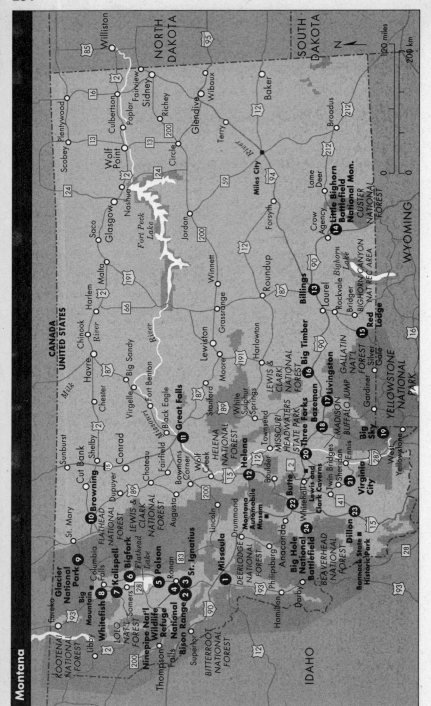

the side of the road. A boardwalk protects the abundant wildflowers and spongy tundra on the hike up to prime wildlife-viewing spots, where it is not uncommon to glimpse a grizzly. Note the changing landscape as you drop over the mountains to the east side of the park, where the forest thins, the vistas grow broader, and a gradual transition to the plains begins. Spend the night in 🏨 **Many Glacier.**

The next day, head for **Browning** ⑩ to enhance your appreciation for the first residents of this landscape at the **Museum of the Plains Indian.** Then it's on to 🏨 **Helena** ⑫, where you can explore the **Montana Historical Society Museum.** Amble down to **Last Chance Gulch** for window-shopping and dinner.

On day four, stop in at the **Holter Museum of Art** before heading back across the Continental Divide. For a fly-fishing experience cast a nymph on the **Blackfoot River,** then continue west back to 🏨 **Missoula** ①, where you can stroll along the downtown river paths and take a ride on the old-fashioned carousel before settling in for the night. If you have extra time, explore Missoula, including the **Historical Museum at Fort Missoula.**

IF YOU HAVE 7 DAYS
Start as for the four-day itinerary, from Missoula through Glacier, possibly spending the second night in 🏨 **East Glacier** or St. Mary. On day three, enjoy a last wander in Glacier before heading southeast to 🏨 **Great Falls** ⑪ and the **C. M. Russell Museum.**

Get an early start the next day for the trek east through Montana's wide-open ranch land to Lewistown, then south to 🏨 **Billings** ⑬. The journey through rolling plains and tiny communities takes about four hours, bringing you to the "Magic City" in time for lunch. Shop for a custom-fitted hat or other western accessory in downtown Billings, then learn about the culture and history of the area at the **Western Heritage Center.** Next, journey southeast to the famed **Little Bighorn Battlefield National Monument** ⑭, exploring the site and interpretive displays that examine both sides of the conflict. Return to Billings for a sunset drive along the buckskin-color rimrocks.

The fifth day sends you southwest to charming **Red Lodge** ⑮ and one of the West's most scenic drives, the Beartooth Scenic Highway, which leads over **Beartooth Pass** to the Silver Gate entrance to **Yellowstone National Park.** This route brings you into Yellowstone's famed Lamar Valley of wolves as you traverse the northern reaches of the park before heading out of its north gate at Gardiner, Montana. Head north through the beautiful Paradise Valley and along the **Yellowstone River,** a route dotted with tempting spots to fish, picnic, or just relax and enjoy the spectacular views. When you reach 🏨 **Livingston** ⑰, check out the art and architecture of the old **Northern Pacific Depot.** Spend the night here or in nearby 🏨 **Bozeman** ⑱.

The next morning, visit Bozeman's outstanding **Museum of the Rockies** for impressive displays on dinosaurs and more recent residents of this region. Head west through **Three Forks** ⑳, perhaps retracing Lewis and Clark's steps at **Missouri Headwaters State Park,** where three rivers join to form the Missouri River. Following a picnic lunch, your next stop should be the extensive subterranean passages of **Lewis and Clark Caverns.** A scenic drive south of the caverns will bring you to **Virginia City** ㉑ and Nevada City, lovingly restored remnants of Montana's frontier days. Tour the sites where gold was struck and vigilantes took the law—and suspects' necks—in their hands. Next, head back to I-90 and 🏨 **Butte** ㉒. Peer into the gigantic **Berkeley Open Pit Mine** and wander the historic downtown area before settling in for a meal and a night's rest.

On the final day of the tour, journey southwest from Butte to the **Big Hole National Battlefield** ㉔ for a vivid glimpse at one of the battles between Chief Joseph's Nez Percé and the U.S. Army. From Big Hole, travel briefly west, then north on U.S. 93 through the lush Bitterroot Valley back to 🔀 **Missoula** ①. Enjoy the Garden City's charms with a walk along the Clark Fork River, a ride on a hand-carved steed on **A Carousel for Missoula,** and, if there's time, a trek to an old homestead in the **Rattlesnake Wilderness.**

When to Tour Montana

Summer and early fall are the most popular times to visit Montana, when most of the state's attractions are open, mountain roads are passable, and high-country wildflowers put on gorgeous displays. In Glacier National Park, the spectacular Going-to-the-Sun Road across the Continental Divide is generally closed by snow from late October until early June, but off-season visitors to the park are rewarded by no crowds, winter wildlife viewing, and snowshoe or ski treks. A Montana winter offers powder skiing, inspiring snow-flocked vistas, and the longest dogsled race in the lower 48 states, the Race to the Sky. Festivals and celebrations are scattered throughout the year, from Butte's rollicking St. Patrick's Day celebration in March to the Crow Fair and Rodeo on the Crow Indian Reservation each August. Rodeos, powwows, and festivals abound in the summer, while Christmas strolls and winter carnivals brighten up the cold months.

MISSOULA TO HELENA

This trip starts in Missoula and makes its way through the heart of western Montana's Rocky Mountains and Mission and Flathead valleys, highlighted by Glacier National Park. The park's deep, pristine lakes and towering cedars, pines, and aspens frame the snow-mottled peaks of the Rocky Mountain front range. You'll pass 2.7 million acres of roadless wilderness as you continue toward Great Falls and Helena, the state capital. Thirty percent of Montana is publicly owned land, and the national park, national forests, and state parks on this drive offer numerous campgrounds and hiking and biking trails.

Missoula

❶ *115 mi west of Helena, via U.S 12 to I–90.*

In a fertile valley and hemmed by mountains, the aptly nicknamed "Garden City" is the largest in western Montana with a population of 57,000. Maple trees line the residential streets, the **Clark Fork River** slices through the center of town, and the University of Montana cozies up against the slopes of Mt. Sentinel. A 6-mi-long riverside trail passes the university's campus en route to Hellgate Canyon; it is ideal for walking and cycling.

In downtown Caras Park along the Clark Fork River, kids saddle up to hand-carved steeds on **A Carousel for Missoula.** The horses and chariots ride on a lovingly restored 1918 carousel frame, accompanied by tunes from the largest band organ in continuous use in the United States. The Dragon Hollow play area next to the Carousel features a dragon, a castle, and many play structures, at no charge. ✉ *1 Caras Park,* ☎ *406/549–8382,* 🌐 *www.carrousel.com.* 💲 *Adults $1 per ride, children 50¢.* ☉ *Memorial Day–Labor Day, daily 11–7; Labor Day–Memorial Day, daily 11–5:30.*

The **Art Museum of Missoula** has changing exhibits of contemporary work and a small permanent collection. ✉ *335 N. Pattee St., 1 block*

from the intersection with W. Broadway, ☎ 406/728–0447, WEB www.
artmissoula.org. 💵 $2; under 18 free ⊙ Tues. noon–8, Wed.–Sat.
noon–6.

The **Rocky Mountain Elk Foundation Wildlife Visitor Center** features
natural-history displays, films, art, taxidermied animals and world-
record elk display. ⊠ 2291 W. Broadway, ☎ 406/523–4545 or 800/
225–5355, WEB www.rmef.org. 💵 Donations accepted. ⊙ Memorial
Day–Labor Day, weekdays 8–6; Labor Day–Memorial Day, weekdays
8–5, weekends 10–4.

The **Historical Museum at Fort Missoula,** at the western edge of town,
sits at the center of Historic Fort Missoula that was established in 1877
at the height of the U.S. Army's conflict with the Nez Percé, led by Chief
Joseph. Indoor and outdoor exhibits, including 13 historic structures
relocated from nearby sites, recount the early settlement and industry
of Missoula County. The black 25th Infantry of bicycle soldiers arrived
in 1888 to test bicycles for military use. They ultimately rode one-speed
bicycles from Missoula to St. Louis, Missouri. The fort was used to
house prisoners of war from Axis nations during World War II. Guided
tours are available by appointment. ⊠ Bldg. 32, Fort Missoula, ☎ 406/
728–3476, WEB www.montana.com/ftmslamuseum. 💵 $3. ⊙ Memo-
rial Day–Labor Day, Mon.–Sat. 10–5, Sun. noon–5; Labor Day–
Memorial Day, Tues.–Sat. noon–5.

The **Smokejumper Visitor Center** has exhibits, videos, and murals that
detail and explain wildland fire ecology and behavior, fire-fighting technique, and smoke-jumping history, which began here in 1942. From
Memorial Day through Labor Day, the center offers five tours daily
by firefighter guides who provide firsthand accounts of jumping into
blazing forests. ⊠ 5765 Old Hwy. 10 W, 6 mi west of town, on Hwy.
10 next to the airport, ☎ 406/329–4934, WEB www.smokejumpers.com.
💵 Donations accepted. ⊙ Memorial Day–Labor Day, daily 8:30–5,
tours on the hr 10–11 and 2–4; by appointment the rest of the yr.

Dining and Lodging

$$–$$$ ✗ **Guy's Lolo Creek Steakhouse.** For a real taste of Montana, head for
★ this steak house in a rustic log structure 8 mi south of Missoula, in
Lolo. The dining room has a hunting-lodge atmosphere, replete with
taxidermied wildlife on the walls. Although most diners opt for one
of Guy's signature sirloins—cooked over a crackling open-pit barbecue and available in three sizes—there are other well-prepared meat,
chicken, and seafood dishes from which to choose. ⊠ 6600 U.S. 12
W, Lolo, ☎ 406/273–2622. AE, D, MC, V. Closed Mon. No lunch.

$$–$$$ ✗ **Marianne's at the Wilma.** Patio seating overlooks the Clark Fork
★ River in this smartly remodeled 1920s complex that includes a 1,000-
seat theater, two smaller theaters, a bar, and an opulent art deco dining room. Entrées range from mushroom baklava, a delicate pastry
stuffed with wild mushrooms and herbs, to New York Strip au poivre
with rosemary roasted potatoes. Breakfast is served on weekends until
2 PM. ⊠ 131 S. Higgins Ave., ☎ 406/728–8549. AE, D, DC, MC, V.

$–$$ ✗ **Zimorino's Red Pies over Montana.** Some of the best pizza that has
ever been tossed anywhere is served here. The pasta and bruschetta are
top-notch, too. Eat in, take out, or call for a delivery. Beer and wine
are served. ⊠ 424 N. Higgins Ave., ☎ 406/549–7434. AE, D, MC, V.
No lunch.

$ ✗ **Bernice's Bakery.** Indoors, outdoors, and on the Clark Fork River,
Missoula's best bakery features buttery croissants and other treats
plus a tempting array of desserts, breads, and coffee 6 AM–10 PM. ⊠
190 S. 3rd W, ☎ 406/728–1358. No credit cards.

$ ✕ **Food For Thought.** Next to the university, locals, professors, and students hang out, study, and eat wholesome food here. Sandwiches to go and bakery goods fill backpacks of day hikers and bikers en route to trailheads. ✉ *540 Daly Ave.,* ☎ *406/721–6033. AE, D, DC, MC, V. No dinner in Jan., July, or Aug.*

$$$$ ▦ **Triple Creek Ranch.** This ranch is definitely off the beaten path—about a 90-minute drive from Missoula—-but it's well worth the effort for those seeking utter seclusion and indulgence. Luxurious log cabins tucked into ponderosa forest offer the kind of privacy and pampering that attracts celebrities to this year-round, adults-only resort. The humblest accommodations share a hot tub amid the trees, while the others (mostly one-bedroom suites) have roomy indoor Jacuzzis or hot tubs on decks overlooking the Bitterroot Range. Massive log beds, fireplaces, and his-and-her bathroom suites with steam showers grace cabins decorated in rich greens and reds. All meals and drinks, whether taken in the main lodge or in your cabin, are included in the per-couple rate, as are on-ranch trail rides, fly-casting instruction, snowshoeing, and cross-country skiing. The staff has that rare blend of friendliness and discretion. ✉ *5551 W. Fork Stage Rte., Darby 59829,* ☎ *406/821–4600,* FAX *406/821–4666,* WEB *www.triplecreekranch.com. 19 cabins. Restaurant, bar, in-room data ports, in-room VCRs, kitchenettes, minibars, pool, hot tubs, massage, putting green, tennis court, hiking, horseback riding, fishing, cross-country skiing, snowmobiling, library, laundry service, business services, meeting room, airport shuttle. AE, D, DC, MC, V. FAP.*

$$–$$$ ▦ **C'mon Inn.** This new hotel near Snowbowl Ski Area and at the bottom of Grant Creek features a spacious, tree-filled indoor courtyard with a pool, baby pool, five hot tubs, and a relaxing waterfall. With easy access to recreation and business in Missoula, the inn is a family-friendly lodge that serves free Continental breakfast. ✉ *2775 Expo Parkway, 59808, off I–90,* ☎ *888/989–5569,* FAX *406/543–4664,* WEB *www.cmoninn.com. 119 rooms. Indoor pool, 5 hot tubs, gym, business services. AE, DC, MC, V. CP.*

$$ ▦ **Goldsmith's Bed and Breakfast.** Built in 1911 for the first presi-
★ dent of the University of Montana, this lodging is on the shore of the Clark Fork River, at the end of a footbridge that leads to the campus. Within the prairie-style building, with big white eaves and a huge porch, are period furnishings, wool carpets, and fresh flowers. Each private room is unique, and public rooms include a library and TV sitting area. A bonus to staying at this B&B is that it's within walking and biking distance to the university and downtown. Enjoy French toast or crêpes in the dining room or on the deck overlooking the Clark Fork River. ✉ *809 E. Front St., 59801,* ☎ *406/728–1585,* FAX *406/543–0045,* WEB *www.goldsmithsinn.com. 3 rooms, 4 suites. Library. D, MC, V. BP.*

$$ ▦ **Holiday Inn Missoula–Parkside.** The Missoula member of this chain is a large, comfortable hotel with a lush atrium in the center and modern rooms. Sunday brunch is served in the atrium. The property's most valued asset is its location in Missoula's riverfront park, a stone's throw from the Clark Fork River and across the river from the university and next to Caras Park. ✉ *200 S. Pattee St., 59802,* ☎ *406/721–8550 or 800/399–0408,* FAX *406/728–3472,* WEB *www. park-side.com. 200 rooms. Restaurant, bar, indoor pool, hot tub, gym. AE, D, DC, MC, V.*

Outdoor Activities and Sports

CYCLING

The folks at **Adventure Cycling** (✉ 150 E. Pine St., ☎ 880/755–2453 or 406/721–1776, WEB www.adv-cycling.org) in downtown Missoula have good suggestions for nearby bike routes and an extensive selection of regional and national bike maps for sale.

GOLF

Highlands Golf Club (⌧ 102 Ben Hogan Dr., ☎ 406/728–7360) has nine holes, and provides the best view of Missoula from the restaurant-bar Shadows Keep. **Larchmont Golf Course** (⌧ 3200 Old Fort Rd., ☎ 406/721–4416) has 18 holes.

SKIING

Montana Snowbowl (⌧ Grant Creek Rd., ☎ 406/549–9696 or 406/549–9777, WEB www.montanasnowbowl.com) is for advanced skiers who are hooked on steep, challenging runs and powdery views of nearby Rattlesnake Wilderness. Telemarkers and geländesprung alpine ski jumpers are a colorful element of the local ski scene. Groomed beginner and intermediate runs make up over half the trails on the 950 acres, 12 mi northwest of Missoula. Services include a restaurant, bar, and Geländesprung Lodge in the base area.

Shopping

Take a break while touring downtown Missoula and have a cappuccino or a glass of fresh-squeezed orange juice at **Butterfly Herbs** (⌧ 232 N. Higgins Ave., ☎ 406/728–8780). If you can't decide what you fancy, try the "Butterfly Coffee Soda"—a cold drink with multiple layers of sweetness. The shop also sells baked goods, candies, soaps, candles, china, and other odds and ends.

Flowers, fresh fruits and vegetables, and unique handmade goods are displayed at the **Missoula Farmers Market** (⌧ N. Higgins Ave. on Railroad and Alder Sts.) on Market Plaza, a two-block area downtown. It takes place Saturday May–October, 9–noon, and Tuesday evenings July–August, 6–7:30. **People's Market** (⌧ Pine St. between Higgins Ave. and Pattee St.) is an outdoor bazaar selling locally made crafts. It's open on Saturday, May–October.

Rockin' Rudy's (⌧ 237 Blaine St., ☎ 406/542–0077) could be called the store that has everything, including new and used records, CDs, and tapes; T-shirts; imported dresses, hats, and accessories; incense; greeting cards; and other gifts.

National Bison Range

➋ *49 mi north of Missoula, via U.S. 93 north to Ravalli, Rte. 200 west, and Rte. 212 north.*

The 19-mi Red Sleep Mountain Drive at the National Bison Range allows close-up views of bison, elk, pronghorn, deer, and mountain sheep. The gravel road rises 2,000 ft and takes about two hours to complete; motorists must begin the drive no later than 6 PM to finish the loop before the gate closes at dark. The 19,000-acre refuge at the foot of the Mission Mountains was established in 1908 by President Theodore Roosevelt. Today the U.S. Fish and Wildlife Service ranches a herd of 400 bison. A visitor center explains the history, habits, and habitat of the bison. To reach the bison range, follow the signs west, then north from the junction of U.S. 93 and Route 200 in Ravalli. ⌧ *132 Bison Range Rd., Moiese,* ☎ *406/644–2211,* WEB *www.refugenet.org/nbr.* ⌧ *$4 per vehicle.* ☉ *Mid-May–Sept., daily 7–9; Oct.–mid-May, weekdays 8–4:30.*

St. Ignatius

❸ *40 mi north of Missoula, via U.S. 93 north.*

The **St. Ignatius Mission**—a church, cabin, and collection of other buildings—was built in the 1890s with bricks made of local clay by missionaries and Native Americans. The 58 murals on the walls and ceilings of the church were used to teach Bible stories to the natives. In the St. Ignatius Mission Museum, an old log cabin, is an exhibit of early artifacts and arts and crafts. In St. Ignatius, take Main Street south to Mission Drive. ⊠ *1 Catholic Mission Dr.,* ☎ *406/745–2768.* ✉ *Donations accepted.* ☼ *Mid-Mar.–mid Oct., daily 9–9; mid-Oct.–mid-Mar., daily 9–5; Sun. 9:15 Mass.*

Ninepipe National Wildlife Refuge

❹ *9 mi north of St. Ignatius via U.S. 93; 49 mi north of Missoula, via U.S. 93.*

Sprawling Ninepipe is *the* place for bird-watchers. This 2,000-acre wetland complex in the shadow of the Mission Mountains is home to everything from marsh hawks to kestrels to red-winged blackbirds. It features rookeries for double-crested cormorants and great blue herons; bald eagles fish here in the winter. Roads through the center of the refuge are closed March through mid-July during nesting season, but you can drive along the periphery throughout the year. Maps are available from the nearby National Bison Range, which manages Ninepipe. ⊠ U.S. 93, ☎ 406/644–2211, WEB *www.r6.fws.gov/refuges/ninepipe/.*

Polson

❺ *18 mi north of Ninepipe National Wildlife Refuge via U.S. 93.*

This quiet community of 4,000 on Flathead Lake sits under the morning shadow of the jagged Mission Mountains. It's the largest town on the Flathead Indian Reservation, which is home to Confederated Salish and Kootenai tribes and the Pend d'Oreille peoples. Picnic spots, lake access, and playgrounds are found at Boettcher, Sacajawea, and Riverside parks. Some other parks are for tribal members only; signs identify picnic areas that are closed to the public. With 180 mi of shoreline, **Flathead Lake** is the largest natural freshwater lake in the western United States and is a wonderful place for sailing, fishing, or swimming. Wildhorse Island State Park is home to bighorn sheep and other wildlife; the 2,165-acre island can only be accessed by private boat. Cherry groves line the lake's shores, and toward the end of July, farmers harvest them and sell them at roadside stands.

The **SQELIX'U/AQFSMAKNI-K Cultural Center (The People's Center)** exhibits the collections of the Salish, Kootenai, and Pend d'Oreille people. Their stories and way of life are shown through 100-year-old photographs, artifacts, and recordings. The People's Center offers educational programs, guided interpretive tours, outdoor traditional lodges, and annual festivals. A gift shop highlights local artists and craftsmen's traditional and non-traditional work. ⊠ *53253 Hwy. 93 W, Pablo, 6 mi south of Polson,* ☎ *406/883–5344 or 800/883–5344,* WEB *www.peoplescenter.org.* ✉ *$3.* ☼ *Weekdays 9–5, weekends 10–5.*

Lodging

$$–$$$ ▦ **Mountain Lake Lodge.** This resort perched above crystalline Flat-
   ★   head Lake offers 30 well-appointed suites surrounding an outdoor pool. Guests enjoy sweeping views of the lake and surrounding mountains from their rooms. The hotel is well situated for hiking, golfing, rafting, and lake cruises. The log-accented dining room is designed to let

you watch the sunset while enjoying smoked pheasant and other delicacies. The dining room is open seasonally; the bar serves light dinners year-round. ⊠ *1950 Sylvan Dr. at Hwy. 35 mile marker 26.5, Bigfork 59911, 29 mi north of Polson,* ☎ *406/837–3800 or 877/823–4923,* FAX *406/837–3861,* WEB *www.mountainlakelodge.com. 30 suites. Restaurant, bar, pool, hot tub. AE, DC, MC, V.*

Outdoor Activities and Sports

Eight white-water miles of the lower Flathead River is the turf of **Flathead Raft Co.** (⊠ 1501 Hwy. 93. S, ☎ 406/883–5838 or 800/654–4359, WEB www.flatheadraftco.com), providing wild rafting adventures, whitewater kayaking, lake and river sea kayaking, and Native American interpretive trips between Kerr Dam and Buffalo Bridge, from June through September.

The 27 holes of the **Polson Country Club** (⊠ 111 Bayview Dr., ☎ 406/883–8230 or 800/392–9795, WEB www.golfmontana.net) are the valley's only ones on the shores of Flathead Lake. Every hole offers views of the Mission and Swan mountain ranges and the lake.

Bigfork

❻ *34 mi north of Polson on Rte. 35.*

The Swan River empties into Flathead Lake at the small, idyllic resort community of Bigfork, which celebrated its centennial in 2001. The small town is filled with shops, galleries, restaurants, and a cultural center. Many summer events are so popular that you should make dinner and playhouse reservations a month in advance. This is a great spot to browse after boating, hiking, horseback riding, golf, mountain biking, or cross-country skiing. The rotating gallery in **Bigfork Art and Cultural Center** (⊠ 525 Electric Ave., ☎ 406/837–6927) displays bronzes, paintings, and other media works by Montana artists.

Dining and Lodging

$$–$$$ ✕ **La Provence.** The garden dining here offers a flower-studded view down Bigfork's main street. Local artists' work decorates the whitewashed walls. The owner-chef combines dishes like French onion soup with Gruyère cheese served inside a large onion, and venison tenderloin with figs and Bordeaux sauce from his hometown, Avignon, France. An international wine list and a traditional chocolate soufflé round off the Mediterranean meals. ⊠ *408 Bridge St.,* ☎ *406/837–2923. AE, MC, V. Closed Sun.*

$$–$$$ ✕ **Showthyme!** In the town's former bank building, a brick structure
★ built in 1908 (see the brick makers' fingerprints in the walls), diners opt for street- or bay-side seating, or a table in the snug bank vault. Signature dishes include fresh ahi tuna with sweet soy ginger and wasabi over jasmine rice. Save room for Benedictine chocolate truffle pie. ⊠ *548 Electric Ave.,* ☎ *406/837–0707. AE, DC, MC, V. No lunch.*

$–$$ ✕ **Swan River Café and Dinner House.** This relaxed yet elegant eatery serves dishes such as rack of lamb, pork tenderloin, pastas, and fondues (which require advance reservation) inside or on the terrace overlooking Bigfork Bay. The Sunday brunch and dinner buffets attract hungry locals. ⊠ *360 Grand Ave.,* ☎ *406/837–2220. AE, D, MC, V.*

$$$$ 🏨 **Averill's Flathead Lake Lodge.** Since 1945 Averill's has been providing families a wholesome and active Western getaway. The beautiful green grounds are on the shore of the lake, where beach fires, canoeing, and sailing take place. The lodge, accommodations, and other buildings are all log and stone structures. Horseback rides set out both in the morning and evening, and you can learn to rope in the rodeo arena. Many activities such as rafting and guided fishing trips are available for an extra cost. It's BYOB at the bar. ✉ *Box 248, 59911,* ☎ *406/837–4391,* FAX *406/837–6977,* WEB *www.averills.com. 20 rooms, 20 cottages. Dining room, lake, pool, 4 tennis courts, hiking, horseback riding, horseshoes, volleyball, beach, boating, waterskiing, fishing, children's programs (3 and up), laundry, airport shuttle. AE, MC, V. Closed Oct.–May. MAP.*

$$ 🏨 **O'Duach'ain Country Inn Bed & Breakfast.** In a quiet lodgepole-pine forest outside of Bigfork, this cozy and comfy B&B consists of two log cabins. The main house is light-filled and has two stone fireplaces and a wraparound terrace—horses graze next door. Each of the rooms are individually decorated in Old West–style. The room in the main house has a step-up Queen Ann bed. Full breakfasts are served at a long dining room table. ✉ *675 Ferndale Dr., 59911,* ☎ *406/837–6851,* FAX *406/ 837–0778,* WEB *www.MontanaInn.com. 4 rooms, 1 suite; 4 with bath. Dining room, hot tub, hiking. AE, MC, V. BP.*

Nightlife and the Arts

From late June through Labor Day, the repertory group **Bigfork Summer Playhouse** (✉ 526 Electric Ave., Box 456, 59911, ☎ 406/837–4886, WEB www.bigfork.org) presents Broadway musicals and comedies each night except Sunday in the Bigfork Center for the Performing Arts. Phone orders for tickets are available from mid-May to the end of August, or by mail beginning in April. Children's workshops and theater are held in the same facility.

Outdoor Activities and Sports

HIKING

Jewel Basin Hiking Area (✉ 10 mi east of Bigfork, via Rte. 83 east for 2.7 mi then north on Echo Lake Rd. and follow signs) provides 35 mi of well-maintained trails among 27 trout-filled alpine lakes. You'll find the nearest phone and hearty to-go trail lunch at the Echo Lake Cafe at the junction of Route 83 and Echo Lake Road. The U.S. Forest Service office (✉ 200 Ranger Station Rd., ☎ 406/837–7500) in Bigfork sells hiking maps.

Shopping

Bigfork's Electric Avenue is lined with galleries and eclectic gift shops and is recognized for unparalleled dining and goodies for the sweet-toothed traveler. Try the soft cookies and hot-out-of-the-oven cinnamon rolls baked daily and even shipped nationwide from **Brookies Cookies** (✉ 191 Mill S, ☎ 406/837–2447).

Filled to the brim with Montana history, regional travel, and other unique books, **Electric Avenue Books** (✉ 490 Electric Ave., ☎ 406/837–6072) is a comfortable setting in which to browse. The shopkeeper offers hot tips on local events, restaurants, and out-of-the-way places.

Electric Avenue Gifts (✉ 459 Electric Ave., ☎ 406/837–4994) carries folk-art gifts and souvenirs. See award-winning sculptor Eric Thorsen at work during daily tours of his studio which is across the street from the gallery, **Eric Thorsen Fine Art Gallery** (✉ 547 Electric Ave., ☎ 406/837–4366). You can pick up the tiniest jar of Huckleberry jam or honey at **Eva Gates Homemade Preserves** (✉ 456 Electric Ave., ☎ 406/837–4356), or have their family-size jars of various berry flavors shipped back home.

En Route Two scenic routes lead north from Bigfork, over the Flathead River (look for osprey nests atop poles), past fields of mint, seed potato, hay, and tree nurseries. When the last glacier receded 10,000 years ago it left a 100-ft depth of fertile soil called glacier loam. Like a bridal bouquet, the **Gatiss Gardens** (✉ 4790 Hwy. 35 at Broeder Loop Rd., Creston, 8 mi north of Bigfork, ☎ 406/755–2418) offers a 1.25-mi gentle trail past hundreds of perennials, bulbs, and shrubs.

Kalispell

❼ *15 mi from Bigfork, via Rte. 82 west and U.S. 93 north; 105 mi north of Missoula via U.S. 93 north.*

Two major highways, U.S. 2 and U.S. 93 meet at a busy downtown intersection in this century-old city. Kalispell is the Flathead County seat and a regional business and shopping center for folks around Northwest Montana. A town highlight is the **Conrad Mansion National Historic Site Museum,** a 26-room Norman-style mansion that was the home of C. E. Conrad, the manager of a freighter on the Missouri River and the founder of Kalispell. Come Christmas, the mansion is lavishly decorated and filled with the wares of local artisans. ⊠ *4th St., between 6th and Woodland Aves.,* ☎ *406/755–2166.* ☞ *$7.* ☉ *Guided tours mid-May–mid-June, daily 10–5:30; mid-June–mid-Sept., daily 9–8; mid-Sept.–mid-Oct., daily 10–5:30.*

The **Hockaday Center for the Arts,** housed in the renovated Carnegie Library, presents contemporary art exhibits. ⊠ *302 2nd Ave. E, at 3rd St.,* ☎ *406/755–5268.* ☞ *Free.* ☉ *Tues.–Fri. 10–5, Sat. 10–3.*

Dining and Lodging

$$–$$$ ✕ **Cafe Max.** The menu changes frequently in this cozy Main Street café where appetizers are likely to have a French influence, like Camembert fritters with brandied apricots. Entrées have a Montana twist, like the Buffalo Osso Buco with bison, or fresh wild salmon coated with black and white sesame seeds, broiled, and topped with huckleberry chutney. ⊠ *121 Main St.,* ☎ *406/755–7687. AE, MC, V. Closed Mon.*

$$ ✕ **Painted Horse Grill.** Though the decor is unusually bland, what is delivered to your table is definitely attention grabbing. The calamari tempura is wonderfully tender, and cumin in the chile rellenos gives the southwestern appetizer an Indian twist. Catch up on your vegetable intake here as the salad greens are the freshest in the area, and the vegetables are nicely steamed. You can't go wrong with this creative menu, including the roast curried duck. ⊠ *110 Main St.,* ☎ *406/257–7035. AE, MC, V. Closed Sun. No lunch Sat.*

$$–$$$ 🛏 **The Keith House.** This impeccable 1911 home could be the cover girl
★ of any home decorating magazine and is the choice of both honeymooners and repeat business travelers. Each room is individually decorated with antiques and exquisite fabrics. Sterling silver and English bone china are set on the dining room table for breakfast. ⊠ *538 5th Ave., 59901,* ☎ *406/752–7913 or 800/972–7913,* FAX *406/752–7933,* WEB *www. keithhousebb.com. 4 rooms, 2 suites. Dining room. AE, MC, V. Closed Oct.–Apr. BP.*

$$–$$$ 🛏 **WestCoast Kalispell Center Hotel.** Attached to the downtown Kalispell Center Mall, this hotel has large, modern rooms and a solarium pool. The restaurant is well lit by an atrium ceiling. ⊠ *N. 20 Main, 59901,* ☎ *406/751–5050 or 800/325–4000,* FAX *406/751–5051,* WEB *www.westcoasthotels.com. 132 rooms. Restaurant, lounge, indoor pool, casino, business services, meeting rooms, free parking. AE, D, DC MC, V.*

$$ 🛏 **Hampton Inn Kalispell.** One mi west of downtown, this new hotel features an indoor 24-hour guest pool and free extended buffet breakfast. ⊠ *1140 U.S. 2 W, 59901,* ☎ *406/755–7900 or 800/426–7866,* FAX *406/755–5056,* WEB *www.northwestinns.com. 120 rooms. In-room VCRs, refrigerators, indoor pool. AE, D, DC, MC, V. BP.*

Nightlife

Cowboy boots and sneakers shift the sawdust on the floor at **Moose's Saloon** (⊠ 173 N. Main, ☎ 406/755–2337). Choose a tune from the

jukebox that will please the raucous crowd, and order some pizza to
go with those suds.

Whitefish/Big Mountain Resort

8 *15 mi north of Kalispell via U.S. 93.*

The sporty resort town of 5,000 is recognized as a mecca for golfing,
lake recreation, hiking, mountain biking, and skiing. Early settlers
came a century ago to farm or join the timber and railroad industries.
Named for the 2-by-7-mi Whitefish Lake where Native Americans caught
and dried whitefish, the town sits at the base of Big Mountain Ski and
Summer Resort. Nine lifts access 3,000 acres of powder skiing, and
provide outstanding winter and summer views into Glacier National
Park and the Canadian Rockies.

If you want to check out a cross-section of American life, drop by the
Whitefish train station at 6 AM, as a sleepy collection of farmers, cowboys, and skiers awaits the arrival of Amtrak's *Empire Builder,* en route
from Seattle to Chicago. Next to the half-timber depot is the **Stump-
town Historical Society's Museum.** The focus here is the Great Northern Railway, the nation's first unsubsidized transcontinental railway
that passed through Whitefish. In addition to lanterns, old posters, and
crockery are reminders of locals' history, such as the books of author
Dorothy M. Johnson and the Whitefish football team photos from 1922
through 1954. Pick up a walking tour map of Whitefish's historic district. ⊠ *500 Depot St.,* ☎ *406/862–0067.* 🖭 *Donation.* ☾ *June–
Sept., Mon.–Sat. 10–4; Oct.–May, Mon.–Sat. 11–3.*

Dining

WHITEFISH

$$–$$$ ✕ **Tupelo Grille.** In homage to Louisiana, native son and chef/owner
Pat Carloss cooks up fine dishes such as crawfish cakes, fried catfish,
Acadian-style orange roughy, and creole chicken and dumplings. Carloss rotates his well-chosen art collection in the dining room and further enlivens the atmosphere with piped-in New Orleans jazz, Dixieland,
or zyedco music. ⊠ *17 Central Ave.,* ☎ *406/862–6136. AE, MC, V.
No lunch.*

$$–$$$ ✕ **Wasabi Sushi Bar.** Not your typical western ski-town eatery,
Wasabi proves the Rocky Mountains are no obstacle to fresh sushi
lovers. Like the eye-watering wasabi, the setting is stimulating, with
wasabi-green walls, a salmon-egg-orange ceiling, and a rock-and-roll
and reggae music sound track. Other than raw fish, there's a tem-
pura-fried soft-shell crab Bento box, which is a traditional Japanese
lunch box item. For more conservative tastebuds there's the chicken
teriyaki and rice. ⊠ *419 E. 2nd St.,* ☎ *406/863–9283. AE, MC, V.
Closed Mon. No lunch.*

$ ✕ **Truby's.** Individual-sized, wood-fired gourmet pizzas are the specialty
here, but there's also choices like the Gorgonzola burger or hickory smoked
baby back ribs. On a warm day, diners fill the patio garden area. The
smoke-free bar has seven beers on tap, from the local Black Star brews
to Guinness. ⊠ *15 Central Ave.,* ☎ *406/862–4979. No lunch Sun.*

BIG MOUNTAIN

$$–$$$$ ✕ **Cafe Kandahar.** This small, rustic dining room serves the finest
meals on the mountain. In addition to dressed-up standards like tourne-
dos of beef and New York strip steak, you can choose from game dishes
such as roast quail and elk rib chops. Nightly specials such as buffalo
or venison fill out the menu. ⊠ *3824 Big Mountain Rd.,* ☎ *406/862–
6247. Reservations essential. AE, D, MC, V. No lunch. Closed late Sept.–
mid-Dec.*

$ ✕ **Big Drift.** You just want something quick between ski or mountain bike runs? Big Drift serves up espresso drinks, deli sandwiches, and bakery goodies in a petite log cabin in the Village area on Big Mountain. ⊠ *3901 Big Mountain Rd.,* ☎ *406/862–3777. No credit cards. Closed early Apr.–mid-June; late Sept.–Thanksgiving.*

Lodging

For lodging at the base of the Big Mountain Ski and Summer Resort, contact **central reservations** (☎ 800/858–4152), which handles everything from upscale Kandahar Lodge to dormitorylike Alpinglow Inn and various condominiums.

WHITEFISH

$$–$$$ 🏠 **Grouse Mountain Lodge.** On the edge of Whitefish, people check in here, and then go out and *do* something, whatever the season. Public tennis courts and cross-country trails border the lodge, and a 36-hole golf course is just down the street. Off-season you can book some bargain activity packages. The thoroughly modern lodge has a sunny lounge area with a lacquered slate floor, elk horn chandeliers, soft-cushioned furniture, and a tall fireplace. Guest rooms have standard, modern furnishings, cable TV, and coffeemakers. The loft units with kitchenettes are good choices for families. ⊠ *2 Fairway Dr., 59937,* ☎ *406/862–3000 or 800/321–8822,* FAX *406/862–0326,* WEB *www.grmtlodge.com. 133 rooms, 12 suites. Restaurant, bar, lounge, indoor pool, hot tubs, bicycles, recreation room, baby-sitting, business services, meeting rooms, airport shuttle, car rental. AE, D, DC, MC, V.*

$$ 🏠 **Garden Wall Inn.** Most of what you see in this 1923 home is antique, ★ from the Glacier National Park first edition books to bed linens with lace borders. All rooms are individually decorated and have feather down duvets. Special extras include a wake-up coffee tray delivered to your room and afternoon beverages and hors d'oeuvres in front of the fireplace. The three-course breakfast in the dining room is served on china from a Glacier National Park lodge. The innkeeper lives on the premises and shares cooking with the vivacious owner. The Snow bus to the ski resort stops one block away. ⊠ *504 Spokane Ave., 59937,* ☎ *406/862–3440 or 888/530–1700,* WEB *www.gardenwallinn.com. 3 rooms, 1 suite. Breakfast room, bicycles. AE, D, MC, V. BP.*

$$ 🏠 **Hidden Moose Lodge.** At the foot of the road that climbs to Big Mountain, this two-story log cabin makes a great place for unwinding. Some of the rooms have their own Jacuzzis, and there's one outdoors as well. Rooms are individually decorated with rough hewn pine furniture and ironwork, and each has its own entrance off a small deck. The living room's vaulted ceiling creates space for plenty of light and a 20-ft-high fireplace. In the evening, a glass of wine or bottle of locally brewed beer is on the house, which can be quite social, especially in summer. ⊠ *1735 E. Lakeshore Dr., 59937,* ☎ *406/862–6516,* FAX *406/862–6514,* WEB *www.hiddenmooselodge.com. 8 rooms. Breakfast room, in-room VCRs, refrigerators, hot tub, bicycles. AE, D, MC, V. BP.*

Nightlife and the Arts

The **O'Shaughnessy Cultural Arts Center** (⊠ 1 Central Ave., ☎ 406/862–5371) hosts a variety of year-round performances in an intimate theater setting.

The après-ski crowd dances in ski boots and rides the center-stage mechanical bucking bull at **The Bier Stube** (⊠ Big Mountain Village, ☎ 406/862–1993). Be sure to ask for your free ring—everyone gets one. **The Dire Wolf Pub** (⊠ 845 Wisconsin Ave., ☎ 406/862–4500) serves up herb-crust pizza, regional microbrews, and a rockin' good time with live funk and reggae most weekends. The pub is smoke free. The brewery **Great Northern Brewing** (⊠ 2 Central Ave., ☎ 406/863–1000) is open for free tastings of seven different brews like the Black Star Wild Huckleberry. In winter it's open Monday through Saturday, 3–7, and in summer Monday through Saturday, noon–6.

Whether the owner's band is playing on the stage or cowboys are serenading a sparse crowd of locals during karoake, the **Blue Moon Nite Club, Casino and Grill** (⊠ Junction of Hwy. 40 and Hwy. 2, Columbia Falls, ☎ 406/892–9925) is a hoot. The wooden dance floor gets a good scuffing on Western dance and country swing nights. Two stuffed grizzly bears rear up near the entrance, and other species decorate the large saloon as well.

Outdoor Activities and Sports

BICYCLING

Of the 2,000 mi of county roads, only 400 mi are paved, leaving dirt and gravel roads and innumerable trails open for discovery. Rent two-wheeled steeds (reservations suggested) at **Glacier Cyclery** (⊠ 326 E. 2nd St., ☎ 406/862–6446, WEB www.glaciercyclery.com). Monday-night group rides begin at the shop courtyard and lead to a variety of trails and a choice of difficulty. Bike maps, gear, and free air are available at this full-service shop.

DOGSLEDDING

Travel at the speed of dogs raring to run, with **Dog Sled Adventures** (⊠ Hwy. 93, 20 mi north of Whitefish, 2 mi north of Olney, ☎ 406/881–2275). Your friendly musher will take care to make the ride suit anyone from kids to seniors. Bundled up in a cozy sled, you'll be whisked through Stillwater State Forest on 1½-hour rides, over a 12-mi trail.

GOLF

The **Whitefish Lake Golf Club** (⊠ 1200 Hwy 93 W., ☎ 406/862–4000 or 406/862–5960), now at 27 holes, had its modest beginning as an airstrip built to aid in the protection of the country. The airstrip was seldom used, but games did have to be interrupted occasionally. The golf course requires reservations for the championship course.

ICE FISHING

Dangling a line through a sawed hole in the ice isn't the world's most aerobic sport, but because of the many lakes in the Whitefish area, it's a popular pastime. Whitefish Lake is the obvious place to start. The **Tally Lake Ranger District** (☎ 406/863–5400) can recommend good spots. The best place for ice-fishing gear in Whitefish is **Lakestream Fly Fishing Shop** (⊠ 15 Central Ave., ☎ 406/862–1298). Guided trips to secluded private lakes, equipment, and fly-fishing gear are sold at the shop. Advice is free.

SNOWMOBILING

There are over 200 groomed snowmobile trails in the Flathead region. **J & L RV and Snowmobile Rentals** (⊠ 1805 U.S. 2 W, Columbia Falls, ☎ 406/892–7666 or 800/531–3511) rents machines and clothing and also leads guided tours to the top of the Big Mountain, trails outside Glacier National Park, and state lands near Olney.

Downhill Skiing and Snowboarding

The **Big Mountain Ski and Summer Resort** has aspirations of bigness beyond the mountain itself. Why hasn't the Big Mountain, with ski-area roots that date back to 1930s, grown much? Perhaps for lack of a sexy name, for starters: the Big Mountain, near Whitefish, on Flathead National Forest—how enticing does that sound? The ski resort is 8 mi from Whitefish and remains comfortably small, popular among train travelers from the Pacific Northwest and the upper Midwest.

The mountain's most distinctive features are its widely spaced trees, which—when encased in snow—are known as snow ghosts. With 3,000 skiable acres, plus out-of-bounds areas for Sno-Cat skiing, the Big Mountain offers a lot of terrain to explore and many different lines to discover among those widely spaced trees. The pleasure of exploration and discovery—such as the finding of a fresh cache of powder many days after a snowstorm—is perhaps the main reason to ski the Big Mountain. Easy discovery comes in the form of free mountain tours by mountain ambassadors. They meet intermediate skiers near the bottom of the main quad chair, Glacier Chaser, at 10:30 AM and 1:30 PM daily.

In general, the pitch is in the intermediate to advanced-intermediate range; there's not a whole lot of super-steep or super-easy skiing. A sameness in pitch, however, doesn't mean a sameness in skiing. With trails falling away on all sides of the mountain, there is a tremendous variation in exposure and hence in snow texture; also take into consideration the number of trees to deal with and the views (the best being northeast toward Glacier National Park).

One of the Big Mountain's best features is its long high-speed quad (the "Glacier Chaser"), meaning that runs using most of the mountain's 2,300-ft vertical are interrupted by less than 10 minutes of lift-riding time. A negative is weather; foggy days are not uncommon, and that's when you're thankful that those snow ghosts are around as points of visual reference.

Summer on the Big Mountain attracts hikers for the Danny On Trail to the mountain summit, which can be accessed on the Glacier Chaser chairlift. Mountain bike trails, a nature center, and a few gift shops and restaurants remain open June–September. ⊠ *Box 1400, Whitefish 59937,* ☎ *406/862–1900 or 800/858–4152,* FAX *406/862–2922,* WEB *www.skiwhitefish.com.* ☉ *Thanksgiving–early Apr., daily 9–4:30.*

FACILITIES
2,500-ft vertical drop; 3,000 skiable acres; 25% beginner, 50% intermediate, 25% advanced; 2 high-speed quad chairs, 1 quad chair, 5 triple chairs, 1 double chair, 2 surface lifts. **Snow report:** (☎ 406/862–SNOW or 800/847–4868).

LESSONS AND PROGRAMS
Group instruction in downhill is offered for $30 for a half day (plus a lift ticket); cross-country, telemark skiing, and snowboarding lessons are also available. Specialty clinics such as racing, mogul, and telemark techniques are provided, as well as children's programs. For information call the **ski school** (☎ 406/862–2909).

LIFT TICKETS
$47. $14 night skiing (mid-December–March, Wednesday–Saturday, 4:30–9).

RENTALS
Full rental packages (skis, boots, and poles) start at $22 per day. Snowboard rentals start at $28 per day.

Nordic Skiing
BACKCOUNTRY SKIING
Because of an unusually liberal policy regarding skiing out-of-bounds, backcountry tours are possible from the top of the Big Mountain. For the most part, the Big Mountain ski patrol does not prevent skiers from crossing ski-area boundary ropes, although if you do so and get into trouble, you're responsible for paying rescue costs. Although the avalanche danger (*very* relatively speaking) is usually not high around

the Big Mountain, the chances of getting lost are. It is very easy to ski too far down the wrong drainage, creating the prospect of a tiring and excruciating bushwhack back to the base. For an intro to the nearby backcountry, you might want to try the Big Mountain's Snow-Cat-skiing operation, in the Ski and Snowboard School, which takes skiers for as little as $45 per person plus a lift ticket on a four-hour off-piste adventure.

TRACK SKIING

There are two machine-groomed track systems in the Whitefish area: both systems serve their purpose well enough, but don't expect inspiring views or a sense of wilderness seclusion. One advantage that **Glacier Nordic Touring Center** (✉ 1200 Hwy. 93 W., ☎ 406/881–4230 for snow report) on Whitefish Lake Golf Course has is that 2.8 km (1.6 mi) of its 12 km (7 mi) of groomed trail is for night skiing. A $3-per-person donation is suggested. Rentals, lessons, and trail maps are available at the **Outback Ski Shack** (☎ 406/862–9498). The **Big Mountain Nordic Center** (☎ 406/862–2946) has its own 16 km (9.6 mi) of groomed trails; the daily fee is $5. Rentals and trail maps are available at **Outpost on Big Mountain** lodge (☎ 406/862–2946). Arrangements for cross-country lessons can be made through the ski school office.

Hungry Horse

15 mi east of Whitefish.

Hungry Horse is one large roadside attraction featuring several wildlife, recreation, and tourism outlets. The kid in you, or your kids, might not let you drive past **Big Sky Waterpark and Miniature Golf.** Besides the ten waterslides and golf course, there's a carousel, arcade games, and bumper cars. ✉ 7211 Hwy. 2 E, junction of U.S. 2 and Rte. 206, ☎ 406/892–5025 or 406/892–2139, WEB *www.bigskywaterslide.com.* 🎟 $15.50. ⊙ *Memorial Day–Labor Day, daily 10–8.*

You've found the vortex of Montana at the **House of Mystery,** a hilarious jaunt through unusual gravitational energies and mystifying phenomena. ✉ 7800 U.S. 2 E, Columbia Falls, ☎ 406/892–1210. 🎟 $4. ⊙ *Apr.–Oct., daily 9–dark.*

Huckleberry Patch Restaurant & Gift Shop (✉ 8868 U.S. 2 E, ☎ 406/837–5000) has been the huckleberry headquarters of the state for nearly 50 years, selling the purple wild berry encased in fudge and in canned goodies.

Get lost in the maze at the **Amazing Fun Center**—and find yourself negotiating the mind-boggling walkways. Other attractions include Bankshot Basketball, go-carts, 18-hole miniature golf, bumper boats in a pond, and a picnic area. ✉ 10265 U.S. 2 E, Coram, ☎ 406/387–5902. 🎟 $5. ⊙ *Memorial Day–mid-Sept., daily 9:30–8:30.*

You're guaranteed to spot several black bears (rescued from circus acts) at **Great Bear Adventure,** a drive-through enclosure where your car is your cage. Look for the orange fencing and fort with guard towers on the west side of the highway. ✉ 10555 U.S. 2 E, Coram, ☎ 406/387–4662. 🎟 $5. ⊙ *Memorial Day–Labor Day, daily.*

OFF THE
BEATEN PATH

WILD EYES – This unusual facility is mainly for photographers, but day visitors can get up close to the numerous animals, too. Choose three animals to spend time with—you can touch young ones, but it's hands-off viewing of adult residents like the Siberian tiger. While young children can participate, all visitors must follow strict rules. It's a joy just to see the affectionate relationship the handlers have with the black panther, spotted leopard, wolves, and other furry friends. Call in advance for an appointment. ✉ *894 Lake Dr., Columbia Falls,* ☎ *406/387–5391 or 888/330–5391,* WEB *www.wildeyes-USA.com.*

Glacier National Park

❾ *27 mi east of Whitefish; 11 mi east of Hungry Horse (to town of Apgar), east on U.S. 2.*

The view into Glacier National Park's interior from Apgar, at the foot of Lake McDonald, has few equals: its majestic, snowcapped peaks look like an illusion rising out of the lake. Motorized access to the park is limited, but the few roads can take the traveler through a range of settings—from densely forested lowlands to craggy heights. Going-to-the-Sun Road, which snakes through the precipitous center of Glacier National Park, is one of the most dizzying rides on the North American continent. Navigating the narrow, curving highway, built from 1922 to 1932, you will understand why access is restricted. Vehicles more than 21 ft long and 8 ft wide (including mirrors) are not allowed to drive over Logan Pass—a restriction that is enforced at checkpoints at the east and west entrances. Most development and services are concentrated around St. Mary Lake, on the east side of the park, and Lake McDonald, on the west side. Other islands of development occur in Many Glacier, in the northeastern part of Glacier; Logan Pass Visitor Center; Apgar village; and West Glacier. The northern boundary of Glacier National Park coincides with the international border and the southern boundary of Canada's Waterton Lakes National Park. Together, the two parks are called Waterton/Glacier International Peace Park. ✉ *Glacier National Park Headquarters, West Glacier 59936,* ☎ *406/888–7800,* WEB *www.nps.gov/glac.* ✑ *$10 per vehicle for a 7-day permit.* ☉ *Park: year-round. Going-to-the-Sun Road's midsection closed over Logan Pass Oct.–June. Limited services in winter. Visitor centers: St. Mary mid-May–late Oct.; Logan Pass mid-June–late Oct.; Apgar mid-May–late Oct.; Many Glacier late May–late Sept.; headquarters weekdays year-round.*

Glacier is known as the "Crown of the Continent," for good reason. About 100 million years ago, continents collided and this part of the world was thrust skyward. The last of the massive Ice Age glaciers swept through here 10,000 years ago, acting like a giant rasp on the landscape, moving huge amounts of soil and rock and etching details such as waterfalls, some 200 lakes, knife-edge ridges, and spires into the mountains. Rivers, gravity, and the yearly cycle of freezing and thawing put the finishing touches on the landscape. The 50 glaciers that remain here now are relatively tiny year-round patches of ice and snow, hidden, like refugees, in the dark, cool, high-altitude recesses of the northern mountains. Triple Divide Peak in the backcountry north of the park is a real curiosity. When the snow from most mountains melts, the water drains to either the Pacific or Atlantic. This peak provides water to the Atlantic, Pacific, and Arctic oceans.

In spring and summer, the alpine wildflowers make up for their short season with an unmatched intensity of color. As the sun warms Glacier in the spring, lilies grow up next to the lip of receding snowbanks. Then the mountain meadows explode in pink and red devil's paintbrush, white phlox, lavender shooting stars, pale blue wild irises, moss campion, and mountain heather—all blooming together in a high-mountain Impressionist painting. Later in the summer, the fragrant white balls of bear grass bloom, each looking like a lightbulb on the end of a stick.

Glacier is one of the last enclaves of the grizzly bear, and the wild country in and around the park is home to the largest population of grizzlies—about 400—in the lower 48 states. Snow-white mountain goats, with their wispy white beards and curious stares, are often seen in alpine areas, and surefooted bighorn sheep graze the high meadows during the short summers.

A haven for outdoor enthusiasts, Glacier National Park offers whitewater river rafting, horseback riding, bird-watching, and scenery gazing, to name a few activities. Glacier is also a backpacker's heaven, and more than 700 mi of maintained trails twist and switchback through towering pines, steel-gray mountains, and valleys; past turquoise high-alpine lakes; and over wind-whipped ridges that command vast expanses of wilderness.

Head east along the shore of finger-shape Lake McDonald on the serpentine, 52-mi, Going-to-the-Sun Road, one of the most scenic drives in the world. If you want a little exercise, stop near **Avalanche Creek,** where you can pick up a 3-mi trail leading to **Avalanche Lake,** one of many mountain-ringed lakes in the park. The walk is relatively easy, making this one of the most accessible backcountry lakes in the park.

At **Logan Pass,** at the summit of Going-to-the-Sun Road, there's a **visitor center.** Follow the boardwalk from its parking lot to crystalline Hidden Lake. Mountain goats climb rocky cliffs at the lake, wildflowers bloom, and ribbons of water pour off the rocks. Before you set out on any hike in the park, however, remember to grab a jacket: snow can fall any month of the year. There's another visitor center at the park's east entrance. Visitation to the park peaks the last week of July and the first week of August.

Dining and Lodging

During the summer only, park lodges offer both formal dining and casual cafés in Apgar Village, Lake McDonald, St. Mary area, East Glacier, Many Glacier, and in Canada, Prince of Wales. Restaurants and cafés outside the park are less expensive (like The Villager in East Glacier), offer imaginative menus (try Two Sisters Café in Babb), and often have extended spring and fall service (like Johnsons Café in St. Mary) after the park's lodges have closed.

$$ 🗒 **Izaak Walton Inn.** Built as a dormitory for railroad workers in 1939, the inn honors its history with handmade bedding stenciled with the Great Northern Railway logo—Rocky, the mountain goat—bed lamps fashioned from rail spikes, and the artwork of Winold Reiss, which was commissioned by the railroad. Amtrak trains stop right outside the inn, making it a convenient lodging for outdoor enthusiasts without a car. Just outside the front door are more than 18 mi of groomed cross-country ski trails. For train buffs, four cabooses have been renovated and are available for cabin-style lodging. The inn is off U.S. 2, which crosses the Marias Pass along the southern boundary of the park, between East and West Glacier. Activity packages are available. ⊠ *123 Izaak Walton Rd., Box 653, Essex 59916,* ☎ *406/888–5700,* FAX *406/888–5200,* WEB *www.izaakwaltoninn.com. 30 rooms, 3 suites. Restaurant, bar, sauna, hiking, ice-skating, cross-country skiing, recreation room, coin laundry. MC, V.*

GLACIER NATIONAL PARK PROPERTIES

The park's three massive stone and timber lodges were built in the early part of the 20th century by the Great Northern Railroad, and today are operated by **Glacier Park, Inc.,** which also handles the motel-like properties in the park. The lodges are available June–September and should be reserved three–six months in advance, though you can check

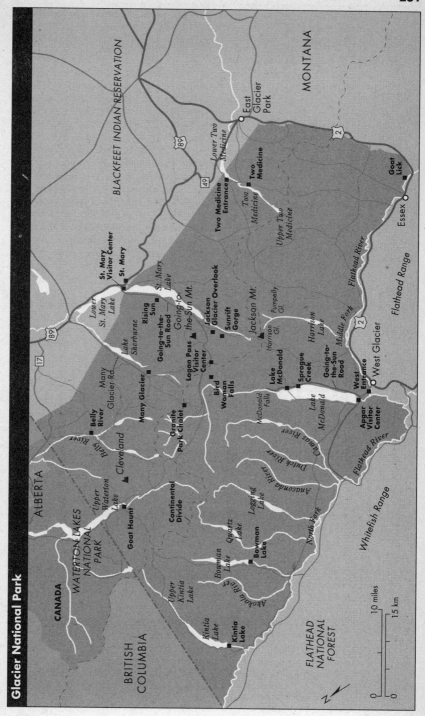

Glacier National Park

CANADA

ALBERTA

BRITISH COLUMBIA

BLACKFEET INDIAN RESERVATION

MONTANA

WATERTON LAKES NATIONAL PARK

FLATHEAD NATIONAL FOREST

Whitefish Range

Flathead Range

US 89

17

49

2

East Glacier Park

Essex

Goat Lick

Two Medicine Entrance

Two Medicine

Lower Two Medicine

Two Medicine

Upper Two Medicine

St. Mary Visitor Center

St. Mary

St. Mary Lake

Lower St. Mary Lake

Rising Sun

Going-to-the-Sun Road

Going-to-the-Sun Mt.

Jackson Glacier Overlook

Sunrift Gorge

Jackson Mt.

Pumpelly Gl.

Harrison Gl.

Harrison Lake

Lake Sherburne

Many Glacier

Many Glacier Rd.

Logan Pass Visitor Center

Bird Woman Falls

Sprague Creek

Lake McDonald

McDonald Falls

Lake McDonald

Going-to-the-Sun Road

West Entrance

West Glacier

Apgar Visitor Center

Middle Fork

Flathead River

Flathead River

Belly River

Belly River

Granite Park Chalet

Cleveland

Goat Haunt

Upper Waterton Lake

Continental Divide

Quartz Lake

Bowman Lake

Logging Lake

Camas Creek

Dutch River

Anaconda River

North Fork

Flathead River

Bowman Lake

Kintla Lake

Upper Kintla Lake

Kintla Lake

Akokala River

0 10 miles

0 15 km

for last-minute cancellations. ⊠ *Box 2025, Columbia Falls, MT 59912,* ☎ *406/892–2525,* FAX *406/892–1375,* WEB *www.glacierparkinc.com. AE, DC, MC, V.*

$$$–$$$$ 🏨 **Glacier Park Lodge.** On the east side of the park and across from the Amtrak station is this beautiful hotel built in 1913. This full-service lodge is supported by 500- to 800-year-old fir and 3-ft-thick cedar logs. If you golf on the spectacular course, watch out for moose. ⊠ *Off U.S. 2, East Glacier,* ☎ *406/226–9311,* FAX *406/226–9152. 154 rooms. Restaurant, bar, snack bar, pool, 9-hole golf course, playground.*

$$–$$$ 🏨 **Many Glacier Hotel.** The most isolated of the grand hotels—it's on Swiftcurrent Lake on the northeast side of the park—this is also one of the most scenic, especially if you nab one of the balcony rooms. There are several hiking trails nearby, and a large wrought-iron fireplace in the lobby where guests gather on chilly mornings. ⊠ *Many Glacier Rd., 12 mi west of Babb,* ☎ *406/732–4411,* FAX *406/732–5522. 211 rooms. Restaurant, bar, ice cream parlor, hiking.*

$$ 🏨 **Lake McDonald Complex.** This former hunting lodge on the shore of lovely Lake McDonald offers cabins, which sleep up to four and don't have kitchens; motel rooms, which are the largest; and units in the lodge itself. The lobby is decorated with mounts of wild animals. ⊠ *Going-to-the-Sun Rd.,* ☎ *406/888–5431. 30 rooms; 13 cabins. Restaurant, bar, coffee shop, hiking, boating, fishing.*

$$ 🏨 **Village Inn.** On Lake McDonald at Apgar Village, the motel could use some updating but is very popular and offers a view of the lake and surrounding peaks. It's near the lake outlet and good fishing. A restaurant, bar, and coffee shop are nearby. ⊠ *Apgar Village,* ☎ FAX *406/756–2444. 36 rooms. Hiking, boating, fishing.*

Outdoor Activities and Sports

The Glacier Institute, based inside the park near West Glacier at the Field Camp and on the remote western boundary at the Big Creek Outdoor Education Center, offers year-round field courses for youth, adults, teachers, and groups. Experts in wildlife biology, native plants and peoples, and river ecology lead educational treks into Glacier's backcountry on day and multiday programs. ⊠ *Box 7457, Kalispell 59901,* ☎ *406/755–1211,* WEB *www.glacierinstitute.org.* 🎟 *$45 and up per day.* 🕙 *Year-round.*

A nearly all-purpose outfitter for the park is **Glacier Wilderness Guides and Montana Raft Company** which operates daylong to weeklong trips that can combine hiking, rafting, and horseback expeditions.

FISHING

Within Glacier National Park is an unlimited range of fishing possibilities, with a catch-and-release policy encouraged. The sportfishing species include burbot (ling); northern pike; whitefish; kokanee salmon; grayling; and cutthroat, rainbow, lake (mackinaw), and brook trout. You can fish in most waters of the park, but the best fishing is generally in the least accessible spots. A fishing license is free, but it is expected that you familiarize yourself with all park fishing regulations before you use any facilities. Stop by a park office to pick up a copy of the regulations and speak with a ranger. If you want a guide for fly-fishing or hiking, contact Glacier Wilderness Guides and Montana Raft Company.

GOLF

Glacier Park Lodge (☎ 406/226–9311), in East Glacier, has a nine-hole, par-36 course, as well as a nine-hole pitch-and-putt course. **Glacier View Golf Course** (☎ 406/888–5471), in West Glacier, is an 18-hole course. On the Canadian side of the park, you could play nine holes at the **Waterton golf course** (☎ 403/859–2114), just outside town. Don't be surprised if you see moose, elk, deer, bighorn sheep, and other wildlife on the greens while playing.

HIKING AND BACKPACKING

Maps for hiking are available at the **Apgar Visitor Center** (☎ 406/888–5441) near the western entrance of Glacier. If you want to backpack, you must pick up a backcountry permit there. Cross-country skiers and snowshoers can pick up a map here too.

Hiking trails of various lengths and levels are well marked within the park. Novices and those who want the help of an experienced guide can sign up with **Glacier Wilderness Guides and Montana Raft Company.** The most spectacular hiking-and-lodging adventure in the state is the gentle 7-mi Highline Trail from Logan Pass to Granite Park Chalet, a National Historic Landmark, which is open for rustic lodging ($60 per night; reservations through Glacier Wilderness Guides) late July–mid September. Built in 1914 by the Great Northern Railway, the chalet was one of nine backcountry lodges of which only two remain, including Sperry Chalet (operated by Belton Chalets, Inc., ☎ 888/345–2649 or 406/387–5654).

HORSEBACK RIDING

Mule Shoe Outfitters (☎ 406/888–5010 or 406/888–5121, WEB www.muleshoe.com) runs the horseback riding concession in Glacier from early June to September 15, as the weather allows. Stables are at Apgar, Lake McDonald, and Many Glacier. Different trips, all led by a guide who provides information on the national park, are for beginning to advanced riders and cover country both flat and mountainous. Rates run from $25 for an hour to $120 for a full day.

RAFTING

Glacier Wilderness Guides and Montana Raft Company (✉ 11970 U.S. 2 E, West Glacier 59936, 1 mi south of West Glacier, ☎ 406/387–5555 or 800/521–7238, WEB www.glacierguides.com) will take you on raft trips through the stomach-churning white water of the Middle Fork of the Flathead and combine it with a hike or horseback ride. Two river outfitters working out of resorts that also rent cabins with kitchens are: **Glacier Raft Company** (✉ 11957 U.S. 2 E and inside West Glacier, #6 Going-to-the-Sun Rd. next to Exxon [summers only], West Glacier 59936, ☎ 406/888–5454 or 800/235–6781, WEB www.glacierraftco.com), which also rents bikes, snowshoes, and cabins and has a full-service fly-fishing shop; and **Great Northern Whitewater** (✉ 12127 U.S. 2 E, 1 mi south of West Glacier, West Glacier 59936, ☎ 406/387–5340 or 800/735–7897, WEB www.gnwhitewater.com), which offers daily whitewater, kayaking, and fishing trips and rents Swiss-style chalets with views of Glacier's peaks.

SKIING

Cross-country ski excursions reveal mountain views, frozen lakes and streams, and wildlife like moose, deer, and bald eagles. Glacier National Park distributes a free pamphlet entitled "Ski Trails of Glacier National Park," which describes 16 ski trails. On scenic trails like Autumn Creek near the Continental Divide, **Glacier Park Ski Tours** (☎ 800/646–6043 Ext. 3724) guides custom day trips and winter camping in snow huts or tents.

The 32 km (19 mi) of groomed track at **Izaak Walton Inn** (✉ U.S. 2, Essex, ☎ 406/888–5700, WEB www.izaakwaltoninn.com), at the edge of Glacier National Park, nicely combine the pleasures of groomed-trail skiing with the spirit of backcountry skiing with views into the park and the Great Bear Wilderness. Because it's alongside the railroad tracks, it is also accessible from Whitefish by train. Track, touring, and

telemark rentals and multiday packages including skiing, lodging, and
meals are available. Be careful when crossing the highway between trails.

En Route The fastest route east from West Glacier and Apgar to Browning (and
the only route in winter, when Going-to-the-Sun Road is closed) is U.S.
2. Near Essex is the **Goat Lick**—a natural salt formation along the highway that attracts mountain goats (the off-highway Goat Lick Overlook parking area is a safe place to watch these animals). The highway
travels over Marias Pass. At 5,216 ft, this is the lowest major pass over
the Rocky Mountains, and the spot where the Great Northern Railroad crossed the Great Divide in 1891.

Browning

⑩ *12 mi east of Glacier National Park via U.S. 2.*

Browning, just east of the Continental Divide, is the center of the
Blackfeet Nation, whose name is thought to have been derived from
the color of their painted or dyed black moccasins. Until the late 19th
century, the Blackfeet hunted the great northern buffalo, moving with
them across the vast northern plains. At one time, the Blackfeet homeland stretched all the way from the Missouri River north to the Bow
and Red Deer rivers in Canada, and from the Rocky Mountains 300
mi east. Rugged terrain and remoteness left Blackfeet territory some
of the last Native American country in the contiguous United States
to be opened to whites. The 1.5 million-acre reservation was established
in 1851, and currently has about 13,000 enrolled tribal members.
Outstanding fly-fishing opportunities exist on the reservation. A tribal
fishing permit is required.

The **Museum of the Plains Indian,** on the north end of town, has been
in operation since the 1930s. The museum houses a stunning collection of ancient artifacts from the Blackfeet who have lived in the region for 7,000 years, and other Plains peoples. ☒ *Junction of U.S. 2
and U.S. 89,* ☏ *406/338–2230.* ☑ *$4.* ☉ *June–Sept., daily 9–4:45;
Oct.–May, weekdays 10–4:30.*

During the second week of July, the Blackfeet host **North American Indian Days** (☏ 406/338–7276) in Browning. This gathering of tribes is
a pageant of drumming, chanting, traditional games, and tepees as far
as the eye can see.

Lodging

$$ 🏠 **Inn Dupuyer B&B.** This 100-year-old, hand-hewn log homestead house
is in the tiny ranching town of Dupuyer. Rooms are done in period decor
and have panoramic mountain views. Guests can join horse-drawn car-
riage rides or just sit on the porch and watch the sun set over the Rock-
ies. Nearby outfitters offer cattle drives and trail rides. Innkeepers can
point you in the right direction for biking (bring your own bike), hik-
ing, fishing, bird watching, and wildlife viewing. ☒ *11 Jones Ave. W.,
Dupuyer 59432, 26 mi south of Browning,* ☏ *406/472–3241. 5 rooms.
Dining room, refrigerators, fishing, library. MC, V. BP.*

En Route Two routes lead from Browning and Glacier National Park toward Great
Falls and Helena, both scenic. Interstate 15 speeds through prairie ranch
lands with glimpses of the snowcapped wilderness to the west. The road
less traveled is Route 89, which snugs up to the base of the Rocky Moun-
tain Front Range. Numerous fish-filled lakes, wildlife management areas,
and dinosaur digs are along this route, as well as the real cowboy towns
of **Dupuyer, Choteau,** and **Augusta.**

Great Falls

⑪ *127 mi south of Browning via I–15.*

Great Falls is the state's third-largest city and was named for the mighty Missouri River waterfalls that were a formidable barrier to early navigation. Lewis and Clark spent nearly a month portaging around the falls during their upriver travels in 1805. Dams smothered the falls; however, much of the river below Great Falls heading north and east remains unaltered. Bikers, walkers, and cross-country skiers take advantage of the popular 13-mi River's Edge Trail paved path. Famed cowboy artist Charles M. Russell (1864–1926) made his home and studio here, and the community celebrates his work the third weekend of March with a three-day C. M. Russell Art Auction.

Russell's original home and log studio, replete with the artist's tools and work, is open to the public. Next door, the **C. M. Russell Museum** complex, a 46,000-square-ft facility, displays watercolors, sculptures, oil paintings, and illustrated notes and letters from the prolific and often humorous artist. You can also see works by O. C. Seltzer, Joseph Henry Sharp, and Edward Curtis. Russell completed 4,000 works of art, primarily portraying the vanishing era of the Old West. ✉ *400 13th St. N,* ☎ *406/727–8787,* WEB *www.cmrussell.org.* 🎟 *$6.* ☉ *May–Sept., Mon.–Sat 9–6, Sun. noon–5; Oct.–May 1, Tues.–Sat. 10–5; Sun. 1–5.*

Trace the trail that the Corps of Discovery traveled almost 200 years ago (1804–06) in search of an overland route to the Pacific Ocean, and experience their struggles and successes at the **Lewis and Clark National Historic Trail Interpretive Center.** Next to the Missouri River, the new center exhibits materials used by travelers and Native Americans of the era through features films, a self-guided tour, and costumed interpreters who conduct demonstrations daily. ✉ *4201 Giant Springs Rd.,* ☎ *406/727–8733,* WEB *www.fs.fed.us/r1/lewisclark/lcic.htm.* 🎟 *$5.* ☉ *Memorial Day weekend–Sept. 30, daily 9–6; Oct.–Memorial Day weekend, Tues.–Sat 9–5, Sun. noon–5.*

OFF THE BEATEN PATH | **Virgelle Merc and Missouri River Canoe Co.** – This canoe outfitter is 75 mi northeast of Great Falls. The Virgelle Merc itself is a restored homestead-era settlement with comfortable accommodations, in homestead cabins, B&B rooms, and even a sheep-herders's wagon under the stars ($30–$120 per night). The river outfitter offers historic eco-tours of one to 10 days, guided in canoes or kayaks following Lewis and Clark's river trail. The Missouri River flows from its headwaters near Bozeman and across the prairie to North Dakota. Boaters float sections of the river from the almost-a-ghost-town, Virgelle, where one of the state's last river-crossing cable ferries operates. ✉ *7485 Virgelle Ferry Rd. N, Loma 59460,* ☎ *800/426–2926,* WEB *www.canoemontana.com. AE, DC, MC, V.*

Lodging

$$–$$$ 🏨 **Hawthorn Suites.** New to the city, this is the only hotel on the Missouri River, with access to the River's Edge Trail. The trail leads 5 leisurely mi to the Lewis and Clark Interpretative Center. Rental bicycles are available at the hotel, which is just three blocks from the downtown business area. A free Continental breakfast is included. ✉ *600 River Dr. S, 59405,* ☎ *800/527–1133 or 406/761–2600,* FAX *406/761–2267. 71 rooms. Dining room, indoor pool, hot tub, sauna, gym. AE, D, DC, MC, V. CP.*

$$ 🏨 **Charlie Russell Manor.** This newly restored 1916 B&B is in the original, historic Great Falls town site. The spacious rooms have TVs and antique furnishings. Breakfasts are hearty and there is on-site catering for special parties. ✉ *825 4th Ave. N, 59401,* ☎ *877/207–6131 or*

406/455–1400, FAX 406/727–3771. 6 rooms. Dining room, in-room data ports, no-smoking rooms, meeting rooms. AE, MC, V. BP.

Helena

12 89 mi south of Great Falls via I–15.

This jewel of a town, where the prairie meets the mountains, started as a rowdy mining camp in 1864 and became a banking and commerce center in the Montana Territory. A century ago, Helena had more millionaires per capita than any other town in the country. With statehood came a fight between the towns of Anaconda and Helena over which would be the capital. In a notoriously corrupt campaign in which both sides bought votes, Helena won. The iron ball of urban renewal robbed the town of much of its history, but Helena still has ornate brick and granite historic buildings along the Last Chance Gulch, of early mining fame. Walk a few blocks down 6th Avenue to the center of historic downtown Helena, and ask at the **Downtown Helena Office** (⊠ 121 N. Last Chance Gulch, ☎ 406/442–9869) for a self-guided walking tour brochure.

On the corner of Last Chance Gulch and Lawrence Street, the lobby of the **Wells Fargo Bank** displays a collection of gold nuggets, including one nugget worth $600,000, taken from area diggings. ⊠ 350 N. Last Chance Gulch, ☎ 406/447–2000. ☜ Free. ☉ Weekdays 9–4.

The **Holter Museum of Art,** a block off Last Chance Gulch, houses both permanent and changing exhibits of visual arts. The emphasis is on Montana artists, folk art, crafts, photography, painting, and sculpture. ⊠ 12 E. Lawrence Ave., ☎ 406/442–6400, WEB www.holtermusuem.org. ☜ Donations accepted. ☉ Memorial Day–Labor Day, Mon.–Sat. 10–5, Sun. noon–5; Labor Day–Memorial Day, Tues.–Fri. 11:30–5, Sat.–Sun. 12–5.

The Greek Renaissance **state capitol building** boasts a dome of Montana copper and Charlie Russell's largest painting, a 12-ft-by-25-ft depiction of Lewis and Clark. Guided tours are offered on the hour in summer from 9 to 4. ⊠ 6th and Montana Sts., ☎ 406/444–2511 or 800/243–9900. ☜ Free. ☉ Daily 8–5.

The **Montana Historical Society Museum** displays one of the most important collections of Charlie Russell's work in its MacKay Gallery. Early black-and-white photos of Yellowstone National Park taken by F. Jay Haynes are on display in the Haynes Gallery. The expansive Montana Homeland exhibit, which features nearly 2,000 historical artifacts, documents, and photographs, gives visitors a thorough look at Montana from the time of the first native settlers to the present. The venue also hosts special events and "family days" during the summer, including programs on folk music, Native American culture, and cowboys. Call ahead for information on upcoming events. ⊠ 225 N. Roberts St., across from the State Capitol, ☎ 406/444–2694 or 800/243–9900, WEB www.montanahistoricalsociety.org. ☜ Donations accepted. ☉ Memorial Day–Labor Day, weekdays 8–6, weekends 9–5; Labor Day–Memorial Day, weekdays 8–5, Sat. 9–5.

Out in front of the Historical Society Museum, catch the **Last Chance Train Tour** for an hour-long tour that threads through Helena's historic neighborhoods of miners' mansions on the west side to the site where four miners made their first gold discovery on the gulch. ⊠ Roberts St., ☎ 406/442–1023 or 888/432–1023, WEB www.lctours.com. ☜ $6.50. ☉ May–June, Sept., daily 10–3; July–Aug., daily 10–6. Tours on the hr.

For an old-fashioned sweet treat, pull up a stool at the **Parrot** (⊠ 42 N. Last Chance Gulch, ☎ 406/442–1470), a soda fountain and candy store built in the 1920s that sells everything from chocolate malts with homemade ice cream to hand-dipped chocolates and a regional favorite, a cherry phosphate.

Dining and Lodging

$$–$$$ ✕ **On Broadway.** Wooden booths, discreet lighting, and brick walls contribute to the comfortable ambience at this Italian restaurant. Popular dishes include New York strip steak and pasta puttanesca (sautéed Greek olive, artichoke heart, red bell pepper, red onion, capers, and pine nuts). When the state legislature is in session, members of congress make this a boisterous place. ⊠ *106 Broadway,* ☎ *406/443–1929. Reservations not accepted. AE, D, DC, MC, V. No lunch. Closed Sun.*

$$–$$$ ✕ **Windbag Saloon & Grill.** This historic restaurant in the heart of down-
★ town was called Big Dorothy's until 1973, when a crusading county attorney forced Dorothy to close up her house of ill repute. Now it's a family restaurant, named for the political debates you're likely to hear while dining on burgers, quiche, salads, and sandwiches. A bounty of cherrywood gives the place a warm, comfortable feel. It also has a large selection of imported beer, on tap and in bottles. ⊠ *19 S. Last Chance Gulch,* ☎ *406/443–9669. AE, D, MC, V. Closed Sun.*

$$ ☷ **Holiday Inn Express.** This newer hotel resembles the chain yet is staffed
★ with pleasant locals who know the region and just may share a favorite fishing spot with visitors. At the junction of Route 12 and I–15, the motel provides easy access to those just needing to sleep for the night. ⊠ *701 Washington, 59601,* ☎ *406/449–4000 or 800/465–4329,* ⴹ *406/449–4522. 75 rooms, 7 suites. Gym. AE, DC, MC, V.*

$$ ☷ **Sanders-Helena Bed and Breakfast.** This three-story Victorian man-
★ sion was built in 1875 by Colonel Wilbur Sanders, the prosecuting attorney at some of the summary trials hosted by the Montana vigilantes. The colonel's rock collection is still in the front hall, and the B&B has retained his furnishings. Most of the rooms have views overlooking mountain-ringed downtown Helena. Breakfasts are a work of art: Grand Marnier french toast, orange soufflé, or gingerbread waffles. ⊠ *328 N. Ewing St., 59601,* ☎ *406/442–3309,* ⴹ *406/443–2361,* ⵣ *www.sandersbb.com. 7 rooms, 6 with bath. AE, MC, V. BP.*

Nightlife and the Arts

In Helena, an oasis for the arts is the **Myrna Loy Center for the Performing Arts** (⊠ 15 N. Ewing St., ☎ 406/443–0287, ⵣ www. myrnaloycenter.com). In a remodeled historic jail, the center—named after the Montana-born actress—offers live performances by nationally and internationally recognized musicians and dance troupes. Two theaters show foreign and independent films, usually two films per night.

Outdoor Activities and Sports

To stretch your legs, consider taking an hour-long hike to the top of Mt. Helena, which towers over the Last Chance Gulch Mall on the west edge of town. From the summit, you'll have panoramic views of Helena, the Helena Valley, and the Rocky Mountains to the west.

CYCLING

Old logging roads like the McDonald Pass area, 20 mi west of town on the Continental Divide, offer challenging mountain biking. Other trails closer to town lead toward mining towns and thick forests. For route information, call the **Helena National Forest** (☎ 406/449–5201).

FISHING

High Plains Outfitters of Helena (⊠ 31 Division St., ☎ 406/442–9671) offers guided trips on various rivers in Montana, including the Missouri, the Big Hole, and the Blackfoot, and wading on smaller rivers and streams.

Shopping

For 50 years, many of the nation's best ceramic artists have come to work in residency at the **Archie Bray Foundation** (⊠ 2915 Country Club Ave., ☎ 406/443–3502, WEB www.archiebray.org). Wander near the five antiquated, 8-ft-high, dome-shape brick kilns on a self-guided walking tour, and visit the gift shop, which sells work produced by foundation artists. It's open Monday through Saturday 9–5 and Sunday 1–5.

Missoula to Helena A to Z

AIRPORTS

Missoula International Airport, on U.S. 93 just west of Missoula, is served by Big Sky, Delta, Horizon, Northwest, SkyWest, and United Express/SkyWest. Glacier Park International Airport, 8 mi northeast of Kalispell and 11 mi southeast of Whitefish on U.S. 2, is serviced by Big Sky, Delta, Horizon, and Northwest. Helena Regional Airport offers flights on Big Sky, Delta, and Horizon. Great Falls Airport is served by Big Sky, Delta, Horizon, and Northwest.

➤ AIRPORT INFORMATION: **Glacier Park International Airport** (☎ 406/257–5994). **Great Falls Airport** (☎ 406/727–3404). **Helena Regional Airport** (☎ 406/442–2821). **Missoula International Airport** (☎ 406/728–4381).

BUS TRAVEL

Greyhound Lines serves east–west travel from the North Dakota border along I–94 and I–90, to the Idaho border. In Montana, Rimrock Trailways stops in most larger communities from Billings to Missoula, Helena, Great Falls, Kalispell, and Whitefish. A winter-only free shuttle bus runs between the Big Mountain resort and Whitefish 7 AM–10 PM, but a car—especially if you want to explore Glacier National Park—is more convenient.

➤ BUS INFORMATION: **Greyhound Lines** (☎ 800/231–2222). **Rimrock Trailways** (☎ 800/555–7655). **SNOW Bus** (⊠ Whitefish, ☎ 406/862–2900).

CAR TRAVEL

Interstate 90 and U.S. 93 pass through Missoula. U.S. 93 and Route 35 lead off I–90 to Kalispell in the Flathead Valley; from there, U.S. 2 heads to Glacier National Park. If you're traveling to Glacier from the east, take I–15 to Great Falls and U.S. 89 to the east entrance to the park.

ROAD CONDITIONS
➤ CONTACT: ☎ 406/449–4000.

EMERGENCIES

Note that emergency 911 works in most locations but not all. Some rural areas still rely on local phone calls to a sheriff office. Cell phone coverage is patchworked across the state and most often does not work in the mountains.

➤ CONTACTS: **Kalispell: Kalispell Regional Hospital** (⊠ 310 Sunnyview La., Kalispell, ☎ 406/752–5111). **Missoula: St. Patrick Hospital** (⊠ 500 W. Broadway, Missoula, ☎ 406/543–7271).

TOURS

Glacier Park, Inc. operates a fleet of vans that navigate along the Going-to-the-Sun Road and other routes and inroads of Glacier. The vintage-1930s red-and-black buses are being upgraded and rehabilitated for use once again. Sun Tours offers Blackfeet cultural and historical interpretive tours of Glacier from comfortable minibuses.

Interpretive tours highlighting the Blackfeet Nation follow traditional trade and hunting routes in Montana and Canada with Blackfeet tribal historians of Blackfeet Historical Site Tours. Trips between June and September range from a half day to 10 days.

➤ CONTACTS: **Blackfeet Historical Site Tours** (✉ Box 2038, Browning 59417, ☎ 406/338–2058). **Glacier Park, Inc.** (☎ 406/226–5666, WEB www.glacierparkinc.com). **Kruger Helicop-Tours** (✉ 11892 U.S. 2 E, West Glacier, ☎ 406/387–4565). **Sun Tours** (☎ 406/226–9220 or 800/786–9220).

TRAIN TRAVEL
Amtrak's *Empire Builder* runs between Portland, Seattle, and Chicago and makes stops in Whitefish, West Glacier, Essex, East Glacier Park, and Browning.

➤ TRAIN INFORMATION: **Amtrak** (☎ 800/872–7245).

VISITOR INFORMATION
➤ TOURIST INFORMATION: **Blackfeet Nation** (✉ 1 Government Sq., Box 850, Browning 59417, ☎ 406/338–7276). **Flathead Convention and Visitors Bureau** (☎ 406/756–9091 or 800/543–3105).**Glacier Country Tourism** (✉ Box 1035, Bigfork 59911–1035, ☎ 406/837–6211 or 800/338–5072, WEB www.glacier.visitmt.com).**Glacier National Park** (✉ West Glacier 59936, ☎ 406/888–7800, WEB www.nps.gov/glac). **Great Falls Chamber of Commerce** (✉ 710 1st Ave. N, 59403, ☎ 406/761–4434 or 800/735–8535, WEB www.travel.mt.us/greatfallscvb). **Helena Chamber of Commerce** (✉ 225 Cruse Ave., Suite A, 59601, ☎ 406/442–4120 or 800/743–5362, WEB www.helenachamber.com). **Missoula Chamber of Commerce** (✉ Box 7577, 59807), ☎ 406/543–6623 or 800/526–3465, WEB www.missoulachamber.com).**Russell Country Tourism** (✉ Box 3166, Great Falls 59807, ☎ 406/761–5036 or 800/527–5348, WEB www.russell.visitmt.com).**Whitefish Chamber of Commerce** (✉ 6475 U.S. 93 S in the Mountain Mall, 59937, ☎ 406/862–3501 or 877/862–3548, WEB www.whitefishchamber.org).

BILLINGS TO BIG HOLE

This tour captures some of the diversity of Montana, moving from the rolling, grassy plains and rimrocks of eastern Montana to the Rocky Mountain Front and across the Continental Divide to southwestern Montana. The route follows I-90 along the meandering Yellowstone River before heading up U.S. 287 toward the timber-draped mountains of the west. Along the way it reveals much of Montana's history, from gold strikes to Indian wars. Mining towns and resort communities, cowboys and capitalists blend effortlessly in the heart of Big Sky Country.

Billings

⓭ *224 mi from Helena, south via U.S. 12/287 and east via I-90.*

Billings, the regional capital of the coal and oil industry, is, with 90,000 residents, not only the largest city in Montana but also the largest city for 500 mi in any direction. The "Magic City" was developed in 1882 with the coming of the railroad and was named after a member of its board of directors, Frederick Billings. Billings is in the middle of the rolling plains of eastern Montana, at the foot of buckskin-color cliffs dubbed the rimrocks, and along the Yellowstone River. Near here are the eerie badlands and dinosaur finds of Makoshika state park, east at Glendive.

Moss Mansion was built in 1903 for businessman P. B. Moss by Dutch architect Henry Hardenbergh (designer of the original Waldorf-Astoria Hotel in New York City). It contains many of the elaborate original furnishings, ranging in style from Moorish to Art Nouveau Empire. Guided tours are offered on the hour. ⊠ *914 Division St.,* ☎ *406/256–5100,* WEB *www.mossmansion.com.* 🎫 *$6.* ☉ *June–Sept. 15, Mon.–Sat. 9–4, Sun. 1–4; Sept. 16–May 31, daily 1–3.*

A worthwhile attraction that offers insight into the history and culture of the Yellowstone River region is the **Western Heritage Center,** on the corner of 29th and Montana avenues. Its permanent exhibit includes oral histories, artifacts, and kid-friendly interactive displays tracing the lives of Native Americans, ranchers, homesteaders, immigrants, and railroad workers during the period 1880–1940. Native American interpretive programs and Museum Without Walls courses are available. ⊠ *2822 Montana Ave.,* ☎ *406/256–6809,* WEB *www.ywhc.org.* 🎫 *Donations accepted.* ☉ *Tues.–Sat. 10–5.*

The **Yellowstone Art Museum,** in the original county jail, features a permanent collection of western art along with changing exhibitions of regional artists' works. ⊠ *401 N. 27th St.,* ☎ *406/256–6804,* WEB *www. yellowstoneartmuseum.org.* 🎫 *$5.* ☉ *Tues.–Sat. 10–5, Sun. noon–5.*

OFF THE
BEATEN PATH

MILES CITY – History buffs may want to travel east from Billings (145 mi via I-94) to the ranch town of Miles City (population 8,400), at the confluence of the cottonwood-lined Tongue and Yellowstone rivers. The federal Treaty of 1868 said this would be "Indian country as long as the grass is green and the sky is blue." That promise changed, however, when gold was found in the Black Hills of South Dakota to the east, and white settlers streamed into this part of the world. Ranchers eventually took over, and in 1884, the last of the great herds of buffalo was slaughtered near here to make room for cattle. Ranching has been a way of life ever since. During the third weekend in May, Miles City holds the **Bucking Horse Sale** (☎ 406/232–2890), a three-day event with a rodeo and a giant block party where rodeo stock contractors come from all over the country to buy the spirited horses. The **Range Riders Museum** (⊠ Old Hwy. 10, across the Tongue River Bridge on west end of Main St., Exit 135 off I-94, ☎ 406/232–4483 or 406/232–6146) is built on the site of the 1846 Fort Keogh. It is open daily 8–6, from April through October and costs $5. It's jammed to the rafters with saddles, chaps, spurs, guns, and other cowboy paraphernalia.

PICTOGRAPH CAVE STATE PARK – Just 7 mi east of town, off I-90 (follow the signs from the Lockwood exit), is this rock outcropping and caves with ocher and black-and-white early drawings of figures, tepees, and wildlife. The complex of three caves was home to generations of prehistoric hunters dating back 10,000 years. More than 30,000 artifacts have been identified from the park. Rock paintings in Pictograph Cave, the largest of the three, can be viewed from a short paved trail. Be on the lookout for rattlesnakes; stay on the path and do not overturn any rocks. ☎ 406/245–0227 or 406/247–2940. 🎫 $4 per car. ☉ May 15–Sept. 30, daily 8–8.

Dining and Lodging

$–$$$ ✕ **Enzo Bistro.** Come to this attractive chalet-style building for new Mediterranean specialities like the Mediterranean meat loaf with basil, cumin, and kalamata olives, and kid favorites like pizzas and pastas. ⊠ *1502 Rehberg La., at Grand,* ☎ *406/651–0999. AE, DC, MC, V. No lunch.*

$ ✕ **Thai Orchid.** One of the few ethnic restaurants around, this Thai gem downtown features spices previously unknown to Montana. ⊠ *2924 2nd Ave. N,* ☎ *406/256–2206. MC, V. Closed weekends.*

$–$$ 🏨 **C'mon Inn.** Five hot tubs and an indoor pool attract families to this new lodging near the major roads and the interstate. Even in winter, it's a garden inside the woodsy, tropical courtyard. Continental breakfast is included. ⊠ *2020 Overland Ave., 59102,* ☎ *406/655–1100 or 800/655–1170,* ℻ *406/652–7672,* WEB *www.cmoninn.com. 80 rooms, 8 suites. Indoor pool, 5 hot tubs, gym, recreation room, meeting rooms. AE, D, DC, MC, V. CP.*

$–$$ 🏨 **Radisson Northern Hotel.** This historic 1905 building in downtown Billings was destroyed by fire in 1940, then rebuilt. Although remodeled, it still provides a sense of the city's past. Rooms follow an American West theme, with woven rugs, bedspreads, and a gaming table. Views are glorious. The massive fireplace is the centerpiece of a comfortable lobby—a common gathering place for guests and locals. The Golden Belle serves Continental cuisine in an atmosphere that's fancier than usual for Montana. ⊠ *19 Broadway at 28th St., 59101,* ☎ *406/ 245–5121 or 800/333–3333,* ℻ *406/259–9862,* WEB *www.radisson.com. 160 rooms. Restaurant, bar. AE, D, DC, MC, V.*

Nightlife and the Arts

The **Alberta Bair Theater for the Performing Arts** (⊠ 2801 3rd Ave. N, ☎ 406/256–6052 or 877/321–2074, WEB www.albertabairtheater.org) presents music, theater, dance, and other cultural events.

Outdoor Activities and Sports

Lake Hills (⊠ 1930 Clubhouse Way, ☎ 406/252–9244) has 18 holes of golf.

Shopping

Al's Bootery and Repair Shop (⊠ 1820 1st Ave. N, ☎ 406/245–4827) corrals your toes into fancy cowboy boots ranging from $50 to $1,800.

Rand's Custom Hats (⊠ 2205 1st Ave. N, ☎ 406/248–7688 or 800/ 346–9815) creates cowboy hats for working cowboys as well as the celluloid variety and will custom-fit a felt fur hat. Prices range from $300 to $2,000. Rand's also sells leather carrying cases.

Little Bighorn Battlefield National Monument

⑭ *60 mi southeast of Billings via I–90 to U.S. 212.*

When the smoke cleared on June 25, 1876, neither Lieutenant Colonel George Armstrong Custer nor his 200 or so blue-shirted troopers were alive to tell the story of their battle against several thousand Northern Plains natives on this windswept prairie along the Little Bighorn River. It was a Pyrrhic victory for the tribes; the loss would force the U.S. government to redouble its efforts to clear them off the plains. Now a national monument, and formerly called Custer's Last Stand, the site, on the Crow Indian Reservation, has a new interpretive display that includes material from recent archaeological excavations. The display explains what led to the momentous clash of two cultures and speculates on what might have happened during the battle. There are rattlesnakes around the area and also beware of touching the flesh-piercing yucca plants. ⊠ *U.S. 212, 15 mi from I–90, Exit 510, 3 mi south of Crow Agency,* ☎ *406/638–2621,* WEB *www.nps.gov/libi.* ⊡ *$10 per vehicle.* ☉ *Memorial Day–Labor Day, daily 8–9; Sept., Apr., and May, daily 8–6; Oct.–Mar., daily 8–4:30.*

The **Crow Fair and Rodeo** (☎ 406/638–2601) takes place in August in Crow Agency—the self-styled tepee capital of the world.

Red Lodge

⑮ *60 mi southwest of Billings via U.S. 212.*

Nestled against the foot of the pine-draped Pryor Mountains, Red Lodge
was named for a band of Cheyenne who marked their settlement with
paintings of red earth. It became a town in the late 1880s when the
Northern Pacific Railroad laid tracks here to take coal back to Billings.
At one time, "Liver Eatin' " Jeremiah Johnson, subject of much western lore and a Robert Redford movie, was sheriff here. Now the historic little burg is listed on the National Register of Historic Places and
is in the process of becoming a full-blown resort town, complete with
a ski area, trout fishing, horseback riding, and a golf course.

Each August, Red Lodge holds an eight-day **Festival of Nations** (☎ 406/
446–1718) to celebrate the numerous ethnic heritages of people who
worked in the mines nearby.

From Red Lodge, you can continue south on U.S. 212 over the precipitous **Beartooth Pass,** which winds its way through lush alpine
country to the "back door" of Yellowstone National Park in Wyoming.
The highway is usually open from May to September, but wintery
weather can close it at any time of the year.

Dining and Lodging

$–$$$ ✕ **Bridge Creek Backcountry Kitchen & Wine Bar.** This casual restau-
rant prepares gourmet dinners using all Montana naturally raised beef.
For lunch, try one of the three soup de jours such as smoked turkey
bisque, country dijon vegetable chowder, or clam chowder. ⊠ *116 S.
Broadway,* ☎ *406/446–9900. AE, DC, MC, V.*

$$–$$$$ ✕▥ **Pollard Hotel.** This 1893 landmark in the heart of Red Lodge's
  ★   historic district has been restored to the charms of an earlier era when
the likes of Calamity Jane and Liver Eatin' Johnson frequented the hotel.
Enjoy a drink in the History Room surrounded by photos recalling the
hotel's past. Reproduction Victorian furniture throughout vivifies a fin
de siècle feeling. Public rooms have handsome oak paneling and green,
brown, and gold flocked wallpapers. Balconies overlook the gallery and
fireplace. Arthur's restaurant ($$–$$$) specializes in steaks, chops, and
exotic game such as ostrich. The sautéed steelhead trout is served with
crayfish crème fraîche sauce and saffron-spinach rice. ⊠ *2 N. Broadway, 59068,* ☎ *406/446–0001 or 800/765–5273,* ₣Ａ₭ *406/446–0002.
39 rooms. Restaurant, bar, no-smoking rooms, hot tub, sauna, gym,
racquetball. AE, D, DC, MC, V. BP.*

$$–$$$$ ▥ **Rock Creek Resort.** After negotiating the cliff-hanging Beartooth Pass
Highway between the lodge and Yellowstone National Park, this re-
sort is a welcome respite. It's set along a babbling, rock-strewn creek
and is decorated in a southwestern motif. A historic old cabin holds
the wonderful restaurant—the Old Piney Dell. The menu features sim-
ple American, Mexican, and regional food. ⊠ *U.S. 212, on the
Beartooth Hwy., 59068, 4½ mi south of Red Lodge,* ☎ *406/446–
1111 or 800/667–1119,* ₣Ａ₭ *406/446–3688. 87 rooms. 2 restaurants,
2 bars, indoor pool, sauna, 4 tennis courts, basketball, soccer, volley-
ball, fishing, cross-country skiing, playground. AE, D, DC, MC, V.*

Outdoor Activities and Sports

While summer visitors swarm into Yellowstone National Park just to
the south, relatively few (except for dedicated backcountry travelers)
come to the Absaroka-Beartooth Wilderness. One reason is that, un-
like Yellowstone, the wilderness area has no paved roads leading into
it, although a four-wheel-drive vehicle is not essential for access. Mon-
tana's highest mountains, including 12,799-ft Granite Peak, are en-
compassed by the wilderness boundaries; because of that, the prime

hiking season (August) is relatively short. High-mountain lakes may remain partially frozen even into August. Perhaps the most popular hiking is in the East Fork–Rosebud Creek area (35 mi one-way), featuring numerous lakes in alpine basins above 9,000 ft. Hikes are moderate to strenuous, and remember, this is bear country. You can get information and permits from Custer National Forest in Billings, or Gallatin National Forest in Bozeman.

In winter, there are 40 km (25 mi) of skiing trails and a 2,350-ft vertical drop at **Red Lodge Mountain** (⊠ 101 Ski Run Rd., ☎ 406/446–2610).

The 18-hole **Red Lodge Mountain Golf Course** (⊠ 828 Upper Continental St., ☎ 406/446–3344) offers a beautiful view of the mountains.

Shopping
Magpie Toymakers (⊠ 115 N. Broadway, ☎ 406/446–3044) sells a dizzying array of dizzying toys, many handcrafted locally.

Big Timber

⓰ *81 mi west of Billings via I–90; 88 mi from Red Lodge via Rte. 78 north and I–90 west.*

People come to Big Timber to shop at its galleries and antiques shops, flyfish the blue-ribbon trout streams, or unwind in front of the Crazy Mountains (so called because supposedly a woman homesteader went crazy from living in such a remote setting). Explore the Boulder Valley and drop by the **Yellowstone River Trout Hatchery** (☎ 406/932–4434) to gaze at cutthroat trout. The **Sweet Grass Chamber of Commerce** (☎ 406/932–5131, WEB www.bigtimber.com) can provide information about sightseeing (a prairie-dog town and a natural bridge) in the region.

Dining and Lodging
$ ✕▥ **Grand Hotel.** This classic western hotel in the middle of downtown Big Timber features fine dining and an 1890s saloon. The rooms ★ are small, clean, and comfortable, and furnished with antiques—the kind of accommodations you might find over the Longbranch Saloon in *Gunsmoke*. A full breakfast is included in the daily room rate. The romantic restaurant ($$$) serves lunch, dinner, and decadent desserts. ⊠ 139 McLeod St., 59011, ☎ 406/932–4459, FAX 406/932–4248, WEB *www.thegrand-hotel.com. 10 rooms, 4 with full bath. Bar, dining room, meeting room. D, MC, V. BP.*

Livingston

⓱ *35 mi west of Big Timber via I–90; 116 mi west of Billings via I–90.*

The stunning mountain backdrop to this town was once Crow territory, and a chief called Arapooish said about it: "The Crow country is good country. The Great Spirit has put it in exactly the right place. When you are in it, you fare well; when you go out of it, you fare worse."

The railroads brought white settlers, and Livingston, along the banks of the beautiful Yellowstone River, was built to serve the railroad. The railroad has been replaced by small businesses that cater to tourists, but the town of 12,000 has retained much of its turn-of-the-20th-century flavor. Perhaps you'll recognize it from Robert Redford's movie *A River Runs Through It,* which was filmed here.

The old **Livingston Depot Center in the Northern Pacific Depot** is now a museum with displays on western and railroad history and works by artists from the region and around the country. The 1902 depot, an Italian villa–style structure, has mosaic trim, a terrazzo floor, and wrought-iron ticket windows. ⊠ *200 W. Park St., Exit 333 off I–90 and turn right onto Park St.,* ☎ *406/222–2300.* ⊞ *$3.* ☽ *Mid-May–Oct., Mon.–Sat. 9–5, Sun. 1–5.*

The **Yellowstone Gateway Museum,** on the north side of town in a turn-of-the-20th-century schoolhouse, holds an old caboose, a sheep wagon, a stagecoach, and other pioneer memorabilia. ⊠ *118 W. Chinook St.,* ☎ *406/222–4184.* ⊞ *$3.* ☽ *June–Labor Day, daily 10–7.*

OFF THE BEATEN PATH	**YELLOWSTONE RIVER –** Just south of Livingston and north of Yellowstone National Park, the Yellowstone River comes roaring down the Yellowstone Plateau and flows through Paradise Valley. Primitive public campsites (available on a first-come, first-served basis) and fishing access sites can be found at various places along the river, which is especially popular for trout fishing, rafting, and canoeing. U.S. 89 follows the west bank of the river, while East River Road runs along the east side.

Dining and Lodging

$$–$$$$ ✕ **Chathams Livingston Bar and Grill.** The enlightened Continental dining and the elegant artwork of landscapes create a comfortable experience in this old western town. Owner Russell Chatham is best known for his original drawings and lithographs displayed in the restaurant and down the block at Chatham Fine Art. ⊠ *130 N. Main St.,* ☎ *406/222–7909. DC, MC, V.*

$$$$ ▨ **63 Ranch.** This 2,000-acre dude ranch is one of Montana's oldest and has been owned by the same family since 1929. A full range of activities is offered by the working cattle ranch, from horseback riding to fishing to pack trips, but only weeklong packages are available. The eight rustic cabins are commodious yet comfortable, with log furniture and private bath. ⊠ *12 mi southeast of Livingston, Box MA979, 59047,* ☎ *406/222–0570,* ℻ *406/222-9446 or 406/222-6363,* ⒲ *www.63ranch.com. 8 cabins. Dining room, pond, horseback riding, fishing, coin laundry. No credit cards. FAP. Closed mid-Sept.–mid-June.*

$$$$ ▨ **B Bar Ranch.** For spectacular winter adventures in cross-country ski-
★   ing and wildlife tracking, this 20,000-acre working cattle ranch hosts guests in winter only. The ranch shares a 6-mi boundary with Yellowstone National Park, in Tom Miner Basin, 36 mi south of Livingston. Some of the 40 km (24 mi) of impeccably groomed trails are tracked by rare Suffolk Punch draft horses from the country's largest herd, here on the B Bar. Sleigh rides and naturalist-led trips into Yellowstone are some of the activities. Rates are per night, all inclusive, and require a two-night minimum stay. ⊠ *818 Tom Miner Creek Rd., Emigrant 59027,* ☎ *406/848–7523,* ℻ *406/847–7793. 6 cabins, 2 lodge rooms. Dining room. No credit cards. FAP. Closed Mar.–mid-Dec.*

$$$$ ▨ **Mountain Sky Guest Ranch.** This full-service guest ranch resort in the middle of scenic Paradise Valley and 30 mi north of Yellowstone National Park is a family favorite. Log cabins feel luxurious after a day in the saddle. The children's program for infants through teens offers age-appropriate activities like hiking, swimming, crafts, hay rides, campfires, and a talent show. Dinners range from Western barbecues to gourmet treats like grilled lamb loin topped with fig-and-port-wine glaze. Everyone learns to dance the two-step to a local band. There's a seven-night minimum stay in summer and a three-night minimum in spring and fall. ⊠ *Big Creek Rd., Emigrant, U.S. 89 29 mi south of I–90, west on Big Creek Rd.; mailing address Box 1128, Bozeman 59715,* ☎ *406/587–1244 or 800/548–3392,* ℻ *406/587–3977 or 406/333–4911,* ⒲ *www.mtnsky.com. 27 cabins. Dining room, pool,* *sauna, 2 tennis courts, hiking, horseback riding, fishing, children's program (all ages). MC, V. FAP.*

$–$$ ▣ **Murray Hotel.** In the old days, this downtown Livingston hotel
★   catered to Yellowstone visitors who came by train. Guests included Will
Rogers and the Queen of Denmark. Remodeled for comfort yet retaining
a distinctly western flavor, the simple, elegant dining room, the Winchester Cafe, is known for delicacies such as buffalo tenderloin. Public spaces re-create the hotel's 1904 beginnings with old photos and
memorabilia. Antiques reflect a different theme in each guest room.
One room has furnishings used in the film *A River Runs Through It.*
Another room commemorates the five years that director Sam Peckinpah lived at the Murray; it's decorated with movie posters and furnishings from the director's room. ⊠ *20 W. Park St., 59047,* ☎ *406/222–1350,* ⅎ͞A͞X *406/222–2752,* W͞E͞B *www.murrayhotel.com. 32 rooms with bath. Restaurant, bar, no-smoking rooms, hot tubs, gym, casino, meeting room. AE, D, MC, V.*

Shopping

ART GALLERIES

Livingston's beauty has inspired artists, as evidenced by the many fine
art galleries in town. The **Danforth Gallery** (⊠ 106 N. Main St., ☎
406/222–6510) is a community art center that displays and sells works
by local and regional artists. **Visions West Gallery** (⊠ 108 S. Main St.,
☎ 406/222–0337) specializes in western and wildlife art, including a
wide range of works on the fly-fishing theme, from paintings and
bronzes to hand-carved flies.

BOOKS

The floorboards creak as you walk through **Sax and Fryer's** (⊠ 109
W. Callender St., ☎ 406/222–1421), an old-time bookstore specializing in western literature. It's the oldest store in Livingston and also sells
gifts.

Bozeman

⓲   *25 mi west of Livingston via I–90.*

In 1864, a trader named John Bozeman led his wagon train through
this valley en route to the booming goldfields at Virginia City and southwest Montana. For several years it was the site of Ft. Ellis, established
to protect settlers making their way west along the Bozeman Trail, which
extended into Montana Territory. Recently the city has become a recreation capital for everything from trout fishing to white-water river rafting to backcountry mountain biking. The arts have also flowered here,
in the home of Montana State University.

The town has a strong western heritage, as displayed at local muse-
☙   ums, downtown galleries, and even the airport. The **Museum of the
Rockies** celebrates the history of the Rockies region. Eclectic exhibits
include everything from prehistory to pioneers and a planetarium.
Visitors can watch workers clean dinosaur fossils and see dinosaur displays of bones and eggs excavated in Montana. Children love the
hands-on science activities in the Martin Discovery Room and the
Tensley Homestead, with home-crafts demonstrations including butter churning, weaving, and blacksmithing. ⊠ *600 W. Kagy Blvd., south end of university campus,* ☎ *406/994–3466 or 406/994–2251,* W͞E͞B *www.museum.montana.edu.* ▣ *$7.* ☉ *Memorial Day–Labor Day, daily 8–8; Labor Day–Memorial Day, Mon.–Sat. 9–5, Sun. 12:30–5.*

Dining and Lodging

$$–$$$$ ✕ **Looie's Downunder.** In the historic downtown area Looie's is pop-
★   ular for both the atmosphere (casual and intimate) and for the food

(try the nightly specials like curried halibut with sushi and seaweed salad). ⊠ *101 E. Main St.,* ☎ *406/522–8814. AE, D, MC, V. No lunch.*

$$–$$$ ✕ **Spanish Peaks Brewing Co.** Plenty of cheery noise fills the cavernous hall of this brewery, a favorite hangout with the university's faculty and students. This is the home of award-winning Black Dog Ale and it serves brick-oven pizza, pasta dishes, and fresh seafood. ⊠ *14 N. Church St. at E. Main St.,* ☎ *406/585–2296. AE, DC, MC, V.*

$$–$$$ ⌂ **Gallatin Gateway Inn.** Built by the Milwaukee Railroad as a stopping-off point for visitors to Yellowstone National Park, this sumptuous inn is conveniently situated 10 mi from town on U.S. 191 and 30 minutes from Big Sky Ski Resort. It did have its dog days, however, when it fell into disrepair and became a seedy bar that featured female Jell-O wrestling (honest). Since 1987, the inn has recaptured its reputation. The uniquely furnished rooms have contemporary, modern western décor and are painted in soothing pastels. The bathrooms, with original tile work and brass fixtures, exude simple elegance. Crisp white linens and candlelight set the formal tone in the wonderful restaurant, which serves regional cuisine, while the Baggage Room Pub's casual fare compliments a day of recreation. ⊠ *U.S. 191, Box 376, Gallatin Gateway 59730,* ☎ *406/763–4672 or 800/676–3522,* ℻ *406/763–4672,* WEB *www.gallatingatewayinn.com. 34 rooms, 32 with bath. Restaurant, pub, pool, tennis court. AE, DC, MC, V.*

$$ ⌂ **Voss Inn.** This B&B occupies an elegant 1883 Victorian house and
★ is lavishly furnished with antiques and knickknacks. Stop by the parlor for afternoon tea or to catch up on the news with other guests who drop in to watch TV or to chat. Huge breakfasts are served in rooms or in the parlor. The lovely English garden makes a great spot for a quiet conversation. ⊠ *319 S. Willson Ave., 59715,* ☎ *406/587–0982,* ℻ *406/585–2964,* WEB *www.bozeman-vossinn.com. 6 rooms. MC, V. BP.*

Outdoor Activities and Sports

Backcountry Bicycle Tours of Bozeman (⊠ Box 4209, 59772, ☎ 406/586–3556) offers touring in the Gallatin Valley and all over the state.

Montana Whitewater (⊠ Box 1552, 59771, ☎ 406/763–4465 or 800/799–4465) provides guided raft trips and horseback/raft packages on the Gallatin and Yellowstone rivers.

SKIING

Bridger Bowl (⊠ 15795 Bridger Canyon Rd., ☎ 406/587–2111 or 800/223–9609, WEB www.bridgerbowl.com) is known for the "cold smoke," light, dry powder skiing. The terrain, from steep, rocky chutes to gentle slopes and meadows, is the headline act at this city-owned mountain, where lift tickets are half the price of upscale resorts. Every October, the ski area hosts the Bridger Raptor Festival to celebrate the golden eagle flyway along the mountain-range crest. Some days, over 200 goldens are spotted gliding the thermals.

Using Sno-Cat or helicopter services, **Montana Powder Guides** (⊠ 15792 Bridger Canyon Rd., 59715, ☎ 406/587–3096) leads expeditions into the snowy backcountry for untracked powder skiing and snowboarding.

Big Sky

⓳ *43 mi south of Bozeman via U.S. 191 and west on Big Sky Rd.*

Lone Peak, the mountain that looms over the isolated community beneath Big Sky, is an appropriate metaphor for the **Big Sky Ski and Summer Resort,** conceived over 25 years ago by the renowned TV newscaster Chet Huntley. Three village areas make up a solitary node of civilization in otherwise undeveloped country, between Bozeman and West

Yellowstone. One is in the canyon area along the Gallatin River and U.S. 191, and another, the Meadow Village, radiates from the 18-hole Big Sky Golf Course. The third enclave, 9 mi west of U.S. 191, is the full-service ski resort itself, looking into rugged wilderness areas, huge open ranches, and Yellowstone National Park. The 1,200 locals are used to driving nearly 50 mi to Bozeman for such simple pleasures as a fresh head of lettuce.

This is not to suggest that Big Sky is uncivilized. Indeed, being just a few decades old and still growing, the resort is quite modern in its design and amenities. It's not as if you can't get a daily newspaper, cable TV, or a substantial, well-prepared meal. Still, Big Sky is one of the most remote major ski resorts in the country. Getting to Big Sky invariably means at least one plane change en route to Bozeman and about an hour's drive to the resort. However, once you're here, a true wilderness awaits you. Yellowstone National Park is visible from the upper mountain ski runs. The park's western entrance at West Yellowstone is 40 mi from the town of Big Sky along a route frequented by elk, moose, and bison (use caution when driving Highway 191).

There's a lack of crowds amongst all this rugged nature, but you don't even have to give up the creature comforts of a warm bed and a good meal. Some major real-estate development around Big Sky may impinge upon that resort-in-the-wild atmosphere in the next few years, though. ⊠ *Westfork Meadows, Box 160100, Big Sky 59716,* ☎ *406/995–5000 or 800/548–4486,* WEB *bigskyresort.com.* ☉ *Thanksgiving–Easter, daily, 9:30–4.*

Dining and Lodging

$$–$$$$ ✕ **Buck's T-4 Lodge and Restaurant.** Within the historic log lodge and bar, this restaurant is known for its wild game (try the antelope satay) and steaks for dinner, and it's live jitterbug music after dark. ⊠ *U.S. 191,* ☎ *406/995–4111. MC, V. Closed mid-Apr.–May.*

$$$$ ✕▦ **Lone Mountain Ranch.** On mostly one-week packages, this resort offers just about any seasonal activity you'd like, including naturalist-guided trips to Yellowstone. The ranch maintains 75 km (45 mi) of groomed trails for classic cross-country skiing and skate skiing. There's an additional 4 trails totalling 10 km (6 mi) for snowshoers only. Downhill skiers catch a free shuttle to the alpine ski resort. Some activities are extra, like the fly-fishing with world-renowned, Orvis-endorsed guide Gary Lewis. Lodging ranges from rustic log cabins to new and elegant log homes. Nonguests are welcome in the log lodge dining room (try the bison steak or free-range chicken with gourmet ingredients), or to partake in a backcountry sleigh-ride, dinner, and entertainment. ⊠ *Box 160069, Big Sky 59716, 4 mi west of U.S. 191, 6 mi from Big Sky resort, and ½ mi down gravel ranch road,* ☎ *406/995–4644 or 800/514–4644,* FAX *406/995–4670,* WEB *www.lmranch.com. 23 cabins, 7 rooms. Restaurant, bar, no-smoking rooms, hot tub, hiking, horseback riding, fishing, cross-country skiing, Nordic school, sleigh rides, shop, recreation room, children's programs, travel services, airport shuttle. D, MC, V. Closed Oct., Nov., Apr., and May. FAP.*

$$$$ ▦ **The Big EZ.** Atop a mountain at 7,500-ft elevation, the Big EZ over-
★ looks the Gallatin River Drainage and mountains. Each luxury suite is appointed with western-style furnishings, an eclectic collection of fine art, and state-of-the-art technology including laptop computers and high-speed Internet access. The property includes an 18-hole, par-72 championship putting course and one of the state's largest outdoor hot tubs. Dinners are unusual, elegant, and savory: try pan-roasted caribou loin or African pheasant and save room for Tasmanian honey crème brûlée. The ranch is 17 mi from Big Sky and all sorts of outdoor activities can

be arranged. ⊠ *7000 Beaver Creek Rd., Big Sky 59716,* ☎ *406/995–7000 or 877/244–3299,* 𝖥𝖠𝖷 *406/995–7007,* 𝖶𝖤𝖡 *www.bigezlodge.com. 13 suites. Restaurant, in-room data ports, putting course, outdoor hot tub, business services. AE, MC, V. FAP.*

$$$$ ⊟ **Summit at Big Sky.** This slope-side and full-service hotel has rooms
★   that take in the full view of Lone Mountain and many of the ski runs. Spacious rooms and suites decorated with a Euro-western flavor fit the discriminating business and family traveler looking for lodging at the center of the mountain action. The best things about the Summit just may be the underground, heated parking garage, unusual in Montana, and the outdoor, year-round soaking pool. ⊠ *1 Lone Mountain Trail, 59716,* ☎ *406/995–5000 or 800/548–4486,* 𝖥𝖠𝖷 *406/995–8095,* 𝖶𝖤𝖡 *www.bigskyresort.com. 213 rooms, 8 suites. 2 restaurants, bar, kitchenettes, minibars, no-smoking rooms, refrigerators, room service, outdoor pool, massage, spa, golf privileges, gym, mountain bikes, downhill ski school, downhill skiing, ski shop, ski storage, shops, baby-sitting, children's programs, concierge, business services, meeting rooms, airport shuttle. AE, D, MC, V.*

Outdoor Activities and Sports

For cross-country ski gear, bicycling and hiking equipment, free advice, and coffee drinks and goodies all year-round, try **Free Heel and Wheel** (⊠ 40 Yellowstone Ave., West Yellowstone, ☎ 406/646–7744, 𝖶𝖤𝖡 www.freeheelandwheel.com), located just outside the park entrance gate.

A quieter way than snowmobiling to sight buffalo herds, trophy-size bull elk, moose, and other winter wildlife is within a comfortable van of the **Yellowstone Alpen Guides Co.** (☎ 406/646–9591 or 800/858–3502, 𝖶𝖤𝖡 www.yellowstoneguides.com). The naturalist guides also lead cross-country ski trips and summer trips in and around the park.

FISHING

On almost any day of the winter, no matter how bitter or nasty the weather, usually a dozen or more die-hard anglers lay out lines in the Gallatin River, which runs along U.S. 191. Rivers such as the Madison (one valley west), the Yellowstone (one valley east), and the Gallatin have made southwestern Montana famous among fly fishermen, most of whom visit during the nonwinter months. However, that's not to say the trout stop biting in winter.

Over 2,000 mi of rivers and streams, and hundreds of lakes flow within a 50-mi radius of West Yellowstone, where **Blue Ribbon Flies** (⊠ 309 Canyon St., West Yellowstone, MT 59758, ☎ 406/646–7642, 𝖶𝖤𝖡 www.blueribbonflies.com) has offered guiding, retail, and advice on fly-fishing for two decades.

Outfitting, flies, rods and reels, equipment rentals, and clothing are available at **Gallatin Riverguides** (⊠ U.S. 191, ☎ 406/995–2290 or 888/707–1505, 𝖶𝖤𝖡 www.montanaflyfishing.com), ½ mi south of the Big Sky entrance. Rental equipment and guide service is offered by **Lone Mountain Ranch** (☎ 406/995–4644 or 800/514–4644).

SNOWMOBILING

Far and away the most popular nonskiing activity in the region is snowmobiling into and around Yellowstone National Park. West Yellowstone (50 mi south of Big Sky) prides itself on being the "Snowmobile Capital of the World," and in winter there are more snowmobiles in town than cars. The most popular excursion is the 60-mi round-trip between West Yellowstone and Old Faithful which reveals only a small portion of the 2.2-million-acre park. **Yellowstone Tour & Travel** (⊠ 211 Yellowstone Ave., West Yellowstone 59758, ☎ 800/221–1151) offers an option of renting the low-emission, four-stroke-engine snowmobiles which are most suitable to the park and its 45-mi-per-hour speed limit. Longer-term rental packages include lodging in West Yellowstone.

Downhill Skiing and Snowboarding

For many years, the attitude of more advanced skiers toward Big Sky was "big deal." There wasn't nearly enough challenging skiing to keep expert skiers interested for long, and certainly not for an entire ski week. As a remedy, the Big Sky people strung up the Challenger chairlift, one of the steepest in the country, and then installed a tram to the summit of Lone Peak, providing access to an array of steep chutes, open bowls, and at least one scary-steep couloir. The tram also gave Big Sky the right to claim the greatest vertical drop—4,350 ft—of any resort in the country. Those changes now provide big action for experts.

None of that, however, has diminished Big Sky's otherwise easy-skiing reputation. There is, indeed, a good deal of intermediate and lower-intermediate terrain, a combination of wide-open bowl skiing higher up and trail skiing lower down. And as on the Challenger terrain, the skiing on these slopes is pretty unpopulated. There are 75 mi (45 km) of groomed downhill and cross-country skiing trails nearby at Lone Mountain Ranch.

The other plus about skiing Big Sky is its wide variety of exposures. Ski areas tend to be built on north-facing slopes where snow usually stays fresher longer, protected from the sun. In addition to these, Big Sky also has plenty of runs facing south and east, and the differing snow textures as a result make for more interesting skiing.

FACILITIES

4,350-ft vertical drop; 3,600 skiable acres; 10% beginner, 47% intermediate, 43% advanced; 1 aerial tram, one 4-passenger gondola, 3 high-speed quads, 1 quad chair, 4 triple chairs, 4 double chairs, 4 surface lifts.

LESSONS AND PROGRAMS

Half-day group-lesson rates at the **ski school** (☎ 406/995–5743 or 800/ 548–4486) are $35; a learn-to-ski package (half-day lesson, equipment rentals, and restricted lift ticket) is $50. Racing, powder, mogul, and snowboarding clinics are also available.

LIFT TICKETS

$55. Multiday tickets (up to six of seven days) are available, with savings of up to $5 per day. Kids 10 and under ski free with an adult who has purchased a lift ticket.

RENTALS

The resort's **Big Sky Ski Rentals** (☎ 406/995–5841) at the base of the mountain offers rental packages at $25, and performance ski packages at $39. Moderate rental packages (starting at $16 per day) are available from **Mad Wolf Ski & Sport** (✉ U.S. 191, 8 mi from ski area, ☎ 406/995–4369).

Nordic Skiing

BACKCOUNTRY SKIING

Lone Mountain Ranch (☎ 406/995–4644 or 800/514–4644) offers guided cross-country ski and snowshoe tours in the nearby backcountry as well as in Yellowstone National Park. Tours near Big Sky tend to cover steeper terrain, with opportunities for telemarking, backcountry skiing, and snowboarding and are best for experienced skiers. Tours in Yellowstone generally cover flat or gently rolling terrain, for which little or no cross-country skiing experience is necessary. In some cases, snow "coaches" (essentially, snow buses) take skiers from West Yellowstone to scenic parts of the park for skiing.

Cat ski adventures from Big Sky in the nearby yet remote Moonlight Basin run daily in winter by **Montana Backcountry Adventures** (⊠ 1 mi west of the resort at Moonlight Basin Ranch, in log cabin, ☎ 406/ 995–3880, WEB www.skimba.com) and access 1,800 acres of untracked powder ski terrain with views into the Lee Metcalf Wilderness Area.

TRACK SKIING

Lone Mountain Ranch (☎ 406/995–4644 or 800/514–4644) is a rare bird in cross-country circles. Not only are there 68 km (42 mi) of groomed trails, but the network is superb, with everything from a flat, open, golf-course layout to tree-lined trails with as much as 1,600 ft of elevation gain (and loss). Much of the trail network provides a genuine sense of woodsy mountain seclusion. If there is a drawback, it is that moose sometimes wander onto the trails, causing pockmarked tracks and occasional moose-skier confrontations. Another Nordic ski area, **Mountain Meadows Guest Ranch** (☎ 406/995–4997 or 888/644–6647, WEB www.mountainmeadowsranch.com), has 30 km (18 mi) of groomed cross-country and snowshoe trails as well as lodging in a beautiful new log facility on a mountaintop above Big Sky.

Three Forks

㉘ *29 mi west of Bozeman via I–90.*

Sacajawea, famed for helping Lewis and Clark, lived in the Three Forks area with the Shoshone before she was kidnapped as a child by a rival tribe. A plaque in the city park commemorates her contribution to the expedition's success.

The Madison, Jefferson, and Gallatin rivers come together to form the mighty Missouri River within **Missouri Headwaters State Park,** a National Historic Landmark. The Missouri is the country's second-longest river at 2,315 mi. Lewis and Clark named the three forks after Secretary of the Treasury Albert Gallatin, Secretary of State James Madison, and President Thomas Jefferson. The park has historical exhibits, interpretive signs, picnic sites, hiking trails, and camping. ⊠ *Trident Rd., 3 mi northeast of Three Forks on I–90, exit at the Three Forks off ramp, then go east on 205, and 3 mi north on 286,* ☎ *406/994– 4042,* WEB *www.fwp.state.mt.us.* 🎫 *$4 per vehicle (includes admission to Madison Buffalo Jump).* ☉ *Daily dawn–dusk.*

Within **Madison Buffalo Jump** historic site is the cliff where Plains natives stampeded bison to their deaths for more than 2,000 years until the arrival of European's guns in the West. An interpretive center explains how the technique enabled Native Americans to gather food and hides. Picnic areas provide a restful break from touring. Be on the lookout for rattlesnakes here, and avoid wandering off the paths; do not turn over any rocks or logs where the rattlers often hide. ⊠ *Buffalo Jump Rd., 5 mi east of Three Forks on I–90, exiting at Logan, then 7 mi south on Buffalo Jump Rd.,* ☎ *406/994–4042,* WEB *www.fwp.state.mt.us.* 🎫 *$4 per vehicle (includes admission to Missouri Headwaters State Park).* ☉ *Daily dawn–dusk.*

Lewis and Clark Caverns, Montana's oldest state park, offers some of the most beautiful underground landscape in the nation. Two-hour tours lead through narrow passages and vaulted chambers past colorful, intriguingly varied limestone formations. The temperature stays in the 50s year-round; jackets and rubber-sole shoes are recommended. The hike to the cavern entrance is mildly strenuous. The cave trip involves lots of bending and stooping. Bring a flashlight, although each cave area is lit during the tour. A campground sits at the lower end of the

park. ✉ *Rte. 2, 19 mi west of Three Forks,* ☎ *406/287–3541.* 🎫 *$8.*
🕐 *June–Labor Day, daily 9–6:30; May and Sept., daily 9–4:30.*

Dining and Lodging

$ ✕ **Wheat Montana.** One of the best lunch meals in the state is grown,
baked, and built where a local ranching family grinds their wheat into
sandwich bread and bakery items (try the gigantic cinnamon rolls). For
their efforts, Wheat Montana was named the nation's top farm in 2001.
Also for sale is grind-your-own flour from several kinds of wheat including "prairie gold whole wheat" and "bronze chief hard red spring
wheat." ✉ *I–90 at Exit 274,* ☎ *406/285–3614 or 800/535–2798. MC,
V. No dinner.*

Virginia City

㉑ *66 mi from Three Forks, via I–90 west, U.S. 287 south, and (at Ennis)
Rte. 287 west.*

Remnants of Montana's frontier days, Virginia City and its smaller
neighbor **Nevada City** are two of the most unusual attractions in the
state, with partially restored historic buildings, a boardwalk, and
stores stocked with 19th-century goods. When miners stampeded
into the state a month after the May 26, 1863 discovery of gold, one
of the places where the diggings were rich was in Virginia City's Alder
Gulch; the city prospered and eventually became the capital of Montana Territory. The success of the city enticed criminals, who held up
miners; in turn, vigilance committees—eager to maintain order—
grew, held lightning-fast trials, and strung up the bad guys. Some of
the graves of those hung by vigilantes remain atop Boot Hill overlooking
town. Nevada City has a smaller collection of historic buildings, a music
hall with fascinating coin-operated instruments, and all sorts of restaurants and shops. You can visit two towns on an old-time narrow-gauge
steam train, the **Baldwin Locomotive No. 12,** Montana's only operating steam locomotive run by volunteer crews. ☎ *406/843–5247,* 🌐
www.virginiacitychamber.com/train. 🎫 *$10 roundtrip.* 🕐 *Five trips
daily Memorial Day–Labor Day, select weekends.*

Butte

㉒ *53 mi west of Three Forks via I–90; 79 mi northwest of Virginia City
via Rte. 287 and Rte. 55.*

Dubbed the "Richest Hill on Earth," Butte was once a wealthy and
rollicking copper-, gold-, and silver-mining town, which during its heyday had an international population of 100,000, and by 1880, had
generated about $22 billion in mineral wealth. Today about 34,000
people live in the Butte-Silver Bow Country and cheer on a revival of
the historic district. Downtown Butte, a National Historic Landmark
area, has numerous ornate buildings reminiscent of the Old West
days. While meandering through the streets, consider this: Butte has
the dubious distinction of containing the largest toxic waste site in
the country—thanks to the old mining wastes. The city maintains a
strong Irish flavor, and its St. Patrick's Day celebration is one of the
region's finest.

The underground copper mines were dug up in the 1950s, creating the
Berkeley Open Pit Mine, which stretches 1½ by 1 mi and reaches 1,800
ft deep (and is filled with toxic water some 800 ft deep). A viewing
platform allows you to look into the now-abandoned, mammoth pit.
✉ *Continental Dr. at Park St.,* ☎ *406/723–3177 or 800/735–6814.*
🎫 *Free.* 🕐 *Daily 8–dusk, weather permitting.*

Keeping watch over Butte—as seen from the east ridge of the Rocky Mountains—is **Our Lady of the Rockies,** a 90-ft-tall, 80-ton statue of the Virgin Mary on the Continental Divide; it's lit at night. For a 2½-hour bus tour, stop by the visitor center, a nonprofit, nondenominational organization. ⊠ *3100 Harrison Ave., at the Butte Plaza Mall,* ☎ *406/782–1221 or 800/800–5239,* WEB *www.ourladyoftherockies.org.* ⊡ *Bus tour $10.* ⊙ *June–Sept., Mon.–Sat. 10 and 2, Sun. 11 and 2, weather permitting.*

OFF THE BEATEN PATH   **MONTANA AUTOMOBILE MUSEUM –** Part of a complex of museums based around the old state penitentiary, this one is a car buff's delight, formerly known as the Towe Ford Museum. Displays include more than 100 vintage Fords and Lincolns dating from 1903 to the 1970s, including such rarities as a Fordson tractor and a Model A snowmobile. Admission here also grants you passage to the Old Montana Prison, Frontier Montana Museum, and Yesterday's Playthings doll and toy museum. ⊠ *1106 Main St., Deer Lodge, 41 mi west of Butte via I–90,* ☎ *406/846–3111.* ⊡ *$9.* ⊙ *Memorial Day–Labor Day, daily 8 AM–8 PM; Sept.–Oct. and Apr.–May, daily 8:30–5:30. Hrs vary at other times of the year.*

Dining and Lodging

$–$$$ ✕ **Uptown Café.** Fresh seafood, steaks (try the Cajun prime rib), poultry, and pasta are served in this informal, smoke-free café. ⊠ *47 E. Broadway,* ☎ *406/723–4735. AE, D, MC, V.*

$ ✕ **Town Talk Bakery.** No visit to Butte is complete without trying a famous Butte pasty (pronounced "paste-ee"), a traditional miner's dinner of meat, potatoes, and onion baked inside a pastry shell. Several eateries serve these pocket-size meals, generally to go. ⊠ *611 E. Front,* ☎ *406/782–4985. No credit cards. Closed Mon.*

$$–$$$$ ⌂ **Fairmont Hot Springs.** If you have children, bring them to this re-
★ sort near Anaconda and 15 mi west of Butte. Although not much as far as architecture goes, it has naturally heated indoor and outdoor swimming pools, a 350-ft water slide, a playground, and a wildlife zoo in a beautiful setting. There's an 18-hole golf course on the grounds. ⊠ *1500 Fairmont Rd., Anaconda 59711,* ☎ *406/797–3241 or 800/ 332–3272,* FAX *406/797–3337. 152 rooms and suites. Restaurant, bar, coffee shop, 2 pools (1 indoor), massage, 18-hole golf course, 2 tennis courts, volleyball, playground. AE, D, DC, MC, V.*

$$ ⌂ **Scott Bed and Breakfast.** Once a miner's boardinghouse, this three-story, redbrick building has had its furnishings changed. Careful renovation left woodwork, doors, banisters, and many windows intact, yet the baths and furnishings are new. This cushy yet affordable B&B is Butte's oldest accommodation and provides extraordinary views of the historic district, the Rockies, and the Highland Mountain range. Early 20th-century boarders probably didn't get to appreciate the view—they slept three to a room for an eight-hour stay. ⊠ *15 W. Copper Ave., 59701,* ☎ *406/723–7030 or 800/844–2952,* FAX *406/782–1415,* WEB *www.butteamerica.com/scott. 7 rooms. Breakfast room, lounge, in-room VCRs. AE, D, MC, V. BP.*

Dillon

❷❸   *65 mi south of Butte, via I–90 west and I–15 south.*

Dillon is a capital of southwestern Montana's ranch country and the seat of the state's largest county, Beaverhead. Dillon began as a shipping point between Utah and the gold fields of Montana. Later, the Union Pacific Railroad shipped cattle and sheep from here to processing. Hiking and mountain biking lead into the nearby Ruby and Tendoy mountains. Blue-ribbon trout fishing on the Beaverhead River attracts thousands of flies and fisherman year-round. The **Beaverhead County Museum** exhibits Native American artifacts; ranching and mining memorabilia; a homesteader's cabin; mining equipment and agricultural artifacts; and a boardwalk imprinted with the area's ranch brands. ✉ *15 S. Montana St.,* ☎ *406/683–5027.* ◷ *Donations accepted.* ◷ *Memorial Day–Labor Day, weekdays 8:30–8, Sat. 12–4; Labor Day–Memorial Day, weekdays 8:30–5.*

OFF THE BEATEN PATH	**BANNACK STATE HISTORIC PARK –** Bannack was Montana's first territorial capital and the site of the state's first major gold strike in 1862. This frontier boomtown is now a state park and features historic structures lining the main street, and picnic and camping spots. Montana's vigilantes terrorized Bannack, led by the most notorious renegade, Sheriff Henry Plummer. The gallows on which he was hanged still stands. Rumors persist that Plummer's stash of stolen gold was hidden somewhere in the mountains near here and never found. To get to Bannack, follow Route 278 21 mi west out of Dillon and watch for a sign just before Badger Pass; take the well-maintained gravel road for 3 mi. ☎ 406/834–3413. ◷ $4 per vehicle. ◷ Park daily dawn–dusk; visitor center Memorial Day–Labor Day, daily 10–6; Sept.–May daily 8–5.

Big Hole National Battlefield

㉔ *87 mi southwest of Butte, via I–90 west, I–15 south, and Rte. 43 west; 10 mi west of Wisdom.*

One of the West's greatest and most tragic stories played out on this battlefield. In 1877, Nez Percé warriors in central Idaho killed some white settlers as retribution for earlier killings by whites. The Nez Percé, knowing the army would make no distinction between the guilty and innocent, fled—the beginning of a 1,500-mi odyssey. They engaged 10 separate U.S. commands in 13 battles and skirmishes. One of the fiercest of these was here at Big Hole Battlefield, where both sides suffered serious losses. From here, the Nez Percé headed toward Yellowstone. A visitor center overlooks the meadows of the Big Hole, which remain as they were at the time of the battle. Tepee poles erected by the park service mark the site of the Nez Percé village and serve as haunting reminders of what transpired here. Ranger-led programs for groups or individuals can be arranged with advance request. The park remains open for winter snowshoeing and cross-country skiing on a groomed trail through the battlefield's sights. ☎ *406/689–3155,* ⟪WEB⟫ *www.nps.gov/biho.* ✉ *$5 per vehicle Memorial Day–Labor Day; free rest of year.* ◷ *May–Labor Day, daily 9–6; Labor Day–Apr., daily 9–5.*

En Route If you're heading back to Missoula from Big Hole, take Route 43 west 16 mi to U.S. 93 for an 80-mi drive through the beautiful **Bitterroot Valley.** The route is flanked by scenic peaks—the Bitterroot Range to your left, the Sapphire Range to your right—and signs along the road mark abundant hiking trails. If you're in need of refreshment, stop in the small town of Victor at **The Hamilton, A Public House** (✉ 104 Main St., ☎ 406/642–6644), an authentic Scottish pub replete with fish-and-chips and a kilt-wearing owner.

Billings to Big Hole A to Z

AIRPORTS

Logan Field International Airport in Billings is the largest in the state and is served by Big Sky, Delta, Horizon, Northwest, Sky West, and United. Farther west, in Bozeman, Gallatin Field Airport is served by

Delta, Horizon, Northwest, and Sky West. Butte's Bert Mooney Airport is served by Horizon and Sky West.

➤ AIRPORT INFORMATION: **Bert Mooney Airport** (☎ 406/494–3771). **Gallatin Field Airport** (☎ 406/388–6632). **Logan Field International Airport** (☎ 406/657–8495).

BUS TRAVEL

Greyhound Lines serves communities along I–94 and I–90, east to west. Rimrock Stages serve most smaller cities from Billings to Helena, Great Falls, Missoula, Kalispell, and Whitefish. Karst Stage runs between Bozeman, Livingston, Billings, and Yellowstone. The 4 x 4 Stage makes custom summer runs and winter daily shuttles from Bozeman to Yellowstone National Park and points in between.

➤ BUS INFORMATION: **4 x 4 Stage** (☎ 406/388–6404 or 800/517–8243). **Karst Stage** (☎ 406/586–8567 or 800/332–0504). **Rimrock Stages** (☎ 406/442–5860).

CAR TRAVEL

Use I–90 for Billings, Livingston, Bozeman, and Butte. U.S. 89 and U.S. 212 link this region with Yellowstone National Park. Big Sky is 45 mi south of Bozeman and 50 mi north of West Yellowstone on U.S. 191.

EMERGENCIES

➤ CONTACTS: **Billings Deaconess Medical Center** (✉ 2800 10th Ave. N, Billings, ☎ 406/255–8400). **Bozeman Deaconess Medical Center** (✉ 915 Highland Blvd., Bozeman, ☎ 406/585–5000). **St. Peter's Community Hospital** (✉ 2475 Broadway, Helena, ☎ 406/442–2480).

TAXIS

City Cab serves Billings and All Valley Cab operates in and around Bozeman.

➤ LOCAL COMPANIES: **All Valley Cab** (☎ 406/388–9999). **City Cab** (☎ 406/252–8700 or 800/625–4838).

TOURS

Off the Beaten Path operates world-wide custom trips including naturalist-guided trips in Montana and Yellowstone, where guests stay at the region's finest lodging and guest-ranch facilities. Karst Stage in Bozeman conducts group tours of the state and one-day tours of Yellowstone National Park for individuals.

➤ CONTACTS: **Karst Stage** (☎ 406/586–8567 or 800/332–0504). **Off the Beaten Path** (✉ 27 E. Main St., 59715, ☎ 406/586–1311 or 800/445–2995, WEB www.offthebeatenpath.com).

VISITOR INFORMATION

➤ TOURIST INFORMATION: **Big Sky Ski and Summer Resort** (✉ Box 160001, Big Sky 59716, ☎ 406/995–5000 or 800/548–4486, WEB bigskyresort.com). **Big Sky Snow report:** ☎ 406/995–5900. **Billings Chamber of Commerce** (✉ 815 S. 27th St., Box 31177, 59107, ☎ 406/245–4111 or 800/735–2635, WEB www.wtp.net/bacc). **Bozeman Convention and Visitors Bureau** (✉ 2000 Commerce Dr., 59715, ☎ 406/586–5421 or 800/228–4224, WEB www.bozemanchamber.com). **Butte Chamber Visitor and Transportation Center** (✉ 1000 George St., 59701, ☎ 406/723–3177 or 800/735–6814, WEB www.butteinfo.org). **Livingston Chamber of Commerce** (✉ 303 E. Park St., 59047, ☎ 406/222–0850, WEB www.livingston.avicom.net). **Miles City Chamber of Commerce** (✉ 315 Main St., 59301, ☎ 406/232–2890). **Red Lodge Chamber of Commerce** (✉ 601 N. Broadway, Box 998, 59068, ☎ 406/446–1718, WEB www.redlodge.com). **Virginia City Chamber of Com-**

merce (⊠ Box 218, 59755, ☎ 406/843–5555 or 800/829–2969, WEB www.goldwest.visitmt.com or www.virginiacitychamber.com).

MONTANA A TO Z

To research prices, get advice from other travelers, and book travel arrangements, visit www.fodors.com.

AIRPORTS

Billings's Logan Field International Airport is the largest in the state. Gallatin Field Airport is just outside Bozeman. Glacier Park International Airport is in Kalispell, and has the best gift shop for Montana-made items. Missoula International Airport is the fourth major facility in the state.

➤ AIRPORT INFORMATION: **Gallatin Field Airport** (☎ 406/388–6632). **Glacier Park International Airport** (☎ 406/257–5994). **Logan Field International Airport** (☎ 406/657–8495). **Missoula International Airport** (☎ 406/728–4381).

BUS TRAVEL

Greyhound Lines carries passengers into Montana from all neighboring states. Rimrock Stages runs regular bus service between Missoula, Bozeman, and Billings.

➤ BUS INFORMATION: **Greyhound Lines** (☎ 800/231–2222). **Rimrock Stages** (☎ 406/549–2339 or 800/255–7655).

CAR TRAVEL

Primary routes into Montana from Idaho include I–90, I–15, U.S 2, and scenic U.S. 12. Interstate 90 enters the state from Wyoming. Interstate 95, U.S. 2, and U.S. 12 are popular access routes from North Dakota, and U.S. 212 is the route from the Black Hills of South Dakota.

Speeds are limited to 65 mph in urban areas and 75 in the wide open spaces. At night, the speed limit is 65. Going east to west, I–94 runs from the North Dakota border and into I–90 near Billings, where it becomes I–90 all the way to the Idaho border. Interstate 90, meanwhile, comes up from Wyoming to join I–94. From north to south, I–15 comes into southern Montana from Idaho, and it runs through Dillon, Butte, Helena, and Great Falls on its way to the Canadian border.

In Montana you may make a right turn at a red light, after stopping, unless there is a sign posted forbidding it.

EMERGENCIES

➤ CONTACT: **Montana Highway Patrol** can be reached at ☎ 406/444–7000.

LODGING
CAMPING

The Montana state highway map, which is free from gas stations, hotels, and Travel Montana, lists many of the state's campgrounds. The U.S. Forest Service and any of the national forest offices around the state can provide information on camping in Montana's forests.

➤ CONTACT: **The U.S. Forest Service, Northern Region Office** (⊠ Box 7669 Missoula 59807, ☎ 406/329–3511, WEB www.fs.fed.us/r1/).

OUTDOOR ACTIVITIES AND SPORTS
FISHING

Licenses are required for fishing. An annual, nonresident season license costs $45 and is good through February of the season it was purchased. A two-day license is $10 plus a required $5 conservation license for the first two days and $10 for every two days after that. A special tribal fishing license is required for both the Blackfeet and Flathead Indian Reservations. For more information, contact the Montana Department of Fish, Wildlife, and Parks.

➤ FISHING INFORMATION: **Montana Department of Fish, Wildlife, and Parks** (✉ 1420 E. 6th Ave., Helena 59620, ☎ 406/444–2535, WEB www.fwp.state.mt.us).

TOURS

Glacier Wilderness Guides and its affiliate Montana Raft Company lead trips through stomach-churning white water, and they often combine the adventure with horseback riding or hiking.

Big Wild Horizon Adventures is a wilderness guide service that specializes in one- to eight-day backpack trips into some of Montana's remotest wild places, like the Selway-Bitterroot Wilderness, Yellowstone, and the Sapphire Mountains. Expert guides discuss the plants, wildlife, and geology.

➤ CONTACTS: **Big Wild Adventures** (✉ 5663 W. Fork Rd., Darby 59829, ☎ 406/821–3747, WEB www.bigwildadventures.com). **Glacier Wilderness Guides and Montana Raft Company** (✉ 11970 U.S. 2 E, West Glacier 59936, ☎ 406/387–5555 or 800/521–7238, WEB www.glacierguides.com). **Montana Board of Outfitters** (✉ Dept. of Commerce, 111 N. Jackson St., Helena, MT 59620, ☎ 406/444–3738).

TRAIN TRAVEL

Amtrak's *Empire Builder* runs east–west across Montana's Highline, the most northern part of the state, on its way from Chicago to Portland and Seattle. Major stops along the route, which parallels U.S. 2, include Havre, Shelby, Glacier National Park—at East Glacier, Essex, and West Glacier—and Whitefish.

VISITOR INFORMATION

Travel Montana provides information and free publications, including a comprehensive directory of lodgings, guest ranches, campgrounds, outfitters, and special events. Get information and permits before hiking and camping in national parks.

➤ TOURIST INFORMATION: **Montana Department of Fish, Wildlife, and Parks** (✉ 1420 E. 6th Ave., Helena 59620, ☎ 406/444–2535, WEB www.fwp.state.mt.us). **Travel Montana** (✉ Dept. of Commerce, 1424 9th Ave., Helena 59620-0533, ☎ 406/444–2654 or 800/847–4868, WEB www.visitmt.com or www.wintermt.com).

➤ NATIONAL FORESTS: **Custer National Forest** (✉ 2602 1st Ave. N, Box 2556, Billings, MT 59103, ☎ 406/657–6200). **Gallatin National Forest** (✉ Federal Bldg., Box 130, Bozeman, MT 59771, ☎ 406/522–2520).

5   UTAH

Although 10 other states exceed Utah's 84,990-square-mi area, few, if any, can match the breadth and diversity of its topography. Around virtually every bend, mountains pierce the skyline. Oceans of sagebrush roll out to the horizon. Improbable canyons score the earth. Snow-white salt flats shimmer, lush evergreen forests rim alpine meadows, and azure lakes glisten in the sun.

Updated by
Kate Boyes
and Janet Lowe

GIVEN THAT SPECTACULAR SCENERY pervades virtually every corner of Utah, visitors can be thankful that much of the state falls under public domain. Federally owned lands include five national parks, seven national monuments, a national historic site, two national recreation areas, seven national forests, and more than 22 million acres held by the Bureau of Land Management (BLM). Add to this nearly four dozen state parks, and it's easy to see why there are unlimited opportunities to enjoy the great outdoors. Whatever your pleasure, you can do it in Utah.

Prior to 1847, Utah shared a history similar to many other western areas. It was home to the Ute, Navajo, Paiute, Gosiute, and Shoshone Indians. It had witnessed the birth and eventual disappearance of the Fremont and ancestral Puebloan peoples. Spanish expeditions had come and gone, and streams and river valleys were stalked by rough-and-ready mountain men. But on July 24, 1847, an event took place that would set Utah on a unique course. On that day, a small band of Mormons led by Brigham Young got its first look at the Great Salt Lake valley. Casting his gaze over the arid land, Young declared to his followers: "This is the place." Within hours the pioneers began planting crops and diverting water for irrigation, and within days Brigham Young drew up plans for what would become one of the most successful social experiments ever.

As members of the relatively new Church of Jesus Christ of Latter-day Saints (LDS), these pioneers had migrated west to escape religious intolerance. Establishing a new promised land adjacent to the Great Salt Lake, they were joined by tens of thousands of other Mormons in the two decades that followed. Many settled in Salt Lake City, while others were directed by Young to establish smaller towns in distant corners of the territory. To populate this particularly harsh land took an effort that was no less than heroic, but the reward was to be a society free from outside influence and control. Or so the pioneers had hoped.

Although the Mormons were determined to keep to themselves, their land of Zion was not to be. In 1862, U.S. troops were dispatched to Salt Lake City to keep an eye on them. In 1868, the discovery of silver in the nearby Wasatch Mountains led to a flood of prospectors and miners and, as a result, to the growth of riotous mining camps. In the year following, the completion of the first transcontinental railroad ushered in additional waves of non-Mormon ("gentile" in LDS terminology) settlers. By the turn of the 20th century, Utah's religious and social homogeneity had been effectively destroyed.

Today, because about 75% of all Utahns count themselves as members of the Mormon church, Utah is decidedly conservative. Utah was, for instance, the only state in the nation that placed Bill Clinton third behind George Bush and Ross Perot in the 1992 presidential election. Politics aside, Utah is not nearly as provincial as many nonresidents have come to believe. When it comes to hotels, restaurants, the arts, and other worldly pleasures, places such as Salt Lake City, Park City, and Ogden have no shortage of excellent options. A legislative overhaul has taken some of the sting out of Utah's infamous drinking laws, although many nightspots require that you purchase a temporary membership (the cost is about $5) before you can order liquor. Combine the state's burgeoning sophistication with its natural splendor, wealth of recreational opportunities, and a growing list of guest services and facilities, and it can safely be said that having fun is not prohibited in Utah.

Pleasures and Pastimes

Dining

There are a growing number of fine restaurants in Salt Lake and Park City, and culinary jewels are cropping up in various other areas. But generally, options lean toward more traditional, family-style eateries serving up meat and potatoes (and a little fresh fish). Having a drink with dinner is not a problem in many of Utah's metropolitan and ski resort restaurants, nor, at most places, is getting a table. Men might want to wear a jacket at the more expensive restaurants in Salt Lake City; otherwise, dress is casual.

CATEGORY	COST*
$$$$	over $30
$$$	$20–$30
$$	$15–$20
$	under $15

*per person for a main course at dinner, excluding drinks, service, and approximately 6½% sales tax (rates vary depending on location)

Lodging

Chains are everywhere. Other than that, accommodations are varied—from entire ski villages under one roof at some of the resorts; the tall, modern business hotels in downtown Salt Lake City; and historic bed-and-breakfast inns and modest motels that simply provide a good place to rest after a day of sightseeing.

CATEGORY	COST*
$$$$	over $225
$$$	$150–$225
$$	$75–$150
$	under $75

*Prices are for a standard double room in high season, not including the 4% tax and service.

Outdoor Activities and Sports

During winter, consistent powder snow brings skiers from all over the world to Utah's first-class resorts. Any of several ski shops in the Salt Lake City area offer reasonably priced rental packages, some for less than $10 a day for skis, boots, and poles. All resorts have rental equipment, but the prices are often one-quarter to one-half cheaper at outside rental companies, and the equipment is better. You're sure to get exactly what you want if you rent in advance from a nonresort company.

In the summer, Utah is filled with hikers, campers, and, increasingly, mountain bikers, and the same companies that outfit skiers in winter can supply summer travelers with everything from golf equipment to bikes. Perhaps most surprising in this second-driest state, boating on the many lakes, rafting on the rivers in the south and east, and fishing (for bass, pike, kokanee salmon, and cutthroat trout), are extremely popular activities. Golf courses are throughout the state, and reservations are generally necessary.

Parks

Utah has five national parks—more than any other state except Alaska and California. Though Bryce and Zion are the best known, fascinating landscape can be seen at Arches, Canyonlands, and Capitol Reef national parks. Utah's 45 state parks range from historic monuments to recreation areas, many of which have public lakes, often reservoirs, that are popular spots for camping as well as boating and other water sports. Officially, national and state parks are open 24 hours a day, but visitor centers are usually open 8–sunset.

Exploring Utah

Utah's landscape is remarkably diverse. Salt Lake City sprawls at the western base of the Wasatch Range. It's the largest in a string of cities known locally as the Wasatch Front. The Wasatch Mountains themselves form a rugged divider spanning the center of the state for 160 mi from north to south. East of the Wasatch Range, the landscape is dominated by the east/west-oriented Uinta Mountains and their foothills, which give way to the rural and ranching country of the Uinta Basin. Millions of years ago, dinosaurs rumbled through this part of the state. Today, their remnants have earned this region the moniker, "Dinosaurland."

All of Utah's national parks are in the southern reaches of the state, which typically offer a climate much more mild and dry year-round than northern Utah's. The geologic division known as the Colorado Plateau dominates the red-rock country of southeastern Utah, where the ancient Fremont and ancestral Puebloan cultures once made their homes. In the southwestern portion of the state, colorful deserts mingle with forested mountains and stretch north to meet the Great Basin.

Numbers in the text correspond to numbers in the margin and on the Utah, Salt Lake City, and Salt Lake City Vicinity maps.

Great Itineraries

IF YOU HAVE 3 DAYS

You'll have little trouble filling a day in and around **Salt Lake City** ①–㉖. Begin at the Great Salt Lake's south shore. During spring and fall migrations there will be hundreds of shore and wading birds. Back in the city, enjoy an early lunch at the historic Lamb's Grill Café, and then do some shopping at the ZCMI Center or Crossroads Plaza. Walk across the street to take a tour of **Temple Square** ① or to simply enjoy the beautiful grounds. A casual dinner at **Trolley Square** ⑲ could be followed by a movie, unless you'd rather take in a Utah Jazz basketball game at the **Delta Center** ⑮. In the morning drive to **Park City** ㉚ and spend the day skiing, golfing, pampering yourself at a spa, or browsing the shops on historic Main Street. Visit the Winter Sports Park to watch would-be Olympians train, or maybe try a ski jump or bobsled run yourself. In the evening, enjoy one of Park City's fine restaurants or clubs. On day three, swing down Provo Canyon to experience "rustic chic" at **Sundance Resort** ㊴, do a little shopping or golfing at Thanksgiving Point, then return to Salt Lake City in the evening for a horse-drawn carriage ride and an elegant dinner at the Metropolitan.

IF YOU HAVE 7 DAYS

It's difficult to experience all of Utah's best in only one week—better to choose specific parts of the state and give them your full attention. The two itineraries that follow do just that. The first begins in Salt Lake City and explores southeastern Utah. The second begins in Las Vegas and highlights the attractions of southwestern Utah.

After a morning of sightseeing and a light lunch in **Salt Lake City** ①–㉖, head toward **Park City** ㉚, stopping at the Factory Stores just outside town before checking into one of Park City's hotels or inns. Splurge on an elegant dinner at Deer Valley Resort's Glitretind or Park City's Grappa. Spend the next morning skiing, golfing, or just relaxing, then drive to **Sundance Resort** ㊴ for dinner and evening entertainment. Spend the night in one of the resort's elegant mountain cabins. After breakfast, drive south to **Capitol Reef National Park** (68). You should have an entire afternoon to hike and explore the park.

During late summer and early fall you can pick fruit in the pioneer orchards along the Fremont River. Overnight in nearby Torrey, dining at one of the tiny town's surprisingly good restaurants. In the morning, pick up some freshly baked bread and other picnic staples at the small store on Route 24, and drive east and north from Torrey to I–70 eastbound, then south on U.S. 191 to **Moab** (51). Choose a spot along the Colorado River to enjoy your picnic lunch beneath soaring sandstone cliffs. After lunch, head north on U.S. 191 and west on Route 313 to enjoy the view from **Dead Horse Point State Park** and the Island in the Sky District of **Canyonlands National Park.** The Colorado and Green rivers, thousands of feet below, flow through the incredible landscape they have carved. Toward evening, head back to Moab for dinner and a good night's sleep. On day five, join a day trip on the Colorado River, rent a bicycle, or head into the surrounding red-rock landscapes on foot, or with a guide in a four-wheel-drive vehicle. End your day with the guided Canyonlands by Night, a relaxing after-dark float on the Colorado, and overnight again in Moab. After breakfast and a stop at one of Moab's well-stocked grocery stores for lunch fixings, head north to **Arches National Park.** Between the stunning scenic drive, and the myriad hiking opportunities, there is plenty here to fill your day. On your final day, pick up a few souvenirs in Moab's various gift shops, or browse for southwestern art in any of several galleries. Then head north east from Moab along the **Colorado River Scenic Byway** (Route 128) to I–70, then west to the town of Green River. Grab a burger at Ray's Tavern, guaranteed to satisfy your appetite all the way back to Salt Lake City.

If you choose to explore southwestern Utah, embarking from Las Vegas via I–15, it is a 158–mi drive to Springdale, a small town at the southern entrance to **Zion National Park** (63). Remember to adjust your watch as Utah is one hour ahead of Nevada time. Spend your first two days hiking in Zion. On your third day, skirt through Zion's east side on Route 9, then follow U.S. 89 north to Route 14 and west to **Cedar City** (62). During the summer, don't miss the Utah Shakespearean Festival, including a Royal Feaste for dinner. If the festival is not going on during your visit, drive Route 14 through Cedar Canyon to visit **Cedar Breaks National Monument** (61), and have a meal at Milt's Stage Stop on your way back to Cedar City for the night. In the morning, take Route 14 and Route 143 to Panguitch, then continue east on Route 12 to **Bryce Canyon National Park** (65). You should arrive in plenty of time to explore the amphitheaters of Bryce on foot or horseback. Don't miss the spectacle of sunset on the colorful formations. From April to October, you can sign up for a chuck-wagon dinner at Best Western Ruby's Inn, then take in the nightly rodeo. Spend the night in the historic Bryce Canyon Lodge. From Bryce on day five, follow Route 12 east to **Escalante** (66) and across the **Grand Staircase–Escalante National Monument** to Calf Creek Falls, a perfect place to picnic. Continue north on Route 12, over Boulder Mountain. Take time to stop and savor the incredible views along the way. The town of Torrey sits at the junction of Route 12 and Route 24; overnight here, and in the morning, take Route 24 east to **Capitol Reef National Park** (68). Spend the day hiking and discovering the history of the Fremont Culture and the 19th-century pioneers, who both settled along the banks of the Fremont River, which runs through the park. Overnight again in Torrey. On day seven, travel back to Salt Lake City via Route 24, U.S. 50, and I–15, detouring across the **Nebo Loop Scenic Byway** (42) for an alpine diversion before rejoining the interstate.

Utah

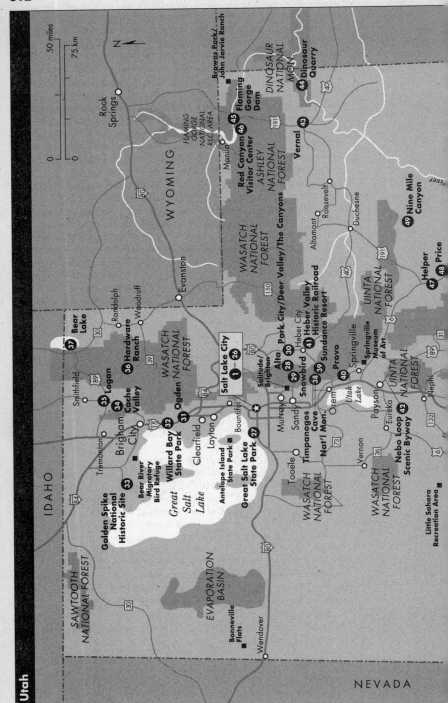

50 miles
75 km
0

N

IDAHO

SAWTOOTH
NATIONAL
FOREST

30

NEVADA

WYOMING

Rock
Springs

80

Evanston

Woodruff
Randolph

30

37 **Bear
Lake**

Smithfield
89
35 **Logan**
34 **Cache
Valley**

Tremonton
84
**Brigham
City**

Bear River
Migratory
Bird Refuge

33

32 **Willard Bay
State Park**
31 **Ogden**
15

WASATCH NATIONAL FOREST

39

36 **Hardware
Ranch**

**Golden Spike
National
Historic Site**

*Great
Salt
Lake*

Antelope Island
State Park

**Great Salt Lake
State Park**

Layton
Clearfield

Bountiful
84

27

Murray
Sandy

EVAPORATION
BASIN

Bonneville
Flats

Wendover

80

Tooele

WASATCH
NATIONAL
FOREST

73

Vernon

Manila

FLAMING GORGE
NATIONAL
REC AREA

45 **Flaming
Gorge Dam**
46 **Red Canyon
Visitor Center**

ASHLEY
NATIONAL
FOREST

191

DINOSAUR
NATIONAL
MON.

**Browns Park/
John Jarvie Ranch**

44 **Dinosaur
Quarry**

40

43 **Vernal**

Roosevelt

Altamont

Duchesne

UINTA
NATIONAL
FOREST

40

6

191

49 **Nine Mile
Canyon**

47 **Helper**
48 **Price**

150

Park City/Deer Valley/The Canyons

Salt Lake City
1–26

Solitude/
Brighton
28
29
30
Alta
Snowbird

**Timpanogos
Cave
Nat'l Mon.**

**Heber Valley
Historic Railroad**
11
Heber City
Sundance Resort
38 39

Orem
Provo
40
*Utah
Lake*

Payson

42 **Nebo Loop
Scenic Byway**

Eureka

132

6

89

31

Nephi

UINTA
NATIONAL
FOREST

**Springville
Museum
of Art**
Springville

36

WASATCH
NATIONAL
FOREST

Little Sahara
Recreation Area

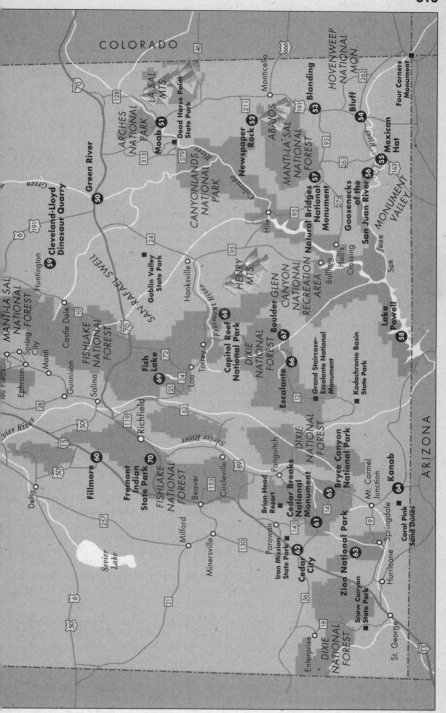

COLORADO

LA SAL MTS

ARCHES NATIONAL PARK

Moab **51**

Dead Horse Point State Park

Green River **50**

Cleveland-Lloyd Dinosaur Quarry **59**

Monticello

Blanding **53**

HOVENWEEP NATIONAL MON.

Bluff **54**

Four Corners Monument

Newspaper Rock **52**

ABAJOS

MANTI-LA SAL NATIONAL FOREST

Mexican Hat **55**

Natural Bridges National Monument **57**

Goosenecks of the San Juan River **56**

MONUMENT VALLEY

CANYONLANDS NATIONAL PARK

Hite

Hall's Crossing

Bullfrog

Lake Powell **58**

MANTI-LA SAL NATIONAL FOREST

Huntington

SAN RAFAEL SWELL

Goblin Valley State Park

Hanksville

HENRY MTS

GLEN CANYON NATIONAL RECREATION AREA

FISHLAKE NATIONAL FOREST

Castle Dale

Spring City

Manti

Gunnison

Salina

Mt. Pleasant

Ephraim

Fish Lake **69**

Torrey

Loa

Capitol Reef National Park **68**

Boulder **67**

DIXIE NATIONAL FOREST

Escalante **66**

Grand Staircase-Escalante National Monument

Kodachrome Basin State Park

Richfield

Delta

Sevier Lake

Fillmore **60**

Fremont Indian State Park **70**

FISHLAKE NATIONAL FOREST

Beaver

Circleville

Panguitch

Bryce Canyon National Park

Mt. Carmel Junction

Kanab **64**

Milford

Minersville

Brian Head Resort

Cedar Breaks National Monument **65**

61

Parowan

Iron Mission State Park **62**

Cedar City

ARIZONA

Snow Canyon State Park

Zion National Park **63**

Springdale

Coral Pink Sand Dunes

Hurricane

Enterprise

DIXIE NATIONAL FOREST

St. George

ARIZONA

When to Tour Utah

Given the different elevations and climates in the state, there's something to experience in Utah year-round, whether hiking the southern canyons in spring or fall, skiing in the mountains in winter, or doing anything outside of the desert in summer. The national parks can become crowded during the summer (and also hot). Early to mid-October is when you can have many of the trails and vistas to yourself and see the cottonwood trees turn a brilliant yellow.

SALT LAKE CITY

Nestled at the foot of the rugged Wasatch Mountains and extending to the south shore of the body of water for which it's named, Salt Lake City features one of the most scenic backdrops in the country, and is emerging as a prominent population and economic center of the Rocky Mountains. Within the last decade, the number of people living in the Salt Lake valley has climbed to more than 800,000. As a reflection of this growth, a dynamic skyline has sprouted, along with ever-widening rings of suburbia. Smog occasionally bedevils the town, and crime is present, but Salt Lake is working hard to maintain the charm of a small, personable city, and it is still an easy place to get around.

Just as Salt Lake has grown considerably in recent years, so too has it come of age. The downtown now features several high-rise hotels, Salt Lake restaurants serve up a whole world of tastes, and there is nightlife worthy of discussion. The Salt Lake arts scene is as prodigious as you'd expect to find in a city twice its size. All over town, fashionable retail enclaves are springing up. The community takes great pride in its NBA team, the Utah Jazz, and in the role it played as host of the 2002 Olympic Winter Games.

As with most Utah municipalities, Salt Lake City is based on a grid plan that was devised by Brigham Young in the 19th century. Most street names have a directional and a numerical designation, which describes their location in relation to one of two axes. Streets with "East" or "West" in their names are east or west of (and parallel to) Main Street, which runs north–south, while "North" and "South" streets run parallel to South Temple Street. The numbers tell how far the streets are from the axes. (For example, 200 East Street is two blocks east of Main Street.) Addresses typically include two directional references and two numerical references; 320 East 200 South Street, for instance, is in the east 300 block of 200 South Street. Three of Salt Lake's most prominent streets are named after the Mormon Temple: North Temple, South Temple, and West Temple, indicating that the streets run parallel to the north, south, and west borders of Temple Square. Main Street borders the square's east side.

The pervasiveness of the Mormon religion notwithstanding, Salt Lake City is not devoid of representation by other faiths. In the blocks east of downtown are three impressive houses of worship and mansions of the early Salt Lake's well-to-do. Dating back to 1871, the Episcopal **Cathedral Church of St. Mark** (⊠ 231 E. 100 South St.) is Salt Lake's oldest non-Mormon church. The Gothic-inspired **Catholic Cathedral of the Madeleine** (⊠ 331 E. South Temple St.) features twin spires, gargoyles, and plenty of stained-glass windows. The **First Presbyterian Church** (⊠ 371 E. South Temple St.) features beautifully crafted red sandstone construction.

Downtown Salt Lake

Although businesses and homes stretch in all directions, the core of downtown Salt Lake City is a compact, four-block-by-four-block area that includes several buildings central to Mormonism, two large shopping malls, historic buildings, and entertainment venues.

A Good Walk

If for no other reason than to orient yourself to Salt Lake's street system, **Temple Square** ① is a good place to begin a walking tour of the city. Across West Temple Street are two Mormon-owned and -operated institutions: the **Museum of Church History and Art** ② and the **Family History Library** ③. East of Temple Square across Main Street is the **Joseph Smith Memorial Building** ④. Dominating the block east of Temple Square is the **LDS Church Office Building** ⑤. Farther east, just across State Street, are **Brigham Young Historic Park and City Creek Park** ⑥. Two blocks south on State Street is **Beehive House** ⑦, Brigham Young's official residence. Many fine buildings stretch east on South Temple Street, a 15-minute walk which brings you to **Kearns Mansion** ⑧, now the Utah governor's residence. The tour of the residence and walk along the way make the detour worthwhile. A half block south of the Beehive House is **Hansen Planetarium** ⑨. A block and a half south, on the west side of State Street at 200 South Street, is the **Gallivan Center** ⑩, an outdoor gathering place with year-round activities. Continue south on State Street to the middle of the 300 South block, and turn right to see the **Exchange Place Historic District** ⑪. One-half block south on State Street, you can picnic or take a rest on the beautiful grounds of the **City and County Building** ⑫.

Salt Lake City's two enormous train stations underscore the two railways' fierce competition for dominance in the region at the time they were built. The **Rio Grande Depot** ⑬ is at the west end of 300 South Street. From there, head up 400 West Street for three blocks to get to the **Union Pacific Railroad Depot** ⑭. Heading back toward Temple Square, you'll see the modern **Delta Center** ⑮ at 300 West and South Temple Street and the **Salt Palace** ⑯ just south of South Temple Street on West Temple Street. These are the current and former homes, respectively, of the Utah Jazz. Each offers visitor information and brochures, as well as an opportunity to purchase good-quality Utah souvenirs.

TIMING

Allot half a day to enjoy this part of the city, not because it's a big area (it's not) but because it's historic, interesting, and pretty in any season.

Sights to See

❼ **Beehive House.** Brigham Young's home, a national historic landmark, was constructed in 1854 and is topped with a replica of a beehive, symbolizing industry. The Beehive House is open for tours throughout the year, and plans are underway to extend tour hours beginning in the summer of 2002. Many furnishings are original, giving visitors a fascinating glimpse of life in an upper-class polygamist household in the late 1800s. Young built the Lion House next door to house his 27 wives and 56 children; now a social center and restaurant, it isn't open for tours. ⊠ *67 E. South Temple St.,* ☎ *801/240–2672.* ⊠ *Free.* ☉ *Mon.–Sat. 9:30–4:30, Sun. 10–1.*

❻ **Brigham Young Historic Park and City Creek Park.** These tiny, twin parks divided by Second Avenue are a pretty diversion from the cityscape. Paths are inlaid with the footprints and names of native animals and birds, and a stone-lined stream drives a lazy mill wheel. ⊠ *East side of State St. at North Temple St.*

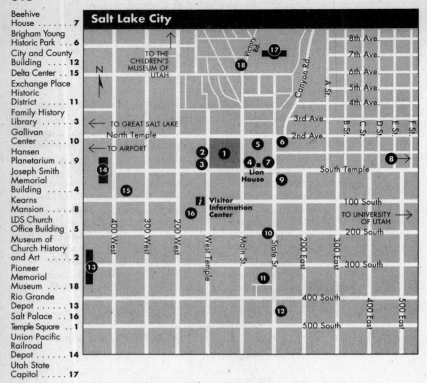

OFF THE
BEATEN PATH

CHILDREN'S MUSEUM OF UTAH – The goal of this museum is to "create the love of learning through hands-on experience," and that's exactly what it does. Children can pilot a jetliner, draw with computers, or dig for mammoth bones as part of the many interactive exhibits. ⊠ *840 N. 300 West St.,* ☎ *801/328-3383,* WEB *www.childmuseum.org.* 🖾 *$3.75; free after 5 PM on Fri.* ☉ *Mon.–Thurs. and Sat. 10–6, Fri. 10–8.*

12 **City and County Building.** This seat of city government is on Washington Square, the site where the original Mormon settlers circled their wagons on their first night in the Salt Lake valley. Said to be modeled after the London City Hall, the massive building has ornate details common to the Romanesque Revival style. Construction began in 1892 and took two years to complete. When Utah achieved statehood in 1896, the building served as the state capitol for 19 years until the current capitol was constructed. Hundreds of trees, including species from around the world, and many winding paths and shady seating areas make the grounds a cool downtown oasis. ⊠ *State St., between 400 and 500 South Sts.*

15 **Delta Center.** From the outside, this structure, built in the early 1990s, resembles an enormous block of ice. But from the inside, the views of the surrounding city and the Wasatch Mountains are stunning. The Delta Center arena seats 20,000 and is home court for the Utah Jazz and the WNBA Utah Starzz. Concerts, rodeos, ice shows, and other touring entertainments are also held here. An information desk and a gift shop are open daily. The gift shop stocks the city's best assortment of Utah Jazz basketball paraphernalia. ⊠ *300 W. South Temple St.,* ☎ *801/ 325-7328.*

THE MORMON INFLUENCE

FROM ITS BEGINNINGS IN 1830 with just six members, the Church of Jesus Christ of Latter-day Saints has evolved into one of the fastest growing religions in the world. There are more than 10 million members in more than 160 countries and territories. The church was conceived and founded in New York by Joseph Smith, who said God the Father and his son, Jesus Christ, came to him in a vision when he was a young boy. Smith said he also saw a resurrected entity named Moroni, who led him to two metal plates that were engraved with the religious history of an ancient American civilization. In 1827, Smith translated this record into the Book of Mormon, which was named for a prophet.

Not long after the Church's creation, religious persecution forced Smith and his followers to flee New York, and they traveled first to Ohio, and then Missouri, before settling in Nauvoo, Illinois, in 1839. But even here the fledgling church was ostracized, and Smith was killed by a mob in June 1844 in Carthage, Illinois. To escape the mounting oppression, Brigham Young, who ascended to the Church's leadership following Smith's death, led a pilgrimage to Utah, then a territory, with the first group arriving in the Salt Lake Valley on July 24, 1847. Here, under Young's guidance, the Church quickly grew and flourished.

In keeping with the Church's emphasis on proselytizing, Young laid plans to both colonize Utah and spread the Church's word. This work led to the founding of small towns not only throughout the territory but from southern Canada to Mexico. Today the Church continues that work through its young people, with most taking time out from college or careers to spend two years abroad on a mission.

Latter-day Saints believe that they are guided by divine revelations received from God by the Church president, who is viewed as a modern-day prophet in the same sense as other biblical leaders. The Book of Mormon is viewed as divinely inspired scripture and is used side-by-side with the Holy Bible. Families are highly valued in the Church, and marriages performed in the Church's temples are thought to continue through eternity. Though Mormons were originally polygamists, the Church ended the practice in order to gain statehood for the territory in the 1890s. Excommunication is the consequence for those continuing polygamy. In 2001, after publicizing his five-wife family on national talk shows, Tom Green learned that Utah authorities could in fact be moved to prosecute polygamy. Since the 1950s, Utah law enforcement had held a "don't ask, don't tell" policy regarding polygamy. Green's 2001 trial was the state's first polygamy trial since the 1950s.

Under the Church's guidance, Utah has evolved into a somewhat progressive, albeit conservative, state where the good of the Church is placed above most other concerns. Despite most states' belief that church and government should be separate, in Utah legislative leaders regularly consult with Church officials on key legislation. And the Church's opposition to alcoholic products has led to the state's peculiar liquor laws. To enter a bar that sells liquor, you first must purchase a "membership," usually for $5. Beer bars, however, do not require such memberships, nor do restaurants that serve food with liquor.

The population of Utah was 2,233,169 in 2000. While only about 50% of Salt Lake City residents belong to the Church, statewide the number is closer to 75% of Utah's population. The Church's influence has created a largely tight-knit state, where people generally are willing to help friends and strangers alike without hesitation.

— Kurt Repanshek

⑪ Exchange Place Historic District. With columns, carved figures, and both angled and curved corners, the massive stone buildings of Exchange Place are reminiscent of those of the Chicago Stock Exchange and New York City's Wall Street historic districts. This cluster of buildings reaching 11 stories includes Salt Lake's first skyscrapers, the Boston and Newhouse buildings. In the early 1900s this was one of the West's leading business centers, and Salt Lake City's center for non-Mormon commerce. Today, the quiet street has restaurants, small shops, and an art gallery. These "skyscrapers" of the past are easily dwarfed by surrounding structures. ⊠ *Between State and Main Sts. at 350 South St. Access is from State St. only.*

❸ Family History Library. Genealogy is important to Mormons because they believe in baptizing their ancestors, even after death. This library houses the largest collection of genealogical data in the world. Mormons and non-Mormons alike visit the facility to make use of the records for research. ⊠ *35 N. West Temple St.,* ☎ *801/240–2331 or 800/537–9703,* WEB *www.familysearch.org.* ☜ *Free.* ☉ *Mon. 7:30–5, Tues.–Sat. 7:30–10.*

❿ Gallivan Center. This outdoor plaza hosts daily entertainments including an ice rink, a giant outdoor chessboard, farmers' markets, lunchtime and evening concerts, and unique art projects for all ages. ⊠ *36 E. 200 South St.,* ☎ *801/532–0459.* ☜ *Free.* ☉ *Daily 7 AM–10 PM.*

❾ Hansen Planetarium. This stargazer's delight features various exhibits, including a moon rock display. There is a great book and gift shop and, of course, a domed theater. Special events include laser shows set to music and live stage performances. ⊠ *15 S. State St.,* ☎ *801/538–2104,* WEB *www.hansenplanetarium.org.* ☜ *Free; shows $2.50–$7.50.* ☉ *Mon.–Thurs. 9 AM–10 PM, Fri. and Sat. 9:30 AM–midnight, Sun. 11:30–6.*

❹ Joseph Smith Memorial Building. Once the Hotel Utah, this building on the National Historic Register is now owned and operated by the Mormon church. Visitors can use a computer program to learn how to do genealogical research or watch an hour-long film on early Mormon history and the emigration of Mormons to the Salt Lake valley in the mid-19th century. The center also has two restaurants and an elegantly restored lobby. ⊠ *South Temple and Main Sts.,* ☎ *801/240–1266 or 800/537–9703.* ☜ *Free.* ☉ *Mon.–Sat. 9–9.*

❽ Kearns Mansion. Built by silver-mining tycoon Thomas Kearns in 1902, this impressive French Chateauesque structure, built of oolitic limestone and sporting numerous turrets and balconies, is now the official residence of Utah's governor. In its early days, the mansion was visited by President Theodore Roosevelt and by dignitaries from around the world. A devastating Christmas fire in 1993 destroyed and damaged much of the mansion's interior. Restoration took three years and included faithful recreation of the colors and patterns used in the original decor, and of the golden dome that illuminates the multistory central stairwell. ⊠ *603 E. South Temple St.,* ☎ *801/538–1005.* ☜ *Free.* ☉ *Tours Apr.–Nov., Tues. and Thurs. 2–4.*

❺ LDS Church Office Building. Standing 28 stories high, this is one of Salt Lake's tallest structures. Although there is not a lot to see here, tours do include a visit to an observation deck on the 26th floor. Separate tours of the lovely gardens on the building's plaza are offered spring through fall. Indicative of the breadth of the church's business dealings, this building has its own zip code just to deal with the volume of mail it receives. ⊠ *50 E. North Temple St.,* ☎ *801/240–2190.* ☜ *Free.* ☉ *June–Aug., Mon.–Sat. 9–4:30; Sept.–May, weekdays 9–4:30.*

❷ Museum of Church History and Art. The museum houses a variety of artifacts and works of art related to the history and doctrine of the Mormon faith, including belongings of church leaders Joseph Smith, Brigham Young, and others. There are also samples of Mormon coins and scrip used as standard commerce in Utah during the 1800s, and beautiful examples of quilting, embroidery, and other handwork. Upstairs galleries exhibit the works of Mormon artists from all over the world, on both religious and secular themes. ⌧ *45 N. West Temple St.,* ☎ *801/240–3310.* ⊡ *Free.* ⊙ *Weekdays 9–9, weekends 10–7.*

❸ Rio Grande Depot. This 1910 depot was built to compete with the showy Union Pacific Railroad Depot three blocks north. It houses the **Utah State Historical Society Museum,** which has rotating exhibits on various aspects of the history of Utah and of the West. An eclectic gift shop is packed with tidbits of history, from Victorian paper-doll reproductions to scholarly tomes and sepia-tone photographs printed from the Historical Society's extensive collection. ⌧ *300 S. Rio Grande St.,* ☎ *801/533–3500.* ⊡ *Free.* ⊙ *Weekdays 8–5, Sat. 10–3.*

❻ Salt Palace. The former home of the National Basketball Association's Utah Jazz has received a massive face-lift and expansion, and it is now an elegant convention center that includes a ballroom. Frequently the site of large consumer shows, community events, and factory-outlet sales, it also has a conveniently located visitor information outlet and a gift shop offering Utah-theme books and gifts of better than average quality. ⌧ *100 S. West Temple St.,* ☎ *801/534–4777,* WEB *www.saltpalace.com.*

❶ Temple Square. Brigham Young chose this spot for a temple upon arriving in the Salt Lake valley, but work on the building did not begin for another six years. Constructed with blocks of granite hauled by oxen and then by train from Little Cottonwood Canyon, the Mormon Temple took 40 years to the day to complete. Its walls measure 16 ft thick at the base. Perched 210 ft above ground level is a golden statue of the trumpeting angel Moroni. Off-limits to all but faithful followers of the Mormon religion, the temple is used for marriages, baptisms, and other religious functions. Non-Mormons can learn more about the activities within the temple at the North and South visitor centers. Dioramas, photos of the temple interior, a baptismal font, and other displays offer considerable insight into the Mormon religion.

Other buildings of interest at Temple Square include the **Assembly Hall,** which was completed in 1882 with leftover granite from the temple, and the **Tabernacle,** home of the world-renowned Mormon Tabernacle Choir. This unusual dome-shape structure was built in the 1860s as a meeting place. Void of interior supports, the 8,000-seat building is known for its exquisite acoustics.

As impressive as the architectural trappings of Temple Square are, don't forget to enjoy the quiet environs of the 10-acre grounds themselves. Don't be surprised if a member of the church politely inquires about any interest you might have in learning more about Mormonism. ⌧ *50 W. North Temple St.,* ☎ *801/240–2534.* ⊡ *Free.* ⊙ *Daily 9 AM–9 PM.*

❹ Union Pacific Railroad Depot. This now-vacant depot, built in 1909 at a cost of $300,000, is a vivid monument to the importance that the railroad played in the settling of Utah and the West. The black, slate-shingle mansard roof sets a distinctive French Second Empire tone for the exterior. Inside, western-theme murals and stained-glass windows create a setting rich with color and texture. ⌧ *South Temple and 400 West Sts.*

Capitol Hill and the University of Utah

A Good Tour

North of downtown but still within walking distance is the **Utah State Capitol** ⑰, one of the nation's finest examples of Renaissance Revival architecture. Also on Capitol Hill is the **Pioneer Memorial Museum** ⑱. The next stops are best reached by car. About 10 blocks south of Capitol Hill at 600 South, then six blocks east on 700 East Street, is another of the town's historical treasures, **Trolley Square** ⑲, now a shopping, restaurant, and entertainment complex. From here, head south on 700 East to 900 South Street to get to expansive Liberty Park and the **Tracy Aviary** ⑳. Continue east on 900 South Street and then turn north on 1300 East to reach the campus of the **University of Utah** and its **Utah Museum of Natural History** ㉑ and **Utah Museum of Fine Art** ㉒.

Next to the University of Utah Medical Center, on the east side of campus, is **Ft. Douglas** ㉓, set up by Union-loyal westerners to keep an eye on the Mormon settlers during the Civil War. Take Connor Road, which begins on the south side of the medical center, for a six-block tour of the fort complex. Stay on Connor Road for one long block beyond the fort to reach **Red Butte Garden and Arboretum** ㉔. Past the gardens, turn west on Wakara Way, follow it one block to Arapeen Drive, then turn south on Arapeen Drive and follow it for half a mile to Sunnyside Avenue; at Sunnyside Avenue, turn east and continue on for half a mile to **This Is The Place Heritage Park** ㉕, which commemorates the Mormons' arrival in Salt Lake. Directly south across Sunnyside Avenue, just east of the state park entrance, is **Utah's Hogle Zoo** ㉖.

TIMING

Though it is somewhat spread out, the points of interest are in clusters, and their diversity make for a wonderful way to spend an entire day. Try exploring the Capitol Hill attractions in the morning and save Trolley Square, the aviary, or the zoo for the lunch hour, as they are the most likely spots to find a meal or snack. Visit the museums at the University of Utah in the afternoon because fewer students attend in the afternoon than in the morning, so parking is more plentiful. Because of its location in the eastern foothills of the city, early evening is a good time to visit the zoo and Red Butte Gardens and Arboretum; watch for the sunset alpenglow on the Wasatch Mountains. In the evenings at This Is The Place Heritage Park, there are special activities, such as Dutch-oven cookouts, hay rides, or candlelight tours during the holiday season.

Sights to See

㉓ **Ft. Douglas.** Established in 1862, this former military post resulted from strained relations between the U.S. government and the Mormon settlers. Acting on the assumption that Brigham Young might side with the Confederates during the Civil War, a brigade of California and Nevada Union volunteers set up shop on this site to keep an eye on things. During their free time, the soldiers took to prospecting in the nearby mountains, which in turn led to the establishment of such mining camps as Park City. Today Ft. Douglas showcases several examples of military architecture spread out across manicured grounds. There's also a small museum highlighting the fort's military history. ⊠ *East side of Wasatch Blvd. at 300 South St.,* ☎ *801/581–1710,* WEB *www.fortdouglas.org.* ☉ *Grounds: daily dawn till dusk; museum: Tues.–Sat. noon–4.*

⑱ **Pioneer Memorial Museum.** Featuring four floors of exhibits, many of which relate to Mormon pioneers, the museum has one of the most extensive collections of settlement-era relics in the West. The museum's

Salt Lake City Vicinity

38 rooms, plus carriage house, include clothing, household furnishings, tools, wagons, carriages, and farm machinery. ⊠ *300 N. Main St.,* ☎ *801/538–1050.* 🖾 *Free, but donations accepted.* ☉ *Mon.–Sat. 9–5.*

24 Red Butte Garden and Arboretum. With 25 acres of gardens and 125 undeveloped acres, the grounds provide many pleasurable hours of strolling through flora from around the world. Of special interest are the Perennial, Fragrance, and Medicinal gardens, the Daylily Collection, the Water Pavilion, and the children's garden. Lectures for gardeners—on bugs and gardening in arid climates, among other topics—and concerts take place regularly. Trails access the natural areas that were closed to the public for more than a century when Ft. Douglas was an active military base. The vegetation was protected, and the areas give you a clear idea of what northern Utah looked like before extensive human occupation tailored it to its purposes. The trails also access nearby mountain terrain. ⊠ *Enter on Wakara Way, east of Foothill Dr.,* ☎ *801/585–0556,* 🌐 *www.redbutte.utah.edu.* 🖾 *$5.* ☉ *May–Sept., Mon.–Sat. 9–8, Sun. 9–5; Oct.–Apr., Tues.–Sun. 10–5.*

25 This Is The Place Heritage Park. Certainly Utah's premier historic park, this compound includes Old Deseret Village, a re-created community typical of Utah in the mid- to late 1800s, where almost 200 volunteers dressed in period clothing show visitors what life was like during pioneer days. Artisans and craftspeople demonstrate their skills in historic buildings, and carriage rides and daily events are offered. An impressive monument depicts Brigham Young and other Mormon settlers entering the valley that was to become their home; around it a ring of smaller stone pedestals are topped with statues of Native Americans, explorers of the West, and mountain men. ⊠ *2601 Sunnyside Ave.,* ☎ *801/584–8391,* 🌐 *parks.state.ut.us.* 🖾 *$6 per vehicle.* ☉ *Daily 7:30–dusk; some special evening activities offered.*

⑳ Tracy Aviary. Set on 7½ acres, this facility features some 133 species of birds from around the globe: ostriches, bald eagles, flamingos, parrots, several types of waterfowl, and many more. There are two free-flight bird shows daily during the summer. ⊠ *600 E. 900 South St.,* ☎ *801/596–8500,* WEB *www.tracyaviary.org.* ⊡ *$3.* ☉ *Nov.–Mar., daily 9–4:30; Apr.–Oct., daily 9–6.*

⑲ Trolley Square. From 1908 to 1945, this sprawling redbrick structure housed nearly 150 trolleys and electric trains for the Utah Light and Railway Company. In the face of more contemporary modes of transport, however, the facility was closed. After a complete overhaul, the mission-style edifice reopened in 1972 and today is home to a collection of more than 100 boutiques, shops, and restaurants, making it one of the more intriguing retail centers in the West. ⊠ *600 S. 700 East St.,* ☎ *801/521–9877.* ☉ *Mon.–Sat. 10–9, Sun. 12–5.*

㉒ Utah Museum of Fine Art. In the spring of 2001, this museum moved into a new 74,000-square-ft facility, giving it twice as much space and over 20 galleries. Special exhibits are mounted regularly and the permanent collection includes ancient Egyptian, Grecian, and Roman relics; Italian Renaissance paintings; Chinese ceramics and scrolls; traditional Japanese screens; sculptures from Cambodia and Thailand; Navajo rugs; and works from Europe, Africa, and Latin America. A new endowment for 20th century American art has brought in works by Jasper Johns and Helen Frankenthaler, among others. Other new features include a café and sculpture court. ⊠ *410 Campus Center Dr. (a continuation of 400 South St.), just south of Marriott Library,* ☎ *801/581–7332,* WEB *www.utah.edu/umfa.* ⊡ *Free.* ☉ *Weekdays 10–5, weekends noon–5.*

㉑ Utah Museum of Natural History. Any kid or hobbyist who has spent some idle moments searching for arrowheads will be well rewarded here. With over 750,000 pieces—many gained during the 1800s—that represent almost 3,000 archaeological sites, the anthropology collection is one of the best in the West. Exhibits focus on the prehistoric inhabitants of the Colorado Plateau and Great Basin areas and other southwestern locations. The dry climate of Utah preserved for centuries not only the houses and religious structures of these peoples, but also their clothing, foodstuffs, toys, weapons, and fragile ceremonial objects. The dryness preserves dinosaur bones and fossils just as well. In the basement are thousands of specimens, dominated by creatures from the Late Jurassic period, many from the Cleveland-Lloyd quarry. Collections of rocks, minerals, and other fossils round out the museum. Utah wildlife is also well represented, and you can even learn why modern-day residents of this state are so enamored of seagulls. ⊠ *1340 E. 200 South St., on President's Circle,* ☎ *801/581–4303,* WEB *www.umnh.utah.edu.* ⊡ *$4.* ☉ *Mon.–Sat. 9:30–5:30, Sun. noon–5.*

☾ ㉖ Utah's Hogle Zoo. The zoo houses more than 1,400 animals, big and small, from all over the world. Most visitors are drawn at once to the outdoor polar bear exhibit, where one of the zoo's newest additions, Anana, a cub born at the zoo in 2000, stays close to her mother's side. In the primate forest, spider, colobus, and capuchin monkeys romp back and forth between an indoor and outdoor area. A children's zoo, an outdoor Discovery Area with interactive exhibits, and frequent live presentations about animals and the zoo's species preservation efforts make visits informative and engaging for both adults and children. During the summer, youngsters enjoy riding the miniature train, which takes them on a tour of the zoo. ⊠ *2600 E. Sunnyside Ave.,* ☎ *801/582–1631.* ⊡ *$7.* ☉ *Daily 9–5.*

⓱ **Utah State Capitol.** In 1912, after the state happened upon $800,000 in inheritance taxes from the estate of Union Pacific Railroad president Edward Harriman, work was begun on the marvelous Renaissance Revival structure that tops Capitol Hill. Beneath the 165-ft-high rotunda is a series of murals, commissioned as part of the WPA project during the Depression, that depict the state's history. Tours provide background information about the Capitol building and its exhibits, and allow visitors to enter the House and Senate chambers and other areas of the building that are generally off limits, including the State Reception Room, nicknamed the Gold Room because of its decor. From the steps outside the Capitol, you get a marvelous view of the entire Salt Lake valley. ✉ *Capitol Hill, 400 N. State St.,* ☎ *801/538–3000.* 🎫 *Free.* ☉ *Daily 8 AM–8 PM; tours weekdays 9–4, every ½ hr.*

OFF THE BEATEN PATH

WHEELER HISTORIC FARM – Come here to experience 1890s-era farm life by taking an "afternoon chores tour," trying your hand at milking a cow, or riding a draft horse–drawn wagon. ✉ *6351 S. 900 East St.,* ☎ *801/264–2212,* 🌐 *www.wheelerfarm.com.* 🎫 *Free; $1 for special events.* ☉ *Mon.–Sat. 10–5.*

Side Trips from Salt Lake City

Depending on your point of view, the **Bingham Canyon Copper Mine** is either a marvel of human engineering or simply a great big eyesore. This enormous open-pit mine measures nearly 2½ mi across and ½ mi deep—the result of removing 5 billion tons of rock. Since operations began nearly 90 years ago by the Kennecott Utah Copper company, more than 12 million tons of copper have been produced. Visitors may view the mine from an overlook, but be sure to check on hours before making the 22-mi trip out there (take I–15 to the 7200 South exit; drive south to 7800 South, then west to Route 48, which leads to the mine). At the visitor center, exhibits and multimedia presentations explain the history and present-day operation of the mine. Outside, cranes the size of large dinosaurs and trucks as tall as some apartment buildings continue to tear down and reshape the mountain. ✉ *Rte. 48, Copperton,* ☎ *801/252–3234.* 🎫 *$2 per vehicle.* ☉ *Apr.–Oct., daily 8 AM–8 PM.*

⓱ As one of the West's most unusual natural features, the Great Salt Lake is second only to the Dead Sea in saltiness. (It is up to eight times saltier than the ocean.) Ready access to this wonder is possible at the **Great Salt Lake State Park,** 16 mi west of Salt Lake City, on the lake's south shore. Here a marina allows you to set sail across the buoyant water on group or charter tours, some that include meals, ranging from one to six hours or more in length—with a range of reasonable prices to match. **Salt Island Adventures** (Marina store, ☎ 801/252–9336, 🌐 www.gslcruises.com) runs cruises weekdays from 9 to 5 and weekends from 10 to 5, between March and December. This is primarily a park for boaters; if you want to test the buoyancy of the water by swimming, try the beaches at Antelope Island State Park. What makes the lake so salty? Because there is no outlet to the ocean, salts and other minerals carried down by rivers and streams become concentrated in this enormous evaporation pond. ✉ *Frontage Rd., 2 mi east of I–80, Exit 104,* ☎ *801/250–1898.* 🎫 *Free.* ☉ *Daily 7 AM–10 PM.*

Jordan River State Park, a 5-mi riverside walkway and outdoor activity area accessed from North Temple Street at Redwood Road (1700 West St.), runs from North Temple Street to 2200 North Street. It has jogging paths, canoeing, picnic facilities, a golf course, and bicycling areas. Like the river in the Middle East for which it's named, Utah's Jordan River runs from fresh water (Utah Lake) to salt (Great Salt Lake).

✉ *1084 N. Redwood Rd., Salt Lake City,* ☏ *801/533–4496.* ✉ *Free.* ☉ *Daily dawn–dusk.*

Calling itself the largest amusement park between Kansas City and the West Coast, **Lagoon** includes all the rides and attractions you'd expect, plus the adjacent Lagoon-A-Beach water park. In operation for more than a century, Lagoon is a Utah landmark. The Sky Scraper, Colossus, and Cliffhanger rides, along with the Pioneer Village and a fine concert series, draw visitors back again and again. Amusement park veterans can pump up their adrenaline at the X-venture Zone "adventures" that fuse extreme sports challenges with traditional amusement park rides. ✉ *375 N. Lagoon Dr., Farmington, 14 mi north of Salt Lake City, Exit 326 off I–15,* ☏ *801/451–8000 or 800/748–5246,* WEB *www.lagoonpark.com.* ✉ *$24–$30.* ☉ *June–late Aug., daily 10* AM–*midnight; May, late Aug–Oct., days and hours vary, call ahead.*

From I–15, **Antelope Island State Park** appears to be a desolate and deserted, water-bound mountain. In reality, this largest island in the Great Salt Lake is home to a variety of wildlife, including a herd of 600 bison, descendants from a group of 12 placed on the island in 1893. In 1983, the Great Salt Lake's level rose dramatically and flooded the 7-mi causeway that leads to the island. The water has since receded, and the 28,000-acre island's beaches, campground, and hiking areas are again accessible. This is the best area to come to for swimming. A concessionaire, **R&G Horseback** (☏ *801/782–4946*), rents horses for island explorations. ✉ *Rte. 127, Syracuse, 7 mi west of I–15, Exit 335, 30 mi north of Salt Lake City,* ☏ *801/773–2941.* ✉ *$7 per vehicle, including fee for causeway; $9 camping per night.* ☉ *Daily 7* AM–*10* PM.

Dining

American

$–$$ ✕ **Lamb's Grill Café.** Having opened its doors in 1919, Lamb's claims to be Utah's oldest restaurant. The decor is reminiscent of a classy 1930s diner, and this is where most of Salt Lake City's "movers and shakers" convene for breakfast. The lunch and dinner menus have beef, chicken, and seafood dishes, plus a selection of sandwiches. ✉ *169 S. Main St.,* ☏ *801/364–7166. AE, D, DC, MC, V. Closed Sun.*

$ ✕ **Squatter's Pub Brewery.** It might seem a guilty pleasure to quaff home-brewed beer in such a conservative state as Utah, but that's exactly what's encouraged in this lively pub in the old Boston Hotel. Regulars and visitors alike chow down on the popular Squatterburger, the Margherita pizza, or the generous plate of fish-and-chips. Anglophiles gravitate to the great bread pudding and one of the eight ales on tap. Because it bases production on demand, the pub promises the freshest brew in town. From pale ale to cream stout, no preservatives are used. ✉ *147 W. Broadway,* ☏ *801/363–2739. Reservations not accepted. AE, D, DC, MC, V.*

Contemporary

$$$–$$$$ ★   ✕ **Metropolitan.** Many Utahns believe there is no finer place to dine than the Metropolitan, which won four major state and national dining awards in 2001. Specialties feature wild game, European delicacies, and absolutely fresh seafood. Try the roasted young chicken with caramelized onions and apple stuffing, sunflower sprouts, and cherry glaze. In the bistro area you can sample the tasting menu. Save room for dessert—rhubarb and strawberry tart with sorbet, panna cotta, or the caramel soufflé with macadamia sauce. The setting is comfortably urban, the staff have the time and knowledge necessary to make each dining experience memorable, and the live jazz on Saturday nights cre-

ates a festive atmosphere. ✉ *173 W. Broadway,* ☎ *801/364–3472. AE, D, MC, V.*

$$–$$$$ ✕ **Log Haven.** Near the head of Millcreek Canyon, just south of Salt
★ Lake City, this 80-year-old rustic retreat in the pines has lured the likes
of Margaret Thatcher and pampered members of the International
Olympics Committee for dinner. Chef David Jones has fused the world's
finest cuisines into his own unique creation, with dishes influenced by
the Pacific Rim, California, the Southwest, and France. House specialties
include coriander-rubbed ahi tuna, pepper-seared filet mignon, and
Cajun-spiced duck confit. ✉ *4 mi up Millcreek Canyon. From I–15,
take I–80 East to I–215 South. Take exit for 39th South, turn left at
the end of the ramp, left onto Wasatch Blvd., then turn right at 3800
South traffic light,* ☎ *801/272–8255. AE, D, DC, MC, V.*

French

$$$$ ✕ **La Caille.** It's hard to imagine a dining experience as interesting and
★ delectable as the one here. Start with the escargots à la Bourguignonne,
followed by the best wilted-spinach salad anywhere. Then choose from
such treats as fresh Norwegian silver salmon baked in parchment or
Châteaubriand served with béarnaise sauce and brittle pommes frites.
Add personable servers dressed in period costume, the stately sur-
roundings of an 18th-century French château replica, and a 22-acre
nature preserve. The result is a dinner worth every penny. ✉ *9565
Wasatch Blvd.,* ☎ *801/942–1751. Reservations essential. AE, D, DC,
MC, V.*

Italian

$–$$$ ✕ **Tuscany.** Nestled among mature trees in a quiet part of the city, Tus-
★ cany has six candlelit dining areas, including a cellar and two wrought-
iron balconies. The detailed appetizer descriptions deliver what they
promise, such as herb-crusted beef carpaccio with caper vinaigrette and
shaved Parmesan. The creative entrées include pesto salmon with
toasted vegetable couscous. Even more unusual are the manageable slices
of a 7-ft chocolate layer cake served in honor of retired Utah Jazz center, Mark Eaton, one of the restaurant's owners. Tuscany boasts one
of the best wine cellars in the city. ✉ *2832 E. 6200 South St.,* ☎ *801/
277–9919. AE, D, DC, MC, V.*

$ ✕ **Tucci's.** Don't let the reasonable prices fool you: the food, service,
and ambience here are far above the ordinary. From the chicken breasts
topped with shrimp and artichokes to the veal with Portobello mushrooms in marsala sauce, every dish is bountiful and delicious, and the
desserts—try the gratino custard or the chocolate mousse—are exquisite.
The staff genuinely enjoys providing a pleasant dining experience. A
variety of seating areas make the restaurant suitable for any occasion,
from a business lunch or romantic dinner to a casual family meal (special dishes are available for children). ✉ *515 S. 700 East St.,* ☎ *801/
533–9111. AE, D, DC, MC, V.*

Seafood

$$–$$$$ ✕ **Market Street Grill.** Known for its fresh and well-prepared seafood,
★ you can count on every entrée being a winner, but be sure to check the
daily fish specials before ordering. The lively restaurant is owned by
Gastronomy, Inc., a Salt Lake chain that transforms historic buildings
into tasteful dining spots. ✉ *48 Market St.,* ☎ *801/322–4668. Reser-
vations not accepted. AE, D, DC, MC, V.*

Southwestern

$$ ✕ **Santa Fe Restaurant.** This restaurant, in scenic Emigration Canyon,
has earned acclaim for its cuisine. The extensive menu offers appetiz-
ers that turn up the heat by combining meats and seafood with chilies
and fresh salsas. Salads of fresh, local baby greens are accompanied by

the crunch of pumpkin or pomegranate seeds. Regional entrées, such as Utah rainbow trout, and traditional southwestern fare, range from mild to hot. The food is plentiful and carefully prepared, and the warm bread, served with all meals, is outstanding. Brunch is served on Sunday. ⊠ *2100 Emigration Canyon,* ☎ *801/582–5888. AE, D, MC, V.*

$–$$ ✕ **Café Pierpont.** Tasty southwestern cuisine is served in a family-oriented setting. Children small enough to walk through the wrought-iron cactus at the door eat for free. The menu includes several fajita and enchilada plates, plus plenty of combination options where you can choose from beef, chicken, and seafood. ⊠ *122 W. Pierpont Ave.,* ☎ *801/364–1222. AE, D, DC, MC, V. No lunch weekends.*

Thai

$–$$ ✕ **Bangkok Thai.** Superb food and excellent service win this restaurant awards year after year. Curry, rice and noodle, vegetarian, and
★ vegan dishes are mainstays, and the wide variety of entrées featuring fresh fish and seafood are a real treat. The spice level of the carefully prepared food ranges from mild to wild and is tailored to suit the diner's taste. ⊠ *1400 S. Foothill Dr.,* ☎ *801/582–8424 or 888/852–8424. AE, D, DC, MC, V. No lunch Sun.*

Lodging

Downtown

$$$$ 🏨 **Grand America.** This downtown hotel, which opened in 2001, is more
★ a destination than a place to spend the night. The 24-story white granite building is set on 20 acres and its gardens, pools, shops, ballrooms, and meeting rooms nearly make up a small village. The European flavor is thanks to English wool carpets, French furniture and tapestries, Italian marble, Irish crystal, and stonework by the master artisans of Spain. The lobby demonstrates a world where quality, elegance, and the beauty of natural materials are still valued. Guest rooms are charming, spacious, and include high-speed T1 data ports. Original art pieces throughout the hotel make a stroll around the building a pleasant way to pass an afternoon. ⊠ *555 S. Main St., 84111,* ☎ *801/258–6000 or 800/621–4505,* ☎ *801/258–6911,* 🌐 *www.grandamerica.com. 810 rooms. 2 restaurants, lounge, in-room data ports, in-room safes, refrigerators, room service, 3 pools, sauna, spa, health club, shops, laundry service, concierge floor, business services, convention center, meeting rooms, airport shuttle, free parking. AE, D, DC, MC, V.*

$$$ 🏨 **Hilton–Salt Lake City Center.** This hotel, the old Doubletree, became part of the Hilton chain in 2001 and is still one of the city's largest and best-appointed places to stay. Within walking distance of many downtown attractions and great restaurants, it also caters to skiers, offering complimentary ski storage. ⊠ *255 S. West Temple St., 84101,* ☎ *801/328–2000,* ☎ *801/532–1953. 499 rooms. 2 restaurants, bar, pool, massage, sauna, health club, free parking. AE, D, DC, MC, V.*

$$–$$$ 🏨 **Hotel Monaco Salt Lake City.** Ensconced in the former Continental Bank Building, this downtown hotel caters to business travelers and skiers. Outside, the 14-story corner building retains its classical cornice, cartouches, and carved stone faces of Norse gods. Inside, the 1940s Hollywood atmosphere is casually elegant, upbeat, and fun. Early evening gatherings in the lobby give guests a chance to mingle in front of the fireplace, or to receive a stress-reducing head, neck, or back massage in a quiet corner of the lobby set up as a sultan's tent. For a small fee, guests can participate in weeknight and weekend outings with all equipment and transportation provided. Amenities for skiers include ski storage and transportation to the slopes. There's even an unusual program that allows you to adopt a goldfish during your stay. ⊠ *15 W. 200 South St., 84101,* ☎ *801/595–0000 or 877/294–9710,*

FAX *801/532–8500,* WEB *www.monaco–saltlakecity.com. 187 rooms, 38 suites. Restaurant, bar, in-room data ports, room service, health club, laundry service, meeting room, free parking. AE, D, DC, MC, V.*

$$–$$$ ⌂ **Little America Hotel.** Inside this 17-story hotel are such niceties as
★ lobby fireplaces, brass railings, chandeliers, and marble tubs. Close attention has been paid to details in service and in the decor of guest rooms, which lean toward elegance, with textured fabrics, plush seating, and variable lighting. The hotel's high level of service and world-class amenities convinced the International Organizing Committee for the Olympics to stay here during the 2002 Winter Games. ⊠ *500 S. Main St., 84101,* ☎ *801/363–6781 or 800/453–9450,* FAX *801/596–5911,* WEB *www.littleamerica.com. 850 rooms. Restaurant, coffee shop, piano bar, room service, indoor-outdoor pool, hot tub, sauna, health club, coin laundry, dry cleaning, laundry service, business services, airport shuttle, free parking. AE, D, DC, MC, V.*

$$–$$$ ⌂ **Saltair Bed & Breakfast.** This 1903 Victorian home is listed on the state and national registers of historic places. Fine oak woodwork and period antiques lend elegance to the rooms. Sitting in the formal parlor with a book before a roaring fire is the perfect way to end the day. Suites with fireplaces and kitchens are available, and families or groups can choose to stay in one of the small houses on the property. Breakfast, which features hearty American fare, is served in the dining room. ⊠ *164 S. 900 East St., 84102,* ☎ *801/533–8184 or 800/733–8184,* FAX *801/595–0332,* WEB *www.saltlakebandb.com. 7 rooms, 9 suites. Dining room, kitchenettes (some), free parking. AE, D, DC, MC, V. BP.*

$$ ⌂ **Anton Boxrud Bed & Breakfast.** Antiques and unusual furnishings from all over the world fill the rooms of this elegant, yet casual, Victorian manor just down the street from the Governor's mansion and a 15-minute stroll from the city center. The complimentary evening snacks and beverages served near the parlor's bay window are as delicious as the bountiful breakfasts that guests enjoy at the dining room table. ⊠ *57 S. 600 East St., 84102,* ☎ *801/363–8035 or 800/524–5511,* FAX *801/ 596–1316,* WEB *www.bbiu.org/antonboxrud. 7 rooms. Dining room, hot tub. AE, D, DC, MC, V. BP.*

$$ ⌂ **Brigham Street Inn.** If you love historic B&Bs, this is the place to stay. On East South Temple (formerly Brigham Street), this turn-of-the-20th-century mansion was carefully restored by Salt Lake architect John Pace. Each of the superbly appointed guest rooms was decorated by a different interior designer. Some are decorated in pastels, with the visual focus being the inn's large tree-shaded windows; others offer jewel-tone furniture and recessed lighting; most have king-size beds and fireplaces. The original woodwork has been preserved throughout, one example of the special attention paid to preserving the home's character. The breakfast is Continental. ⊠ *1135 E. South Temple St., 84102,* ☎ *801/364–4461 or 800/417–4461,* FAX *801/521–3201,* WEB *www.brighamstreetinn.citysearch.com. 9 rooms. Breakfast room. AE, D, DC, MC, V. CP.*

$$ ⌂ **Shilo Inn.** A couple of blocks from Temple Square, this hotel combines the convenience of a downtown location with good rates. Service is reasonable, and the amenities, such as the complimentary breakfast buffet, pool and fitness room, and the outside glass elevator that gives guests a spectacular view of the city, are much better than what you'd expect for the price. ⊠ *206 S. West Temple St., 84101,* ☎ *801/521–9500,* FAX *801/359–6527,* WEB *www.shiloinns.com. 200 rooms. 2 restaurants, bar, pool, hot tub, sauna, gym, coin laundry, airport shuttle, free parking. AE, D, DC, MC, V. CP.*

$–$$ ⌂ **Ramada Inn–Downtown.** All rooms and facilities circle an enclosed courtyard in this downtown hotel, a design that makes this a remarkably pleasant place to stay. The courtyard's casual, tropical atmosphere is created by a pool and hot tub, several gardenlike seating areas, large plants, and cages of finches and parakeets. The rooms are clean and airy, and the amenities—fitness center, billiards, sauna, lounge—combined with the reasonable price might make you want to stay an extra day. ⊠ *230 W. 600 South St., 84103,* ☎ *801/364–5200,* ℻ *801/364–0974,* WEB *www.ramadainnslc.com. 120 rooms. Restaurant, bar, pool, hot tub, sauna, health club, billiards, recreation room, coin laundry, laundry services, meetings rooms, airport shuttle, free parking. AE, D, DC, MC, V.*

Airport and Greater Salt Lake Valley

$$–$$$$ 🏨 **La Europa Royale.** Set on a large, wooded lot in South Salt Lake,
★   this small, elegant hotel pampers its guests. For skiers, there's easy access to the resorts in Big and Little Cottonwood canyons, individual ski lockers on the property, and gas fireplaces in each room. For business travelers, rooms come with data-grade phone systems, data ports, and desks. The comfortable guest rooms, which include Jacuzzis, are individually decorated but not fussy. Outside, two landscaped acres invite after-meal walks. Complimentary sit-down breakfasts are creative and well prepared. ⊠ *1135 E. Vine St., 84121,* ☎ *801/263–7999 or 800/523–8767,* ℻ *801/263–8090,* WEB *www.laeuropa.com. 8 rooms. Dining room, in-room data ports, gym, laundry service and dry cleaning, airport shuttle. AE, D, DC, MC, V. BP.*

$$ 🏨 **Radisson Hotel Airport.** This very comfortable hotel is the best lodging near the airport. Rooms include a wet bar and refrigerator. Try the free Continental breakfast and the Club Room for fun dining possibilities. ⊠ *2177 W. North Temple St., 84116,* ☎ *801/364–5800,* ℻ *801/364–5823,* WEB *www.radisson.com. 127 rooms. Restaurant, refrigerators, pool, hot tub, gym, airport shuttle. AE, D, DC, MC, V. CP.*

$–$$ 🏨 **Hampton Inn–Sandy.** Pleasant rooms, nice furnishings, and a moderate price make this a worthwhile place to stay if you're just passing through. The hotel is close to I–15, and there are movie theaters, several restaurants, and a shopping mall within 1 mi. ⊠ *10690 S. Holiday Park Dr., Sandy 84070,* ☎ *801/571–0800,* ℻ *801/572–0708. 131 rooms. Indoor pool, hot tub, coin laundry. AE, D, DC, MC, V.*

$–$$ 🏨 **Reston Hotel.** This property is just 10 minutes from downtown and 15 minutes from the airport. The three-story hotel offers an indoor pool and hot tub, and a café that serves a deluxe, complimentary Continental breakfast. ⊠ *5335 College Dr., Murray 84123,* ☎ *801/264–1054 or 800/231–9710,* ℻ *801/264–1054,* WEB *www.restonhotelslc.com. 98 rooms. Café, indoor pool, hot tub, meeting rooms. AE, D, DC, MC, V. CP.*

Nightlife and the Arts

BARS AND LOUNGES
The **Bay** (⊠ 404 S. West Temple St., ☎ 801/363–2623) is a smoke- and alcohol-free club with three dance floors. The **Hard Rock Café** (⊠ 505 South, 600 East, ☎ 801/532–7625) features burgers and rock-and-roll memories. A good place for spotting Utah Jazz basketball players and their visiting competitors is **Port O' Call** (⊠ 78 W. 400 South St., ☎ 801/521–0589), a sports bar with 14 satellite dishes and 26 TVs.

DANCE
Salt Lake's three main dance companies perform at the historic **Capitol Theatre** (⊠ 50 W. 200 South St., ☎ 801/355–2787). **Ballet West** (☎ 801/355–2787) is considered one of the nation's top ballet companies, performing both classical and original works. **Repertory Dance Theatre** (☎ 801/534–1000) presents modern-dance performances. **Ririe-Woodbury Dance Company** (☎ 801/328–1062) is Salt Lake's

premier modern-dance troupe. It's recognized for its innovation and commitment to community education.

MUSIC

The **Mormon Tabernacle Choir** (✉ Temple Sq., ☎ 801/240–2534) may be heard in performance in the Tabernacle on Sunday morning at 9:30 (be seated by 9:15) or during rehearsals on Thursday at 8 PM. The choir, which includes men and women of all ages from around the intermountain region, many of whom drive for hours several times a week just to attend rehearsals, performs sacred music, with some secular—classical and patriotic—works. The **Utah Symphony** (✉ 123 W. South Temple St., ☎ 801/533–6683) performs 260 concerts annually, both at home in the acoustically acclaimed Maurice Abravanel Concert Hall (part of the Salt Palace convention center) and in cities across the nation and abroad.

NIGHTCLUBS

The **Dead Goat Saloon** (✉ 165 S. West Temple St., ☎ 801/328–4628) features live music nightly. The tempo is upbeat, and the grill is fired up every day for lunch and dinner. **Green Street Social Club** (✉ 602 E. 500 South St., ☎ 801/532–4200) is a fine spot to meet or make friends while enjoying light food, live music, and dancing. The art deco **Zephyr Club** (✉ 301 S. West Temple St., ☎ 801/355–5646) showcases both local and nationally recognized bands.

OPERA

Utah Opera Company (✉ Capitol Theatre, 50 W. 200 South St., ☎ 801/355–2787) produces four operas a year, which often feature nationally recognized stars. Even if you don't care for opera, check out the ornate facade of the Capitol Theatre.

THEATER

Off Broadway Theatre (✉ 272 S. Main St., ☎ 801/355–4628) puts on musicals, plays, comedy shows, and improvisational comedy events. **Pioneer Theatre Company** (✉ 300 S. 1400 East St., ☎ 801/581–6961) features classic and contemporary musicals and plays during its season, which runs from September through May. **Salt Lake Acting Company** (✉ 168 W. 500 North St., ☎ 801/363–7522) is nationally recognized for its development of new plays. Performances run year-round.

Outdoor Activities and Sports

Salt Lake City is a gateway to the excellent ski resorts strung along the Wasatch Range. Seven of these are accessible in less than ½ hour from Salt Lake.

Participant Sports

CYCLING

Salt Lake City is a comparatively easy city to tour by bicycle, thanks to its extra-wide streets and not-so-frenetic traffic. An especially good route is **City Creek Canyon,** east of the state capitol. On odd-number days from mid-May through September the road is closed to motor vehicles. Liberty Park, Sugarhouse Park, and Jordan River State Park also have good cycling (and jogging) paths.

GOLF

Less than five minutes from downtown you can tee off at the 18-hole **Rose Park Golf Course** (✉ 1386 N. Redwood Rd., ☎ 801/596–5030). A championship course and spectacular scenery await golfers at the **South Mountain Golf Club** (✉ 1247 E. Rambling Rd., Draper, ☎ 801/495–0500). **Stonebridge Golf Club** (✉ 4415 Links Dr., West Valley City,

☎ 801/908–7888) is a five-minute drive from the Salt Lake International Airport, and it offers a Johnny Miller signature design course. If you're near the east bench of the city, try the **University of Utah Golf Course** (✉ 102 Fieldhouse Dr., ☎ 801/581–6511).

SKIING

Advance equipment and clothing rental reservations are available from **Utah Ski&Golf** (✉ 134 W. 600 South St., ☎ 801/355–9088 or 801/539–8660, 🌐 www.utahskigolf.com). The company has a downtown Salt Lake City location and locations at both terminals of the Salt Lake International Airport, and provides free shuttle service from your downtown hotel to their store.

Spectator Sports

BASEBALL

The Pacific Coast League, Triple A **Salt Lake Buzz** (✉ 77 W. 1300 South St., ☎ 801/485–3800) play at Franklin Covey Field, which has the Wasatch Range for a backdrop.

BASKETBALL

The **Utah Jazz** (✉ 301 W. South Temple St., ☎ 801/355–3865) is Salt Lake City's NBA team and a real crowd-pleaser. Home games are played at the Delta Center. The WNBA **Utah Starzz** (✉ 301 W. South Temple St., ☎ 801/358–7328) share the Delta Center with the Utah Jazz.

HOCKEY

Turner Cup Champions for 1995 and 1996, the **Utah Grizzlies** (✉ 3200 S. Decker Lake Dr., West Valley City, ☎ 801/988–8000) play IHL hockey on the E Center ice.

Shopping

Crossroads Plaza (✉ 50 S. Main St., ☎ 801/531–1799) is an all-inclusive downtown shopping experience. Among its 140 stores and restaurants are Nordstrom and Mervyn's.

East of I–15 in the south end of the city, **Factory Stores of America** (✉ 12101 S. Factory Outlet Dr., ☎ 801/571–2933) offers outlet discounts on everything from cookware and coats to luggage, books, and Doc Martens.

Under the commission of Brigham Young, dedicated polygamist Archibald Gardner (11 wives) built a flour mill in 1877. Today you can visit the mill and stroll among over 30 specialty shops in the adjacent **Gardner Village** (✉ 1100 W. 7800 South St., ☎ 801/566–8903). Items for sale include furniture, collectibles, and knickknacks.

The wares at **Trolley Square** (✉ 600 S. 700 East St., ☎ 801/521–9877) run the gamut from estate jewelry and designer clothes to bath products, baskets, and saltwater taffy. Stores include Laura Ashley, the Gap, Williams-Sonoma, and Banana Republic.

Founded by Brigham Young in 1868, the Zion's Cooperative Mercantile Institution (ZCMI) was America's first department store. Although the ZCMI stores have now become part of the Meier & Frank chain, the name lives on at the **ZCMI Center Mall** (✉ South Temple and Main St., ☎ 801/321–8745), which dates back to 1902. This thoroughly modern shopping center features over 90 stores, including Eddie Bauer and Godiva. The center is closed Sunday.

ANTIQUES

Visit **R. M. Kennard Antiques** (✉ 65 W. 300 South St., ☎ 801/328–9796) in the heart of the downtown area for fine American and European art, furniture, and dishes. The vicinity of **300 South and 300**

East streets has several small shops specializing in antique jewelry, furnishings, art, and collectibles. The accent at **Elementé** (⊠ 353 W. Pierpont Ave., ☎ 801/355–7400) is on unique and unusual period pieces. Don't miss the Bargain Basementé. Just a short walk from the downtown area you'll find **Moriarty's Antiques & Curiosities** (⊠ 959 S. West Temple St., ☎ 801/521–7207), which specializes in furnishings for the home and garden; it will ship gifts nationwide.

BOOKS
Deseret Book (⊠ 36 S. State St., ☎ 801/321–8745), purveyor of books and materials related to the Mormon church and its doctrine, has several Salt Lake locations, the largest of which is in the ZCMI Center. In a rambling house, with room after room filled with books, **The King's English** (⊠ 1511 S. 1500 East St., ☎ 801/484–9100) is a fun place to browse. **Sam Weller's Zion Book Store** (⊠ 254 S. Main St., ☎ 801/328–2586 or 800/333–7269) stocks more than half a million new and used books.

CRAFTS
Mormon Handicraft (⊠ Main St. at South Temple, ☎ 801/355–2141 or 800/843–1480) sells exquisite quilts, crafts, and children's clothing made by Utah residents. **The Quilted Bear** (⊠ 145 W. 7200 South St., ☎ 801/566–5454) is a co-op with gifts, home accessories, and collectibles created by more than 600 different craftspeople.

Salt Lake City A to Z

AIRPORTS & TRANSFERS
Salt Lake City International Airport is 7 mi northwest of downtown Salt Lake City. It is served by American, America West, Continental, Delta, Northwest, Southwest, TWA, and United.

All major car-rental agencies have desks at Salt Lake International. From the airport, drive 7 mi east on I–80 to North Temple Street, which will take you directly to the city center. The Utah Transit Authority runs buses regularly between the airport and downtown. Most downtown hotels offer free airport pickup for guests. Yellow Cab provides 24-hour service to all of the Salt Lake valley. The cost of a ride into town is about $15.
➤ AIRPORT INFORMATION: **Salt Lake City International Airport** (☎ 801/575–2400).
➤ TAXIS AND SHUTTLES: **City Cab Company** (☎ 801/363–8400 or 801/363–5550). **Utah Transit Authority** (☎ 801/743–3882 or 888/743–3882). **Ute Cab Company** (☎ 801/359–7788). **Yellow Cab** (☎ 801/521–2100, 801/521–1862, or 800/826–4746).

BUS TRAVEL TO AND FROM SALT LAKE CITY
Greyhound Lines runs several buses each day to the terminal at 160 West South Temple Street.
➤ BUS INFORMATION: **Greyhound Lines** (☎ 801/355–9579).

CAR TRAVEL
With the reconstruction of I–15 completed in 2001, highway travel around the area is now quick and easy. From I–80, take I–15 north to 600 South Street to reach the city center. Salt Lake City's streets are extra wide and typically not congested. Most are two-way.

EMERGENCIES
➤ HOSPITALS: **Columbia St. Mark's Hospital** (⊠ 1200 E. 3900 South St., ☎ 801/268–7111). **LDS Hospital** (⊠ 8th Ave. and C St., ☎ 801/408–1100). **Primary Children's Medical Center** (⊠ 100 N. Medical

Dr., ☎ 801/588–2000). **Salt Lake Regional Medical Center** (✉ 1050
E. South Temple St., ☎ 801/350–4111). **University Hospital and Clin-
ics** (✉ 50 N. Medical Dr., ☎ 801/581–2121).
➤ PHARMACIES: **Broadway Pharmacy** (✉ 242 E. 300 South St., ☎ 801/
363–3939), open until 9 PM. **Harmon's Supermarket** (✉ 3270 S. 1300
East St., ☎ 801/487–5461), open until midnight.

TOURS

Innsbrook Tours provides tours of Salt Lake City, the Great Salt Lake,
and the Bingham Canyon Copper Mine; most tours include lunch at
Brigham Young's historic living quarters. Lewis Brothers Stages conducts tours of Salt Lake City sights in *Old Salty,* an open-air, rubber-
tire train. Tours depart from Temple and Trolley squares. Utah Heritage
Foundation offers the most authoritative tours of Salt Lake's historic
sights.
➤ CONTACTS: **Innsbrook Tours** (✉ 3353 S. Main St., ☎ 801/534–1001).
Lewis Brothers Stages (✉ 549 W. 500 South St., ☎ 801/359–8677 or
800/826–5844). **Utah Heritage Foundation** (✉ 485 Canyon Rd., ☎
801/533–0858).

TRAIN TRAVEL

Amtrak serves the area daily out of Amtrak Passenger Station.
➤ TRAIN INFORMATION: **Amtrak Passenger Station** (✉ 340 S. 600 West
St., ☎ 801/322–3510).

TRANSPORTATION AROUND SALT LAKE CITY

Salt Lake has a very workable public transportation system. A Free Fare
Zone for travel by bus covers a 15-block area downtown and on Capitol Hill. Round-trip bus service to the ski resorts (Solitude, Brighton,
Snowbird, or Alta) costs $1.75 each way; most other bus routes cost
$1 per ride. A light rail system, called TRAX, moves passengers quickly
around the city, and to the small cities south of Salt Lake. The north–
south light rail route begins at the Delta Center and ends at 9800 South;
there are 16 stations along the way, and 11 have free park-and-ride
lots. The east–west route begins at the University of Utah and ends at
Main Street; it is scheduled for completion in early 2002. For $2, you
can buy an all-day ticket, good for unlimited rides on both the bus and
TRAX. Exact change is required for rides on both the bus and TRAX
systems.
➤ INFORMATION: **Utah Transit Authority** (☎ 801/743–3882 or 888/
743–3882, WEB www.rideuta.com).

VISITOR INFORMATION

The Salt Lake Convention and Visitors Bureau is open weekdays 8:30–
5 and weekends 9–5.
➤ TOURIST INFORMATION: **Salt Lake Convention and Visitors Bureau** (✉
90 S. West Temple St., 84101, ☎ 801/521–2822, WEB www.saltlake.org).

THE WASATCH RANGE

Rising to elevations of more than 11,000 ft and stretching some 160
mi from the Idaho border to central Utah, the Wasatch Range is an
imposing and important geographic feature in the western United
States. From a geologic perspective, the mountains are a complex assemblage of igneous, sedimentary, and metamorphic formations. From
a demographic one, the western base of these mountains—a corridor
known as the Wasatch Front—is home to three-quarters of all Utahns.
Not only Salt Lake City residents but also those in Ogden, Logan, and
Provo wake up each morning to a spectacular view of the Wasatch.

Scientific and social implications aside, the Wasatch Range is one of the nation's premier mountain playgrounds. Uppermost in many visitors' minds is the legendary skiing found at resorts such as Snowbird, Alta, and Park City. On the back side of the Wasatch Range, Park City is Utah's only real ski town, and because it's a mere 40-minute drive from Salt Lake International Airport, it is the most accessible ski town in the country. What many outdoor enthusiasts don't realize is that these same ski towns double as wonderful summer destinations. Picturesque mountain communities, miles of hiking and bicycling trails, bright blue lakes, and truly spectacular alpine scenery add up to a vacation that's hard to beat.

Water-sports enthusiasts will find a surprising number of places to boat, windsurf, water-ski, and sail. The most popular of these spots are state park facilities. They include Bear Lake, Willard Bay and Pineview Reservoir near Ogden, Rockport Reservoir, Deer Creek Reservoir, Hyrum Reservoir, Jordanelle Reservoir in the Heber Valley, and Utah Lake. Fishers head to Bear Lake, the Logan and Blacksmith Fork rivers, outside Logan; Willard Bay and Pineview Reservoir; the Provo River and Deer Creek Reservoir, northeast of Provo; and Jordanelle Reservoir.

Alta

28 *28 mi from Salt Lake City via I–15 south, I–215 east, and Rte. 210 south.*

Within Little Cottonwood Canyon, the nation's second-oldest ski area started out as a silver-mining camp in the 1800s. So frenzied was the pace back then that the year-round population topped 8,000. The eventual crash of the silver market, however, left the canyon virtually empty until it was recognized for its potential as a winter sports area. A lift was pieced together from an old mine tram, and in January 1939 the Alta Lifts Company was in business. Today Alta is widely acclaimed for both what it has and what it doesn't have. The ski area promises a generous helping of Wasatch powder—up to 500 inches a year. What you won't find is the glitz and pomp that other resorts exude. From the lifts to lodging, everything here is unpretentious. Duct tape on ripped nylon pants is Alta chic, and trail signs are exceedingly rare, since only interloping tourists don't know their way around. Alta is so retro that it is one of the few ski areas left in the country that disallows snowboarding. Alta also prides itself in being a preternaturally local ski area.

Dining and Lodging

The **central reservations** number for Alta lodgings is ☎ 888/782–9258.

$$$–$$$$ ✕ **Shallow Shaft.** For fine beef, seafood, poultry, and pasta dishes, Alta's only base-area sit-down restaurant that is not part of a lodging property is the place to go. The small interior is cozy and decorated in funky southwestern style with a sandy color scheme and walls adorned with 19th-century mining tools found on the mountain. The menu is also southwestern, with adventurous specials including lamb chops grilled and served in ancho-chili sauce and pork medallions braised in apple cider. The restaurant makes its own ice cream daily. Homemade pizza is also served, as is liquor. ⊠ *Across from the Alta Lodge,* ☎ *801/742–2177. AE, D, MC, V.*

$$$$ 🏨 **Rustler Lodge.** The fanciest lodge in Alta most resembles a traditional full-service hotel. The interior is decidedly upscale, with dark wood paneling, burgundy chairs and couches, handsome wooden backgammon tables, and a grand piano dominating a small sitting room

off the main lobby. Guest quarters are handsomely decorated with dark woods, white brick walls, and richly colored fabrics. Larger rooms have sofas and seating areas. All but three units have a private bathroom. As at all of Alta's lodges, breakfast and dinner are included in the price. ⊠ *Box 8030, 84092,* ☎ *801/742–2200 or 888/532–2582,* FAX *801/742– 3832,* WEB *www.rustlerlodge.com. 85 rooms, 82 with bath; 4 dorms. Restaurant, bar, lobby lounge, outdoor pool, indoor hot tub, 2 saunas, spa, ski shop, children's programs (ages 4–14), coin laundry. No credit cards. MAP.*

$$–$$$
★   **Alta Peruvian Lodge.** Comfortably rustic is the best way to describe the Alta Peruvian. You'll first enter the plant-filled lobby, where a large stone fireplace dominates a room with handcrafted blond-wood furniture, books, and hotel guests relaxing after an intense day on the slopes. A picture window overlooks the outdoor swimming pool and hot tub, with the mountain in the background. This is the quintessential classic ski lodge where après-ski means hot chocolate, apple cider, and brownies set out on tables around the room. The family-style dining room and the bar upstairs are equally cozy, but the rooms can be tiny, and more than half have shared bathrooms down the hall. Guest rooms range from simple dormitory style to simply furnished two-bedroom suites. Three meals a day at the in-house restaurant are included in the price of lodging. Combine this meal plan with complimentary lift tickets, and you have one-stop shopping—Alta style. ⊠ *Box 8017, 84092,* ☎ *801/742– 3000 or 800/453–8488,* FAX *801/742–3007,* WEB *www.altaperuvian.com. 65 rooms, 30 with bath; 20 suites; 4 dorms. Restaurant, bar, pool, outdoor hot tub, sauna, coin laundry, ski shop. AE, D, MC, V. FAP.*

Outdoor Activities and Sports

CYCLING AND HIKING

Many cycling and hiking trails access the higher reaches of the Wasatch–Cache National Forest from Alta. The trails over Catherine Pass will put you at the head of Big Cottonwood Canyon at the Brighton Ski Area. The hike to Catherine Pass is relatively easy and quite scenic.

Downhill Skiing

You can return to **Alta** year after year and still discover places to ski you never knew existed before. It's a ski area made to be explored but hard to get around. There are few trail signs. The lift system seems antiquated and poorly laid out, and a lot of trails seem to flatten out quickly or lead nowhere. This is a complex package of terrain, and the more you explore Alta, the richer your rewards.

Alta sprawls across two large basins, Albion and Wildcat, comprising mostly open bowls and meadows but with some trail skiing, too. There is no clear, easily readable fall line as there is at Snowbird; fall lines drop and roll away in many directions and angles. Furthermore, much of the best skiing (for advanced or expert skiers) requires finding obscure traverses or some hiking.

The only solution is simply to stick with it. One day—one run, even—will be your epiphany, and suddenly Alta will explode upon you with possibilities. On the lower slopes of Albion Basin, Alta has a terrific expanse of novice and lower-intermediate terrain. Rolling meadows combine as perhaps the best place in the country for lesser-skilled skiers to learn to ski powder. ⊠ *Box 8007, 84092,* ☎ *801/359–1078,* WEB *www.alta.com or www.altaskiarea.com.*

FACILITIES

2,100-ft vertical drop; 2,200 skiable acres; 25% novice, 40% intermediate, 35% advanced; 6 double chairs, 2 triple chairs. **Snow report:** ☎ 801/572–3939.

Half-day group lessons for adults and children are available (two-hour lessons start at $30).

Lift tickets are $35.

Snowbird

29 *1 mi from Alta via Rte. 210 west.*

Since the early 1970s, "the Bird" has taken skiing to new heights. The Snowbird Ski and Summer Resort, which shares Little Cottonwood Canyon with Alta, is one of the nation's most modern ski facilities. Its fast tram quietly whisks skiers in stylish powder suits to the summit, and there are plenty of trail signs, most with Japanese translations. At the base area a cluster of modern structures house elegant guest rooms, exquisite restaurants, and fun nightclubs. The largest of these buildings, the Cliff Lodge, is like an entire ski town under one roof. Weekly live jazz performances, festivals that focus on food and wine, murder mystery dinner theater events, games, and holiday celebrations provide entertainment during breaks from skiing or in the evening. During the summer, Little Cottonwood Canyon is still the place to be for outdoor fun. From Memorial Day weekend to October, Snowbird fires up its tram to ferry sightseers and hikers to the top. From here you get one of the most spectacular views in the West.

Dining and Lodging

The **central reservations** number for lodging in Snowbird is ☎ 800/232–9542.

$$$–$$$$ ✕ **Aerie.** In what may be Utah's most scenic dining spot, this 10th-floor
★ restaurant atop the Cliff Lodge serves sumptuous cuisine. Try the grilled free-range chicken with winter vegetable pastina or the aged New York strip steak with cognac peppercorn sauce. In keeping with the elegance of its setting, much attention is paid to preparation and presentation. There is a sushi bar, and even if you are staying for only one night, it's worth dining here simply to be able to select from the impressive wine list. ✉ *9900 E. Little Cottonwood Canyon Rd.,* ☎ *801/521–6040 Ext. 5500. AE, D, DC, MC, V.*

$$$$ ⌂ **Cliff Lodge.** This is one of the finest ski-resort accommodations in
★ the Rocky Mountains, with a friendly and helpful staff. To some, the large, 10-story structure with bare concrete walls initially looks bland, but it doesn't take long to realize that the real beauty of its design is that it blends with the scenery. Every window looks out to a wonderful view, and rooms are decorated mainly in mountain colors and desert pastels. The Cliff Spa is on the top two floors, with a rooftop pool, massage rooms, hot tubs, and steam rooms. In addition, you have your choice of several fine restaurants, one in the Cliff Lodge and several close by in other lodges. Camp Snowbird provides summer activities for children. ✉ *9900 E. Little Cottonwood Canyon Rd., Snowbird Ski and Summer Resort, 84092,* ☎ *801/742–2222 or 800/453–3000,* FAX *801/947–8227,* WEB *www.snowbird.com. 464 rooms, 47 suites. 4 restaurants, 6 bars, 2 pools, hair salon, 4 hot tubs, sauna, spa, health club, babysitting, children's programs (ages 3–12), coin laundry, dry cleaning, laundry service, convention center, meeting room. AE, D, DC, MC, V.*

Nightlife and the Arts

Snowbird Special Events Department (☎ 801/933–2110) mounts a variety of events throughout the year, such as performances by the Utah Symphony, outdoor concerts, a jazz and blues festival, and murder mystery weekends. As a guest at Snowbird, you receive a complimentary membership to the **"Club at Snowbird"** and can enjoy a drink at any of several lounges spread about the base area.

Outdoor Activities and Sports

CYCLING AND HIKING

Off-road cyclists are discovering that Snowbird's ski slopes make for some excellent, if strenuous, riding. Down the canyon from Snowbird is the trailhead for the Red Pine Lake and White Pine Lake trails. Located 3½ mi and 5 mi in, respectively, these mountain lakes make for great day hikes.

ROCK CLIMBING AND MOUNTAINEERING

Formed by the tireless path of an ancient glacier, **Little Cottonwood Canyon** cuts an enormous swath through the Wasatch–Cache National Forest. Canyon walls are composed mostly of striated granite and traditional climbing routes of varied difficulty abound. There are a few bolted routes as well. For information and permits for climbing in Little Cottonwood, contact **Wasatch–Cache National Forest** (⊠ 8236 Federal Bldg., Salt Lake City, UT 84138, ☎ 801/524–5030). **Snowbird Ski and Summer Resort** (☎ 801/521–6040) has a competition-class outdoor climbing wall open to the public.

Downhill Skiing

An expert's dream and a novice skier's nightmare, **Snowbird Ski and Summer Resort** has plenty of powder-filled chutes, bowls, and meadow areas. Like its neighbor, Alta, it's known for its expert runs; 45% of Snowbird is black diamond terrain. In contrast, however, an extra $19 for a lift ticket will get you the speed, convenience, and impressive vertical drop (3,240 ft in one fell swoop) that only Snowbird's 125-passenger aerial tram can provide.

Its open bowls, such as Little Cloud and Regulator Johnson, are challenging, while chutes from the Upper Cirque and the Gad Chutes can be positively hair-raising. On deep-powder days—not uncommon at the 'Bird—those chutes can also be exhilarating for skiers who like that sense of a cushioned free fall with every turn. If you're looking for intermediate cruising runs, however, there's the long, meandering Chips, a few runs from the Gad chairlifts. ⊠ Box 929000, 9000 Little Cottonwood Canyon Rd., Snowbird 84092, ☎ 801/742–2222 or 800/385–2002, FAX 801/947–8227, WEB www.snowbird.com.

FACILITIES

3,240-ft vertical drop; 2,500 skiable acres; 25% novice, 30% intermediate, 45% advanced; 125-passenger tram, 2 quad lifts, 7 double chairs. **Snow report:** ☎ 801/933–2100.

LESSONS AND PROGRAMS

Of note is Snowbird's Mountain Experience Program, a combination of guidance and instruction for expert skiers in challenging, off-slope terrain and variable snow conditions. Full-day workshops start at $85. The 2½-hour lessons begin at $52.

LIFT TICKETS

Tickets are $54 for tram and chairs; $45 for chairlift-only.

Brighton

25 mi from Snowbird via Rte. 210 north and Rte. 190 east; 30 mi from Salt Lake City via I–15 south, I–215 east, Rte. 210 south, and Rte. 190 east.

North of Snowbird in Big Cottonwood Canyon is a small, locally treasured gem—**Brighton Ski Resort.** Brighton offers a perfect combination:

all the fluffy powder of Alta and Snowbird and all the quiet charm many large resorts have left behind. This is a great place for families; it was the first resort in Utah to offer a kids-ski-free program, and it has received many awards for its service to children and parents. If you're looking for excitement, over one-third of the runs are for advanced skiers, and lifts provide access to extensive backcountry areas for the real experts.

Value is a keyword at Brighton. All-day lift tickets cost $37 for adults; two-hour group lessons are $26. The emphasis on value extends to Brighton Lodge, which is quiet, comfortable, and so reasonably priced (keep in mind that children 10 and under stay free) you might be able to stretch your ski weekend into a full week of fun. ✉ *Star Route, Brighton 84121,* ☎ *801/532–4731 or 800/873–5512,* FAX *435/649–1787,* WEB *www.skibrighton.com.*

Facilities
1,745-ft vertical drop; 850 skiable acres; 21% beginner, 40% intermediate, 39% advanced/expert; 3 high-speed quad chairs, 1 triple chair, 3 double chairs. **Snow report:** ☎ 801/532–4731 or 800/873–5512.

Solitude

3 mi from Brighton via Rte. 190 west; 27 mi from Salt Lake City via I–15 south, I–215 east, Rte. 210 south, and Rte. 190 east.

The history of mining and skiing in Utah often go hand-in-hand, and that's certainly true of **Solitude Mountain Resort.** The Solitude area was named by miners, who came to Big Cottonwood Canyon in the early 1900s in search of silver. In the 1950s, a man who had made his fortune elsewhere in mining decided to retire in the Wasatch Mountains and take up skiing. He left a local resort in a huff one day when he was denied use of the bathrooms, which were reserved for lodging guests. In revenge, he built a rival resort. The result is Solitude, which has served skiers since 1957 and now rivals many resorts in the West.

During the past decade, Solitude has grown into a village, with lodges, condominiums, a luxury hotel, and award-winning restaurants. The emphasis is on comfort and on the creation of memorable experiences. A perfect example is the yurt dinner: after a guided snowshoe or cross-country ski tour through the forest, guests enjoy a five-course gourmet dinner at a Mongolian hut.

Downhill skiing and snowboarding are the main attractions at Solitude; $39 buys an all-day lift pass, and a half-day group lesson costs a modest $40. However, there are also miles of snowshoe and cross-country trails at the **Nordic Center** (☎ 801/536–5774). For $10, adults can use the trails all day; for $40, they receive an all-day trail pass and a one-hour private lesson. ✉ *12000 Big Cottonwood Canyon, Solitude 84121,* ☎ *801/534–1400 or 800/748–4754,* FAX *435/649–5276,* WEB *www.skisolitude.com.*

Facilities
2,047-ft vertical drop; 1,200 skiable acres; 20% beginner, 50% intermediate, 30% advanced; 1 high-speed quad chair, 2 triple chairs, 4 double chairs. **Snow report:** ☎ 801/536–5777.

Park City/Deer Valley/The Canyons

30 *33 mi from Salt Lake City via I–80 east (to Exit 145) and Rte. 224 south.*

Park City was a rip-roaring mining town like no other. Silver was discovered here in 1868, and in the years immediately following, the town's population grew by leaps and bounds. In the process it earned the nickname "Sin City." Certainly, it was uncommon for any municipality within spitting distance of Salt Lake to have more than two dozen saloons and a thriving red-light district. Despite the generosity of the mountains, Park City eventually fell victim to depressed silver prices. It was not until 1946 that its current livelihood began to take shape in the form of the small Snow Park ski hill, which opened a few miles south. In 1963, Treasure Mountain Resort began operations with its skier's subway—an underground train and hoist system that ferried skiers to the mountain's top via old mining tunnels. In the years since, facilities were upgraded, and Treasure Mountain became the Park City Mountain Resort. Although it has a mind-numbing collection of condominiums, at its heart is a historic downtown district that rings with authenticity and reminds visitors that Park City is a real town with real roots.

Most visitors come to Park City to ski, but the town also serves as an excellent base camp for summer activities. Hiking trails are plentiful. A scenic drive over Guardsman Pass (via a gravel road that is passable for most vehicles) reveals incredible mountain vistas and a plethora of alpine wildflowers. There are some acclaimed golf greens, hot-air ballooning is available, and mountain bikers find the ski slopes truly exceptional pedaling.

With so much to offer both summer and winter visitors, the town now includes three resorts, each with its own unique qualities. The emphasis at the original Park City Mountain Resort is on skiing and socializing in town. At Deer Valley, located in a more secluded area on the edge of Park City, visitors revel in the quiet and in the great food and amenities. The Canyons, opened in 1997, is a rapidly growing destination resort just north of town; it ranks in the top five resorts in America in terms of overall ski area, and it combines luxury with a casual atmosphere. A free shuttle-bus system serves the town of Park City, the three resort areas, and the many surrounding hotels. Although the shuttle is efficient, the Park City area is fairly spread out, so a car can be helpful.

The **Alpine Slide** (⊠ 1345 Lowell Ave., Park City, ☎ 435/649–8111 or 800/222–7275) is a big attraction during the summer at the Park City Mountain Resort. Children of all ages can fly down the curving track on a sled that is easy to control. The **Utah Winter Sports Park** (⊠ 3000 Bear Hollow Dr., Park City, ☎ 435/658–4200) was the official site of the 2002 Olympic bobsled, luge, and ski-jumping events. Anyone who dreams of Olympic glory can take recreational ski-jumping lessons or bobsled rides on actual Olympic courses. The Winter Sports Park also serves as a year-round training site for members of the U.S. Ski Team and other athletes training for amateur competition. In summer, check out the freestyle ski jumpers who practice their form on a special jump with a splash pool at the bottom.

Dining

$$$-$$$$ ✕ **Glitretind.** The Glitretind is posh without being ostentatious, gracious without being overbearing, exemplary in service, and impeccable in decor, with handsome wood trim, cranberry tablecloths, crystal glasses, hand-painted china, and fresh-cut flowers. It is, in a word, exquisite. Dishes are prepared with a creative selection of ingredients. How does pepper-crusted duck breast sound? For dessert, the Chocolate Trio, with its warm, creamy chocolate sauce, is divine, and most desserts feature delicate sugar work. This restaurant received awards in 2001 for the best brunch and the best wine list in the Park City area. ⊠ *Stein Eriksen Lodge, Deer Valley,* ☎ *435/645–6455. Reservations essential. AE, DC, MC, V.*

$$$–$$$$
★
✕ **Grappa.** In Park City's old town district, this restaurant specializes in ambience and northern Italian dishes. Heavy floor tiles, bricks, and timbers lend a rustic, warm, farmhouse feel. Tables on the wraparound balcony overlook those on the first floor. The menus, which change seasonally, offer appetizers such as homemade duck prosciutto with a summer pear and balsamic vinegar salad, and fried calamari served with basil aioli and fresh marinara. Innovative entrées include crisp, pan-fried game hen with spinach tortellini and roasted garlic velouté, as well as pancetta-wrapped chicken fricassee filled with spinach and mushroom risotto. ⊠ *151 Main St., Park City,* ☎ *435/ 645–0636. AE, D, MC, V.*

$$–$$$$ ✕ **Riverhorse Café.** The two large upper-level warehouse rooms that make up this café resemble an ultramodern big-city supper club, with exposed beams, polished hardwood floors, black-and-white furnishings, and walls adorned with work by contemporary Utah artists. Musicians entertain on most nights. For your meal, choose from ahi tuna, charred rack of lamb, or macadamia-crusted Alaskan halibut, their signature dish. Don't miss the restaurant's famous mashed potatoes. ⊠ *540 Main St., Park City,* ☎ *435/649–3536. Reservations essential. AE, D, MC, V.*

$$–$$$ ✕ **Zoom.** Owned by Robert Redford, this "western chic" eatery's specialty is . . . drum roll, please . . . macaroni and cheese! Suffice it to say it's nothing like the stuff in the box. The rest of the menu offers other comfort foods, but always kicked up a notch. Locals favor the tri-tip steak served with grits disguised by garlic and Asiago cheese, or the beefed-up, but totally meatless, Portobello mushroom burger. Leave room for the chocolate mousse cake with raspberry sauce. ⊠ *660 Main St., Park City,* ☎ *435/649–9108. AE, D, DC, MC, V.*

$–$$ ✕ **Café Terigo.** This airy café serves several well-prepared pasta and seafood dishes using only fresh ingredients. Good picks include almond-encrusted salmon or smoked chicken with sun-dried tomatoes over fettuccine. Desserts like bread pudding or mud pie can top off the meal. ⊠ *424 Main St., Park City,* ☎ *435/645–9555. AE, D, MC, V.*

$–$$ ✕ **Nacho Mamma's.** Located in Prospector Square just a few minutes from Main Street, this local favorite features southwestern dishes that will test the temperature at which your taste buds explode. The chiles rellenos, which come with chicken, beef, or shrimp, push the upper limits of spicy, while the beef *chipotle,* with its thinly sliced beef and tangy sauce, will sate any meat-lover's appetite. ⊠ *1821 Sidewinder Dr., Park City,* ☎ *435/645–8226. AE, D, MC, V.*

$ ✕ **Burgie's.** Burgers, grilled chicken, and New York steak are a few of the classic American favorites served at this eatery on Park City's historic Main Street. Saturday is salsa night, with music and dancing in a hall above the restaurant. ⊠ *570 Main St., Park City,* ☎ *435/649– 0011. AE, D, MC, V.*

$ ✕ **El Chubasco.** For a quick and hearty meal of traditional Mexican food, this new—and instantly popular—place is perfect. Favorites are shrimp fajitas, *posole* (a rich soup that combines pork and dried corn in a chili-laden tomato base), fish tacos, and warm empanadas. The low-key atmosphere is part of the charm. ⊠ *1890 Bonanza Dr., Park City,* ☎ *435/645–9114. AE, D, DC, MC, V.*

Lodging

Central reservations: ☎ 800/558–3337 for Deer Valley; 800/222– 7275 for Park City; 888/226–9667 for the Canyons.

$$$–$$$$ ☷ **Marriott Hotel.** As one of Park City's largest, this hotel includes a full array of amenities, including underground parking, which makes it the preferred hotel of athletes who participate in the annual World Cup competition. The motif is western, and the decor includes items from Park City's mining era. On the premises is a restaurant plus a nice atrium area with a pool. It's an easy walk from here to the shops and restaurants of downtown Park City. ⊠ *1895 Sidewinder Dr., Box 4439, Park City 84060,* ☎ *435/649–2900 or 800/234–9003,* FAX *435/ 649–4852,* WEB *www.parkcityutah.com. 199 rooms. Restaurant, bar, coffee shop, indoor pool, hot tub, sauna, gym, bicycles, mountain bikes, ski shop, laundry services, convention center, meetings rooms. AE, D, DC, MC, V.*

$$$–$$$$ 🏨 **Shadow Ridge Resort.** Few other hotels in town can match the Shadow Ridge for convenience and comfort. Just a few feet from the Park City Mountain Resort, you can amble to the slopes in less time than it takes to warm up your car. Accommodations are in one- or two-bedroom condominium suites. With full kitchens, these suites are a sweet deal for families. All rooms have sturdy furnishings in the colors of a mountain summer. The staff here is friendly and experienced. ⊠ *50 Shadow Ridge St., Box 1820, Park City 84060,* ☎ *435/655–3315 or 800/451–3031,* FAX *435/649–5951,* WEB *www.shadowridgepc.com. 100 suites. Bar, pool, hot tub, sauna, coin laundry, laundry services, meeting rooms. AE, D, DC, MC, V.*

$$–$$$$ 🏨 **Washington School Inn.** This inn off of Main Street proves an old school-
★ house (1889) can make a great B&B. The school closed in the mid-1930s and the three-story stone structure was carefully restored in the 1980s to make way for the guest rooms, kitchen, and common areas. The interior is spacious and designer-perfect, with high, vaulted ceilings, cherrywood wainscoting, and a stunning center staircase leading to the bell tower. The large rooms and suites have Victorian-era furnishings and are individually decorated, with features such as country-style wall coverings, handwoven area rugs, tile-and-stone flooring or carpeting, clawfoot tubs, and, in some rooms, four-poster canopy beds. Breakfast including omelets, quiches, or soufflés is served buffet-style in the dining room. At the free afternoon tea, drinks and appetizers are served. ⊠ *543 Park Ave., Box 536, Park City 84060,* ☎ *435/649–3800 or 800/ 824–1672,* FAX *435/649–3802,* WEB *www.washingtonschoolinn.com. 12 rooms, 3 suites. Dining room, hot tub, sauna, gym, laundry room. AE, D, DC, MC, V. BP.*

$$–$$$ 🏨 **Best Western Landmark Inn.** Out by the interstate, this property makes a great stopover for travelers. The rooms are nicely furnished, and the location is convenient if you want to split your time between Park City and Salt Lake. A Continental breakfast is included in the price of a room, and there is a small convenience store on the property. ⊠ *6560 N. Landmark Dr., 84098,* ☎ *435/649–7300 or 800/548–8824,* FAX *435/649– 1760,* WEB *www.bestwestern.com. 106 rooms. Restaurant, indoor pool, hot tub, gym, coin laundry. AE, D, DC, MC, V. CP.*

$$ 🏨 **Holiday Inn Express.** With fireplaces and log furniture, this new hotel near the highway manages to keep up the warm feel of a rustic cabin. A free shuttle service provides rides to and from the Park City area resorts during the winter. A free Continental breakfast is provided. ⊠ *1501 W. Ute Blvd., Park City 84098,* ☎ *435/658–1600 or 888/870– 4386,* FAX *435/658–1600,* WEB *www.basshotels.com. 76 rooms. Indoor pool, hot tub, sauna. AE, D, DC, MC, V. CP.*

Nightlife and the Arts

Park City hosts a variety of performing-arts events throughout the summer. The historic **Egyptian Theatre** (⊠ 328 Main St., ☎ 435/649–9371), in downtown Park City, stages many different plays by local groups and national touring companies. The **Park City International Chamber Music Festival** (☎ 435/649–5309) runs from early July through mid-August. Deer Valley Resort's outdoor **Summer Concert Series** (☎ 435/ 649–1000) includes everything from classical to country music. The

Summit Institute (☎ 435/649–2315) at Deer Valley puts on musical and dance events throughout the summer. Included are performances by the Ririe-Woodbury Dance Company, a String Chamber Music Festival, and several artist-in-residence programs.

Among Park City's lively bars is **Cicero's** (✉ 306 Main St., ☎ 435/649–5044), which offers live music on most evenings and also serves good Italian and American food.

Outdoor Activities and Sports

Rockport State Park (✉ 9040 N. Rte. 302, Peoa, 7 mi south of Wanship on Rte. 32, ☎ 435/336–2241) is northeast of Park City and is quite nice for boating and fishing. There are eight camping areas for either developed or primitive camping.

CYCLING

Several mountain bike trails are accessible from the **Guardsman Pass Road** in Park City. Both Deer Valley Ski Resort and the Park City Mountain Resort run lifts in the summer to facilitate fun descents by bike. The Canyons also has cycling trails on the resort property. The **Historic Union Pacific Rail Trail** is a 28-mi trail popular with cyclists. It begins at Park City and follows I–80 to Echo Reservoir.

GOLF

The **Park City Municipal Golf Course** (✉ 1541 Thaynes Canyon Dr., ☎ 435/615–5800) has 18 holes.

HOT-AIR BALLOONING

Park City Balloon Adventures (☎ 435/645–8787 or 800/396–8787) offers half-hour and one-hour scenic flights daily, weather permitting. Fliers meet at a local hotel and are shuttled to the takeoff site, which varies from day to day. A Continental breakfast is served during the flight, and a champagne or nonalcoholic toast is offered on touchdown. Reservations are required.

Downhill Skiing and Snowboarding

The skiing might not be as dramatic as Alta and Snowbird, and the natural snow not quite as plentiful (about 300 inches in a winter, compared with about 500 inches in neighboring Big Cottonwood and Little Cottonwood canyons), but there is a lot of skiing for all levels. If your youngsters do not ski, the city has several licensed child-care agencies. Your resort or the Park City Chamber of Commerce/Visitors Bureau can point you to providers.

Snow reports: ☎ 435/615–3308 for the Canyons; 435/649–2000 for Deer Valley; 435/647–5449 or 800/222–7275 for Park City.

With a vertical drop of 3,190 ft, **The Canyons** has similar mountain terrain to that of neighboring Park City, but intermediates will find somewhat longer cruising runs here. Above-tree-line bowls feed into some fine tree skiing for experts. The resort has 3,625 acres in skiable terrain and is building a year-round base resort. There are 11 lifts, including an eight-passenger gondola, and several on-mountain restaurants. As the first Park City mountain to allow snowboarding (only Deer Valley prohibits it now) this resort is popular with younger crowds. ✉ *4000 The Canyons Resort Dr., Park City 84098,* ☎ *435/649–5400 or 888/226–9667,* FAX *435/649–7374,* WEB *www.thecanyons.com.*

Two miles south of Park City, **Deer Valley** broke new ground in the ski industry by providing such amenities as ski valets, on-slope telephones, grooming fit for a king, and slope-side dining of the highest caliber. For such pampering, the resort has won rave reviews from virtually every ski and travel magazine. While Deer Valley has elevated grooming to an art, it also offers extreme terrain in Empire Canyon.

Deer Valley's forte is wide, meticulously groomed intermediate runs. It is a ski area for those who want to believe that they can ski with the grace of Stein Eriksen. The moderate pitch of the terrain and the quality of the grooming leads to skiing's version of ballroom dancing. Part of the Deer Valley experience includes a two- to three-hour midday interlude of feasting on the Silver Lake Lodge buffet and catching major rays on the snow-covered meadow in front of the lodge—an area known appropriately as McHenry's Beach. The skiing experience, in other words, fits right in with the resort's overall image. After a while, however, a certain sense of sameness can set in. That's why it's nice having Park City Mountain Resort right next door. ⊠ *Box 1525, Park City 84060,* ☎ *435/649–1000 or 800/424–3337,* FAX *435/645–6538,* WEB *www.deervalley.com.*

With 100 trails and 3,300 acres of skiable terrain, including 650 acres of open bowls, the **Park City Mountain Resort** is one of Utah's largest ski complexes. The mountain is accessed by 14 chairlifts, four of which are six-person chairs. Roughly half of Park City's terrain is rated as intermediate, but the slopes that line Jupiter Peak are revered by experts as well. The east face of Jupiter features some truly hairy, rock-lined chutes, and Portuguese Gap is an elevator shaft lined by trees. A "six-pack" chair in McConkey's bowl provides access to additional steeps. Snowmaking covers 475 acres, and night skiers will delight in Pay Day, the longest lighted run in the Rockies.

Park City's main drawback isn't lack of steepness but lack of length; despite a vertical drop of 3,100 ft, it's hard putting together a run of more than about 1,400 vertical ft. The ski area is laid out as a series of segments rather than a single unit. That said, however, Park City probably has the best overall terrain mix of any ski area in Utah, enough to keep skiers of all abilities happy for several days. ⊠ *Box 39, Northstar Dr., 84060,* ☎ *435/649–8111 or 800/222–7275,* WEB *www.parkcitymountain.com.*

FACILITIES

The Canyons: 3,190-ft vertical drop; 3,625 skiable acres; 14% beginner, 44% intermediate, 42% advanced; 1 8-passenger gondola, 4 high-speed quad chairs, 4 quad chairs, 1 triple chair, 1 double chair, 1 surface lift. **Deer Valley:** 3,000-ft vertical drop; 1,750 skiable acres; 15% beginner, 50% intermediate, 35% advanced; 1 high-speed gondola, 4 high-speed quad chairs, 2 quad chairs, 9 triple chairs, 2 double chairs. **Park City:** 3,100-ft vertical drop; 3,300 skiable acres; 18% beginner, 43% intermediate, 39% advanced; 4 high-speed 6-passenger chairs, 1 high-speed quad chair, 5 triple chairs, 4 double chairs.

LESSONS AND PROGRAMS

The Perfect Turn program at **The Canyons** (☎ 435/615–8040 or 888/226–9667) bills itself as a "coaching" program rather than an instructional program, for skiers and snowboarders of all ages. One-hour private clinics start at $57 per person and $90 for two. At **Deer Valley Resort** (☎ 435/649–1000), five-hour adult group lessons start at $65. Private lessons start at $72 an hour. **Park City Mountain Resort** (☎ 435/649–8111 or 800/227–7275) has a two-hour adult group lesson that starts at $48. The resort's popular snowboarding lessons are similarly priced. Children's programs are available. Park City also has an excellent instructional program for skiers with disabilities and group programs for senior citizens or women only.

LIFT TICKETS

The Canyons: $59. **Deer Valley:** $63. **Park City:** $60. A Silver Passport, which allows skiers to use the lifts at all three resorts, is available in multiday increments beginning at $58 per day.

RENTALS

Several shops in the Park City area rent equipment packages, some for as little as $10 a day. Advance rental reservations are available from **Breeze Ski Rentals** (⊠ 1284 Lowell, Park City, near Pay Day lift, ☎ 435/649–2736 or 800/525–0314; ⊠ 1415 Lowell, Park City, near ice rink, ☎ 435/649–1902; ⊠ 4343 N. Hwy. 224, The Canyons, ☎ 435/655–7066, WEB www.skirentals.com), which has two Park City locations and one in The Canyons. Rates range between $12 and $43 per day, depending on equipment and store. **Jan's Mountain Outfitters** (⊠ 1600 Park Ave., Park City, ☎ 435/649–4949 or 800/745–1020) offers not only equipment packages ($18 per day; $28 for high-performance) but also clothing-rental packages starting at $27 per day.

Utah Ski & Golf (⊠ 698 Park Ave., Park City, ☎ 435/649–3020; ⊠ 1255 Empire Ave., Park City, in the Sweetwater Condo, ☎ 435/655–8367, WEB www.utahskigolf.com) has two locations in Park City in addition to locations at both terminals of the Salt Lake International Airport, and they offer downhill and cross-country equipment, snowshoes, and clothing. Rates for downhill ski equipment range from $10 to $30 per day; complete ski packages, which include equipment and clothing, are $35 per day.

Nordic Skiing

BACKCOUNTRY SKIING

Skiers who want to do some unguided skiing on their own can climb the Guardsman's Pass Road, which is between Deer Valley and Park City and is closed to traffic in winter. Strong intermediates and better can reserve a three-canyon tour with **Ski Utah Interconnect Adventure Tour** (☎ 801/534–1907).

TRACK SKIING

The only set tracks in the Park City area are at the **White Pine Ski Touring Center,** between Park City and The Canyons. The 12 groomed mi are on a flat golf course that's nothing special as far as either scenery or terrain variation is concerned, but adequate for anyone seeking a quick aerobic workout. Lessons and rentals are available. ⊠ *Box 680068, Park City 84068,* ☎ *801/649–8710 or 801/649–8701.* ☞ *Trail fee $12.*

Shopping

Within the colorful structures that line Park City's Main Street are a number of clothing boutiques, sporting-goods stores, and gift shops. **Christmas on Main Street** (⊠ 442 Main St., Park City, ☎ 435/645–8115) carries ornaments year-round. Visit **Jan's Mountain Outfitters** (⊠ 1600 Park Ave., Park City, ☎ 435/649–4949) to pick up skiing, bicycling, camping, and fly-fishing gear. A few miles north of Park City, next to I–80, are the **Factory Stores at Park City** (⊠ 6699 N. Landmark Dr., ☎ 435/645–7078 or 888/746–7333). Represented in this collection of 47 outlets are Nike, Brooks Brothers, Eddie Bauer, Guess, and Corning, among others.

Ogden

③①   *35 mi from Salt Lake City via I–15 north.*

With a population of more than 65,000, Ogden combines a small-town feel with the infrastructure of a larger city. Upon the site of a stockade and trading post built by mountain man Miles Goodyear, Brigham Young directed the settlement of Ogden in 1850. Despite its Mormon roots, however, Ogden was to change radically with the arrival of the transcontinental railroad in the area in 1869. The town quickly became a major western crossroads, and it received a great influx of non-Mormons. With the advent of World War II, the military began to have a considerable presence in town, which, with Hill Air Force Base nearby, it still has today. Ogden is also a college town; Weber State University is within the city limits.

On your way into town from the south are Hill Air Force Base and the **Hill Aerospace Museum.** Among the many interesting planes housed in this large hangar are the SR-71 Blackbird (a reconnaissance aircraft that made a transatlantic flight in less than two hours), a B-17 Flying Fortress, 40 WWII aircraft, and a plane first flown in 1911. ⊠ *Hill Air Force Base, Exit 341 off I–15,* ☎ *801/777–6868,* WEB *www.hill.af.mil/museum.* ▣ *Free.* ☉ *Daily 9–4:30.*

Ogden has a number of vintage buildings and museums. The best of the latter are found in the **Ogden Union Station.** Built in 1924, this impressive Spanish Revival structure demonstrates the considerable esteem railroad travel once enjoyed and houses some interesting museums: the Utah State Railroad Museum, the Browning-Kimball Car Museum, and the Browning Firearms Museum. (Browning is a renowned gun manufacturer.) ⊠ *25th St. and Wall Ave.,* ☎ *801/629–8444.* ▣ *$3 (combined ticket to museums).* ☉ *Mon.–Sat. 10–6, Sun. 11–3.*

The **Eccles Community Art Center** displays a permanent art collection and hosts special showings in an impressive Victorian mansion. The permanent collection focuses on contemporary artists, such as LeConte Stewart, Henri Mosher, Pilar Pobil, David Jackson, and Richard Van Wagoner, and monthly exhibits feature works by emerging Utah artists. A new sculpture plaza opened in 2001. ⊠ *2580 Jefferson Ave.,* ☎ *801/ 392–6935.* ▣ *Free.* ☉ *Weekdays 9–5, Sat. 9–3.*

Highlighting a chapter in history that unfolded decades prior to the railroad era, **Ft. Buenaventura State Park** is a 32-acre tract with exact replicas of the stockade and cabins that Miles Goodyear built in 1846. Guides in period costume interpret the ways of the early trappers, and hundreds of mountain-man enthusiasts rendezvous at the fort in September, at Thanksgiving, and over Easter weekend. Camping and picnicking facilities are available. ⊠ *2450 A Ave.,* ☎ *801/621–4808.* ▣ *$4 per vehicle.* ☉ *June–Sept., daily 8 AM–8 PM; Oct.–May, daily 8–5.*

In downtown Ogden, the **Ogden River Parkway** follows the banks of the Ogden River for 3 mi to the mouth of Ogden Canyon. A real people place, this urban greenway hosts a number of outdoor activities, including bicycling, walking, jogging, tennis, baseball, and fishing, all free and open to the public. What really distinguishes the Ogden River Parkway, however, are the two parks found along the way. The **MTC Learning Park** has botanical gardens and pavilion facilities; the **George S. Eccles Dinosaur Park** charges a small fee for visitors to view dozens of life-size dinosaur replicas in one of the largest collections of its kind in the nation. ⊠ *1544 E. Park Blvd.,* ☎ *801/393–3466.* ▣ *Dinosaur Park $3.50.* ☉ *Dinosaur Park hrs vary by season and according to the weather.*

With the Ogden River Parkway pointing the way, follow Route 39 (a designated scenic byway) into Ogden Canyon. A few miles beyond the canyon mouth, the mountains open up to make room for **Pineview Reservoir.** During the summer, this 2,000-acre lake is festooned with colorful sailboards and the graceful arcs of water-skiers. The fishing is

When you pack your MCI Calling Card, it's like packing your loved ones along too.

Your MCI Calling Card is the easy way to stay in touch when you travel. Use it to call to and from over 125 countries. Plus, every time you call, you can earn frequent flier miles. So wherever your travels take you, call home with your MCI Calling Card. It's even easy to get one. Just visit **www.mci.com/worldphone.**

EASY TO CALL WORLDWIDE

1. Just enter the WorldPhone® access number of the country you're calling from.
2. Enter or give the operator your MCI Calling Card number.
3. Enter or give the number you're calling.

Aruba ✣	800-888-8
Bahamas ✣	1-800-888-8000
Barbados ✣	1-800-888-8000
Bermuda ✣	1-800-888-8000
British Virgin Islands ✣	1-800-888-8000
Canada	1-800-888-8000
Mexico	01-800-021-8000
Puerto Rico	1-800-888-8000
United States	1-800-888-8000
U.S. Virgin Islands	1-800-888-8000

✣ Limited availability.

EARN FREQUENT FLIER MILES

MCI®

SEE THE WORLD
IN FULL COLOR

Fodor's Exploring Guides bring all the great sights vividly to life with hundreds of photographs, fascinating historical background, and colorful anecdotes. Detailed maps and practical information keep you headed in the right direction.

Pair a **Fodor's** Exploring Guide with your trusted Gold Guide for a complete planning package.

good, and some beaches, campgrounds, and marinas dot the shore. **Anderson Cove,** along the southern end of the lake, is quite popular, as is **Middle Inlet,** along the eastern shore. During the winter, Ogden Canyon reveals some great (and inexpensive) alternatives to the Salt Lake City ski scene, including Snowbasin and Powder Mountain.

㉜ Willard Bay State Park, about 10,000 acres in size, is actually a freshwater arm of the Great Salt Lake. Fed by canals in the spring, it is effectively protected from saltwater intrusion by dikes, and because it is freshwater, Willard Bay is a popular fishing, boating, and bird-watching area. Facilities include a marina, group areas, concession stands, and shady picnic spots for day use. Bald and golden eagles are spotted frequently in tall trees that grow along the park's Eagle Beach. ⊠ *15 mi north of Ogden off I–15,* ☎ *435/734–9494.* ⌑ *$6 per vehicle.* ◷ *Daily 6 AM–10 PM.*

If you happen to be passing through in the late summer or early fall, drive up U.S. 89/91 from Ogden to Brigham City to enjoy Utah's **Fruitway.** You'll find many produce stands and peach, apple, cherry, plum, pear, and apricot orchards.

Dining and Lodging

$$–$$$$ ✕ **Gray Cliff Lodge Restaurant.** Set in scenic Ogden Canyon, this local favorite features Utah trout, prime rib, lamb, and seafood. Small touches, such as lace tablecloths and linen napkins, and a wall of windows that offers views of mountains and forests, create a quiet, romantic atmosphere. ⊠ *508 Ogden Canyon,* ☎ *801/392–6775. AE, D, DC, MC, V.*

$–$$$ ✕ **Rooster's.** Located on historic 25th Street, this brewpub offers ex-
★ cellent food, and libations brewed on-site. Pizzas, prime rib, and daily seafood specials are popular, as is the spicy seafood jambalaya. Wash down your meal with a tall Golden Spike Ale, or any of the Brewmaster's Specials, which vary by season. Sunday brunch at Rooster's is a lazy pleasure. ⊠ *253 25th St.,* ☎ *801/627–6171. AE, D, DC, MC, V.*

$–$$ ✕ **Bavarian Chalet.** For the finest German food in Utah, served in a setting suitably old-world, the Bavarian is it. The menu includes traditional favorites, such as Wiener schnitzel and sauerbraten, along with a few updated surprises. A sampler plate, with smaller portions of at least three different dishes, is popular, as is the Black Forest cake. ⊠ *4387 Harrison Blvd.,* ☎ *801/479–7561. AE, D, MC, V.*

$–$$ ✕ **Maddox Ranch House.** Down-home western food—steak, chicken, bison—and portions big enough to satisfy a ranch hand make this place, located 12 mi north of Ogden, plenty popular. Every item is made from scratch, and people drive here from surrounding states just for a piece of the fresh peach pie. The friendly service is a delight. ⊠ *1900 S. U.S. 89, Perry,* ☎ *435/723–8545. AE, D, DC, MC, V.*

$ ✕ **Shooting Star Saloon.** For what some consider to be the best burger in the country (the menu doesn't stray from burgers and beer), as well as a frontier bar atmosphere, visit this Huntsville tavern. From the dollar bills pinned to the ceiling to the stuffed head of a 300-pound St. Bernard on the wall to the graffiti in the bathrooms, there is something to look at in every corner. ⊠ *7350 E. 200 South St., Huntsville, 17 mi from Ogden via Rte. 39,* ☎ *801/745–2002. No credit cards.*

$ ✕☷ **Best Western High Country Inn.** This motel off I–15 is spacious and comfortable, and the rustic western motif and friendly staff give the place a cozy feel. Jeremiah's, the hotel's restaurant, is a popular dining place for locals and has won the "Best Breakfast in Utah" award for the past eight years. The restaurant also serves hearty American lunches and dinners. The hotel is within easy walking distance of a nature center with several trails, and it's close to the George S. Eccles Dinosaur Park. ⊠ *1335 W. 12th St., 84404,* ☎ *801/394–9474 or 800/594–8979,* FAX *801/392–6589,* WEB *www.bestwestern.com. 111 rooms. Restaurant, refrigerators, pool, hot tub, gym, coin laundry. AE, D, DC, MC, V.*

$$–$$$ 🛏 **Historic Ben Lomond Hotel.** Listed on the National Register of His-
★ toric Places, the hotel is one of Ogden's most prominent structures and is worth a peek inside just for its hand-painted ceiling tiles and chandeliers. All accommodations are elegant suites, furnished with cherrywood furniture, refrigerators, data ports, and two televisions. Monthly rates are available and are remarkably reasonable, making this a great base from which to mount an extended exploration of northern Utah. A club on the premises features live music, a Manager's Social is held in the lobby on weekday evenings, and a full breakfast is included. ⊠ *2510 Washington Blvd., 84401,* ☎ *801/627–1900,* FAX *801/394–5342,* WEB *www.benlomondhotel.com. 144 suites. Restaurant, bar, in-room data ports, refrigerators, gym, nightclub, laundry services, free parking. AE, D, DC, MC, V. BP.*

$–$$ 🛏 **Snowberry Inn.** Overlooking Pineview Reservoir in the Wasatch Mountains above Ogden, this cozy inn is everything a rural B&B should be. The quiet environment and views enhance the experience, as do the rustic yet comfortable rooms. The vegetarian breakfast is complete and country good. The inn is near three ski areas. ⊠ *1315 N. Hwy. 158, Box 795, Eden 84310,* ☎ *801/745–2634. 5 rooms, 2 suites. Hot tub, coin laundry. AE, D, MC, V. BP.*

Nightlife and the Arts

The **Club Esquire: House of Blues** (⊠ 2510 Washington Blvd., ☎ 801/612–3060) in the Historic Ben Lomond Hotel, is a great place to relax and hear live blues bands. The **Perry Egyptian Theater** (⊠ 2415 Washington Blvd., ☎ 801/395–3200) is an art deco jewel where live theater is staged. Occasionally, films, such as those screened at the Sundance Film Festival, are shown. **Weber State University** (⊠ 3750 Harrison Blvd., ☎ 801/626–6000) regularly offers theater, music, and dance performances by students and visiting artists at the Val A. Browning Center for the Performing Arts.

Outdoor Activities and Sports

GOLF

There are three 18-hole courses in the area. The **Ben Lomond Golf Course** (⊠ 1800 N. Hwy. 89, Harrisville, ☎ 801/782–7754) has a serene setting with beautiful views of the Wasatch Mountains. The **Mount Ogden Golf Course** (⊠ 3000 Taylor Ave., ☎ 801/629–0699) is one of the prettiest courses in Utah, and the view of Ogden Valley is stunning. Just minutes from downtown Ogden, the **Riverside Golf Course** (⊠ 460 S. Weber Dr., ☎ 801/399–4636) winds along the scenic Ogden River.

RAFTING

For a white-water adventure the whole family can enjoy, try rafting the Weber River on a tour with **Park City Rafting** (⊠ 1105 N. Taggert La., Morgan, ☎ 435/655–3800). The relatively gentle two-hour trip is a great way to experience a rugged canyon, and there are several mild rapids (Class II–III) to provide excitement. All equipment is provided.

Downhill Skiing

Rising north of Ogden Canyon's Pineview Reservoir is **Powder Mountain** (⊠ Hwy. 158, Eden, ☎ 801/745–3772). As the name suggests, Powder Mountain receives a generous helping of the white stuff for which Utah is known. It offers just under 2,000 vertical ft, three chairlifts, and three surface tows. Skiable acreage totals 1,800, and two slopeside eateries provide après-ski diversions.

A vertical drop of 2,950 ft made **Snowbasin** (⊠ Hwy. 226, Huntsville, 17 mi from Ogden, ☎ 801/399–1135) the perfect site for the downhill ski races during the 2002 Olympic Winter Games. With nine chairlifts accessing more than 3,000 acres of skiable terrain, this is one of Utah's largest ski resorts. Snowbasin has no base-area accommodations.

Shopping

East of the train depot in Ogden, 25th Street first served as a center for immigrants before becoming the town's shadiest avenue in the 1870s. Today the historic street is a shopping district. Behind the old brick fronts that once housed gambling halls, saloons, opium dens, and the like are antiques shops, gift boutiques, and restaurants.

OFF THE BEATEN PATH | **BEAR RIVER MIGRATORY BIRD REFUGE** – Thirty-seven miles from Ogden via I–15 north (to Exit 366 at Brigham City) and Forest Street (which becomes Bird Refuge Road) west, this was originally a series of freshwater lagoons ideally suited for waterfowl; however, in 1983 the 74,000-acre preserve was inundated by the rising Great Salt Lake. Ice floes destroyed all facilities at the refuge, but a considerable amount of work by the U.S. Fish and Wildlife Service has resurrected a 12-mi driving tour that follows various dikes. The habitat has been reclaimed, and the refuge once again hosts seasonal influxes of ducks, geese, and shorebirds. Plans for a new visitor center are in the works, along with a proposed expansion of the acreage. ⊠ *Bird Refuge Rd., 16 mi west of Brigham City,* ☎ *435/723–5887.* ☜ *Free.* ⊙ *Daily dawn–dusk.*

Golden Spike National Historic Site

③③ *54 mi from Ogden via I–15 north (to Exit 368 at Brigham City), Rte. 83 west.*

The Union Pacific and Central Pacific railroads met here at Promontory Summit on May 10, 1869, completing the first transcontinental route. Under the auspices of the National Park Service, Golden Spike features a visitor center, an auto tour, some vintage locomotives on display, and several locomotives that are still running. Every May 10 (and on Saturdays and holidays during the summer), a reenactment of the driving of the golden spike is held. ⊠ *Rte. 83, 32 mi west of Brigham City,* ☎ *435/471–2209,* WEB *www.nps.gov/gosp/home.* ☜ *$7 per vehicle.* ⊙ *June–Aug., daily 8–4:30; Sept.–May, daily 8–6.*

Cache Valley

③④ *18 mi from Brigham City via U.S. 89/91 north.*

East of Brigham City, U.S. 89/91 tops Sardine Summit in Wellsville Canyon before dropping into the highly scenic Cache Valley. Walled in on the west by the imposing Wellsville Mountains (often touted as the steepest incline of any range in the country) and by the Bear River Range (a sub-range of the Wasatch) to the east, Cache Valley is 15 mi wide and 60 mi long. The valley was originally home to bands of Northwestern Shoshone. During the 1820s, it became a favorite haunt for Jim Bridger and other mountain men, who held many rendezvous in the area. The trappers often stashed, or "cached," their furs in the valley. Mormon pioneers, led by Peter Maughan, arrived in 1856 and created permanent settlements. Today Cache Valley is one of the most important agricultural regions in Utah. Topping the list of foods produced here is cheese. One of three cheese factories in the valley, Cache Valley Cheese is the nation's largest producer of Swiss cheese.

To learn about Cache Valley's history from 1820 to 1920, visit the **American West Heritage Center,** which features a 1917 living historical farm, a pioneer site, and a Shoshone encampment. Construction of mountain man and military displays will begin in 2002. On the farm, numerous antique farm implements are on display, draft horses still pull their weight, workers dressed in period clothing demonstrate such tasks as sheepshearing and quilting, and special events take place throughout the year. The Festival of the American West, held at the Center in July, includes additional displays and reenactments, along with food booths, cowboy poetry readings, and concerts. ⊠ *4025 S. U.S. 89/91, Wellsville,* ☎ *435/245–6050 or 800/225–3378,* WEB *www.americanwestcenter.org.* ☎ *$3–$5.* ☉ *Memorial Day–Labor Day, Mon.–Sat. 10–5.*

Logan

35 *25 mi from Brigham City via U.S. 89/91 north.*

Logan is home to **Utah State University** (☎ 435/797–1000), a land-grant college that began in 1888. Today, USU has an enrollment of well over 20,000 and is a leader in such diverse fields as agriculture, natural resources, and space technology. Just east of downtown Logan, the USU campus is best toured by starting at the historic **Old Main** administration building—look for the bell tower. Across campus, the Chase Fine Arts Center includes the **Nora Eccles Art Museum** (☎ 435/797–1414; ☎ free; ☉ weekdays 10:30–4:30), which features exhibits by local, nationally, and internationally recognized artists. No visit to USU would be complete without a stop at the **Food Science Building** (⊠ 1200 East and 750 North Sts.) for a scoop of the university's famous ice cream. You can also get breakfast and a lunch or dinner of soup and sandwiches here.

The twin towers of Logan's **Mormon Temple** (⊠ 100 North and 200 East Sts.) remind all that this college town is also a conservative community with Mormon roots. Rising from a grassy knoll, this impressive limestone edifice took settlers seven years to complete. The site was chosen by Brigham Young in 1877, and the work was directed by architect Truman O. Angell, designer of the Salt Lake temple. As with all Mormon temples, this structure is open only to followers of the faith.

Historic **Main Street** is best explored by a walking tour; an illustrated brochure, available from the **Chamber of Commerce** (⊠ 160 N. Main St.), guides you along both sides of Main Street and up a few cross streets. The more interesting buildings include the LDS Tabernacle (open to non-Mormons); St. John's Episcopal Church, representing Cache Valley's first non-Mormon denomination; the Ellen Eccles and Lyric theaters; the Cache County Courthouse, with its restored cupola; and the Bluebird Restaurant. Stop in at the **Bluebird** (⊠ 19 N. Main St., ☎ 435/752–3155) to admire the early 1900s decor and to enjoy handcrafted chocolates, a cool drink, or an ice-cream treat at the soda fountain.

If you pass through in the winter, be sure to drive up Blacksmith Fork Canyon to **Hardware Ranch.** Here the state Division of Wildlife Resources feeds several hundred head of elk throughout the snowy months. A 20-minute sleigh ride takes you up close to the majestic creatures for some great pictures; call ahead (☎ 435/753–6168) to combine your sleigh ride with an excellent barbecue dinner. There is also a visitor center and café. ⊠ *Rte. 101, 24 mi southeast of Logan via U.S. 165 and Rte. 101, Hyrum,* ☎ *435/753–6206,* WEB *www.hardwareranch.com.* ☎ *Sleigh rides $6.* ☉ *Mid-Dec.–mid-Mar., daily 10–5, snow conditions permitting.*

Dining and Lodging

$ ✕ **Callaway's.** The cuisine here is what a fine chef from Italy might develop after visiting southern California and the Southwest. Ravioli, linguine, fettuccine—they're all served, but with an eclectic approach. Santa Fe Alfredo is a good example, as are the dishes that feature bison. The chicken and rosemary ravioli, with a buttery basil sauce, is excellent. Hot bread sticks and a dipping sauce are served with each meal; those and a bowl of delicately seasoned soup will satisfy diners with smaller appetites. If you have room for dessert, try the decadent chocolate cake. The food is definitely worth the 6-mi drive from Logan (north on U.S. 91). ✉ *54 N. Main St., Smithfield,* ☎ *435/563–9179. AE, MC, V.*

$ ✕ **Gia's Italian Restaurant.** Upstairs you will find sit-down service and carefully prepared Italian dishes. Downstairs, in the Factory, the service is strictly cafeteria style, the food includes pizza and sandwiches, and the atmosphere is lively. As any college student will tell you, the basement is where you go to meet friends for a beer, while upstairs is reserved for entertaining a date or parents. ✉ *119 S. Main St.,* ☎ *435/752–8384. AE, D, MC, V.*

$ ✕ **Tanpopo.** In a small shopping plaza off Main Street, this family-run restaurant serves Japanese food that has both taste and visual appeal. Begin lunch or dinner with an item from the sushi bar—dragon rolls are popular, along with the shrimp tempura and California rolls—or try a gyoza appetizer. Favorite entrées include salmon teriyaki, and shrimp and vegetable tempura. For special occasions, reserve a private dining room, where seating and service follow the traditional Japanese style. ✉ *55 W. 1000 North St.,* ☎ *435/750–7099. AE, D, MC, V.*

$$–$$$ 🏨 **Anniversary Inn.** This wonderful B&B on Logan's most prestigious
★ historic boulevard is actually three separate buildings on one city lot, including a 22-room mansion that dates to the late 1800s, a carriage house, and the White House. Guest rooms, called fantasy suites, range from smaller models to full suites, each with a different look. The Honeymoon Suite is elaborately romantic, and the Jesse James Hideout and the Swiss Family Robinson suites accurately hint at their decor. All rooms have two-person jetted tubs. A Continental breakfast is delivered to your room, and there is no smoking in the rooms. ✉ *169 E. Center St., 84321,* ☎ *435/752–3443 or 800/574–7605,* WEB *www.anniversaryinn.com. 21 rooms. AE, D, MC, V. CP.*

$–$$ 🏨 **Baugh Best Western Motel.** These basic, yet comfortable, accommodations are one of the best deals in town. Because it is locally owned, the service is personable enough to make up for the standard motel-style furnishings. ✉ *153 S. Main St., 84321,* ☎ *435/752–5220 or 800/462–4154,* FAX *435/752–3251. 78 rooms. Restaurant, pool. AE, D, DC, MC, V.*

Nightlife and the Arts

Thanks to both the presence of Utah State University and the community's keen interest in the arts, Logan is home to many fine productions. USU's theater and music departments host a variety of exciting performances. The **Ellen Eccles Theatre** (✉ 43 S. Main St., ☎ 435/752–0026) presents Broadway musicals, Celtic music, and a yearly series of performances appropriate for children. The **Lyric Theatre** (✉ 28 W. Center St., ☎ 435/797–0305) features performances by the university's repertory company. The **Utah Festival Opera Company** (☎ 435/750–0300 or 800/262–0074) performs a five-week season between July and August at the Ellen Eccles Theatre.

Outdoor Activities and Sports

Hyrum State Park (✉ 405 W. 300 South St., in the northwest corner of Hyrum, ☎ 435/245–6866) has a 450-acre reservoir that draws local boaters during the summer and fall. Shady picnic areas, a peaceful rural setting, and great views of the Wellsville Mountains and the Bear River Range make this a popular spot for family gatherings. During the winter, ice fishing is the sport of choice.

CANOEING

Although you can canoe on virtually any body of water in the region, the best places include **Tony Grove Lake** in Logan Canyon and the **Bear River,** northwest of Logan. Winding in serpentine fashion through Cache Valley, the Bear River features several nice stretches, including a particularly satisfying one that runs 11 mi between Amalga and Tremonton. Canoeists pass a blue heron rookery along the way, so this is a good float for bird-watchers.

CYCLING AND HIKING

Road cyclists pedal out into scenic Cache Valley on its long, flat country roads or venture up Logan and Blacksmith Fork canyons. Mountain bikers can spend an afternoon on the 9-mi round-trip from Wood Camp, in Logan Canyon, to the 3,200-year-old Jardine juniper tree that grows on a high ridge offering views of Wyoming and Idaho. Mountain bikers and hikers alike can access a prime wilderness area via the 3-mi route from Tony Grove Lake to the summit of Naomi Peak. The Limber Pine Trail is a popular and easy hike (1-mi round-trip) at the summit between Logan Canyon and Bear Lake. In the Wellsville Mountains, a 2-mi trail climbs steeply from Maple Bench to Stewart Pass, a lofty ridge top along the annual migration route of eagles and hawks; on a clear day, the view from the ridge extends for over 80 mi.

GOLF

The 18 holes of the **Logan River Municipal Golf Course** (⊠ 1000 S. U.S. 89/91, Logan, ☎ 435/750–0123) are surrounded by wetlands, shady groves of trees alongside the river, and wildlife viewing areas.

OFF THE
BEATEN PATH

LOGAN CANYON – From Logan, U.S. 89 continues for 30 mi up the scenic Logan Canyon before topping out at the crest of the Bear River range. Within the canyon are a number of campgrounds and picnic areas administered by the Wasatch–Cache National Forest. For a particularly satisfying excursion, drive the 7-mi side road (marked) to Tony Grove Lake. At more than 8,000 ft, this subalpine jewel is surrounded by cliffs, alpine meadows, and, during the summer, a visually stunning profusion of wildflowers. A short trail circles the lake, and other backcountry routes enter the Mt. Naomi Wilderness Area to the west.

Bear Lake

 41 mi from Logan (to Garden City) via U.S. 89 north.

Eight miles wide and 20 mi long, Bear Lake is an unusual shade of blue, thanks to tiny bits of limestone in the water. It is home to five species of fish found nowhere else, including the Bonneville cisco, which draws fishermen during spawning in January. Among the lake's more discreet inhabitants is the Bear Lake Monster, which, like its Loch Ness counterpart, lurks somewhere in the depths of the lake, according to local lore.

There are three state park facilities on the lake. **Bear Lake State Park-Marina** (⊠ U.S. 89, 2 mi north of Garden City, ☎ 435/946–3343 or 800/322–3770) contains a marina, beach, picnic area, campground, and visitor center with information on all area parks. At **Eastside State Park** (⊠ 10 mi north of Laketown), the lake bottom drops off quickly, making this site a favorite among anglers and scuba divers. Facilities include a primitive campground and boat ramp. **Rendezvous Beach State**

Park (✉ Rte. 30, near Laketown) is on the south shore of Bear Lake and has more than a mile of sandy beaches, three campgrounds, and picnic areas. Getting its name from the mountain-man gatherings that took place here in 1827 and 1828, Rendezvous Beach hosts a reenactment of the events each September.

Dining and Lodging

The Bear Lake area's signature cuisine centers around raspberries, which grow abundantly in this mountain valley. The town celebrates this abundance during Bear Lake Raspberry Days, held each year at the beginning of August. Throughout the summer, several fast-food stands offer huge fresh raspberry shakes along with typical fast-food fare. Year-round restaurants are few and far between here, and though the food is plentiful, it is also pretty standard. Several small resorts provide condominium-style lodging with beachfront access to Bear Lake and nightly or weekly rates.

$$–$$$ ✕🏨 **Harbor Village Resort.** This resort has direct access to 300 mi of snowmobile trails (many area businesses rent vehicles). Condo sizes vary and they are pleasantly furnished. Resort guests mingle with locals and campers at Harbor Village's restaurant ($–$$$), open Friday and Saturday. ✉ *900 N. Bear Lake Blvd., Box 201, Garden City 84028,* ☎ *435/946–3448,* FAX *435/946–2819,* WEB *www.harborvillagerealty.com. 40 condos. Restaurant, 2 pools (1 indoor), hot tub, sauna, gym. AE, D, DC, MC, V.*

Outdoor Activities and Sports

CYCLING

In addition to the mountain bike trails minutes away in Logan Canyon, a 48-mi loop trail circles Bear Lake. Cyclists of all abilities can enjoy all, or any portion, of this fairly level ride. The paved **Lakeside Bicycle Path** curves from Bear Lake Marina south and east along the shore, with several rest stops. Interpretive signs contain stories about Bear Lake's history, as well as tales from local lore.

GOLF

Bear Lake Golf Course (✉ Garden City, ☎ 435/946–8742) offers nine holes in a charming, lakeside setting.

Timpanogos Cave National Monument

🚩 *36 mi from Salt Lake City via I–15 south and Rte. 92 east.*

Soaring, 11,750-ft **Mt. Timpanogos** is the centerpiece of a wilderness area of the same name and towers over Timpanogos Cave National Monument, along Route 92 within American Fork Canyon. After a strenuous hike up a steep 1½-mi trail to the cave entrance, you may explore three caves connected by two man-made tunnels. A variety of stalactites and stalagmites, plus other formations, make the round-trip hike and tour, which take about three hours, well worth the effort. No water is available on the trail or at the cave, and the cave temperature is 45°F throughout the year, so bring water and warm clothes. Although there is some lighting inside the caves, flashlights can be useful; they make exploring the caves more interesting and are handy for walking down the trail after dark. These popular tours are often sold out; to guarantee your place, purchase tickets in advance. ✉ *Rte. 92, 3 mi from American Fork,* ☎ *801/756–5239 for cave information; 801/756–5238 to buy tickets in advance,* WEB *www.nps.gov/tica.* 🎫 *Tours $6.* ☉ *Early May–Oct., daily 7 AM–5:30.*

OFF THE
BEATEN PATH

ALPINE LOOP SCENIC BYWAY – Beyond Timpanogos Cave, Route 92 continues up American Fork Canyon before branching off to climb behind

Mt. Timpanogos itself. Designated the Alpine Loop Scenic Byway, this twisting mountain road reveals some stunning mountain scenery before dropping into Provo Canyon to the south. The 9-mi Timpooneke Trail and the 8-mi Aspen Trail, both off the byway, reach the summit of Mt. Timpanogos. Closed in winter, the Alpine Loop is not recommended for motor homes and trucks pulling trailers. While the Alpine Loop Scenic Byway provides a roundabout way to get to scenic Provo Canyon from I-15, a more direct route follows U.S. 189 east from Orem.

Sundance Resort

39 *51 mi from Salt Lake City via I–15 south and Rte. 52 east.*

The small but distinctive Sundance Resort, best accessed from Provo Canyon, came into being when Robert Redford purchased a ski hill in 1969. Reflecting the actor's interests in the environment, the arts, and outdoor recreation, the resort was designed to blend in with the natural surroundings. In the summer, a number of hiking and biking trails, as well as theater productions, entice visitors. In winter, the yearly Sundance Film Festival holds several activities that draw a wide audience. The festival has become an internationally recognized venue for showing important low-budget films produced outside the mainstream studio system.

Dining and Lodging

$$$–$$$$ ✕ **Tree Room.** In addition to serving up great Continental cuisine,
★   such as the black bass with morels in a truffle sauce, this restaurant has a special ambience. The place is filled with exquisite Native American art and western memorabilia collected by Robert Redford. The man does have good taste. ⊠ *Sundance Resort,* ☎ *801/223–4200. AE, D, DC, MC, V.*

$$–$$$ ✕ **Foundry Grill.** Wood-oven cooked pizzas, double-cut pork chops with
★   mashed potatoes, and spit-roasted chickens are among the hearty staples served up at the resort's other full-service restaurant. The view of alplike Mount Timpanogos isn't bad, either. ⊠ *Sundance Resort,* ☎ *801/223–4220. AE, D, DC, MC, V.*

$$$$ ⌂ **Sundance Cottages.** Ranging in size from one to three bedrooms,
★   these self-sufficient cottages lie in an appealing forest setting. All rooms feature natural wood trim and handmade furniture, and suites have rock fireplaces, decks, and kitchenettes. Jetted tubs are available in some accommodations. A new spa offers herbal wraps, facials, massages, exercise equipment, and an aerobics work-out area, among other amenities. This is a great getaway place, especially in summer. ⊠ *R.R. 3, Box A-1, 84604,* ☎ *801/225–4107 or 800/892–1600,* FAX *801/226–1937,* WEB *www.sundanceresort.com. 20 rooms, 77 suites. Restaurant, bar, in-room VCRs, kitchenettes, massage, spa, aerobics, laundry service. AE, D, DC, MC, V.*

Nightlife and the Arts

Like the mind-set labeled the "Sundance ethic," nightlife at the resort is low-key. Many guests opt to spend the evenings relaxing in their cottages. For a little more action, Sundance's **Owl Bar** (☎ 801/225–4107) has an ornate western bar (bullet holes and all) that was originally in a Thermopolis, Wyoming, establishment frequented by the "Hole in the Wall" outlaws. There is live music nightly.

In January the Sundance Institute (☎ 801/225–4107 or 800/892–1600) presents the **Sundance Film Festival,** a renowned showcase for independent filmmakers with screenings and workshops at Sundance, and in Salt Lake City, Ogden, and Park City. Sundance Resort hosts the **Sundance Summer Theatre** from mid-June through August. Broadway musicals are staged under the stars in a spectacular outdoor theater. The summer **Children's Theatre** (✉ Sundance Resort, ☏ 801/225–4107 or 800/892–1600) features outdoor musicals for the little ones.

Outdoor Activities and Sports

Skiers at **Sundance Resort** (✉ R.R. 3, Box A-1, Sundance 84604, off Rte. 52, ☏ 801/225–4107 or 800/892–1600) will find 42 runs across 450 acres of terrain and four lifts that access the mountain's 2,150 vertical ft. In the summer, the mountain trails can be explored on bike or on foot.

Shopping

The General Store (✉ Sundance Resort, ☏ 801/225–4107) is home base for the award-winning Sundance catalog and features distinctive home furnishings, clothing, and jewelry reflecting the Sundance ethic and taste. Most practical for cozy evenings indoors is the good selection of beer, wine, and other spirits.

Provo

㊵ *15 mi from Sundance via Rte. 52 west; 45 mi from Salt Lake City via I–15 south.*

Provo, with a population of over 100,000, is one of the fastest-growing cities in the country. With the towering peak of Mt. Timpanogos above the city on the east and Utah Lake below it on the west, it's also one of the prettiest. The historic downtown section includes many small shops and family restaurants; the newer sections, stretching ever farther to the north and south of the city center, contain malls, factory outlet stores, a wide variety of eateries, and the headquarters for several large corporations.

Although the scenic resources in and around Utah Valley are considerable, Provo and the entire region are probably best known as the home of **Brigham Young University** (✉ 1230 North St. and Campus Dr.). The university was established by the Mormon church in 1875 as the Brigham Young Academy, with a mandate to combine teaching about the sacred and the secular. It has grown into one of the largest religiously affiliated universities in the world, and it still reflects the conservative nature of the Mormon church. Students must adhere to a strict dress and honor code, and they are supposed to refrain from alcohol, tobacco, and caffeine. The university is known for a variety of undergraduate and graduate programs, is a considerable force in regional athletics, and serves as a cultural center for the southern Wasatch area. Heading up BYU attractions is a quartet of museums.

The collection of more than 14,000 works at the **Museum of Art at Brigham Young University** focuses primarily on American artists, such as Maynard Dixon, Dorothea Lange, Albert Bierstadt, and Robert Henri, and emphasizes the Hudson River School and the American Impressionists. Utah artists are represented by work from the Mormon pioneer era to the present. Rembrandt, Monet, and Rubens are also in the collection, along with some fine Far Eastern selections. ✉ *N. Campus Dr., southeast of Cougar Stadium,* ☏ *801/378–2787,* WEB *www.byu.edu/moa.* ⌦ *Free.* ☉ *Mon. and Thurs. 10–9; Tues., Wed., Fri. 10–6; Sat. noon–5.*

♺ The **Monte L. Bean Life Science Museum** of Brigham Young University includes exhibits on wildlife from around the world plus live reptile displays. ✉ *1430 North St., north of the bell tower,* ☏ *801/378–5051.* ⌦ *Free.* ☉ *Weekdays 10–9, Sat. 10–5.*

♺ BYU's **Earth Sciences Museum** features dinosaur bones, fossils, tours for adults and children, and various hands-on activities, including a table of artifacts that children can touch. ⊠ *1683 N. Canyon Rd., across from Cougar Stadium,* ☎ *801/378–3680.* 🖃 *Free.* ⊙ *Weekdays 9–5, Sat. noon–4.*

The **Museum of Peoples and Cultures** at BYU is an interesting student-curated collection of artifacts relating to cultures from all over the world, housed in two galleries. Most exhibits focus on peoples and cultures of the Americas. ⊠ *700 N. 100 East St.,* ☎ *801/378–6112.* 🖃 *Free.* ⊙ *Weekdays 9–5.*

In downtown Provo, the **McCurdy Historical Doll Museum** displays over 3,000 dolls from around the world in a private collection started by Laura McCurdy Clark. The facility also includes a doll hospital (for repairs) and a gift shop. ⊠ *246 N. 100 East St.,* ☎ *801/377–9935.* 🖃 *$2.* ⊙ *Tues.–Sat. noon–5.*

Dining and Lodging

$$–$$$ ✕ **Magelby's.** This award-winning restaurant offers fine dining in a building that also serves as an art gallery. Paintings, sculptures, and other artwork are displayed throughout. The steaks, seafood, and chicken are excellent, and the nearly three dozen homemade desserts are famous. ⊠ *1675 N. 200 West St.,* ☎ *801/374–6249. AE, D, MC, V. Closed Sun.*

$–$$$ ✕ **Restaurant Roy.** Freshly made pastas, meat dishes, and seafood, accompanied by a wide variety of wines, are served in this fine-dining establishment. Both the pepper steak and macadamia-encrusted halibut are popular. Classical music, an intimate atmosphere, and views of the Utah Valley and the Wasatch Mountains through French windows make this the perfect place for a romantic meal. ⊠ *2005 S. State St., Orem,* ☎ *801/235–9111. AE, D, DC, MC, V. Closed Sun. and Mon.*

$$ 🏨 **Provo Marriott Hotel.** A large facility, this hotel close to the downtown area offers good service. The guest rooms and common areas have more sophisticated furnishings than many properties in this price range. The hotel's newly opened Seasons Lounge, one of the few private clubs in Provo, is the place to go for drinks and music. ⊠ *101 W. 100 North St., 84601,* ☎ *801/377–4700 or 800/777–7144,* FAX *801/377–4708,* WEB *www.marriott.com. 331 rooms. Restaurant, bar, indoor pool, outdoor pool, hot tub, sauna, gym. AE, D, DC, MC, V.*

$–$$ 🏨 **Best Western Cottontree Inn.** Close to Brigham Young University as well as downtown, this is a good choice for moderately priced lodging. There are indoor and outdoor pools on-site, and you can get a pass to a nearby gym to work out. A Continental breakfast is included in the rate. ⊠ *2230 N. University Pkwy., 84604,* ☎ *801/373–7044,* FAX *801/375–5240. 80 rooms. In-room data ports, indoor pool, outdoor pool, laundry facilities. AE, D, DC, MC, V. CP.*

Nightlife and the Arts

Although Provo is not completely "dry," the standards of Brigham Young University are very evident in the city's dearth of nightlife options. Local bands, bands with national reputations, and DJs keep **Atchafalaya** (⊠ 210 W. Center St., just off I–15 at the Center St. exit, ☎ 801/373–9014) hopping. Between dances and turns and karaoke, sample some spicy Cajun food. Specialties of the bar's Cajun Café are the shrimp and crawfish. The new **Seasons Lounge** in the Provo Marriott Hotel (⊠ 101 W. 100 North St., ☎ 801/377–4700) is a casual gathering spot. The music is generally soft and in the background, making this the place for quiet conversations.

Because **Brigham Young University** (☎ 801/378–4636) has a considerable interest in the arts, Provo is a great place to catch a play, dance performance, or musical production. There are a dozen performing groups in all. Of special note are the BYU International Folk Dancers and Ballroom Dancers.

Outdoor Activities and Sports

CYCLING

In the Provo area, road cyclists may make a 100-mi circumnavigation of Utah Lake or tackle U.S. 189 through Provo Canyon or the Alpine Loop Scenic Byway.

FISHING

Provo Canyon's reputation for great fishing on one of the best trout streams in North America is a reputation many locals regard dubiously. They claim to know better places in Utah to fish, and they complain that the reputation has resulted in overfishing. Maybe they're right, but believers are out there year-round in their waders, laying out lines. They are presumably pulling something out of the river to make that immersion in cold water worthwhile. A heavily used canyon road parallels the river, and the location—just a few miles from downtown Provo—makes this the sort of river where businesspeople can pull on waders over suit trousers and make a few casts after work. **Onstream Outfitters: Flyfishing Consultants** (⊠ 1151 E. 230 South St., Provo, UT 84606, ☎ 801/371–0891 or 888/593–4900, WEB www.flyfishingutah.com) offers fishing excursions on the Provo River; they provide all the equipment and do everything except buy the fishing license for you. **Provo River Outfitters Flyfishing Guide Service** (⊠ 916 E. 1150 North St., Pleasant Grove, UT 84062, ☎ 801/785–5260 or 888/776–8824, WEB www.utahflyfishing.com) has years of experience and will tailor a trip to fit your level of ability.

GOLF

The 27 holes at **East Bay Golf Course** (⊠ 1860 S. East Bay Blvd., ☎ 801/373–6262) near Utah Lake give golfers a chance to meander along ponds and wetlands, and to spot the birds that frequent this riparian area.

There's something for everyone at **Thanksgiving Point** (⊠ 3003 N. Thanksgiving Way, Lehi, ☎ 801/768–2300 or 888/672–6040)—for golfers and those who must wait for them. Aside from the 18-hole championship course designed by Johnny Miller there are greenhouses, gardens, and a barnyard animal park. Two large gift shops feature furniture, home decor items, and jewelry. The North American Museum of Ancient Life is on the property; it includes dinosaur exhibits, activities for children, and an IMAX theater. The grounds are a pleasant place to have a picnic.

ICE SKATING

Peaks Ice Arena includes a double ice sheet, open throughout the year for figure skating, hockey, and parties. One rink hosted hockey matches during the 2002 Winter Olympics. ⊠ *100 N. Seven Peaks Blvd.,* ☎ *801/370–0452,* FAX *801/373–8711,* WEB *www.peaksarena.com.* ☞ *$4.* ☉ *Hrs vary; call for current information.*

ROCK CLIMBING AND MOUNTAINEERING

American Fork Canyon, 10 mi north of Provo in the Uinta National Forest, has northern Utah's best sport climbing with dozens of fixed routes. The canyon's steep walls also offer face, slab, and crack climbs. For information and permits for climbing, contact **Uinta National Forest** ⊠ 88 W. 100 North St., Box 1428, Provo, UT 84601, ☎ 801/377–5780). **The Wilderness School** (⊠ 72 W. 500 North St., Orem, UT 84057, ☎ 801/221–0398, WEB www.highangletechnologies.com) offers climbing classes and guided climbing trips to American Fork Canyon and to other climbing areas in central and southeastern Utah.

Around Point of the Mountain (a popular hang-gliding haven and site of the Utah State Prison), I–15 drops into Utah Valley, much of which is covered by **Utah Lake.** Although Utah's largest freshwater lake is 11 mi wide and 24 mi long, it averages a scant 9 ft deep. Boating and fishing are popular, but the cloudy (some would say polluted) water makes swimming questionable. On the east shore, **Utah Lake State Park** (✉ 4400 W. Center St., ☎ 801/375–0731) is the lake's best access point. In addition to three boat ramps, campgrounds, picnic areas, and a marina, the park has a wheelchair-accessible fishing area. **Deer Creek State Park** (✉ 11 mi northeast of Provo on U.S. 189, ☎ 435/654–0171) is popular with anglers and boaters, and it offers a quieter alternative to Utah Lake.

OFF THE BEATEN PATH	**SPRINGVILLE MUSEUM OF ART –** Springville, 10 mi south of Provo on I–15 or U.S. 89, is known for its support of the arts, and the Springville Museum of Art is a must stop for fine-arts fans. Beginning as a warehouse for works produced at the local high school, the museum later began to accept gifts from major artists. The present facility was built in 1937 and features mostly works by Utahns, such as Gary Lee Price, Richard Van Wagoner, and James T. Harwood, but it also has a collection of Soviet working-class Impressionism. ✉ *126 E. 400 South St., ☎ 801/489–2727.* ⊡ *Free.* ☉ *Tues., Thurs., Fri., and Sat. 10–5; Wed. 10–9; Sun. 3–6.*

The Heber Valley

30 mi from Provo (to Heber City) via U.S. 189 north; 20 mi from Park City via U.S. 40.

In April of 1859, 11 men struggled their way through a snowslide in Provo Canyon to settle the verdant Heber Valley. Today this area, with several small towns, including Heber City and Midway, still bears a resemblance to the farm valley of those settlers' dreams. It truly seems a world away from the sophisticated sprawl of Park City to the north.

The railroad tracks running along U.S. 189 are part of the scenic **④①** **Heber Valley Historic Railroad.** Following a line that first ran in 1899, trains take passengers on a nostalgic trip through beautiful Provo Canyon. Each car has been carefully restored, and two of the engines—Number 618 and Number 1907—are fully operational, steam-powered locomotives. ✉ *450 S. 600 West St., Heber City, ☎ 435/654–5601,* WEB *www.hebervalleyrr.org.* ⊡ *$12 and up.* ☉ *Daily 10–5.*

Jordanelle State Park has two recreation areas on a large mountain reservoir. The **Hailstone Area** is 10 mi north of Heber City via U.S. 40, with tent and RV camping, and day-use areas. There are also boat ramps, a children's playground, a visitor center, and a marina store where water toys (wave runners, and the like) can be rented. To the east, across the reservoir on Route 32, the **Rock Cliff** facilities are near the Provo River. This is a quiet area known for excellent wildlife watching, particularly along a series of elevated boardwalks winding through the aspen forest. The 50 campsites here are all "walk-ins." The Rock Cliff Nature Center provides interpretation of the area's natural history. ☎ *435/649–9540 Hailstone; 435/783–3030 Rock Cliff.* ⊡ *$6 per vehicle.* ☉ *May–Sept., daily 6–10; Oct.–Apr., daily 8–5.*

Utah's largest state park, **Wasatch Mountain State Park** (✉ 1281 Warmsprings Dr., off Rte. 224, Midway, ☎ 435/654–1791) is known for its 27-hole golf course but also offers hiking and riding trails in the summer and Nordic skiing in the winter. Olympic cross-country skiers competed here during the 2002 Winter Games.

At the south end of the Heber Valley, U.S. 189 passes **Deer Creek Reservoir** (☎ 435/654–0171) where folks head for boating, swimming, and camping.

Dining and Lodging

$$$-$$$$　✕▣ **The Homestead.** The Homestead combines the facilities of a com-
★　　plete resort with the charm of a country inn. The centerpiece is a nat-
ural hot spring once popular with the silver miners of Park City (and
now used by guests). The site was first developed in 1886 as an inn
and restaurant. An expansion in 1952 turned the property into a rus-
tic yet elegant year-round resort where today you can enjoy a cham-
pionship golf course, cross-country ski touring, hot-air ballooning,
snowmobiling, and exceptionally fine dining. The menu at Simon's,
the upscale restaurant ($$–$$$, reservations essential), includes such
dishes as pan-roasted Alaskan halibut and rack of lamb. The Home-
stead is in Midway, 4 mi west of Heber City via Midway Lane. ⊠ *700
N. Homestead Dr., Box 99, Midway 84049, ☎ 435/654–1102 or
800/327–7220, ℻ 435/654–5087, ᵂᴱᴮ www.homesteadresort.com.
140 rooms. 2 restaurants, bar, pool, hot tub, sauna, 18-hole golf
course, 2 tennis courts, gym, horseback riding, cross-country skiing,
convention center. AE, D, DC, MC, V.*

Nephi

*30 mi from Springville via I–15 south; 50 mi from Springville via
Nebo Loop Scenic Byway (Forest Service Rd. 15).*

South of Springville on I–15, you will soon leave behind the more pop-
ulated area of the state for more rural surroundings. Towering over
this area is Mt. Nebo, which at 11,877 ft is the tallest peak in the Wasatch
❷ Range. From the town of Payson, the 43-mi **Nebo Loop Scenic Byway**
circles east of Mt. Nebo's summit to access impressive panoramas of
Utah Valley, the Wasatch Range, and many canyons, small lakes,
forests, and some alluring hiking trails. A ¼-mi walk leads to the
Devil's Kitchen Geologic Area, a collection of strangely eroded spires
and ridges. The Nebo Loop Scenic Byway returns to I–15 at Nephi, a
small town that provides basic services.

Outdoor Activities and Sports

The laborious grades of the Nebo Loop Scenic Byway provide a test of
endurance for cyclists. A challenging 6-mi hiking route climbs Mt. Nebo
from a trailhead at the Andrews Canyon parking lot along the Nebo Loop
Scenic Byway. It is administered by the **Uinta National Forest** (☎ 801/
377–5780); because snow can fall at this elevation any month of the year
and trails can be washed out by spring runoff or heavy rainstorms, it's
a good idea to call for current trail conditions before beginning this climb.

OFF THE　　**LITTLE SAHARA RECREATION AREA** – These expansive sand dunes origi-
BEATEN PATH　nated as sandbars in Lake Bonneville, but they have moved 150 mi in
the 10,000 years since the lake receded. Although much of this 60,000-
acre sandbox is popular with off-road vehicle enthusiasts, the BLM has
established three campgrounds and an area especially for children.
Nine thousand acres have been set aside as a nature preserve. ⊠ *From
Nephi, follow Rte. 132 west for 13 mi; then turn north and follow a
paved BLM road 8 mi to Jericho Junction, ☎ 435/743–4116. ⊡ $6
per vehicle. ⊙ Daily, 24 hrs.*

The Wasatch Range A to Z

BUS TRAVEL
Greyhound Lines serves many towns along the Wasatch Front: Tremonton, Logan, Brigham City, Ogden, and Provo. The Utah Transit Authority has frequent service to all of Salt Lake valley, Davis and Weber counties, and Utah Valley. Buses, with ski racks, also make several runs a day to the ski areas in Little and Big Cottonwood canyons.
➤ BUS INFORMATION: **Greyhound Lines** (☎ 800/231–2222). **Utah Transit Authority** (☎ 801/743–3882 or 888/743–3882).

CAR TRAVEL
If you're driving into the area, chances are you'll be coming on either I–15 or I–80. Even if you fly into Salt Lake City, it's a good idea to rent a car at the airport and drive to the section of the Wasatch you want to visit.

The main thoroughfare along the Wasatch Mountains is I–15. From this trunk, I–80 heads east toward Park City, U.S. 89 branches to the north and south, U.S. 189 runs up Provo Canyon, and Route 132 winds into Sanpete County. All these routes feature spectacular mountain views. Winter visitors should be versed in driving on snowy roads; cars should be equipped with snow tires or chains. Although not far from Alta and Snowbird as the crow flies, Park City, and its three ski resorts, is best accessed by following I–80 east from Salt Lake City through Parley's Canyon.

EMERGENCIES
➤ CONTACTS: **Logan: Logan Regional Hospital** (✉ 1400 N. 500 East St., Logan, ☎ 435/752–2050). **Ogden: Columbia-Ogden Regional Medical Center** (✉ 5475 S. 500 East St., Ogden, ☎ 801/479–2111). **Park City: Family Health and Emergency Center** (✉ 1665 Bonanza Dr., Park City, ☎ 435/649–7640). **Provo: Utah Valley Regional Medical Center** (✉ 1034 N. 500 West St., Provo, ☎ 801/373–7850).

LODGING
CAMPING
Across the Wasatch–Cache and Uinta national forests are a number of wonderful campgrounds. Between Big and Little Cottonwood canyons there are four higher-elevation camping facilities. Of the nine facilities in Logan Canyon, Guinavah-Malibu and Tony Grove campgrounds are the nicest. Near Nephi a pair of campgrounds are found along the Nebo Loop Scenic Byway. All 11 campgrounds in the Huntsville area in Ogden Canyon offer swimming and fishing. In the Provo area, American Fork, Provo Canyon, and the Hobble Creek drainage hold dozens of possibilities. In Sanpete County, most campground facilities are found to the east in the Manti–La Sal National Forest. Additional campgrounds are at the region's state parks and national monuments and at the Little Sahara Recreation Area.

TAXI AND SHUTTLES
Several companies provide transportation between Salt Lake City and the ski resorts for about $55 round-trip. A free and efficient shuttle-bus system in Park City serves all the resort and local hotels in that area.
➤ CONTACTS: **Canyon Transportation** (☎ 801/255–1841 or 800/255–1841). **Express Shuttle** (☎ 801/596–1600 or 800/397–0773). **Lewis Bros. Stages** (☎ 801/359–8677 or 800/826–5844). **Park City Transportation** (☎ 435/649–8567 or 800/637–3803).

TOURS

The guided Ski Utah Interconnect Adventure Tour is a combination of lift-serviced and backcountry skiing that connects Utah's three major skiing areas: Big Cottonwood, Little Cottonwood, and Park City. The trip can be negotiated either on telemark skis or with regular alpine gear. About half of the skiing is within ski resort boundaries. For the most part, however, avalanche risks make backcountry skiing ill-advised for all but those with the proper safety equipment and considerable backcountry experience. The fee is $150, and that includes lunch and transportation.

Heli-skiing is an experience most enjoyable for strong intermediate and advanced skiers. Whether in search of powder, or for the solitude of the backcountry, Wasatch Powderbird Guides has permits for several thousand acres of skiable terrain, mostly in the basins and drainages on the periphery of Alta and Snowbird. In general, tours cost $490–$595 per person per day, depending on the season, and reservations are required.

➤ Ski Tours: **Ski Utah Interconnect Adventure Tour** (⊠ c/o Ski Utah, 150 W. 500 South St., Salt Lake City 84101, ☎ 801/534–1907). **Wasatch Powderbird Guides** (⊠ Box 920057, Snowbird 84092, ☎ 801/742–2800).

TRAIN TRAVEL

Amtrak has service to Ogden and Provo.

VISITOR INFORMATION

➤ Tourist Information: **Bridgerland** (⊠ 160 N. Main St., Logan 84321, ☎ 435/752–2161 or 800/882–4433). **Brigham City Chamber of Commerce** (⊠ 6 N. Main St., Brigham City 84302, ☎ 435/723–3931). **Golden Spike Empire** (⊠ 2501 Wall Ave., Ogden 84401, ☎ 801/627–8288 or 800/255–8824, WEB www.ogdencvb.org). **Great Salt Lake Country** (⊠ 90 S. West Temple St., Salt Lake City 84101, ☎ 801/521–2822). **Heber Valley County Chamber of Commerce** (⊠ 475 N. Main St., Heber 84032, ☎ 435/654–3666, WEB www.hebervalleycc.org). **Mountainland** (⊠ 586 E. 800 North St., Orem 84097, ☎ 801/229–3800, WEB www.mountainland.org). **Panoramaland** (⊠ 4 S. Main St., Box 71, Nephi 84648, ☎ 435/623–5203 or 800/748–4361). **Park City Chamber of Commerce/Convention and Visitors Bureau** (⊠ Box 1630, Park City 84060, ☎ 435/649–6100 or 800/453–1360, WEB www.parkcityinfo.com). **Ski Utah** (⊠ 150 W. 500 South St., Salt Lake City 84101, ☎ 801/534–1779, WEB www.skiutah.com). **Springville Chamber of Commerce** (⊠ 50 S. Main St., Springville 84663, ☎ 801/489–4681).**Utah County Convention and Visitors Bureau** (⊠ 51 S. University Ave., Suite 111, Provo 84601, ☎ 801/370–8393 or 800/222–8824, WEB www.utahvalley.org/cvb).

NORTHEASTERN UTAH

With the western portion of Dinosaur National Monument within its borders, northeastern Utah counts the remains of Jurassic giants as its primary attraction. While the monument and related sites provide a glimpse into the lives of long-extinct creatures, the region also showcases colorful slickrock canyons and deserts, a scenic stretch of the Green River, the Uinta Mountains—Utah's highest mountain range, and the sprawling Uinta Basin. (Uinta is pronounced *You-in-tah*.) Boating, waterskiing, and windsurfing are popular at Flaming Gorge Reservoir, Red Fleet Reservoir, Starvation Reservoir, Steinaker Lake, and Strawberry Reservoir, all of which have boat-ramp facilities. Add to these natural wonders some Fremont rock art, relics of 19th-century pioneers and outlaws, challenging hiking and horse pack trips in the mountains, and the cultural offerings of the Uintah and Ouray Indian Reservation, which is the second-largest reservation in the United States, and you have a worthwhile tour to a remote corner of the West.

Uinta Mountains

49 mi (to Kamas) from Salt Lake City via I–80 and Rte. 32 south.

Although the Wasatch may be Utah's best-known mountain range, the Uinta Mountains, the only major east–west mountain range in the Rockies, are its tallest, topped by 13,528-ft Kings Peak. The quickest, easiest (read: paved) route to Uinta country is the Mirror Lake Scenic Byway, which begins in Kamas. The 65-mi drive follows Route 150 into the heavily wooded canyons of the **Wasatch–Cache National Forest** (⊠ 50 E. Center St., Box 68, Kamas, ☎ 435/783–4338), cresting at 10,687-ft Bald Mountain Pass. At nearby Mirror Lake, campgrounds provide a base for hikes into the surrounding mountains, and Highline Trail accesses the 460,000-acre High Uintas Wilderness Area to the east.

The Uinta Mountains area, particularly in the High Uintas Wilderness where no vehicles are allowed, is prime country for pack trips and horseback day rides between late June and September. The Uintas are ribboned with streams, and they have hundreds of small lakes set in rolling meadows. Several ranches clustered on the south slopes of the range offer riding on Uinta trails; the **Utah Travel Council** (☎ 800/200–1160) publishes a directory.

The Uinta Basin

116 mi (to Duchesne) from Salt Lake City via I–80 and U.S. 40 east.

The Uinta Basin is a vast area of gently rolling land bordered by the Uinta Mountains to the north, the Wasatch Mountains to the west, and a series of high plateaus and cliffs to the south. With more rivers, reservoirs, and lakes than many sections of the arid West, this is a prime agricultural area, and farms and ranches are scattered across the region. Small towns—some with populations of a few hundred people or less, without stoplights, and with no amenities other than a gas station and post office (sometimes located in the same building)—tend to be clustered around the three major rivers that cut through the basin. The land, not the amenities, draws people here, for this is the kind of wide open space, with high country in the distance, that most visitors imagine when they think of the West.

Nearly 1 million acres in size, the sovereign land of the **Uintah and Ouray Indian Reservation** spreads out across the Uinta Basin and northeastern Utah to the eastern edge of the state. Visitors are asked to stay on the main roads, although camping and hiking are allowed with a permit that can be obtained by writing to the Ute tribe (⊠ Box 190, Fort Duchesne 84026). The Ute tribe hosts the Northern Ute Indian Pow Wow in early July at **tribal headquarters** (☎ 435/722–5141) in Fort Duchesne.

Accessible by dirt roads from the reservation are several recreation areas in the **Ashley National Forest** (⊠ 244 W. U.S. 40, Roosevelt, ☎ 435/722–5018). One of these, Moon Lake, features a U.S. Forest Service campground, a private resort, and trails that lead to the High Uintas Wilderness Area.

The first major town one hits while driving east on U.S. 40 is **Duchesne,** a county seat just north of a portion of the reservation. It was settled in the early 1900s when parts of the Ute Indians' Uintah and Ouray Reservation were opened to Anglo settlement by President Theodore

Roosevelt. Duchesne was originally called Theodore in honor of the president, but the community eventually adopted the name of a French nun instead. Anglers cast for walleye, German brown trout, and bass at 3,520-acre **Starvation Reservoir** (⊠ 4 mi northwest of Duchesne on U.S. 40, ☏ 435/738–2326), which also has camping facilities.

On the south slope of the Uinta Mountains (17 mi north and east of Duchesne on Route 87), **Altamont** is where the far-flung ranchers of the Uinta Basin come for church services, to pick up mail, or have a look at the people who have stopped to get directions on their way to the several guest ranches in the area.

Dining and Lodging

$–$$ ★ ✕ **Frontier Grill.** Affiliated with a locally owned motel, this family restaurant is known for its great sandwiches and salads during the noon hour, its prime rib and seafood at night, and its homemade pies any time of the day. ⊠ 65 S. 200 East St., Roosevelt, off U.S. 40, ☏ 435/722–3669. AE, DC, MC, V.

$$$ ✕▥ **Falcon's Ledge Lodge.** This modern lodge in pristine Stillwater Canyon offers multiday luxury sporting packages, featuring falconry, fly-fishing, and trips into the High Uintas Wilderness, as well as overnight lodging. Guest rooms are luxurious; some have vault ceilings and Jacuzzis. The spacious lobby has sweeping views of the high desert scenery. The five- to seven-course meals ($$$) are the best in the area. Specialties include filet mignon with cracked pepper sauce, and bacon-wrapped halibut. Fresh home-baked bread is served at every meal. Nonguests must make advance reservations for the restaurant. A full breakfast gives guests plenty of energy for the many outdoor activities the lodge offers. ⊠ Stillwater Canyon, Box 67, Altamont 84001, ☏ 435/454–3737, FAX 435/454–3392, WEB www.falconsledge.com. 9 rooms. Restaurant, fishing, horseback riding. AE, MC, V. BP.

$ ▥ **Best Western Inn.** Clean and comfortable rooms, plus a pool and a coffee shop make this the place to stay in Roosevelt. There's also a restaurant nearby. ⊠ Rte. 1, Box 2860, E. Hwy. 40, Roosevelt 84066, ☏ 435/722–4644, FAX 435/722–0179. 40 rooms. Coffee shop, pool, hot tub. AE, D, DC, MC, V.

Outdoor Activities and Sports

Anglers will enjoy trying their luck at **Strawberry Reservoir** (⊠ 25 mi south of Heber City on U.S. 40, ☏ 435/548–2321), which covers 17,000 acres. Construction on the original reservoir, part of a federal project designed to bring water from the Colorado River basin to the Wasatch Front, began in 1906. In 1973, the Soldier Creek Dam was built downstream, and the original Strawberry Reservoir dam was eventually removed. The result was a much larger storage facility, which boaters and anglers alike now relish. Ice fishing is also popular. Four U.S. Forest Service campgrounds and four marinas dot the lakeshore.

Campgrounds abound in the **Ashley National Forest** (⊠ 244 W. U.S. 40, Roosevelt, ☏ 435/722–5018) north of Duchesne and Roosevelt and west of Flaming Gorge. **Flaming Gorge National Recreation Area** (administered by the Ashley National Forest) contains more than a dozen campgrounds within the Utah portion, including those in the Dutch John and Antelope Flat areas. Several commercial campgrounds are also in the area.

Vernal

43 30 mi from Roosevelt via U.S. 40 east.

The largest town (population 6,800) in the northeast corner of the state, Vernal serves as a hub for visiting the area, which was frequented by mountain man William Ashley in the 1820s and first settled during the 1870s. Two museums feature relics and memorabilia from Vernal's yesteryear. **The Daughters of Utah Pioneers Museum** (⊠ 158 S. 500 West St., ☎ 435/789–0352. ☞ Free; ◷ Memorial Day–Labor Day, Mon.–Sat. noon–6) offers some perspective on what pioneer life was like. The **Western Heritage Museum** (⊠ 302 E. 200 South St., ☎ 435/789–7399) highlights, among other Old West themes, 19th-century outlaws of the Vernal area. To leaf through the history of outlaws, pioneers, and other characters drop in at the **Uintah County Library** (⊠ 155 E. Main St., ☎ 435/789–0091. ◷ Mon.–Thurs. 10–9, Fri. and Sat. 10–6), which houses an excellent regional history research center. The library also displays an extensive collection of dolls in period costumes.

Because Vernal was so isolated in its early days, shipping was expensive. To avoid high freight costs, one businessman had a bank facade shipped in brick by brick by U.S. mail. Nicknamed the **Parcel Post Bank** (⊠ 3 W. Main St.), the 1916 structure still stands and is part of the Zions First National Bank building in downtown Vernal. The **1877 log post office and store** (⊠ 1255 W. 2000 North St.), one of the few buildings of this kind in the region, is still structurally sound. You can admire it from outside while the restoration project within continues.

☺ One hundred and fifty million years ago, this land was the stomping ground of dinosaurs. At **Utah Field House of Natural History State Park** a large mural depicts the last 2.7 billion years of the Uinta Basin's geologic history, and Fremont and Ute artifacts offer insight into the early presence of humans in the area. Numerous rock samples and fossils (including dinosaur bones) are also on display. The outdoor Dinosaur Garden features 18 life-size dinosaur models in a primordial setting, models of other prehistoric creatures, and a path that leads to a shady picnic area with a group pavilion and a public playground. ⊠ 235 E. Main St., ☎ 435/789–3799. ☞ $5. ◷ June–Sept., daily 8 AM–9 PM; Oct.–May, daily 9–5.

44 Dinomania rules at Dinosaur National Monument, which straddles the Utah-Colorado border. Inside the astounding enclosure of the **Dinosaur Quarry** are some 2,000 dinosaur bones encased in a 200-ft-long sandstone face. This collection of fossils resulted when floods brought the bodies of several dinosaurs to rest on a sandbar; subsequent deposits covered the carcasses where they lay, becoming part of the Morrison Formation. The cache of paleontological treasures was discovered by Earl Douglass in 1909. Today visitors must ride a shuttle bus from the visitor center to the quarry during busy times of the year.

Although most people visit Dinosaur National Monument to see dinosaur bones, this 200,000-acre park also offers a generous supply of alluring backcountry. An especially scenic drive runs 6 mi east from the quarry to the **Josie Morris Cabin**. A rugged individualist, Ms. Morris kept company with the likes of Butch Cassidy. Along the drive, watch for ancient rock art, geological formations, and hiking trails that begin at the side of the road. Another nice drive with wonderful vistas of the Utah-Colorado border is along the Harpers Corner Road. The drive into Rainbow Park not only passes some impressive Fremont petroglyph panels but also reaches a put-in point for rafters, who toss about on the white water of the Green and Yampa rivers. ⊠ 20 mi east of Vernal on Rte. 149, ☎ 435/781–7700 quarry. ☞ $10 per vehicle. ◷ Memorial Day–Labor Day, daily 8–7; Oct.–May, daily 8–4:30.

Boating and waterskiing enthusiasts will love **Steinaker Lake State Park** (⊠ 7 mi north of Vernal on U.S. 191, ☎ 435/789–4432). More than

2 mi long, Steinaker Reservoir also relinquishes a fair number of large-mouth bass and rainbow trout. Hiking and biking trails begin at the park, and there are wildlife viewing areas nearby. Camping sites for tents and trailers, and covered group pavilions, make this a popular park.

Red Fleet State Park (⊠ 10 mi north of Vernal off U.S. 191, ☎ 435/789–4432), like the other reservoirs in the region, is great for boat and bait. What really attracts visitors are the colorful sandstone formations in which the lake is nestled. In addition, a section of 200-million-year-old dinosaur tracks can be reached by a short hike or by boat.

OFF THE
BEATEN PATH

BROWNS PARK AND THE JOHN JARVIE RANCH – If visiting the back of beyond is your interest, then drive 65 mi northeast from Vernal on U.S. 191 to Browns Park. Lying along a quieter stretch of the Green River and extending into Colorado, this area features plenty of high desert scenery and a fascinating historic site, the John Jarvie Ranch (follow signs off Rte. 191). Operated by the BLM, the ranch includes four original buildings constructed by Scotsman John Jarvie more than a century ago. Jarvie was a storekeeper, an accomplished musician, and a prospector. His even-handed treatment of his customers earned respect from the area's ranchers and from the many outlaws who frequented the area en route to more remote hideouts. Because the road into Browns Park can be rough at times, be sure to check with the BLM's Vernal office (☎ 435/789–1362) about road conditions, or call the Jarvie Ranch directly (☎ 435/885–3307).

Dining and Lodging

$–$$
★
✕ **Curry Manor.** The diverse menu includes entrées such as Parmesan-pesto chicken, baked salmon stuffed with crab, and pork tenderloin with wild-berry sauce. At lunch, the restaurant serves dishes such as prime rib sandwiches, tortellini, and chicken Caesar salad. ⊠ 189 S. Vernal Ave., ☎ 435/789–2289. AE, D, MC, V.

$
✕ **Casa Rios.** If you're in search of south-of-the-border flavors, this is a good bet. Try the special beef burrito or the chimichangas. ⊠ 2015 W. Rte. 40, ☎ 435/789–0103. MC, V. Closed Sun. and Mon.

$
✕ **7-11 Ranch Restaurant.** No, this restaurant is not associated in any way with the convenience store chain that bears part of the name. Specialties are prime rib, steaks, and homemade soups and pies, and the food is so good that businesses frequently hold lunch meetings here or have the restaurant cater special events. A gift shop sells souvenirs from the area, and it's just a quick walk from the restaurant to local museums. ⊠ 77 E. Main St., ☎ 435/789–1170. AE, D, MC, V.

$$–$$$
🖭 **Landmark Inn Bed&Breakfast.** In a former Baptist church building, this lovely inn has a homey feel. Rooms are individually decorated with quilts and western Americana, and suites—popular for honeymoons and anniversaries—have four-poster beds, gas fireplaces, and jetted tubs. A light breakfast of cereals, breads, yogurts, fruits, and juices is served in the dining room, and guests are welcome to congregate around the living room fireplace in the evening. The building is wheelchair accessible. ⊠ 288 E. 100 South St., 84078, ☎ 435/781–1800 or 888/738–1800, WEB www.landmark-inn.com. 7 rooms, 3 suites. Dining room. AE, D, DC, MC, V. CP.

$–$$
🖭 **Best Western Antlers Motel.** Locals rate this as Vernal's best accommodations. The motel offers good-size rooms decorated in quiet colors, and the staff is friendly and helpful. A wading pool and playground delight young guests. ⊠ 423 W. Main St., 84078, ☎ 435/789–1202 or 888/791–2929, FAX 435/789–4979, WEB www.bestwestern.com. 44 rooms. Restaurant, pool, hot tub, playground. AE, D, DC, MC, V.

Outdoor Activities and Sports

CAMPING

Dinosaur National Monument (⊠ 4545 U.S. 40, Dinosaur, CO 81610, ☎ 970/374–3000 or 435/781–7700) has two campgrounds near the quarry on the Utah side. Reservations are not accepted from individuals, but sites are available on a first-come, first-served basis.

RAFTING

White-water enthusiasts find challenging stretches on the Green and Yampa rivers in Dinosaur National Monument. Joining forces near Echo Park in Colorado, the two waterways have each carved spectacular canyons through several aeons' worth of rock, and they are still at it in rapids such as Whirlpool Canyon, SOB, Disaster Falls, and Hell's Half Mile. Day-trippers will enjoy a float down the Green River below the Flaming Gorge Dam. The **Utah Travel Council** (☎ 800/200–1160) can provide a directory detailing river routes and which outfitters run them.

En Route   For more recreational opportunities, return to Vernal and head north on U.S. 191 to Steinaker Lake and Red Fleet state parks. Both have reservoirs ideally suited to water sports and fishing. Past Red Fleet Reservoir, U.S. 191 begins to ascend the eastern flank of the Uinta uplift. This section of the tour follows what is known as the **Drive Through the Ages.** Within a distance of 30 mi, the road passes 19 geologic formations, including the billion-year-old exposed core of the Uinta Mountains, with signs identifying and describing them. This route also provides plenty of opportunity for wildlife watching. A road guide is available at the Northeastern Utah Visitor Center (⊠ Utah Fieldhouse of Natural History, 235 E. Main St., Vernal, ☎ 435/789–7894).

Flaming Gorge National Recreation Area

40 mi from Vernal (to Flaming Gorge Dam) via U.S. 191 north.

In May of 1869, during his mapping expedition on the Green and Colorado rivers, explorer John Wesley Powell named this canyon Flaming Gorge for its "flaming, brilliant red" color. Powell was not the first traveler to be in awe of the landscape. The first recorded visitors were fur trappers who set up a long-term camp in 1825. By the late 1800s, scores of cattlemen and farmers, followed by rustlers and outlaws, had come to live in the area. The people came, but not the conveniences that generally follow. Flaming Gorge remained one of Utah's most remote and least-developed inhabited areas well into the 1950s. In 1964, Flaming Gorge Canyon and the Green River running through it were plugged with a 500-ft-high wall of concrete. The result is a 90-mi-long reservoir that twists and turns among canyon walls. Although much of the lake stretches north into Wyoming, most facilities lie south of the state line in Utah.

45   Upon reaching Greendale Junction, 36 mi north of Vernal, stay right on U.S. 191 if you wish to visit the **Flaming Gorge Dam.** Displays at the nearby visitor center explain aspects of this engineering marvel, and the dam is open for self-guided tours Memorial Day–Labor Day, daily 9–5.

46   Inside the **Red Canyon Visitor Center** are displays covering the geology, flora and fauna, and human history of the Flaming Gorge area, but the most magnificent thing about the center is its location atop a cliff that towers 1,300 ft above the lake. The views here are outstanding, and you can enjoy them while having a picnic on the grounds. ⊠ *Turn left onto Rte. 44 at Greendale Junction and follow signs to visitor center turnoff,* ☎ *435/889–3713.* ☉ *Memorial Day–Labor Day, daily 10–5.*

Numerous hiking trails, most of them up the steep, rugged sides of canyons, and a scenic drive traverse the **Sheep Creek Canyon Geological Area** (✉ Sheep Creek Canyon Loop Rd., 28 mi west of U.S. 191 and Rte. 44 junction, ☎ 435/784–3445), which is full of upturned layers of rock. Watch for wild horses, bighorn sheep, and a bat cave alongside the road. In the fall, salmon return to Sheep Creek to spawn; a viewing kiosk and several bridges provide unobtrusive locations from which to watch the spawning runs.

Dining and Lodging

$–$$$ 🏨 **Flaming Gorge Lodge.** Probably the best accommodations in the vicinity of Flaming Gorge, the lodge has a great restaurant, plus a store, raft rentals, and fishing guide service. Rooms are simple but not spartan. Condos include a bedroom (two queen beds and one twin bed), living room, dining room, and full kitchen. The emphasis here is on comfort, not frills, although all accommodations include televisions and VCRs. ✉ *Greendale, U.S. 191, Dutch John 84023,* ☎ *435/889–3773,* FAX *435/889–3788,* WEB *www.fglodge.com. 21 rooms, 24 condos. Restaurant, in-room VCRs, travel services. AE, D, MC, V.*

$–$$ 🏨 **Red Canyon Lodge.** Three comfort levels of cabins compose this property. The basic difference between them is bathroom facilities. "Frontier" means a shared shower house and rest room. Each "Rustic" cabin has its own full bathroom. "Luxury" cabins are bigger, with living room, vault ceilings, kitchenette, and full bathrooms. Although none of the options are truly luxurious, the plain but functional accommodations feel just fine in this wild setting. ✉ *790 Red Canyon Rd., Dutch John 84023,* ☎ *435/889–3759,* FAX *435/889–5106,* WEB *www.redcanyonlodge.com. 20 cabins. Restaurant. AE, D, MC, V.*

Outdoor Activities and Sports

CYCLING

Because it mixes high desert vegetation—blooming sage, rabbit brush, cactus, and wildflowers—and red-rock terrain with a cool climate, Flaming Gorge National Recreation Area is an ideal destination for road and trail biking. The 3-mi-round-trip **Bear Canyon–Bootleg ride** begins south of the dam off U.S. 191 at the Firefighters' Memorial Campground and runs west to an overview of the reservoir. A free brochure, *Flaming Gorge Trails,* describes this and other cycling routes. The brochure is distributed at area visitor centers.

FISHING

Fishers can try their luck at all of this region's reservoirs, but old-timers maintain that Flaming Gorge provides the best lake fishing. For the best river fishing, experts suggest the Green River below Flaming Gorge Dam. Fed by cold water from the bottom of the lake, this stretch has been identified as one of the best trout fisheries in the world.

WATER SPORTS

In the Flaming Gorge area, three marinas offer boat rentals and supplies. The **Buckboard Marina** (✉ HCR 65, Box 100, Green River, ☎ 307/875–6927) is handy for boaters who approach the reservoir from the Wyoming side. **Cedar Springs Marina** (✉ Box 337, Dutch John, ☎ 435/889–3795) is close to the dam. The **Lucerne Valley Marina** (✉ Box 10, Manila, ☎ 435/784–3483) offers a wide range of services to boaters at the northwestern edge of the Flaming Gorge area.

En Route   The quickest route from Flaming Gorge to Salt Lake City cuts northwest across Wyoming to I–80.

Northeastern Utah A to Z

BUS TRAVEL
Greyhound Lines serves Vernal.

CAR TRAVEL
Both U.S. 40 and U.S. 191 are well maintained; however, there are some curvy, mountainous stretches. If you're headed for the wilderness, be prepared for dirt roads.

EMERGENCIES
➤ CONTACTS: **Roosevelt: Uinta Basin Medical Center** (✉ 250 W. 300 North St., Roosevelt, ☎ 435/722–4691). **Vernal: Ashley Valley Medical Center** (✉ 151 W. 200 North St., Vernal, ☎ 435/789–3342).

TOURS
Dinaland Aviation offers flights over Dinosaur National Monument, Flaming Gorge, and the canyons of the Green River. Prices range from $29 to $69 per person.

Guided river trips are available from Adrift Adventures–Dinosaur, Hatch River Expeditions, and Holiday Expeditions. Trips run one to six days and cost $63 and up.

J/L Ranch Outfitters and Guides leads weeklong pack trips into the Uintas and the Ashley National Forest. One thing that sets this operation apart is the extra care taken to assess each rider's ability in a casual way, then offer gentle instruction.
➤ CONTACTS: **Adrift Adventures–Dinosaur** (✉ Box 192, Jensen 84035, ☎ 435/789–3600 or 800/824–0150, WEB www.adrift.com). **Dinaland Aviation** (✉ 830 E. 500 South St., Vernal, ☎ 435/789–4612). **Hatch River Expeditions** (✉ 55 E. Main St., Box 1150, Vernal 84078, ☎ 435/789–4316 or 800/342–8243, FAX 435/789–8513). **Holiday Expeditions** (✉ 793 S. 1500 East, Vernal 84078, ☎ 435/789–4586 or 800/624–6323.) **J/L Ranch Outfitters and Guides** (✉ Box 129, Whiterocks, UT 84085, ☎ 801/353–4049).

VISITOR INFORMATION
➤ TOURIST INFORMATION: **Dinosaurland Travel Board** (✉ 25 E. Main St., Vernal 84078, ☎ 800/477–5558, WEB www.dinoland.com). **Duchesne County Chamber of Commerce** (✉ 50 E. 200 South St., #35–11, Duchesne 84066, ☎ 435/722–4598). **Flaming Gorge Chamber of Commerce** (✉ General Delivery, Manila 84046, ☎ 435/784–3582). **Northeastern Utah Visitor Center** (✉ Utah Fieldhouse of Natural History, 235 E. Main St., Vernal 84078, ☎ 435/789–7894). **Utah Welcome Center–Jensen** (✉ off U.S. 40 at the Jensen exit, ☎ 435/789–4002). **Vernal Chamber of Commerce** (✉ 134 W. Main St., Vernal 84078, ☎ 435/789–1352).

SOUTHEASTERN UTAH

The first thing travelers to southeastern Utah notice is the color. Red, orange, purple, pink, creamy ivory, deep chocolate, and even shades of turquoise paint the landscape. Unlikely patterns such as candy-cane stripes jump from the rocks, which themselves jut and tilt first one way, then another. No flat, colorful canvas, the landscape has near vertical walls standing in the way of easy route-finding. Deep canyons, carved by wild western rivers, crisscross the area. Rocks teeter on slim columns or burst like mushrooms from the ground. Snowcapped mountains stand in the distant horizon no matter which direction you look. The sky is more often blue in a region that receives only about 8 inches of rain a year. When thunderstorms do build, the sky turns a dramatic gun-metal gray, bringing deep orange cliffs into sharp relief.

Embroidered through the region is evidence of the people who came before rock climbers and Mormons. Rock art as old as 4,000 years is etched or painted on canyon walls. The most familiar of these ancient dwellers are the ancestral Puebloans, formerly known as Anasazi, who occupied the area between 700 and 2,000 years ago.

The southeast, generally known as canyonlands, calls out to the adventurous traveler. There is surprise around every corner whether you explore the region by car, by raft, by foot, by bicycle, or in a rugged 4×4 vehicle. On the trail you'll discover cactus or a lush garden of ferns created by precious springs or seeps. On the river, hawks float overhead. On the road, you'll encounter trading posts that have been selling Native American art for decades or, nearer Navajo land, you can purchase art from its makers. Enter these lands with a mind as open as the skies. Be a curious, willing traveler in one of the wildest regions left in America. Also be a prepared traveler. This is the area that invented the term "you can't get there from here," so plan your journey by using all or part of the suggested route. Although the region has shown a large growth in visitors, and services are generally plentiful, it's a good idea to keep your gas tank topped off. Carry water and snacks. Whatever you do, don't forget your camera and lots of film; you're sure to use twice what you think you will.

Helper

47 *63 mi from Provo via U.S. 6 south.*

If you're headed into the area from the north, making a brief stop in Helper yields a worthwhile tribute to the local area's history. The **Western Mining and Railroad Museum,** housed in a former hotel that is part of a national historic district, features displays on the development of mining in Castle Country, Depression-era paintings, an archive room for researchers, and an outdoor display of trains and mining equipment. ⊠ *296 S. Main St.,* ☎ *435/472–3009.* ⊠ *$2.* ☉ *May–Sept., Mon.–Sat. 10–6; Oct.–Apr., Tues.–Sat. 11–4.*

Price

48 *11 mi from Helper via U.S. 6 south.*

Price is the hub of Utah's Castle Country (so called because many rock formations resemble castles). As with virtually every other community in southern Utah, Price began as a Mormon farming enclave in the late 19th century. Shortly after it was established, however, the town took on a noticeably different character. In 1883 the railroad arrived, bringing with it immigrants from around the world. Nearby coal reserves were tapped, and the town has counted mining as its primary industry ever since. Today, because many of Price's nearly 10,000 residents are still employed in the coalfields, there are strong labor union ties in the community, a fact that makes Price and nearby Helper bastions of liberalism and the Democratic party in an otherwise conservative state.

The **Price Mural** in the Municipal Building (⊠ 185 E. Main St.) narrates the modern history of Price and surrounding Carbon County, beginning with the first white settlers. A Works Progress Administration project, this 200-ft-long mural was painted between 1938 and 1941 by native Lynn Fausett.

☾ As in other parts of Utah, the past in Castle Country extends at least a few years prior to the arrival of Mormon farmers in the 19th century—to about 150 million years ago. Housing one of the best collections of dinosaur memorabilia in the region is the **College of Eastern Utah Prehistoric Museum,** next to the Price Municipal Building. Front and center in the museum's Hall of Dinosaurs are several complete dinosaur skeletons, and that of an 11,000-year-old mammoth excavated locally. A rare dinosaur egg is on display, as are dinosaur tracks unearthed by miners in nearby coal beds. ⊠ *155 E. Main St.,* ☎ *435/ 637–5060.* ⊋ *$3 suggested donation.* ☉ *Apr.–Sept., daily 9–6; Oct.– Mar., Mon.–Sat. 9–5.*

Outdoor Activities and Sports

CAMPING

Price Canyon Recreation Area (⊠ 18 mi northwest of Price along U.S. 6, ☎ 435/636–3600) is operated by the BLM, and with RV and tent camping sites, picnic tables, and flush toilets, is more accommodating than most BLM facilities.

GOLF

The **Carbon Country Club Golf Course** (⊠ Between Helper and Price on U.S. 6, ☎ 435/637–2388) is the oldest in the eastern half of the state, and it's one of the most unusual. Golfers will encounter ancient Native American rock art, a family cemetery, and gorgeous views of the Price River while they play the 18-hole course.

Nine Mile Canyon

❹❾ *7½ mi from Price via U.S. 6/191 south.*

Nine Mile Canyon, an enormous gallery of hundreds of petroglyphs etched into its boulders and cliffs, is the handiwork of the Fremont Indians, who lived in much of what is now Utah from AD 300 to 1250. The meaning of these images is one of the most mystifying puzzles of the area, but almost as confounding is how a canyon 40 mi long came to be named "Nine Mile." One explanation points to John Wesley Powell's epic float down the nearby Green River in 1869. It seems the expedition's mapmaker drew up a 9-mi triangulation, which he titled Nine Mile Creek. The canyon has the remnants of many homesteads, stage stops, and ranches. However, the petroglyphs and pictographs are the main draw. It's important not to disturb the fragile rock art in any way. Because most of this 80-mi round-trip is on a gravel road, plan to take most of a day to complete it. A brochure detailing significant sites is available at visitor centers in Price. Without it, many panels will go unnoticed. Of course, the best way to experience Nine Mile Canyon is to go with a guide. **Reflections on the Ancients** (⊠ Box 444, Wellington, UT 84542, ☎ 435/637–5801 or 800/468–4060) offers archaeologist-led tours. General information is available from the BLM office in Price.

En Route   Southeast of the turnoff for Nine Mile Canyon, U.S. 6/191 continues into some of the most desolate terrain anywhere. Known as the **San Rafael Desert,** this stark, open landscape can be a bit overwhelming, but views of the Book Cliffs to the east may make you feel less agoraphobic. Because this drive includes some lengthy straightaways, you may find yourself developing a heavy foot, but beware: the Utah Highway Patrol watches this stretch closely.

Green River

❺⓿ *65 mi from Price via U.S. 6/191 south and I–70 east.*

The highway bypasses Green River, but the mostly sleepy little town does offer a quiet alternative to busier tourist destinations nearby. Thanks to irrigation water siphoned from the river of the same name, the town is known for its watermelons and its annual **Melon Days** celebration. Held the third weekend in September, this small-town event features a parade and fair, plenty of music, thousands of pounds of melons, and a canoe race.

Several river-running outfits base themselves here—and for good reason. The Green River flows through some of the most wildly beautiful desert landscape in the American West and to the north of town has carved two spectacular canyons, Desolation and Gray. Within Desolation, there is a sense of complete separation from the civilized world. The only reminders of people having ever been in this area are occasional pictographs and abandoned homesteads. Be prepared in midsummer to encounter desert heat—although the cool river water is never far away.

South of town, the river drifts at a lazier pace through Labyrinth and Stillwater canyons, and the 68-mi stretch of river that runs south to Mineral Bottom in Canyonlands National Park is best suited to canoes and motorized boats.

Adventurers have run Utah's wild waterways for more than a century. The largest tributary of the Colorado River, the Green was the last major river in the continental United States to be explored. John Wesley Powell and a party of nine men checked it off the list with an epic voyage in 1869. Commemorating this feat is the **John Wesley Powell River History Museum.** In addition to various exhibits, artifacts, and works of art concerning 19th-century western exploration, it also houses the River Runner's Hall of Fame, a tribute to those who have followed in Powell's wake. In 2001, a fine art gallery, **The River Gallery,** opened to display art related to the region. ⊠ *885 E. Main St., on the Green River,* ☎ *435/564–3427.* ☞ *$2.* ☉ *June–Sept., daily 8–8; Oct.–May, daily 9–5.*

To get a real taste of the deserted lands beyond the highway, drive out to **Crystal Geyser,** 10 mi south of town on good, graded road. The geyser erupts every 14 to 16 hours for about 30 minutes, with water shooting 80 to 100 ft high. Mineral deposits have created a dramatic orange "terrace" surrounding the eruption site. The staff at the Green River Information Center, which is in the John Wesley Powell River History Museum, can provide detailed directions and updated road conditions.

Dining and Lodging

$–$$ ✕ **Tamarisk Restaurant.** This sit-down eatery features homemade pies and fudge in addition to a full dinner menu specializing in steaks, as well as Mexican and vegetarian dishes. The riverside setting makes dining here a treat. ⊠ *870 E. Main St.,* ☎ *435/564–8109. AE, D, DC, MC, V.*

$ ✕ **Ray's Tavern.** Ray's is something of a western legend and a favorite ★ hangout for river runners. Stop here for great tales about working on the river as well as the best all-beef hamburger in two counties. ⊠ *25 S. Broadway,* ☎ *435/564–3511. AE, D, MC, V.*

$–$$ 🏨 **Best Western River Terrace Hotel.** The setting, on the bank of the Green River, is conducive to a good night's rest. Comfortable rooms are furnished with large beds, and the premises are clean. Be sure to ask for a river-view room to take best advantage of this property. ⊠ *880 E. Main St., 84525,* ☎ *435/564–3401,* 𝖥𝖠𝖷 *435/564–3403,* 𝖶𝖤𝖡 *www.bestwestern.com. 51 rooms. Pool, hot tub. AE, D, DC, MC, V.*

Outdoor Activities and Sports

CYCLING AND FOUR-WHEELING

West of Green River, the **San Rafael Swell,** north and south of I–70, presents a wild landscape where outlaws once camped in twisting canyons, and cowboys galloped across vast tracts of desert grazing land. In modern times, off-road vehicle trails carved the area, providing easy access for cyclists. A cult classic among four-wheelers, the swell's routes such as Buckhorn Draw, Hidden Splendor, and the Copper Globe Loop are favored destinations.

A free bike-trail guide is available from the Castle Country Travel Region. There are no reliable water sources in the desert, so carry plenty of water on any ride or hike. Another great place to explore on a bicycle is **Nine Mile Canyon.** Contact the BLM in Price for maps of the area and trip suggestions.

RAFTING AND CANOEING

May through September, raft trips on the Green River, both above and below the town of the same name, are generally arranged by companies headquartered in Vernal or Moab. The annual Raft Utah directory available from the Utah Travel Council has descriptions of the river canyons and information on guides and outfitters. No rapids are over Class III, making the river an excellent option for kayakers just beginning to get the feel for paddling. Dvorak Expeditions runs a six-day trip on the Green River.

Green River City serves as a put-in point for those headed into **Labyrinth Canyon.** Here canoeists are king, for there is barely a ripple along the entire route. For information, contact the BLM in Price.

GOLF

The nine-hole **Green River State Park Golf Course** (☎ 435/564–8882) meanders along the scenic bank of the river.

Moab and Environs

51 *52 mi from Green River via I–70 east and U.S. 191 south.*

The first attempt at settling Moab in 1855 by a group of Mormon pioneers ended unsuccessfully. The verdant valley near the Colorado River had always been common ground for Navajo and Ute people, and peace between these Native Americans and the newcomers was always tenuous. When a confusing and unplanned battle erupted into the tragic death of two missionaries, the Mormon settlers abandoned their Elk Mountain Mission. After that, few people ventured into the area until the 1880s when cowboys and ranchers began taking an interest in the area for cattle grazing. This time, the settlers stayed and the town was named Moab.

A number of theories about how Moab got its name float around bookstores and coffee shops. The most accepted is the biblical derivation. In the Bible, the name Moab occurs frequently referring to a dry, mountainous area east of the Dead Sea and southeast of Jerusalem. This explanation seems to fit in both Moab's geographical relationship to Salt Lake City, the Great Salt Lake, and the geologic characteristics of the area.

Mining has historically been the major local economic activity with vanadium being discovered nearby in 1912. The first of a boom bust cycle began in 1920 with the discovery of uranium, but it was not until Charlie Steen, a down-on-his-luck prospector, wandered into town in the 1950s and made a dramatic uranium strike that Moab changed character forever. Moab was known as a wild, rough-and-tumble town filled with hardworking and hard-playing miners. The town was overflowing with people living in tents and other makeshift homes. Bars were plentiful as were barroom brawls. But in 1964 when the demand for uranium decreased, the largest mine closed and thousands of workers lost their jobs. The wealth and freewheeling ways of Moab disappeared as the town entered into almost two decades of economic downturn.

Moab is still one of the more lively small towns in Utah, but tourism has replaced mining as the economic resource. Arches and Canyonlands national parks lure nearly a million people to the area every year. The unique and colorful geology of the area also calls out to mountain bikers who love to ride their bicycles over the humps of "slickrock" which act like natural highways in the wilderness. Thousands more people take four-wheel-drive vehicles into the backcountry to drive the challenging network of roads left from mining days. Still others flock to the shores of the Colorado River where they set out in rafts to tackle some of the largest white-water rapids in the country. The city has learned to accommodate guests to the area by building many new motels, restaurants, and other visitor services. What was a sleepy, depressed town in the 1970s and '80s has become the hub of activity and a major tourist destination in the United States.

Moab's diverse population makes it a culturally fascinating place to visit. Environmentalists must learn to coexist with ranchers; pro-development factions come up against anti-growth forces; and Mormon church leaders struggle with value issues in a predominantly non-Mormon community.

Arches National Park, a few miles north of Moab, is a geologic wonderland unlike any other, with giant pinnacles and balanced rocks teetering throughout the "rockscape." The park holds the largest collection of natural arches in the world. Although the process by which these spans of red rock were formed is complex, geologists do point to an underlying bed of salt as the main impetus. As this material shifted, fissures formed in the overlying layer of sandstone. Wind and water then eroded this rock into freestanding fins, which were in turn sculpted into the arches and formations seen today. Many of the park's premier sights, including the Courthouse Towers, Balanced Rock, the Windows, and Skyline Arch, are found along the park's 21-mi paved road. Others, such as Delicate Arch, the Fiery Furnace, and Devil's Garden, are accessible only by foot. Other than the visitor center at the park entrance and the 50-site Devil's Garden Campground, which lies at road's end, there are no services in Arches. ✉ *5 mi north of Moab on U.S. 191,* ☎ *435/259–8161,* WEB *www.nps.gov/arch/home.htm.* ✈ *$10 per vehicle.* ☉ *Visitor center daily 8–sunset.*

For a small taste of history in the Moab area, stop by the **Dan O'Laurie Museum.** Ancient and historic Native Americans are remembered in exhibits of sandals, baskets, pottery, and other artifacts. Other displays chronicle the early Spanish expeditions into the area and the history of uranium discovery and exploration. ✉ *118 E. Center St.,* ☎ *435/259–7985.* ✈ *$2.* ☉ *Apr.–Oct., Mon.–Sat. 1–8; Nov.–Mar., Mon.–Thurs. 3–7, Fri. and Sat. 1–7.*

☾ **Hole 'n the Rock** is a 14-room, 5,000-square-ft home carved into a solid rock wall. It would be just another funky roadside attraction if it didn't represent 20 years of toil for Albert and Gladys Christensen. ✉ *15 mi south of Moab on U.S. 191,* ☎ *435/686–2250.* ✈ *$2.50.* ☉ *June–Sept., daily 8–8; Oct.–May, daily 9–5.*

Encompassing some 500 square mi of rugged desert terrain, **Canyonlands National Park** is naturally divided by the Colorado and Green rivers into three districts. Although the Needles and Maze districts are accessible from points farther south and west, the **Island in the Sky District** is reached from Moab. As the name suggests, this portion of the park features a high plateau ringed by thousand-foot cliffs. A favorite among photographers is Mesa Arch, which is reached by hiking a ¼-mi trail. The arch frames the canyons that stretch to the horizon as far as the eye can see. Spires and castles rise out of the desert, just as canyons carve deep recesses into the earth. Peer off the edge of rock beneath the arch and you're looking down about 1,000 ft. A number of scenic overlooks, each of which is precariously perched at land's end, are accessed by 20 mi of paved road. From the Shafer Canyon Overlook, you gaze down upon the twisted Shafer Trail—an early 1900s cattle route that was later upgraded for high-clearance vehicles. From Grand View Point, you can take in spectacular views of the meandering Colorado and Green rivers, the sandstone pinnacles of the Needles District far to the south, and the labyrinths of the Maze District to the southwest. ⊠ *33 mi from Moab via U.S. 191 north and Rte. 313 west,* ☎ *435/259–7164,* WEB *www.nps.gov/cany/home.htm.* ☎ *$10 per vehicle.* ⊙ *Visitor center daily 8–sunset.*

Dead Horse Point State Park, one of the finest of Utah's state parks, overlooks a sweeping oxbow of the Colorado River, some 2,000 ft below, and the upside-down landscapes of Canyonlands National Park. Dead Horse Point itself is a small peninsula connected to the main mesa by a narrow neck of land. As the story goes, cowboys used to drive wild horses onto the point and pen them there with a brush fence. Some were accidentally forgotten and left to perish. Facilities at the park include a modern visitor center and museum, a 21-site campground with drinking water, and an overlook. ⊠ *34 mi from Moab at the end of Rte. 313,* ☎ *435/259–2614; 800/322–3770 for campground reservations,* WEB *parks.state.ut.us.* ☎ *$6 per vehicle.* ⊙ *Daily 8–6.*

One of the most scenic drives in the country is found along Route 128, 2 mi north of Moab off U.S. 191. The **Colorado River Scenic Byway** runs along the Colorado River northeast to I–70. First passing through a high-walled corridor, the drive eventually breaks out into Professor Valley, home of the monoliths of Fisher Towers and Castle Rock, which you may recognize from various car commercials. The byway also passes the single-lane Dewey Bridge, in use from 1916 to 1986. Near the end of the 44-mi drive is the tiny town of Cisco.

For close-up views of the Colorado River and opportunity to see ancient Native American rock art, travel the **Potash Scenic Byway.** Potash Road, or Route 279, is north of the Colorado River bridge and stretches for about 15 mi before the pavement ends. The steep canyon walls that hug the road are also a favorite of rock climbers, so caution must be used when driving this route. At the end of the pavement is the Moab Salt Plant that extracts salt and potash from deposits hundreds of feet below. The evaporation ponds can be seen from several overlooks in the area. Beyond the plant, a rough dirt road, not suitable for passenger cars, continues into Canyonlands National Park's Island in the Sky district.

Although Moab is best known for its slickrock desert, it is also the gateway to the second-highest mountain range in the state—the 12,000-ft La Sal Mountains. Beginning 8 mi south of Moab, the 62-mi **La Sal Mountain Loop** climbs over the western flank of the range before connecting to Route 128 to the north. Long a favorite stomping ground of locals, the often snowcapped La Sal Mountains have been discovered by out-of-towners as a welcome retreat from the summer heat.

Moab's Skyway chairlift that you to the top of the Moab Rim. The views are spectacular and you can access hiking and biking trails from here. Sunset is particularly popular, when white clouds turn tangerine. ⊠ *985 W. Kane Creek Blvd.,* ☎ *435/259–7799.* ☎ *$9.* ⊙ *Mar.–Thanksgiving, daily 9 AM until after dark; Feb., weekends 9 AM–dark.*

OFF THE
BEATEN PATH

CANYON RIMS RECREATION AREA – With a few hours to spare, you can enjoy two remarkable canyon-country vistas. Turn off U.S. 191 at a point centered between Moab and Monticello (about 27 mi south of Moab, and 26 mi north of Monticello), and the paved Needles Overlook Road runs 22 mi west to Needles Overlook, which takes in the southern end of Canyonlands National Park. Less than 20 mi farther on a good, graded road is the Anticline Overlook, which encompasses the Colorado River, Dead Horse Point, and other locales to the north. For more information, contact the Moab district office of the BLM. ⊠ *BLM office, 82 E. Dogwood St., Moab 84532,* ☎ *435/259–6111,* WEB *www.blm.gov/utah/moab/canyon_rims.html.*

Dining and Lodging

$–$$$ ✕ **Buck's Grill House.** For a real taste of the American West, try the buffalo meat loaf or venison stew served at this popular dinner spot. The meats are thick and tender and the gravies are finger-licking good. A selection of southwestern entrées including duck tamales and buffalo chorizo tacos round out the menu. You'll definitely find something on the wine list to complement your meal. ⊠ *1393 N. Hwy. 191,* ☎ *435/259–5201. AE, D, MC, V. No lunch.*

$$–$$$ ✕ **Center Café.** Multiple awards have been bestowed upon this little
★ jewel in the desert. In 2001 it moved into a quiet, off-street location with a courtyard for outdoor dining. Inside is a fireplace and Spanish Mediterranean decor. Whether grilled black Angus beef tenderloin with caramelized onion and Gorgonzola, or roasted eggplant lasagna with feta cheese and Moroccan olive marinara, there is always something to make your taste buds sigh. Be sure to ask for the impressive wine list. ⊠ *60 N. 100 West St.,* ☎ *435/259–4295. D, MC, V.*

$–$$$ ✕ **Sorrel River Grill.** The most scenic dining experience in Moab is 17
★ mi down the Colorado River Road (Highway 128) at the Sorrel River Ranch. Outdoor dining gives you views of the Colorado River, the La Sal Mountains, and the red-rock spires and towers that surround the ranch. Start with the artichoke fondue and then select from a diverse menu including a tender, juicy fillet or beautifully prepared salmon, shrimp, or scallops. The owner is vegetarian, so the menu has plentiful veggie entrées. Unlike many contemporary restaurants, portions here are generous, but save room for their homemade pie or cheesecake. Breakfast is also served. ⊠ *Hwy. 128 Mile Marker 17.5,* ☎ *435/259–4642. AE, MC, V. No lunch.*

$–$$ ✕ **Eddie McStiff's.** This casual restaurant and microbrewery serves up pizzas and zesty Italian specialties to go with 13 freshly brewed concoctions such as raspberry and blueberry wheat beer and a smooth cream ale. ⊠ *57 S. Main St.,* ☎ *435/259–2337. MC, V.*

$–$$ ✕ **Poplar Place.** This local landmark for fun and lively dining is known for its appetizers, pizzas, and sandwiches. Rooftop dining is perfect for warm summer evenings. ⊠ *11 E. 100 N. Main St.,* ☎ *435/259–6018. MC, V.*

$ ✕ **Eklecticafe.** One of the more creative restaurants in Moab, breakfast and lunch items include a variety of burritos and wraps, scrambled tofu, Polish sausage, Indonesian satay kebabs, or one of many fresh, organic salads. On nice days, you can take your meal outside to the large covered patio. Winter days you'll want to stay inside by the wood-burning stove. ⊠ *352 N. Main St.,* ☎ *435/259–6896. MC, V. No dinner.*

$ ✕ **Jail House Café.** Breakfast here will keep you going long into the afternoon. From eggs Benedict to waffles, the menu is guaranteed to fill you up. Housed in what once was the county courthouse, the building held prisoners in the past. ⊠ *101 N. Main St.,* ☎ *435/259–3900. MC, V. Closed Nov.–Mar. No lunch or dinner.*

$ ✕ **La Hacienda.** This family-owned and -operated restaurant serves good south-of-the-border meals at an equally good price. The helpings are generous and the service is friendly. And yes, you can order a margarita, too. ⊠ *574 N. Main St.,* ☎ *435/259–6319. AE, D, MC, V.*

$$$–$$$$ ▦ **Pack Creek Ranch.** A real treat, this out-of-the-way (and glad of it) guest ranch sits beneath the snowcapped summits of the La Sal Mountains. Horses graze in the pastures and mule deer frequent the grounds. Cabins, with one to four bedrooms, are spacious and luxurious, including woven rugs, bent-willow furnishings, and full kitchens; most have stone fireplaces. There are no TVs or phones to disturb the peace and quiet. A full breakfast is included in the price of the room. The ranch's lodge can be rented by groups and will prepare dinner with advance arrangements. The pool, hot tub, and sauna are within earshot of the creek. ⊠ *La Sal Mountain Loop, 20 mi from Moab; Box 1270, Moab 84532,* ☎ *435/259–5505,* FAX *435/259–8879,* WEB *www.packcreekranch.com. 11 cabins, 1 house. Pool, hot tub, massage, sauna, horseback riding. AE, D, MC, V. BP.*

$$$–$$$$ ▦ **Sorrel River Ranch.** The ultimate getaway is this luxury ranch about
   ★   24 mi from town. The ranch is on the banks of the Colorado River and all rooms offer either a river or mountain view. No matter which way you look, the vista is spectacular in a landscape studded with towering red cliffs, buttes, and spires. Rooms are carefully decorated with a distinct western flair featuring log furnishings, and have a kitchenette. Most rooms have claw-foot jetted tubs. Some have fireplaces. To preserve the ranch feel and views, cars are not allowed near the rooms. Guests may ride a shuttle in or take a short walk from the parking area. An on-site preschool will accept guests' children for the day. ⊠ *Box K, Hwy. 128 Mile Marker 17.5, 84532,* ☎ *435/259–4642 or 877/359–2715,* FAX *435/259–3016,* WEB *www.sorrelriver.com. 33 rooms. Restaurant, kitchenettes, pool, hot tub, massage, health club, basketball, horseback riding, playground, laundry service, meeting room. AE, MC, V.*

$$–$$$ ▦ **Gonzo Inn.** The closest thing to a hotel in Moab is this interesting in-town luxury motel. Careful attention was given to design, color, and art when creating this eclectic inn. The furnishings are all decidedly contemporary, using much metal and steel. Some rooms have jetted tubs and fireplaces. Others feature large concrete showers that make you feel like you're showering in an elegant spa. The pool, hot tub, and courtyard overlook a local pathway used for strolling or jogging. Each room has either a private balcony or patio. A complimentary Continental breakfast is included and an espresso bar is available for serious coffee drinkers. ⊠ *100 W. 200 South St., 84532,* ☎ *435/259–2515 or 800/791–4044,* FAX *435/259–6992,* WEB *www.gonzoinn.com. 43 rooms. Breakfast room, pool, hot tub. AE, D, MC, V. CP.*

$$–$$$ ▦ **Sunflower Hill Bed and Breakfast.** This turn-of-the-20th-century dwelling is tucked away on a quiet neighborhood street and managed by a family that truly values its guests. A charming country feel is accomplished with antiques and farmhouse treasures, and well-tended gardens and pathways. The newer rooms have jetted tubs and private porches where you can lounge in the fluffy white robes provided. The buffet-style breakfast features a vegetable frittata, side meats, and home-baked pastries. Evening refreshments are offered when you return from exploring the parks and canyons. ⊠ *185 N. 3rd East St., 84532,* ☎ *435/259–2974,* FAX *435/259–3065,* WEB *www.sunflowerhill.com. 10 rooms, 2 suites. Dining room. AE, D, MC, V. BP.*

$$ ▦ **Dreamkeeper Inn.** Serenity is just a few breaths away at this classy bed-and-breakfast in a quiet Moab neighborhood. The home was originally built during the uranium boom days and is a one-level ranch

house. The rooms line a hallway, and each opens onto the pool, patio, and courtyard area where you may want to have your morning coffee. The large, shady grounds are filled with flower and vegetable gardens. Each room is uniquely decorated with antiques or southwestern-style log furnishings. Two cottages off the main house offer a bit more privacy. A full breakfast in the sunny dining area starts your day just right. The owners of this inn are warm and generous people. ⊠ *191 S. 200 East St., 84532,* ☎ *435/259–5998,* FAX *435/259–3912,* WEB *www.dreamkeeperinn.com. 6 rooms, 2 cottages. Dining room, pool, hot tub. AE, D, MC, V. BP.*

$ 🖃 **Red Stone Inn.** Truly one of the best bargains in Moab, this one-story motel offers small but adequate rooms in a location convenient to restaurants and shops. Log furniture and knotty-pine walls give it more character than you'll find at other rooms in this price range. The emphasis here is clearly on service. Mountain bikes are allowed in rooms. The motel provides a bicycle work stand and service station. Guests can cook on the gas grill in the picnic area and use the pool at the sister motel across the street. The motel has 16 rooms where pets are allowed. ⊠ *535 S. Main St., 84532,* ☎ *435/259–3500 or 800/722–1972,* FAX *435/259–2717,* WEB *www.moabredstone.com. 52 rooms. Coin laundry. AE, D, MC, V.*

Nightlife

At **Eddie McStiff's** (⊠ 57 S. Main St., ☎ 435/259–2337), several televisions draw a crowd to the separate barroom. The creative house brews on tap may help patrons participate in "open mike" performances later in the night. On weekends, there's live music at **Rio Colorado Restaurant** (⊠ 2 S. 100 West St., ☎ 435/259–6666). The **Sportsman's Lounge** (⊠ 1991 S. Hwy. 191, ☎ 435/259–9972) has a big dance floor and live music every weekend.

Operating from April to October, **Canyonlands by Night** (⊠ on U.S. 191, just north of the Colorado River bridge, ☎ 435/259–5261) offers an unusual two-hour boat ride on the Colorado River after dark. Using 40,000 watts of illumination that lights the canyon walls, the trip includes music and narration highlighting Moab's history, Native American legends, and geologic formations along the river.

Outdoor Activities and Sports

CAMPING

There are abundant commercial campgrounds in and around Moab both for RV and tent campers. Some are open year-round, others close from November to March, and most accept reservations. The Moab Information Center has a complete listing of commercial campgrounds and current availability status of public campgrounds.

Of the many appealing public campgrounds, Devil's Garden in Arches National Park, Squaw Flat in the Needles District of Canyonlands National Park, and Dead Horse Point State Park are the best bets for finding good facilities in gorgeous settings and close to hiking trails. These campgrounds fill early in the day April through October. The BLM hosts public camping along the Colorado River on Highway 128. Another nice spot is the Wind Whistle Campground in the BLM's Canyon Rims Recreation Area, 32 mi south of Moab. None of the public campgrounds accept reservations for individual campers.

🔺 **Canyonlands Campground.** This downtown camp park is convenient to all local amenities, and is still a shady retreat. ⊠ *555 S. Main St., Moab,* ☎ *435/259–6848 or 888/522–6848,* WEB *www.moab-utah.com/canyonlands/rv.html. 130 sites. Flush toilets, dump station, some full hook-ups, some partial hookups, drinking water, laundry facilities,* *showers, grills, picnic tables, electricity, public telephone, general store, service station, swimming. AE, D, MC, V*

⚠ **Slickrock Campground.** One of Moab's older campgrounds, you'll find lots of mature shade trees and all the basic amenities here plus three hot tubs where adults have the priority. Just about 3 mi from Arches National Park and next to a fabulous restaurant, you can easily make this your home base. ⊠ *1301½ N. Hwy. 191, Moab,* ☎ *435/259–7660 or 800/448–8873,* FAX *435/259–7776,* WEB *www.slickrockcampground.com. 198 sites. Flush toilets, dump station, drinking water, laundry facilities, showers, grills, picnic tables, snack bar, electricity, public telephone, general store, swimming. MC, V.*

⚠ **Up the Creek Campground.** This neighborhood campground is nestled under big cottonwoods on the banks of Mill Creek. Even though it's near downtown, you'll feel like you're in the woods. Camping is limited to walk-in tent sites only. ⊠ *210 E. 300 South St.,* ☎ *435/259–6995. 20 sites. Flush toilets, drinking water, showers, picnic tables, grills. No credit cards. Closed Nov.–mid-Mar.*

CYCLING

Mountain biking draws people of all ages off the pavement and onto rugged four-wheel-drive roads and trails. One of the many popular routes is the Slickrock Trail, a stunning area of steep slickrock dunes a few miles east of Moab. Beginners should master the 2½-mi practice loop before attempting the longer, and very challenging, 10½-mi loop. More moderate rides can be found on the Gemini Bridges or Monitor and Merrimac trails, both off of U.S. 191 north of Moab. Backcountry permits are required for the vigorous 100-mi White Rim Trail in Canyonlands National Park. The Moab Information Center carries a free biking trail guide.

Poison Spider Bicycles (⊠ 497 N. Main St., ☎ 435/259–7882 or 800/635–1792) is a fully loaded shop staffed by young, friendly bike experts. For full-suspension bike rentals, sales, solid advice on trails, parts, equipment and gear, visit the oldest bike shop in town, **Rim Cyclery** (⊠ 94 W. 100 South St., ☎ 435/259–5333).

Several companies offer shuttles to and from trailheads including **Roadrunner Shuttle** (☎ 435/259–9402).

FOUR-WHEELING

There are thousands of miles of four-wheel-drive roads in and around Moab. The rugged terrain with its hair-raising ledges, steep climbs, and smooth expanses of slickrock is the perfect place for drivers to test their metal. For 35 years, Moab has been the home of the annual Jeep Safari when nearly 2,000 off-road enthusiasts hit the backcountry roads. There are abundant trails suitable for all levels of drivers. Seasoned 4X4 drivers might tackle the daunting Moab Rim, Elephant Hill, or Poison Spider Mesa. Novice drivers will be happier touring Long Canyon, Hurrah Pass, or, for those not afraid of precipitous cliff edges, the famous Shafer Trail. All of the routes offer spectacular scenery in the vast desert lands surrounding Moab. Guided 4×4 tours are offered by many outfitters. Maps and guidebooks for off-pavement driving are available at many stores including **TI Maps** (⊠ 29 E. Center St., ☎ 435/259–5529).

For people without four-wheel-drive vehicles, rentals are available at **Farabee 4×4 Rentals** (⊠ 401 N. Main St., ☎ 435/259–7494 or 800/806–5337). **Highpoint Hummer Tours** (⊠ 281 N. Main St., ☎ 435/259–2972 or 877/486–6833) hosts guests in unique, open-air Hummer vehicles. **Raven Rock Art Tours** (⊠ ☎ 435/259–4510 or 888/799–5293) combines mellow off-road travel with visits to ancient Native American rock-art sites. **Tag-A-Long Expeditions** (✉ 452 N. Main St., ☎ 435/259–8946 or 800/453–3292) holds permits to take guests into the interior of Canyonlands National Park.

GOLF

Moab Golf Course (✉ 2705 S. East Bench Rd., ☎ 435/259–6488) has 18 holes. This unusual course has lush greens set against a red-rock sandstone backdrop, a lovely visual combination that's been known to distract even the most focused golfer.

NORDIC SKIING

Once snow flies, portions of the **La Sal Mountain Loop** road are impassable, but a well-maintained hut-to-hut system, operated by Tag-A-Long Expeditions (✉ ☎ 435/259–8946 or 800/453–3292), make this a wonderful place to cross-country ski.

RAFTING

As it flows through Moab, the Colorado River is misleadingly calm; white-water adventures await rafters both upstream and down. Up-river, near the Colorado state line, is **Westwater Canyon,** an exciting one- or two-day float with Class III–IV (on a I–VI scale) rapids. Moab's **Daily** river run, which begins along Route 128, offers somewhat tamer waters just out of town. Downstream from Moab, in the heart of Canyonlands National Park, is **Cataract Canyon,** which manages more than two dozen legendary rapids up to Class V in a 14-mi stretch. A permit is required from the BLM in Moab to run Westwater, and a trip down Cataract Canyon requires one from Canyonlands National Park.

The best way to enjoy a white-water rafting trip is to hook up with one of the many experienced raft-outfitting companies. These outfitters already hold the permits, the equipment, and guides who can take you safely through the rapids.

Shopping

In Moab, shopping opportunities are plentiful from March until the end of October, with art galleries, jewelry stores, and shops carrying T-shirts and souvenirs on every block. A visit to Moab is not complete without a stop at **Back of Beyond Books** (✉ 83 N. Main St., ☎ 435/259–5154). This anything-but-mainstream store has the largest selection of guidebooks, Native American studies, environmental, and regional titles you'll find anywhere in the Rockies. The **Moab Rock Shop** (✉ 600 N. Main St., ☎ 435/259–7312) has one of the most interesting rock collections in the state. For irresistible photographic images of the landscape you'll be seeing, visit **Tom Till Gallery** (✉ 61 N. Main St., ☎ 435/259–9808). To take a step back in time, visit one of Moab's more unique stores, **Western Image** (✉ 79 N. Main St., ☎ 435/259–3006). The shop is packed with antique cowboy and western collectibles along with cowboy hats and clothing.

Newspaper Rock

52 *51 mi from Moab via U.S. 191 south and Rte. 211 west.*

Beginning 2,000 years ago, inhabitants of this region began etching cryptic images on a large rock face. In the centuries following, subsequent chapters of an undecipherable history were added, resulting in an impressive collection of petroglyphs that archaeologists cite as one of the most comprehensive in the Southwest. An interpretive trail and small campground are provided. ✉ *12 mi west of U.S. 191 on Rte. 211,* ☎ *435/587–2141.* ✆ *Free.*

Blanding

53   *25 mi from Monticello via U.S. 191 south.*

Conservative Blanding is dry: that is, there's no state liquor store, and no alcohol is sold at stores or in restaurants. What Blanding does offer, however, is the **Edge of the Cedars State Park.** Here, one of the nation's foremost museums dedicated to the ancestral Puebloan Indians displays a variety of pots, baskets, spear points, and such. Interestingly, many of these artifacts were donated by guilt-ridden pot hunters, or archaeological looters. Behind the museum, you can visit an actual ancestral Puebloan ruin. ⊠ *660 W. 400 North St.,* ☎ *435/ 678–2238,* WEB *parks.state.ut.us.* ☞ *$5 per vehicle.* ☉ *May–Oct., daily 8–8; Nov.–Apr., daily 9–5.*

Road-weary travelers, especially children, will enjoy a stop at the **Dinosaur Museum.** Skeletons, fossil logs, footprints, and scientifically replicated dinosaur skin are all on display. Hallways hold a collection of movie posters featuring Godzilla and other dinosaur-like monsters dating back to the 1930s. ⊠ *754 S. 200 West St.,* ☎ *435/678–3454.* ☞ *$2.* ☉ *Apr.–Oct., Mon.–Sat. 9–5.*

The antiques shop **Ol' West Traders** (⊠ *1949 S. Main St., 105-12,* ☎ *435/678–2568*) specializes in old cowboy paraphernalia.

OFF THE BEATEN PATH

HOVENWEEP NATIONAL MONUMENT – For anyone with an abiding interest in the ancient Anasazi Indians, now called ancestral Puebloans, a visit to this monument is a must. Along a remote stretch of the Utah-Colorado border southeast of Blanding, Hovenweep features several unusual tower structures that may have been used for making astronomical observations. By marking the summer solstice, these early farmers knew the best times of the year to plant their crops. A half-mile walking tour, or a more rigorous 1½-mi hike into the canyon, allows you to see the ancient dwellings. A 32-site campground is available for overnighters in tents or small vehicles. ⊠ *28 mi east of U.S. 191 on Rte. 262,* ☎ *970/562–4282,* WEB *nps.gov/hove/.* ☞ *$6.* ☉ *Daily 8 AM–sunset.*

Dining and Lodging

$–$$ ✕ **Homestead Steak House.** Breakfast, lunch, and dinner are served at this classic American restaurant. These folks specialize in authentic Navajo fry bread and Navajo tacos. The big Sheepherder's Sandwich is also made with fry bread, filled with your choice of meat. ⊠ *121 E. Center St.,* ☎ *435/678–3456. AE, D, MC, V. No breakfast on weekends.*

$–$$ ☷ **Comfort Inn.** One of the newer properties in Blanding, this chain motel offers a variety of amenities that may not be found elsewhere in in Monticello. A complimentary Continental breakfast is included. ⊠ *711 S. Main St., 84511,* ☎ *435/678–3271 or 800/622–3250,* FAX *435/ 678–3217. 52 rooms. Indoor pool, hot tub, gym, coin laundry. AE, D, DC, MC, V. CP.*

$ ☷ **Four Corners Inn.** This family-owned motel offers clean, large rooms and a Continental breakfast. If you're lucky, you'll meet up with the owner who tells stories about historical Blanding. The gift shop sells handmade quilts and trading-post items. One room comes with a kitchenette. ⊠ *131 East Center (Hwy. 191), 84535,* ☎ *435/ 678–3257 or 800/574–3150,* FAX *435/678–3186. 32 rooms. AE, D, MC, V. CP.*

Bluff

54 *25 mi from Blanding via U.S. 191 south.*

Bluff, settled in 1880, is one of southeastern Utah's oldest towns. Mormon pioneers built a ranching empire that made the town at one time the richest per capita in the state. Although this early period of affluence has passed, several historic Victorian-style homes remain and can be seen on a short walking tour of the town. Bluff is something of a supply point for residents of the Navajo Indian Nation, the largest Native American reservation, which lies just beyond the San Juan River. Bluff is a quiet town which has deliberately avoided development that many nearby towns pursued. Hundreds of people travel to Bluff each year to launch river trips onto the San Juan River from Sand Island Recreation Site. The San Juan River and surrounding area holds strong evidence of population by ancient Native American Indians. The river corridor and nearby canyons are rich with rock art, dwellings, and other archaeological sites.

OFF THE BEATEN PATH

FOUR CORNERS MONUMENT – Head south from Bluff on U.S. 191 for about 35 mi, to its junction with U.S. 160. (The U.S. 191/U.S. 160 junction is south of the Utah/Arizona border in the Navajo Nation.) Drive east on U.S. 160 for about 30 mi. At this point, U.S. 160 curves north to the only place in the country where four states, Utah, Arizona, New Mexico, and Colorado, meet. Administered by the Navajo Nation, Four Corners offers not only a geography lesson but also a great opportunity to buy Native American jewelry and other traditional crafts directly from Navajo artisans. Bring cash, as credit cards and checks may not be accepted, particularly when buying from roadside displays or other impromptu marketplaces.

Dining and Lodging

$–$$ ✕ **Cow Canyon Trading Post.** This tiny, but absolutely charming, restaurant next to a classic trading post serves three dinner entrées daily. Meals are creative and diverse with a touch of ethnic flair. There is usually a grilled meat with plenty of fresh vegetables and you can order beer or wine with your meal. ⊠ *Intersection of Hwy. 191 and Hwy. 163,* ☎ *435/672–2208. AE, MC, V. Closed Nov.–Mar. No lunch.*

$$ ⬚ **Desert Rose Inn and Cabins.** Bluff's largest motel is truly a rose in the desert. Its attractive log-cabin style with a front porch gives it a nostalgic touch, and all rooms are spacious and clean with uncommonly large bathrooms. The cabins have small refrigerators and microwaves. ⊠ *701 West Hwy. 191, 84512,* ☎ *435/672–2303 or 888/475–7673,* FAX *435/672–2217,* WEB *www.desertroseinn.com. 30 rooms, 6 cabins. Hot tub. AE, D, MC, V.*

$ ⬚ **Recapture Lodge.** This lodge is regionally renowned, so call ahead for reservations. Known for its friendliness, the motel offers guided tours into the surrounding canyon country. Slide shows examining local geology, art, and history are presented at night. The plain, clean rooms come at good prices. ⊠ *U.S. 191, Box 309, 84512,* ☎ *435/ 672–2281,* FAX *435/672–2284. 28 rooms. Pool, hot tub, travel services. AE, D, MC, V.*

Outdoor Activities and Sports

Three miles west of Bluff, the **Sand Island Recreation Site** is the launch site for San Juan River trips. This BLM facility includes a primitive campground and a large panel of ancestral Puebloan rock art. The panel includes several large images of Kokopelli, the mischief maker from Pueblo Indian lore. While somewhat calmer than the Colorado, the San Juan River offers some truly exceptional scenery and abundant opportunity to visit archaeological sites. It can be run in two sections: from Bluff to Mexican Hat, and from Mexican Hat to Lake Powell. For permits, contact the **BLM** (✉ San Juan Resource Area, Box 7, Monticello 84535, ☎ 435/587–1544). If you don't have your own rafts or kayaks, **Wild River Expeditions** (✉ 101 Main St., Bluff, ☎ 435/672–2244 or 800/422–7654) will take you on the San Juan River. This reliable outfitter is known for educational trips which emphasize the geology, natural history, and archaeological wonders of the San Juan and its canyons.

Mexican Hat

🟡 *20 mi from Bluff via U.S. 163 south.*

Small Mexican Hat lies on the north bank of the San Juan River. Named for a nearby rock formation, which you can't miss on the way into town, Mexican Hat is a jumping-off point for visiting two geological wonders.

By crossing the San Juan River and driving 21 mi south of Mexican Hat on U.S. 163 across Navajo land, you will reach the **Monument Valley Tribal Park.** Thanks to its striking red-rock spires, buttes, and mesas, Monument Valley has earned international recognition as the setting for dozens of movies and television commercials. Just as memorable as the scenery, though, is the taste of Navajo culture you can get here. In addition to visiting the historic **Gouldings Trading Post** and shopping at its rows of arts and crafts booths, plan to take a Navajo-guided tour of the valley. These informative excursions invariably include a stop at a hogan, the traditional Navajo home. Guide services can be acquired at the **Tribal Park headquarters** (☎ 435/727–3287), which is on a paved spur off U.S. 163 at the Utah-Arizona border. The costs for guided tours in Monument Valley vary based on the length of the tour and the season of the year. The headquarters office is open daily, 10 AM–sunset.

🟡 From the overlook at **Goosenecks of the San Juan River** (✉ 10 mi northwest of Mexican Hat off Rte. 261) you can peer down upon what geologists claim is the best example of an "entrenched meander" in the world. The river's serpentine course resembles the necks of geese in spectacular 1,000-ft-deep chasms. Although the Goosenecks of the San Juan River is actually a state park, no facilities other than pit toilets are provided, and no fee is charged.

Lodging

$–$$ 🏨 **Gouldings Lodge.** This is the best place from which to tour Monument Valley and the surrounding Navajo Nation. Rooms are better than those at most motels this far out of the way. Most rooms have stunning views, and the service here is quite friendly. Part of the 1923 Gouldings Trading Post, the lodge gives guests a good feel for the history of the area. The shop has a great selection of Native American arts and crafts. ✉ *Box 360001, Monument Valley, 84536, off U.S. 163,* ☎ *435/727–3231,* FAX *435/727–3344,* WEB *www.gouldings.com. 77 rooms. Restaurant, pool, shop. AE, D, DC, MC, V.*

$–$$ 🏨 **San Juan Inn.** The highlight of this property is its location on a bluff overlooking the San Juan River. The rooms all face the river and are clean and generally large. There is a small grocery store for supplies and a nearby café that serves cold beer. ✉ *U.S. 163 and the San Juan River,* ☎ *435/683–2220,* FAX *435/683–2210. 39 rooms. Grocery, hot tub, gym. AE, D, DC, MC, V.*

Shopping

When in Monument Valley, be sure to stop at **Gouldings Trading Post** (✉ off Hwy. 163, ☎ 435/727–3231) for a wide selection of fine handcrafted jewelry, Navajo rugs, and pottery. The store started in a tent in the 1920s and its reputation for selling only authentic Native American art is solid. **Oljato Trading Post** (✉ Kayenta, AZ, off Hwy. 163, ☎ 435/727–3210), 7.6 beautiful miles past Gouldings Trading Post, was opened in 1905 by John Wetherill and is registered with the Utah Historical Society. Since baskets are used by the local Navajo population, there is a good selection here. The current building dates from 1921.

En Route   From the turnoff for the Goosenecks, Route 261 heads north toward what looks to be an impregnable 1,200-ft wall of rock. The road climbs this obstacle in a steep, 3-mi ascent known as the Moki Dugway. Unpaved but well graded, the series of tight curves is manageable by passenger cars, but not recommended for RVs or towed vehicles. Be sure to stop at an overlook near the top for a superb view into **Monument Valley.** At the top of the Moki Dugway, the drive returns to pavement as Route 261 tracks north across Cedar Mesa—relatively flat terrain that is thick with piñon and juniper, but not cedar. Deep canyons divide this plateau land. Once home to ancestral Puebloan Indians, these drainages feature hundreds, if not thousands, of their cliff dwellings. Grand Gulch, the largest of these drainages, is protected as a primitive area and is a popular destination for backpackers.

Natural Bridges National Monument

57 *33 mi from Mexican Hat via Rtes. 261 and 275 north; 38 mi from Blanding via Rtes. 95 and 275 east.*

When Elliot McClure, an early visitor to Natural Bridges National Monument, drove his car through the park in 1931, his car slowly disintegrated. First his headlights fell off. Next, his doors dropped off. Finally, his bumpers worked loose, and the radiator broke away. Today a journey to see the three stone bridges is far less hazardous. All roads are paved and a scenic 9-mi route takes you to stops that overlook Sipapu, Owachomo, and Kachina bridges. You'll need just an hour or two to drive to overlooks of the natural bridges and remains of an ancestral Puebloan structure, but if you have more time you can also hike to each of the bridges on the uncrowded trails that are fragrant with the smell of sage. Sipapu and Kachina are fairly strenuous, with steep trails dropping into the canyon. Owachomo is an easy walk. For the scientists among you, be sure to stop by the monument's solar panels. Once the largest array of solar panels in the world, the solar energy helps keep Natural Bridges National Monument clean and quiet. There is also a small 13-site primitive campground. ✉ *Rte. 275 off Rte. 95*, ☎ *435/692–1234*, WEB *www.nps.gov/nabr/.* 🎫 *$6 per vehicle.* ☉ *Daily 7 AM–sunset.*

Lodging

$$ 🏨 **Fry Canyon Lodge.** There's not much to do at this lodge other than watch the cliffs change color at sunset or listen for the whir of a hummingbird nearby, but a stay here is unforgettable. Originally built in 1955, the lodge was lovingly renovated in the mid-1990s. A sturdy porch is handy for gazing or reading. Some rooms have writing desks or tables. The older rooms feature vintage chests of drawers and cheery quilts. Perhaps the biggest surprise is the restaurant menu that features a 2-inch-thick pork loin with apple-chili chutney or an oh-so-tender filet mignon. The wine list is impressive, especially in the middle of nowhere. A stay here is more like a special event than a night of lodging. While guests do get priority, if you'd like to try the great restaurant, call ahead or drop in to see if seating is available. ✉ *Hwy. 95 Mile Post 71, 84533*, ☎ *435/259–5334*, FAX *435/259–4101*, WEB *www.frycanyon.com. 10 rooms. Restaurant. MC, V. Closed Nov.–Mar.*

Lake Powell

③ *50 mi from Natural Bridges Monument (to Hall's Crossing) via Rte. 95 east to Rte. 276 west for 40 mi.*

Lake Powell, the recreational focus of the 1,255,400-acre Glen Canyon National Recreation Area, is the second-largest man-made lake in the United States. To explore its 1,900 mi of shoreline fully would take years. If you don't have that kind of time and must move on northward, a bridge at Hite Crossing on Route 95 will give you a glimpse of the lake. The most pleasurable way to see the lake, its inlets, and the curvaceous sandstone cliffs that ring it is to rent a houseboat at any of the lake's marinas. However, guided day tours are also available. A popular full-day or half-day excursion sets out from the Bullfrog and Hall's Crossing marinas to **Rainbow Bridge.** The largest natural bridge in the world, this 290-ft-high, 275-ft-wide span is breathtaking. Lake Powell is also known for its bass fishing. A Utah fishing license and further information may be obtained at any of the marinas. For rentals and tours, contact **Lake Powell Reservations** (✉ Box 56909, Phoenix, AZ 85079, ☎ 800/528–6154, WEB www.visitlakepowell.com). Houseboat rentals begin at $1,031 for three days; a day trip to Rainbow Bridge starts at $106.

Hall's Crossing Marina is the eastern terminus of the **Lake Powell Ferry.** From here the 150-ft *John Atlantic Burr* or *Charles Hall* will float you and your car across a 3-mi stretch of the lake to the Bullfrog Basin Marina, from which it's an hour's drive north to rejoin Route 95. Ferries run seven days a week and depart on the even hour from Hall's Crossing and on the odd hour from Bullfrog. ✉ *Hall's Crossing Marina, Rte. 276,* ☎ *435/684–7000. Reservations not accepted.* 🖃 *$12 per car.* ☉ *May 15–Sept. 30, 8–7; Oct. 1–Oct. 31, 8–5; Nov. 1–Apr. 14, 8–3; Apr. 15–May 14, 8–5.*

Lodging

All of Lake Powell's major marinas have a gas station, campground, lodging, a general store, and boat docks.

$$ 🏨 **Defiance House Lodge.** At the Bullfrog marina, this cliff-top lodge has comfortable and clean rooms, but the real draw is the view. An on-site restaurant also serves three meals a day. Families can take advantage of the 3-bedroom units with full kitchens. ✉ *Box 4055, Lake Powell 84533,* ☎ *435/684–2233 or 800/528–6154,* FAX *435/684–3114,* WEB *visitlakepowell.com/lodging/defiance.htm. 48 rooms, 8 suites. Restaurant. AE, D, MC, V.*

Hanksville

95 mi from Natural Bridges National Monument via Rte. 95 north.

If you don't have the time to cross Lake Powell by ferry, simply follow Route 95 to Hite Crossing. (Just before the bridge, a left turn leads to Hite Marina—the only services for miles around.) Upon crossing the bridge, continue north past the 11,000-ft Henry Mountains to Hanksville, a good place to gas up. Here, pick up Route 24, and head northeast toward I–70. Signs point the way to **Goblin Valley State Park.** As the name implies, the area is filled with hundreds of gnomelike rock formations. Short, easy trails wind through the goblins (to the delight of children), and there's a small, but dusty, campground with modern rest rooms and showers. ✉ *12 mi north of Hanksville via Rte. 24,* ☎ *435/ 564–3633,* WEB *parks.state.ut.us.* 🖃 *$4 per vehicle.* ☉ *Daily 8–sunset.*

OFF THE
BEATEN PATH

THE MAZE – Of the three districts within Canyonlands National Park, the Maze is by far the most remote. Requiring a four-wheel-drive vehicle and a steady hand at the wheel, the signed, but unimproved, route into the Maze begins 50 mi north of Hanksville, almost exactly east of the paved route leading west from Highway 24 to Goblin Valley State Park. It crosses nearly 50 mi of high-clearance dirt road before reaching its second stage, the incredibly rugged Flint Trail. At the journey's end, intrepid travelers will find not only a wonderful view of the Maze but also a trail of sorts that runs to the bottom. A scrambled collection of sandstone canyons, the Maze is one of the most appropriately named features in southern Utah. If you do make the drive into the Maze, consider a visit to nearby Horseshoe Canyon. Featuring larger-than-life-size pictographs that may date back several thousand years, this isolated annex of Canyonlands National Park is well worth the bumpy ride and the 4-mi hike to the canyon. ☎ 435/259–7164, WEB www.nps.gov/cany/hom/htm. ✑ *$10 per vehicle.*

En Route A bit north of Goblin Valley you may notice a long line of flatiron-shape cliffs jutting from the desert floor to the west. This is the San Rafael Reef—the front of the 80-mi-long **San Rafael Swell.** Rugged and quite expansive, the San Rafael Swell is a popular destination for outdoors lovers. After turning west on I–70, you can get an up-close look at this impressive landform from a turnoff where the interstate passes through the sawtooth ridge. A little more than 50 mi west of the Route 24 interchange, turn north on Route 10. After passing through the small towns of Emery (the first outpost of civilization since Hanksville) and Ferron, you'll reach Castle Dale.

Huntington

9 mi from Castle Dale via Rte. 10 north.

As a nearby power plant suggests, the town of Huntington counts its coal reserves as its most valuable resource. It is also home to Huntington State Park, with a 237-acre reservoir. Having produced more complete skeletons than any other site in the world, **Cleveland-Lloyd Dinosaur Quarry** is one of the state's premier destinations for dinosaur aficionados and paleontologists. Remains here are mostly from the Late Jurassic (the carnivorous Allosaurus is a frequent find). Reached by Route 155 and a series of graded roads, the enclosed, active quarry has a visitor center and an outdoor nature trail. ✉ *20 mi east of Huntington via Rte. 155,* ☎ *435/636–3600,* WEB *www.blm.gov/uta/price/quarry.htm.* ✑ *$3.* ☉ *Late Mar.–Memorial Day, Fri., Sat., Sun. 10–5; Memorial Day–Labor Day, daily 10–5; Sept., Fri., Sat., Sun. 10–5.*

Southeastern Utah A to Z

AIRPORTS
The nearest airport to southeastern Utah is Walker Field Airport in Grand Junction, Colorado, 110 mi from Moab. It is served by America West, Sky West, and United Express. Rental cars are available at the airport. ➤ AIRPORT INFORMATION: **Walker Field Airport** (✉ Grand Junction, CO, ☎ 970/244–9100).

CAR TRAVEL
To reach southeastern Utah, take I–15 to U.S. 6 from Salt Lake City and the northwest, I–70 or U.S. 666 from Colorado and the east, and U.S. 191 from Wyoming and the northeast or Arizona and the south. Most roads are well-maintained two-lane highways. Be sure your car is in good working order, as there are long stretches of empty road between towns, and keep the gas tank topped off.

EMERGENCIES

➤ CONTACTS: **Allen Memorial Hospital** (⊠ 719 W. 4th North St., Moab, ☎ 435/259–7191). **Blanding Medical Center** (⊠ 930 N. 400 West St., Blanding, ☎ 435/678–3434). **San Juan County Hospital** (⊠ 364 W. 1st North St., Monticello, ☎ 435/587–2116).

LODGING

CONDOS

Some of the best values in Moab are condominiums. Cedar Breaks Condominiums is an in-town condo with a grassy lawn, hot tub, grills, and outdoor tables and chairs. There's plenty of room here for the kids to play. These units have full kitchens, large bathrooms, and each apartment has its own balcony or patio. A homey, one-story apartment complex tucked on a dead-end street has two bedrooms. The grounds are shady and relaxing with hammocks strung between trees. The luxury Golf Course Condominiums sit on the fairway of the Moab Golf Club a few miles south of town. Views into the red-rock cliffs and La Sal Mountains make this a particularly enjoyable stay. The very professional Moab Lodging and Central Reservations handles reservations for these units and dozens of other motels, condos, and B&Bs in all price ranges.

➤ RESERVATIONS: **Moab Lodging and Central Reservations** (⊠ 50 E. Center St., Moab, ☎ 435/259–5125, 800/505–5343, or 800/748–4386, FAX 435/259–6079, WEB www.moabutahlodging.com).

TOURS

Moab offers a multitude of guide services. Whether you are interested in a 4×4 expedition into the rugged backcountry, a river-rafting trip, a jet-boat tour on calm water, bicycle tours, rock-art tours, or a scenic air flight, outfitters are available to accommodate your needs. It is always best to make reservations, but don't hesitate to call if you make a last-minute decision to join an expedition. Cancellations or unfilled trips sometimes make it possible to jump on a tour with short notice. Tag-A-Long Expeditions offers both rafting and 4×4 expeditions. Highpoint Hummer & ATV Tours provides trips into the backcountry. Raven Rock Art Tours will take you to hidden archaeological sites. Slickrock Air Guides has years of experience as pilots flying over the region.

CYCLING

Rim Tours offers guided day trips around Moab and extended trips in southern Utah. Western Spirit Cycling also offers fully supported multiday tours throughout the region, including the 140-mi Kokopelli Trail, and the White Rim Trail in Canyonlands National Park.

RAFTING

Sheri Griffith Expeditions leads multiday raft trips into Cataract Canyon, Westwater Canyon, and on the Green River. Tag-A-Long Expeditions has been in Moab for over 35 years and has a good reputation. It runs single or multiday raft trips on the Colorado and Green rivers. For people who want to stay dry, you can run scenic calm-water stretches of the Colorado in a large, comfortable jet boat. Canyon Voyages Adventure Co. is a good choice for day trips and also offers multiday trips into Westwater Canyon. This friendly company is also the only outfitter to operate a kayak school for those who want to learn how to run the rapids on their own.

➤ CONTACTS: **Adrift Adventures** (⊠ 378 N. Main St., Box 577, Moab 84532, ☎ 435/259–8594 or 800/874–4483). **Canyon Voyages Adventure Co.** (⊠ 211 N. Main St., Moab 84532, ☎ 435/259–6007 or 800/733–6007, FAX 435/259–9391). **Highpoint Hummer** (⊠ 281 N. Main

St., Moab 84532, ☎ 435/259–2972 or 877/486–6833). **Holiday Ex-peditions** (✉ 1055 E. Main St., Green River 84525, ☎ 435/564–3273 or 800/624–6323). **Raven Rock Art Tours** (✉ Moab 84532, ☎ 435/ 259–4510 or 888/799–5293). **Rim Tours** (✉ 1233 S. Hwy. 191, Moab 84532, ☎ 435/259–5223 or 800/626–7335). **Sheri Griffith Expeditions** (✉ 2231 S. Hwy 191, Box 1324, Moab 84532, ☎ 435/259–8229 or 800/332–2439). **Slickrock Air Guides** (✉ 2231 S. Hwy. 191, Moab 84532, ☎ 435/259–6216 or 800/332–2439). **Tag-A-Long Expeditions** (✉ 452 N. Main St., Box 1206, Moab 84532, ☎ 435/259–8946 or 800/453–3292). **Western Spirit Cycling** (✉ 478 Mill Creek Dr., Moab, ☎ 435/259–8732 or 800/845–2453). **Wild River Expeditions** (✉ 101 Main St., Bluff, ☎ 435/672–2244 or 800/422–7654).

TRAIN TRAVEL
Amtrak has service to Helper and Thompson Springs.

VISITOR INFORMATION
For many scenic drives, hikes, and biking areas, you can get information on land usage and facilities from a BLM office. The Moab Information Center is *the* center for information in Moab and has complete listings of tour operators, campgrounds, and other recreational activities. The friendly staff also has brochures and catalogs to activities in all of southeastern Utah. In Green River, information is available at the John Wesley Powell History Museum (Green River Information Center). Canyonlands Natural History Association operates a bookstore there where you can purchase educational books and maps to the region.
➤ TOURIST INFORMATION: **BLM** (✉ 900 N. 700 East St., Price 84501, ☎ 435/636–3600; ✉ Grand Resource Area, Box M, Moab 84532, ☎ 435/259–8193, WEB www.ut.blm.gov). **Castle Country Travel Region** (✉ 90 N. 100 East St., Box 1037, Price 84501, ☎ 435/637–3009 or 800/842–0789, WEB www.castlecountry.com). **Green River Information Center** (✉ 885 E. Main St., on the Green River, Green River 84525, ☎ 435/564–3427, FAX 435/564–8470). **Moab Information Center** (✉ Center and Main Sts., Moab 84532, ☎ 435/259–8825 or 800/635–6622, WEB www.discovermoab.com). **San Juan County Visitor Services** (✉ 117 S. Main St., Box 490, Monticello 84535, ☎ 435/587–3235 or 800/574–4386, WEB www.southeastutah.com).

SOUTHWESTERN UTAH

As you travel through southwestern Utah you will be treated to wild, colorful canyons and mountain peaks that reach for the sky. The region is a diverse one, offering the best of a desert ecosystem, and the best of an alpine terrain with its cool summer temperatures. In winter, higher elevations become snow-covered wonderlands. Red-rock canyons are dusted in white and clouds drop deeply into the canyons profoundly impacting the colors of the rock. When the sun comes out, creamy ivory, copper, gold, and platinum cliffs catch the light, contrasting against the deep reds and pinks. Blue-green juniper, pine, and spruce pop out in relief against the naked rock. Here you will encounter things called "hoodoos," vertical columns of colorful rock eroded into strange shapes, and rocks that look like temples and thrones. The most adventurous travelers tackle the remote canyons of the Grand Staircase–Escalante National Monument. Throughout the southwestern territories of Utah, athletes challenge themselves on rock, through the mountains, on narrow raging rivers, and, a bit more tamely, on the stunning golf courses of St. George. In southwestern Utah—"Dixie"—you can do it all.

Utah's Dixie—including St. George and surrounding areas—is so
named because it started out as cotton farming territory during Mormon settlement in the 1860s. This area is realizing the largest growth
in the state, no doubt because of the temperate weather. While the need
for cotton farms in Utah disappeared with the introduction of the
transcontinental railway, constant sunshine has kept the economy
growing. As snowbirds flock here to live and play the links, St. George
is quickly gaining a reputation as a premiere retirement community.

There are so many beautiful parks, historical sights, and intriguing destinations to explore in this half of the state, it may be difficult to
choose among them all. Once you see Zion, Bryce Canyon, or Capitol Reef national park, a wish to linger may alter your plans.

Fillmore

60 *56 mi from Nephi via I–15 south.*

Given its central location, Fillmore was designated the territorial capital by Brigham Young in 1851, before the town even existed. Though
the town did manage to complete the first wing of the capitol in 1855,
local problems and the booming population in Salt Lake City led to
the legislature reseating itself in Salt Lake City. Its first statehouse was
never completed, but the portion that does stand is counted as Utah's
oldest government building. The **Territorial Statehouse State Park** includes a collection of settlement-era relics housed in the statehouse, outdoor interpretive displays, parklike grounds, and a rose garden. ⊠ *50
W. Capitol Ave.,* ☎ *435/743–5316,* WEB *parks/state.ut.us.* ☞ *$5 per
vehicle.* ⊙ *Memorial Day–Labor Day, Mon.–Sat. 8–8, Sun. 9–6; Labor
Day–Memorial Day, Mon.–Sat. 9–6.*

Brian Head

50 mi from Beaver via I–15 and Rte. 143 south.

With an abundance of biking trails and other activities, the ski-resort
town of Brian Head is also a favorite summertime retreat. Five miles
beyond Brian Head is one of the region's better-known scenic won-
61 ders, **Cedar Breaks National Monument.** Cutting deep into the western end of the lofty Markagunt Plateau, uplift and erosion by wind,
rain, and river have etched an amphitheater awash in shades of pink,
gold, and lavender. Two especially nice backcountry strolls (each 2 mi
long) follow the Spectra Point and Alpine Pond trails, and although
winter snows do close the road, the monument is a favorite among cross-
country skiers. Road cyclists will enjoy stretches of Routes 14, 143,
and 148. There are no cedars at Cedar Breaks—early pioneers misiden-
tified junipers growing in the area. ⊠ *Rte. 143,* ☎ *435/586–9451,* WEB
www.nps.gov/cebr/. ☞ *$4 per vehicle.* ⊙ *May–Oct., daily 8–sunset.*

Dining and Lodging

$–$$$ ✕ **The Edge.** This is the place to eat lunch and dinner in Brian Head.
The Edge Burger is a half-pound monstrosity draped with cheese. Din-
ners include steaks, seafood, soups, and salads. The views of the sur-
rounding pink and white cliffs, hoodoos, and alpine forests make any
meal special here. ⊠ *406 S. Rte. 143,* ☎ *435/677–3343. AE, MC, V.*

$$–$$$ ⊡ **Cedar Breaks Lodge.** On the north end of town, this casual resort
features large studio rooms with kitchenettes. The lodge is nestled
among aspen and pine trees for a truly alpine stay. ⊠ *223 Hunter Ridge
Rd./Rte. 143, Box 190248, 84719,* ☎ *435/677–3000 or 888/282–3327,*
FAX *435/677–2211,* WEB *www.cedarbreakslodge.com. 121 units. Restau-
rant, bar, kitchenettes, hot tub, gym. AE, D, MC, V.*

Outdoor Activities and Sports

CYCLING

Brian Head is a good place to base cycling excursions. The area's most popular ride is the 12-mi Bunker Creek Trail, which winds its way through forests and meadows to Panguitch Lake. Five mi south of Brian Head, road cyclists can explore Cedar Breaks National Monument and vicinity. Brian Head Resort runs one of its ski lifts in summer, providing access to several mountain-bike trails. A shuttle service takes riders to other trails on the resort property.

DOWNHILL SKIING

Known for its abundance of snow, **Brian Head Resort** (⊠ off Rte. 143, Brian Head, ☎ 435/677–2035 or 800/272–7426, WEB www.brianhead.com) is a favorite among California skiers weary of the crowded mega-resorts of their own state. Six lifts service 53 runs and a vertical drop of 1,707 ft. There's nothing quite like skiing with snow-studded red-rock cliffs as the backdrop. The resort is pretty evenly divided among beginner, intermediate, and expert slopes.

Cedar City

62 *34 mi from Brian Head via Rte. 143 north and I–15 south; or 30 mi from Brian Head via Rte. 143 south, Rte. 148 south, and Rte. 14 west.*

With a population of about 21,000, Cedar City is southern Utah's second-largest community. The town was settled in 1851 by Mormons sent to mine iron-ore deposits. The mining chapter of the town's history is today embodied at the **Iron Mission State Park.** It displays the usual collection of pioneer artifacts, plus a number of horse-drawn wagons. ⊠ *635 N. Main St.,* ☎ *435/586–9290,* WEB *parks.state.ut.us.* ⌖ *$4 per vehicle.* ◷ *Daily 9–sunset.*

From late June through the first week of September, the **Utah Shakespearean Festival** (☎ 435/586–7880, WEB www.bard.org) which involves much more than just Shakespeare, draws tens of thousands. The outdoor theater at Southern Utah University is a replica of the Old Globe Theatre from Shakespeare's time, showcasing Shakespearean costume and set displays during the season.

Dining and Lodging

$$–$$$$ ★ ✕ **Milt's Stage Stop.** This inviting spot in beautiful Cedar Canyon is known for its terrific 12-ounce rib-eye steak, its prime rib, and its fresh crab, lobster, and shrimp dishes. In winter, deer feed in front of the restaurant as a fireplace blazes away inside. Hunting trophies decorate the rustic building's interior, and splendid views of mountains delight patrons year-round. ⊠ *Cedar Canyon, 5 mi east of town on Rte. 14,* ☎ *435/586–9344. AE, D, DC, MC, V. No lunch.*

$$–$$$ ▦ **Baker House Bed and Breakfast.** An authentic replica of a Queen Ann Victorian mansion, this three-story home is a delight. Built in 1998, it has all the shine and polish of a new facility, but all the ambience of the Victorian period. Each room is named after a writer and has a fireplace and hot tub. Lord Byron is the luxury room and occupies an entire floor. Breakfast might include quiche, fruit tarts, and muffins. Within 2 mi of the Globe Theatre, it is a perfect place to stay during the Shakespeare Festival. ⊠ *1800 Royal Hunte Dr., 84720,* ☎ *435/867–5695 or 888/611–8181,* FAX *435/867–5694,* WEB *www.bbhost.com/bakerhouse. 5 rooms. Dining room, hot tubs. AE, D, DC, MC, V. CP.*

$$ ▦ **Bard's Inn Bed and Breakfast.** Rooms in this turn-of-the-20th-century house are named after heroines in Shakespeare's plays—perfect for those attending the Utah Shakespearean Festival, which is within walking distance. There are wonderful antiques throughout and hand-

crafted quilts grace the beds. A full breakfast includes fresh home-baked breads, fruit, juices, and oven-shirred eggs. ✉ *150 S. 100 West St., 84720,* ☎ *435/586–6612. 7 rooms. Dining room. AE, MC, V. BP.*

Nightlife and the Arts

You can take a few turns on the dance floor to soft rock or country music at the **Playhouse** (✉ 1027 N. Main St., ☎ 435/586–9010). The college crowd tends to gather at the **Sportsmen's Lounge** (✉ 900 S. Main St., ☎ 435/586–6552) for hard rock, rap tunes, and dancing.

St. George

53 mi from Cedar City via I–15 south.

Three hundred Mormon families were sent to St. George in 1861 to grow cotton. St. Georgians now number over 50,000, of whom a burgeoning number are retirees. The **St. George Chamber of Commerce** (✉ 97 E. St. George Blvd., ☎ 435/628–1658, WEB www.stgeorgechamber.com) has a self-guided walking tour flyer and can help plan a tour of the area. **Zion Factory Stores** (✉ 245 N. Red Cliffs Dr., I–15 Exit 8, ☎ 435/674–9800 or 800/269–8687) is southern Utah's only factory-outlet center.

Outdoor Activities and Sports

One of St. George's several golf courses, the 18-hole **Entrada at Snow Canyon** (✉ 2511 W. Entrada Trail, ☎ 435/674–7500) is the newest and is Utah's first Johnny Miller Signature Course. A cap of volcanic rock tops the red Navajo sandstone walls of **Snow Canyon State Park** (✉ 11 mi northwest of St. George on Rte. 18, ☎ 435/628–2255, WEB parks.state.ut.us), which has short trails and small desert canyons to explore.

Hurricane

13 mi from St. George via I–15 north and Rte. 9 east.

Once a sleepy pioneer town on the Virgin River, this area has recently experienced enormous growth, probably owing to St. George's popularity. Hurricane has one of the state's most scenic 18-hole golf courses, **Sky Mountain** (✉ 1000 N. 2600 West St., ☎ 435/635–7888). The course, nestled against the colorful red rock, looks out on nearby Pine Valley mountain and its 10,000-ft peak. **Chums Company Store** (✉ 120 S. Main St., ☎ 435/635–9836 or 800/323–3707) is the factory outlet for Hello Wear, a line of sturdy outdoor clothing designed and manufactured in Hurricane.

Zion National Park

🔞 *40 mi from St. George via I–15 north and Rte. 9 east.*

This humbling collection of vividly colored canyons and monoliths was first established as Mukuntuweap National Monument in 1909. A decade later it became Zion National Park. In Zion Canyon, the centerpiece of this relatively small park, vertical sandstone cliffs tower nearly 3,000 ft above the canyon floor. Places such as Angel's Landing climb so high, only the intrepid make it to the top. Zion is a surprise at every turn: wildflowers hanging from cliff sides, swamps in the desert, and deposits of petrified wood all occupy this rare desert sanctuary. The park's palette of ivory, copper, and rich pink changes shade with every movement of clouds or sun. A sudden rainfall can bring spectacular flash floods and waterfalls.

Winding through the canyon is the Virgin River, the powerful force that carved the gorge through the implacable rock walls. At road's end is the Gateway to the Narrows. Here the river continues its journey

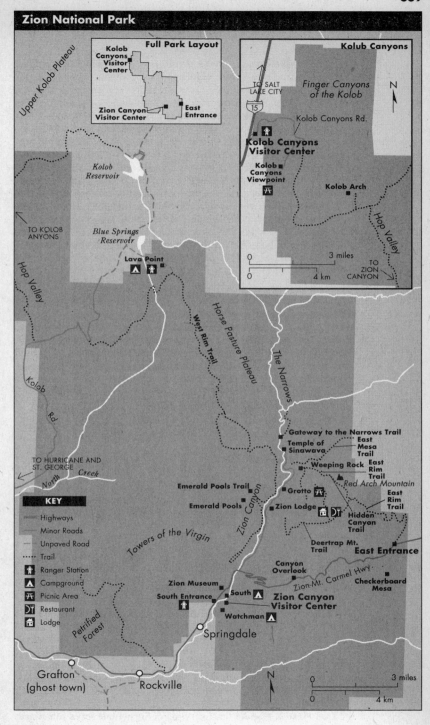

Zion National Park

Full Park Layout

Kolob Canyons Visitor Center

Zion Canyon Visitor Center — East Entrance

Kolub Canyons

N

TO SALT LAKE CITY

15

Finger Canyons of the Kolob

Kolob Canyons Rd.

Kolob Canyons Visitor Center

Kolob Canyons Viewpoint

Kolob Arch

Hop Valley

0   3 miles
0   4 km

TO ZION CANYON

Upper Kolob Plateau

Kolob Reservoir

TO KOLOB ANYONS

Blue Springs Reservoir

Lava Point

Hop Valley

Kolob Rd.

West Rim Trail

Horse Pasture Plateau

The Narrows

TO HURRICANE AND ST. GEORGE

North Creek

Gateway to the Narrows Trail

Temple of Sinawava

East Mesa Trail

Weeping Rock

East Rim Trail

Red Arch Mountain

Emerald Pools Trail

Grotto

Zion Canyon

East Rim Trail

Emerald Pools

Zion Lodge

Hidden Canyon Trail

Deertrap Mt. Trail

East Entrance

Towers of the Virgin

Canyon Overlook

Zion-Mt. Carmel Hwy.

Checkerboard Mesa

KEY

— Highways
— Minor Roads
- - Unpaved Road
· · · Trail
☗ Ranger Station
⊼ Campground
🎑 Picnic Area
🍴 Restaurant
🏠 Lodge

Zion Museum

South Entrance

South

Zion Canyon Visitor Center

Watchman

Petrified Forest

Springdale

Grafton (ghost town)

Rockville

N

0   3 miles
0   4 km

through the wilderness, creating passageways only a few feet wide in places.

A shuttle system and new visitor center, both completed in 2000, help accommodate the nearly 3 million visitors who come to Zion National Park each year. The park's scenic drive is closed to private vehicles April–October. You may leave your car at the visitor center inside the park, but the lot is usually full from 10 AM to 3 PM daily. A free shuttle from the town of Springdale makes several pickups throughout town where parking is also available. The shuttle system is easy to use and has returned the park to a quiet sanctuary. Many animals that had left the area are returning as the traffic and related noise and pollution disappear. Hikes to the Emerald Pools are especially popular as is the 1-mi paved walk along the Virgin River to the Narrows. The short hike to Weeping Rock guarantees some cooling sprinkles of water overhead from a waterfall. If you see a small speck moving on a distant canyon wall, it's probably one of the many expert rock climbers that frequent the park. Check with the visitor center for a complete list of hiking trails, rock-climbing routes (most are for advanced climbers), and permits. ⊠ *30 mi east of I–15 on Rte. 9, Springdale,* ☎ *435/772–3256,* WEB *www.nps.gov/zion.* ☞ *$10 per individual (arriving by bicycle, motorcycle, on foot [not to exceed $20 per family group]); $20 per vehicle.* ☉ *Daily 8–sunset.*

Dining and Lodging

$$–$$$ ★ ✕ **Bit and Spur Restaurant and Saloon.** This restaurant has been a legend in Utah for decades. Tell anyone you've been to Zion National Park or Springdale and they'll ask if you ate at the Bit and Spur. A seasonal menu offers a variety of classic Mexican entrées including burritos, tacos, and tostadas, but it also gets creative. Try the sweet potato tamale with tomatillo salsa, or the *puerco relleno,* grilled pork tenderloin filled with walnuts, apples, Gorgonzola, and raisins. Whatever you do, make an effort to get there early so you can eat outside and enjoy the grounds and great views. ⊠ *1212 Zion Park Blvd., Springdale,* ☎ *435/772–3498. D, MC, V.*

$–$$ ✕ **Spotted Dog Cafe at Flanigan's Inn.** Dinner at this restaurant is worthy of any special occasion. The atmosphere is refined and quiet with eclectic music playing in the background. You might hear Harry Belafonte or Audie Murphy as you dine. Entrées include lamb, chicken, steak, and, of course, locally grown trout, encrusted in pumpkin seed and pan-seared. The restaurant really struts its stuff with the pork tenderloin with apple-almond sauce and mango chutney. Gaze out the windowed wall for a view onto the creamy cliffs washed in the pink and orange so common in Zion Canyon. ⊠ *428 Zion Park Blvd., Springdale,* ☎ *435/772–3244. AE, DC, MC, V.*

$ ✕ **Sol Foods.** For a quick, healthy breakfast, lunch, or dinner, stop for some delicious, affordable flavors at this convenient restaurant just outside the park entrance. Daily specials include spanakopita, quiche, lasagna, and a variety of salads. The staff also prepares picnic baskets or box lunches. Vegetarians will be more than happy here and so will folks wanting a cold beer or a hot espresso. Nearby is the ice-cream parlor that serves hand-dipped ice creams, banana splits, and more espresso. Patio dining near the Virgin River with views into the park is plentiful. ⊠ *95 Zion Park Blvd., Springdale,* ☎ *435/772–0277. MC, V. Closed Jan.*

$ ✕ **Zion Pizza & Noodle Co.** Everyone in Springdale loves this place, and it's easy to understand why. Creative pizzas such as a Thai chicken pizza or a hot and spicy burrito pizza put the punch back into dough, tomato paste, and cheese. The pastas are cooked right every single time. Try the linguine with grilled chicken, peanuts, and teriyaki sauce or the homemade pasta marinara with or without meatballs. The restaurant is in an old church and you can dine indoors, outdoors, or in the beer garden. Folks in search of wine or cocktails will have to look elsewhere; only microbrews are served here. ✉ *868 Zion Park Blvd., Springdale,* ☎ *435/772–3815. No credit cards. Closed Dec.–Feb.*

$$ 🏨 **Best Western Zion Park Inn.** This spacious and modern facility meets every basic traveling need and then some. Large rooms, a big swimming pool to cool you in the summer, and a hot tub to relieve your aches and pains after a long hike in the park all make a stay here satisfying. The inn is even a shuttle stop, so one step out the door and you're on your way to Zion National Park. ✉ *1215 Zion Park Blvd., Springdale 84767,* ☎ *435/772–3200 or 800/934–7275,* FAX *435/772–2449,* WEB *www.zionparkinn.com. 120 rooms. Restaurant, pool, hot tub, shops, coin laundry. AE, D, DC, MC, V.*

$$ 🏨 **Cliffrose Lodge and Gardens.** Poppies, iris, and honeysuckle, along with dozens of other flowers, adorn the 5-acre grounds of this friendly, charming lodge. From your balcony, you can drink in views of the towering, colorful cliffs for which Zion is famous. The Virgin River is just outside your door and you can picnic or barbecue there. Children will be more than happy tumbling in the lush green grass, running through the sprinkler, or playing with the multitude of toys provided for their delight. The Cliffrose is within walking distance of the Zion National Park visitor center and shuttle stop. Restaurants, shops, and the giant-screen movie theater are nearby. Large, comfy rooms will let you stretch out after a long hike. ✉ *281 Zion Park Blvd., Box 510, Springdale, 84767,* ☎ *435/772–3234 or 800/243–8824,* FAX *435/772–3900,* WEB *www.cliffroselodge.com. 36 rooms. Pool, hot tub. AE, D, MC, V.*

$$ 🏨 **Desert Pearl Inn.** By all means, stay at the Desert Pearl when you
★ visit Zion National Park, but be forewarned: you won't want to leave. Rooms are spacious with vaulted ceilings and thickly padded carpets that hold down noise. The attentive owners have added extra touches such as cushy throw pillows, Roman shades, oversize windows, a bidet, and tiled showers with deep tubs. The pool area is exceptionally beautiful with a large, creatively shaped pool, a double-size hot tub with a waterfall nearby, and showers and rest rooms at poolside. Large balconies or patios accompany each room and overlook either the Virgin River or the pool. At night, crank open your windows and listen to the river flow by; that will be the only sound you hear. Every room is a suite here and you get spalike facilities at standard room prices. This is truly a rare pearl in the desert. ✉ *707 Zion Park Blvd., Springdale 84767,* ☎ *435/772–8888 or 888/828–0898,* FAX *435/772–8889,* WEB *www.desertpearl.com. 60 suites. In-room data ports, in-room safes, in-room VCRs, kitchenettes, pool, hot tub. AE, D, MC, V.*

$$ 🏨 **Harvest House.** This B&B is on the edge of Zion National Park. Along with three rooms and a suite with two bedrooms and a living room, this property has cactus gardens and a pond swimming with koi. A covered veranda winds a third of the way around the house. Breakfasts might include eggs Florentine or apple pancakes. ✉ *29 Canyon View Dr., Springdale 84767,* ☎ *435/772–3880,* FAX *435/772–3327,* WEB *www.harvesthouse.com. 3 rooms, 1 suite. Dining room, hot tub. MC, V. BP.*

$$ 🏨 **Snow Family Guest Ranch.** Just 15 minutes from Zion National Park,
★ this B&B is a western-theme oasis filled with comfortable surprises, like window seats with excellent views, inviting common areas—both indoors and out—and breakfasts worth lingering over. You'll certainly enjoy the warm, gracious hospitality at this quiet getaway outside the hustle-bustle of Springdale. ✉ *633 E. Hwy. 9, Box 790190, Virgin*

84779, ☎ *435/635–2500 or 877/655–7669,* FAX *435/635–4720,* WEB
*www.snowfamilyranch.com. 9 rooms. Dining room, pool, hot tub. AE,
D, MC, V. BP.*

$$ ⬛ **Zion Canyon Lodge.** Although the original burned down in 1925,
this lodge recreates the classic look of the old inn. Knotty-pine wood-
work and log and wicker furnishings accent the lobby. Rooms are mod-
ern but not fancy. This is a place of quiet retreat, so there are no
televisions. Kids can play outside on the abundant grassy lawns. You
might be happier in one of the historic western cabins which date from
the 1930s and have gas-log fireplaces. The lodge is within walking dis-
tance of trailheads, horseback riding, and the shuttle stop. Reserva-
tions are recommended at least six months in advance. ⊠ *Zion National
Park, 84767,* ☎ *435/772–3213 or 303/297–2757,* FAX *435/772–2001,*
WEB *www.amfac.com. 81 rooms, 40 cabins. Restaurant, shop. AE, D,
DC, MC, V.*

Shopping

Even a tiny town like Springdale has some great shopping. **Canyon Of-
ferings** (⊠ 933 Zion Park Blvd., Springdale, ☎ 435/772–3456 or 800/
788–2443) is packed with original jewelry, wind chimes, garden or-
naments, and a hundred other things to make you smile. **Ranch Road
Fine Art** (⊠ 205 Zion Park Blvd., Springdale, ☎ 435/772–0465) dis-
plays the work of local ceramic artists and limited-edition giclee photo-
graph prints that are a joy to behold. **Tribal Arts Zion** (⊠ 291 Zion
Park Blvd., Springdale, ☎ 435/772–3353) has one of the largest se-
lections of Native American jewelry in the area, as well as pottery, rugs,
and other handiwork. The **Worthington Gallery** (⊠ 789 Park Blvd.,
Springdale, ☎ 435/772–3446 or 800/626–9973) has a wide selection
of pottery and other ceramic art created by Utah artisans.

En Route   From the depths of Zion Canyon, the **Zion–Mount Carmel Highway**
(Route 9) climbs eastward through one of the more impressive scenic
drives in the Southwest. Sandstone cliffs and dunes in shades of white,
copper, and pink are to the left and right. After several switchbacks,
the road enters a one-mi-long tunnel, complete with portals. Con-
structed in 1930, the tunnel is too small for large RVs or tour buses
to pass without having rangers stop traffic; RV and bus drivers pay a
fee of $10 and up for this service. Beyond the tunnel's east entrance,
Route 9 continues out of the park to Mount Carmel Junction, pass-
ing through the park's slickrock territory, including Checkerboard
Mesa, which resembles an enormous sandstone playing board. From
here, U.S. 89 heads south for 17 mi to Kanab.

Kanab

64 *40 mi from Zion National Park's east entrance via Rte. 9 east and U.S.
89 south.*

Kanab serves as a gateway to portions of the Grand Staircase–Escalante
National Monument, but the picturesque town merits its own bragging
rights. The welcoming sign at city limits reads "Greatest Earth on
Show" and Kanab has been used as a setting in more than 100 movies
and television shows. **Frontier Movie Town** is jam-packed with Old
West movie memorabilia. Some of the buildings in its replica of a fron-
tier town were actually used in movie sets, and photos on the walls in-
side reveal many familiar faces. ⊠ *297 W. Center St.,* ☎ *435/644–5337.*
⬛ *Free.* ☉ *May–Oct., daily 9 AM–10 PM; Nov.–Apr., daily 10–6.*

Coral Pink Sand Dunes State Park is a giant playland of tinted sand.
Big kids play on the dunes with their all-terrain vehicles, but an area
has been set aside for families to explore. There is a 22-site campground.

✉ *Yellowjacket and Hancock Rds., 12 mi west of Kanab via U.S. 89,* ☎ *435/648–2800,* WEB *parks.state.ut.us.* 🎫 *$4 per vehicle.* ☉ *Year-round.*

Dining and Lodging

$ ✕ **Chef's Palace.** This restaurant is a local favorite for rib-eye steaks, prime rib, and seafood. For added cowboy atmosphere, dine in the Dude Room. ✉ *176 W. Center St.,* ☎ *435/644–5052. AE, D, DC, MC, V.*

$ 🏨 **Parry Lodge.** Back in the 1930s, movie stars stayed here. The names of who slept in each room are listed above the doors of the older units, and Hollywood-related photos decorate the lobby. Despite the age of the hotel, rooms are well maintained and comfortable. ✉ *89 E. Center St., 84741,* ☎ *435/644–2601 or 800/748–4104,* FAX *435/644–2605. 89 rooms. Restaurant, pool. AE, D, MC, V.*

Bryce Canyon National Park

⑥⑤ *77 mi from Kanab via Rte. 9 west, U.S. 89 north (at Mount Carmel Junction), and Rte. 12 east.*

Not actually a canyon, Bryce Canyon is a set of amphitheaters carved into the eastern rim of the colorful Paunsaugunt Plateau. As gullies widen to become canyons, fins of rock are exposed and become subject to further erosion. Freezing and thawing of water, which has collected in vertical cracks, eventually erodes the fin leaving vertical columns of rocks. These pink "hoodoos" are what draws 1½ million visitors to the park each year. Much of the park is visible from the many overlooks along the park's 35 mi of paved road. Among the stunning sights are the **Silent City**, named for the eerie rock profiles and figures, and the "chessmen" of **Queen's Garden**. Because early- and late-day sunlight casts such an unusual glow on these rock formations, many folks count Bryce as their favorite of Utah's national parks. Given its nearly 8,000-ft elevation, winter turns the area into a wonderland for cross-country skiers. The 11-mi, level **Rim Trail** features nonstop scenery, while the **Fairyland Loop** and **Queen's Garden** trails lead hikers down into the amphitheater for an intimate walk among the hoodoos. All trails into the park's interior require fairly strenuous descents and ascents. Queen's Garden Trail is the easiest access into the amphitheater, but it is still equivalent to climbing down and up a 32-story building. ✉ *Bryce Canyon, Hwy. 63,* ☎ *435/834–5322.* 🎫 *$20 per vehicle.* ☉ *Daily 8 AM–sunset.*

Lodging

$$ 🏨 **Best Western Ruby's Inn.** With its large restaurant and gift shop just north of the park entrance, this is Grand Central Station for Bryce. A nightly rodeo and chuck-wagon cookout take place nearby. Rooms vary in age, with sprawling wings added as the park gained popularity. All of the guest rooms are consistently comfortable and attractive, however. The lobby has rough-hewn log beams and poles, and a decor heavy on "southwestern chic." If you'd rather camp, Ruby's also offers over a hundred sites for RVs and tents nearby. There are also cabins that sleep up to four, and teepees that accommodate up to eight, available at the nearby campground. ✉ *Rte. 63, Box 1, Bryce 84764,* ☎ *435/ 834–5341 or 800/468–8660,* FAX *435/834–5265,* WEB *www.rubysinn.com. 368 rooms. Restaurant, 2 pools, hot tub, shop, coin laundry. AE, D, DC, MC, V.*

$$ 🏨 **Bryce Canyon Lodge.** Just a few feet from the rim views and hiking trailheads is this circa-1920s lodge designed by Stanley Gilbert Underwood for the Union Pacific Railroad. A National Historic Landmark, the lodge has been faithfully restored, right down to the lobby's huge limestone fireplace, its log-and-wrought-iron chandelier, and bark-covered hickory furniture, which was built by the same company that cre-

Bryce Canyon National Park

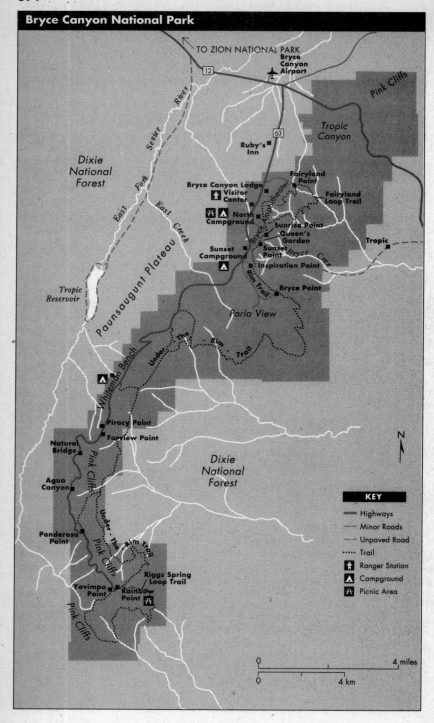

TO ZION NATIONAL PARK

Bryce Canyon Airport

12

63

Pink Cliffs

Tropic Canyon

Dixie National Forest

Ruby's Inn

Sevier River

East Fork

East Creek

Bryce Canyon Lodge
Visitor Center

North Campground

Fairyland Point

Fairyland Loop Trail

Sunrise Point

Queen's Garden

Bryce Amphitheater

Tropic

Sunset Campground

Sunset Point

Inspiration Point

Bryce Creek

Bryce Point

Tropic Reservoir

Paunsaugunt Plateau

Paria View

The

Rim

Trail

Under

Rim Trail

Whiteman Bench

Piracy Point

Fairview Point

Natural Bridge

Pink Cliffs

Agua Canyon

Dixie National Forest

Ponderosa Point

Under-The Pink Cliffs

Riggs Spring Loop Trail

Yovimpa Point

Rainbow Point

Pink Cliffs

N

KEY

▬▬	Highways
—	Minor Roads
– –	Unpaved Road
⋯	Trail
🏠	Ranger Station
⛺	Campground
⛲	Picnic Area

0 ——————— 4 miles

0 ——————— 4 km

ated the originals. Guests have their choice of motel-style rooms with either a balcony or porch; suites on the lodge's second level; or cozy lodgepole-pine cabins, some with cathedral ceilings and gas fireplaces. Reservations are hard to come by: call several months ahead, or, if you're feeling lucky, call the day before your arrival—cancellations occasionally make last-minute bookings possible. Horseback rides into the park's interior can be arranged in the lobby. ⊠ *2 mi south of park entrance on Rte. 63, Box 400, Cedar City 84720,* ☎ *435/834–5361; 303/ 297–2757 for advance reservations,* FAX *435/834–5464. 75 rooms, 39 cabins, 3 suites. Restaurant. AE, D, DC, MC, V. Closed Nov.–Apr.*

OFF THE
BEATEN PATH

KODACHROME BASIN STATE PARK – Among the spectacular but little-known geological displays at this park are peculiar formations called sand pipes. The basin was named for Kodak's classic color film after pictures of it appeared in a 1949 *National Geographic* article. Several hiking trails take you to natural arches. The park is surrounded by the Grand Staircase–Escalante National Monument. ⊠ *Take Rte. 12 22 mi east from the eastern entrance to Bryce Canyon National Park and Kodachrome Basin Rd. 9 mi south; or from Escalante, 33 mi on Rte. 12 to basin road,* ☎ *435/679–8562.* 🎟 *$4 per vehicle.* ☉ *Daily 8–sunset.*

Outdoor Activities and Sports

See the park by helicopter, van, or buggy with **Bryce Canyon Tours** (⊠ Hwy. 63, just outside the park entrance, ☎ 435/834–5341). The company has an office inside Best Western Ruby's Inn. **Canyon Trail Rides** (☎ 435/679–8665) will take you on the ride of your life into the amphitheater of Bryce Canyon National Park. Meet in the lobby of Bryce Canyon Lodge, 2 mi south of park entrance on Route 63. **Ruby's Red Canyon Horseback Rides** (☎ 800/468–8660) retraces trails taken by outlaw Butch Cassidy in Red Canyon, outside the park. It's office is also in Best Western Ruby's Inn.

Escalante

 50 mi from Bryce Canyon National Park (eastern edge) via Rte. 12 east.

Escalante is the primary gateway community for the **Grand Staircase– Escalante National Monument.** Created in September 1996, the huge monument covers 1.7 million acres. It was named for a series of geologic formations creating a staircase effect, and for the scenic gorges carved by the Escalante River. There are more than 300 archaeological sites within it, as well as myriad mazelike canyons. Services and facilities inside the monument are virtually nonexistent. Outfitters can take you on horseback riding trips, hikes, or car tours from the area gateways of Escalante, Kanab, Boulder, and Tropic. This monument is administered by the Bureau of Land Management, rather than the National Park Service. ⊠ *Entrances off Rte. 12 or Hwy. 63. Monument office: 755 W. Main St.,* ☎ *435/826–5499,* WEB *www.ut.blm.gov/monument/.*

Camping, swimming, boating, and fishing for rainbow trout on the 30-acre Wide Hollow Reservoir of **Escalante State Park** (⊠ 710 N. Reservoir Rd., off of Rte. 12, ☎ 435/826–4466, WEB parks.state.ut.us), make this a diverse destination. Its natural wonder is its collection of rainbow-color, 150-million-year-old petrified wood.

Outdoor Activities and Sports

In the northern section of the monument, east of the town of Escalante, Route 12 crosses the Escalante River, which has carved an extensive canyon system highly favored by backpackers. While en route to southeastern Utah in 1879, Mormon pioneers chipped and blasted a narrow passageway in solid rock, through which they lowered their wagons. This **Hole in the Rock Trail,** now a 60-mi gravel road, leads from Escalante to the actual hole-in-the-rock site in Glen Canyon Recreation Area. Much of the original passageway has been flooded by the waters of Lake Powell.

A good long-distance mountain-bike ride in the isolated Escalante region follows the 44-mi **Hell's Backbone Road** from Escalante to Boulder. The grade is steep, but the views of **Box Death Hollow** make it worthwhile. Mountain bikers may want to pedal a portion of the **Burr Trail,** a 66-mi backcountry route (usable by most vehicles when dry) that crosses east through the monument into the southern portion of Capitol Reef National Park.

En Route Make sure your camera is loaded and ready as you travel over Route 12. This amazing road passes through Grand Staircase–Escalante National Monument on one of the most scenic drives in America. Don't get distracted, though: the paved road is twisting and steep, and at times climbs over a hogback with sheer drop-offs on both sides. Instead of trying to view the mind-boggling scenes from your car, take time to pull over at the viewpoints. Along the way, you'll encounter the **Calf Creek Recreation Area,** highlighted by 126-ft Calf Creek Falls. The 5½-mi round-trip hike to the falls is fairly level, but much of the trail is in deep sand, making it somewhat strenuous. A small, pleasant campground is near the creek, but fills each day by noon April–October.

Boulder

67 *29 mi from Escalante via Rte. 12 north.*

How remote is Boulder? So remote that only in the 1940s did it stop receiving its mail by mule. Boulder is home to **Anasazi State Park.** Believed to be one of the largest ancestral Puebloan (formerly known as Anasazi) sites west of the Colorado River, the village is largely unexcavated. A paved outdoor trail leads to the protected ruins of a surface pueblo pit house that predates AD 1200. Within a reproduction of an ancient dwelling is a museum featuring interactive exhibits and views into the climate-controlled environment where artifacts are stored. ⊠ *460 N. Rte. 12,* ☎ *435/335–7308,* WEB *parks.state.ut.us.* ⊠ *$5 per vehicle.* ☉ *Daily 8–sunset.*

Dining and Lodging

$–$$$ ✕ **Hell's Backbone Grill.** This remote spot is worth the drive from any
★ distance. Owners Blake Campbell and Jen Castle use only local organic foods that have a historical foundation in the area, so you might find buffalo on the menu, but never salmon. Their creations are inspired by Native American, western range, southwestern, or Mormon pioneer recipes. Your salad might contain such goodies as strawberries, jicama, pine nuts, and dried corn topped with their especially surprising dressing. Outdoor dining overlooking the pond is a treat. Because of a desire to integrate into the conservative, rural community, no alcohol is served. ⊠ *Boulder Mountain Lodge, 20 N. Hwy. 12,* ☎ *435/335–7464. DC, MC, V. Closed Nov.–Mar. No lunch.*

$$ ▥ **Boulder Mountain Lodge.** A 5-acre pond serves as sanctuary to ducks,
★ coots, and other waterfowl at this wonderfully pastoral lodge. Large, modern rooms, with either balconies or patios, all have gorgeous views of the wetlands. Horses graze nearby. The main lodge contains a great room with fireplace and library. There is also a fine-art gallery and restaurant on the premises. The service and care given guests here is impeccable. ⊠ *Junction of Hwy. 12 and the Burr Trail, Boulder 84716,* ☎ *435/335–7460 or 800/556–3446,* FAX *435/335–7461,*

WEB *www.boulder-utah.com. 20 rooms. Lobby, kitchenettes (some), library. DC, MC, V. Closed Nov.–Mar.*

En Route North of Boulder, Route 12 continues up and over **Boulder Mountain,** in the Dixie National Forest. As this stretch of scenic byway reaches 9,200 ft, it encounters some lush pine, spruce, and aspen forests. In addition, magnificent views of the Escalante River canyons to the south and the Henry Mountains to the east open up along the way. It is definitely worth your time to stop at the overlooks.

Capitol Reef National Park

68 *45 mi from Boulder via Rte. 12 north and Rte. 24 east.*

Some of the most dramatic color in the West is found at Capitol Reef National Park, which gets its name from the dome-shape rocks that populate the area. The dominant Moenkopi formation is a rich, red-chocolate hue, but every shade of purple, coral, red, and ivory paints the landscape. The park is literally a reef in the desert—a giant fold in the earth that stretches for more than 100 mi. The best news is that this park is far less crowded than nearby Bryce and Zion national parks.

Winding through the north part of the park is the Fremont River, which supports the valley's fruit orchards. This northern area receives the most visitation, but the southern reaches known as the **Waterpocket Fold,** should not be overlooked if you have the time. Reached by the 66-mi Burr Trail, the area is accessible to most vehicles during dry weather. The northernmost tip of the park offers a 58-mi scenic drive through spectacular **Cathedral Valley.** The area is remote and the road unpaved, so do not enter without a high-clearance vehicle, some planning, and a cell phone. Check at the visitor center, located 11 mi east of Torrey on U.S. 24, for road conditions and a self-guided auto tour brochure.

The visitor center can also provide information about abundant hiking trails in the park or direct you to the 71-site campground. Open all year for tents and recreational vehicles, the campground is on a first-come, first-served basis. It fills by mid-afternoon during spring, summer, and fall. Located in the historic Fruita district of the park, it is bordered by the Fremont River on one side, and fruit orchards on another. The fruit can be picked during harvest time.

While in the Fruita area, stop by the **Gifford Homestead,** a vignette of early 20th-century life on the farm. The small house, decorated with original furnishings of the period, depicts the typical spartan nature of rural Utah farm homes of the early 1900s. A gift shop run by the Capitol Reef Natural History Association sells jellies, soaps, looped rugs, and Roseville pottery. ⊠ *Hwy. 24, Torrey,* ☎ *435/425–3791.* 📠 *Free; scenic drive $5 per vehicle.* ☉ *Daily 8–sunset.*

Dining and Lodging

There are many lodging options near the park. Torrey, 11 mi west of the park's east entrance on Route 24, offers the largest variety.

$$–$$$ ✕ **Café Diablo.** This popular Torrey restaurant keeps getting better and ★ better. Innovative southwestern entrées include buffalo tenderloin, quail and rabbit sausage, black bean falafel, or local trout crusted with pumpkin seeds and served with a cilantro lime sauce. If you're really adventurous, try the rattlesnake cakes—free-range desert rattler served with ancho-rosemary aioli. ⊠ *599 W. Main St., Torrey,* ☎ *435/425–3070. MC, V. Closed Nov.–Apr.*

$–$$$ ✕ **Rim Rock Restaurant.** This restaurant sits high on a cliff and offers 360-degree views of the "land of sleeping rainbow." The meals generally feature beef, fish, and game and are accented with creative sauces. You will eat every bite of the mixed-grill plate. ⊠ *2523 E. Hwy. 24 between Torrey and Capitol Reef National Park,* ☎ *435/425–3388. AE, DC, MC, V. Closed Nov.–Mar.*

$$–$$$ ⊞ **SkyRidge Bed and Breakfast.** Among the guest comments about this colorful, three-story inn is "I dream about SkyRidge." It is not hard to understand why. The textured walls are hung with the works of local artists. Unusual furniture—each piece chosen for its look and feel—makes the guest rooms and common areas both stimulating and comfortable. Each of the inn's windows offers an exceptional view of the desert and mountains surrounding Capitol Reef National Park. Meals here are excellent, including dinners in the winter, when area restaurants are closed. A full breakfast is included. ⊠ *950 E. Hwy. 24, Box 750220, Torrey 84775,* ☎ *435/425–3222,* FAX *435/425–3222,* WEB *www.bbiu.org/skyridge. 6 rooms. Dining room, hot tub. MC, V. BP.*

$$ ⊞ **Lodge at Red River Ranch.** You'll swear you've walked into one
★ of the great lodges of western legend when you walk through the doors. The great room is decorated with wagon-wheel chandeliers, Native American rugs, leather furniture, and Frederick Remington sculptures. Chess tables await willing players. A giant fireplace warms one wall. Guest rooms, each with fireplace, are meticulously and individually decorated with fine antiques and art. Massive beams crisscross the ceilings, and most rooms have a patio or balcony overlooking the grounds. The dining area features a train that runs around the ceiling. This lodge is all about atmosphere. ⊠ *2900 W. Hwy. 24, Box 69, Teasdale 84773,* ☎ *435/425–3322 or 800/205–6343,* FAX *435/425–3329,* WEB *www.redriverranch.com. 15 rooms. Restaurant. AE, DC, MC, V. Closed Nov.–Mar.*

$$ ⊞ **Muley Twist Inn.** Quiet classical music plays in the great room while you sit in a rocking chair on the porch and watch the cliffs change color in the evening sun at this splendid B &B. The innkeepers are refined and educated and a delight to get to know. ⊠ *125 S. 250 West, Teasdale 84773,* ☎ *435/425–3511 or 800/530–1038,* FAX *435/425–3641,* WEB *www. go-utah.com/muleytwist. 5 rooms. Breakfast room. AE, MC, V. BP.*

$–$$ ⊞ **Chuck Wagon Lodge.** Zane Grey, the famous western novelist, used to rent an 1892 cabin on the grounds of this interesting complex. The owner has taken great care to create comfortable accommodations where once there was nothing but an RV park. The outdoor pool is especially nice and one of the larger ones in the southern half of the state. There are standard rooms, cabins, and some real economy rooming above the old general store. Foremost at this lodge is friendly service. ⊠ *12 W. Main St., Torrey 84773,* ☎ *435/425–3335 or 800/863–3288,* FAX *435/425–3434,* WEB *www.austinschuckwagonmotel.com. 25 rooms, 3 cabins. Grocery, pool, hot tub. AE, DC, MC, V. Closed Nov.–Mar.*

$ **Cactus Hill Motel.** One of the best-kept secrets in southern Utah, this small motel is on a working sheep ranch and alfalfa farm in Teasdale. The setting amid fields of alfalfa with red-and-white cliffs as a backdrop is stunning. It's a real bargain, too. ⊠ *830 S. 1000 East, Teasdale 84773,* ☎ *435/425–3578 or 800/507–2624,* FAX *435/425–3578,* WEB *www.cactushillmotel.com. 5 rooms, 1 cabin. AE, D, MC, V.*

$ ⊞ **Pine Shadows Cabins.** These full-housekeeping cabins are tucked against the pink-and-white cliffs and surrounded by pine trees. The cabins are large, clean, and fully equipped with a kitchen, VCR, bathroom, one or two beds, and a futon. ⊠ *125 S. 195 West St., Teasdale 84773,* ☎ *435/425–3939 or 800/708–1223,* FAX *435/425–3651,* WEB *www.go-utah.com/pineshadows. 6 cabins. In-room VCRs, kitchenettes. MC, V.*

Outdoor Activities and Sports

Hondoo Rivers and Trails (⊠ Rte. 24, Torrey, ☎ 435/425–3519 or 800/ 332–2696) has rapidly built a reputation for innovative adventures on horseback or via four-wheel-drive vehicle into the mountains and deserts surrounding Capitol Reef National Park.

Fish Lake

⑥⑨ *26 mi from Loa via Rte. 24 west and Rte. 25 north.*

Fish Lake, 8,800 ft high, 1 mi wide, and 6 mi long, is known for its fishing, but you needn't have tackle box in hand to enjoy its beautiful environs. Mountain scenery and a quiet setting are the real draw. Some great hikes explore the higher reaches of the area (one trail leads to the 11,633-ft summit of Fish Lake Hightop Plateau). Cyclists enjoy fall and summer rides on forest service roads or along Route 12, a designated Scenic Byway that circles the east and north ends of the lake. There are several campgrounds as well as some wonderful lodges. The lake's depth averages 85 ft. It is stocked annually with lake trout, rainbow trout, mackinaw, and splake. A large population of brown trout are native to the lake. This is a destination so impressive that the 1.4-million-acre **Fishlake National Forest** (☎ 435/896–9233) was named after it.

Lodging

$–$$ 🛏 **Fish Lake Lodge.** This large, lakeside lodge built in 1932 exudes rustic charm and character and has great views. It houses a restaurant, a gift shop, a game room for the kids, and even a dance hall. Guests stay in cabins that sleep two to 18 people. The larger cabins are the newest, but all focus on function rather than cute amenities. The lodge, general store, and restaurant are closed from early September to late May, while cabins are available year-round. ⊠ *HC80, Rte. 25, 84701,* ☎ *435/638–1000,* 🖷 *435/638–1001. 45 cabins. Restaurant. D, MC, V.*

Richfield

43 mi from Fish Lake via Rte. 25 south, Rte. 24 north, Rte. 119 west, and I–70 south.

Route 119 winds through the fertile farmlands of the Sevier River valley to the town of Richfield, on I–70 and the only major town for miles. There's no attractions here, but you might welcome the opportunity to shop for supplies or grab a bite to eat. The Sevier River, which flows north through Richfield and Salina, is known for trout fishing.

⑦⓪ **Fremont Indian State Park,** 21 mi south of Richfield via I–70, in Clear Creek Canyon, has a visitor center, campground, paved interpretive trails, and hiking trails to rock-art panels. Originally the site included a village of pit houses, but it was destroyed in the 1980s by construction of I–70 (after archaeologists completed excavation). Most of the 800 rock-art panels can be reached via the park's 12 mi of trails. This is also home to the World Atlal Tournament where folks compete at spear-throwing. The event is held the third week of June every year. ⊠ *11550 Clear Creek Canyon Rd.,* ☎ *435/527–4631.* 🖾 *$5.* ☉ *Daily 9–sunset.*

OFF THE
BEATEN PATH

PIUTE COUNTY – Heavily traveled Route 89 (which leads to Bryce Canyon and also the Grand Canyon) courses through tiny Piute County. South of Femont Indian State Park, you'll pass the butterscotch-color Big Rock Candy Mountain, a landmark made famous in a song by Burl Ives. Blink, and you'll miss it and its campsite and gift shop. **Piute State Park** (⊠ 12 mi south of Marysvale off U.S. 89, ☎ 435/624–3268) has excellent fishing and boating on a 3,360-acre reservoir, but is not scenic.

In the town of Junction, you can't miss the bright-red **Piute County Courthouse.** Built in 1902, the adobe structure is on the National Register of Historic Places. Robert LeRoy Parker—alias Butch Cassidy—grew up near the small town of **Circleville** just south of Junction. **Otter Creek State Park** (⊠ 4 mi north of Antimony on Rte. 22, ☎ 435/624–3268) has a 3,120-acre lake known for rainbow trout.

$ ▣ **Travelodge.** This is the motel locals recommend to their friends. It provides consistently nice, though not necessarily surprising, rooms in a good location. The rooms were remodeled in 2000. Pets are allowed for a fee. ⊠ *647 S. Main St., Richfield 84701,* ☎ *435/896–9271 or 800/549–8208,* FAX *435/896–6864. 39 rooms. Restaurant, heated indoor pool, hot tub. AE, D, DC, MC, V.*

Southwestern Utah A to Z

AIR TRAVEL
SkyWest flies to Cedar City and St. George municipal airports. United Express also flies to St. George. Las Vegas's McCarran International Airport is 116 mi from St. George, Utah—the St. George Shuttle makes nine trips a day between it and St. George.
➤ SHUTTLE VAN: **St. George Shuttle** (⊠ 1245 S. Main St., ☎ 435/628–8320 or 800/933–8320, WEB www.stgshuttle.com).

BUS TRAVEL
Greyhound Lines runs buses along the I–15 corridor, making stops in Beaver, Parowan, Cedar City, and St. George.
➤ BUS INFORMATION: **Beaver** (⊠ El Bambi Café, 935 N. Main St., ☎ 435/438–2983). **Cedar City** (⊠ 1355 S. Main St., ☎ 435/586–9465). **St. George** (⊠ McDonald's, 1235 S. Bluff St.).

CAR TRAVEL
Interstate 15 is the main route into the region, from Las Vegas to the southwest and Salt Lake City to the northeast. At the town of Cove Fort, I–70 heads east from I–15. Highway 89, which leads to Bryce Canyon, is a good, well-traveled road with a few interesting sights, gas stations, and convenience stores. Other various well-maintained two-lane highways traverse southwestern Utah. Some mountain curves can be expected, and winter months may see hazardous conditions in the higher elevations. Be sure that your car is in good working order, and keep the gas tank topped off.

CAR RENTAL
St. George has major car rental agencies both at its airport and within town.

EMERGENCIES
➤ CONTACTS: **Beaver Valley Hospital** (⊠ 85 N. 400 East St., Beaver, ☎ 435/438–2531). **Cedar City: Valley View Medical Center** (⊠ 595 S. 75 East St., Cedar City, ☎ 435/586–6587). **Kanab: Kane County Hospital** (⊠ 355 N. Main St., Kanab, ☎ 435/644–5811). **St. George: Dixie Regional Medical Center** (⊠ 544 S. 400 East St., St. George, ☎ 435/634–4000).

LODGING
CAMPING
In this region of Utah, campers have their choice from low-desert to high-mountain facilities and more than 100 commercial campgrounds. Campgrounds in Bryce, Capitol Reef, and Zion national parks fill up fast. Most of the area's state parks have camping facilities, and the re-

gion's two national forests offer many wonderful sites. In the Dixie National Forest, the Panguitch Lake, Pine Valley, and Boulder Mountain areas are especially nice. In Fishlake National Forest, Beaver Canyon, and Fish Lake are good picks.

➤ CAMPSITES: **Dixie National Forest** (⊠ 82 N. 100 East St., Cedar City 84720, ☎ 435/865–3700). **Fishlake National Forest** (⊠ 115 E. 900 North St., Richfield 84701, ☎ 435/896–9233).

TOURS

Boulder Mountain Lodge and Hondoo River and Trails arrange hiking and four-wheel-drive tours into portions of the Grand Staircase–Escalante National Monument. Canyon Trail Rides operates mule and horseback riding tours in Bryce Canyon and Zion national parks as well as the North Rim of the Grand Canyon. Pedal Pusher Tours leads cycling tours in Capitol Reef National Park and vicinity.

➤ CONTACTS: **Boulder Mountain Lodge** (⊠ Box 1397, Boulder 84716, ☎ 435/335–7460 or 800/556–3446). **Canyon Trail Rides** (⊠ Box 128, Tropic 84776, ☎ 435/679–8665). **Hondoo River and Trails** (⊠ 95 E. Main St., Box 98, Torrey 84775, ☎ 435/425–3519 or 800/332–2696). **Pedal Pusher Tours** (⊠ 151 W. Main St., Box 750101, Torrey 84775, ☎ 435/425–3378).

TRAIN TRAVEL

Milford, west of I–70, receives limited Amtrak service at the Union Pacific facility just off Main Street.

VISITOR INFORMATION

➤ TOURIST INFORMATION: **Beaver County Travel Council** (⊠ Box 1060, Beaver 84713, ☎ 435/438–5384, WEB www.beavercountyutahtc.com). **Capitol Reef Country** (⊠ Rte. 24, Box 7, Teasdale 84773, ☎ 800/858–7951, WEB www.capitolreef.org.). **Color Country** (⊠ 906 N. 1400 West St., Box 1550, St. George 84771, ☎ 435/628–4171 or 800/233–8824, WEB www.colorcountry.org). **Garfield County Travel Council** (⊠ 55 S. Main St., Panguitch 84074, ☎ 800/444–6689, WEB www. brycecanyoncountry.com). **Iron County Tourism and Convention Bureau** (⊠ Box 1007, Cedar City 84721, ☎ 435/586–5124 or 800/354–4849). **Kane County Travel Council** (⊠ Box 728, Kanab 84741, ☎ 435/644–5033). **Panoramaland** (⊠ 4 S. Main St., Box 71, Nephi 84648, ☎ 435/623–5203 or 800/748–4361). **Piute Tourism Board** (⊠ Piute County Courthouse, Junction 84740, ☎ 435/577–2949). **Sevier Travel Council** (⊠ 220 N. 600 West St., Richfield 84701, ☎ 435/896–8898 or 800/662–8898). **Washington County Travel and Convention Bureau** (⊠ 425 S. 700 East St., St. George 84770, ☎ 435/634–5747 or 800/869–6635).

UTAH A TO Z

To research prices, get advice from other travelers, and book travel arrangements, visit www.fodors.com.

AIR TRAVEL
CARRIERS
Commuter service between Salt Lake City and smaller Utah cities, such as St. George, Cedar City, and Vernal, is available through SkyWest.
➤ AIRLINES AND CONTACTS: **SkyWest** (☎ 801/575–2508 or 800/453–9417).

BUS TRAVEL
Greyhound Lines runs several buses each day through Salt Lake City. In addition, there are terminals in Beaver, Brigham City, Cedar City, Logan, Ogden, Price, Provo, St. George, Tremonton, and Vernal.

CAR TRAVEL
Interstate 80 crosses Utah east to west, and I–15 runs the length of the state, from Idaho to Arizona. These two routes intersect in Salt Lake City. U.S. 191 accesses eastern Utah, and U.S. 666 enters the southeast from Colorado. Front-wheel drive is suggested on the snowy roads of winter.

It is legal in Utah to make a right turn on a red light, after coming to a complete stop. Maximum speeds in urban areas may be as low as 55 mi per hour, even on major highways. Away from the cities, maximum speed is usually 75 mi per hour. State highways are usually 65 mi per hour. Seat belts are required. Helmets must be worn by motorcyclists and passengers under the age of 18.

EMERGENCIES
In most towns, call 911 for police, fire, and ambulance service. In rural areas, the Utah Highway Patrol has jurisdiction, as do county sheriff departments. Major towns have hospitals with emergency rooms. Outside Salt Lake, pharmacies don't tend to stay open late, but major supermarket chains have pharmacy departments that are often open to 10 PM or so.
➤ CONTACTS: **Utah Highway Patrol** (☎ 801/965–4676).

TOURS
GrayLine Motor Tours offers statewide tours in summer, and tours of northern Utah year-round.
➤ CONTACTS: **GrayLine Motor Tours** (✉ 553 W. 100 South St., Salt Lake City 84101, ☎ 801/521–7060 or 800/309–2352).

TRAIN TRAVEL
Amtrak has daily service from the Rio Grande Depot in Salt Lake City and also serves Helper, Milford, Ogden, Provo, and Thompson Springs.

VISITOR INFORMATION
Fishing licenses are available from the Utah Division of Wildlife Resources. The Utah Division of Parks and Recreation operates all state parks. Use fees, between $4 and $5, are charged at all state parks. Most state parks accept reservations for campsites but also have some sites available on a first-come, first-served basis.
➤ TOURIST INFORMATION: **Utah Division of Parks and Recreation** (✉ 1594 W. North Temple St., Suite 116, Salt Lake City 84116, ☎ 801/538–7220, WEB parks.state.ut.us). **Utah Division of Wildlife Resources** (✉ 1596 W. North Temple St., Salt Lake City 84116, ☎ 801/538–4700, WEB www.nr.state.ut.us/dwr/dwr.htm). **Utah State Parks Reservation Center** (☎ 800/322–3770). **Utah Travel Council** (✉ Council Hall, Capitol Hill, Salt Lake City 84114, ☎ 801/538–1030 or 800/200–1160, WEB www.utah.com).

6 WYOMING

Wyoming is a land of wide-open spaces, soaring mountains, plains, prairie, high desert—and historical and cultural sites dating back thousands of years. Yellowstone and Grand Teton national parks and the gateway communities of Jackson and Cody are the state's greatest attractions, but Wyoming has cowboys—and rodeos— in nearly every town or city, plus miners, loggers, and high-tech business executives. Wilderness, resort, or city, the lifestyle is casual and friendly.

Revised and
updated by
Candy
Moulton

SOARING SNOWCAPPED PEAKS AND LUSH MOUNTAIN MEADOWS
mark the backbone of America as the Rockies cut across
Wyoming. In most people's minds, wild Wyoming is synonymous
with its northwest section and its cluster of parks, forests, and ski resorts. Yellowstone National Park, where geysers spout, elk bugle, mud
pots boil, and larkspur blooms, is justly the state's most popular destination. Just to the south, the Grand Tetons rise abruptly from the Snake
River plain, above the lively community of Jackson and the surrounding
Jackson Hole, where efforts are being made to retain working ranches
and open space in the face of a tide of "second-homers" that include
the likes of Sandra Bullock, Harrison Ford, and Vice President Dick
Cheney.

Incomparable as the rocky crags and alpine valleys of the Northwest
are, there is much more to Wyoming. The mountains smooth into prairie
and plains on the east side of the state and have a few pockets of desert
in the southwest. The other most-visited regions of the state, the northeast and southeast, blend mountain and plain, mine and ranch, and
country towns and western cities. In the southeast, the museums, festivals, and parks of Cheyenne and Laramie ensure that Wyoming's heritage as a frontier territory has its place in contemporary life. The Bighorn
Mountains in the northeast attract hikers and fishermen eager to avoid
the more visited sites in the northwest.

Besides diverse terrain, you'll also see a wide array of life, from the
immense herds of antelope, deer, and elk, to dozens of small towns where
you'll find ranchers rubbing elbows with telecommuting investors.
You can find a rodeo somewhere in Wyoming every day throughout
the summer, including the daddy of 'em all, Cheyenne's Frontier Days,
the last full week in July. Ride a horse, float a wild river, fish for trout,
or visit an art gallery. Gaze off into the distance at a sunset unmarred
by houses and development, or walk the route of the overland emigrants who traveled on the Oregon, California, and Mormon trails in
the 1800s.

Culture in Wyoming tends to be low key. There are symphonies and
music festivals ranging from country to jazz and classical, as well as
stage performances like plays and melodramas. You can also attend
Plains Indian powwows, mountain man rendezvous, or brewfests. The
state has some incredibly well-done small museums (Old West Museum
in Cheyenne, and Trail Town in Cody) as well as the world-class Buffalo Bill Historical Center in Cody that is constantly expanding and
which now has five major exhibit areas.

People who live in Wyoming, and those who come to visit, know that
it's a tough country. Winters can be long, cold, and snowy; spring is
mainly mud, rain, and more snow; summer is short and so packed with
activities you can barely catch your breath; while fall is spectacular.
But it has a laid-back attitude that attracts people who want to shrug
off the pressures of big-city living. The space and solitude also draws
artistic types: writers, musicians, and artists who create in a variety of
media. Wyoming residents know that the state's most valuable resource is the same wild and unspoiled country that astonished explorers
50, 100, and 200 years ago. Of that, there is no shortage.

The closest Wyoming comes to big cities is Cheyenne and Casper, neither of which has more than 70,000 residents. Wyoming has fewer full-
time residents (493,782) than any other state, but you'll find no
inferiority complex. Whether they're riding the tram at Teton Village's
world-class ski resort or haying the horses at a ranch in the Sierra Madre

Mountains, Wyoming residents take ornery pride in being just specks on an uncluttered landscape, five people per square mile. They know they have something that is fast disappearing elsewhere in the world, and, with a hint of pride on a weather-beaten face, they're willing to share it. All that means visitors can experience great diversity when traveling across the state with an average elevation that's second highest in the nation (behind only Colorado). Locals often say whenever they leave Wyoming it's a downhill trip.

Pleasures and Pastimes

Dining

The greatest variety of fine dining is in Jackson, and no other community in Wyoming comes close. There the possibilities range from a cookout with tables in tepees to an open-grilled meal in a massive log restaurant. In almost every small town, however, you'll find a place that does wonders with the regional specialties: steak and prime rib, buffalo, and trout. Vegetarians will find the choices somewhat limited in most areas of the state. Wyoming dining is casual; jackets and ties are not needed except in a couple of Jackson's finer restaurants.

CATEGORY	COST*
$$$$	over $30
$$$	$20–$30
$$	$10–$20
$	under $10

per person for a main course at dinner

Dude Ranches and Pack Trips

No state in the Union exalts cowboy life as Wyoming does. The concept of the dude-ranch vacation started here at a ranch that's still operating, and some of the best ranches in the West truly are in Wyoming. The state had more than 80 at last count.

You'll find places to play cowboy all across Wyoming from Pinedale, Jackson, and Dubois south of Grand Teton National Park, to Cody on the eastern side of Yellowstone National Park, Sheridan (where it all started at Eaton's Ranch) and Buffalo east of the Bighorn Mountains, and down south in the Snowy Range and Sierra Madres near Saratoga and Encampment. In almost all cases, dude ranching is supplemented by pack trips that take you into high, rugged corners of the state.

Some of Wyoming's best guest ranches are Brush Creek Ranch near Saratoga, Paradise Ranch near Buffalo, and T Cross Ranch near Dubois.

Fishing

Lake and stream fishing in Wyoming is legendary. Record trout have been taken at Jackson Lake, on Flaming Gorge Reservoir, and at Pathfinder Reservoir, plus the trout population in Yellowstone Lake has been revived. Inside and outside the national parks, the rivers are teeming with rainbow, native cutthroat, brook, brown, and Mackinaw trout, as well as whitefish and catfish at some lower elevations. The Snake River has its own unique cutthroat strain. Fishing aficionados often trek south into the Wind River mountains, where glacier-fed lakes yield all of the above plus golden trout.

For good reason, most visitors to the Jackson Hole area cast their attention westward to the Tetons. For that reason, such waters as Jackson and Jenny lakes and the Snake River are heavily fished, especially at the height of the summer tourist season. That's why many local anglers prefer heading eastward into the Wind River range of Bridger-Teton National Forest. The scenic grandeur of the Bridger Wilderness Area here includes 1,300 lakes and more than 800 mi of streams teeming with fish. This is high country—including Gannett Peak, at 13,804 ft the highest point in Wyoming—meaning that some lakes may remain partially frozen even into July. If the Wind River range has a drawback, it is lack of easy access: roads lead only to the region, not through it; for the best fishing, you should be prepared to do some hiking.

The North Platte River upstream from Saratoga is a blue-ribbon water with excellent fishing for trout. Local outfitters take guided trips, or can provide you with information about access and what type of flies and lures to use. The North Platte upstream from Casper has a section known as the Miracle Mile, for its abundance of large trout. High-mountain lake and stream fishing is also abundant in the Bighorn Mountains. For lake or reservoir fishing try Flaming Gorge Reservoir near Green River, and Pathfinder or Seminoe reservoirs near Casper.

Check at tackle shops or sporting goods stores for recommended fishing spots, but don't necessarily expect to get a straight answer. These are waters Wyomingites would prefer to keep for themselves.

Lodging

Accommodations in Wyoming range from practical roadside motels to exclusive dude-ranch retreats. The *Wyoming Visitor Directory,* available from the Wyoming Division of Tourism, provides listings of motels, bed-and-breakfasts, dude ranches, and campgrounds and RV parks, along with major attractions. Summer traffic slackens after Labor Day, and many motels drop their fees from then until June. (In Jackson, however, prices go up again from late December through March, for the ski season.) Summer reservations for the better accommodations in Yellowstone National Park, Jackson, and Cody should be made three months in advance; make Cheyenne reservations during Frontier Days at least six months ahead. The accommodations around Yellowstone are growing exponentially, and the few remaining older, bare-bones establishments (bathrooms down the hall, no air-conditioning) are being refurbished. In Yellowstone itself, lodging is generally less expensive than what you'll find in nearby communities and most park lodging has been upgraded substantially in recent years, with the addition of telephones in many rooms.

CATEGORY	COST*
$$$$	over $200
$$$	$130–$200
$$	$75–$130
$	under $75

Prices are for a standard double room in high season, not including tax and service.

Outdoor Activities

There are no shortages of mountains and rivers and all kinds of trails for the intrepid traveler. Jackson and the parks just to the north are the focus of intensive recreation, whether it's bagging peaks in the Tetons in August or Sno-Cat skiing in the fresh powder at Grand Targhee. Wintertime opportunities are outstanding with downhill ski areas, cross-country ski and snowmobile trails that are among the best in the region, and activities ranging from ice fishing to horse-drawn chariot racing or dogsledding. There is a lot of outdoors in Wyoming, however, and the adventurous visitor may want to try some less well-known areas and activities, from dude ranching around Sheridan and Cody to camping in national forests throughout the state.

Exploring Wyoming

Wyoming's two national parks lie in northwest Wyoming, both along the Continental Divide. Yellowstone National Park, with its geothermal wonders, is the state's most popular destination. Just to the south, Grand Teton National Park protects the spectacular Tetons, which jut along the skyline above the Snake River. Their adjacent gateway towns are Jackson, Pinedale, and Dubois to the south and Cody on the east. This entire region is mountain country with high peaks (some of them remaining snowcapped year-round) and deep valleys.

In the northeast, along the eastern flank of the Bighorn Mountains, are the communities of Sheridan, Big Horn, and Buffalo, where ranching (both cattle and dude) is the main use of the land. Farther to the east the land switches to grassland and rolling hills, with occasional buttes and other landforms such as the unique Devils Tower, the country's first National Monument. Gillette and surrounding environs is energy country with huge open-pit coal mines and an ever-widening web of coal-bed methane gas wells.

Almost dead center in the state, Casper is a high-plains landscape and an energy country as well, situated along the North Platte River and the corridor of the national historic trails that pioneers followed to Oregon and California in the 1800s.

Cheyenne and Laramie anchor the southeast as the plains and prairies around those cities morph into the Medicine Bow and Snowy Range mountains near Saratoga. In the southwest, Rock Springs, Green River, and Evanston lie within or at the edge of the Little Colorado Desert where wild horses roam freely as they have for centuries.

Numbers in the text correspond to numbers in the margin and on the Wyoming map.

Great Itineraries

IF YOU HAVE 3 DAYS

The most popular section of Wyoming, the northwest, will more than fill a three-day trip, so plan to pack your time as completely as possible to see amazing scenery and wildlife in a unique landscape. Because it has the best air service, begin your trip in 🖼 **Jackson** ① and plan to spend the first full day touring the community and **Grand Teton National Park** ⑦. Be sure to visit the National Wildlife Art Museum and the National Elk Refuge, where you'll see elk by the thousands in the winter and other wildlife such as trumpeter swans in the summer. Head north on U.S. 191 to **Moose.** Stop at the Grand Teton National Park visitor center, then visit Menor's Ferry and the Chapel of the Transfiguration, before continuing north on Teton Park Road to lunch at either Jenny Lake or Jackson Lake. Spend the afternoon fishing, boating, or hiking. For a great view of Jackson Hole, drive to the top of **Signal Mountain** before returning to Jackson for the evening. For a western meal and program, try dinner at the Bar J Chuckwagon, then kick up your heels at one of Jackson's great western bars.

Early on your second day take U.S. 191 north through **Grand Teton National Park** ⑦ to Moran Junction, then head toward 🖼 **Yellowstone National Park** ⑧. Once in the park go first to Old Faithful. Plan to spend the morning there, walking the geyser basin boardwalks and watching the eruption of Old Faithful. Have lunch before continuing north toward Norris Geyser Basin. Expect some travel delays due to highway construction between Madison and Norris, but rest assured there is plenty to see if you must wait. At Norris spend some time walking the boardwalks, where it's easy to lose track of time as you pon-

Wyoming

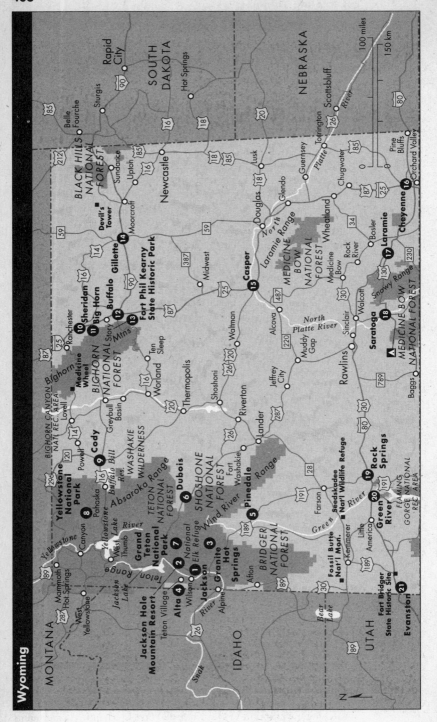

SOUTH DAKOTA

NEBRASKA

MONTANA

IDAHO

UTAH

Rapid City

Sturgis

Hot Springs

Belle Fourche

Sundance

Upton

Newcastle

Scottsbluff

Torrington

Pine Bluffs

Orchard Valley

Moorcroft

Devil's Tower

Gillette

BLACK HILLS NATIONAL FOREST

Lusk

Guernsey

Chugwater

Cheyenne 16

Laramie 17

230

Douglas

Glendo

Wheatland

Bosler

Rock River

Medicine

Bow

Buffalo 12

Sheridan 10

Big Horn 11

Fort Phil Kearny State Historic Park 13

14

Ranchester

Story

Medicine Wheel

Mtns

BIGHORN NATIONAL FOREST

Midwest

Casper 15

Medicine Bow

LARAMIE RANGE

MEDICINE BOW NATIONAL FOREST

Snowy Range

Saratoga 18

Walcott

Sinclair

Rawlins

Baggs

Ten Sleep

Worland

Thermopolis

Shoshoni

Wolfman

Alcova

Muddy Gap

Jeffrey City

North Platte River

BIGHORN CANYON NAT. REC. AREA

Lovell

Greybull

Basin

Powell

Cody 9

Pohaska

Buffalo Bill Res.

WASHAKIE WILDERNESS

Absaroka Range

Dubois 6

SHOSHONE NATIONAL FOREST

Fort Washakie

Lander

Riverton

Wind River Range

Pinedale 5

Farson

Seedskadee Nat'l Wildlife Refuge

Rock Springs 19

Green River 20

FLAMING GORGE NATIONAL REC. AREA

Yellowstone National Park

Yellowstone Lake

West Thumb

Canyon

Grand Teton National Park

National Elk Refuge

Teton Range

Jackson Hole Mountain Resort

Teton Village

Alta 4

Wilson

Jackson 1

Granite Hot Springs 3

Afton

Alpine

BRIDGER NATIONAL FOREST

Kemmerer

Fossil Butte Nat'l Mon.

LaBarge

Little America

Fort Bridger State Historic Site

Evanston 21

Mammoth Hot Springs

West Yellowstone

Snake River

Bear Lake

TETON NATIONAL FOREST

7

2

8

100 miles

150 km

N

der the marvels of Yellowstone's underground plumbing. After you leave Norris head east to Canyon Village. Plan to spend the rest of the afternoon and evening at the Grand Canyon of the Yellowstone. Hike to the lookout points for the Yellowstone Falls.

On your third day, you have a choice to make. You could complete the Yellowstone loop, taking time to stop at Yellowstone Lake Hotel for a snack or even lunch and return to Grand Teton National Park and Jackson, where shopping opportunities abound. Or, head east over Sylvan Pass and take U.S. 14/16/20 to 🔲 **Cody** ⑨. If flying into Jackson and out of Cody isn't a problem or if you are driving, then heading to Cody is the recommended direction. Visit Trail Town in the morning, have lunch at the Irma Hotel, then devote your entire afternoon to the Buffalo Bill Historical Center with its five museums. In the evening you could head out to the Cody Night Rodeo.

IF YOU HAVE 7 DAYS

You can easily spend a full week exploring the sights in the three-day itinerary, spending several nights in Jackson or staying in Grand Teton before heading on to Yellowstone. If you want to see more of Wyoming's varied regions, however, start in Cheyenne. This suggested tour begins in southeastern Wyoming, and takes you from the area dominated by the Union Pacific Railroad to central Wyoming, marked by the ruts of the Oregon–California–Mormon trails. Then you can continue toward the northeast and the lands dominated historically by the Northern Plains Indians, before touring the two national parks.

Get to know Wyoming's cowboy and Old West heritage on your first morning in **Cheyenne** ⑯ at the Old West Museum. Then take Route 210 to **Laramie** ⑰, where you can visit the Laramie Plains Museum and do some shopping in the restored Landmark Square downtown. Have lunch, then continue west on the Snowy Range Scenic Byway (Route 130) to 🔲 **Saratoga** ⑱. Have dinner at the Wolf Hotel, then spend the evening relaxing in the hot mineral Hobo Pool. In winter Route 130 closes so take I–80 or U.S. 30 west from Laramie and then head south on Route 130 to Saratoga.

Leave Saratoga early on your second day, taking Route 130 to I–80. Head west to Rawlins, then turn north on U.S. 287 and Route 220. Stop to visit sites on the Oregon and Mormon trails, including Independence Rock and the Martin's Cove Visitor Center at the Handcart Ranch. You may want to take a lunch or at least some snacks; there is no dining offered at the Handcart Ranch and it takes about three hours to drive from Saratoga to 🔲 **Casper** ⑮, without stops. Spend the afternoon and evening at **Fort Caspar Historic Site,** at the **National Historic Trails Interpretive Center.**

On your third day, venture into the region where the greatest Plains Indian wars of the 1860s occurred. Take I–25 north to **Buffalo** ⑫, where you can visit the Jim Gatchell Memorial Museum, an unusually interesting local institution with collections of Native American artifacts. Have lunch in Buffalo then continue 12 mi north of Buffalo to Exit 44. Three miles on U.S. 87 and Route 193 will bring you to **Fort Phil Kearny State Historic Site** ⑬. Once you've had a chance to tour the visitor center and fort location, you might want to visit nearby sites of the Fetterman Massacre and the Wagon Box Fight (the visitor center can provide detailed directions). Take U.S. 87 north to Story and detour on Route 332 to **Big Horn** ⑪, where you can visit the Bradford Brinton Memorial, one of the West's finest ranches, which has an unparalleled collection of western art including originals by Charles M. Russell and Frederic Remington. Then return to U.S. 87 and drive north to ⚄ **Sheridan** ⑩. Spend the late afternoon shopping at the museum of King Ropes and Saddlery or at the Trail End State Historic Site.

On day four, head north on I–90 from Sheridan to Ranchester, then take scenic byway Alternate U.S. 14 west over the Bighorns. Take the time to visit the **Medicine Wheel,** a site sacred to Native Americans, from which you can see the entire Bighorn Basin. Once you've visited the Medicine Wheel, continue west down the hairpin turns of Alternate U.S. 14, possibly stopping for lunch at Lovell or Powell before heading in to ⚄ **Cody** ⑨. The eastern part of Alternate U.S. 14 (through Bighorn National Forest) is closed in winter; then, you'll have to take the also scenic U.S. 14 from Sheridan to Cody. Plan to spend the late afternoon and evening touring the Buffalo Bill Historical Center.

If you like, explore Cody on the morning of your fifth day, then head toward **Yellowstone National Park** ⑧ on U.S. 14/16/20, driving up the North Fork of the Shoshone River. You'll cross Sylvan Pass, a spectacular high-mountain road that's been recently reconstructed, and travel along Yellowstone Lake. Turn north at Fishing Bridge toward Canyon Village where you can experience the wonders of the Grand Canyon of the Yellowstone.

As an alternate out of Cody take Route 120 north to Route 196, the Chief Joseph Scenic Byway, and follow it to Cooke City, Montana, and Yellowstone's northeast gate. Proceed to Mammoth Hot Springs for lunch, then head south toward Norris and Old Faithful, spending the afternoon exploring the two geyser basins. Spend the night at ⚄ **Old Faithful.**

From Old Faithful take the western loop road over Craig Pass south to West Thumb and Grant Village for a final break and view of geyser basins in Yellowstone before you continue south along U.S. 89/191/287 to **Grand Teton National Park** ⑦. Have lunch at the Jackson Lake Lodge in Grand Teton then spend your afternoon exploring Grand Teton, hiking near Jenny Lake, boating on Jackson Lake, or visiting historic sites, such as Menor's Ferry and the Chapel of the Transfiguration. Arrive in ⚄ **Jackson** ① by early evening for dinner and perhaps dancing at one of the town's western watering holes.

Spend your final day in Jackson or take a drive over to Wilson and the Teton Village area, where you can ride the tram to the top of the peaks for a spectacular view of the region.

When to Tour Wyoming

The best time to tour Wyoming is summer or fall, because the high-mountain country gets lots of snow in the winter, and spring hardly exists. July and August are your best bets for avoiding snowstorms, but even then be aware that it can and does snow every month of the year in the mountains. In fall the crowds have diminished, the days are warm, and the nights are cool. Mid-September usually brings the first snowstorm of the season, followed by an Indian summer of calm days and cool temperatures. Some mountain passes, such as the Snowy Range Scenic Byway, close in the winter. Many of Wyoming's museums also close or have limited fall and winter hours. Yellowstone National Park roads generally close by early October and don't reopen until late April or early May. Winter activities on snowmobiles, snow coaches, and cross-country skis are allowed generally from mid-December through February. Grand Teton National Park also closes by late fall and doesn't reopen until May. Before Memorial Day, services in both parks are limited.

Summertime abounds in local celebrations and rodeos. Mountain men and women hold rendezvous (named for the gatherings of fur trappers) along the Green River near Pinedale in mid-July and on the Blacks Fork at Fort Bridger over Labor Day. The Fort Bridger rendezvous is one of the largest in the entire Rocky Mountain region. For snowmobilers and skiers, the winter season is the main attraction. Ice fishing is popular in January on lakes near Saratoga and Casper.

NORTHWEST WYOMING

Yellowstone's appeal is as strong today as it was in 1872, when the region became the first national park. The numbers of people touring Yellowstone is increasing in both the summer and winter seasons, leading park officials to consider future restrictions on visitation. Though there are plans to restrict snowmobiling in the park, that sport is still open at least through the winter season ending in March 2003. Many outfitters and AmFac Parks and Resorts have switched to snowmobiles with four-stroke engines that are quieter and cleaner than older machines.

Much of what draws more than 3 million people to the Yellowstone region each year are the natural wonders: bubbling mud pots, spouting geysers, rushing rivers, spectacular waterfalls, and most of all, the diversity of wildlife. Long known for its elk and buffalo herds, Yellowstone in 1995 again became home for North American wolves, in an expensive experimental repopulation program. The last wild wolves to roam the region had been killed by hunters during the 1930s, so the return of the carnivore drew worldwide attention. There are presently about 170 wolves in the park that are part of several different packs. They are thriving and you can participate in special tours designed to provide a glimpse of the elusive animals.

Travelers are recognizing that the wild beauty extends beyond the artificial boundaries of the park. They hike in June among the colorful explosions of wildflowers near Togwotee Pass in the Bridger-Teton National Forest north of Dubois, or ride horses in the Wapiti Valley near Cody. They raft down the white water of the Hoback River south of Jackson and view the herds of elk that gather at the National Elk Refuge.

Yellowstone's so-called "gateway" towns, including Jackson and Pinedale to the south, Cody to the east, and Dubois to the southeast, have developed their own attractions, some of them cultural, and have improved their accommodations as well. The effort to find a balance between saving the untrammeled wonders of the region and playing host to a curious and enthusiastic tide of visitors is one of the civic challenges here, but there is a definite move to establish conservation easements on open lands remaining.

Jackson

❶ *33 mi south of Grand Teton National Park's Colter Bay Visitor Center on U.S. 89/191/287.*

The largest number of visitors to northwest Wyoming come to Jackson, which remains a small western town, "howdy" in the daytime and hopping in the evening. For active types, it's a place to stock up on supplies before heading for outdoor adventures. For those resting their feet a while, there's a wealth of galleries and western-wear shops and, at night, varied cuisines and no shortage of bars and music. By the way, Jackson is the town, while Jackson Hole is the valley, which encompasses Grand Teton National Park and the town itself. (It's a hole because it is completely surrounded by mountain peaks.)

Jackson's charm and popularity put it at risk. On busy summer days, traffic can slow to a crawl where the highway doglegs through downtown. Proposals for new motels and condominiums sprout like the purple asters in the spring, as developers vie for a share of the vacation market. Old-timers suggest that the town—in fact, the entire Jackson Hole—has already lost the dusty charm it had when horses stood at hitch rails around the Town Square. However, with national parks and forests and state lands occupying some of the most beautiful real estate in the country, there's only so much ground on which to build. These limitations, along with the cautious approach of locals, may keep Jackson on a human scale.

The **Town Square** has tall shade trees and, at the corners, arches woven from hundreds of elk antlers. In the winter, Christmas lights adorn the arches, and during the summer, there's a melodramatic "shoot-out" every evening at 6:30. Stagecoach rides originate here during the day.

For local history, visit the **Jackson Hole Museum** where you can get acquainted with who the early settlers were and how Dead Man's Bar got its name. ⊠ *Corner of Glenwood and Deloney Ave.,* ☎ *307/733–2414.* ⚑ *$3.* ☉ *Weekdays 8–5.*

Dining and Lodging
You can make reservations for most motels in Jackson through two **reservation services**: Central Reservations (☎ 800/443–6931) and Jackson Hole Vacations (☎ 800/223–4059).

$$–$$$ ★ ✕ **The Blue Lion.** Consistently excellent fare is the rule at this blue clapboard house two blocks from the Town Square. Dishes range from rack of lamb to grilled elk to fresh seafood. Lunch on the deck is a treat in summer. The restaurant is entirely no-smoking. ⊠ *160 N. Millward St.,* ☎ *307/733–3912. AE, D, MC, V.*

$$–$$$ ✕ **Off Broadway.** Stop here for seafood and pasta (Cajun shrimp with black linguine), with a little Thai, wild game, and snazzy neon thrown in. There's both indoor and outdoor seating. ⊠ *30 King St.,* ☎ *307/733–9777. AE, MC, V. No lunch.*

$$–$$$ ✕ **Sweetwater Restaurant.** Mediterranean meals are served up in a log-cabin atmosphere, and nothing is lost in the translation. Start with smoked buffalo carpaccio or roasted red pepper hummus; then go on to roast duckling, venison tenderloin, or yellowfin tuna. ⊠ *85 S. King St.,* ☎ *307/733–3553. AE, D, MC, V.*

$$ ✕ **Nani's Genuine Pasta House.** The ever-changing menu (it has different regional menus each month) at this cozy, almost cramped, restaurant may contain braised veal shanks with saffron risotto or other regional Italian cooking. Almost hidden behind a motel, it's designed to attract gourmets, not tourists. You'll also find vegan dishes and you can dine in or take out. ⊠ *242 N. Glenwood St.,* ☎ *307/733–3888. MC, V.*

$–$$ ✕ **Billy's Giant Hamburgers.** Sharing an entrance with the Cadillac Grille, Billy's is casual, noisy, and the portions are just plain huge. There are a few booths, more tall tables with stools, and you can sit at the bar. Choose from a variety of sandwiches, or one of Billy's specialties, a really big burger that is really, really good. ⊠ *55 N. Cache Dr.,* ☎ *307/733–3279. AE, MC, V.*

$–$$ ★ ✕ **The Bunnery.** Lunch and dinner are served here in the summer, but it's the breakfasts that are irresistible, whether it's an omelet or a home-baked pastry. It's elbow-to-elbow inside and a brief wait to be seated on busy mornings, but any inconvenience is well worth it. You can also find a decent vegetarian selection here. ⊠ *130 N. Cache St., Hole-in-the-Wall Mall,* ☎ *307/733–5474. Reservations not accepted. MC, V.*

$–$$ ✕ **Jedediah's House of Sourdough.** This restaurant, a block east of the Town Square, makes breakfast and lunch for the big appetite. There are plenty of "sourjacks" (sourdough flapjacks) and biscuits and gravy, and it has a friendly, noisy, elbow-knocking atmosphere. Burgers are mountain-man size and dinners include trout, barbecue chicken, and steak. ⊠ *135 E. Broadway Ave.,* ☎ *307/733–5671. Reservations not accepted. AE, D, MC, V. No dinner Labor Day–Memorial Day.*

$ ✗ **Vista Grande.** You'll get a generous portion of Mexican-style food here, though it's a little bland if you like spicy dishes. Service can be a bit on the slow side, but gazing at the Tetons from the window or from the deck makes a great way to pass the time. Because it's a popular place, it can get crowded and noisy. ⊠ *Teton Village Rd. near Wilson turnoff,* ☎ *307/733–6964. Reservations not accepted. AE, MC, V.*

$$$$ ✗🏠 **Wort Hotel.** This brick Victorian hotel near the Town Square
★ seems to have been around as long as the Tetons, but it feels fresh inside. A fireplace warms the lobby, and a sitting area is just up the stairs. Each room has locally made, western-style furniture, including pole beds and pine dressers, with carpets, drapes, and bedcoverings in warm, muted tones such as blues and mauves. You can sip a drink in the Silver Dollar Bar—aptly named for the 2,032 silver dollars imbedded on top of the bar—or sit down for a fine meal ($–$$). Try the mixed grill of buffalo and elk medallions or the nightly veal special. ⊠ *50 N. Glenwood St., 83001,* ☎ *307/733–2190 or 800/322–2727,* FAX *307/733–2067,* WEB *www.worthotel.com. 60 rooms. Restaurant, bar, hot tub, gym, meeting room. AE, D, DC, MC, V.*

$$$–$$$$ 🏠 **Days Inn.** Like other chains, this motel is something familiar, but the lodgepole swing out front, the lobby's elk-antler chandelier, and the rooms' Teton-, Wind River–, or Snake River–range views remind you where you are. Some rooms have microwaves and fridges, and a Continental breakfast is included. There are ski boot and glove dryers in the lobby, plus in-room ski racks and safes. ⊠ *350 S. Hwy. 89, 83001,* ☎ *307/739–9010,* FAX *307/733–0044. 91 rooms. Breakfast room, no-smoking rooms, some refrigerators, hot tub, sauna, ski storage. AE, D, DC, MC, V. CP.*

$$$ 🏠 **Parkway Inn.** Each room has a distinctive look, with oak or wicker furniture, and all are filled with antiques, from 19th-century pieces onward. The overall effect is homey and delightful, especially appealing if you plan to stay several days or longer. ⊠ *125 N. Jackson St., 83001,* ☎ *307/733–3143 or 800/247–8390,* FAX *307/733–0955,* WEB *www.parkwayinn.com. 37 rooms, 12 suites. Breakfast room, no-smoking rooms, indoor pool, hot tub, gym. AE, D, DC, MC, V. CP.*

$$–$$$ 🏠 **Cowboy Village Resort.** Stay in your own small log cabin with covered decks and barbecue grills. There is a ski wax room, and both the START Bus and Targhee Express buses that service the ski areas stop on the property. Continental breakfast is served in winter. ⊠ *120 S. Flat Creek, 83001,* ☎ *307/733–3121 or 800/962–4988,* FAX *307/739–1955. 82 cabins. Kitchenettes (some), no-smoking rooms, hot tub, coin laundry. AE, D, MC, V.*

$$ 🏠 **Antler Motel.** Like real estate agents say, location, location, location, and no motel in Jackson is more convenient to the Town Square than the Antler, just one block south. Some rooms have fireplaces, but they are otherwise standard motel rooms. Pets are allowed. ⊠ *43 W. Pearl St., 83001,* ☎ *307/733–2535 or 800/483–8667,* FAX *307/733–2002,* WEB *www.townsquraeinns.com. 110 rooms. Hot tub, sauna, gym, coin laundry, meeting room. AE, D, MC, V.*

Nightlife

There is never a shortage of live music in Jackson, where local performers play country, rock, and folk. Some of the most popular bars are on the Town Square. At the **Million Dollar Cowboy Bar** (⊠ 25 N. Cache St., ☎ 307/733–2207), everyone dresses up in cowboy garb and tries to two-step into the Old West. There is live music most nights at the **Rancher Bar** (⊠ 20 E. Broadway Ave., ☎ 307/733–3886).

A special treat is down the road from Jackson at the **Stagecoach Bar** (✉ Rte. 22, Wilson, ☎ 307/733–4407), which fills to bursting Sunday when the house band—a motley bunch that includes a novelist, the first man to ski down the Grand Teton, and a changing cast of guitar aces—is playing.

Shopping

Jackson's peaceful Town Square is surrounded by storefronts with a mixture of specialty and outlet shops—most of them small-scale—with moderate to expensive prices. Just north of Jackson's center, on Cache Street, is a small cluster of fine shops in Gaslight Alley.

BOOKS

One of Gaslight Alley's best shops is **Valley Bookstore** (✉ 125 N. Cache St., ☎ 307/733–4533). It ranks among the top bookstores in the region, with a big selection and salespeople who can talk Tolstoy while guiding you to the best publications on local subjects.

CLOTHING

At the south edge of town, **Cattle Kate** (✉ 3530 S. Park Dr., ☎ 800/332–5382) produces some of the best designs in contemporary western wear for women on the market today. The store also carries a few men's accessories. **Hide Out Leather** (✉ 40 N. Center St., ☎ 307/733–2422) carries many local designs and has a diverse selection of coats, vests, and accessories such as pillows and throws. Try **Jackson Hole Clothiers** (✉ 45 E. Deloney Ave., ☎ 307/733–7211) for women's western wear and hand-knit sweaters.

CRAFT AND ART GALLERIES

Jackson's art galleries serve a range of tastes. The fine nature photography of Tom Mangelson is displayed at his **Images of Nature Gallery** (✉ 170 N. Cache St., ☎ 307/733–9752). **Trailside Galleries** (✉ 105 N. Center St., ☎ 307/733–3186) sells traditional western art and jewelry.

SPORTING GOODS

Jackson is well stocked with the best in outdoor equipment, winter and summer, including standout **Jack Dennis Sports** (✉ 50 E. Broadway Ave., ☎ 307/733–3270), Jackson's premier sports shop, an internationally known fishing and sporting headquarters. It also has a store at Teton Village. **Skinny Skis** (✉ 65 W. Deloney Ave., ☎ 307/733–6094) offers everything a cross-country skier might need. **Teton Mountaineering** (✉ 170 N. Cache, ☎ 307/733–3595) specializes in Nordic skiing, climbing, and hiking equipment and clothing. **Westbank Anglers** (✉ 3670 N. Moose-Wilson Rd., ☎ 307/733–6483) fulfills fly-fishing dreams.

Jackson Hole

11 mi from Jackson to Teton Village and Jackson Hole Ski Resort via Rte. 22 and Teton Village Rd.

Completely surrounded by mountain peaks, Jackson Hole encompasses Grand Teton National Park, private homes and ranches, the Bridger-Teton National Forest, and Jackson Hole Ski Area. Though you might headquarter in Jackson, most of the outdoor activities in the region occur in Jackson Hole. Named for fur trapper David Jackson in 1829, the valley has a world-class ski mountain, hiking and biking trails, and the Snake River, with its attendant opportunities to fish or float, runs right through the middle of it.

Jackson Hole is potentially the best ski resort area in the United States. The expanse and variety of terrain are awesome. There are literally thousands of ways of getting from top to bottom, and not all of them are hellishly steep, despite Jackson's reputation. The ski resort is at Teton Village on the west side of the valley.

2 There are two reasons why **Jackson Hole Mountain Resort** might not *absolutely* be the country's best ski resort. The first has to do with the base Teton Village, a functional but rather ordinary cluster of buildings. Improvements and upgrades of the base-area facilities in recent years include new lodging options, but compared with many other major resorts around the country, this is a relatively spartan place. A big reason the base area remains meagerly developed is that it is closely circumscribed by protected land (Grand Teton National Park). In the winter ski season, it can be less expensive to stay in Jackson, about 20 minutes away; during summer it is generally cheaper to stay at Teton Village.

Three miles north of Jackson, the **National Wildlife Art Museum** is just what it sounds like. Among the paintings and sculptures of bighorn sheep, elk, and other animals of the West are works by famous artists such as George Catlin and Charles M. Russell. You can stand on the deck and gaze across the National Elk Refuge, where, particularly in winter, you will see wildlife in a natural habitat. ⊠ *2820 Rungius Rd.,* ☎ *307/733–5771,* WEB *www.wildlifeart.org.* ⌧ *$6.* ☉ *Nov.–Sept., daily 8–5; Oct., Mon.–Sat. 9–5, Sun. 1–5.*

More than 7,000 elk, many with enormous antler racks, winter on the **National Elk Refuge,** just north of Jackson. You can take a horse-drawn sleigh ride to visit the huge herd in the winter. The elk stand or eat calmly as sleighs loaded with families and alfalfa pellets move in their midst. Dress warmly. Throughout the year, visitors drive up Refuge Road (well east of the herd in winter) for a view of Teton Valley, and sometimes camp at Curtis Creek Campground. ⊠ *Elk Refuge Visitor Center, 2820 Rungius Rd., 3 mi north of Jackson at the National Wildlife Art Museum,* ☎ *307/733–5771,* WEB *www. nationalelkrefuge.fws.gov.* ⌧ *Free; sleigh rides $8.* ☉ *Year-round; sleigh rides, mid–Dec.–Apr.*

South of Jackson Hole, concerted local and national efforts have preserved both the wildlands and the ranches that dot the Teton Valley floor. The Snake River turns west and the contours steepen; by Hoback Junction there's white-water excitement. The highway provides good views of the river's twists and turns and the life-jacketed rafters and kayakers who float the canyon. About 13 mi south of Jackson at Hoback Junction, turn east on U.S. 189/191 and follow the Hoback River south up its beautiful canyon. A tributary canyon 10 mi south of the junction is

3 followed by a well-maintained and marked gravel road to **Granite Hot Springs,** in the Bridger-Teton National Forest, 10 mi east of U.S. 189/191 on Granite Creek Road. Visitors come for the shady, creek-side campground, the pool fed by hot springs, and moderate hikes up Granite Canyon to passes with panoramic views. In the winter, there is a popular snowmobile and dogsled trail from the highway.

Dining and Lodging

$$ ✕ **Bar J Chuckwagon.** At the best bargain in the Jackson Hole area, ★ you'll get a true western meal along with some of the best western entertainment in the region. The meal, served on a tin plate, includes barbecued roast beef, chicken, or rib-eye steak; potatoes; beans; biscuits; applesauce; spice cake; and ranch coffee or lemonade. The multitalented Bar J Wranglers sing, play instruments, share cowboy stories and poetry, and even yodel. "Lap-size" children eat free. ⊠ *4200 Bar J Chuckwagon Rd., Wilson,* ☎ *307/733–3370. D, MC, V.*

$–$$ ✕ **Mangy Moose.** Folks pour in off the ski slopes for a lot of food and talk at this two-level restaurant plus bar with an outdoor deck. The place is adorned with antiques, including a full-size stuffed caribou and sleigh suspended from the ceiling. There's a high noise level but decent food of the steaks and burgers variety at fair prices. ✉ *Teton Village,* ☎ *307/733–4913. AE, MC, V.*

$$$–$$$$ ✕ 🏨 **Spring Creek Ranch.** Outside Jackson on Gros Ventre Butte, this luxury resort offers beautiful views of the Tetons and a number of amenities, including cooking in some units, horseback riding, and tennis, as well as cross-country skiing and sleigh rides in winter. Aside from 36 hotel rooms, there's a changing mix of studios, suites, and condos with lofts, called "Choates." Rooms have wood-burning fireplaces. There are steps to the lower-level restaurant, the **Granary** ($$$–$$$$; reservations essential), which serves fine food and is slightly more expensive than the resort; lead off with Dungeness crab and Havarti cheese wrapped in phyllo dough, followed by poached salmon with a cucumber dill sauce and wild rice. ✉ *1800 Spirit Dance Rd., Box 4780, 83001,* ☎ *307/733–8833 or 800/443–6139,* 🆒 *307/733–1524,* 🌐 *www.springcreekranch.com. 36 rooms, 76 studios and suites. Restaurant, kitchenettes, outdoor pool, 2 tennis courts, horseback riding, cross-country skiing, sleigh rides. AE, D, DC, MC, V.*

$$$–$$$$ 🏨 **Alpenhof Lodge.** This small Austrian-style hotel is in the heart of the Jackson Hole Ski Resort, next to the tram. The deluxe rooms have balconies, hand-carved Bavarian furniture, and cream-color walls; some have fireplaces and Jacuzzis. Standard rooms are smaller, and don't have balconies, but they do have the hand-carved Bavarian furniture. Entrées such as wild game loaf is served in the dining room, and Dietrich's Bar and Bistro is a relatively quiet nightclub that also offers casual dining. ✉ *3255 W. McCollister Dr., Teton Village 83025,* ☎ *307/733–3242 or 800/732–3244,* 🆒 *307/739–1516,* 🌐 *www.alpehnoflodge.com. 42 rooms. Dining room, bar, pool, massage, ski storage, nightclub. AE, D, DC, MC, V. Closed Oct., Nov., and mid-Apr.–May.*

$$$$ 🏨 **Amangani.** This exclusive resort of sandstone and redwood melds ★   into the landscape of Gros Ventre Butte, enjoying beautiful views of Spring Creek valley from its cliff. The warm hospitality is western, but the setting is that of Eastern simplicity, with tall ceilings, clean lines, and rooms with platform beds, large soaking tubs, and plenty of space. The amenities here are the best in Jackson Hole and include horseback riding, tennis, and cross-country skiing and sleigh rides in winter. ✉ *1535 N.E. Butte Rd., Box 15030, 83002,* ☎ *307/734–7333 or 877/734–7333,* 🆒 *307/734–7332. 40 suites. Restaurant, lobby lounge, in-room data ports, in-room safes, in-room VCRs, minibars, no-smoking rooms, refrigerators, room service, pool, hot tub, massage, sauna, spa, steam room, 2 tennis courts, health club, horseback riding, cross-country skiing, sleigh rides, library, dry cleaning, concierge, meeting room, airport shuttle. AE, D, DC, MC, V.*

$$$$ 🏨 **R Lazy S Ranch.** Jackson Hole, with the spectacle of the Tetons in the background, is true dude-ranch country and the R Lazy S is one of the largest dude ranches in the area. Horseback riding and instruction is the primary activity, with a secondary emphasis on fishing, either in private waters on the ranch or at other rivers and streams. Guests stay in log-cabin guest cottages and gather for meals in the large main lodge. ✉ *Teton Village, Box 308, Teton Village, WY 83025,* ☎ *307/733–2655,* 🆒 *307/734–1120,* 🌐 *www.rlazys.com. Accommodations for 45. Dining room, horseback riding, fishing. No credit cards. Closed Oct.–mid June. FAP.*

$$$$ 🏨 **The Painted Porch Bed and Breakfast.** Cozy, clean, and comfortable, this traditional red-and-white farmhouse built in 1901 is nestled on 3½ acres of pine and aspen about midway between Jackson and Teton Village. Both rooms have private entrances. ⊠ *3755 N. Moose-Wilson Rd., 83002,* ☎ *307/733–1981,* FAX *307/733–1564,* WEB *www.jacksonholebedandbreakfast.com. 2 rooms. Breakfast room, library. AE, D, MC, V. BP.*

Outdoor Activities and Sports

CAMPING

There's great camping in **Bridger-Teton National Forest** (⊠ 340 N. Cache St., Box 1888, Jackson 83001, ☎ 307/739–5500, FAX 307/739–5010, WEB www.fs.fed.us/btnf/), including **Curtis Canyon,** east of the National Elk Refuge, and **Granite Creek,** just below the hot springs near the Hoback River.

CANOEING, KAYAKING, AND RAFTING

South of Jackson, where the Hoback joins the Snake River and the canyon walls become steep, there are lively white-water sections. But the Snake is a river for those who value scenery over white-water thrills. For the most part, floating rather than taking on rapids is the theme of running the Snake (with trips usually incorporating Jackson Lake); as such, it is a good choice for families with younger children. What makes the trip special is the Teton Range, looming as much as 8,000 ft above the river. This float trip can also be combined with two or more days of sea kayaking on Jackson Lake, at the foot of the Tetons. Raft trips take place between June and September. Experienced paddlers run the Hoback, too.

The Snake River, whose rating is Class I–Class II, has earned a strange footnote in history as the river that Evel Knievel tried (and failed miserably) to jump over on a rocket-powered motorcycle.

If you want instruction in the fine art of paddling, contact **Snake River Kayak and Canoe** (☎ 307/733–3127 or 800/529–2501) in Jackson. Take lessons or rent canoes and kayaks from **Teton Aquatics** (⊠ 155 W. Gill Ave., Jackson, ☎ 307/733–3127). If you'd rather be a passenger, traveling the peaceful parts of the river looking for wildlife, contact **Barker-Ewing Scenic Float Trips** (⊠ Box 100–J, Moose 83012, ☎ 307/733–1800 or 800/365–1800). **Triangle X Float Trips** (⊠ Moose 83012, ☎ 307/733–5500 or 307/733–6445) offers more subdued river trips including sunrise and sunset wildlife floats and a 10-mi scenic float. For wet and wild stretches of river, get in touch with **Lewis & Clark Expeditions** (⊠ 145 W. Gill St., Box 720, Jackson 83001, ☎ 307/733–4022 or 800/824–5375). **Barker-Ewing Float Trips** (⊠ 45 W. Broadway, Box 3032, Jackson 83001, ☎ 800/448–4204) tackles the wilder stuff. **Mad River Boat Trips** (⊠ 1060 S. U.S. 89, Box 2222, Jackson 83001, ☎ 307/733–6203 or 800/458–7238), which worked on *A River Runs Through It* (directed by Robert Redford), leads a variety of white-water trips.

CYCLING

Cyclists ride the **Spring Gulch Road,** part pavement, part dirt, off Route 22, along the base of Gros Ventre Butte, rejoining U.S. 26/89/191 near the Gros Ventre River. The trip up to **Lower Slide Lake,** north of town, is a favorite. Turn east off U.S. 26/89/191 to Kelly, and then take the Slide Lake Road. Bike rentals and sales are available at **Teton Cyclery** (⊠ 175 N. Glenwood St., ☎ 307/733–4386). **Hoback Sports** (⊠ 40 S. Millward St., ☎ 307/733–5335) has bike rentals and tours including family-style outings to the National Elk Refuge, or intermediate or advanced tours from the top of Snow King Mountain.

DOGSLEDDING

Dogsledding excursions are available through **Iditarod Sled Dog Tours** (☎ 307/733–7388 or 800/554–7388, WEB www.jhsleddog.com). Frank

Teasley, a veteran Iditarod racer, leads half-day introductory trips or full-day trips to Granite Hot Springs.

GOLF

Jackson Hole Golf and Tennis Club (✉ 5000 Spring Gulch Rd., ☎ 307/733–3111, WEB www.gtlc.com) is a championship 18-hole course near the Jackson Hole Airport, with tennis, fly-fishing, horseback riding, and swimming facilities. The 18-hole **Teton Pines Golf Club** (✉ 3450 N. Clubhouse St., ☎ 307/733–1733, WEB www.tetonpines.com) is just south of the Jackson Hole Ski Resort.

HIKING

The plus here is that much of the uphill legwork can be dispensed with by aerial tram, the same one that carries Jackson Hole skiers upward in winter. From the top, you can walk through high-mountain basins filled with wildflowers in summer, or along cliff-line ridges, all the while with the stunning facade of the Tetons as a backdrop. The weather and wildflowers are best between July and August. A loop of about 30 mi can be made by picking up the Teton Crest Trail, then branching off on the Death Canyon Trail. Don't necessarily expect solitude; most of the time you're in Grand Teton National Park, an exceedingly popular tourist destination. However, this route keeps you well away from the visitor crush at the park's main gate, so you aren't likely to encounter hiker traffic jams, either.

Permits for backcountry use of the forest are needed only by groups and commercial operators such as outfitters. Camping permits are needed for most developed areas of the **Bridger-Teton National Forest** (✉ Box 1888, 340 N. Cache St., Jackson, WY 83001, ☎ 307/739–5500, WEB www.fs.fed.us/btnf), but not for remote areas of the forest such as wilderness areas. Generally camping permits are $15 for a developed campsite and some picnic areas also have a $5 fee. In all cases there are limits on the number of days you may stay in one area. You can take part in wilderness camping, climbing, and exploration of alpine areas with experienced guides on day trips, overnight excursions, or as part of regular classes offered by **Jackson Hole Mountain Guides** (✉ Box 7477, Jackson, WY 83001, ☎ 307/733–4979, WEB www.jhmg.com).

ICE CLIMBING

Among North American climbers, the Tetons are considered a must before hanging up one's ropes and pitons. The mountaineering action continues into winter. Anyone interested in climbing, or learning to climb, can contact **Jackson Hole Mountain Guides** (✉ Box 7477, Jackson, WY 83001, ☎ 307/733–4979, WEB www.jhmg.com) for half-day lessons to multiday trips.

OUTDOOR TOURS

For leisurely appreciation of the area, try a multiday covered wagon and horseback trip with **Teton Wagon Train and Horse Adventure** (✉ Box 10307, Jackson 83002, ☎ 888/734–6101, WEB www.tetonwagontrain.com). **Wild West Jeep Tours** (✉ Box 7506, Jackson 83002, ☎ 307/733–9036, WEB www.wildwestjeeptours.com) has naturalist guides who will show you the backcountry.

SLEIGH RIDES

Sleigh rides into the National Elk Refuge last about 45 minutes and leave from in front of the National Wildlife Art Museum (✉ 2820 Rungius Rd., ☎ 307/733–5771) daily in winter, 10–4, about every 20 minutes. Dinner sleigh rides are offered at **Spring Creek Ranch** (✉ 1800 Spirit Dance Rd., ☎ 307/733–8833 or 800/443–6139), with dinner at its Granary restaurant.

Information on snowmobile rentals and guides is available from the Jackson Hole Chamber of Commerce.

Numerous companies in the Jackson area rent snowmobiles. **Rocky Mountain Snowmobile Tours** (✉ 1050 S. Hwy. 89, Box 820, Jackson, WY 83001, ☎ 307/733–2237 or 800/647–2561, WEB www.snowmobiletours.net) guides one- to five-day trips. Featured destinations are Granite Hot Springs and Yellowstone National Park.

Downhill Skiing and Snowboarding

Because of **Jackson Hole Mountain Resort**'s location on the eastern flanks of the Tetons, it gets on average about 20 ft less snow in a season than does Grand Targhee, a much smaller resort on the western slope. That predominantly eastern exposure often results in snow conditions (at least on the lower half of the mountain) that are less than ideal, either mushy or crusty.

But when the snow is right, this is truly one of the great skiing experiences in America. Jackson is a place to appreciate both as a skier and a voyeur. World-class racers like Olympic champion skier Tommy Moe and snowboarder Rob Kingwill regularly train here. As Kingwill puts it, "nothing really compares to Jackson Hole. I really crave the type of terrain Jackson Hole has. This place has the most consistently steep terrain. You can spend years and years here and never cross your trail."

On the resort map, about 60 squiggly lines designate named trails, but this does not even begin to suggest the thousands of different skiable routes from top to bottom. The resort claims 2,500 skiable acres, a figure that seems unduly conservative. And although Jackson is best known for its advanced to extreme skiing, it is also a place where imaginative intermediates can go exploring and have the time of their lives. A word of warning, though. High snowfall some winters can lead to extreme avalanche danger in spite of efforts by the Ski Patrol to make the area as safe as possible. Before venturing from known trails and routes, check with the Ski Patrol for conditions; ski with a friend, and carry an emergency locator device.

The tram to the summit of Rendezvous Peak provides access to 4,139 vertical ft of skiing, resulting in arguably the longest continuous runs in the United States. The immediate possibilities from the top are somewhat limited: the choice is either Rendezvous Bowl, wide open and moderately steep; or Corbett's Couloir, perhaps the most famous extreme run in America. You must jump into Corbett's or rappel in by rope. If you don't make that first turn, you don't make any; it can be a long and injurious slide to the bottom. The vast majority of skiers choose Rendezvous Bowl, and thereafter, many, many possibilities unfold. There is so much skiing (most of it expert and advanced) that one whole side of the mountain (the Hobacks) is generally opened only on fresh powder days.

Most of Jackson's intermediate skiing is from Après Vous Mountain and in Casper Bowl, between Rendezvous and Après Vous. Casper Bowl tends to attract more skiers, and Après Vous is surprisingly underskied (in part because the chair is long and slow). Après Vous is a great place for intermediates to ski groomed runs and to explore off the beaten track. From the chairlifts on Rendezvous Mountain, Gros Ventre (known by locals simply as GV) is flat-out one of the best intermediate runs in the country—about 2,800 vertical ft of big-turn cruising, with a good, consistent pitch most of the way.

Jackson is not a good place for novice skiers. A small cluster of trails near the base is serviceable, but that's about it. The only way novices get to see the summit is to ride the tram to the top, take in the view (which on a clear day is awesome), and ride the tram down. ✉ *Box 290, Teton Village 83025,* ☎ *307/733–2292 or 800/333–7766,* WEB *www.jacksonhole.com.* ✇ *$32.* ☺ *Early Dec.–mid-Apr., daily 9–4; Tram Tours May–late-Sept., daily 9–5; June–Aug., daily 9–7.*

FACILITIES

4,139-ft vertical drop; 2,500 skiable acres; 10% beginner, 40% intermediate, 50% expert; 1 aerial tram, 1 gondola, 3 quad chairs, 1 triple chair, 3 double chairs, 1 surface lift.

LESSONS AND PROGRAMS

Half-day group lessons at the **Jackson Hole Ski School** (☎ 307/733–2292 or 800/450–0477) start at $50. There are extensive children's programs, including lessons for kids 6 to 13 years old and day care. Nordic skiing lessons start at $45. For expert skiers, the **Wild West Adrenaline Camps** (☎ 307/739–2791 or 800/450–0477), headed by such expert skiers as Tommy Moe, the 1994 Olympic gold medalist, and Pepi Steigler, run for five days, teaching everything from big-mountain free-skiing to racing techniques. The cost is $600 per person. Snowboarders can get expert advice from world-class snowboarder Rob Kingwill and other extreme champions during week-long courses that cost $675 per person.

LIFT TICKETS

$56. Savings of about 10% on five- to seven-day tickets.

RENTALS

Equipment can be rented at ski shops in the town of Jackson. **Jackson Hole Sports** (☎ 307/733–4005 or 800/443–6931), at the Bridger Center at the ski area, offers ski and snowboard rental packages starting at $20 a day.

HELI-SKIING

In general, a good time to go is when there has been relatively little recent snowfall. For two or three days after a storm, good powder skiing can usually be found within the ski area. Daily trips can be arranged through **High Mountain Helicopter Skiing** (☎ 307/733–3274, WEB www.heliskijackson.com) in Teton Village Sports.

Nordic Skiing

With lots of public lands, Nordic skiing opportunities are outstanding in Jackson Hole. You can enjoy the trails in Grand Teton National Park, at Spring Creek Ranch, and within the Bridger-Teton and Shoshone national forests. Among the best places is **Togwotee Pass,** east of Jackson and north of Dubois on U.S. 26/287, in Bridger-Teton and Shoshone national forests. Lessons and groomed trails are available for a fee at **Spring Creek Ranch** (✉ 1800 Spirit Dance Rd., ☎ 307/733–8833 or 800/443–6139).

BACKCOUNTRY SKIING

Few areas in North America can compete with Jackson Hole when it comes to the breadth, beauty, and variety of backcountry opportunities. For touring skiers, one of the easier areas (because of flatter routes) is along the base of the Tetons toward Jenny and Jackson lakes. In summer, this area can become crowded with national park visitors; solitude is more the order of things in winter. Telemark skiers (or even skiers on alpine gear) can find numerous downhill routes by skiing in from Teton Pass, snow stability permitting. A guide isn't required for tours to the national park lakes but might be helpful for those unfamiliar with the lay of the land; trails and trail markers set in summer can become obscured by winter snows. When you are touring elsewhere, a guide familiar with the area and avalanche danger is a virtual necessity. The Tetons are big country, and the risks are commensurately large as well.

The **Jackson Hole Nordic Center** (☎ 307/733–2292 or 800/450–0477) at Teton Village has cross-country, telemark, and snowshoe rentals and track and telemark lessons. The resort has naturalist tours into the backcountry. Rental packages begin at $18. **Alpine Guides** (☎ 307/739–2663) leads half-day and full-day backcountry tours into the national parks and other areas near the resort, for more downhill-minded skiers. Arrangements can also be made through the Jackson Hole Ski School. **Jackson Hole Mountain Guides** (✉ Box 7477, Jackson 83001, ☎ 307/733–4979, WEB www.jhmg.com) leads more strenuous backcountry tours.

TRACK SKIING

The **Jackson Hole Nordic Center** (✉ Teton Village, ☎ 307/739–2292 or 800/450–0477, WEB www.jacksonhole.com) is at the ski-resort base. The scenic 17 km (10 ½ mi) of groomed track is relatively flat. Because the Nordic Center and the downhill ski area are under the same management, downhill skiers with multiday passes can switch over to Nordic skiing in the afternoon for no extra charge. Rentals and lessons are available; alpine lift tickets are also good at the Nordic Center.

Nightlife and the Arts
Every summer the **Grand Teton Music Festival** (✉ Box 490, Teton Village Resort, 83025, ☎ 307/733–1128) presents more than 40 concerts featuring symphonic and chamber music both at Walk Festival Hall and outdoors. From January through March performances are held at the National Wildlife Art Museum.

Shopping
In Teton Village, the **Mountainside Mall,** not to be mistaken for a big suburban mall (to its credit), you can find goggles, snowboards, or skis, or clothing ranging from parkas to swimsuits.

Alta

④ *31 mi northwest of Jackson, Rte. 22 to Rte. 33 (in Idaho) to Alta cutoff (back to Wyoming).*

Alta is home to the Grand Targhee Ski and Summer Resort, famed for its deep powder and family atmosphere. The slopes never feel crowded. But to experience complete solitude, try a day of Sno-Cat skiing in untracked powder. There are three lifts and one rope tow, and a vertical drop of 2,200 ft.

Dining and Lodging

$$–$$$$ ✗ **Skadi's.** This roomy and relaxing place has southwestern-style decor, high ceilings, and good lighting. On the menu are tenderloin beef with *poblano* chili sauce and regional game dishes including venison and pheasant. ✉ *Grand Targhee Ski and Summer Resort, Ski Hill Rd., Alta,* ☎ *307/353–2300 or 800/827–4433. AE, D, MC, V.*

$$–$$$$ ✗▥ **Grand Targhee Ski and Summer Resort.** Perched on the west side of the Tetons, this small but modern facility has a handsome, naturalwood look and the atmosphere of an alpine village. The motel-style rooms are simply furnished and clustered around common areas with fireplaces; the condominium rooms are brighter and more spacious. You won't find crowds and there are four lifts at the ski area and more expansion is on the drawing board. Skadi's is the resort's foremost restaurant ($$–$$$); the Cactus Kitchen has quicker, less expensive food.

✉ *Box SKI, Alta 83422,* ☎ *307/353–2300 or 800/827–4433,* WEB *www.grandtarghee.com. 65 motel-style rooms, 32 condos. 5 restaurants, pool, hot tub, outdoor hot tub, cross-country skiing, airport shuttle. AE, D, MC, V.*

Pinedale

❺ *77 mi south of Jackson on Rte. 189.*

Fur trappers gathered on the Green River near what is now Pinedale for seven rendezvous during the 1800s, and modern-day buckskinners also hold a rendezvous in the area. Pinedale is a southern gateway to Jackson Hole, but has much to offer on its own. To the east are millions of acres of Bridger-Teton National Forest, much of it off limits to all but foot and horse traffic. The peaks reach higher than 13,000 ft, and the area is liberally sprinkled with more than a thousand high-mountain lakes where fishing is generally excellent. Contact the **Bridger-Teton National Forest Pinedale Ranger District** (✉ 29 E. Fremont Rd., Pinedale, WY 82941, ☎ 307/367–4326, WEB www.fs.fed.us/btnfeast) for more information.

The **Museum of the Mountain Man** depicts the trapper heritage of the area and also has an exhibit devoted to pioneer and ranch history of Sublette County. ✉ *700 E. Hennick Rd.,* ☎ *307/367–4101,* WEB *www.museumofthemountainman.com.* 🎫 *$4.* ☉ *May–Sept., daily 10–6; call for winter hrs.*

Dining and Lodging

$–$$ ✕ **McGregors Pub.** Built in 1905, this converted hotel has a classic western interior with a restaurant on the ground floor. Local folks like the steaks and seafood, though the menu also has Italian dishes and there is a kid's menu. You can eat inside or outside on the patio. ✉ *21 N. Franklin St.,* ☎ *307/367–4443. D, DC, MC, V. Closed weekends. No lunch.*

$–$$ ✕ **Moose Creek Trading Company.** As the name suggests, the theme here is moose, from the wrought-iron bar tables depicting moose to the stuffed animals in the gift shop. Upbeat and eclectic, this downtown restaurant does well with prime rib, seafood, and lobster dishes, and has homemade pies and desserts. Try the chunky chicken salad for a light summer meal. ✉ *44 W. Pine St.,* ☎ *307/367–4616. AE, D, DC, MC, V.*

$$–$$$$ ⊡ **Best Western Pinedale Inn.** On the north side of town and within three blocks of downtown shopping and restaurants, the rooms aren't large, but they have contemporary furniture. Exercise equipment is available and pets are allowed. ✉ *850 W. Pine St., 82941,* ☎ *307/367–6869,* FAX *307/367–6897. 58 rooms. Some refrigerators, indoor pool, hot tub. AE, D, DC, MC, V. CP.*

$$ ⊡ **Window on the Winds B & B.** This modern yet rustic home of wood, stone, and glass gets its name from the huge windows that allow stunning views of the Gros Ventre Mountain range, the Wind River mountains, and Gannett Peak, the state's highest point. Rooms have lodgepole pine beds, jewel- or earth-tone southwestern quilts and rugs, and mountain views. Children and pets are welcome at this family-oriented, homey place. ✉ *10151 U.S. 191, 82941,* ☎ *307/367–2600 or 888/367–1345,* FAX *307/367–2395,* WEB *www.windowonthewinds.com. 4 rooms, 2 with shared bath. Breakfast room, hot tub. AE, D, DC, MC, V. BP.*

Dubois

❻ *86 mi east of Jackson on U.S. 26 and U.S. 287.*

The mountains around Dubois attracted explorers as early as 1811, when members of the Wilson Price Hunt party crossed through the region en route to Fort Astoria. These high peaks still attract folks who like to hike, climb, ride horses, camp, and experience wilderness. The largest herd of free-ranging bighorn sheep in the country lives here, roaming the high country in summer and wintering just above town on Whiskey Mountain.

Just south and east of Grand Teton and Yellowstone, Dubois is the least well known of the "gateway" communities to the parks, but the town of 1,000 provides all the services a visitor in Jackson or Cody might need. You can still get a room during the peak summer season without making a reservation months in advance, though it is a good idea to call a week or so before you arrive.

The **Wind River Historical Center** has displays related to Wind River tie hacks (individuals who cut ties for railroads), local geology, and archaeology of the Mountain Shoshone, or Sheep Eater Indians. Outbuildings include the town's first schoolhouse, a saddle shop, a homestead house, and a bunkhouse. The center also offers Elderhostel programs. ⊠ *909 W. Ramshorn Ave.,* ☎ *307/455–2284,* WEB *www.windriverhistory.org.* ⊠ *$1.* ⊙ *June–Sept., daily 9–5.*

Learn about bighorn sheep, including the Rocky Mountain bighorn, at the **National Bighorn Sheep Interpretive Center** on the north side of Dubois. There are mounted specimens such as a "super slam" that has one of each type of wild sheep in the world, and two bighorn rams fighting during the rut. Hands-on exhibits illustrate a bighorn's body language, characteristics, and habitat. Winter tours to Whiskey Mountain provide an opportunity to see the wild sheep in their natural habitat. ⊠ *907 Ramshorn Ave.,* ☎ *307/455–3429 or 888/209–2795,* WEB *www.bighorn.org.* ⊠ *$2.* ⊙ *Memorial Day–Labor Day, daily 9–8; Labor Day–Memorial Day, daily (hrs subject to change); wildlife viewing tours mid-Nov.–Mar.*

Outdoor Activities and Sports

ROCK CLIMBING AND MOUNTAINEERING

Much of the appeal of the Wind River range is the relatively difficult access to major peaks, the most significant of which is Gannett Peak, at 13,804 ft the highest mountain in Wyoming. The trip into the base of the mountain can take two days, with considerable ups and downs and stream crossings that can be dangerous in late spring and early summer. The reward for such effort, however, is seclusion: climbing Gannett Peak might not be as dramatic as climbing the Grand Teton to the west, but you won't have to face the national park crowds at the beginning or end of the climb. Wind River is a world of granite and glaciers, the latter (though small) being among the last active glaciers in the U.S. Rockies. Other worthy climbs in the Wind River range are Gannett's neighbors Mt. Sacajawea and Fremont Peak. **Jackson Hole Mountain Guides** (⊠ Box 7477, Jackson, WY 83001, ☎ 307/733–4979, WEB www.jhmg.com) leads trips in the area.

Dining and Lodging

$–$$ ✕ **Rustic Pine Steakhouse.** The bar here is one of Wyoming's more memorable spots, where locals and visitors congregate to share news about hunting or hiking, and the adjoining steak house serves mouthwatering steak and seafood in a quiet atmosphere. Get your greens in at the salad bar. ⊠ *123 Ramshorn Ave.,* ☎ *307/455–2772. MC, V. No lunch.*

$ ✕ **Cowboy Cafe.** This small restaurant in downtown Dubois serves homemade food including sandwiches and steaks, buffalo burgers, chicken, pork, and fish. ⊠ *115 Ramshorn Ave.,* ☎ *307/455–2595. MC, V.*

$ ✕ **Ramshorn Bagel and Deli.** This deli serves breakfast and lunch, including bagels, soup, and sandwiches. ⊠ *202 E. Ramshorn,* ☎ *307/455–2400. No credit cards. No dinner.*

$$$$ ⊡ **Absaroka Ranch.** Traditional guest-ranch activities like horseback riding, hiking, fishing, or relaxing take place in this mountain setting. Five Mile Creek runs through the property, 16 mi west of Dubois. There are special programs for children and you can take an overnight pack trip deep into the mountain country. The ranch takes weeklong bookings only. ⊠ *Box 929, 82513,* ☎ *307/455–2275,* FAX *307/455–2275,* WEB *www.dteworld.com/absaroka. 4 cabins. Dining room, hiking, horseback riding, fishing, recreation room, children's programs. No credit cards. No smoking. Closed mid-Sept.–mid-June. FAP.*

$$$$ ⊡ **T Cross Ranch.** In an isolated valley 15 mi north of Dubois, the T Cross is a traditional guest ranch where cozy cabins have porches with rocking chairs, fireplaces or woodstoves, and handmade log furniture. You can snuggle under a down quilt or spend your days riding horses. Hosts Ken and Garey Neal have been in the guest ranch business for decades and they know how to match people to horses. Only weeklong stays are available. ⊠ *Box 638 KRW, 15 mi north of Dubois, 82513,* ☎ *307/455–2206,* FAX *307/455–2720,* WEB *www.ranchweb.com/tcross. 8 cabins. Dining room, no-smoking rooms, hot tub, hiking, horseback riding, fishing, recreation room, library, children's programs (ages 6 and up), playground. No credit cards. Closed mid-Sept.–mid-June.*

$$$–$$$$ ⊡ **Brooks Lake Lodge.** This mountain resort and sporting lodge gives you scenery with service. The lodge, originally built in 1922, has massive open beam ceilings with log and wicker furnishings, subtle lighting, and lots of space. Each of the lodge bedrooms and cabins has handcrafted lodgepole furniture. Take a canoe out on the lake in summer or in the winter you can take dogsled rides with outfitters. ⊠ *458 Brooks Lake Rd., 82513,* ☎ *307/455–2121,* FAX *307/455–2121,* WEB *www.brookslake.com. 6 rooms, 6 cabins. Restaurant, bar, lake, hiking, horseback riding, fishing, cross-country skiing, snowmobiling, tobogganing. AE, MC, V. FAP.*

$$ ⊡ **Stagecoach Motor Inn.** This locally owned downtown motel has a large backyard with a picnic area and playground equipment, and even a replica stagecoach for kids to climb on. But the play area is bordered by Pretty Horse Creek, so young children need some supervision. More fun is provided by the heated pool. Some rooms have full kitchens; many have refrigerators. ⊠ *103 E. Ramshorn, 82513,* ☎ *307/455–2303 or 800/455–5090,* FAX *307/455–3903,* WEB *www.dteworld.com/stagecoach. 42 rooms, 6 suites. Refrigerators, pool, playground, coin laundry. AE, D, MC, V.*

Grand Teton National Park

❼ *2 mi north of Jackson on U.S. 191; 55 mi north of Dubois on U.S. 26/287.*

One might think this smaller park with a shorter history is dwarfed by its northern neighbor—Yellowstone—but nothing overshadows peaks like these. Presumably no translation of the French is necessary. The peaks—Mt. Moran, Teewinot Mountain, Mt. Owen, the Grand, and Middle Teton—form a magnificent and dramatic front along the west side of the Teton Valley. Lakes large and small are strung along the range's base, draining north into Jackson Lake, which in turn drains south into the Snake River. Grand Teton was put together from ranches John D. Rockefeller, Jr., bought up in the 1930s. It has a few oddities within its boundaries, such as a commercial airport and a dam to hold water for Idaho irrigators, but for fishing, hiking, climbing, boating, and rugged beauty, it's hard to match.

Exploration of Grand Teton National Park generally occurs either from the south—Jackson—or from the north at Yellowstone National

Park. By starting from the south you can make your first stop at **Moose,** which is park headquarters and site of a visitor center, where you can get a good, quick overview of the park.

Just north of the Moose visitor center turn east to **Menor's Ferry.** The ferry on display is not the original, but it is an accurate re-creation of the one built by Bill Menor in the 1890s and demonstrates how people once crossed the Snake River. Several cabins, including the home and store used by Bill Menor, who also operated the ferry, remain at the site; the Menor home holds a park gift shop. There is an historic photo collection in one of the cabins.

One parking lot serves both Menor's Ferry and the nondenominational **Chapel of the Transfiguration,** where the view of the Tetons brings couples from all over the world to say their vows.

Jenny Lake is right below the Grand Teton. You can hike on an easy–moderate trail 2 mi around the lake from the parking area at the south end to Hidden Falls. The trail is steeper from there to Inspiration Point, but then it levels off. The views are increasingly spectacular as you hike the canyon. The trail continues to Lake Solitude, but it's 9 mi from the trailhead to the lake, so be sure to allow plenty of time. You can make the walk miles shorter by taking a boat ride from the dock near the parking area to the Cascade Canyon Trailhead.

There are many easy hikes heading off toward the mountains from Teton Park Road. (They're shown on the map in *Teewinot,* the free publication handed out at the entrances.) One of the nicest, south of Jenny Lake, is to Taggart Lake. The **Taggart Lake Trail** is an easy–moderate 1.6-mi hike from the trailhead to the lake. If you continue around the lake, the terrain is steeper near Beaver Creek and the entire loop is 4 mi. There are views of Avalanche Canyon, and you will probably see moose along the route; be sure to keep your distance. Hikers as well as canoeists enjoy **Leigh and String lakes,** which have short hikes to and around them, just north of Jenny Lake; turn west at North Jenny Lake Junction.

At the north end of the park is **Jackson Lake.** The biggest of the park's glacier-scooped lakes, it was made larger still by a dam, farther south, built in 1909. The lake is popular with sailors, anglers, and even windsurfers. Campgrounds and lodges dot the shore. Near Jackson Lake Junction, the Snake River emerges from the Jackson Lake Dam and winds east and then south through the park. Whether you're on the water or on shore, **Oxbow Bend,** below the dam, is an excellent place to see waterfowl and other wildlife.

U.S. 26/89/191 does run the full length of the park, with the Tetons on display all the way, but at this point (Jackson Lake Junction), a better, more leisurely route is the smaller **Teton Park Road,** which runs south to Moose, where it rejoins the highway heading to Jackson.

Not far south of Jackson Lake Junction on the Teton Park Road, you can take a brief side trip up narrow **Signal Mountain Road** to its summit, where you can see the valley and mountains on all sides. ⊠ *National Park Service, Moose 83012,* ☎ *307/739–3300; 307/733–2053 TTY,* WEB *www.nps.gov/grte.* ⊠ *7-day pass good for both Yellowstone and Grand Teton national parks: $20 per motor vehicle, $10 nonmotorized entry permit, $15 motorcycle or snowmobile.*

Dining and Lodging

$$ ✕ **Dornan's Chuckwagon.** This popular local hangout has Old West decor and mountain views. In the summer, it cooks up an outdoor Dutch-oven buffet (roast beef, ribs, and cowboy beans) and a friendly

Grand Teton National Park

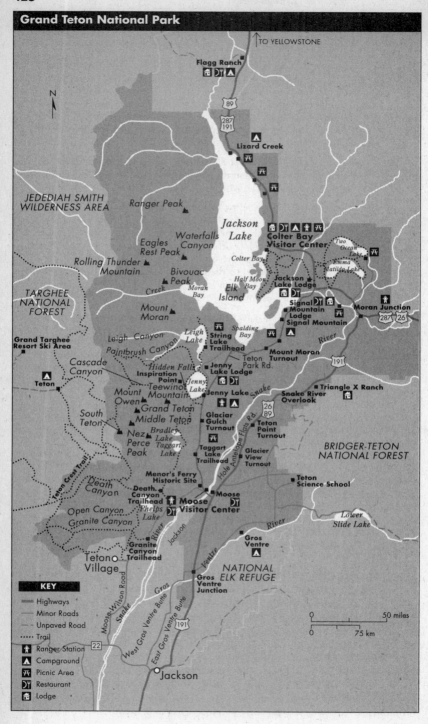

TO YELLOWSTONE

Flagg Ranch

89

287
191

Lizard Creek

JEDEDIAH SMITH
WILDERNESS AREA

Ranger Peak

Jackson
Lake

Colter Bay
Visitor Center

Two
Ocean
Lake

Eagles
Rest Peak

Waterfalls
Canyon

Colter Bay

Emma
Matilde Lake

Rolling Thunder
Mountain

Bivouac
Peak

Half Moon
Bay

Jackson
Lake Lodge

TARGHEE
NATIONAL
FOREST

Creek

Moran
Bay

Elk
Island

Signal
Mountain
Lodge
Signal Mountain

Moran Junction

Mount
Moran

Grand Targhee
Resort Ski Area

Leigh Canyon

Paintbrush Canyon

Leigh
Lake

Spalding
Bay

String
Lake
Trailhead

287 26

River

Cascade
Canyon

Hidden Falls

Inspiration
Point

Teton
Park Rd.

Mount Moran
Turnout

Teton

Jenny
Lake Lodge

191

Jenny
Lake

Triangle X Ranch

Mount
Owen

Teewinot
Mountain

Jenny Lake

Snake

Snake River
Overlook

South
Teton

Grand Teton
Middle Teton

Glaciar
Gulch
Turnout

26
89

Nez
Perce
Peak

Bradley
Lake
Taggart
Lake

Teton
Point
Turnout

BRIDGER-TETON
NATIONAL FOREST

Taggart
Lake
Trailhead

Glacier
View
Turnout

Teton Crest Trail

Death
Canyon

Menor's Ferry
Historic Site

Teton
Science School

Death
Canyon
Trailhead

Moose

Open Canyon

Phelps
Lake

Moose
Visitor Center

Lower
Slide Lake

Granite Canyon

River

Jackson

Gros
Ventre

Teton
Village

Granite
Canyon
Trailhead

Moose-Wilson Road

NATIONAL
ELK REFUGE

Gros
Ventre
Junction

Gros

Ventre

22

Snake

West Gros Ventre Butte

East Gros Ventre Butte

191

River

Jackson

KEY

— Highways
— Minor Roads
- - Unpaved Road
···· Trail
🛉 Ranger Station
▲ Campground
🛱 Picnic Area
🍴 Restaurant
🏠 Lodge

0   50 miles
0   75 km

atmosphere to go with it. On Wednesdays and Saturdays you can also get steak, prime rib, and grilled chicken. Meals are served outside and can be eaten at picnic tables or inside tepees. Alcohol is BYOB—A good wine shop·is adjacent. ⊠ *U.S. 191, Moose,* ☎ *307/733–2415. MC, V.*

$$–$$$$ ✕▥ **Jackson Lake Lodge.** Outside, the resort has a 1950s look, dark brown and low-slung. Inside, two large fireplaces adorn the lounge, Native American designs decorate the walls, and huge picture windows look out at Willow Flats, below Jackson Lake Dam. There are 30 smaller rooms in the main lodge; the others, in one-story motor-lodge–style buildings, are preferable. Some rooms have Teton views and a higher price tag as a result. You can arrange for horseback riding, float trips, and boating excursions that depart from the lodge, and swim in the park's only pool. Rotating four dinner menus, the Mural Room ($$–$$$$) often features buffalo, as well as local game dishes, such as venison or antelope. ⊠ *U.S. 89 north of Jackson Lake Junction, Grand Teton Lodge Co., Box 250, Moran 83013,* ☎ *307/733–3100 or 800/ 628–9988,* FAX *307/543–3143,* WEB *www.gtlc.com. 385 rooms. 2 restaurants, bar, pool, hiking, horseback riding, boating, recreation room, business services, meeting rooms, airport shuttle. AE, DC, MC, V. Closed late Oct.–mid-May.*

$–$$ ✕▥ **Colter Bay Village.** Less expensive than its posher cousins, the Colter Bay Village, near Jackson Lake, has splendid views and an excellent marina and beach for the windsurfing crowd. (You'll need a wet suit.) The cabins have a western style. The 66 tent cabins aren't fancy, but they do keep the wind and rain off (and share rest-room facilities). There is also a 112-space RV park with showers, a service station, and marina. The Chuckwagon restaurant ($–$$) is family oriented, serving lasagna, trout, and barbecue spareribs. ⊠ *Off U.S. 89; mailing address: Grand Teton Lodge Co., Box 250, Moran 83013,* ☎ *307/733–3100 or 800/628–9988,* FAX *307/543–3143. 166 cabins, 66 tent cabins, 112 RV spaces. 2 restaurants, bar, hiking, boating, camping, shops, coin laundry. AE, DC, MC, V. Closed late Sept.–late May (tent cabins have slightly shorter season).*

$$$$ ▥ **Jenny Lake Lodge.** In this most exclusive of the park's resorts, ele-★ gant yet rustic cabins are bedecked with handmade quilts, down comforters, and electric blankets. You can have a phone in your room on request. All activities are included in the price along with breakfast and dinner. Located in a pine forest, a wildfire in 2000 burned to a point just across the road from the lodge. The lodge dining room ($$$$) serves a set dinner menu with a choice of entrées emphasizing Rocky Mountain cuisine, including roast prime rib of buffalo or breast of pheasant with pheasant sausage. Jackets are requested for evening dining. ⊠ *Jenny Lake Rd., Grand Teton Lodge Co., Box 250, Moran 83013,* ☎ *307/ 733–3100 or 800/628–9988,* FAX *307/543–3143,* WEB *www.gtlc.com. 37 rooms. Restaurant, bar, horseback riding, boating, bicycles. AE, DC, MC, V. Closed mid-Oct.–early June. MAP.*

$$–$$$ ▥ **Signal Mountain Lodge.** Built of volcanic stone and pine shingles, the lodge sits on the eastern shore of Jackson Lake. The lobby has a fireplace, a piano, and Adirondack furniture, and guest rooms are clustered in cabinlike units, some with kitchenettes. You can rent boats, take scenic float trips, or fish. The Peaks restaurant ($–$$) offers up views of the lake and the Tetons as well as a menu with elk medallions and shrimp linguine. The Trapper Grill, where you can eat indoors or out on the deck, serves sandwiches and even a Rocky Mountain elk chili burger. ⊠ *Teton Park Rd., Box 50, Moran 83013,* ☎ *307/543–2831. 79 rooms. Restaurant, bar, kitchenettes, boating, fishing, shops. AE, DC, MC, V. Closed mid-Oct.–early May.*

Outdoor Activities and Sports

The **Teton Science School** (⊠ Box 68, Kelly 83011, ☎ 307/733–4765) offers field courses on ecology, park history, and wildlife.

CAMPING

Grand Teton has five public campgrounds. The most popular is at **Jenny Lake** (⊠ Teton Park Rd. at S. Jenny Lake), which has 49 tent sites. The most luxurious camp site is **Colter Bay** (⊠ On Jackson Lake, 7 mi north of Jackson Lake Lodge), which has 350 sites, showers, RV hookups, and laundry facilities. **Gros Ventre Campground** (⊠ 4 mi east of U.S. 26/89/191 at Gros Ventre Junction), on the far eastern side of the park, is so large (360 sites) that it doesn't fill up as fast as the others; it also has an RV dump. Fees are $12 per night.

CANOEING, KAYAKING, AND RAFTING

For river runners, there are peaceful, scenic stretches of the upper **Snake River** in Grand Teton National Park, including the beautiful Oxbow. You can navigate them yourself by canoe or kayak, or float as a passenger on a guided raft. Be sure to check current conditions and ability recommendations with park rangers before you launch. Companies listed under Jackson Hole serve the park as well.

ROCK CLIMBING AND MOUNTAINEERING

In many ways, the 13,770-ft Grand Teton is the most obvious U.S. mountain to climb: 8,000 vertical ft of jagged, exposed rock—more photographed, perhaps, than any other mountain in the nation. It is far from the easiest mountain to climb, however, and there are at least two days of steep rock to deal with on the ascent and rappels of 100 ft (or more) to negotiate on the descent. It is hard to believe that a fellow named Bill Briggs actually skied down the Grand Teton. Fortunately for less experienced climbers, there are other good options in the park, notably 12,325-ft Teewinot Mountain, a more moderate challenge that combines rock, ice, and scrambling. Regardless of the mountain (or route) chosen, the views are as good as they come in the Rockies.

Jenny Lake Ranger Station (☎ 307/739–3300) is the center for climbing information from June to mid-September. **Exum Mountain Guides** (⊠ South end of Jenny Lake, Box 56, Moose, ☎ 307/733–2297) lead climbs.

WATER SPORTS

Boats must be licensed by the parks. Seven-day permits, good in Grand Teton and Yellowstone parks, cost $10 for motorboats and $5 for non-motorized boats. Obtain permits at Moose Visitor's Center or Colter Bay Visitor Center year-around, and at Flagg Information Station, or the Signal Mountain and Buffalo Ranger Stations during summer. You can hire canoes and powerboats at **Colter Bay Marina** (⊠ North of Jackson Lake Junction, ☎ 307/733–3100). **Signal Mountain Marina** (⊠ Teton Park Rd. at the south end of the lake, ☎ 307/543–2831) rents boats.

For boat rides on Jenny Lake contact **Teton Boating Inc.** (☎ 307/733–2703). Rides across the lake lasting about 30 minutes cost $4. The boats run early June–mid-September, daily 8–6. They load from the south end of the parking lot.

Yellowstone National Park

❽ *52 mi from Cody (to east entrance) via North Fork Hwy. (U.S. 14/16/20).*

Few places in the world can match Yellowstone National Park's collection of accessible wonders, from grazing bison and cruising trumpeter swans to rainbow-color hot springs and thundering geysers. As

Yellowstone National Park

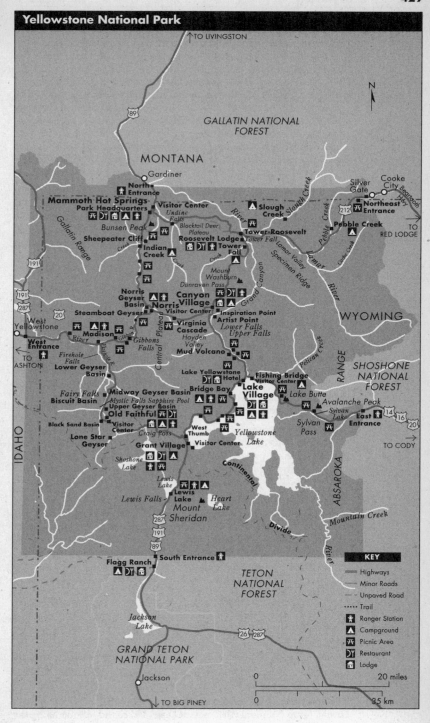

↑ TO LIVINGSTON

GALLATIN NATIONAL FOREST

MONTANA

Gardiner

North Entrance

Mammoth Hot Springs
Park Headquarters

Visitor Center

Undine Falls

Slough Creek

Silver Gate

Cooke City

Northeast Entrance

Bunsen Peak

Blacktail Deer Plateau

Pebble Creek

TO RED LODGE

Sheepeater Cliff

Roosevelt Lodge

Tower-Roosevelt

Gallatin Range

Indian Creek

Tower Fall

Tower Fall

Lamar Valley

Specimen Ridge

Lamar River

WYOMING

Norris Geyser Basin

Mount Washburn

Dunraven Pass

Canyon Village

Grand Canyon

Steamboat Geyser

Norris Visitor Center

Madison

Central Plateau

Virginia Cascade

Inspiration Point

Artist Point

Lower Falls Upper Falls

Hayden Valley

SHOSHONE NATIONAL FOREST

West Yellowstone

West Entrance

Gibbons Falls

Mud Volcano

Firehole Falls

Lower Geyser Basin

Lake Yellowstone Hotel

Fishing Bridge Visitor Center

Lake Village

Lake Butte

Avalanche Peak

TO ASHTON

Fairy Falls

Biscuit Basin

Midway Geyser Basin

Mystic Falls Sapphire Pool

Upper Geyser Basin

Bridge Bay

Pelican Creek

Sylvan Lake

East Entrance

IDAHO

Black Sand Basin

Old Faithful

Visitor Center

Craig Pass

West Thumb

Yellowstone Lake

Sylvan Pass

TO CODY

Lone Star Geyser

Visitor Center

Grant Village

ABSAROKA RANGE

Shoshone Lake

Continental

Lewis Lake

Lewis Lake

Heart Lake

Mount Sheridan

Lewis Falls

Divide

Mountain Creek

Flagg Ranch

South Entrance

TETON NATIONAL FOREST

Jackson Lake

GRAND TETON NATIONAL PARK

Jackson

↓ TO BIG PINEY

KEY

Highways
Minor Roads
Unpaved Road
Trail
Ranger Station
Campground
Picnic Area
Restaurant
Lodge

0   20 miles

0   35 km

you visit the park's hydrothermal areas, you'll be walking on top of the Yellowstone Caldera—a 28-by-47-mi collapsed volcanic cone, which last erupted about 600,000 years ago. The park's geyser basins, hot mud pots, fumaroles (steam vents), and hot springs are kept bubbling by an underground pressure cooker filled with magma. One geophysicist describes Yellowstone as "a window on the earth's interior." There are two major seasons in Yellowstone: summer (May–September), when by far the majority of visitors come, and winter (mid-December–February), when fewer people venture into the region, though it is no less spectacular a time and there are adequate services and facilities to meet all needs. Some roads may open later or close earlier due to snowfall. The park has numerous picnic areas and campgrounds, as well as restaurants and lodgings, and there are warming huts for winter users.

Before you start visiting the sights, assess your desires and abilities. If time is limited, pick a single area, such as the Grand Canyon of the Yellowstone or the Norris Geyser Basin, and don't try to do everything. The 370 mi of public roads in the park are both a blessing and a curse, and one of the things that will definitely determine your routes as you visit the park. The park has been upgrading roads during the past decade and now there are wider, smoother routes in many areas of the park. Significantly, the construction over Sylvan Pass between Fishing Bridge and the East Entrance is now complete, as is construction of U.S. 14/16/20 from the East Entrance to Cody. However, work is now beginning on the park road from Madison to Norris so expect some short (30-minute) delays there from late May to late August until 2003. That road will close for construction each year in late August. Also, plans are in the works to begin reconstruction of the park road between Tower and Canyon over Dunraven Pass in 2002. Once that project starts, that stretch of park road will be closed to all travel throughout the summer season. Check with park rangers to determine where you'll encounter construction delays, then give yourself plenty of time and enjoy the scenery and wildlife.

There are summer-staffed visitor centers throughout the park and a busy schedule of guided hikes, evening talks, and campfire programs, which are detailed in the park newsletter, *Discover Yellowstone.* In winter some centers and warming huts are open and distribute information about trails and activities. Pamphlets describing hot-spring basins are available for 50¢ at each site or visitor center.

As you explore the park keep this important thought in mind: this is not an amusement park. It is a wild place. The animals may seem docile or tame, but they are wild and every year careless visitors are injured, sometimes even killed, when they venture too close. Particularly dangerous are female animals with their young, and bison, which can turn and charge in an instant. (Watch their tails, when they are standing up or crooked like a question mark, the bison is agitated.) ✉ *Box 168, Yellowstone National Park, WY 82190,* ☎ *307/344–7381; 307/344–2386 TTD,* ℻ *307/344–2005,* 🕸 *www.nps.gov/yell.* 💲 *7-day pass good for both Yellowstone and Grand Teton National Parks: $20 per motor vehicle, $10 nonmotorized entry permit, $10 hike or bicycle, $15 motorcycle or snowmobile.* ⊘ *Year-round to Mammoth; open early May–Sept. in other areas; open winter season mid-Dec.–Feb. to over-snow vehicles and transportation methods (skis/snowshoes) only.*

The **South Entrance Road** to Yellowstone National Park enters from Grand Teton National Park, passes Lewis Lake, and follows along the sometimes steep-sided path of the Lewis River. At **West Thumb,** you reach Yellowstone Lake. The park's roads are in a figure-eight pattern and you can follow them in any direction. (Each entrance road links up to the 142-mi figure-eight Grand Loop Road, which includes both the Upper Loop and Lower Loop roads.) We recommend turning toward the northwest at West Thumb and heading toward the geyser basins.

The drive over **Craig Pass,** between West Thumb and Old Faithful, has been upgraded and widened.

The **Upper Geyser Basin** and its centerpiece, **Old Faithful,** is is one of Yellowstone's most popular locations in any season. The mysterious plumbing of Yellowstone has lengthened the geyser's cycle somewhat in recent years, but Old Not-So-Faithful spouts a powerful 140-ft spume that pleases spectators every 88 minutes or so. A visitor center nearby posts the approximate time of the next eruption. Marked trails and bridges lead across the river to **Geyser Hill.** You can wander downriver, too, away from crowds, to **Castle Geyser** and **Morning Glory Pool.** Also in the Old Faithful area are two geysers famous for huge, but very rare, eruptions: **Giantess Geyser** and **Giant Geyser.**

At the heart of the tourist attractions and amenities at Old Faithful is **Old Faithful Inn,** worth a visit even if you aren't staying here. An architectural marvel built in the winter of 1903 and later expanded, the log building has a six-story lobby with a huge rock fireplace and wraparound balconies high in the rafters. Note the oil painting in the dining room of Old Faithful geyser by artist Paco Young of Bozeman, Montana, which was dedicated in May 2001 as the first piece sponsored by Yellowstone National Art Trust. The Art Trust organized to provide for the creation and donation of original art by leading American artists and to encourage the use of the park as a setting in which to paint, draw, photograph, or sculpt.

Along the Lower Loop north of Old Faithful, there are two distinct geyser areas, beginning with the Old Faithful basin. The **Midway Geyser Basin** has some beautiful, richly colored, bottomless pools: former geysers Grand Prismatic Spring and Excelsior Geyser Crater. **Lower Geyser Basin** features the fumaroles, blue pools, pink mud pots, and minigeysers of **Fountain Paint Pots** (small in scale but great in variety) as well as the **Great Fountain Geyser.**

North of Lower Geyser Basin the Lower Loop follows the steaming Firehole River, providing views at times of elk and bison in the distance. A one-way circuit branches off (headed south) through the **Firehole River canyon,** which features a spring-warmed swimming hole. If you decide to go swimming, be sure to stay on the trails; two park employees were severely burned in 2000 when they ventured off them. At **Madison Junction,** traffic from the popular West Entrance joins the Lower Loop Road. The Lower and Upper Loop roads join here. On the road connecting Madison Junction with the Grand Canyon of the Yellowstone you'll see the remains of the North Fork Fire, which left a moonscape on this plateau. More than a decade after the fire, the effects are still clearly visible in the form of dead standing trees, though young trees are rapidly taking over.

At **Norris Geyser Basin,** the hottest and oldest geyser basin in the park, changes occur every year: new geysers erupt, steam vents hiss to life, hot springs suddenly stop flowing. The names of the features—Whirligig Geyser, Whale's Mouth, Emerald Spring, and Arch Steam Vent—are often apt descriptions. Rangers can tell you what new formations to look for. Walk west through **Back Basin,** where the huge, unpredictable **Steamboat Geyser** has come dramatically to life in recent years, but don't wait for it: it blows 300 ft about once a year. To the east, the smaller, colorful **Porcelain Basin** has a 1-mi boardwalk and, usually, a lot of people. You can sometimes see the whitish basin floor bulge and pulsate from underground pressure.

North of Norris on the Upper Loop is **Mammoth Hot Springs.** Many travelers skip this section of the loop, though it includes some spectacular views, including those of **Roaring Mountain,** which looks like a giant pile of melted vanilla ice cream. Mammoth is the gateway for the North Entrance. Here you'll find full services; the colony of old, stone military buildings that are now the park headquarters; and the **Horace Albright Visitor Center,** with the park's largest assemblage of information, exhibits, and publications as well as historic archives for researchers. Antlered elk wander on the grass, and during the fall, bugling bulls collect their harems. The hot springs drop down terraces on the mountainside just west of the headquarters and hotel. Though the springs' flow has diminished in recent years, the **Minerva Terrace** is worth a look. You can hike a boardwalk from the top to the bottom of the huge white hot-spring constructions.

Continue clockwise on the Upper Loop. You'll pass the 60-ft **Undine Falls.** Farther along the Upper Loop, a short trail leads to the huge stump of a petrified redwood tree. Soon you reach **Tower-Roosevelt.** Here you can take the Northeast Entrance Road up the **Lamar River valley,** a favorite haunt of bison and wolves.

If you drive a short way east up Chittenden Road, which intersects the Upper Loop midway between Tower-Roosevelt Junction and Canyon, you can hike 3 mi to the top of **Mt. Washburn** (10,243 ft) for an unparalleled view of the region. You'll have a view toward the Grand Canyon of the Yellowstone, the Beartooth Mountains to the northeast, and the mosaic created by forest fires in 1988. South of Chittenden Road, the Upper Loop crosses over **Dunraven Pass**; in recent years, grizzlies have often been seen in a meadow here, however a road improvement project slated to begin in 2002 will close this road for about three years. From the junction of the Upper and Lower loops just north of **Canyon,** you can turn south toward Yellowstone Lake or head west again to Norris and south toward Madison Junction.

The magnificent **Grand Canyon of the Yellowstone** formed where water draining from Yellowstone Lake cut deep into an ancient lava flow. Just south of Canyon is a road to the 109-ft **Upper Falls,** not as high as the more spectacular Lower Falls, but well worth a visit. You can also drive across Chittenden Bridge above the Upper Falls to view the canyon from a paved road that runs about 2 mi along the South Rim. A short hike brings you to **Artist Point,** and adventurous hikers can go farther along the South Rim on various trails. The Grand Loop Road continues along the North Rim to **Canyon,** where there is a lodge and campground. From here you can backtrack along the one-way North Rim Drive to see more of the canyon. Short paths lead to scenic overlooks, including **Inspiration Point,** that provide great views of the canyon and of the breathtaking 308-ft **Lower Falls.** From Inspiration Point, you can also hike 3 mi along the **North Rim Trail,** with still more river and falls views.

The Lower Loop leads from Canyon south to **Fishing Bridge,** where the Yellowstone River drains Yellowstone Lake. Although you can't fish here anymore—it's too popular with grizzly bears—it's a nice place for a stroll, though do make a little noise to let bears know you are in the area. The East Entrance Road heads east from Fishing Bridge over **Sylvan Pass** to Cody. In the winter, this is a favorite, if rather harrowing, entrance for snowmobilers, who ride the park's snow-packed roads. There are plans to restrict snowmobiling in the park, but it is still possible to snowmobile through at least March of 2003, and possibly longer depending on the outcome of an ongoing study. Park outfitters have begun using cleaner, quieter four-stroke snowmobiles.

THE CHANGING WORLD OF YELLOWSTONE

YELLOWSTONE IS DEFINITELY NOT a sleepy world of natural wonders. The park does, truly, feel alive when you see mud pots, steam vents, fumaroles, and paint pots—all different aspects of the park's geyser basins, and all intriguing. Beyond the geyser activity, seasonal changes in wildlife and vegetation make Yellowstone fascinating to visit over and over again.

Though Old Faithful continues to spew routinely, even it has changed in recent years due to various factors. The geyser now erupts about every 88 minutes (up from about every 78 minutes in 1990), and it may look different each time. Monitoring shows Old Faithful almost always spews forth the same amount of water at each eruption, but how it does so varies. Sometimes it shoots higher and faster, while other times it lasts longer, but doesn't reach so high into the sky.

Other geyser basin features aren't so reliable. The force and nature of the various geysers depends on several factors, including the complex underground plumbing at Yellowstone. Rangers say the greatest threats to the geyser basin activity are earthquakes (which occur regularly in the region, though they are usually very small tremors), and the impact caused by people. In past years, for example, people threw hundreds of coins into the bright blue Morning Glory Pool. The coins eventually clogged the pool's water vents, causing it to turn from a bright blue color to a sickly green. Though it has been cleaned and people are warned not to throw anything into it, the Morning Glory Pool has never regained its pristine color.

Besides its unique geology related to geyser basins, Yellowstone has many other faces to present to visitors. There are petrified forests and fossil remains of both plants and animals. The ongoing ecological development of the region draws widespread interest. Efforts to control movement of bison—to keep them from wandering out of the park during the winter months to seek food—and the reintroduction of wolves to the ecosystem are just two examples of issues that quickly polarize people living in, or visiting, the region around Yellowstone.

Wolves were returned to Yellowstone in 1995. They acclimated so well that they quickly formed several packs, some of which have ventured outside the park's boundaries. Their presence has had lasting effects on wildlife populations. The wolves feed on both elk and buffalo, and park rangers have reported a significant decline in the Yellowstone coyote population. Since the wolves are bigger and stronger than coyotes, they kill coyotes or force them to find a new range.

When massive fires tore through Yellowstone in 1988, some believed it would take generations to undo the destruction, yet the park has restored itself from the effects of those fires already. However, additional wildfires in 2000 and 2001 mean more years to regenerate both trees and undergrowth. Certainly when you visit Yellowstone now you will see reminders of fires—vast areas of stark, dead trees. But you will also see the new growth. Lodgepole pine forests need fire to release their seeds and once seeds get a start, trees grow quickly. The new growth provides excellent hiding cover for animals, making it harder for visitors to see wildlife like elk or deer.

The constant changes in Yellowstone, created by shifts in underground plumbing at the geyser basins, the territorial movements of animals, and the regeneration of plant life, make the park a new experience every time you visit.

— Candy Moulton

Yellowstone Lake was formed by glaciers. From Bridge Bay, at the lake's northern end, you can take a boat cruise, with fine views of the Absaroka Mountains and the **Lake Yellowstone Hotel.** The hotel (built in 1891, with renovations and additions through the 1920s and a centennial restoration in 1991) is the oldest surviving lodging in any national park. Columns, gables, and decorative moldings give it a distinctive neo-Colonial air.

The Lower Loop follows the west shore of the lake south from Bridge Bay back to **West Thumb** and the South Entrance Road.

OFF THE
BEATEN PATH

BEARTOOTH HIGHWAY – A scenic side trip outside the park at the northeast entrance is the 68-mi Beartooth Highway, U.S. 212. The highest highway in Montana, it runs in and out of Montana and Wyoming and over 10,947-ft Beartooth Pass. To return to Yellowstone, you'll have to backtrack. Plan to spend about three hours, round-trip. Switchbacks cut into steep cliffs allow cars up to spectacular views of granite peaks, snowfields, and lakes. You can make the trip even better, and longer, by taking the Chief Joseph Scenic Highway, Route 296, south from the Beartooth Highway toward Cody. There are no services, but you'll see the beautiful Sunlight Basin and the dramatic gorge carved by the Clarks Fork of the Yellowstone River.

Dining and Lodging

The park has six areas with lodges and full-scale restaurants open during the summer, and two areas open during the winter. They are operated by **AmFac Parks and Resorts** (✉ Yellowstone National Park, Box 165, Mammoth 82190, ☎ 307/344–7311; 307/344–7901 to contact a guest, FAX 307/344–7456, WEB www.travelyellowstone.com) and all accept major credit cards. Ask about size of beds, bathrooms, thickness of walls, and room location when you book, especially in the older hotels, where accommodations vary and upgrades are ongoing. Telephones have been put in some rooms, but there are no TVs. All park lodging is no-smoking and there are no roll-away beds.

All 11 campgrounds (under $12) have both RV and tent sites. Reservations should be made for Bridge Bay, Canyon, Grant Village, and Madison campgrounds, and for Fishing Bridge RV Park ($28) by contacting AmFac Parks and Resorts. The sites are open mid-May–late-September with some variations.

$$–$$$ ✕▥ **Lake Yellowstone Hotel.** Built in 1889 on the north end of Yellowstone Lake, the pale yellow hotel with neoclassical Greek columns
★ and huge lakefront windows is the oldest and most elegant park resort. Afternoon chamber music in the sunny lobby provides a refreshing reminder of old-style luxury tourism in the "wilderness." The color scheme throughout the hotel and its annex is varying shades of pinks from palest rose to melon. You can stay in a somewhat primitive cabin, with pine beds and paneling, or at the hotel in a room with wicker furniture and brass beds. There are phones in the hotel rooms, but not in the cabins. The restaurant ($–$$$$) is casual, with a menu that includes Thai curry shrimp and fettuccine with smoked salmon and snow peas. Restaurant reservations are required. ✉ *Lake Village. 193 rooms, 1 suite, 102 cabins. Restaurant, bar, lounge, some in-room data ports, no-smoking rooms, lake, hiking, boating, fishing, shops, piano, travel services. AE, D, DC, MC, V. Closed Oct.–mid-May.*

$$–$$$ ✕▥ **Old Faithful Inn.** You can loll in front of the lobby's roaring fire
★ and look up at wooden balconies that seem to disappear into the night sky; on those deep balconies, guests play cards, scribble at writing desks, or just relax above the hubbub. Guest-room decor ranges from brass

beds to Victorian cherrywood to inexpensive motel-style furniture. More expensive rooms face the geyser. Room phones are available in east- and west-wing rooms only. The restaurant ($$–$$$) is a huge hall centered on a fireplace of volcanic stone, and offers up shrimp scampi and chicken Forestière. Restaurant reservations are required. ⊠ *Old Faithful. 327 rooms, 79 with shared bath; 9 suites. Restaurant, bar, some in-room data ports, no-smoking rooms, hot springs, hiking, shops, piano, travel services. AE, D, DC, MC, V. Closed mid-Oct.–early May.*

$$ ✕⊞ **Mammoth Hot Springs Hotel.** Sharing its grounds with park headquarters, this is farther from some of the park's favorite attractions than other hotels, but it's also less crowded. Rooms are small, and they can be rather warm in summer, though there are fans and you can open the window. Many of the hotel rooms have been refurnished and include in-room showers; others share bathrooms down the hall. The cabins have lush lawns and are arranged around "auto courts," a 1950s touch. Some have outdoor hot tubs and all share rest-room facilities. The lobby and the restaurant ($$–$$$), which serves such regional American dishes as prime rib and chicken with Brie and raspberry sauce, have art deco motifs. Elk sometimes graze between the hotel and the Terrace Grill, an airy room with large windows offering cafeteria-style service. ⊠ *Mammoth. 97 rooms, 68 with bath; 115 cabins, 72 with bath. 2 restaurants, bar, fans, hiking, horseback riding, cross-country skiing, ice-skating, snowmobiling, shops, piano, travel services. AE, D, DC, MC, V. Closed early Oct.–mid-Dec. and mid-Mar.–early May.*

$$$ ✕⊞ **Old Faithful Snow Lodge.** Built in 1998, this lodge establishes a new standard for winter lodging in Yellowstone and it brings back the grand tradition of classic park lodges with huge beams, western furnishings, a fireplace in the spacious lobby and another between the bar and restaurant, and a long sitting room with Molesworth-style writing desks and overstuffed chairs. The small mezzanine has wicker chairs and gives a view of the lobby; it's a great place for people watching. This is one of only two lodging facilities open during the winter months and there are wheelchair accessible rooms as well as phones in the rooms. Cabins near the lodge are less expensive, though they have no phones and are spartan. ⊠ *Off Old Faithful bypass Rd., next to visitor center. 100 rooms, 34 cabins. Restaurant, bar, hiking, cross-country skiing, ski shop, snowmobiling, snowshoeing, shops, solarium, travel services. AE, D, DC, MC, V. Closed mid-Oct.–mid-Dec. and mid-Mar.–early-May.*

$$ ⊞ **Canyon Lodge.** Canyon has the largest selection of lodging in the park. The Dunraven and Cascade lodges perch above the Grand Canyon of Yellowstone in the pine forest. Rooms in the lodges are truly pleasant and have telephones, light wood furniture, pine wainscoting, and brown carpeting. Some rooms are wheelchair accessible. The Canyon cabins, also in the forest, are plain duplex or fourplex units on stilts with brown wood siding and no style whatsoever. Most of them share bathroom facilities. To get to the restaurant and cafeteria from any of the lodging requires either an uphill drive or a fairly long hike of about a mile. The cafeteria fills up with a lunchtime crowd interested in sandwiches, chili, and lasagna, and the restaurant (where dinner reservations are required) features pastas, prime rib, and trout almandine. ⊠ *Canyon. 81 rooms, 532 cabins. Restaurant, bar, cafeteria, hiking, horseback riding, shops, travel services. AE, D, DC, MC, V. Closed early Sept.–late May.*

$$ ⊞ **Grant Village.** The least appetizing accommodation in the park is dull and gray and in standard motel style, but it is near the lake. You can even see the lake from some rooms, though you have to peer through the pines to do so. There are phones in the rooms, and some rooms are wheelchair accessible. The Grant Village dining room (reser-

vations required) serves steak, chicken, and seafood. It has a deck for outdoor dining. ⊠ *Grant Village. 300 rooms. Restaurant, bar, hiking, lake, boating, shops, travel services. AE, D, DC, MC, V. Closed late-Sept.–late-May.*

$–$$ ⊞ **Lake Lodge.** Behind the regal Lake Yellowstone Hotel, the lodge offers motel-style rooms and cabins. The lodge rooms are decent as are the refurbished cabins, but other cabins are shabby with peeling paint, though if all you need is a place to sleep, they are a real bargain. There are no phones and pets are allowed. ⊠ *Lake Village. 186 rooms. Bar, cafeteria, lake, hiking, coin laundry. AE, D, DC, MC, V. Closed mid-Sept.–mid-June.*

$–$$ ⊞ **Roosevelt Lodge.** Near the beautiful Lamar Valley in the park's northeast corner, this is a simple, log-cabin alternative to more expensive accommodations. The dining-room restaurant, which looks like an Old West hunting lodge, dishes up barbecued ribs, Roosevelt beans, and other western fare. There is a convenience store and gas station, and you can take a stagecoach ride. ⊠ *Tower-Roosevelt. 80 cabins, 8 with bath. Restaurant, bar, grocery, hiking, horseback riding, travel services. AE, D, DC, MC, V. Closed early Sept.–early June.*

Outdoor Activities and Sports

CYCLING

Though many people do enjoy Yellowstone via bicycle, many of the roads are narrow, with little or no shoulder and heavy traffic, making bike riding somewhat hazardous. The road from Grant Village over **Craig Pass** to Old Faithful is roomier and in better shape than most other park roads, but there is no designated bike path. The park does allow only bicycling, roller blading, roller skis, hiking, and jogging on the road between West Entrance and Mammoth Hot Springs from mid-March through late-April, so you can ride then without sharing the road with automobiles.

SNOWMOBILING

In Yellowstone, **AmFac Parks and Resorts** rents snowmobiles at the Mammoth Hot Springs Hotel or Old Faithful Snow Lodge for $95 per day; there is a $15 per week user fee.

WATER SPORTS

On Yellowstone Lake, boaters embark from **Bridge Bay** (☎ 307/344–7311); rentals are available with rowboats costing $7 per hour, and outboards renting for $30 per hour. Fishing is allowed in Yellowstone waters with an appropriate license.

Cody

❾ *52 mi from Yellowstone via U.S. 14/16/20 east.*

Cody, founded in 1896 and named for Pony Express rider, army scout, and entertainer William F. "Buffalo Bill" Cody, lies 52 mi from the East Entrance to Yellowstone National Park. The North Fork Highway, as the route is locally known, traverses a spectacular region, following the North Fork of the Shoshone River and offering views of amazing rock formations. The winding road has been completely rebuilt so you can concentrate on the views, not the driving. Cody is within easy reach of Shoshone National Forest, the Absaroka Range, the Washakie Wilderness, and the Buffalo Bill Reservoir. A brochure with a self-guided walking tour of the town's historic sites, such as the Irma Hotel, is available from the Chamber of Commerce for a $1 donation.

At the west end of this quiet little gateway town is one of the finest museums in the West: the **Buffalo Bill Historical Center.** The center houses five museums in one: the Whitney Gallery of Western Art, with works by traditional western artists, including Charlie Russell and Frederic Remington; the Buffalo Bill Historical Center, which has memorabilia of the scout and showman; the Plains Indian Museum, housing art and artifacts of the Plains tribes; the Cody Firearms Museum, with the world's largest collection of American firearms; and the Draper Museum of Natural History. ☒ *720 Sheridan Ave.,* ☎ *307/587–4771,* WEB *www.bbhc.org.* ☒ *$10 (2 days).* ☉ *Apr., daily 10–5; May, daily 8–8; June–mid-Sept., daily 7 AM–8 PM; mid-Sept.–Oct., daily 8–5; Nov.–Mar., daily 10–3.*

☺ **Cody Nite Rodeo,** more dusty and intimate than such big rodeos as Frontier Days, offers children's events, such as goat roping, in addition to the regular adult events. Contact the Cody Chamber of Commerce for information. ☒ *$10 and $12; seat prices vary with location.* ☉ *June–Aug., daily 8:30 PM.*

On Cody's western outskirts, just off the West Yellowstone Highway, is **Trail Town,** a collection of historic buildings from Wyoming's frontier days. It features a cemetery of famous local mountain men, as well as Native American and pioneer artifacts. ☒ *1831 Demaris Dr.,* ☎ *307/587–5302,* WEB *www.nezperce.com/trltown.html.* ☒ *$4.* ☉ *May–Sept., daily 8–8.*

Dining and Lodging

$–$$ ✕ **Proud Cut Saloon.** At this popular downtown eatery and watering hole, owner Del Nose serves what locals call "kick-ass cowboy cuisine": steaks, prime rib, shrimp, fish, and chicken. The western decor includes paintings, vintage photographs of Cody country, and large game mounts. ☒ *1227 Sheridan Ave.,* ☎ *307/527–6905. D, MC, V.*

$ ✕ **La Comida.** Making no claim to authentic Mexican cooking, this restaurant nevertheless has received high honors, and has been reviewed in numerous national newspapers and magazines. The owners prefer to describe their recipes as "Cody-Mex." You can order enchiladas, burritos, tacos, and chile rellenos, though it's not as spicy as similar foods would be in the Southwest. The decor is authentic Mexican and the atmosphere festive. ☒ *1385 Sheridan Ave.,* ☎ *307/587–9556. AE, D, DC, MC, V.*

$$–$$$$ ⊡ **Cody Guest Houses.** You have several options here, from a Victorian ★ guest house with lace curtains and antique furnishings to a four-bedroom lodge with a fireplace. Choose from 10 different guest houses (one- to four-bedrooms), all of them lovingly restored and elegantly decorated. These houses are meant to make you feel truly at home, so you'll find refrigerators, full kitchens, outdoor barbecue grills, and children's play areas at most of them. ☒ *1525 Beck Ave., 82414,* ☎ *307/587–6000 or 800/587–6560,* FAX *307/587–8048,* WEB *www.codyguesthouses.com. 10 houses. AE, D, MC, V.*

$$–$$$ ⊡ **Buffalo Bill Village.** This downtown development comprises three lodgings, which share many facilities. The Buffalo Bill Village Resort, consisting of log cabins with modern interiors, and the Holiday Inn Convention Center, a typical two-story brick hotel, are most noteworthy. The downtown shopping district begins just one block to the west and there is a grocery store a block away as well. ☒ *1701 Sheridan Ave., 82414,* ☎ *307/587–5544,* WEB *www.blairhotels.com. Resort 83 cabins; Inn 184 rooms. Restaurant, bar, pool, gym, meeting room, airport shuttle. AE, D, DC, MC, V.*

$$ ⊡ **Pahaska Teepee Resort.** Two mi from Yellowstone's East Entrance, these cabins in a pine forest are a good base for summer and winter recreation, both inside and outside the park. This was Buffalo Bill's original getaway in the high country. If you have a big family or group of friends traveling together, consider renting the Reunion Lodge. Some of the cabins stand alone while others are grouped in a duplex or fourplex. An extensive cross-country ski trail network has a trail-head at Pahaska and there is also a gas station and convenience store. ✉ *183 Yellowstone Hwy., 82414,* ☎ *307/527–7701 or 800/628–7791,* FAX *307/527–4019,* WEB *www.pahaska.com. 48 two-, four-, and six-room cabins. Restaurant, bar, hiking, horseback riding, cross-country skiing, ski shop, snowmobiling, travel services. D, MC, V.*

$–$$ 🛏 **Irma Hotel.** Named for Buffalo Bill's daughter, this hotel retains some frontier charm with with brass beds and period furniture in many rooms, a large restaurant, and an elaborate cherrywood bar. If you want true history be sure to stay in the hotel (which has 15 rooms) and not in the annex, which are standard contemporary rooms. During the summer, locals stage a gunfight on the porch Tuesday–Saturday at 7 PM. ✉ *1192 Sheridan Ave., 82414,* ☎ *307/587–4221 or 800/745–4762,* FAX *307/587–1775,* WEB *www.irmahotel.com. 40 rooms. Restaurant, bar. AE, D, DC, MC, V.*

Outdoor Activities and Sports

CANOEING, KAYAKING, AND RAFTING

Family river trips on the Shoshone River are offered by **River Runners** (✉ 1491 Sheridan Ave., 82801, ☎ 307/527–7238). **Wyoming River Trips** (✉ Buffalo Bill Village, Box 1541-TC, 82414, ☎ 307/587–6661 or 800/586–6661) also arranges Shoshone River trips.

GOLF

Olive Glenn Golf and Country Club (✉ 802 Meadow La., ☎ 307/587–5551 or 307/587–5308) is a highly rated 18-hole course open to the public; a Jacuzzi, pool, and two tennis courts are also on site.

Shopping

Flight West (✉ 1155 Sheridan Ave., ☎ 307/527–7800) offers designer western women's wear, leather goods for men and women, as well as books, gifts, and jewelry. Women shop at the **Plush Pony** (✉ 1350 Sheridan Ave., ☎ 307/587–4677) for "uptown western clothes" ranging from the best leather belts to the most stylish skirts, jackets, and dresses.

Northwest Wyoming A to Z

AIRPORTS AND TRANSFERS

East of Yellowstone, at Cody, Yellowstone Regional Airport is served by commuter airlines out of Denver. There is also service to the Yellowstone area through Bozeman and West Yellowstone, both in Montana.

Jackson Hole Airport lies north of Jackson in Grand Teton National Park, about 40 mi south of Yellowstone National Park. American, Sky-West, United, and United Express provide multiple flights daily, with connections in Denver, Salt Lake City, and Chicago. Scheduled jet service increases during the ski season. Flights may also be booked—often at a discount—through Jackson Hole Central Reservations.

Many lodgings have free shuttle-bus service to and from the Jackson Hole airport.

➤ AIRPORT INFORMATION: **Jackson Hole Airport** (☎ 307/733–7682, 307/733–4005, or 800/443–6931). **Yellowstone Regional Airport** (☎ 307/587–5096).

➤ TRANSFER INFORMATION: **All Star Transportation** (☎ 307/733–2888). **Alltrans** (☎ 307/733–3135 or 800/443–6133). **Jackson Hole Transportation** (☎ 307/733–3135).

BIKE TRAVEL

Wyoming roads do not offer wide shoulders, but that doesn't stop cyclists from pedaling the area's two-lane highways, either in the midst of cross-country tours or on day trips. Bikers need to be alert for motorists, who are often distracted and sometimes negligent. In addition, mountain bikes are increasingly climbing the trails that hikers favor, and there are sometimes conflicts. Various outfitters guide and supply bicyclists, and provide advice and trail maps as well.

BUS TRAVEL

During ski season, START buses operate between Jackson and the Jackson Hole Ski Resort. The fare is $4 one-way and the buses operate from 6 AM to 11 PM. During the summer season the START buses are free, operating from 6 AM to 10:30 PM. They pick up at more than 40 locations. Reservations 48 hours in advance are necessary for buses equipped for people with disabilities. The Targhee Express runs between Jackson and the Grand Targhee Ski Resort with pickups at various lodging properties in Jackson and Teton Village. Combination shuttle/Grand Targhee lift tickets are $56. Shuttle service only is $20 per day. Advance reservations are required. Nightly shuttle-bus between Jackson and Teton Village is provided by All Star Transportation.

➤ BUS INFORMATION: **ADA buses** (☎ 307/733–4521). **All Star Transportation** (☎ 307/733–2888). **Jackson Hole Express** (☎ 307/733–1719 or 800/652–9510) provides shuttle service between Jackson and the Salt Lake City Airport or Idaho Falls Airport. **START** (☎ 307/733–4521). **Targhee Express** (☎ 307/734–9754 or 307/733–3101).

CAR RENTAL

If you didn't drive to Wyoming, rent a car once you arrive. Jackson Hole Airport has major car-rental agencies, which offer four-wheel-drive vehicles and ski racks. Local rental agencies include Aspen Rent-A-Car, which rents cars, full-size vans, and sports utility vehicles, and Eagle Rent-A-Car, which has autos and also rents sport utility vehicles and snowmobiles as a package.

➤ CONTACTS: **Aspen Rent-A-Car** (⌧ 345 W. Broadway Jackson Hole, ☎ 307/733–9224 or 877/222–7736). **Eagle Rent-A-Car** (⌧ 375 N. Cache Dr. Jackson Hole, ☎ 307/739–9999 or 800/582–2128).

CAR TRAVEL

The Yellowstone area is well away from the interstates, so drivers make their way here on two-lane highways that are long on miles and scenery. From I–80, take U.S. 191 north from Rock Springs; it's about 177 mi to Jackson. From I–90, drive west from Sheridan on U.S. 14 or 14A to Cody, and cross over beautiful Sylvan Pass to Yellowstone's East Entrance. Be forewarned, however, that construction has been causing delays in the Sylvan Pass area. Check in Cody for current road information. It's about 200 mi from Sheridan to the park. Alternatively, you can take U.S. 89 from the north or U.S. 191/287 from the west, both from Montana. Be extremely cautious in the winter when whiteouts and ice are not uncommon.

ROAD INFORMATION AND EMERGENCY SERVICES

Contact the Wyoming Department of Transportation for road and travel reports October–April. For emergency situations dial 911 or contact the Wyoming Highway Patrol.

➤ CONTACTS: **Grand Teton Park Road Conditions** (☎ 307/739–3300). **Wyoming Department of Transportation** (☎ 800/WYO–ROAD). **Wyoming Highway Patrol** (☎ 800/442–9090). **Yellowstone Road Conditions** (☎ 307/344–7381).

EMERGENCIES

In Yellowstone, the Lake Clinic and Hospital is open May 21–September 15. Clinics are also in Mammoth (open year-around, weekdays), and at Old Faithful (open May 11–October 14). Grand Teton Medical Clinic is open May 23–October 3.

➤ CONTACTS: **Grand Teton Medical Clinic** (⊠ next to Jackson Lake Lodge, ☎ 307/543–2514). **Lake Clinic and Hospital** (⊠ behind the Lake Hotel, ☎ 307/242–7241). **Mammoth** (⊠ next to the post office, Mammoth, ☎ 307/344–7965). **Old Faithful Clinic and Pharmacy** (⊠ back of the parking lot behind Old Faithful Inn and next to the Post Office, ☎ 307/545–7325). **St. John's Hospital** (⊠ 625 E. Broadway Ave., Jackson, ☎ 307/733–3636). **West Park Hospital** (⊠ 707 Sheridan Ave., Cody, ☎ 307/527–7501).

FISHING

Limits and restrictions on fishing in the parks change from year to year. Anglers age 16 and older must obtain a fishing permit, $10 for a 10-day permit or $20 for a season permit. Youths ages 12–15 must obtain a free park license. The permits are available at ranger stations, visitor centers, and Hamilton Stores. Children age 11 and younger may fish for free if they are accompanied by an adult. Outside the parks on state, private, or national forest lands, Wyoming fishing licenses are required and are usually available at sporting-goods stores. The Wind River Indian Reservation has some of the best fishing in the Rockies. A separate license is required here. Contact Shoshone and Arapaho Tribes.

➤ LICENSES AND OUTFITTERS: **Shoshone and Arapaho Tribes** (⊠ Fish and Game Dept., 1 Washakie, Fort Washakie 82520, ☎ 307/332–7207). **Skinner Brothers Guides and Outfitters** (⊠ Box 859, Pinedale, WY 82941, ☎ 307/367–2270 or 800/237–9138).

LODGING

APARTMENT & CABIN RENTALS

Rendezvous Mountain Rentals handles condominiums and homes for vacation rentals in the Jackson Hole area, including properties at Jackson Hole Racquet Club, Teton Pines, and Teton Village. Vacation Condo Rental has town-house-style condominiums near Jackson with four bedrooms, three baths, a Jacuzzi, and fully equipped kitchen.

➤ LOCAL AGENTS: **Rendezvous Mountain Rentals** (⊠ Box 11338, Jackson, 83002, ☎ 307/739–9050 or 888/739–2565, FAX 307/734–2677, WEB www.rmrentals.com). **Vacation Condo Rental** (⊠ 175 S. King, Box 2228, Jackson 83001, ☎ 800/992–9948, FAX 307/739–1686).

CAMPING

In the national parks, most campgrounds are open June through September. In Grand Teton, campsites are available by advanced reservation. Fees are $12 for developed campgrounds. You can reserve a backcountry site for a $20 nonrefundable fee, but you can also take a chance that the site you want will be open and pay no fee. For campsite reservations in Yellowstone, call AmFac Parks and Resorts. There are no reservations taken for most campgrounds in the Bridger-Teton National Forest and the Targhee National Forest, and most of these fill up more slowly than in the national parks. Reservations can be made for some national forest campgrounds near Jackson through U.S. Forest Reservations.

➤ CONTACTS: **AmFac Parks and Resorts** (☎ 307/344–7311). **Bridger-Teton National Forest** (☎ 307/739–5500). **Grand Teton** (☎ 307/739–3300). **Targhee National Forest** (☎ 208/624–3151). **U.S. Forest Reservations** (☎ 800/280–2267).

SAFETY

You can encounter a grizzly bear, mountain lion, wolf, or other wild animal (like a mad female moose) anywhere in the Yellowstone ecosys-

tem that encompasses the mountains and valleys around Pine,
Dubois, Jackson, Cody, and both Grand Teton and Yellowstone
tional parks. If you are hiking on any backcountry trails, carry be
repellent, make noise, and don't travel alone. Check with forest or park
rangers for other tips to protect yourself. (There are different tactics
depending on animal species.) Always let someone know where you
are going and when you plan to return. There have been few fatal encounters with grizzlies and black bears in the region, though almost
every summer there are incidents involving bears.

Of greater concern to most people are female animals, particularly moose,
with young by their side. Those animal mothers are fiercely protective
of their offspring. Buffalo can and do charge visitors every year. The
best safety rule with all animals is to give them plenty of space.

TOURS AND EDUCATION

AmFac Parks and Resorts offers lodging and bus tours as well as multiday guided hiking tours of Yellowstone in the summer; in the winter, packages include snowmobiling, skiing, snowshoeing, and group
tours by motorized snow coach. There are special tours to view wild
wolves. They also offer one-hour narrated boat tours of northern Yellowstone Lake.

Absaroka Outfitters, from its scenic ranch, guides hunting and horseback-riding trips in the remote wilderness to the southeast of Yellowstone. Backcountry Bicycle Tours leads mountain bike tours in the area's
parks and forests, mixing in rafting and hiking for variety. Barker-Ewing
Scenic Float Trips conducts gentle scenic floats or white-water trips,
either half-day journeys or longer trips that include cookouts and
camping. For bouncier guided white-water trips, contact the similarly
named Barker-Ewing Float Trips. Flagg Ranch Village, between Grand
Teton and Yellowstone parks, runs snowmobiling and fishing trips. Cowboy Village at Togwotee Mountain has a large snowmobile-guiding operation in the winter and switches to horse pack trips in summer.

The Yellowstone Institute is based in the pastoral Lamar Valley and
offers a wide range of summer and winter courses about the ecology,
history, and wildlife of Yellowstone. Search with a historian for the trail
the Nez Perce took in their flight a century ago, or get tips from professional photographers on how to capture a trumpeter swan on film.
Facilities are fairly primitive—guests do their own cooking and stay
in heated log cabins or camp—but prices are reasonable and there's
no better way to get out from behind the windshield and learn what
makes the park tick. Some programs are specifically designed for
young people and families.

➤ CONTACTS: **Absaroka Outfitters** (✉ Box 929, Dubois 82513, ☎ 307/
455–2275). **AmFac Parks and Resorts** (✉ Yellowstone National Park,
Mammoth 82190, ☎ 307/344–7901). **Backcountry Bicycle Tours** (✉
Box 4029, Bozeman, MT 59772, ☎ 406/586–3556). **Barker-Ewing Float
Trips** (✉ 45 W. Broadway, Box 3032, Jackson 83001, ☎ 800/448–
4202). **Barker-Ewing Scenic Float Trips** (✉ Box 100-J, Moose 83012,
☎ 307/733–1800 or 800/365–1800). **Cowboy Village at Togwotee
Mountain** (✉ Box 91, Moran 83013, ☎ 307/543–2847; 800/543–2847
outside WY). **Flagg Ranch Village** (✉ Box 187, Moran 83013, ☎ 307/
543–2861 or 800/443–2311). **Yellowstone Institute** (✉ Box 117, Yellowstone National Park 82190, ☎ 307/344–2294).

VISITOR INFORMATION

➤ TOURIST INFORMATION: **Cody Chamber of Commerce** (✉ 836 Sheridan Ave., Box 2777, Cody 82414, ☎ 307/587–2297, FAX 307/527–6228,
WEB www.codychamber.org). **Dubois Chamber of Commerce** (✉ Box

632, Dubois 82513, ☎ 307/455–2556, FAX 307/455–3168, WEB www.
dteworld.com/duboiscc). **Jackson Hole Chamber of Commerce** (✉ 990
W. Broadway, Box E, Jackson 83001, ☎ 307/733–3316, FAX 307/733–
5585, WEB www.jacksonholeinfo.com). **Jackson Hole Ski Resort** (✉ Box
290, Teton Village 83025, ☎ 307/733–2292 or 800/443–6931, FAX 307/
733–2660, WEB www.jacksonhole.com). **Pinedale Chamber of Commerce**
(✉ 32 E. Pine St., Pinedale 82941, ☎ 307/367–2242, FAX 307/367–6830,
WEB www.pinedalechamber.com). **Snow report** (☎ 307/733–4005).

NORTHEAST WYOMING

Separated from Yellowstone by the Bighorn Basin, the Bighorn Mountains should not be overlooked by lovers of high places. Topped by the
200,000-acre Cloud Peak Wilderness Area, the mountains offer good
fishing, good hiking (the terrain is often very rocky, the result of glacia-
tion), plenty of wildlife, and some fascinating relics of ancient aboriginal
residents. Friendly little towns dot the Bighorns' eastern slope, but the
"big" town is Sheridan.

The area has not been heavily promoted, though it has a rich history,
especially of 19th-century warfare between the frontier military and
Native Americans. Even richer is its lode of coal, which lies just below
the surface mostly east of Sheridan and near Gillette, that has brought
multinational companies in to operate strip mines. More recently coal-
bed methane reserves are being developed in the region. It's the top-
soil above the coal seams, however, that maintains the area's most
characteristic and enduring element—ranches. Dude ranching had its
start here, and many of the dudes were so loyal to this country that
they married locals and moved west permanently.

This is the heart of energy-boom country, surrounded by coal mines
and oil fields. Farther to the east, the Black Hills rise from the Powder River basin and lead into South Dakota.

Sheridan

🔟 *149 mi from Cody via U.S. 14 east.*

The country's first dude ranches opened for business around Sheridan
in the early 1900s. Sheridan is what you'd expect a western town to
be. Main Street, unlike so many downtowns, is still vital and bustling,
crowded with false-front stone and brick buildings, some of which date
back to the turn of the 20th century. The refurbished art deco **Wyo
Theater** (✉ 42 N. Main St., ☎ 307/672–9048) hosts special events from
time to time. A narrow storefront on Main holds **King Ropes and Saddlery** (✉ 184 N. Main St.), and behind it is a free museum with a collection of cowboy memorabilia assembled by owner Don King.

The **Trail End State Historic Site** is the former home of Wyoming governor, U.S. senator, and rancher John B. Kendrick and is the closest
Sheridan comes to a historical museum. Built in the Flemish Revival
style, the 1913 house features elegant hand-carved woodwork and a
third-floor ballroom. Turn-of-the-20th-century furnishings and
Kendrick's memorabilia decorate the house. Out back is a sod-roof log
cabin built in 1878. ✉ *400 Clarendon Ave.,* ☎ *307/674–4589,* WEB
www.trailend.org. 🎟 *$2.* ⊙ *Apr.–May, daily 1–4 except Memorial week-
end, 10–5; June–Aug., daily 9–6; Sept.–mid-Dec., daily 1–4.*

Not far from the center of town is the **Sheridan Inn,** with 69 gables
sprouting all over its long roof. On the National Register of Historic
Places, the inn was once considered the finest between Chicago and
the Pacific, luring the likes of Herbert Hoover, Will Rogers, and Ernest

Hemingway. Cowboys no longer ride their horses into the bar. Lunch is served year-around. There's also a gift shop, and tours are led by volunteers. ⊠ *856 Broadway,* ☎ *307/674–5440.* ☉ *Weekdays 11–2 and 5–9, weekends 11–2 and 5–10.*

In the Bighorn Mountains, 70 mi west of Sheridan along scenic U.S. 14 and Alternate U.S. 14 (the roads fork at Burgess Junction), is the **Medicine Wheel,** a site sacred to Native Americans, from which you can see the entire Bighorn Basin. The origin of the Medicine Wheel is unknown. It is made of rocks arranged in the shape of a hub and spokes, and it attracts Native Americans from many tribes. To protect the area, access to the wheel is restricted to foot travel (1½-mi hike to the site), except for individuals with physical disabilities, who are allowed to drive in from the highway. Alternate U.S. 14 is open only from about June through September.

Dining and Lodging

$$–$$$$ ★ ✕ **Ciao Bistro.** Nine tables are squeezed into this European-style café's cramped quarters. There's an impressive array of fine food on the menu. Try the lamb shanks, Chilean sea bass, or horseradish-crusted halibut. ⊠ *120 N. Main St.,* ☎ *307/672–2838. No credit cards.*

$ ✕ **Silver Spur.** You have to look closely to spot this breakfast place. It may appear a little dingy, but the helpings are cowboy-size and the omelets are well prepared. ⊠ *832 N. Main St.,* ☎ *307/672–2749. No credit cards. No dinner.*

$$$$ 🏠 **Eaton's Guest Ranch.** This is the place credited with creating the dude ranch, and it's still going strong after more than a century as a working cattle ranch. West of Sheridan on the edge of the Bighorn National Forest, it offers horseback riding, fishing, cookouts, and pack trips. The ranch can accommodate 125 guests, and reservations should be made by March. The facilities are a collection of cabins and the main lodge. All meals are included. ⊠ *270 Eaton's Ranch Rd., Wolf 82844,* ☎ *307/655–9285 or 800/210–1049,* FAX *307/655–9269,* WEB *www.eatonsranch.com. 51 cabins. Dining room, pool, hiking, horseback riding, fishing. MC, V. Closed Oct.–May. FAP.*

$$–$$$ ★ 🏠 **Spahn's Big Horn Mountain Bed and Breakfast.** Ron and Bobbie Spahn have guest rooms and cabins at their soaring log home 15 mi west of Sheridan. The rooms have tongue-and-groove woodwork and peeled-log beams. Ruffled curtains and peeled-log beds complete the look. They offer far more than a traditional B&B: horseback riding, cookouts, and guided tours that include a "moose safari." Full breakfasts are provided, and other meals are available by arrangement. ⊠ *Box 579, Big Horn 82833,* ☎ *307/674–8150,* WEB *www.bighorn-wyoming.com. 4 rooms. Dining room, horseback riding, travel services. MC, V. BP.*

$$ 🏠 **Best Western Sheridan Center Motor Inn.** A favorite with bus tours, this motel has four buildings connected by a sky bridge over Main Street. These rooms are typical motel, but some have pole furniture and blue and green tones. ⊠ *612 N. Main St., 82801,* ☎ *307/674–7421,* FAX *307/672–3018,* WEB *www.bestwestern.com/sheridancenter. 138 rooms. 2 restaurants, bar, indoor pool, sauna, spa, recreation room. AE, D, DC, MC, V.*

$$ 🏠 **Sheridan Holiday Inn.** This five-floor lodging with a western theme is five minutes from the center of town. The lobby's soaring four-story atrium is accented with plants. From the overstuffed couches and chairs you can watch and listen to a waterfall that cascades from the second story. ⊠ *1809 Sugarland Dr., 82801,* ☎ *307/672–8931 or 800/465–4329,* FAX *307/672–6388,* WEB *www.holiday-inn.com. 212 rooms, 7 sites. Restaurant, bar, indoor pool, hair salon, hot tub, sauna, putting green, gym, racquetball, business services, convention center, meeting room, airport shuttle. AE, D, DC, MC, V.*

$ ▣ **Mill Inn.** An old mill by a bridge is incorporated into this motel on the east side of town. The building has six stories, but the top four floors are business offices. The furniture in the remodeled guest rooms came from a dude ranch, so it has a definite western style. ⊠ *2161 Coffeen Ave., 82801,* ☎ *307/672–6401 or 888/357–6455,* ℻ *307/672–6401,* WEB *www.sheridanmillinn.com. 45 rooms. Breakfast room, gym. AE, D, MC, V. CP.*

CAMPING

Bighorn National Forest has several campgrounds, but you can camp anywhere away from the highways for free; contact the **Bighorn National Forest** (⊠ 1969 S. Sheridan Ave., Sheridan 82801, ☎ 307/672–0751, WEB www.fs.fed.us/r2/bighorn) for more information. Like many Wyoming towns, Sheridan makes campers welcome for a night of free tenting in **Washington Park,** along Little Goose Creek along Coffeen Avenue. The **Big Horn Mountain KOA Campground** (⊠ 63 Decker Rd., Box 35A, Sheridan 82801, ☎ 307/674–8766) has 35 tent sites, two Kamper Kabins that sleep four, and 80 trailer slots.

Shopping

The suburban malls that have drained so many downtowns are absent in Sheridan, where Main Street is lined with fascinating, mostly home-grown, businesses. Don't miss **King Ropes and Saddlery** (⊠ 184 N. Main St., ☎ 307/672–2702 or 800/443–8919), where hard-core cowboys the world over shop for the tools of the trade. From Stetson hats to bridle bits, you can get an entire rancher's repertoire, including a hand-carved saddle costing thousands of dollars. Enormous racks in the back hold every kind of rope imaginable, and professional cowboys are often here trying out the hemp on a dummy steer. For an excellent selection of both local and general-interest books, try the **Book Shop** (⊠ 117 N. Main St., ☎ 307/672–6505). Anglers will want to visit the **Fly Shop of the Big Horns** (⊠ 377 Coffeen Ave., ☎ 307/672–5866).

Big Horn

❶ *10 mi south of Sheridan on Rte. 335.*

If you're not staying at a ranch and you want to get a look at one of the West's finest, visit the **Bradford Brinton Memorial** on the old Quarter Circle A Ranch. It's near Big Horn, a small town with tree-lined streets and mountain views. The Brinton family didn't exactly rough it in this 20-room clapboard home, complete with libraries, fine furniture, and silver and china services. A reception gallery hangs changing exhibits from the Brinton art collection, which features such western artists as Charles M. Russell and Frederic Remington. ⊠ *239 Brinton Rd.,* ☎ *307/672–3173.* ☜ *$3.* ☉ *May 15–Labor Day, daily 9:30–5.*

Sheridan and Big Horn are access points to the **Bighorn National Forest,** which has a variety of hiking trails and camping spots for use in the summer, and which is a popular snowmobiling area in the winter. ⊠ *1969 S. Sheridan Ave.,* ☎ *307/672–0751,* WEB *www.fs.fed.us/r2/bighorn.*

OFF THE
BEATEN PATH
BIG HORN EQUESTRIAN CENTER – Continue west beyond the town of Big Horn on Route 28 and you'll come to a huge expanse of green fields where locals play polo—yes, polo—on Sunday in the summer. English and Scottish families brought polo to this area in the 1890s, and now the Big Horn Polo Club is opening its 65 acres of turf to other summer events as well, from youth soccer to bronc riding. It's free to watch, and you can almost always find someone willing to explain the sport. ⊠ *Near state bird farm, on Rte. 28,* ☎ *800/453–3650.*

Buffalo

12 *25 mi south of Big Horn via I–90, U.S. 87, and Rte. 335.*

Buffalo is a trove of history and a hospitable little town in the foothills below Big Horn Pass. This is the area where cattle barons who wanted free grazing and homesteaders who wanted to build fences fought it out in the Johnson County Invasion of 1892. Nearby are the sites of several skirmishes between the U.S. military and Native Americans along the Bozeman Trail.

The **Jim Gatchell Memorial Museum** is the kind of small-town museum that's worth stopping for. It contains Native American, military, outlaw, and ranching artifacts collected by a local druggist who was a close friend of area Native Americans. ✉ *100 Fort St.,* ☎ *307/684–9331,* WEB *www.jimgathcell.com.* 🎫 *$4.* ☼ *Mid-Apr.–Dec., Mon–Sat. 9–8, Sun. noon–5.*

The **Fetterman Massacre Monument** (✉ 12 mi north of Buffalo, just off I–90, obtain directions at Fort Phil Kearny) is a rock monolith dedicated to the memory of Lt. William J. Fetterman and his 80 men, who died in a December 21, 1866 battle with Lakota warriors led by Red Cloud.

13 The frontier army occupied **Fort Phil Kearny** for only a couple of years in the mid-1860s to protect travelers headed to Montana's gold fields. The region became bitterly contested by the army and the Plains Indians. No original buildings remain at the state historic site (they were burned as soon as the military abandoned the fort in 1868), but the fort site is marked and the visitor center has good details. The stockade around the fort has been re-created. ✉ *12 mi north of Buffalo on I–90,* ☎ *307/684–7629 or 307/777–7014,* WEB *www.philkearny.vcn.com.* 🎫 *$1.* ☼ *Mid-May–Sept., daily 8–6.*

Dining and Lodging

$$–$$$ ✗ **Winchester Steak House.** You can tie up your car in front of the hitch
★ racks before this western-style eatery in a false-front building. The menu has steak, and more steak, plus a large rock fireplace and small bar. Locals rave about the place. ✉ *117 Hwy. 16 E,* ☎ *307/684–8636. MC, V.*

$ ✗ **Colonel Bozemans.** Literally on the Bozeman Trail, Colonel Boze-
★ man's serves decent food amid western memorabilia. Local favorites include buffalo steak and prime rib. You can dine outdoors on the deck. ✉ *675 E. Hart St.,* ☎ *307/684–5555. AE, D, MC, V.*

$ ✗ **Tom's Main Street Diner.** This tiny place dishes up huge burgers and
★ sandwiches in short order. ✉ *41 N. Main St.,* ☎ *307/684–7444. AE, D, MC, V.*

$$$$ 🏨 **Paradise Guest Ranch.** The children's programs at Paradise are outstanding, and there's plenty for adults as well, including some incredible country through which to horseback ride. All rooms are in log cabins that stair-step their way up the hillside above French Creek. Cabins have kitchenettes, and some have fireplaces and washers and dryers. When not out riding, you can hike mountain trails, take part in the excellent fly-fishing program, or relax by the pool. Nightly activities range from picnics to square dancing. Youths ages 13–17 take an overnight pack trip, and adults or families can take several-day pack trips to high-mountain lakes. September is adults only; one week is geared toward women. There are no phones or TVs here—and not even cell phone service. ✉ *Hunter Creek Rd., of U.S. 16, 82834,* ☎ *307/684–7876,* FAX *307/684–9054,* WEB *www.paradiseranch.com. 18 cabins. Bar, dining room, kitchenettes, pool, pond, hot tub, massage, basketball, hiking, horseback riding, horseshoes, fishing, shops, piano, recreation* room, library, children's programs (all ages), playground, coin laundry, meeting rooms, travel services, airport shuttle. No credit cards. Closed Oct.–Apr. MAP.

$$ ⊡ **Comfort Inn.** Several blocks from downtown, this motel is along the city's bike and walking path. ⊠ 65 U.S. 16 E, 82834, ☎ 307/684–9564 or 800/228–5150, WEB www.comfortinn.com. 41 rooms. Breakfast room, hot tub. AE, D, DC, MC, V. CP.

$ ⊡ **Blue Gables Motel.** The cabins of this highway-side motel cluster in a U-shape. The motel is a homey place with Old West collectibles and quilts. Rooms do not have phones. ⊠ 662 N. Main St., 82834, ☎ 307/684–2574 or 800/684–2574. 17 rooms. No-smoking rooms, pool. D, MC, V.

En Route Driving across the **Powder River basin** between Buffalo and Gillette may bore people more accustomed to four lanes of bumper-to-bumper traffic. It helps to read the history in the landscape: the draws where the Sioux hunted and hid from white interlopers, the uplifts where coal seams rise to the surface, and the ranches where cattle barons once grazed their stock. If this is the sort of thing that appeals to you, you may want to take the longer route to Gillette and forsake I–90 for U.S. 16/14. The rolling countryside may look as if it's been turned back to the deer and antelope, but on these back roads and around eye-blink towns such as Ucross and Spotted Horse, some of the country's wealthiest people have built ranch retreats.

Gillette

⑭ *70 mi from Buffalo on I–90.*

Gillette has worked hard to make itself presentable, but you don't have to go far to find a shovel bigger than a house at one of the giant strip mines nearby. Seventeen miles south of Gillette at the **Eagle Butte Coal Mine,** shovels and haul trucks dwarf anything in a science-fiction movie. There's a surprising amount of wildlife, from falcons to deer to bobcats, dwelling in and around the huge pits. Register for the summer tours at the Gillette Visitors Center. ⊠ *Gillette Visitors Center, Flying J Travel Plaza, 1810 S. Douglas Hwy.,* ☎ *307/686–0040 or 800/544–6136.* ⊠ *Free.* ⊙ *Tours June–Aug., daily 9–11.*

OFF THE BEATEN PATH   **DEVILS TOWER** – Sixty miles east of Gillette, I–90 begins rising into the Black Hills. A side trip north takes in Devils Tower, a butte that juts upward 1,280 ft above the plain of the Belle Fourche River. Native American legend has it that the tower was corrugated by the claws of a bear trying to reach some children on top, but geologists say it's the core of a defunct volcano. The tower was a tourist magnet long before a spaceship landed here in the movie *Close Encounters of the Third Kind.* Teddy Roosevelt made it the nation's first national monument in 1906. ⊠ *Rte. 24, 6 mi off U.S. 14,* ☎ *307/467–5283,* WEB *www.nps.gov/deto.* ⊠ *$4.* ⊙ *Visitor center June–Labor Day, daily 8–8.*

Dining and Lodging

$$ ✕ **Packard's Grill.** This family restaurant is a cross between a brewpub and a sports bar, with sports team memorabilia on the walls. Sandwiches are the standard fare. ⊠ *408 S. Douglas Hwy.,* ☎ *307/686–5149. AE, D, DC, MC, V.*

$–$$ ✕ **Bailey's Bar & Grill.** This handsome, shadow-filled restaurant in an ★ old brick building turns out delicious sandwiches and burgers for lunch, and dinners that include steak, seafood, and chicken. Sit at tall tables or at the long bar and enjoy a good selection of tap beers. ⊠ *301 S. Gillette Ave.,* ☎ *307/686–7678. AE, D, MC, V.*

$$ ⊞ **Best Western Tower West Lodge.** On the west side of town, you can find large rooms here done in beige and teal. Public space is aplenty too with an outdoor courtyard and a lobby with leather couches and chairs grouped around the fireplace. ⊠ *109 N. U.S. 14/16, 82716,* ☎ *307/686–2210,* FAX *307/682–5105. 189 rooms. Restaurant, bar, indoor pool, gym, hot tub. AE, D, DC, MC, V.*

$$ ⊞ **Clarion Western Plaza.** Travelers with a yen for exercise will appreciate
★ the pool of lap-swimming proportions in this motel where everything is under one roof. Rooms are decorated in soft teal and mauve. Steak and seafood are served at the Sierra Café. ⊠ *2009 S. Douglas Hwy., 82718,* ☎ *307/686–3000 or 800/686–3368,* FAX *307/686–4018. 159 rooms. Restaurant, indoor pool, sauna, gym. AE, D, DC, MC, V.*

$ ⊞ **Quality Inn.** Right off I–90, this motel has large rooms but no frills, except for a free Continental breakfast. Antelope often graze nearby. ⊠ *1004 E. U.S. 14/16, 82716,* ☎ *307/682–2616 or 800/621–2182,* FAX *307/687–7002. 80 rooms. Breakfast room. AE, D, DC, MC, V. CP.*

Nightlife and the Arts

Pop and country performers make occasional appearances at Gillette's **Camplex** (⊠ 1635 Reata Dr., ☎ 307/682–0552 or 307/682–8802, WEB www.cam-plex.com). A variety of horse, livestock, and rodeo events also are held at the facility.

En Route The route from Gillette to Casper goes through the Thunder Basin National Grasslands and then crosses the Teapot Dome area, which gave its name to an oil-leasing scandal in the 1920s.

Northeast Wyoming A to Z

AIRPORTS

Sheridan and Gillette are served by United Express out of Denver.
➤ AIRPORT INFORMATION: **Campbell County Airport** (⊠ 2000 Airport Rd., Suite 108 Gillette, ☎ 307/686–1042).

BUS TRAVEL

The northeast corner, like central Wyoming, is well served by Powder River Transportation.
➤ BUS INFORMATION: **Powder River Transportation** (⊠ 1700 E. U.S. 14/16, Gillette, ☎ 307/682–0960 or 800/237–7211).

CAR TRAVEL

Two interstates join at Buffalo: I–25 comes up from Denver, Cheyenne, Casper, and points south; I–90 comes from South Dakota and the Black Hills in the east and from Montana to the north.

EMERGENCIES

➤ CONTACTS: Gillette: **Campbell County Memorial Hospital** (⊠ 501 S. Burma St., Gillette, ☎ 307/682–8811). Sheridan: **Sheridan County Memorial Hospital** (⊠ 1401 W. 5th St., Sheridan, ☎ 307/672–1000).

VISITOR INFORMATION

➤ TOURIST INFORMATION: **Buffalo Chamber of Commerce** (⊠ 55 N. Main, Buffalo 82834, ☎ 307/684–5544 or 800/227–5122, WEB www.buffalowyo.org). **Campbell County Chamber of Commerce** (⊠ 314 S. Gillette Ave., Gillette 82716, ☎ 307/682–3673, WEB www.gillette.org). **Gillette Convention and Visitor's Bureau** (⊠ 59 1810 S. Douglas Hwy., Gillette 82718, ☎ 307/686–0040 or 800/544–6136, FAX 307/686–1258, WEB www.visitgillette.net). **Sheridan Chamber of Commerce** (⊠ Box 707, Sheridan 82801, ☎ 307/672–2485, WEB www.sheridanwyo.com).

CENTRAL WYOMING

Central Wyoming encompasses the North Platte River valley. Several pioneer trails converged along the Platte and the Sweetwater rivers and through South Pass, the easiest pass in the Rockies for covered wagons to negotiate. The North Platte River valley is one of Wyoming's important agricultural areas, but the wealth of modern central Wyoming is based on its deposits of oil, uranium, and bentonite.

Casper

🔟 *136 mi south of Gillette via Rte. 59 south, Rte. 387 west, and I–25 south; 112 mi south of Buffalo on I–25.*

Nearly in the center of Wyoming, Casper is the state's largest city. Its growth is related primarily to oil and gas exploration, although sheep and cattle ranchers run their stock on lands all around the city. Five major pioneer trails passed near or through Casper in the period 1843–70. The best known are the Oregon Trail and the Mormon Trail, both of which crossed the North Platte River in the vicinity of today's Casper. The early history of the trails and the military's role in central Wyoming is interpreted at the **National Historic Trails Interpretive Center.** Projected onto a series of screens 11 ft high and 55 ft wide, a film shows Wyoming trail sites and scenes of wagon travelers. You can climb into a wagon to see what it was like to cross the river, or learn about Mormon pioneers who traveled west with Handcarts in 1856. ⊠ *1501 N. Poplar,* ☎ *307/265–8030, www.trib.com/~rlund/NHTIC.html.* 🎟 *$6.* ☺ *Year-round.*

The early military history in the region is interpreted at **Fort Caspar Historic Site,** which has living history with mountain men, and military re-enactors during the Fort Caspar Rendezvous in June and at the Platte Bridge Encampment in July. ⊠ *4001 Fort Caspar Rd.,* ☎ *307/235–8462,* WEB *www.fortcasparwyoming.com.* 🎟 *Free.* ☺ *Site open year-round; museum mid-May–mid-Sept., Mon.–Sat. 8–7, Sun. noon–7; mid-Sept.–mid-May, weekdays 8–5.*

The **Casper Planetarium** (⊠ 904 N. Poplar St., ☎ 307/577–0310, 🎟 $2.50) has multimedia programs on astronomy and space subjects. **Werner Wildlife Museum** (⊠ 405 E. 15th St., ☎ 307/235–2108, 🎟 free, ☺ mid-May–Labor Day, daily, 10–5; Labor Day–mid-May, weekdays, 2–5) has displays of birds and animals indigenous to Wyoming. The **Tate Earth Science Center and Geological Museum** (⊠ Casper College campus, ☎ 307/268–2447, 🎟 free, ☺ weekdays, 9–5; Sat. 10–4) has displays of fossils, rocks, jade, and the fossilized parts of a brontosaurus, plus other dinosaur bones.

OFF THE
BEATEN PATH
🐾

HANDCART RANCH – The Martin's Cove Visitor Center here is operated by the Church of Jesus Christ of Latter-day Saints and has exhibits on the Sun family and ranching operation, which took place here from 1872 until the church bought the Sun Ranch in 1997. The Oregon, California, and Mormon Trails cross the ranch and it is particularly important to the Mormons because two groups of pioneers traveling with handcarts to Salt Lake City became stranded in the area by snowstorms in 1856. They had left the area along the Missouri River near Omaha, Nebraska, too late in the year to cross the mountains before winter set in. A 3½-mi trail leads to Martin's Cove, where the handcart pioneers found shelter from the cold. Visitors can push one of 100 handcarts up the trail to get a feel for this mode of transportation. The carts are loaned free, on a first-come, first-served basis; none is loaned after 3:30 and none on Sunday. ⊠ Rte. 220, 60 mi southwest of Casper, ☎ 307/328–2953, WEB www.handcart.com. 🎟 Free. ☺ Daily 8–7.

Dining and Lodging

$$–$$$$ ✕ **Poor Boys Steakhouse.** Reminiscent of a frontier mining camp or western town, this steak house at the Parkway Plaza has blue-and-white-check tablecloths and chair backs, quick service, and large portions of steak, seafood, or chicken. Salad comes in a bucket and is served with fresh, hot bread. Try the Moonshine Mama (grilled chicken breast smothered in mushrooms and Monterey Jack and cheddar cheeses); or enjoy a tantalizingly tender filet mignon and shrimp. For dessert there is Dutch apple pie and Ashley's Avalanche—a huge plate of ice cream, white-chocolate brownie, cherry-pie filling, chocolate sauce, and whipped cream. ⊠ *123 W. "E" St.,* ☎ *307/235–1777. AE, D, DC, MC, V.*

$$–$$$ ✕ **Armor's.** A quiet atmosphere with cozy booths and tables makes this a popular place for a special dinner. In addition to standards such as steaks and prime rib are blackened and Cajun entrées. ⊠ *3422 S. Energy La.,* ☎ *307/235–3000. AE, D, DC, MC, V.*

$–$$ ✕ **El Jarro.** Usually crowded, and always noisy, this place serves hearty portions of Mexican cuisine and makes a mighty fine margarita. ⊠ *500 W. "F" St.,* ☎ *307/577–0538. AE, MC, V.*

$–$$ ✕ **Sanfords Grub and Pub.** This lively spot may be a brewery, but children are welcome here in the heart of downtown. The menu is extensive and the place is decorated with 20th-century memorabilia. For those who don't eat meat, this is the Casper restaurant with the greatest variety of dishes, including pastas, pizzas, and calzones. ⊠ *241 S. Center St.,* ☎ *307/234–4555. AE, D, DC, MC, V.*

$$ 🏨 **Hampton Inn.** This is a clean and very quiet lodging, with coffeemakers and large cable TVs in rooms that have neutral walls, dark floral spreads, and an easy chair with ottoman. There's a small restaurant, Cafe José's, that serves authentic Mexican food, including enchiladas, flautas, and chimichangas. ⊠ *400 W. "F" St., 82601,* ☎ *307/235–6668,* FAX *307/235–2027. 122 rooms. Restaurant, pool, sauna. AE, D, DC, MC, V. CP.*

$ 🏨 **Parkway Plaza.** With a large convention center, the Parkway is one of Casper's busiest motels. The rooms are quiet and large, with double vanities, one inside the bathroom, and one outside. Furnishings are contemporary in the rooms, but western in the public areas. The pool has wading and diving sections. ⊠ *123 W. Center St., 82601,* ☎ *307/235–1777 or 800/270–7829,* FAX *307/235–8068,* WEB *www.parkwayplaza.net. 295 rooms. Restaurant, bar, coffee shop, indoor/outdoor pool, hot tub, sauna, gym, playground, business services, convention center, meeting rooms. AE, D, MC, V.*

$ 🏨 **Radisson.** Just off I–25, this full-service location has everything you need under one roof. The large rooms are decorated in contemporary style with muted colors. ⊠ *800 N. Poplar St., 82601,* ☎ *307/266–6000,* FAX *307/473–1010. 229 rooms. Restaurant, bar, café, indoor pool, hot tub, business services, convention center, meeting room. AE, D, DC, MC, V.*

Nightlife and the Arts

Both the Casper Symphony Orchestra and the Casper College Theater Department perform at the 465-seat **Gertrude Krampert Theater** (Casper College, ⊠ 125 College Dr., ☎ 307/268–2500). **Stage III Community Theater** (⊠ 4080 S. Poplar St., ☎ 307/234–0946) provides entertainment such as plays and other dramatic performances at various times.

Outdoor Activities and Sports

The **Platte River Parkway path** is a hiking trail adjacent to the North Platte River in downtown Casper. Access points are at Amoco Park at 1st and Poplar streets; or at Crosswinds Park, on North Poplar Street near the Casper Events Center. **Edness Kimball Wilkins State Park**

(⊠ I–25, 6 mi east of Casper, ☎ 307/577–5150) is a day-use area with picnicking, swimming, fishing, and a walking path.

Central Wyoming A to Z

AIRPORTS
Casper is served by United Express out of Denver and Delta/Skywest from Salt Lake City.
➤ AIRPORT INFORMATION: **Natrona County International Airport** (⊠ 8500 Airport Pkwy., Casper, ☎ 307/472–6688).

BUS TRAVEL
The central part of Wyoming is well served by Powder River Transportation, which connects with Greyhound Lines in Cheyenne.
➤ BUS INFORMATION: **Greyhound Lines** (☎ 307/634–7744 or 800/231–2222). **Powder River Transportation** (⊠ 1700 E. U.S. 14/16, Gillette, ☎ 307/682–0960).

EMERGENCIES
➤ CONTACT: **Wyoming Medical Center** (⊠ 1233 E. 2nd St., Casper, ☎ 307/577–7201, WEB www.wmcnet.org).

VISITOR INFORMATION
➤ TOURIST INFORMATION: **Casper Chamber of Commerce** (⊠ 500 N. Center St., 82601, ☎ 307/234–5311 or 800/852–1889, FAX 307/265–2643, WEB www.casperwyoming.org). **Casper Convention and Visitors Bureau** (⊠ 330 S. Center St., 82602, ☎ 307/234–5362 or 800/852–1889, FAX 307/261–9928, WEB www.casperwyoming.org).

SOUTHEAST WYOMING

The high plains morph into the mountains in southeast Wyoming as the rolling grasslands around Cheyenne rise to the Laramie and Medicine Bow mountain ranges at the west side of the region. Communities such as Cheyenne and Laramie still have strong western roots along with their western names.

Cheyenne sits apart from the mountainous magnet of western Wyoming. Some detractors say it's more a part of Colorado's Front Range, which runs south across the nearby border, but the area is no Colorado wanna-be. Cheyenne is a dynamic city, thriving on a mixture of state government, the military, and new industry. The University of Wyoming, the state's only four-year university, is just over the Medicine Bow Mountains in Laramie, and outside the city limits, cattle grazing on rolling hills are a reminder that the area's century-old ranching community still survives.

Cheyenne

16 *178 mi south of Casper via I–25; 110 mi north of Denver via I–25.*

Born in 1867 as the Union Pacific Railroad inched its way across the plains, Cheyenne began as a rowdy camp for railroad gangs, cowboys, prospectors heading for the Black Hills, and soldiers. It more than lived up to its nickname: "Hell on Wheels." In the late 19th century, the region's enormously wealthy cattle barons, many of them English, settled in Cheyenne. They sipped brandy at the Cheyenne Club and hired hard cases like Tom Horn to take care of their competitors on the open range. Nineteenth-century Cheyenne is remembered in the area slogan "Live the Legend" and is celebrated in July with western élan in Frontier Days.

During Frontier Days, Cheyenne is up to its neck in bucking broncs and bulls and joyful bluster. There are pancake breakfasts put on by locals, parades and pageantry, and parties that require the endurance of a cattle hand on a weeklong drive. The century-old event is now the world's largest outdoor rodeo extravaganza, dubbed the "Daddy of 'Em All."

The **Old West Museum** at Frontier Park has 30,000 pieces in all, including 125 carriages. Guided tours are geared toward children. During Frontier Days, the museum hosts the Governor's Invitational Western Art Show and Sale, in which top western wildlife and landscape artists from around the country exhibit. ⊠ *4501 N. Carey Ave.,* ☎ *307/778–7290 or 800/266–2696,* WEB *www.oldwestmuseum.org.* 🖼 *$5.* ⊙ *Sept.–May, weekdays 9–5, Sat. 11–4; June–Aug., weekdays 9–7, weekends 10–5; extended hrs during Frontier Days.*

The **Wyoming State Capitol** is a Corinthian-style structure, authorized by the Ninth Territorial Legislative Assembly in 1886 and now on the National Register of Historic Places. The dome, covered in 24-carat gold leaf and visible from all roads leading into the city, is 50 ft in diameter at the base and 146 ft high. Standing in front is a statue of Esther Hobart Morris, a proponent of women's suffrage. Wyoming is nicknamed the "Equality State" because it was the first state to give women the vote. As a result of Wyoming's small population and informal ways, it's not unusual to find the governor wandering the halls of the capitol. You can take a self-guided tour of state offices and the senate and house chambers. ⊠ *Capitol Ave.,* ☎ *307/777–7220,* WEB *www.state.wy.us.* 🖼 *Free.* ⊙ *Weekdays 8–5; May–Aug. also Sat. 9–5.*

The **Historic Governor's Mansion** was the residence of 19 Wyoming first families from 1905 to 1976, when the state built a new residence for the governor. Ornate chandeliers in nearly every room are just some of the interesting appointments. ⊠ *300 E. 21st St.,* ☎ *307/777–7878,* WEB *http://spacr.state.wy.us/sphs/govern1.htm.* 🖼 *Free.* ⊙ *Tues.–Sat. 9–5.*

One of Wyoming's nicknames is the "Cowboy State," and the premiere cowboy event is **Cheyenne Frontier Days,** held the last full week of July every year since 1897. Leading contenders in the Professional Rodeo Cowboys Association compete at Cheyenne, and there is a variety of other activities including chuck-wagon races, an Indian village and dancing, free pancake breakfasts that feed up to 12,000 people in two hours, and nightly concerts featuring top country entertainers. Reservations are a must. ⊠ *Box 2477, Cheyenne 82003,* ☎ *307/778–7222 or 800/227–6336; 800/543–2339 in WY,* WEB *www.cfdrodeo.com.* 🖼 *Rodeo $10–$22; concerts $16–$30; package plans $28–$50.*

Dining and Lodging

$$–$$$ ✕ **Little Bear Steakhouse.** Locals rave about this classic American
★ steak house with western decor. Try the New York strip steak or the rib eye. Non-steak eaters will also find seafood on the menu. ⊠ *1700 Little Bear Rd.,* ☎ *307/634–3684. AE, D, DC, MC, V.*

$–$$ ✕ **The Albany.** Historic photos of early-day Cheyenne set the tone for this downtown icon, a place that seems as old as the city itself. It's a bit dark, and the booths a bit shabby, but the American food is solid. Now if only you could get the walls to tell their stories. No doubt they've heard it all as many of the movers and shakers in Cheyenne's past (and a few in its present) have eaten here. ⊠ *1506 Capitol Ave.,* ☎ *307/638–3507. AE, D, DC, MC, V.*

$–$$ ✕ **Lexie's Café.** In the oldest home in Cheyenne, a brick building more
★ than a century old, the café has delightful breakfast and lunch menus and offers heaping platters of Mexican, Italian, and American food.

✉ *216 E. 17th St.,* ☎ *307/638–8712. AE, D, DC, MC, V. Closed Sun. No dinner.*

$–$$ ✕ **Los Amigos.** Mexican decorations on the walls complement the south-of-the-border food at this local favorite south of downtown. ✉ *620 Central Ave.,* ☎ *307/638–8591. MC, V. Closed Sun.*

$–$$$ ✕▥ **Best Western Hitching Post Inn.** State legislators frequent this hotel, known to locals as "The Hitch." It books country-western performers in the lounge. With its dark wood walls, this hotel has an elegance not found elsewhere in Cheyenne. The Cheyenne Cattle Company restaurant serves steak and other dishes in a quiet, relaxed atmosphere. Next door are opportunities for minigolf and ice-skating. ✉ *1700 W. Lincolnway, 82001,* ☎ *307/638–3301,* ℻ *307/778–7194. 166 rooms. Restaurant, coffee shop, lobby lounge, in-room data ports, refrigerators, room service, indoor and outdoor pool, gym, shop, dance club, laundry service, business services, convention center, meeting room, airport shuttle. AE, D, DC, MC, V.*

$$–$$$ ▥ **Little America Hotel and Resort.** At the intersection of I–80 and I–25, the resort's highlight is its executive golf course. Most guest rooms are in several buildings clustered around the swimming pool, and some are attached to the common public areas via a glassed-in breezeway. ✉ *2800 W. Lincolnway, 82001,* ☎ *307/775–8400 or 800/445–6945,* ℻ *307/775–8425,* 🌐 *www.littleamerica.com. 188 rooms. Restaurant, bar, coffee shop, dining room, lounge, air-conditioning, in-room data ports, some minibars, refrigerators, room service, pool, 9-hole golf course, gym, shops, nightclub, laundry service, business services, convention center, meeting rooms, airport shuttle. AE, D, DC, MC, V.*

$–$$$ ▥ **A. Drummond's Ranch Bed and Breakfast.** Halfway between Cheyenne and Laramie and bordered by Curt Gowdy State Park lands, this B&B is on 120 acres and has a 100-mi view of the Laramie Range and the Colorado Rockies. Guests include cross-country skiers and mountain bikers (the ranch conducts two- to six-hour tours for both), runners who want to train at the 7,500-ft elevation, and horseback riders (stalls are available to board a horse or other pets during your stay). Lunch and dinner can be provided for an extra charge; special diets can be accommodated. ✉ *399 Happy Jack Rd., Cheyenne 82007,* ☎ ℻ *307/634–6042,* 🌐 *www.cruising-america.com/drummond.html. 4 rooms, 2 with bath. Dining room, outdoor hot tub, library. MC, V. BP.*

$$ ▥ **Nagel Warren Mansion.** This historic mansion, built in 1888, has gorgeous woodwork, ornate staircases, period furniture and wallpaper, and lavish rooms decorated with antiques. The location is close to downtown, within walking distance of shops, and adjacent to two restaurants. Some rooms have gas fireplaces, and a full breakfast is included. ✉ *222 E. 17th St., 82001,* ☎ *307/637–3333 or 800/811–2610,* ℻ *307/638–6879. 12 rooms. Dining room, in-room data ports, no-smoking rooms, hot tub, gym, piano, library, meeting rooms. AE, MC, V. BP.*

$$ ▥ **Rainsford Inn.** Elegant surroundings and a B&B atmosphere welcome you on historic "Cattleman's Row" in the heart of downtown Cheyenne. The Cattle Baron Corner has masculine decor and overlooks 17th Street, where Cheyenne's cattle barons lived in the late 1800s. One room is suitable for people with disabilities and includes a roll-in shower. The third-floor "Grandma's Attic" is a very private retreat. All rooms have whirlpool tubs, one has a gas fireplace, and a full breakfast is included. ✉ *219 E. 18th St., 82001,* ☎ *307/638–2337,* ℻ *307/634–4506. 7 rooms. Dining room, no-smoking rooms, library. AE, MC, V. BP.*

Nightlife

For an evening of live country music and shuffling your feet along a large dance floor, try the **Cheyenne Club** (✉ 1617 Capitol Ave., ☎ 307/

635–7777). There's also live music, dancing, and drinks at the **Cowboy South** (⊠ 312 S. Greeley Hwy., ☏ 307/637–3800).

Outdoor Activities and Sports

CAMPING

As everywhere in Wyoming, camping opportunities are abundant. Cheyenne has the **Terry Bison Ranch** (⊠ I–25 Service Rd. near the Colorado state line, ☏ 307/634–4171). Besides a full-service campground and RV park (100 tent sites, 90 RV sites, 300 picnic sites, and 88 full hookups), the bison ranch—yes, there are nearly 2,000 head on the property—has a restaurant and occasional entertainment. The **Wyoming Campground and Mobile Home Park** (⊠ I–80, Exit 377, ☏ 307/547–2244) is a basic, no-frills camping area.

GOLF

The **Airport Course** (⊠ 4801 Central Ave., ☏ 307/637–6418) has 18 holes. There's a nine-hole course at **Little America Hotel and Resort** (⊠ 2800 W. Lincolnway, ☏ 307/775–8400). Play 18-holes of golf at **Prairie View** (⊠ 3601 Windmill Rd., ☏ 307/637–6420).

Shopping

Cheyenne's **Frontier Mall** (⊠ 1400 Dell Range Blvd., ☏ 307/638–2290) houses 75 specialty shops and four major department stores. It's as typical an American mall as you'll find.

Wrangler (⊠ 16th and Capitol Sts., ☏ 307/634–3048) offers a full line of traditional western clothes, ranging from Wrangler and Rocky Mountain jeans to Panhandle Slim shirts, Resistol hats, and Laredo boots. There are sizes and styles for the entire family.

En Route On your way west, midway between Cheyenne and Laramie, north of I–80 and south of Happy Jack Road (Route 210), is **Vedauwoo,** a particularly unusual area and a great place for a picnic. Springing out of high plains and open meadows are glacial remnants in the form of huge granite boulders piled skyward with reckless abandon. These one-of-a-kind rock formations, dreamscapes of gray stone, provide opportunities for hiking, climbing, and photography.

Laramie

🔟 *45 mi west of Cheyenne via I–80 and Rte. 210.*

Laramie, nestled in a valley between the Medicine Bow Mountains and the Laramie Range, was first settled when the railroad reached here in 1867. For a time it was a tough "end-of-the-rail" town. Vigilantes took care of lawbreakers, hanging them from convenient telegraph poles. Laramie today is the home of the University of Wyoming and is in the center of open-plains ranching country. Many of the historic downtown buildings hold retail shops and restaurants.

Perhaps because of the bedlam of the early days, Laramie became the site of the Wyoming Territorial Prison in 1872. Until 1903, it was the region's federal and state penal facility, locking down Butch Cassidy and other infamous frontier outlaws. Today the restored prison is the gem of **Wyoming Territorial Park,** giving life to the legends of frontier law and justice. In addition, the park contains a 19th-century railroad display, a U.S. marshals' museum, a replica of a frontier town, a living-history program, and the Horse Barn Dinner Theater. ⊠ *975 Snowy Range Rd.,* ☏ *307/745–6161 or 800/845–2287,* WEB *www.wyoprisonpark.org.* ☞ *Park only $12; dinner theater $29.95; combination ticket $35.95.* ☉ *Park Memorial Day–Labor Day, daily 9–6; dinner theater June–Aug., Wed.–Sun. 6 PM.*

For more area history, visit the **Laramie Plains Museum,** in the Ivinson mansion. Built in 1892 by Edward Ivinson, a businessman and philanthropist and one of Laramie's first settlers, the estate houses a growing collection of historical artifacts from the Laramie plains area. ✉ *603 Ivinson Ave.,* ☎ *307/742–4448,* WEB *www.laramiemuseum.org.* ⚏ *$4.* ◷ *June–Aug., Mon.–Sat. 9–6, Sun. 1–4; Sept.–May, Mon.–Sat. 1–4.*

The **University of Wyoming** (✉ 13th St. and Ivinson Ave., WEB www. uwyo.edu) offers year-round events—from concerts to football—and a number of attractions. The best place to start, for a tour or just for information, is the **UW Visitor Center** (✉ 14th St. and Grand Ave., ☎ 307/766–4075). Depending on your interests, you might want to visit the **Anthropology Museum** (☎ 307/766–5136, WEB http:// uwadmnweb.uwyo.edu/anth/museum.html), **Art Museum** (☎ 307/ 766–6622, WEB http://uwadmnweb.wyo.edu/artmuseum), **planetarium** (☎ 307/766–6514), **Entomology Museum** (☎ 307/766–2298, WEB www.uwyo.edu/ag/psisci/braconid/museum.htm), **Rocky Mountain Herbarium** (☎ 307/766–2236), or other campus museums of note.

The **University of Wyoming Geological Museum,** in a building with a dinosaur statue out front, contains the skeleton of an apatosaurus 15 ft high and 75 ft long and believed to have weighed 30 tons. Other exhibits explore the dinosaur family tree, meteorites, fossils, and earthquakes. ✉ *Northwest corner of University of Wyoming campus,* ☎ *307/766–2646 or 307/766–4218,* WEB *www.uwyo.edu/geomuseum.* ⚏ *Free.* ◷ *Weekdays 8–5, weekends 10–3.*

The **American Heritage Center** houses more than 10,000 photographs, rare books, collections of papers, and memorabilia related to such subjects as American and western history, the petroleum industry, conservation movements, transportation, and the performing arts. ✉ *2111 Willet Dr.,* ☎ *307/766–4114,* WEB *uwadmnweb.uwyo.edu/ahc.* ⚏ *Free.* ◷ *Sept.–May, weekdays 8–5, Sat. 11–5; June–Aug., weekdays 7:30–4:30.*

The **Wyoming Children's Museum and Nature Center** is a hands-on place in which children ages 3–12 and families can explore, make noise, experiment, play, imagine, discover, and invent. Emphasis is on wildlife and nature. ✉ *968 N. 9th,,* ☎ *307/745–6332.* ⚏ *$2.* ◷ *Tues.–Thurs. 9–4, Sat. 10–4; also Fri. 1–5 in summer.*

Dining and Lodging

$$–$$$$ ✗ **Cavalryman Supper Club.** It's the food, not the look of the place, that attracts people to this restaurant on the plains, 1 mi south of Laramie on U.S. 287. There is a lounge area with dining on the upper and lower floors. Prime rib, steak, and lobster are on the menu. ✉ *4425 S. 3rd St.,* ☎ *307/745–5551. AE, DC, MC, V. No lunch.*

$ ✗ **Café Jacques 3rd Street Bar and Grill.** This casual bar and grill serves sandwiches and 70 beers including microbrews, domestic, and imported brands. ✉ *220 Grand Ave.,* ☎ *307/742–5522. AE, DC, MC, V.*

$ ✗ **Overland Restaurant.** This restaurant in the historic district, right on the railroad tracks, cooks up breakfast, lunch, and dinner. Patio dining and a superb wine list enhance the food: pasta, chicken, quiche, beef, and seafood. For Sunday brunch, you might find such entrées as yellowfin tuna and eggs, a buffalo chili omelet, or avocados Benedict. ✉ *100 Ivinson Ave.,* ☎ *307/721–2800. AE, D, MC, V.*

$–$$ ⌂ **Best Western Foster's Country Corner.** This white-brick Best Western is on the western edge of town, at the Snowy Range Road exit off I–80. The property includes a convenience store, 24-hour restaurant, and liquor store. The rooms are basic, with contemporary furnishings. ✉ *Box 580, Exit 311 off I–80, 1561 Jackson St., 82070,* ☎ *307/742–*

8371, FAX 307/742–0884. 112 rooms. Restaurant, bar, indoor pool, hot tub. AE, D, DC, MC, V.

$ ★ ⊡ **Annie Moore's Guest House.** This historic home across from the University of Wyoming campus has been a fraternity, a sorority, and an apartment building, and now it's a B&B. Terra-cotta tiles, hardwood floors, the sounds of nesting owls, and a cat named Archina, who greets guests, make it cozy. Continental breakfast with homemade goodies comes with good conversation. ⊠ *819 University, 82070,* ☎ *307/721–4177. 6 rooms with 3 shared baths. Dining room, recreation room, library. AE, D, MC, V. CP.*

$ ⊡ **Laramie Comfort Inn.** On busy Grand Avenue, three blocks from War Memorial Stadium at the University of Wyoming, this motel has a full wheelchair-accessible room with the only roll-in shower in the city. One of the three suites has a whirlpool. ⊠ *3420 Grand Ave., 82070,* ☎ *307/721–8856 or 800/228–5150. 55 rooms, 3 suites, 1 efficiency apartment. Indoor pool, hot tub, gym. AE, D, DC, MC, V. CP.*

Nightlife and the Arts

The **University of Wyoming's fine arts program** (☎ 307/766–5249) regularly holds concerts featuring classical and popular performers. The **UW Department of Theater and Dance** presents periodic productions on the main stage of the UW Fine Arts Center (☎ 307/766–3327).

Dinner theater is performed at the **Horse Barn Dinner Theater** (⊠ 975 Snowy Range Rd., ☎ 307/745–6161 or 800/845–2287).

Country-and-western nightlife is found at the **Buckhorn** (⊠ 114 Ivinson Ave., ☎ 307/742–3554). Kick up your heels on the dance floor at the **Cowboy Saloon** (⊠ 108 S. 2nd St., ☎ 307/721–3165). The younger set often congregates at the **Drawbridge Tavern** (⊠ 1622 Grand Ave., ☎ 307/745–3490), which also hosts rock bands. Hang with the college students at **Mingles** (⊠ 3206 Grand Ave., ☎ 307/721–2005). For rock, head to **Shooters Saloon** (⊠ 303 S. 3rd St., ☎ 307/745–7676).

Outdoor Activities and Sports

CAMPING

Laramie has a **KOA** (⊠ I–80 at Curtis St. exit, ☎ 307/742–6553) campground. **Curt Gowdy State Park** (⊠ off Happy Jack Rd.) is a good camping spot about 20 mi east of the city. In rolling hill country with pine forest and a profusion of wildflowers during spring and summer months, the park has picnic sites and areas for swimming and boating.

CYCLING

Mountain biking trails are scattered throughout the Medicine Bow National Forest and the Happy Jack recreation area, located east of Laramie. For information, trail maps, and rentals, see Mike or Doug Lowham at the **Pedal House** (⊠ 207 S. 1st St., Laramie, ☎ 307/742–5533).

GOLF

Enjoy the links at the 18-hole **Jacoby Park Golf Course** (⊠ off N. 30th St., ☎ 307/745–3111).

SKIING

Downhill and cross-country skiing are available 32 mi southwest of Laramie at the **Snowy Range Ski Area** (⊠ 1420 Thomas St., Laramie 82070, ☎ 307/745–5750 or 800/602–7669, WEB www.snowyrange.com, ⌨ $30 full-day lift tickets; $16 full-day adult ski rental). Cross-country trails are scattered throughout the Medicine Bow National Forest and the Happy Jack recreation area. For information and rentals, contact **Cross Country Connection** (⊠ 117 Grand Ave., Laramie 82070, ☎ 307/721–2851).

Shopping

Laramie's most unusual shopping is found in a shopping district called
Landmark Square along Ivinson Avenue and Grand Avenue. Stores offer
artwork, clothing, and handcrafted items. **Curiosity Shoppe** (✉ 206 S.
2nd St., ☎ 307/745–4760) sells antiques, pottery, and hand-embroi-
dered and -crocheted items. **A Touch of Country** (✉ 312 S. 2nd St., ☎
307/721–2171) features folk art, pottery, baskets, country pine furniture, and a year-round Christmas Shoppe.

BOOKS

Chickering Bookstore (✉ 203 S. 2nd St., ☎ 307/742–8609) features
regional authors, self-help, and a good selection of children's titles. **The
Grand Newsstand** (✉ 214 Grand Ave., ☎ 307/742–5127) has the best
selection of western and regional titles in the city. **The Second Story**
(✉ 105 Ivinson Ave., ☎ 307/745–4423), in an old, antiques-laden upstairs suite of offices, stocks only "personally recommended books,"
some of them signed by visiting authors.

SPECIALTY FOODS

Laramie's **Whole Earth Granary** (✉ 111 Ivinson Ave., ☎ 307/745–4268)
sells organic whole grains and flours, 50 varieties of coffee, herbal extracts, essential oils, and fresh seafood flown in weekly, including live
Maine lobster.

En Route   In the summer, you can get away from the interstates by taking Route
130, the **Snowy Range Scenic Byway,** west of Laramie. This paved road
in excellent condition runs over 10,847-ft Snowy Range Pass through
the Medicine Bow National Forest, providing views of Medicine Bow
Peak. Along the way, there are 10 campgrounds (six right on the road),
10 hiking trails (from 1½- to 8-mi long), and 100 alpine lakes and streams.
The more adventurous can take any of the several gravel roads that
lead into the forest. Maps are available from the Medicine Bow National Forest office.

Saratoga

⑱   *79 mi west of Laramie via Rte. 130, summer only; or 98 mi via I–80
west to Walcott Junction and Rte. 130/230 south.*

Tucked away in a valley formed by the Snowy Range and Sierra Madre
mountains, with the North Platte River bisecting the region, Saratoga
is a rarely visited treasure. Fine shopping and dining combine with elegant lodging facilities and outstanding recreational opportunities
such as river floating and fishing, and cross-country skiing and snowmobiling. The town first went by the name Warm Springs, but it was
changed to Saratoga in 1884 (for Saratoga Springs, New York). The
Hobo Pool Hot Springs and the adjacent swimming pool heated by the
springs are main attractions. ✉ *201 S. River St.,* ☎ *307/326–5417.*
🎫 *Free.* ☺ *Springs year-round, 24 hrs; pool Memorial Day–Labor Day,
daily 9–8; sometimes closed for lessons.*

Dining and Lodging

$–$$ ✕ **Lazy River Cantina.** Mexican sombreros and music greet you in this
downtown restaurant that also includes a bar and lounge where locals
and visitors take their shot at darts. The entrées include tacos, enchiladas, burritos, and chimichangas, served in one of two small rooms.
You can sit in a booth and watch folks and traffic on busy Bridge Street.
✉ *110 E. Bridge St.,* ☎ *307/326–8472. MC, V.*

$–$$ ✕🏨 **Wolf Hotel.** This downtown 1893 hotel on the National Register
of Historic Places is well maintained by its proud owners. The guest
rooms are on the second and third floors; there is no elevator. Though
some rooms are small, all have Victorian charm. The downstairs din-

ing room ($–$$$), bar, and lounge have Victorian furnishings, including dark green wallpaper, antique oak tables, crystal chandeliers, and lacy drapes. There is fine dining at lunch and dinner; prime rib and steaks are real specialties. ✉ *101 E. Bridge St., 82331,* ☎ *307/326–5525. 5 rooms, 4 suites. Restaurant, bar. AE, DC, MC, V.*

$$–$$$ 🛏 **Saratoga Inn.** With leather couches in the common areas, pole-style beds, and western art, this inn is as nice as any place in Wyoming. Some rooms are in the main lodge, which has a double fireplace lounge that opens both to the central sitting room and the back porch; other rooms are in separate buildings surrounding a large expanse of lawn and a hot mineral water swimming pool. Some of the five outdoor hot tubs (also hot mineral water) are covered with Indian tepees for more privacy. There's a nine-hole public golf course, where cottonwoods, conifers, and the North Platte River also come into play. The inn coordinates year-round activities with a local guest ranch. ✉ *E. Pic-Pike Rd., 82331,* ☎ *307/326–5261,* FAX *307/326–5109. 50 rooms. Dining room, bar, lobby lounge, hot springs, outdoor hot tub, driving range, 9-hole golf course, 2 tennis courts. AE, DC, MC, V.*

$$ 🛏 **Spirit West River Lodge.** Beside the Encampment River, 18 mi south of Saratoga, this massive log structure has walls of lichen-covered rocks and large, scenic-view windows. The lodge is full of stained glass and most of the western artwork is by owner R. G. Finney (known for his wildlife bronzes and paintings). His wife Lynn, who serves the full breakfast, is a Senior Olympic gold medalist in cycling and a native of the area. She can tell you the best cycling routes and cross-country ski trails. There is a mile of private access fishing on the Encampment River and each room has a private entrance off a deck overlooking the river. ✉ *18 mi south of Saratoga and ¼ mi east of Riverside on Rte. 230, Box 605, Encampment 82325,* ☎ *307/326–5753,* FAX *307/327–5753. 4 rooms, 1 cabin. Bar, breakfast room, gym, pond, fishing, bicycles, piano. MC, V. BP.*

Outdoor Activities and Sports

CANOEING AND RAFTING

Great Rocky Mountain Outfitters (✉ 216 E. Walnut St., 82331, ☎ 307/326–8750, WEB www.grmo.com) offers guided canoe and raft expeditions on the North Platte River and rental packages.

FISHING

Brook trout are prevalent in the lakes and streams of Medicine Bow National Forest, but you can find rainbow, golden, cutthroat, and brown trout, as well as splake. Anglers can also drop a fly in the North Platte River. **Great Rocky Mountain Outfitters** (✉ 216 E. Walnut St., Saratoga, ☎ 307/326–8750, WEB www.grmo.com) rent tackle and runs fishing trips on the Upper North Platte. They are an efficient, well-run company that has dominated the market for years.

SKIING AND SNOWMOBILING

Extensive trail networks in the Medicine Bow National Forest include opportunities for novice or experienced cross-country skiers and snowmobilers. For trail conditions, contact the **Hayden/Brush Creek Ranger District** (☎ 307/326–5258 or 307/327–5481, WEB www.fs.fed.us/r2/mbr) of the Medicine Bow National Forest.

For ski rentals and sales, as well as trail information contact Mark Rauterkus at the **Trading Post** (✉ Junction Hwys. 70 and 230, Encampment 82325, ☎ 307/327–5720, WEB www.wyomingcarboncounty.com/trading.htm). Snowmobile rentals, including full- or half-day guided treks into the Snowy Range or Sierra Madre, are available from **Platte Valley Outfitters** (✉ 1st St. and Bridge Ave., Saratoga, ☎ 307/326–5750).

Southeast Wyoming A to Z

AIRPORTS

Cheyenne Airport is served by United Express. Many visitors prefer to fly into Denver International Airport and drive the 90 mi north to Cheyenne. If you only need to get to and from the airport or bus station and the capitol area, you can make do with cabs.

➤ AIRPORT INFORMATION: **Cheyenne Airport** (✉ 200 E. 8th Ave., ☎ 307/634–7071).

➤ TAXIS: **Checker Cab** (☎ 307/635–5555). **Yellow Cab** (☎ 307/638–3333).

BUS TRAVEL

Greyhound Lines connects Cheyenne to such hubs as Denver and Salt Lake City.

➤ BUS INFORMATION: **Greyhound Lines** (✉ 1503 Capitol Ave., ☎ 307/634–7744 or 800/231–2222).

CAR RENTAL

➤ LOCAL AGENCIES: **Avis Rent A Car** (✉ municipal airport, Cheyenne, ☎ 307/632–9371; ✉ municipal airport, Laramie, ☎ 307/745–7156). **Dollar Rent A Car** (✉ 300 E. 8th Ave., Cheyenne, ☎ 307/632–2422; ✉ 555 General Breeze Rd., Laramie, ☎ 307/742–8805). **Enterprise Rent A Car** (✉ 800 W. Lincolnway, Cheyenne, ☎ 307/632–1907; ✉ 2208 Grand Ave., Laramie, ☎ 307/721–9876). **Hertz** (✉ municipal airport, Cheyenne, ☎ 307/634–2131).

EMERGENCIES

➤ CONTACTS: **Cheyenne: United Medical Center** (✉ 300 E. 23rd St., Cheyenne, ☎ 307/634–2273).**Laramie: Ivinson Memorial Hospital** (✉ 255 N. 30th St., Laramie, ☎ 307/742–2141).

TOURS

The Cheyenne Trolley takes a $6, two-hour tour of the historic downtown area and Frances E. Warren Air Force Base, including 20–25 minutes at the Old West Museum. The trolley runs from mid-May to mid-September, Monday–Saturday at 10 and 1:30, Sunday at 11:30. Tickets are sold at the Cheyenne Area Convention and Visitors Bureau on weekdays and at the Wrangler shop on weekends. For a self-guided walking tour of the downtown and capitol area in Cheyenne, contact the Cheyenne Area Convention and Visitors Bureau.

Platte Valley Shuttles and Tours has standard tours of the Snowy Range or Battle Mountain scenic highways; statewide tours that take in the Oregon Trail; and custom tours for all of Wyoming. The company also provides shuttle service for snowmobilers, cross-country skiers, horseback riders, and fishermen or river float trips. They will shuttle you to a site or trailhead, or shuttle your vehicle (including pickups and horse or snowmobile trailers), to and from regional airports.

➤ CONTACTS: **Cheyenne Trolley Ticket Sales:** at the Cheyenne Area Convention and Visitors Bureau (✉ 309 W. Lincolnway, ☎ 307/778–3133); Wrangler shop (✉ 16th and Capitol Sts.).**Platte Valley Shuttles and Tours** (✉ Box 1652, Saratoga 82331, ☎ 307/326–5582, WEB www.plattevalleyshuttles.com).

Visitor Information

➤ TOURIST INFORMATION: **Albany County Tourism Board (Laramie)** (✉ 800 S. 3rd St., Laramie 82070, ☎ 307/745–7339 or 800/445–5303, FAX 307/745–4624, WEB www.laramie-tourism.org). **Cheyenne Area Convention and Visitors Bureau** (✉ 309 W. Lincolnway/16th St., Cheyenne 82001, ☎ 307/778–3133 or 800/426–5009, WEB www.cheyenne.org).

Medicine Bow National Forest (✉ 2468 Snowy Range Rd., Laramie, ☎ 307/745–8971, WEB www.fs.fed.us/r2/mbr). **Saratoga-Platte Valley Chamber of Commerce** (✉ Box 1095, Saratoga 82331, ☎ 307/326–8855, FAX 307/326–8855, WEB www.trib.com/SPVCC).

SOUTHWEST WYOMING

Known as the Red or Little Colorado Desert, this is a unique area of Wyoming with a combination of badlands, desert, and mountains. The region is known for its mineral resources and for its dinosaurs. The far corner of southwestern Wyoming has close ties to Utah. Not only are many communities predominantly Mormon, but with Salt Lake City just over an hour away, Evanston residents also shop and attend cultural events there.

Rock Springs

⑲ *150 mi west of Saratoga via 130 and I–80.*

Coal mining has always defined the community of Rock Springs, established when the Union Pacific Railroad pushed through the area in the late 1860s. The mines drew laborers from a variety of nationalities, making this a real melting pot of cultures. Sprawled at the base of White Mountain, Rock Springs, population 24,000, is the site of Western Wyoming College, a facility known for its paleontological resources.

The Little Colorado Desert to the north and east is home to hundreds of wild horses; you can often catch a glimpse of them from area highways. Locals are working to establish a driving loop tour that will provide information—and sometimes views—of the wild horses.

Dinosaurs are among the prehistoric animal and plant specimens on display at **Western Wyoming Community College Natural History Museum.** Species range in age from 180 million to 67 million years old. Look out for the fossilized fish and the baby alligator. The dinosaurs are placed throughout the building and the museum has rotating exhibits. ✉ *2500 College Dr.,* ☎ *307/382–1600.* 🎫 *Free.* ☉ *Daily 8–7.*

Dining and Lodging

$–$$ ✕ **Bitter Creek Brewery.** Choose from 16 different burgers and wash it down with Bob, a local brew that has won awards at brewfests in Denver and Laramie, or try a Coal Porter (a dark beer that symbolizes the coal mining heritage of this community). There are other food items besides burgers on the menu as well. The brewery is in a long, narrow room with a cement floor and blond oak furniture. ✉ *604 Broadway,* ☎ *307/362–4782. AE, MC, V.*

$ ✕ **Boschetto's European Market.** Rock Springs's population has been a melting pot of nationalities since its earliest settlement as a coal mining town. Boschetto's, a European-style market and deli, with its varieties of cheese, sausage, spaghetti, and other foods, caters to the variety of folks living in the city. The setting sparkles with a tile floor, black and white chairs, and small white linen–covered tables. RV travelers can stock the refrigerator or cooler, and diners can order a meal to eat in. The owners cook tantalizing steak sandwiches on an outdoor grill. ✉ *6717 Broadway,* ☎ *307/362–2350. AE, D, DC, MC, V.*

$ ✕ **Grubs Drive-In.** There isn't a lot of room in this tiny diner where you sit at a horseshoe-shape counter elbow-to-elbow with the other diners. The specialty is burgers with fries and the same family has been dishing them up for more than 50 years. ✉ *415 Paulson St.,* ☎ *307/362–6634. MC, V.*

$$ ☒ **Holiday Inn.** A fireplace in the lobby sets the mood at this Holiday Inn on the west side of town. An indoor pool has its own space in a separate room to the left side of the lobby. Guest rooms have light-color furniture including a chair and ottoman for relaxing. Ground-floor rooms have exterior entrances. Pets are allowed for a $10 fee. ☒ *1675 Sunset Dr., 82902,* ☎ *307/382–9200,* FAX *307/632–1064,* WEB *www. holidayinn.com. 113 rooms, 1 suite. Restaurant, bar, some refrigerators, indoor pool, hot tub, gym, meeting rooms, airport shuttle. AE, D, DC, MC, V.*

$ ☒ **Ramada Limited.** Cherrywood furniture including a desk, end tables, and easy chair is the look here. Free Continental breakfast is served by the fireplace in the breakfast room. Located on the west side of town, take Exit 102 off of I–80, and you will be just one block from the city's White Mountain Mall. Pets are allowed. ☒ *2717 Dewar Dr., 82902,* ☎ *307/362–1770; 888/307–7890 reservations only,* FAX *307/362–2830,* WEB *www.ramada.com. 129 rooms, 2 suites. Breakfast room, in-room data ports, outdoor pool, gym, laundry service. AE, D, DC, MC, V. CP.*

Green River

❷⓿ *12 mi west of Rock Springs via I–80.*

Of all the towns along the Union Pacific Railroad, Green River is the only one that predated the rails arrival in the late 1860s. It began as a Pony Express and stage station on the Overland Trail. In 1869 and again in 1871, John Wesley Powell launched expeditions down the Green and Colorado rivers from sites near Green River. The town of more than 13,000 attracts those who want to explore the waterways of the Green River drainage.

The Flaming Gorge Reservoir of the **Flaming Gorge National Recreation Area** straddles the border between Wyoming and Utah, though most of the park's visitor services are in Utah. The water flow comes from the Green River and is held back by Flaming Gorge Dam. You can boat and fish, as well as watch for wildlife. The area is as rich in history as it is spectacularly beautiful. Mountain men like Jim Bridger and outlaws like Butch Cassidy found haven here, and in 1869, on his first exploration down the Green River, John Wesley Powell named many local landmarks: Flaming Gorge, Horseshoe Canyon, Red Canyon, and the Gates of Lodore. You'll find marinas, lodging, food, and campgrounds, places to rent horses and snowmobiles, and trails for mountain bikes as well. The Ashley National Forest administers the area. ☒ *20 mi south of Green River on Rte. 530 or U.S. 191,* ☎ *801/784–3445; 800/277–7571 for information on reservoir elevations and river flows; 877/444–6677 or TDD 877/833–6777 for campground reservations,* WEB *www.fs.fed.us/r4/ashley/fg_html_aw.html.*

The 25,000 acres of **Seedskadee National Wildlife Refuge** are inhabited by prairie falcons, peregrine falcons, Canada geese, and various species of hawks and owls. Trumpeter swans occasionally use the area. Within or near the refuge, you'll find homestead and ranch sites, Oregon Trail crossings, and ferry sites over the Green River, as well as the place where Jim Bridger and Henry Fraeb built a trading post in 1839. Visitor information and restrooms are available 24 hours. ☒ *37 mi north of green River on Rte. 372,* ☎ *307/875–2187,* WEB *www.r6.fws.gov/refuges/ seedskad.* ☒ *Free.*

Dining and Lodging

$–$$ ✕ **Denali Grill and Bakery.** The Mt. Denali theme is evident in this down-home restaurant with artificial pine trees galore, twig curtain rods, pictures of moose and bears, and iron caribou silhouettes on the walls.

The owners pride themselves on their homemade breads, soups, and sandwiches. Local favorites are the baby back barbecued ribs and salmon fillet. Bread pudding, pecan torte, and lemon crunch pie are on the list of homemade desserts. ✉ *375 Uinta Dr.,* ☎ *307/875–4654. AE, D, MC, V.*

$–$$ ✕ **Penny's Diner.** The name pretty much says it all—a 1950s-style 24-hour diner with a bright shiny look, reminiscent of a railcar, and flashing neon lights. Try a burger, fries, and milk shake. The diner is part of the Oak Tree Inn. ✉ *1172 W. Flaming Gorge Way,* ☎ *307/875–3500. AE, D, DC, MC, V.*

$$–$$$$ ▥ **Little America.** This one-stop facility sits alone in the Little Colorado Desert, and it can be a real haven if the weather becomes inclement. The hotel, founded in 1934, is the original of the small chain. The rooms are large and comfortable, some have in-room data ports and refrigerators. There is also a full-service fuel station and convenience store. ✉ *I–80, 20 mi west of Green River, 82929,* ☎ *307/875–2400 or 800/634–2401,* ℻ *307/872–2666,* 🕸 *www.littleamerica.com. 140 rooms, 18 with shower only. Restaurant, bar, pool, gym, playground, laundry facilities, business services. AE, D, DC, MC, V.*

$ ▥ **Oak Tree Inn.** A completely no-smoking facility, this two-story inn on the west side of town is 20 mi from Flaming Gorge and has views of unique rock outcroppings above the city. Pets are allowed. ✉ *1170 W. Flaming Gorge Way, 82935,* ☎ *307/875–3500,* ℻ *307/875–4889. 192 rooms. Restaurant, no-smoking rooms, some refrigerators, gym, hot tub, coin laundry. AE, D, DC, MC, V.*

Evanston

㉑ *86 mi west of Green River on I–80; 80 mi east of Salt Lake City, Utah, on I–80.*

Like other raucous towns established as the Union Pacific laid its tracks across Wyoming, Evanston started as a tent city. Many of the rail workers were Chinese. Today Evanston celebrates that railroad and Chinese history at Depot Square, with the UP Railroad Depot and a replica of a Chinese joss house.

With the 2002 Winter Olympics in Park City and Salt Lake City, Evanston became a gateway community and it lived up to its interest in the games by becoming the North American Training Center for the Jamaican bobsled teams. After a local man in Evanston saw the movie *Cool Runnings* and when Salt Lake got the Olympic bid, he contacted the Jamaicans and invited them to Evanston. It was a great cultural exchange for the community.

Started in 1842 as a trading post by mountain man Jim Bridger and his partner Louis Vasquez, **Fort Bridger State Historic Site** was under the domination of Mormons by 1853 after they either purchased the fort or forced the original owners to leave—historians aren't sure which scenario occurred. As the U.S. Army approached during a conflict known as the Mormon War of 1857, the Mormons deserted the area and burned the original Bridger post. Fort Bridger then became a frontier military post until it was abandoned in 1890. Many of the military-era buildings remain and the Bridger post has been rebuilt and is staffed by a mountain man and woman. You can attend interpretive programs and living-history demonstrations during the summer. The largest mountain man rendezvous in the intermountain West occurs annually at Fort Bridger over Labor Day Weekend, attracting hundreds of buckskinners and Native Americans plus thousands of visitors. ✉ *34 mi east of Evanston on I–80, at 37000 Business Loup,* ☎ *307/782–3842,* 🕸 *www.spacr.state.wy.us/sphs/bridger1.htm.* ▣ *$2 Wyoming* *residents; $5 nonresidents.* ⊙ *Grounds year-round, daily 8–sunset; museum Apr. and Oct. weekends 9–4:30, May–Sept. daily 9–5:30; Bridger/Vasquez Trading Co. May–Sept., daily 9–5.*

A unique concentration of creatures is embedded in the natural outcrop **Fossil Butte National Monument,** indicating clearly that this area was once an inland sea. The monument was established on October 23, 1972. You can hike the fossil trails and unwind at the picnic area. ✉ *50 mi north of Evanston on U.S. 189, then 15 mi west on U.S. 30,* ☎ *307/877–4457,* WEB *www.nps.gov/fobu.*

Dining and Lodging

$–$$ ✕ **Don Pedro's Family Mexican Restaurant.** You don't find it more authentic than this small, family-owned Mexican restaurant. As you soak in the ambience of sombreros, serapes, and Mexican music, try the sizzling fajitas, or the special *molcajete,* a stew of beef and chicken. ✉ *909 Front St.,* ☎ *307/789–2944. AE, D, DC, MC, V.*

$–$$ ✕ **Legal Tender.** Within the Best Western Dunmar Inn, this restaurant has the most "upscale" atmosphere in the community even though it isn't pretentious. It's quiet with lots of faux greenery and a floral carpet. There is a full salad bar and a varied menu with steak, seafood, chicken, and pasta. ✉ *1601 Harrison Dr.,* ☎ *307/789–3770. AE, D, DC, MC, V.*

$ ✕ **Hunan Garden.** Evanston's Chinese culture comes through in this restaurant with green walls and Chinese lamps that serves Hunan, Szechuan, and Mandarin. Among the house specialities on the extensive menu are walnut prawns, double face noodles (chicken, prawns, and beef sautéed with vegetables), and black pepper beef or lamb. You can also order gourmet dinners for two or more diners including combinations of hot and sour soup, cheese puffs, barbecue pork egg rolls, sweet and sour prawns, Hunan chicken, and Mongolian beef. ✉ *933 Front St.,* ☎ *307/789–3908. MC, V.*

$–$$ ☷ **Best Western Dunmar Inn.** This large motel is spread over a big area that's a bit mazelike as you drive or walk to your room from the main lobby and restaurant area. The rooms are large with a desk and separate table and easy chairs. ✉ *1601 Harrison Dr., Box 0768, 82931,* ☎ *307/789–3770 or 800/654–6509,* FAX *307/789–3758. 165 rooms. Restaurant, bar, no-smoking rooms, business services, meeting rooms. AE, D, MC, V.*

$–$$ ☷ **Days Inn.** On the west side of town, this motel has one suite with a hot tub. Other rooms have a table and two easy chairs. Pets are allowed for a $10 charge. ✉ *339 Wasatch Rd., 82931,* ☎ *307/789–2220,* FAX *307/789–4122,* WEB *www.daysinn.com. 113 rooms, 1 suite. Restaurant, bar, laundry, sauna, hot tub. AE, D, DC, MC, V.*

$–$$ ☷ **Pine Gables Inn B&B.** This house, the only B&B in town, is on the National Register of Historic Places and is in a quiet neighborhood three blocks from downtown. The rooms have murals, hand-painted by the house owner, antique furnishings, and nooks and crannies that are a fun part of the house's architecture. There is a large Jacuzzi in one suite, and a kitchenette in another. All rooms have TV and telephones; some rooms have fireplaces and claw-foot tubs. ✉ *1049 Center St., 82930,* ☎ *307/789–2069 or 800/789–2069,* WEB *www.cruising-america.com/ pinegables. 3 rooms, 2 suites. Breakfast room, library. AE, MC, V. BP.*

$ ☷ **High Country Inn.** This hotel on the west side of town got a complete face-lift in 2001 so the rooms are fresh and inviting with neutral-tone walls, mauve and green accents, and dark green carpeting. The lobby has lots of oak trim and an aquarium. The exterior doors are shielded by an enclosed walkway. You can even participate in off-track betting at this site. ✉ *1936 Harrison Dr., 82930,* ☎ *307/789–2810,* FAX *307/789–5506. 110 rooms, 2 suites. Restaurant, bar, pool. AE, D, DC, MC, V.*

Southwest Wyoming A to Z

AIRPORTS

United Express serves the local airports.

➤ AIRPORT INFORMATION: **Evanston Municipal Airport** (⊠ 2160 Airport Rd., Evanston, ☎ 307/789–2256). **Sweetwater County Airport** (⊠ 382 Rte. 370, Rock Springs, ☎ 307/352–6880).

BUS TRAVEL

➤ BUS INFORMATION: **Greyhound Lines** (⊠ 1936 W. Lincoln Hwy., Evanston, ☎ 307/789–2810 or 800/231–2222; ⊠ 1655 Sunset Dr., Rock Springs, ☎ 307/362–293 or 800/231–2222).

CAR TRAVEL

You'll need a car to get around in this region and can find rental agencies at airports or in each community.

EMERGENCIES

➤ CONTACTS: **Evanston Regional Hospital** (⊠ 190 Arrowhead Dr., Evanston, ☎ 307/789–3636 or 800/244–3537). **Rock Springs: Memorial Hospital of Sweetwater County** (⊠ 1200 College Dr., Rock Springs, ☎ 307/362–3711).

TOURS

The Bear River Outdoor Recreation Alliance has a series of trails used for mountain biking and hiking in the summer and as Nordic ski trails during the winter. There is also a system of yurts for overnight stays. The trails are a cooperative project of the Alliance, the U.S. Forest Service, Evanston Parks and Recreation Department, and the Wyoming and Utah state parks divisions. Information is available at the Depot Square Visitors Information Center, Wasatch National Forest, Evanston Ranger Station, or by writing Bear River Outdoor Recreation Alliance.

VISITOR INFORMATION

➤ TOURIST INFORMATION: **Visitors Information Center/Depot Square** (⊠ 920 Front St., Evanston 82930, ☎ 307/789–1472). **Bear River Outdoor Recreation Alliance** (⊠ Box 2600, Evanston 82930, ☎ 307/789–1770). **Evanston Chamber of Commerce** (⊠ 36 Tenth St., Evanston 82931, ☎ 307/783–0370, WEB www.etownchamber.com). **Wasatch National Forest, Evanston Ranger Station** (⊠ 1565 S. Rte. 150, Evanston 82930, ☎ 307/789–3194, WEB www.fs.fed.us/wcnf).

WYOMING A TO Z

To research prices, get advice from other travelers, and book travel arrangements, visit www.fodors.com.

AIR TRAVEL

An oddity of Wyoming is that you can fly directly from Jackson to Chicago, but to get a commercial flight from Jackson to Casper, within the state, requires a change of planes in Salt Lake City. Commuter airlines connect a few towns, but these intrastate routes and the airlines serving them change fairly often. Great Lakes Aviation Limited serves several Wyoming cities.

➤ SMALL CARRIERS: **Great Lakes Aviation Limited** (⊠ 901 W. Brundage La., Sheridan, ☎ 307/672–7794).

CAR TRAVEL

I–80 crosses Wyoming's southern tier, connecting Cheyenne to Salt Lake City; watch the weather in winter and spring, when wind and snow can cause major problems. Entering the northeast corner from the east,

I–90 passes through Gillette and Sheridan before exiting north into Montana. I–25 runs north from Denver through Cheyenne and Casper to join I–90 at Buffalo. Major natural attractions are some distance from the interstates, however, so travelers can expect to cross Wyoming's wide-open spaces on smaller, well-maintained highways. Snowplows do a herculean job of keeping most roads clear in winter.

Making a right turn on a red light (after coming to a complete stop) is legal in Wyoming.

EMERGENCIES

In most areas, call 911 for police, fire, and medical emergencies. Call the Wyoming Highway Patrol for accidents.

➤ CONTACTS: **Poison Control** (☎ 800/955–9119). **Wyoming Highway Patrol** (☎ 800/442–9090).

FISHING

Limits and restrictions on fishing in national parks in Wyoming change from year to year. A free national park license is required. Outside the parks, on state, private, or national forest lands, Wyoming fishing licenses are required and are usually available at sporting-goods stores and drugstores. Nonresidents can purchase a one-day license for $10 and $65 for the season. You must also purchase a $5 conservation stamp. Children under 14 may fish without a license when with a licensed adult. Contact the Wyoming Game and Fish Department for information.

➤ LICENSES: **Wyoming Game and Fish Department** (✉ 5400 Bishop Blvd., Cheyenne 82006, ☎ 307/777–4600, WEB http://gf.state.wy.us).

SNOWMOBILING

Snowmobiling is allowed on snow-packed roads within Yellowstone Park, at least until March of 2003, and perhaps longer depending on the outcome of an ongoing study. The state of Wyoming has over 2,000 mi of groomed and ungroomed trails. The state grooms an extensive network of trails in the forests of the Northwest, including the Continental Divide Snowmobile Trail, which runs from Lander through Grand Teton. Among the bigger snowmobile operations in the Northwest are Flagg Ranch Village and Togwotee Mountain Lodge. The state also maintains trails in the Bighorn mountains, in the Black Hills in northeastern Wyoming, and in the Sierra Madre and Snowy ranges in the south-central part of the state. Maps and trail conditions are available from the state program. All snowmobiles must have a state registration decal, which costs $15 for nonresidents.

➤ TRAIL INFORMATION: **Wyoming State Snowmobile Program** (☎ 307/777–7550, WEB http://wyoparks.state.wy.us/snow/popup.htm).

TOURS

Platte Valley Shuttles and Tours has local service in the Saratoga area, and also does statewide tours that focus on arts and culture, historic trails, state parks, or wildlife. They will customize a tour to suit your needs. Equitour coordinates equestrian rambles the world over, but home base is in Wyoming, where trips explore areas such as Butch Cassidy's Hole in the Wall country and the route of the Pony Express. Bridger Wilderness Outfitters run pack trips out of Pinedale.

Off the Beaten Path specializes in individualized vacations throughout Wyoming. They're well connected with the outdoor recreation community and offer both preplanned and custom guided tours throughout Wyoming, Montana, and the Canadian Rockies. Rocky Mountain Holiday Tours sells various packages of lodging, transportation, and tours with a range of itineraries, including Grand Teton and Yellowstone national parks and the Oregon Trail.

➤ CONTACTS: **Bridger Wilderness Outfitters** (✉ Box 561T, Pinedale 82941, ☎ 307/367–2268 or 888/803–7316, WEB www.bwo.com). **Equitour** (✉ 24 Birchfield La., Lander 82520, ☎ 800/572–1230, WEB www.horseriders.com). **Off the Beaten Path** (✉ 27 E. Main St., Bozeman, MT 59715, ☎ 406/586–1311 or 800/455–2995, FAX 406/587–4147, WEB www.offbeatenpath.com). **Platte Valley Shuttles and Tours** (✉ Box 1652, Saratoga 82331, ☎ 307/326–5582, WEB www.plattevalleyshuttles.com). **Rocky Mountain Holiday Tours** (✉ Box 2063, Fort Collins, CO 80522, ☎ 800/237–7211, FAX 970/482–5815, WEB www.rmhtours.com).

VISITOR INFORMATION

➤ TOURIST INFORMATION: **Division of Parks and Cultural Resources** (✉ Barrett Bldg., 24th St. and Central Ave., Cheyenne 82002, ☎ 307/777–7013, WEB spacr.state.wy.us/sphs/index1.htm). **Wyoming Division of Tourism** (✉ I–25 at College Dr., Cheyenne 82002, ☎ 307/777–7777 or 800/225–5996, FAX 307/777–6904, WEB www.wyomingtourism.org).

INDEX

Icons and Symbols

★ Our special recommen-
  dations

✕ Restaurant

🏨 Lodging establishment

✕🏨 Lodging establishment
  whose restaurant war-
  rants a special trip

🐥 Good for kids (rubber
  duck)

☞ Sends you to another
  section of the guide for
  more information

✉ Address

☎ Telephone number

🕐 Opening and closing
  times

💳 Admission prices

Numbers in white and black
circles ③ ❸ that appear on
the maps, in the margins, and
within the tours correspond
to one another.